C++11 for Programmers Second Edition

Deitel® Developer Series

The publisher offers excellent discounts on this book when ordered in quantity for bulk purchases or special sales, which may include electronic versions and/or custom covers and content particular to your business, training goals, marketing focus, and branding interests. For more information, please contact:

U. S. Corporate and Government Sales
(800) 382-3419
corpsales@pearsontechgroup.com

For sales outside the U. S., please contact:

International Sales
international@pearsoned.com

Visit us on the Web: informit.com/ph

Library of Congress Cataloging-in-Publication Data

On file

ISBN-13: 978-0-13-343985-4
ISBN-10: 0-13-343985-2

Text printed in the United States at RR Donnelley in Crawfordsville, Indiana..
First printing, February 2013

C++11 for Programmers
Second Edition
Deitel® Developer Series

Paul Deitel
Deitel & Associates, Inc.

Harvey Deitel
Deitel & Associates, Inc.

Upper Saddle River, NJ • Boston • Indianapolis • San Francisco
New York • Toronto • Montreal • London • Munich • Paris • Madrid
Capetown • Sydney • Tokyo • Singapore • Mexico City

Trademarks

To our review team:

Dean Michael Berris
Danny Kalev
Linda M. Krause
James P. McNellis
Robert C. Seacord
José Antonio González Seco

We are grateful for your guidance and expertise.

Paul and Harvey Deitel

Contents

Chapter 24 and Appendices F–K are PDF documents posted online at
`www.informit.com/title/9780133439854`

Online Chapters and Appendices

Chapter 24 and Appendices F–K are PDF documents posted online at `www.informit.com/title/9780133439854`

[*Note:* The test drives for Windows and Linux are in Chapter 1.]

Preface

"The chief merit of language is clearness ..."
—Galen

Welcome to *C++11 for Programmers*! This book presents leading-edge computing technologies for software developers.

We focus on software engineering best practices. At the heart of the book is the Deitel signature "live-code approach"—concepts are presented in the context of complete working programs, rather than in code snippets. Each complete code example is accompanied by live sample executions. All the source code is available at

```
www.deitel.com/books/cpp11fp
```

As you read the book, if you have questions, we're easy to reach at

```
deitel@deitel.com
```

We'll respond promptly. For book updates, visit `www.deitel.com/books/cpp11fp`. Join our social media communities on Facebook (`www.deitel.com/DeitelFan`), Twitter (`@deitel`), Google+ (`gplus.to/deitel`) and LinkedIn (`bit.ly/DeitelLinkedIn`), and subscribe to the *Deitel® Buzz Online* newsletter (`www.deitel.com/newsletter/subscribe.html`).

Features

Here are the key features of *C++11 for Programmers*.

C++11 Standard

The new C++11 standard, published in 2011, motivated us to write *C++11 for Programmers.* Throughout the book, each new C++11 feature we discuss is marked with the "11" icon you see here in the margin. These are some of the key C++11 features of this new edition:

- ***Conforms to the new C++11 standard.*** Extensive coverage of many of the key new C++11 features (Fig. 1).
- ***Code thoroughly tested on three popular industrial-strength C++11 compilers.*** We tested the code examples on GNU™ C++ 4.7, Microsoft® Visual C++® 2012 and Apple® LLVM in Xcode® 4.5.
- ***Smart pointers.*** Smart pointers help you avoid dynamic memory management errors by providing additional functionality beyond that of built-in pointers. We discuss `unique_ptr` in Chapter 17, and `shared_ptr` and `weak_ptr` in Chapter 24.

C++11 features in *C++11 for Programmers*		
`all_of` algorithm `any_of` algorithm `array` container `auto` for type inference `begin`/`end` functions `cbegin`/`cend` container member functions Compiler fix for >> in template types `copy_if` algorithm `copy_n` algorithm `crbegin`/`crend` container member functions `decltype` Default type arguments in function templates `default`ed member functions Delegating constructors `delete`d member functions `explicit` conversion operators `final` classes `final` member functions `find_if_not` algorithm `forward_list` container Immutable keys in associative containers In-class initializers	Inheriting base-class constructors `insert` container member functions return iterators `is_heap` algorithm `is_heap_until` algorithm Keywords new in C++11 Lambda expressions List initialization of key–value `pair`s List initialization of `pair` objects List initialization of return values List initializing a dynamically allocated array List initializing a `vector` List initializers in constructor calls `long long int` type `min` and `max` algorithms with `initializer_list` parameters `minmax` algorithm `minmax_element` algorithm `move` algorithm Move assignment operators `move_backward` algorithm Move constructors `noexcept`	Non-deterministic random number generation `none_of` algorithm Numeric conversion functions `nullptr` `override` keyword Range-based `for` statement Regular expressions Rvalue references Scoped `enums` `shared_ptr` smart pointer `shrink_to_fit` `vector`/`deque` member function Specifying the type of an `enum`'s constants `static_assert` objects for file names `string` objects for file names `swap` non-member function Trailing return types `for` functions `tuple` variadic template `unique_ptr` smart pointer Unsigned `long long int` `weak_ptr` smart pointer

Fig. 1 | A sampling of C++11 features in *C++11 for Programmers*.

- ***Earlier coverage of template-based Standard Library containers, iterators and algorithms, enhanced with C++11 capabilities.*** We moved the treatment of Standard Library containers, iterators and algorithms from Chapter 20 in the previous edition to Chapters 15 and 16 and enhanced it with new C++11 features. The vast majority of your data structure needs can be fulfilled by *reusing* these Standard Library capabilities.
- ***Online Chapter 24, C++11: Additional Topics.*** In this chapter, we present additional C++11 topics. The new C++11 standard has been available since 2011, but not all C++ compilers have fully implemented the features. If all three of our key compilers already implemented a particular C++11 feature at the time we wrote this book, we generally integrated a discussion of that feature into the text with a live-code example. If any of these compilers had *not* implemented that feature, we included a bold italic heading followed by a brief discussion of the feature. Many of those discussions will be expanded in online Chapter 24 as the features are implemented. Placing the chapter online allows us to evolve it dynamically. This

chapter includes discussions of regular expressions, the `shared_ptr` and `weak_ptr` smart pointers, move semantics and more. You can access this chapter at:

```
www.informit.com/title/9780133439854
```

- ***Random Number generation, simulation and game playing.*** To help make programs more secure (see Secure C++ Programming on the next page), we now discuss C++11's new non-deterministic random-number generation capabilities.

Object-Oriented Programming

- ***Early-objects approach.*** The book introduces the basic concepts and terminology of object technology in Chapter 1. You'll develop your first customized C++ classes and objects in Chapter 3.
- ***C++ Standard Library*** **`string`*.*** C++ offers *two* types of strings—`string` class objects (which we begin using in Chapter 3) and C strings (from the C programming language). We've replaced most occurrences of C strings with instances of C++ class `string` to make programs more robust and eliminate many of the security problems of C strings. We discuss C strings later in the book to prepare you for working with the legacy code in industry. In new development, you should favor `string` objects.
- ***C++ Standard Library*** **`array`*.*** Our primary treatment of arrays now uses the Standard Library's `array` class template instead of built-in, C-style, pointer-based arrays. We also cover built-in arrays because they still have some uses in C++ and so that you'll be able to read legacy code. C++ offers *three* types of arrays—class templates `array` and `vector` (which we start using in Chapter 7) and C-style, pointer-based arrays which we discuss in Chapter 8. As appropriate, we use class template `array` and occasionally, class template `vector`, instead of C arrays throughout the book. In new development, you should favor class templates `array` and `vector`.
- ***Crafting valuable classes.*** A key goal of this book is to prepare you to build valuable reusable C++ classes. In the Chapter 10 case study, you'll build your own custom `Array` class. Chapter 10 begins with a test-drive of class template `string` so you can see an elegant use of operator overloading before you implement your own customized class with overloaded operators.
- ***Case studies in object-oriented programming.*** We provide case studies that span multiple sections and chapters and cover the software development lifecycle. These include the `GradeBook` class in Chapters 3–7, the `Time` class in Chapter 9 and the `Employee` class in Chapters 11–12. Chapter 12 contains a detailed diagram and explanation of how C++ can implement polymorphism, `virtual` functions and dynamic binding "under the hood."
- ***Optional case study: Using the UML to develop an object-oriented design and C++ implementation of an ATM.*** The UML™ (Unified Modeling Language™) is the industry-standard graphical language for modeling object-oriented systems. We introduce the UML in the early chapters. Chapters 22 and 23 include an *optional* case study on object-oriented design using the UML. We design and implement the software for a simple automated teller machine (ATM). We analyze a typical requirements document that specifies the system to be built. We determine the classes

needed to implement that system, the attributes the classes need to have, the behaviors the classes need to exhibit and we specify how the classes must interact with one another to meet the system requirements. From the design we produce a complete C++ implementation. Readers often report that the case study "ties it all together" and helps them achieve a deeper understanding of object orientation.

- ***Exception handling.*** We integrate basic exception handling *early* in the book. You can easily pull more detailed material forward from Chapter 17, Exception Handling: A Deeper Look.
- ***Key programming paradigms.*** We discuss *object-oriented programming* and *generic programming*.

Pedagogic Features

- ***Examples.*** We include a broad range of example programs selected from computer science, business, simulation, game playing and other topics.
- ***Illustrations and figures.*** Abundant tables, line drawings, UML diagrams, programs and program outputs are included.

Other Features

- ***Pointers.*** We provide thorough coverage of the built-in pointer capabilities and the intimate relationship among built-in pointers, C strings and built-in arrays.
- ***Debugger appendices.*** We provide three debugger appendices—Appendix H, Using the Visual Studio Debugger, Appendix I, Using the GNU C++ Debugger and Appendix J, Using the Xcode Debugger.

Secure C++ Programming

It's difficult to build industrial-strength systems that stand up to attacks from viruses, worms, and other forms of "malware." Today, via the Internet, such attacks can be instantaneous and global in scope. Building security into software from the beginning of the development cycle can greatly reduce vulnerabilities.

The CERT® Coordination Center (`www.cert.org`) was created to analyze and respond promptly to attacks. CERT—the Computer Emergency Response Team—is a government-funded organization within the Carnegie Mellon University Software Engineering Institute™. CERT publishes and promotes secure coding standards for various popular programming languages to help software developers implement industrial-strength systems that avoid the programming practices that leave systems open to attacks.

We'd like to thank Robert C. Seacord, Secure Coding Manager at CERT and an adjunct professor in the Carnegie Mellon University School of Computer Science. Mr. Seacord was a technical reviewer for our book, *C How to Program, 7/e*, where he scrutinized our C programs from a security standpoint, recommending that we adhere to the *CERT C Secure Coding Standard*.

We've done the same for *C++11 for Programmers*, adhering to key *CERT C++ Secure Coding Standard* guidelines (as appropriate for a book at this level), which you can find at:

```
www.securecoding.cert.org
```

We were pleased to discover that we've already been recommending many of these coding practices in our books since the early 1990s. If you'll be building industrial-strength C++ systems, *Secure Coding in C and C++, Second Edition* (Robert Seacord, Addison-Wesley Professional) is a must read.

Training Approach

C++11 for Programmers stresses program clarity and concentrates on building well-engineered software.

Live-Code Approach. The book includes hundreds of "live-code" examples—each new concept is presented in the context of a complete working C++ program that is immediately followed by one or more actual executions showing the program's inputs and outputs.

Syntax Shading. For readability, we syntax shade the code, similar to the way most integrated-development environments and code editors syntax color the code. Our syntax-shading conventions are:

```
comments appear like this
keywords appear like this
constants and literal values appear like this
all other code appears in black
```

Code Highlighting. We place light-gray rectangles around each program's key code segments.

Using Fonts for Emphasis. We place the key terms and the index's page reference for each defining occurrence in ***bold italic*** text for easier reference. We emphasize on-screen components in the **bold Helvetica** font (e.g., the **File** menu) and emphasize C++ program text in the `Lucida` font (e.g., `int x = 5`).

Web Access. All of the source-code examples can be downloaded from:

```
www.deitel.com/books/cpp11fp
```

Objectives. The chapter opening quotations are followed by a list of chapter objectives.

Programming Tips. We include hundreds of programming tips to help you focus on important aspects of program development. These tips and practices represent the best we've gleaned from a combined eight decades of programming and teaching experience.

Good Programming Practice

The Good Programming Practices *call attention to techniques that will help you produce programs that are clearer, more understandable and more maintainable.*

Common Programming Error

Pointing out these Common Programming Errors *reduces the likelihood that you'll make them.*

Error-Prevention Tip

These tips contain suggestions for exposing and removing bugs from your programs; many of the tips describe aspects of C++ that prevent bugs from getting into your programs.

Performance Tip

These tips highlight opportunities for making your programs run faster or minimizing the amount of memory that they occupy.

Portability Tip

The Portability Tips *help you write code that will run on a variety of platforms.*

Software Engineering Observation

The Software Engineering Observations *highlight architectural and design issues that affect the construction of software systems, especially large-scale systems.*

Online Chapter and Appendices

The following chapter and appendices are available online:

- Chapter 24, C++11: Additional Features
- Appendix F, C Legacy Code Topics
- Appendix G, UML 2: Additional Diagram Types
- Appendix H, Using the Visual Studio Debugger
- Appendix I, Using the GNU C++ Debugger
- Appendix J, Using the Xcode Debugger
- Appendix K, Test Driving a C++ Program on Mac OS X

To access the online chapter and appendices, go to:

```
www.informit.com/register
```

You must register for an an InformIT account and then login. After you've logged into your account, you'll see the **Register a Product** box. Enter the book's ISBN (9780133439854) to access the page with the online chapter and appendices.

Obtaining the Software Used in *C++11 for Programmers*

We wrote the code examples in *C++11 for Programmers* using the following C++ development tools:

- Microsoft's free Visual Studio Express 2012 for Windows Desktop, which includes Visual C++ and other Microsoft development tools. This runs on Windows 7 and 8 and is available for download at

```
www.microsoft.com/express
```

- GNU's free GNU C++ (`gcc.gnu.org/install/binaries.html`), which is already installed on most Linux systems and can also be installed on Mac OS X and Windows systems.
- Apple's free Xcode, which OS X users can download from the Mac App Store.

C++11 Fundamentals: Parts I, II, III and IV LiveLessons Video Training Product

Our *C++11 Fundamentals: Parts I, II, III and IV* LiveLessons video training product shows you what you need to know to start building robust, powerful software with C++. It includes 20+ hours of expert training synchronized with *C++11 for Programmers*. For additional information about Deitel LiveLessons video products, visit

```
www.deitel.com/livelessons
```

or contact us at `deitel@deitel.com`. You can also access our LiveLessons videos if you have a subscription to Safari Books Online (`www.safaribooksonline.com`). These LiveLessons will be available in the Summer of 2013.

Acknowledgments

We'd like to thank Abbey Deitel and Barbara Deitel of Deitel & Associates, Inc. for long hours devoted to this project. Abbey co-authored Chapter 1 and this Preface, and she and Barbara painstakingly researched the new capabilities of C++11.

We're fortunate to have worked on this project with the dedicated publishing professionals at Prentice Hall/Pearson. We appreciate the extraordinary efforts and mentorship of our friend and professional colleague Mark L. Taub, Editor-in-Chief of Pearson Technology Group. Carole Snyder did a great job recruiting distinguished members of the C++ community to review the manuscript. Chuti Prasertsith designed the cover with creativity and precision—we gave him our vision for the cover and he made it happen. John Fuller does a superb job managing the production of all of our Deitel Developer Series books and LiveLessons video products.

Reviewers

We wish to acknowledge the efforts of the reviewers whose constructive criticisms helped us shape the recent editions of this content. They scrutinized the text and the programs and provided countless suggestions for improving the presentation: Dean Michael Berris (Google, Member ISO C++ Committee), Danny Kalev (C++ expert, certified system analyst and former member of the C++ Standards Committee), Linda M. Krause (Elmhurst College), James P. McNellis (Microsoft Corporation), Robert C. Seacord (Secure Coding Manager at SEI/CERT, author of *Secure Coding in C and C++*); José Antonio González Seco (Parliament of Andalusia), Virginia Bailey (Jackson State University), Thomas J. Borrelli (Rochester Institute of Technology), Ed Brey (Kohler Co.), Chris Cox (Adobe Systems), Gregory Dai (eBay), Peter J. DePasquale (The College of New Jersey), John Dibling (SpryWare), Susan Gauch (University of Arkansas), Doug Gregor (Apple, Inc.), Jack Hagemeister (Washington State University), Williams M. Higdon (University of Indiana), Anne B. Horton (Lockheed Martin), Terrell Hull (Logicalis Integration Solutions), Ed James-Beckham (Borland), Wing-Ning Li (University of Arkansas), Dean Mathias (Utah State University), Robert A. McLain (Tidewater Community College), Robert Myers (Florida State University), Gavin Osborne (Saskatchewan Institute of Applied Science and Technology), Amar Raheja (California State Polytechnic University, Pomona), April Reagan (Microsoft), Raymond Stephenson (Microsoft), Dave Topham (Ohlone College), Anthony Williams (author and C++ Standards Committee member) and Chad Willwerth (University Washington, Tacoma).

As you read the book, we'd sincerely appreciate your comments, criticisms and suggestions for improving the text. Please address all correspondence to:

```
deitel@deitel.com
```

We'll respond promptly. We enjoyed writing *C++11 for Programmers.* We hope you enjoy reading it!

Paul Deitel
Harvey Deitel

About the Authors

Paul Deitel, CEO and Chief Technical Officer of Deitel & Associates, Inc., is a graduate of MIT, where he studied Information Technology. Through Deitel & Associates, Inc., he has delivered hundreds of programming courses to industry, government and military clients, including Cisco, IBM, Siemens, Sun Microsystems, Dell, Fidelity, NASA at the Kennedy Space Center, the National Severe Storm Laboratory, White Sands Missile Range, Rogue Wave Software, Boeing, SunGard Higher Education, Nortel Networks, Puma, iRobot, Invensys and many more. He and his co-author, Dr. Harvey M. Deitel, are the world's best-selling programming-language textbook/professional book/video authors.

Dr. Harvey Deitel, Chairman and Chief Strategy Officer of Deitel & Associates, Inc., has more than 50 years of experience in computing. Dr. Deitel earned B.S. and M.S. degrees in Electrical Engineering from MIT and a Ph.D. in Mathematics from Boston University. In the 1960s, through Advanced Computer Techniques and Computer Usage Corporation, he worked on the teams building various IBM operating systems. In the 1970s, he built commercial software systems. He has extensive college teaching experience, including earning tenure and serving as the Chairman of the Computer Science Department at Boston College before founding Deitel & Associates, Inc., in 1991 with his son, Paul Deitel. The Deitels' publications have earned international recognition, with translations published in Chinese, Korean, Japanese, German, Russian, Spanish, French, Polish, Italian, Portuguese, Greek, Urdu and Turkish. Dr. Deitel has delivered hundreds of programming courses to corporate, academic, government and military clients.

Deitel® Dive-Into® Series Corporate Training

Deitel & Associates, Inc., founded by Paul Deitel and Harvey Deitel, is an internationally recognized authoring and corporate training organization, specializing in computer programming languages, object technology, mobile app development and Internet and web software technology. The company's clients include many of the world's largest corporations, government agencies, branches of the military, and academic institutions. The company offers instructor-led training courses delivered at client sites worldwide on major programming languages and platforms, including C++, Visual C++®, C, Java™, Visual C#®, Visual Basic®, XML®, Python®, object technology, Internet and web programming, Android app development, Objective-C and iOS app development and a growing list of additional programming and software development courses.

Through its 37-year publishing partnership with Prentice Hall/Pearson, Deitel & Associates, Inc., publishes leading-edge programming professional books, college textbooks and *LiveLessons* video courses. Deitel & Associates, Inc. and the authors can be reached at:

```
deitel@deitel.com
```

To learn more about Deitel *Dive-Into® Series* Corporate Training curriculum, visit:

```
www.deitel.com/training
```

To request a proposal for worldwide on-site, instructor-led training at your organization, e-mail `deitel@deitel.com`.

Individuals wishing to purchase Deitel books and *LiveLessons* video training can do so through `www.deitel.com`. Bulk orders by corporations, the government, the military and academic institutions should be placed directly with Pearson. For more information, visit

```
www.informit.com/store/sales.aspx
```

1

Introduction

Objectives

In this chapter you'll:

- Review object-technology concepts.
- Learn the elements of a typical C++ program-development environment.
- Test-drive a C++ application.

Outline

1.1 Introduction

Welcome to C++—a powerful computer programming language that's appropriate for technically oriented people with little or no programming experience, and for experienced programmers to use in building substantial information systems.

You'll learn *object-oriented programming in C++*. You'll create many *C++ software objects* that model *things* in the real-world.

11 C++ is one of today's most popular software development languages. This text provides an introduction to programming in C++11—the latest version standardized through the **International Organization for Standardization** (**ISO**) and the **International Electrotechnical Commission** (**IEC**).

1.2 C++

C++ evolved from C, which was developed by Dennis Ritchie at Bell Laboratories. C is available for most computers and is hardware independent. With careful design, it's possible to write C programs that are **portable** to most computers.

The widespread use of C with various kinds of computers (sometimes called **hardware platforms**) unfortunately led to many variations. A standard version of C was needed. The American National Standards Institute (ANSI) cooperated with the International Organization for Standardization (ISO) to standardize C worldwide; the joint standard document was published in 1990 and is referred to as *ANSI/ISO 9899: 1990.*

C11 is the latest ANSI standard for the C programming language. It was developed to evolve the C language to keep pace with increasingly powerful hardware and ever more demanding user requirements. C11 also makes C more consistent with C++. For more information on C and C11, see our book *C How to Program, 7/e* and our C Resource Center (located at `www.deitel.com/C`).

C++, an extension of C, was developed by Bjarne Stroustrup in 1979 at Bell Laboratories. Originally called "C with Classes", it was renamed to C++ in the early 1980s. C++ provides a number of features that "spruce up" the C language, but more importantly, it provides capabilities for object-oriented programming.

You'll begin developing customized, reusable classes and objects in Chapter 3, Introduction to Classes, Objects and Strings. The book is object oriented, where appropriate, from the start and throughout the text.

We also provide an *optional* automated teller machine (ATM) case study in Chapters 22–23, which contains a complete C++ implementation. The case study presents a carefully paced introduction to object-oriented design using the UML—an industry-standard graphical modeling language for developing object-oriented systems. We guide you through a friendly design experience intended for the novice.

C++ Standard Library

C++ programs consist of pieces called **classes** and **functions.** You can program each piece yourself, but most C++ programmers take advantage of the rich collections of classes and functions in the **C++ Standard Library**. Thus, there are really two parts to learning the C++ "world." The first is learning the C++ language itself; the second is learning how to use the classes and functions in the C++ Standard Library. We discuss many of these classes and functions. Most compiler vendors provide online C++ Standard Library reference documentation. You can also learn about the C++ Standard library at:

```
www.cppreference.com
```

In addition to the C++ Standard Library, many special-purpose class libraries are supplied by independent software vendors and by the open-source community.

Software Engineering Observation 1.1

Use a "building-block" approach to create programs. Avoid reinventing the wheel. Use existing pieces wherever possible. Called ***software reuse****, this practice is central to object-oriented programming.*

Software Engineering Observation 1.2

When programming in C++, you typically will use the following building blocks: classes and functions from the C++ Standard Library, classes and functions you and your colleagues create and classes and functions from various popular third-party libraries.

The advantage of creating your own functions and classes is that you'll know exactly how they work. You'll be able to examine the C++ code. The disadvantage is the time-consuming and complex effort that goes into designing, developing and maintaining new functions and classes that are correct and that operate efficiently.

Performance Tip 1.1

Using C++ Standard Library functions and classes instead of writing your own versions can improve program performance, because they're written carefully to perform efficiently. This technique also shortens program development time.

Portability Tip 1.1

Using C++ Standard Library functions and classes instead of writing your own improves program portability, because they're included in every C++ implementation.

1.3 Object Technology

Building software quickly, correctly and economically remains an elusive goal at a time when demands for new and more powerful software are soaring. *Objects*, or more precisely—as we'll see in Chapter 3—the *classes* objects come from, are essentially *reusable* software components. There are date objects, time objects, audio objects, video objects, automobile objects, people objects, etc. Almost any *noun* can be reasonably represented as a software object in terms of *attributes* (e.g., name, color and size) and *behaviors* (e.g., calculating, moving and communicating). Software developers have discovered that using a modular, object-oriented design-and-implementation approach can make software-development groups much more productive than was possible with earlier techniques—object-oriented programs are often easier to understand, correct and modify.

The Automobile as an Object

Let's begin with a simple analogy. Suppose you want to *drive a car and make it go faster by pressing its accelerator pedal.* What must happen before you can do this? Well, before you can drive a car, someone has to *design* it. A car typically begins as engineering drawings, similar to the *blueprints* that describe the design of a house. These drawings include the design for an accelerator pedal. The pedal *hides* from the driver the complex mechanisms that actually make the car go faster, just as the brake pedal hides the mechanisms that slow the car, and the steering wheel *hides* the mechanisms that turn the car. This enables people with little or no knowledge of how engines, braking and steering mechanisms work to drive a car easily.

Before you can drive a car, it must be *built* from the engineering drawings that describe it. A completed car has an *actual* accelerator pedal to make the car go faster, but even that's not enough—the car won't accelerate on its own (hopefully!), so the driver must *press* the pedal to accelerate the car.

Member Functions and Classes

Let's use our car example to introduce some key object-oriented programming concepts. Performing a task in a program requires a **member function**. The member function houses the program statements that actually perform its task. It hides these statements from its user, just as the accelerator pedal of a car hides from the driver the mechanisms of making the car go faster. In C++, we create a program unit called a **class** to house the set of member functions that perform the class's tasks. For example, a class that represents a bank account might contain one member function to *deposit* money to an account, another to *withdraw* money from an account and a third to *inquire* what the account's current balance is. A class is similar in concept to a car's engineering drawings, which house the design of an accelerator pedal, steering wheel, and so on.

Instantiation

Just as someone has to *build a car* from its engineering drawings before you can actually drive a car, you must *build an object* from a class before a program can perform the tasks that the class's methods define. The process of doing this is called *instantiation.* An object is then referred to as an **instance** of its class.

Reuse

Just as a car's engineering drawings can be *reused* many times to build many cars, you can *reuse* a class many times to build many objects. Reuse of existing classes when building new classes and programs saves time and effort. Reuse also helps you build more reliable and effective systems, because existing classes and components often have gone through extensive *testing, debugging* and *performance tuning.* Just as the notion of *interchangeable parts* was crucial to the Industrial Revolution, reusable classes are crucial to the software revolution that has been spurred by object technology.

Messages and Member Function Calls

When you drive a car, pressing its gas pedal sends a *message* to the car to perform a task—that is, to go faster. Similarly, you *send messages to an object*. Each message is implemented as a **member function call** that tells a member function of the object to perform its task. For example, a program might call a particular bank account object's *deposit* member function to increase the account's balance.

Attributes and Data Members

A car, besides having capabilities to accomplish tasks, also has *attributes*, such as its color, its number of doors, the amount of gas in its tank, its current speed and its record of total miles driven (i.e., its odometer reading). Like its capabilities, the car's attributes are represented as part of its design in its engineering diagrams (which, for example, include an odometer and a fuel gauge). As you drive an actual car, these attributes are carried along with the car. Every car maintains its *own* attributes. For example, each car knows how much gas is in its own gas tank, but *not* how much is in the tanks of *other* cars.

An object, similarly, has attributes that it carries along as it's used in a program. These attributes are specified as part of the object's class. For example, a bank account object has a *balance attribute* that represents the amount of money in the account. Each bank account object knows the balance in the account it represents, but *not* the balances of the *other* accounts in the bank. Attributes are specified by the class's **data members.**

Encapsulation

Classes **encapsulate** (i.e., wrap) attributes and member functions into objects—an object's attributes and member functions are intimately related. Objects may communicate with one another, but they're normally not allowed to know how other objects are implemented—implementation details are *hidden* within the objects themselves. This **information hiding**, as we'll see, is crucial to good software engineering.

Inheritance

A new class of objects can be created quickly and conveniently by **inheritance**—the new class absorbs the characteristics of an existing class, possibly customizing them and adding unique characteristics of its own. In our car analogy, an object of class "convertible" certainly *is an* object of the more *general* class "automobile," but more *specifically*, the roof can be raised or lowered.

Object-Oriented Analysis and Design (OOAD)

Soon you'll be writing programs in C++. How will you create the **code** (i.e., the program instructions) for your programs? Perhaps, like many programmers, you'll simply turn on your computer and start typing. This approach may work for small programs (like the ones we present in the early chapters of the book), but what if you were asked to create a software system to control thousands of automated teller machines for a major bank? Or suppose you were asked to work on a team of thousands of software developers building the next U.S. air traffic control system? For projects so large and complex, you should not simply sit down and start writing programs.

To create the best solutions, you should follow a detailed **analysis** process for determining your project's **requirements** (i.e., defining *what* the system is supposed to do) and developing a **design** that satisfies them (i.e., deciding *how* the system should do it). Ideally, you'd go through this process and carefully review the design (and have your design reviewed by other software professionals) before writing any code. If this process involves analyzing and designing your system from an object-oriented point of view, it's called an **object-oriented analysis and design (OOAD) process**. Languages like C++ are object oriented. Programming in such a language, called **object-oriented programming (OOP)**, allows you to implement an object-oriented design as a working system.

The UML (Unified Modeling Language)
Although many different OOAD processes exist, a single graphical language for communicating the results of *any* OOAD process has come into wide use. This language, known as the Unified Modeling Language (UML), is now the most widely used graphical scheme for modeling object-oriented systems. We present our first UML diagrams in Chapters 3 and 4, then use them in our deeper treatment of object-oriented programming through Chapter 12. In our *optional* ATM Software Engineering Case Study in Chapters 22–23 we present a simple subset of the UML's features as we guide you through an object-oriented design experience.

1.4 Typical C++ Development Environment

C++ systems generally consist of three parts: a program development environment, the language and the C++ Standard Library. C++ programs typically go through six phases: edit, preprocess, compile, link, load and execute. The following discussion explains a typical C++ program development environment.

Phase 1: Editing a Program
Phase 1 consists of editing a file with an *editor program*, normally known simply as an *editor* (Fig. 1.1). You type a C++ program (typically referred to as **source code**) using the editor, make any necessary corrections and save the program on a secondary storage device, such as your hard drive. C++ source code filenames often end with the `.cpp`, `.cxx`, `.cc` or `.C` extensions (note that `C` is in uppercase) which indicate that a file contains C++ source code. See the documentation for your C++ compiler for more information on file-name extensions.

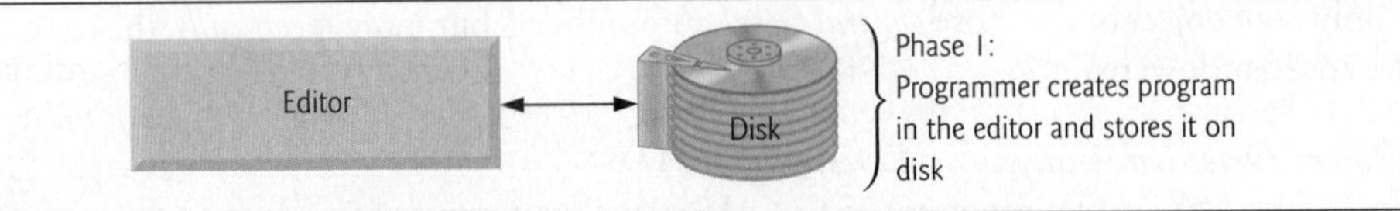

Fig. 1.1 | Typical C++ development environment—editing phase.

Two editors widely used on Linux systems are `vi` and `emacs`. C++ software packages for Microsoft Windows such as Microsoft Visual C++ (`microsoft.com/express`) have editors integrated into the programming environment. You can also use a simple text editor, such as Notepad in Windows, to write your C++ code.

For organizations that develop substantial information systems, **integrated development environments (IDEs)** are available from many major software suppliers. IDEs provide tools that support the software-development process, including editors for writing and editing programs and debuggers for locating **logic errors**—errors that cause programs to execute incorrectly. Popular IDEs include Microsoft® Visual Studio 2012 Express Edition, Dev C++, NetBeans, Eclipse, Apple's Xcode and CodeLite.

Phase 2: Preprocessing a C++ Program

In Phase 2, you give the command to **compile** the program (Fig. 1.2). In a C++ system, a **preprocessor** program executes automatically before the compiler's translation phase begins (so we call preprocessing Phase 2 and compiling Phase 3). The C++ preprocessor obeys commands called **preprocessing directives,** which indicate that certain manipulations are to be performed on the program before compilation. These manipulations usually include other text files to be compiled, and perform various text replacements. The most common preprocessing directives are discussed in the early chapters; a detailed discussion of preprocessor features appears in Appendix E, Preprocessor.

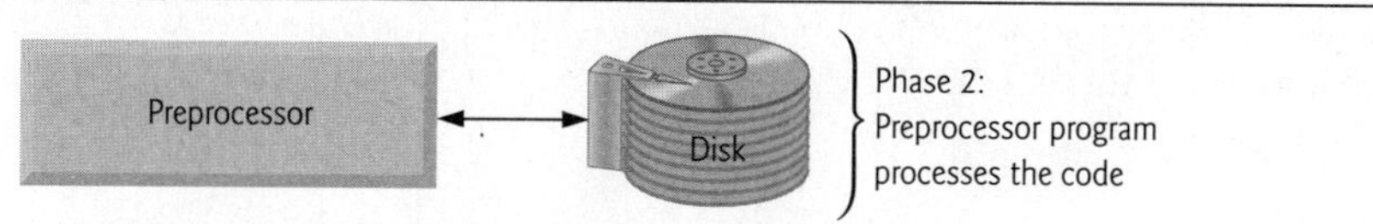

Fig. 1.2 | Typical C++ development environment—preprocessor phase.

Phase 3: Compiling a C++ Program

In Phase 3, the compiler translates the C++ program into machine-language code—also referred to as object code (Fig. 1.3).

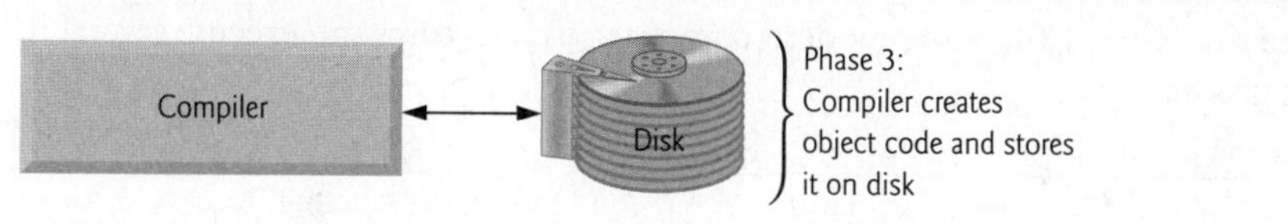

Fig. 1.3 | Typical C++ development environment—compilation phase.

Phase 4: Linking

Phase 4 is called **linking.** C++ programs typically contain references to functions and data defined elsewhere, such as in the standard libraries or in the private libraries of groups of programmers working on a particular project (Fig. 1.4). The object code produced by the C++ compiler typically contains "holes" due to these missing parts. A **linker** links the object code with the code for the missing functions to produce an **executable program** (with no missing pieces). If the program compiles and links correctly, an executable image is produced.

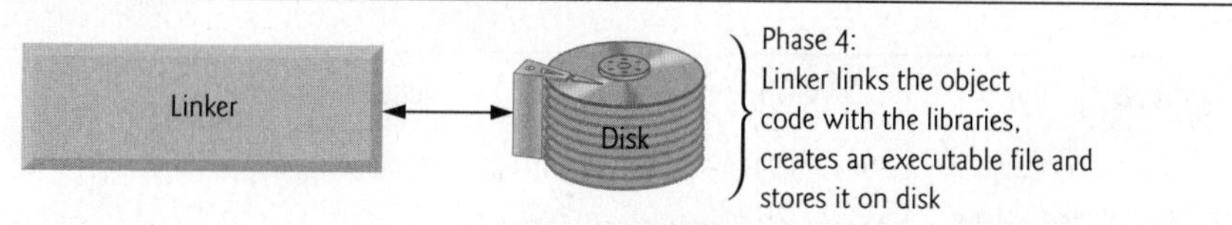

Fig. 1.4 | Typical C++ development environment—linking phase.

Phase 5: Loading

Phase 5 is called **loading.** Before a program can be executed, it must first be placed in memory (Fig. 1.5). This is done by the **loader,** which takes the executable image from disk and transfers it to memory. Additional components from shared libraries that support the program are also loaded.

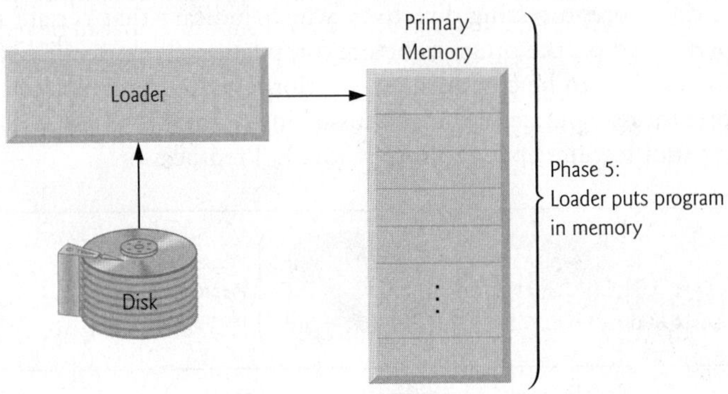

Fig. 1.5 | Typical C++ development environment—loading phase.

Phase 6: Execution

Finally, the computer, under the control of its CPU, **executes** the program one instruction at a time (Fig. 1.6). Some modern computer architectures can execute several instructions in parallel.

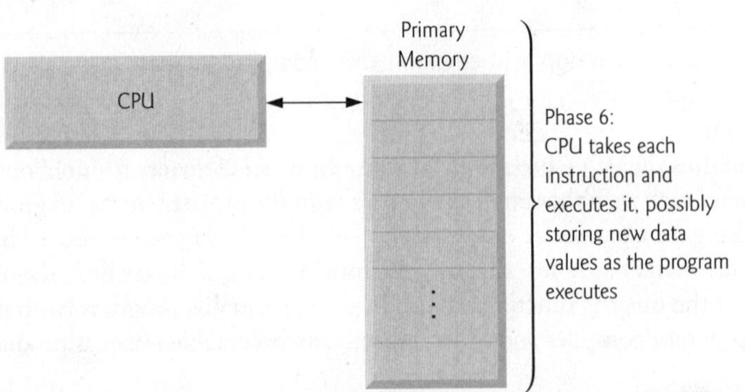

Fig. 1.6 | Typical C++ development environment—execution phase.

Problems That May Occur at Execution Time

Programs might not work on the first try. Each of the preceding phases can fail because of various errors that we'll discuss throughout this book. For example, an executing program might try to divide by zero (an illegal operation for integer arithmetic in C++). This would cause the C++ program to display an error message. If this occurred, you'd have to return to the edit phase, make the necessary corrections and proceed through the remaining phases again to determine that the corrections fixed the problem(s). [*Note:* Most programs in C++ input or output data. Certain C++ functions take their input from `cin` (the **standard input stream**; pronounced "see-in"), which is normally the keyboard, but `cin` can be redirected to another device. Data is often output to `cout` (the **standard output stream**; pronounced "see-out"), which is normally the computer screen, but `cout` can be redirected to another device. When we say that a program prints a result, we normally mean that the result is displayed on a screen. Data may be output to other devices, such as disks and hardcopy printers. There is also a **standard error stream** referred to as **cerr.** The `cerr` stream (normally connected to the screen) is used for displaying error messages.

Common Programming Error 1.1

*Errors such as division by zero occur as a program runs, so they're called **runtime errors** or **execution-time errors. Fatal runtime errors** cause programs to terminate immediately without having successfully performed their jobs. **Nonfatal runtime errors** allow programs to run to completion, often producing incorrect results.*

1.5 Test-Driving a C++ Application

In this section, you'll run and interact with your first C++ application. You'll begin by running an entertaining guess-the-number game, which picks a number from 1 to 1000 and prompts you to guess it. If your guess is correct, the game ends. If your guess is not correct, the application indicates whether your guess is higher or lower than the correct number. There is no limit on the number of guesses you can make. [*Note:* Normally this application randomly selects the correct answer as you execute the program. This test-drive version of the application uses the same correct answer every time the program executes (though this may vary by compiler), so you can use the *same* guesses we use in this section and see the *same* results as we walk you through interacting with your first C++ application.]

We'll demonstrate running a C++ application using the Windows **Command Prompt** and a shell on Linux. The application runs similarly on both platforms. Many development environments are available in which you can compile, build and run C++ applications, such as GNU™ C++, Microsoft® Visual C++®, Apple® Xcode®, NetBeans®, Eclipse™, etc.

We use fonts to distinguish between features you see on the screen (e.g., the **Command Prompt**) and elements that are not directly related to the screen. We emphasize screen features like titles and menus (e.g., the **File** menu) in a semibold **sans-serif Helvetica** font and emphasize filenames, text displayed by an application and values you should enter into an application (e.g., `GuessNumber` or `500`) in a `sans-serif Lucida` font. As you've noticed, the **defining occurrence** of each term is set in bold type. For the figures in this section, we point out significant parts of the application. To make these features more visible, we've modified the background color of the **Command Prompt** window (for the Windows test drive only). To modify the **Command Prompt** colors on your system, open a **Command Prompt** by selecting **Start > All Programs > Accessories > Command Prompt**, then right click the title bar and select **Properties.** In the **"Command Prompt" Properties** dialog box that appears, click the **Colors** tab, and select your preferred text and background colors.

Running a C++ Application from the Windows Command Prompt

1. ***Checking your setup.*** It's important to read the Before You Begin section at `www.deitel.com/books/cpp11fp/` to make sure that you've copied the book's examples to your hard drive correctly.
2. ***Locating the completed application.*** Open a **Command Prompt** window. To change to the directory for the completed **GuessNumber** application, type **`cd C:\examples\ch01\GuessNumber\Windows`**, then press *Enter* (Fig. 1.7). The command `cd` is used to change directories.

Fig. 1.7 | Opening a **Command Prompt** window and changing the directory.

3. ***Running the*** **GuessNumber** ***application.*** Now that you are in the directory that contains the **GuessNumber** application, type the command **`GuessNumber`** (Fig. 1.8) and press *Enter*. [*Note:* `GuessNumber.exe` is the actual name of the application; however, Windows assumes the `.exe` extension by default.]

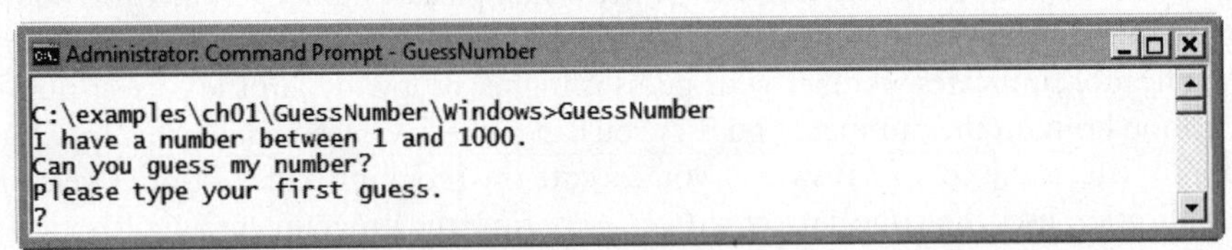

Fig. 1.8 | Running the **GuessNumber** application.

4. ***Entering your first guess.*** The application displays `"Please type your first guess."`, then displays a question mark (`?`) as a prompt on the next line (Fig. 1.8). At the prompt, enter **`500`** (Fig. 1.9).

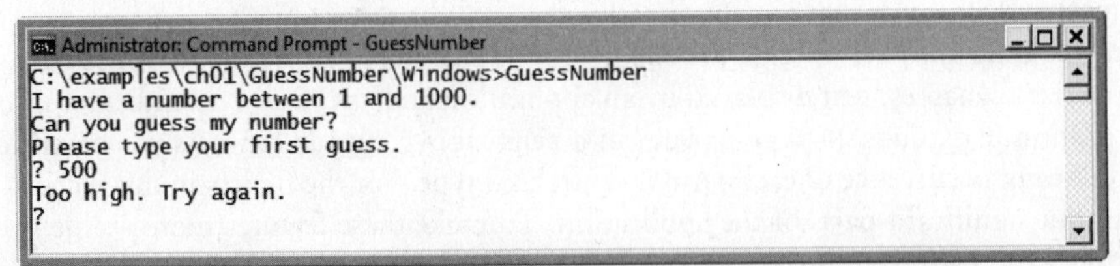

Fig. 1.9 | Entering your first guess.

5. ***Entering another guess.*** The application displays `"Too high. Try again."`, meaning that the value you entered is greater than the number the application chose as

the correct guess. So, you should enter a lower number for your next guess. At the prompt, enter **250** (Fig. 1.10). The application again displays "Too high. Try again.", because the value you entered is still greater than the number that the application chose as the correct guess.

```
Administrator: Command Prompt - GuessNumber
C:\examples\ch01\GuessNumber\Windows>GuessNumber
I have a number between 1 and 1000.
Can you guess my number?
Please type your first guess.
? 500
Too high. Try again.
? 250
Too high. Try again.
?
```

Fig. 1.10 | Entering a second guess and receiving feedback.

6. ***Entering additional guesses.*** Continue to play the game by entering values until you guess the correct number. The application will display "Excellent! You guessed the number!" (Fig. 1.11).

```
Administrator: Command Prompt - GuessNumber
Too high. Try again.
? 125
Too low. Try again.
? 187
Too high. Try again.
? 156
Too high. Try again.
? 140
Too high. Try again.
? 132
Too high. Try again.
? 128
Too low. Try again.
? 130
Too low. Try again.
? 131

Excellent! You guessed the number!
Would you like to play again (y or n)?
```

Fig. 1.11 | Entering additional guesses and guessing the correct number.

7. ***Playing the game again or exiting the application.*** After you guess correctly, the application asks if you'd like to play another game (Fig. 1.11). At the "Would you like to play again (y or n)?" prompt, entering the one character **y** causes the application to choose a new number and displays the message "Please type your first guess." followed by a question mark prompt (Fig. 1.12) so you can make your first guess in the new game. Entering the character **n** ends the application and returns you to the application's directory at the **Command Prompt** (Fig. 1.13). Each time you execute this application from the beginning (i.e., *Step 3*), it will choose the same numbers for you to guess.

8. *Close the* Command Prompt *window.*

```
Administrator: Command Prompt - GuessNumber

Excellent! You guessed the number!
Would you like to play again (y or n)? y

I have a number between 1 and 1000.
Can you guess my number?
Please type your first guess.
?
```

Fig. 1.12 | Playing the game again.

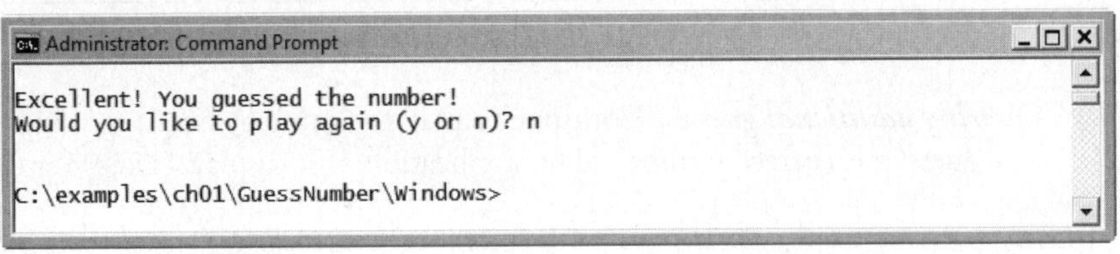

Fig. 1.13 | Exiting the game.

Running a C++ Application Using GNU C++ with Linux

For this test drive, we assume that you know how to copy the examples into your home directory. Also, for the figures in this section, we use a bold highlight to point out the user input required by each step. The prompt in the shell on our system uses the tilde (~) character to represent the home directory, and each prompt ends with the dollar sign ($) character. The prompt will vary among Linux systems.

1. ***Locating the completed application.*** From a Linux shell, change to the completed **GuessNumber** application directory (Fig. 1.14) by typing

```
cd Examples/ch01/GuessNumber/GNU_Linux
```

then pressing *Enter*. The command `cd` is used to change directories.

```
~$ cd examples/ch01/GuessNumber/GNU_Linux
~/examples/ch01/GuessNumber/GNU_Linux$
```

Fig. 1.14 | Changing to the **GuessNumber** application's directory.

2. ***Compiling the*** GuessNumber ***application.*** To run an application on the GNU C++ compiler, you must first compile it by typing

```
g++ GuessNumber.cpp -o GuessNumber
```

as in Fig. 1.15. This command compiles the application and produces an executable file called `GuessNumber`.

```
~/examples/ch01/GuessNumber/GNU_Linux$ g++ GuessNumber.cpp -o GuessNumber
~/examples/ch01/GuessNumber/GNU_Linux$
```

Fig. 1.15 | Compiling the **GuessNumber** application using the g++ command.

3. ***Running the*** **GuessNumber** ***application.*** To run the executable file `GuessNumber`, type `./GuessNumber` at the next prompt, then press *Enter* (Fig. 1.16).

```
~/examples/ch01/GuessNumber/GNU_Linux$ ./GuessNumber
I have a number between 1 and 1000.
Can you guess my number?
Please type your first guess.
?
```

Fig. 1.16 | Running the **GuessNumber** application.

4. ***Entering your first guess.*** The application displays `"Please type your first guess."`, then displays a question mark (?) as a prompt on the next line (Fig. 1.16). At the prompt, enter **500** (Fig. 1.17). [*Note:* This is the same application that we modified and test-drove for Windows, but the outputs could vary based on the compiler being used.]

```
~/examples/ch01/GuessNumber/GNU_Linux$ ./GuessNumber
I have a number between 1 and 1000.
Can you guess my number?
Please type your first guess.
? 500
Too high. Try again.
?
```

Fig. 1.17 | Entering an initial guess.

5. ***Entering another guess.*** The application displays `"Too high. Try again."`, meaning that the value you entered is greater than the number the application chose as the correct guess (Fig. 1.17). At the next prompt, enter **250** (Fig. 1.18). This time the application displays `"Too low. Try again."`, because the value you entered is less than the correct guess.

```
~/examples/ch01/GuessNumber/GNU_Linux$ ./GuessNumber
I have a number between 1 and 1000.
Can you guess my number?
Please type your first guess.
? 500
Too high. Try again.
? 250
Too low. Try again.
?
```

Fig. 1.18 | Entering a second guess and receiving feedback.

6. ***Entering additional guesses.*** Continue to play the game (Fig. 1.19) by entering values until you guess the correct number. When you guess correctly, the application displays "`Excellent! You guessed the number.`"

```
Too low. Try again.
? 375
Too low. Try again.
? 437
Too high. Try again.
? 406
Too high. Try again.
? 391
Too high. Try again.
? 383
Too low. Try again.
? 387
Too high. Try again.
? 385
Too high. Try again.
? 384
Excellent! You guessed the number.
Would you like to play again (y or n)?
```

Fig. 1.19 | Entering additional guesses and guessing the correct number.

7. ***Playing the game again or exiting the application.*** After you guess the correct number, the application asks if you'd like to play another game. At the "`Would you like to play again (y or n)?`" prompt, entering the one character **`y`** causes the application to choose a new number and displays the message "`Please type your first guess.`" followed by a question mark prompt (Fig. 1.20) so you can make your first guess in the new game. Entering the character **`n`** ends the application and returns you to the application's directory in the shell (Fig. 1.21). Each time you execute this application from the beginning (i.e., *Step 3*), it will choose the same numbers for you to guess.

```
Excellent! You guessed the number.
Would you like to play again (y or n)? y

I have a number between 1 and 1000.
Can you guess my number?
Please type your first guess.
?
```

Fig. 1.20 | Playing the game again.

```
Excellent! You guessed the number.
Would you like to play again (y or n)? n

~/examples/ch01/GuessNumber/GNU_Linux$
```

Fig. 1.21 | Exiting the game.

1.6 Operating Systems

Popular desktop operating systems include Linux, Windows and OS X (formerly called Mac OS X)—we used all three in developing this book. Popular mobile operating systems used in smartphones and tablets include Google's Android, Apple's iOS (for iPhone, iPad and iPod Touch devices), BlackBerry OS and Windows Phone. You can develop applications in C++ for all of the following key operating systems, including several of the latest mobile operating systems.

1.6.1 Windows—A Proprietary Operating System

In the mid-1980s, Microsoft developed the **Windows operating system**, consisting of a graphical user interface built on top of DOS—an enormously popular personal-computer operating system that users interacted with by *typing* commands. Windows borrowed from many concepts (such as icons, menus and windows) developed by Xerox PARC and popularized by early Apple Macintosh operating systems. Windows 8 is Microsoft's latest operating system—its features include enhancements to the user interface, faster startup times, further refinement of security features, touch-screen and multitouch support, and more. Windows is a *proprietary* operating system—it's controlled by Microsoft exclusively. Windows is by far the world's most widely used desktop operating system.

1.6.2 Linux—An Open-Source Operating System

The Linux operating system is perhaps the greatest success of the *open-source* movement. **Open-source software** departs from the *proprietary* software development style that dominated software's early years. With open-source development, individuals and companies *contribute* their efforts in developing, maintaining and evolving software in exchange for the right to use that software for their own purposes, typically at *no charge*. Open-source code is often scrutinized by a much larger audience than proprietary software, so errors often get removed faster. Open source also encourages innovation. Enterprise systems companies, such as IBM, Oracle and many others, have made significant investments in Linux open-source development.

Some key organizations in the open-source community are the Eclipse Foundation (the Eclipse Integrated Development Environment helps programmers conveniently develop software), the Mozilla Foundation (creators of the Firefox web browser), the Apache Software Foundation (creators of the Apache web server used to develop web-based applications) and SourceForge (which provides tools for managing open-source projects—it has hundreds of thousands of them under development). Rapid improvements to computing and communications, decreasing costs and open-source software have made it much easier and more economical to create a software-based business now than just a decade ago. A great example is Facebook, which was launched from a college dorm room and built with open-source software.

The **Linux** kernel is the core of the most popular open-source, freely distributed, full-featured operating system. It's developed by a loosely organized team of volunteers and is popular in servers, personal computers and embedded systems. Unlike that of proprietary operating systems like Microsoft's Windows and Apple's OS X, Linux source code (the program code) is available to the public for examination and modification and is free to download and install. As a result, Linux users benefit from a community of developers actively debugging and improving the kernel, and the ability to customize the operating system to meet specific needs.

A variety of issues—such as Microsoft's market power, the small number of user-friendly Linux applications and the diversity of Linux distributions, such as Red Hat Linux, Ubuntu Linux and many others—have prevented widespread Linux use on desktop computers. Linux has become extremely popular on servers and in embedded systems, such as Google's Android-based smartphones.

1.6.3 Apple's OS X; Apple's iOS for iPhone®, iPad® and iPod Touch® Devices

Apple, founded in 1976 by Steve Jobs and Steve Wozniak, quickly became a leader in personal computing. In 1979, Jobs and several Apple employees visited Xerox PARC (Palo Alto Research Center) to learn about Xerox's desktop computer that featured a graphical user interface (GUI). That GUI served as the inspiration for the Apple Macintosh, launched with much fanfare in a memorable Super Bowl ad in 1984.

The Objective-C programming language, created by Brad Cox and Tom Love at Stepstone in the early 1980s, added capabilities for object-oriented programming (OOP) to the C programming language. At the time of this writing, Objective-C was comparable in popularity to C++.[1] Steve Jobs left Apple in 1985 and founded NeXT Inc. In 1988, NeXT licensed Objective-C from StepStone and developed an Objective-C compiler and libraries which were used as the platform for the NeXTSTEP operating system's user interface and Interface Builder—used to construct graphical user interfaces.

Jobs returned to Apple in 1996 when Apple bought NeXT. Apple's OS X operating system is a descendant of NeXTSTEP. Apple's proprietary operating system, **iOS**, is derived from Apple's OS X and is used in the iPhone, iPad and iPod Touch devices.

1.6.4 Google's Android

Android—the fastest growing mobile and smartphone operating system—is based on the Linux kernel and Java. Experienced Java programmers can quickly dive into Android development. One benefit of developing Android apps is the openness of the platform. The operating system is open source and free.

The Android operating system was developed by Android, Inc., which was acquired by Google in 2005. In 2007, the Open Handset Alliance™—a consortium of 34 companies initially and 84 by 2011—was formed to continue developing Android. As of June 2012, more than 900,000 Android devices were being activated each day![2] Android smartphones are now outselling iPhones in the United States.[3] The Android operating system is used in numerous smartphones (such as the Motorola Droid, HTC One S, Samsung Galaxy Nexus and many more), e-reader devices (such as the Kindle Fire and Barnes and Noble Nook™), tablet computers (such as the Dell Streak and the Samsung Galaxy Tab), in-store touch-screen kiosks, cars, robots, multimedia players and more.

---

1. www.tiobe.com/index.php/content/paperinfo/tpci/index.html.
2. mashable.com/2012/06/11/900000-android-devices/.
3. www.pcworld.com/article/196035/android_outsells_the_iphone_no_big_surprise.html.

1.7 C++11 and the Open Source Boost Libraries

C++11 (formerly called C++0x)—the latest C++ programming language standard—was published by ISO/IEC in 2011. Bjarne Stroustrup, the creator of C++, expressed his vision for the future of the language—the main goals were to make C++ easier to learn, improve library building capabilities and increase compatibility with the C programming language. The new standard extends the C++ Standard Library and includes several features and enhancements to improve performance and security. The major C++ compiler vendors have already implemented many of the new C++11 features (Fig. 1.22). Throughout the book, we discuss various key features of C++11. For more information, visit the C++ Standards Committee website at `www.open-std.org/jtc1/sc22/wg21/` and `isocpp.org`. Copies of the C++11 language specification (ISO/IEC 14882:2011) can be purchased at:

```
http://bit.ly/CPlusPlus11Standard
```

C++ Compiler	URL of C++11 feature descriptions
C++11 features implemented in each of the major C++ compilers.	`wiki.apache.org/stdcxx/C%2B%2B0xCompilerSupport`
Microsoft® Visual C++	`msdn.microsoft.com/en-us/library/hh567368.aspx`
GNU Compiler Collection (g++)	`gcc.gnu.org/projects/cxx0x.html`
Intel® C++ Compiler	`software.intel.com/en-us/articles/c0x-features-supported-by-intel-c-compiler/`
IBM® XL C/C++	`www.ibm.com/developerworks/mydeveloperworks/blogs/5894415f-be62-4bc0-81c5-3956e82276f3/entry/xlc_compiler_s_c_11_support50?lang=en`
Clang	`clang.llvm.org/cxx_status.html`
EDG ecpp	`www.edg.com/docs/edg_cpp.pdf`

Fig. 1.22 | C++ compilers that have implemented major portions of C++11.

Boost C++ Libraries

The **Boost C++ Libraries** are free, open-source libraries created by members of the C++ community. They are peer reviewed and portable across many compilers and platforms. Boost has grown to over 100 libraries, with more being added regularly. Today there are thousands of programmers in the Boost open source community. Boost provides C++ programmers with useful libraries that work well with the existing C++ Standard Library. The Boost libraries can be used by C++ programmers working on a wide variety of platforms with many different compilers.

Some of the new C++11 Standard Library features were derived from corresponding Boost libraries. We overview the libraries and provide code examples for the "regular expression" and "smart pointer" libraries, among others.

Regular expressions are used to match specific character patterns in text. They can be used to validate data to ensure that it's in a particular format, to replace parts of one string with another, or to split a string.

Many common bugs in C and C++ code are related to pointers, a powerful programming capability that C++ absorbed from C. As you'll see, **smart pointers** help you avoid errors associated with traditional pointers.

1.8 Web Resources

This section provides links to our C++ and related Resource Centers that will be useful to you as you learn C++. These include blogs, articles, whitepapers, compilers, development tools, downloads, FAQs, tutorials, webcasts, wikis and links to C++ game programming resources. For updates on Deitel publications, Resource Centers, training courses, partner offers and more, follow us on Facebook® at `www.facebook.com/deitelfan/`, Twitter® `@deitel`, Google+ at `gplus.to/deitel` and LinkedIn at `bit.ly/DeitelLinkedIn`.

Deitel & Associates Websites

`www.deitel.com/books/cpp11fp/`

The Deitel & Associates *C++11 for Programmers* site. Here you'll find links to the book's examples and other resources.

`www.deitel.com/cplusplus/`
`www.deitel.com/visualcplusplus/`
`www.deitel.com/codesearchengines/`
`www.deitel.com/programmingprojects/`

Check these Resource Centers for compilers, code downloads, tutorials, documentation, books, e-books, articles, blogs, RSS feeds and more that will help you develop C++ applications.

`www.deitel.com`

Check this site for updates, corrections and additional resources for all Deitel publications.

`www.deitel.com/newsletter/subscribe.html`

Subscribe here to the *Deitel® Buzz Online* e-mail newsletter to follow the Deitel & Associates publishing program, including updates and errata to *C++11 for Programmers*.

2

Introduction to C++ Programming, Input/Output and Operators

Objectives

In this chapter you'll:

- Write simple C++ programs.
- Write input and output statements.
- Use fundamental types.
- Use arithmetic operators.
- Learn the precedence of arithmetic operators.
- Write decision-making statements.

Outline

2.1 Introduction

We now introduce C++ programming. We show how to display messages on the screen and obtain data from the user at the keyboard for processing. We explain how to perform *arithmetic calculations* and save their results for later use. We demonstrate *decision-making* by showing you how to *compare* two numbers, then display messages based on the comparison results.

Compiling and Running Programs

At `www.deitel.com/books/cpp11fp`, we've posted videos that demonstrate compiling and running programs in Microsoft Visual C++, GNU C++ and Xcode.

2.2 First Program in C++: Printing a Line of Text

Consider a simple program that prints a line of text (Fig. 2.1). This program illustrates several important features of the C++ language. The line numbers are *not* part of the source code.

```
1  // Fig. 2.1: fig02_01.cpp
2  // Text-printing program.
3  #include <iostream> // allows program to output data to the screen
4
5  // function main begins program execution
6  int main()
7  {
8     std::cout << "Welcome to C++!\n"; // display message
9
10    return 0; // indicate that program ended successfully
11 } // end function main
```

```
Welcome to C++!
```

Fig. 2.1 | Text-printing program.

Comments

Lines 1 and 2

```
// Fig. 2.1: fig02_01.cpp
// Text-printing program.
```

each begin with `//`, indicating that the remainder of each line is a **comment**. The comment `Text-printing program` describes the purpose of the program. A comment beginning with

// is called a **single-line comment** because it terminates at the end of the current line. [*Note:* You also may use comments containing one or more lines enclosed in /* and */.]

#include Preprocessing Directive

Line 3

```
#include <iostream> // allows program to output data to the screen
```

is a **preprocessing directive**, which is a message to the C++ preprocessor (introduced in Section 1.4). Lines that begin with # are processed by the preprocessor *before* the program is compiled. This line notifies the preprocessor to include in the program the contents of the **input/output stream header <iostream>**. This header is a file containing information used by the compiler when compiling any program that outputs data to the screen or inputs data from the keyboard using C++'s stream input/output. The program in Fig. 2.1 outputs data to the screen, as we'll soon see. We discuss headers in more detail in Chapter 6 and explain the contents of <iostream> in Chapter 13.

Common Programming Error 2.1

Forgetting to include the <iostream> header in a program that inputs data from the keyboard or outputs data to the screen causes the compiler to issue an error message.

Blank Lines and White Space

Line 4 is simply a *blank line*. Together, blank lines, *space characters* and *tab characters* are known as **whitespace**. Whitespace characters are normally *ignored* by the compiler.

The main Function

Line 5

```
// function main begins program execution
```

is another single-line comment indicating that program execution begins at the next line.

Line 6

```
int main()
```

is a part of every C++ program. The parentheses after main indicate that **main** is a program building block called a **function**. C++ programs typically consist of one or more functions and classes (as you'll learn in Chapter 3). Exactly *one* function in every program *must* be named main. Figure 2.1 contains only one function. C++ programs begin executing at function main, even if main is *not* the first function defined in the program. The keyword int to the left of main indicates that main returns an integer value. The complete list of C++ keywords can be found in Fig. 4.2. We'll say more about return a value when we demonstrate how to create your own functions in Section 3.3. For now, simply include the keyword int to the left of main in each of your programs.

The **left brace**, **{**, (line 7) must *begin* the **body** of every function. A corresponding **right brace**, **}**, (line 11) must *end* each function's body.

An Output Statement

Line 8

```
std::cout << "Welcome to C++!\n"; // display message
```

instructs the computer to perform an action—namely, to print the characters contained between the double quotation marks. Together, the quotation marks and the characters between them are called a **string**, a **character string** or a **string literal**. In this book, we refer to characters between double quotation marks simply as strings. Whitespace characters in strings are not ignored by the compiler.

The entire line 8, including `std::cout`, the `<<` **operator**, the string `"Welcome to C++!\n"` and the **semicolon** (`;`), is called a **statement**. Most C++ statements end with a semicolon, also known as the **statement terminator** (we'll see some exceptions to this soon). Preprocessing directives (like `#include`) do not end with a semicolon. Typically, output and input in C++ are accomplished with **streams** of characters. Thus, when the preceding statement is executed, it sends the stream of characters `Welcome to C++!\n` to the **standard output stream object**—**`std::cout`**—which is normally "connected" to the screen.

Good Programming Practice 2.1

Indent the body of each function one level within the braces that delimit the function's body. This makes a program's functional structure stand out and makes the program easier to read.

Good Programming Practice 2.2

Set a convention for the size of indent you prefer, then apply it uniformly. The tab key may be used to create indents, but tab stops may vary. We prefer three spaces per level of indent.

The `std` Namespace

The `std::` before `cout` is required when we use names that we've brought into the program by the preprocessing directive `#include <iostream>`. The notation `std::cout` specifies that we are using a name, in this case `cout`, that belongs to namespace `std`. The names `cin` (the standard input stream) and `cerr` (the standard error stream)—introduced in Chapter 1—also belong to namespace `std`. Namespaces are an advanced C++ feature that we discuss in depth in Chapter 21, Other Topics. For now, you should simply remember to include `std::` before each mention of `cout`, `cin` and `cerr` in a program. This can be cumbersome—the next example introduces `using` declarations and the `using` directive, which will enable you to omit `std::` before each use of a name in the `std` namespace.

The Stream Insertion Operator and Escape Sequences

In the context of an output statement, the `<<` operator is referred to as the **stream insertion operator**. When this program executes, the value to the operator's right, the right **operand,** is inserted in the output stream. Notice that the operator points in the direction of where the data goes. A string literal's characters *normally* print exactly as they appear between the double quotes. However, the characters `\n` are *not* printed on the screen (Fig. 2.1). The backslash (\) is called an **escape character**. It indicates that a "special" character is to be output. When a backslash is encountered in a string of characters, the next character is combined with the backslash to form an **escape sequence**. The escape sequence `\n` means **newline.** It causes the screen cursor to move to the beginning of the next line on the screen. Some common escape sequences are listed in Fig. 2.2.

Escape sequence	Description
`\n`	Newline. Position the screen cursor to the beginning of the next line.
`\t`	Horizontal tab. Move the screen cursor to the next tab stop.
`\r`	Carriage return. Position the screen cursor to the beginning of the current line; do not advance to the next line.
`\a`	Alert. Sound the system bell.
`\\`	Backslash. Used to print a backslash character.
`\'`	Single quote. Used to print a single quote character.
`\"`	Double quote. Used to print a double quote character.

Fig. 2.2 | Escape sequences.

The `return` *Statement*

Line 10

```
return 0; // indicate that program ended successfully
```

is one of several means we'll use to **exit a function**. When the **`return` statement** is used at the end of `main`, as shown here, the value `0` indicates that the program has *terminated successfully*. The right brace, `}`, (line 11) indicates the end of function `main`. According to the C++ standard, if program execution reaches the end of `main` without encountering a `return` statement, it's assumed that the program terminated successfully—exactly as when the last statement in main is a `return` statement with the value `0`. For that reason, we *omit* the `return` statement at the end of `main` in subsequent programs.

2.3 Modifying Our First C++ Program

We now present two examples that modify the program of Fig. 2.1 to print text on one line by using multiple statements and to print text on several lines by using a single statement.

Printing a Single Line of Text with Multiple Statements

`Welcome to C++!` can be printed several ways. For example, Fig. 2.3 performs stream insertion in multiple statements (lines 8–9), yet produces the same output as the program of Fig. 2.1. [*Note:* From this point forward, we use a *light gray background* to highlight the key features each program introduces.] Each stream insertion resumes printing where the previous one stopped. The first stream insertion (line 8) prints `Welcome` followed by a space, and because this string did not end with `\n`, the second stream insertion (line 9) begins printing on the *same* line immediately following the space.

```
1 // Fig. 2.3: fig02_03.cpp
2 // Printing a line of text with multiple statements.
3 #include <iostream> // allows program to output data to the screen
4
```

Fig. 2.3 | Printing a line of text with multiple statements. (Part 1 of 2.)

```
// function main begins program execution
int main()
{
   std::cout << "Welcome ";
   std::cout << "to C++!\n";
} // end function main
```

```
Welcome to C++!
```

Fig. 2.3 | Printing a line of text with multiple statements. (Part 2 of 2.)

Printing Multiple Lines of Text with a Single Statement

A single statement can print multiple lines by using newline characters, as in line 8 of Fig. 2.4. Each time the `\n` (newline) escape sequence is encountered in the output stream, the screen cursor is positioned to the beginning of the next line. To get a blank line in your output, place two newline characters back to back, as in line 8.

```
1  // Fig. 2.4: fig02_04.cpp
2  // Printing multiple lines of text with a single statement.
3  #include <iostream> // allows program to output data to the screen
4
5  // function main begins program execution
6  int main()
7  {
8     std::cout << "Welcome\nto\n\nC++!\n";
9  } // end function main
```

```
Welcome
to

C++!
```

Fig. 2.4 | Printing multiple lines of text with a single statement.

2.4 Another C++ Program: Adding Integers

Our next program obtains two integers typed by a user at the keyboard, computes the sum of these values and outputs the result using `std::cout`. Figure 2.5 shows the program and sample inputs and outputs. In the sample execution, we highlight the user's input in bold. The program begins execution with function `main` (line 6). The left brace (line 7) begins `main`'s body and the corresponding right brace (line 22) ends it.

```
1  // Fig. 2.5: fig02_05.cpp
2  // Addition program that displays the sum of two integers.
3  #include <iostream> // allows program to perform input and output
```

Fig. 2.5 | Addition program that displays the sum of two integers. (Part 1 of 2.)

```
4
5   // function main begins program execution
6   int main()
7   {
8      // variable declarations
9      int number1 = 0; // first integer to add (initialized to 0)
10     int number2 = 0; // second integer to add (initialized to 0)
11     int sum = 0; // sum of number1 and number2 (initialized to 0)
12
13     std::cout << "Enter first integer: "; // prompt user for data
14     std::cin >> number1; // read first integer from user into number1
15
16     std::cout << "Enter second integer: "; // prompt user for data
17     std::cin >> number2; // read second integer from user into number2
18
19     sum = number1 + number2; // add the numbers; store result in sum
20
21     std::cout << "Sum is " << sum << std::endl; // display sum; end line
22  } // end function main
```

```
Enter first integer: 45
Enter second integer: 72
Sum is 117
```

Fig. 2.5 | Addition program that displays the sum of two integers. (Part 2 of 2.)

Variable Declarations

Lines 9–11

```
int number1 = 0; // first integer to add (initialized to 0)
int number2 = 0; // second integer to add (initialized to 0)
int sum = 0; // sum of number1 and number2 (initialized to 0)
```

are **declarations**. The identifiers `number1`, `number2` and `sum` are the names of **variables**. These declarations specify that the variables `number1`, `number2` and `sum` are data of type **`int`**, meaning that these variables will hold integer values. The declarations also initialize each of these variables to `0`.

Error-Prevention Tip 2.1

Although it's not always necessary to initialize every variable explicitly, doing so will help you avoid many kinds of problems.

All variables *must* be declared with a *name* and a *data type before* they can be used in a program. Several variables of the same type may be declared in one declaration or in multiple declarations. We could have declared all three variables in one declaration by using a **comma-separated list** as follows:

```
int number1 = 0, number2 = 0, sum = 0;
```

This makes the program less readable and prevents us from providing comments that describe each variable's purpose.

Good Programming Practice 2.3

Declare only one variable in each declaration and provide a comment that explains the variable's purpose in the program.

Fundamental Types

We'll soon discuss the type `double` for specifying *real numbers*, and the type `char` for specifying *character data*. Real numbers are numbers with decimal points, such as 3.4, 0.0 and –11.19. A `char` variable may hold only a single lowercase letter, a single uppercase letter, a single digit or a single special character (e.g., `$` or *). Types such as `int`, `double` and `char` are called **fundamental types**. Fundamental-type names consist of one or more *keywords* and therefore *must* appear in all lowercase letters. Appendix C contains the complete list of fundamental types.

Identifiers

A variable name (such as `number1`) is any valid **identifier** that is *not* a keyword. An identifier is a series of characters consisting of letters, digits and underscores (_) that does *not* begin with a digit. C++ is **case sensitive**—uppercase and lowercase letters are *different*, so `a1` and `A1` are *different* identifiers.

Portability Tip 2.1

C++ allows identifiers of any length, but your C++ implementation may restrict identifier lengths. Use identifiers of 31 characters or fewer to ensure portability.

Good Programming Practice 2.4

Choosing meaningful identifiers makes a program ***self-documenting***—*a person can understand the program simply by reading it rather than having to refer to program comments or documentation.*

Good Programming Practice 2.5

Avoid using abbreviations in identifiers. This improves program readability.

Good Programming Practice 2.6

Do not use identifiers that begin with underscores and double underscores, because C++ compilers may use names like that for their own purposes internally. This will prevent the names you choose from being confused with names the compilers choose.

Placement of Variable Declarations

Declarations of variables can be placed almost anywhere in a program, but they *must* appear *before* their corresponding variables are used in the program. For example, in the program of Fig. 2.5, the declaration in line 9

```
int number1 = 0; // first integer to add (initialized to 0)
```

could have been placed immediately before line 14

```
std::cin >> number1; // read first integer from user into number1
```

Obtaining the First Value from the User

Line 13

```
std::cout << "Enter first integer: "; // prompt user for data
```

displays `Enter first integer:` followed by a space. This message is called a **prompt** because it directs the user to take a specific action. We like to pronounce the preceding statement as "`std::cout` *gets* the string `"Enter first integer: "`." Line 14

```
std::cin >> number1; // read first integer from user into number1
```

uses the **standard input stream object `cin`** (of namespace `std`) and the **stream extraction operator**, `>>`, to obtain a value from the keyboard. Using the stream extraction operator with `std::cin` takes character input from the standard input stream, which is usually the keyboard. We like to pronounce the preceding statement as, "`std::cin` *gives* a value to `number1`" or simply "`std::cin` *gives* `number1`."

When the computer executes the preceding statement, it waits for the user to enter a value for variable `number1`. The user responds by typing an integer (as characters), then pressing the *Enter* key (sometimes called the *Return* key) to send the characters to the computer. The computer converts the character representation of the number to an integer and assigns (i.e., copies) this number (or **value**) to the variable `number1`. Any subsequent references to `number1` in this program will use this same value.

The `std::cout` and `std::cin` stream objects facilitate interaction between the user and the computer.

Users can, of course, enter *invalid* data from the keyboard. For example, when your program is expecting the user to enter an integer, the user could enter alphabetic characters, special symbols (like # or @) or a number with a decimal point (like 73.5), among others. In these early programs, we assume that the user enters *valid* data. As you progress through the book, you'll learn various techniques for dealing with the broad range of possible data-entry problems.

Obtaining the Second Value from the User

Line 16

```
std::cout << "Enter second integer: "; // prompt user for data
```

prints `Enter second integer:` on the screen, prompting the user to take action. Line 17

```
std::cin >> number2; // read second integer from user into number2
```

obtains a value for variable `number2` from the user.

Calculating the Sum of the Values Input by the User

The assignment statement in line 19

```
sum = number1 + number2; // add the numbers; store result in sum
```

adds the values of variables `number1` and `number2` and assigns the result to variable `sum` using the **assignment operator** `=`. We like to read this statement as, "`sum` *gets* the value of `number1 + number2`." Most calculations are performed in assignment statements. The `=` operator and the `+` operator are **binary operators**—each has *two* operands. In the case of the `+` operator, the two operands are `number1` and `number2`. In the case of the preceding `=` operator, the two operands are `sum` and the value of the expression `number1 + number2`.

Good Programming Practice 2.7

Place spaces on either side of a binary operator. This makes the operator stand out and makes the program more readable.

Displaying the Result

Line 21

```
std::cout << "Sum is " << sum << std::endl; // display sum; end
line
```

displays the character string `Sum is` followed by the numerical value of variable `sum` followed by `std::endl`—a **stream manipulator**. The name `endl` is an abbreviation for "end line" and belongs to namespace `std`. The `std::endl` stream manipulator outputs a newline, then "flushes the output buffer." This simply means that, on some systems where outputs accumulate in the machine until there are enough to "make it worthwhile" to display them on the screen, `std::endl` forces any accumulated outputs to be displayed at that moment. This can be important when the outputs are prompting the user for an action, such as entering data.

The preceding statement outputs multiple values of different types. The stream insertion operator "knows" how to output each type of data. Using multiple stream insertion operators (<<) in a single statement is referred to as **concatenating**, **chaining** or **cascading stream insertion operations.**

Calculations can also be performed in output statements. We could have combined the statements in lines 19 and 21 into the statement

```
std::cout << "Sum is " << number1 + number2 << std::endl;
```

thus eliminating the need for the variable `sum`.

A powerful feature of C++ is that you can create your own data types called classes (we introduce this capability in Chapter 3 and explore it in depth in Chapter 9). You can then "teach" C++ how to input and output values of these new data types using the >> and << operators (this is called **operator overloading**—a topic we explore in Chapter 10).

2.5 Arithmetic

Most programs perform arithmetic calculations. Figure 2.6 summarizes the C++ **arithmetic operators.** The **asterisk** (*) indicates *multiplication* and the **percent sign** (**%**) is the *modulus operator* that will be discussed shortly. The arithmetic operators in Fig. 2.6 are all *binary* operators, i.e., operators that take two operands. For example, the expression `number1 + number2` contains the binary operator + and the two operands `number1` and `number2`.

Integer division (i.e., where both the numerator and the denominator are integers) yields an integer quotient; for example, the expression `7 / 4` evaluates to `1` and the expression `17 / 5` evaluates to `3`. *Any fractional part in integer division is* ***truncated****—no rounding occurs.*

C++ provides the **modulus operator**, `%`, that yields the *remainder after integer division.* The modulus operator can be used *only* with integer operands. The expression `x % y` yields the *remainder* after `x` is divided by `y`. Thus, `7 % 4` yields `3` and `17 % 5` yields `2`. In later chapters, we discuss many interesting applications of the modulus operator, such as determining whether one number is a *multiple* of another (a special case of this is determining whether a number is *odd* or *even*).

C++ operation	C++ arithmetic operator	Algebraic expression	C++ expression
Addition	+	$f + 7$	`f + 7`
Subtraction	-	$p - c$	`p - c`
Multiplication	*	bm or $b \cdot m$	`b * m`
Division	/	x / y or $\frac{x}{y}$ or $x \div y$	`x / y`
Modulus	%	$r \bmod s$	`r % s`

Fig. 2.6 | Arithmetic operators.

Arithmetic Expressions in Straight-Line Form

Arithmetic expressions in C++ must be entered into the computer in **straight-line form.** Thus, expressions such as "a divided by b" must be written as a / b, so that all constants, variables and operators appear in a straight line. The algebraic notation

$$\frac{a}{b}$$

is generally *not* acceptable to compilers, although some special-purpose software packages do support more natural notation for complex mathematical expressions.

Parentheses for Grouping Subexpressions

Parentheses are used in C++ expressions in the same manner as in algebraic expressions. For example, to multiply a times the quantity b + c we write a * (b + c).

Rules of Operator Precedence

C++ applies the operators in arithmetic expressions in a precise order determined by the following **rules of operator precedence**, which are generally the same as those in algebra:

1. Operators in expressions contained within pairs of *parentheses* are evaluated first. Parentheses are at the highest level of precedence. In cases of **nested**, or **embedded, parentheses**, such as

   ```
   ( a * ( b + c ) )
   ```

   the operators in the *innermost* pair of parentheses are applied first.

2. Multiplication, division and modulus operations are applied next. If an expression contains several multiplication, division and modulus operations, operators are applied from *left to right.* Multiplication, division and modulus are on the *same* level of precedence.

3. Addition and subtraction operations are applied last. If an expression contains several addition and subtraction operations, operators are applied from *left to right.* Addition and subtraction also have the *same* level of precedence.

The rules of operator precedence define the order in which C++ applies operators. When we say that certain operators are applied from left to right, we are referring to the **associativity** of the operators. For example, the addition operators (+) in the expression

```
a + b + c
```

associate from left to right, so a + b is calculated first, then c is added to that sum to determine the whole expression's value. We'll see that some operators associate from *right to left*. Figure 2.7 summarizes these rules of operator precedence. We expand this table as we introduce additional C++ operators. Appendix A contains the complete precedence chart.

Operator(s)	Operation(s)	Order of evaluation (precedence)
( )	Parentheses	Evaluated first. If the parentheses are *nested*, such as in the expression a * (b + c / d + e)), the expression in the *innermost* pair is evaluated first. [*Caution:* If you have an expression such as (a + b) * (c - d) in which two sets of parentheses are not nested, but appear "on the same level," the C++ Standard does *not* specify the order in which these parenthesized subexpressions will be evaluated.]
* / %	Multiplication Division Modulus	Evaluated second. If there are several, they're evaluated left to right.
+ -	Addition Subtraction	Evaluated last. If there are several, they're evaluated left to right.

Fig. 2.7 | Precedence of arithmetic operators.

Sample Algebraic and C++ Expressions

Now consider several expressions in light of the rules of operator precedence. Each example lists an algebraic expression and its C++ equivalent. The following is an example of an arithmetic mean (average) of five terms:

Algebra: $m = \frac{a + b + c + d + e}{5}$

C++:
```
m = ( a + b + c + d + e ) / 5;
```

The parentheses are required because division has *higher* precedence than addition. The *entire* quantity (a + b + c + d + e) is to be divided by 5.

The following is an example of the equation of a straight line:

Algebra: $y = mx + b$

C++:
```
y = m * x + b;
```

No parentheses are required. The multiplication is applied first because multiplication has a *higher* precedence than addition.

The following example contains modulus (%), multiplication, division, addition, subtraction and assignment operations:

Algebra: $z = pr\%q + w/x - y$

C++:
```
z = p * r % q + w / x - y;
  6   1   2   4   3   5
```

The circled numbers indicate the order in which C++ applies the operators. The multiplication, modulus and division are evaluated *first* in left-to-right order (i.e., they associate from left to right) because they have *higher precedence* than addition and subtraction. The addition and subtraction are applied next. These are also applied left to right. The assignment operator is applied *last* because its precedence is *lower* than that of any of the arithmetic operators.

Evaluation of a Second-Degree Polynomial

To develop a better understanding of the rules of operator precedence, consider the evaluation of a second-degree polynomial $y = ax^2 + bx + c$:

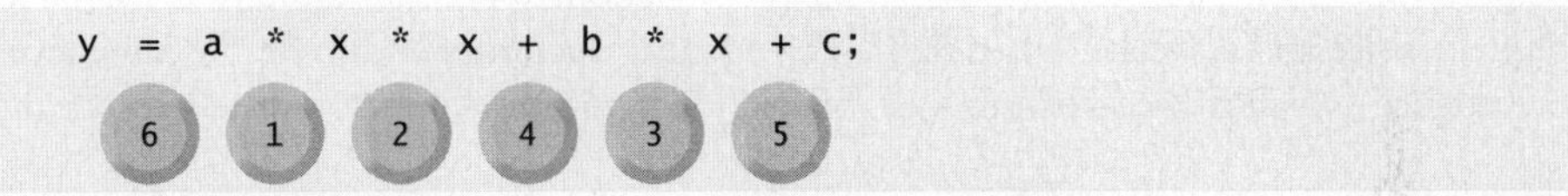

The circled numbers indicate the order in which C++ applies the operators. *There is no arithmetic operator for exponentiation in C++*, so we've represented x^2 as x * x. In Chapter 5, we'll discuss the standard library function pow ("power") that performs exponentiation.

Suppose variables a, b, c and x in the preceding second-degree polynomial are initialized as follows: a = 2, b = 3, c = 7 and x = 5. Figure 2.8 illustrates the order in which the operators are applied and the final value of the expression.

```
Step 1.  y = 2 * 5 * 5 + 3 * 5 + 7;      (Leftmost multiplication)
             2 * 5 is 10

Step 2.  y = 10 * 5 + 3 * 5 + 7;         (Leftmost multiplication)
             10 * 5 is 50

Step 3.  y = 50 + 3 * 5 + 7;             (Multiplication before addition)
                  3 * 5 is 15

Step 4.  y = 50 + 15 + 7;                (Leftmost addition)
             50 + 15 is 65

Step 5.  y = 65 + 7;                     (Last addition)
             65 + 7 is 72

Step 6.  y = 72                          (Last operation—place 72 in y)
```

Fig. 2.8 | Order in which a second-degree polynomial is evaluated.

Redundant Parentheses

As in algebra, it's acceptable to place *unnecessary* parentheses in an expression to make the expression clearer. These are called **redundant parentheses.** For example, the preceding assignment statement could be parenthesized as follows:

```
y = ( a * x * x ) + ( b * x ) + c;
```

2.6 Decision Making: Equality and Relational Operators

We now introduce a simple version of C++'s **`if` statement** that allows a program to take alternative action based on whether a **condition** is true or false. If the condition is *true*, the statement in the body of the `if` statement *is* executed. If the condition is *false*, the body statement *is not* executed. We'll see an example shortly.

Conditions in `if` statements can be formed by using the **relational operators** and **equality operators** summarized in Fig. 2.9. The relational operators all have the same level of precedence and associate left to right. The equality operators both have the same level of precedence, which is *lower* than that of the relational operators, and associate left to right.

Algebraic relational or equality operator	C++ relational or equality operator	Sample C++ condition	Meaning of C++ condition
Relational operators			
$>$	`>`	`x > y`	`x` is greater than `y`
$<$	`<`	`x < y`	`x` is less than `y`
$\geq$	`>=`	`x >= y`	`x` is greater than or equal to `y`
$\leq$	`<=`	`x <= y`	`x` is less than or equal to `y`
Equality operators			
$=$	`==`	`x == y`	`x` is equal to `y`
$\neq$	`!=`	`x != y`	`x` is not equal to `y`

Fig. 2.9 | Relational and equality operators.

Common Programming Error 2.2

Reversing the order of the pair of symbols in the operators `!=`, `>=` and `<=` (by writing them as `=!`, `=>` and `=<`, respectively) is normally a syntax error. In some cases, writing `!=` as `=!` will not be a syntax error, but almost certainly will be a ***logic error*** *that has an effect at execution time. You'll understand why when you learn about logical operators in Chapter 5. A* ***fatal logic error*** *causes a program to fail and terminate prematurely. A* ***nonfatal logic error*** *allows a program to continue executing, but usually produces incorrect results.*

Common Programming Error 2.3

Confusing the equality operator `==` with the assignment operator `=` results in logic errors. We like to read the equality operator as "is equal to" or "double equals," and the assignment operator as "gets" or "gets the value of" or "is assigned the value of." As you'll see in Section 5.9, confusing these operators may not necessarily cause an easy-to-recognize syntax error, but may cause subtle logic errors.

Using the `if` Statement

The following example (Fig. 2.10) uses six `if` statements to compare two numbers input by the user. If the condition in any of these `if` statements is satisfied, the output statement associated with that `if` statement is executed.

```
// Fig. 2.13: fig02_13.cpp
// Comparing integers using if statements, relational operators
// and equality operators.
#include <iostream> // allows program to perform input and output

using std::cout; // program uses cout
using std::cin; // program uses cin
using std::endl; // program uses endl

// function main begins program execution
int main()
{
   int number1 = 0; // first integer to compare (initialized to 0)
   int number2 = 0; // second integer to compare (initialized to 0)

   cout << "Enter two integers to compare: "; // prompt user for data
   cin >> number1 >> number2; // read two integers from user

   if ( number1 == number2 )
      cout << number1 << " == " << number2 << endl;

   if ( number1 != number2 )
      cout << number1 << " != " << number2 << endl;

   if ( number1 < number2 )
      cout << number1 << " < " << number2 << endl;

   if ( number1 > number2 )
      cout << number1 << " > " << number2 << endl;

   if ( number1 <= number2 )
      cout << number1 << " <= " << number2 << endl;

   if ( number1 >= number2 )
      cout << number1 << " >= " << number2 << endl;
} // end function main
```

```
Enter two integers to compare: 3 7
3 != 7
3 < 7
3 <= 7
```

```
Enter two integers to compare: 22 12
22 != 12
22 > 12
22 >= 12
```

```
Enter two integers to compare: 7 7
7 == 7
7 <= 7
7 >= 7
```

Fig. 2.10 | Comparing integers using `if` statements, relational operators and equality operators.

using Declarations

Lines 6–8

```
using std::cout; // program uses cout
using std::cin; // program uses cin
using std::endl; // program uses endl
```

are **using declarations** that eliminate the need to repeat the `std::` prefix as we did in earlier programs. We can now write `cout` instead of `std::cout`, `cin` instead of `std::cin` and `endl` instead of `std::endl`, respectively, in the remainder of the program.

In place of lines 6–8, many programmers prefer to provide the **using directive**

```
using namespace std;
```

which enables a program to use *all* the names in any standard C++ header (such as `<iostream>`) that a program might include. From this point forward in the book, we'll use the preceding directive in our programs. In Chapter 21, Other Topics, we'll discuss some issues with `using` directives in large-scale systems.

Variable Declarations and Reading the Inputs from the User

Lines 13–14

```
int number1 = 0; // first integer to compare (initialized to 0)
int number2 = 0; // second integer to compare (initialized to 0)
```

declare the variables used in the program and initializes them to `0`.

The program uses cascaded stream extraction operations (line 17) to input two integers. Remember that we're allowed to write `cin` (instead of `std::cin`) because of line 7. First a value is read into variable `number1`, then a value is read into variable `number2`.

Comparing Numbers

The `if` statement in lines 19–20

```
if ( number1 == number2 )
   cout << number1 << " == " << number2 << endl;
```

compares the values of variables `number1` and `number2` to test for equality. If the values are equal, the statement in line 20 displays a line of text indicating that the numbers are equal. If the conditions are `true` in one or more of the `if` statements starting in lines 22, 25, 28, 31 and 34, the corresponding body statement displays an appropriate line of text.

Each `if` statement in Fig. 2.10 has a single statement in its body and each body statement is indented. In Chapter 4 we show how to specify `if` statements with multiple-statement bodies (by enclosing the body statements in a pair of braces, `{ }`, creating what's called a **compound statement** or a **block**).

Common Programming Error 2.4

Placing a semicolon immediately after the right parenthesis after the condition in an `if` statement is often a logic error (although not a syntax error). The semicolon causes the body of the `if` statement to be empty, so the `if` statement performs no action, regardless of whether or not its condition is true. Worse yet, the original body statement of the `if` statement now becomes a statement in sequence *with the `if` statement and* always *executes, often causing the program to produce incorrect results.*

White Space

Recall that whitespace characters, such as tabs, newlines and spaces, are normally ignored by the compiler. So, statements may be split over several lines and may be spaced according to your preferences. It's a syntax error to split identifiers, strings (such as `"hello"`) and constants (such as the number `1000`) over several lines.

Good Programming Practice 2.8

A lengthy statement may be spread over several lines. If a single statement must be split across lines, choose meaningful breaking points, such as after a comma in a comma-separated list, or after an operator in a lengthy expression. If a statement is split across two or more lines, indent all subsequent lines and left-align the group of indented lines.

Operator Precedence

Figure 2.11 shows the precedence and associativity of the operators introduced in this chapter. The operators are shown top to bottom in decreasing order of precedence. All these operators, with the exception of the assignment operator `=`, associate from left to right. Addition is left-associative, so an expression like `x + y + z` is evaluated as if it had been written `(x + y) + z`. The assignment operator `=` associates from *right to left*, so an expression such as `x = y = 0` is evaluated as if it had been written `x = (y = 0)`, which, as we'll soon see, first assigns `0` to `y`, then assigns the *result* of that assignment—`0`—to `x`.

Operators	Associativity	Type
`()`	*[See caution in Fig. 2.7]*	grouping parentheses
`*` `/` `%`	left to right	multiplicative
`+` `-`	left to right	additive
`<<` `>>`	left to right	stream insertion/extraction
`<` `<=` `>` `>=`	left to right	relational
`==` `!=`	left to right	equality
`=`	right to left	assignment

Fig. 2.11 | Precedence and associativity of the operators discussed so far.

Good Programming Practice 2.9

Refer to the operator precedence and associativity chart (Appendix A) when writing expressions containing many operators. Confirm that the operators in the expression are performed in the order you expect. If you're uncertain about the order of evaluation in a complex expression, break the expression into smaller statements or use parentheses to force the order of evaluation, exactly as you'd do in an algebraic expression. Be sure to observe that some operators such as assignment (=) associate right to left rather than left to right.

2.7 Wrap-Up

You learned many important basic features of C++ in this chapter, including displaying data on the screen, inputting data from the keyboard and declaring variables of fundamental types. In particular, you learned to use the output stream object `cout` and the input stream object `cin` to build simple interactive programs. We explained how variables are stored in and retrieved from memory. You also learned how to use arithmetic operators to perform calculations. We discussed the order in which C++ applies operators (i.e., the rules of operator precedence), as well as the associativity of the operators. You also learned how C++'s `if` statement allows a program to make decisions. Finally, we introduced the equality and relational operators, which you use to form conditions in `if` statements.

The non-object-oriented applications presented here introduced you to basic programming concepts. As you'll see in Chapter 3, C++ applications typically contain just a few lines of code in function `main`—these statements normally create the objects that perform the work of the application, then the objects "take over from there." In Chapter 3, you'll learn how to implement your own classes and use objects of those classes in applications.

3

Introduction to Classes, Objects and Strings

Objectives

In this chapter you'll:

- Define a class and use it to create an object.
- Implement a class's behaviors as member functions.
- Implement a class's attributes as data members.
- Call a member function of an object to perform a task.
- Learn the differences between data members of a class and local variables of a function.
- Use a constructor to initialize an object's data when the object is created.
- Engineer a class to separate its interface from its implementation and encourage reuse.
- Use objects of class `string`.

Outline

3.1 Introduction

In this chapter, you'll begin writing programs that employ the basic concepts of *object-oriented programming* that we introduced in Section 1.3. One common feature of every program in Chapter 2 was that all the statements that performed tasks were located in function `main`. Typically, the programs you develop in this book will consist of function `main` and one or more *classes*, each containing *data members* and *member functions*. If you become part of a development team in industry, you might work on software systems that contain hundreds, or even thousands, of classes. In this chapter, we develop a simple, well-engineered framework for organizing object-oriented programs in C++.

We present a carefully paced sequence of complete working programs to demonstrate creating and using your own classes. These examples begin our integrated case study on developing a grade-book class that instructors can use to maintain student test scores. We also introduce the C++ standard library class `string`.

3.2 Defining a Class with a Member Function

We begin with an example (Fig. 3.1) that consists of class `GradeBook` (lines 8–16)—which, when it's fully developed in Chapter 7, will represent a grade book that an instructor can use to maintain student test scores—and a `main` function (lines 19–23) that creates a `GradeBook` object. Function `main` uses this object and its `displayMessage` member function (lines 12–15) to display a message on the screen welcoming the instructor to the grade-book program.

```
1  // Fig. 3.1: fig03_01.cpp
2  // Define class GradeBook with a member function displayMessage,
3  // create a GradeBook object, and call its displayMessage function.
4  #include <iostream>
5  using namespace std;
6
7  // GradeBook class definition
8  class GradeBook
9  {
```

Fig. 3.1 | Define class `GradeBook` with a member function `displayMessage`, create a `GradeBook` object and call its `displayMessage` function. (Part 1 of 2.)

```
10 public:
11    // function that displays a welcome message to the GradeBook user
12    void displayMessage() const
13    {
14       cout << "Welcome to the Grade Book!" << endl;
15    } // end function displayMessage
16 }; // end class GradeBook
17
18 // function main begins program execution
19 int main()
20 {
21    GradeBook myGradeBook; // create a GradeBook object named myGradeBook
22    myGradeBook.displayMessage(); // call object's displayMessage function
23 } // end main
```

```
Welcome to the Grade Book!
```

Fig. 3.1 | Define class `GradeBook` with a member function `displayMessage`, create a `GradeBook` object and call its `displayMessage` function. (Part 2 of 2.)

Class GradeBook

Before function `main` (lines 19–23) can create a `GradeBook` object, we must tell the compiler what member functions and data members belong to the class. The `GradeBook` **class definition** (lines 8–16) contains a member function called `displayMessage` (lines 12–15) that displays a message on the screen (line 14). We need to make an object of class `GradeBook` (line 21) and call its `displayMessage` member function (line 22) to get line 14 to execute and display the welcome message. We'll soon explain lines 21–22 in detail.

The class definition begins in line 8 with the keyword `class` followed by the class name `GradeBook`. By convention, the name of a user-defined class begins with a capital letter, and for readability, each subsequent word in the class name begins with a capital letter. This capitalization style is often referred to as **Pascal case**, because the convention was widely used in the Pascal programming language. The occasional uppercase letters resemble a camel's humps. More generally, **camel case** capitalization style allows the first letter to be either lowercase or uppercase (e.g., `myGradeBook` in line 21).

Every class's **body** is enclosed in a pair of left and right braces (`{` and `}`), as in lines 9 and 16. The class definition terminates with a semicolon (line 16).

Common Programming Error 3.1

Forgetting the semicolon at the end of a class definition is a syntax error.

Recall that the function `main` is always called automatically when you execute a program. Most functions do *not* get called automatically. As you'll soon see, you must call member function `displayMessage` *explicitly* to tell it to perform its task.

Line 10 contains the keyword **`public`**, which is an **access specifier**. Lines 12–15 define member function `displayMessage`. This member function appears *after* access specifier `public:` to indicate that the function is "available to the public"—that is, it can be called by other functions in the program (such as `main`), and by member functions of other classes (if there are any). Access specifiers are always followed by a colon (`:`). For the remainder of the text, when we refer to the access specifier `public` in the text, we'll omit the colon as we did in this sentence. Section 3.4 introduces the access specifier `private`. Later in the book we'll study the access specifier `protected`.

When you define a function, you must specify a **return type** to indicate the type of the value returned by the function when it completes its task. In line 12, keyword **`void`** to the left of the function name `displayMessage` is the function's return type. Return type `void` indicates that `displayMessage` will *not* return any data to its **calling function** (in this example, line 22 of `main`, as we'll see in a moment) when it completes its task. In Fig. 3.5, you'll see an example of a function that *does* return a value.

The name of the member function, `displayMessage`, follows the return type (line 12). By convention, our function names use the *camel case* style with a lowercase first letter. The parentheses after the member function name indicate that this is a *function*. An empty set of parentheses, as shown in line 12, indicates that this member function does *not* require additional data to perform its task. You'll see an example of a member function that *does* require additional data in Section 3.3.

We declared member function `displayMessage` **`const`** in line 12 because in the process of displaying `"Welcome to the Grade Book!"` the function *does not*, and *should not*, modify the `GradeBook` object on which it's called. Declaring `displayMessage const` tells the compiler, "this function should *not* modify the object on which it's called—if it does, please issue a compilation error." This can help you locate errors if you accidentally insert code in `displayMessage` that *would* modify the object. Line 12 is commonly referred to as a **function header**.

Every function's *body* is delimited by left and right braces (`{` and `}`), as in lines 13 and 15. The *function body* contains statements that perform the function's task. In this case, member function `displayMessage` contains one statement (line 14) that displays the message `"Welcome to the Grade Book!"`. After this statement executes, the function has completed its task.

Testing Class **GradeBook**

Next, we'd like to use class `GradeBook` in a program. As you saw in Chapter 2, the function `main` (lines 19–23) begins the execution of every program.

In this program, we'd like to call class `GradeBook`'s `displayMessage` member function to display the welcome message. Typically, you cannot call a member function of a class until you *create an object* of that class. (As you'll learn in Section 9.14, `static` member functions are an exception.) Line 21 creates an object of class `GradeBook` called `myGradeBook`. The variable's type is `GradeBook`—the class we defined in lines 8–16. When we declare variables of type `int`, as we did in Chapter 2, the compiler knows what `int` is—it's a *fundamental type* that's "built into" C++. In line 21, however, the compiler does *not* automatically know what type `GradeBook` is—it's a **user-defined type**. We tell the compiler what `GradeBook` is by including the *class definition* (lines 8–16). If we omitted these lines, the compiler would issue an error message. Each class you create becomes a new *type* that can be used to create objects. You can define new class types as needed; this is one reason why C++ is known as an **extensible programming language**.

Line 22 *calls* the member function `displayMessage` using variable `myGradeBook` followed by the **dot operator** (`.`), the function name `displayMessage` and an empty set of parentheses. This call causes the `displayMessage` function to perform its task. At the beginning of line 22, "`myGradeBook.`" indicates that `main` should use the `GradeBook` object that was created in line 21. The *empty parentheses* in line 12 indicate that member function `displayMessage` does *not* require additional data to perform its task, which is why we called this function with empty parentheses in line 22. (In Section 3.3, you'll see how to pass data to a function.) When `displayMessage` completes its task, the program reaches the end of `main` (line 23) and terminates.

UML Class Diagram for Class **GradeBook**

Recall from Section 1.3 that the UML is a standardized graphical language used by software developers to represent their object-oriented systems. In the UML, each class is modeled in a **UML class diagram** as a *rectangle* with three *compartments*. Figure 3.2 presents a class diagram for class `GradeBook` (Fig. 3.1). The *top compartment* contains the class's name centered horizontally and in boldface type. The *middle compartment* contains the class's attributes, which correspond to data members in C++. This compartment is currently empty, because class `GradeBook` does not yet have any attributes. (Section 3.4 presents a version of class `GradeBook` with an attribute.) The *bottom compartment* contains the class's operations, which correspond to member functions in C++. The UML models operations by listing the operation name followed by a set of parentheses. Class `GradeBook` has only one member function, `displayMessage`, so the bottom compartment of Fig. 3.2 lists one operation with this name. Member function `displayMessage` does *not* require additional information to perform its tasks, so the parentheses following `displayMessage` in the class diagram are *empty*, just as they are in the member function's header in line 12 of Fig. 3.1. The *plus sign (+)* in front of the operation name indicates that `displayMessage` is a *public* operation in the UML (i.e., a `public` member function in C++).

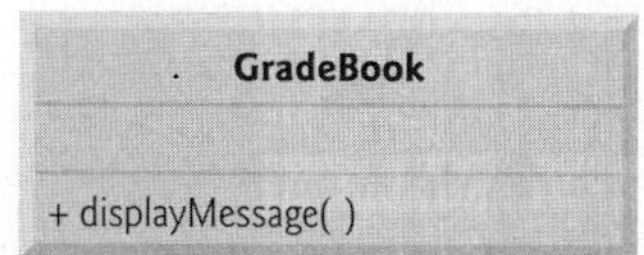

Fig. 3.2 | UML class diagram indicating that class `GradeBook` has a public `displayMessage` operation.

3.3 Defining a Member Function with a Parameter

In our car analogy from Section 1.3, we mentioned that pressing a car's gas pedal sends a *message* to the car to perform a task—make the car go faster. But *how fast* should the car accelerate? As you know, the farther down you press the pedal, the faster the car accelerates. So the message to the car includes *both* the *task to perform* and *additional information that helps the car perform the task*. This additional information is known as a **parameter**—the *value* of the parameter helps the car determine how fast to accelerate. Similarly, a member function can require one or more parameters that represent additional data it needs to perform its task. A function call supplies values—called **arguments**—for each of the function's parameters. For example, to make a deposit into a bank account, suppose a `deposit` member function of an `Account` class specifies a parameter that represents the *deposit amount*. When the `deposit` member function is called, an argument value representing the deposit amount is copied to the member function's parameter. The member function then adds that amount to the account balance.

Defining and Testing Class **GradeBook**

Our next example (Fig. 3.3) redefines class `GradeBook` (lines 9–18) with a `displayMessage` member function (lines 13–17) that displays the course name as part of the welcome message. The new version of `displayMessage` requires a *parameter* (`courseName` in line 13) that represents the course name to output.

```
1  // Fig. 3.3: fig03_03.cpp
2  // Define class GradeBook with a member function that takes a parameter,
3  // create a GradeBook object and call its displayMessage function.
4  #include <iostream>
5  #include <string> // program uses C++ standard string class
6  using namespace std;
7
8  // GradeBook class definition
9  class GradeBook
10 {
11 public:
12    // function that displays a welcome message to the GradeBook user
13    void displayMessage( string courseName ) const
14    {
15       cout << "Welcome to the grade book for\n" << courseName << "!"
16          << endl;
17    } // end function displayMessage
18 }; // end class GradeBook
19
20 // function main begins program execution
21 int main()
22 {
23    string nameOfCourse; // string of characters to store the course name
24    GradeBook myGradeBook; // create a GradeBook object named myGradeBook
25
26    // prompt for and input course name
27    cout << "Please enter the course name:" << endl;
28    getline( cin, nameOfCourse ); // read a course name with blanks
29    cout << endl; // output a blank line
30
31    // call myGradeBook's displayMessage function
32    // and pass nameOfCourse as an argument
33    myGradeBook.displayMessage( nameOfCourse );
34 } // end main
```

```
Please enter the course name:
CS101 Introduction to C++ Programming

Welcome to the grade book for
CS101 Introduction to C++ Programming!
```

Fig. 3.3 | Define class `GradeBook` with a member function that takes a parameter, create a `GradeBook` object and call its `displayMessage` function.

Before discussing the new features of class `GradeBook`, let's see how the new class is used in `main` (lines 21–34). Line 23 creates a variable of type **`string`** called `nameOfCourse` that will be used to store the course name entered by the user. A variable of type `string` represents a string of characters such as "`CS101 Introduction to C++ Programming`". A string is actually an *object* of the C++ Standard Library class `string`. This class is defined in **header `<string>`**, and the name `string`, like `cout`, belongs to namespace `std`. To enable lines 13 and 23 to compile, line 5 *includes* the `<string>` header. The `using` directive in line 6 allows us to simply write `string` in line 23 rather than `std::string`. For now, you can think of `string` variables like variables of other types such as `int`. You'll learn additional `string` capabilities in Section 3.8 and in Chapter 19.

Line 24 creates an object of class `GradeBook` named `myGradeBook`. Line 27 prompts the user to enter a course name. Line 28 reads the name from the user and assigns it to the `nameOfCourse` variable, using the library function **`getline`** to perform the input. Before we explain this line of code, let's explain why we cannot simply write

```
cin >> nameOfCourse;
```

to obtain the course name.

In our sample program execution, we use the course name "`CS101 Introduction to C++ Programming`," which contains multiple words *separated by blanks*. (Recall that we highlight user-entered data in bold.) When reading a `string` with the stream extraction operator, `cin` reads characters *until the first white-space character is reached*. Thus, only "`CS101`" would be read by the preceding statement. The rest of the course name would have to be read by subsequent input operations.

In this example, we'd like the user to type the complete course name and press *Enter* to submit it to the program, and we'd like to store the *entire* course name in the `string` variable `nameOfCourse`. The function call `getline( cin, nameOfCourse )` in line 28 reads characters (*including* the space characters that separate the words in the input) from the standard input stream object `cin` (i.e., the keyboard) until the *newline* character is encountered, places the characters in the `string` variable `nameOfCourse` and *discards* the newline character. When you press *Enter* while entering data, a newline is inserted in the input stream. The `<string>` header must be included in the program to use function `getline`, which belongs to namespace `std`.

Line 33 calls `myGradeBook`'s `displayMessage` member function. The `nameOfCourse` variable in parentheses is the *argument* that's passed to member function `displayMessage` so that it can perform its task. The value of variable `nameOfCourse` in `main` is *copied* to member function `displayMessage`'s parameter `courseName` in line 13. When you execute this program, member function `displayMessage` outputs as part of the welcome message the course name you type (in our sample execution, `CS101 Introduction to C++ Programming`).

More on Arguments and Parameters

To specify in a function definition that the function requires data to perform its task, you place additional information in the function's **parameter list**, which is located in the parentheses following the function name. The parameter list may contain *any* number of parameters, including *none at all* (represented by empty parentheses as in Fig. 3.1, line 12) to indicate that a function does *not* require any parameters. The `displayMessage` member function's parameter list (Fig. 3.3, line 13) declares that the function requires one parameter. Each parameter specifies a *type* and an *identifier*. The type `string` and the identifier courseName indicate that member function displayMessage requires a string to perform its task. The member function body uses the parameter courseName to access the value that's passed to the function in the function call (line 33 in main). Lines 15–16 display parameter courseName's value as part of the welcome message. The parameter variable's name (courseName in line 13) can be the *same* as or *different* from the argument variable's name (nameOfCourse in line 33)—you'll learn why in Chapter 6.

A function can specify multiple parameters by separating each from the next with a comma. The number and order of arguments in a function call *must match* the number and order of parameters in the parameter list of the called member function's header. Also, the argument types in the function call must be consistent with the types of the corresponding parameters in the function header. (As you'll learn in subsequent chapters, an argument's type and its corresponding parameter's type need not always be *identical*, but they must be "consistent.") In our example, the one string argument in the function call (i.e., nameOfCourse) *exactly matches* the one string parameter in the member-function definition (i.e., courseName).

Updated UML Class Diagram for Class GradeBook

The UML class diagram of Fig. 3.4 models class GradeBook of Fig. 3.3. Like the class GradeBook defined in Fig. 3.1, this GradeBook class contains public member function displayMessage. However, this version of displayMessage has a *parameter*. The UML models a parameter by listing the parameter name, followed by a colon and the parameter type in the parentheses following the operation name. The UML has its *own* data types *similar* to those of C++. The UML is *language independent*—it's used with many different programming languages—so its terminology does not exactly match that of C++. For example, the UML type String corresponds to the C++ type string. Member function displayMessage of class GradeBook (Fig. 3.3, lines 13–17) has a string parameter named courseName, so Fig. 3.4 lists courseName : String between the parentheses following the operation name displayMessage. This version of the GradeBook class still does *not* have any data members.

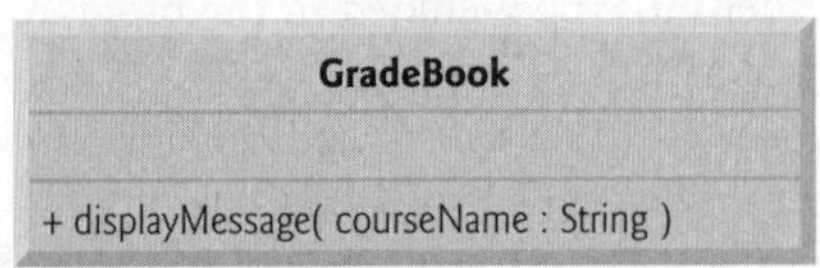

Fig. 3.4 | UML class diagram indicating that class GradeBook has a public displayMessage operation with a courseName parameter of UML type String.

3.4 Data Members, *set* Member Functions and *get* Member Functions

In Chapter 2, we declared all of a program's variables in its main function. Variables declared in a function definition's body are known as **local variables** and can be used *only* from the line of their declaration in the function to the closing right brace (}) of the block in which they're declared. A local variable must be declared *before* it can be used in a function. A local variable cannot be accessed *outside* the function in which it's declared. *When* *a function terminates, the values of its local variables are lost.* (You'll see an exception to this in Chapter 6 when we discuss `static` local variables.)

A class normally consists of one or more member functions that manipulate the attributes that belong to a particular object of the class. Attributes are represented as variables in a class definition. Such variables are called **data members** and are declared *inside* a class definition but *outside* the bodies of the class's member-function definitions. Each object of a class maintains its own attributes in memory. These attributes exist throughout the life of the object. The example in this section demonstrates a `GradeBook` class that contains a `courseName` data member to represent a particular `GradeBook` object's course name. If you create more than one `GradeBook` object, each will have its own `courseName` data member, and these can contain *different* values.

`GradeBook` Class with a Data Member, and set *and* get *Member Functions*

In our next example, class `GradeBook` (Fig. 3.5) maintains the course name as a *data member* so that it can be *used* or *modified* throughout a program's execution. The class contains member functions `setCourseName`, `getCourseName` and `displayMessage`. Member function `setCourseName` *stores* a course name in a `GradeBook` data member. Member function `getCourseName` *obtains* the course name from that data member. Member function `displayMessage`—which now specifies *no parameters*—still displays a welcome message that includes the course name. However, as you'll see, the function now *obtains* the course name by calling another function in the same class—`getCourseName`.

```
// Fig. 3.5: fig03_05.cpp
// Define class GradeBook that contains a courseName data member
// and member functions to set and get its value;
// Create and manipulate a GradeBook object with these functions.
#include <iostream>
#include <string> // program uses C++ standard string class
using namespace std;

// GradeBook class definition
class GradeBook
{
public:
   // function that sets the course name
   void setCourseName( string name )
   {
      courseName = name; // store the course name in the object
   } // end function setCourseName

   // function that gets the course name
   string getCourseName() const
   {
      return courseName; // return the object's courseName
   } // end function getCourseName

```

Fig. 3.5 | Defining and testing class `GradeBook` with a data member and *set* and *get* member functions. (Part 1 of 2.)

```
25      // function that displays a welcome message
26      void displayMessage() const
27      {
28         // this statement calls getCourseName to get the
29         // name of the course this GradeBook represents
30         cout << "Welcome to the grade book for\n" << getCourseName() << "!"
31            << endl;
32      } // end function displayMessage
33   private:
34      string courseName; // course name for this GradeBook
35   }; // end class GradeBook
36
37   // function main begins program execution
38   int main()
39   {
40      string nameOfCourse; // string of characters to store the course name
41      GradeBook myGradeBook; // create a GradeBook object named myGradeBook
42
43      // display initial value of courseName
44      cout << "Initial course name is: " << myGradeBook.getCourseName()
45         << endl;
46
47      // prompt for, input and set course name
48      cout << "\nPlease enter the course name:" << endl;
49      getline( cin, nameOfCourse ); // read a course name with blanks
50      myGradeBook.setCourseName( nameOfCourse ); // set the course name
51
52      cout << endl; // outputs a blank line
53      myGradeBook.displayMessage(); // display message with new course name
54   } // end main
```

```
Initial course name is:

Please enter the course name:
CS101 Introduction to C++ Programming

Welcome to the grade book for
CS101 Introduction to C++ Programming!
```

Fig. 3.5 | Defining and testing class GradeBook with a data member and *set* and *get* member functions. (Part 2 of 2.)

A typical instructor teaches *several* courses, each with its own course name. Line 34 declares that courseName is a variable of type string. Because the variable is declared in the class definition (lines 10–35) but outside the bodies of the class's member-function definitions (lines 14–17, 20–23 and 26–32), the variable is a *data member*. Every instance (i.e., object) of class GradeBook contains each of the class's data members—if there are two GradeBook objects, each has its *own* courseName (one per object), as you'll see in the example of Fig. 3.7. A benefit of making courseName a data member is that *all* the member functions of the class can manipulate any data members that appear in the class definition (in this case, courseName).

Access Specifiers **public** *and* **private**

Most data-member declarations appear after the **private** access specifier. Variables or functions declared after access specifier private (and *before* the next access specifier if there is one) are accessible only to member functions of the class for which they're declared (or to "friends" of the class, as you'll see in Chapter 9). Thus, data member courseName can be used *only* in member functions setCourseName, getCourseName and displayMessage of class GradeBook (or to "friends" of the class, if there are any).

Error-Prevention Tip 3.1

Making the data members of a class private *and the member functions of the class* public *facilitates debugging because problems with data manipulations are localized to either the class's member functions or the friends of the class.*

Common Programming Error 3.2

An attempt by a function, which is not a member of a particular class (or a friend of that class) to access a private *member of that class is a compilation error.*

The *default access* for class members is private so all members *after* the class header and *before* the first access specifier (if there are any) are private. The access specifiers public and private may be repeated, but this is unnecessary and can be confusing.

Declaring data members with access specifier private is known as **data hiding.** When a program creates a GradeBook object, data member courseName is *encapsulated* (hidden) in the object and can be accessed only by member functions of the object's class. In class GradeBook, member functions setCourseName and getCourseName manipulate the data member courseName directly.

Member Functions **setCourseName** *and* **getCourseName**

Member function setCourseName (lines 14–17) does not *return* any data when it completes its task, so its return type is void. The member function *receives* one parameter—name—which represents the course name that will be passed to it as an argument (as we'll see in line 50 of main). Line 16 assigns name to data member courseName, thus *modifying* the object—for this reason, we do *not* declare setCourseName const. In this example, setCourseName does not *validate* the course name—i.e., the function does *not* check that the course name adheres to any particular format or follows any other rules regarding what a "valid" course name looks like. Suppose, for instance, that a university can print student transcripts containing course names of only 25 characters or fewer. In this case, we might want class GradeBook to ensure that its data member courseName never contains more than 25 characters. We discuss validation in Section 3.8.

Member function getCourseName (lines 20–23) *returns* a particular GradeBook object's courseName, *without* modifying the object—for this reason, we declare getCourseName const. The member function has an *empty parameter list*, so it does *not* require additional data to perform its task. The function specifies that it returns a string. When a function that specifies a return type other than void is called and completes its task, the function uses a **return statement** (as in line 22) to *return a result* to its calling function. For example, when you go to an automated teller machine (ATM) and request your account balance, you expect the ATM to give you a value that represents your balance. Similarly, when a statement calls member function getCourseName on a GradeBook object, the statement expects to receive the `GradeBook`'s course name (in this case, a `string`, as specified by the function's return type).

If you have a function `square` that returns the square of its argument, the statement

```
result = square( 2 );
```

returns `4` from function `square` and assigns to variable `result` the value `4`. If you have a function `maximum` that returns the largest of three integer arguments, the statement

```
biggest = maximum( 27, 114, 51 );
```

returns `114` from function `maximum` and assigns this value to variable `biggest`.

The statements in lines 16 and 22 each use variable `courseName` (line 34) even though it was *not* declared in any of the member functions. We can do this because `courseName` is a *data member* of the class and data members are accessible from a class's member functions.

Member Function `displayMessage`

Member function `displayMessage` (lines 26–32) does *not* return any data when it completes its task, so its return type is `void`. The function does *not* receive parameters, so its parameter list is empty. Lines 30–31 output a welcome message that includes the value of data member `courseName`. Line 30 calls member function `getCourseName` to obtain the value of `courseName`. Member function `displayMessage` could also access data member `courseName` directly, just as member functions `setCourseName` and `getCourseName` do. We explain shortly why it's preferable from a software engineering perspective to call member function `getCourseName` to obtain the value of `courseName`.

Testing Class `GradeBook`

The `main` function (lines 38–54) creates one object of class `GradeBook` and uses each of its member functions. Line 41 creates a `GradeBook` object named `myGradeBook`. Lines 44–45 display the initial course name by calling the object's `getCourseName` member function. The first line of the output does not show a course name, because the object's `courseName` data member (i.e., a `string`) is initially empty—by default, the initial value of a `string` is the so-called **empty string**, i.e., a string that does not contain any characters. Nothing appears on the screen when an empty string is displayed.

Line 48 prompts the user to enter a course name. Local `string` variable `nameOfCourse` (declared in line 40) is set to the course name entered by the user, which is obtained by the call to the `getline` function (line 49). Line 50 calls object `myGradeBook`'s `setCourseName` member function and supplies `nameOfCourse` as the function's argument. When the function is called, the argument's value is copied to parameter `name` (line 14) of member function `setCourseName`. Then the parameter's value is assigned to data member `courseName` (line 16). Line 52 skips a line; then line 53 calls object `myGradeBook`'s `displayMessage` member function to display the welcome message containing the course name.

Software Engineering with Set *and* Get *Functions*

A class's `private` data members can be manipulated *only* by member functions of that class (and by "friends" of the class as you'll see in Chapter 9). So a **client of an object**—that is, any statement that calls the object's member functions from *outside* the object—calls the class's `public` member functions to request the class's services for particular objects of the class. This is why the statements in function `main` call member functions `setCourseName`, `getCourseName` and `displayMessage` on a `GradeBook` object. Classes often provide `public` member functions to allow clients of the class to ***set*** (i.e., assign values to) or ***get*** (i.e., obtain the values of) `private` data members. These member function names need not begin with `set` or `get`, but this naming convention is common. In this example, the member function that *sets* the `courseName` data member is called `setCourseName`, and the member function that *gets* the value of the `courseName` data member is called `getCourseName`. *Set* functions are sometimes called **mutators** (because they mutate, or change, values), and *get* functions are also called **accessors** (because they access values).

Recall that declaring data members with access specifier `private` enforces data hiding. Providing `public` *set* and *get* functions allows clients of a class to access the hidden data, but only *indirectly*. The client knows that it's attempting to modify or obtain an object's data, but the client does *not* know *how* the object performs these operations. In some cases, a class may *internally* represent a piece of data one way, but expose that data to clients in a different way. For example, suppose a `Clock` class represents the time of day as a `private` `int` data member `time` that stores the number of seconds since midnight. However, when a client calls a `Clock` object's `getTime` member function, the object could return the time with hours, minutes and seconds in a `string` in the format `"HH:MM:SS"`. Similarly, suppose the `Clock` class provides a *set* function named `setTime` that takes a `string` parameter in the `"HH:MM:SS"` format. Using `string` capabilities presented in Chapter 19, the `setTime` function could convert this `string` to a number of seconds, which the function stores in its `private` data member. The *set* function could also check that the value it receives represents a valid time (e.g., `"12:30:45"` is valid but `"42:85:70"` is not). The *set* and *get* functions allow a client to interact with an object, but the object's `private` data remains safely *encapsulated* (i.e., hidden) in the object itself.

The *set* and *get* functions of a class also should be used by other member functions *within* the class to manipulate the class's `private` data, even though these member functions *can* access the `private` data directly. In Fig. 3.5, member functions `setCourseName` and `getCourseName` are `public` member functions, so they're accessible to clients of the class, as well as to the class itself. Member function `displayMessage` calls member function `getCourseName` to obtain the value of data member `courseName` for display purposes, even though `displayMessage` can access `courseName` directly—accessing a data member via its *get* function creates a better, more robust class (i.e., a class that's easier to maintain and less likely to malfunction). If we decide to change the data member `courseName` in some way, the `displayMessage` definition will *not* require modification—only the bodies of the *get* and *set* functions that directly manipulate the data member will need to change. For example, suppose we want to represent the course name as two separate data members—`courseNumber` (e.g., `"CS101"`) and `courseTitle` (e.g., `"Introduction to C++ Programming"`). Member function `displayMessage` can still issue a single call to member function `getCourseName` to obtain the full course name to display as part of the welcome message. In this case, `getCourseName` would need to build and return a `string` containing the `courseNumber` followed by the `courseTitle`. Member function `displayMessage` could continue to display the complete course title "`CS101 Introduction to C++ Programming`." The benefits of calling a *set* function from another member function of the same class will become clearer when we discuss validation in Section 3.8.

Good Programming Practice 3.1

Always try to localize *the effects of changes to a class's data members by accessing and manipulating the data members through their corresponding* get *and* set *functions.*

Software Engineering Observation 3.1

Write programs that are clear and easy to maintain. Change is the rule rather than the exception. You should anticipate that your code will be modified, and possibly often.

GradeBook's *UML Class Diagram with a Data Member and* set *and* get *Functions*

Figure 3.6 contains an updated UML class diagram for the version of class `GradeBook` in Fig. 3.5. This diagram models `GradeBook`'s data member `courseName` as an attribute in the middle compartment. The UML represents data members as attributes by listing the attribute name, followed by a colon and the attribute type. The UML type of attribute `courseName` is `String`, which corresponds to `string` in C++. Data member `courseName` is `private` in C++, so the class diagram lists a *minus sign (–)* in front of the corresponding attribute's name. Class `GradeBook` contains three `public` member functions, so the class diagram lists three operations in the third compartment. Operation `setCourseName` has a `String` parameter called `name`. The UML indicates the *return type* of an operation by placing a colon and the return type after the parentheses following the operation name. Member function `getCourseName` of class `GradeBook` has a `string` return type in C++, so the class diagram shows a `String` return type in the UML. Operations `setCourseName` and `displayMessage` do not return values (i.e., they return `void` in C++), so the UML class diagram does not specify a return type after the parentheses of these operations.

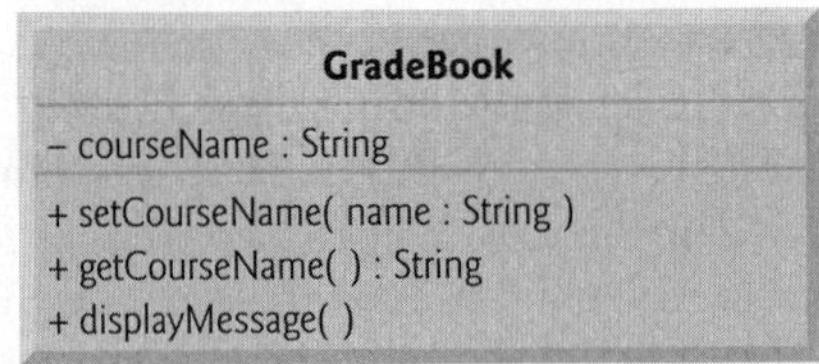

Fig. 3.6 | UML class diagram for class `GradeBook` with a private `courseName` attribute and public operations `setCourseName`, `getCourseName` and `displayMessage`.

3.5 Initializing Objects with Constructors

As mentioned in Section 3.4, when an object of class `GradeBook` (Fig. 3.5) is created, its data member `courseName` is initialized to the empty string by default. What if you want to provide a course name when you *create* a `GradeBook` object? Each class you declare can provide one or more **constructors** that can be used to initialize an object of the class when the object is created. A constructor is a special member function that must be defined with the *same name as the class*, so that the compiler can distinguish it from the class's other member functions. An important difference between constructors and other functions is that *constructors cannot return values*, so they *cannot* specify a return type (not even `void`). Normally, constructors are declared `public`. In the early chapters, our classes will generally have one constructor—in later chapters, you'll see how to create classes with more that one constructor using the technique of *function overloading*, which we introduce in Section 6.17.

C++ automatically calls a constructor for each object that's created, which helps ensure that objects are initialized properly before they're used in a program. The constructor call occurs when the object is created. If a class does not *explicitly* include constructors, the compiler provides a **default constructor** with *no* parameters. For example, when line 41 of Fig. 3.5 creates a `GradeBook` object, the default constructor is called. The default constructor provided by the compiler creates a `GradeBook` object without giving any initial values to the object's fundamental type data members. For data members that are objects of other classes, the default constructor implicitly calls each data member's default constructor to ensure that the data member is initialized properly. This is why the `string` data member `courseName` (in Fig. 3.5) was initialized to the empty string—the default constructor for class `string` sets the `string`'s value to the empty string.

In the example of Fig. 3.7, we specify a course name for a `GradeBook` object when the object is created (e.g., line 47). In this case, the argument `"CS101 Introduction to C++ Programming"` is passed to the `GradeBook` object's constructor (lines 14–18) and used to initialize the `courseName`. Figure 3.7 defines a modified `GradeBook` class containing a constructor with a `string` parameter that receives the initial course name.

```
1  // Fig. 3.7: fig03_07.cpp
2  // Instantiating multiple objects of the GradeBook class and using
3  // the GradeBook constructor to specify the course name
4  // when each GradeBook object is created.
5  #include <iostream>
6  #include <string> // program uses C++ standard string class
7  using namespace std;
8
9  // GradeBook class definition
10 class GradeBook
11 {
12 public:
13    // constructor initializes courseName with string supplied as argument
14    explicit GradeBook( string name )
15       : courseName( name ) // member initializer to initialize courseName
16    {
17       // empty body
18    } // end GradeBook constructor
19
20    // function to set the course name
21    void setCourseName( string name )
22    {
23       courseName = name; // store the course name in the object
24    } // end function setCourseName
25
26    // function to get the course name
27    string getCourseName() const
28    {
```

Fig. 3.7 | Instantiating multiple objects of the `GradeBook` class and using the `GradeBook` constructor to specify the course name when each `GradeBook` object is created. (Part 1 of 2.)

```
29         return courseName; // return object's courseName
30      } // end function getCourseName
31
32      // display a welcome message to the GradeBook user
33      void displayMessage() const
34      {
35         // call getCourseName to get the courseName
36         cout << "Welcome to the grade book for\n" << getCourseName()
37            << "!" << endl;
38      } // end function displayMessage
39   private:
40      string courseName; // course name for this GradeBook
41   }; // end class GradeBook
42
43   // function main begins program execution
44   int main()
45   {
46      // create two GradeBook objects
47      GradeBook gradeBook1( "CS101 Introduction to C++ Programming" );
48      GradeBook gradeBook2( "CS102 Data Structures in C++" );
49
50      // display initial value of courseName for each GradeBook
51      cout << "gradeBook1 created for course: " << gradeBook1.getCourseName()
52         << "\ngradeBook2 created for course: " << gradeBook2.getCourseName()
53         << endl;
54   } // end main
```

```
gradeBook1 created for course: CS101 Introduction to C++ Programming
gradeBook2 created for course: CS102 Data Structures in C++
```

Fig. 3.7 | Instantiating multiple objects of the GradeBook class and using the GradeBook constructor to specify the course name when each GradeBook object is created. (Part 2 of 2.)

Defining a Constructor

Lines 14–18 of Fig. 3.7 define a constructor for class GradeBook. The constructor has the *same* name as its class, GradeBook. A constructor specifies in its parameter list the data it requires to perform its task. When you create a new object, you place this data in the parentheses that follow the object name (as we did in lines 47–48). Line 14 indicates that class GradeBook's constructor has a string parameter called name. We declared this constructor **explicit**, because it takes a *single* parameter—this is important for subtle reasons that you'll learn in Section 10.13. For now, just declare *all* single-parameter constructors explicit. Line 14 does *not* specify a return type, because constructors *cannot* return values (or even void). Also, constructors cannot be declared const (because initializing an object modifies it).

The constructor uses a **member-initializer list** (line 15) to initialize the courseName data member with the value of the constructor's parameter name. *Member initializers* appear between a constructor's parameter list and the left brace that begins the constructor's body. The member initializer list is separated from the parameter list with a *colon (:)*. A member initializer consists of a data member's *variable name* followed by parentheses containing the member's *initial value*. In this example, `courseName` is initialized with the value of the parameter `name`. If a class contains more than one data member, each data member's initializer is separated from the next by a comma. The member initializer list executes *before* the body of the constructor executes. You can perform initialization in the constructor's body, but you'll learn later in the book that it's more efficient to do it with member initializers, and some types of data members must be initialized this way.

Notice that both the constructor (line 14) and the `setCourseName` function (line 21) use a parameter called `name`. You can use the *same* parameter names in *different* functions because the parameters are *local* to each function—they do *not* interfere with one another.

Testing Class **`GradeBook`**

Lines 44–54 of Fig. 3.7 define the `main` function that tests class `GradeBook` and demonstrates initializing `GradeBook` objects using a constructor. Line 47 creates and initializes `GradeBook` object `gradeBook1`. When this line executes, the `GradeBook` constructor (lines 14–18) is called with the argument `"CS101 Introduction to C++ Programming"` to initialize `gradeBook1`'s course name. Line 48 repeats this process for `GradeBook` object `gradeBook2`, this time passing the argument `"CS102 Data Structures in C++"` to initialize `gradeBook2`'s course name. Lines 51–52 use each object's `getCourseName` member function to obtain the course names and show that they were indeed initialized when the objects were created. The output confirms that each `GradeBook` object maintains its *own* data member `courseName`.

Ways to Provide a Default Constructor for a Class

Any constructor that takes *no* arguments is called a default constructor. A class can get a default constructor in one of several ways:

1. The compiler *implicitly* creates a default constructor in every class that does *not* have any user-defined constructors. The default constructor does *not* initialize the class's data members, but *does* call the default constructor for each data member that's an object of another class. An uninitialized variable contains an undefined ("garbage") value.
2. You *explicitly* define a constructor that takes no arguments. Such a default constructor will call the default constructor for each data member that's an object of another class and will perform additional initialization specified by you.
3. *If you define any constructors with arguments, C++ will not implicitly create a default constructor for that class.* We'll show later that C++11 allows you to force the compiler to create the default constructor even if you've defined non-default constructors.

For each version of class `GradeBook` in Fig. 3.1, Fig. 3.3 and Fig. 3.5 the compiler *implicitly* defined a default constructor.

Error-Prevention Tip 3.2

Unless no initialization of your class's data members is necessary (almost never), provide constructors to ensure that your class's data members are initialized with meaningful values when each new object of your class is created.

Software Engineering Observation 3.2

Data members can be initialized in a constructor, or their values may be set later after the object is created. However, it's a good software engineering practice to ensure that an object is fully initialized before *the client code invokes the object's member functions. You should not rely on the client code to ensure that an object gets initialized properly.*

Adding the Constructor to Class ***GradeBook****'s UML Class Diagram*

The UML class diagram of Fig. 3.8 models the `GradeBook` class of Fig. 3.7, which has a constructor with a `name` parameter of type `string` (represented by type `String` in the UML). Like operations, the UML models constructors in the third compartment of a class in a class diagram. To distinguish a constructor from a class's operations, the UML places the word "constructor" between guillemets (« and ») before the constructor's name. By convention, you list the class's constructor *before* other operations in the third compartment.

GradeBook
– courseName : String
«constructor» + GradeBook(name : String) + setCourseName(name : String) + getCourseName( ) : String + displayMessage( )

Fig. 3.8 | UML class diagram indicating that class `GradeBook` has a constructor with a `name` parameter of UML type `String`.

3.6 Placing a Class in a Separate File for Reusability

One of the benefits of creating class definitions is that, when packaged properly, your classes can be *reused* by other programmers. For example, you can *reuse* C++ Standard Library type `string` in any C++ program by including the header `<string>` (and, as you'll see, by being able to link to the library's object code).

Programmers who wish to use our `GradeBook` class cannot simply include the file from Fig. 3.7 in another program. As you learned in Chapter 2, function `main` begins the execution of every program, and every program must have *exactly one* `main` function. If other programmers include the code from Fig. 3.7, they get extra "baggage"—our `main` function—and their programs will then have two `main` functions. Attempting to compile a program with two `main` functions produces an error. So, placing `main` in the same file with a class definition *prevents that class from being reused* by other programs. In this section, we demonstrate how to make class `GradeBook` reusable by *separating it into another file* from the `main` function.

Headers

Each of the previous examples in the chapter consists of a single `.cpp` file, also known as a **source-code file**, that contains a `GradeBook` class definition and a `main` function. When building an object-oriented C++ program, it's customary to define *reusable* source code (such as a class) in a file that by convention has a `.h` filename extension—known as a **header**. Programs use `#include` preprocessing directives to include headers and take advantage of reusable software components, such as type `string` provided in the C++ Standard Library and user-defined types like class `GradeBook`.

Our next example separates the code from Fig. 3.7 into two files—`GradeBook.h` (Fig. 3.9) and `fig03_10.cpp` (Fig. 3.10). As you look at the header in Fig. 3.9, notice that it contains only the `GradeBook` class definition (lines 7–38) and the headers on which the class depends. The `main` function that *uses* class `GradeBook` is defined in the source-code file `fig03_10.cpp` (Fig. 3.10) in lines 8–18. To help you prepare for the larger programs you'll encounter later in this book and in industry, we often use a separate source-code file containing function `main` to test our classes (this is called a **driver program**). You'll soon learn how a source-code file with `main` can use the class definition found in a header to create objects of a class.

```
1  // Fig. 3.9: GradeBook.h
2  // GradeBook class definition in a separate file from main.
3  #include <iostream>
4  #include <string> // class GradeBook uses C++ standard string class
5
6  // GradeBook class definition
7  class GradeBook
8  {
9  public:
10    // constructor initializes courseName with string supplied as argument
11    explicit GradeBook( std::string name )
12       : courseName( name ) // member initializer to initialize courseName
13    {
14       // empty body
15    } // end GradeBook constructor
16
17    // function to set the course name
18    void setCourseName( std::string name )
19    {
20       courseName = name; // store the course name in the object
21    } // end function setCourseName
22
23    // function to get the course name
24    std::string getCourseName() const
25    {
26       return courseName; // return object's courseName
27    } // end function getCourseName
28
29    // display a welcome message to the GradeBook user
30    void displayMessage() const
31    {
32       // call getCourseName to get the courseName
33       std::cout << "Welcome to the grade book for\n" << getCourseName()
34          << "!" << std::endl;
35    } // end function displayMessage
36 private:
37    std::string courseName; // course name for this GradeBook
38 }; // end class GradeBook
```

Fig. 3.9 | `GradeBook` class definition in a separate file from `main`.

```
1  // Fig. 3.10: fig03_10.cpp
2  // Including class GradeBook from file GradeBook.h for use in main.
3  #include <iostream>
4  #include "GradeBook.h" // include definition of class GradeBook
5  using namespace std;
6
7  // function main begins program execution
8  int main()
9  {
10    // create two GradeBook objects
11    GradeBook gradeBook1( "CS101 Introduction to C++ Programming" );
12    GradeBook gradeBook2( "CS102 Data Structures in C++" );
13
14    // display initial value of courseName for each GradeBook
15    cout << "gradeBook1 created for course: " << gradeBook1.getCourseName()
16       << "\ngradeBook2 created for course: " << gradeBook2.getCourseName()
17       << endl;
18 } // end main
```

```
gradeBook1 created for course: CS101 Introduction to C++ Programming
gradeBook2 created for course: CS102 Data Structures in C++
```

Fig. 3.10 | Including class `GradeBook` from file `GradeBook.h` for use in `main`.

Use `std::` with Standard Library Components in Headers

Throughout the header (Fig. 3.9), we use `std::` when referring to `string` (lines 11, 18, 24 and 37), `cout` (line 33) and `endl` (line 34). For subtle reasons that we'll explain in a later chapter, headers should *never* contain `using` directives or `using` declarations (Section 2.6).

Including a Header That Contains a User-Defined Class

A header such as `GradeBook.h` (Fig. 3.9) cannot be used as a complete program, because it does not contain a `main` function. To test class `GradeBook` (defined in Fig. 3.9), you must write a separate source-code file containing a `main` function (such as Fig. 3.10) that instantiates and uses objects of the class.

The compiler doesn't know what a `GradeBook` is because it's a user-defined type. In fact, the compiler doesn't even know the classes in the C++ Standard Library. To help it understand how to use a class, we must explicitly provide the compiler with the class's definition—that's why, for example, to use type `string`, a program must include the `<string>` header. This enables the compiler to determine the amount of memory that it must reserve for each `string` object and ensure that a program calls a `string`'s member functions correctly.

To create `GradeBook` objects `gradeBook1` and `gradeBook2` in lines 11–12 of Fig. 3.10, the compiler must know the *size* of a `GradeBook` object. While objects conceptually contain data members and member functions, C++ objects actually contain *only* data. The compiler creates only *one* copy of the class's member functions and *shares* that copy among all the class's objects. Each object, of course, needs its own data members, because their contents can vary among objects (such as two different `BankAccount` objects having two different balances). The member-function code, however, is *not modifiable*, so it can be shared among all objects of the class. Therefore, the size of an object depends on the amount of memory required to store the class's data members. By including `GradeBook.h` in line 4, we give the compiler access to the information it needs (Fig. 3.9, line 37) to determine the size of a `GradeBook` object and to determine whether objects of the class are used correctly (in lines 11–12 and 15–16 of Fig. 3.10).

Line 4 instructs the C++ preprocessor to replace the directive with a copy of the contents of `GradeBook.h` (i.e., the `GradeBook` class definition) *before* the program is compiled. When the source-code file `fig03_10.cpp` is compiled, it now contains the `GradeBook` class definition (because of the `#include`), and the compiler is able to determine how to create `GradeBook` objects and see that their member functions are called correctly. Now that the class definition is in a header (without a `main` function), we can include that header in *any* program that needs to reuse our `GradeBook` class.

How Headers Are Located

Notice that the name of the `GradeBook.h` header in line 4 of Fig. 3.10 is enclosed in quotes (" ") rather than angle brackets (< >). Normally, a program's source-code files and user-defined headers are placed in the *same* directory. When the preprocessor encounters a header name in quotes, it attempts to locate the header in the same directory as the file in which the `#include` directive appears. If the preprocessor cannot find the header in that directory, it searches for it in the same location(s) as the C++ Standard Library headers. When the preprocessor encounters a header name in angle brackets (e.g., `<iostream>`), it assumes that the header is part of the C++ Standard Library and does *not* look in the directory of the program that's being preprocessed.

Error-Prevention Tip 3.3

To ensure that the preprocessor can locate headers correctly, `#include` preprocessing directives should place user-defined headers names in quotes (e.g., `"GradeBook.h"`) and place C++ Standard Library headers names in angle brackets (e.g., `<iostream>`).

Additional Software Engineering Issues

Now that class `GradeBook` is defined in a header, the class is *reusable*. Unfortunately, placing a class definition in a header as in Fig. 3.9 still *reveals the entire implementation of the class to the class's clients*—`GradeBook.h` is simply a text file that anyone can open and read. Conventional software engineering wisdom says that to use an object of a class, the client code needs to know only what member functions to call, what arguments to provide to each member function and what return type to expect from each member function. *The client code does not need to know how those functions are implemented.*

If client code *does* know how a class is implemented, the programmer might write client code based on the class's implementation details. Ideally, if that implementation changes, the class's clients should not have to change. *Hiding the class's implementation details makes it easier to change the class's implementation while minimizing, and hopefully eliminating, changes to client code.*

In Section 3.7, we show how to break up the `GradeBook` class into two files so that

1. the class is *reusable*,
2. the clients of the class know what member functions the class provides, how to call them and what return types to expect, and
3. the clients do *not* know how the class's member functions are implemented.

3.7 Separating Interface from Implementation

In the preceding section, we showed how to promote software reusability by separating a class definition from the client code (e.g., function `main`) that uses the class. We now introduce another fundamental principle of good software engineering—**separating interface from implementation.**

Interface of a Class

Interfaces define and standardize the ways in which things such as people and systems interact with one another. For example, a radio's controls serve as an interface between the radio's users and its internal components. The controls allow users to perform a limited set of operations (such as changing the station, adjusting the volume, and choosing between AM and FM stations). Various radios may implement these operations differently—some provide push buttons, some provide dials and some support voice commands. The interface specifies *what* operations a radio permits users to perform but does not specify *how* the operations are implemented inside the radio.

Similarly, the **interface of a class** describes *what* services a class's clients can use and how to *request* those services, but not *how* the class carries out the services. A class's `public` interface consists of the class's `public` member functions (also known as the class's **public services**). For example, class `GradeBook`'s interface (Fig. 3.9) contains a constructor and member functions `setCourseName`, `getCourseName` and `displayMessage`. `GradeBook`'s clients (e.g., `main` in Fig. 3.10) *use* these functions to request the class's services. As you'll soon see, you can specify a class's interface by writing a class definition that lists *only* the member-function names, return types and parameter types.

Separating the Interface from the Implementation

In our prior examples, each class definition contained the complete definitions of the class's `public` member functions and the declarations of its `private` data members. However, it's better software engineering to define member functions *outside* the class definition, so that their implementation details can be *hidden* from the client code. This practice *ensures* that you do not write client code that depends on the class's implementation details.

The program of Figs. 3.11–3.13 separates class `GradeBook`'s interface from its implementation by splitting the class definition of Fig. 3.9 into two files—the header `GradeBook.h` (Fig. 3.11) in which class `GradeBook` is defined, and the source-code file `GradeBook.cpp` (Fig. 3.12) in which `GradeBook`'s member functions are defined. By convention, member-function definitions are placed in a source-code file of the same base name (e.g., `GradeBook`) as the class's header but with a `.cpp` filename extension. The source-code file `fig03_13.cpp` (Fig. 3.13) defines function `main` (the client code). The code and output of Fig. 3.13 are identical to that of Fig. 3.10. Figure 3.14 shows how this three-file program is compiled from the perspectives of the `GradeBook` class programmer and the client-code programmer—we'll explain this figure in detail.

`GradeBook.h`: Defining a Class's Interface with Function Prototypes

Header `GradeBook.h` (Fig. 3.11) contains another version of `GradeBook`'s class definition (lines 8–17). This version is similar to the one in Fig. 3.9, but the function definitions in Fig. 3.9 are replaced here with **function prototypes** (lines 11–14) that *describe the class's* `public` *interface without revealing the class's member-function implementations.* A function prototype is a *declaration* of a function that tells the compiler the function's name, its return type and the types of its parameters. Also, the header still specifies the class's `private` data member (line 16) as well. Again, the compiler *must* know the data members of the class to determine how much memory to reserve for each object of the class. Including the header `GradeBook.h` in the client code (line 5 of Fig. 3.13) provides the compiler with the information it needs to ensure that the client code calls the member functions of class `GradeBook` correctly.

```
1  // Fig. 3.11: GradeBook.h
2  // GradeBook class definition. This file presents GradeBook's public
3  // interface without revealing the implementations of GradeBook's member
4  // functions, which are defined in GradeBook.cpp.
5  #include <string> // class GradeBook uses C++ standard string class
6
7  // GradeBook class definition
8  class GradeBook
9  {
10 public:
11    explicit GradeBook( std::string ); // constructor initialize courseName
12    void setCourseName( std::string ); // sets the course name
13    std::string getCourseName() const; // gets the course name
14    void displayMessage() const; // displays a welcome message
15 private:
16    std::string courseName; // course name for this GradeBook
17 }; // end class GradeBook
```

Fig. 3.11 | `GradeBook` class definition containing function prototypes that specify the interface of the class.

The function prototype in line 11 (Fig. 3.11) indicates that the constructor requires one `string` parameter. Recall that constructors don't have return types, so no return type appears in the function prototype. Member function `setCourseName`'s function prototype indicates that `setCourseName` requires a `string` parameter and does not return a value (i.e., its return type is `void`). Member function `getCourseName`'s function prototype indicates that the function does not require parameters and returns a `string`. Finally, member function `displayMessage`'s function prototype (line 14) specifies that `displayMessage` does not require parameters and does not return a value. These function prototypes are the same as the first lines of the corresponding function definitions in Fig. 3.9, except that the parameter names (which are *optional* in prototypes) are not included and each function prototype *must* end with a semicolon.

Good Programming Practice 3.2

Although parameter names in function prototypes are optional (they're ignored by the compiler), many programmers use these names for documentation purposes.

`GradeBook.cpp`: Defining Member Functions in a Separate Source-Code File

Source-code file `GradeBook.cpp` (Fig. 3.12) *defines* class `GradeBook`'s member functions, which were *declared* in lines 11–14 of Fig. 3.11. The definitions appear in lines 9–33 and are nearly identical to the member-function definitions in lines 11–35 of Fig. 3.9. Note that the `const` keyword *must* appear in *both* the function prototypes (Fig. 3.11, lines13–14) and the function definitions for functions `getCourseName` and `displayMessage` (lines 22 and 28).

```
1  // Fig. 3.12: GradeBook.cpp
2  // GradeBook member-function definitions. This file contains
3  // implementations of the member functions prototyped in GradeBook.h.
4  #include <iostream>
5  #include "GradeBook.h" // include definition of class GradeBook
6  using namespace std;
7
8  // constructor initializes courseName with string supplied as argument
9  GradeBook::GradeBook( string name )
10    : courseName( name ) // member initializer to initialize courseName
11 {
12    // empty body
13 } // end GradeBook constructor
14
15 // function to set the course name
16 void GradeBook::setCourseName( string name )
17 {
18    courseName = name; // store the course name in the object
19 } // end function setCourseName
20
21 // function to get the course name
22 string GradeBook::getCourseName() const
23 {
24    return courseName; // return object's courseName
25 } // end function getCourseName
26
27 // display a welcome message to the GradeBook user
28 void GradeBook::displayMessage() const
29 {
30    // call getCourseName to get the courseName
31    cout << "Welcome to the grade book for\n" << getCourseName()
32       << "!" << endl;
33 } // end function displayMessage
```

Fig. 3.12 | `GradeBook` member-function definitions represent the implementation of class `GradeBook`.

Each member-function name (lines 9, 16, 22 and 28) is preceded by the class name and `::`, which is known as the **scope resolution operator**. This "ties" each member function to the (now separate) `GradeBook` class definition (Fig. 3.11), which declares the class's member functions and data members. Without "`GradeBook::`" preceding each function name, these functions would *not* be recognized by the compiler as member functions of class `GradeBook`—the compiler would consider them "free" or "loose" functions, like `main`. These are also called *global functions*. Such functions cannot access `GradeBook`'s `private` data or call the class's member functions, without specifying an object. So, the compiler would *not* be able to compile these functions. For example, lines 18 and 24 in Fig. 3.12 that access variable `courseName` would cause compilation errors because `courseName` is not declared as a local variable in each function—the compiler would not know that `courseName` is already declared as a data member of class `GradeBook`.

Common Programming Error 3.3

When defining a class's member functions outside *that class, omitting the class name and scope resolution operator (`::`) preceding the function names causes errors.*

To indicate that the member functions in `GradeBook.cpp` are part of class `GradeBook`, we must first include the `GradeBook.h` header (line 5 of Fig. 3.12). This allows us to access the class name `GradeBook` in the `GradeBook.cpp` file. When compiling `GradeBook.cpp`, the compiler uses the information in `GradeBook.h` to ensure that

1. the first line of each member function (lines 9, 16, 22 and 28) matches its prototype in the `GradeBook.h` file—for example, the compiler ensures that `getCourseName` accepts no parameters and returns a `string`, and that
2. each member function knows about the class's data members and other member functions—for example, lines 18 and 24 can access variable `courseName` because it's declared in `GradeBook.h` as a data member of class `GradeBook`, and line 31 can call function `getCourseName`, because it's declared as a member function of the class in `GradeBook.h` (and because the call conforms with the corresponding prototype).

Testing Class GradeBook

Figure 3.13 performs the same `GradeBook` object manipulations as Fig. 3.10. Separating `GradeBook`'s interface from the implementation of its member functions does *not* affect the way that this client code uses the class. It affects only how the program is compiled and linked, which we discuss in detail shortly.

```
// Fig. 3.13: fig03_13.cpp
// GradeBook class demonstration after separating
// its interface from its implementation.
#include <iostream>
#include "GradeBook.h" // include definition of class GradeBook
using namespace std;

// function main begins program execution
int main()
{
   // create two GradeBook objects
   GradeBook gradeBook1( "CS101 Introduction to C++ Programming" );
   GradeBook gradeBook2( "CS102 Data Structures in C++" );

   // display initial value of courseName for each GradeBook
   cout << "gradeBook1 created for course: " << gradeBook1.getCourseName()
      << "\ngradeBook2 created for course: " << gradeBook2.getCourseName()
      << endl;
} // end main
```

Fig. 3.13 | GradeBook class demonstration after separating its interface from its implementation. (Part 1 of 2.)

```
gradeBook1 created for course: CS101 Introduction to C++ Programming
gradeBook2 created for course: CS102 Data Structures in C++
```

Fig. 3.13 | GradeBook class demonstration after separating its interface from its implementation. (Part 2 of 2.)

As in Fig. 3.10, line 5 of Fig. 3.13 includes the `GradeBook.h` header so that the compiler can ensure that `GradeBook` objects are created and manipulated correctly in the client code. Before executing this program, the source-code files in Fig. 3.12 and Fig. 3.13 must both be compiled, then linked together—that is, the member-function calls in the client code need to be tied to the implementations of the class's member functions—a job performed by the linker.

The Compilation and Linking Process

The diagram in Fig. 3.14 shows the compilation and linking process that results in an executable `GradeBook` application that can be used by instructors. Often a class's interface and implementation will be created and compiled by one programmer and used by a separate programmer who implements the client code that uses the class. So, the diagram shows what's required by both the class-implementation programmer and the client-code programmer. The dashed lines in the diagram show the pieces required by the class-implementation programmer, the client-code programmer and the `GradeBook` application user, respectively. [*Note:* Figure 3.14 is *not* a UML diagram.]

A class-implementation programmer responsible for creating a reusable `GradeBook` class creates the header `GradeBook.h` and the source-code file `GradeBook.cpp` that `#include`s the header, then compiles the source-code file to create `GradeBook`'s object code. To hide the class's member-function implementation details, the class-implementation programmer would provide the client-code programmer with the header `GradeBook.h` (which specifies the class's interface and data members) and the `GradeBook` object code (i.e., the machine code instructions that represent `GradeBook`'s member functions). The client-code programmer is *not* given `GradeBook.cpp`, so the client remains unaware of how `GradeBook`'s member functions are implemented.

The client code programmer needs to know only `GradeBook`'s interface to use the class and must be able to link its object code. Since the interface of the class is part of the class definition in the `GradeBook.h` header, the client-code programmer must have access to this file and must `#include` it in the client's source-code file. When the client code is compiled, the compiler uses the class definition in `GradeBook.h` to ensure that the `main` function creates and manipulates objects of class `GradeBook` correctly.

To create the executable `GradeBook` application, the last step is to link

1. the object code for the `main` function (i.e., the client code),
2. the object code for class `GradeBook`'s member-function implementations and
3. the C++ Standard Library object code for the C++ classes (e.g., `string`) used by the class-implementation programmer and the client-code programmer.

The linker's output is the *executable* `GradeBook` application that instructors can use to manage their students' grades. Compilers and IDEs typically invoke the linker for you after compiling your code.

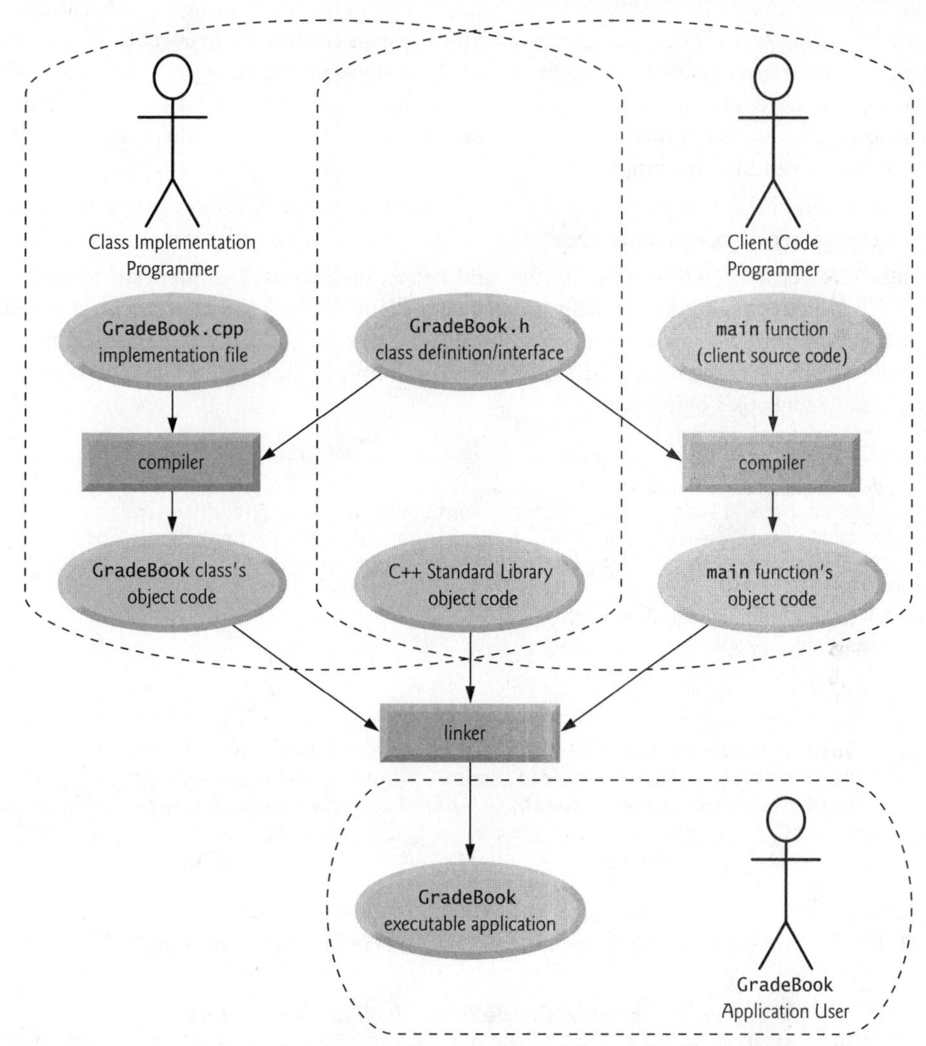

Fig. 3.14 | Compilation and linking process that produces an executable application.

For further information on compiling multiple-source-file programs, see your compiler's documentation. We provide links to various C++ compilers in our C++ Resource Center at `www.deitel.com/cplusplus/`.

3.8 Validating Data with *set* Functions

In Section 3.4, we introduced *set* functions for allowing clients of a class to modify the value of a `private` data member. In Fig. 3.5, class `GradeBook` defines member function `setCourseName` to simply assign a value received in its parameter `name` to data member `courseName`. This member function does not ensure that the course name adheres to any particular format or follows any other rules regarding what a "valid" course name looks like. Suppose that a university can print student transcripts containing course names of only 25 characters or less. If the university uses a system containing GradeBook objects to generate the transcripts, we might want class GradeBook to ensure that its data member courseName never contains more than 25 characters. The program of Figs. 3.15–3.17 enhances class GradeBook's member function setCourseName to perform this **validation** (also known as **validity checking**).

GradeBook Class Definition

GradeBook's class definition (Fig. 3.15)—and hence, its interface—is identical to that of Fig. 3.11. Since the interface remains unchanged, clients of this class need not be changed when the definition of member function setCourseName is modified. This enables clients to take advantage of the improved GradeBook class simply by linking the client code to the updated GradeBook's object code.

```
// Fig. 3.15: GradeBook.h
// GradeBook class definition presents the public interface of
// the class. Member-function definitions appear in GradeBook.cpp.
#include <string> // program uses C++ standard string class

// GradeBook class definition
class GradeBook
{
public:
   explicit GradeBook( std::string ); // constructor initialize courseName
   void setCourseName( std::string ); // sets the course name
   std::string getCourseName() const; // gets the course name
   void displayMessage() const; // displays a welcome message
private:
   std::string courseName; // course name for this GradeBook
}; // end class GradeBook
```

Fig. 3.15 | GradeBook class definition presents the public interface of the class.

Validating the Course Name with **GradeBook** *Member Function* **setCourseName**

The changes to class GradeBook are in the definitions of the constructor (Fig. 3.16, lines 9–12) and setCourseName (lines 16–29). Rather than using a member initializer, the constructor now calls setCourseName. In general, *all* data members should be initialized with *member initializers*. However, sometimes a constructor must also *validate* its argument(s)—often, this is handled in the constructor's body (line 11). The call to setCourseName *validates* the constructor's argument and *sets* the data member courseName. Initially, courseName's value will be set to the empty string *before* the constructor's body executes, then setCourseName will *modify* courseName's value.

In setCourseName, the if statement in lines 18–19 determines whether parameter name contains a *valid* course name (i.e., a string of 25 or fewer characters). If the course name is valid, line 19 stores it in data member courseName. Note the expression name.size() in line 18. This is a member-function call just like myGradeBook.displayMessage(). The C++ Standard Library's string class defines a member function **size** that returns the number of characters in a string object. Parameter name is a string object, so the call `name.size()` returns the number of characters in `name`. If this value is less than or equal to 25, `name` is valid and line 19 executes.

```
1  // Fig. 3.16: GradeBook.cpp
2  // Implementations of the GradeBook member-function definitions.
3  // The setCourseName function performs validation.
4  #include <iostream>
5  #include "GradeBook.h" // include definition of class GradeBook
6  using namespace std;
7
8  // constructor initializes courseName with string supplied as argument
9  GradeBook::GradeBook( string name )
10 {
11    setCourseName( name ); // validate and store courseName
12 } // end GradeBook constructor
13
14 // function that sets the course name;
15 // ensures that the course name has at most 25 characters
16 void GradeBook::setCourseName( string name )
17 {
18    if ( name.size() <= 25 ) // if name has 25 or fewer characters
19       courseName = name; // store the course name in the object
20
21    if ( name.size() > 25 ) // if name has more than 25 characters
22    {
23       // set courseName to first 25 characters of parameter name
24       courseName = name.substr( 0, 25 ); // start at 0, length of 25
25
26       cerr << "Name \"" << name << "\" exceeds maximum length (25).\n"
27          << "Limiting courseName to first 25 characters.\n" << endl;
28    } // end if
29 } // end function setCourseName
30
31 // function to get the course name
32 string GradeBook::getCourseName() const
33 {
34    return courseName; // return object's courseName
35 } // end function getCourseName
36
37 // display a welcome message to the GradeBook user
38 void GradeBook::displayMessage() const
39 {
40    // call getCourseName to get the courseName
41    cout << "Welcome to the grade book for\n" << getCourseName()
42       << "!" << endl;
43 } // end function displayMessage
```

Fig. 3.16 | Member-function definitions for class `GradeBook` with a *set* function that validates the length of data member `courseName`.

The `if` statement in lines 21–28 handles the case in which `setCourseName` receives an *invalid* course name (i.e., a name that is more than 25 characters long). Even if parameter `name` is too long, we still want to leave the `GradeBook` object in a **consistent state**—that is, a state in which the object's data member `courseName` contains a valid value (i.e., a `string` of 25 characters or less). Thus, we truncate the specified course name and assign the first 25 characters of `name` to the `courseName` data member (unfortunately, this could truncate the course name awkwardly). Standard class `string` provides member function **`substr`** (short for "substring") that returns a new `string` object created by copying part of an existing `string` object. The call in line 24 (i.e., `name.substr(0, 25)`) passes two integers (`0` and `25`) to `name`'s member function `substr`. These arguments indicate the portion of the string `name` that `substr` should return. The first argument specifies the *starting position* in the original `string` from which characters are copied—the first character in every string is considered to be at position 0. The second argument specifies the *number of characters to copy*. Therefore, the call in line 24 returns a 25-character substring of `name` starting at position 0 (that is, the first 25 characters in `name`). For example, if `name` holds the value `"CS101 Introduction to Programming in C++"`, `substr` returns `"CS101 Introduction to Pro"`. After the call to `substr`, line 24 assigns the substring returned by `substr` to data member `courseName`. In this way, `setCourseName` ensures that `courseName` is always assigned a string containing 25 or fewer characters. If the member function has to truncate the course name to make it valid, lines 26–27 display a warning message using `cerr`, as mentioned in Chapter 1.

The `if` statement in lines 21–28 contains two body statements—one to set the `courseName` to the first 25 characters of parameter `name` and one to print an accompanying message to the user. Both statements should execute when `name` is too long, so we place them in a pair of braces, `{ }`. Recall from Chapter 2 that this creates a *block*. You'll learn more about placing multiple statements in a control statement's body in Chapter 4.

The statement in lines 26–27 could also appear without a stream insertion operator at the start of the second line of the statement, as in:

```
cerr << "Name \"" << name << "\" exceeds maximum length (25).\n"
   "Limiting courseName to first 25 characters.\n" << endl;
```

The C++ compiler combines adjacent string literals, even if they appear on separate lines of a program. Thus, in the statement above, the C++ compiler would combine the string literals `"\" exceeds maximum length (25).\n"` and `"Limiting courseName to first 25 characters.\n"` into a single string literal that produces output identical to that of lines 26–27 in Fig. 3.16. This behavior allows you to print lengthy strings by breaking them across lines in your program without including additional stream insertion operations.

Testing Class **GradeBook**

Figure 3.17 demonstrates the modified version of class `GradeBook` (Figs. 3.15–3.16) featuring validation. Line 12 creates a `GradeBook` object named `gradeBook1`. Recall that the `GradeBook` constructor calls `setCourseName` to initialize data member `courseName`. In previous versions of the class, the benefit of calling `setCourseName` in the constructor was not evident. Now, however, *the constructor takes advantage of the validation* provided by `setCourseName`. The constructor simply calls `setCourseName`, *rather than duplicating* its validation code. When line 12 of Fig. 3.17 passes an initial course name of `"CS101 Introduction to Programming in C++"` to the `GradeBook` constructor, the constructor passes this value to `setCourseName`, where the actual initialization occurs. Because this course name contains more than 25 characters, the body of the second `if` statement executes, causing `courseName` to be initialized to the truncated 25-character course name

"CS101 Introduction to Pro" (the truncated part is highlighted in line 12). The output in Fig. 3.17 contains the warning message output by lines 26–27 of Fig. 3.16 in member function setCourseName. Line 13 creates another GradeBook object called gradeBook2—the valid course name passed to the constructor is exactly 25 characters.

```
1  // Fig. 3.17: fig03_17.cpp
2  // Create and manipulate a GradeBook object; illustrate validation.
3  #include <iostream>
4  #include "GradeBook.h" // include definition of class GradeBook
5  using namespace std;
6
7  // function main begins program execution
8  int main()
9  {
10    // create two GradeBook objects;
11    // initial course name of gradeBook1 is too long
12    GradeBook gradeBook1( "CS101 Introduction to Programming in C++" );
13    GradeBook gradeBook2( "CS102 C++ Data Structures" );
14
15    // display each GradeBook's courseName
16    cout << "gradeBook1's initial course name is: "
17       << gradeBook1.getCourseName()
18       << "\ngradeBook2's initial course name is: "
19       << gradeBook2.getCourseName() << endl;
20
21    // modify gradeBook1's courseName (with a valid-length string)
22    gradeBook1.setCourseName( "CS101 C++ Programming" );
23
24    // display each GradeBook's courseName
25    cout << "\ngradeBook1's course name is: "
26       << gradeBook1.getCourseName()
27       << "\ngradeBook2's course name is: "
28       << gradeBook2.getCourseName() << endl;
29 } // end main
```

```
Name "CS101 Introduction to Programming in C++" exceeds maximum length (25).
Limiting courseName to first 25 characters.

gradeBook1's initial course name is: CS101 Introduction to Pro
gradeBook2's initial course name is: CS102 C++ Data Structures

gradeBook1's course name is: CS101 C++ Programming
gradeBook2's course name is: CS102 C++ Data Structures
```

Fig. 3.17 | Creating and manipulating a GradeBook object in which the course name is limited to 25 characters in length.

Lines 16–19 of Fig. 3.17 display the truncated course name for gradeBook1 (we highlight this in the program output) and the course name for gradeBook2. Line 22 calls gradeBook1's setCourseName member function directly, to change the course name in the GradeBook object to a shorter name that does not need to be truncated. Then, lines 25–28 output the course names for the GradeBook objects again.

Additional Notes on Set *Functions*

A `public` *set* function such as `setCourseName` should carefully scrutinize any attempt to modify the value of a data member (e.g., `courseName`) to ensure that the new value is appropriate for that data item. For example, an attempt to *set* the day of the month to 37 should be rejected, an attempt to *set* a person's weight to zero or a negative value should be rejected, an attempt to *set* a grade on an exam to 185 (when the proper range is zero to 100) should be rejected, and so on.

Software Engineering Observation 3.3

Making data members `private` *and controlling access, especially write access, to those data members through* `public` *member functions helps ensure data integrity.*

Error-Prevention Tip 3.4

The benefits of data integrity are not automatic simply because data members are made `private`*—you must provide appropriate validity checking and report the errors.*

A *set* function could return a value indicating that an attempt was made to assign invalid data to an object of the class. A client could then test the return value of the *set* function to determine whether the attempt to modify the object was successful and to take appropriate action if not. We will do that in later chapters after we introduce a bit more programming technology. In C++, clients of objects also can be notified of problems via the *exception-handling mechanism*, which we begin discussing in Chapter 7 and present in-depth in Chapter 17.

3.9 Wrap-Up

In this chapter, you created user-defined classes, and created and used objects of those classes. We declared data members of a class to maintain data for each object of the class. We also defined member functions that operate on that data. You learned that member functions that do not modify a class's data should be declared `const`. We showed how to call an object's member functions to request the services the object provides and how to pass data to those member functions as arguments. We discussed the difference between a local variable of a member function and a data member of a class. We also showed how to use a constructor and a member-initializer list to ensure that every object is initialized properly. You learned that a single-parameter constructor should be declared `explicit`, and that a constructor cannot be declared `const` because it modifies the object being initialized. We demonstrated how to separate the interface of a class from its implementation to promote good software engineering. You learned that `using` directives and `using` declarations should never be placed in headers. We presented a diagram that shows the files that class-implementation programmers and client-code programmers need to compile the code they write. We demonstrated how *set* functions can be used to validate an object's data and ensure that objects are maintained in a consistent state. UML class diagrams were used to model classes and their constructors, member functions and data members. In the next chapter, we begin our introduction to control statements, which specify the order in which a function's actions are performed.

4

Control Statements: Part 1; Assignment, ++ and -- Operators

Objectives

In this chapter you'll:

- Use the `if` and `if...else` selection statements to choose among alternative actions.
- Use the `while` repetition statement to execute statements in a program repeatedly.
- Implement counter-controlled repetition and sentinel-controlled repetition.
- Use the increment, decrement and assignment operators.

Outline

4.1 Introduction

In this chapter, we introduce C++'s `if`, `if...else` and `while` control statements. We devote a portion of this chapter (and Chapters 5–7) to further developing the `GradeBook` class. We add a member function that uses control statements to calculate the average of a set of student grades and we introduce C++'s assignment, increment and decrement operators.

4.2 Control Structures

Normally, statements in a program execute one after the other in the order in which they're written. This is called **sequential execution**. Various C++ statements we'll soon discuss enable you to specify that *the next statement to execute may be other than the next one in sequence*. This is called **transfer of control**.

During the 1960s, it became clear that the indiscriminate use of transfers of control was the root of much difficulty experienced by software development groups. Blame was pointed at the **goto statement**, which allows you to specify a transfer of control to one of a wide range of possible destinations in a program (creating what's often called "spaghetti code"). The notion of so-called **structured programming** became almost synonymous with "**goto elimination.**"

Böhm and Jacopini's[1] research demonstrated that all programs could be written in terms of only three **control structures**, namely, the **sequence structure**, the **selection structure** and the **repetition structure.** The term "control structures" comes from the field of computer science. When we introduce C++'s implementations of control structures, we'll refer to them in the terminology of the C++ standard document as "control statements."

Sequence Structure in C++

The *sequence structure* is built into C++. Unless directed otherwise, the computer executes C++ statements one after the other in the order in which they're written—that is, in sequence. The UML **activity diagram** of Fig. 4.1 illustrates a typical sequence structure in which two calculations are performed in order. C++ allows you to have as many actions as you want in a sequence structure. As you'll soon see, anywhere a *single action* may be placed, you may place *several actions in sequence.*

In this figure, the two statements add a grade to a `total` variable and add the value 1 to a `counter` variable. Such statements might appear in a program that *averages* several student grades. To calculate an average, the *total of the grades* being averaged is divided by

1. Böhm, C., and G. Jacopini, "Flow Diagrams, Turing Machines, and Languages with Only Two Formation Rules," *Communications of the ACM*, Vol. 9, No. 5, May 1966, pp. 366–371.

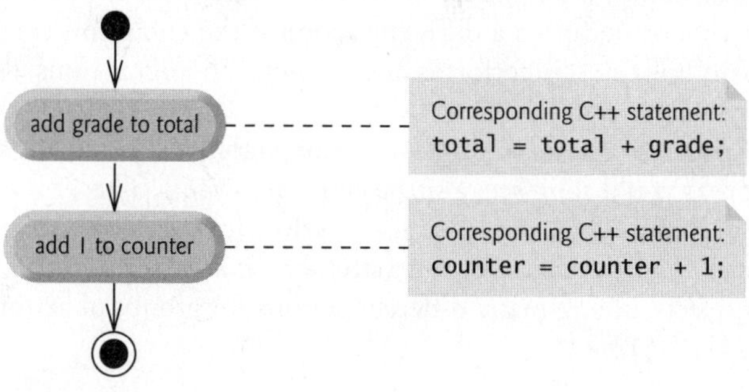

Fig. 4.1 | Sequence-structure activity diagram.

the *number of grades*. A counter variable would be used to keep track of the number of values being averaged. You'll see similar statements in the program of Section 4.6.

An activity diagram models the **workflow** (also called the **activity**) of a portion of a software system. Such workflows may include a portion of an algorithm, such as the sequence structure in Fig. 4.1. Activity diagrams are composed of special-purpose symbols, such as **action state symbols** (a rectangle with its left and right sides replaced with arcs curving outward), **diamonds** and **small circles**; these symbols are connected by **transition arrows**, which represent the flow of the activity.

Activity diagrams clearly show how control structures operate. Consider the sequence-structure activity diagram of Fig. 4.1. It contains two **action states** that represent actions to perform. Each action state contains an **action expression**—e.g., "add grade to total" or "add 1 to counter"—that specifies a particular action to perform. Other actions might include calculations or input/output operations. The arrows in the activity diagram are called transition arrows. These arrows represent **transitions**, which indicate the *order* in which the actions represented by the action states occur—the program that implements the activities illustrated by the activity diagram in Fig. 4.1 first adds `grade` to `total`, then adds `1` to `counter`.

The **solid circle** at the top of the diagram represents the activity's **initial state**—the *beginning* of the workflow *before* the program performs the modeled activities. The solid circle surrounded by a hollow circle that appears at the bottom of the activity diagram represents the **final state**—the *end* of the workflow *after* the program performs its activities.

Figure 4.1 also includes rectangles with the upper-right corners folded over. These are called **notes** in the UML—explanatory remarks that describe the purpose of symbols in the diagram. Figure 4.1 uses UML notes to show the C++ code associated with each action state in the activity diagram. A **dotted line** connects each note with the element that the note describes. Activity diagrams normally do not show the C++ code that implements the activity. We use notes for this purpose here to illustrate how the diagram relates to C++ code. For more information on the UML, see the ATM case study in Chapters 22–23.

Selection Statements in C++

C++ provides three types of selection statements (discussed in this chapter and Chapter 5). The `if` selection statement either performs (selects) an action if a condition is true or skips the action if the condition is false. The `if...else` selection statement performs an action if a condition is true or performs a different action if the condition is false. The `switch` selection statement (Chapter 5) performs one of *many* different actions, depending on the value of an integer expression.

The `if` selection statement is a **single-selection statement** because it selects or ignores a *single action* (or, as you'll soon see, a *single group of actions*). The `if...else` statement is called a **double-selection statement** because it selects between two different actions (or groups of actions). The `switch` selection statement is called a **multiple-selection statement** because it selects among many different actions (or groups of actions).

Repetition Statements in C++

C++ provides three types of repetition statements (also called **looping statements** or **loops**) for performing statements repeatedly while a condition (called the **loop-continuation condition**) remains true. These are the **`while`**, **`do...while`** and **`for`** statements. (Chapter 5 presents the `do...while` and `for` statements, and Chapter 7 presents a specialized version of the `for` statement that's used with arrays and containers.) The `while` and `for` statements perform the action (or group of actions) in their bodies zero or more times—if the loop-continuation condition is initially false, the action (or group of actions) will *not* execute. The `do...while` statement performs the action (or group of actions) in its body *at least once.*

Each of the words `if`, `else`, `switch`, `while`, `do` and `for` is a C++ keyword. Keywords *cannot* be used as identifiers, such as variable names, and must be spelled with only lowercase letters. Figure 4.2 provides a complete list of C++ keywords.

C++ Keywords				
Keywords common to the C and C++ programming languages				
auto	break	case	char	const
continue	default	do	double	else
enum	extern	float	for	goto
if	int	long	register	return
short	signed	sizeof	static	struct
switch	typedef	union	unsigned	void
volatile	while			
C++-only keywords				
and	and_eq	asm	bitand	bitor
bool	catch	class	compl	const_cast
delete	dynamic_cast	explicit	export	false
friend	inline	mutable	namespace	new
not	not_eq	operator	or	or_eq
private	protected	public	reinterpret_cast	static_cast
template	this	throw	true	try
typeid	typename	using	virtual	wchar_t
xor	xor_eq			

Fig. 4.2 | C++ keywords. (Part 1 of 2.)

C++ Keywords				
C++11 keywords				
`alignas`	`alignof`	`char16_t`	`char32_t`	`constexpr`
`decltype`	`noexcept`	`nullptr`	`static_assert`	`thread_local`

Fig. 4.2 | C++ keywords. (Part 2 of 2.)

Summary of Control Statements in C++

C++ has only three kinds of control structures, which from this point forward we refer to as control statements: the *sequence statement*, *selection statements* (three types—`if`, `if...else` and `switch`) and *repetition statements* (three types—`while`, `for` and `do...while`). Each program combines as many of each of these control statements as appropriate for the algorithm the program implements. We can model each control statement as an activity diagram with initial and final states representing that control statement's entry and exit points, respectively. These **single-entry/single-exit control statements** make it easy to build programs—control statements are attached to one another by connecting the exit point of one to the entry point of the next. We call this **control-statement stacking.** There's only one other way to connect control statements—called **control-statement nesting**, in which one control statement is contained *inside* another.

Software Engineering Observation 4.1

Any C++ program can be constructed from only seven different types of control statements (sequence, `if`, `if...else`, `switch`, `while`, `do...while` and `for`) combined in only two ways (control-statement stacking and control-statement nesting).

4.3 `if` Selection Statement

Programs use selection statements to choose among alternative courses of action. For example, suppose the passing grade on an exam is 60. The statement

```
if ( grade >= 60 )
   cout << "Passed";
```

determines whether the condition `grade >= 60` is `true` or `false`. If the condition is `true`, `"Passed"` is printed and the next statement in order is performed. If the condition is `false`, the output statement is ignored and the next statement in order is performed. The indentation of the second line is optional, but it's recommended because it emphasizes the inherent structure of the program.

It's important to note here that we're casually assuming that `grade` contains a valid value—an integer in the range 0 to 100. Throughout the book, we'll introduce many important validation techniques.

Error-Prevention Tip 4.1

In industrial-strength code, always validate all inputs.

Figure 4.3 illustrates the single-selection `if` statement. It contains what is perhaps *the* most important symbol in an activity diagram—the diamond or **decision symbol**, which indicates that a *decision* is to be made. A decision symbol indicates that the workflow will continue along a path determined by the symbol's associated **guard conditions**, which can be true or false. Each transition arrow emerging from a decision symbol has a guard condition specified in *square brackets* above or next to the transition arrow. If a particular guard condition is true, the workflow enters the action state to which that transition arrow points. In Fig. 4.3, if the grade is greater than or equal to 60, the program prints "Passed" to the screen, then transitions to the final state of this activity. If the grade is less than 60, the program immediately transitions to the final state without displaying a message.

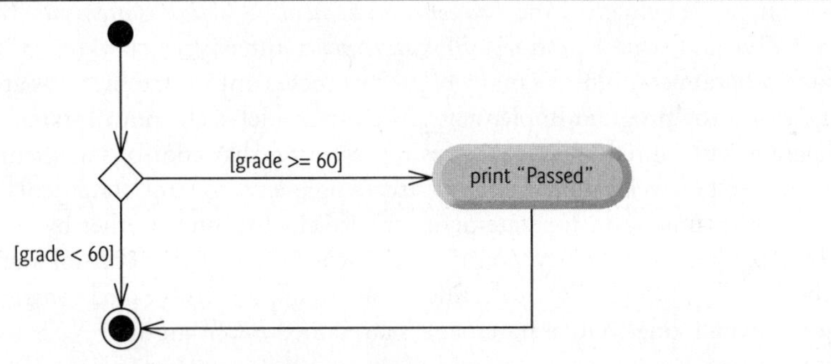

Fig. 4.3 | `if` single-selection statement activity diagram.

You saw in Chapter 2 that decisions can be based on conditions containing relational or equality operators. Actually, in C++, a decision can be based on *any* expression—if the expression evaluates to *zero*, it's treated as *false*; if the expression evaluates to *nonzero*, it's treated as *true*. C++ provides the data type **`bool`** for variables that can hold only the values **`true`** and **`false`**—each of these is a C++ keyword.

Portability Tip 4.1

For compatibility with earlier versions of C, which used integers for Boolean values, the `bool` *value* `true` *also can be represented by any* nonzero *value (compilers typically use 1) and the* `bool` *value* `false` *also can be represented as the value* zero.

The `if` statement is a *single-entry/single-exit* statement. We'll see that the activity diagrams for the remaining control statements also contain initial states, transition arrows, action states that indicate actions to perform, decision symbols (with associated guard conditions) that indicate decisions to be made and final states.

4.4 `if...else` Double-Selection Statement

The `if` single-selection statement performs an indicated action only when the condition is true; otherwise the action is skipped. The `if...else` double-selection statement allows you to specify an action to perform when the condition is true and a different action to perform when the condition is false. For example, the statement

```
if ( grade >= 60 )
   cout << "Passed";
else
   cout << "Failed";
```

displays "Passed" if grade >= 60, but displays "Failed" if the student's grade is less than 60. In either case, the next statement in sequence is then performed. The body of the else is also indented. Figure 4.4 illustrates the the if...else statement's flow of control.

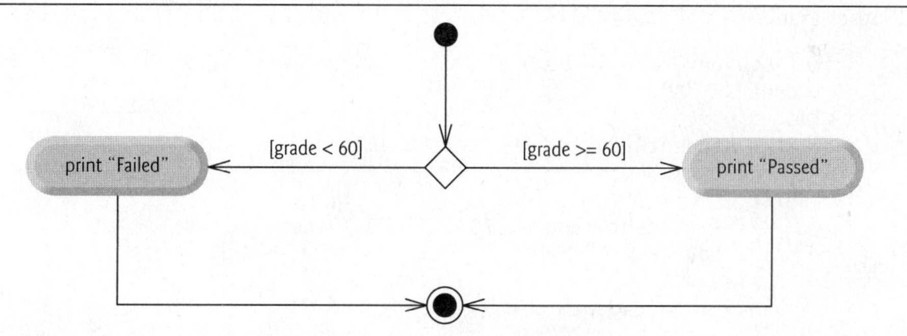

Fig. 4.4 | if...else double-selection statement activity diagram.

Conditional Operator (?:)

C++ provides the **conditional operator** (?:), which is closely related to the if...else statement. The conditional operator is C++'s only **ternary operator**—it takes three operands. The operands, together with the conditional operator, form a **conditional expression**. The first operand is a condition, the second operand is the value for the entire conditional expression if the condition is true and the third operand is the value for the entire conditional expression if the condition is false. For example, the output statement

```
cout << ( grade >= 60 ? "Passed" : "Failed" );
```

contains a conditional expression, grade >= 60 ? "Passed" : "Failed", that evaluates to the string "Passed" if the condition grade >= 60 is true, but evaluates to "Failed" if the condition is false. Thus, the statement with the conditional operator performs essentially the same as the preceding if...else statement. As we'll see, the precedence of the conditional operator is low, so the parentheses in the preceding expression are required.

Error-Prevention Tip 4.2

To avoid precedence problems (and for clarity), place conditional expressions (that appear in larger expressions) in parentheses.

The values in a conditional expression also can be actions to execute. For example, the following conditional expression also prints "Passed" or "Failed":

```
grade >= 60 ? cout << "Passed" : cout << "Failed";
```

The preceding conditional expression is read, "If grade is greater than or equal to 60, then cout << "Passed"; otherwise, cout << "Failed"." This, too, is comparable to the preceding `if...else` statement. Conditional expressions can appear in some program contexts where `if...else` statements cannot.

Nested `if...else` *Statements*

Nested `if...else` statements test for multiple cases by placing `if...else` selection statements *inside* other `if...else` selection statements. For example, the following `if...else` statement displays `A` for exam grades greater than or equal to 90, `B` for grades in the range 80 to 89, `C` for grades in the range 70 to 79, `D` for grades in the range 60 to 69 and `F` for all other grades:

```
if ( studentGrade >= 90 ) // 90 and above gets "A"
   cout << "A";
else
   if ( studentGrade >= 80 ) // 80-89 gets "B"
      cout << "B";
   else
      if ( studentGrade >= 70 ) // 70-79 gets "C"
         cout << "C";
      else
         if ( studentGrade >= 60 ) // 60-69 gets "D"
            cout << "D";
         else // less than 60 gets "F"
            cout << "F";
```

If `studentGrade` is greater than or equal to 90, the first four conditions are true, but only the statement after the first test executes. Then, the program skips the `else`-part of the "outermost" `if...else` statement.

Many programmers write the preceding statement as

```
if ( studentGrade >= 90 ) // 90 and above gets "A"
   cout << "A";
else if ( studentGrade >= 80 ) // 80-89 gets "B"
   cout << "B";
else if ( studentGrade >= 70 ) // 70-79 gets "C"
   cout << "C";
else if ( studentGrade >= 60 ) // 60-69 gets "D"
   cout << "D";
else // less than 60 gets "F"
   cout << "F";
```

The two forms are identical except for the spacing and indentation, which the compiler ignores. The latter form is popular because it avoids deep indentation of the code to the right, which can force lines to wrap.

Performance Tip 4.1

A nested `if...else` statement can perform much faster than a series of single-selection `if` statements because of the possibility of early exit after one of the conditions is satisfied.

Performance Tip 4.2

In a nested `if...else` statement, test the conditions that are more likely to be `true` at the beginning of the nested statement. This will enable the nested `if...else` statement to run faster by exiting earlier than if infrequently occurring cases were tested first.

Dangling-else Problem

The compiler always associates an else with the *immediately preceding* if unless told to do otherwise by the placement of braces ({ and }). This behavior can lead to what's referred to as the **dangling-else problem**. For example,

```
if ( x > 5 )
   if ( y > 5 )
      cout << "x and y are > 5";
else
   cout << "x is <= 5";
```

appears to indicate that if x is greater than 5, the nested if statement determines whether y is also greater than 5. If so, "x and y are > 5" is output. Otherwise, it appears that if x is not greater than 5, the else part of the if...else outputs "x is <= 5".

Beware! This nested if...else statement does not execute as it appears. The compiler actually interprets the statement as

```
if ( x > 5 )
   if ( y > 5 )
      cout << "x and y are > 5";
   else
      cout << "x is <= 5";
```

in which the body of the first if is a nested if...else. The outer if statement tests whether x is greater than 5. If so, execution continues by testing whether y is also greater than 5. If the second condition is true, the proper string—"x and y are > 5"—is displayed. However, if the second condition is false, the string "x is <= 5" is displayed, even though we know that x is greater than 5.

To force the nested if...else statement to execute as originally intended, we can write it as follows:

```
if ( x > 5 )
{
   if ( y > 5 )
      cout << "x and y are > 5";
}
else
   cout << "x is <= 5";
```

The braces ({}) indicate to the compiler that the second if statement is in the body of the first if and that the else is associated with the first if.

Blocks

The if selection statement expects *only one* statement in its body. Similarly, the if and else parts of an if...else statement each expect *only one* body statement. To include *several* statements in the body of an if or in either part of an if...else, enclose the statements in braces ({ and }). A set of statements contained within a pair of braces is called a **block**.

Software Engineering Observation 4.2

A block can be placed anywhere in a program that a single statement can be placed.

The following example includes a block in the `else` part of an `if...else` statement.

```
if ( studentGrade >= 60 )
   cout << "Passed.\n";
else
{
   cout << "Failed.\n";
   cout << "You must take this course again.\n";
}
```

In this case, if `studentGrade` is less than 60, the program executes *both* statements in the body of the `else` and prints

```
Failed.
You must take this course again.
```

Notice the braces surrounding the two statements in the `else` clause. These braces are important. Without the braces, the statement

```
cout << "You must take this course again.\n";
```

would be *outside* the body of the `else` part of the `if` and would execute regardless of whether the grade was less than 60. This is a logic error.

Just as a block can be placed anywhere a single statement can be placed, it's also possible to have no statement at all, which is called a **null statement** or an **empty statement**. The null statement is represented by placing a semicolon (;) where a statement would normally be.

Common Programming Error 4.1

Placing a semicolon after the condition in an `if` *statement leads to a logic error in single-selection* `if` *statements and a syntax error in double-selection* `if...else` *statements (when the* `if` *part contains an actual body statement).*

4.5 `while` Repetition Statement

As an example of C++'s `while` repetition statement, consider a program segment designed to find the first power of 3 larger than 100. Suppose the integer variable `product` has been initialized to 3. When the following `while` repetition statement finishes executing, `product` contains the result:

```
int product = 3;

while ( product <= 100 )
   product = 3 * product;
```

When the `while` statement begins execution, `product`'s value is 3. Each repetition multiplies `product` by 3, so `product` takes on the values 9, 27, 81 and 243 successively. When `product` becomes 243, the `while` statement condition (`product <= 100`) becomes `false`. This terminates the repetition, so the final value of `product` is 243. At this point, program execution continues with the next statement after the `while` statement.

The UML activity diagram of Fig. 4.5 illustrates the flow of control that corresponds to the preceding `while` statement. Once again, the symbols in the diagram (besides the initial state, transition arrows, a final state and three notes) represent an action state and a decision. This diagram also introduces the UML's **merge symbol**, which joins two flows of activity into one flow of activity. The UML represents *both* the merge symbol and the decision symbol as diamonds. In this diagram, the merge symbol joins the transitions from the initial state and from the action state, so they *both* flow into the decision that determines whether the loop should begin (or continue) executing. The decision and merge symbols can be distinguished by the number of incoming and outgoing transition arrows. A decision symbol has one transition arrow pointing *to* the diamond and two or more transition arrows pointing out *from* the diamond to indicate possible transitions from that point. In addition, each transition arrow pointing out of a decision symbol has a guard condition next to it. A merge symbol has two or more transition arrows pointing *to* the diamond and only one transition arrow pointing *from* the diamond, to indicate multiple activity flows merging to continue the activity. Unlike the decision symbol, the merge symbol does *not* have a counterpart in C++ code.

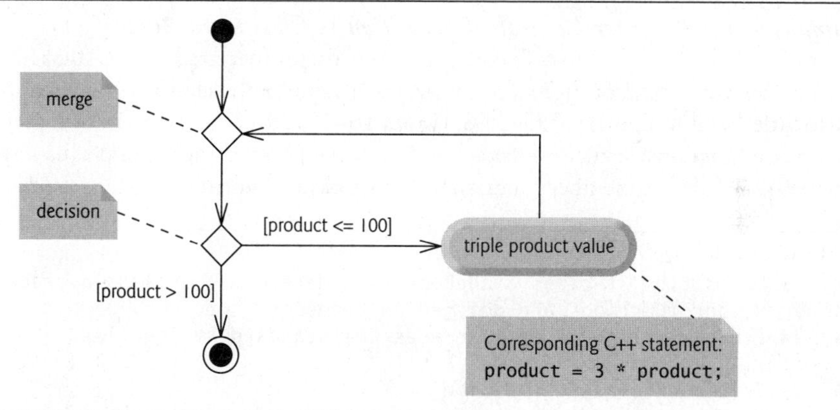

Fig. 4.5 | `while` repetition statement UML activity diagram.

The diagram of Fig. 4.5 clearly shows the repetition of the `while` statement discussed earlier in this section. The transition arrow emerging from the action state points to the merge, which transitions back to the decision that's tested each time through the loop until the guard condition `product > 100` becomes true. Then the `while` statement exits (reaches its final state) and control passes to the next statement in sequence in the program.

4.6 Counter-Controlled Repetition

This section and Section 4.7 solve two variations of a class average problem. Consider the following problem statement:

> *A class of ten students took a quiz. The grades (0 to 100) for this quiz are available to you. Calculate and display the total of the grades and the class average.*

The class average is equal to the sum of the grades divided by the number of students. The algorithm for solving this problem on a computer must input each of the grades, calculate the average and print the result. We use **counter-controlled repetition** to input the grades one at a time.

This section presents a version of class `GradeBook` (Figs. 4.6–4.7) that implements the algorithm in a C++ member function, and an application (Fig. 4.8) that demonstrates the algorithm in action.

Enhancing GradeBook *Validation*

Let's consider an enhancement we made to class `GradeBook`. In Fig. 3.16, our `setCourseName` member function validated the course name by testing whether the course name's length was less than or equal to 25 characters, using an `if` statement. If this was true, the course name would be set. This code was followed by an `if` statement that tested whether the course name's length was larger than 25 characters (in which case the course name would be shortened). The second `if` statement's condition is the exact opposite of the first `if` statement's condition. If one condition evaluates to `true`, the other must evaluate to `false`. Such a situation is ideal for an `if...else` statement, so we've modified our code, replacing the two `if` statements with one `if...else` statement, as shown in lines 18–25 of Fig. 4.7).

Implementing Counter-Controlled Repetition in Class GradeBook

Class `GradeBook` (Figs. 4.6–4.7) contains a constructor (declared in line 10 of Fig. 4.6 and defined in lines 9–12 of Fig. 4.7) that assigns a value to the class's data member `courseName` (declared in line 16 of Fig. 4.6). Lines 16–26, 29–32 and 35–39 of Fig. 4.7 define member functions `setCourseName`, `getCourseName` and `displayMessage`, respectively. Lines 42–64 define member function `determineClassAverage`.

```
1  // Fig. 4.6: GradeBook.h
2  // Definition of class GradeBook that determines a class average.
3  // Member functions are defined in GradeBook.cpp
4  #include <string> // program uses C++ standard string class
5
6  // GradeBook class definition
7  class GradeBook
8  {
9  public:
10    explicit GradeBook( std::string ); // initializes course name
11    void setCourseName( std::string ); // set the course name
12    std::string getCourseName() const; // retrieve the course name
13    void displayMessage() const; // display a welcome message
14    void determineClassAverage() const; // averages user-entered grades
15 private:
16    std::string courseName; // course name for this GradeBook
17 }; // end class GradeBook
```

Fig. 4.6 | Class average problem using counter-controlled repetition: `GradeBook` header.

```
1  // Fig. 4.7: GradeBook.cpp
2  // Member-function definitions for class GradeBook that solves the
3  // class average program with counter-controlled repetition.
4  #include <iostream>
5  #include "GradeBook.h" // include definition of class GradeBook
```

Fig. 4.7 | Class average problem using counter-controlled repetition: `GradeBook` source code file. (Part 1 of 3.)

```
using namespace std;

// constructor initializes courseName with string supplied as argument
GradeBook::GradeBook( string name )
{
   setCourseName( name ); // validate and store courseName
} // end GradeBook constructor

// function to set the course name;
// ensures that the course name has at most 25 characters
void GradeBook::setCourseName( string name )
{
   if ( name.size() <= 25 ) // if name has 25 or fewer characters
      courseName = name; // store the course name in the object
   else // if name is longer than 25 characters
   { // set courseName to first 25 characters of parameter name
      courseName = name.substr( 0, 25 ); // select first 25 characters
      cerr << "Name \"" << name << "\" exceeds maximum length (25).\n"
         << "Limiting courseName to first 25 characters.\n" << endl;
   } // end if...else
} // end function setCourseName

// function to retrieve the course name
string GradeBook::getCourseName() const
{
   return courseName;
} // end function getCourseName

// display a welcome message to the GradeBook user
void GradeBook::displayMessage() const
{
   cout << "Welcome to the grade book for\n" << getCourseName() << "!\n"
      << endl;
} // end function displayMessage

// determine class average based on 10 grades entered by user
void GradeBook::determineClassAverage() const
{
   // initialization phase
   int total = 0; // sum of grades entered by user
   unsigned int gradeCounter = 1; // number of grade to be entered next

   // processing phase
   while ( gradeCounter <= 10 ) // loop 10 times
   {
      cout << "Enter grade: "; // prompt for input
      int grade = 0; // grade value entered by user
      cin >> grade; // input next grade
      total = total + grade; // add grade to total
      gradeCounter = gradeCounter + 1; // increment counter by 1
   } // end while
```

Fig. 4.7 | Class average problem using counter-controlled repetition: GradeBook source code file. (Part 2 of 3.)

```
57
58       // termination phase
59       int average = total / 10; // ok to mix declaration and calculation
60
61       // display total and average of grades
62       cout << "\nTotal of all 10 grades is " << total << endl;
63       cout << "Class average is " << average << endl;
64    } // end function determineClassAverage
```

Fig. 4.7 | Class average problem using counter-controlled repetition: `GradeBook` source code file. (Part 3 of 3.)

Because the `gradeCounter` variable (Fig. 4.7, line 46) is used to count from 1 to 10 in this program (all positive values), we declared the variable as an **`unsigned int`**, which can store only *non-negative* values (that is, 0 and higher). Local variables `total` (Fig. 4.7, line 45), `grade` (line 52) and `average` (line 59) to be of type `int`. Variable `grade` stores the user input. Notice that the preceding declarations appear in the body of member function `determineClassAverage`. Also, variable `grade` is declared in the `while` statement's body because it's used *only* in the loop—in general, variables should be declared just before they're used. We initialize `grade` to `0` (line 52) as a good practice, even though a new value is immediately input for grade in line 53.

In this chapter's versions of class `GradeBook`, we simply read and process a set of grades. The averaging calculation is performed in member function `determineClassAverage` using *local variables*—we do not preserve any information about student grades in the class's data members. In Chapter 7, we modify class `GradeBook` to maintain the grades in memory using a data member that refers to an array. This allows a `GradeBook` object to perform various calculations on a set of grades without requiring the user to enter the grades multiple times.

Lines 45–46 initialize `total` to `0` and `gradeCounter` to `1` before they're used in calculations. Line 49 indicates that the `while` statement should continue looping (also called **iterating**) as long as `gradeCounter`'s value is less than or equal to `10`. While this condition remains true, the `while` statement repeatedly executes the statements between the braces that delimit its body (lines 49–56).

Line 51 displays the prompt `"Enter grade: "`. Line 53 reads the grade entered by the user and assigns it to variable `grade`. Line 54 adds the new grade entered by the user to the `total` and assigns the result to `total`, which replaces its previous value.

Line 55 adds `1` to `gradeCounter` to indicate that the program has processed the current grade and is ready to input the next grade from the user. Incrementing `gradeCounter` eventually causes `gradeCounter` to exceed `10`. At that point the `while` loop terminates because its condition (line 49) becomes false.

When the loop terminates, line 59 performs the averaging calculation and assigns its result to the variable `average`. Line 62 displays the text `"Total of all 10 grades is "` followed by variable `total`'s value. Line 63 then displays the text `"Class average is "` followed by variable `average`'s value. Member function `determineClassAverage` then returns control to the calling function (i.e., `main` in Fig. 4.8).

Demonstrating Class **GradeBook**

Figure 4.8 contains this application's `main` function, which creates an object of class `GradeBook` and demonstrates its capabilities. Line 9 of Fig. 4.8 creates a new `GradeBook` object called `myGradeBook`. The string in line 9 is passed to the `GradeBook` constructor (lines 9–12 of Fig. 4.7). Line 11 of Fig. 4.8 calls `myGradeBook`'s `displayMessage` member function to display a welcome message to the user. Line 12 then calls `myGradeBook`'s `determineClassAverage` member function to allow the user to enter 10 grades, for which the member function then calculates and prints the average.

```
1  // Fig. 4.8: fig04_08.cpp
2  // Create GradeBook object and invoke its determineClassAverage function.
3  #include "GradeBook.h" // include definition of class GradeBook
4
5  int main()
6  {
7     // create GradeBook object myGradeBook and
8     // pass course name to constructor
9     GradeBook myGradeBook( "CS101 C++ Programming" );
10
11    myGradeBook.displayMessage(); // display welcome message
12    myGradeBook.determineClassAverage(); // find average of 10 grades
13 } // end main
```

```
Welcome to the grade book for
CS101 C++ Programming
Enter grade: 67
Enter grade: 78
Enter grade: 89
Enter grade: 67
Enter grade: 87
Enter grade: 98
Enter grade: 93
Enter grade: 85
Enter grade: 82
Enter grade: 100

Total of all 10 grades is 846
Class average is 84
```

Fig. 4.8 | Class average problem using counter-controlled repetition: Creating a `GradeBook` object (Fig. 4.6–Fig. 4.7) and invoking its `determineClassAverage` member function.

Notes on Integer Division and Truncation

The averaging calculation performed in response to the function call in line 12 of Fig. 4.8 produces an integer result. The sample execution indicates that the sum of the grade values is 846, which, when divided by 10, should yield 84.6—a number with a decimal point. However, the result of the calculation `total / 10` (line 59 of Fig. 4.7) is the integer 84, because `total` and 10 are both integers. Dividing two integers results in integer division—any fractional part of the calculation is *truncated*. We'll see how to obtain a result that includes a decimal point from the averaging calculation in the next section.

Common Programming Error 4.2

Assuming that integer division rounds (rather than truncates) can lead to incorrect results. For example, 7 ÷ 4, yields 1.75 in conventional arithmetic, but truncates the floating-point part (.75) in integer arithmetic. So the result is 1. Similarly, –7 ÷ 4, yields –1.

In Fig. 4.7, if line 59 used `gradeCounter` rather than 10, the output for this program would display an incorrect value, 76. This would occur because in the final iteration of the `while` statement, `gradeCounter` was incremented to the value 11 in line 55.

A Note About Arithmetic Overflow

In Fig. 4.7, line 54

```
total = total + grade; // add grade to total
```

added each `grade` entered by the user to the `total`. Even this simple statement has a *potential* problem—adding the integers could result in a value that's *too large* to store in an `int` variable. This is known as **arithmetic overflow** and causes *undefined behavior*, which can lead to unintended results (`en.wikipedia.org/wiki/Integer_overflow#Security_ramifications`). Figure 2.5's addition program had the same issue in line 19, which calculated the sum of two `int` values entered by the user:

```
sum = number1 + number2; // add the numbers; store result in sum
```

The maximum and minimum values that can be stored in an `int` variable are represented by the constants `INT_MAX` and `INT_MIN`, respectively, which are defined in the header `<climits>`. There are similar constants for the other integral types and for floating-point types. You can see your platform's values for these constants by opening the headers `<climits>` and `<cfloat>` in a text editor (you can search your file system for these files).

It's considered a good practice to ensure that *before* you perform arithmetic calculations like the ones in line 54 of Fig. 4.7 and line 19 of Fig. 2.5, they will *not* overflow. The code for doing this is shown on the CERT website `www.securecoding.cert.org`—just search for guideline "INT32-CPP." The code uses the `&&` (logical AND) and `||` (logical OR) operators, which are introduced in Chapter 5. In industrial-strength code, you should perform checks like these for *all* calculations.

A Deeper Look at Receiving User Input

Any time a program receives input from the user various problems might occur. For example, in line 53 of Fig. 4.7

```
cin >> grade; // input next grade
```

we assume that the user will enter an integer grade in the range 0 to 100. However, the person entering a grade could enter an integer less than 0, an integer greater than 100, an integer outside the range of values that can be stored in an `int` variable, a number containing a decimal point or a value containing letters or special symbols that's not even an integer.

To ensure that the user's input is valid, industrial-strength programs must test for all possible erroneous cases. As you progress through the book, you'll learn various techniques for dealing with the broad range of possible input problems.

4.7 Sentinel-Controlled Repetition

Let's generalize the class average problem. Consider the following problem:

> *Develop a class average program that processes grades for an* arbitrary *number of students each time it's run.*

In the previous example, the problem statement specified the number of students, so the number of grades (10) was known in advance. In this example, no indication is given of how many grades the user will enter during the program's execution. The program must process an *arbitrary* number of grades. How can the program determine when to stop the input of grades? How will it know when to calculate and print the class average?

To solve this problem, we can use a special value called a **sentinel value** (also called a **signal value**, a **dummy value** or a **flag value**) to indicate "end of data entry." After typing the legitimate grades, the user types the sentinel value to indicate that the last grade has been entered.

The sentinel value must be chosen so that it's not confused with an acceptable input value. Grades are normally nonnegative integers, so –1 is an acceptable sentinel value. Thus, a run of the program might process inputs such as 95, 96, 75, 74, 89 and –1. The program would then compute and print the class average for the grades 95, 96, 75, 74 and 89. Since –1 is the sentinel value, it should not enter into the averaging calculation.

Implementing Sentinel-Controlled Repetition in Class **GradeBook**

Figures 4.9–4.10 show class `GradeBook` containing member function `determineClassAverage` (this class is demonstrated in Fig. 4.11). Although each grade entered is an integer, the averaging calculation is likely to produce a number with a decimal point—in other words, a real number or **floating-point number** (e.g., 7.33, 0.0975 or 1000.12345). C++ provides several data types for storing floating-point numbers in memory, including **`float`** and **`double`**. The primary difference between these types is that, compared to `float` variables, `double` variables can typically store numbers with larger magnitude and finer detail (i.e., more digits to the right of the decimal point—also known as the number's **precision**). This program introduces a special operator called a **cast operator** to *force* the averaging calculation to produce a floating-point numeric result.

```
// Fig. 4.9: GradeBook.h
// Definition of class GradeBook that determines a class average.
// Member functions are defined in GradeBook.cpp
#include <string> // program uses C++ standard string class

// GradeBook class definition
class GradeBook
{
public:
   explicit GradeBook( std::string ); // initializes course name
   void setCourseName( std::string ); // set the course name
   std::string getCourseName() const; // retrieve the course name
```

Fig. 4.9 | Class average using sentinel-controlled repetition: `GradeBook` header. (Part 1 of 2.)

```
   void displayMessage() const; // display a welcome message
   void determineClassAverage() const; // averages user-entered grades
private:
   std::string courseName; // course name for this GradeBook
}; // end class GradeBook
```

Fig. 4.9 | Class average using sentinel-controlled repetition: GradeBook header. (Part 2 of 2.)

```
// Fig. 4.10: GradeBook.cpp
// Member-function definitions for class GradeBook that solves the
// class average program with sentinel-controlled repetition.
#include <iostream>
#include <iomanip> // parameterized stream manipulators
#include "GradeBook.h" // include definition of class GradeBook
using namespace std;

// constructor initializes courseName with string supplied as argument
GradeBook::GradeBook( string name )
{
   setCourseName( name ); // validate and store courseName
} // end GradeBook constructor

// function to set the course name;
// ensures that the course name has at most 25 characters
void GradeBook::setCourseName( string name )
{
   if ( name.size() <= 25 ) // if name has 25 or fewer characters
      courseName = name; // store the course name in the object
   else // if name is longer than 25 characters
   { // set courseName to first 25 characters of parameter name
      courseName = name.substr( 0, 25 ); // select first 25 characters
      cerr << "Name \"" << name << "\" exceeds maximum length (25).\n"
         << "Limiting courseName to first 25 characters.\n" << endl;
   } // end if...else
} // end function setCourseName

// function to retrieve the course name
string GradeBook::getCourseName() const
{
   return courseName;
} // end function getCourseName

// display a welcome message to the GradeBook user
void GradeBook::displayMessage() const
{
   cout << "Welcome to the grade book for\n" << getCourseName() << "!\n"
      << endl;
} // end function displayMessage

```

Fig. 4.10 | Class average problem using sentinel-controlled repetition: GradeBook source code file. (Part 1 of 2.)

```
// determine class average based on 10 grades entered by user
void GradeBook::determineClassAverage() const
{
   // initialization phase
   int total = 0; // sum of grades entered by user
   unsigned int gradeCounter = 0; // number of grades entered
   // processing phase
   // prompt for input and read grade from user
   cout << "Enter grade or -1 to quit: ";
   int grade = 0; // grade value
   cin >> grade; // input grade or sentinel value
   // loop until sentinel value read from user
   while ( grade != -1 ) // while grade is not -1
   {
      total = total + grade; // add grade to total
      gradeCounter = gradeCounter + 1; // increment counter
      // prompt for input and read next grade from user
      cout << "Enter grade or -1 to quit: ";
      cin >> grade; // input grade or sentinel value
   } // end while
   // termination phase
   if ( gradeCounter != 0 ) // if user entered at least one grade...
   {
      // calculate average of all grades entered
      double average = static_cast< double >( total ) / gradeCounter;
      // display total and average (with two digits of precision)
      cout << "\nTotal of all " << gradeCounter << " grades entered is "
         << total << endl;
      cout << setprecision( 2 ) << fixed;
      cout << "Class average is " << average << endl;
   } // end if
   else // no grades were entered, so output appropriate message
      cout << "No grades were entered" << endl;
} // end function determineClassAverage
```

Fig. 4.10 | Class average problem using sentinel-controlled repetition: `GradeBook` source code file. (Part 2 of 2.)

```
// Fig. 4.11: fig04_11.cpp
// Create GradeBook object and invoke its determineClassAverage function.
#include "GradeBook.h" // include definition of class GradeBook
int main()
{
```

Fig. 4.11 | Class average problem using sentinel-controlled repetition: Creating a `GradeBook` object and invoking its `determineClassAverage` member function. (Part 1 of 2.)

```
    // create GradeBook object myGradeBook and
    // pass course name to constructor
    GradeBook myGradeBook( "CS101 C++ Programming" );

    myGradeBook.displayMessage(); // display welcome message
    myGradeBook.determineClassAverage(); // find average of 10 grades
} // end main
```

```
Welcome to the grade book for
CS101 C++ Programming

Enter grade or -1 to quit: 97
Enter grade or -1 to quit: 88
Enter grade or -1 to quit: 72
Enter grade or -1 to quit: -1

Total of all 3 grades entered is 257
Class average is 85.67
```

Fig. 4.11 | Class average problem using sentinel-controlled repetition: Creating a `GradeBook` object and invoking its `determineClassAverage` member function. (Part 2 of 2.)

This example stacks control statements on top of one another—the `while` statement (lines 56–64 of Fig. 4.10) is immediately followed by an `if...else` statement (lines 67–79) in sequence. Much of the code in this program is identical to the code in Fig. 4.7, so we concentrate on the new features and issues.

Lines 46–47 initialize variables `total` and `gradeCounter` to `0`, because no grades have been entered yet. Remember that this program uses sentinel-controlled repetition. To keep an accurate record of the number of grades entered, the program increments variable `gradeCounter` *only* when the user enters a grade value that is *not* the sentinel value and the program completes the processing of the grade. We declared and initialized variables `grade` (line 52) and `average` (line 70) where they are used. Notice that line 70 declares the variable `average` as type `double`. Recall that we used an `int` variable in the preceding example to store the class average. Using type `double` in the current example allows us to store the class average calculation's result as a floating-point number. Finally, notice that both input statements (lines 53 and 63) are preceded by an output statement that prompts the user for input.

Program Logic for Sentinel-Controlled Repetition vs. Counter-Controlled Repetition

Compare the program logic for sentinel-controlled repetition with that for counter-controlled repetition in Fig. 4.7. In counter-controlled repetition, each iteration of the `while` statement (lines 49–56 of Fig. 4.7) reads a value from the user, for the specified number of iterations. In sentinel-controlled repetition, the program reads the first value (lines 51–53 of Fig. 4.10) before reaching the `while`. This value determines whether the program's flow of control should enter the body of the `while`. If the condition is false, the user entered the sentinel value, so the body does not execute (i.e., no grades were entered). If, on the other hand, the condition is true, the body begins execution, and the loop adds the `grade` value to the `total` (line 58) and increments `gradeCounter` (line 59). Then lines 62–63 in the loop's body prompt for and input the next value from the user. Next, program control reaches the closing right brace (}) of the while's body in line 64, so execution continues with the test of the while's condition (line 56). The condition uses the most recent grade input by the user to determine whether the loop's body should execute again. The value of variable grade is always input from the user immediately before the program tests the while condition. This allows the program to determine whether the value *just input* is the sentinel value *before* the program processes that value (i.e., adds it to the total and increments gradeCounter). If the sentinel value is input, the loop terminates, and the program does not add the value –1 to the total.

After the loop terminates, the if...else statement (lines 67–79) executes. The condition in line 67 determines whether any grades were entered. If none were, the else part (lines 78–79) of the if...else statement executes and displays the message "No grades were entered" and the member function returns control to the calling function.

Notice the block in the while loop in Fig. 4.10. Without the braces, the last three statements in the body of the loop would fall outside the loop, causing the computer to interpret this code incorrectly, as follows:

```
// loop until sentinel value read from user
while ( grade != -1 )
   total = total + grade; // add grade to total
gradeCounter = gradeCounter + 1; // increment counter

// prompt for input and read next grade from user
cout << "Enter grade or -1 to quit: ";
cin >> grade;
```

This would cause an infinite loop in the program if the user did not input -1 for the first grade (in line 53).

Floating-Point Number Precision and Memory Requirements

Variables of type float represent **single-precision floating-point numbers** and have approximately seven significant digits on most of today's systems. Variables of type double represent **double-precision floating-point numbers.** These require twice as much memory as float variables and provide approximately 15 significant digits on most of today's systems—approximately double the precision of float variables. Most programmers represent floating-point numbers with type double. In fact, C++ treats all floating-point numbers you type in a program's source code (such as 7.33 and 0.0975) as double values by default. Such values in the source code are known as **floating-point literals**. See Appendix C, Fundamental Types, for the ranges of values for floats and doubles.

In conventional arithmetic, floating-point numbers often arise as a result of division—when we divide 10 by 3, the result is 3.3333333..., with the sequence of 3s repeating infinitely. The computer allocates only a *fixed* amount of space to hold such a value, so clearly the stored floating-point value can be only an *approximation.*

Due to the imprecise nature of floating-point numbers, type double is preferred over type float, because double variables can represent floating-point numbers more accurately. For this reason, we use type double throughout the book.

Converting Between Fundamental Types Explicitly and Implicitly

The variable average is declared to be of type double (line 70 of Fig. 4.10) to capture the fractional result of our calculation. However, total and gradeCounter are both integer variables. Recall that dividing two integers results in integer division, in which any fractional part of the calculation is lost truncated). In the following statement:

```
double average = total / gradeCounter;
```

the division occurs *first*—the result's fractional part is lost *before* it's assigned to average. To perform a floating-point calculation with integers, we must create *temporary* floating-point values. C++ provides the **static_cast operator** to accomplish this task. Line 70 uses the cast operator `static_cast<double>(total)` to create a *temporary* floating-point copy of its operand in parentheses—`total`. Using a cast operator in this manner is called **explicit conversion**. The value stored in `total` is still an integer.

The calculation now consists of a floating-point value (the temporary `double` version of `total`) divided by the integer `gradeCounter`. The compiler knows how to evaluate *only* expressions in which the operand types are *identical*. To ensure that the operands are of the same type, the compiler performs an operation called **promotion** (also called **implicit conversion**) on selected operands. For example, in an expression containing values of data types `int` and `double`, C++ **promotes** `int` operands to `double` values. In our example, we are treating `total` as a `double` (by using the `static_cast` operator), so the compiler promotes `gradeCounter` to `double`, allowing the calculation to be performed—the result of the floating-point division is assigned to `average`. In Chapter 6, Functions and an Introduction to Recursion, we discuss all the fundamental data types and their order of promotion.

Cast operators are available for use with every data type and with class types as well. The `static_cast` operator is formed by following keyword `static_cast` with angle brackets (< and >) around a data-type name. The `static_cast` operator is a **unary operator**—an operator that takes only one operand. In Chapter 2, we studied the binary arithmetic operators. C++ also supports unary versions of the plus (+) and minus (-) operators, so that you can write such expressions as `-7` or `+5`. Cast operators have higher precedence than other unary operators, such as unary + and unary -. This precedence is higher than that of the **multiplicative operators** *, / and %, and lower than that of parentheses. We indicate the cast operator with the notation `static_cast<`*type*`>()` in our precedence charts.

Formatting for Floating-Point Numbers

The formatting capabilities in Fig. 4.10 are discussed here briefly and explained in depth in Chapter 13, Stream Input/Output: A Deeper Look. The call to **setprecision** in line 75 (with an argument of 2) indicates that `double` variable `average` should be printed with *two* digits of **precision** to the right of the decimal point (e.g., 92.37). This call is referred to as a **parameterized stream manipulator** (because of the 2 in parentheses). Programs that use these calls must contain the preprocessing directive (line 5)

```
#include <iomanip>
```

The manipulator `endl` is a **nonparameterized stream manipulator** (because it isn't followed by a value or expression in parentheses) and does *not* require the `<iomanip>` header. If the precision is not specified, floating-point values are normally output with *six* digits of precision (i.e., the **default precision** on most of today's systems), although we'll see an exception to this in a moment.

The stream manipulator **`fixed`** (line 75) indicates that floating-point values should be output in so-called **fixed-point format**, as opposed to **scientific notation**. Scientific notation is a way of displaying a number as a floating-point number between the values of 1.0 and 10.0, multiplied by a power of 10. For instance, the value 3,100.0 would be displayed in scientific notation as 3.1×10^3. Scientific notation is useful when displaying values that are very large or very small. Formatting using scientific notation is discussed further in Chapter 13. Fixed-point formatting, on the other hand, is used to force a floating-point number to display a specific number of digits. Specifying fixed-point formatting also forces the decimal point and trailing zeros to print, even if the value is a whole number amount, such as 88.00. Without the fixed-point formatting option, such a value prints in C++ as 88 *without* the trailing zeros and *without* the decimal point. When the stream manipulators `fixed` and `setprecision` are used in a program, the *printed* value is **rounded** to the number of decimal positions indicated by the value passed to `setprecision` (e.g., the value `2` in line 75), although the value in memory remains unaltered. For example, the values 87.946 and 67.543 are output as 87.95 and 67.54, respectively. It's also possible to *force* a decimal point to appear by using stream manipulator **`showpoint`**. If `showpoint` is specified without `fixed`, then trailing zeros will not print. Like `endl`, stream manipulators `fixed` and `showpoint` do not use parameters, nor do they require the `<iomanip>` header. Both can be found in header `<iostream>`.

Lines 75 and 76 of Fig. 4.10 output the class average *rounded* to the nearest hundredth and with *exactly* two digits to the right of the decimal point. The parameterized stream manipulator (line 75) indicates that variable `average`'s value should be displayed with *two* digits of precision to the right of the decimal point—as indicated by `setprecision(2)`. The three grades entered during the execution of the program in Fig. 4.11 total 257, which yields the average 85.666… and prints with rounding as 85.67.

A Note About Unsigned Integers

In Fig. 4.7, line 46 declared the variable `gradeCounter` as an `unsigned int` because it can assume only the values from 1 through 11 (11 terminates the loop), which are all positive values. In general, counters that should store only non-negative values should be declared with `unsigned` types. Variables of `unsigned` integer types can represent values from 0 to approximately *twice the positive range* of the corresponding signed integer types. You can determine your platform's maximum `unsigned int` value with the constant `UINT_MAX` from `<climits>`.

Figure 4.7 could have also declared as `unsigned int` the variables `grade`, `total` and `average`. Grades are normally values from 0 to 100, so the `total` and `average` should each be greater than or equal to 0. We declared those variables as `int`s because we can't control what the user actually enters—the user could enter *negative* values. Worse yet, the user could enter a value that's not even a number. (We'll show how to deal with such erroneous inputs later in the book.)

Sometimes sentinel-controlled loops use *intentionally* invalid values to terminate a loop. For example, in line 56 of Fig. 4.10, we terminate the loop when the user enters the sentinel `-1` (an invalid grade), so it would be improper to declare variable `grade` as an `unsigned int`. As you'll see, the end-of-file (`EOF`) indicator—which is introduced in the next chapter and is often used to terminate sentinel-controlled loops—is also normally implemented internally in the compiler as a negative number.

4.8 Nested Control Statements

We've seen that control statements can be *stacked* on top of one another (in sequence). Here, we examine the only other structured way control statements can be connected, namely, by **nesting** one control statement within another. Consider the following problem statement:

> *A college offers a course that prepares students for the state licensing exam for real estate brokers. Last year, ten of the students who completed this course took the exam. The college wants to know how well its students did on the exam. You've been asked to write a program to summarize the results. You've been given a list of these 10 students. Next to each name is written a 1 if the student passed the exam or a 2 if the student failed.*
>
> *Your program should analyze the results of the exam as follows:*
>
> 1. *Input each test result (i.e., a 1 or a 2). Display the prompting message "Enter result" each time the program requests another test result.*
> 2. *Count the number of test results of each type.*
> 3. *Display a summary of the test results indicating the number of students who passed and the number who failed.*
> 4. *If more than eight students passed the exam, print the message "Bonus to instructor!"*

After reading the problem statement carefully, we make the following observations:

1. The program must process test results for 10 students. A *counter-controlled loop* can be used because the number of test results is known in advance.
2. Each test result is a number—either a 1 or a 2. Each time the program reads a test result, the program must determine whether the number is a 1 or a 2. For simplicity, we test only for a 1 in our algorithm. If the number is not a 1, we assume that it's a 2.
3. Two counters are used to keep track of the exam results—one to count the number of students who passed the exam and one to count the number of students who failed the exam.
4. After the program has processed all the results, it must decide whether more than eight students passed the exam.

Program That Solves Examination Results

The program that solves the examination-results prolem is shown in Fig. 4.12. This example does *not* contain a class—it contains just a source code file with function `main` performing all the application's work. In this chapter and in Chapter 3, you've seen examples consisting of one class (including the header and source code files for this class), as well as another source code file testing the class. This source code file contained function `main`, which created an object of the class and called its member functions. Occasionally, when it does not make sense to try to create a *reusable* class to demonstrate a concept, we'll use an example contained entirely within the `main` function of a *single* source code file.

Lines 9–11 and 18 declare and initialize the variables used to process the examination results. Looping programs sometimes require initialization at the beginning of *each* repetition; such reinitialization would be performed by assignment statements rather than in declarations or by moving the declarations inside the loop bodies.

```
// Fig. 4.12: fig04_12.cpp
// Examination-results problem: Nested control statements.
#include <iostream>
using namespace std;

int main()
{
   // initializing variables in declarations
   unsigned int passes = 0; // number of passes
   unsigned int failures = 0; // number of failures
   unsigned int studentCounter = 1; // student counter

   // process 10 students using counter-controlled loop
   while ( studentCounter <= 10 )
   {
      // prompt user for input and obtain value from user
      cout << "Enter result (1 = pass, 2 = fail): ";
      int result = 0; // one exam result (1 = pass, 2 = fail)
      cin >> result; // input result

      // if...else nested in while
      if ( result == 1 )          // if result is 1,
         passes = passes + 1;     // increment passes;
      else                        // else result is not 1, so
         failures = failures + 1; // increment failures

      // increment studentCounter so loop eventually terminates
      studentCounter = studentCounter + 1;
   } // end while

   // termination phase; display number of passes and failures
   cout << "Passed " << passes << "\nFailed " << failures << endl;

   // determine whether more than eight students passed
   if ( passes > 8 )
      cout << "Bonus to instructor!" << endl;
} // end main
```

```
Enter result (1 = pass, 2 = fail): 1
Enter result (1 = pass, 2 = fail): 2
Enter result (1 = pass, 2 = fail): 2
Enter result (1 = pass, 2 = fail): 1
Enter result (1 = pass, 2 = fail): 1
Enter result (1 = pass, 2 = fail): 1
Enter result (1 = pass, 2 = fail): 2
Enter result (1 = pass, 2 = fail): 1
Enter result (1 = pass, 2 = fail): 1
Enter result (1 = pass, 2 = fail): 2
Passed 6
Failed 4
```

Fig. 4.12 | Examination-results problem: Nested control statements. (Part 1 of 2.)

```
Enter result (1 = pass, 2 = fail): 1
Enter result (1 = pass, 2 = fail): 1
Enter result (1 = pass, 2 = fail): 1
Enter result (1 = pass, 2 = fail): 1
Enter result (1 = pass, 2 = fail): 2
Enter result (1 = pass, 2 = fail): 1
Enter result (1 = pass, 2 = fail): 1
Enter result (1 = pass, 2 = fail): 1
Enter result (1 = pass, 2 = fail): 1
Enter result (1 = pass, 2 = fail): 1
Passed 9
Failed 1
Bonus to instructor!
```

Fig. 4.12 | Examination-results problem: Nested control statements. (Part 2 of 2.)

The `while` statement (lines 14–29) loops 10 times. Each iteration inputs and processes one exam result. The `if...else` statement (lines 22–25) for processing each result is nested in the `while` statement. If the `result` is `1`, the `if...else` statement increments `passes`; otherwise, it assumes the `result` is `2` and increments `failures`. Line 28 increments `studentCounter` before the loop condition is tested again in line 15. After 10 values have been input, the loop terminates and line 32 displays the number of `passes` and the number of `failures`. The `if` statement in lines 35–36 determines whether more than eight students passed the exam and, if so, outputs the message `"Bonus to instructor!"`.

Figure 4.12 shows the input and output from two sample executions of the program. At the end of the second sample execution, the condition in line 35 is true—more than eight students passed the exam, so the program outputs a message indicating that the instructor should receive a bonus.

C++11 List Initialization

C++11 introduces a new variable initialization syntax. **List initialization** (also called uniform initialization) enables you to use one syntax to initialize a variable of *any* type. Consider line 11 of Fig. 4.12

```
unsigned int studentCounter = 1;
```

In C++11, you can write this as

```
unsigned int studentCounter = { 1 };
```

or

```
unsigned int studentCounter{ 1 };
```

The braces ({ and }) represent the *list initializer*. For a fundamental-type variable, you place only one value in the list initializer. For an object, the list initializer can be a *comma-separated list* of values that are passed to the object's constructor. For example, consider an `Employee` class that contains an employee's first name, last name and salary. Assuming the class defines a constructor that receives `strings` for the first and last names and a `double` for the salary, you could initialize `Employee` objects as follows:

```
Employee employee1{ "Bob", "Blue", 1234.56 };
Employee employee2 = { "Sue", "Green", 2143.65 };
```

For fundamental-type variables, list-initialization syntax also *prevents* so-called **narrowing conversions** that could result in *data loss*. For example, previously you could write

```
int x = 12.7;
```

which attempts to assign the `double` value `12.7` to the `int` variable `x`. A `double` value is converted to an `int`, by *truncating* the floating-point part (`.7`), which results in a *loss* of information—a *narrowing conversion*. The actual value assigned to `x` is `12`. Many compilers generate a *warning* for this statement, but still allow it to compile. However, using list initialization, as in

```
int x = { 12.7 };
```

or

```
int x{ 12.7 };
```

yields a *compilation error*, thus helping you avoid a potentially subtle logic error. For example, Apple's Xcode LLVM compiler gives the error

```
Type 'double' cannot be narrowed to 'int' in initializer list
```

We'll discuss additional list-initializer features in later chapters.

4.9 Assignment Operators

C++ provides several **assignment operators** for abbreviating assignment expressions. For example, the statement

```
c = c + 3;
```

can be abbreviated with the **addition assignment operator** `+=` as

```
c += 3;
```

which adds the value of the expression on the operator's right to the value of the variable on the operator's left and stores the result in the left-side variable. Any statement of the form

variable = *variable operator expression*;

in which the same *variable* appears on both sides of the assignment operator and *operator* is one of the binary operators +, -, *, /, or % (or a few others we'll discuss later in the text), can be written in the form

variable operator= *expression*;

Thus the assignment `c += 3` adds `3` to `c`. Figure 4.13 shows the arithmetic assignment operators, sample expressions using these operators and explanations.

Assignment operator	Sample expression	Explanation	Assigns
Assume: `int c = 3, d = 5, e = 4, f = 6, g = 12;`			
`+=`	`c += 7`	`c = c + 7`	10 to `c`

Fig. 4.13 | Arithmetic assignment operators. (Part 1 of 2.)

Assignment operator	Sample expression	Explanation	Assigns
-=	d -= 4	d = d - 4	1 to d
*=	e *= 5	e = e * 5	20 to e
/=	f /= 3	f = f / 3	2 to f
%=	g %= 9	g = g % 9	3 to g

Fig. 4.13 | Arithmetic assignment operators. (Part 2 of 2.)

4.10 Increment and Decrement Operators

In addition to the arithmetic assignment operators, C++ also provides two unary operators for adding 1 to or subtracting 1 from the value of a numeric variable. These are the unary **increment operator**, ++, and the unary **decrement operator**, --, which are summarized in Fig. 4.14. A program can increment by 1 the value of a variable called c using the increment operator, ++, rather than the expression c = c + 1 or c += 1. An increment or decrement operator that's prefixed to (placed *before*) a variable is referred to as the **prefix increment** or **prefix decrement operator**, respectively. An increment or decrement operator that's postfixed to (placed *after*) a variable is referred to as the **postfix increment** or **postfix decrement operator**, respectively.

Operator	Called	Sample expression	Explanation
++	preincrement	++a	Increment a by 1, then use the new value of a in the expression in which a resides.
++	postincrement	a++	Use the current value of a in the expression in which a resides, then increment a by 1.
--	predecrement	--b	Decrement b by 1, then use the new value of b in the expression in which b resides.
--	postdecrement	b--	Use the current value of b in the expression in which b resides, then decrement b by 1.

Fig. 4.14 | Increment and decrement operators.

Using the prefix increment (or decrement) operator to add (or subtract) 1 from a variable is known as **preincrementing** (or **predecrementing**) the variable. Preincrementing (or predecrementing) causes the variable to be incremented (decremented) by 1, then the new value of the variable is used in the expression in which it appears. Using the postfix increment (or decrement) operator to add (or subtract) 1 from a variable is known as **postincrementing** (or **postdecrementing**) the variable. Postincrementing (or postdecrementing) causes the *current* value of the variable to be used in the expression in which it appears, then the variable's value is incremented (decremented) by 1.

Figure 4.15 demonstrates the difference between the prefix increment and postfix increment versions of the ++ increment operator. The decrement operator (--) works similarly.

```
1  // Fig. 4.15: fig04_15.cpp
2  // Preincrementing and postincrementing.
3  #include <iostream>
4  using namespace std;
5
6  int main()
7  {
8     // demonstrate postincrement
9     int c = 5; // assign 5 to c
10    cout << c << endl; // print 5
11    cout << c++ << endl; // print 5 then postincrement
12    cout << c << endl; // print 6
13
14    cout << endl; // skip a line
15
16    // demonstrate preincrement
17    c = 5; // assign 5 to c
18    cout << c << endl; // print 5
19    cout << ++c << endl; // preincrement then print 6
20    cout << c << endl; // print 6
21 } // end main
```

```
5
5
6

5
6
6
```

Fig. 4.15 | Preincrementing and postincrementing.

Line 9 initializes c to 5, and line 10 outputs c's initial value. Line 11 outputs the value of the expression c++. This postincrements the variable c, so c's original value (5) is output, then c's value is incremented. Thus, line 11 outputs c's initial value (5) again. Line 12 outputs c's new value (6) to prove that the variable's value was incremented in line 11.

Line 17 resets c's value to 5, and line 18 outputs that value. Line 19 outputs the value of the expression ++c. This expression preincrements c, so its value is incremented, then the new value (6) is output. Line 20 outputs c's value again to show that the value of c is still 6 after line 19 executes.

The arithmetic assignment operators and the increment and decrement operators can be used to simplify program statements. The three assignment statements in Fig. 4.12

```
passes = passes + 1;
failures = failures + 1;
studentCounter = studentCounter + 1;
```

can be written more concisely with assignment operators as

```
passes += 1;
failures += 1;
studentCounter += 1;
```

with prefix increment operators as

```
++passes;
++failures;
++studentCounter;
```

or with postfix increment operators as

```
passes++;
failures++;
studentCounter++;
```

When you increment (++) or decrement (--) an integer variable in a statement by itself, the preincrement and postincrement forms have the same logical effect, and the predecrement and postdecrement forms have the same logical effect. It's only when a variable appears in the context of a larger expression that preincrementing the variable and postincrementing the variable have different effects (and similarly for predecrementing and postdecrementing).

Common Programming Error 4.3

Attempting to use the increment or decrement operator on an expression other than a modifiable variable name, e.g., writing `++(x + 1)`*, is a syntax error.*

Figure 4.16 shows the precedence and associativity of the operators introduced to this point. The operators are shown top-to-bottom in decreasing order of precedence. The second column indicates the associativity of the operators at each level of precedence. Notice that the conditional operator (?:), the unary operators preincrement (++), predecrement (--), plus (+) and minus (-), and the assignment operators =, +=, -=, *=, /= and %= associate from *right to left*. All other operators in Fig. 4.16 associate from *left to right*. The third column names the various groups of operators.

Operators	Associativity	Type
:: ()	left to right *[See caution in Fig. 2.7 regarding grouping parentheses.]*	primary
++ -- **static_cast**<*type*>()	left to right	postfix
++ -- + -	right to left	unary (prefix)
* / %	left to right	multiplicative
+ -	left to right	additive
<< >>	left to right	insertion/extraction
< <= > >=	left to right	relational

Fig. 4.16 | Operator precedence for the operators encountered so far in the text. (Part 1 of 2.)

Operators	Associativity	Type
`==` `!=`	left to right	equality
`?:`	right to left	conditional
`=` `+=` `-=` `*=` `/=` `%=`	right to left	assignment

Fig. 4.16 | Operator precedence for the operators encountered so far in the text. (Part 2 of 2.)

4.11 Wrap-Up

In this chapter, you learned that only three types of control structures—sequence, selection and repetition—are needed to develop any algorithm. We demonstrated two of C++'s selection statements—the `if` single-selection statement and the `if...else` double-selection statement. The `if` statement is used to execute a set of statements based on a condition—if the condition is true, the statements execute; if it isn't, the statements are skipped. The `if...else` double-selection statement is used to execute one set of statements if a condition is true, and another set of statements if the condition is false. We then discussed the `while` repetition statement, where a set of statements are executed repeatedly as long as a condition is true. We used control-statement stacking to total and compute the average of a set of student grades with counter-controlled and sentinel-controlled repetition, and we used control-statement nesting to analyze and make decisions based on a set of exam results. We introduced assignment operators that can be used for abbreviating statements. We presented the increment and decrement operators, which can be used to add or subtract the value 1 from a variable. In the next chapter, we continue our discussion of control statements, introducing the `for`, `do...while` and `switch` statements.

5

Control Statements: Part 2; Logical Operators

Objectives

In this chapter you'll:

- Use `for` and `do...while` to execute statements in a program repeatedly.
- Implement multiple selection using the `switch` selection statement.
- Learn how `break` and `continue` alter the flow of control.
- Use the logical operators to form complex conditional expressions in control statements.
- Learn to avoid the consequences of confusing the equality and assignment operators.

Outline

5.1 Introduction

In this chapter, we present C++'s remaining control statements. The control statements we study here and those you learned in Chapter 4 will help you build and manipulate objects. We continue our early emphasis on object-oriented programming.

In this chapter, we demonstrate the `for`, `do...while` and `switch` statements. Through examples using `while` and `for`, we explore counter-controlled repetition. We expand the `GradeBook` class to use a `switch` statement to count the number of A, B, C, D and F grades in a set of letter grades entered by the user. We introduce the `break` and `continue` program control statements. We discuss the logical operators, which enable you to use more powerful conditional expressions. We also examine the common error of confusing the equality (==) and assignment (=) operators, and how to avoid it.

5.2 Essentials of Counter-Controlled Repetition

This section uses the `while` repetition statement to formalize the elements required to perform counter-controlled repetition:

1. the **name of a control variable** (or loop counter)
2. the **initial value** of the control variable
3. the **loop-continuation condition** that tests for the **final value** of the control variable (i.e., whether looping should continue)
4. the **increment** (or **decrement**) by which the control variable is modified each time through the loop.

The program in Fig. 5.1 prints the numbers from 1 to 10. The declaration in line 8 *names* the control variable (`counter`), declares it to be an `unsigned int`, reserves space for it in memory and sets it to an *initial value* of `1`. Declarations that require initialization are *executable* statements. In C++, it's more precise to call a variable declaration that also reserves memory a **definition**. Because definitions are declarations, too, we'll use the term "declaration" except when the distinction is important.

```
1  // Fig. 5.1: fig05_01.cpp
2  // Counter-controlled repetition.
3  #include <iostream>
```

Fig. 5.1 | Counter-controlled repetition. (Part 1 of 2.)

```
4  using namespace std;
5
6  int main()
7  {
8     unsigned int counter = 1; // declare and initialize control variable
9
10    while ( counter <= 10 ) // loop-continuation condition
11    {
12       cout << counter << " ";
13       ++counter; // increment control variable by 1
14    } // end while
15
16    cout << endl; // output a newline
17 } // end main
```

```
1 2 3 4 5 6 7 8 9 10
```

Fig. 5.1 | Counter-controlled repetition. (Part 2 of 2.)

Line 13 *increments* the loop counter by 1 each time the loop's body is performed. The loop-continuation condition (line 10) in the `while` statement determines whether the value of the control variable is less than or equal to `10` (the final value for which the condition is `true`). The body of this `while` executes even when the control variable is `10`. The loop terminates when the control variable is greater than `10` (i.e., when `counter` is `11`).

Figure 5.1 can be made more concise by initializing `counter` to `0` and by replacing the `while` statement with

```
counter = 0;
while ( ++counter <= 10 ) // loop-continuation condition
   cout << counter << " ";
```

This code saves a statement, because the incrementing is done in the `while` condition *before* the condition is tested. Also, the code eliminates the braces around the body of the `while`, because the `while` now contains only *one* statement. Coding in such a condensed fashion can lead to programs that are more difficult to read, debug, modify and maintain.

Error-Prevention Tip 5.1

Floating-point values are approximate, so controlling counting loops with floating-point variables can result in imprecise counter values and inaccurate tests for termination. Control counting loops with integer values. Separately, `++` *and* `--` *can be used only with integer operands.*

5.3 for Repetition Statement

In addition to `while`, C++ provides the **`for` repetition statement**, which specifies the counter-controlled repetition details in a single line of code. To illustrate the power of `for`, let's rewrite the program of Fig. 5.1. The result is shown in Fig. 5.2.

When the `for` statement (lines 10–11) begins executing, the control variable `counter` is declared and initialized to 1. Then, the loop-continuation condition (line 10 between

```
1  // Fig. 5.2: fig05_02.cpp
2  // Counter-controlled repetition with the for statement.
3  #include <iostream>
4  using namespace std;
5
6  int main()
7  {
8     // for statement header includes initialization,
9     // loop-continuation condition and increment.
10    for ( unsigned int counter = 1; counter <= 10; ++counter )
11       cout << counter << " ";
12
13    cout << endl; // output a newline
14 } // end main
```

```
1 2 3 4 5 6 7 8 9 10
```

Fig. 5.2 | Counter-controlled repetition with the `for` statement.

the semicolons) `counter <= 10` is checked. The initial value of `counter` is 1, so the condition is satisfied and the body statement (line 11) prints the value of `counter`, namely 1. Then, the expression `++counter` increments control variable `counter` and the loop begins again with the loop-continuation test. The control variable is now 2, so the final value is not exceeded and the program performs the body statement again. This process continues until the loop body has executed 10 times and the control variable `counter` is incremented to 11—this causes the loop-continuation test to fail, so repetition terminates. The program continues by performing the first statement after the `for` statement (in this case, the output statement in line 13).

`for` Statement Header Components

Figure 5.3 takes a closer look at the `for` statement header (line 10) of Fig. 5.2. Notice that the `for` statement header "does it all"—it specifies each of the items needed for counter-controlled repetition with a control variable. If there's more than one statement in the body of the `for`, braces are required to enclose the body of the loop. Typically, `for` statements are used for counter-controlled repetition and `while` statements are used for sentinel-controlled repetition.

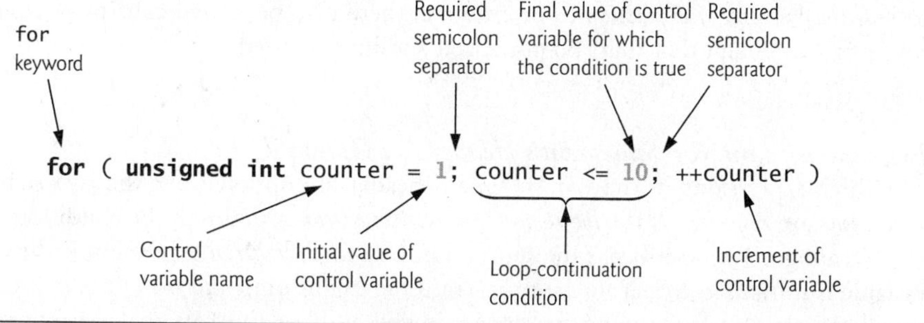

Fig. 5.3 | `for` statement header components.

Off-By-One Errors

If you incorrectly wrote `counter < 10` as the loop-continuation condition in Fig. 5.2, then the loop would execute only 9 times. This is a common **off-by-one error**.

General Format of a `for` *Statement*

The general form of the `for` statement is

```
for ( initialization; loopContinuationCondition; increment )
    statement
```

where the *initialization* expression initializes the loop's control variable, *loopContinuationCondition* determines whether the loop should continue executing and *increment* increments the control variable. In most cases, the `for` statement can be represented by an equivalent `while` statement, as follows:

```
initialization;

while ( loopContinuationCondition )
{
    statement
    increment;
}
```

There's an exception to this rule, which we'll discuss in Section 5.7.

If the *initialization* expression declares the control variable (i.e., its type is specified before its name), the control variable can be used *only* in the body of the `for` statement—the control variable will be unknown *outside* the `for` statement. This restricted use of the control variable name is known as the variable's **scope**. The scope of a variable specifies *where* it can be used in a program. Scope is discussed in detail in Chapter 6.

Comma-Separated Lists of Expressions

The *initialization* and *increment* expressions can be comma-separated lists of expressions. The commas, as used in these expressions, are **comma operators**, which guarantee that lists of expressions evaluate from left to right. The comma operator has the lowest precedence of all C++ operators. *The value and type of a comma-separated list of expressions is the value and type of the rightmost expression.* The comma operator is often used in `for` statements, where its primary application is to enable you to use *multiple initialization expressions* and/or *multiple increment expressions*. For example, there may be several control variables in a single `for` statement that must be initialized and incremented.

Expressions in the `for` *Statement's Header Are Optional*

The three expressions in the `for` statement header are optional but the two semicolon separators are *required*. If the *loopContinuationCondition* is omitted, the condition is true, thus creating an *infinite loop*. One might omit the *initialization* expression if the control variable is initialized earlier in the program. One might omit the *increment* expression if the increment is calculated by statements in the body of the `for` or if no increment is needed.

Increment Expression Acts Like a Standalone Statement

The increment expression in the for statement acts like a standalone statement at the end of for statement's body. Therefore, for integer counters, the expressions

```
counter = counter + 1
counter += 1
++counter
counter++
```

are all equivalent in the *increment* expression (when no other code appears there). The integer variable being incremented here does not appear in a larger expression, so both preincrementing and postincrementing actually have the *same* effect.

Common Programming Error 5.1

Placing a semicolon immediately to the right of the right parenthesis of a for *header makes the body of that* for *statement an empty statement. This is usually a logic error.*

***for** Statement: Notes and Observations*

The initialization, loop-continuation condition and increment expressions of a for statement can contain arithmetic expressions. For example, if x = 2 and y = 10, and x and y are not modified in the loop body, the for header

```
for ( unsigned int j = x; j <= 4 * x * y; j += y / x )
```

is equivalent to

```
for ( unsigned int j = 2; j <= 80; j += 5 )
```

The "increment" of a for statement can be negative, in which case it's really a *decrement* and the loop actually counts *downward* (as shown in Section 5.4).

If the loop-continuation condition is *initially false*, the body of the for statement is not performed. Instead, execution proceeds with the statement following the for.

Frequently, the control variable is printed or used in calculations in the body of a for statement, but this is not required. It's common to use the control variable for controlling repetition while never mentioning it in the body of the for statement.

Error-Prevention Tip 5.2

Although the value of the control variable can be changed in the body of a for *statement, avoid doing so, because this can lead to subtle logic errors.*

***for** Statement UML Activity Diagram*

The for repetition statement's UML activity diagram is similar to that of the while statement (Fig. 4.5). Figure 5.4 shows the activity diagram of the for statement in Fig. 5.2. The diagram makes it clear that initialization occurs once *before* the loop-continuation test is evaluated the first time, and that incrementing occurs *each time* through the loop *after* the body statement executes. Note that (besides an initial state, transition arrows, a merge, a final state and several notes) the diagram contains only *action states* and a *decision*.

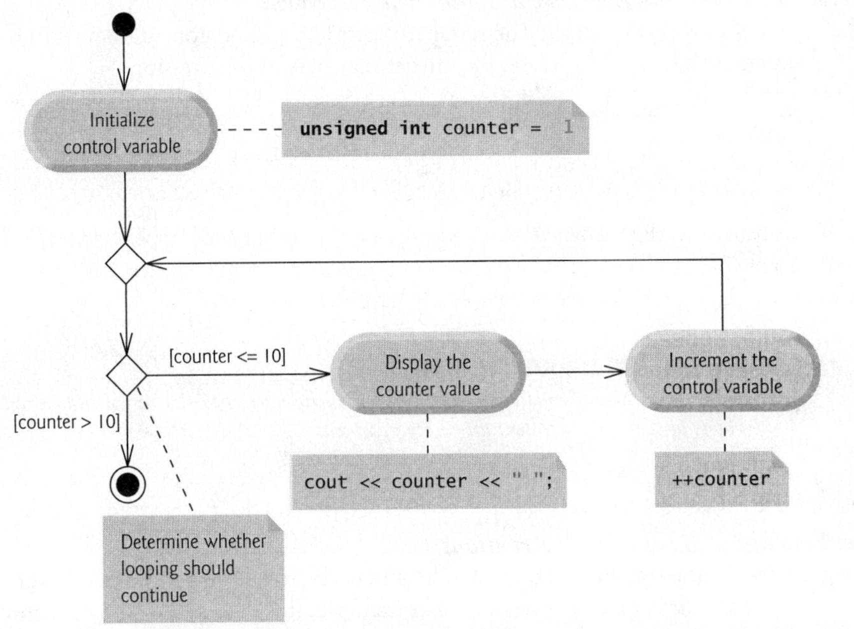

Fig. 5.4 | UML activity diagram for the `for` statement in Fig. 5.2.

5.4 Examples Using the for Statement

The following examples show methods of varying the control variable in a `for` statement. In each case, we write the appropriate `for` statement header. Note the change in the relational operator for loops that *decrement* the control variable.

a) Vary the control variable from `1` to `100` in increments of `1`.

```
for ( unsigned int i = 1; i <= 100; ++i )
```

b) Vary the control variable from `100` down to `0` in decrements of `1`. Notice that we used type `int` for the control variable in this `for` header. The condition does not become false until control variable `i` contains `-1`, so the control variable must be able to store both positive and negative numbers.

```
for ( int i = 100; i >= 0; --i )
```

c) Vary the control variable from `7` to `77` in steps of `7`.

```
for ( unsigned int i = 7; i <= 77; i += 7 )
```

d) Vary the control variable from `20` down to `2` in steps of `-2`.

```
for ( unsigned int i = 20; i >= 2; i -= 2 )
```

e) Vary the control variable over the following sequence of values: `2`, `5`, `8`, `11`, `14`, `17`.

```
for ( unsigned int i = 2; i <= 17; i += 3 )
```

f) Vary the control variable over the following sequence of values: 99, 88, 77, 66, 55.

```
for ( unsigned int i = 99; i >= 55; i -= 11 )
```

Common Programming Error 5.2

Not using the proper relational operator in the loop-continuation condition of a loop that counts downward (such as incorrectly using `i <= 1` instead of `i >= 1` in a loop counting down to 1) is a logic error that yields incorrect results when the program runs.

Common Programming Error 5.3

Do not use equality operators (`!=` or `==`) in a loop-continuation condition if the loop's control variable increments or decrements by more than 1. For example consider the `for` statement header `for ( unsigned int counter = 1; counter != 10; counter += 2 )`. The loop-continuation test `counter != 10` never becomes false (resulting in an infinite loop*).*

Application: Summing the Even Integers from 2 to 20

The program of Fig. 5.5 uses a `for` statement to sum the even integers from 2 to 20. Each iteration of the loop (lines 11–12) adds control variable `number`'s value to variable `total`.

```
1  // Fig. 5.5: fig05_05.cpp
2  // Summing integers with the for statement.
3  #include <iostream>
4  using namespace std;
5
6  int main()
7  {
8     unsigned int total = 0; // initialize total
9
10    // total even integers from 2 through 20
11    for ( unsigned int number = 2; number <= 20; number += 2 )
12       total += number;
13
14    cout << "Sum is " << total << endl; // display results
15 } // end main
```

```
Sum is 110
```

Fig. 5.5 | Summing integers with the `for` statement.

The body of the `for` statement in Fig. 5.5 actually could be merged into the increment portion of the `for` header by using the *comma operator* as follows:

```
for ( unsigned int number = 2; // initialization
      number <= 20; // loop continuation condition
      total += number, number += 2 ) // total and increment
   ; // empty body
```

Good Programming Practice 5.1

Although statements preceding a `for` and statements in the body of a `for` often can be merged into the `for` header, doing so can make the program more difficult to read, maintain, modify and debug.

Application: Compound Interest Calculations

Consider the following problem statement:

> *A person invests $1000.00 in a savings account yielding 5 percent interest. Assuming that all interest is left on deposit in the account, calculate and print the amount of money in the account at the end of each year for 10 years. Use the following formula for determining these amounts:*
>
> $$a = p\,(\,1 + r\,)^n$$
>
> *where*
>
> p *is the original amount invested (i.e., the principal),*
> r *is the annual interest rate,*
> n *is the number of years and*
> a *is the amount on deposit at the end of the* n*th* *year.*

The `for` statement (Fig. 5.6, lines 21–28) performs the indicated calculation for each of the 10 years the money remains on deposit, varying a control variable from 1 to 10 in increments of 1. C++ does *not* include an exponentiation operator, so we use the **standard library function `pow`** (line 24). The function `pow(x, y)` calculates the value of `x` raised to the yth power. In this example, the algebraic expression $(1 + r)^n$ is written as `pow(1.0 + rate, year)`, where variable `rate` represents r and variable `year` represents n. Function `pow` takes two arguments of type `double` and returns a `double` value.

```
1  // Fig. 5.6: fig05_06.cpp
2  // Compound interest calculations with for.
3  #include <iostream>
4  #include <iomanip>
5  #include <cmath> // standard math library
6  using namespace std;
7
8  int main()
9  {
10    double amount; // amount on deposit at end of each year
11    double principal = 1000.0; // initial amount before interest
12    double rate = .05; // annual interest rate
13
14    // display headers
15    cout << "Year" << setw( 21 ) << "Amount on deposit" << endl;
16
17    // set floating-point number format
18    cout << fixed << setprecision( 2 );
19
20    // calculate amount on deposit for each of ten years
21    for ( unsigned int year = 1; year <= 10; ++year )
22    {
23       // calculate new amount for specified year
24       amount = principal * pow( 1.0 + rate, year );
25
26       // display the year and the amount
27       cout << setw( 4 ) << year << setw( 21 ) << amount << endl;
28    } // end for
29 } // end main
```

Fig. 5.6 | Compound interest calculations with `for`. (Part 1 of 2.)

```
Year    Amount on deposit
   1              1050.00
   2              1102.50
   3              1157.63
   4              1215.51
   5              1276.28
   6              1340.10
   7              1407.10
   8              1477.46
   9              1551.33
  10              1628.89
```

Fig. 5.6 | Compound interest calculations with `for`. (Part 2 of 2.)

This program will not compile without including header `<cmath>` (line 5). Function `pow` requires two `double` arguments. Variable `year` is an integer. Header `<cmath>` includes information that tells the compiler to convert the value of `year` to a temporary `double` representation before calling the function. This information is contained in `pow`'s function prototype. Chapter 6 summarizes other math library functions.

Common Programming Error 5.4

Forgetting to include the appropriate header when using standard library functions (e.g., `<cmath>` *in a program that uses math library functions) is a compilation error.*

A Caution about Using Type `float` or `double` for Monetary Amounts

Lines 10–12 declare the `double` variables `amount`, `principal` and `rate`. We did this for simplicity because we're dealing with fractional parts of dollars, and we need a type that allows decimal points in its values. Unfortunately, this can cause trouble. Here's a simple explanation of what can go wrong when using `float` or `double` to represent dollar amounts (assuming `setprecision(2)` is used to specify two digits of precision when printing): Two dollar amounts stored in the machine could be 14.234 (which prints as 14.23) and 18.673 (which prints as 18.67). When these amounts are added, they produce the internal sum 32.907, which prints as 32.91. Thus your printout could appear as

```
  14.23
+ 18.67
-------
  32.91
```

but a person adding the individual numbers as printed would expect the sum 32.90! You've been warned! [*Note:* Some third-party vendors sell C++ class libraries that perform precise monetary calculations.]

Using Stream Manipulators to Format Numeric Output

The output statement in line 18 before the `for` loop and the output statement in line 27 in the `for` loop combine to print the values of the variables `year` and `amount` with the formatting specified by the parameterized stream manipulators `setprecision` and **`setw`** and the nonparameterized stream manipulator `fixed`. The stream manipulator `setw(4)` specifies that the next value output should appear in a **field width** of 4—i.e., `cout` prints the value with *at least* 4 character positions. If the value to be output is *less* than 4 character positions wide, the value is **right justified** in the field by default. If the value to be output is *more* than 4 character positions wide, the field width is extended *rightward* to accommodate the entire value. To indicate that values should be output **left justified**, simply output nonparameterized stream manipulator **`left`** (found in header `<iostream>`). Right justification can be restored by outputting nonparameterized stream manipulator **`right`**.

The other formatting in the output statements indicates that variable `amount` is printed as a fixed-point value with a decimal point (specified in line 18 with the stream manipulator `fixed`) right justified in a field of 21 character positions (specified in line 27 with `setw(21)`) and two digits of precision to the right of the decimal point (specified in line 18 with manipulator `setprecision(2)`). We applied the stream manipulators `fixed` and `setprecision` to the output stream (i.e., `cout`) before the `for` loop because these format settings remain in effect until they're changed—such settings are called **sticky settings** and they do *not* need to be applied during each iteration of the loop. However, the field width specified with `setw` applies *only* to the *next* value output. We discuss C++'s powerful input/output formatting capabilities in Chapter 13, Stream Input/Output: A Deeper Look.

The calculation `1.0 + rate`, which appears as an argument to the `pow` function, is contained in the body of the `for` statement. In fact, this calculation produces the *same* result during each iteration of the loop, so repeating it is wasteful—it should be performed once before the loop.

Performance Tip 5.1

Avoid placing expressions whose values do not change inside loops. Even if you do, many of today's sophisticated optimizing compilers will automatically place such expressions outside *the loops in the generated machine code.*

Performance Tip 5.2

Many compilers contain optimization features that improve the performance of the code you write, but it's still better to write good code from the start.

5.5 do...while Repetition Statement

The `do...while` repetition statement is similar to the `while` statement. In the `while` statement, the loop-continuation condition test occurs at the beginning of the loop *before* the body of the loop executes. The `do...while` statement tests the loop-continuation condition *after* the loop body executes; therefore, *the loop body always executes at least once.*

Figure 5.7 uses a `do...while` statement to print the numbers 1–10. Upon entering the `do...while` statement, line 12 outputs `counter`'s value and line 13 increments `counter`. Then the program evaluates the loop-continuation test at the bottom of the loop (line 14). If the condition is true, the loop continues from the first body statement in the `do...while` (line 12). If the condition is false, the loop terminates and the program continues with the next statement after the loop (line 16).

```
// Fig. 5.7: fig05_07.cpp
// do...while repetition statement.
#include <iostream>
using namespace std;

int main()
{
   unsigned int counter = 1; // initialize counter

   do
   {
      cout << counter << " "; // display counter
      ++counter; // increment counter
   } while ( counter <= 10 ); // end do...while

   cout << endl; // output a newline
} // end main
```

```
1 2 3 4 5 6 7 8 9 10
```

Fig. 5.7 | do...while repetition statement.

do...while Statement UML Activity Diagram

Figure 5.8 contains the do...while statement's UML activity diagram, which makes it clear that the loop-continuation condition is not evaluated until *after* the loop performs its body at least once.

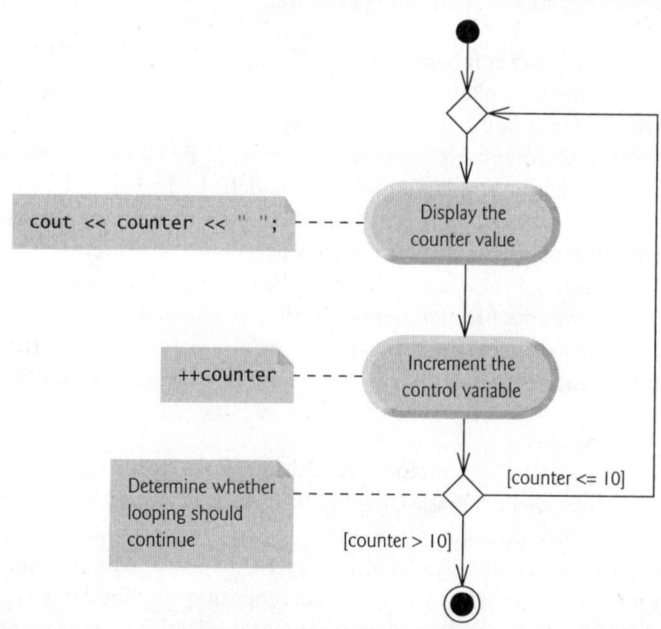

Fig. 5.8 | UML activity diagram for the do...while repetition statement of Fig. 5.7.

Braces in a do...while *Statement*

It's not necessary to use braces in the do...while statement if there's only one statement in the body; however, most programmers include the braces to avoid confusion between the while and do...while statements. For example,

```
while ( condition )
```

normally is regarded as the header of a while statement. A do...while with no braces around the single statement body appears as

```
do
   statement
while ( condition );
```

which can be confusing. You might misinterpret the last line—while(*condition*);—as a while statement containing as its body an empty statement. Thus, the do...while with one statement often is written as follows to avoid confusion:

```
do
{
   statement
} while ( condition );
```

5.6 switch Multiple-Selection Statement

C++ provides the **switch multiple-selection** statement to perform many different actions based on the possible values of a variable or expression. Each action is associated with the value of an **integral constant expression** (i.e., any combination of character and integer constants that evaluates to a constant integer value).

GradeBook *Class with* switch *Statement to Count A, B, C, D and F Grades*

This next version of the GradeBook class asks the user to enter a set of letter grades, then displays a summary of the number of students who received each grade. The class uses a switch to determine whether each grade entered is an A, B, C, D or F and to increment the appropriate grade counter. Class GradeBook is defined in Fig. 5.9, and its member-function definitions appear in Fig. 5.10. Figure 5.11 shows sample inputs and outputs of the main program that uses class GradeBook to process a set of grades.

Like earlier versions of the class definition, the GradeBook class definition (Fig. 5.9) contains function prototypes for member functions setCourseName (line 11), getCourseName (line 12) and displayMessage (line 13), as well as the class's constructor (line 10). The class definition also declares private data member courseName (line 17).

GradeBook *Class Header*

Class GradeBook (Fig. 5.9) now contains five additional private data members (lines 18–22)—counter variables for each grade category (i.e., A, B, C, D and F). The class also contains two additional public member functions—inputGrades and displayGradeReport. Member function inputGrades (declared in line 14) reads an arbitrary number of letter grades from the user using sentinel-controlled repetition and updates the appropriate grade counter for each grade entered. Member function displayGradeReport (declared in line 15) outputs a report containing the number of students who received each letter grade.

```
// Fig. 5.9: GradeBook.h
// GradeBook class definition that counts letter grades.
// Member functions are defined in GradeBook.cpp
#include <string> // program uses C++ standard string class

// GradeBook class definition
class GradeBook
{
public:
   explicit GradeBook( std::string ); // initialize course name
   void setCourseName( std::string ); // set the course name
   std::string getCourseName() const; // retrieve the course name
   void displayMessage() const; // display a welcome message
   void inputGrades(); // input arbitrary number of grades from user
   void displayGradeReport() const; // display report based on user input
private:
   std::string courseName; // course name for this GradeBook
   unsigned int aCount; // count of A grades
   unsigned int bCount; // count of B grades
   unsigned int cCount; // count of C grades
   unsigned int dCount; // count of D grades
   unsigned int fCount; // count of F grades
}; // end class GradeBook
```

Fig. 5.9 | GradeBook class definition that counts letter grades.

GradeBook Class Source-Code File

Source-code file GradeBook.cpp (Fig. 5.10) contains the member-function definitions for class GradeBook. Lines 11–15 in the constructor initialize the five grade counters to 0—when a GradeBook object is first created, no grades have been entered yet. These counters will be incremented in member function inputGrades as the user enters grades. The definitions of member functions setCourseName, getCourseName and displayMessage are identical to those in the earlier versions of class GradeBook.

```
1  // Fig. 5.10: GradeBook.cpp
2  // Member-function definitions for class GradeBook that
3  // uses a switch statement to count A, B, C, D and F grades.
4  #include <iostream>
5  #include "GradeBook.h" // include definition of class GradeBook
6  using namespace std;
7
8  // constructor initializes courseName with string supplied as argument;
9  // initializes counter data members to 0
10 GradeBook::GradeBook( string name )
11    : aCount( 0 ), // initialize count of A grades to 0
12      bCount( 0 ), // initialize count of B grades to 0
13      cCount( 0 ), // initialize count of C grades to 0
14      dCount( 0 ), // initialize count of D grades to 0
15      fCount( 0 )  // initialize count of F grades to 0
16 {
```

Fig. 5.10 | GradeBook class uses switch statement to count letter grades. (Part 1 of 3.)

```
   setCourseName( name );
} // end GradeBook constructor

// function to set the course name; limits name to 25 or fewer characters
void GradeBook::setCourseName( string name )
{
   if ( name.size() <= 25 ) // if name has 25 or fewer characters
      courseName = name; // store the course name in the object
   else // if name is longer than 25 characters
   { // set courseName to first 25 characters of parameter name
      courseName = name.substr( 0, 25 ); // select first 25 characters
      cerr << "Name \"" << name << "\" exceeds maximum length (25).\n"
         << "Limiting courseName to first 25 characters.\n" << endl;
   } // end if...else
} // end function setCourseName

// function to retrieve the course name
string GradeBook::getCourseName() const
{
   return courseName;
} // end function getCourseName

// display a welcome message to the GradeBook user
void GradeBook::displayMessage() const
{
   // this statement calls getCourseName to get the
   // name of the course this GradeBook represents
   cout << "Welcome to the grade book for\n" << getCourseName() << "!\n"
      << endl;
} // end function displayMessage

// input arbitrary number of grades from user; update grade counter
void GradeBook::inputGrades()
{
   int grade; // grade entered by user

   cout << "Enter the letter grades." << endl
      << "Enter the EOF character to end input." << endl;

   // loop until user types end-of-file key sequence
   while ( ( grade = cin.get() ) != EOF )
   {
      // determine which grade was entered
      switch ( grade ) // switch statement nested in while
      {
         case 'A': // grade was uppercase A
         case 'a': // or lowercase a
            ++aCount; // increment aCount
            break; // necessary to exit switch

```

Fig. 5.10 | GradeBook class uses switch statement to count letter grades. (Part 2 of 3.)

```
67             case 'B': // grade was uppercase B
68             case 'b': // or lowercase b
69                ++bCount; // increment bCount
70                break; // exit switch
71
72             case 'C': // grade was uppercase C
73             case 'c': // or lowercase c
74                ++cCount; // increment cCount
75                break; // exit switch
76
77             case 'D': // grade was uppercase D
78             case 'd': // or lowercase d
79                ++dCount; // increment dCount
80                break; // exit switch
81
82             case 'F': // grade was uppercase F
83             case 'f': // or lowercase f
84                ++fCount; // increment fCount
85                break; // exit switch
86
87             case '\n': // ignore newlines,
88             case '\t': // tabs,
89             case ' ': // and spaces in input
90                break; // exit switch
91
92             default: // catch all other characters
93                cout << "Incorrect letter grade entered."
94                   << " Enter a new grade." << endl;
95                break; // optional; will exit switch anyway
96          } // end switch
97       } // end while
98    } // end function inputGrades
99
100   // display a report based on the grades entered by user
101   void GradeBook::displayGradeReport() const
102   {
103      // output summary of results
104      cout << "\n\nNumber of students who received each letter grade:"
105         << "\nA: " << aCount // display number of A grades
106         << "\nB: " << bCount // display number of B grades
107         << "\nC: " << cCount // display number of C grades
108         << "\nD: " << dCount // display number of D grades
109         << "\nF: " << fCount // display number of F grades
110         << endl;
111   } // end function displayGradeReport
```

Fig. 5.10 | GradeBook class uses switch statement to count letter grades. (Part 3 of 3.)

Reading Character Input

The user enters letter grades for a course in member function `inputGrades` (lines 49–98). In the `while` header, in line 57, the parenthesized assignment `(grade = cin.get())` executes first. The `cin.get()` function reads one character from the keyboard and stores that character in integer variable `grade` (declared in line 51). Normally, characters are stored in variables of type `char`; however, characters can be stored in any integer data type, because types `short`, `int`, `long` and `long long` are guaranteed to be at least as big as type `char`. Thus, we can treat a character either as an integer or as a character, depending on its use. For example, the statement

```
cout << "The character (" << 'a' << ") has the value "
   << static_cast< int > ( 'a' ) << endl;
```

prints the character a and its integer value as follows:

```
The character (a) has the value 97
```

The integer 97 is the character's numerical representation in the computer. Appendix B shows the characters and decimal equivalents from the **ASCII (American Standard Code for Information Interchange) character set.**

Generally, assignment statements have the value that's assigned to the variable on the left side of the =. Thus, the value of the assignment expression `grade = cin.get()` is the same as the value returned by `cin.get()` and assigned to the variable `grade`.

The fact that assignment expressions have values can be useful for assigning the same value to *several* variables. For example,

```
a = b = c = 0;
```

first evaluates `c = 0` (because the = operator associates from right to left). The variable `b` is then assigned the value of `c = 0` (which is 0). Then, a is assigned the value of `b = (c = 0)` (which is also 0). In the program, the value of `grade = cin.get()` is compared with the value of `EOF` (a symbol whose acronym stands for "end-of-file"). We use `EOF` (which normally has the value –1) as the sentinel value. *However, you do not type the value –1, nor do you type the letters EOF as the sentinel value.* Rather, you type a *system-dependent keystroke combination* that means "end-of-file" to indicate that you have no more data to enter. `EOF` is a symbolic integer constant that is included into the program via the `<iostream>` header.[1] If the value assigned to `grade` is equal to `EOF`, the `while` loop (lines 57–97) terminates. We've chosen to represent the characters entered into this program as `int`s, because `EOF` has type `int`.

Entering the EOF Indicator

On OS X/Linux/UNIX systems and many others, end-of-file is entered by typing

<*Ctrl*> *d*

on a line by itself. This notation means to press and hold down the *Ctrl* key, then press the *d* key. On other systems such as Microsoft Windows, end-of-file can be entered by typing

<*Ctrl*> *z*

[*Note:* In some cases, you must press *Enter* after the preceding key sequence. Also, the characters `^Z` sometimes appear on the screen to represent end-of-file, as shown in Fig. 5.11.]

Portability Tip 5.1

The keystroke combinations for entering end-of-file are system dependent.

1. To compile this program, some compilers require the header `<cstdio>` which defines `EOF`.

Portability Tip 5.2

Testing for the symbolic constant EOF rather than -1 makes programs more portable. The C standard, from which C++ adopts the definition of EOF, states that EOF is a negative integral value, so EOF could have different values on different systems.

In this program, the user enters grades at the keyboard. When the user presses the *Enter* (or the *Return*) key, the characters are read by the `cin.get()` function, one character at a time. If the character entered is not end-of-file, the flow of control enters the `switch` statement (Fig. 5.10, lines 60–96), which increments the appropriate letter-grade counter.

switch Statement Details

The `switch` statement consists of a series of **case labels** and an optional **default** case. These are used in this example to determine which counter to increment, based on a grade. When the flow of control reaches the `switch`, the program evaluates the expression in the parentheses (i.e., `grade`) following keyword `switch` (line 60). This is called the **controlling expression**. The `switch` statement compares the value of the controlling expression with each `case` label. Assume the user enters the letter `C` as a grade. The program compares `C` to each `case` in the `switch`. If a match occurs (`case 'C':` in line 72), the program executes the statements for that `case`. For the letter `C`, line 74 increments `cCount` by `1`. The `break` statement (line 75) causes program control to proceed with the first statement after the `switch`—in this program, control transfers to line 97. This line marks the end of the body of the `while` loop that inputs grades (lines 57–97), so control flows to the `while`'s condition (line 57) to determine whether the loop should continue executing.

The `case`s in our `switch` explicitly test for the lowercase and uppercase versions of the letters A, B, C, D and F. Note the `case`s in lines 62–63 that test for the values `'A'` and `'a'` (both of which represent the grade A). Listing `case`s consecutively with no statements between them enables the `case`s to perform the same set of statements—when the controlling expression evaluates to either `'A'` or `'a'`, the statements in lines 64–65 will execute. Each `case` can have multiple statements. The `switch` selection statement does not require braces around multiple statements in each `case`.

Without `break` statements, each time a match occurs in the `switch`, the statements for that `case` *and* subsequent `case`s execute until a `break` statement or the end of the `switch` is encountered.

Common Programming Error 5.5

Forgetting a `break` statement when one is needed in a `switch` statement is a logic error.

Common Programming Error 5.6

Omitting the space between the word `case` and the integral value tested in a `switch` statement—e.g., writing `case3:` instead of `case 3:`—is a logic error. The `switch` statement will not perform the appropriate actions when the controlling expression has a value of 3.

Providing a default Case

If *no* match occurs between the controlling expression's value and a `case` label, the `default` case (lines 92–95) executes. We use the `default` case in this example to process all controlling-expression values that are neither valid grades nor newline, tab or space characters. If no match occurs, the `default` case executes, and lines 93–94 print an error message indicating that an incorrect letter grade was entered. If no match occurs in a `switch` statement that does not contain a `default` case, program control continues with the first statement after the `switch`.

Error-Prevention Tip 5.3

Provide a `default` case in `switch` statements. Cases not explicitly tested in a `switch` statement without a `default` case are ignored. Including a `default` case focuses you on the need to process exceptional conditions. There are situations in which no `default` processing is needed. Although the `case` clauses and the `default` case clause in a `switch` statement can occur in any *order, it's common practice to place the `default` clause last.*

Good Programming Practice 5.2

The last `case` in a `switch` statement does not require a `break` statement. Nevertheless, include this `break` for clarity and for symmetry with other cases.

Ignoring Newline, Tab and Blank Characters in Input

Lines 87–90 in the `switch` statement of Fig. 5.10 cause the program to skip newline, tab and blank characters. Reading characters one at a time can cause problems. To have the program read the characters, we must send them to the computer by pressing the *Enter* key. This places a newline character in the input after the character we wish to process. Often, this newline character must be specially processed. By including these `case`s in our `switch` statement, we prevent the error message in the `default` case from being printed each time a newline, tab or space is encountered in the input.

*Testing Class **GradeBook***

Figure 5.11 creates a `GradeBook` object (line 8). Line 10 invokes its `displayMessage` member function to output a welcome message to the user. Line 11 invokes member function `inputGrades` to read a set of grades from the user and keep track of how many students received each grade. The output window in Fig. 5.11 shows an error message displayed in response to entering an invalid grade (i.e., `E`). Line 12 invokes `GradeBook` member function `displayGradeReport` (defined in lines 101–111 of Fig. 5.10), which outputs a report based on the grades entered (as in the output in Fig. 5.11).

```
1  // Fig. 5.11: fig05_11.cpp
2  // Creating a GradeBook object and calling its member functions.
3  #include "GradeBook.h" // include definition of class GradeBook
4
5  int main()
6  {
7     // create GradeBook object
8     GradeBook myGradeBook( "CS101 C++ Programming" );
9
10    myGradeBook.displayMessage(); // display welcome message
11    myGradeBook.inputGrades(); // read grades from user
12    myGradeBook.displayGradeReport(); // display report based on grades
13 } // end main
```

Fig. 5.11 | Creating a `GradeBook` object and calling its member functions. (Part 1 of 2.)

```
Welcome to the grade book for
CS101 C++ Programming!

Enter the letter grades.
Enter the EOF character to end input.
a
B
c
C
A
d
f
C
E
Incorrect letter grade entered. Enter a new grade.
D
A
b
^Z


Number of students who received each letter grade:
A: 3
B: 2
C: 3
D: 2
F: 1
```

Fig. 5.11 | Creating a GradeBook object and calling its member functions. (Part 2 of 2.)

switch Statement UML Activity Diagram

Figure 5.12 shows the UML activity diagram for the general switch multiple-selection statement. Most switch statements use a break in each case to terminate the switch statement after processing the case. Figure 5.12 emphasizes this by including break statements in the activity diagram. Without the break statement, control would not transfer to the first statement after the switch statement after a case is processed. Instead, control would transfer to the next case's actions.

The diagram makes it clear that the break statement at the end of a case causes control to exit the switch statement immediately. Again, note that (besides an initial state, transition arrows, a final state and several notes) the diagram contains action states and decisions. Also, the diagram uses merge symbols to merge the transitions from the break statements to the final state.

Each case can be used to test only an integral *constant* expression—any combination of character constants and integer constants that evaluates to a constant integer value. A character constant is represented as the specific character in single quotes, such as 'A'. An integer constant is simply an integer value. Also, each case label can specify only one integral constant expression.

Common Programming Error 5.7

Providing case *labels with identical values in a* switch *statement is a compilation error.*

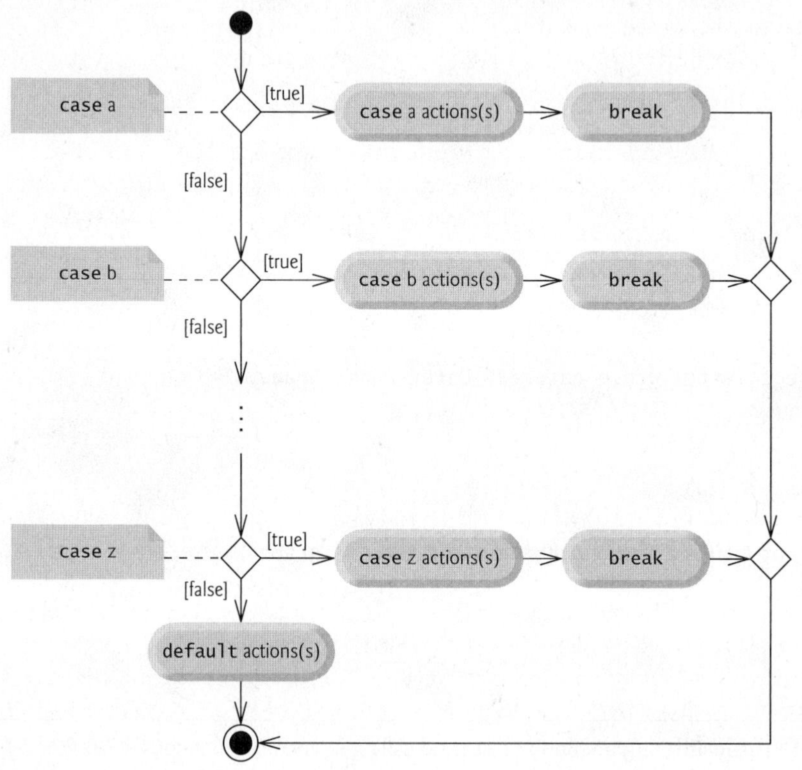

Fig. 5.12 | `switch` multiple-selection statement UML activity diagram with `break` statements.

Notes on Data Types

C++ has *flexible data type sizes* (see Appendix C, Fundamental Types). Different applications, for example, might need integers of different sizes. C++ provides several integer types. The range of integer values for each type is platform dependent. In addition to the types `int` and `char`, C++ provides the types `short` (an abbreviation of `short int`), `long` (an abbreviation of `long int`) and `long long` (an abbreviation of `long long int`). The minimum range of values for `short` integers is –32,767 to 32,767. For the vast majority of integer calculations, `long` integers are sufficient. The minimum range of values for `long` integers is –2,147,483,647 to 2,147,483,647. On most computers, `int`s are equivalent either to `short` or to `long`. The range of values for an `int` is at least the same as that for `short` integers and no larger than that for `long` integers. The data type `char` can be used to represent any of the characters in the computer's character set. It also can be used to represent small integers.

C++11 In-Class Initializers

C++11 allows you to provide a default value for a data member when you declare it in the class declaration. For example, lines 18–22 of Fig. 5.9 could have initialized data members `aCount`, `bCount`, `cCount`, `dCount` and `fCount` to `0` as follows:

```
unsigned int aCount = 0; // count of A grades
unsigned int bCount = 0; // count of B grades
unsigned int cCount = 0; // count of C grades
unsigned int dCount = 0; // count of D grades
unsigned int fCount = 0; // count of F grades
```

rather than initializing them in the class's constructor (Fig. 5.10, lines 10–18). In later chapters, we'll continue discussing in-class initializers and show how they enable you to perform certain data member initializations that were not possible in earlier C++ versions.

5.7 break and continue Statements

C++ also provides statements `break` and `continue` to alter the flow of control. The preceding section showed how `break` can be used to terminate a `switch` statement's execution. This section discusses how to use `break` in a repetition statement.

break Statement

The **`break` statement**, when executed in a `while`, `for`, `do...while` or `switch` statement, causes immediate exit from that statement. Program execution continues with the next statement. Common uses of the `break` statement are to escape early from a loop or to skip the remainder of a `switch` statement. Figure 5.13 demonstrates the `break` statement (line 13) exiting a `for` repetition statement.

When the `if` statement detects that `count` is `5`, the `break` statement executes. This terminates the `for` statement, and the program proceeds to line 18 (immediately after the `for` statement), which displays a message indicating the control variable value that terminated the loop. The `for` statement fully executes its body only four times instead of 10. The control variable `count` is defined outside the `for` statement header, so that we can use the control variable both *in* the loop's body and *after* the loop completes its execution.

```
1   // Fig. 5.13: fig05_13.cpp
2   // break statement exiting a for statement.
3   #include <iostream>
4   using namespace std;
5
6   int main()
7   {
8      unsigned int count; // control variable also used after loop terminates
9
10     for ( count = 1; count <= 10; ++count ) // loop 10 times
11     {
12        if ( count == 5 )
13           break; // break loop only if count is 5
14
15        cout << count << " ";
16     } // end for
17
18     cout << "\nBroke out of loop at count = " << count << endl;
19  } // end main
```

Fig. 5.13 | `break` statement exiting a `for` statement. (Part 1 of 2.)

```
1 2 3 4
Broke out of loop at count = 5
```

Fig. 5.13 | break statement exiting a for statement. (Part 2 of 2.)

continue Statement

The **continue statement**, when executed in a while, for or do...while statement, skips the remaining statements in the body of that statement and proceeds with the next iteration of the loop. In while and do...while statements, the loop-continuation test evaluates immediately after the continue statement executes. In the for statement, the increment expression executes, then the loop-continuation test evaluates.

Figure 5.14 uses the continue statement (line 11) in a for statement to skip the output statement (line 13) when the nested if (lines 10–11) determines that the value of count is 5. When the continue statement executes, program control continues with the increment of the control variable in the for header (line 8) and loops five more times.

```
1  // Fig. 5.14: fig05_14.cpp
2  // continue statement terminating an iteration of a for statement.
3  #include <iostream>
4  using namespace std;
5
6  int main()
7  {
8     for ( unsigned int count = 1; count <= 10; ++count ) // loop 10 times
9     {
10       if ( count == 5 ) // if count is 5,
11          continue;      // skip remaining code in loop
12
13       cout << count << " ";
14    } // end for
15
16    cout << "\nUsed continue to skip printing 5" << endl;
17 } // end main
```

```
1 2 3 4 6 7 8 9 10
Used continue to skip printing 5
```

Fig. 5.14 | continue statement terminating an iteration of a for statement.

In Section 5.3, we stated that the while statement could be used in most cases to represent the for statement. The one exception occurs when the increment expression in the while statement follows the continue statement. In this case, the increment does not execute before the program tests the loop-continuation condition, and the while does not execute in the same manner as the for.

5.8 Logical Operators

So far we've studied only **simple conditions**, such as counter <= 10, total > 1000 and number != sentinelValue. We expressed these conditions in terms of the relational operators

>, <, >= and <=, and the equality operators == and !=. Each decision tested precisely one condition. To test multiple conditions while making a decision, we performed these tests in separate statements or in nested if or if...else statements.

C++ provides **logical operators** that are used to form more complex conditions by combining simple conditions. The logical operators are && (logical AND), || (logical OR) and ! (logical NOT, also called logical negation).

Logical AND (&&) Operator

Suppose that we wish to ensure that two conditions are *both* true before we choose a certain path of execution. In this case, we can use the **&& (logical AND)** operator, as follows:

```
if ( gender == FEMALE && age >= 65 )
   ++seniorFemales;
```

This if statement contains two simple conditions. The condition gender == FEMALE is used here to determine whether a person is a female. The condition age >= 65 determines whether a person is a senior citizen. The simple condition to the left of the && operator evaluates first. If necessary, the simple condition to the right of the && operator evaluates next. As we'll discuss shortly, the right side of a logical AND expression is evaluated *only* if the left side is true. The if statement then considers the combined condition

```
gender == FEMALE && age >= 65
```

This condition is true if and only if *both* of the simple conditions are true. Finally, if this combined condition is indeed true, the statement in the if statement's body increments the count of seniorFemales. If either (or both) of the simple conditions are false, then the program skips the incrementing and proceeds to the statement following the if. The preceding combined condition can be made more readable by adding redundant parentheses:

```
( gender == FEMALE ) && ( age >= 65 )
```

Common Programming Error 5.8

Although 3 < x < 7 is a mathematically correct condition, it does not evaluate as you might expect in C++. Use (3 < x && x < 7) to get the proper evaluation in C++.

Figure 5.15 summarizes the && operator. The table shows all four possible combinations of false and true values for *expression1* and *expression2*. Such tables are often called **truth tables**. C++ evaluates to false or true all expressions that include relational operators, equality operators and/or logical operators.

expression1	expression2	expression1 && expression2
false	false	false
false	true	false
true	false	false
true	true	true

Fig. 5.15 | && (logical AND) operator truth table.

Logical OR (||) Operator

Now let's consider the || (**logical OR**) operator. Suppose we wish to ensure that either *or* both of two conditions are true before we choose a certain path of execution. In this case, we use the || operator, as in the following program segment:

```
if ( ( semesterAverage >= 90 ) || ( finalExam >= 90 ) )
   cout << "Student grade is A" << endl;
```

which contains two simple conditions. The simple condition semesterAverage >= 90 evaluates to determine whether the student deserves an "A" in the course because of a solid performance throughout the semester. The simple condition finalExam >= 90 evaluates to determine whether the student deserves an "A" in the course because of an outstanding performance on the final exam. The if statement then considers the combined condition

```
( semesterAverage >= 90 ) || ( finalExam >= 90 )
```

and awards the student an "A" if *either or both* of the simple conditions are true. The message "Student grade is A" prints unless *both* of the simple conditions are false. Figure 5.16 is a truth table for the logical OR operator (||).

expression1	expression2	expression1 || expression2
false	false	false
false	true	true
true	false	true
true	true	true

Fig. 5.16 | || (logical OR) operator truth table.

The && operator has a higher precedence than the || operator. Both operators associate from left to right. An expression containing && or || operators evaluates only until the truth or falsehood of the expression is known. Thus, evaluation of the expression

```
( gender == FEMALE ) && ( age >= 65 )
```

stops immediately if gender is not equal to FEMALE (i.e., the entire expression is false) and continues if gender is equal to FEMALE (i.e., the entire expression could still be true if the condition age >= 65 is true). This performance feature for the evaluation of logical AND and logical OR expressions is called **short-circuit evaluation.**

Performance Tip 5.3

In expressions using operator &&, if the separate conditions are independent of one another, make the condition most likely to be false *the leftmost condition. In expressions using operator* ||, *make the condition most likely to be* true *the leftmost condition. This use of short-circuit evaluation can reduce a program's execution time.*

Logical Negation (!) Operator

C++ provides the ! (**logical NOT**, also called **logical negation**) operator to "reverse" a condition's meaning. The unary logical negation operator has only a single condition as an operand. The unary logical negation operator is placed *before* a condition when we are interested in choosing a path of execution if the original condition (without the logical negation operator) is `false`, such as in the following program segment:

```
if ( !( grade == sentinelValue ) )
   cout << "The next grade is " << grade << endl;
```

The parentheses around the condition `grade == sentinelValue` are needed because the logical negation operator has a higher precedence than the equality operator.

You can often avoid the `!` operator by using an appropriate relational or equality operator. For example, the preceding `if` statement also can be written as follows:

```
if ( grade != sentinelValue )
   cout << "The next grade is " << grade << endl;
```

This flexibility often can help you express a condition in a more "natural" or convenient manner. Figure 5.17 is a truth table for the logical negation operator (`!`).

expression	!expression
false	true
true	false

Fig. 5.17 | ! (logical negation) operator truth table.

Logical Operators Example

Figure 5.18 demonstrates the logical operators by producing their truth tables. The output shows each expression that's evaluated and its `bool` result. By default, `bool` values `true` and `false` are displayed by `cout` and the stream insertion operator as `1` and `0`, respectively. We use **stream manipulator `boolalpha`** (a *sticky* manipulator) in line 9 to specify that the value of each `bool` expression should be displayed as either the word "true" or the word "false." For example, the result of the expression `false && false` in line 10 is `false`, so the second line of output includes the word "false." Lines 9–13 produce the truth table for `&&`. Lines 16–20 produce the truth table for `||`. Lines 23–25 produce the truth table for `!`.

```
1  // Fig. 5.18: fig05_18.cpp
2  // Logical operators.
3  #include <iostream>
4  using namespace std;
5
6  int main()
7  {
8     // create truth table for && (logical AND) operator
9     cout << boolalpha << "Logical AND (&&)"
10       << "\nfalse && false: " << ( false && false )
11       << "\nfalse && true: " << ( false && true )
12       << "\ntrue && false: " << ( true && false )
13       << "\ntrue && true: " << ( true && true ) << "\n\n";
```

Fig. 5.18 | Logical operators. (Part 1 of 2.)

```
   // create truth table for || (logical OR) operator
   cout << "Logical OR (||)"
      << "\nfalse || false: " << ( false || false )
      << "\nfalse || true: " << ( false || true )
      << "\ntrue || false: " << ( true || false )
      << "\ntrue || true: " << ( true || true ) << "\n\n";

   // create truth table for ! (logical negation) operator
   cout << "Logical NOT (!)"
      << "\n!false: " << ( !false )
      << "\n!true: " << ( !true ) << endl;
} // end main
```

```
Logical AND (&&)
false && false: false
false && true: false
true && false: false
true && true: true

Logical OR (||)
false || false: false
false || true: true
true || false: true
true || true: true

Logical NOT (!)
!false: true
!true: false
```

Fig. 5.18 | Logical operators. (Part 2 of 2.)

Summary of Operator Precedence and Associativity

Figure 5.19 adds the logical and comma operators to the operator precedence and associativity chart. The operators are shown from top to bottom, in decreasing order of precedence.

Operators	Associativity	Type
:: ()	left to right *[See caution in Fig. 2.7 regarding grouping parentheses.]*	primary
++ -- **static_cast**< *type* >()	left to right	postfix
++ -- + - !	right to left	unary (prefix)
* / %	left to right	multiplicative
+ -	left to right	additive
<< >>	left to right	insertion/extraction
< <= > >=	left to right	relational

Fig. 5.19 | Operator precedence and associativity. (Part 1 of 2.)

Operators	Associativity	Type
`==` `!=`	left to right	equality
`&&`	left to right	logical AND
`||`	left to right	logical OR
`?:`	right to left	conditional
`=` `+=` `-=` `*=` `/=` `%=`	right to left	assignment
`,`	left to right	comma

Fig. 5.19 | Operator precedence and associativity. (Part 2 of 2.)

5.9 Confusing the Equality (==) and Assignment (=) Operators

There's one error that C++ programmers, no matter how experienced, tend to make so frequently that we feel it requires a separate section. That error is accidentally swapping the operators == (equality) and = (assignment). What makes this so damaging is that it ordinarily does *not* cause *syntax errors*—statements with these errors tend to compile correctly and the programs run to completion, often generating incorrect results through *runtime logic errors*. Some compilers issue a *warning* when = is used in a context where == is expected.

Two aspects of C++ contribute to these problems. One is that *any expression that produces a value can be used as a condition*—if the value of the expression is zero, it's treated as `false`, and if the value is nonzero, it's treated as `true`. The second is that assignments produce a value—namely, the value assigned to the variable on the left side of the assignment operator. For example, suppose we intend to write

```
if ( payCode == 4 ) // good
   cout << "You get a bonus!" << endl;
```

but we accidentally write

```
if ( payCode = 4 ) // bad
   cout << "You get a bonus!" << endl;
```

The first `if` statement properly awards a bonus to the person whose `payCode` is equal to 4. The second one—which contains the error—evaluates the assignment expression in the `if` condition as the value 4. *Any nonzero value is interpreted as* `true`, so this condition always evaluates as `true` and the person *always* receives a bonus regardless of what the actual paycode is! Even worse, the paycode has been *modified* when it was only supposed to be *examined!*

Error-Prevention Tip 5.4

Programmers normally write conditions such as `x == 7` *with the variable name on the left and the constant on the right. By placing the constant on the left, as in* `7 == x`*, you'll be protected by the compiler if you accidentally replace the* `==` *operator with* `=`*. The compiler treats this as a compilation error, because you can't change the value of a constant. This will prevent the potential devastation of a runtime logic error.*

lvalues *and* rvalues

Variable names are said to be ***lvalues*** (for "left values") because they can be used on the *left* side of an assignment operator. Constants are said to be ***rvalues*** (for "right values") because they can be used on only the *right* side of an assignment operator. *Lvalues* can also be used as *rvalues*, but not vice versa.

There's another equally unpleasant situation. Suppose you want to assign a value to a variable with a simple statement like

```
x = 1;
```

but instead write

```
x == 1;
```

Here, too, this is *not* a syntax error. Rather, the compiler simply evaluates the conditional expression. If `x` is equal to `1`, the condition is `true` and the expression evaluates to the value `true`. If `x` is not equal to `1`, the condition is `false` and the expression evaluates to the value `false`. Regardless of the expression's value, there's no assignment operator, so the value simply is lost. The value of `x` remains unaltered, probably causing an execution-time logic error. Unfortunately, we do not have a handy trick to help you with this problem!

Error-Prevention Tip 5.5

Use your text editor to search for all occurrences of = in your program and check that you have the correct assignment operator or logical operator in each place.

5.10 Wrap-Up

We've now completed our introduction to control statements. This chapter demonstrated the `for`, `do...while` and `switch` statements. We showed that any algorithm can be developed using combinations of the sequence structure, the three types of selection statements—`if`, `if...else` and `switch`—and the three types of repetition statements—`while`, `do...while` and `for`. We discussed how you can combine these building blocks. You used the `break` and `continue` statements to alter a repetition statement's flow of control. We also introduced logical operators, which enable you to use more complex conditional expressions in control statements. Finally, we examined the common errors of confusing the equality and assignment operators and provided suggestions for avoiding these errors. In Chapter 6, we examine functions in greater depth.

6

Functions and an Introduction to Recursion

Objectives

In this chapter you'll:

- Construct programs modularly from functions.
- Use common math library functions.
- Pass data to functions and return results.
- Learn how the function call and return mechanism is supported by the function call stack and activation records.
- Use random number generation to implement game-playing applications.
- Learn how the visibility of identifiers is limited to specific regions of programs.
- Write and use recursive functions.

Outline

6.1 Introduction

In this chapter, we discuss functions, beginning with an overview of a portion of the C++ Standard Library's math functions. Next, you'll learn how to declare a function with more than one parameter. We'll also present additional information about function prototypes and how the compiler uses them to convert the type of an argument in a function call to the type specified in a function's parameter list, if necessary.

Next, we'll take a brief diversion into simulation techniques with random number generation and develop a version of a popular casino dice game that uses most of the C++ capabilities we've discussed.

We then present storage-class specifiers and scope rules. These determine the period during which an object exists in memory and where its identifier can be referenced in a program. You'll learn how C++ keeps track of which function is currently executing, how parameters and other local variables of functions are maintained in memory and how a function knows where to return after it completes execution. We discuss topics that help improve program performance—inline functions that can eliminate the overhead of a function call and reference parameters that can be used to pass large data items to functions efficiently.

Many of the applications you develop will have more than one function of the same name. This technique, called function overloading, is used to implement functions that perform similar tasks for arguments of different types or possibly for different numbers of arguments. We consider function templates—a mechanism for defining a family of overloaded functions. The chapter concludes with a discussion of recursive functions—functions that call themselves, either directly, or indirectly through other functions.

6.2 Math Library Functions

Sometimes functions, such as `main`, are *not* members of a class. Such functions are called **global functions**. Like a class's member functions, the function prototypes for global functions are placed in headers, so that the global functions can be reused in any program that includes the header and that can link to the function's object code. For example, recall that we used function `pow` of the `<cmath>` header to raise a value to a power in Fig. 5.6. We introduce various functions from the `<cmath>` header here to present the concept of global functions that do not belong to a particular class.

The `<cmath>` header provides a collection of functions that enable you to perform common mathematical calculations. For example, you can calculate the square root of `900.0` with the function call

```
sqrt( 900.0 )
```

The preceding expression evaluates to `30.0`. Function `sqrt` takes an argument of type `double` and returns a `double` result. There's no need to create any objects before calling function `sqrt`. Also, *all* functions in the `<cmath>` header are *global* functions—therefore, each is called simply by specifying the name of the function followed by parentheses containing the function's arguments. If you call `sqrt` with a negative argument, the function sets a global variable named `errno` to the constant value `EDOM`. The variable `errno` and the constant `EDOM` are defined in the `<cerrno>` header. We'll discuss global variables in Section 6.9.

Error-Prevention Tip 6.1

Do not call `sqrt` with a negative argument. For industrial-strength code, always check that the arguments you pass to math functions are valid.

Function arguments may be constants, variables or more complex expressions. If `c = 13.0`, `d = 3.0` and `f = 4.0`, then the statement

```
cout << sqrt( c + d * f ) << endl;
```

displays the square root of `13.0 + 3.0 * 4.0 = 25.0`—namely, `5.0`. Some math library functions are summarized in Fig. 6.1. In the figure, the variables `x` and `y` are of type `double`.

Function	Description	Example
`ceil( x )`	rounds *x* to the smallest integer not less than *x*	`ceil( 9.2 )` is `10.0` `ceil( -9.8 )` is `-9.0`
`cos( x )`	trigonometric cosine of *x* (*x* in radians)	`cos( 0.0 )` is `1.0`
`exp( x )`	exponential function e^x	`exp( 1.0 )` is `2.718282` `exp( 2.0 )` is `7.389056`

`fabs( x )`	absolute value of *x*	`fabs( 5.1 )` is `5.1`
		`fabs( 0.0 )` is `0.0`
		`fabs( -8.76 )` is `8.76`

`floor( x )`	rounds *x* to the largest integer not greater than *x*	`floor( 9.2 )` is `9.0` `floor( -9.8 )` is `-10.0`
`fmod( x, y )`	remainder of *x/y* as a floating-point number	`fmod( 2.6, 1.2 )` is `0.2`

Fig. 6.1 | Math library functions. (Part 1 of 2.)

Function	Description	Example
`log( x )`	natural logarithm of *x* (base *e*)	`log( 2.718282 )` is `1.0` `log( 7.389056 )` is `2.0`
`log10( x )`	logarithm of *x* (base 10)	`log10( 10.0 )` is `1.0` `log10( 100.0 )` is `2.0`
`pow( x, y )`	*x* raised to power *y* (x^y)	`pow( 2, 7 )` is `128` `pow( 9, .5 )` is `3`
`sin( x )`	trigonometric sine of *x* (*x* in radians)	`sin( 0.0 )` is `0`
`sqrt( x )`	square root of *x* (where *x* is a nonnegative value)	`sqrt( 9.0 )` is `3.0`
`tan( x )`	trigonometric tangent of *x* (*x* in radians)	`tan( 0.0 )` is `0`

Fig. 6.1 | Math library functions. (Part 2 of 2.)

6.3 Function Definitions with Multiple Parameters

Let's consider functions with *multiple* parameters. Figures 6.2–6.4 modify class `GradeBook` by including a user-defined function called `maximum` that determines and returns the largest of three `int` grades. When the application executes, the `main` function (lines 5–13 of Fig. 6.4) creates one `GradeBook` object (line 8) and calls its `inputGrades` member function (line 11) to read three integer grades from the user. In class `GradeBook`'s implementation file (Fig. 6.3), lines 52–53 of member function `inputGrades` prompt the user to enter three integer values and read them from the user. Line 56 calls member function `maximum` (defined in lines 60–73). Function `maximum` determines the largest value, then the `return` statement (line 72) returns that value to the point at which function `inputGrades` invoked `maximum` (line 56). Member function `inputGrades` then stores `maximum`'s return value in data member `maximumGrade`. This value is then output by calling function `displayGradeReport` (line 12 of Fig. 6.4). [*Note:* We named this function `displayGradeReport` because subsequent versions of class `GradeBook` will use this function to display a complete grade report, including the maximum and minimum grades.] In Chapter 7, we'll enhance class `GradeBook` to process sets of grades.

```
// Fig. 6.2: GradeBook.h
// Definition of class GradeBook that finds the maximum of three grades.
// Member functions are defined in GradeBook.cpp
#include <string> // program uses C++ standard string class

// GradeBook class definition
class GradeBook
{
public:
   explicit GradeBook( std::string ); // initializes course name
```

Fig. 6.2 | Definition of class `GradeBook` that finds the maximum of three grades. (Part 1 of 2.)

```
   void setCourseName( std::string ); // set the course name
   std::string getCourseName() const; //retrieve the course name
   void displayMessage() const; // display a welcome message
   void inputGrades(); // input three grades from user
   void displayGradeReport() const; // display report based on the grades
   int maximum( int, int, int ) const; // determine max of 3 values
private:
   std::string courseName; // course name for this GradeBook
   int maximumGrade; // maximum of three grades
}; // end class GradeBook
```

Fig. 6.2 | Definition of class **GradeBook** that finds the maximum of three grades. (Part 2 of 2.)

```
// Fig. 6.3: GradeBook.cpp
// Member-function definitions for class GradeBook that
// determines the maximum of three grades.
#include <iostream>
using namespace std;

#include "GradeBook.h" // include definition of class GradeBook

// constructor initializes courseName with string supplied as argument;
// initializes maximumGrade to 0
GradeBook::GradeBook( string name )
   : maximumGrade( 0 ) // this value will be replaced by the maximum grade
{
   setCourseName( name ); // validate and store courseName
} // end GradeBook constructor

// function to set the course name; limits name to 25 or fewer characters
void GradeBook::setCourseName( string name )
{
   if ( name.size() <= 25 ) // if name has 25 or fewer characters
      courseName = name; // store the course name in the object
   else // if name is longer than 25 characters
   { // set courseName to first 25 characters of parameter name
      courseName = name.substr( 0, 25 ); // select first 25 characters
      cerr << "Name \"" << name << "\" exceeds maximum length (25).\n"
         << "Limiting courseName to first 25 characters.\n" << endl;
   } // end if...else
} // end function setCourseName

// function to retrieve the course name
string GradeBook::getCourseName() const
{
   return courseName;
} // end function getCourseName

// display a welcome message to the GradeBook user
void GradeBook::displayMessage() const
{
```

Fig. 6.3 | Member-function definitions for class **GradeBook** that determines the maximum of three grades. (Part 1 of 2.)

```
   // this statement calls getCourseName to get the
   // name of the course this GradeBook represents
   cout << "Welcome to the grade book for\n" << getCourseName() << "!\n"
      << endl;
} // end function displayMessage

// input three grades from user; determine maximum
void GradeBook::inputGrades()
{
   int grade1; // first grade entered by user
   int grade2; // second grade entered by user
   int grade3; // third grade entered by user

   cout << "Enter three integer grades: ";
   cin >> grade1 >> grade2 >> grade3;

   // store maximum in member maximumGrade
   maximumGrade = maximum( grade1, grade2, grade3 );
} // end function inputGrades

// returns the maximum of its three integer parameters
int GradeBook::maximum( int x, int y, int z ) const
{
   int maximumValue = x; // assume x is the largest to start

   // determine whether y is greater than maximumValue
   if ( y > maximumValue )
      maximumValue = y; // make y the new maximumValue

   // determine whether z is greater than maximumValue
   if ( z > maximumValue )
      maximumValue = z; // make z the new maximumValue

   return maximumValue;
} // end function maximum

// display a report based on the grades entered by user
void GradeBook::displayGradeReport() const
{
   // output maximum of grades entered
   cout << "Maximum of grades entered: " << maximumGrade << endl;
} // end function displayGradeReport
```

Fig. 6.3 | Member-function definitions for class GradeBook that determines the maximum of three grades. (Part 2 of 2.)

```
// Fig. 6.4: fig06_04.cpp
// Create GradeBook object, input grades and display grade report.
#include "GradeBook.h" // include definition of class GradeBook

int main()
{
```

Fig. 6.4 | Create GradeBook object, input grades and display grade report. (Part 1 of 2.)

```
    // create GradeBook object
    GradeBook myGradeBook( "CS101 C++ Programming" );

    myGradeBook.displayMessage(); // display welcome message
    myGradeBook.inputGrades(); // read grades from user
    myGradeBook.displayGradeReport(); // display report based on grades
} // end main
```

```
Welcome to the grade book for
CS101 C++ Programming!

Enter three integer grades: 86 67 75
Maximum of grades entered: 86
```

```
Welcome to the grade book for
CS101 C++ Programming!

Enter three integer grades: 67 86 75
Maximum of grades entered: 86
```

```
Welcome to the grade book for
CS101 C++ Programming!

Enter three integer grades: 67 75 86
Maximum of grades entered: 86
```

Fig. 6.4 | Create `GradeBook` object, input grades and display grade report. (Part 2 of 2.)

Software Engineering Observation 6.1

The commas used in line 56 of Fig. 6.3 to separate the arguments to function `maximum` *are* not *comma operators as discussed in Section 5.3. The comma operator guarantees that its operands are evaluated left to right. The order of evaluation of a function's arguments, however, is* not *specified by the C++ standard. Thus, different compilers can evaluate function arguments in different orders. The C++ standard* does *guarantee that all arguments in a function call are evaluated* before *the called function executes.*

Portability Tip 6.1

Sometimes when a function's arguments are expressions, such as those with calls to other functions, the order in which the compiler evaluates the arguments could affect the values of one or more of the arguments. If the evaluation order changes between compilers, the argument values passed to the function could vary, causing subtle logic errors.

Error-Prevention Tip 6.2

If you have doubts about the order of evaluation of a function's arguments and whether the order would affect the values passed to the function, evaluate the arguments in separate assignment statements before the function call, assign the result of each expression to a local variable, then pass those variables as arguments to the function.

Function Prototype for `maximum`

Member function `maximum`'s prototype (Fig. 6.2, line 16) indicates that the function returns an integer value, has the name `maximum` and requires three integer parameters to perform its task. The function's first line (Fig. 6.3, line 60) matches the function prototype and indicates that the parameter names are `x`, `y` and `z`. When `maximum` is called (Fig. 6.3, line 56), the parameter `x` is initialized with the value of the argument `grade1`, the parameter `y` is initialized with the value of the argument `grade2` and the parameter `z` is initialized with the value of the argument `grade3`. There must be one argument in the function call for each parameter (also called a **formal parameter**) in the function definition.

Notice that multiple parameters are specified in both the function prototype and the function header as a comma-separated list. The compiler refers to the function prototype to check that calls to `maximum` contain the correct number and types of arguments and that the types of the arguments are in the correct order. In addition, the compiler uses the prototype to ensure that the value returned by the function can be used correctly in the expression that called the function (e.g., a function call that returns `void` *cannot* be used as the right side of an assignment statement). Each argument must be *consistent* with the type of the corresponding parameter. For example, a parameter of type `double` can receive values like 7.35, 22 or –0.03456, but not a string like `"hello"`. If the arguments passed to a function do *not* match the types specified in the function's prototype, the compiler attempts to convert the arguments to those types. Section 6.4 discusses this conversion.

Common Programming Error 6.1

Declaring function parameters of the same type as `double x, y` *instead of* `double x, double y` *is a syntax error—a type is required for each parameter in the parameter list.*

Common Programming Error 6.2

Compilation errors occur if the function prototype, header and calls do not all agree in the number, type and order of arguments and parameters, and in the return type. Linker errors and other types of errors can occur as well as you'll see later in the book.

Software Engineering Observation 6.2

A function that has many parameters may be performing too many tasks. Consider dividing the function into smaller functions that perform the separate tasks. Limit the function header to one line if possible.

Logic of Function `maximum`

To determine the maximum value (lines 60–73 of Fig. 6.3), we begin with the assumption that parameter `x` contains the largest value, so line 62 of function `maximum` declares local variable `maximumValue` and initializes it with the value of parameter `x`. Of course, it's possible that parameter `y` or `z` contains the actual largest value, so we must compare each of these values with `maximumValue`. The `if` statement in lines 65–66 determines whether `y` is greater than `maximumValue` and, if so, assigns `y` to `maximumValue`. The `if` statement in lines 69–70 determines whether `z` is greater than `maximumValue` and, if so, assigns `z` to `maximumValue`. At this point the largest of the three values is in `maximumValue`, so line 72 returns that value to the call in line 56. When program control returns to the point in the program where `maximum` was called, `maximum`'s parameters `x`, `y` and `z` are no longer accessible to the program.

Returning Control from a Function to Its Caller

There are several ways to return control to the point at which a function was invoked. If the function does *not* return a result (i.e., it has a `void` return type), control returns when the program reaches the function-ending right brace, or by execution of the statement

```
return;
```

If the function *does* return a result, the statement

```
return expression;
```

evaluates *expression* and returns the value of *expression* to the caller. Some compilers issue errors and others issue warnings if you do *not* provide an appropriate `return` statement in a function that's supposed to return a result.

6.4 Function Prototypes and Argument Coercion

A function prototype (also called a **function declaration**) tells the compiler the name of a function, the type of data it returns, the number of parameters it expects to receive, the types of those parameters and the order in which the parameters of those types are expected.

Software Engineering Observation 6.3

Function prototypes are required unless the function is defined before it is used. Use `#include` preprocessing directives to obtain function prototypes for the C++ Standard Library functions from the headers of the appropriate libraries (e.g., the prototype for `sqrt` is in header `<cmath>`; a partial list of C++ Standard Library headers appears in Section 6.5). Also use `#include` to obtain headers containing function prototypes written by you or other programmers.

Common Programming Error 6.3

If a function is defined before *it's invoked, then its definition also serves as the function's prototype, so a separate prototype is unnecessary. If a function is invoked* before *it's defined, and that function does not have a function prototype, a compilation error occurs.*

Software Engineering Observation 6.4

Always provide function prototypes, even though it's possible to omit them when functions are defined before *they're used. Providing the prototypes avoids tying the code to the order in which functions are defined (which can easily change as a program evolves).*

Function Signatures

The portion of a function prototype that includes the *name of the function* and the *types of its arguments* is called the **function signature** or simply the **signature**. The function signature does not specify the function's return type. *Functions in the same scope must have unique signatures.* The scope of a function is the region of a program in which the function is known and accessible. We'll say more about scope in Section 6.10.

In Fig. 6.2, if the function prototype in line 16 had been written

```
void maximum( int, int, int );
```

the compiler would report an error, because the `void` return type in the function prototype would differ from the `int` return type in the function header. Similarly, such a prototype would cause the statement

```
cout << maximum( 6, 7, 0 );
```

to generate a compilation error, because that statement depends on `maximum` to return a value to be displayed.

Argument Coercion

An important feature of function prototypes is **argument coercion**—i.e., forcing arguments to the appropriate types specified by the parameter declarations. For example, a program can call a function with an integer argument, even though the function prototype specifies a `double` argument—the function will still work correctly.

Argument Promotion Rules and Implicit Conversions[1]

Sometimes, argument values that do not correspond precisely to the parameter types in the function prototype can be converted by the compiler to the proper type before the function is called. These conversions occur as specified by C++'s **promotion rules**. The promotion rules indicate the *implicit conversions* that the compiler can perform between fundamental types. An `int` can be converted to a `double`. A `double` can also be converted to an `int` but the fractional part of the `double` value is *truncated*. Keep in mind that `double` variables can hold numbers of much greater magnitude than `int` variables, so the loss of data may be considerable. Values may also be modified when converting large integer types to small integer types (e.g., `long` to `short`), signed to unsigned or unsigned to signed. Unsigned integers range from 0 to approximately twice the positive range of the corresponding signed type.

The promotion rules apply to expressions containing values of two or more data types; such expressions are also referred to as **mixed-type expressions.** The type of each value in a mixed-type expression is promoted to the "highest" type in the expression (actually a *temporary* version of each value is created and used for the expression—the original values remain unchanged). Promotion also occurs when the type of a function argument does *not* match the parameter type specified in the function definition or prototype. Figure 6.5 lists the arithmetic data types in order from "highest type" to "lowest type."

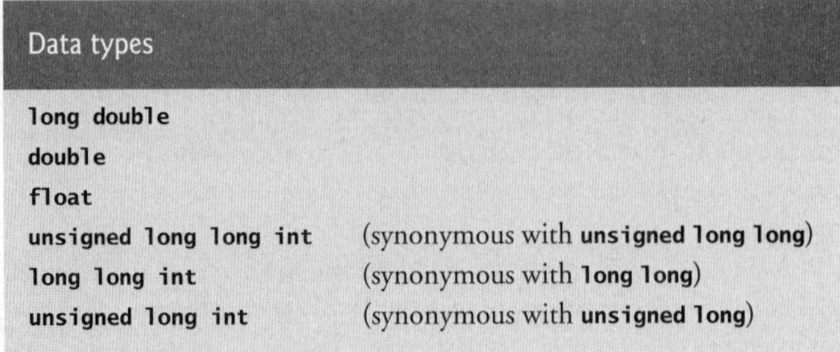

Data types	
`long double`	
`double`	
`float`	
`unsigned long long int`	(synonymous with **`unsigned long long`**)
`long long int`	(synonymous with **`long long`**)
`unsigned long int`	(synonymous with **`unsigned long`**)

Fig. 6.5 | Promotion hierarchy for arithmetic data types. (Part 1 of 2.)

1. Promotions and conversions are complex topics discussed in Section 4 and the beginning of Section 5 of the C++ standard. You can purchase a copy of the standard at `bit.ly/CPlusPlus11Standard`.

Data types	
`long int`	(synonymous with `long`)
`unsigned int`	(synonymous with `unsigned`)
`int`	
`unsigned short int`	(synonymous with `unsigned short`)
`short int`	(synonymous with `short`)
`unsigned char`	
`char` and `signed char`	
`bool`	

Fig. 6.5 | Promotion hierarchy for arithmetic data types. (Part 2 of 2.)

Conversions Can Result in Incorrect Values

Converting values to *lower* fundamental types can result in incorrect values. Therefore, a value can be converted to a lower fundamental type only by *explicitly* assigning the value to a variable of lower type (some compilers will issue a warning in this case) or by using a *cast operator* (see Section 4.7). Function argument values are converted to the parameter types in a function prototype as if they were being assigned directly to variables of those types. If a `square` function that uses an integer parameter is called with a floating-point argument, the argument is converted to `int` (a lower type), and `square` could return an incorrect value. For example, `square(4.5)` returns `16`, not `20.25`.

Common Programming Error 6.4

It's a compilation error if the arguments in a function call do not match the number and types of the parameters declared in the corresponding function prototype. It's also an error if the number of arguments in the call matches, but the arguments cannot be implicitly converted to the expected types.

6.5 C++ Standard Library Headers

The C++ Standard Library is divided into many portions, each with its own header. The headers contain the function prototypes for the related functions that form each portion of the library. The headers also contain definitions of various class types and functions, as well as constants needed by those functions. A header "instructs" the compiler on how to interface with library and user-written components. Figure 6.6 lists some common C++ Standard Library headers, most of which are discussed later in the book. The term "macro" that's used several times in Fig. 6.6 is discussed in detail in Appendix E, Preprocessor.

Header	Explanation
`<iostream>`	Contains function prototypes for the C++ standard input and output functions, introduced in Chapter 2, and is covered in more detail in Chapter 13, Stream Input/Output: A Deeper Look.

Fig. 6.6 | C++ Standard Library headers. (Part 1 of 3.)

Header	Explanation
`<iomanip>`	Contains function prototypes for stream manipulators that format streams of data. This header is first used in Section 4.7 and is discussed in more detail in Chapter 13, Stream Input/Output: A Deeper Look.
`<cmath>`	Contains function prototypes for math library functions (Section 6.2).
`<cstdlib>`	Contains function prototypes for conversions of numbers to text, text to numbers, memory allocation, random numbers and various other utility functions. Portions of the header are covered in Section 6.6; Chapter 10, Operator Overloading; Class `string`; Chapter 17, Exception Handling: A Deeper Look; Chapter 20, Bits, Characters, C Strings and `struct`s; and Appendix F, C Legacy Code Topics.
`<ctime>`	Contains function prototypes and types for manipulating the time and date. This header is used in Section 6.6.
`<array>`, `<vector>`, `<list>`, `<forward_list>`, `<deque>`, `<queue>`, `<stack>`, `<map>`, `<unordered_map>`, `<unordered_set>`, `<set>`, `<bitset>`	These headers contain classes that implement the C++ Standard Library containers. Containers store data during a program's execution. The `<vector>` header is first introduced in Chapter 7, Class Templates `array` and `vector`; Catching Exceptions. We discuss all these headers in Chapter 15, Standard Library Containers and Iterators.
`<cctype>`	Contains function prototypes for functions that test characters for certain properties (such as whether the character is a digit or a punctuation), and function prototypes for functions that can be used to convert lowercase letters to uppercase letters and vice versa. These topics are discussed in Chapter 20, Bits, Characters, C Strings and `struct`s.
`<cstring>`	Contains function prototypes for C-style string-processing functions. This header is used in Chapter 10, Operator Overloading; Class `string`.
`<typeinfo>`	Contains classes for runtime type identification (determining data types at execution time). This header is discussed in Section 12.8.
`<exception>`, `<stdexcept>`	These headers contain classes that are used for exception handling (discussed in Chapter 17, Exception Handling: A Deeper Look).
`<memory>`	Contains classes and functions used by the C++ Standard Library to allocate memory to the C++ Standard Library containers. This header is used in Chapter 17, Exception Handling: A Deeper Look.
`<fstream>`	Contains function prototypes for functions that perform input from and output to files on disk (discussed in Chapter 14, File Processing).
`<string>`	Contains the definition of class `string` from the C++ Standard Library (discussed in Chapter 19, Class `string` and String Stream Processing).
`<sstream>`	Contains function prototypes for functions that perform input from strings in memory and output to strings in memory (discussed in Chapter 19, Class `string` and String Stream Processing).

Fig. 6.6 | C++ Standard Library headers. (Part 2 of 3.)

Header	Explanation
`<functional>`	Contains classes and functions used by C++ Standard Library algorithms. This header is used in Chapter 15.
`<iterator>`	Contains classes for accessing data in the C++ Standard Library containers. This header is used in Chapter 15.
`<algorithm>`	Contains functions for manipulating data in C++ Standard Library containers. This header is used in Chapter 15.
`<cassert>`	Contains macros for adding diagnostics that aid program debugging. This header is used in Appendix E, Preprocessor.
`<cfloat>`	Contains the floating-point size limits of the system.
`<climits>`	Contains the integral size limits of the system.
`<cstdio>`	Contains function prototypes for the C-style standard input/output library functions.
`<locale>`	Contains classes and functions normally used by stream processing to process data in the natural form for different languages (e.g., monetary formats, sorting strings, character presentation, etc.).
`<limits>`	Contains classes for defining the numerical data type limits on each computer platform.
`<utility>`	Contains classes and functions that are used by many C++ Standard Library headers.

Fig. 6.6 | C++ Standard Library headers. (Part 3 of 3.)

6.6 Case Study: Random Number Generation

[*Note:* The random-number generation techniques shown in this section and Section 6.7
are included for readers who are not yet using C++11 compilers. In Section 6.8, we'll pres- 11
ent C++11's improved random-number capabilities.]

We now take a brief and hopefully entertaining diversion into a popular programming application, namely simulation and game playing. In this and the next section, we develop a game-playing program that includes multiple functions.

The element of chance can be introduced into computer applications by using the C++ Standard Library function **rand**. Consider the following statement:

```
i = rand();
```

The function `rand` generates an unsigned integer between 0 and `RAND_MAX` (a symbolic constant defined in the `<cstdlib>` header). You can determine the value of `RAND_MAX` for your system simply by displaying the constant. If `rand` truly produces integers at random, every number between 0 and `RAND_MAX` has an equal *chance* (or probability) of being chosen each time `rand` is called.

The range of values produced directly by the function `rand` often is different than what a specific application requires. For example, a program that simulates coin tossing might require only 0 for "heads" and 1 for "tails." A program that simulates rolling a six-sided die would require random integers in the range 1 to 6. A program that randomly predicts the next type of spaceship (out of four possibilities) that will fly across the horizon in a video game might require random integers in the range 1 through 4.

Rolling a Six-Sided Die

To demonstrate `rand`, Fig. 6.7 simulates 20 rolls of a six-sided die and displays the value of each roll. The function prototype for the `rand` function is in `<cstdlib>`. To produce integers in the range 0 to 5, we use the modulus operator (%) with `rand` as follows:

```
rand() % 6
```

This is called **scaling**. The number 6 is called the **scaling factor**. We then **shift** the range of numbers produced by adding 1 to our previous result. Figure 6.7 confirms that the results are in the range 1 to 6. If you execute this program more than once, you'll see that it produces the same "random" values each time. We'll show how to fix this in Figure 6.9.

```cpp
// Fig. 6.7: fig06_07.cpp
// Shifted, scaled integers produced by 1 + rand() % 6.
#include <iostream>
#include <iomanip>
#include <cstdlib> // contains function prototype for rand
using namespace std;

int main()
{
   // loop 20 times
   for ( unsigned int counter = 1; counter <= 20; ++counter )
   {
      // pick random number from 1 to 6 and output it
      cout << setw( 10 ) << ( 1 + rand() % 6 );

      // if counter is divisible by 5, start a new line of output
      if ( counter % 5 == 0 )
         cout << endl;
   } // end for
} // end main
```

```
         6         6         5         5         6
         5         1         1         5         3
         6         6         2         4         2
         6         2         3         4         1
```

Fig. 6.7 | Shifted, scaled integers produced by `1 + rand() % 6`.

Rolling a Six-Sided Die 6,000,000 Times

To show that the numbers produced by `rand` occur with approximately equal likelihood, Fig. 6.8 simulates 6,000,000 rolls of a die. Each integer in the range 1 to 6 should appear approximately 1,000,000 times. This is confirmed by the program's output.

```
// Fig. 6.8: fig06_08.cpp
// Rolling a six-sided die 6,000,000 times.
#include <iostream>
#include <iomanip>
#include <cstdlib> // contains function prototype for rand
using namespace std;

int main()
{
   unsigned int frequency1 = 0; // count of 1s rolled
   unsigned int frequency2 = 0; // count of 2s rolled
   unsigned int frequency3 = 0; // count of 3s rolled
   unsigned int frequency4 = 0; // count of 4s rolled
   unsigned int frequency5 = 0; // count of 5s rolled
   unsigned int frequency6 = 0; // count of 6s rolled

   // summarize results of 6,000,000 rolls of a die
   for ( unsigned int roll = 1; roll <= 6000000; ++roll )
   {
      unsigned int face = 1 + rand() % 6; // random number from 1 to 6

      // determine roll value 1-6 and increment appropriate counter
      switch ( face )
      {
         case 1:
            ++frequency1; // increment the 1s counter
            break;
         case 2:
            ++frequency2; // increment the 2s counter
            break;
         case 3:
            ++frequency3; // increment the 3s counter
            break;
         case 4:
            ++frequency4; // increment the 4s counter
            break;
         case 5:
            ++frequency5; // increment the 5s counter
            break;
         case 6:
            ++frequency6; // increment the 6s counter
            break;
         default: // invalid value
            cout << "Program should never get here!";
      } // end switch
   } // end for

   cout << "Face" << setw( 13 ) << "Frequency" << endl; // output headers
   cout << "   1" << setw( 13 ) << frequency1
      << "\n   2" << setw( 13 ) << frequency2
      << "\n   3" << setw( 13 ) << frequency3
      << "\n   4" << setw( 13 ) << frequency4
```

Fig. 6.8 | Rolling a six-sided die 6,000,000 times. (Part 1 of 2.)

```
53        << "\n  5" << setw( 13 ) << frequency5
54        << "\n  6" << setw( 13 ) << frequency6 << endl;
55  } // end main
```

```
Face    Frequency
   1       999702
   2      1000823
   3       999378
   4       998898
   5      1000777
   6      1000422
```

Fig. 6.8 | Rolling a six-sided die 6,000,000 times. (Part 2 of 2.)

As the output shows, we can simulate the rolling of a six-sided die by scaling and shifting the values produced by `rand`. The program should *never* get to the `default` case (lines 43–44) in the `switch` structure, because the `switch`'s controlling expression (`face`) *always* has values in the range 1–6; however, we provide the `default` case as a matter of good practice. After we study arrays in Chapter 7, we show how to replace the entire `switch` structure in Fig. 6.8 elegantly with a single-line statement.

Error-Prevention Tip 6.3

Provide a `default` case in a `switch` to catch errors even if you are absolutely, positively certain that you have no bugs!

Randomizing the Random Number Generator

Executing the program of Fig. 6.7 again produces

```
      6        6        5        5        6
      5        1        1        5        3
      6        6        2        4        2
      6        2        3        4        1
```

The program prints exactly the *same* sequence of values shown in Fig. 6.7. How can these be random numbers? *When debugging a simulation program, this repeatability is essential for proving that corrections to the program work properly.*

Function `rand` actually generates **pseudorandom numbers**. Repeatedly calling `rand` produces a sequence of numbers that appears to be random. However, the sequence *repeats* itself each time the program executes. Once a program has been thoroughly debugged, it can be conditioned to produce a *different* sequence of random numbers for each execution. This is called **randomizing** and is accomplished with the C++ Standard Library function **`srand`**. Function `srand` takes an `unsigned` integer argument and **seeds** the `rand` function to produce a different sequence of random numbers for each execution. C++11 provides additional random number capabilities that can produce **nondeterministic random numbers**—a set of random numbers that can't be predicted. Such random number generators are used in simulations and security scenarios where predictability is undesirable. Section 6.8 introduces C++11 random-number generation capabilities.

Good Programming Practice 6.1

Ensure that your program seeds the random number generator differently *(and* only once*) each time the program executes; otherwise, an attacker would easily be able to determine the sequence of pseudorandom numbers that would be produced.*

Seeding the Random Number Generator with `srand`

Figure 6.9 demonstrates function `srand`. The program uses the data type `unsigned int`. An `int` is represented by at least two bytes, is typically four bytes on 32-bit systems and can be as much as eight bytes on 64-bit systems. An `int` can have positive and negative values. A variable of type `unsigned int` is also stored in at least two bytes of memory. A four-byte `unsigned int` can have only *nonnegative* values in the range 0–4294967295. Function `srand` takes an `unsigned int` value as an argument. The function prototype for the `srand` function is in header `<cstdlib>`.

```
// Fig. 6.9: fig06_09.cpp
// Randomizing the die-rolling program.
#include <iostream>
#include <iomanip>
#include <cstdlib> // contains prototypes for functions srand and rand
using namespace std;

int main()
{
   unsigned int seed = 0; // stores the seed entered by the user

   cout << "Enter seed: ";
   cin >> seed;
   srand( seed ); // seed random number generator

   // loop 10 times
   for ( unsigned int counter = 1; counter <= 10; ++counter )
   {
      // pick random number from 1 to 6 and output it
      cout << setw( 10 ) << ( 1 + rand() % 6 );

      // if counter is divisible by 5, start a new line of output
      if ( counter % 5 == 0 )
         cout << endl;
   } // end for
} // end main
```

```
Enter seed: 67
         6         1         4         6         2
         1         6         1         6         4
```

```
Enter seed: 432
         4         6         3         1         6
         3         1         5         4         2
```

Fig. 6.9 | Randomizing the die-rolling program. (Part 1 of 2.)

```
Enter seed: 67
        6         1         4         6         2
        1         6         1         6         4
```

Fig. 6.9 | Randomizing the die-rolling program. (Part 2 of 2.)

The program produces a *different* sequence of random numbers each time it executes, provided that the user enters a *different* seed. We used the *same* seed in the first and third sample outputs, so the *same* series of 10 numbers is displayed in each of those outputs.

Seeding the Random Number Generator with the Current Time

To randomize *without* having to enter a seed each time, we may use a statement like

```
srand( static_cast<unsigned int>( time( 0 ) ) );
```

This causes the computer to read its *clock* to obtain the value for the seed. Function **time** (with the argument 0 as written in the preceding statement) typically returns the current time as the number of seconds since January 1, 1970, at midnight Greenwich Mean Time (GMT). This value (which is of type time_t) is converted to an unsigned int and used as the seed to the random number generator—the static_cast in the preceding statement eliminates a compiler warning that's issued if you pass a time_t value to a function that expects an unsigned int. The function prototype for time is in <ctime>.

Scaling and Shifting Random Numbers

Previously, we simulated the rolling of a six-sided die with the statement

```
face = 1 + rand() % 6;
```

which always assigns an integer (at random) to variable face in the range 1 ≤face ≤6. The width of this range (i.e., the number of consecutive integers in the range) is 6 and the starting number in the range is 1. Referring to the preceding statement, we see that the width of the range is determined by the number used to scale rand with the modulus operator (i.e., 6), and the starting number of the range is equal to the number (i.e., 1) that is added to the expression rand % 6. We can generalize this result as

```
number = shiftingValue + rand() % scalingFactor;
```

where ***shiftingValue*** is equal to the *first number* in the desired range of consecutive integers and ***scalingFactor*** is equal to the *width* of the desired range of consecutive integers.

6.7 Case Study: Game of Chance; Introducing enum

One of the most popular games of chance is a dice game known as "craps," which is played in casinos and back alleys worldwide. The rules of the game are straightforward:

> *A player rolls two dice. Each die has six faces. These faces contain 1, 2, 3, 4, 5 and 6 spots. After the dice have come to rest, the sum of the spots on the two upward faces is calculated. If the sum is 7 or 11 on the first roll, the player wins. If the sum is 2, 3 or 12 on the first roll (called "craps"), the player loses (i.e., the "house" wins). If the sum is 4, 5, 6, 8, 9 or 10 on the first roll, then that sum becomes the player's "point." To win, you must continue rolling the dice until you "make your point." The player loses by rolling a 7 before making the point.*

The program in Fig. 6.10 simulates the game. In the rules, notice that the player must roll two dice on the first roll and on all subsequent rolls. We define function `rollDice` (lines 62–74) to roll the dice and compute and print their sum. The function is defined once, but called from lines 20 and 44. The function takes no arguments and returns the sum of the two dice, so empty parentheses and the return type `unsigned int` are indicated in the function prototype (line 8) and function header (line 62).

```
1  // Fig. 6.10: fig06_10.cpp
2  // Craps simulation.
3  #include <iostream>
4  #include <cstdlib> // contains prototypes for functions srand and rand
5  #include <ctime> // contains prototype for function time
6  using namespace std;
7
8  unsigned int rollDice(); // rolls dice, calculates and displays sum
9
10 int main()
11 {
12    // enumeration with constants that represent the game status
13    enum Status { CONTINUE, WON, LOST }; // all caps in constants
14
15    // randomize random number generator using current time
16    srand( static_cast<unsigned int>( time( 0 ) ) );
17
18    unsigned int myPoint = 0; // point if no win or loss on first roll
19    Status gameStatus = CONTINUE; // can contain CONTINUE, WON or LOST
20    unsigned int sumOfDice = rollDice(); // first roll of the dice
21
22    // determine game status and point (if needed) based on first roll
23    switch ( sumOfDice )
24    {
25       case 7: // win with 7 on first roll
26       case 11: // win with 11 on first roll
27          gameStatus = WON;
28          break;
29       case 2: // lose with 2 on first roll
30       case 3: // lose with 3 on first roll
31       case 12: // lose with 12 on first roll
32          gameStatus = LOST;
33          break;
34       default: // did not win or lose, so remember point
35          gameStatus = CONTINUE; // game is not over
36          myPoint = sumOfDice; // remember the point
37          cout << "Point is " << myPoint << endl;
38          break; // optional at end of switch
39    } // end switch
40
41    // while game is not complete
42    while ( CONTINUE == gameStatus ) // not WON or LOST
43    {
44       sumOfDice = rollDice(); // roll dice again
```

Fig. 6.10 | Craps simulation. (Part 1 of 3.)

```cpp

      // determine game status
      if ( sumOfDice == myPoint ) // win by making point
         gameStatus = WON;
      else
         if ( sumOfDice == 7 ) // lose by rolling 7 before point
            gameStatus = LOST;
   } // end while

   // display won or lost message
   if ( WON == gameStatus )
      cout << "Player wins" << endl;
   else
      cout << "Player loses" << endl;
} // end main

// roll dice, calculate sum and display results
unsigned int rollDice()
{
   // pick random die values
   unsigned int die1 = 1 + rand() % 6; // first die roll
   unsigned int die2 = 1 + rand() % 6; // second die roll

   unsigned int sum = die1 + die2; // compute sum of die values

   // display results of this roll
   cout << "Player rolled " << die1 << " + " << die2
      << " = " << sum << endl;
   return sum; // end function rollDice
} // end function rollDice
```

```
Player rolled 2 + 5 = 7
Player wins
```

```
Player rolled 6 + 6 = 12
Player loses
```

```
Player rolled 1 + 3 = 4
Point is 4
Player rolled 4 + 6 = 10
Player rolled 2 + 4 = 6
Player rolled 6 + 4 = 10
Player rolled 2 + 3 = 5
Player rolled 2 + 4 = 6
Player rolled 1 + 1 = 2
Player rolled 4 + 4 = 8
Player rolled 4 + 3 = 7
Player loses
```

Fig. 6.10 | Craps simulation. (Part 2 of 3.)

```
Player rolled 3 + 3 = 6
Point is 6
Player rolled 5 + 3 = 8
Player rolled 4 + 5 = 9
Player rolled 2 + 1 = 3
Player rolled 1 + 5 = 6
Player wins
```

Fig. 6.10 | Craps simulation. (Part 3 of 3.)

enum Type Status

The player may win or lose on the first roll or on any subsequent roll. The program uses variable `gameStatus` to keep track of this. Variable `gameStatus` is declared to be of new type `Status`. Line 13 declares a user-defined type called an **enumeration** that's introduced by the keyword **enum** and followed by a **type name** (in this case, `Status`) and a set of integer constants represented by identifiers. The values of these **enumeration constants** start at `0`, unless specified otherwise, and increment by `1`. In the preceding enumeration, the constant `CONTINUE` has the value 0, `WON` has the value 1 and `LOST` has the value 2. The identifiers in an `enum` must be *unique*, but separate enumeration constants *can* have the same integer value.

Good Programming Practice 6.2

Capitalize the first letter of an identifier used as a user-defined type name.

Good Programming Practice 6.3

Use only uppercase letters in enumeration constant names. This makes these constants stand out in a program and reminds you that enumeration constants are not *variables.*

Variables of user-defined type `Status` can be assigned only one of the three values declared in the enumeration. When the game is won, the program sets variable `gameStatus` to `WON` (lines 27 and 48). When the game is lost, the program sets variable `gameStatus` to `LOST` (lines 32 and 51). Otherwise, the program sets variable `gameStatus` to `CONTINUE` (line 35) to indicate that the dice must be rolled again.

Common Programming Error 6.5

Assigning the integer equivalent of an enumeration constant (rather than the enumeration constant, itself) to a variable of the enumeration type is a compilation error.

Another popular enumeration is

```
enum Months { JAN = 1, FEB, MAR, APR, MAY, JUN, JUL, AUG,
   SEP, OCT, NOV, DEC };
```

which creates user-defined type `Months` with enumeration constants representing the months of the year. The first value in the preceding enumeration is explicitly set to `1`, so the remaining values increment from `1`, resulting in the values `1` through `12`. Any enumeration constant can be assigned an integer value in the enumeration definition, and subsequent enumeration constants each have a value 1 higher than the preceding constant in the list until the next explicit setting.

Error-Prevention Tip 6.4

Use unique values for an `enum`*'s constants to help prevent hard-to-find logic errors.*

Winning or Losing on the First Roll

After the first roll, if the game is won or lost, the program skips the body of the `while` statement (lines 42–52) because `gameStatus` is not equal to `CONTINUE`. The program proceeds to the `if...else` statement in lines 55–58, which prints `"Player wins"` if `gameStatus` is equal to `WON` and `"Player loses"` if `gameStatus` is equal to `LOST`.

Continuing to Roll

After the first roll, if the game is not over, the program saves the sum in `myPoint` (line 36). Execution proceeds with the `while` statement, because `gameStatus` is equal to `CONTINUE`. During each iteration of the `while`, the program calls `rollDice` to produce a new `sum`. If `sum` matches `myPoint`, the program sets `gameStatus` to `WON` (line 48), the `while`-test fails, the `if...else` statement prints `"Player wins"` and execution terminates. If `sum` is equal to 7, the program sets `gameStatus` to `LOST` (line 51), the `while`-test fails, the `if...else` statement prints `"Player loses"` and execution terminates.

The craps program uses two functions—`main` and `rollDice`—and the `switch`, `while`, `if...else`, nested `if...else` and nested `if` statements.

C++11—Scoped `enum`*s*

In Fig. 6.10, we introduced `enum`s. One problem with `enum`s (also called *unscoped* `enum`*s*) is that multiple `enum`s may contain the *same* identifiers. Using such `enum`s in the same program can lead to naming collisions and logic errors. To eliminate these problems, C++11 introduces so-called **scoped** `enum`**s**, which are declared with the keywords **`enum class`** (or the synonym **`enum struct`**). For example, we can define the `Status` `enum` of Fig. 6.10 as:

```
enum class Status { CONTINUE, WON, LOST };
```

To reference a scoped `enum` constant, you *must* qualify the constant with the scoped `enum`'s type name (`Status`) and the scope-resolution operator (`::`), as in `Status::CONTINUE`. This *explicitly identifies* `CONTINUE` as a constant in the *scope* of `enum class Status`. Thus, if another scoped `enum` contains the same identifier for one of its constants, it's always clear which version of the constant is being used.

Error-Prevention Tip 6.5

Use scoped `enum`*s to avoid potential naming conflicts and logic errors from unscoped* `enum`*s that contain the same identifiers.*

C++11—Specifying the Type of an `enum`*'s Constants*

The constants in an `enum` are represented as integers. By default, an unscoped `enum`'s underlying integral type depends on its constants' values—the type is guaranteed to be large enough to store the constant values specified. By default, a scoped `enum`'s underlying integral type is `int`. C++11 allows you to specify an `enum`'s underlying integral type by following the `enum`'s type name with a colon (`:`) and the integral type. For example, we can specify that the constants in the `enum class Status` should have type `unsigned int`, as in

```
enum class Status : unsigned int { CONTINUE, WON, LOST };
```

Common Programming Error 6.6

A compilation error occurs if an enum *constant's value is outside the range that can be represented by the* enum*'s underlying type.*

6.8 C++11 Random Numbers

According to CERT, function rand does not have "good statistical properties" and can be predictable, which makes programs that use rand less secure (CERT guideline MSC30-CPP). As we mentioned in Section 6.6, C++11 provides a new, *more secure* library of random-number capabilities that can produce nondeterministic random numbers for simulations and security scenarios where predictability is undesirable. These new capabilities are located in the C++ Standard Library's <random> header.

Random-number generation is a mathematically sophisticated topic for which mathematicians have developed many random-number generation algorithms with different statistical properties. For flexibility based on how random numbers are used in programs, C++11 provides many classes that represent various random-number generation *engines* and *distributions*. An engine implements a random-number generation algorithm that produce pseudorandom numbers. A distribution controls the range of values produced by an engine, the types of those values (e.g., int, double, etc.) and the statistical properties of the values. In this section, we'll use the default random-number generation engine—**default_random_engine**—and a **uniform_int_distribution**, which *evenly* distributes pseudorandom integers over a specified range of values. The default range is from 0 to the maximum value of an int on your platform.

Rolling a Six-Sided Die

Figure 6.11 uses the default_random_engine and the uniform_int_distribution to roll a six-sided die. Line 14 creates a default_random_engine object named engine. Its constructor argument *seeds* the random-number generation engine with the current time. If you don't pass a value to the constructor, the default seed will be used and the program will produce the *same* sequence of numbers each time it executes. Line 15 creates randomInt—a uniform_int_distribution object that produces unsigned int values (as specified by <unsigned int>) in the range 1 to 6 (as specified by the constructor arguments). The expression randomInt(engine) (line 21) returns one unsigned int value in the range 1 to 6.

```
1  // Fig. 6.11: fig06_11.cpp
2  // Using a C++11 random-number generation engine and distribution
3  // to roll a six-sided die.
4  #include <iostream>
5  #include <iomanip>
6  #include <random> // contains C++11 random number generation features
7  #include <ctime>
8  using namespace std;
9
```

Fig. 6.11 | Using a C++11 random-number generation engine and distribution to roll a six-sided die. (Part 1 of 2.)

```
10  int main()
11  {
12     // use the default random-number generation engine to
13     // produce uniformly distributed pseudorandom int values from 1 to 6
14     default_random_engine engine( static_cast<unsigned int>( time(0) ) );
15     uniform_int_distribution<unsigned int> randomInt( 1, 6 );
16
17     // loop 10 times
18     for ( unsigned int counter = 1; counter <= 10; ++counter )
19     {
20        // pick random number from 1 to 6 and output it
21        cout << setw( 10 ) << randomInt( engine );
22
23        // if counter is divisible by 5, start a new line of output
24        if ( counter % 5 == 0 )
25           cout << endl;
26     } // end for
27  } // end main
```

```
         2         1         2         3         5
         6         1         5         6         4
```

Fig. 6.11 | Using a C++11 random-number generation engine and distribution to roll a six-sided die. (Part 2 of 2.)

The notation `<unsigned int>` in line 15 indicates that `uniform_int_distribution` is a *class template*. In this case, any integer type can be specified in the angle brackets (< and >). In Chapter 18, we discuss how to create class templates and various other chapters show how to use existing class templates from the C++ Standard Library. For now, you should feel comfortable using class template `uniform_int_distribution` by mimicking the syntax shown in the example.

6.9 Storage Classes and Storage Duration

The programs you've seen so far use identifiers for variable names and functions. The attributes of variables include *name, type, size* and *value*. Each identifier in a program also has other attributes, including **storage duration**, scope and **linkage**.

C++ provides five **storage-class specifiers** that determine a variable's storage duration: **`register`**, **`extern`**, **`mutable`** and **`static`**. This section discusses storage-class specifiers `register`, `extern` and `static`. Storage-class specifier `mutable` is used exclusively with classes and `thread_local` is used in multithreaded applications—these are discussed in Chapters 21 and 24, respectively.

Storage Duration

An identifier's *storage duration* determines the period during which that identifier *exists in memory.* Some exist briefly, some are repeatedly created and destroyed and others exist for a program's entire execution. First we discuss the storage durations **static** and **automatic.**

Scope
An identifier's *scope* is where *the identifier can be referenced* in a program. Some identifiers can be referenced throughout a program; others can be referenced from only limited portions of a program. Section 6.10 discusses the scope of identifiers.

Linkage
An identifier's *linkage* determines whether it's known only in the *source file where it's declared* or *across multiple files that are compiled, then linked together*. An identifier's *storage-class specifier* helps determine its storage duration and linkage.

Storage Duration
The storage-class specifiers can be split into four storage durations: *automatic*, *static*, *dynamic* and *thread*. Automatic and static storage duration are discussed below. In Chapter 10, you'll see how to request additional memory in your program dynamically at execution time. Variables allocated dynamically have *dynamic storage duration*.

Local Variables and Automatic Storage Duration
Variables with *automatic storage duration* include:

- local variables declared in functions
- function parameters
- local variables or function parameters declared with `register`

Such variables are created when program execution enters the block in which they're defined, they exist while the block is active and they're destroyed when the program exits the block. An automatic variable exists only in the *nearest enclosing pair of curly braces* within the body of the function in which the definition appears, or for the entire function body in the case of a function parameter. Local variables are of automatic storage duration by *default*. For the remainder of the text, we refer to variables of automatic storage duration simply as *automatic variables*.

Performance Tip 6.1

Automatic storage is a means of conserving memory, because automatic storage duration variables exist in memory only when the block in which they're defined is executing.

Software Engineering Observation 6.5

Automatic storage is an example of the ***principle of least privilege****. In the context of an application, the principle states that code should be granted* only *the amount of privilege and access that it needs to accomplish its designated task,* but no more. *Why should we have variables stored in memory and accessible when they're* not *needed?*

Good Programming Practice 6.4

Declare variables as close to where they're first used as possible.

Register Variables
Data in the machine-language version of a program is normally loaded into registers for calculations and other processing.

The compiler might ignore `register` declarations. For example, there might not be a sufficient number of registers available. The following definition *suggests* that the `unsigned int` variable `counter` be placed in one of the computer's registers; regardless of whether the compiler does this, `counter` is initialized to 1:

```
register unsigned int counter = 1;
```

The `register` keyword can be used *only* with local variables and function parameters.

Performance Tip 6.2

The storage-class specifier `register` *can be placed before an automatic variable declaration to suggest that the compiler maintain the variable in one of the computer's high-speed hardware registers rather than in memory. If intensely used variables such as counters or totals are kept in hardware registers, the overhead of repeatedly loading the variables from memory into the registers and storing the results back into memory is eliminated.*

Performance Tip 6.3

Often, `register` *is unnecessary. Today's optimizing compilers can recognize frequently used variables and may place them in registers without needing a* `register` *declaration.*

Static Storage Duration

Keywords `extern` and `static` declare identifiers for variables with *static storage duration* and for functions. Variables with static storage duration exist in memory from the point at which the program begins execution and until the program terminates. Such a variable is *initialized once when its declaration is encountered.* For functions, the name of the function exists when the program begins execution. Even though function names and static-storage-duration variables exist from the start of program execution, their identifiers cannot necessarily be used throughout the program. Storage duration and scope (where a name can be used) are separate issues, as we'll see in Section 6.10.

Identifiers with Static Storage Duration

There are two types of identifiers with *static storage duration*—external identifiers (such as global variables) and local variables declared with the storage-class specifier `static`. **Global variables** are created by placing variable declarations *outside* any class or function definition. Global variables retain their values throughout a program's execution. Global variables and global functions can be referenced by any function that follows their declarations or definitions in the source file.

Software Engineering Observation 6.6

Declaring a variable as global rather than local allows unintended side effects *to occur when a function that does not need access to the variable accidentally or maliciously modifies it. This is another example of the principle of least privilege—in general, except for truly global resources such as* `cin` *and* `cout`*, the use of global variables should be avoided unless there are unique performance requirements.*

Software Engineering Observation 6.7

Variables used only in a particular function should be declared as local variables in that function rather than as global variables.

`static` *Local Variables*

Local variables declared `static` are still known only in the function in which they're declared, but, unlike automatic variables, *`static` local variables retain their values when the function returns to its caller*. The next time the function is called, the `static` local variables contain the values they had when the function last completed execution. The following statement declares local variable `count` to be `static` and to be initialized to 1:

```
static unsigned int count = 1;
```

All numeric variables of static storage duration are *initialized to zero by default*, but it's nevertheless a good practice to explicitly initialize all variables.

Storage-class specifiers `extern` and `static` have special meaning when they're applied explicitly to external identifiers such as global variables and global function names. In Appendix F, C Legacy Code Topics, we discuss using `extern` and `static` with external identifiers and multiple-source-file programs.

6.10 Scope Rules

The portion of the program where an identifier can be used is known as its *scope*. For example, when we declare a local variable in a block, it can be referenced only in that block and in blocks nested within that block. This section discusses **block scope**, **function scope**, **global namespace scope** and **function-prototype scope**. Later we'll see two other scopes—**class scope** (Chapter 9) and **namespace scope** (Chapter 21).

Block Scope

Identifiers declared *inside* a block have *block scope*, which begins at the identifier's declaration and ends at the terminating right brace (`}`) of the block in which the identifier is declared. Local variables have block scope, as do function parameters. Any block can contain variable declarations. When blocks are nested and an identifier in an outer block has the same name as an identifier in an inner block, the identifier in the outer block is "hidden" until the inner block terminates. The inner block "sees" its own local identifier's value and not that of the enclosing block's identically named identifier. Local variables declared `static` still have block scope, even though they exist from the time the program begins execution. Storage duration does *not* affect an identifier's scope.

Common Programming Error 6.7

Accidentally using the same name for an identifier in an inner block that's used for an identifier in an outer block, when in fact you want the identifier in the outer block to be active for the duration of the inner block, is typically a logic error.

Error-Prevention Tip 6.6

Avoid variable names that hide names in outer scopes.

Function Scope

Labels (identifiers followed by a colon such as `start:` or a `case` label in a `switch` statement) are the only identifiers with *function scope*. Labels can be used *anywhere* in the function in which they appear, but cannot be referenced *outside* the function body.

Global Namespace Scope

An identifier declared *outside* any function or class has *global namespace scope.* Such an identifier is "known" in all functions from the point at which it's declared until the end of the file. Global variables, function definitions and function prototypes placed outside a function all have global namespace scope.

Function-Prototype Scope

The only identifiers with *function-prototype scope* are those used in the parameter list of a function prototype. As mentioned previously, function prototypes do *not* require names in the parameter list—only types are required. Names appearing in the parameter list of a function prototype are *ignored* by the compiler. Identifiers used in a function prototype can be reused elsewhere in the program without ambiguity.

Scope Demonstration

The program of Fig. 6.12 demonstrates scoping issues with global variables, automatic local variables and `static` local variables. Line 10 declares and initializes global variable `x` to 1. This global variable is hidden in any block (or function) that declares a variable named `x`. In `main`, line 14 displays the value of global variable `x`. Line 16 declares a local variable `x` and initializes it to 5. Line 18 outputs this variable to show that the global `x` is hidden in `main`. Next, lines 20–24 define a new block in `main` in which another local variable `x` is initialized to 7 (line 21). Line 23 outputs this variable to show that it *hides* `x` in the outer block of `main` as well as the global `x`. When the block exits, the variable `x` with value 7 is destroyed automatically. Next, line 26 outputs the local variable `x` in the outer block of `main` to show that it's *no longer hidden.*

```
1  // Fig. 6.12: fig06_12.cpp
2  // Scoping example.
3  #include <iostream>
4  using namespace std;
5
6  void useLocal(); // function prototype
7  void useStaticLocal(); // function prototype
8  void useGlobal(); // function prototype
9
10 int x = 1; // global variable
11
12 int main()
13 {
14    cout << "global x in main is " << x << endl;
15
16    int x = 5; // local variable to main
17
18    cout << "local x in main's outer scope is " << x << endl;
19
20    { // start new scope
21       int x = 7; // hides both x in outer scope and global x
22
23       cout << "local x in main's inner scope is " << x << endl;
24    } // end new scope
```

Fig. 6.12 | Scoping example. (Part 1 of 3.)

```

   cout << "local x in main's outer scope is " << x << endl;

   useLocal(); // useLocal has local x
   useStaticLocal(); // useStaticLocal has static local x
   useGlobal(); // useGlobal uses global x
   useLocal(); // useLocal reinitializes its local x
   useStaticLocal(); // static local x retains its prior value
   useGlobal(); // global x also retains its prior value

   cout << "\nlocal x in main is " << x << endl;
} // end main

// useLocal reinitializes local variable x during each call
void useLocal()
{
   int x = 25; // initialized each time useLocal is called

   cout << "\nlocal x is " << x << " on entering useLocal" << endl;
   ++x;
   cout << "local x is " << x << " on exiting useLocal" << endl;
} // end function useLocal

// useStaticLocal initializes static local variable x only the
// first time the function is called; value of x is saved
// between calls to this function
void useStaticLocal()
{
   static int x = 50; // initialized first time useStaticLocal is called

   cout << "\nlocal static x is " << x << " on entering useStaticLocal"
      << endl;
   ++x;
   cout << "local static x is " << x << " on exiting useStaticLocal"
      << endl;
} // end function useStaticLocal

// useGlobal modifies global variable x during each call
void useGlobal()
{
   cout << "\nglobal x is " << x << " on entering useGlobal" << endl;
   x *= 10;
   cout << "global x is " << x << " on exiting useGlobal" << endl;
} // end function useGlobal
```

```
global x in main is 1
local x in main's outer scope is 5
local x in main's inner scope is 7
local x in main's outer scope is 5

local x is 25 on entering useLocal
local x is 26 on exiting useLocal
```

Fig. 6.12 | Scoping example. (Part 2 of 3.)

```
local static x is 50 on entering useStaticLocal
local static x is 51 on exiting useStaticLocal

global x is 1 on entering useGlobal
global x is 10 on exiting useGlobal

local x is 25 on entering useLocal
local x is 26 on exiting useLocal

local static x is 51 on entering useStaticLocal
local static x is 52 on exiting useStaticLocal

global x is 10 on entering useGlobal
global x is 100 on exiting useGlobal

local x in main is 5
```

Fig. 6.12 | Scoping example. (Part 3 of 3.)

To demonstrate other scopes, the program defines three functions, each of which takes no arguments and returns nothing. Function `useLocal` (lines 39–46) declares automatic variable `x` (line 41) and initializes it to 25. When the program calls `useLocal`, the function prints the variable, increments it and prints it again before the function returns program control to its caller. Each time the program calls this function, the function *recreates* automatic variable `x` and *reinitializes* it to 25.

Function `useStaticLocal` (lines 51–60) declares `static` variable `x` and initializes it to 50. Local variables declared as `static` retain their values even when they're out of scope (i.e., the function in which they're declared is not executing). When the program calls `useStaticLocal`, the function prints `x`, increments it and prints it again before the function returns program control to its caller. In the next call to this function, `static` local variable `x` contains the value 51. The *initialization* in line 53 *occurs only once*—the first time `useStaticLocal` is called.

Function `useGlobal` (lines 63–68) does not declare any variables. Therefore, when it refers to variable `x`, the global `x` (line 10, preceding `main`) is used. When the program calls `useGlobal`, the function prints the global variable `x`, multiplies it by 10 and prints it again before the function returns program control to its caller. The next time the program calls `useGlobal`, the global variable has its modified value, 10. After executing functions `useLocal`, `useStaticLocal` and `useGlobal` twice each, the program prints the local variable `x` in `main` again to show that none of the function calls modified the value of `x` in `main`, because the functions all referred to variables in other scopes.

6.11 Function Call Stack and Activation Records

To understand how C++ performs function calls, we first need to consider a data structure (i.e., collection of related data items) known as a **stack**. Stacks are known as **last-in, first-out (LIFO) data structures**—the last item pushed (inserted) on the stack is the first item popped (removed) from the stack.

Function-Call Stack

One of the most important mechanisms for programmers to understand is the **function call stack** (sometimes referred to as the **program execution stack**). This data structure—working "behind the scenes"—supports the function call/return mechanism. It also supports the creation, maintenance and destruction of each called function's automatic variables. As we'll see in Figs. 6.14–6.16, last-in, first-out (LIFO) behavior is *exactly* what a function needs in order to return to the function that called it.

Stack Frames

As each function is called, it may, in turn, call other functions, which may, in turn, call other functions—all *before* any of the functions return. Each function eventually must return control to the function that called it. So, somehow, we must keep track of the *return addresses* that each function needs to return control to the function that called it. The function call stack is the perfect data structure for handling this information. Each time a function calls another function, an entry is *pushed* onto the stack. This entry, called a **stack frame** or an **activation record**, contains the *return address* that the called function needs in order to return to the calling function. It also contains some additional information we'll soon discuss. If the called function returns, instead of calling another function before returning, the stack frame for the function call is *popped*, and control transfers to the return address in the popped stack frame.

The beauty of the call stack is that each called function always finds the information it needs to return to its caller at the *top* of the call stack. And, if a function makes a call to another function, a stack frame for the new function call is simply *pushed* onto the call stack. Thus, the return address required by the newly called function to return to its caller is now located at the *top* of the stack.

Automatic Variables and Stack Frames

The stack frames have another important responsibility. Most functions have automatic variables—parameters and any local variables the function declares. Automatic variables need to exist while a function is executing. They need to remain active if the function makes calls to other functions. But when a called function returns to its caller, the called function's automatic variables need to "go away." The called function's stack frame is a perfect place to reserve the memory for the called function's automatic variables. That stack frame exists as long as the called function is active. When that function returns—and no longer needs its local automatic variables—its stack frame is *popped* from the stack, and those local automatic variables are no longer known to the program.

Stack Overflow

Of course, the amount of memory in a computer is finite, so only a certain amount of memory can be used to store activation records on the function call stack. If more function calls occur than can have their activation records stored on the function call stack, a fatal error known as **stack overflow** occurs.

Function Call Stack in Action

Now let's consider how the call stack supports the operation of a `square` function called by `main` (lines 9–14 of Fig. 6.13). First the operating system calls `main`—this pushes an activation record onto the stack (shown in Fig. 6.14). The activation record tells `main` how to return to the operating system (i.e., transfer to return address R1) and contains the space for main's automatic variable (i.e., a, which is initialized to 10).

```
// Fig. 6.13: fig06_13.cpp
// square function used to demonstrate the function
// call stack and activation records.
#include <iostream>
using namespace std;

int square( int ); // prototype for function square

int main()
{
   int a = 10; // value to square (local automatic variable in main)

   cout << a << " squared: " << square( a ) << endl; // display a squared
} // end main

// returns the square of an integer
int square( int x ) // x is a local variable
{
   return x * x; // calculate square and return result
} // end function square
```

```
10 squared: 100
```

Fig. 6.13 | square function used to demonstrate the function call stack and activation records.

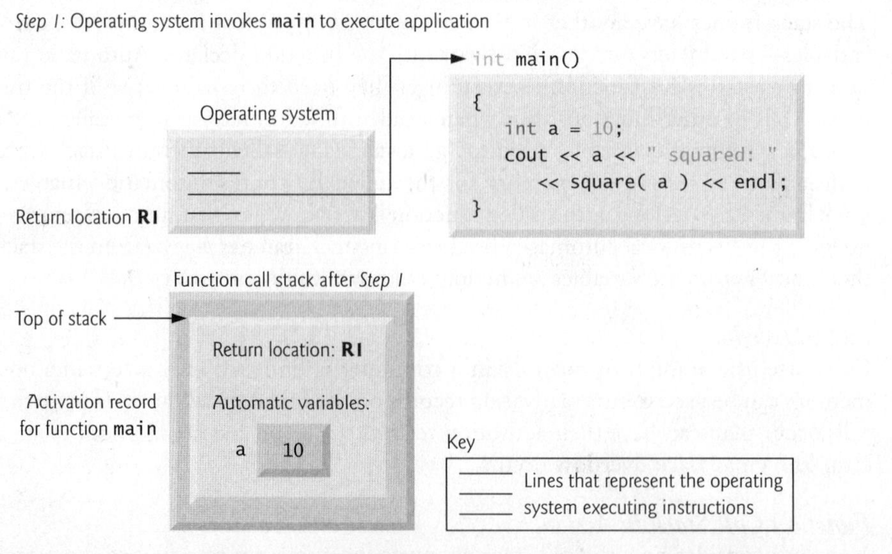

Fig. 6.14 | Function call stack after the operating system invokes main to execute the program.

Function main—before returning to the operating system—now calls function square in line 13 of Fig. 6.13. This causes a stack frame for square (lines 17–20) to be pushed onto the function call stack (Fig. 6.15). This stack frame contains the return address that square needs to return to main (i.e., R2) and the memory for square's automatic variable (i.e., x).

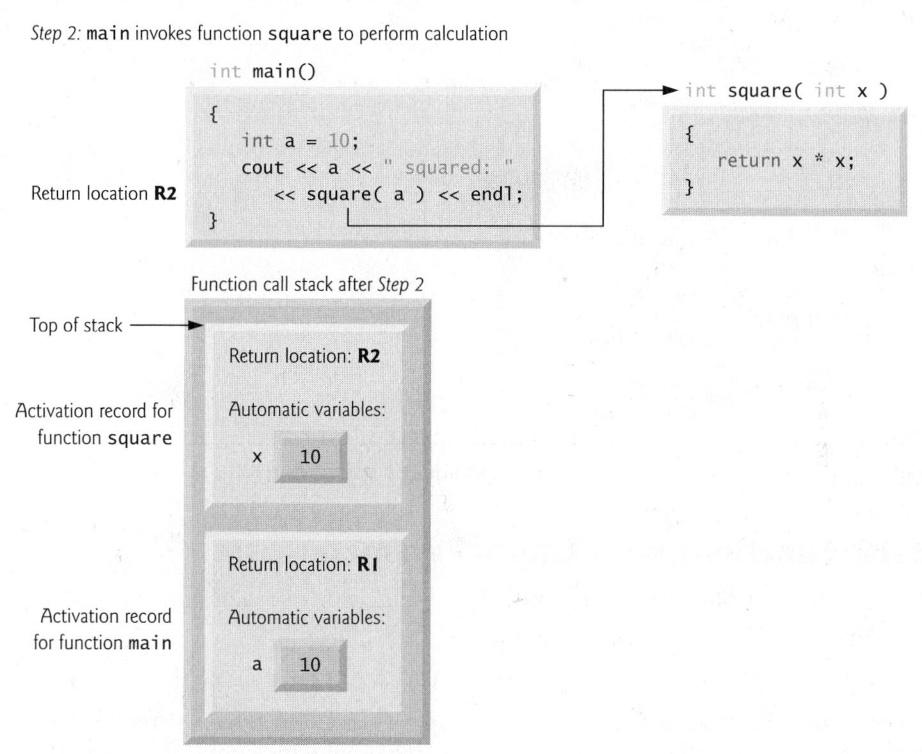

Fig. 6.15 | Function call stack after main invokes square to perform the calculation.

After square calculates the square of its argument, it needs to return to main—and no longer needs the memory for its automatic variable x. So square's stack frame is *popped* from the stack—giving square the return location in main (i.e., R2) and losing square's automatic variable. Figure 6.16 shows the function call stack *after* square's activation record has been popped.

Function main now displays the result of calling square (Fig. 6.13, line 13). Reaching the closing right brace of main causes its stack frame to be *popped* from the stack, gives main the address it needs to return to the operating system (i.e., R1 in Fig. 6.14)—at this point, main's automatic variable (i.e., a) no longer exists.

You've now seen how valuable the stack data structure is in implementing a key mechanism that supports program execution. Data structures have many important applications in computer science.

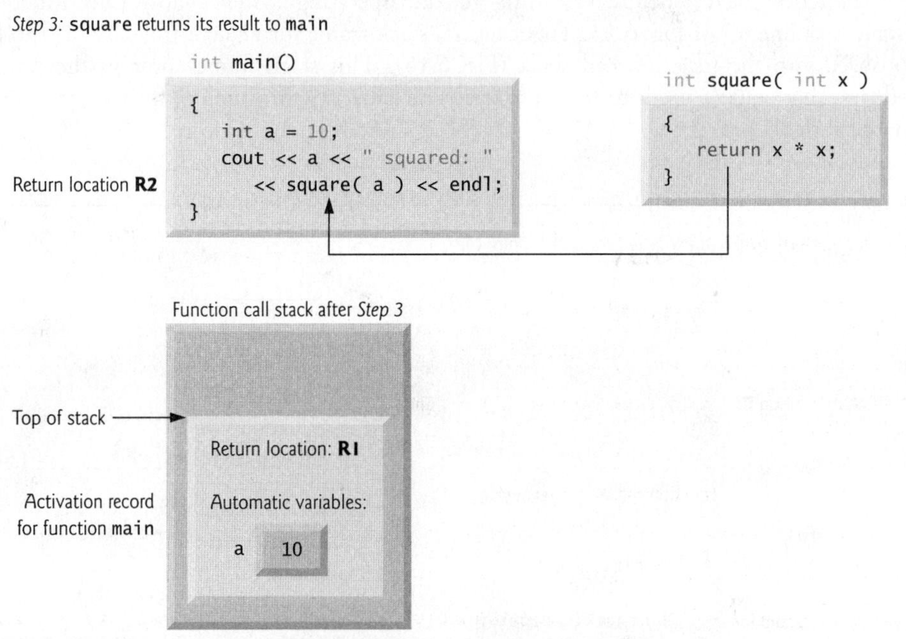

Fig. 6.16 | Function call stack after function `square` returns to `main`.

6.12 Functions with Empty Parameter Lists

In C++, an *empty parameter list* is specified by writing either `void` or nothing at all in parentheses. The prototype

```
void print();
```

specifies that function `print` does *not* take arguments and does *not* return a value. Figure 6.17 shows both ways to declare and use functions with empty parameter lists.

```
// Fig. 6.17: fig06_17.cpp
// Functions that take no arguments.
#include <iostream>
using namespace std;

void function1(); // function that takes no arguments
void function2( void ); // function that takes no arguments

int main()
{
   function1(); // call function1 with no arguments
   function2(); // call function2 with no arguments
} // end main

```

Fig. 6.17 | Functions that take no arguments. (Part 1 of 2.)

```
// function1 uses an empty parameter list to specify that
// the function receives no arguments
void function1()
{
   cout << "function1 takes no arguments" << endl;
} // end function1

// function2 uses a void parameter list to specify that
// the function receives no arguments
void function2( void )
{
   cout << "function2 also takes no arguments" << endl;
} // end function2
```

```
function1 takes no arguments
function2 also takes no arguments
```

Fig. 6.17 | Functions that take no arguments. (Part 2 of 2.)

6.13 Inline Functions

Implementing a program as a set of functions is good from a software engineering standpoint, but function calls involve execution-time overhead. C++ provides **inline functions** to help reduce function call overhead. Placing the qualifier **`inline`** before a function's return type in the function definition *advises* the compiler to generate a copy of the function's body code in *every* place where the function is called (when appropriate) to avoid a function call. This often makes the program *larger*. The compiler can *ignore* the `inline` qualifier and generally does so for all but the *smallest* functions. Reusable `inline` functions are typically placed in headers, so that their definitions can be included in each source file that uses them.

Software Engineering Observation 6.8

If you change the definition of an `inline` function, you should recompile all of that function's clients.

Performance Tip 6.4

Compilers can inline code for which you have not explicitly used the `inline` keyword. Today's optimizing compilers are so sophisticated that it's best to leave inlining decisions to the compiler.

Figure 6.18 uses `inline` function `cube` (lines 9–12) to calculate the volume of a cube. Keyword **`const`** in function `cube`'s parameter list (line 9) tells the compiler that the function does *not* modify variable `side`. This ensures that `side`'s value is *not* changed by the function during the calculation. (Keyword `const` is discussed in detail in Chapters 7–9.)

Software Engineering Observation 6.9

The `const` qualifier should be used to enforce the principle of least privilege. Using the principle of least privilege to properly design software can greatly reduce debugging time and improper side effects and can make a program easier to modify and maintain.

```
// Fig. 6.18: fig06_18.cpp
// inline function that calculates the volume of a cube.
#include <iostream>
using namespace std;

// Definition of inline function cube. Definition of function appears
// before function is called, so a function prototype is not required.
// First line of function definition acts as the prototype.
inline double cube( const double side )
{
   return side * side * side; // calculate cube
} // end function cube

int main()
{
   double sideValue; // stores value entered by user
   cout << "Enter the side length of your cube: ";
   cin >> sideValue; // read value from user

   // calculate cube of sideValue and display result
   cout << "Volume of cube with side "
      << sideValue << " is " << cube( sideValue ) << endl;
} // end main
```

```
Enter the side length of your cube: 3.5
Volume of cube with side 3.5 is 42.875
```

Fig. 6.18 | `inline` function that calculates the volume of a cube.

6.14 References and Reference Parameters

Two ways to pass arguments to functions in many programming languages are **pass-by-value** and **pass-by-reference**. When an argument is passed by value, a *copy* of the argument's value is made and passed (on the function call stack) to the called function. Changes to the copy do *not* affect the original variable's value in the caller. This prevents the *accidental side effects* that so greatly hinder the development of correct and reliable software systems. So far, each argument in the book has been passed by value.

Performance Tip 6.5

One disadvantage of pass-by-value is that, if a large data item is being passed, copying that data can take a considerable amount of execution time and memory space.

Reference Parameters

This section introduces reference parameters—the first of the two means C++ provides for performing pass-by-reference. With *pass-by-reference*, the caller gives the called function the ability to *access the caller's data directly*, and to *modify* that data.

Performance Tip 6.6

Pass-by-reference is good for performance reasons, because it can eliminate the pass-by-value overhead of copying large amounts of data.

Software Engineering Observation 6.10

Pass-by-reference can weaken security; the called function can corrupt the caller's data.

Later, we'll show how to achieve the performance advantage of pass-by-reference while *simultaneously* achieving the software engineering advantage of protecting the caller's data from corruption.

A **reference parameter** is an *alias* for its corresponding argument in a function call. To indicate that a function parameter is passed by reference, simply follow the parameter's type in the function prototype by an *ampersand (&)*; use the same convention when listing the parameter's type in the function header. For example, the following declaration in a function header

```
int &count
```

when read from *right to left* is pronounced "`count` is a reference to an `int`." In the function call, simply mention the variable by name to pass it by reference. Then, mentioning the variable by its parameter name in the body of the called function actually refers to the *original variable* in the calling function, and the original variable can be *modified* directly by the called function. As always, the function prototype and header must agree.

Passing Arguments by Value and by Reference

Figure 6.19 compares pass-by-value and pass-by-reference with reference parameters. The "styles" of the arguments in the calls to function `squareByValue` and function `squareByReference` are identical—both variables are simply mentioned by name in the function calls. *Without checking the function prototypes or function definitions, it isn't possible to tell from the calls alone whether either function can modify its arguments.* Because function prototypes are mandatory, the compiler has no trouble resolving the ambiguity.

Common Programming Error 6.8

Because reference parameters are mentioned only by name in the body of the called function, you might inadvertently treat reference parameters as pass-by-value parameters. This can cause unexpected side effects if the original variables are changed by the function.

```
// Fig. 6.19: fig06_19.cpp
// Passing arguments by value and by reference.
#include <iostream>
using namespace std;

int squareByValue( int ); // function prototype (value pass)
void squareByReference( int & ); // function prototype (reference pass)

int main()
{
   int x = 2; // value to square using squareByValue
   int z = 4; // value to square using squareByReference

```

Fig. 6.19 | Passing arguments by value and by reference. (Part 1 of 2.)

```
14      // demonstrate squareByValue
15      cout << "x = " << x << " before squareByValue\n";
16      cout << "Value returned by squareByValue: "
17         << squareByValue( x ) << endl;
18      cout << "x = " << x << " after squareByValue\n" << endl;
19
20      // demonstrate squareByReference
21      cout << "z = " << z << " before squareByReference" << endl;
22      squareByReference( z );
23      cout << "z = " << z << " after squareByReference" << endl;
24   } // end main
25
26   // squareByValue multiplies number by itself, stores the
27   // result in number and returns the new value of number
28   int squareByValue( int number )
29   {
30      return number *= number; // caller's argument not modified
31   } // end function squareByValue
32
33   // squareByReference multiplies numberRef by itself and stores the result
34   // in the variable to which numberRef refers in function main
35   void squareByReference( int &numberRef )
36   {
37      numberRef *= numberRef; // caller's argument modified
38   } // end function squareByReference
```

```
x = 2 before squareByValue
Value returned by squareByValue: 4
x = 2 after squareByValue

z = 4 before squareByReference
z = 16 after squareByReference
```

Fig. 6.19 | Passing arguments by value and by reference. (Part 2 of 2.)

Chapter 8 discusses *pointers*; pointers enable an alternate form of pass-by-reference in which the style of the call clearly indicates pass-by-reference (and the potential for modifying the caller's arguments).

Performance Tip 6.7

For passing large objects, use a constant *reference parameter to simulate the appearance and security of pass-by-value and avoid the overhead of passing a copy of the large object.*

To specify that a reference should not be allowed to modify the argument, place the `const` qualifier *before* the type specifier in the parameter declaration. Note the placement of `&` in function `squareByReference`'s parameter list (line 35, Fig. 6.19). Some C++ programmers prefer to write the equivalent form `int& numberRef`.

References as Aliases within a Function

References can also be used as aliases for other variables *within* a function (although they typically are used with functions as shown in Fig. 6.19). For example, the code

```
int count = 1; // declare integer variable count
int &cRef = count; // create cRef as an alias for count
++cRef; // increment count (using its alias cRef)
```

increments variable `count` by using its alias `cRef`. Reference variables *must* be initialized in their declarations and cannot be reassigned as *aliases* to other variables. Once a reference is *declared* as an alias for another variable, all operations supposedly performed on the *alias* (i.e., the reference) are actually performed on the *original* variable. The alias is simply another name for the original variable. Unless it's a reference to a constant, a reference argument must be an *lvalue* (e.g., a variable name), not a constant or *rvalue* expression (e.g., the result of a calculation).

Returning a Reference from a Function

Functions can return references, but this can be dangerous. When returning a reference to a variable declared in the called function, unless that variable is declared `static`, the reference refers to an automatic variable that's *discarded* when the function terminates. An attempt to access such a variable yields *undefined behavior*. References to undefined variables are called **dangling references**.

Common Programming Error 6.9

Returning a reference to an automatic variable in a called function is a logic error. Compilers typically issue a warning when this occurs. For industrial-strength code, always *eliminate all compilation warnings before producing executable code.*

6.15 Default Arguments

It's common for a program to invoke a function repeatedly with the *same* argument value for a particular parameter. In such cases, you can specify that such a parameter has a **default argument**, i.e., a default value to be passed to that parameter. When a program *omits* an argument for a parameter with a default argument in a function call, the compiler rewrites the function call and inserts the default value of that argument.

Default arguments *must* be the rightmost (trailing) arguments in a function's parameter list. When calling a function with two or more default arguments, if an omitted argument is *not* the rightmost argument in the argument list, then all arguments to the right of that argument also *must* be omitted. Default arguments must be specified with the *first* occurrence of the function name—typically, in the function prototype. If the function prototype is omitted because the function definition also serves as the prototype, then the default arguments should be specified in the function header. Default values can be any expression, including constants, global variables or function calls. Default arguments also can be used with `inline` functions.

Figure 6.20 demonstrates using default arguments to calculate a box's volume. The function prototype for `boxVolume` (line 7) specifies that all three parameters have been given default values of `1`. We provided variable names in the function prototype for readability. As always, variable names are *not* required in function prototypes.

The first call to `boxVolume` (line 13) specifies no arguments, thus using all three default values of 1. The second call (line 17) passes only a `length` argument, thus using default values of 1 for the `width` and `height` arguments. The third call (line 21) passes arguments for only `length` and `width`, thus using a default value of 1 for the `height` argu-

```
1  // Fig. 6.20: fig06_20.cpp
2  // Using default arguments.
3  #include <iostream>
4  using namespace std;
5
6  // function prototype that specifies default arguments
7  unsigned int boxVolume( unsigned int length = 1, unsigned int width = 1,
8     unsigned int height = 1 );
9
10 int main()
11 {
12    // no arguments--use default values for all dimensions
13    cout << "The default box volume is: " << boxVolume();
14
15    // specify length; default width and height
16    cout << "\n\nThe volume of a box with length 10,\n"
17       << "width 1 and height 1 is: " << boxVolume( 10 );
18
19    // specify length and width; default height
20    cout << "\n\nThe volume of a box with length 10,\n"
21       << "width 5 and height 1 is: " << boxVolume( 10, 5 );
22
23    // specify all arguments
24    cout << "\n\nThe volume of a box with length 10,\n"
25       << "width 5 and height 2 is: " << boxVolume( 10, 5, 2 )
26       << endl;
27 } // end main
28
29 // function boxVolume calculates the volume of a box
30 unsigned int boxVolume( unsigned int length, unsigned int width,
31    unsigned int height )
32 {
33    return length * width * height;
34 } // end function boxVolume
```

```
The default box volume is: 1

The volume of a box with length 10,
width 1 and height 1 is: 10

The volume of a box with length 10,
width 5 and height 1 is: 50

The volume of a box with length 10,
width 5 and height 2 is: 100
```

Fig. 6.20 | Using default arguments.

ment. The last call (line 25) passes arguments for `length`, `width` and `height`, thus using no default values. Any arguments passed to the function explicitly are assigned to the function's parameters from left to right. Therefore, when `boxVolume` receives one argument, the function assigns the value of that argument to its `length` parameter (i.e., the leftmost parameter in the parameter list). When `boxVolume` receives two arguments, the function assigns the values of those arguments to its `length` and `width` parameters in that order. Finally, when `boxVolume` receives all three arguments, the function assigns the values of those arguments to its `length`, `width` and `height` parameters, respectively.

Good Programming Practice 6.5

Using default arguments can simplify writing function calls. However, some programmers feel that explicitly specifying all arguments is clearer.

6.16 Unary Scope Resolution Operator

It's possible to declare local and global variables of the same name. C++ provides the **unary scope resolution operator** (`::`) to access a global variable when a local variable of the same name is in scope. The unary scope resolution operator cannot be used to access a *local* variable of the same name in an outer block. A global variable can be accessed directly without the unary scope resolution operator if the name of the global variable is not the same as that of a local variable in scope.

Figure 6.21 shows the unary scope resolution operator with local and global variables of the same name (lines 6 and 10). To emphasize that the local and global versions of variable `number` are distinct, the program declares one variable `int` and the other `double`.

```
1  // Fig. 6.21: fig06_21.cpp
2  // Unary scope resolution operator.
3  #include <iostream>
4  using namespace std;
5
6  int number = 7; // global variable named number
7
8  int main()
9  {
10    double number = 10.5; // local variable named number
11
12    // display values of local and global variables
13    cout << "Local double value of number = " << number
14       << "\nGlobal int value of number = " << ::number << endl;
15 } // end main
```

```
Local double value of number = 10.5
Global int value of number = 7
```

Fig. 6.21 | Unary scope resolution operator.

Good Programming Practice 6.6

Always using the unary scope resolution operator (`::`) to refer to global variables makes it clear that you're intending to access a global variable rather than a nonglobal variable.

Software Engineering Observation 6.11

Always using the unary scope resolution operator (`::`) to refer to global variables makes programs easier to modify by reducing the risk of name collisions with nonglobal variables.

Error-Prevention Tip 6.7

Always using the unary scope resolution operator (::) to refer to a global variable eliminates logic errors that might occur if a nonglobal variable hides the global variable.

Error-Prevention Tip 6.8

Avoid using variables of the same name for different purposes in a program. Although this is allowed in various circumstances, it can lead to errors.

6.17 Function Overloading

C++ enables several functions of the same name to be defined, as long as they have different signatures. This is called **function overloading**. The C++ compiler selects the proper function to call by examining the number, types and order of the arguments in the call. Function overloading is used to create several functions of the *same* name that perform similar tasks, but on *different* data types. For example, many functions in the math library are overloaded for different numeric types—the C++ standard requires `float`, `double` and `long double` overloaded versions of the math library functions discussed in Section 6.2.

Good Programming Practice 6.7

Overloading functions that perform closely related tasks can make programs more readable and understandable.

Overloaded `square` *Functions*

Figure 6.22 uses overloaded `square` functions to calculate the square of an `int` (lines 7–11) and the square of a `double` (lines 14–18). Line 22 invokes the `int` version of function `square` by passing the literal value `7`. C++ treats whole number literal values as type `int`. Similarly, line 24 invokes the `double` version of function `square` by passing the literal value `7.5`, which C++ treats as a `double`. In each case the compiler chooses the proper function to call, based on the type of the argument. The last two lines of the output window confirm that the proper function was called in each case.

```
1  // Fig. 6.22: fig06_22.cpp
2  // Overloaded square functions.
3  #include <iostream>
4  using namespace std;
5
6  // function square for int values
7  int square( int x )
8  {
9     cout << "square of integer " << x << " is ";
10    return x * x;
11 } // end function square with int argument
12
```

Fig. 6.22 | Overloaded `square` functions. (Part 1 of 2.)

```
// function square for double values
double square( double y )
{
   cout << "square of double " << y << " is ";
   return y * y;
} // end function square with double argument

int main()
{
   cout << square( 7 ); // calls int version
   cout << endl;
   cout << square( 7.5 ); // calls double version
   cout << endl;
} // end main
```

```
square of integer 7 is 49
square of double 7.5 is 56.25
```

Fig. 6.22 | Overloaded `square` functions. (Part 2 of 2.)

How the Compiler Differentiates Among Overloaded Functions

Overloaded functions are distinguished by their *signatures*. A signature is a combination of a function's name and its parameter types (in order). The compiler encodes each function identifier with the types of its parameters (sometimes referred to as **name mangling** or **name decoration**) to enable **type-safe linkage**. Type-safe linkage ensures that the proper overloaded function is called and that the types of the arguments conform to the types of the parameters.

Figure 6.23 was compiled with GNU C++. Rather than showing the execution output of the program (as we normally would), we show the mangled function names produced in assembly language by GNU C++. Each mangled name (other than `main`) begins with two underscores (__) followed by the letter `Z`, a number and the function name. The number that follows `Z` specifies how many characters are in the function's name. For example, function `square` has 6 characters in its name, so its mangled name is prefixed with `__Z6`. The function name is then followed by an encoding of its parameter list. In the parameter list for function `nothing2` (line 25; see the fourth output line), `c` represents a `char`, `i` represents an `int`, `Rf` represents a `float &` (i.e., a reference to a `float`) and `Rd` represents a `double &` (i.e., a reference to a `double`). In the parameter list for function `nothing1`, `i` represents an `int`, `f` represents a `float`, `c` represents a `char` and `Ri` represents an `int &`. The two `square` functions are distinguished by their parameter lists; one specifies `d` for `double` and the other specifies `i` for `int`. The return types of the functions are *not* specified in the mangled names. *Overloaded functions can have different return types, but if they do, they must also have different parameter lists.* Again, you *cannot* have two functions with the *same* signature and *different* return types. Function-name mangling is compiler specific. Also, function `main` is *not* mangled, because it *cannot* be overloaded.

Common Programming Error 6.10

Creating overloaded functions with identical parameter lists and different return types is a compilation error.

```
// Fig. 6.23: fig06_23.cpp
// Name mangling to enable type-safe linkage.

// function square for int values
int square( int x )
{
   return x * x;
} // end function square

// function square for double values
double square( double y )
{
   return y * y;
} // end function square

// function that receives arguments of types
// int, float, char and int &
void nothing1( int a, float b, char c, int &d )
{
   // empty function body
} // end function nothing1

// function that receives arguments of types
// char, int, float & and double &
int nothing2( char a, int b, float &c, double &d )
{
   return 0;
} // end function nothing2

int main()
{
} // end main
```

```
__Z6squarei
__Z6squared
__Z8nothing1ifcRi
__Z8nothing2ciRfRd
main
```

Fig. 6.23 | Name mangling to enable type-safe linkage.

The compiler uses only the parameter lists to distinguish between overloaded functions. Such functions need *not* have the same number of parameters. Use caution when overloading functions with default parameters, because this may cause ambiguity.

Common Programming Error 6.11

A function with default arguments omitted might be called identically to another overloaded function; this is a compilation error. For example, having a program that contains both *a function that explicitly takes no arguments and a function of the same name that contains all default arguments results in a compilation error when an attempt is made to use that function name in a call passing no arguments. The compiler cannot determine which version of the function to choose.*

Overloaded Operators

In Chapter 10, we discuss how to overload *operators* to define how they should operate on objects of user-defined data types. (In fact, we've been using many overloaded operators to this point, including the stream insertion << and the stream extraction >> operators, which are overloaded for *all* the fundamental types. We say more about overloading << and >> to be able to handle objects of user-defined types in Chapter 10.)

6.18 Function Templates

Overloaded functions are normally used to perform similar operations that involve different program logic on different data types. If the program logic and operations are *identical* for each data type, overloading may be performed more compactly and conveniently by using **function templates**. You write a single function template definition. Given the argument types provided in calls to this function, C++ automatically generates separate **function template specializations** to handle each type of call appropriately. Thus, defining a single function template essentially defines a whole family of overloaded functions.

Figure 6.24 defines a `maximum` function template (lines 3–17) that determines the largest of three values. All function template definitions begin with the **`template` keyword** (line 3) followed by a **template parameter list** to the function template enclosed in angle brackets (< and >). Every parameter in the template parameter list (often referred to as a **formal type parameter**) is preceded by keyword `typename` or keyword `class` (they are synonyms in this context). The formal type parameters are placeholders for fundamental types or user-defined types. These placeholders, in this case, `T`, are used to specify the types of the function's parameters (line 4), to specify the function's return type (line 4) and to declare variables within the body of the function definition (line 6). A function template is defined like any other function, but uses the formal type parameters as placeholders for actual data types.

```
1  // Fig. 6.24: maximum.h
2  // Function template maximum header.
3  template < typename T >  // or template< class T >
4  T maximum( T value1, T value2, T value3 )
5  {
6     T maximumValue = value1; // assume value1 is maximum
7
8     // determine whether value2 is greater than maximumValue
9     if ( value2 > maximumValue )
10       maximumValue = value2;
11
12    // determine whether value3 is greater than maximumValue
13    if ( value3 > maximumValue )
14       maximumValue = value3;
15
16    return maximumValue;
17 } // end function template maximum
```

Fig. 6.24 | Function template `maximum` header.

The function template declares a single formal type parameter `T` (line 3) as a placeholder for the type of the data to be tested by function `maximum`. The name of a type parameter must be unique in the template parameter list for a particular template definition. When the compiler detects a `maximum` invocation in the program source code, the *type of* the data passed to `maximum` is substituted for `T` throughout the template definition, and C++ creates a complete function for determining the maximum of three values of the specified data type—all three must have the same type, since we use only one type parameter in this example. Then the newly created function is compiled—templates are a means of *code generation.*

Figure 6.25 uses the `maximum` function template to determine the largest of three `int` values, three `double` values and three `char` values, respectively (lines 17, 27 and 37). Separate functions are created as a result of the calls in lines 17, 27 and 37—expecting three `int` values, three `double` values and three `char` values, respectively.

```
1  // Fig. 6.25: fig06_25.cpp
2  // Function template maximum test program.
3  #include <iostream>
4  #include "maximum.h" // include definition of function template maximum
5  using namespace std;
6
7  int main()
8  {
9     // demonstrate maximum with int values
10    int int1, int2, int3;
11
12    cout << "Input three integer values: ";
13    cin >> int1 >> int2 >> int3;
14
15    // invoke int version of maximum
16    cout << "The maximum integer value is: "
17       << maximum( int1, int2, int3 );
18
19    // demonstrate maximum with double values
20    double double1, double2, double3;
21
22    cout << "\n\nInput three double values: ";
23    cin >> double1 >> double2 >> double3;
24
25    // invoke double version of maximum
26    cout << "The maximum double value is: "
27       << maximum( double1, double2, double3 );
28
29    // demonstrate maximum with char values
30    char char1, char2, char3;
31
32    cout << "\n\nInput three characters: ";
33    cin >> char1 >> char2 >> char3;
34
35    // invoke char version of maximum
36    cout << "The maximum character value is: "
37       << maximum( char1, char2, char3 ) << endl;
38 } // end main
```

Fig. 6.25 | Function template `maximum` test program. (Part 1 of 2.)

```
Input three integer values: 1 2 3
The maximum integer value is: 3

Input three double values: 3.3 2.2 1.1
The maximum double value is: 3.3

Input three characters: A C B
The maximum character value is: C
```

Fig. 6.25 | Function template `maximum` test program. (Part 2 of 2.)

The function template specialization created for type `int` replaces each occurrence of `T` with `int` as follows:

```
int maximum( int value1, int value2, int value3 )
{
   int maximumValue = value1; // assume value1 is maximum

   // determine whether value2 is greater than maximumValue
   if ( value2 > maximumValue )
      maximumValue = value2;

   // determine whether value3 is greater than maximumValue
   if ( value3 > maximumValue )
      maximumValue = value3;

   return maximumValue;
} // end function template maximum
```

C++11—Trailing Return Types for Functions

11

C++11 introduces **trailing return types** for functions. To specify a trailing return type you place the keyword `auto` before the function name, then follow the function's parameter list with `->` and the return type. For example, to specify a trailing return type for function template `maximum` (Fig. 6.24), you'd write

```
template < typename T >
auto maximum( T x, T y, T z ) -> T
```

As you build more complex function templates, there are cases for which only trailing return types are allowed. Such complex function templates are beyond this book's scope.

6.19 Recursion

A **recursive function** is a function that calls itself, either directly, or indirectly (through another function). [*Note:* The C++ standard document indicates that `main` should not be called within a program or recursively. Its sole purpose is to be the starting point for program execution.]

Recursion Concepts

We first consider recursion conceptually, then examine programs containing recursive functions. Recursive problem-solving approaches have a number of elements in common. A recursive function is called to solve a problem. The function knows how to solve only the *simplest case(s)*, or so-called **base case(s)**. If the function is called with a base case, the function simply returns a result. If the function is called with a more complex problem, it typically divides the problem into two conceptual pieces—a piece that the function knows how to do and a piece that it does not know how to do. To make recursion feasible, the latter piece *must* resemble the original problem, but be a slightly simpler or smaller version. This new problem looks like the original, so the function calls a copy of itself to work on the smaller problem—this is referred to as a **recursive call** and is also called the **recursion step**. The recursion step often includes the keyword `return`, because its result will be combined with the portion of the problem the function knew how to solve to form the result passed back to the original caller, possibly `main`.

Common Programming Error 6.12

Omitting the base case or writing the recursion step incorrectly so that it does not converge on the base case causes an infinite recursion error, typically causing a stack overflow. This is analogous to the problem of an infinite loop in an iterative (nonrecursive) solution.

The recursion step executes while the original call to the function is still "open," i.e., it has not yet finished executing. The recursion step can result in many more such recursive calls, as the function keeps dividing each new subproblem with which the function is called into two conceptual pieces. In order for the recursion to eventually terminate, each time the function calls itself with a slightly simpler version of the original problem, this sequence of smaller and smaller problems must eventually *converge* on the base case. At that point, the function recognizes the base case and returns a result to the previous copy of the function, and a sequence of returns ensues up the line until the original call eventually returns the final result to `main`. This sounds quite exotic compared to the kind of problem solving we've been using to this point. As an example of these concepts at work, let's write a recursive program to perform a popular mathematical calculation.

Factorial

The factorial of a nonnegative integer n, written $n!$ (and pronounced "n factorial"), is the product

$$n \cdot (n-1) \cdot (n-2) \cdot \ldots \cdot 1$$

with 1! equal to 1, and 0! defined to be 1. For example, 5! is the product $5 \cdot 4 \cdot 3 \cdot 2 \cdot 1$, which is equal to 120.

Iterative Factorial

The factorial of an integer, `number`, greater than or equal to 0, can be calculated **iteratively** (nonrecursively) by using a `for` statement as follows:

```
factorial = 1;
for ( unsigned int counter = number; counter >= 1; --counter )
   factorial *= counter;
```

Recursive Factorial

A *recursive* definition of the factorial function is arrived at by observing the following algebraic relationship:

$$n! = n \cdot (n-1)!$$

For example, 5! is clearly equal to 5 * 4! as is shown by the following:

$$5! = 5 \cdot 4 \cdot 3 \cdot 2 \cdot 1$$
$$5! = 5 \cdot (4 \cdot 3 \cdot 2 \cdot 1)$$
$$5! = 5 \cdot (4!)$$

Evaluating 5!

The evaluation of 5! would proceed as shown in Fig. 6.26, which illustrates how the succession of recursive calls proceeds until 1! is evaluated to be 1, terminating the recursion. Figure 6.26(b) shows the values returned from each recursive call to its caller until the final value is calculated and returned.

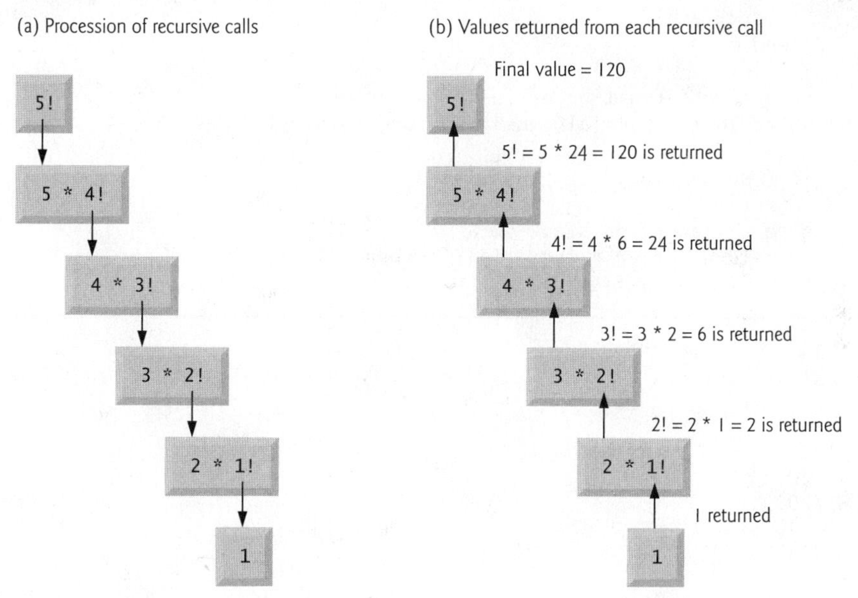

Fig. 6.26 | Recursive evaluation of 5!.

Using a Recursive `factorial` Function to Calculate Factorials

Figure 6.27 uses recursion to calculate and print the factorials of the integers 0–10. (The choice of the data type `unsigned long` is explained momentarily.) The recursive function `factorial` (lines 18–24) first determines whether the terminating condition `number <= 1` (line 20) is true. If `number` is less than or equal to 1, the `factorial` function returns 1 (line 21), no further recursion is necessary and the function terminates. If `number` is greater than 1, line 23 expresses the problem as the product of `number` and a recursive call to `factorial` evaluating the factorial of `number - 1`, which is a slightly simpler problem than the original calculation `factorial(number)`.

Why We Chose Type `unsigned long` in This Example

Function `factorial` has been declared to receive a parameter of type `unsigned long` and return a result of type `unsigned long`. This is shorthand notation for `unsigned long int`. The C++ standard requires that a variable of type `unsigned long int` be *at least as big as* an `int`.

```
// Fig. 6.27: fig06_27.cpp
// Recursive function factorial.
#include <iostream>
#include <iomanip>
using namespace std;

unsigned long factorial( unsigned long ); // function prototype

int main()
{
   // calculate the factorials of 0 through 10
   for ( unsigned int counter = 0; counter <= 10; ++counter )
      cout << setw( 2 ) << counter << "! = " << factorial( counter )
         << endl;
} // end main

// recursive definition of function factorial
unsigned long factorial( unsigned long number )
{
   if ( number <= 1 ) // test for base case
      return 1; // base cases: 0! = 1 and 1! = 1
   else // recursion step
      return number * factorial( number - 1 );
} // end function factorial
```

```
 0! = 1
 1! = 1
 2! = 2
 3! = 6
 4! = 24
 5! = 120
 6! = 720
 7! = 5040
 8! = 40320
 9! = 362880
10! = 3628800
```

Fig. 6.27 | Recursive function `factorial`.

Typically, an `unsigned long int` is stored in at least four bytes (32 bits); such a variable can hold a value in the range 0 to at least 4,294,967,295. (The data type `long int` is also typically stored in at least four bytes and can hold a value at least in the range –2,147,483,647 to 2,147,483,647.) As can be seen in Fig. 6.27, factorial values become large quickly. We chose the data type `unsigned long` so that the program can calculate factorials greater than 7! on computers with small (such as two-byte) integers. Unfortunately, the function `factorial` produces large values so quickly that even `unsigned long` does not help us compute many factorial values before even the size of an `unsigned long` variable is exceeded.

C++11 Type `unsigned long long int`

C++11's new `unsigned long long int` type (which can be abbreviated as `unsigned long long`) on some systems enables you to store values in 8 bytes (64 bits) which can hold numbers as large as 18,446,744,073,709,551,615.

Representing Even Larger Numbers
Variables of type `double` could be used to calculate factorials of larger numbers. This points to a weakness in many programming languages, namely, that the languages are not easily extended to handle the unique requirements of various applications. As we'll see when we discuss object-oriented programming in more depth, C++ is an *extensible* language that allows us to create classes that can represent arbitrarily large integers if we wish. Such classes already are available in popular class libraries.

6.20 Example Using Recursion: Fibonacci Series

The Fibonacci series

0, 1, 1, 2, 3, 5, 8, 13, 21, …

begins with 0 and 1 and has the property that each subsequent Fibonacci number is the sum of the previous two Fibonacci numbers.

The series occurs in nature and, in particular, describes a form of spiral. The ratio of successive Fibonacci numbers converges on a constant value of 1.618…. This number frequently occurs in nature and has been called the **golden ratio** or the **golden mean.** Humans tend to find the golden mean aesthetically pleasing. Architects often design windows, rooms and buildings whose length and width are in the ratio of the golden mean. Postcards are often designed with a golden mean length/width ratio.

Recursive Fibonacci Definition
The Fibonacci series can be defined recursively as follows:

$$\text{fibonacci}(0) = 0$$
$$\text{fibonacci}(1) = 1$$
$$\text{fibonacci}(n) = \text{fibonacci}(n - 1) + \text{fibonacci}(n - 2)$$

The program of Fig. 6.28 calculates the nth Fibonacci number recursively by using function `fibonacci`. Fibonacci numbers tend to become large quickly, although slower than factorials do. Therefore, we chose the data type `unsigned long` for the parameter type and the return type in function `fibonacci`. Figure 6.28 shows the execution of the program, which displays the Fibonacci values for several numbers.

The application begins with a `for` statement that calculates and displays the Fibonacci values for the integers 0–10 and is followed by three calls to calculate the Fibonacci values of the integers 20, 30 and 35 (lines 16–18). The calls to `fibonacci` (lines 13 and 16–18) from `main` are *not* recursive calls, but the calls from line 27 of `fibonacci` are recursive. Each time the program invokes `fibonacci` (lines 22–28), the function immediately tests the base case to determine whether `number` is equal to `0` or `1` (line 24). If this is true, line 25 returns `number`. Interestingly, if `number` is greater than 1, the recursion step (line 27) generates *two* recursive calls, each for a slightly smaller problem than the original call to `fibonacci`.

```
1  // Fig. 6.28: fig06_28.cpp
2  // Recursive function fibonacci.
3  #include <iostream>
```

Fig. 6.28 | Recursive function `fibonacci`. (Part 1 of 2.)

```
using namespace std;

unsigned long fibonacci( unsigned long ); // function prototype

int main()
{
   // calculate the fibonacci values of 0 through 10
   for ( unsigned int counter = 0; counter <= 10; ++counter )
      cout << "fibonacci( " << counter << " ) = "
         << fibonacci( counter ) << endl;

   // display higher fibonacci values
   cout << "\nfibonacci( 20 ) = " << fibonacci( 20 ) << endl;
   cout << "fibonacci( 30 ) = " << fibonacci( 30 ) << endl;
   cout << "fibonacci( 35 ) = " << fibonacci( 35 ) << endl;
} // end main

// recursive function fibonacci
unsigned long fibonacci( unsigned long number )
{
   if ( ( 0 == number ) || ( 1 == number ) ) // base cases
      return number;
   else // recursion step
      return fibonacci( number - 1 ) + fibonacci( number - 2 );
} // end function fibonacci
```

```
fibonacci( 0 ) = 0
fibonacci( 1 ) = 1
fibonacci( 2 ) = 1
fibonacci( 3 ) = 2
fibonacci( 4 ) = 3
fibonacci( 5 ) = 5
fibonacci( 6 ) = 8
fibonacci( 7 ) = 13
fibonacci( 8 ) = 21
fibonacci( 9 ) = 34
fibonacci( 10 ) = 55

fibonacci( 20 ) = 6765
fibonacci( 30 ) = 832040
fibonacci( 35 ) = 9227465
```

Fig. 6.28 | Recursive function `fibonacci`. (Part 2 of 2.)

Evaluating `fibonacci(3)`

Figure 6.29 shows how function `fibonacci` would evaluate `fibonacci(3)`. This figure raises some interesting issues about the *order* in which C++ compilers evaluate the operands of operators. This is a *separate* issue from the order in which operators are applied to their operands, namely, the order dictated by the rules of operator precedence and associativity. Figure 6.29 shows that evaluating `fibonacci(3)` causes two recursive calls, namely, `fibonacci(2)` and `fibonacci(1)`. In what order are these calls made?

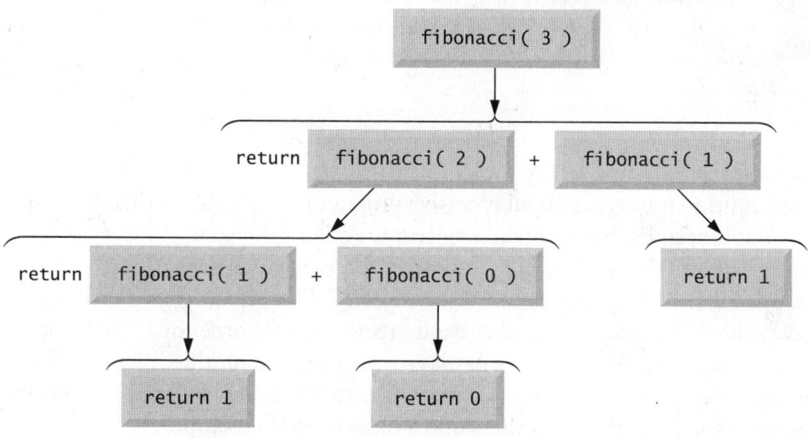

Fig. 6.29 | Set of recursive calls to function `fibonacci`.

Order of Evaluation of Operands

Most programmers simply assume that the operands are evaluated left to right. C++ does *not* specify the order in which the operands of most operators (including +) are to be evaluated. Therefore, you must make no assumption about the order in which these calls execute. The calls could in fact execute `fibonacci(2)` first, then `fibonacci(1)`, or they could execute in the reverse order: `fibonacci(1)`, then `fibonacci(2)`. In this program and in most others, it turns out that the final result would be the same. However, in some programs the evaluation of an operand can have **side effects** (changes to data values) that could affect the final result of the expression.

C++ specifies the order of evaluation of the operands of only *four* operators—`&&`, `||`, comma (`,`) and `?:`. The first three are binary operators whose two operands are guaranteed to be evaluated left to right. The last operator is C++'s only *ternary* operator—its leftmost operand is always evaluated first; if it evaluates to *true*, the middle operand evaluates next and the last operand is ignored; if the leftmost operand evaluates to *false*, the third operand evaluates next and the middle operand is ignored.

Portability Tip 6.2

Programs that depend on the order of evaluation of the operands of operators other than `&&`, `||`, `?:` *and the comma* (`,`) *operator can function differently with different compilers and can lead to logic errors.*

Common Programming Error 6.13

Writing programs that depend on the order of evaluation of the operands of operators other than `&&`, `||`, `?:` *and the comma* (`,`) *operator can lead to logic errors.*

Error-Prevention Tip 6.9

Do not depend on the order in which operands are evaluated. To ensure that side effects are applied in the correct order, break complex expressions into separate statements.

Common Programming Error 6.14

Recall that the `&&` *and* `||` *operators use short-circuit evaluation. Placing an expression with a side effect on the right side of a* `&&` *or* `||` *operator is a logic error if that expression should always be evaluated.*

Exponential Complexity

A word of caution is in order about recursive programs like the one we use here to generate Fibonacci numbers. Each level of recursion in function `fibonacci` has a *doubling* effect on the number of function calls; i.e., the number of recursive calls that are required to calculate the nth Fibonacci number is on the order of 2^n. This rapidly gets out of hand. Calculating only the 20th Fibonacci number would require on the order of 2^{20} or about a million calls, calculating the 30th Fibonacci number would require on the order of 2^{30} or about a billion calls, and so on. Computer scientists refer to this as **exponential complexity**. Problems of this nature humble even the world's most powerful computers!

Performance Tip 6.8

Avoid Fibonacci-style recursive programs that result in an exponential "explosion" of calls.

6.21 Recursion vs. Iteration

This section compares the recursive and iterative problem-solving approaches and discusses why you might choose one over the other in a particular situation.

- Both iteration and recursion are *based on a control statement*: Iteration uses a *repetition structure*; recursion uses a *selection structure.*
- Both iteration and recursion involve *repetition*: Iteration explicitly uses a *repetition structure*; recursion achieves repetition through *repeated function calls.*
- Iteration and recursion each involve a *termination test*: Iteration terminates when the *loop-continuation condition fails*; recursion terminates when a *base case is recognized.*
- Iteration with counter-controlled repetition and recursion each *gradually approach termination*: Iteration *modifies a counter* until the counter assumes a value that makes the loop-continuation condition fail; recursion produces *simpler versions of the original problem* until the base case is reached.
- Both iteration and recursion *can occur infinitely*: An *infinite loop* occurs with iteration if the loop-continuation test never becomes false; *infinite recursion* occurs if the recursion step does not reduce the problem during each recursive call in a manner that converges on the base case.

Iterative Factorial Implementation

To illustrate the differences between iteration and recursion, let's examine an iterative solution to the factorial problem (Fig. 6.30). A repetition statement is used (lines 23–24 of Fig. 6.30) rather than the selection statement of the recursive solution (lines 20–23 of

Fig. 6.27). Both solutions use a termination test. In the recursive solution, line 20 (Fig. 6.27) tests for the base case. In the iterative solution, line 23 (Fig. 6.30) tests the loop-continuation condition—if the test fails, the loop terminates. Finally, instead of producing simpler versions of the original problem, the iterative solution uses a counter that is modified until the loop-continuation condition becomes false.

```
1  // Fig. 6.30: fig06_30.cpp
2  // Iterative function factorial.
3  #include <iostream>
4  #include <iomanip>
5  using namespace std;
6
7  unsigned long factorial( unsigned int ); // function prototype
8
9  int main()
10 {
11    // calculate the factorials of 0 through 10
12    for ( unsigned int counter = 0; counter <= 10; ++counter )
13       cout << setw( 2 ) << counter << "! = " << factorial( counter )
14          << endl;
15 } // end main
16
17 // iterative function factorial
18 unsigned long factorial( unsigned int number )
19 {
20    unsigned long result = 1;
21
22    // iterative factorial calculation
23    for ( unsigned int i = number; i >= 1; --i )
24       result *= i;
25
26    return result;
27 } // end function factorial
```

```
 0! = 1
 1! = 1
 2! = 2
 3! = 6
 4! = 24
 5! = 120
 6! = 720
 7! = 5040
 8! = 40320
 9! = 362880
10! = 3628800
```

Fig. 6.30 | Iterative function `factorial`.

Negatives of Recursion

Recursion has negatives. It repeatedly invokes the mechanism, and consequently the *overhead, of function calls.* This can be expensive in both processor time and memory space. Each recursive call causes *another copy of the function variables* to be created; this can consume considerable memory. Iteration normally occurs within a function, so the overhead of repeated function calls and extra memory assignment is omitted. So why choose recursion?

Software Engineering Observation 6.12

Any problem that can be solved recursively can also be solved iteratively (nonrecursively). A recursive approach is normally chosen when the recursive approach more naturally mirrors the problem and results in a program that's easier to understand and debug. Another reason to choose a recursive solution is that an iterative solution is not apparent.

Performance Tip 6.9

Avoid using recursion in performance situations. Recursive calls take time and consume additional memory.

Common Programming Error 6.15

Accidentally having a nonrecursive function call itself, either directly or indirectly (through another function), is a logic error.

6.22 Wrap-Up

In this chapter, you learned more about function declarations, including function prototypes, function signatures, function headers and function bodies. We overviewed the math library functions. You learned about argument coercion, or the forcing of arguments to the appropriate types specified by the parameter declarations of a function. We demonstrated how to generate random numbers and use them in a game-playing application. We showed how to define sets of constants with `enum`s. You also learned about the scope of variables, storage-class specifiers and storage duration. Two different ways to pass arguments to functions were covered—pass-by-value and pass-by-reference. For pass-by-reference, references are used as an alias to a variable. We showed how to implement inline functions and functions that receive default arguments. You learned that multiple functions in one class can be overloaded by providing functions with the same name and different signatures. Such functions can be used to perform the same or similar tasks, using different types or different numbers of parameters. We demonstrated a simpler way of overloading functions using function templates, where a function is defined once but can be used for several different types. We discussed recursion, where a function calls itself, either directly or indirectly through another function, to solve a problem.

In Chapter 7, you'll learn how to maintain lists and tables of data in `array` and `vector` objects. You'll see enhanced versions of the `GradeBook` class that use `array`s to store the actual grades entered.

7

Class Templates **array** and **vector**; Catching Exceptions

Objectives

In this chapter you'll:

- Use C++ Standard Library class template `array`—a fixed-size collection of related data items.
- Use `array`s to store, sort and search lists and tables of values.
- Declare `array`s, initialize `array`s and refer to the elements of `array`s.
- Use the range-based `for` statement.
- Pass `array`s to functions.
- Declare and manipulate multidimensional `array`s.
- Use C++ Standard Library class template `vector`—a variable-size collection of related data items.

Outline

7.1 Introduction

This chapter discusses **arrays**, which are *fixed-size* collections consisting of data items of the *same* type, and **vectors** which are collections (also of data items of the *same* type) that can grow and shrink *dynamically* at execution time. Both array and vector are C++ standard library class templates. To use them, you must include the <array> and <vector> headers respectively.

After discussing how arrays are declared, created and initialized, we present examples that demonstrate several common array manipulations. We show how to *search* arrays to find particular elements and *sort* arrays to put their data in *order*.

We enhance the GradeBook class by using both one- and two-dimensional arrays to maintain a set of grades in memory and analyze the grades from multiple exams. We introduce the *exception-handling* mechanism and use it to allow a program to continue executing when the program attempts to access an array or vector element that does not exist.

7.2 arrays

An array is a *contiguous* group of memory locations that all have the *same* type. To refer to a particular location or element in the array, we specify the name of the array and the **position number** of the particular element in the array.

Figure 7.1 shows an integer array called c that contains 12 **elements**. You refer to any one of these elements by giving the array name followed by the particular element's position number in square brackets ([]). The position number is more formally called a **subscript** or **index** (this number specifies the number of elements from the beginning of the array). The first element has **subscript 0 (zero)** and is sometimes called the **zeroth element.** Thus, the elements of array c are c[0] (pronounced "c sub zero"), c[1], c[2] and so on. The highest subscript in array c is 11, which is 1 less than the number of elements in the array (12). array names follow the same conventions as other variable names.

A subscript must be an integer or integer expression (using any integral type). If a program uses an expression as a subscript, then the program evaluates the expression to deter-

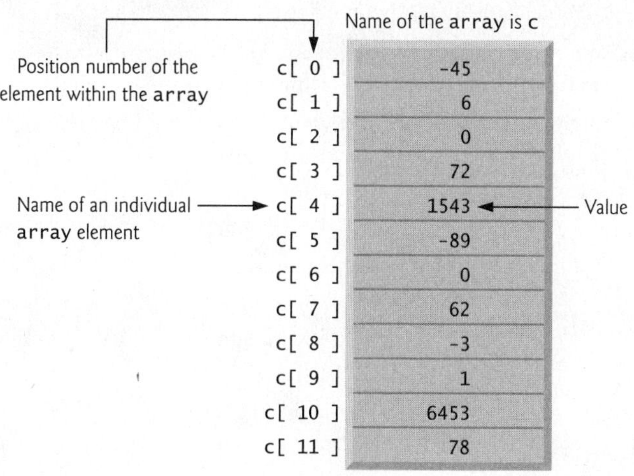

Fig. 7.1 | array of 12 elements.

mine the subscript. For example, if we assume that variable a is equal to 5 and that variable b is equal to 6, then the statement

```
c[ a + b ] += 2;
```

adds 2 to array element c[11]. A subscripted array name is an *lvalue*—it can be used on the left side of an assignment, just as non-array variable names can.

Let's examine array c in Fig. 7.1 more closely. The **name** of the entire array is c. Each array *knows its own size*, which can be determined by calling its **size** member function as in c.size(). Its 12 elements are referred to as c[0] to c[11]. The **value** of c[0] is -45, the value of c[7] is 62 and the value of c[11] is 78. To print the sum of the values contained in the first three elements of array c, we'd write

```
cout << c[ 0 ] + c[ 1 ] + c[ 2 ] << endl;
```

To divide the value of c[6] by 2 and assign the result to the variable x, we would write

```
x = c[ 6 ] / 2;
```

The brackets that enclose a subscript are actually an *operator* that has the same precedence as parentheses. Figure 7.2 shows the precedence and associativity of the operators introduced so far. The operators are shown top to bottom in decreasing order of precedence with their associativity and type.

Operators	Associativity	Type
:: ()	left to right *[See caution in Fig. 2.7 regarding grouping parentheses.]*	primary

Fig. 7.2 | Precedence and associativity of the operators introduced to this point. (Part 1 of 2.)

Operators	Associativity	Type
`()` `[]` `++` `--` `static_cast<type>(operand)`	left to right	postfix
`++` `--` `+` `-` `!`	right to left	unary (prefix)
`*` `/` `%`	left to right	multiplicative
`+` `-`	left to right	additive
`<<` `>>`	left to right	insertion/extraction
`<` `<=` `>` `>=`	left to right	relational
`==` `!=`	left to right	equality
`&&`	left to right	logical AND
`||`	left to right	logical OR
`?:`	right to left	conditional
`=` `+=` `-=` `*=` `/=` `%=`	right to left	assignment
`,`	left to right	comma

Fig. 7.2 | Precedence and associativity of the operators introduced to this point. (Part 2 of 2.)

7.3 Declaring arrays

arrays occupy space in memory. To specify the type of the elements and the number of elements required by an array use a declaration of the form:

```
array< type, arraySize > arrayName;
```

The notation <*type*, *arraySize*> indicates that array is a class template. The compiler reserves the appropriate amount of memory based on the *type* of the elements and the *arraySize.* (Recall that a declaration which reserves memory is more properly known as a *definition.*) The *arraySize* must be an unsigned integer. To tell the compiler to reserve 12 elements for integer array c, use the declaration

```
array< int, 12 > c; // c is an array of 12 int values
```

arrays can be declared to contain values of most data types. For example, an array of type string can be used to store character strings.

7.4 Examples Using arrays

The following examples demonstrate how to declare, initialize and manipulate arrays.

7.4.1 Declaring an array and Using a Loop to Initialize the array's Elements

The program in Fig. 7.3 declares five-element integer array n (line 10). Line 5 includes the <array> header, which contains the definition of class template array. Lines 13–14 use a for statement to initialize the array elements to zeros. Like other automatic variables, automatic arrays are *not* implicitly initialized to zero although static arrays are.

The first output statement (line 16) displays the column headings for the columns printed in the subsequent `for` statement (lines 19–20), which prints the `array` in tabular format. Remember that `setw` specifies the field width in which only the *next* value is to be output.

```
1  // Fig. 7.3: fig07_03.cpp
2  // Initializing an array's elements to zeros and printing the array.
3  #include <iostream>
4  #include <iomanip>
5  #include <array>
6  using namespace std;
7
8  int main()
9  {
10    array< int, 5 > n; // n is an array of 5 int values
11
12    // initialize elements of array n to 0
13    for ( size_t i = 0; i < n.size(); ++i )
14       n[ i ] = 0; // set element at location i to 0
15
16    cout << "Element" << setw( 13 ) << "Value" << endl;
17
18    // output each array element's value
19    for ( size_t j = 0; j < n.size(); ++j )
20       cout << setw( 7 ) << j << setw( 13 ) << n[ j ] << endl;
21 } // end main
```

```
Element        Value
      0            0
      1            0
      2            0
      3            0
      4            0
```

Fig. 7.3 | Initializing an `array`'s elements to zeros and printing the `array`.

In this program, the control variables `i` (line 13) and `j` (line 19) that specify `array` subscripts are declared to be of type **`size_t`**. According to the C++ standard `size_t` represents an unsigned integral type. This type is recommended for any variable that represents an `array`'s size or an `array`'s subscripts. Type `size_t` is defined in the `std` namespace and is in header `<cstddef>`, which is included by various other headers. If you attempt to compile a program that uses type `size_t` and receive errors indicating that it's not defined, simply include `<cstddef>` in your program.

7.4.2 Initializing an array in a Declaration with an Initializer List

The elements of an `array` also can be initialized in the `array` declaration by following the `array` name with an equals sign and a brace-delimited comma-separated list of **initializers**. The program in Fig. 7.4 uses an **initializer list** to initialize an integer `array` with five values (line 11) and prints the `array` in tabular format (lines 13–17).

```
// Fig. 7.4: fig07_04.cpp
// Initializing an array in a declaration.
#include <iostream>
#include <iomanip>
#include <array>
using namespace std;

int main()
{
   // use list initializer to initialize array n
   array< int, 5 > n = { 32, 27, 64, 18, 95 };

   cout << "Element" << setw( 13 ) << "Value" << endl;

   // output each array element's value
   for ( size_t i = 0; i < n.size(); ++i )
      cout << setw( 7 ) << i << setw( 13 ) << n[ i ] << endl;
} // end main
```

```
Element        Value
      0           32
      1           27
      2           64
      3           18
      4           95
```

Fig. 7.4 | Initializing an array in a declaration.

If there are *fewer* initializers than array elements, the remaining array elements are initialized to zero. For example, the elements of array n in Fig. 7.3 could have been initialized to zero with the declaration

```
array< int, 5 > n = {}; // initialize elements of array n to 0
```

which initializes the elements to zero, because there are fewer initializers (none in this case) than array elements. This technique can be used only in the array's declaration, whereas the initialization technique shown in Fig. 7.3 can be used repeatedly during program execution to "reinitialize" an array's elements.

If the array size and an initializer list are specified in an array declaration, the number of initializers must be less than or equal to the array size. The array declaration

```
array< int, 5 > n = { 32, 27, 64, 18, 95, 14 };
```

causes a compilation error, because there are six initializers and only five array elements.

7.4.3 Specifying an array's Size with a Constant Variable and Setting array Elements with Calculations

Figure 7.5 sets the elements of a 5-element array s to the even integers 2, 4, 6, 8 and 10 (lines 15–16) and prints the array in tabular format (lines 18–22). These numbers are generated (line 16) by multiplying each successive value of the loop counter by 2 and adding 2.

```
1  // Fig. 7.5: fig07_05.cpp
2  // Set array s to the even integers from 2 to 10.
3  #include <iostream>
4  #include <iomanip>
5  #include <array>
6  using namespace std;
7
8  int main()
9  {
10    // constant variable can be used to specify array size
11    const size_t arraySize = 5; // must initialize in declaration
12
13    array< int, arraySize > s; // array s has 5 elements
14
15    for ( size_t i = 0; i < s.size(); ++i ) // set the values
16       s[ i ] = 2 + 2 * i;
17
18    cout << "Element" << setw( 13 ) << "Value" << endl;
19
20    // output contents of array s in tabular format
21    for ( size_t j = 0; j < s.size(); ++j )
22       cout << setw( 7 ) << j << setw( 13 ) << s[ j ] << endl;
23 } // end main
```

```
Element        Value
      0            2
      1            4
      2            6
      3            8
      4           10
```

Fig. 7.5 | Set array s to the even integers from 2 to 10.

Line 11 uses the **const qualifier** to declare a **constant variable** arraySize with the value 5. A constant variable that's used to specify array's size *must* be initialized with a constant expression when it's declared and *cannot* be modified thereafter (as shown in Fig. 7.6 and Fig. 7.7). Constant variables are also called **named constants** or **read-only variables.**

Common Programming Error 7.1

Not initializing a constant variable when it's declared is a compilation error.

Common Programming Error 7.2

Assigning a value to a constant variable in an executable statement is a compilation error.

```
// Fig. 7.6: fig07_06.cpp
// Using a properly initialized constant variable.
#include <iostream>
using namespace std;
```

Fig. 7.6 | Using a properly initialized constant variable. (Part 1 of 2.)

```

int main()
{
   const int x = 7; // initialized constant variable

   cout << "The value of constant variable x is: " << x << endl;
} // end main
```

```
The value of constant variable x is: 7
```

Fig. 7.6 | Using a properly initialized constant variable. (Part 2 of 2.)

```
// Fig. 7.7: fig07_07.cpp
// A const variable must be initialized.

int main()
{
   const int x; // Error: x must be initialized

   x = 7; // Error: cannot modify a const variable
} // end main
```

Microsoft Visual C++ compiler error message:

```
error C2734: 'x' : const object must be initialized if not extern
error C3892: 'x' : you cannot assign to a variable that is const
```

GNU C++ compiler error message:

```
fig07_07.cpp:6:14: error: uninitialized const ‘x’ [-fpermissive]
fig07_07.cpp:8:8: error: assignment of read-only variable ‘x’
```

LLVM compiler error message:

```
Default initialization of an object of const type 'const int'
```

Fig. 7.7 | A `const` variable must be initialized.

In Fig. 7.7, the compilation error produced by Microsoft Visual C++ refers to the `int` variable `x` as a "`const` object." The C++ standard defines an "object" as any "region of storage." Like class objects, fundamental-type variables also occupy space in memory, so they're often referred to as "objects."

Constant variables can be placed anywhere a constant expression is expected. In Fig. 7.5, constant variable `arraySize` specifies the size of `array` `s` in line 13.

7.4.4 Summing the Elements of an array

Often, the elements of an `array` represent a series of values to be used in a calculation. For example, if the elements of an `array` represent exam grades, a professor may wish to total the elements of the `array` and use that sum to calculate the class average for the exam.

The program in Fig. 7.8 sums the values contained in the four-element integer `array` `a`. The program declares, creates and initializes the `array` in line 10. The `for` statement (lines 14–15) performs the calculations. The values being supplied as initializers for `array` `a` also could be read into the program from the user at the keyboard, or from a file on disk (see Chapter 14, File Processing). For example, the `for` statement

```
for ( size_t j = 0; j < a.size(); ++j )
   cin >> a[ j ];
```

reads one value at a time from the keyboard and stores the value in element `a[j]`.

```
1  // Fig. 7.8: fig07_08.cpp
2  // Computing the sum of the elements of an array.
3  #include <iostream>
4  #include <array>
5  using namespace std;
6
7  int main()
8  {
9     const size_t arraySize = 4; // specifies size of array
10    array< int, arraySize > a = { 10, 20, 30, 40 };
11    int total = 0;
12
13    // sum contents of array a
14    for ( size_t i = 0; i < a.size(); ++i )
15       total += a[ i ];
16
17    cout << "Total of array elements: " << total << endl;
18 } // end main
```

```
Total of array elements: 100
```

Fig. 7.8 | Computing the sum of the elements of an `array`.

7.4.5 Using Bar Charts to Display array Data Graphically

Many programs present data to users in a graphical manner. For example, numeric values are often displayed as bars in a bar chart. In such a chart, longer bars represent proportionally larger numeric values. One simple way to display numeric data graphically is with a bar chart that shows each numeric value as a bar of asterisks (*).

Professors often like to examine grade distributions on an exam. A professor might graph the number of grades in each of several categories to visualize the grade distribution. Suppose the grades were 87, 68, 94, 100, 83, 78, 85, 91, 76 and 87. There was one grade of 100, two grades in the 90s, four grades in the 80s, two grades in the 70s, one grade in the 60s and no grades below 60. Our next program (Fig. 7.9) stores this data in an `array` of 11 elements, each corresponding to a grade category. For example, `n[0]` indicates the number of grades in the range 0–9, `n[7]` indicates the number of grades in the range 70–79 and `n[10]` indicates the number of grades of 100. The `GradeBook` versions in Figs. 7.15–7.16 and Figs. 7.22–7.23 contain code that calculates these grade frequencies based on a set of grades. For now, we manually create the `array` by looking at the set of grades.

```
1  // Fig. 7.9: fig07_09.cpp
2  // Bar chart printing program.
3  #include <iostream>
4  #include <iomanip>
5  #include <array>
6  using namespace std;
7
8  int main()
9  {
10    const size_t arraySize = 11;
11    array< unsigned int, arraySize > n =
12       { 0, 0, 0, 0, 0, 0, 1, 2, 4, 2, 1 };
13
14    cout << "Grade distribution:" << endl;
15
16    // for each element of array n, output a bar of the chart
17    for ( size_t i = 0; i < n.size(); ++i )
18    {
19       // output bar labels ("0-9:", ..., "90-99:", "100:" )
20       if ( 0 == i )
21          cout << "  0-9: ";
22       else if ( 10 == i )
23          cout << "  100: ";
24       else
25          cout << i * 10 << "-" << ( i * 10 ) + 9 << ": ";
26
27       // print bar of asterisks
28       for ( unsigned int stars = 0; stars < n[ i ]; ++stars )
29          cout << '*';
30
31       cout << endl; // start a new line of output
32    } // end outer for
33 } // end main
```

```
Grade distribution:
  0-9:
10-19:
20-29:
30-39:
40-49:
50-59:
60-69: *
70-79: **
80-89: ****
90-99: **
  100: *
```

Fig. 7.9 | Bar chart printing program.

The program reads the numbers from the array and graphs the information as a bar chart, displaying each grade range followed by a bar of asterisks indicating the number of grades in that range. To label each bar, lines 20–25 output a grade range (e.g., "70-79: ") based on the current value of counter variable i. The *nested* for statement (lines 28–29) outputs the bars. Note the loop-continuation condition in line 28 (`stars < n[i]`). Each time the program reaches the *inner* `for`, the loop counts from `0` up to `n[i]`, thus using a value in `array n` to determine the number of asterisks to display. In this example, `n[0]`–`n[5]` contain zeros because no students received a grade below 60. Thus, the program displays no asterisks next to the first six grade ranges.

7.4.6 Using the Elements of an array as Counters

Sometimes, programs use counter variables to summarize data, such as the results of a survey. In Fig. 6.8, we used separate counters in our die-rolling program to track the number of occurrences of each side of a die as the program rolled the die 6,000,000 times. An `array` version of this program is shown in Fig. 7.10. This version also uses the new C++11 random-number generation capabilities that were introduced in Section 6.8.

Figure 7.10 uses the `array frequency` (line 18) to count the occurrences of each side of the die. *The single statement in line 22 of this program replaces the* `switch` *statement in lines 23–45 of Fig. 6.8.* Line 22 uses a random value to determine which `frequency` element to increment during each iteration of the loop. The calculation in line 22 produces a random subscript from 1 to 6, so `array frequency` must be large enough to store six counters. However, we use a seven-element `array` in which we ignore `frequency[0]`—it's clearer to have the die face value 1 increment `frequency[1]` than `frequency[0]`. Thus, each face value is used directly as a subscript for `array frequency`. We also replace lines 49–54 of Fig. 6.8 by looping through `array frequency` to output the results (Fig. 7.10, lines 27–29).

```
1  // Fig. 7.10: fig07_10.cpp
2  // Die-rolling program using an array instead of switch.
3  #include <iostream>
4  #include <iomanip>
5  #include <array>
6  #include <random>
7  #include <ctime>
8  using namespace std;
9
10 int main()
11 {
12    // use the default random-number generation engine to
13    // produce uniformly distributed pseudorandom int values from 1 to 6
14    default_random_engine engine( static_cast< unsigned int >( time(0) ) );
15    uniform_int_distribution< unsigned int > randomInt( 1, 6 );
16
17    const size_t arraySize = 7; // ignore element zero
18    array< unsigned int, arraySize > frequency = {}; // initialize to 0s
19
20    // roll die 6,000,000 times; use die value as frequency index
21    for ( unsigned int roll = 1; roll <= 6000000; ++roll )
22       ++frequency[ randomInt( engine ) ];
23
24    cout << "Face" << setw( 13 ) << "Frequency" << endl;
25
```

Fig. 7.10 | Die-rolling program using an `array` instead of `switch`. (Part 1 of 2.)

```
      // output each array element's value
      for ( size_t face = 1; face < frequency.size(); ++face )
         cout << setw( 4 ) << face << setw( 13 ) << frequency[ face ]
            << endl;
} // end main
```

```
Face    Frequency
   1      1000167
   2      1000149
   3      1000152
   4       998748
   5       999626
   6      1001158
```

Fig. 7.10 | Die-rolling program using an array instead of switch. (Part 2 of 2.)

7.4.7 Using arrays to Summarize Survey Results

Our next example uses arrays to summarize the results of data collected in a survey. Consider the following problem statement:

> *Twenty students were asked to rate on a scale of 1 to 5 the quality of the food in the student cafeteria, with 1 being "awful" and 5 being "excellent." Place the 20 responses in an integer array and determine the frequency of each rating.*

This is a popular type of array-processing application (Fig. 7.11). We wish to summarize the number of responses of each type (that is, 1–5). The array responses (lines 15–16) is a 20-element integer array of the students' responses to the survey. The array responses is declared const, as its values do not (and should not) change. We use a six-element array frequency (line 19) to count the number of occurrences of each response. Each element of the array is used as a counter for one of the survey responses and is initialized to zero. As in Fig. 7.10, we ignore frequency[0].

```
1  // Fig. 7.11: fig07_11.cpp
2  // Poll analysis program.
3  #include <iostream>
4  #include <iomanip>
5  #include <array>
6  using namespace std;
7
8  int main()
9  {
10    // define array sizes
11    const size_t responseSize = 20; // size of array responses
12    const size_t frequencySize = 6; // size of array frequency
13
14    // place survey responses in array responses
15    const array< unsigned int, responseSize > responses =
16       { 1, 2, 5, 4, 3, 5, 2, 1, 3, 1, 4, 3, 3, 3, 2, 3, 3, 2, 2, 5 };
17
```

Fig. 7.11 | Poll analysis program. (Part 1 of 2.)

```
18      // initialize frequency counters to 0
19      array< unsigned int, frequencySize > frequency = {};
20
21      // for each answer, select responses element and use that value
22      // as frequency subscript to determine element to increment
23      for ( size_t answer = 0; answer < responses.size(); ++answer )
24         ++frequency[ responses[ answer ] ];
25
26      cout << "Rating" << setw( 17 ) << "Frequency" << endl;
27
28      // output each array element's value
29      for ( size_t rating = 1; rating < frequency.size(); ++rating )
30         cout << setw( 6 ) << rating << setw( 17 ) << frequency[ rating ]
31            << endl;
32   } // end main
```

```
Rating          Frequency
     1                  3
     2                  5
     3                  7
     4                  2
     5                  3
```

Fig. 7.11 | Poll analysis program. (Part 2 of 2.)

The first for statement (lines 23–24) takes the responses one at a time from the array responses and increments one of the five counters in the frequency array (frequency[1] to frequency[5]). The key statement in the loop is line 24, which increments the appropriate frequency counter, depending on the value of responses[answer].

Let's consider several iterations of the for loop. When control variable answer is 0, the value of responses[answer] is the value of responses[0] (i.e., 1 in line 16), so the program interprets ++frequency[responses[answer]] as

```
++frequency[ 1 ]
```

which increments the value in array element 1. To evaluate the expression, start with the value in the *innermost* set of square brackets (answer). Once you know answer's value (which is the value of the loop control variable in line 23), plug it into the expression and evaluate the expression in the next outer set of square brackets (i.e., responses[answer], which is a value selected from the responses array in lines 15–16). Then use the resulting value as the subscript for the frequency array to specify which counter to increment.

When answer is 1, responses[answer] is the value of responses[1], which is 2, so the program interprets ++frequency[responses[answer]] as

```
++frequency[ 2 ]
```

which increments array element 2.

When answer is 2, responses[answer] is the value of responses[2], which is 5, so the program interprets ++frequency[responses[answer]] as

```
++frequency[ 5 ]
```

which increments array element 5, and so on. Regardless of the number of responses processed in the survey, the program requires *only* a six-element array (ignoring element zero) to summarize the results, because all the response values are between 1 and 5 and the subscript values for an six-element array are 0 through 5.

Bounds Checking for **array** *Subscripts*
If the data in responses contained an invalid value, such as 13, the program would have attempted to add 1 to frequency[13], which is *outside* the bounds of the array. *When you use the [] operator to access an* array *element, C++ provides no automatic* array ***bounds checking*** *to prevent you from referring to an element that does not exist.* Thus, an executing program can "walk off" either end of an array without warning. In Section 7.10, we demonstrate the class template vector's at function, which performs bounds checking for you. Class template array also has an at function.

It's important to ensure that every subscript you use to access an array element is within the array's bounds—that is, greater than or equal to 0 and less than the number of array elements.

Allowing programs to read from or write to array elements outside the bounds of arrays are common *security flaws*. Reading from out-of-bounds array elements can cause a program to crash or even appear to execute correctly while using bad data. Writing to an out-of-bounds element (known as a *buffer overflow*) can corrupt a program's data in memory, crash a program and allow attackers to exploit the system and execute their own code. For more information on buffer overflows, see en.wikipedia.org/wiki/Buffer_overflow.

Common Programming Error 7.3

Referring to an element outside the array *bounds is an* execution-time *logic error. It isn't a syntax error.*

Error-Prevention Tip 7.1

When looping through an array*, the index should never go below 0 and should always be less than the total number of* array *elements (one less than the size of the* array*). Make sure that the loop-termination condition prevents accessing elements outside this range. In Chapters 15–16, you'll learn about iterators, which can help prevent accessing elements outside an* array*'s (or other container's) bounds.*

7.4.8 Static Local arrays and Automatic Local arrays

Chapter 6 discussed the storage-class specifier static. A static local variable in a function definition exists for the program's duration but is visible *only* in the function's body.

Performance Tip 7.1

We can apply static *to a local* array *declaration so that it's* not *created and initialized each time the program calls the function and is* not *destroyed each time the function terminates. This can improve performance, especially when using large* arrays.

A program initializes static local arrays when their declarations are first encountered. If a static array is not initialized explicitly by you, each element of that array is initialized to *zero* by the compiler when the array is created. Recall that C++ does *not* perform such default initialization for automatic variables.

Figure 7.12 demonstrates function staticArrayInit (lines 24–40) with a static local array (line 27) and function automaticArrayInit (lines 43–59) with an automatic local array (line 46).

```
1  // Fig. 7.12: fig07_12.cpp
2  // static array initialization and automatic array initialization.
3  #include <iostream>
4  #include <array>
5  using namespace std;
6
7  void staticArrayInit(); // function prototype
8  void automaticArrayInit(); // function prototype
9  const size_t arraySize = 3;
10
11 int main()
12 {
13    cout << "First call to each function:\n";
14    staticArrayInit();
15    automaticArrayInit();
16
17    cout << "\n\nSecond call to each function:\n";
18    staticArrayInit();
19    automaticArrayInit();
20    cout << endl;
21 } // end main
22
23 // function to demonstrate a static local array
24 void staticArrayInit( void )
25 {
26    // initializes elements to 0 first time function is called
27    static array< int, arraySize > array1; // static local array
28
29    cout << "\nValues on entering staticArrayInit:\n";
30
31    // output contents of array1
32    for ( size_t i = 0; i < array1.size(); ++i )
33       cout << "array1[" << i << "] = " << array1[ i ] << "  ";
34
35    cout << "\nValues on exiting staticArrayInit:\n";
36
37    // modify and output contents of array1
38    for ( size_t j = 0; j < array1.size(); ++j )
39       cout << "array1[" << j << "] = " << ( array1[ j ] += 5 ) << "  ";
40 } // end function staticArrayInit
41
42 // function to demonstrate an automatic local array
43 void automaticArrayInit( void )
44 {
45    // initializes elements each time function is called
46    array< int, arraySize > array2 = { 1, 2, 3 }; // automatic local array
47
48    cout << "\n\nValues on entering automaticArrayInit:\n";
```

Fig. 7.12 | static array initialization and automatic array initialization. (Part 1 of 2.)

```
49
50      // output contents of array2
51      for ( size_t i = 0; i < array2.size(); ++i )
52         cout << "array2[" << i << "] = " << array2[ i ] << "  ";
53
54      cout << "\nValues on exiting automaticArrayInit:\n";
55
56      // modify and output contents of array2
57      for ( size_t j = 0; j < array2.size(); ++j )
58         cout << "array2[" << j << "] = " << ( array2[ j ] += 5 ) << "  ";
59   } // end function automaticArrayInit
```

```
First call to each function:

Values on entering staticArrayInit:
array1[0] = 0  array1[1] = 0  array1[2] = 0
Values on exiting staticArrayInit:
array1[0] = 5  array1[1] = 5  array1[2] = 5

Values on entering automaticArrayInit:
array2[0] = 1  array2[1] = 2  array2[2] = 3
Values on exiting automaticArrayInit:
array2[0] = 6  array2[1] = 7  array2[2] = 8

Second call to each function:

Values on entering staticArrayInit:
array1[0] = 5  array1[1] = 5  array1[2] = 5
Values on exiting staticArrayInit:
array1[0] = 10  array1[1] = 10  array1[2] = 10

Values on entering automaticArrayInit:
array2[0] = 1  array2[1] = 2  array2[2] = 3
Values on exiting automaticArrayInit:
array2[0] = 6  array2[1] = 7  array2[2] = 8
```

Fig. 7.12 | static array initialization and automatic array initialization. (Part 2 of 2.)

Function staticArrayInit is called twice (lines 14 and 18). The static local array1 is *initialized to zero* by the compiler the first time the function is called. The function prints the array, adds 5 to each element and prints the array again. The second time the function is called, the static array contains the *modified* values stored during the first function call.

Function automaticArrayInit also is called twice (lines 15 and 19). Automatic local array2's elements are initialized (line 46) with the values 1, 2 and 3. The function prints the array, adds 5 to each element and prints the array again. The second time the function is called, the array elements are *reinitialized* to 1, 2 and 3. The array has *automatic storage duration*, so the array is recreated and reinitialized during each call to automaticArrayInit.

7.5 Range-Based for Statement

As we've shown, it's common to process *all* the elements of an array. The new C++11 **range-based for statement** allows you to do this *without using a counter*, thus avoiding the possibility of "stepping outside" the array and eliminating the need for you to implement your own bounds checking.

Error-Prevention Tip 7.2

When processing all elements of an array, if you don't need access to an array element's subscript, use the range-based for statement.

The syntax of a range-based for statement is:

```
for ( rangeVariableDeclaration : expression )
    statement
```

where *rangeVariableDeclaration* has a type and an identifier (e.g., `int item`), and *expression* is the array through which to iterate. The type in the *rangeVariableDeclaration* must be *consistent* with the type of the array's elements. The identifier represents successive array element values on successive iterations of the loop. You can use the range-based for statement with most of the C++ Standard Library's prebuilt data structures (commonly called *containers*), including classes array and vector.

Figure 7.13 uses the range-based for to display an array's contents (lines 13–14 and 22–23) and to multiply each of the array's element values by 2 (lines 17–18).

```
1  // Fig. 7.13: fig07_13.cpp
2  // Using range-based for to multiply an array's elements by 2.
3  #include <iostream>
4  #include <array>
5  using namespace std;
6
7  int main()
8  {
9     array< int, 5 > items = { 1, 2, 3, 4, 5 };
10
11    // display items before modification
12    cout << "items before modification: ";
13    for ( int item : items )
14       cout << item << " ";
15
16    // multiply the elements of items by 2
17    for ( int &itemRef : items )
18       itemRef *= 2;
19
20    // display items after modification
21    cout << "\nitems after modification: ";
22    for ( int item : items )
23       cout << item << " ";
24
25    cout << endl;
26 } // end main
```

```
items before modification: 1 2 3 4 5
items after modification: 2 4 6 8 10
```

Fig. 7.13 | Using range-based for to multiply an array's elements by 2.

Using the Range-Based for *to Display an* array*'s Contents*

The range-based for statement simplifies the code for iterating through an array. Line 13 can be read as "for each iteration, assign the next element of items to int variable item, then execute the following statement." Thus, for each iteration, identifier item represents one element in items. Lines 13–14 are equivalent to the following counter-controlled repetition:

```
for ( int counter = 0; counter < items.size(); ++counter )
   cout << items[ counter ] << " ";
```

Using the Range-Based for *to Modify an* array*'s Contents*

Lines 17–18 use a range-based for statement to multiply each element of items by 2. In line 17, the *rangeVariableDeclaration* indicates that itemRef is an int *reference* (&). Recall that a reference is an alias for another variable in memory—in this case, one of the array's elements. We use an int reference because items contains int values and we want to *modify* each element's value—because itemRef is declared as a *reference*, any change you make to itemRef *changes* the corresponding element value in the array.

Using an Element's Subscript

The range-based for statement can be used in place of the counter-controlled for statement whenever code looping through an array does *not* require access to the element's subscript. For example, totaling the integers in an array (as in Fig. 7.8) requires access only to the element values—the elements' subscripts are irrelevant. However, if a program must use subscripts for some reason other than simply to loop through an array (e.g., to print a subscript number next to each array element value, as in the examples early in this chapter), you should use the counter-controlled for statement.

7.6 Case Study: Class GradeBook Using an array to Store Grades

This section further evolves class GradeBook, introduced in Chapter 3 and expanded in Chapters 4–6. Recall that this class represents a grade book used by a professor to store and analyze student grades. Previous versions of the class process grades entered by the user, but *do not* maintain the individual grade values in the class's data members. Thus, repeat calculations require the user to reenter the grades. One way to solve this problem would be to store each grade entered in an individual data member of the class. For example, we could create data members grade1, grade2, …, grade10 in class GradeBook to store 10 student grades. However, the code to total the grades and determine the class average would be cumbersome. In this section, we solve this problem by storing grades in an array.

Storing Student Grades in an array *in Class* GradeBook

Figure 7.14 shows the output that summarizes the 10 grades we store in an object of the next version of class GradeBook (Figs. 7.15–7.16), which uses an array of integers to store the grades of 10 students for a single exam. This eliminates the need to repeatedly input the same set of grades. array grades is declared as a data member in line 28 of Fig. 7.15—therefore, each GradeBook object maintains its own set of grades.

```
Welcome to the grade book for
CS101 Introduction to C++ Programming!

The grades are:

Student  1:  87
Student  2:  68
Student  3:  94
Student  4: 100
Student  5:  83
Student  6:  78
Student  7:  85
Student  8:  91
Student  9:  76
Student 10:  87

Class average is 84.90
Lowest grade is 68
Highest grade is 100

Grade distribution:
  0-9:
10-19:
20-29:
30-39:
40-49:
50-59:
60-69: *
70-79: **
80-89: ****
90-99: **
  100: *
```

Fig. 7.14 | Output of the GradeBook example that stores grades in an array.

```
// Fig. 7.15: GradeBook.h
// Definition of class GradeBook that uses an array to store test grades.
// Member functions are defined in GradeBook.cpp
#include <string>
#include <array>

// GradeBook class definition
class GradeBook
{
public:
   // constant -- number of students who took the test
   static const size_t students = 10; // note public data

   // constructor initializes course name and array of grades
   GradeBook( const std::string &, const std::array< int, students > & );

   void setCourseName( const std::string & ); // set the course name
   string getCourseName() const; // retrieve the course name
```

Fig. 7.15 | Definition of class GradeBook that uses an array to store test grades. (Part 1 of 2.)

```
   void displayMessage() const; // display a welcome message
   void processGrades() const; // perform operations on the grade data
   int getMinimum() const; // find the minimum grade for the test
   int getMaximum() const; // find the maximum grade for the test
   double getAverage() const; // determine the average grade for the test
   void outputBarChart() const; // output bar chart of grade distribution
   void outputGrades() const; // output the contents of the grades array
private:
   std::string courseName; // course name for this grade book
   std::array< int, students > grades; // array of student grades
}; // end class GradeBook
```

Fig. 7.15 | Definition of class GradeBook that uses an array to store test grades. (Part 2 of 2.)

```
// Fig. 7.16: GradeBook.cpp
// GradeBook class member functions manipulating
// an array of grades.
#include <iostream>
#include <iomanip>
#include "GradeBook.h" // GradeBook class definition
using namespace std;

// constructor initializes courseName and grades array
GradeBook::GradeBook( const string &name,
   const array< int, students > &gradesArray )
   : courseName( name ), grades( gradesArray )
{
} // end GradeBook constructor

// function to set the course name
void GradeBook::setCourseName( const string &name )
{
   courseName = name; // store the course name
} // end function setCourseName

// function to retrieve the course name
string GradeBook::getCourseName() const
{
   return courseName;
} // end function getCourseName

// display a welcome message to the GradeBook user
void GradeBook::displayMessage() const
{
   // this statement calls getCourseName to get the
   // name of the course this GradeBook represents
   cout << "Welcome to the grade book for\n" << getCourseName() << "!"
      << endl;
} // end function displayMessage

```

Fig. 7.16 | GradeBook class member functions manipulating an array of grades. (Part 1 of 3.)

```
// perform various operations on the data
void GradeBook::processGrades() const
{
   // output grades array
   outputGrades();

   // call function getAverage to calculate the average grade
   cout << setprecision( 2 ) << fixed;
   cout << "\nClass average is " << getAverage() << endl;

   // call functions getMinimum and getMaximum
   cout << "Lowest grade is " << getMinimum() << "\nHighest grade is "
      << getMaximum() << endl;

   // call function outputBarChart to print grade distribution chart
   outputBarChart();
} // end function processGrades

// find minimum grade
int GradeBook::getMinimum() const
{
   int lowGrade = 100; // assume lowest grade is 100

   // loop through grades array
   for ( int grade : grades )
   {
      // if current grade lower than lowGrade, assign it to lowGrade
      if ( grade < lowGrade )
         lowGrade = grade; // new lowest grade
   } // end for

   return lowGrade; // return lowest grade
} // end function getMinimum

// find maximum grade
int GradeBook::getMaximum() const
{
   int highGrade = 0; // assume highest grade is 0

   // loop through grades array
   for ( int grade : grades )
   {
      // if current grade higher than highGrade, assign it to highGrade
      if ( grade > highGrade )
         highGrade = grade; // new highest grade
   } // end for

   return highGrade; // return highest grade
} // end function getMaximum

// determine average grade for test
double GradeBook::getAverage() const
{
```

Fig. 7.16 | GradeBook class member functions manipulating an array of grades. (Part 2 of 3.)

```
   int total = 0; // initialize total

   // sum grades in array
   for ( int grade : grades )
      total += grade;

   // return average of grades
   return static_cast< double >( total ) / grades.size();
} // end function getAverage

// output bar chart displaying grade distribution
void GradeBook::outputBarChart() const
{
   cout << "\nGrade distribution:" << endl;

   // stores frequency of grades in each range of 10 grades
   const size_t frequencySize = 11;
   array< unsigned int, frequencySize > frequency = {}; // init to 0s

   // for each grade, increment the appropriate frequency
   for ( int grade : grades )
      ++frequency[ grade / 10 ];

   // for each grade frequency, print bar in chart
   for ( size_t count = 0; count < frequencySize; ++count )
   {
      // output bar labels ("0-9:", ..., "90-99:", "100:" )
      if ( 0 == count )
         cout << "  0-9: ";
      else if ( 10 == count )
         cout << "  100: ";
      else
         cout << count * 10 << "-" << ( count * 10 ) + 9 << ": ";

      // print bar of asterisks
      for ( unsigned int stars = 0; stars < frequency[ count ]; ++stars )
         cout << '*';

      cout << endl; // start a new line of output
   } // end outer for
} // end function outputBarChart

// output the contents of the grades array
void GradeBook::outputGrades() const
{
   cout << "\nThe grades are:\n\n";

   // output each student's grade
   for ( size_t student = 0; student < grades.size(); ++student )
      cout << "Student " << setw( 2 ) << student + 1 << ": " << setw( 3 )
         << grades[ student ] << endl;
} // end function outputGrades
```

Fig. 7.16 | GradeBook class member functions manipulating an array of grades. (Part 3 of 3.)

The size of the array in line 28 of Fig. 7.15 is specified by public static const data member students (declared in line 12), which is public so that it's accessible to the class's clients. We'll soon see an example of a client program using this constant. Declaring students with the const qualifier indicates that this data member is constant—its value cannot be changed after being initialized.

Keyword static in this variable declaration indicates that the data member is *shared by all objects of the class*—so in this particular implementation of class GradeBook, all GradeBook objects store grades for the same number of students. Recall from Section 3.4 that when each object of a class maintains its own copy of an attribute, the variable that represents the attribute is known as a data member—each object (instance) of the class has a *separate copy* of the variable in memory. There are variables for which each object of a class does *not* have a separate copy. That is the case with **static data members**, which are also known as **class variables**. When objects of a class containing static data members are created, all the objects share one copy of the class's static data members. A static data member can be accessed within the class definition and the member-function definitions like any other data member. As you'll soon see, a public static data member can also be accessed outside of the class, *even when no objects of the class exist*, using the class name followed by the scope resolution operator (::) and the name of the data member. You'll learn more about static data members in Chapter 9.

Constructor

The class's constructor (declared in line 15 of Fig. 7.15 and defined in lines 10–14 of Fig. 7.16) has two parameters—the course name and a reference to an array of grades. When a program creates a GradeBook object (e.g., line 15 of Fig. 7.17), the program passes an existing int array to the constructor, which copies the array's values into the data member grades (line 12 of Fig. 7.16). The grade values in the passed array could have been input from a user or read from a file on disk (as we discuss in Chapter 14, File Processing). In our test program, we simply initialize an array with a set of grade values (Fig. 7.17, lines 11–12). Once the grades are stored in data member grades of class GradeBook, all the class's member functions can access the grades array as needed to perform various calculations. Note that the constructor receives both the string and the array by reference—this is more efficient than receiving copies of the original string and array. The constructor does not need to modify either the original string or array, so we also declared each parameter as const to ensure that the constructor does not accidentally modify the originald data in the caller. We also modified function setCourseName to receive its string argument by reference.

Member Function **processGrades**

Member function processGrades (declared in line 20 of Fig. 7.15 and defined in lines 38–53 of Fig. 7.16) contains a series of member function calls that output a report summarizing the grades. Line 41 of Fig. 7.16 calls member function outputGrades to print the contents of the array grades. Lines 138–140 in member function outputGrades use a for statement to output each student's grade. Although array indices start at 0, a professor would typically number students starting at 1. Thus, lines 139–140 output student + 1 as the student number to produce grade labels "Student 1: ", "Student 2: ", and so on.

Member Function getAverage

Member function processGrades next calls member function getAverage (line 45) to obtain the average of the grades. Member function getAverage (declared in line 23 of Fig. 7.15 and defined in lines 88–98 of Fig. 7.16) totals the values in array grades before calculating the average. The averaging calculation in line 97 uses grades.size() to determine the number of grades being averaged.

Member Functions getMinimum *and* getMaximum

Lines 48–49 in processGrades call member functions getMinimum and getMaximum to determine the lowest and highest grades of any student on the exam, respectively. Let's examine how member function getMinimum finds the *lowest* grade. Because the highest grade allowed is 100, we begin by assuming that 100 is the lowest grade (line 58). Then, we compare each of the elements in the array to the lowest grade, looking for smaller values. Lines 61–66 in member function getMinimum loop through the array, and line 64 compares each grade to lowGrade. If a grade is less than lowGrade, lowGrade is set to that grade. When line 68 executes, lowGrade contains the lowest grade in the array. Member function getMaximum (lines 72–85) works similarly to member function getMinimum.

Member Function outputBarChart

Finally, line 52 in member function processGrades calls member function outputBarChart to print a distribution chart of the grade data using a technique similar to that in Fig. 7.9. In that example, we manually calculated the number of grades in each category (i.e., 0–9, 10–19, …, 90–99 and 100) by simply looking at a set of grades. In this example, lines 110–111 use a technique similar to that in Fig. 7.10 and Fig. 7.11 to calculate the frequency of grades in each category. Line 107 of Fig. 7.16 declares and creates array frequency of 11 unsigned ints to store the frequency of grades in each grade category. For each grade in array grades, lines 110–111 increment the appropriate element of the frequency array. To determine which element to increment, line 111 divides the current grade by 10 using integer division. For example, if grade is 85, line 111 increments frequency[8] to update the count of grades in the range 80–89. Lines 114–129 next print the bar chart (see Fig. 7.17) based on the values in array frequency. Like lines 28–29 of Fig. 7.9, lines 125–126 of Fig. 7.16 use a value in array frequency to determine the number of asterisks to display in each bar.

Testing Class GradeBook

The program of Fig. 7.17 creates an object of class GradeBook (Figs. 7.15–7.16) using the int array grades (declared and initialized in lines 11–12). The scope resolution operator (::) is used in the expression "GradeBook::students" (line 11) to access class GradeBook's static constant students. We use this constant here to create an array that's the same size as the array stored as a data member in class GradeBook. Line 13 declares a string representing the course name. Line 15 passes the course name and the array of grades to the GradeBook constructor. Line 16 displays a welcome message, and line 17 invokes the GradeBook object's processGrades member function.

```
// Fig. 7.17: fig07_17.cpp
// Creates GradeBook object using an array of grades.
#include <array>
#include "GradeBook.h" // GradeBook class definition
using namespace std;

// function main begins program execution
int main()
{
   // array of student grades
   const array< int, GradeBook::students > grades =
      { 87, 68, 94, 100, 83, 78, 85, 91, 76, 87 };
   string courseName = "CS101 Introduction to C++ Programming";

   GradeBook myGradeBook( courseName, grades );
   myGradeBook.displayMessage();
   myGradeBook.processGrades();
} // end main
```

Fig. 7.17 | Creates a `GradeBook` object' using an `array` of grades, then invokes member function `processGrades` to analyze them.

7.7 Sorting and Searching arrays

In this section, we use the built-in C++ Standard Library **sort** function to arrange the elements in an `array` into ascending order and the built-in **binary_search** function to determine whether a value is in the `array`.

Sorting

Sorting data—placing it into ascending or descending order—is one of the most important computing applications. A bank sorts all checks by account number so that it can prepare individual bank statements at the end of each month. Telephone companies sort their phone directories by last name; and within all entries with the *same* last name, sorting those by first name to make it easy to find phone numbers. Virtually every organization must sort some data and, in many cases, massive amounts of it. Sorting data is an intriguing problem that has attracted some of the most intense research efforts in the field of computer science.

Searching

Often it may be necessary to determine whether an `array` contains a value that matches a certain **key value**. The process of finding a particular element of an `array` is called **searching**.

Demonstrating Functions `sort` *and* `binary_search`

Figure 7.18 begins by creating an unsorted `array` of `string`s (lines 13–14) and displaying the contents of the `array` (lines 17–19). Next, line 21 uses C++ Standard Library function `sort` to sort the elements of the `array` `colors` into ascending order. The `sort` function's arguments specify the range of elements that should be sorted—in this case, the entire array. We'll discuss the complete details of class template array's begin and end functions in later chapters. As you'll see, function sort can be used to sort the elements of several different types of data structures. Lines 24–26 display the contents of the sorted array.

Lines 29 and 34 demonstrate use binary_search to determine whether a value is in the array. The sequence of values must be sorted in ascending order first—binary_search does *not* verify this for you. The function's first two arguments represent the range of elements to search and the third is the *search key*—the value to locate in the array. The function returns a bool indicating whether the value was found. In Chapter 16, we'll use a C++ Standard function find to obtain the location of the search key in an array.

```
1  // Fig. 7.18: fig07_18.cpp
2  // Sorting and searching arrays.
3  #include <iostream>
4  #include <iomanip>
5  #include <array>
6  #include <string>
7  #include <algorithm> // contains sort and binary_search
8  using namespace std;
9
10 int main()
11 {
12    const size_t arraySize = 7; // size of array colors
13    array< string, arraySize > colors = { "red", "orange", "yellow",
14       "green", "blue", "indigo", "violet" };
15
16    // output original array
17    cout << "Unsorted array:\n";
18    for ( string color : colors )
19       cout << color << " ";
20
21    sort( colors.begin(), colors.end() ); // sort contents of colors
22
23    // output sorted array
24    cout << "\nSorted array:\n";
25    for ( string item : colors )
26       cout << item << " ";
27
28    // search for "indigo" in colors
29    bool found = binary_search( colors.begin(), colors.end(), "indigo" );
30    cout << "\n\n\"indigo\" " << ( found ? "was" : "was not" )
31       << " found in colors" << endl;
32
33    // search for "cyan" in colors
34    found = binary_search( colors.begin(), colors.end(), "cyan" );
35    cout << "\"cyan\" " << ( found ? "was" : "was not" )
36       << " found in colors" << endl;
37 } // end main
```

Fig. 7.18 | Sorting and searching arrays. (Part 1 of 2.)

```
Unsorted array:
red orange yellow green blue indigo violet
Sorted array:
blue green indigo orange red violet yellow

"indigo" was found in colors
"cyan" was not found in colors
```

Fig. 7.18 | Sorting and searching arrays. (Part 2 of 2.)

7.8 Multidimensional arrays

You can use arrays with two dimensions (i.e., subscripts) to represent **tables of values** consisting of information arranged in **rows** and **columns**. To identify a particular table element, we must specify two subscripts—by convention, the first identifies the element's *row* and the second identifies the element's *column*. arrays that require two subscripts to identify a particular element are called **two-dimensional arrays** or **2-D arrays**. arrays with two or more dimensions are known as **multidimensional arrays** and can have more than two dimensions. Figure 7.19 illustrates a two-dimensional array, a. The array contains three rows and four columns, so it's said to be a 3-by-4 array. In general, an array with *m* rows and *n* columns is called an ***m*-by-*n* array**.

	Column 0	Column 1	Column 2	Column 3
Row 0	a[0][0]	a[0][1]	a[0][2]	a[0][3]
Row 1	a[1][0]	a[1][1]	a[1][2]	a[1][3]
Row 2	a[2][0]	a[2][1]	a[2][2]	a[2][3]

Column subscript
Row subscript
array name

Fig. 7.19 | Two-dimensional array with three rows and four columns.

Every element in array a is identified in Fig. 7.19 by an element name of the form a[i][j], where a is the name of the array, and i and j are the subscripts that uniquely identify each element in a. Notice that the names of the elements in row 0 all have a first subscript of 0; the names of the elements in column 3 all have a second subscript of 3.

Common Programming Error 7.4

Referencing a two-dimensional array element a[x][y] incorrectly as a[x, y] is an error. Actually, a[x, y] is treated as a[y], because C++ evaluates the expression x, y (containing a comma operator) simply as y (the last *of the comma-separated expressions).*

Figure 7.20 demonstrates initializing two-dimensional arrays in declarations. Lines 13–14 each declare an arrays of arrays with two rows and three columns. Notice the nested array type declaration. In each array, the type of its elements is specified as

```
array< int, columns >
```

indicating that each array contains as its elements three-element arrays of int values—the constant columns has the value 3.

```
1  // Fig. 7.20: fig07_20.cpp
2  // Initializing multidimensional arrays.
3  #include <iostream>
4  #include <array>
5  using namespace std;
6
7  const size_t rows = 2;
8  const size_t columns = 3;
9  void printArray( const array< array< int, columns >, rows> & );
10
11 int main()
12 {
13    array< array< int, columns >, rows > array1 = { 1, 2, 3, 4, 5, 6 };
14    array< array< int, columns >, rows > array2 = { 1, 2, 3, 4, 5 };
15
16    cout << "Values in array1 by row are:" << endl;
17    printArray( array1 );
18
19    cout << "\nValues in array2 by row are:" << endl;
20    printArray( array2 );
21 } // end main
22
23 // output array with two rows and three columns
24 void printArray( const array< array< int, columns >, rows> & a )
25 {
26    // loop through array's rows
27    for ( auto const &row : a )
28    {
29       // loop through columns of current row
30       for ( auto const &element : row )
31          cout << element << ' ';
32
33       cout << endl; // start new line of output
34    } // end outer for
35 } // end function printArray
```

```
Values in array1 by row are:
1 2 3
4 5 6

Values in array2 by row are:
1 2 3
4 5 0
```

Fig. 7.20 | Initializing multidimensional arrays.

The declaration of array1 (line 13) provides six initializers. The compiler initializes the elements of row 0 followed by the elements of row 1. So, the first three values initialize row 0's elements to 1, 2 and 3, and the last three initialize row 1's elements to 4, 5 and 6.

The declaration of array2 (line 14) provides only five initializers. The initializers are assigned to row 0, then row 1. Any elements that do not have an explicit initializer are initialized to *zero*, so array2[1][2] is 0.

The program calls function printArray to output each array's elements. Notice that the function prototype (line 9) and definition (lines 24–35) specify that the function receives a two row and three column array. The parameter receives the array by reference and is declared const because the function does not modify the array's elements.

Nested Range-Based for *Statements*

To process the elements of a two-dimensional array, we use a nested loop in which the *outer* loop iterates through the *rows* and the *inner* loop iterates through the *columns* of a given row. Function printArray's nested loop is implemented with range-based for statements. Lines 27 and 30 introduce the C++11 **auto** keyword, which tells the compiler to infer (determine) a variable's data type based on the variable's initializer value. The outer loop's range variable row is initialized with an element from the parameter a. Looking at the array's declaration, you can see that the array contains elements of type

11

```
array< int, columns >
```

so the compiler infers that row refers to a three-element array of int values (again, columns is 3). The const & in row's declaration indicates that the reference *cannot* be used to modify the rows and prevents each row from being *copied* into the range variable. The inner loop's range variable element is initialized with one element of the array represented by row, so the compiler infers that element refers to an int because each row contains three int values. In an IDE, you can typically hover your mouse over a variable declared with auto and the IDE will display the variable's inferred type. Line 31 displays the value from a given row and column.

Nested Counter-Controlled for *Statements*

We could have implemented the nested loop with counter-controlled repetition as follows:

```
for ( size_t row = 0; row < a.size(); ++row )
{
   for ( size_t column = 0; column < a[ row ].size(); ++column )
      cout << a[ row ][ column ] << ' ';

   cout << endl;
} // end outer for
```

Other Common array *Manipulations*

Many common array manipulations use for statements. For example, the following for statement sets all the elements in row 2 of array a in Fig. 7.19 to zero:

```
for ( size_t column = 0; column < 4; ++column )
   a[ 2 ][ column ] = 0;
```

The for statement varies only the second subscript (i.e., the column subscript). The preceding for statement is equivalent to the following assignment statements:

```
a[ 2 ][ 0 ] = 0;
a[ 2 ][ 1 ] = 0;
a[ 2 ][ 2 ] = 0;
a[ 2 ][ 3 ] = 0;
```

The following nested counter-controlled for statement determines the total of *all* the elements in array a in Fig. 7.19:

```
total = 0;

for ( size_t row = 0; row < a.size(); ++row )
   for ( size_t column = 0; column < a[ row ].size(); ++column )
      total += a[ row ][ column ];
```

The for statement totals the elements of the array one row at a time. The outer for statement begins by setting row (i.e., the row subscript) to 0, so the elements of row 0 may be totaled by the inner for statement. The outer for statement then increments row to 1, so the elements of row 1 can be totaled. Then, the outer for statement increments row to 2, so the elements of row 2 can be totaled. When the nested for statement terminates, total contains the sum of all the array elements. This nested loop can be implemented with range-based for statements as:

```
total = 0;

for ( auto row : a ) // for each row
   for ( auto column : row ) // for each column in row
      total += column;
```

7.9 Case Study: Class GradeBook Using a Two-Dimensional array

In Section 7.6, we presented class GradeBook (Figs. 7.15–7.16), which used a one-dimensional array to store student grades on a single exam. In most semesters, students take several exams. Professors are likely to want to analyze grades across the entire semester, both for a single student and for the class as a whole.

Storing Student Grades in a Two-Dimensional **array** *in Class* **GradeBook**

Figure 7.21 shows the output that summarizes 10 students grades on three exams. We store the grades as a two-dimensional array in an object of the next version of class GradeBook Figures 7.22–7.23. Each row of the array represents a single student's grades for the entire course, and each column represents all the grades the students earned for one particular exam. A client program, such as Fig. 7.24, passes the array as an argument to the GradeBook constructor. Since there are 10 students and three exams, we use a ten-by-three array to store the grades.

```
Welcome to the grade book for
CS101 Introduction to C++ Programming!

The grades are:

            Test 1  Test 2  Test 3  Average
Student  1      87      96      70    84.33
Student  2      68      87      90    81.67
Student  3      94     100      90    94.67
```

Fig. 7.21 | Output of GradeBook that uses two-dimensional arrays. (Part 1 of 2.)

```
Student  4     100      81      82    87.67
Student  5      83      65      85    77.67
Student  6      78      87      65    76.67
Student  7      85      75      83    81.00
Student  8      91      94     100    95.00
Student  9      76      72      84    77.33
Student 10      87      93      73    84.33

Lowest grade in the grade book is 65
Highest grade in the grade book is 100

Overall grade distribution:
  0-9:
10-19:
20-29:
30-39:
40-49:
50-59:
60-69: ***
70-79: ******
80-89: ***********
90-99: *******
  100: ***
```

Fig. 7.21 | Output of GradeBook that uses two-dimensional arrays. (Part 2 of 2.)

```
// Fig. 7.22: GradeBook.h
// Definition of class GradeBook that uses a
// two-dimensional array to store test grades.
// Member functions are defined in GradeBook.cpp
#include <array>
#include <string>

// GradeBook class definition
class GradeBook
{
public:
   // constants
   static const size_t students = 10; // number of students
   static const size_t tests = 3; // number of tests

   // constructor initializes course name and array of grades
   GradeBook( const std::string &,
      std::array< std::array< int, tests >, students > & );

   void setCourseName( const std::string & ); // set the course name
   std::string getCourseName() const; // retrieve the course name
   void displayMessage() const; // display a welcome message
   void processGrades() const; // perform operations on the grade data
   int getMinimum() const; // find the minimum grade in the grade book
   int getMaximum() const; // find the maximum grade in the grade book
```

Fig. 7.22 | Definition of class GradeBook that uses a two-dimensional array to store test grades. (Part 1 of 2.)

```
   double getAverage( const std::array< int, tests > & ) const;
   void outputBarChart() const; // output bar chart of grade distribution
   void outputGrades() const; // output the contents of the grades array
private:
   std::string courseName; // course name for this grade book
   std::array< std::array< int, tests >, students > grades; // 2D array
}; // end class GradeBook
```

Fig. 7.22 | Definition of class GradeBook that uses a two-dimensional array to store test grades. (Part 2 of 2.)

```
// Fig. 7.23: GradeBook.cpp
// Member-function definitions for class GradeBook that
// uses a two-dimensional array to store grades.
#include <iostream>
#include <iomanip> // parameterized stream manipulators
using namespace std;

// include definition of class GradeBook from GradeBook.h
#include "GradeBook.h" // GradeBook class definition

// two-argument constructor initializes courseName and grades array
GradeBook::GradeBook( const string &name,
   std::array< std::array< int, tests >, students > &gradesArray )
   : courseName( name ), grades( gradesArray )
{
} // end two-argument GradeBook constructor

// function to set the course name
void GradeBook::setCourseName( const string &name )
{
   courseName = name; // store the course name
} // end function setCourseName

// function to retrieve the course name
string GradeBook::getCourseName() const
{
   return courseName;
} // end function getCourseName

// display a welcome message to the GradeBook user
void GradeBook::displayMessage() const
{
   // this statement calls getCourseName to get the
   // name of the course this GradeBook represents
   cout << "Welcome to the grade book for\n" << getCourseName() << "!"
      << endl;
} // end function displayMessage
```

Fig. 7.23 | Member-function definitions for class GradeBook that uses a two-dimensional array to store grades. (Part 1 of 4.)

```

// perform various operations on the data
void GradeBook::processGrades() const
{
   // output grades array
   outputGrades();

   // call functions getMinimum and getMaximum
   cout << "\nLowest grade in the grade book is " << getMinimum()
      << "\nHighest grade in the grade book is " << getMaximum() << endl;

   // output grade distribution chart of all grades on all tests
   outputBarChart();
} // end function processGrades

// find minimum grade in the entire gradebook
int GradeBook::getMinimum() const
{
   int lowGrade = 100; // assume lowest grade is 100

   // loop through rows of grades array
   for ( auto const &student : grades )
   {
      // loop through columns of current row
      for ( auto const &grade : student )
      {
         // if current grade less than lowGrade, assign it to lowGrade
         if ( grade < lowGrade )
            lowGrade = grade; // new lowest grade
      } // end inner for
   } // end outer for

   return lowGrade; // return lowest grade
} // end function getMinimum

// find maximum grade in the entire gradebook
int GradeBook::getMaximum() const
{
   int highGrade = 0; // assume highest grade is 0

   // loop through rows of grades array
   for ( auto const &student : grades )
   {
      // loop through columns of current row
      for ( auto const &grade : student )
      {
         // if current grade greater than highGrade, assign to highGrade
         if ( grade > highGrade )
            highGrade = grade; // new highest grade
      } // end inner for
   } // end outer for
```

Fig. 7.23 | Member-function definitions for class GradeBook that uses a two-dimensional array to store grades. (Part 2 of 4.)

```

   return highGrade; // return highest grade
} // end function getMaximum

// determine average grade for particular set of grades
double GradeBook::getAverage( const array<int, tests> &setOfGrades ) const
{
   int total = 0; // initialize total

   // sum grades in array
   for ( int grade : setOfGrades )
      total += grade;

   // return average of grades
   return static_cast< double >( total ) / setOfGrades.size();
} // end function getAverage

// output bar chart displaying grade distribution
void GradeBook::outputBarChart() const
{
   cout << "\nOverall grade distribution:" << endl;

   // stores frequency of grades in each range of 10 grades
   const size_t frequencySize = 11;
   array< unsigned int, frequencySize > frequency = {}; // init to 0s

   // for each grade, increment the appropriate frequency
   for ( auto const &student : grades )
      for ( auto const &test : student )
         ++frequency[ test / 10 ];

   // for each grade frequency, print bar in chart
   for ( size_t count = 0; count < frequencySize; ++count )
   {
      // output bar label ("0-9:", ..., "90-99:", "100:" )
      if ( 0 == count )
         cout << "  0-9: ";
      else if ( 10 == count )
         cout << "  100: ";
      else
         cout << count * 10 << "-" << ( count * 10 ) + 9 << ": ";

      // print bar of asterisks
      for ( unsigned int stars = 0; stars < frequency[ count ]; ++stars )
         cout << '*';

      cout << endl; // start a new line of output
   } // end outer for
} // end function outputBarChart

```

Fig. 7.23 | Member-function definitions for class GradeBook that uses a two-dimensional array to store grades. (Part 3 of 4.)

```
139 // output the contents of the grades array
140 void GradeBook::outputGrades() const
141 {
142    cout << "\nThe grades are:\n\n";
143    cout << "            "; // align column heads
144
145    // create a column heading for each of the tests
146    for ( size_t test = 0; test < tests; ++test )
147       cout << "Test " << test + 1 << "  ";
148
149    cout << "Average" << endl; // student average column heading
150
151    // create rows/columns of text representing array grades
152    for ( size_t student = 0; student < grades.size(); ++student )
153    {
154       cout << "Student " << setw( 2 ) << student + 1;
155
156       // output student's grades
157       for ( size_t test = 0; test < grades[ student ].size(); ++test )
158          cout << setw( 8 ) << grades[ student ][ test ];
159
160       // call member function getAverage to calculate student's average;
161       // pass row of grades as the argument
162       double average = getAverage( grades[ student ] );
163       cout << setw( 9 ) << setprecision( 2 ) << fixed << average << endl;
164    } // end outer for
165 } // end function outputGrades
```

Fig. 7.23 | Member-function definitions for class GradeBook that uses a two-dimensional array to store grades. (Part 4 of 4.)

*Overview of Class **GradeBook**'s Functions*

Five member functions (declared in lines 24–28 of Fig. 7.22) perform array manipulations to process the grades. Each of these member functions is similar to its counterpart in the earlier one-dimensional array version of class GradeBook (Figs. 7.15–7.16). Member function getMinimum (defined in lines 54–71 of Fig. 7.23) determines the lowest grade of all students for the semester. Member function getMaximum (defined in lines 74–91 of Fig. 7.23) determines the highest grade of all students for the semester. Member function getAverage (lines 94–104 of Fig. 7.23) determines a particular student's semester average. Member function outputBarChart (lines 107–137 of Fig. 7.23) outputs a bar chart of the distribution of all student grades for the semester. Member function outputGrades (lines 140–165 of Fig. 7.23) outputs the two-dimensional array in a tabular format, along with each student's semester average.

*Functions **getMinimum** and **getMaximum***

Member functions getMinimum, getMaximum, outputBarChart and outputGrades each loop through array grades by using nested range-based for or counter-controlled for statements. For example, consider the nested for statement (lines 59–68) in member function getMinimum. The outer for statement loops through the rows that represent each student and the inner for loops through the grades of a given student. Each grade is compared with variable lowGrade in the body of the inner for statement. If a grade is less than lowGrade, lowGrade is set to that grade. This repeats until all rows and columns of grades have been traversed. When execution of the nested statement is complete, lowGrade contains the smallest grade in the two-dimensional array. Member function getMaximum works similarly to member function getMinimum.

Function outputBarChart

Member function outputBarChart in Fig. 7.23 is nearly identical to the one in Fig. 7.16. However, to output the overall grade distribution for a whole semester, the function uses a nested for statement (lines 116–118) to increment the elements of the one-dimensional array frequency based on all the grades in the two-dimensional array. The rest of the code in each of the two outputBarChart member functions that displays the chart is identical.

Function outputGrades

Member function outputGrades (lines 140–165) uses nested counter-controlled for statements to output values of the array grades, in addition to each student's semester average. The output in Fig. 7.21 shows the result, which resembles the tabular format of a professor's physical grade book. Lines 146–147 print the column headings for each test. We use a counter-controlled for statement so that we can identify each test with a number. Similarly, the for statement in lines 152–164 first outputs a row label using a counter variable to identify each student (line 154). Although array indices start at 0, lines 147 and 154 output test + 1 and student + 1, respectively, to produce test and student numbers starting at 1 (see Fig. 7.21). The inner for statement in lines 157–158 uses the outer for statement's counter variable student to loop through a specific row of array grades and output each student's test grade. Finally, line 162 obtains each student's semester average by passing the current row of grades (i.e., grades[student]) to member function getAverage.

Function getAverage

Member function getAverage (lines 94–104) takes as an argument a one-dimensional array of test results for a particular student. When line 162 calls getAverage, the first argument is grades[student], which specifies that a particular row of the two-dimensional array grades should be passed to getAverage. For example, based on the array created in Fig. 7.24, the argument grades[1] represents the three values (a one-dimensional array of grades) stored in row 1 of the two-dimensional array grades. A two-dimensional array's elements are one-dimensional arrays. Member function getAverage calculates the sum of the array elements, divides the total by the number of test results and returns the floating-point result as a double value (line 103).

Testing Class GradeBook

The program in Fig. 7.24 creates an object of class GradeBook (Figs. 7.22–7.23) using the two-dimensional array of ints named grades (declared and initialized in lines 11–21). Line 11 accesses class GradeBook's static constants students and tests to indicate the size of each dimension of array grades. Lines 23–24 pass a course name and grades to the GradeBook constructor. Lines 25–26 then invoke myGradeBook's displayMessage and processGrades member functions to display a welcome message and obtain a report summarizing the students' grades for the semester, respectively.

```
// Fig. 7.24: fig07_24.cpp
// Creates GradeBook object using a two-dimensional array of grades.
#include <array>
#include "GradeBook.h" // GradeBook class definition
using namespace std;

// function main begins program execution
int main()
{
   // two-dimensional array of student grades
   array< array< int, GradeBook::tests >, GradeBook::students > grades =
      { 87, 96, 70,
        68, 87, 90,
        94, 100, 90,
        100, 81, 82,
        83, 65, 85,
        78, 87, 65,
        85, 75, 83,
        91, 94, 100,
        76, 72, 84,
        87, 93, 73 };

   GradeBook myGradeBook(
      "CS101 Introduction to C++ Programming", grades );
   myGradeBook.displayMessage();
   myGradeBook.processGrades();
} // end main
```

Fig. 7.24 | Creates a GradeBook object using a two-dimensional array of grades, then invokes member function processGrades to analyze them.

7.10 Introduction to C++ Standard Library Class Template vector

We now introduce C++ Standard Library class template **vector**, which is similar to class template array, but also supports dynamic resizing. Except for the features that modify a vector, the other features shown in Fig. 7.25 also work for arrays. Standard class template vector is defined in header <vector> (line 5) and belongs to namespace std. Chapter 15 discusses the full functionality of vector. At the end of this section, we'll demonstrate class vector's bounds checking capabilities and introduce C++'s exception-handling mechanism, which can be used to detect and handle an out-of-bounds vector index.

```
1 // Fig. 7.25: fig07_25.cpp
2 // Demonstrating C++ Standard Library class template vector.
3 #include <iostream>
4 #include <iomanip>
5 #include <vector>
6 #include <stdexcept>
7 using namespace std;
```

Fig. 7.25 | Demonstrating C++ Standard Library class template vector. (Part 1 of 4.)

```

void outputVector( const vector< int > & ); // display the vector
void inputVector( vector< int > & ); // input values into the vector

int main()
{
   vector< int > integers1( 7 ); // 7-element vector< int >
   vector< int > integers2( 10 ); // 10-element vector< int >

   // print integers1 size and contents
   cout << "Size of vector integers1 is " << integers1.size()
      << "\nvector after initialization:" << endl;
   outputVector( integers1 );

   // print integers2 size and contents
   cout << "\nSize of vector integers2 is " << integers2.size()
      << "\nvector after initialization:" << endl;
   outputVector( integers2 );

   // input and print integers1 and integers2
   cout << "\nEnter 17 integers:" << endl;
   inputVector( integers1 );
   inputVector( integers2 );

   cout << "\nAfter input, the vectors contain:\n"
      << "integers1:" << endl;
   outputVector( integers1 );
   cout << "integers2:" << endl;
   outputVector( integers2 );

   // use inequality (!=) operator with vector objects
   cout << "\nEvaluating: integers1 != integers2" << endl;

   if ( integers1 != integers2 )
      cout << "integers1 and integers2 are not equal" << endl;

   // create vector integers3 using integers1 as an
   // initializer; print size and contents
   vector< int > integers3( integers1 ); // copy constructor

   cout << "\nSize of vector integers3 is " << integers3.size()
      << "\nvector after initialization:" << endl;
   outputVector( integers3 );

   // use overloaded assignment (=) operator
   cout << "\nAssigning integers2 to integers1:" << endl;
   integers1 = integers2; // assign integers2 to integers1

   cout << "integers1:" << endl;
   outputVector( integers1 );
   cout << "integers2:" << endl;
   outputVector( integers2 );
```

Fig. 7.25 | Demonstrating C++ Standard Library class template vector. (Part 2 of 4.)

```
   // use equality (==) operator with vector objects
   cout << "\nEvaluating: integers1 == integers2" << endl;

   if ( integers1 == integers2 )
      cout << "integers1 and integers2 are equal" << endl;

   // use square brackets to use the value at location 5 as an rvalue
   cout << "\nintegers1[5] is " << integers1[ 5 ];

   // use square brackets to create lvalue
   cout << "\n\nAssigning 1000 to integers1[5]" << endl;
   integers1[ 5 ] = 1000;
   cout << "integers1:" << endl;
   outputVector( integers1 );

   // attempt to use out-of-range subscript
   try
   {
      cout << "\nAttempt to display integers1.at( 15 )" << endl;
      cout << integers1.at( 15 ) << endl; // ERROR: out of range
   } // end try
   catch ( out_of_range &ex )
   {
      cerr << "An exception occurred: " << ex.what() << endl;
   } // end catch

   // changing the size of a vector
   cout << "\nCurrent integers3 size is: " << integers3.size() << endl;
   integers3.push_back( 1000 ); // add 1000 to the end of the vector
   cout << "New integers3 size is: " << integers3.size() << endl;
   cout << "integers3 now contains: ";
   outputVector( integers3 );
} // end main

// output vector contents
void outputVector( const vector< int > &array )
{
   for ( int item : items )
      cout << item << " ";

   cout << endl;
} // end function outputVector

// input vector contents
void inputVector( vector< int > &array )
{
   for ( int &item : items )
      cin >> item;
} // end function inputVector
```

Fig. 7.25 | Demonstrating C++ Standard Library class template vector. (Part 3 of 4.)

```
Size of vector integers1 is 7
vector after initialization:
0 0 0 0 0 0 0

Size of vector integers2 is 10
vector after initialization:
0 0 0 0 0 0 0 0 0 0

Enter 17 integers:
1 2 3 4 5 6 7 8 9 10 11 12 13 14 15 16 17

After input, the vectors contain:
integers1:
1 2 3 4 5 6 7
integers2:
8 9 10 11 12 13 14 15 16 17

Evaluating: integers1 != integers2
integers1 and integers2 are not equal

Size of vector integers3 is 7
vector after initialization:
1 2 3 4 5 6 7

Assigning integers2 to integers1:
integers1:
8 9 10 11 12 13 14 15 16 17
integers2:
8 9 10 11 12 13 14 15 16 17

Evaluating: integers1 == integers2
integers1 and integers2 are equal

integers1[5] is 13

Assigning 1000 to integers1[5]
integers1:
8 9 10 11 12 1000 14 15 16 17

Attempt to display integers1.at( 15 )
An exception occurred: invalid vector<T> subscript

Current integers3 size is: 7
New integers3 size is: 8
integers3 now contains: 1 2 3 4 5 6 7 1000
```

Fig. 7.25 | Demonstrating C++ Standard Library class template vector. (Part 4 of 4.)

Creating vector *Objects*

Lines 14–15 create two vector objects that store values of type int—integers1 contains seven elements, and integers2 contains 10 elements. By default, all the elements of each vector object are set to 0. Like arrays, vectors can be defined to store most data types, by replacing int in vector<int> with the appropriate type.

vector *Member Function* size*; Function* outputVector

Line 18 uses vector member function **size** to obtain the size (i.e., the number of elements) of integers1. Line 20 passes integers1 to function outputVector (lines 96–102), which uses a range-based for statement to obtain the value in each element of the `vector` for output. As with class template `array`, you can also do this using a counter-controlled loop and the subscript (`[]`) operator. Lines 23 and 25 perform the same tasks for `integers2`.

Function `inputVector`

Lines 29–30 pass `integers1` and `integers2` to function `inputVector` (lines 105–109) to read values for each `vector`'s elements from the user. The function uses a range-based `for` statement with a range variable that is a reference to an `int` to form *lvalues* that are used to store the input values in each `vector` element.

Comparing `vector` *Objects for Inequality*

Line 41 demonstrates that `vector` objects can be compared with one another using the `!=` operator. If the contents of two `vector`s are not equal, the operator returns `true`; otherwise, it returns `false`.

Initializing One `vector` *with the Contents of Another*

The C++ Standard Library class template `vector` allows you to create a new `vector` object that's initialized with the contents of an existing `vector`. Line 46 creates a `vector` object `integers3` and initializes it with a copy of `integers1`. This invokes `vector`'s so-called *copy constructor* to perform the copy operation. You'll learn about copy constructors in detail in Chapter 10. Lines 48–50 output the size and contents of `integers3` to demonstrate that it was initialized correctly.

Assigning `vector`*s and Comparing* `vector`*s for Equality*

Line 54 assigns `integers2` to `integers1`, demonstrating that the assignment (=) operator can be used with `vector` objects. Lines 56–59 output the contents of both objects to show that they now contain identical values. Line 64 then compares `integers1` to `integers2` with the equality (==) operator to determine whether the contents of the two objects are equal after the assignment in line 54 (which they are).

Using the `[]` *Operator to Access and Modify* `vector` *Elements*

Lines 68 and 70 use square brackets (`[]`) to obtain a `vector` element and use it as an *rvalue* and as an *lvalue*, respectively. Recall from Section 5.9 that an *rvalue* cannot be modified, but an *lvalue* can. As is the case with `array`s, *C++ is not required to perform bounds checking when* `vector` *elements are accessed with square brackets.*[1] Therefore, you must ensure that operations using `[]` do not accidentally attempt to manipulate elements outside the bounds of the `vector`. Standard class template `vector` does, however, provide bounds checking in its member function `at` (as does class template `array`), which we use at line 80 and discuss shortly.

Exception Handling: Processing an Out-of-Range Subscript

An **exception** indicates a problem that occurs while a program executes. The name "exception" suggests that the problem occurs infrequently—if the "rule" is that a statement normally executes correctly, then the problem represents the "exception to the rule." **Exception handling** enables you to create **fault-tolerant programs** that can resolve (or

---

1. Some compilers have options for bounds checking to help prevent buffer overflows.

handle) exceptions. In many cases, this allows a program to continue executing as if no problems were encountered. For example, Fig. 7.25 still runs to completion, even though an attempt was made to access an out-of-range subscript. More severe problems might prevent a program from continuing normal execution, instead requiring the program to notify the user of the problem, then terminate. When a function detects a problem, such as an invalid array subscript or an invalid argument, it **throws** an exception—that is, an exception occurs. Here we introduce exception handling briefly. We'll discuss it in detail in Chapter 17, Exception Handling: A Deeper Look.

The `try` *Statement*

To handle an exception, place any code that might throw an exception in a **`try` statement** (lines 77–85). The **`try` block** (lines 77–81) contains the code that might *throw* an exception, and the **`catch` block** (lines 82–85) contains the code that *handles* the exception if one occurs. As you'll see in Chapter 17, you can have many `catch` blocks to handle different types of exceptions that might be thrown in the corresponding `try` block. If the code in the `try` block executes successfully, lines 82–85 are ignored. The braces that delimit `try` and `catch` blocks' bodies are required.

The `vector` member function **`at`** provides bounds checking and throws an exception if its argument is an invalid subscript. By default, this causes a C++ program to terminate. If the subscript is valid, function `at` returns the element at the specified location as a modifiable *lvalue* or a nonmodifiable *lvalue*. A nonmodifiable *lvalue* is an expression that identifies an object in memory (such as an element in a `vector`), but cannot be used to modify that object. If `at` is called on a `const array` or via a reference that's declared `const`, the function returns a nonmodifiable *lvalue*.

Executing the `catch` *Block*

When the program calls `vector` member function `at` with the argument `15` (line 80), the function attempts to access the element at location 15, which is *outside* the `vector`'s bounds—`integers1` has only 10 elements at this point. Because bounds checking is performed at execution time, `vector` member function `at` generates an exception—specifically line 80 throws an **`out_of_range`** exception (from header `<stdexcept>`) to notify the program of this problem. At this point, the `try` block terminates immediately and the `catch` block begins executing—if you declared any variables in the `try` block, they're now out of scope and are not accessible in the `catch` block.

The `catch` block declares a type (`out_of_range`) and an exception parameter (`ex`) that it receives as a reference. The `catch` block can handle exceptions of the specified type. Inside the block, you can use the parameter's identifier to interact with a caught exception object.

`what` *Member Function of the Exception Parameter*

When lines 82–85 *catch* the exception, the program displays a message indicating the problem that occurred. Line 84 calls the exception object's **`what`** member function to get the error message that is stored in the exception object and display it. Once the message is displayed in this example, the exception is considered handled and the program continues with the next statement after the `catch` block's closing brace. In this example, lines 88–92 execute next. We use exception handling again in Chapters 9–12 and Chapter 17 presents a deeper look at exception handling.

Changing the Size of a `vector`

One of the key differences between a `vector` and an `array` is that a `vector` can dynamically grow to accommodate more elements. To demonstrate this, line 88 shows the current size of `integers3`, line 89 calls the `vector`'s **`push_back`** member function to add a new element containing 1000 to the end of the `vector` and line 90 shows the new size of `integers3`. Line 92 then displays `integers3`'s new contents.

C++11: List Initializing a `vector`

Many of the `array` examples in this chapter used list initializers to specify the initial `array` element values. C++11 also allows this for `vector`s (and other C++ Standard Library data structures). At the time of this writing, list initializers were not yet supported for `vector`s in Visual C++.

7.11 Wrap-Up

This chapter explored the use of C++ Standard Library class templates `array` and `vector` to store data in and retrieve data from lists and tables of values. The chapter examples demonstrated how to declare an `array`, initialize an `array` and refer to individual elements of an `array`. We passed `array`s to functions by reference and used the `const` qualifier to prevent the called function from modifying the `array`'s elements, thus enforcing the principle of least privilege. You learned how to use C++11's new range-based `for` statement to manipulate all the elements of an `array`. We also showed how to use C++ Standard Library functions `sort` and `binary_search` to sort and search an `array`, respectively. You learned how to declare and manipulate multidimensional `array`s of `array`s. We used nested counter-controlled and nested range-based `for` statements to iterate through all the rows and columns of a two-dimensional `array`. We also showed how to use `auto` to infer a variable's type based on its initializer value. Finally, we demonstrated the capabilities of C++ Standard Library class template `vector`. In that example, we discussed how to access `array` and `vector` elements with bounds checking and demonstrated basic exception-handling concepts. In later chapters, we'll continue our coverage of data structures.

We've now introduced the basic concepts of classes, objects, control statements, functions and `array` objects. In Chapter 8, we present one of C++'s most powerful features—the pointer. Pointers keep track of where data and functions are stored in memory, which allows us to manipulate those items in interesting ways. As you'll see, C++ also provides a language element called an array (different from the class template `array`) that is closely related to pointers. In contemporary C++ code, its considered better practice to use C++11's `array` class template rather than traditional arrays.

8

Pointers

Objectives

In this chapter you'll:

- Learn what pointers are.
- Learn the similarities and differences between pointers and references.
- Use pointers to pass arguments to functions by reference.
- Understand the close relationships between pointers and built-in arrays.
- Use pointer-based strings.
- Use built-in arrays.
- Use C++11 capabilities, including `nullptr` and Standard Library functions `begin` and `end`.

Outline

8.1 Introduction

This chapter discusses *pointers*—one of the most powerful, yet challenging to use, C++ capabilities. Our goals here are to help you determine when it's appropriate to use pointers, and show how to use them *correctly* and *responsibly*.

In Chapter 6, we saw that references can be used to perform pass-by-reference. Pointers also enable pass-by-reference and can be used to create and manipulate dynamic data structures that can grow and shrink, such as linked lists, queues, stacks and trees. This chapter explains basic pointer concepts.

We also show the intimate relationship among *built-in arrays* and pointers. C++ inherited built-in arrays from the C programming language. As we saw in Chapter 7, the C++ Standard Library classes `array` and `vector` provide implementations of arrays as full-fledged objects—in fact, `array` and `vector` each store their elements in built-in arrays. *In new software development projects, you should favor* `array` *and* `vector` *objects to built-in arrays.*

Similarly, C++ actually offers two types of strings—`string` class objects (which we've been using since Chapter 3) and *C-style, pointer-based strings* (*C strings*). This chapter briefly introduces C strings to deepen your knowledge of pointers and built-in arrays. C strings were widely used in older C and C++ software. We discuss C strings in depth in Appendix F. *In new software development projects, you should favor* `string` *class objects.*

We'll examine the use of pointers with class objects in Chapter 12, where we'll see that the so-called "polymorphic processing" associated with object-oriented programming is performed with pointers and references.

8.2 Pointer Variable Declarations and Initialization

Indirection

Pointer variables contain *memory addresses* as their values. Normally, a variable *directly* contains a specific value. A pointer contains the *memory address* of a variable that, in turn, contains a specific value. In this sense, a variable name **directly references a value**, and a pointer **indirectly references a value** (Fig. 8.1). Referencing a value through a pointer is called **indirection**. Diagrams typically represent a pointer as an *arrow* from the *variable that contains an address* to the *variable located at that address* in memory.

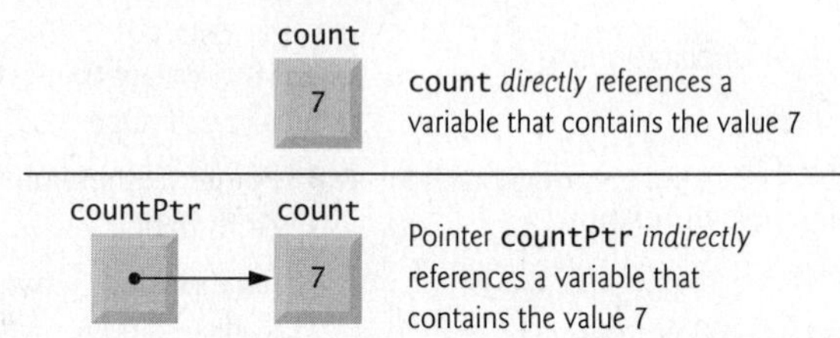

Fig. 8.1 | Directly and indirectly referencing a variable.

Declaring Pointers

Pointers, like any other variables, must be declared *before* they can be used. For example, for the pointer `countPtr` in Fig. 8.1, the declaration

```
int *countPtr, count;
```

declares the variable `countPtr` to be of type `int *` (i.e., a pointer to an `int` value) and is read (*right to left*), "`countPtr` is a pointer to `int`." Also, variable `count` in the preceding declaration is declared to be an `int`, *not* a pointer to an `int`. The `*` in the declaration applies *only* to `countPtr`. Each variable being declared as a pointer *must* be preceded by an asterisk (`*`). For example, the declaration

```
double *xPtr, *yPtr;
```

indicates that both `xPtr` and `yPtr` are pointers to `double` values. When `*` appears in a declaration, it's *not* an operator; rather, it indicates that the variable being declared is a pointer. Pointers can be declared to point to objects of *any* data type.

Common Programming Error 8.1

Assuming that the `*` used to declare a pointer distributes to all names in a declaration's comma-separated list of variables can lead to errors. Each pointer must be declared with the `*` prefixed to the name (with or without spaces in between). Declaring only one variable per declaration helps avoid these types of errors and improves program readability.

Good Programming Practice 8.1

Although it's not a requirement, including the letters `Ptr` in a pointer variable name makes it clear that the variable is a pointer and that it must be handled accordingly.

Initializing Pointers

Pointers should be initialized to **`nullptr`** (new in C++11) or an address of the corresponding type either when they're declared or in an assignment. A pointer with the value `nullptr` "points to nothing" and is known as a **null pointer**. From this point forward, when we refer to a "null pointer" we mean a pointer with the value `nullptr`.

Error-Prevention Tip 8.1

Initialize all pointers to prevent pointing to unknown or uninitialized areas of memory.

Null Pointers Prior to C++11

In earlier versions of C++, the value specified for a null pointer was `0` or `NULL`. `NULL` is defined in several standard library headers to represent the value `0`. Initializing a pointer to `NULL` is equivalent to initializing a pointer to `0`, but prior to C++11, `0` was used by convention. The value `0` is the *only* integer value that can be assigned directly to a pointer variable without first *casting* the integer to a pointer type.

8.3 Pointer Operators

Address (&) Operator

The **address operator (&)** is a unary operator that *obtains the memory address of its operand.* For example, assuming the declarations

```
int y = 5; // declare variable y
int *yPtr = nullptr; // declare pointer variable yPtr
```

the statement

```
yPtr = &y; // assign address of y to yPtr
```

assigns the address of the variable `y` to pointer variable `yPtr`. Then variable `yPtr` is said to "point to" `y`. Now, `yPtr` *indirectly* references variable `y`'s value. The use of the `&` in the preceding statement is *not* the same as the use of the `&` in a *reference variable declaration*, which is *always* preceded by a data-type name. When declaring a reference, the `&` is part of the type. In an expression like `&y`, the `&` is the *address operator.*

Figure 8.2 shows a representation of memory after the preceding assignment. The "pointing relationship" is indicated by drawing an arrow from the box that represents the pointer `yPtr` in memory to the box that represents the variable `y` in memory.

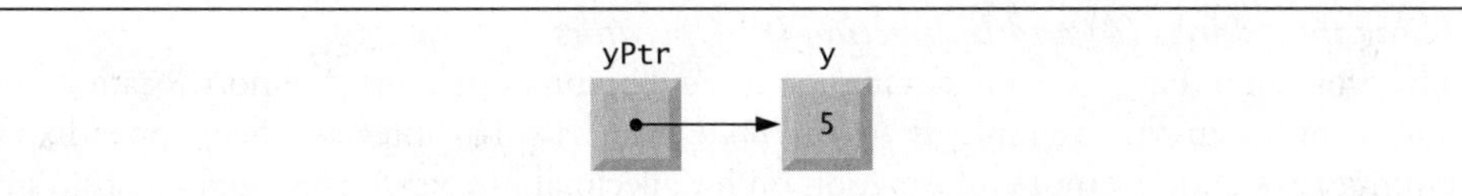

Fig. 8.2 | Graphical representation of a pointer pointing to a variable in memory.

Figure 8.3 shows another pointer representation in memory with integer variable `y` stored at memory location `600000` and pointer variable `yPtr` stored at location `500000`. The operand of the address operator must be an *lvalue*—the address operator *cannot* be applied to constants or to expressions that result in temporary values (like the results of calculations).

yPtr
location 500000
600000
y
location 600000
5

Fig. 8.3 | Representation of `y` and `yPtr` in memory.

Indirection (*) Operator

The unary * **operator**—commonly referred to as the **indirection operator** or **dereferencing operator**—*returns an lvalue representing the object to which its pointer operand points.* For example (referring again to Fig. 8.2), the statement

```
cout << *yPtr << endl;
```

displays the value of variable y, namely, 5, just as the statement

```
cout << y << endl;
```

would. Using * in this manner is called **dereferencing a pointer**. A *dereferenced pointer* may also be used on the *left* side of an assignment statement, as in

```
*yPtr = 9;
```

which would assign 9 to y in Fig. 8.3. The *dereferenced pointer* may also be used to receive an input value as in

```
cin >> *yPtr;
```

which places the input value in y.

Common Programming Error 8.2

Dereferencing an uninitialized pointer results in undefined behavior that could cause a fatal execution-time error. This could also lead to accidentally modifying important data, allowing the program to run to completion, possibly with incorrect results.

Error-Prevention Tip 8.2

Dereferencing a null pointer results in undefined behavior and typically is a fatal execution-time error, so you should ensure that a pointer is not null before *dereferencing it.*

Using the Address (&) and Indirection (*) Operators

The program in Fig. 8.4 demonstrates the & and * pointer operators. Memory locations are output by << in this example as *hexadecimal* (i.e., base-16) integers. (See Appendix D, Number Systems, for more information on hexadecimal integers.) The memory addresses output by this program are *platform dependent*, so you may get different results when you run the program. The address of a (line 11) and the value of aPtr (line 12) are identical in the output, confirming that the address of a is indeed assigned to the pointer variable aPtr.

```
1  // Fig. 8.4: fig08_04.cpp
2  // Pointer operators & and *.
3  #include <iostream>
4  using namespace std;
5
6  int main()
7  {
8     int a = 7; // assigned 7 to a
9     int *aPtr = &a; // initialize aPtr with the address of int variable a
10
```

Fig. 8.4 | Pointer operators & and *. (Part 1 of 2.)

```
   cout << "The address of a is " << &a
      << "\nThe value of aPtr is " << aPtr;
   cout << "\n\nThe value of a is " << a
      << "\nThe value of *aPtr is " << *aPtr << endl;
} // end main
```

```
The address of a is 002DFD80
The value of aPtr is 002DFD80

The value of a is 7
The value of *aPtr is 7
```

Fig. 8.4 | Pointer operators & and *. (Part 2 of 2.)

Precedence and Associativity of the Operators Discussed So Far

Figure 8.5 lists the precedence and associativity of the operators introduced to this point. The address (&) and dereferencing operator (*) are *unary operators* on the fourth level.

Operators	Associativity	Type
`::` `()`	left to right *[See caution in Fig. 2.7 regarding grouping parentheses.]*	primary
`()` `[]` `++` `--` static_cast<*type*>(*operand*)	left to right	postfix
`++` `--` `+` `-` `!` `&` `*`	right to left	unary (prefix)
`*` `/` `%`	left to right	multiplicative
`+` `-`	left to right	additive
<< >>	left to right	insertion/extraction
< <= > >=	left to right	relational
`==` `!=`	left to right	equality
`&&`	left to right	logical AND
||	left to right	logical OR
`?:`	right to left	conditional
`=` `+=` `-=` `*=` `/=` `%=`	right to left	assignment
`,`	left to right	comma

Fig. 8.5 | Operator precedence and associativity of the operators discussed so far.

8.4 Pass-by-Reference with Pointers

There are three ways in C++ to pass arguments to a function—pass-by-value, pass-by-reference with reference arguments and **pass-by-reference with pointer arguments**. Chapter 6 compared and contrasted pass-by-reference with reference arguments and pass-by-value. Here, we explain pass-by-reference with pointer arguments.

Chapter 6 showed that `return` can return *one value* from a called function or simply return *control*. You also learned that arguments can be passed to a function using reference parameters, which enable the called function to *modify the original values of the arguments in the caller.* Reference parameters also enable programs to pass *large data objects* to a function and avoid the overhead of passing the objects by value (which, of course, copies the object). Pointers, like references, also can be used to modify one or more variables in the caller or to pass pointers to large data objects to avoid the overhead of passing the objects by value.

You can use pointers and the indirection operator (*) to accomplish pass-by-reference (exactly as pass-by-reference is done in C programs—C does not have references). When calling a function with an argument that should be modified, the *address* of the argument is passed. This is normally accomplished by applying the address operator (&) to the name of the variable whose value will be modified.

An Example of Pass-By-Value

Figure 8.6 and Fig. 8.7 present two versions of a function that cubes an integer. Figure 8.6 passes variable `number` *by value* (line 14) to function `cubeByValue` (lines 19–22), which cubes its argument and passes the new value back to `main` using a `return` statement (line 21). The new value is assigned to `number` (line 14) in `main`. The calling function has the opportunity to examine the function call's result *before* modifying variable `number`'s value. For example, we could have stored the result of `cubeByValue` in another variable, examined its value and assigned the result to `number` only after determining that the returned value was reasonable.

```
1  // Fig. 8.6: fig08_06.cpp
2  // Pass-by-value used to cube a variable's value.
3  #include <iostream>
4  using namespace std;
5
6  int cubeByValue( int ); // prototype
7
8  int main()
9  {
10    int number = 5;
11
12    cout << "The original value of number is " << number;
13
14    number = cubeByValue( number ); // pass number by value to cubeByValue
15    cout << "\nThe new value of number is " << number << endl;
16 } // end main
17
18 // calculate and return cube of integer argument
19 int cubeByValue( int n )
20 {
21    return n * n * n; // cube local variable n and return result
22 } // end function cubeByValue
```

```
The original value of number is 5
The new value of number is 125
```

Fig. 8.6 | Pass-by-value used to cube a variable's value.

An Example of Pass-By-Reference with Pointers

Figure 8.7 passes the variable `number` to function `cubeByReference` using *pass-by-reference with a pointer argument* (line 15)—the *address* of `number` is passed to the function. Function `cubeByReference` (lines 21–24) specifies parameter `nPtr` (a pointer to `int`) to receive its argument. The function *uses the dereferenced pointer* to cube the value to which `nPtr` points (line 23). This *directly* changes the value of `number` in `main` (line 11). Line 23 is equivalent to

```
*nPtr = (*nPtr) * (*nPtr) * (*nPtr); // cube *nPtr
```

```
1  // Fig. 8.7: fig08_07.cpp
2  // Pass-by-reference with a pointer argument used to cube a
3  // variable's value.
4  #include <iostream>
5  using namespace std;
6
7  void cubeByReference( int * ); // prototype
8
9  int main()
10 {
11    int number = 5;
12
13    cout << "The original value of number is " << number;
14
15    cubeByReference( &number ); // pass number address to cubeByReference
16
17    cout << "\nThe new value of number is " << number << endl;
18 } // end main
19
20 // calculate cube of *nPtr; modifies variable number in main
21 void cubeByReference( int *nPtr )
22 {
23    *nPtr = *nPtr * *nPtr * *nPtr; // cube *nPtr
24 } // end function cubeByReference
```

```
The original value of number is 5
The new value of number is 125
```

Fig. 8.7 | Pass-by-reference with a pointer argument used to cube a variable's value.

A function receiving an *address* as an argument must define a *pointer parameter* to *receive* the address. For example, the header for function `cubeByReference` (line 21) specifies that `cubeByReference` receives the address of an `int` variable (i.e., a pointer to an `int`) as an argument, stores the address in `nPtr` and does *not* return a value.

Function `cubeByReference`'s prototype (line 7) contains `int *` in parentheses. As with other types, it isn't necessary to include the *names* of pointer parameters in prototypes. Parameter names included for documentation purposes are *ignored* by the compiler.

Insight: All Arguments Are Passed By Value

In C++, *all* arguments are *always* passed by value. Passing a variable by reference with a pointer *does not actually pass anything by reference*—a pointer to that variable is *passed by value* and is *copied* into the function's corresponding pointer parameter. The called function can then access that variable in the caller simply by dereferencing the pointer, thus accomplishing *pass-by-reference.*

Graphical Analysis of Pass-By-Value and Pass-By-Reference

Figures 8.8–8.9 analyze graphically the execution of Fig. 8.6 and Fig. 8.7, respectively. In the diagrams, the values in rectangles above a given expression or variable represent the value of that expression or variable. Each diagram's right column shows functions `cubeByValue` (Fig. 8.6) and `cubeByReference` (Fig. 8.7) *only* when they're executing.

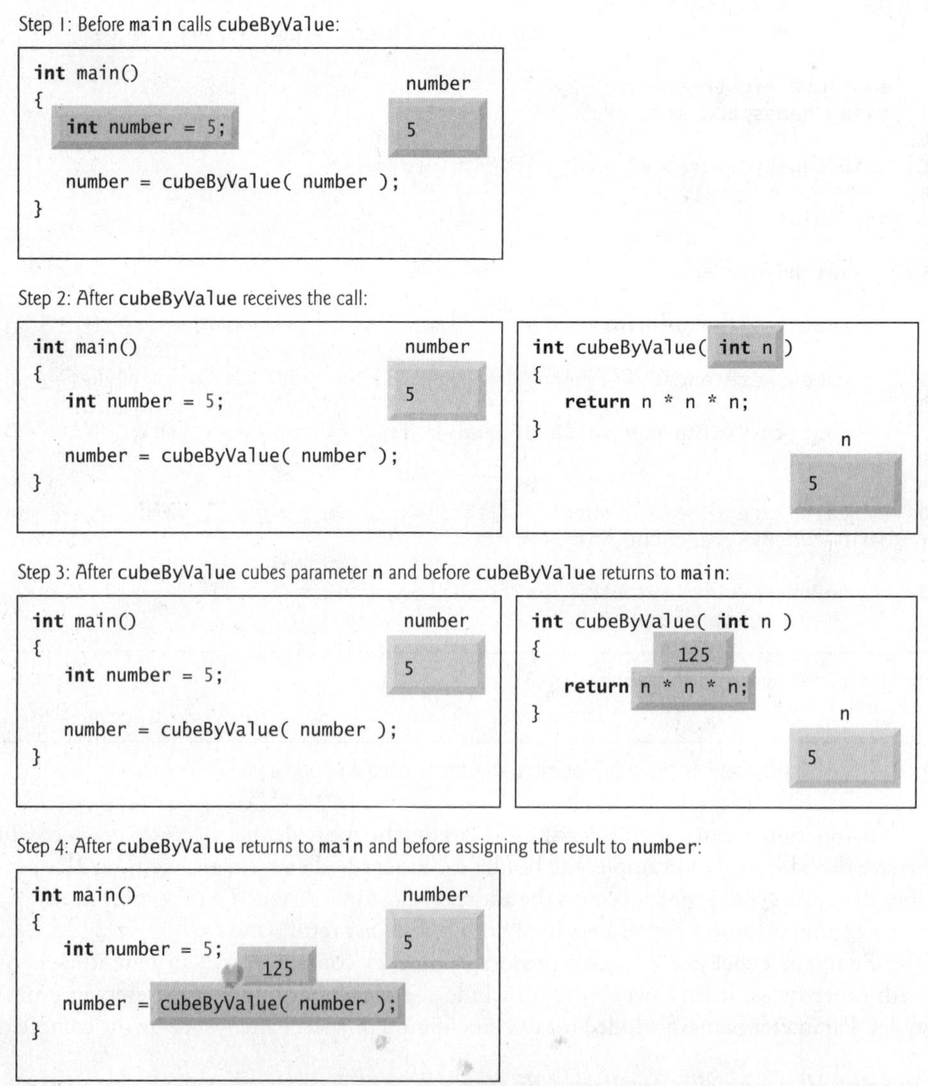

Step 1: Before `main` calls `cubeByValue`:

```
int main()                          number
{
   int number = 5;                     5

   number = cubeByValue( number );
}
```

Step 2: After `cubeByValue` receives the call:

```
int main()                          number
{
   int number = 5;                     5

   number = cubeByValue( number );
}
```

```
int cubeByValue( int n )
{
   return n * n * n;
}
                          n
                          5
```

Step 3: After `cubeByValue` cubes parameter `n` and before `cubeByValue` returns to `main`:

```
int main()                          number
{
   int number = 5;                     5

   number = cubeByValue( number );
}
```

```
int cubeByValue( int n )
{            125
   return n * n * n;
}
                          n
                          5
```

Step 4: After `cubeByValue` returns to `main` and before assigning the result to `number`:

```
int main()                          number
{
   int number = 5;                     5
               125
   number = cubeByValue( number );
}
```

Fig. 8.8 | Pass-by-value analysis of the program of Fig. 8.6. (Part 1 of 2.)

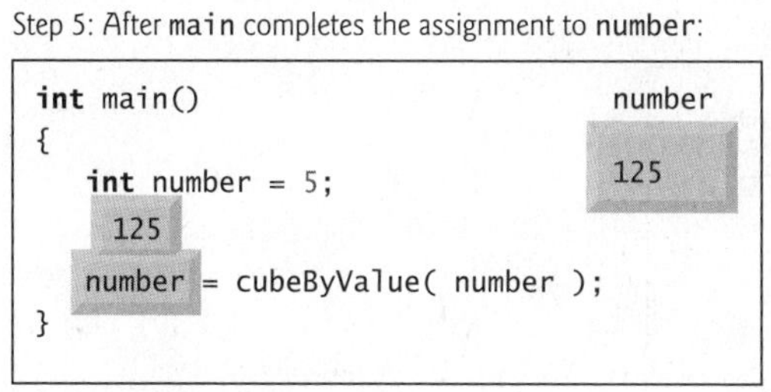

Step 5: After `main` completes the assignment to `number`:

```
int main()                                  number
{                                           125
   int number = 5;
   125
   number = cubeByValue( number );
}
```

Fig. 8.8 | Pass-by-value analysis of the program of Fig. 8.6. (Part 2 of 2.)

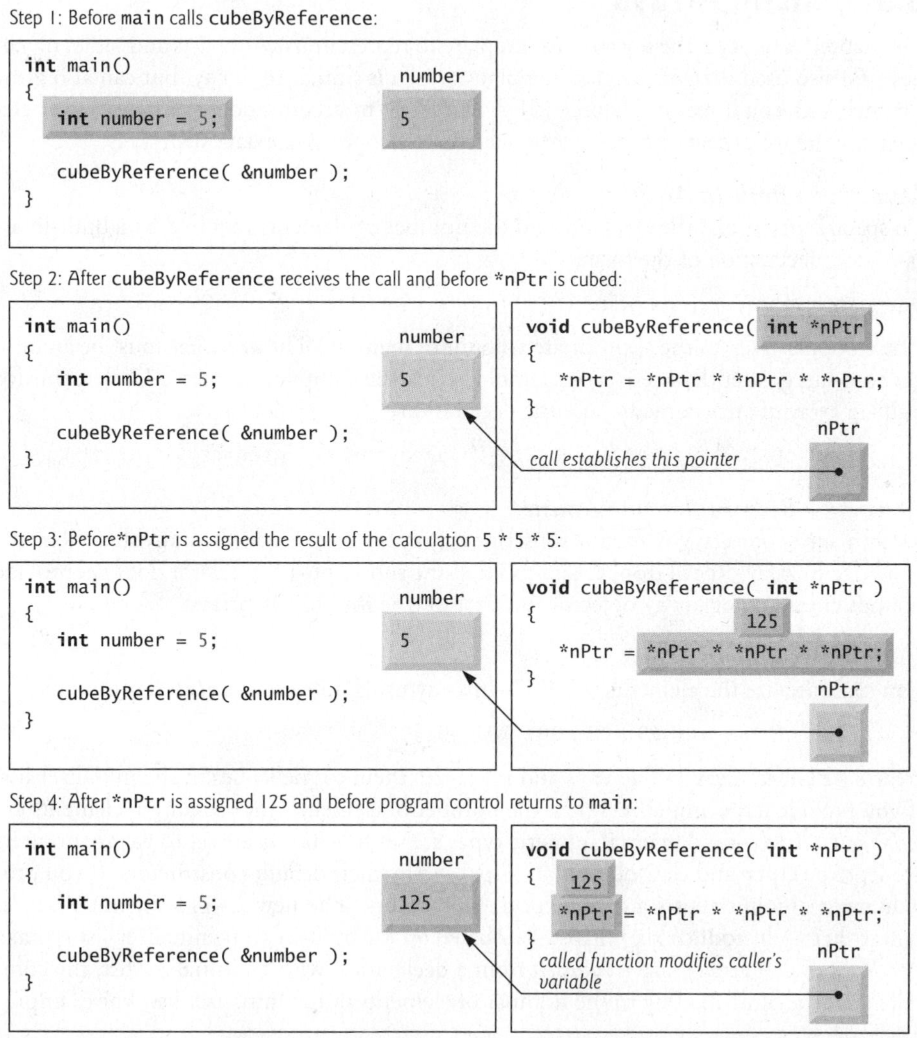

Step 1: Before `main` calls `cubeByReference`:

```
int main()                                  number
{                                           5
   int number = 5;

   cubeByReference( &number );
}
```

Step 2: After `cubeByReference` receives the call and before `*nPtr` is cubed:

```
int main()                          number      void cubeByReference( int *nPtr )
{                                   5           {
   int number = 5;                                 *nPtr = *nPtr * *nPtr * *nPtr;
                                                }
   cubeByReference( &number );                                              nPtr
}                                               call establishes this pointer
```

Step 3: Before`*nPtr` is assigned the result of the calculation 5 * 5 * 5:

```
int main()                          number      void cubeByReference( int *nPtr )
{                                   5           {                 125
   int number = 5;                                 *nPtr = *nPtr * *nPtr * *nPtr;
                                                }
   cubeByReference( &number );                                              nPtr
}
```

Step 4: After `*nPtr` is assigned 125 and before program control returns to `main`:

```
int main()                          number      void cubeByReference( int *nPtr )
{                                   125         {  125
   int number = 5;                                 *nPtr = *nPtr * *nPtr * *nPtr;
                                                }
   cubeByReference( &number );                  called function modifies caller's   nPtr
}                                               variable
```

Fig. 8.9 | Pass-by-reference analysis of the program of Fig. 8.7. (Part 1 of 2.)

Step 5: After `cubeByReference` returns to `main`:

```
int main()
{
   int number = 5;

   cubeByReference( &number );
}
```


Fig. 8.9 | Pass-by-reference analysis of the program of Fig. 8.7. (Part 2 of 2.)

8.5 Built-In Arrays

In Chapter 7, we used the `array` class template to represent *fixed-size* lists and tables of values. We also used the `vector` class template, which is similar to `array`, but can also grow (or shrink as you'll see in Chapter 15) dynamically to accommodate more or fewer elements. Here we present *built-in arrays,* which are also *fixed-size* data structures.

Declaring a Built-In Array

To specify the type of the elements and the number of elements required by a built-in array, use a declaration of the form:

```
type arrayName[ arraySize ];
```

The compiler reserves the appropriate amount of memory. The *arraySize* must be an integer constant greater than zero. For example, to tell the compiler to reserve 12 elements for built-in array of `int`s named `c`, use the declaration

```
int c[ 12 ]; // c is a built-in array of 12 integers
```

Accessing a Built-In Array's Elements

As with `array` objects, you use the subscript (`[]`) operator to access the individual elements of a built-in array. Recall from Chapter 7 that the subscript (`[]`) operator does *not* provide bounds checking for `array` objects—this is also true for built-in arrays.

Initializing Built-In Arrays

You can initialize the elements of a built-in array using an *initializer list.* For example,

```
int n[ 5 ] = { 50, 20, 30, 10, 40 };
```

creates a built-in array of five `int`s and initializes them to the values in the initializer list. If you provide fewer initializers than the number of elements, the remaining elements are *value initialized*—fundamental numeric types are set to `0`, `bool`s are set to `false`, pointers are set to `nullptr` and class objects are initialized by their default constructors. If you provide too many initializers a compilation error occurs. The new C++11 list-initialization syntax that we introduced in Chapter 4 is based on the built-in array initializer-list syntax.

If a built-in array's size is *omitted* from a declaration with an initializer list, the compiler sizes the built-in array to the number of elements in the initializer list. For example,

```
int n[] = { 50, 20, 30, 10, 40 };
```

creates a five-element `array`.

Error-Prevention Tip 8.3

Always specify a built-in array's size, even when providing an initializer list. This enables the compiler to ensure that you do not provide too many initializers.

Passing Built-In Arrays to Functions

The value of a built-in array's name is implicitly convertible to the address of the built-in array's first element. So `arrayName` is implicitly convertible to `&arrayName[0]`. For this reason, you don't need to take the address (&) of a built-in array to pass it to a function—you simply pass the built-in array's name. As you saw in Section 8.4, a function that receives a pointer to a variable in the caller can *modify* that variable in the caller. For built-in arrays, this means that the called function can modify *all* the elements of a built-in array in the caller—unless the function precedes the corresponding built-in array parameter with `const` to indicate that the elements should *not* be modified.

Software Engineering Observation 8.1

Applying the `const` *type qualifier to a built-in array parameter in a function definition to prevent the original built-in array from being modified in the function body is another example of the principle of least privilege. Functions should not be given the capability to modify a built-in array unless it's absolutely necessary.*

Declaring Built-In Array Parameters

You can declare a built-in array parameter in a function header, as follows:

```
int sumElements( const int values[], const size_t numberOfElements )
```

which indicates that the function's first argument should be a one-dimensional built-in array of `int`s that should *not* be modified by the function. Unlike `array` objects, built-in arrays don't know their own size, so a function that processes a built-in array should have parameters to receive both the built-in array *and* its size.

The preceding header can also be written as:

```
int sumElements( const int *values, const size_t numberOfElements )
```

The compiler does not differentiate between a function that receives a pointer and a function that receives a built-in array. This, of course, means that the function must "know" when it's receiving a built-in array or simply a single variable that's being passed by reference. When the compiler encounters a function parameter for a one-dimensional built-in array of the form `const int values[]`, the compiler converts the parameter to the pointer notation `const int *values` (that is, "`values` is a pointer to an integer constant"). These forms of declaring a one-dimensional built-in array parameter are interchangeable—for *clarity* you should use the `[]` notation when the function expects a built-in array argument.

C++11: Standard Library Functions `begin` *and* `end`

In Section 7.7, we showed how to sort an `array` object with the C++ Standard Library function `sort`. We sorted an `array` of `string`s called `colors` as follows:

```
sort( colors.begin(), colors.end() ); // sort contents of colors
```

The `array` class's `begin` and `end` functions specified that the entire `array` should be sorted. Function `sort` (and many other C++ Standard Library functions) can also be applied to built-in arrays. For example, to sort the built-in array `n` shown earlier in this section, you can write:

```
sort( begin( n ), end( n ) ); // sort contents of built-in array n
```

C++11's new **`begin`** and **`end`** functions (from header `<iterator>`) each receive a built-in array as an argument and return a pointer that can be used to represent ranges of elements to process in C++ Standard Library functions like `sort`.

Built-In Array Limitations

Built-in arrays have several limitations:

- They *cannot be compared* using the relational and equality operators—you must use a loop to compare two built-in arrays element by element.
- They *cannot be assigned* to one another.
- They *don't know their own size*—a function that processes a built-in array typically receives *both* the built-in array's *name* and its *size* as arguments.
- They *don't provide automatic bounds checking*—you must ensure that array-access expressions use subscripts that are within the built-in array's bounds.

Objects of class templates `array` and `vector` are safer, more robust and provide more capabilities than built-in arrays.

Sometimes Built-In Arrays Are Required

In contemporary C++ code, you should use the more robust `array` (or `vector`) objects to represent lists and tables of values. However, there are cases in which built-in arrays *must* be used, such as processing a program's **command-line arguments**. You supply command-line arguments to a program by placing them after the program's name when executing it from the command line. Such arguments typically pass options to a program. For example, on a Windows computer, the command

```
dir /p
```

uses the `/p` argument to list the contents of the current directory, pausing after each screen of information. Similarly, on Linux or OS X, the following command uses the `-la` argument to list the contents of the current directory with details about each file and directory:

```
ls -la
```

Command-line arguments are passed to `main` as a built-in array of pointer-based strings (Section 8.10). Appendix F shows how to process command-line arguments.

8.6 Using `const` with Pointers

Recall that `const` enables you to inform the compiler that the value of a particular variable should *not* be modified. Many possibilities exist for using (or *not* using) `const` with function parameters, so how do you choose the most appropriate? Let the *principle of least privilege* be your guide. Always give a function *enough* access to the data in its parameters to accomplish its specified task, *but no more*. This section discusses how to combine const with pointer declarations to enforce the principle of least privilege.

Chapter 6 explained that when an argument is passed by value, a *copy* of the argument is passed to the function. If the copy is *modified* in the *called* function, the original value in the caller *does not change*. In some instances, even the copy of the argument's value should *not* be altered in the called function.

Consider a function that takes a pointer to the initial element of a built-in array and the array's size as arguments and subsequently displays the built-in array's elements. Such a function should loop through the elements and output each individually. The built-in array's size is used in the function's body to determine the highest subscript so the loop can terminate when the displaying completes. The size does not need to change in the function body, so it should be declared const to *ensure* that it will not change. Because the built-in array is only being displayed, it, too, should be declared const. This is especially important because built-in arrays are *always* passed by reference and could easily be changed in the called function. An attempt to modify a const value is a *compilation* error.

Software Engineering Observation 8.2

If a value does not (or should not) change in the body of a function to which it's passed, the parameter should be declared const.

Error-Prevention Tip 8.4

Before using a function, check its function prototype to determine the parameters that it can and cannot modify.

There are four ways to pass a pointer to a function: a *nonconstant pointer to nonconstant data*, a *nonconstant pointer to constant data* (Fig. 8.10), a *constant pointer to nonconstant data* (Fig. 8.11) and a *constant pointer to constant data* (Fig. 8.12). Each combination provides a different level of access privilege.

8.6.1 Nonconstant Pointer to Nonconstant Data

The highest access is granted by a **nonconstant pointer to nonconstant data**—the *data can be modified* through the dereferenced pointer, and the *pointer can be modified* to point to other data. Such a pointer's declaration (e.g., int *countPtr) does *not* include const.

8.6.2 Nonconstant Pointer to Constant Data

A **nonconstant pointer to constant data** is a pointer that can be modified to point to *any* data item of the appropriate type, but the data to which it points *cannot* be modified through that pointer. Such a pointer might be used to *receive* a built-in array argument to a function that should be allowed to read the elements, but *not* modify them. Any attempt to modify the data in the function results in a compilation error. The declaration for such a pointer places const to the *left* of the pointer's type, as in

```
const int *countPtr;
```

The declaration is read from *right to left* as "countPtr is a pointer to an integer *constant*" or more precisely, "countPtr is a *non-constant* pointer to an integer *constant*."

Figure 8.10 demonstrates GNU C++'s compilation error message produced when attempting to compile a function that receives a *nonconstant pointer* to *constant data*, then tries to use that pointer to modify the data.

```
// Fig. 8.10: fig08_10.cpp
// Attempting to modify data through a
// nonconstant pointer to constant data.

void f( const int * ); // prototype

int main()
{
   int y = 0;

   f( &y ); // f will attempt an illegal modification
} // end main

// constant variable cannot be modified through xPtr
void f( const int *xPtr )
{
   *xPtr = 100; // error: cannot modify a const object
} // end function f
```

GNU C++ compiler error message:

```
fig08_10.cpp: In function 'void f(const int*)':
fig08_10.cpp:17:12: error: assignment of read-only location '* xPtr'
```

Fig. 8.10 | Attempting to modify data through a nonconstant pointer to `const` data.

When a function is called with a built-in array as an argument, its contents are effectively passed by reference because the built-in array's name is implicitly convertible to the address of the built-in array's first element. However, *by default, objects such as* `array`*s and* `vector`*s are passed by value—a copy of the entire object is passed.* This requires the execution-time overhead of making a *copy* of each data item in the object and storing it on the function call stack. When a pointer to an object is passed, only a copy of the *address* of the object must be made—the *object itself is not copied.*

Performance Tip 8.1

If they do not need to be modified by the called function, pass large objects using pointers to constant data or references to constant data, to obtain the performance benefits of pass-by-reference and avoid the copy overhead of pass-by-value.

Software Engineering Observation 8.3

Passing large objects using pointers to constant data, or references to constant data offers the security of pass-by-value.

Software Engineering Observation 8.4

Use pass-by-value to pass fundamental-type arguments (e.g., ints, doubles, etc.) to a function unless the caller explicitly *requires that the called function be able to directly modify the value in the caller. This is another example of the principle of least privilege.*

8.6.3 Constant Pointer to Nonconstant Data

A **constant pointer to nonconstant data** is a pointer that always points to the same memory location, and the data at that location *can* be modified through the pointer. Pointers that are declared const *must be initialized when they're declared*, but if the pointer is a function parameter, it's *initialized with the pointer that's passed to the function*.

The program of Fig. 8.11 attempts to modify a constant pointer. Line 11 declares pointer ptr to be of type int * const. The declaration is read from *right to left* as "ptr is a constant pointer to a nonconstant integer." The pointer is *initialized* with the address of integer variable x. Line 14 attempts to *assign* the address of y to ptr, but the compiler generates an error message. No error occurs when line 13 assigns the value 7 to *ptr—the nonconstant value to which ptr points *can* be modified using the dereferenced ptr, even though ptr itself has been declared const.

```
1  // Fig. 8.11: fig08_11.cpp
2  // Attempting to modify a constant pointer to nonconstant data.
3
4  int main()
5  {
6     int x, y;
7
8     // ptr is a constant pointer to an integer that can
9     // be modified through ptr, but ptr always points to the
10    // same memory location.
11    int * const ptr = &x; // const pointer must be initialized
12
13    *ptr = 7; // allowed: *ptr is not const
14    ptr = &y; // error: ptr is const; cannot assign to it a new address
15 } // end main
```

Microsoft Visual C++ compiler error message:

```
you cannot assign to a variable that is const
```

Fig. 8.11 | Attempting to modify a constant pointer to nonconstant data.

8.6.4 Constant Pointer to Constant Data

The *minimum* access privilege is granted by a **constant pointer to constant data**. Such a pointer *always* points to the *same* memory location, and the data at that location *cannot* be modified via the pointer. This is how a built-in array should be passed to a function that *only reads* from the built-in array, using array subscript notation, and *does not modify* the built-in array. The program of Fig. 8.12 declares pointer variable ptr to be of type const int * const (line 13). This declaration is read from *right to left* as "ptr is a *constant pointer* *to an integer constant.*" The figure shows the Xcode LLVM compiler's error messages that are generated when an attempt is made to modify the data to which `ptr` points (line 17) and when an attempt is made to modify the address stored in the pointer variable (line 18)—these show up on the lines of code with the errors in the Xcode text editor. In line 15, no errors occur when the program attempts to dereference `ptr`, or when the program attempts to output the value to which `ptr` points, because *neither* the pointer *nor* the data it points to is being modified in this statement.

```
1  // Fig. 8.12: fig08_12.cpp
2  // Attempting to modify a constant pointer to constant data.
3  #include <iostream>
4  using namespace std;
5
6  int main()
7  {
8     int x = 5, y;
9
10    // ptr is a constant pointer to a constant integer.
11    // ptr always points to the same location; the integer
12    // at that location cannot be modified.
13    const int *const ptr = &x;
14
15    cout << *ptr << endl;
16
17    *ptr = 7; // error: *ptr is const; cannot assign new value
18    ptr = &y; // error: ptr is const; cannot assign new address
19 } // end main
```

Xcode LLVM compiler error message:

```
Read-only variable is not assignable
Read-only variable is not assignable
```

Fig. 8.12 | Attempting to modify a constant pointer to constant data.

8.7 `sizeof` Operator

The *compile time* unary operator **`sizeof`** determines the size in bytes of a built-in array or of any other data type, variable or constant *during program compilation*. When applied to a built-in array's *name*, as in Fig. 8.13 (line 13), the `sizeof` operator returns the *total number of bytes in the array* as a value of type `size_t`. The computer we used to compile this program stores variables of type `double` in 8 bytes of memory, and `numbers` is declared to have 20 elements (line 11), so it uses 160 bytes in memory. When applied to a *pointer parameter* (line 22) in a function that *receives a built-in array as an argument*, the `sizeof` operator returns the size of the *pointer* in bytes (4 on the system we used)—*not* the built-in array's size.

Common Programming Error 8.3

Using the `sizeof` operator in a function to find the size in bytes of a built-in array parameter results in the size in bytes of a pointer, not the size in bytes of the built-in array.

```
// Fig. 8.13: fig08_13.cpp
// Sizeof operator when applied to a built-in array's name
// returns the number of bytes in the built-in array.
#include <iostream>
using namespace std;

size_t getSize( double * ); // prototype

int main()
{
   double numbers[ 20 ]; // 20 doubles; occupies 160 bytes on our system

   cout << "The number of bytes in the array is " << sizeof( numbers );

   cout << "\nThe number of bytes returned by getSize is "
      << getSize( numbers ) << endl;
} // end main

// return size of ptr
size_t getSize( double *ptr )
{
   return sizeof( ptr );
} // end function getSize
```

```
The number of bytes in the array is 160
The number of bytes returned by getSize is 4
```

Fig. 8.13 | sizeof operator when applied to a built-in array's name returns the number of bytes in the built-in array.

The number of *elements* in a built-in array can be determined using the results of two sizeof operations. For example, to determine the number of elements in the built-in array numbers, use the following expression (which is evaluated at *compile time*):

```
sizeof numbers / sizeof( numbers[ 0 ] )
```

The expression divides the number of bytes in numbers (160, assuming 8 byte doubles) by the number of bytes in the built-in array's zeroth element (8)—resulting in the number of elements in numbers (20).

Determining the Sizes of the Fundamental Types, a Built-In Array and a Pointer

Figure 8.14 uses sizeof to calculate the number of bytes used to store many of the standard data types. The output was produced using the default settings in Visual C++ 2012 on a Windows 7 computer. Type sizes are *platform dependent*. On another system, for example, double and long double may be of different sizes.

```
// Fig. 8.14: fig08_14.cpp
// sizeof operator used to determine standard data type sizes.
#include <iostream>
```

Fig. 8.14 | sizeof operator used to determine standard data type sizes. (Part 1 of 2.)

```
using namespace std;

int main()
{
   char c; // variable of type char
   short s; // variable of type short
   int i; // variable of type int
   long l; // variable of type long
   long ll; // variable of type long long
   float f; // variable of type float
   double d; // variable of type double
   long double ld; // variable of type long double
   int array[ 20 ]; // built-in array of int
   int *ptr = array; // variable of type int *

   cout << "sizeof c = " << sizeof c
      << "\tsizeof(char) = " << sizeof( char )
      << "\nsizeof s = " << sizeof s
      << "\tsizeof(short) = " << sizeof( short )
      << "\nsizeof i = " << sizeof i
      << "\tsizeof(int) = " << sizeof( int )
      << "\nsizeof l = " << sizeof l
      << "\tsizeof(long) = " << sizeof( long )
      << "\nsizeof ll = " << sizeof ll
      << "\tsizeof(long long) = " << sizeof( long long )
      << "\nsizeof f = " << sizeof f
      << "\tsizeof(float) = " << sizeof( float )
      << "\nsizeof d = " << sizeof d
      << "\tsizeof(double) = " << sizeof( double )
      << "\nsizeof ld = " << sizeof ld
      << "\tsizeof(long double) = " << sizeof( long double )
      << "\nsizeof array = " << sizeof array
      << "\nsizeof ptr = " << sizeof ptr << endl;
} // end main
```

```
sizeof c = 1    sizeof(char) = 1
sizeof s = 2    sizeof(short) = 2
sizeof i = 4    sizeof(int) = 4
sizeof l = 4    sizeof(long) = 4
sizeof ll = 8   sizeof(long long) = 8
sizeof f = 4    sizeof(float) = 4
sizeof d = 8    sizeof(double) = 8
sizeof ld = 8   sizeof(long double) = 8
sizeof array = 80
sizeof ptr = 4
```

Fig. 8.14 | `sizeof` operator used to determine standard data type sizes. (Part 2 of 2.)

Portability Tip 8.1

The number of bytes used to store a particular data type may vary among systems. When writing programs that depend on data type sizes, always use `sizeof` *to determine the number of bytes used to store the data types.*

Operator `sizeof` can be applied to any expression or type name. When `sizeof` is applied to a variable name (which is not a built-in array's name) or other expression, the number of bytes used to store the specific type of the expression is returned. The parentheses used with `sizeof` are required *only* if a type name (e.g., `int`) is supplied as its operand. The parentheses used with `sizeof` are *not* required when `sizeof`'s operand is an expression. Remember that `sizeof` is a *compile-time* operator, so `sizeof`'s operand is not evaluated.

8.8 Pointer Expressions and Pointer Arithmetic

This section describes the operators that can have *pointers* as operands and how these operators are used with pointers. C++ enables **pointer arithmetic**—a few arithmetic operations may be performed on pointers. *Pointer arithmetic is appropriate only for pointers that point to built-in array elements.*

A pointer may be incremented (++) or decremented (--), an integer may be added to a pointer (+ or +=) or subtracted from a pointer (- or -=), or one pointer may be subtracted from another of the same type—this particular operation is appropriate only for two pointers that point to elements of the *same* built-in array.

Portability Tip 8.2

Most computers today have four-byte or eight-byte integers. Because the results of pointer arithmetic depend on the size of the objects a pointer points to, pointer arithmetic is machine dependent.

Assume that `int v[5]` has been declared and that its first element is at memory location 3000. Assume that pointer `vPtr` has been initialized to point to `v[0]` (i.e., the value of `vPtr` is 3000). Figure 8.15 diagrams this situation for a machine with four-byte integers. Variable `vPtr` can be initialized to point to `v` with either of the following statements (because a built-in array's name evaluates to the address of its zeroth element):

```
int *vPtr = v;
int *vPtr = &v[ 0 ];
```

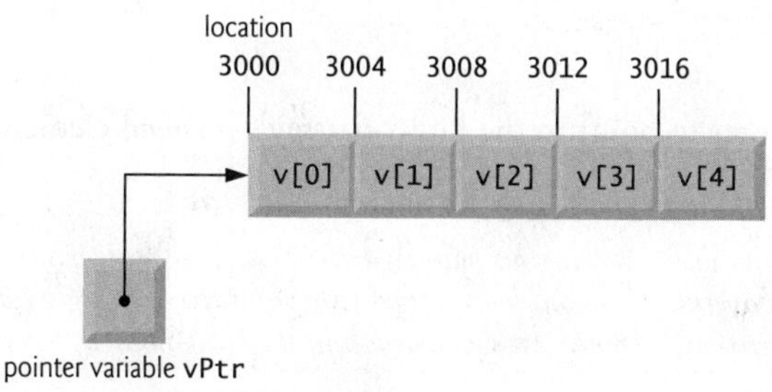

Fig. 8.15 | Built-in array `v` and a pointer variable `int *vPtr` that points to `v`.

Adding Integers to and Subtracting Integers from Pointers

In conventional arithmetic, the addition 3000 + 2 yields the value 3002. This is normally *not* the case with pointer arithmetic. When an integer is added to, or subtracted from, a pointer, the pointer is *not* simply incremented or decremented by that integer, but by that integer *times the size of the object to which the pointer refers.* The number of bytes depends on the object's data type. For example, the statement

```
vPtr += 2;
```

would produce 3008 (from the calculation 3000 + 2 * 4), assuming that an `int` is stored in four bytes of memory. In the built-in array `v`, `vPtr` would now point to `v[2]` (Fig. 8.16). If an integer is stored in eight bytes of memory, then the preceding calculation would result in memory location 3016 (3000 + 2 * 8).

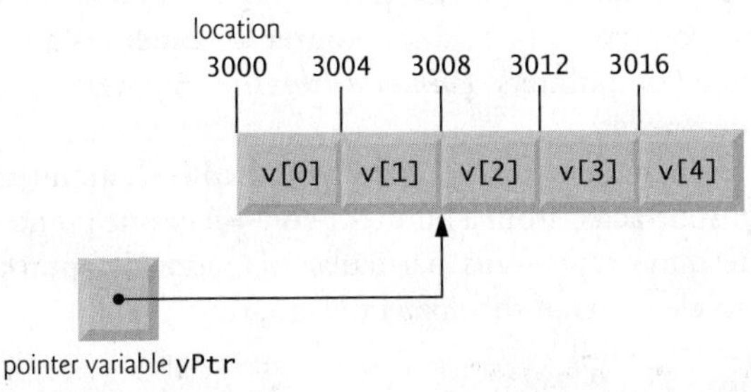

Fig. 8.16 | Pointer `vPtr` after pointer arithmetic.

If `vPtr` had been incremented to 3016, which points to `v[4]`, the statement

```
vPtr -= 4;
```

would set `vPtr` back to 3000—the beginning of the built-in array. If a pointer is being incremented or decremented by one, the increment (++) and decrement (--) operators can be used. Each of the statements

```
++vPtr;
vPtr++;
```

increments the pointer to point to the built-in array's *next* element. Each of the statements

```
--vPtr;
vPtr--;
```

decrements the pointer to point to the built-in array's *previous* element.

Error-Prevention Tip 8.5

There's no bounds checking on pointer arithmetic. You must ensure that every pointer arithmetic operation that adds an integer to or subtracts an integer from a pointer results in a pointer that references an element within the built-in array's bounds.

Subtracting Pointers

Pointer variables pointing to the *same* built-in array may be subtracted from one another. For example, if `vPtr` contains the address 3000 and `v2Ptr` contains 3008, the statement

```
x = v2Ptr - vPtr;
```

would assign to `x` the *number of built-in array elements* from `vPtr` to `v2Ptr`—in this case, 2. *Pointer arithmetic is meaningful only on a pointer that points to a built-in array.* We cannot assume that two variables of the same type are stored contiguously in memory unless they're adjacent elements of a built-in array.

Common Programming Error 8.4

Subtracting or comparing two pointers that do not refer to elements of the same *built-in array is a logic error.*

Pointer Assignment

A pointer can be assigned to another pointer if both pointers are of the *same* type. Otherwise, a cast operator (normally a `reinterpret_cast`; discussed in Section 14.7) must be used to convert the value of the pointer on the right of the assignment to the pointer type on the left of the assignment. The exception to this rule is the **pointer to `void`** (i.e., `void *`), which is a generic pointer capable of representing *any* pointer type. *Any pointer to a fundamental type or class type can be assigned to a pointer of type* `void *` *without casting.* However, a pointer of type `void *` *cannot* be assigned directly to a pointer of another type—the pointer of type `void *` must first be *cast* to the proper pointer type.

Cannot Dereference a `void *`

A `void *` pointer *cannot* be dereferenced. For example, the compiler "knows" that a pointer to `int` refers to four bytes of memory on a machine with four-byte integers, but a pointer to `void` simply contains a memory address for an *unknown* data type—the compiler does *not* know the precise number of bytes to which the pointer refers and the data type. The compiler must know the data type to determine the number of bytes to dereference for a particular pointer—for a pointer to `void`, this number of bytes *cannot* be determined.

Common Programming Error 8.5

Assigning a pointer of one type to a pointer of another (other than `void *`*) without using a cast (normally a* `reinterpret_cast`*) is a compilation error.*

Common Programming Error 8.6

*The allowed operations on void * pointers are: comparing* `void *` *pointers with other pointers, casting* `void *` *pointers to other pointer types and assigning addresses to* `void *` *pointers. All other operations on* `void *` *pointers are compilation errors.*

Comparing Pointers

Pointers can be compared using equality and relational operators. Comparisons using relational operators are meaningless unless the pointers point to elements of the *same* built-in array. Pointer comparisons compare the *addresses* stored in the pointers. A comparison of two pointers pointing to the same built-in array could show, for example, that one pointer points to a higher numbered element of the built-in array than the other pointer does. A common use of pointer comparison is determining whether a pointer has the value `nullptr`, `0` or `NULL` (i.e., the pointer does not point to anything).

8.9 Relationship Between Pointers and Built-In Arrays

Built-in arrays and pointers are intimately related in C++ and may be used *almost* interchangeably. Pointers can be used to do any operation involving array subscripting.

Assume the following declarations

```
int b[ 5 ]; // create 5-element int array b; b is a const pointer
int *bPtr; // create int pointer bPtr, which isn't a const pointer
```

We can set `bPtr` to the address of the first element in the built-in array `b` with the statement

```
bPtr = b; // assign address of built-in array b to bPtr
```

This is equivalent to assigning the address of the first element as follows:

```
bPtr = &b[ 0 ]; // also assigns address of built-in array b to bPtr
```

Pointer/Offset Notation

Built-in array element `b[3]` can alternatively be referenced with the pointer expression

```
*( bPtr + 3 )
```

The `3` in the preceding expression is the **offset** to the pointer. When the pointer points to the beginning of a built-in array, the offset indicates which built-in array element should be referenced, and the offset value is identical to the subscript. This notation is referred to as **pointer/offset notation**. The parentheses are necessary, because the precedence of * is higher than that of +. Without the parentheses, the preceding expression would add `3` to a copy of `*bPtr`'s value (i.e., `3` would be added to `b[0]`, assuming that `bPtr` points to the beginning of the built-in array).

Just as the built-in array element can be referenced with a pointer expression, the *address*

```
&b[ 3 ]
```

can be written with the pointer expression

```
bPtr + 3
```

Pointer/Offset Notation with the Built-In Array's Name as the Pointer

The built-in array name can be treated as a pointer and used in pointer arithmetic. For example, the expression

```
*( b + 3 )
```

also refers to the element `b[3]`. In general, all subscripted built-in array expressions can be written with a pointer and an offset. In this case, pointer/offset notation was used with the built-in array's name as a pointer. The preceding expression does *not* modify the built-in array's name; `b` still points to the built-in array's first element.

Pointer/Subscript Notation

Pointers can be subscripted exactly as built-in arrays can. For example, the expression

```
bPtr[ 1 ]
```

refers to `b[1]`; this expression uses **pointer/subscript notation**.

The Name of a Built-In Array Is Not Modifiable

The expression

```
b += 3
```

causes a compilation error, because it attempts to *modify* the value of the built-in array's name with pointer arithmetic.

Good Programming Practice 8.2

For clarity, use built-in array notation instead of pointer notation when manipulating built-in arrays.

Demonstrating the Relationship Between Pointers and Built-In Arrays

Figure 8.17 uses the four notations discussed in this section for referring to built-in array elements—*array subscript notation, pointer/offset notation with the built-in array's name as a pointer, pointer subscript notation* and *pointer/offset notation with a pointer*—to accomplish the same task, namely displaying the four elements of the built-in array of `int`s named `b`.

```
// Fig. 8.17: fig08_17.cpp
// Using subscripting and pointer notations with built-in arrays.
#include <iostream>
using namespace std;

int main()
{
   int b[] = { 10, 20, 30, 40 }; // create 4-element built-in array b
   int *bPtr = b; // set bPtr to point to built-in array b

   // output built-in array b using array subscript notation
   cout << "Array b displayed with:\n\nArray subscript notation\n";

   for ( size_t i = 0; i < 4; ++i )
      cout << "b[" << i << "] = " << b[ i ] << '\n';

   // output built-in array b using array name and pointer/offset notation
   cout << "\nPointer/offset notation where "
      << "the pointer is the array name\n";

   for ( size_t offset1 = 0; offset1 < 4; ++offset1 )
      cout << "*(b + " << offset1 << ") = " << *( b + offset1 ) << '\n';

   // output built-in array b using bPtr and array subscript notation
   cout << "\nPointer subscript notation\n";

   for ( size_t j = 0; j < 4; ++j )
      cout << "bPtr[" << j << "] = " << bPtr[ j ] << '\n';

   cout << "\nPointer/offset notation\n";

   // output built-in array b using bPtr and pointer/offset notation
   for ( size_t offset2 = 0; offset2 < 4; ++offset2 )
      cout << "*(bPtr + " << offset2 << ") = "
         << *( bPtr + offset2 ) << '\n';
} // end main
```

Fig. 8.17 | Using subscripting and pointer notations with built-in arrays. (Part 1 of 2.)

```
Array b displayed with:

Array subscript notation
b[0] = 10
b[1] = 20
b[2] = 30
b[3] = 40

Pointer/offset notation where the pointer is the array name
*(b + 0) = 10
*(b + 1) = 20
*(b + 2) = 30
*(b + 3) = 40

Pointer subscript notation
bPtr[0] = 10
bPtr[1] = 20
bPtr[2] = 30
bPtr[3] = 40

Pointer/offset notation
*(bPtr + 0) = 10
*(bPtr + 1) = 20
*(bPtr + 2) = 30
*(bPtr + 3) = 40
```

Fig. 8.17 | Using subscripting and pointer notations with built-in arrays. (Part 2 of 2.)

8.10 Pointer-Based Strings

We've already used the C++ Standard Library `string` class to represent strings as full-fledged objects. For example, the `GradeBook` class case study in Chapters 3–7 represents a course name using a `string` object. Chapter 19 presents class `string` in detail. This section introduces C-style, pointer-based strings (as defined by the C programming language), which we'll simply call **C strings**. *C++'s `string` class is preferred for use in new programs, because it eliminates many of the security problems and bugs that can be caused by manipulating C strings.* We cover C strings here for a deeper understanding of pointers and built-in arrays. Also, if you work with legacy C and C++ programs, you're likely to encounter pointer-based strings. We cover C strings in detail in Appendix F.

Characters and Character Constants

Characters are the fundamental building blocks of C++ source programs. Every program is composed of a sequence of characters that—when grouped together meaningfully—is interpreted by the compiler as instructions used to accomplish a task. A program may contain **character constants**. A character constant is an integer value represented as a character in single quotes. The *value* of a character constant is the integer value of the character in the machine's character set. For example, `'z'` represents the integer value of `z` (122 in the ASCII character set; see Appendix B), and `'\n'` represents the integer value of newline (10 in the ASCII character set).

Strings

A string is a series of characters treated as a single unit. A string may include letters, digits and various **special characters** such as +, -, *, / and $. **String literals**, or **string constants**, in C++ are written in double quotation marks as follows:

```
"John Q. Doe"                  (a name)
"9999 Main Street"             (a street address)
"Maynard, Massachusetts"       (a city and state)
"(201) 555-1212"               (a telephone number)
```

Pointer-Based Strings

A pointer-based string is a built-in array of characters ending with a **null character** (`'\0'`), which marks where the string terminates in memory. A string is accessed via a pointer to its first character. The `sizeof` a string literal is the length of the string *including* the terminating null character. Pointer-based strings are like built-in arrays—a built-in array name is also a pointer to its first element.

String Literals as Initializers

A string literal may be used as an initializer in the declaration of either a built-in array of `char`s or a variable of type `const char *`. The declarations

```
char color[] = "blue";
const char *colorPtr = "blue";
```

each initialize a variable to the string `"blue"`. The first declaration creates a *five-element* built-in array `color` containing the characters `'b'`, `'l'`, `'u'`, `'e'` *and* `'\0'`. The second declaration creates pointer variable `colorPtr` that points to the letter `b` in the string `"blue"` (which ends in `'\0'`) somewhere in memory. String literals have *static storage duration* (they exist for the duration of the program) and may or may not be *shared* if the same string literal is referenced from multiple locations in a program.

Error-Prevention Tip 8.6

If you need to modify the contents of a string literal, store it in a built-in array of `char`s *first.*

Character Constants as Initializers

The declaration `char color[] = "blue";` could also be written

```
char color[] = { 'b', 'l', 'u', 'e', '\0' };
```

which uses character constants in single quotes (`'`) as initializers for each element of the built-in array. When declaring a built-in array of `char`s to contain a string, the built-in array must be large enough to store the string *and* its terminating null character. The compiler determines the size of the built-in array in the preceding declaration, based on the *number of initializers in the initializer list.*

Common Programming Error 8.7

Not allocating sufficient space in a built-in array of `char`s *to store the null character that terminates a string is a logic error.*

Common Programming Error 8.8

Creating or using a C string that does not contain a terminating null character can lead to logic errors.

Error-Prevention Tip 8.7

When storing a string of characters in a built-in array of `char`*s, be sure that the built-in array is large enough to hold the largest string that will be stored. C++ allows strings of* any *length. If a string is longer than the built-in array of* `char`*s in which it's to be stored, characters beyond the end of the built-in array will overwrite data in memory following the built-in array, leading to logic errors and potential security breaches.*

Accessing Characters in a C String

Because a C string is a built-in array of characters, we can access individual characters in a string directly with array subscript notation. For example, in the preceding declaration, `color[0]` is the character `'b'`, `color[2]` is `'u'` and `color[4]` is the null character.

Reading Strings into `char` *Built-In Arrays with* `cin`

A string can be read into a built-in array of `char`s using stream extraction with `cin`. For example, the following statement reads a string into the built-in 20-element array of `char`s named `word`:

```
cin >> word;
```

The string entered by the user is stored in `word`. The preceding statement reads characters until a white-space character or end-of-file indicator is encountered. The string should be no longer than 19 characters to leave room for the terminating null character. The `setw` stream manipulator can be used to *ensure* that the string read into `word` *does not exceed the size of the built-in array*. For example, the statement

```
cin >> setw( 20 ) >> word;
```

specifies that `cin` should read a maximum of 19 characters into `word` and save the 20th location to store the terminating null character for the string. The `setw` stream manipulator is not a sticky setting—it applies *only* to the next value being input. If more than 19 characters are entered, the remaining characters are not saved in `word`, *but they will be in the input stream and can be read by the next input operation.*[1] Of course, any input operation can also fail. We show how to detect input failures in Section 13.8.

Reading Lines of Text into `char` *Built-In Arrays with* `cin.getline`

In some cases, it's desirable to input an *entire line of text* into a built-in array of `char`s. For this purpose, the `cin` object provides the member function **`getline`**, which takes three arguments—a *built-in array of* `char`*s* in which the line of text will be stored, a *length* and a *delimiter character*. For example, the statements

```
char sentence[ 80 ];
cin.getline( sentence, 80, '\n' );
```

1. To learn how to ignore extra characters in the input steam, see the article at: `www.daniweb.com/software-development/cpp/threads/90228/flushing-the-input-stream`.

declare `sentence` as a built-in array of 80 characters and read a line of text from the keyboard into the built-in array. The function stops reading characters when the delimiter character `'\n'` is encountered, when the *end-of-file indicator* is entered or when the number of characters read so far is one less than the length specified in the second argument. The last character in the built-in array is reserved for the *terminating null character*. If the delimiter character is encountered, it's read and *discarded*. The third argument to `cin.getline` has `'\n'` as a default value, so the preceding function call could have been written as:

```
cin.getline( sentence, 80 );
```

Chapter 13, Stream Input/Output: A Deeper Look, provides a detailed discussion of `cin.getline` and other input/output functions.

Displaying C Strings

A built-in array of `char`s representing a null-terminated string can be output with `cout` and <<. The statement

```
cout << sentence;
```

displays the built-in array `sentence`. Like `cin`, `cout` does not care how large the built-in array of `char`s is. The characters are output until a *terminating null character* is encountered; the null character is *not* displayed. [*Note:* `cin` and `cout` assume that built-in array of `char`s should be processed as strings terminated by null characters; `cin` and `cout` do not provide similar input and output processing capabilities for other built-in array types.]

8.11 Wrap-Up

In this chapter we provided a detailed introduction to pointers—variables that contain memory addresses as their values. We began by demonstrating how to declare and initialize pointers. You saw how to use the address operator (&) to assign the address of a variable to a pointer and the indirection operator (*) to access the data stored in the variable indirectly referenced by a pointer. We discussed passing arguments by reference using pointer arguments.

We discussed how to declare and use built-in arrays, which C++ inherited from the C programming language. You learned how to use `const` with pointers to enforce the principle of least privilege. We demonstrated using nonconstant pointers to nonconstant data, nonconstant pointers to constant data, constant pointers to nonconstant data, and constant pointers to constant data. We discussed the compile-time `sizeof` operator, which can be used to determine the sizes of data types and variables in bytes at compile time.

We discussed how to use pointers in arithmetic and comparison expressions. You saw that pointer arithmetic can be used to move from one element of a built-in array to another. We briefly introduced pointer-based strings.

In the next chapter, we begin our deeper treatment of classes. You'll learn about the scope of a class's members and how to keep objects in a consistent state. You'll also learn about using special member functions called constructors and destructors, which execute when an object is created and destroyed, respectively, and we'll discuss when constructors and destructors are called. In addition, we'll demonstrate using default arguments with constructors and using default memberwise assignment to assign one object of a class to another object of the same class. We'll also discuss the danger of returning a reference to a `private` data member of a class.

9

Classes: A Deeper Look; Throwing Exceptions

Objectives

In this chapter you'll:

- Use an include guard.
- Access class members via an object's name, a reference or a pointer.
- Use destructors to perform "termination housekeeping."
- Learn the order of constructor and destructor calls.
- Learn about the dangers of returning a reference to `private` data.
- Assign the data members of one object to those of another object.
- Create objects composed of other objects.
- Use `friend` functions and `friend` classes.
- Use the `this` pointer in a member function to access a non-`static` class member.

Outline

9.1 Introduction

This chapter takes a deeper look at classes. We use an integrated `Time` class case study and other examples to demonstrate several class construction capabilities. We begin with a `Time` class that reviews several of the features presented in preceding chapters. The example also demonstrates using an *include guard* in headers to prevent header code from being included in the same source code file more than once.

We demonstrate how client code can access a class's `public` members via the name of an object, a reference to an object or a pointer to an object. As you'll see, object names and references can be used with the dot (`.`) member selection operator to access a `public` member, and pointers can be used with the arrow (`->`) member selection operator.

We discuss access functions that can read or write an object's data members. A common use of access functions is to test the truth or falsity of conditions—such functions are known as *predicate functions*. We also demonstrate the notion of a utility function (also called a *helper function*)—a `private` member function that supports the operation of the class's `public` member functions, but is *not* intended for use by clients of the class.

We show how to pass arguments to constructors and show how default arguments can be used in constructors to enable client code to initialize objects using a variety of arguments. Next, we discuss a special member function called a *destructor* that's part of every class and is used to perform "termination housekeeping" on an object before it's destroyed. We demonstrate the *order* in which constructors and destructors are called.

We show that returning a reference or pointer to `private` data *breaks the encapsulation of a class*, allowing client code to directly access an object's data. We use default memberwise assignment to assign an object of a class to another object of the same class.

We use `const` objects and `const` member functions to prevent modifications of objects and enforce the principle of least privilege. We discuss *composition*—a form of reuse in which a class can have objects of other classes as members. Next, we use *friendship* to specify that a nonmember function can also access a class's non-`public` members—a technique that's often used in operator overloading (Chapter 10) for performance reasons. We discuss the `this` pointer, which is an *implicit* argument in all calls to a class's non-`static` member functions, allowing them to access the correct object's data members and non-`static` member functions. We motivate the need for `static` class members and show how to use them in your own classes.

9.2 `Time` Class Case Study

Our first example creates class `Time` and tests the class. We demonstrate an important C++ software engineering concept—using an include guard in headers to prevent the code in the header from being included into the same source code file more than once. Since a class can be defined only once, using such preprocessing directives prevents multiple-definition errors.

`Time` Class Definition

The class definition (Fig. 9.1) contains prototypes (lines 13–16) for member functions `Time`, `setTime`, `printUniversal` and `printStandard`, and includes `private unsigned int` members `hour`, `minute` and `second` (lines 18–20). Class `Time`'s `private` data members can be accessed *only* by its member functions. Chapter 11 introduces a third access specifier, `protected`, as we study inheritance and the part it plays in object-oriented programming.

Good Programming Practice 9.1

For clarity and readability, use each access specifier only once in a class definition. Place `public` members first, where they're easy to locate.

Software Engineering Observation 9.1

Each member of a class should have `private` visibility unless it can be proven that the element needs `public` visibility. This is another example of the principle of least privilege.

```
1  // Fig. 9.1: Time.h
2  // Time class definition.
3  // Member functions are defined in Time.cpp
4
5  // prevent multiple inclusions of header
6  #ifndef TIME_H
7  #define TIME_H
8
9  // Time class definition
10 class Time
11 {
12 public:
13    Time(); // constructor
14    void setTime( int, int, int ); // set hour, minute and second
15    void printUniversal() const; // print time in universal-time format
16    void printStandard() const; // print time in standard-time format
17 private:
18    unsigned int hour; // 0 - 23 (24-hour clock format)
19    unsigned int minute; // 0 - 59
20    unsigned int second; // 0 - 59
21 }; // end class Time
22
23 #endif
```

Fig. 9.1 | `Time` class definition.

In Fig. 9.1, the class definition is enclosed in the following **include guard** (lines 6, 7 and 23):

```
// prevent multiple inclusions of header
#ifndef TIME_H
#define TIME_H
   ...
#endif
```

When we build larger programs, other definitions and declarations will also be placed in headers. The preceding include guard prevents the code between **#ifndef** (which means "if not defined") and **#endif** from being included if the name TIME_H has been defined. If the header has *not* been included previously in a file, the name TIME_H is defined by the **#define** directive and the header statements *are* included. If the header has been included previously, TIME_H *is defined* already and the header is *not* included again. Attempts to include a header multiple times (inadvertently) typically occur in large programs with many headers that may themselves include other headers.

Error-Prevention Tip 9.1

Use #ifndef, #define and #endif preprocessing directives to form an include guard that prevents headers from being included more than once in a source-code file.

Good Programming Practice 9.2

By convention, use the name of the header in uppercase with the period replaced by an underscore in the #ifndef and #define preprocessing directives of a header.

Time Class Member Functions

In Fig. 9.2, the Time constructor (lines 11–14) initializes the data members to 0—the universal-time equivalent of 12 AM. Invalid values cannot be stored in the data members of a Time object, because the constructor is called when the Time object is created, and all subsequent attempts by a client to modify the data members are scrutinized by function setTime (discussed shortly). Finally, it's important to note that you can define *overloaded constructors* for a class—we studied overloaded functions in Section 6.17.

```
1  // Fig. 9.2: Time.cpp
2  // Time class member-function definitions.
3  #include <iostream>
4  #include <iomanip>
5  #include <stdexcept> // for invalid_argument exception class
6  #include "Time.h" // include definition of class Time from Time.h
7
8  using namespace std;
9
10 // Time constructor initializes each data member to zero.
11 Time::Time()
12    : hour( 0 ), minute( 0 ), second( 0 )
13 {
14 } // end Time constructor
```

Fig. 9.2 | Time class member-function definitions. (Part 1 of 2.)

```
15
16  // set new Time value using universal time
17  void Time::setTime( int h, int m, int s )
18  {
19     // validate hour, minute and second
20     if ( ( h >= 0 && h < 24 ) && ( m >= 0 && m < 60 ) &&
21        ( s >= 0 && s < 60 ) )
22     {
23        hour = h;
24        minute = m;
25        second = s;
26     } // end if
27     else
28        throw invalid_argument(
29           "hour, minute and/or second was out of range" );
30  } // end function setTime
31
32  // print Time in universal-time format (HH:MM:SS)
33  void Time::printUniversal() const
34  {
35     cout << setfill( '0' ) << setw( 2 ) << hour << ":"
36        << setw( 2 ) << minute << ":" << setw( 2 ) << second;
37  } // end function printUniversal
38
39  // print Time in standard-time format (HH:MM:SS AM or PM)
40  void Time::printStandard() const
41  {
42     cout << ( ( hour == 0 || hour == 12 ) ? 12 : hour % 12 ) << ":"
43        << setfill( '0' ) << setw( 2 ) << minute << ":" << setw( 2 )
44        << second << ( hour < 12 ? " AM" : " PM" );
45  } // end function printStandard
```

Fig. 9.2 | `Time` class member-function definitions. (Part 2 of 2.)

Before C++11, only `static const int` data members (which you saw in Chapter 7) could be initialized where they were declared in the class body. For this reason, data members typically should be initialized by the class's constructor as *there is no default initialization for fundamental-type data members.* As of C++11, you can now use an *in-class initializer* to initialize any data member where it's declared in the class definition.

`Time` Class Member Function `setTime` and Throwing Exceptions

Function `setTime` (lines 17–30) is a `public` function that declares three `int` parameters and uses them to set the time. Lines 20–21 test each argument to determine whether the value is in range, and, if so, lines 23–25 assign the values to the `hour`, `minute` and `second` data members. The `hour` value must be greater than or equal to 0 and less than 24, because universal-time format represents hours as integers from 0 to 23 (e.g., 1 PM is hour 13 and 11 PM is hour 23; midnight is hour 0 and noon is hour 12). Similarly, both `minute` and `second` must be greater than or equal to 0 and less than 60. For values outside these ranges, `setTime` **throws an exception** (lines 28–29) of type **`invalid_argument`** (from header `<stdexcept>`), which notifies the client code that an invalid argument was received. As you learned in Section 7.10, you can use `try...catch` to catch exceptions and attempt to recover from them, which we'll do in Fig. 9.3. The **throw statement** (lines 28–29) creates a new object of type `invalid_argument`. The parentheses following the class name indicate a call to the `invalid_argument` constructor that allows us to specify a custom error message string. After the exception object is created, the `throw` statement immediately terminates function `setTime` and the exception is returned to the code that attempted to set the time.

`Time` Class Member Function `printUniversal`

Function `printUniversal` (lines 33–37 of Fig. 9.2) takes no arguments and outputs the time in universal-time format, consisting of three colon-separated pairs of digits. If the time were 1:30:07 PM, function `printUniversal` would return `13:30:07`. Line 35 uses parameterized stream manipulator **`setfill`** to specify the **fill character** that's displayed when an integer is output in a field *wider* than the number of digits in the value. The fill characters appear to the *left* of the digits in the number, because the number is *right aligned* by default—for *left aligned* values, the fill characters would appear to the right. In this example, if the `minute` value is 2, it will be displayed as 02, because the fill character is set to zero (`'0'`). If the number being output fills the specified field, the fill character will *not* be displayed. Once the fill character is specified with `setfill`, it applies for *all* subsequent values that are displayed in fields wider than the value being displayed—`setfill` is a "sticky" setting. This is in contrast to `setw`, which applies *only* to the next value displayed—`setw` is a "nonsticky" setting.

Error-Prevention Tip 9.2

Each sticky setting (such as a fill character or floating-point precision) should be restored *to its previous setting when it's no longer needed. Failure to do so may result in incorrectly formatted output later in a program. Chapter 13, Stream Input/Output: A Deeper Look, discusses how to reset the fill character and precision.*

`Time` Class Member Function `printStandard`

Function `printStandard` (lines 40–45) takes no arguments and outputs the date in standard-time format, consisting of the `hour`, `minute` and `second` values separated by colons and followed by an AM or PM indicator (e.g., `1:27:06 PM`). Like function `printUniversal`, function `printStandard` uses `setfill('0')` to format the `minute` and `second` as two digit values with leading zeros if necessary. Line 42 uses the conditional operator (`?:`) to determine the value of `hour` to be displayed—if the `hour` is `0` or `12` (AM or PM), it appears as 12; otherwise, the `hour` appears as a value from 1 to 11. The conditional operator in line 44 determines whether AM or PM will be displayed.

Defining Member Functions Outside the Class Definition; Class Scope

Even though a member function declared in a class definition may be defined outside that class definition (and "tied" to the class via the *scope resolution operator*), that member function is still within that **class's scope**—that is, its name is known to other class members referred to via an object of the class, a reference to an object of the class, a pointer to an object of the class or the scope resolution operator. We'll say more about class scope shortly.

If a member function is defined in a class's body, the member function is implicitly declared *inline*. Remember that the compiler reserves the right not to inline any function.

Performance Tip 9.1

Defining a member function inside *the class definition inlines the member function (if the compiler chooses to do so). This can improve performance.*

Software Engineering Observation 9.2

Only the simplest and most stable member functions (i.e., whose implementations are unlikely to change) should be defined in the class header.

Member Functions vs. Global Functions (Also Called Free Functions)

The `printUniversal` and `printStandard` member functions take no arguments, because these member functions implicitly know that they're to print the data members of the particular `Time` object on which they're invoked. This can make member function calls more concise than conventional function calls in procedural programming.

Software Engineering Observation 9.3

Using an object-oriented programming approach often simplifies function calls by reducing the number of parameters. This benefit derives from the fact that encapsulating data members and member functions within a class gives the member functions the right to access the data members.

Software Engineering Observation 9.4

Member functions are usually shorter than functions in non-object-oriented programs, because the data stored in data members have ideally been validated by a constructor or by member functions that store new data. Because the data is already in the object, the member-function calls often have no arguments or fewer arguments than function calls in non-object-oriented languages. Thus, the calls, the function definitions and the function prototypes are shorter. This improves many aspects of program development.

Error-Prevention Tip 9.3

The fact that member function calls generally take either no arguments or substantially fewer arguments than conventional function calls in non-object-oriented languages reduces the likelihood of passing the wrong arguments, the wrong types of arguments or the wrong number of arguments.

Using Class `Time`

Once defined, `Time` can be used as a type in declarations as follows:

```
Time sunset; // object of type Time
array< Time, 5 > arrayOfTimes; // array of 5 Time objects
Time &dinnerTime = sunset; // reference to a Time object
Time *timePtr = &dinnerTime; // pointer to a Time object
```

Figure 9.3 uses class `Time`. Line 11 instantiates a single object of class `Time` called `t`. When the object is instantiated, the `Time` constructor is called to initialize each `private` data member to `0`. Then, lines 15 and 17 print the time in universal and standard formats, respectively, to confirm that the members were initialized properly. Line 19 sets a new time by calling member function `setTime`, and lines 23 and 25 print the time again in both formats.

```
// Fig. 9.3: fig09_03.cpp
// Program to test class Time.
// NOTE: This file must be compiled with Time.cpp.
#include <iostream>
#include <stdexcept> // for invalid_argument exception class
#include "Time.h" // include definition of class Time from Time.h
using namespace std;

int main()
{
   Time t; // instantiate object t of class Time

   // output Time object t's initial values
   cout << "The initial universal time is ";
   t.printUniversal(); // 00:00:00
   cout << "\nThe initial standard time is ";
   t.printStandard(); // 12:00:00 AM

   t.setTime( 13, 27, 6 ); // change time

   // output Time object t's new values
   cout << "\n\nUniversal time after setTime is ";
   t.printUniversal(); // 13:27:06
   cout << "\nStandard time after setTime is ";
   t.printStandard(); // 1:27:06 PM

   // attempt to set the time with invalid values
   try
   {
      t.setTime( 99, 99, 99 ); // all values out of range
   } // end try
   catch ( invalid_argument &e )
   {
      cout << "Exception: " << e.what() << endl;
   } // end catch

   // output t's values after specifying invalid values
   cout << "\n\nAfter attempting invalid settings:"
      << "\nUniversal time: ";
   t.printUniversal(); // 13:27:06
   cout << "\nStandard time: ";
   t.printStandard(); // 1:27:06 PM
   cout << endl;
} // end main
```

```
The initial universal time is 00:00:00
The initial standard time is 12:00:00 AM

Universal time after setTime is 13:27:06
Standard time after setTime is 1:27:06 PM

Exception: hour, minute and/or second was out of range
```

Fig. 9.3 | Program to test class Time. (Part 1 of 2.)

```
After attempting invalid settings:
Universal time: 13:27:06
Standard time: 1:27:06 PM
```

Fig. 9.3 | Program to test class `Time`. (Part 2 of 2.)

Calling `setTime` with Invalid Values

To illustrate that method `setTime` validates its arguments, line 30 calls `setTime` with invalid arguments of `99` for the `hour`, `minute` and `second`. This statement is placed in a `try` block (lines 28–31) in case `setTime` throws an `invalid_argument` exception, which it will do since the arguments are all invalid. When this occurs, the exception is caught at lines 32–35 and line 34 displays the exception's error message by calling its `what` member function. Lines 38–42 output the time again in both formats to confirm that `setTime` did not change the time when invalid arguments were supplied.

Looking Ahead to Composition and Inheritance

Often, classes do not have to be created "from scratch." Rather, they can *include objects of other classes as members* or they may be **derived** from other classes that provide attributes and behaviors the new classes can use. Such software reuse can greatly enhance productivity and simplify code maintenance. Including class objects as members of other classes is called **composition** (or **aggregation**) and is discussed in Section 9.11. Deriving new classes from existing classes is called **inheritance** and is discussed in Chapter 11.

Object Size

People new to object-oriented programming often suppose that objects must be quite large because they contain data members and member functions. *Logically*, this is true—you may think of objects as containing data and functions (and our discussion has certainly encouraged this view); *physically*, however, this is *not* true.

Performance Tip 9.2

Objects contain only data, so objects are much smaller than if they also contained member functions. The compiler creates one copy (only) of the member functions separate from all objects of the class. All objects of the class share *this one copy. Each object, of course, needs its own copy of the class's data, because the data can vary among the objects. The function code is nonmodifiable and, hence, can be shared among all objects of one class.*

9.3 Class Scope and Accessing Class Members

A class's data members and member functions belong to that class's scope. Nonmember functions are defined at *global namespace scope*, by default. (We discuss namespaces in more detail in Section 21.4.)

Within a class's scope, class members are immediately accessible by all of that class's member functions and can be referenced by name. Outside a class's scope, `public` class members are referenced through one of the **handles** on an object—an *object name*, a *reference* to an object or a *pointer* to an object. The type of the object, reference or pointer specifies the interface (e.g., the member functions) accessible to the client. [We'll see in Section 9.13 that an *implicit handle* is inserted by the compiler on every reference to a data member or member function from within an object.]

Class Scope and Block Scope
Variables declared in a member function have *block scope* and are known only to that function. If a member function defines a variable with the same name as a variable with class scope, the class-scope variable is *hidden* in the function by the block-scope variable. Such a hidden variable can be accessed by preceding the variable name with the class name followed by the scope resolution operator (`::`). Hidden global variables can be accessed with the scope resolution operator (see Chapter 6).

Dot (`.`) and Arrow (`->`) Member Selection Operators
The dot member selection operator (`.`) is preceded by an object's name or with a reference to an object to access the object's members. The **arrow member selection operator** (`->`) is preceded by a pointer to an object to access the object's members.

Accessing `public` Class Members Through Objects, References and Pointers
Consider an `Account` class that has a `public` `setBalance` member function. Given the following declarations:

```
Account account; // an Account object

// accountRef refers to an Account object
Account &accountRef = account;

// accountPtr points to an Account object
Account *accountPtr = &account;
```

You can invoke member function `setBalance` using the dot (`.`) and arrow (`->`) member selection operators as follows:

```
// call setBalance via the Account object
account.setBalance( 123.45 );

// call setBalance via a reference to the Account object
accountRef.setBalance( 123.45 );

// call setBalance via a pointer to the Account object
accountPtr->setBalance( 123.45 );
```

9.4 Access Functions and Utility Functions

Access Functions
Access functions can read or display data. Another common use for access functions is to test the truth or falsity of conditions—such functions are often called **predicate functions.** An example of a predicate function would be an `isEmpty` function for any container class—a class capable of holding many objects, like a `vector`. A program might test `isEmpty` before attempting to read another item from the container object. An `isFull` predicate function might test a container-class object to determine whether it has no additional room. Useful predicate functions for our `Time` class might be `isAM` and `isPM`.

Utility Functions
A **utility function** (also called a **helper function**) is a `private` member function that supports the operation of a class's other member functions. Utility functions are declared `private` because they're not intended for use by the class's clients. A common use of a utility function would be to place in a function some common code that would otherwise be duplicated in several other member functions.

9.5 `Time` Class Case Study: Constructors with Default Arguments

The program of Figs. 9.4–9.6 enhances class `Time` to demonstrate how arguments are implicitly passed to a constructor. The constructor defined in Fig. 9.2 initialized `hour`, `minute` and `second` to `0` (i.e., midnight in universal time). Like other functions, constructors can specify *default arguments*. Line 13 of Fig. 9.4 declares the `Time` constructor to include default arguments, specifying a default value of zero for each argument passed to the constructor. The constructor is declared `explicit` because it can be called with one argument. We discuss explicit constructors in detail in Section 10.13.

```
1  // Fig. 9.4: Time.h
2  // Time class containing a constructor with default arguments.
3  // Member functions defined in Time.cpp.
4
5  // prevent multiple inclusions of header
6  #ifndef TIME_H
7  #define TIME_H
8
9  // Time class definition
10 class Time
11 {
12 public:
13    explicit Time( int = 0, int = 0, int = 0 ); // default constructor
14
15    // set functions
16    void setTime( int, int, int ); // set hour, minute, second
17    void setHour( int ); // set hour (after validation)
18    void setMinute( int ); // set minute (after validation)
19    void setSecond( int ); // set second (after validation)
20
21    // get functions
22    unsigned int getHour() const; // return hour
23    unsigned int getMinute() const; // return minute
24    unsigned int getSecond() const; // return second
25
26    void printUniversal() const; // output time in universal-time format
27    void printStandard() const; // output time in standard-time format
28 private:
29    unsigned int hour; // 0 - 23 (24-hour clock format)
30    unsigned int minute; // 0 - 59
31    unsigned int second; // 0 - 59
32 }; // end class Time
33
34 #endif
```

Fig. 9.4 | `Time` class containing a constructor with default arguments.

In Fig. 9.5, lines 10–13 define the new version of the `Time` constructor that receives values for parameters `hour`, `minute` and `second` that will be used to initialize `private` data members `hour`, `minute` and `second`, respectively. The default arguments to the constructor ensure that, even if no values are provided in a constructor call, the constructor still initializes the data members. *A constructor that defaults all its arguments is also a default constructor—that is, a constructor that can be invoked with no arguments. There can be at most one default constructor per class.* The version of class `Time` in this example provides *set* and *get* functions for each data member. The `Time` constructor now calls `setTime`, which calls the `setHour`, `setMinute` and `setSecond` functions to validate and assign values to the data members.

Software Engineering Observation 9.5

Any change to the default argument values of a function requires the client code to be recompiled (to ensure that the program still functions correctly).

```
// Fig. 9.5: Time.cpp
// Member-function definitions for class Time.
#include <iostream>
#include <iomanip>
#include <stdexcept>
#include "Time.h" // include definition of class Time from Time.h
using namespace std;

// Time constructor initializes each data member
Time::Time( int hour, int minute, int second )
{
   setTime( hour, minute, second ); // validate and set time
} // end Time constructor

// set new Time value using universal time
void Time::setTime( int h, int m, int s )
{
   setHour( h ); // set private field hour
   setMinute( m ); // set private field minute
   setSecond( s ); // set private field second
} // end function setTime

// set hour value
void Time::setHour( int h )
{
   if ( h >= 0 && h < 24 )
      hour = h;
   else
      throw invalid_argument( "hour must be 0-23" );
} // end function setHour

// set minute value
void Time::setMinute( int m )
{
   if ( m >= 0 && m < 60 )
      minute = m;
   else
      throw invalid_argument( "minute must be 0-59" );
} // end function setMinute
```

Fig. 9.5 | Member-function definitions for class `Time`. (Part 1 of 2.)

```
40
41  // set second value
42  void Time::setSecond( int s )
43  {
44     if ( s >= 0 && s < 60 )
45        second = s;
46     else
47        throw invalid_argument( "second must be 0-59" );
48  } // end function setSecond
49
50  // return hour value
51  unsigned int Time::getHour() const
52  {
53     return hour;
54  } // end function getHour
55
56  // return minute value
57  unsigned Time::getMinute() const
58  {
59     return minute;
60  } // end function getMinute
61
62  // return second value
63  unsigned Time::getSecond() const
64  {
65     return second;
66  } // end function getSecond
67
68  // print Time in universal-time format (HH:MM:SS)
69  void Time::printUniversal() const
70  {
71     cout << setfill( '0' ) << setw( 2 ) << getHour() << ":"
72        << setw( 2 ) << getMinute() << ":" << setw( 2 ) << getSecond();
73  } // end function printUniversal
74
75  // print Time in standard-time format (HH:MM:SS AM or PM)
76  void Time::printStandard() const
77  {
78     cout << ( ( getHour() == 0 || getHour() == 12 ) ? 12 : getHour() % 12 )
79        << ":" << setfill( '0' ) << setw( 2 ) << getMinute()
80        << ":" << setw( 2 ) << getSecond() << ( hour < 12 ? " AM" : " PM" );
81  } // end function printStandard
```

Fig. 9.5 | Member-function definitions for class `Time`. (Part 2 of 2.)

In Fig. 9.5, line 12 of the constructor calls member function `setTime` with the values passed to the constructor (or the default values). Function `setTime` calls `setHour` to ensure that the value supplied for `hour` is in the range 0–23, then calls `setMinute` and `setSecond` to ensure that the values for `minute` and `second` are each in the range 0–59. Functions `setHour` (lines 24–30), `setMinute` (lines 33–39) and `setSecond` (lines 42–48) each throw an exception if an out-of-range argument is received.

Function main in Fig. 9.6 initializes five Time objects—one with all three arguments defaulted in the implicit constructor call (line 10), one with one argument specified (line 11), one with two arguments specified (line 12), one with three arguments specified (line 13) and one with three invalid arguments specified (line 38). The program displays each object in universal-time and standard-time formats. For Time object t5 (line 38), the program displays an error message because the constructor arguments are out of range.

```
1  // Fig. 9.6: fig09_06.cpp
2  // Constructor with default arguments.
3  #include <iostream>
4  #include <stdexcept>
5  #include "Time.h" // include definition of class Time from Time.h
6  using namespace std;
7
8  int main()
9  {
10    Time t1; // all arguments defaulted
11    Time t2( 2 ); // hour specified; minute and second defaulted
12    Time t3( 21, 34 ); // hour and minute specified; second defaulted
13    Time t4( 12, 25, 42 ); // hour, minute and second specified
14
15    cout << "Constructed with:\n\nt1: all arguments defaulted\n  ";
16    t1.printUniversal(); // 00:00:00
17    cout << "\n  ";
18    t1.printStandard(); // 12:00:00 AM
19
20    cout << "\n\nt2: hour specified; minute and second defaulted\n  ";
21    t2.printUniversal(); // 02:00:00
22    cout << "\n  ";
23    t2.printStandard(); // 2:00:00 AM
24
25    cout << "\n\nt3: hour and minute specified; second defaulted\n  ";
26    t3.printUniversal(); // 21:34:00
27    cout << "\n  ";
28    t3.printStandard(); // 9:34:00 PM
29
30    cout << "\n\nt4: hour, minute and second specified\n  ";
31    t4.printUniversal(); // 12:25:42
32    cout << "\n  ";
33    t4.printStandard(); // 12:25:42 PM
34
35    // attempt to initialize t6 with invalid values
36    try
37    {
38       Time t5( 27, 74, 99 ); // all bad values specified
39    } // end try
40    catch ( invalid_argument &e )
41    {
42       cerr << "\n\nException while initializing t5: " << e.what() << endl;
43    } // end catch
44 } // end main
```

Fig. 9.6 | Constructor with default arguments. (Part 1 of 2.)

```
Constructed with:

t1: all arguments defaulted
  00:00:00
  12:00:00 AM

t2: hour specified; minute and second defaulted
  02:00:00
  2:00:00 AM

t3: hour and minute specified; second defaulted
  21:34:00
  9:34:00 PM

t4: hour, minute and second specified
  12:25:42
  12:25:42 PM

Exception while initializing t5: hour must be 0-23
```

Fig. 9.6 | Constructor with default arguments. (Part 2 of 2.)

Notes Regarding Class `Time`'s Set *and* Get *Functions and Constructor*

`Time`'s *set* and *get* functions are called throughout the class's body. In particular, function `setTime` (lines 16–21 of Fig. 9.5) calls functions `setHour`, `setMinute` and `setSecond`, and functions `printUniversal` and `printStandard` call functions `getHour`, `getMinute` and `getSecond` in line 71–72 and lines 78–80. In each case, these functions could have accessed the class's `private` data directly. However, consider changing the representation of the time from three `int` values (requiring 12 bytes of memory on systems with four-byte `int`s) to a single `int` value representing the total number of seconds that have elapsed since midnight (requiring only four bytes of memory). If we made such a change, only the bodies of the functions that access the `private` data directly would need to change—in particular, the individual *set* and *get* functions for the `hour`, `minute` and `second`. There would be no need to modify the bodies of functions `setTime`, `printUniversal` or `printStandard`, because they do *not* access the data directly. Designing the class in this manner reduces the likelihood of programming errors when altering the class's implementation.

Similarly, the `Time` constructor could be written to include a copy of the appropriate statements from function `setTime`. Doing so may be slightly more efficient, because the extra call to `setTime` is eliminated. However, duplicating statements in multiple functions or constructors makes changing the class's internal data representation more difficult. Having the `Time` constructor call `setTime` and having `setTime` call `setHour`, `setMinute` and `setSecond` enables us to limit the changes to code that validates the `hour`, `minute` or `second` to the corresponding *set* function. This reduces the likelihood of errors when altering the class's implementation.

Software Engineering Observation 9.6

If a member function of a class already provides all or part of the functionality required by a constructor (or other member function) of the class, call that member function from the constructor (or other member function). This simplifies the maintenance of the code and reduces the likelihood of an error if the implementation of the code is modified. As a general rule: Avoid repeating code.

Common Programming Error 9.1

A constructor can call other member functions of the class, such as set *or* get *functions, but because the constructor is initializing the object, the data members may not yet be initialized. Using data members before they have been properly initialized can cause logic errors.*

C++11: Using List Initializers to Call Constructors

11

Recall from Section 4.8 that C++11 now provides a uniform initialization syntax called list initializers that can be used to initialize any variable. Lines 11–13 of Fig. 9.6 can be written using list initializers as follows:

```
Time t2{ 2 }; // hour specified; minute and second defaulted
Time t3{ 21, 34 }; // hour and minute specified; second defaulted
Time t4{ 12, 25, 42 }; // hour, minute and second specified
```

or

```
Time t2 = { 2 }; // hour specified; minute and second defaulted
Time t3 = { 21, 34 }; // hour and minute specified; second defaulted
Time t4 = { 12, 25, 42 }; // hour, minute and second specified
```

The form without the = is preferred.

C++11: Overloaded Constructors and Delegating Constructors

11

Section 6.17 showed how to overload functions. A class's constructors and member functions can also be overloaded. Overloaded constructors typically allow objects to be initialized with different types and/or numbers of arguments. To overload a constructor, provide in the class definition a prototype for each version of the constructor, and provide a separate constructor definition for each overloaded version. This also applies to the class's member functions.

In Figs. 9.4–9.6, the `Time` constructor with three parameters had a default argument for each parameter. We could have defined that constructor instead as four overloaded constructors with the following prototypes:

```
Time(); // default hour, minute and second to 0
Time( int ); // initialize hour; default minute and second to 0
Time( int, int ); // initialize hour and minute; default second to
0
Time( int, int, int ); // initialize hour, minute and second
```

Just as a constructor can call a class's other member functions to perform tasks, C++11 now allows constructors to call other constructors in the same class. The calling constructor is known as a **delegating constructor**—it *delegates* its work to another constructor. This is useful when overloaded constructors have common code that previously would have been defined in a `private` utility function and called by all the constructors.

The first three of the four `Time` constructors declared above can delegate work to one with three `int` arguments, passing 0 as the default value for the extra parameters. To do so, you use a member initializer with the name of the class as follows:

```
Time::Time()
   : Time( 0, 0, 0 ) // delegate to Time( int, int, int )
{
} // end constructor with no arguments
```

```
Time::Time( int hour )
   : Time( hour, 0, 0 ) // delegate to Time( int, int, int )
{
} // end constructor with one argument

Time::Time( int hour, int minute )
   : Time( hour, minute, 0 ) // delegate to Time( int, int, int )
{
} // end constructor with two arguments
```

9.6 Destructors

A **destructor** is another type of special member function. The name of the destructor for a class is the **tilde character** (~) followed by the class name. This naming convention has intuitive appeal, because as we'll see in a later chapter, the tilde operator is the bitwise complement operator, and, in a sense, the destructor is the complement of the constructor. A destructor may not specify parameters or a return type.

A class's destructor is called *implicitly* when an object is destroyed. This occurs, for example, as an object is destroyed when program execution leaves the scope in which that object was instantiated. *The destructor itself does not actually release the object's memory*—it performs **termination housekeeping** before the object's memory is reclaimed, so the memory may be reused to hold new objects.

Even though destructors have not been defined for the classes presented so far, *every class has one destructor*. If you do not *explicitly* define a destructor, the compiler defines an "empty" destructor. [*Note:* We'll see that such an *implicitly* created destructor does, in fact, perform important operations on class-type objects that are created through composition (Section 9.11) and inheritance (Chapter 11).] In Chapter 10, we'll build destructors appropriate for classes whose objects contain dynamically allocated memory (e.g., for arrays and strings) or use other system resources (e.g., files on disk, which we study in Chapter 14). We discuss how to dynamically allocate and deallocate memory in Chapter 10.

9.7 When Constructors and Destructors Are Called

Constructors and destructors are called *implicitly* by the compiler. The order in which these function calls occur depends on the order in which execution enters and leaves the scopes where the objects are instantiated. Generally, destructor calls are made in the *reverse order* of the corresponding constructor calls, but as we'll see in Figs. 9.7–9.9, the storage classes of objects can alter the order in which destructors are called.

Constructors and Destructors for Objects in Global Scope

Constructors are called for objects defined in global scope (also called global namespace scope) *before* any other function (including `main`) in that program begins execution (although the order of execution of global object constructors between files is *not* guaranteed). The corresponding destructors are called when `main` terminates. Function **`exit`** forces a program to terminate immediately and does *not* execute the destructors of local objects. The `exit` function often is used to terminate a program when a fatal unrecoverable error occurs. Function **`abort`** performs similarly to function `exit` but forces the program to terminate *immediately*, without allowing the destructors of any objects to be called. Function abort is usually used to indicate an *abnormal termination* of the program. (See Appendix F for more information on functions exit and abort.)

Constructors and Destructors for Local Objects

The constructor for an local object is called when execution reaches the point where that object is defined—the corresponding destructor is called when execution leaves the object's scope (i.e., the block in which that object is defined has finished executing). Constructors and destructors for local objects are called each time execution enters and leaves the scope of the object. Destructors are not called for local objects if the program terminates with a call to function exit or function abort.

Constructors and Destructors for **static** *Local Objects*

The constructor for a static local object is called only *once*, when execution first reaches the point where the object is defined—the corresponding destructor is called when main terminates or the program calls function exit. Global and static objects are destroyed in the *reverse* order of their creation. Destructors are *not* called for static objects if the program terminates with a call to function abort.

Demonstrating When Constructors and Destructors Are Called

The program of Figs. 9.7–9.9 demonstrates the order in which constructors and destructors are called for objects of class CreateAndDestroy (Fig. 9.7 and Fig. 9.8) of various storage classes in several scopes. Each object of class CreateAndDestroy contains an integer (objectID) and a string (message) that are used in the program's output to identify the object (Fig. 9.7, lines 16–17). This mechanical example is purely for pedagogic purposes. For this reason, line 19 of the destructor in Fig. 9.8 determines whether the object being destroyed has an objectID value 1 or 6 (line 19) and, if so, outputs a newline character. This line makes the program's output easier to follow.

```
1  // Fig. 9.7: CreateAndDestroy.h
2  // CreateAndDestroy class definition.
3  // Member functions defined in CreateAndDestroy.cpp.
4  #include <string>
5  using namespace std;
6
7  #ifndef CREATE_H
8  #define CREATE_H
9
10 class CreateAndDestroy
11 {
12 public:
13    CreateAndDestroy( int, string ); // constructor
14    ~CreateAndDestroy(); // destructor
15 private:
16    int objectID; // ID number for object
17    string message; // message describing object
18 }; // end class CreateAndDestroy
19
20 #endif
```

Fig. 9.7 | CreateAndDestroy class definition.

```
// Fig. 9.8: CreateAndDestroy.cpp
// CreateAndDestroy class member-function definitions.
#include <iostream>
#include "CreateAndDestroy.h"// include CreateAndDestroy class definition
using namespace std;

// constructor sets object's ID number and descriptive message
CreateAndDestroy::CreateAndDestroy( int ID, string messageString )
   : objectID( ID ), message( messageString )
{
   cout << "Object " << objectID << "   constructor runs   "
      << message << endl;
} // end CreateAndDestroy constructor

// destructor
CreateAndDestroy::~CreateAndDestroy()
{
   // output newline for certain objects; helps readability
   cout << ( objectID == 1 || objectID == 6 ? "\n" : "" );

   cout << "Object " << objectID << "   destructor runs    "
      << message << endl;
} // end ~CreateAndDestroy destructor
```

Fig. 9.8 | `CreateAndDestroy` class member-function definitions.

Figure 9.9 defines object `first` (line 10) in global scope. Its constructor is actually called *before* any statements in `main` execute and its destructor is called at program termination *after* the destructors for all objects with automatic storage duration have run.

```
1  // Fig. 9.9: fig09_09.cpp
2  // Order in which constructors and
3  // destructors are called.
4  #include <iostream>
5  #include "CreateAndDestroy.h" // include CreateAndDestroy class definition
6  using namespace std;
7
8  void create( void ); // prototype
9
10 CreateAndDestroy first( 1, "(global before main)" ); // global object
11
12 int main()
13 {
14    cout << "\nMAIN FUNCTION: EXECUTION BEGINS" << endl;
15    CreateAndDestroy second( 2, "(local automatic in main)" );
16    static CreateAndDestroy third( 3, "(local static in main)" );
17
18    create(); // call function to create objects
19
20    cout << "\nMAIN FUNCTION: EXECUTION RESUMES" << endl;
21    CreateAndDestroy fourth( 4, "(local automatic in main)" );
```

Fig. 9.9 | Order in which constructors and destructors are called. (Part 1 of 2.)

```
22      cout << "\nMAIN FUNCTION: EXECUTION ENDS" << endl;
23   } // end main
24
25   // function to create objects
26   void create( void )
27   {
28      cout << "\nCREATE FUNCTION: EXECUTION BEGINS" << endl;
29      CreateAndDestroy fifth( 5, "(local automatic in create)" );
30      static CreateAndDestroy sixth( 6, "(local static in create)" );
31      CreateAndDestroy seventh( 7, "(local automatic in create)" );
32      cout << "\nCREATE FUNCTION: EXECUTION ENDS" << endl;
33   } // end function create
```

```
Object 1   constructor runs   (global before main)

MAIN FUNCTION: EXECUTION BEGINS
Object 2   constructor runs   (local automatic in main)
Object 3   constructor runs   (local static in main)

CREATE FUNCTION: EXECUTION BEGINS
Object 5   constructor runs   (local automatic in create)
Object 6   constructor runs   (local static in create)
Object 7   constructor runs   (local automatic in create)

CREATE FUNCTION: EXECUTION ENDS
Object 7   destructor runs    (local automatic in create)
Object 5   destructor runs    (local automatic in create)

MAIN FUNCTION: EXECUTION RESUMES
Object 4   constructor runs   (local automatic in main)

MAIN FUNCTION: EXECUTION ENDS
Object 4   destructor runs    (local automatic in main)
Object 2   destructor runs    (local automatic in main)

Object 6   destructor runs    (local static in create)
Object 3   destructor runs    (local static in main)

Object 1   destructor runs    (global before main)
```

Fig. 9.9 | Order in which constructors and destructors are called. (Part 2 of 2.)

Function `main` (lines 12–23) declares three objects. Objects `second` (line 15) and `fourth` (line 21) are local objects, and object `third` (line 16) is a `static` local object. The constructor for each of these objects is called when execution reaches the point where that object is declared. The destructors for objects `fourth` then `second` are called—in the *reverse* of the order in which their constructors were called—when execution reaches the end of `main`. Because object `third` is `static`, it exists until program termination. The destructor for object `third` is called *before* the destructor for global object `first`, but *after* all other objects are destroyed.

Function `create` (lines 26–33) declares three objects—`fifth` (line 29) and `seventh` (line 31) as local automatic objects, and `sixth` (line 30) as a `static` local object. The destructors for objects `seventh` then `fifth` are called—the *reverse* of the order in which their constructors were called—when `create` terminates. Because `sixth` is `static`, it exists until program termination. The destructor for `sixth` is called *before* the destructors for `third` and `first`, but *after* all other objects are destroyed.

9.8 Time Class Case Study: A Subtle Trap— Returning a Reference or a Pointer to a private Data Member

A reference to an object is an alias for the name of the object and, hence, may be used on the left side of an assignment statement. In this context, the reference makes a perfectly acceptable *lvalue* that can receive a value. One way to use this capability is to have a `public` member function of a class return a reference to a `private` data member of that class. If a function returns a reference that is declared `const`, the reference is a non-modifiable *lvalue* and cannot be used to modify the data.

The program of Figs. 9.10–9.12 uses a simplified `Time` class (Fig. 9.10 and Fig. 9.11) to demonstrate returning a reference to a `private` data member with member function `badSetHour` (declared in Fig. 9.10 in line 15 and defined in Fig. 9.11 in lines 37–45). Such a reference return actually makes a call to member function `badSetHour` an alias for `private` data member `hour`! The function call can be used in any way that the `private` data member can be used, including as an *lvalue* in an assignment statement, thus *enabling clients of the class to clobber the class's* `private` *data at will!* A similar problem would occur if a pointer to the `private` data were to be returned by the function.

```
1  // Fig. 9.10: Time.h
2  // Time class declaration.
3  // Member functions defined in Time.cpp
4
5  // prevent multiple inclusions of header
6  #ifndef TIME_H
7  #define TIME_H
8
9  class Time
10 {
11 public:
12    explicit Time( int = 0, int = 0, int = 0 );
13    void setTime( int, int, int );
14    unsigned int getHour() const;
15    unsigned int &badSetHour( int ); // dangerous reference return
16 private:
17    unsigned int hour;
18    unsigned int minute;
19    unsigned int second;
20 }; // end class Time
21
22 #endif
```

Fig. 9.10 | Time class declaration.

```
// Fig. 9.11: Time.cpp
// Time class member-function definitions.
#include <stdexcept>
#include "Time.h" // include definition of class Time
using namespace std;

// constructor function to initialize private data; calls member function
// setTime to set variables; default values are 0 (see class definition)
Time::Time( int hr, int min, int sec )
{
   setTime( hr, min, sec );
} // end Time constructor

// set values of hour, minute and second
void Time::setTime( int h, int m, int s )
{
   // validate hour, minute and second
   if ( ( h >= 0 && h < 24 ) && ( m >= 0 && m < 60 ) &&
      ( s >= 0 && s < 60 ) )
   {
      hour = h;
      minute = m;
      second = s;
   } // end if
   else
      throw invalid_argument(
         "hour, minute and/or second was out of range" );
} // end function setTime

// return hour value
unsigned int Time::getHour()
{
   return hour;
} // end function getHour

// poor practice: returning a reference to a private data member.
unsigned int &Time::badSetHour( int hh )
{
   if ( hh >= 0 && hh < 24 )
      hour = hh;
   else
      throw invalid_argument( "hour must be 0-23" );

   return hour; // dangerous reference return
} // end function badSetHour
```

Fig. 9.11 | Time class member-function definitions.

Figure 9.12 declares `Time` object `t` (line 10) and reference `hourRef` (line 13), which is initialized with the reference returned by the call `t.badSetHour(20)`. Line 15 displays the value of the alias `hourRef`. This shows how `hourRef` *breaks the encapsulation of the class*—statements in `main` should not have access to the `private` data of the class. Next, line 16 uses the alias to set the value of `hour` to 30 (an invalid value) and line 17 displays the value returned by function `getHour` to show that assigning a value to `hourRef` actually modifies the `private` data in the `Time` object `t`. Finally, line 21 uses the `badSetHour` function call itself as an *lvalue* and assigns 74 (another invalid value) to the reference returned by the function. Line 26 again displays the value returned by function `getHour` to show that assigning a value to the result of the function call in line 21 modifies the `private` data in the `Time` object `t`.

Software Engineering Observation 9.7

Returning a reference or a pointer to a `private` data member breaks the encapsulation of the class and makes the client code dependent on the representation of the class's data. There are cases where doing this is appropriate—we'll show an example of this when we build our custom `Array` class in Section 10.10.

```
1  // Fig. 9.12: fig09_12.cpp
2  // Demonstrating a public member function that
3  // returns a reference to a private data member.
4  #include <iostream>
5  #include "Time.h" // include definition of class Time
6  using namespace std;
7
8  int main()
9  {
10    Time t; // create Time object
11
12    // initialize hourRef with the reference returned by badSetHour
13    int &hourRef = t.badSetHour( 20 ); // 20 is a valid hour
14
15    cout << "Valid hour before modification: " << hourRef;
16    hourRef = 30; // use hourRef to set invalid value in Time object t
17    cout << "\nInvalid hour after modification: " << t.getHour();
18
19    // Dangerous: Function call that returns
20    // a reference can be used as an lvalue!
21    t.badSetHour( 12 ) = 74; // assign another invalid value to hour
22
23    cout << "\n\n*************************************************\n"
24       << "POOR PROGRAMMING PRACTICE!!!!!!!!\n"
25       << "t.badSetHour( 12 ) as an lvalue, invalid hour: "
26       << t.getHour()
27       << "\n*************************************************" << endl;
28 } // end main
```

```
Valid hour before modification: 20
Invalid hour after modification: 30

*************************************************
POOR PROGRAMMING PRACTICE!!!!!!!!
t.badSetHour( 12 ) as an lvalue, invalid hour: 74
*************************************************
```

Fig. 9.12 | `public` member function that returns a reference to a `private` data member.

9.9 Default Memberwise Assignment

The assignment operator (=) can be used to assign an object to another object of the same class. By default, such assignment is performed by **memberwise assignment** (also called **copy assignment**)—each data member of the object on the *right* of the assignment operator is assigned individually to the *same* data member in the object on the *left* of the assignment operator. Figures 9.13–9.14 define a `Date` class. Line 18 of Fig. 9.15 uses **default memberwise assignment** to assign the data members of `Date` object `date1` to the corresponding data members of `Date` object `date2`. In this case, the `month` member of `date1` is assigned to the `month` member of `date2`, the `day` member of `date1` is assigned to the `day` member of `date2` and the `year` member of `date1` is assigned to the `year` member of `date2`. [*Caution:* Memberwise assignment can cause serious problems when used with a class whose data members contain pointers to dynamically allocated memory; we discuss these problems in Chapter 10 and show how to deal with them.]

```
// Fig. 9.13: Date.h
// Date class declaration.  Member functions are defined in Date.cpp.

// prevent multiple inclusions of header
#ifndef DATE_H
#define DATE_H

// class Date definition
class Date
{
public:
   explicit Date( int = 1, int = 1, int = 2000 ); // default constructor
   void print();
private:
   unsigned int month;
   unsigned int day;
   unsigned int year;
}; // end class Date

#endif
```

Fig. 9.13 | Date class declaration.

```
// Fig. 9.14: Date.cpp
// Date class member-function definitions.
#include <iostream>
#include "Date.h" // include definition of class Date from Date.h
using namespace std;

// Date constructor (should do range checking)
Date::Date( int m, int d, int y )
   : month( m ), day( d ), year( y )
{
} // end constructor Date
```

Fig. 9.14 | Date class member-function definitions. (Part 1 of 2.)

```

// print Date in the format mm/dd/yyyy
void Date::print()
{
   cout << month << '/' << day << '/' << year;
} // end function print
```

Fig. 9.14 | Date class member-function definitions. (Part 2 of 2.)

```
// Fig. 9.15: fig09_15.cpp
// Demonstrating that class objects can be assigned
// to each other using default memberwise assignment.
#include <iostream>
#include "Date.h" // include definition of class Date from Date.h
using namespace std;

int main()
{
   Date date1( 7, 4, 2004 );
   Date date2; // date2 defaults to 1/1/2000

   cout << "date1 = ";
   date1.print();
   cout << "\ndate2 = ";
   date2.print();

   date2 = date1; // default memberwise assignment

   cout << "\n\nAfter default memberwise assignment, date2 = ";
   date2.print();
   cout << endl;
} // end main
```

```
date1 = 7/4/2004
date2 = 1/1/2000

After default memberwise assignment, date2 = 7/4/2004
```

Fig. 9.15 | Class objects can be assigned to each other using default memberwise assignment.

Objects may be passed as function arguments and may be returned from functions. Such passing and returning is performed using pass-by-value by default—a *copy* of the object is passed or returned. In such cases, C++ creates a new object and uses a **copy constructor** to copy the original object's values into the new object. For each class, the compiler provides a default copy constructor that copies each member of the original object into the corresponding member of the new object. Like memberwise assignment, copy constructors can cause serious problems when used with a class whose data members contain pointers to dynamically allocated memory. Chapter 10 discusses how to define customized copy constructors that properly copy objects containing pointers to dynamically allocated memory.

9.10 const Objects and const Member Functions

Let's see how the principle of least privilege applies to objects. Some objects need to be modifiable and some do not. You may use keyword `const` to specify that an object *is not* modifiable and that any attempt to modify the object should result in a compilation error. The statement

```
const Time noon( 12, 0, 0 );
```

declares a `const` object `noon` of class `Time` and initializes it to 12 noon. It's possible to instantiate `const` and non-`const` objects of the same class.

Software Engineering Observation 9.8

Attempts to modify a `const` *object are caught at compile time rather than causing execution-time errors.*

Performance Tip 9.3

Declaring variables and objects `const` *when appropriate can improve performance—compilers can perform optimizations on constants that cannot be performed on non-*`const` *variables.*

C++ disallows member function calls for `const` *objects unless the member functions themselves are also declared* `const`. This is true even for *get* member functions that do *not* modify the object. *This is also a key reason that we've declared as* `const` *all member-functions that do not modify the objects on which they're called.*

As you saw starting with class `GradeBook` in Chapter 3, a member function is specified as `const` *both* in its prototype by inserting the keyword `const` *after* the function's parameter list and, in the case of the function definition, before the left brace that begins the function *body*.

Common Programming Error 9.2

Defining as `const` *a member function that modifies a data member of the object is a compilation error.*

Common Programming Error 9.3

Defining as `const` *a member function that calls a non-*`const` *member function of the class on the same object is a compilation error.*

Common Programming Error 9.4

Invoking a non-`const` *member function on a* `const` *object is a compilation error.*

An interesting problem arises for constructors and destructors, each of which typically modifies objects. A constructor *must* be allowed to modify an object so that the object can be initialized properly. A destructor must be able to perform its termination housekeeping chores before an object's memory is reclaimed by the system. Attempting to declare a constructor or destructor `const` is a compilation error. The "`const`ness" of a `const` object is enforced from the time the constructor *completes* initialization of the object until that object's destructor is called.

Using **const** *and Non-***const** *Member Functions*

The program of Fig. 9.16 uses class `Time` from Figs. 9.4–9.5, but removes `const` from function `printStandard`'s prototype and definition so that we can show a compilation error. We instantiate two `Time` objects—non-`const` object `wakeUp` (line 7) and `const` object `noon` (line 8). The program attempts to invoke non-`const` member functions `setHour` (line 13) and `printStandard` (line 20) on the `const` object `noon`. In each case, the compiler generates an error message. The program also illustrates the three other member-function-call combinations on objects—a non-`const` member function on a non-`const` object (line 11), a `const` member function on a non-`const` object (line 15) and a `const` member function on a `const` object (lines 17–18). The error messages generated for non-`const` member functions called on a `const` object are shown in the output window.

```
1  // Fig. 9.16: fig09_16.cpp
2  // const objects and const member functions.
3  #include "Time.h" // include Time class definition
4
5  int main()
6  {
7     Time wakeUp( 6, 45, 0 ); // non-constant object
8     const Time noon( 12, 0, 0 ); // constant object
9
10                              // OBJECT       MEMBER FUNCTION
11    wakeUp.setHour( 18 );  // non-const    non-const
12
13    noon.setHour( 12 );    // const        non-const
14
15    wakeUp.getHour();      // non-const    const
16
17    noon.getMinute();      // const        const
18    noon.printUniversal(); // const        const
19
20    noon.printStandard();  // const        non-const
21 } // end main
```

Microsoft Visual C++ compiler error messages:

```
C:\examples\ch09\Fig09_16_18\fig09_18.cpp(13) : error C2662:
   'Time::setHour' : cannot convert 'this' pointer from 'const Time' to
   'Time &'
          Conversion loses qualifiers
C:\examples\ch09\Fig09_16_18\fig09_18.cpp(20) : error C2662:
   'Time::printStandard' : cannot convert 'this' pointer from 'const Time' to
   'Time &'
        Conversion loses qualifiers
```

Fig. 9.16 | `const` objects and `const` member functions.

A constructor must be a non-`const` *member function*, but it can still be used to initialize a `const` object (Fig. 9.16, line 8). Recall from Fig. 9.5 that the `Time` constructor's definition calls another non-`const` member function—`setTime`—to perform the initialization of a `Time` object. Invoking a non-`const` member function from the constructor call as part of the initialization of a `const` object is allowed.

Line 20 in Fig. 9.16 generates a compilation error even though member function `printStandard` of class `Time` *does not* modify the object on which it's invoked. The fact that a member function does not modify an object is *not* sufficient—the function must *explicitly* be declared `const`.

9.11 Composition: Objects as Members of Classes

An `AlarmClock` object needs to know when it's supposed to sound its alarm, so why not include a `Time` object as a member of the `AlarmClock` class? Such a capability is called **composition** and is sometimes referred to as a ***has-a* relationship**—*a class can have objects of other classes as members.*

Software Engineering Observation 9.9

A common form of software reusability is composition, in which a class has objects of other types as members.

Previously, we saw how to pass arguments to the constructor of an object we created in `main`. Now we show how *an class's constructor can pass arguments to member-object constructors via member initializers.*

Software Engineering Observation 9.10

Data members are constructed in the order in which they're declared in the class definition (not in the order they're listed in the constructor's member initializer list) and before their enclosing class objects (sometimes called ***host objects****) are constructed.*

The next program uses classes `Date` (Figs. 9.17–9.18) and `Employee` (Figs. 9.19–9.20) to demonstrate composition. Class `Employee`'s definition (Fig. 9.19) contains `private` data members `firstName`, `lastName`, `birthDate` and `hireDate`. Members `birthDate` and `hireDate` are `const` objects of class `Date`, which contains `private` data members `month`, `day` and `year`. The `Employee` constructor's header (Fig. 9.20, lines 10–11) specifies that the constructor has four parameters (`first`, `last`, `dateOfBirth` and `dateOfHire`). The first two parameters are passed via member initializers to the `string` class constructor for the `firstName` and `lastName` data members. The last two are passed via member initializers to the `Date` class constructor for the `birthDate` and `hireDate` data members.

```
// Fig. 9.17: Date.h
// Date class definition; Member functions defined in Date.cpp
#ifndef DATE_H
#define DATE_H

class Date
{
public:
   static const unsigned int monthsPerYear = 12; // months in a year
   explicit Date( int = 1, int = 1, int = 1900 ); // default constructor
   void print() const; // print date in month/day/year format
   ~Date(); // provided to confirm destruction order
```

Fig. 9.17 | Date class definition. (Part 1 of 2.)

```
private:
   unsigned int month; // 1-12 (January-December)
   unsigned int day; // 1-31 based on month
   unsigned int year; // any year

   // utility function to check if day is proper for month and year
   unsigned int checkDay( int ) const;
}; // end class Date

#endif
```

Fig. 9.17 | Date class definition. (Part 2 of 2.)

```
// Fig. 9.18: Date.cpp
// Date class member-function definitions.
#include <array>
#include <iostream>
#include <stdexcept>
#include "Date.h" // include Date class definition
using namespace std;

// constructor confirms proper value for month; calls
// utility function checkDay to confirm proper value for day
Date::Date( int mn, int dy, int yr )
{
   if ( mn > 0 && mn <= monthsPerYear ) // validate the month
      month = mn;
   else
      throw invalid_argument( "month must be 1-12" );

   year = yr; // could validate yr
   day = checkDay( dy ); // validate the day

   // output Date object to show when its constructor is called
   cout << "Date object constructor for date ";
   print();
   cout << endl;
} // end Date constructor

// print Date object in form month/day/year
void Date::print() const
{
   cout << month << '/' << day << '/' << year;
} // end function print

// output Date object to show when its destructor is called
Date::~Date()
{
   cout << "Date object destructor for date ";
   print();
   cout << endl;
} // end ~Date destructor
```

Fig. 9.18 | Date class member-function definitions. (Part 1 of 2.)

```

// utility function to confirm proper day value based on
// month and year; handles leap years, too
unsigned int Date::checkDay( int testDay ) const
{
   static const array< int, monthsPerYear + 1 > daysPerMonth =
      { 0, 31, 28, 31, 30, 31, 30, 31, 31, 30, 31, 30, 31 };

   // determine whether testDay is valid for specified month
   if ( testDay > 0 && testDay <= daysPerMonth[ month ] )
      return testDay;

   // February 29 check for leap year
   if ( month == 2 && testDay == 29 && ( year % 400 == 0 ||
      ( year % 4 == 0 && year % 100 != 0 ) ) )
      return testDay;

   throw invalid_argument( "Invalid day for current month and year" );
} // end function checkDay
```

Fig. 9.18 | Date class member-function definitions. (Part 2 of 2.)

```
// Fig. 9.19: Employee.h
// Employee class definition showing composition.
// Member functions defined in Employee.cpp.
#ifndef EMPLOYEE_H
#define EMPLOYEE_H

#include <string>
#include "Date.h" // include Date class definition

class Employee
{
public:
   Employee( const std::string &, const std::string &,
      const Date &, const Date & );
   void print() const;
   ~Employee(); // provided to confirm destruction order
private:
   std::string firstName; // composition: member object
   std::string lastName; // composition: member object
   const Date birthDate; // composition: member object
   const Date hireDate; // composition: member object
}; // end class Employee

#endif
```

Fig. 9.19 | Employee class definition showing composition.

```
1  // Fig. 9.20: Employee.cpp
2  // Employee class member-function definitions.
3  #include <iostream>
4  #include "Employee.h" // Employee class definition
5  #include "Date.h" // Date class definition
6  using namespace std;
7
8  // constructor uses member initializer list to pass initializer
9  // values to constructors of member objects
10 Employee::Employee( const string &first, const string &last,
11    const Date &dateOfBirth, const Date &dateOfHire )
12    : firstName( first ), // initialize firstName
13      lastName( last ), // initialize lastName
14      birthDate( dateOfBirth ), // initialize birthDate
15      hireDate( dateOfHire ) // initialize hireDate
16 {
17    // output Employee object to show when constructor is called
18    cout << "Employee object constructor: "
19       << firstName << ' ' << lastName << endl;
20 } // end Employee constructor
21
22 // print Employee object
23 void Employee::print() const
24 {
25    cout << lastName << ", " << firstName << "  Hired: ";
26    hireDate.print();
27    cout << "  Birthday: ";
28    birthDate.print();
29    cout << endl;
30 } // end function print
31
32 // output Employee object to show when its destructor is called
33 Employee::~Employee()
34 {
35    cout << "Employee object destructor: "
36       << lastName << ", " << firstName << endl;
37 } // end ~Employee destructor
```

Fig. 9.20 | `Employee` class member-function definitions.

`Employee` Constructor's Member Initializer List

The *colon (:)* following the constructor's header (Fig. 9.20, line 12) begins the *member initializer list*. The member initializers specify the `Employee` constructor parameters being passed to the constructors of the `string` and `Date` data members. Parameters `first`, `last`, `dateOfBirth` and `dateOfHire` are passed to the constructors for objects `firstName` (line 12), `lastName` (line 13), `birthDate` (line 14) and `hireDate` (line 15), respectively. Again, member initializers are separated by commas. The order of the member initializers does not matter. They're executed in the order that the member objects are declared in class `Employee`.

Good Programming Practice 9.3

For clarity, list member initializers in the order that the class's data members are declared.

`Date` *Class's Default Copy Constructor*

As you study class `Date` (Fig. 9.17), notice that the class does *not* provide a constructor that receives a parameter of type `Date`. So, why can the `Employee` constructor's member initializer list initialize the `birthDate` and `hireDate` objects by passing `Date` objects to their `Date` constructors? As we mentioned in Section 9.9, the compiler provides each class with a *default copy constructor* that copies each data member of the constructor's argument object into the corresponding member of the object being initialized. Chapter 10 discusses how you can define *customized* copy constructors.

Testing Classes `Date` *and* `Employee`

Figure 9.21 creates two `Date` objects (lines 10–11) and passes them as arguments to the constructor of the `Employee` object created in line 12. Line 15 outputs the `Employee` object's data. When each `Date` object is created in lines 10–11, the `Date` constructor defined in lines 11–25 of Fig. 9.18 displays a line of output to show that the constructor was called (see the first two lines of the sample output). [*Note:* Line 12 of Fig. 9.21 causes two additional `Date` constructor calls that do not appear in the program's output. When each of the `Employee`'s `Date` member objects is initialized in the `Employee` constructor's member-initializer list (Fig. 9.20, lines 14–15), the default copy constructor for class `Date` is called. Since this constructor is defined implicitly by the compiler, it does not contain any output statements to demonstrate when it's called.]

```
1  // Fig. 9.21: fig09_21.cpp
2  // Demonstrating composition--an object with member objects.
3  #include <iostream>
4  #include "Date.h" // Date class definition
5  #include "Employee.h" // Employee class definition
6  using namespace std;
7
8  int main()
9  {
10    Date birth( 7, 24, 1949 );
11    Date hire( 3, 12, 1988 );
12    Employee manager( "Bob", "Blue", birth, hire );
13
14    cout << endl;
15    manager.print();
16 } // end main
```

```
Date object constructor for date 7/24/1949
Date object constructor for date 3/12/1988
Employee object constructor: Bob Blue

Blue, Bob  Hired: 3/12/1988  Birthday: 7/24/1949
Employee object destructor: Blue, Bob
Date object destructor for date 3/12/1988
Date object destructor for date 7/24/1949
Date object destructor for date 3/12/1988
Date object destructor for date 7/24/1949
```

There are actually five constructor calls when an `Employee` is constructed—two calls to the `string` class's constructor (lines 12–13 of Fig. 9.20), two calls to the `Date` class's default copy constructor (lines 14–15 of Fig. 9.20) and the call to the `Employee` class's constructor.

Fig. 9.21 | Demonstrating composition—an object with member objects.

Class `Date` and class `Employee` each include a destructor (lines 34–39 of Fig. 9.18 and lines 33–37 of Fig. 9.20, respectively) that prints a message when an object of its class is destructed. This enables us to confirm in the program output that objects are constructed from the *inside out* and destroyed in the *reverse* order, from the *outside in* (i.e., the `Date` *member* objects are destroyed after the `Employee` object that *contains* them).

Notice the last four lines in the output of Fig. 9.21. The last two lines are the outputs of the `Date` destructor running on `Date` objects `hire` (Fig. 9.21, line 11) and `birth` (Fig. 9.21, line 10), respectively. These outputs confirm that the three objects created in `main` are destructed in the *reverse* of the order in which they were constructed. The `Employee` destructor output is five lines from the bottom. The fourth and third lines from the bottom of the output window show the destructors running for the `Employee`'s member objects `hireDate` (Fig. 9.19, line 21) and `birthDate` (Fig. 9.19, line 20). The last two lines of the output correspond to the `Date` objects created in lines 11and 10 of Fig. 9.21.

These outputs confirm that the `Employee` object is destructed from the *outside in*—i.e., the `Employee` destructor runs first (output shown five lines from the bottom of the output window), then the member objects are destructed in the *reverse order* from which they were constructed. Class `string`'s destructor does not contain output statements, so we do *not* see the `firstName` and `lastName` objects being destructed. Again, Fig. 9.21's output did not show the constructors running for member objects `birthDate` and `hireDate`, because these objects were initialized with the *default* `Date` class copy constructors provided by the compiler.

What Happens When You Do Not Use the Member Initializer List?

If a member object is *not* initialized through a member initializer, the member object's *default constructor* will be called *implicitly*. Values, if any, established by the default constructor can be overridden by *set* functions. However, for complex initialization, this approach may require significant additional work and time.

Common Programming Error 9.5

A compilation error occurs if a member object is not initialized with a member initializer and the member object's class does not provide a default constructor (i.e., the member object's class defines one or more constructors, but none is a default constructor).

Performance Tip 9.4

Initialize member objects explicitly through member initializers. This eliminates the overhead of "doubly initializing" member objects—once when the member object's default constructor is called and again when set *functions are called in the constructor body (or later) to initialize the member object.*

Software Engineering Observation 9.11

If a data member is an object of another class, making that member object `public` *does not violate the encapsulation and hiding of that member object's* `private` *members. But, it does violate the encapsulation and hiding of the containing class's implementation, so member objects of class types should still be* `private`.

9.12 friend Functions and friend Classes

A **friend function** of a class is a non-member function that has the right to access the public *and* non-public class members. Standalone functions, entire classes or member functions of other classes may be declared to be *friends* of another class.

This section presents a mechanical example of how a friend function works. In Chapter 10 we'll show friend functions that overload operators for use with class objects—as you'll see, sometimes a member function cannot be used for certain overloaded operators.

Declaring a friend

To declare a function as a friend of a class, precede the function prototype in the class definition with keyword friend. To declare all member functions of class ClassTwo as friends of class ClassOne, place a declaration of the form

```
friend class ClassTwo;
```

in the definition of class ClassOne.

Friendship is *granted, not taken*—for class B to be a friend of class A, class A must *explicitly* declare that class B is its friend. Friendship is not *symmetric*—if class A is a friend of class B, you cannot infer that class B is a friend of class A. Friendship is not *transitive*—if class A is a friend of class B and class B is a friend of class C, you cannot infer that class A is a friend of class C.

Modifying a Class's private Data with a Friend Function

Figure 9.22 is a mechanical example in which we define friend function setX to set the private data member x of class Count. As a convention, we place the friend declaration (line 9) *first* in the class definition, even before public member functions are declared. Again, this friend declaration can appear *anywhere* in the class.

Function setX (lines 29–32) is a stand-alone (global) function—it isn't a member function of class Count. For this reason, when setX is invoked for object counter, line 41 passes counter as an argument to setX rather than using a handle (such as the name of the object) to call the function, as in

```
counter.setX( 8 ); // error: setX not a member function
```

If you remove the friend declaration in line 9, you'll receive error messages indicating that function setX cannot modify class Count's private data member x.

```
1  //Fig. 9.22: fig09_22.cpp
2  // Friends can access private members of a class.
3  #include <iostream>
4  using namespace std;
5
6  // Count class definition
7  class Count
8  {
9     friend void setX( Count &, int ); // friend declaration
```

Fig. 9.22 | Friends can access private members of a class. (Part 1 of 2.)

```cpp
public:
   // constructor
   Count()
      : x( 0 ) // initialize x to 0
   {
      // empty body
   } // end constructor Count

   // output x
   void print() const
   {
      cout << x << endl;
   } // end function print
private:
   int x; // data member
}; // end class Count

// function setX can modify private data of Count
// because setX is declared as a friend of Count (line 9)
void setX( Count &c, int val )
{
   c.x = val; // allowed because setX is a friend of Count
} // end function setX

int main()
{
   Count counter; // create Count object

   cout << "counter.x after instantiation: ";
   counter.print();

   setX( counter, 8 ); // set x using a friend function
   cout << "counter.x after call to setX friend function: ";
   counter.print();
} // end main
```

```
counter.x after instantiation: 0
counter.x after call to setX friend function: 8
```

Fig. 9.22 | `Friends` can access `private` members of a class. (Part 2 of 2.)

As we mentioned, Fig. 9.22 is a mechanical example of using the `friend` construct. It would normally be appropriate to define function `setX` as a member function of class `Count`. It would also normally be appropriate to separate the program of Fig. 9.22 into three files:

1. A header (e.g., `Count.h`) containing the `Count` class definition, which in turn contains the prototype of `friend` function `setX`
2. An implementation file (e.g., `Count.cpp`) containing the definitions of class `Count`'s member functions and the definition of `friend` function `setX`
3. A test program (e.g., `fig09_22.cpp`) with `main`.

Overloaded **friend** *Functions*

It's possible to specify overloaded functions as friends of a class. Each function intended to be a friend must be explicitly declared in the class definition as a friend of the class.

Software Engineering Observation 9.12

Even though the prototypes for friend *functions appear in the class definition, friends are* not *member functions.*

Software Engineering Observation 9.13

Member access notions of private, protected *and* public *are not relevant to* friend *declarations, so* friend *declarations can be placed* anywhere *in a class definition.*

Good Programming Practice 9.4

Place all friendship declarations first inside the class definition's body and do not precede them with any access specifier.

9.13 Using the this Pointer

We've seen that an object's member functions can manipulate the object's data. There can be *many* objects of a class, so how do member functions know *which* object's data members to manipulate? Every object has access to its own address through a pointer called **this** (a C++ keyword). The this pointer is *not* part of the object itself—i.e., the memory occupied by the this pointer is not reflected in the result of a sizeof operation on the object. Rather, the this pointer is passed (by the compiler) as an *implicit* argument to each of the object's non-static member functions. Section 9.14 introduces static class members and explains why the this pointer is *not* implicitly passed to static member functions.

Using the **this** *Pointer to Avoid Naming Collisions*

Member functions use the this pointer *implicitly* (as we've done so far) or *explicitly* to reference an object's data members and other member functions. A common *explicit* use of the this pointer is to avoid *naming conflicts* between a class's data members and member-function parameters (or other local variables). Consider the Time class's hour data member and setHour member function in Figs. 9.4–9.5. We could have defined setHour as:

```
// set hour value
void Time::setHour( int hour )
{
   if ( hour >= 0 && hour < 24 )
      this->hour = hour; // use this pointer to access data member
   else
      throw invalid_argument( "hour must be 0-23" );
} // end function setHour
```

In this function definition, setHour's parameter has the *same name* as the data member hour. In setHour's scope, the parameter hour *hides* the data member. However, you can still access the data member hour by qualifying its name with this->. So the following statement assigns the hour parameter's value to the data member hour

```
this->hour = hour; // use this pointer to access data member
```

Error-Prevention Tip 9.4

To make your code clearer and more maintainable, and to avoid errors, never hide data members with local variable names.

Type of the `this` Pointer

The type of the `this` pointer depends on the type of the object and whether the member function in which `this` is used is declared `const`. For example, in a non-`const` member function of class `Employee`, the `this` pointer has the type `Employee *`. In a `const` member function, the `this` pointer has the type `const Employee *`.

Implicitly and Explicitly Using the `this` Pointer to Access an Object's Data Members

Figure 9.23 demonstrates the implicit and explicit use of the `this` pointer to enable a member function of class `Test` to print the `private` data `x` of a `Test` object. In the next example and in Chapter 10, we show some substantial and subtle examples of using `this`.

```
// Fig. 9.23: fig09_23.cpp
// Using the this pointer to refer to object members.
#include <iostream>
using namespace std;

class Test
{
public:
   explicit Test( int = 0 ); // default constructor
   void print() const;
private:
   int x;
}; // end class Test

// constructor
Test::Test( int value )
   : x( value ) // initialize x to value
{
   // empty body
} // end constructor Test

// print x using implicit and explicit this pointers;
// the parentheses around *this are required
void Test::print() const
{
   // implicitly use the this pointer to access the member x
   cout << "        x = " << x;

   // explicitly use the this pointer and the arrow operator
   // to access the member x
   cout << "\n  this->x = " << this->x;

```

Fig. 9.23 | using the `this` pointer to refer to object members. (Part 1 of 2.)

```
33      // explicitly use the dereferenced this pointer and
34      // the dot operator to access the member x
35      cout << "\n(*this).x = " << ( *this ).x << endl;
36   } // end function print
37
38   int main()
39   {
40      Test testObject( 12 ); // instantiate and initialize testObject
41
42      testObject.print();
43   } // end main
```

```
        x = 12
  this->x = 12
(*this).x = 12
```

Fig. 9.23 | using the `this` pointer to refer to object members. (Part 2 of 2.)

For illustration purposes, member function `print` (lines 24–36) first prints `x` by using the `this` pointer *implicitly* (line 27)—only the name of the data member is specified. Then `print` uses two different notations to access `x` through the `this` pointer—the arrow operator (`->`) off the `this` pointer (line 31) and the dot operator (`.`) off the dereferenced `this` pointer (line 35). Note the parentheses around `*this` (line 35) when used with the dot member selection operator (`.`). The parentheses are required because the dot operator has *higher* precedence than the `*` operator. Without the parentheses, the expression `*this.x` would be evaluated as if it were parenthesized as `*(this.x)`, which is a *compilation error*, because the dot operator cannot be used with a pointer.

One interesting use of the `this` pointer is to prevent an object from being assigned to itself. As we'll see in Chapter 10, *self-assignment* can cause serious errors when the object contains pointers to dynamically allocated storage.

Using the `this` Pointer to Enable Cascaded Function Calls

Another use of the `this` pointer is to enable **cascaded member-function calls**—that is, invoking multiple functions in the same statement (as in line 12 of Fig. 9.26). The program of Figs. 9.24–9.26 modifies class `Time`'s *set* functions `setTime`, `setHour`, `setMinute` and `setSecond` such that each returns a reference to a `Time` object to enable cascaded member-function calls. Notice in Fig. 9.25 that the last statement in the body of each of these member functions returns `*this` (lines 23, 34, 45 and 56) into a return type of `Time &`.

The program of Fig. 9.26 creates `Time` object `t` (line 9), then uses it in *cascaded member-function calls* (lines 12 and 24). Why does the technique of returning `*this` as a reference work? The dot operator (`.`) associates from left to right, so line 12 first evaluates `t.setHour(18)`, then returns a reference to object `t` as the value of this function call. The remaining expression is then interpreted as

```
t.setMinute( 30 ).setSecond( 22 );
```

The `t.setMinute(30)` call executes and returns a reference to the object `t`. The remaining expression is interpreted as

```
t.setSecond( 22 );
```

```
// Fig. 9.24: Time.h
// Cascading member function calls.

// Time class definition.
// Member functions defined in Time.cpp.
#ifndef TIME_H
#define TIME_H

class Time
{
public:
   explicit Time( int = 0, int = 0, int = 0 ); // default constructor

   // set functions (the Time & return types enable cascading)
   Time &setTime( int, int, int ); // set hour, minute, second
   Time &setHour( int ); // set hour
   Time &setMinute( int ); // set minute
   Time &setSecond( int ); // set second

   // get functions (normally declared const)
   unsigned int getHour() const; // return hour
   unsigned int getMinute() const; // return minute
   unsigned int getSecond() const; // return second

   // print functions (normally declared const)
   void printUniversal() const; // print universal time
   void printStandard() const; // print standard time
private:
   unsigned int hour; // 0 - 23 (24-hour clock format)
   unsigned int minute; // 0 - 59
   unsigned int second; // 0 - 59
}; // end class Time

#endif
```

Fig. 9.24 | Time class modified to enable cascaded member-function calls.

```
// Fig. 9.25: Time.cpp
// Time class member-function definitions.
#include <iostream>
#include <iomanip>
#include <stdexcept>
#include "Time.h" // Time class definition
using namespace std;

// constructor function to initialize private data;
// calls member function setTime to set variables;
// default values are 0 (see class definition)
Time::Time( int hr, int min, int sec )
{
```

Fig. 9.25 | Time class member-function definitions modified to enable cascaded member-function calls. (Part 1 of 3.)

```
   setTime( hr, min, sec );
} // end Time constructor

// set values of hour, minute, and second
Time &Time::setTime( int h, int m, int s ) // note Time & return
{
   setHour( h );
   setMinute( m );
   setSecond( s );
   return *this; // enables cascading
} // end function setTime

// set hour value
Time &Time::setHour( int h ) // note Time & return
{
   if ( h >= 0 && h < 24 )
      hour = h;
   else
      throw invalid_argument( "hour must be 0-23" );

   return *this; // enables cascading
} // end function setHour

// set minute value
Time &Time::setMinute( int m ) // note Time & return
{
   if ( m >= 0 && m < 60 )
      minute = m;
   else
      throw invalid_argument( "minute must be 0-59" );

   return *this; // enables cascading
} // end function setMinute

// set second value
Time &Time::setSecond( int s ) // note Time & return
{
   if ( s >= 0 && s < 60 )
      second = s;
   else
      throw invalid_argument( "second must be 0-59" );

   return *this; // enables cascading
} // end function setSecond

// get hour value
unsigned int Time::getHour() const
{
   return hour;
} // end function getHour

```

Fig. 9.25 | Time class member-function definitions modified to enable cascaded member-function calls. (Part 2 of 3.)

```
// get minute value
unsigned int Time::getMinute() const
{
   return minute;
} // end function getMinute

// get second value
unsigned int Time::getSecond() const
{
   return second;
} // end function getSecond

// print Time in universal-time format (HH:MM:SS)
void Time::printUniversal() const
{
   cout << setfill( '0' ) << setw( 2 ) << hour << ":"
      << setw( 2 ) << minute << ":" << setw( 2 ) << second;
} // end function printUniversal

// print Time in standard-time format (HH:MM:SS AM or PM)
void Time::printStandard() const
{
   cout << ( ( hour == 0 || hour == 12 ) ? 12 : hour % 12 )
      << ":" << setfill( '0' ) << setw( 2 ) << minute
      << ":" << setw( 2 ) << second << ( hour < 12 ? " AM" : " PM" );
} // end function printStandard
```

Fig. 9.25 | `Time` class member-function definitions modified to enable cascaded member-function calls. (Part 3 of 3.)

Line 24 (Fig. 9.26) also uses cascading. Note that we cannot chain another member-function call after `printStandard` here, because `printStandard` does *not* return a reference to `t`. Placing the call to `printStandard` before the call to `setTime` in line 24 results in a compilation error. Chapter 10 presents several practical examples of using cascaded function calls. One such example uses multiple << operators with `cout` to output multiple values in a single statement.

```
1  // Fig. 9.26: fig09_26.cpp
2  // Cascading member-function calls with the this pointer.
3  #include <iostream>
4  #include "Time.h" // Time class definition
5  using namespace std;
6
7  int main()
8  {
9     Time t; // create Time object
10
11    // cascaded function calls
12    t.setHour( 18 ).setMinute( 30 ).setSecond( 22 );
13
```

Fig. 9.26 | Cascading member-function calls with the `this` pointer. (Part 1 of 2.)

```
    // output time in universal and standard formats
    cout << "Universal time: ";
    t.printUniversal();

    cout << "\nStandard time: ";
    t.printStandard();

    cout << "\n\nNew standard time: ";

    // cascaded function calls
    t.setTime( 20, 20, 20 ).printStandard();
    cout << endl;
} // end main
```

```
Universal time: 18:30:22
Standard time: 6:30:22 PM

New standard time: 8:20:20 PM
```

Fig. 9.26 | Cascading member-function calls with the `this` pointer. (Part 2 of 2.)

9.14 `static` Class Members

There is an important exception to the rule that each object of a class has its own copy of all the data members of the class. In certain cases, only *one* copy of a variable should be *shared* by *all* objects of a class. A **`static` data member** is used for these and other reasons. Such a variable represents "class-wide" information, i.e., data that is shared by *all* instances and is *not* specific to any one object of the class. Recall, for example, that the versions of class `GradeBook` in Chapter 7 use `static` data members to store constants representing the number of grades that all `GradeBook` objects can hold.

Motivating Class-Wide Data

Let's further motivate the need for `static` class-wide data with an example. Suppose that we have a video game with `Martian`s and other space creatures. Each `Martian` tends to be brave and willing to attack other space creatures when the `Martian` is aware that there are at least five `Martian`s present. If fewer than five are present, each `Martian` becomes cowardly. So each `Martian` needs to know the `martianCount`. We could endow each instance of class `Martian` with `martianCount` as a data member. If we do, every `Martian` will have a *separate* copy of the data member. Every time we create a new `Martian`, we'll have to update the data member `martianCount` in all `Martian` objects. Doing this would require every `Martian` object to have, or have access to, handles to all other `Martian` objects in memory. This wastes space with the redundant copies of the `martianCount` and wastes time in updating the separate copies. Instead, we declare `martianCount` to be `static`. This makes `martianCount` class-wide data. Every `Martian` can access `martianCount` as if it were a data member of the `Martian`, but only *one* copy of the `static` variable `martianCount` is maintained in the program. This saves space. We save time by having the `Martian` constructor increment `static` variable `martianCount` and having the `Martian` destructor decrement `martianCount`. Because there's only one copy, we do not have to increment or decrement separate copies of `martianCount` for each `Martian` object.

Performance Tip 9.5

Use `static` data members to save storage when a single copy of the data for all objects of a class will suffice.

Scope and Initialization of `static` Data Members

A class's `static` data members have *class scope*. A `static` data member *must* be initialized *exactly* once. Fundamental-type `static` data members are initialized by default to `0`. Prior to C++11, a `static const` data member of `int` or `enum` type could be initialized in its declaration in the class definition and all other `static` data members had to be defined and intialized *at global namespace scope* (i.e., outside the body of the class definition). Again, 11 C++11's in-class initializers also allow you to initialize these variables where they're declared in the class definition. If a `static` data member is an object of a class that provides a default constructor, the `static` data member need not be initialized because its default constructor will be called.

Accessing `static` Data Members

A class's `private` and `protected static` members are normally accessed through the class's `public` member functions or `friend`s. *A class's `static` members exist even when no objects of that class exist.* To access a `public static` class member when no objects of the class exist, simply prefix the class name and the scope resolution operator (`::`) to the name of the data member. For example, if our preceding variable `martianCount` is `public`, it can be accessed with the expression `Martian::martianCount`, even when there are no `Martian` objects. (Of course, using `public` data is discouraged.)

To access a `private` or `protected static` class member when *no* objects of the class exist, provide a `public` **`static` member function** and call the function by prefixing its name with the class name and scope resolution operator. A `static` member function is a service of the *class*, *not* of a specific *object* of the class.

Software Engineering Observation 9.14

A class's `static` data members and `static` member functions exist and can be used even if no objects of that class have been instantiated.

Demonstrating `static` Data Members

The program of Figs. 9.27–9.29 demonstrates a `private static` data member called `count` (Fig. 9.27, line 24) and a `public static` member function called `getCount` (Fig. 9.27, line 18). In Fig. 9.28, line 8 defines and initializes the data member `count` to zero *at global namespace scope* and lines 12–15 define `static` member function `getCount`. Notice that neither line 8 nor line 12 includes keyword `static`, yet both lines define `static` class members. The `static` keyword cannot be applied to a member definition that appears outside the class definition. Data member `count` maintains a count of the number of objects of class `Employee` that have been instantiated. When objects of class `Employee` exist, member `count` can be referenced through *any* member function of an `Employee` object—in Fig. 9.28, `count` is referenced by both line 22 in the constructor and line 32 in the destructor.

```
// Fig. 9.27: Employee.h
// Employee class definition with a static data member to
// track the number of Employee objects in memory
#ifndef EMPLOYEE_H
#define EMPLOYEE_H

#include <string>

class Employee
{
public:
   Employee( const std::string &, const std::string & ); // constructor
   ~Employee(); // destructor
   std::string getFirstName() const; // return first name
   std::string getLastName() const; // return last name

   // static member function
   static unsigned int getCount(); // return # of objects instantiated
private:
   std::string firstName;
   std::string lastName;

   // static data
   static unsigned int count; // number of objects instantiated
}; // end class Employee

#endif
```

Fig. 9.27 | Employee class definition with a static data member to track the number of Employee objects in memory.

```
// Fig. 9.28: Employee.cpp
// Employee class member-function definitions.
#include <iostream>
#include "Employee.h" // Employee class definition
using namespace std;

// define and initialize static data member at global namespace scope
unsigned int Employee::count = 0; // cannot include keyword static

// define static member function that returns number of
// Employee objects instantiated (declared static in Employee.h)
unsigned int Employee::getCount()
{
   return count;
} // end static function getCount

// constructor initializes non-static data members and
// increments static data member count
Employee::Employee( const string &first, const string &last )
   : firstName( first ), lastName( last )
{
```

Fig. 9.28 | Employee class member-function definitions. (Part 1 of 2.)

```
      ++count; // increment static count of employees
      cout << "Employee constructor for " << firstName
         << ' ' << lastName << " called." << endl;
   } // end Employee constructor

   // destructor deallocates dynamically allocated memory
   Employee::~Employee()
   {
      cout << "~Employee() called for " << firstName
         << ' ' << lastName << endl;
      --count; // decrement static count of employees
   } // end ~Employee destructor

   // return first name of employee
   string Employee::getFirstName() const
   {
      return firstName; // return copy of first name
   } // end function getFirstName

   // return last name of employee
   string Employee::getLastName() const
   {
      return lastName; // return copy of last name
   } // end function getLastName
```

Fig. 9.28 | Employee class member-function definitions. (Part 2 of 2.)

Figure 9.29 uses static member function getCount to determine the number of Employee objects in memory at various points in the program. The program calls Employee::getCount() before any Employee objects have been created (line 12), after two Employee objects have been created (line 23) and after those Employee objects have been destroyed (line 34). Lines 16–29 in main define a *nested scope*. Recall that local variables exist until the scope in which they're defined terminates. In this example, we create two Employee objects in lines 17–18 inside the nested scope. As each constructor executes, it increments class Employee's static data member count. These Employee objects are destroyed when the program reaches line 29. At that point, each object's destructor executes and decrements class Employee's static data member count.

```
 1  // Fig. 9.29: fig09_29.cpp
 2  // static data member tracking the number of objects of a class.
 3  #include <iostream>
 4  #include "Employee.h" // Employee class definition
 5  using namespace std;
 6
 7  int main()
 8  {
 9     // no objects exist; use class name and binary scope resolution
10     // operator to access static member function getCount
11     cout << "Number of employees before instantiation of any objects is "
12        << Employee::getCount() << endl; // use class name
```

Fig. 9.29 | static data member tracking the number of objects of a class. (Part 1 of 2.)

```

   // the following scope creates and destroys
   // Employee objects before main terminates
   {
      Employee e1( "Susan", "Baker" );
      Employee e2( "Robert", "Jones" );

      // two objects exist; call static member function getCount again
      // using the class name and the scope resolution operator
      cout << "Number of employees after objects are instantiated is "
         << Employee::getCount();

      cout << "\n\nEmployee 1: "
         << e1.getFirstName() << " " << e1.getLastName()
         << "\nEmployee 2: "
         << e2.getFirstName() << " " << e2.getLastName() << "\n\n";
   } // end nested scope in main

   // no objects exist, so call static member function getCount again
   // using the class name and the scope resolution operator
   cout << "\nNumber of employees after objects are deleted is "
      << Employee::getCount() << endl;
} // end main
```

```
Number of employees before instantiation of any objects is 0
Employee constructor for Susan Baker called.
Employee constructor for Robert Jones called.
Number of employees after objects are instantiated is 2

Employee 1: Susan Baker
Employee 2: Robert Jones

~Employee() called for Robert Jones
~Employee() called for Susan Baker

Number of employees after objects are deleted is 0
```

Fig. 9.29 | `static` data member tracking the number of objects of a class. (Part 2 of 2.)

A member function should be declared `static` if it does *not* access non-`static` data members or non-`static` member functions of the class. Unlike non-`static` member functions, *a `static` member function does not have a `this` pointer*, because *`static` data members and `static` member functions exist independently of any objects of a class*. The `this` pointer *must* refer to a specific *object* of the class, and when a `static` member function is called, there might *not* be any objects of its class in memory.

Common Programming Error 9.6

Using the `this` pointer in a `static` member function is a compilation error.

Common Programming Error 9.7

Declaring a `static` member function `const` is a compilation error. The `const` qualifier indicates that a function cannot modify the contents of the object *on which it operates, but `static` member functions exist and operate independently of any objects of the class.*

9.15 Wrap-Up

This chapter deepened our coverage of classes, using a `Time` class case study to introduce several new features. We used an include guard to prevent the code in a header (`.h`) file from being included multiple times in the same source code (`.cpp`) file. You learned how to use the arrow operator to access an object's members via a pointer of the object's class type. You learned that member functions have class scope—the member function's name is known only to the class's other members unless referred to by a client of the class via an object name, a reference to an object of the class, a pointer to an object of the class or the scope resolution operator. We also discussed access functions (commonly used to retrieve the values of data members or to test the truth or falsity of conditions) and utility functions (`private` member functions that support the operation of the class's `public` member functions).

You learned that a constructor can specify default arguments that enable it to be called in a variety of ways. You also learned that any constructor that can be called with no arguments is a default constructor and that there can be at most one default constructor per class. We discussed destructors for performing termination housekeeping on an object of a class before that object is destroyed, and demonstrated the order in which an object's constructors and destructors are called.

We demonstrated the problems that can occur when a member function returns a reference or a pointer to a `private` data member, which breaks the encapsulation of the class. We also showed that objects of the same type can be assigned to one another using default memberwise assignment—in Chapter 10, we'll discuss how this can cause problems when an object contains pointer members.

You learned how to specify `const` objects and `const` member functions to prevent modifications to objects, thus enforcing the principle of least privilege. You also learned that, through composition, a class can have objects of other classes as members. We demonstrated how to use `friend` functions.

You learned that the `this` pointer is passed as an implicit argument to each of a class's non-`static` member functions, allowing them to access the correct object's data members and other non-`static` member functions. We used the `this` pointer explicitly to access the class's members and to enable cascaded member-function calls. We motivated the notion of `static` data members and member functions and demonstrated how to declare and use them in your own classes.

In Chapter 10, we continue our study of classes and objects by showing how to enable C++'s operators to work with *class-type objects*—a process called *operator overloading*. For example, you'll see how to overload the << operator so it can be used to output a complete array without explicitly using a repetition statement.

10

Operator Overloading; Class `string`

Objectives

In this chapter you'll:

- Learn how operator overloading can help you craft valuable classes.
- Overload unary and binary operators.
- Convert objects from one class to another class.
- Use overloaded operators and additional features of the `string` class.
- Create `PhoneNumber`, `Date` and `Array` classes that provide overloaded operators.
- Perform dynamic memory allocation with `new` and `delete`.
- Use keyword `explicit` to indicate that a constructor cannot be used for implicit conversions.
- Experience a "light-bulb moment" when you'll truly appreciate the elegance and beauty of the class concept.

Outline

10.1 Introduction

This chapter shows how to enable C++'s operators to work with class objects—a process called **operator overloading**. One example of an overloaded operator built into C++ is <<, which is used *both* as the stream insertion operator *and* as the bitwise left-shift operator (which is discussed in Chapter 20). Similarly, >> also is overloaded; it's used both as the stream extraction operator and the bitwise right-shift operator. Both of these operators are overloaded in the C++ Standard Library. You've been using overloaded operators since early in the book. The overloads are built into the base C++ language itself. For example, C++ overloads the addition operator (+) and the subtraction operator (-) to perform differently, depending on their context in integer, floating-point and pointer arithmetic with data of fundamental types.

You can overload *most* operators to be used with class objects—the compiler generates the appropriate code based on the *types* of the operands. The jobs performed by overloaded operators also can be performed by explicit function calls, but operator notation is often more natural.

Our examples start by demonstrating the C++ Standard Library's class `string`, which has lots of overloaded operators. This enables you to see overloaded operators in use before implementing your own overloaded operators. Next, we create a `PhoneNumber` class that enables us to use overloaded operators << and >> to conveniently output and input fully formatted, 10-digit phone numbers. We then present a `Date` class that overloads the prefix and postfix increment (++) operators to add one day to the value of a `Date`. The class also overloads the += operator to allow a program to increment a `Date` by the number of days specified on the right side of the operator.

Next, we present a capstone case study—an `Array` class that uses overloaded operators and other capabilities to solve various problems with pointer-based arrays. This is one of the most important case studies in the book. Many of our readers have indicated that the `Array` case study is their "light bulb moment" in truly understanding what classes and object technology are all about. As part of this class, we'll overload stream insertion, stream extraction, assignment, equality, relational and subscript operators. Once you master this `Array` class, you'll indeed understand the essence of object technology—crafting, using and reusing valuable classes.

The chapter concludes with discussions of how you can convert between types (incuding class types), problems with certain implicit conversions and how to prevent those problems.

10.2 Using the Overloaded Operators of Standard Library Class string

Figure 10.1 demonstrates many of class string's overloaded operators and several other useful member functions, including empty, substr and at. Function empty determines whether a string is empty, function substr returns a string that represents a portion of an existing string and function at returns the character at a specific index in a string (after checking that the index is in range). Chapter 19 presents class string in detail.

```
// Fig. 10.1: fig10_01.cpp
// Standard Library string class test program.
#include <iostream>
#include <string>
using namespace std;

int main()
{
   string s1( "happy" );
   string s2( " birthday" );
   string s3;

   // test overloaded equality and relational operators
   cout << "s1 is \"" << s1 << "\"; s2 is \"" << s2
      << "\"; s3 is \"" << s3 << '\"'
      << "\n\nThe results of comparing s2 and s1:"
      << "\ns2 == s1 yields " << ( s2 == s1 ? "true" : "false" )
      << "\ns2 != s1 yields " << ( s2 != s1 ? "true" : "false" )
      << "\ns2 >  s1 yields " << ( s2 > s1 ? "true" : "false" )
      << "\ns2 <  s1 yields " << ( s2 < s1 ? "true" : "false" )
      << "\ns2 >= s1 yields " << ( s2 >= s1 ? "true" : "false" )
      << "\ns2 <= s1 yields " << ( s2 <= s1 ? "true" : "false" );

   // test string member-function empty
   cout << "\n\nTesting s3.empty():" << endl;

   if ( s3.empty() )
   {
      cout << "s3 is empty; assigning s1 to s3;" << endl;
      s3 = s1; // assign s1 to s3
      cout << "s3 is \"" << s3 << "\"";
   } // end if

   // test overloaded string concatenation operator
   cout << "\n\ns1 += s2 yields s1 = ";
```

Fig. 10.1 | Standard Library string class test program. (Part 1 of 3.)

```
      s1 += s2; // test overloaded concatenation
      cout << s1;

      // test overloaded string concatenation operator with a C string
      cout << "\n\ns1 += \" to you\" yields" << endl;
      s1 += " to you";
      cout << "s1 = " << s1 << "\n\n";

      // test string member function substr
      cout << "The substring of s1 starting at location 0 for\n"
         << "14 characters, s1.substr(0, 14), is:\n"
         << s1.substr( 0, 14 ) << "\n\n";

      // test substr "to-end-of-string" option
      cout << "The substring of s1 starting at\n"
         << "location 15, s1.substr(15), is:\n"
         << s1.substr( 15 ) << endl;

      // test copy constructor
      string s4( s1 );
      cout << "\ns4 = " << s4 << "\n\n";

      // test overloaded copy assignment (=) operator with self-assignment
      cout << "assigning s4 to s4" << endl;
      s4 = s4;
      cout << "s4 = " << s4 << endl;

      // test using overloaded subscript operator to create lvalue
      s1[ 0 ] = 'H';
      s1[ 6 ] = 'B';
      cout << "\ns1 after s1[0] = 'H' and s1[6] = 'B' is: "
         << s1 << "\n\n";

      // test subscript out of range with string member function "at"
      try
      {
         cout << "Attempt to assign 'd' to s1.at( 30 ) yields:" << endl;
         s1.at( 30 ) = 'd'; // ERROR: subscript out of range
      } // end try
      catch ( out_of_range &ex )
      {
         cout << "An exception occurred: " << ex.what() << endl;
      } // end catch
   } // end main
```

```
s1 is "happy"; s2 is " birthday"; s3 is ""

The results of comparing s2 and s1:
s2 == s1 yields false
s2 != s1 yields true
s2 >  s1 yields false
s2 <  s1 yields true
```

Fig. 10.1 | Standard Library string class test program. (Part 2 of 3.)

```
s2 >= s1 yields false
s2 <= s1 yields true

Testing s3.empty():
s3 is empty; assigning s1 to s3;
s3 is "happy"

s1 += s2 yields s1 = happy birthday

s1 += " to you" yields
s1 = happy birthday to you

The substring of s1 starting at location 0 for
14 characters, s1.substr(0, 14), is:
happy birthday

The substring of s1 starting at
location 15, s1.substr(15), is:
to you

s4 = happy birthday to you

assigning s4 to s4
s4 = happy birthday to you

s1 after s1[0] = 'H' and s1[6] = 'B' is: Happy Birthday to you

Attempt to assign 'd' to s1.at( 30 ) yields:
An exception occurred: invalid string position
```

Fig. 10.1 | Standard Library `string` class test program. (Part 3 of 3.)

Lines 9–11 create three `string` objects—`s1` is initialized with the literal `"happy"`, `s2` is initialized with the literal `" birthday"` and `s3` uses the default `string` constructor to create an empty `string`. Lines 14–15 output these three objects, using `cout` and operator `<<`, which the `string` class designers overloaded to handle `string` objects. Then lines 16–22 show the results of comparing `s2` to `s1` by using class `string`'s overloaded equality and relational operators, which perform lexicographical comparisons (i.e., like a dictionary ordering) using the numerical values of the characters (see Appendix B, ASCII Character Set) in each `string`.

Class `string` provides member function **`empty`** to determine whether a `string` is empty, which we demonstrate in line 27. Member function `empty` returns `true` if the `string` is empty; otherwise, it returns `false`.

Line 30 demonstrates class `string`'s overloaded copy assignment operator by assigning `s1` to `s3`. Line 31 outputs `s3` to demonstrate that the assignment worked correctly.

Line 36 demonstrates class `string`'s overloaded += operator for *string concatenation*. In this case, the contents of `s2` are appended to `s1`. Then line 37 outputs the resulting string that's stored in `s1`. Line 41 demonstrates that a string literal can be appended to a `string` object by using operator +=. Line 42 displays the result.

Class `string` provides member function **`substr`** (lines 47 and 52) to return a *portion* of a string as a `string` object. The call to `substr` in line 47 obtains a 14-character substring (specified by the second argument) of `s1` starting at position 0 (specified by the first argument).The call to `substr` in line 52 obtains a substring starting from position 15 of `s1`. When the second argument is not specified, `substr` returns the *remainder* of the `string` on which it's called.

Line 55 creates `string` object `s4` and initializes it with a copy of `s1`. This results in a call to class `string`'s *copy constructor*. Line 60 uses class `string`'s overloaded copy assignment (=) operator to demonstrate that it handles *self-assignment* properly—we'll see when we build class `Array` later in the chapter that self-assignment can be dangerous and we'll show how to deal with the issues.

Lines 64–65 use class `string`'s overloaded `[]` operator to create *lvalues* that enable new characters to replace existing characters in `s1`. Line 67 outputs the new value of `s1`. *Class `string`'s overloaded `[]` operator does not perform any bounds checking.* Therefore, *you must ensure that operations using standard class `string`'s overloaded `[]` operator do not accidentally manipulate elements outside the bounds of the `string`.* Class `string` *does* provide bounds checking in its member function **`at`**, which throws an exception if its argument is an *invalid* subscript. If the subscript is valid, function `at` returns the character at the specified location as a modifiable *lvalue* or an nonmodifiable *lvalue* (e.g., a `const` reference), depending on the context in which the call appears. Line 73 demonstrates a call to function `at` with an invalid subscript; this throws an `out_of_range` exception.

10.3 Fundamentals of Operator Overloading

As you saw in Fig. 10.1, operators provide a concise notation for manipulating `string` objects. You can use operators with your own user-defined types as well. Although C++ does *not* allow *new* operators to be created, it *does* allow most existing operators to be overloaded so that, when they're used with objects, they have meaning appropriate to those objects.

Operator overloading is *not* automatic—you must write operator-overloading functions to perform the desired operations. An operator is overloaded by writing a non-`static` member function definition or non-member function definition as you normally would, except that the function name starts with the keyword `operator` followed by the symbol for the operator being overloaded. For example, the function name `operator+` would be used to overload the addition operator (+) for use with objects of a particular class (or `enum`). When operators are overloaded as member functions, they must be non-`static`, because *they must be called on an object of the class* and operate on that object.

To use an operator on an object of a class, you must define overloaded operator functions for that class—with three exceptions:

- The *assignment operator (=)* may be used with *most* classes to perform *memberwise assignment* of the data members—each data member is assigned from the assignment's "source" object (on the right) to the "target" object (on the left). *Memberwise assignment is dangerous for classes with pointer members,* so we'll explicitly overload the assignment operator for such classes.
- The *address (&) operator* returns a pointer to the object; this operator also can be overloaded.
- The *comma operator* evaluates the expression to its left then the expression to its right, and returns the value of the latter expression. This operator also can be overloaded.

Operators That Cannot Be Overloaded

Most of C++'s operators can be overloaded. Figure 10.2 shows the operators that cannot be overloaded.[1]

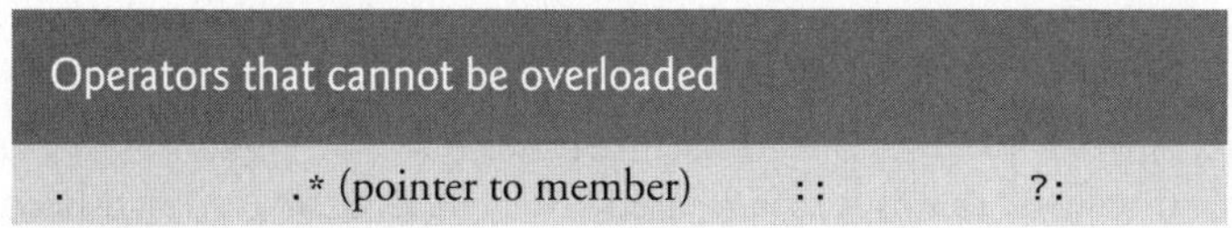

Operators that cannot be overloaded			
.	.* (pointer to member)	::	?:

Fig. 10.2 | Operators that cannot be overloaded.

Rules and Restrictions on Operator Overloading
As you prepare to overload operators for your own classes, there are several rules and restrictions you should keep in mind:

- *The precedence of an operator cannot be changed by overloading.* However, parentheses can be used to *force* the order of evaluation of overloaded operators in an expression.
- *The associativity of an operator cannot be changed by overloading*—if an operator normally associates from left to right, then so do all of its overloaded versions.
- *You cannot change the "arity" of an operator* (that is, the number of operands an operator takes)—overloaded unary operators remain unary operators; overloaded binary operators remain binary operators. Operators &, *, + and - all have both unary and binary versions; these unary and binary versions can be separately overloaded.
- *You cannot create new operators; only existing operators can be overloaded.*
- The meaning of how an operator works on values of fundamental types *cannot* be changed by operator overloading. For example, you cannot make the + operator subtract two `int`s. Operator overloading works only with *objects of user-defined types or with a mixture of an object of a user-defined type and an object of a fundamental type.*
- Related operators, like + and +=, *must* be overloaded separately.
- When overloading `()`, `[]`, `->` or any of the assignment operators, the operator overloading function *must* be declared as a class member. For all other overloadable operators, the operator overloading functions can be member functions or non-member functions.

Software Engineering Observation 10.1
Overload operators for class types so they work as closely as possible to the way built-in operators work on fundamental types.

10.4 Overloading Binary Operators

A binary operator can be overloaded as a non-`static`*member function with one parameter or as a non-member function with two parameters (one of those parameters must be either a class object or a reference to a class object).* A non-member operator function is often declared as `friend` of a class for performance reasons.

1. Although it's possible to overload the address (&), comma (,), && and || operators, you should avoid doing so to avoid subtle errors. For insights on this, see CERT guideline DCL10-CPP.

Binary Overloaded Operators as Member Functions

Consider using < to compare two objects of a String class that you define. When overloading binary operator < as a non-static member function of a String class, if y and z are String-class objects, then y < z is treated as if y.operator<(z) had been written, invoking the operator< member function with one argument declared below:

```
class String
{
public:
   bool operator<( const String & ) const;
   ...
}; // end class String
```

Overloaded operator functions for binary operators can be member functions *only* when the *left* operand is an object of the class in which the function is a member.

Binary Overloaded Operators as Non-Member Functions

As a non-member function, binary operator < *must* take *two* arguments—*one* of which *must* be an object (or a reference to an object) of the class that the overloaded operator is associated with. If y and z are String-class objects or references to String-class objects, then y < z is treated as if the call operator<(y, z) had been written in the program, invoking function operator< which is declared as follows:

```
bool operator<( const String &, const String & );
```

10.5 Overloading the Binary Stream Insertion and Stream Extraction Operators

You can input and output fundamental-type data using the stream extraction operator >> and the stream insertion operator <<. The C++ class libraries overload these binary operators for each fundamental type, including pointers and char * strings. You can also overload these operators to perform input and output for your own types. The program of Figs. 10.3–10.5 overloads these operators to input and output PhoneNumber objects in the format "(000) 000-0000." The program assumes telephone numbers are input correctly.

```
// Fig. 10.3: PhoneNumber.h
// PhoneNumber class definition
#ifndef PHONENUMBER_H
#define PHONENUMBER_H

#include <iostream>
#include <string>

class PhoneNumber
{
```

Fig. 10.3 | PhoneNumber class with overloaded stream insertion and stream extraction operators as friend functions. (Part 1 of 2.)

```
   friend std::ostream &operator<<( std::ostream &, const PhoneNumber & );
   friend std::istream &operator>>( std::istream &, PhoneNumber & );
private:
   std::string areaCode; // 3-digit area code
   std::string exchange; // 3-digit exchange
   std::string line; // 4-digit line
}; // end class PhoneNumber

#endif
```

Fig. 10.3 | PhoneNumber class with overloaded stream insertion and stream extraction operators as friend functions. (Part 2 of 2.)

```
// Fig. 10.4: PhoneNumber.cpp
// Overloaded stream insertion and stream extraction operators
// for class PhoneNumber.
#include <iomanip>
#include "PhoneNumber.h"
using namespace std;

// overloaded stream insertion operator; cannot be
// a member function if we would like to invoke it with
// cout << somePhoneNumber;
ostream &operator<<( ostream &output, const PhoneNumber &number )
{
   output << "(" << number.areaCode << ") "
      << number.exchange << "-" << number.line;
   return output; // enables cout << a << b << c;
} // end function operator<<

// overloaded stream extraction operator; cannot be
// a member function if we would like to invoke it with
// cin >> somePhoneNumber;
istream &operator>>( istream &input, PhoneNumber &number )
{
   input.ignore(); // skip (
   input >> setw( 3 ) >> number.areaCode; // input area code
   input.ignore( 2 ); // skip ) and space
   input >> setw( 3 ) >> number.exchange; // input exchange
   input.ignore(); // skip dash (-)
   input >> setw( 4 ) >> number.line; // input line
   return input; // enables cin >> a >> b >> c;
} // end function operator>>
```

Fig. 10.4 | Overloaded stream insertion and stream extraction operators for class PhoneNumber.

```
// Fig. 10.5: fig10_05.cpp
// Demonstrating class PhoneNumber's overloaded stream insertion
// and stream extraction operators.
#include <iostream>
```

Fig. 10.5 | Overloaded stream insertion and stream extraction operators. (Part 1 of 2.)

```
5  #include "PhoneNumber.h"
6  using namespace std;
7
8  int main()
9  {
10    PhoneNumber phone; // create object phone
11
12    cout << "Enter phone number in the form (123) 456-7890:" << endl;
13
14    // cin >> phone invokes operator>> by implicitly issuing
15    // the non-member function call operator>>( cin, phone )
16    cin >> phone;
17
18    cout << "The phone number entered was: ";
19
20    // cout << phone invokes operator<< by implicitly issuing
21    // the non-member function call operator<<( cout, phone )
22    cout << phone << endl;
23 } // end main
```

```
Enter phone number in the form (123) 456-7890:
(800) 555-1212
The phone number entered was: (800) 555-1212
```

Fig. 10.5 | Overloaded stream insertion and stream extraction operators. (Part 2 of 2.)

Overloading the Stream Extraction (>>) Operator

The stream extraction operator function `operator>>` (Fig. 10.4, lines 21–30) takes the `istream` reference `input` and the `PhoneNumber` reference `number` as arguments and returns an `istream` reference. Operator function `operator>>` inputs phone numbers of the form

```
(800) 555-1212
```

into objects of class `PhoneNumber`. When the compiler sees the expression

```
cin >> phone
```

in line 16 of Fig. 10.5, the compiler generates the *non-member function call*

```
operator>>( cin, phone );
```

When this call executes, reference parameter `input` (Fig. 10.4, line 21) becomes an alias for `cin` and reference parameter `number` becomes an alias for `phone`. The operator function reads as `string`s the three parts of the telephone number into the `areaCode` (line 24), `exchange` (line 26) and `line` (line 28) members of the `PhoneNumber` object referenced by parameter `number`. Stream manipulator `setw` limits the number of characters read into each `string`. *When used with* `cin` *and* `string`*s,* `setw` *restricts the number of characters read to the number of characters specified by its argument* (i.e., `setw(3)` allows three characters to be read). The parentheses, space and dash characters are skipped by calling `istream` member function `ignore` (Fig. 10.4, lines 23, 25 and 27), which discards the specified number of characters in the input stream (one character by default). Function `operator>>` returns `istream` reference `input` (i.e., `cin`). This enables input operations on `PhoneNumber` objects to be *cascaded* with input operations on other `PhoneNumber` objects or other data types. For example, a program can input two `PhoneNumber` objects in one statement as follows:

```
cin >> phone1 >> phone2;
```

First, the expression `cin >> phone1` executes by making the non-member function call

```
operator>>( cin, phone1 );
```

This call then returns a reference to `cin` as the value of `cin >> phone1`, so the remaining portion of the expression is interpreted simply as `cin >> phone2`. This executes by making the *non-member function call*

```
operator>>( cin, phone2 );
```

Good Programming Practice 10.1

Overloaded operators should mimic the functionality of their built-in counterparts—e.g., the + operator should perform addition, not subtraction. Avoid excessive or inconsistent use of operator overloading, as this can make a program cryptic and difficult to read.

Overloading the Stream Insertion (<<) Operator

The stream insertion operator function (Fig. 10.4, lines 11–16) takes an `ostream` reference (`output`) and a `const PhoneNumber` reference (`number`) as arguments and returns an `ostream` reference. Function `operator<<` displays objects of type `PhoneNumber`. When the compiler sees the expression

```
cout << phone
```

in line 22 of Fig. 10.5, the compiler generates the *non-member function call*

```
operator<<( cout, phone );
```

Function `operator<<` displays the parts of the telephone number as `string`s, because they're stored as `string` objects.

Overloaded Operators as Non-Member `friend` Functions

The functions `operator>>` and `operator<<` are declared in `PhoneNumber` as *non-member, `friend` functions* (Fig. 10.3, lines 11–12). They're *non-member functions* because the object of class `PhoneNumber` must be the operator's *right* operand. If these were to be `PhoneNumber` *member functions*, the following awkward statements would have to be used to output and input a `PhoneNumber`:

```
phone << cout;
phone >> cin;
```

Such statements would be confusing to most C++ programmers, who are familiar with `cout` and `cin` appearing as the *left* operands of `<<` and `>>`, respectively.

Overloaded operator functions for binary operators can be member functions only when the *left* operand is an object of the class in which the function is a member. *Overloaded input and output operators are declared as `friend`s if they need to access non-`public` class members directly or because the class may not offer appropriate* get *functions.* Also, the `PhoneNumber` reference in function `operator<<`'s parameter list (Fig. 10.4, line 11) is `const`, because the `PhoneNumber` will simply be output, and the `PhoneNumber` reference in function operator>>'s parameter list (line 21) is non-const, because the PhoneNumber object must be modified to store the input telephone number in the object.

Software Engineering Observation 10.2

New input/output capabilities for user-defined types are added to C++ without modifying standard input/output library classes. This is another example of C++'s extensibility.

Why Overloaded Stream Insertion and Stream Extraction Operators Are Overloaded as Non-Member Functions

The overloaded stream insertion operator (<<) is used in an expression in which the left operand has type ostream &, as in cout << classObject. To use the operator in this manner where the *right* operand is an object of a user-defined class, it must be overloaded as a *non-member function*. To be a member function, operator << would have to be a member of class ostream. This is *not* possible for user-defined classes, since we are *not allowed to modify C++ Standard Library classes*. Similarly, the overloaded stream extraction operator (>>) is used in an expression in which the *left* operand has the type istream &, as in cin >> classObject, and the *right* operand is an object of a user-defined class, so it, too, must be a *non-member function*. Also, each of these overloaded operator functions may require access to the private data members of the class object being output or input, so these overloaded operator functions can be made friend functions of the class for performance reasons.

10.6 Overloading Unary Operators

A unary operator for a class can be overloaded as a non-static member function with no arguments or as a non-member function with one argument that must be an object (or a reference to an object) of the class. Member functions that implement overloaded operators must be non-static so that they can access the non-static data in each object of the class.

Unary Overloaded Operators as Member Functions

Consider overloading unary operator ! to test whether an object of your own String class is empty. Such a function would return a bool result. When a unary operator such as ! is overloaded as a member function with no arguments and the compiler sees the expression !s (in which s is an object of class String), the compiler generates the function call s.operator!(). The operand s is the String object for which the String class member function operator! is being invoked. The function is declared as follows:

```
class String
{
public:
   bool operator!() const;
   ...
}; // end class String
```

Unary Overloaded Operators as Non-Member Functions

A unary operator such as ! may be overloaded as a *non-member function* with one parameter. If s is a String class object (or a reference to a String class object), then !s is treated as if the call operator!(s) had been written, invoking the *non-member* operator! function that's declared as follows:

```
bool operator!( const String & );
```

10.7 Overloading the Unary Prefix and Postfix ++ and -- Operators

The prefix and postfix versions of the increment and decrement operators can all be overloaded. We'll see how the compiler distinguishes between the prefix version and the postfix version of an increment or decrement operator.

To overload the prefix and postfix increment operators, each overloaded operator function must have a distinct signature, so that the compiler will be able to determine which version of ++ is intended. The prefix versions are overloaded exactly as any other prefix unary operator would be. Everything stated in this section for overloading prefix and postfix increment operators applies to overloading predecrement and postdecrement operators. In the next section, we examine a `Date` class with overloaded prefix and postfix increment operators.

Overloading the Prefix Increment Operator

Suppose that we want to add 1 to the day in `Date` object `d1`. When the compiler sees the preincrementing expression `++d1`, the compiler generates the *member-function call*

```
d1.operator++()
```

The prototype for this operator member function would be

```
Date &operator++();
```

If the prefix increment operator is implemented as a *non-member function*, then, when the compiler sees the expression `++d1`, the compiler generates the function call

```
operator++( d1 )
```

The prototype for this non-member operator function would be declared as

```
Date &operator++( Date & );
```

Overloading the Postfix Increment Operator

Overloading the postfix increment operator presents a challenge, because the compiler must be able to distinguish between the signatures of the overloaded prefix and postfix increment operator functions. The *convention* that has been adopted is that, when the compiler sees the postincrementing expression `d1++`, it generates the *member-function call*

```
d1.operator++( 0 )
```

The prototype for this operator member function is

```
Date operator++( int )
```

The argument `0` is strictly a *dummy value* that enables the compiler to distinguish between the prefix and postfix increment operator functions. The same syntax is used to differentiate between the prefix and postfix decrement operator functions.

If the postfix increment is implemented as a *non-member function*, then, when the compiler sees the expression `d1++`, the compiler generates the function call

```
operator++( d1, 0 )
```

The prototype for this function would be

```
Date operator++( Date &, int );
```

Once again, the 0 argument is used by the compiler to distinguish between the prefix and postfix increment operators implemented as non-member functions. Note that the *postfix increment operator* returns Date objects *by value*, whereas the prefix increment operator returns Date objects *by reference*—the postfix increment operator typically returns a temporary object that contains the original value of the object before the increment occurred. C++ treats such objects as *rvalues*, which *cannot be used on the left side of an assignment*. The prefix increment operator returns the actual incremented object with its new value. Such an object *can* be used as an *lvalue* in a continuing expression.

Performance Tip 10.1

The extra object that's created by the postfix *increment (or decrement) operator can result in a performance problem—especially when the operator is used in a loop. For this reason, you should prefer the overloaded* prefix *increment and decrement operators.*

10.8 Case Study: A Date Class

The program of Figs. 10.6–10.8 demonstrates a Date class, which uses overloaded prefix and postfix increment operators to add 1 to the day in a Date object, while causing appropriate increments to the month and year if necessary. The Date header (Fig. 10.6) specifies that Date's public interface includes an overloaded stream insertion operator (line 11), a default constructor (line 13), a setDate function (line 14), an overloaded prefix increment operator (line 15), an overloaded postfix increment operator (line 16), an overloaded += addition assignment operator (line 17), a function to test for leap years (line 18) and a function to determine whether a day is the last day of the month (line 19).

```
1  // Fig. 10.6: Date.h
2  // Date class definition with overloaded increment operators.
3  #ifndef DATE_H
4  #define DATE_H
5
6  #include <array>
7  #include <iostream>
8
9  class Date
10 {
11    friend std::ostream &operator<<( std::ostream &, const Date & );
12 public:
13    Date( int m = 1, int d = 1, int y = 1900 ); // default constructor
14    void setDate( int, int, int ); // set month, day, year
15    Date &operator++(); // prefix increment operator
16    Date operator++( int ); // postfix increment operator
17    Date &operator+=( unsigned int ); // add days, modify object
18    static bool leapYear( int ); // is date in a leap year?
19    bool endOfMonth( int ) const; // is date at the end of month?
20 private:
21    unsigned int month;
22    unsigned int day;
23    unsigned int year;
```

Fig. 10.6 | Date class definition with overloaded increment operators. (Part 1 of 2.)

```

   static const std::array< unsigned int, 13 > days; // days per month
   void helpIncrement(); // utility function for incrementing date
}; // end class Date

#endif
```

Fig. 10.6 | Date class definition with overloaded increment operators. (Part 2 of 2.)

```
// Fig. 10.7: Date.cpp
// Date class member- and friend-function definitions.
#include <iostream>
#include <string>
#include "Date.h"
using namespace std;

// initialize static member; one classwide copy
const array< unsigned int, 13 > Date::days =
   { 0, 31, 28, 31, 30, 31, 30, 31, 31, 30, 31, 30, 31 };

// Date constructor
Date::Date( int month, int day, int year )
{
   setDate( month, day, year );
} // end Date constructor

// set month, day and year
void Date::setDate( int mm, int dd, int yy )
{
   if ( mm >= 1 && mm <= 12 )
      month = mm;
   else
      throw invalid_argument( "Month must be 1-12" );

   if ( yy >= 1900 && yy <= 2100 )
      year = yy;
   else
      throw invalid_argument( "Year must be >= 1900 and <= 2100" );

   // test for a leap year
   if ( ( month == 2 && leapYear( year ) && dd >= 1 && dd <= 29 ) ||
        ( dd >= 1 && dd <= days[ month ] ) )
      day = dd;
   else
      throw invalid_argument(
         "Day is out of range for current month and year" );
} // end function setDate

// overloaded prefix increment operator
Date &Date::operator++()
{
```

Fig. 10.7 | Date class member- and friend-function definitions. (Part 1 of 3.)

```
   helpIncrement(); // increment date
   return *this; // reference return to create an lvalue
} // end function operator++

// overloaded postfix increment operator; note that the
// dummy integer parameter does not have a parameter name
Date Date::operator++( int )
{
   Date temp = *this; // hold current state of object
   helpIncrement();

   // return unincremented, saved, temporary object
   return temp; // value return; not a reference return
} // end function operator++

// add specified number of days to date
Date &Date::operator+=( unsigned int additionalDays )
{
   for ( int i = 0; i < additionalDays; ++i )
      helpIncrement();

   return *this; // enables cascading
} // end function operator+=

// if the year is a leap year, return true; otherwise, return false
bool Date::leapYear( int testYear )
{
   if ( testYear % 400 == 0 ||
      ( testYear % 100 != 0 && testYear % 4 == 0 ) )
      return true; // a leap year
   else
      return false; // not a leap year
} // end function leapYear

// determine whether the day is the last day of the month
bool Date::endOfMonth( int testDay ) const
{
   if ( month == 2 && leapYear( year ) )
      return testDay == 29; // last day of Feb. in leap year
   else
      return testDay == days[ month ];
} // end function endOfMonth

// function to help increment the date
void Date::helpIncrement()
{
   // day is not end of month
   if ( !endOfMonth( day ) )
      ++day; // increment day
   else
      if ( month < 12 ) // day is end of month and month < 12
      {
         ++month; // increment month
```

Fig. 10.7 | Date class member- and friend-function definitions. (Part 2 of 3.)

```
         day = 1; // first day of new month
      } // end if
      else // last day of year
      {
         ++year; // increment year
         month = 1; // first month of new year
         day = 1; // first day of new month
      } // end else
} // end function helpIncrement

// overloaded output operator
ostream &operator<<( ostream &output, const Date &d )
{
   static string monthName[ 13 ] = { "", "January", "February",
      "March", "April", "May", "June", "July", "August",
      "September", "October", "November", "December" };
   output << monthName[ d.month ] << ' ' << d.day << ", " << d.year;
   return output; // enables cascading
} // end function operator<<
```

Fig. 10.7 | Date class member- and friend-function definitions. (Part 3 of 3.)

```
// Fig. 10.8: fig10_08.cpp
// Date class test program.
#include <iostream>
#include "Date.h" // Date class definition
using namespace std;

int main()
{
   Date d1( 12, 27, 2010 ); // December 27, 2010
   Date d2; // defaults to January 1, 1900

   cout << "d1 is " << d1 << "\nd2 is " << d2;
   cout << "\n\nd1 += 7 is " << ( d1 += 7 );

   d2.setDate( 2, 28, 2008 );
   cout << "\n\n  d2 is " << d2;
   cout << "\n++d2 is " << ++d2 << " (leap year allows 29th)";

   Date d3( 7, 13, 2010 );

   cout << "\n\nTesting the prefix increment operator:\n"
      << "  d3 is " << d3 << endl;
   cout << "++d3 is " << ++d3 << endl;
   cout << "  d3 is " << d3;

   cout << "\n\nTesting the postfix increment operator:\n"
      << "  d3 is " << d3 << endl;
   cout << "d3++ is " << d3++ << endl;
   cout << "  d3 is " << d3 << endl;
} // end main
```

Fig. 10.8 | Date class test program. (Part 1 of 2.)

```
d1 is December 27, 2010
d2 is January 1, 1900

d1 += 7 is January 3, 2011

  d2 is February 28, 2008
++d2 is February 29, 2008 (leap year allows 29th)

Testing the prefix increment operator:
  d3 is July 13, 2010
++d3 is July 14, 2010
  d3 is July 14, 2010

Testing the postfix increment operator:
  d3 is July 14, 2010
d3++ is July 14, 2010
  d3 is July 15, 2010
```

Fig. 10.8 | `Date` class test program. (Part 2 of 2.)

Function `main` (Fig. 10.8) creates two `Date` objects (lines 9–10)—`d1` is initialized to December 27, 2010 and `d2` is initialized by default to January 1, 1900. The `Date` constructor (defined in Fig. 10.7, lines 13–16) calls `setDate` (defined in Fig. 10.7, lines 19–38) to validate the month, day and year specified. Invalid values for the month, day or year result in `invalid_argument` exceptions.

Line 12 of `main` (Fig. 10.8) outputs each of the `Date` objects, using the overloaded stream insertion operator (defined in Fig. 10.7, lines 107–114). Line 13 of `main` uses the overloaded operator += (defined in Fig. 10.7, lines 59–65) to add seven days to `d1`. Line 15 in Fig. 10.8 uses function `setDate` to set `d2` to February 28, 2008, which is a leap year. Then, line 17 preincrements `d2` to show that the date increments properly to February 29. Next, line 19 creates a `Date` object, `d3`, which is initialized with the date July 13, 2010. Then line 23 increments `d3` by 1 with the overloaded prefix increment operator. Lines 21–24 output `d3` before and after the preincrement operation to confirm that it worked correctly. Finally, line 28 increments `d3` with the overloaded postfix increment operator. Lines 26–29 output `d3` before and after the postincrement operation to confirm that it worked correctly.

`Date` *Class Prefix Increment Operator*

Overloading the prefix increment operator is straightforward. The prefix increment operator (defined in Fig. 10.7, lines 41–45) calls utility function `helpIncrement` (defined in Fig. 10.7, lines 87–104) to increment the date. This function deals with "wraparounds" or "carries" that occur when we increment the last day of the month. These carries require incrementing the month. If the month is already 12, then the year must also be incremented and the month must be set to 1. Function `helpIncrement` uses function `endOfMonth` to determine whether the end of a month has been reached and increment the day correctly.

The overloaded prefix increment operator returns a reference to the current `Date` object (i.e., the one that was just incremented). This occurs because the current object, `*this`, is returned as a `Date &`. This enables a preincremented `Date` object to be used as an *lvalue*, which is how the built-in prefix increment operator works for fundamental types.

`Date` *Class Postfix Increment Operator*

Overloading the postfix increment operator (defined in Fig. 10.7, lines 49–56) is trickier. To emulate the effect of the postincrement, we must return an *unincremented copy* of the `Date` object. For example, if `int` variable `x` has the value `7`, the statement

```
cout << x++ << endl;
```

outputs the *original* value of variable `x`. So we'd like our postfix increment operator to operate the same way on a `Date` object. On entry to `operator++`, we save the current object (`*this`) in `temp` (line 51). Next, we call `helpIncrement` to increment the current `Date` object. Then, line 55 returns the *unincremented copy* of the object previously stored in `temp`. This function *cannot* return a reference to the local `Date` object `temp`, because a local variable is destroyed when the function in which it's declared exits. Thus, declaring the return type to this function as `Date &` would return a reference to an object that no longer exists.

Common Programming Error 10.1

Returning a reference (or a pointer) to a local variable is a common error for which most compilers will issue a warning.

10.9 Dynamic Memory Management

You can control the *allocation* and *deallocation* of memory in a program for objects and for arrays of any built-in or user-defined type. This is known as **dynamic memory management** and is performed with the operators **`new`** and **`delete`**. We'll use these capabilities to implement our `Array` class in the next section.

You can use the `new` operator to dynamically **allocate** (i.e., reserve) the exact amount of memory required to hold an object or built-in array at execution time. The object or built-in array is created in the **free store** (also called the **heap**)—*a region of memory assigned to each program for storing dynamically allocated objects.*[2] Once memory is allocated in the free store, you can access it via the pointer that operator `new` returns. When you no longer need the memory, you can *return* it to the free store by using the `delete` operator to **deallocate** (i.e., *release*) the memory, which can then be *reused* by future `new` operations.[3]

Obtaining Dynamic Memory with `new`

Consider the following statement:

```
Time *timePtr = new Time();
```

The `new` operator allocates storage of the proper size for an object of type `Time`, calls the default constructor to initialize the object and returns a pointer to the type specified to the right of the `new` operator (i.e., a `Time *`). If `new` is unable to find sufficient space in memory for the object, it indicates that an error occurred by throwing an exception.

---

2. Operator `new` could fail to obtain the needed memory, in which case a `bad_alloc` exception will occur. Chapter 17 shows how to deal with failures when using `new`.
3. Operators `new` and `delete` *can* be overloaded, but this is beyond the scope of the book. If you do overload `new`, then you should overload `delete` in the *same scope* to avoid subtle dynamic memory management errors.

Releasing Dynamic Memory with delete

To destroy a dynamically allocated object and free the space for the object, use the delete operator as follows:

```
delete timePtr;
```

This statement first *calls the destructor for the object to which* timePtr *points, then deallocates the memory associated with the object, returning the memory to the free store.*

Common Programming Error 10.2

*Not releasing dynamically allocated memory when it's no longer needed can cause the system to run out of memory prematurely. This is sometimes called a "**memory leak.**"*

Error-Prevention Tip 10.1

Do not delete memory that was not allocated by new. Doing so results in undefined behavior.

Error-Prevention Tip 10.2

After you delete a block of dynamically allocated memory be sure not to delete the same block again. One way to guard against this is to immediately set the pointer to nullptr*. Deleting a* nullptr *has no effect.*

Initializing Dynamic Memory

You can provide an initializer for a newly created fundamental-type variable, as in

```
double *ptr = new double( 3.14159 );
```

which initializes a newly created double to 3.14159 and assigns the resulting pointer to ptr. The same syntax can be used to specify a comma-separated list of arguments to the constructor of an object. For example,

```
Time *timePtr = new Time( 12, 45, 0 );
```

initializes a new Time object to 12:45 PM and assigns the resulting pointer to timePtr.

Dynamically Allocating Built-In Arrays with new []

You can also use the new operator to allocate built-in arrays dynamically. For example, a 10-element integer array can be allocated and assigned to gradesArray as follows:

```
int *gradesArray = new int[ 10 ]();
```

which declares int pointer gradesArray and assigns to it a pointer to the first element of a dynamically allocated 10-element array of ints. The parentheses following new int[10] value initialize the array's elements—fundamental numeric types are set to 0, bools are set to false, pointers are set to nullptr and class objects are initialized by their default constructors. The size of an array created at compile time must be specified using an integral constant expression; however, a dynamically allocated array's size can be specified using *any* non-negative integral expression that can be evaluated at execution time.

C++11: Using a List Initializer with a Dynamically Allocated Built-In Array

Prior to C++11, when allocating a built-in array of objects dynamically, you *could not* pass arguments to each object's constructor—each object was initialized by its *default* constructor. In C++11, you can use a list initializer to initialize the elements of a dynamically allocated built-in array, as in

```
int *gradesArray = new int[ 10 ]{};
```

The empty set of braces as shown here indicates that *default initialization* should be used for each element—for fundamental types each element is set to 0. The braces may also contain a comma-separated list of initializers for the array's elements.

Releasing Dynamically Allocated Built-In Arrays with `delete []`

To deallocate the memory to which `gradesArray` points, use the statement

```
delete [] gradesArray;
```

If the pointer points to a built-in array of objects, the statement first calls the destructor for every object in the array, then deallocates the memory. If the preceding statement did *not* include the square brackets (`[]`) and `gradesArray` pointed to a built-in array of objects, the result is *undefined—some compilers call the destructor only for the first object in the array. Using* `delete` *or* `delete []` *on a* `nullptr` *has no effect.*

Common Programming Error 10.3

Using `delete` *instead of* `delete []` *for built-in arrays of objects can lead to runtime logic errors. To ensure that every object in the array receives a destructor call, always delete memory allocated as an array with operator* `delete []`*. Similarly, always delete memory allocated as an individual element with operator* `delete`*—the result of deleting a single object with operator* `delete []` *is undefined.*

C++11: Managing Dynamically Allocated Memory with `unique_ptr`

C++11's new `unique_ptr` is a "smart pointer" for managing dynamically allocated memory. When a `unique_ptr` goes out of scope, its destructor *automatically* returns the managed memory to the free store. In Chapter 17, we introduce `unique_ptr` and show how to use it to manage dynamically allocated objects or a dynamically allocated built-in arrays. 11

10.10 Case Study: Array Class

We discussed built-in arrays in Chapter 8. Pointer-based arrays have many problems, including:

- A program can easily "walk off" either end of a built-in array, because *C++ does not check whether subscripts fall outside the range of the array* (though you can still do this explicitly).
- Built-in arrays of size *n* must number their elements 0, …, *n* – 1; alternate subscript ranges are *not* allowed.
- An entire built-in array cannot be input or output at once; each element must be read or written individually (unless the array is a null-terminated C string).
- Two built-in arrays cannot be meaningfully compared with equality or relational operators (because the array names are simply pointers to where the arrays begin in memory and two arrays will always be at different memory locations).

- When a built-in array is passed to a general-purpose function designed to handle arrays of any size, the array's *size* must be passed as an additional argument.
- One built-in array cannot be *assigned* to another with the assignment operator(s).

Class development is an interesting, creative and intellectually challenging activity—always with the goal of *crafting valuable classes*. With C++, you can implement more robust array capabilities via classes and operator overloading as has been done with class templates `array` and `vector` in the C++ Standard Library. In this section, we'll develop our own custom array class that's preferable to built-in arrays. When we refer to "arrays" in this case study, we mean built-in arrays.

In this example, we create a powerful `Array` class that performs range checking to ensure that subscripts remain within the bounds of the `Array`. The class allows one `Array` object to be assigned to another with the assignment operator. `Array` objects know their size, so the size does not need to be passed separately to functions that receive `Array` parameters. Entire `Arrays` can be input or output with the stream extraction and stream insertion operators, respectively. You can compare `Arrays` with the equality operators `==` and `!=`.

10.10.1 Using the Array Class

The program of Figs. 10.9–10.11 demonstrates class `Array` and its overloaded operators. First we walk through `main` (Fig. 10.9) and the program's output, then we consider the class definition (Fig. 10.10) and each of its member-function definitions (Fig. 10.11).

```
// Fig. 10.9: fig10_09.cpp
// Array class test program.
#include <iostream>
#include <stdexcept>
#include "Array.h"
using namespace std;

int main()
{
   Array integers1( 7 ); // seven-element Array
   Array integers2; // 10-element Array by default

   // print integers1 size and contents
   cout << "Size of Array integers1 is "
      << integers1.getSize()
      << "\nArray after initialization:\n" << integers1;

   // print integers2 size and contents
   cout << "\nSize of Array integers2 is "
      << integers2.getSize()
      << "\nArray after initialization:\n" << integers2;

   // input and print integers1 and integers2
   cout << "\nEnter 17 integers:" << endl;
   cin >> integers1 >> integers2;
```

Fig. 10.9 | Array class test program. (Part 1 of 3.)

```

   cout << "\nAfter input, the Arrays contain:\n"
      << "integers1:\n" << integers1
      << "integers2:\n" << integers2;

   // use overloaded inequality (!=) operator
   cout << "\nEvaluating: integers1 != integers2" << endl;

   if ( integers1 != integers2 )
      cout << "integers1 and integers2 are not equal" << endl;

   // create Array integers3 using integers1 as an
   // initializer; print size and contents
   Array integers3( integers1 ); // invokes copy constructor

   cout << "\nSize of Array integers3 is "
      << integers3.getSize()
      << "\nArray after initialization:\n" << integers3;

   // use overloaded assignment (=) operator
   cout << "\nAssigning integers2 to integers1:" << endl;
   integers1 = integers2; // note target Array is smaller

   cout << "integers1:\n" << integers1
      << "integers2:\n" << integers2;

   // use overloaded equality (==) operator
   cout << "\nEvaluating: integers1 == integers2" << endl;

   if ( integers1 == integers2 )
      cout << "integers1 and integers2 are equal" << endl;

   // use overloaded subscript operator to create rvalue
   cout << "\nintegers1[5] is " << integers1[ 5 ];

   // use overloaded subscript operator to create lvalue
   cout << "\n\nAssigning 1000 to integers1[5]" << endl;
   integers1[ 5 ] = 1000;
   cout << "integers1:\n" << integers1;

   // attempt to use out-of-range subscript
   try
   {
      cout << "\nAttempt to assign 1000 to integers1[15]" << endl;
      integers1[ 15 ] = 1000; // ERROR: subscript out of range
   } // end try
   catch ( out_of_range &ex )
   {
      cout << "An exception occurred: " << ex.what() << endl;
   } // end catch
} // end main
```

Fig. 10.9 | Array class test program. (Part 2 of 3.)

```
Size of Array integers1 is 7
Array after initialization:
           0           0           0           0
           0           0           0

Size of Array integers2 is 10
Array after initialization:
           0           0           0           0
           0           0           0           0
           0           0

Enter 17 integers:
1 2 3 4 5 6 7 8 9 10 11 12 13 14 15 16 17

After input, the Arrays contain:
integers1:
           1           2           3           4
           5           6           7
integers2:
           8           9          10          11
          12          13          14          15
          16          17

Evaluating: integers1 != integers2
integers1 and integers2 are not equal

Size of Array integers3 is 7
Array after initialization:
           1           2           3           4
           5           6           7

Assigning integers2 to integers1:
integers1:
           8           9          10          11
          12          13          14          15
          16          17

integers2:
           8           9          10          11
          12          13          14          15
          16          17

Evaluating: integers1 == integers2
integers1 and integers2 are equal

integers1[5] is 13

Assigning 1000 to integers1[5]
integers1:
           8           9          10          11
          12        1000          14          15
          16          17

Attempt to assign 1000 to integers1[15]
An exception occurred: Subscript out of range
```

Fig. 10.9 | Array class test program. (Part 3 of 3.)

Creating **`Array`***s, Outputting Their Size and Displaying Their Contents*
The program begins by instantiating two objects of class `Array`—`integers1` (Fig. 10.9, line 10) with seven elements, and `integers2` (line 11) with the default `Array` size—10 elements (specified by the `Array` default constructor's prototype in Fig. 10.10, line 14). Lines 14–16 in Fig. 10.9 use member function `getSize` to determine the size of `integers1` then output `integers1`'s contents, using the `Array` overloaded stream insertion operator. The sample output confirms that the `Array` elements were set correctly to zeros by the constructor. Next, lines 19–21 output the size of `Array integers2` then output `integers2`'s contents, using the `Array` overloaded stream insertion operator.

Using the Overloaded Stream Insertion Operator to Fill an **`Array`**
Line 24 prompts the user to input 17 integers. Line 25 uses the `Array` overloaded stream extraction operator to read the first seven values into `integers1` and the remaining 10 values into `integers2`. Lines 27–29 output the two arrays with the overloaded `Array` stream insertion operator to confirm that the input was performed correctly.

Using the Overloaded Inequality Operator
Line 34 tests the overloaded inequality operator by evaluating the condition

```
integers1 != integers2
```

The program output shows that the `Array`s are not equal.

Initializing a New **`Array`** *with a Copy of an Existing* **`Array`***'s Contents*
Line 39 instantiates a third `Array` called `integers3` and initializes it with a copy of `Array integers1`. This invokes class `Array`'s **copy constructor** to copy the elements of `integers1` into `integers3`. We discuss the details of the copy constructor shortly. The copy constructor can also be invoked by writing line 39 as follows:

```
Array integers3 = integers1;
```

The equal sign in the preceding statement is *not* the assignment operator. When an equal sign appears in the declaration of an object, it invokes a constructor for that object. This form can be used to pass only a single argument to a constructor—specifically, the value on the right side of the = symbol.

Lines 41–43 output the size of `integers3` then output `integers3`'s contents, using the `Array` overloaded stream insertion operator to confirm that `integers3`'s elements were set correctly by the copy constructor.

Using the Overloaded Assignment Operator
Line 47 tests the overloaded assignment operator (=) by assigning `integers2` to `integers1`. Lines 49–50 display both `Array` objects' contents to confirm that the assignment was successful. `Array integers1` originally held 7 integers, but was resized to hold a copy of the 10 elements in `integers2`. As we'll see, the overloaded assignment operator performs this resizing operation in a manner that's transparent to the client code.

Using the Overloaded Equality Operator
Line 55 uses the overloaded equality operator (==) to confirm that objects `integers1` and `integers2` are indeed *identical* after the assignment in line 47.

Using the Overloaded Subscript Operator

Line 59 uses the overloaded subscript operator to refer to `integers1[5]`—an in-range element of `integers1`. This subscripted name is used as an *rvalue* to print the value stored in `integers1[5]`. Line 63 uses `integers1[5]` as a modifiable *lvalue* on the left side of an assignment statement to assign a new value, `1000`, to element `5` of `integers1`. We'll see that `operator[]` returns a reference to use as the modifiable *lvalue* after the operator confirms that `5` is a valid subscript for `integers1`.

Line 70 attempts to assign the value `1000` to `integers1[15]`—an *out-of-range* element. In this example, `operator[]` determines that the subscript is out of range and throws an `out_of_range` exception.

Interestingly, *the array subscript operator `[]` is not restricted for use only with arrays*; it also can be used, for example, to select elements from other kinds of *container classes*, such as `string`s and dictionaries. Also, when overloaded `operator[]` functions are defined, *subscripts no longer have to be integers*—characters, strings or even objects of user-defined classes also could be used. In Chapter 15, we discuss the Standard Library `map` class that allows `string` subscripts.

10.10.2 Array Class Definition

Now that we've seen how this program operates, let's walk through the class header (Fig. 10.10). As we refer to each member function in the header, we discuss that function's implementation in Fig. 10.11. In Fig. 10.10, lines 34–35 represent the `private` data members of class `Array`. Each `Array` object consists of a `size` member indicating the number of elements in the `Array` and an `int` pointer—`ptr`—that points to the dynamically allocated pointer-based array of integers managed by the `Array` object.

```
1   // Fig. 10.10: Array.h
2   // Array class definition with overloaded operators.
3   #ifndef ARRAY_H
4   #define ARRAY_H
5
6   #include <iostream>
7
8   class Array
9   {
10     friend std::ostream &operator<<( std::ostream &, const Array & );
11     friend std::istream &operator>>( std::istream &, Array & );
12
13  public:
14     explicit Array( int = 10 ); // default constructor
15     Array( const Array & ); // copy constructor
16     ~Array(); // destructor
17     size_t getSize() const; // return size
18
19     const Array &operator=( const Array & ); // assignment operator
20     bool operator==( const Array & ) const; // equality operator
21
```

Fig. 10.10 | Array class definition with overloaded operators. (Part 1 of 2.)

```
   // inequality operator; returns opposite of == operator
   bool operator!=( const Array &right ) const
   {
      return ! ( *this == right ); // invokes Array::operator==
   } // end function operator!=

   // subscript operator for non-const objects returns modifiable lvalue
   int &operator[]( int );

   // subscript operator for const objects returns rvalue
   int operator[]( int ) const;
private:
   size_t size; // pointer-based array size
   int *ptr; // pointer to first element of pointer-based array
}; // end class Array

#endif
```

Fig. 10.10 | Array class definition with overloaded operators. (Part 2 of 2.)

```
// Fig. 10.11: Array.cpp
// Array class member- and friend-function definitions.
#include <iostream>
#include <iomanip>
#include <stdexcept>

#include "Array.h" // Array class definition
using namespace std;

// default constructor for class Array (default size 10)
Array::Array( int arraySize )
   : size( arraySize > 0 ? arraySize :
        throw invalid_argument( "Array size must be greater than 0" ) ),
     ptr( new int[ size ] )
{
   for ( size_t i = 0; i < size; ++i )
      ptr[ i ] = 0; // set pointer-based array element
} // end Array default constructor

// copy constructor for class Array;
// must receive a reference to an Array
Array::Array( const Array &arrayToCopy )
   : size( arrayToCopy.size ),
     ptr( new int[ size ] )
{
   for ( size_t i = 0; i < size; ++i )
      ptr[ i ] = arrayToCopy.ptr[ i ]; // copy into object
} // end Array copy constructor

// destructor for class Array
Array::~Array()
{
```

Fig. 10.11 | Array class member- and friend-function definitions. (Part 1 of 3.)

```
   delete [] ptr; // release pointer-based array space
} // end destructor

// return number of elements of Array
size_t Array::getSize() const
{
   return size; // number of elements in Array
} // end function getSize

// overloaded assignment operator;
// const return avoids: ( a1 = a2 ) = a3
const Array &Array::operator=( const Array &right )
{
   if ( &right != this ) // avoid self-assignment
   {
      // for Arrays of different sizes, deallocate original
      // left-side Array, then allocate new left-side Array
      if ( size != right.size )
      {
         delete [] ptr; // release space
         size = right.size; // resize this object
         ptr = new int[ size ]; // create space for Array copy
      } // end inner if

      for ( size_t i = 0; i < size; ++i )
         ptr[ i ] = right.ptr[ i ]; // copy array into object
   } // end outer if

   return *this; // enables x = y = z, for example
} // end function operator=

// determine if two Arrays are equal and
// return true, otherwise return false
bool Array::operator==( const Array &right ) const
{
   if ( size != right.size )
      return false; // arrays of different number of elements

   for ( size_t i = 0; i < size; ++i )
      if ( ptr[ i ] != right.ptr[ i ] )
         return false; // Array contents are not equal

   return true; // Arrays are equal
} // end function operator==

// overloaded subscript operator for non-const Arrays;
// reference return creates a modifiable lvalue
int &Array::operator[]( int subscript )
{
   // check for subscript out-of-range error
   if ( subscript < 0 || subscript >= size )
      throw out_of_range( "Subscript out of range" );

```

Fig. 10.11 | Array class member- and friend-function definitions. (Part 2 of 3.)

```
   return ptr[ subscript ]; // reference return
} // end function operator[]

// overloaded subscript operator for const Arrays
// const reference return creates an rvalue
int Array::operator[]( int subscript ) const
{
   // check for subscript out-of-range error
   if ( subscript < 0 || subscript >= size )
      throw out_of_range( "Subscript out of range" );

   return ptr[ subscript ]; // returns copy of this element
} // end function operator[]

// overloaded input operator for class Array;
// inputs values for entire Array
istream &operator>>( istream &input, Array &a )
{
   for ( size_t i = 0; i < a.size; ++i )
      input >> a.ptr[ i ];

   return input; // enables cin >> x >> y;
} // end function

// overloaded output operator for class Array
ostream &operator<<( ostream &output, const Array &a )
{
   // output private ptr-based array
   for ( size_t i = 0; i < a.size; ++i )
   {
      output << setw( 12 ) << a.ptr[ i ];

      if ( ( i + 1 ) % 4 == 0 ) // 4 numbers per row of output
         output << endl;
   } // end for

   if ( a.size % 4 != 0 ) // end last line of output
      output << endl;

   return output; // enables cout << x << y;
} // end function operator<<
```

Fig. 10.11 | Array class member- and friend-function definitions. (Part 3 of 3.)

Overloading the Stream Insertion and Stream Extraction Operators as `friend`*s*

Lines 10–11 of Fig. 10.10 declare the overloaded stream insertion operator and the overloaded stream extraction operator as `friend`s of class `Array`. When the compiler sees an expression like `cout << arrayObject`, it invokes *non-member function* `operator<<` with the call

```
operator<<( cout, arrayObject )
```

When the compiler sees an expression like `cin >> arrayObject`, it invokes *non-member function* `operator>>` with the call

```
operator>>( cin, arrayObject )
```

Again, these stream insertion and stream extraction operator functions *cannot* be members of class Array, because the Array object is always mentioned on the *right* side of the stream insertion or stream extraction operator.

Function operator<< (defined in Fig. 10.11, lines 111–126) prints the number of elements indicated by size from the integer array to which ptr points. Function operator>> (defined in Fig. 10.11, lines 102–108) inputs directly into the array to which ptr points. Each of these operator functions returns an appropriate reference to enable *cascaded* output or input statements, respectively. These functions have access to an Array's private data because they're declared as friends of class Array. We could have used class Array's getSize and operator[] functions in the bodies of operator<< and operator>>, in which case these operator functions would not need to be friends of class Array.

You might be tempted to replace the counter-controlled for statement in lines 104–105 and many of the other for statements in class Array's implementation with the C++11 range-based for statement. Unfortunately, range-based for does *not* work with dynamically allocated built-in arrays.

Array Default Constructor

Line 14 of Fig. 10.10 declares the *default constructor* for the class and specifies a default size of 10 elements. When the compiler sees a declaration like line 11 in Fig. 10.9, it invokes class Array's default constructor to set the size of the Array to 10 elements. The default constructor (defined in Fig. 10.11, lines 11–18) validates and assigns the argument to data member size, uses new to obtain the memory for the *internal pointer-based representation* of this Array and assigns the pointer returned by new to data member ptr. Then the constructor uses a for statement to set all the elements of the array to zero. It's possible to have an Array class that does not initialize its members if, for example, these members are to be read at some later time; but this is considered to be a poor programming practice. Arrays, and *objects in general, should be properly initialized as they're created.*

Array Copy Constructor

Line 15 of Fig. 10.10 declares a *copy constructor* (defined in Fig. 10.11, lines 22–28) that initializes an Array by making a copy of an existing Array object. *Such copying must be done carefully to avoid the pitfall of leaving both Array objects pointing to the same dynamically allocated memory.* This is exactly the problem that would occur with *default memberwise copying*, if the compiler is allowed to define a default copy constructor for this class. Copy constructors are invoked whenever a copy of an object is needed, such as in

- passing an object by value to a function,
- returning an object by value from a function or
- initializing an object with a copy of another object of the same class.

The copy constructor is called in a declaration when an object of class Array is instantiated and initialized with another object of class Array, as in the declaration in line 39 of Fig. 10.9.

The copy constructor for Array copies the size of the initializer Array into data member size, uses new to obtain the memory for the internal pointer-based representation of this Array and assigns the pointer returned by new to data member ptr. Then the copy constructor uses a for statement to copy all the elements of the initializer Array into the new Array object. An object of a class can look at the private data of any other object of that class (using a handle that indicates which object to access).

Software Engineering Observation 10.3

The argument to a copy constructor should be a const *reference to allow a* const *object to be copied.*

Common Programming Error 10.4

If the copy constructor simply copied the pointer in the source object to the target object's pointer, then both would point to the same *dynamically allocated memory. The first destructor to execute would delete the dynamically allocated memory, and the other object's* ptr *would point to memory that's no longer allocated, a situation called a* ***dangling pointer****—this would likely result in a serious runtime error (such as early program termination) when the pointer was used.*

Array Destructor

Line 16 of Fig. 10.10 declares the class's destructor (defined in Fig. 10.11, lines 31–34). The destructor is invoked when an object of class Array goes out of scope. The destructor uses delete [] to release the memory allocated dynamically by new in the constructor.

Error-Prevention Tip 10.3

If after deleting dynamically allocated memory, the pointer will continue to exist *in memory, set the pointer's value to* nullptr *to indicate that the pointer no longer points to memory in the free store. By setting the pointer to* nullptr*, the program loses access to that free-store space, which could be reallocated for a different purpose. If you do not set the pointer to* nullptr*, your code could* inadvertently access the reallocated memory, causing subtle, nonrepeatable logic errors. *We did not set* ptr *to* nullptr *in line 33 of Fig. 10.11 because after the destructor executes, the* Array *object no longer exists in memory.*

getSize Member Function

Line 17 of Fig. 10.10 declares function getSize (defined in Fig. 10.11, lines 37–40) that returns the number of elements in the Array.

Overloaded Assignment Operator

Line 19 of Fig. 10.10 declares the overloaded assignment operator function for the class. When the compiler sees the expression integers1 = integers2 in line 47 of Fig. 10.9, the compiler invokes member function operator= with the call

```
integers1.operator=( integers2 )
```

Member function operator='s implementation (Fig. 10.11, lines 44–62) tests for **self-assignment** (line 46) in which an Array object is being assigned to itself. When this is equal to the right operand's address, a *self-assignment* is being attempted, so the assignment is skipped (i.e., the object already is itself; in a moment we'll see why self-assignment is dangerous). If it isn't a self-assignment, then the function determines whether the sizes of the two Arrays are identical (line 50); in that case, the original array of integers in the left-side Array object is *not* reallocated. Otherwise, operator= uses delete [] (line 52) to release the memory originally allocated to the target Array, copies the size of the source Array to the size of the target Array (line 53), uses new to allocate the memory for the target Array and places the pointer returned by new into the Array's ptr member. Then the for statement in lines 57–58 copies the elements from the source Array to the target Array. Regardless of whether this is a self-assignment, the member function returns the current object (i.e., *this in line 61) as a constant reference; this enables cascaded Array assignments such as x = y = z, but prevents ones like (x = y) = z because z cannot be assigned to the const Array reference that's returned by (x = y). If self-assignment occurs, and function operator= did not test for this case, operator= would unnecessarily copy the elements of the Array into itself.

Software Engineering Observation 10.4

11 *A copy constructor, a destructor and an overloaded assignment operator are usually provided as a group for any class that uses dynamically allocated memory. With the addition of move semantics in C++11, other functions should also be provided, as you'll see in Chapter 24.*

Common Programming Error 10.5

Not providing a copy constructor and overloaded assignment operator for a class when objects of that class contain pointers to dynamically allocated memory is a potential logic error.

11 *C++11: Move Constructor and Move Assignment Operator*

C++11 adds the notions of a *move constructor* and a *move assignment operator*. We defer a discussion of these new functions until Chapter 24, C++11: Additional Features. This discussion will affect the two preceding tips.

11 *C++11: Deleting Unwanted Member Functions from Your Class*

Prior to C++11, you could prevent class objects from being *copied* or *assigned* by declaring as private the class's copy constructor and overloaded assignment operator. As of C++11, you can simply *delete* these functions from your class. To do so in class Array, replace the prototypes in lines 15 and 19 of Fig. 10.10 with:

```
Array( const Array & ) = delete;
const Array &operator=( const Array & ) = delete;
```

Though you can delete *any* member function, it's most commonly used with member functions that the compiler can *auto-generate*—the default constructor, copy constructor, assignment operator, and in C++ 11, the move constructor and move assignment operator.

Overloaded Equality and Inequality Operators

Line 20 of Fig. 10.10 declares the overloaded equality operator (==) for the class. When the compiler sees the expression integers1 == integers2 in line 55 of Fig. 10.9, the compiler invokes member function operator== with the call

```
integers1.operator==( integers2 )
```

Member function operator== (defined in Fig. 10.11, lines 66–76) immediately returns false if the size members of the Arrays are not equal. Otherwise, operator== compares each pair of elements. If they're all equal, the function returns true. The first pair of elements to differ causes the function to return false immediately.

Lines 23–26 of Fig. 10.9 define the overloaded inequality operator (!=) for the class. Member function operator!= uses the overloaded operator== function to determine whether one Array is *equal* to another, then returns the *opposite* of that result. Writing operator!= in this manner enables you to *reuse* operator==, which *reduces the amount of code that must be written in the class.* Also, the full function definition for operator!= is in the Array header. This allows the compiler to *inline* the definition of operator!=.

Overloaded Subscript Operators

Lines 29 and 32 of Fig. 10.10 declare two overloaded subscript operators (defined in Fig. 10.11 in lines 80–87 and 91–98, respectively). When the compiler sees the expression integers1[5] (Fig. 10.9, line 59), it invokes the appropriate overloaded operator[] member function by generating the call

```
integers1.operator[]( 5 )
```

The compiler creates a call to the const version of operator[] (Fig. 10.11, lines 91–98) when the subscript operator is used on a const Array object. For example, if you pass an Array to a function that receives the Array as a const Array & named z, then the const version of operator[] is required to execute a statement such as

```
cout << z[ 3 ] << endl;
```

Remember, a program can invoke only the const member functions of a const object.

Each definition of operator[] determines whether the subscript it receives as an argument is *in range* and—if not, each throws an out_of_range exception. If the subscript is in range, the non-const version of operator[] returns the appropriate Array element as a reference so that it may be used as a modifiable *lvalue* (e.g., on the *left* side of an assignment statement). If the subscript is in range, the const version of operator[] returns a copy of the appropriate element of the Array.

C++11: Managing Dynamically Allocated Memory with **unique_ptr**

11

In this case study, class Array's destructor used delete [] to return the dynamically allocated built-in array to the free store. As you recall, C++11 enables you to use unique_ptr to ensure that this dynamically allocated memory is deleted when the Array object goes out of scope. In Chapter 17, we introduce unique_ptr and show how to use it to manage a dynamically allocated objects or dynamically allocated built-in arrays.

C++11: Passing a List Initializer to a Constructor

11

In Fig. 7.4, we showed how to initialize an array object with a comma-separated list of initializers in braces, as in

```
array< int, 5 > n = { 32, 27, 64, 18, 95 };
```

Recall from Section 4.8 that C++11 now allows *any* object to be initialized with a *list initializer* and that the preceding statement can also be written without the =, as in

```
array< int, 5 > n{ 32, 27, 64, 18, 95 };
```

C++11 also allows you to use list initializers when you declare objects of your own classes. For example, you can now provide an Array constructor that would enabled the following declarations:

```
Array integers = { 1, 2, 3, 4, 5 };
```

or

```
Array integers{ 1, 2, 3, 4, 5 };
```

each of which creates an Array object with five elements containing the integers from 1 to 5.

To support list initialization, you can define a constructor that receives an *object* of the class template initializer_list. For class Array, you'd include the <initializer_list> header. Then, you'd define a constructor with the first line:

```
Array::Array( initializer_list< int > list )
```

You can determine the number of elements in the list parameter by calling its size member function. To obtain each initializer and copy it into the Array object's dynamically allocated built-in array, you can use a range-based for as follows:

```
size_t i = 0;

for ( int item : list )
   ptr[ i++ ] = item;
```

10.11 Operators as Member vs. Non-Member Functions

Whether an operator function is implemented as a *member function* or as a *non-member function*, the operator is still used the same way in expressions. So which is best?

When an operator function is implemented as a *member function*, the *leftmost* (or only) operand must be an object (or a reference to an object) of the operator's class. If the left operand *must* be an object of a different class or a fundamental type, this operator function *must* be implemented as a *non-member function* (as we did in Section 10.5 when overloading << and >> as the stream insertion and stream extraction operators, respectively). A *non-member operator function* can be made a friend of a class if that function must access private or protected members of that class directly.

Operator member functions of a specific class are called (*implicitly* by the compiler) only when the *left* operand of a binary operator is specifically an object of that class, or when the *single operand of a unary operator* is an object of that class.

Commutative Operators

Another reason why you might choose a non-member function to overload an operator is to enable the operator to be *commutative*. For example, suppose we have a *fundamental type variable*, number, of type long int, and an *object* bigInteger1, of class HugeInt (a class in which integers may be arbitrarily large rather than being limited by the machine word size of the underlying hardware). The addition operator (+) produces a *temporary* HugeInt object as the sum of a HugeInt and a long int (as in the expression bigInteger1 + number), *or* as the sum of a long int and a HugeInt (as in the expression number + bigInteger1). Thus, we require the addition operator to be *commutative* (exactly as it is with two fundamental-type operands). The problem is that the class object *must* appear on the *left* of the addition operator if that operator is to be overloaded as a *member function*. So, we *also* overload the operator as a *non-member function* to allow the HugeInt to appear on the *right* of the addition. The operator+ function that deals with the HugeInt on the *left* can still be a *member function*. The *non-member function* can simply swap its arguments and call the *member function*.

10.12 Converting Between Types

Most programs process information of many types. Sometimes all the operations "stay within a type." For example, adding an `int` to an `int` produces an `int`. It's often necessary, however, to convert data of one type to data of another type. This can happen in assignments, in calculations, in passing values to functions and in returning values from functions. The compiler knows how to perform certain conversions among fundamental types. You can use *cast operators* to *force* conversions among fundamental types.

But what about user-defined types? The compiler cannot know in advance how to convert among user-defined types, and between user-defined types and fundamental types, so you must specify how to do this. Such conversions can be performed with **conversion constructors**—constructors that can be called with a single argument (we'll refer to these as *single-argument constructors*). Such constructors can turn objects of other types (including fundamental types) into objects of a particular class.

Conversion Operators

A **conversion operator** (also called a *cast operator*) can be used to convert an object of one class to another type. Such a conversion operator must be a *non-*`static` *member function.* The function prototype

```
MyClass::operator char *() const;
```

declares an overloaded cast operator function for converting an object of class `MyClass` into a temporary `char *` object. The operator function is declared `const` because it does *not* modify the original object. The return type of an overloaded **cast operator function** is implicitly the type to which the object is being converted. If `s` is a class object, when the compiler sees the expression `static_cast<char *>(s)`, the compiler generates the call

```
s.operator char *()
```

to convert the operand `s` to a `char *`.

Overloaded Cast Operator Functions

Overloaded cast operator functions can be defined to convert objects of user-defined types into fundamental types or into objects of other user-defined types. The prototypes

```
MyClass::operator int() const;
MyClass::operator OtherClass() const;
```

declare *overloaded cast operator functions* that can convert an object of user-defined type `MyClass` into an integer or into an object of user-defined type `OtherClass`, respectively.

Implicit Calls to Cast Operators and Conversion Constructors

One of the nice features of cast operators and conversion constructors is that, when necessary, the compiler can call these functions *implicitly* to create *temporary* objects. For example, if an object `s` of a user-defined `String` class appears in a program at a location where an ordinary `char *` is expected, such as

```
cout << s;
```

the compiler can call the overloaded cast-operator function `operator char *` to convert the object into a `char *` and use the resulting `char *` in the expression. With this cast operator provided for a `String` class, the stream insertion operator does *not* have to be overloaded to output a `String` using `cout`.

Software Engineering Observation 10.5

When a conversion constructor or conversion operator is used to perform an implicit conversion, *C++ can apply* only one *implicit constructor or operator function call (i.e., a single user-defined conversion) to try to match the needs of another overloaded operator. The compiler will not satisfy an overloaded operator's needs by performing a series of implicit, user-defined conversions.*

10.13 `explicit` Constructors and Conversion Operators

Recall that we've been declaring as `explicit` every constructor that can be called with one argument. With the exception of copy constructors, any constructor that can be called with a *single argument* and is *not* declared `explicit` can be used by the compiler to perform an *implicit conversion*. The constructor's argument is converted to an object of the class in which the constructor is defined. The conversion is automatic and you need not use a cast operator. *In some situations, implicit conversions are undesirable or error-prone.* For example, our `Array` class in Fig. 10.10 defines a constructor that takes a single `int` argument. The intent of this constructor is to create an `Array` object containing the number of elements specified by the `int` argument. However, if this constructor were not declared `explicit` it could be misused by the compiler to perform an *implicit conversion*.

Common Programming Error 10.6

Unfortunately, the compiler might use implicit conversions in cases that you do not expect, resulting in ambiguous expressions that generate compilation errors or result in execution-time logic errors.

Accidentally Using a Single-Argument Constructor as a Conversion Constructor

The program (Fig. 10.12) uses the `Array` class of Figs. 10.10–10.11 to demonstrate an improper implicit conversion. To allow this implicit conversion, we removed the explicit keyword from line 14 in `Array.h` (Fig. 10.10).

Line 11 in `main` (Fig. 10.12) instantiates `Array` object `integers1` and calls the *single-argument constructor* with the `int` value `7` to specify the number of elements in the `Array`. Recall from Fig. 10.11 that the `Array` constructor that receives an `int` argument initializes all the `Array` elements to 0. Line 12 calls function `outputArray` (defined in lines 17–21), which receives as its argument a `const Array &` to an `Array`. The function outputs the number of elements in its `Array` argument and the contents of the `Array`. In this case, the size of the `Array` is `7`, so seven `0`s are output.

Line 13 calls function `outputArray` with the `int` value `3` as an argument. However, this program does *not* contain a function called `outputArray` that takes an `int` argument. So, the compiler determines whether class `Array` provides a *conversion constructor* that can convert an `int` into an `Array`. Since the `Array` constructor receives one `int` argument, the compiler assumes that the constructor is a conversion constructor that can be used to convert the argument `3` into a temporary `Array` object containing three elements. Then, the compiler passes the temporary `Array` object to function `outputArray` to output the

Array's contents. Thus, even though we do not *explicitly* provide an outputArray function that receives an int argument, the compiler is able to compile line 13. The output shows the contents of the three-element Array containing 0s.

```
1  // Fig. 10.12: fig10_12.cpp
2  // Single-argument constructors and implicit conversions.
3  #include <iostream>
4  #include "Array.h"
5  using namespace std;
6
7  void outputArray( const Array & ); // prototype
8
9  int main()
10 {
11    Array integers1( 7 ); // 7-element Array
12    outputArray( integers1 ); // output Array integers1
13    outputArray( 3 ); // convert 3 to an Array and output Array's contents
14 } // end main
15
16 // print Array contents
17 void outputArray( const Array &arrayToOutput )
18 {
19    cout << "The Array received has " << arrayToOutput.getSize()
20       << " elements. The contents are:\n" << arrayToOutput << endl;
21 } // end outputArray
```

```
The Array received has 7 elements. The contents are:
           0           0           0           0
           0           0           0

The Array received has 3 elements. The contents are:
           0           0           0
```

Fig. 10.12 | Single-argument constructors and implicit conversions.

Preventing Implicit Conversions with Single-Argument Constructors

The reason we've been declaring every single-argument contructor preceded by the keyword **explicit** is to *suppress implicit conversions via conversion constructors when such conversions should not be allowed.* A constructor that's declared explicit *cannot* be used in an *implicit* conversion. In the example of Figure 10.13, we use the original version of Array.h from Fig. 10.10, which included the keyword explicit in the declaration of the *single-argument constructor* in line 14

```
explicit Array( int = 10 ); // default constructor
```

Figure 10.13 presents a slightly modified version of the program in Fig. 10.12. When this program in Fig. 10.13 is compiled, the compiler produces an error message indicating that the integer value passed to outputArray in line 13 *cannot* be converted to a const Array &. The compiler error message (from Visual C++) is shown in the output window. Line 14 demonstrates how the explicit constructor can be used to create a temporary Array of 3 elements and pass it to function outputArray.

Error-Prevention Tip 10.4

Always use the `explicit` *keyword on single-argument constructors unless they're intended to be used as conversion constructors.*

```
// Fig. 10.13: fig10_13.cpp
// Demonstrating an explicit constructor.
#include <iostream>
#include "Array.h"
using namespace std;

void outputArray( const Array & ); // prototype

int main()
{
   Array integers1( 7 ); // 7-element Array
   outputArray( integers1 ); // output Array integers1
   outputArray( 3 ); // convert 3 to an Array and output Array's contents
   outputArray( Array( 3 ) ); // explicit single-argument constructor call
} // end main

// print Array contents
void outputArray( const Array &arrayToOutput )
{
   cout << "The Array received has " << arrayToOutput.getSize()
      << " elements. The contents are:\n" << arrayToOutput << endl;
} // end outputArray
```

```
c:\books\2012\cpphtp9\examples\ch10\fig10_13\fig10_13.cpp(13): error C2664:
'outputArray' : cannot convert parameter 1 from 'int' to 'const Array &'
        Reason: cannot convert from 'int' to 'const Array'
        Constructor for class 'Array' is declared 'explicit'
```

Fig. 10.13 | Demonstrating an `explicit` constructor.

C++11: `explicit` *Conversion Operators*

As of C++11, similar to declaring single-argument constructors `explicit`, you can declare conversion operators `explicit` to prevent the compiler from using them to perform implicit conversions. For example, the prototype:

```
explicit MyClass::operator char *() const;
```

declares `MyClass`'s `char *` cast operator `explicit`.

10.14 Overloading the Function Call Operator ()

Overloading the **function call operator** `()` is powerful, because functions can take an *arbitrary* number of comma-separated parameters. In a *customized* `String` class, for example, you could overload this operator to select a substring from a `String`—the operator's two integer parameters could specify the *start location* and the *length of the substring to be selected*. The `operator()` function could check for such errors as a *start location out of range* or a *negative substring length*.

The overloaded function call operator must be a *non-static* member function and could be defined with the first line:

```
String String::operator()( size_t index, size_t length ) const
```

In this case, it should be a const member function because obtaining a substring should *not* modify the original String object.

Suppose string1 is a String object containing the string "AEIOU". When the compiler encounters the expression string1(2, 3), it generates the member-function call

```
string1.operator()( 2, 3 )
```

which returns a String containing "IOU".

Another possible use of the function call operator is to enable an alternate Array subscripting notation. Instead of using C++'s double-square-bracket notation, such as in chessBoard[row][column], you might prefer to overload the function call operator to enable the notation chessBoard(row, column), where chessBoard is an object of a modified two-dimensional Array class. The primary use of the function call operator is to define function objects, which we discuss in Chapter 16.

10.15 Wrap-Up

In this chapter, you learned how to overload operators to work with class objects. We demonstrated standard C++ class string, which makes extensive use of overloaded operators to create a robust, reusable class that can replace C strings. Next, we discussed several restrictions that the C++ standard places on overloaded operators. We then presented a PhoneNumber class that overloaded operators << and >> to conveniently output and input phone numbers. You also saw a Date class that overloaded the prefix and postfix increment (++) operators and we showed a special syntax that's required to differentiate between the prefix and postfix versions of the increment (++) operator.

Next, we introduced the concept of dynamic memory management. You learned that you can create and destroy objects dynamically with the new and delete operators, respectively. Then, we presented a capstone Array class case study that used overloaded operators and other capabilities to solve various problems with pointer-based arrays. This case study helped you truly understand what classes and object technology are all about—crafting, using and reusing valuable classes. As part of this class, you saw overloaded stream insertion, stream extraction, assignment, equality and subscript operators.

You learned reasons for implementing overloaded operators as member functions or as non-member functions. The chapter concluded with discussions of converting between types (including class types), problems with certain implicit conversions defined by single-argument constructors and how to prevent those problems by using explicit constructors.

In the next chapter, we continue our discussion of classes by introducing a form of software reuse called inheritance. We'll see that when classes share common attributes and behaviors, it's possible to define those attributes and behaviors in a common "base" class and "inherit" those capabilities into new class definitions, enabling you to create the new classes with a minimal amount of code.

Object-Oriented Programming: Inheritance

Objectives

In this chapter you'll:

- Learn qhat inheritance is and how it promotes software reuse.
- Understand the notions of base classes and derived classes and the relationships between them.
- Use the `protected` member access specifier.
- Understand the use of constructors and destructors in inheritance hierarchies.
- Learn the order in which constructors and destructors are called in inheritance hierarchies.
- Understand the differences between `public`, `protected` and `private` inheritance.
- Use inheritance to customize existing software.

Outline

11.1 Introduction

This chapter continues our discussion of object-oriented programming (OOP) by introducing **inheritance**—a form of software reuse in which you create a class that absorbs an existing class's capabilities, then *customizes* or enhances them. Software reuse saves time during program development by taking advantage of proven, high-quality software.

When creating a class, instead of writing completely new data members and member functions, you can specify that the new class should **inherit** the members of an existing class. This existing class is called the **base class**, and the new class is called the **derived class**. Other programming languages, such as Java and C#, refer to the base class as the **superclass** and the derived class as the **subclass**. A derived class represents a *more specialized* group of objects.

C++ offers `public`, `protected` and `private` inheritance. In this chapter, we concentrate on `public` inheritance and briefly explain the other two. *With* `public` *inheritance, every object of a derived class is also an object of that derived class's base class.* However, base-class objects are *not* objects of their derived classes. For example, if we have `Vehicle` as a base class and `Car` as a derived class, then all `Car`s are `Vehicle`s, but not all `Vehicle`s are `Car`s—for example, a `Vehicle` could also be a `Truck` or a `Boat`.

We distinguish between the ***is-a*** **relationship** and the *has-a* relationship. The *is-a* relationship represents inheritance. In an *is-a* relationship, an object of a derived class also can be treated as an object of its base class—for example, a `Car` *is a* `Vehicle`, so any attributes and behaviors of a `Vehicle` are also attributes and behaviors of a `Car`. By contrast, the *has-a* relationship represents *composition*, which was discussed in Chapter 9. In a *has-a* relationship, an object *contains* one or more objects of other classes as members. For example, a `Car` has many components—it *has a* steering wheel, *has a* brake pedal, *has a* transmission, etc.

11.2 Base Classes and Derived Classes

Figure 11.1 lists several simple examples of base classes and derived classes. Base classes tend to be *more general* and derived classes tend to be *more specific*.

Base class	Derived classes
Student	GraduateStudent, UndergraduateStudent
Shape	Circle, Triangle, Rectangle, Sphere, Cube
Loan	CarLoan, HomeImprovementLoan, MortgageLoan
Employee	Faculty, Staff
Account	CheckingAccount, SavingsAccount

Fig. 11.1 | Inheritance examples.

Because every derived-class object *is an* object of its base class, and one base class can have *many* derived classes, the set of objects represented by a base class typically is *larger* than the set of objects represented by any of its derived classes. For example, the base class `Vehicle` represents all vehicles, including cars, trucks, boats, airplanes, bicycles and so on. By contrast, derived class `Car` represents a *smaller, more specific* subset of all vehicles.

Inheritance relationships form **class hierarchies**. A base class exists in a hierarchical relationship with its derived classes. Although classes can exist independently, once they're employed in inheritance relationships, they become affiliated with other classes. A class becomes either a base class—supplying members to other classes, a derived class—inheriting its members from other classes, or *both*.

`CommunityMember` Class Hierarchy

Let's develop a simple inheritance hierarchy with five levels (represented by the UML class diagram in Fig. 11.2). A university community has thousands of `CommunityMember`s.

These `CommunityMember`s consist of `Employee`s, `Student`s and alumni (each of class `Alumnus`). `Employee`s are either `Faculty` or `Staff`. `Faculty` are either `Administrator`s or

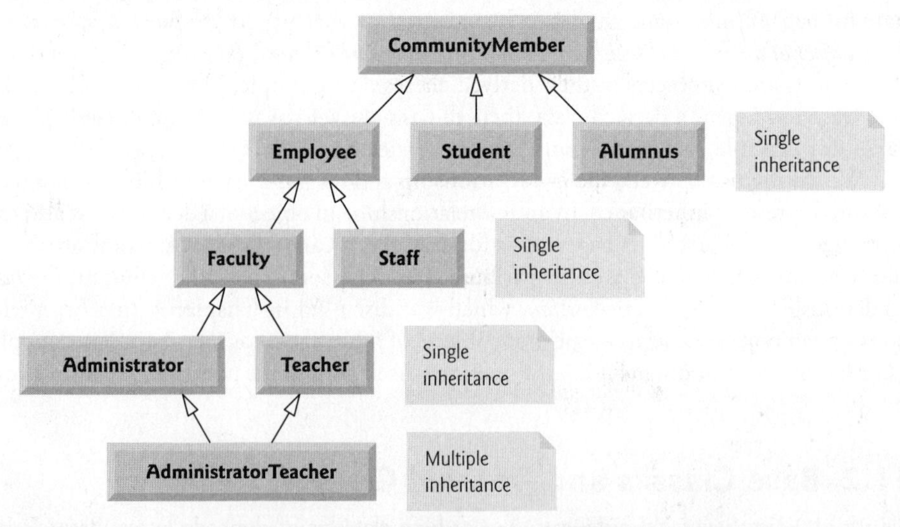

Fig. 11.2 | Inheritance hierarchy for university `CommunityMember`s.

Teachers. Some Administrators, however, are also Teachers. We've used *multiple inheritance* to form class AdministratorTeacher. With **single inheritance**, a class is derived from *one* base class. With **multiple inheritance**, a derived class inherits simultaneously from *two or more* (possibly unrelated) base classes. We discuss multiple inheritance in Chapter 21, Other Topics, but multiple inheritance is generally discouraged.

Each arrow in the hierarchy (Fig. 11.2) represents an *is-a* relationship. For example, as we follow the arrows in this class hierarchy, we can state "an Employee *is a* CommunityMember" and "a Teacher *is a* Faculty member." CommunityMember is the **direct base class** of Employee, Student and Alumnus. In addition, CommunityMember is an **indirect base class** of all the other classes in the diagram. An indirect base class is inherited from two or more levels up the class hierarchy.

Starting from the bottom of the diagram, you can follow the arrows upwards and apply the *is-a* relationship to the topmost base class. For example, an AdministratorTeacher *is an* Administrator, *is a* Faculty member, *is an* Employee and *is a* CommunityMember.

Shape Class Hierarchy

Now consider the Shape inheritance hierarchy in Fig. 11.3. This hierarchy begins with base class Shape. Classes TwoDimensionalShape and ThreeDimensionalShape derive from base class Shape—a Shape *is a* TwoDimensionalShape or *is a* ThreeDimensionalShape. The third level of this hierarchy contains *more specific* types of TwoDimensionalShapes and ThreeDimensionalShapes. As in Fig. 11.2, we can follow the arrows from the bottom of the diagram upwards to the topmost base class in this hierarchy to identify several *is-a* relationships. For instance, a Triangle *is a* TwoDimensionalShape and *is a* Shape, while a Sphere *is a* ThreeDimensionalShape and *is a* Shape.

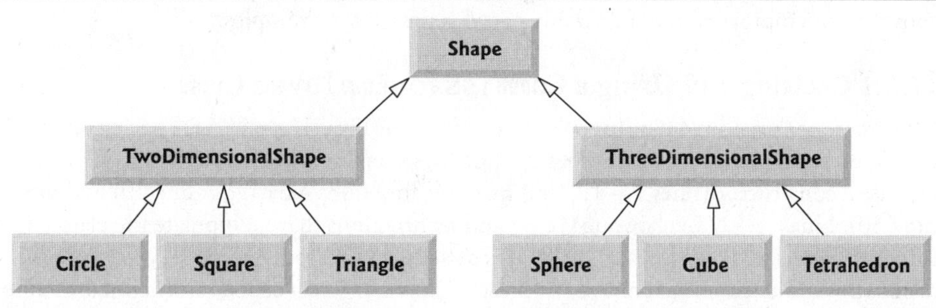

Fig. 11.3 | Inheritance hierarchy for Shapes.

To specify that class TwoDimensionalShape (Fig. 11.3) is derived from (or inherits from) class Shape, class TwoDimensionalShape's definition could begin as follows:

```
class TwoDimensionalShape : public Shape
```

This is an example of **public inheritance**, the most commonly used form. We'll also discuss **private inheritance** and **protected inheritance** (Section 11.5). With all forms of inheritance, private members of a base class are *not* accessible directly from that class's derived classes, but these private base-class members are still inherited (i.e., they're still considered parts of the derived classes). With public inheritance, all other base-class members retain their original member access when they become members of the derived class (e.g., `public` members of the base class become `public` members of the derived class, and, as we'll soon see, `protected` members of the base class become `protected` members of the derived class). Through inherited base-class member functions, the derived class can manipulate `private` members of the base class (if these inherited member functions provide such functionality in the base class). Note that `friend` functions are *not* inherited.

Inheritance is *not* appropriate for every class relationship. In Chapter 9, we discussed the *has-a* relationship, in which classes have members that are objects of other classes. Such relationships create classes by *composition* of existing classes. For example, given the classes `Employee`, `BirthDate` and `TelephoneNumber`, it's improper to say that an `Employee` *is a* `BirthDate` or that an `Employee` *is a* `TelephoneNumber`. However, it is appropriate to say that an `Employee` *has a* `BirthDate` and that an `Employee` *has a* `TelephoneNumber`.

It's possible to treat base-class objects and derived-class objects similarly; their commonalities are expressed in the members of the base class. Objects of all classes derived from a common base class can be treated as objects of that base class (i.e., such objects have an *is-a* relationship with the base class). In Chapter 12, we consider many examples that take advantage of this relationship.

11.3 Relationship between Base and Derived Classes

In this section, we use an inheritance hierarchy containing types of employees in a company's payroll application to discuss the relationship between a base class and a derived class. Commission employees (who will be represented as objects of a base class) are paid a percentage of their sales, while base-salaried commission employees (who will be represented as objects of a derived class) receive a base salary plus a percentage of their sales. We divide our discussion of the relationship between commission employees and base-salaried commission employees into a carefully paced series of five examples.

11.3.1 Creating and Using a `CommissionEmployee` Class

Let's examine `CommissionEmployee`'s class definition (Figs. 11.4–11.5). The `CommissionEmployee` header (Fig. 11.4) specifies class `CommissionEmployee`'s `public` services, which include a constructor (lines 11–12) and member functions `earnings` (line 29) and `print` (line 30). Lines 14–27 declare `public` *get* and *set* functions that manipulate the class's data members (declared in lines 32–36) `firstName`, `lastName`, `socialSecurityNumber`, `grossSales` and `commissionRate`. Member functions `setGrossSales` (defined in lines 57–63 of Fig. 11.5) and `setCommissionRate` (defined in lines 72–78 of Fig. 11.5), for example, validate their arguments before assigning the values to data members `grossSales` and `commissionRate`, respectively.

```
1  // Fig. 11.4: CommissionEmployee.h
2  // CommissionEmployee class definition represents a commission employee.
3  #ifndef COMMISSION_H
4  #define COMMISSION_H
5
6  #include <string> // C++ standard string class
7
```

Fig. 11.4 | `CommissionEmployee` class header. (Part 1 of 2.)

```
class CommissionEmployee
{
public:
   CommissionEmployee( const std::string &, const std::string &,
      const std::string &, double = 0.0, double = 0.0 );

   void setFirstName( const std::string & ); // set first name
   std::string getFirstName() const; // return first name

   void setLastName( const std::string & ); // set last name
   std::string getLastName() const; // return last name

   void setSocialSecurityNumber( const std::string & ); // set SSN
   std::string getSocialSecurityNumber() const; // return SSN

   void setGrossSales( double ); // set gross sales amount
   double getGrossSales() const; // return gross sales amount

   void setCommissionRate( double ); // set commission rate (percentage)
   double getCommissionRate() const; // return commission rate

   double earnings() const; // calculate earnings
   void print() const; // print CommissionEmployee object
private:
   std::string firstName;
   std::string lastName;
   std::string socialSecurityNumber;
   double grossSales; // gross weekly sales
   double commissionRate; // commission percentage
}; // end class CommissionEmployee

#endif
```

Fig. 11.4 | `CommissionEmployee` class header. (Part 2 of 2.)

```
// Fig. 11.5: CommissionEmployee.cpp
// Class CommissionEmployee member-function definitions.
#include <iostream>
#include <stdexcept>
#include "CommissionEmployee.h" // CommissionEmployee class definition
using namespace std;

// constructor
CommissionEmployee::CommissionEmployee(
   const string &first, const string &last, const string &ssn,
   double sales, double rate )
{
   firstName = first; // should validate
   lastName = last; // should validate
   socialSecurityNumber = ssn; // should validate
   setGrossSales( sales ); // validate and store gross sales
```

Fig. 11.5 | Implementation file for `CommissionEmployee` class that represents an employee who is paid a percentage of gross sales. (Part 1 of 3.)

```
   setCommissionRate( rate ); // validate and store commission rate
} // end CommissionEmployee constructor

// set first name
void CommissionEmployee::setFirstName( const string &first )
{
   firstName = first; // should validate
} // end function setFirstName

// return first name
string CommissionEmployee::getFirstName() const
{
   return firstName;
} // end function getFirstName

// set last name
void CommissionEmployee::setLastName( const string &last )
{
   lastName = last; // should validate
} // end function setLastName

// return last name
string CommissionEmployee::getLastName() const
{
   return lastName;
} // end function getLastName

// set social security number
void CommissionEmployee::setSocialSecurityNumber( const string &ssn )
{
   socialSecurityNumber = ssn; // should validate
} // end function setSocialSecurityNumber

// return social security number
string CommissionEmployee::getSocialSecurityNumber() const
{
   return socialSecurityNumber;
} // end function getSocialSecurityNumber

// set gross sales amount
void CommissionEmployee::setGrossSales( double sales )
{
   if ( sales >= 0.0 )
      grossSales = sales;
   else
      throw invalid_argument( "Gross sales must be >= 0.0" );
} // end function setGrossSales

// return gross sales amount
double CommissionEmployee::getGrossSales() const
{
```

Fig. 11.5 | Implementation file for `CommissionEmployee` class that represents an employee who is paid a percentage of gross sales. (Part 2 of 3.)

```
68      return grossSales;
69   } // end function getGrossSales
70
71   // set commission rate
72   void CommissionEmployee::setCommissionRate( double rate )
73   {
74      if ( rate > 0.0 && rate < 1.0 )
75         commissionRate = rate;
76      else
77         throw invalid_argument( "Commission rate must be > 0.0 and < 1.0" );
78   } // end function setCommissionRate
79
80   // return commission rate
81   double CommissionEmployee::getCommissionRate() const
82   {
83      return commissionRate;
84   } // end function getCommissionRate
85
86   // calculate earnings
87   double CommissionEmployee::earnings() const
88   {
89      return commissionRate * grossSales;
90   } // end function earnings
91
92   // print CommissionEmployee object
93   void CommissionEmployee::print() const
94   {
95      cout << "commission employee: " << firstName << ' ' << lastName
96         << "\nsocial security number: " << socialSecurityNumber
97         << "\ngross sales: " << grossSales
98         << "\ncommission rate: " << commissionRate;
99   } // end function print
```

Fig. 11.5 | Implementation file for `CommissionEmployee` class that represents an employee who is paid a percentage of gross sales. (Part 3 of 3.)

`CommissionEmployee` *Constructor*

The `CommissionEmployee` constructor definition *purposely does not use member-initializer syntax* in the first several examples of this section, so that we can demonstrate how `private` and `protected` specifiers affect member access in derived classes. As shown in Fig. 11.5, lines 13–15, we assign values to data members `firstName`, `lastName` and `socialSecurityNumber` in the constructor body. Later in this section, we'll return to using member-initializer lists in the constructors.

We do not validate the values of the constructor's arguments `first`, `last` and `ssn` before assigning them to the corresponding data members. We certainly could validate the first and last names—perhaps by ensuring that they're of a reasonable length. Similarly, a social security number could be validated to ensure that it contains nine digits, with or without dashes (e.g., `123-45-6789` or `123456789`).

`CommissionEmployee` *Member Functions* `earnings` *and* `print`

Member function `earnings` (lines 87–90) calculates a `CommissionEmployee`'s earnings. Line 89 multiplies the `commissionRate` by the `grossSales` and returns the result. Member function `print` (lines 93–99) displays the values of a `CommissionEmployee` object's data members.

Testing Class `CommissionEmployee`

Figure 11.6 tests class `CommissionEmployee`. Lines 11–12 instantiate `CommissionEmployee` object `employee` and invoke the constructor to initialize the object with `"Sue"` as the first name, `"Jones"` as the last name, `"222-22-2222"` as the social security number, `10000` as the gross sales amount and `.06` as the commission rate. Lines 19–24 use `employee`'s *get* functions to display the values of its data members. Lines 26–27 invoke the object's member functions `setGrossSales` and `setCommissionRate` to change the values of data members `grossSales` and `commissionRate`, respectively. Line 31 then calls `employee`'s `print` member function to output the updated `CommissionEmployee` information. Finally, line 34 displays the `CommissionEmployee`'s earnings, calculated by the object's `earnings` member function using the updated values of data members `grossSales` and `commissionRate`.

```
1  // Fig. 11.6: fig11_06.cpp
2  // CommissionEmployee class test program.
3  #include <iostream>
4  #include <iomanip>
5  #include "CommissionEmployee.h" // CommissionEmployee class definition
6  using namespace std;
7
8  int main()
9  {
10    // instantiate a CommissionEmployee object
11    CommissionEmployee employee(
12       "Sue", "Jones", "222-22-2222", 10000, .06 );
13
14    // set floating-point output formatting
15    cout << fixed << setprecision( 2 );
16
17    // get commission employee data
18    cout << "Employee information obtained by get functions: \n"
19       << "\nFirst name is " << employee.getFirstName()
20       << "\nLast name is " << employee.getLastName()
21       << "\nSocial security number is "
22       << employee.getSocialSecurityNumber()
23       << "\nGross sales is " << employee.getGrossSales()
24       << "\nCommission rate is " << employee.getCommissionRate() << endl;
25
26    employee.setGrossSales( 8000 ); // set gross sales
27    employee.setCommissionRate( .1 ); // set commission rate
28
29    cout << "\nUpdated employee information output by print function: \n"
30       << endl;
31    employee.print(); // display the new employee information
32
33    // display the employee's earnings
34    cout << "\n\nEmployee's earnings: $" << employee.earnings() << endl;
35 } // end main
```

Fig. 11.6 | `CommissionEmployee` class test program. (Part 1 of 2.)

```
Employee information obtained by get functions:

First name is Sue
Last name is Jones
Social security number is 222-22-2222
Gross sales is 10000.00
Commission rate is 0.06

Updated employee information output by print function:

commission employee: Sue Jones
social security number: 222-22-2222
gross sales: 8000.00
commission rate: 0.10

Employee's earnings: $800.00
```

Fig. 11.6 | CommissionEmployee class test program. (Part 2 of 2.)

11.3.2 Creating a BasePlusCommissionEmployee Class Without Using Inheritance

We now discuss the second part of our introduction to inheritance by creating and testing (a completely new and independent) class BasePlusCommissionEmployee (Figs. 11.7–11.8), which contains a first name, last name, social security number, gross sales amount, commission rate *and* base salary.

```
// Fig. 11.7: BasePlusCommissionEmployee.h
// BasePlusCommissionEmployee class definition represents an employee
// that receives a base salary in addition to commission.
#ifndef BASEPLUS_H
#define BASEPLUS_H

#include <string> // C++ standard string class

class BasePlusCommissionEmployee
{
public:
   BasePlusCommissionEmployee( const std::string &, const std::string &,
      const std::string &, double = 0.0, double = 0.0, double = 0.0 );

   void setFirstName( const std::string & ); // set first name
   std::string getFirstName() const; // return first name

   void setLastName( const std::string & ); // set last name
   std::string getLastName() const; // return last name

   void setSocialSecurityNumber( const std::string & ); // set SSN
   std::string getSocialSecurityNumber() const; // return SSN

   void setGrossSales( double ); // set gross sales amount
   double getGrossSales() const; // return gross sales amount
```

Fig. 11.7 | BasePlusCommissionEmployee class header. (Part 1 of 2.)

```

   void setCommissionRate( double ); // set commission rate
   double getCommissionRate() const; // return commission rate

   void setBaseSalary( double ); // set base salary
   double getBaseSalary() const; // return base salary

   double earnings() const; // calculate earnings
   void print() const; // print BasePlusCommissionEmployee object
private:
   std::string firstName;
   std::string lastName;
   std::string socialSecurityNumber;
   double grossSales; // gross weekly sales
   double commissionRate; // commission percentage
   double baseSalary; // base salary
}; // end class BasePlusCommissionEmployee

#endif
```

Fig. 11.7 | BasePlusCommissionEmployee class header. (Part 2 of 2.)

```
// Fig. 11.8: BasePlusCommissionEmployee.cpp
// Class BasePlusCommissionEmployee member-function definitions.
#include <iostream>
#include <stdexcept>
#include "BasePlusCommissionEmployee.h"
using namespace std;

// constructor
BasePlusCommissionEmployee::BasePlusCommissionEmployee(
   const string &first, const string &last, const string &ssn,
   double sales, double rate, double salary )
{
   firstName = first; // should validate
   lastName = last; // should validate
   socialSecurityNumber = ssn; // should validate
   setGrossSales( sales ); // validate and store gross sales
   setCommissionRate( rate ); // validate and store commission rate
   setBaseSalary( salary ); // validate and store base salary
} // end BasePlusCommissionEmployee constructor

// set first name
void BasePlusCommissionEmployee::setFirstName( const string &first )
{
   firstName = first; // should validate
} // end function setFirstName

// return first name
string BasePlusCommissionEmployee::getFirstName() const
{
```

Fig. 11.8 | BasePlusCommissionEmployee class represents an employee who receives a base salary in addition to a commission. (Part 1 of 3.)

```
   return firstName;
} // end function getFirstName

// set last name
void BasePlusCommissionEmployee::setLastName( const string &last )
{
   lastName = last; // should validate
} // end function setLastName

// return last name
string BasePlusCommissionEmployee::getLastName() const
{
   return lastName;
} // end function getLastName

// set social security number
void BasePlusCommissionEmployee::setSocialSecurityNumber(
   const string &ssn )
{
   socialSecurityNumber = ssn; // should validate
} // end function setSocialSecurityNumber

// return social security number
string BasePlusCommissionEmployee::getSocialSecurityNumber() const
{
   return socialSecurityNumber;
} // end function getSocialSecurityNumber

// set gross sales amount
void BasePlusCommissionEmployee::setGrossSales( double sales )
{
   if ( sales >= 0.0 )
      grossSales = sales;
   else
      throw invalid_argument( "Gross sales must be >= 0.0" );
} // end function setGrossSales

// return gross sales amount
double BasePlusCommissionEmployee::getGrossSales() const
{
   return grossSales;
} // end function getGrossSales

// set commission rate
void BasePlusCommissionEmployee::setCommissionRate( double rate )
{
   if ( rate > 0.0 && rate < 1.0 )
      commissionRate = rate;
   else
      throw invalid_argument( "Commission rate must be > 0.0 and < 1.0" );
} // end function setCommissionRate

```

Fig. 11.8 | BasePlusCommissionEmployee class represents an employee who receives a base salary in addition to a commission. (Part 2 of 3.)

```
82  // return commission rate
83  double BasePlusCommissionEmployee::getCommissionRate() const
84  {
85     return commissionRate;
86  } // end function getCommissionRate
87
88  // set base salary
89  void BasePlusCommissionEmployee::setBaseSalary( double salary )
90  {
91     if ( salary >= 0.0 )
92        baseSalary = salary;
93     else
94        throw invalid_argument( "Salary must be >= 0.0" );
95  } // end function setBaseSalary
96
97  // return base salary
98  double BasePlusCommissionEmployee::getBaseSalary() const
99  {
100    return baseSalary;
101 } // end function getBaseSalary
102
103 // calculate earnings
104 double BasePlusCommissionEmployee::earnings() const
105 {
106    return baseSalary + ( commissionRate * grossSales );
107 } // end function earnings
108
109 // print BasePlusCommissionEmployee object
110 void BasePlusCommissionEmployee::print() const
111 {
112    cout << "base-salaried commission employee: " << firstName << ' '
113       << lastName << "\nsocial security number: " << socialSecurityNumber
114       << "\ngross sales: " << grossSales
115       << "\ncommission rate: " << commissionRate
116       << "\nbase salary: " << baseSalary;
117 } // end function print
```

Fig. 11.8 | `BasePlusCommissionEmployee` class represents an employee who receives a base salary in addition to a commission. (Part 3 of 3.)

Defining Class `BasePlusCommissionEmployee`

The `BasePlusCommissionEmployee` header (Fig. 11.7) specifies class `BasePlusCommissionEmployee`'s `public` services, which include the `BasePlusCommissionEmployee` constructor (lines 12–13) and member functions `earnings` (line 33) and `print` (line 34). Lines 15–31 declare `public` *get* and *set* functions for the class's `private` data members (declared in lines 36–41) `firstName`, `lastName`, `socialSecurityNumber`, `grossSales`, `commissionRate` *and* `baseSalary`. These variables and member functions encapsulate all the necessary features of a base-salaried commission employee. Note the similarity between this class and class `CommissionEmployee` (Figs. 11.4–11.5)—in this example, we do *not* yet exploit that similarity.

Class `BasePlusCommissionEmployee`'s `earnings` member function (defined in lines 104–107 of Fig. 11.8) computes the earnings of a base-salaried commission employee.

Line 106 returns the result of adding the employee's base salary to the product of the commission rate and the employee's gross sales.

Testing Class **BasePlusCommissionEmployee**

Figure 11.9 tests class `BasePlusCommissionEmployee`. Lines 11–12 instantiate object `employee` of class `BasePlusCommissionEmployee`, passing `"Bob"`, `"Lewis"`, `"333-33-3333"`, `5000`, `.04` and `300` to the constructor as the first name, last name, social security number, gross sales, commission rate *and* base salary, respectively. Lines 19–25 use `BasePlusCommissionEmployee`'s *get* functions to retrieve the values of the object's data members for output. Line 27 invokes the object's `setBaseSalary` member function to change the base salary. Member function `setBaseSalary` (Fig. 11.8, lines 89–95) ensures that data member `baseSalary` is not assigned a negative value, because an employee's base salary cannot be negative. Line 31 of Fig. 11.9 invokes the object's `print` member function to output the updated `BasePlusCommissionEmployee`'s information, and line 34 calls member function `earnings` to display the `BasePlusCommissionEmployee`'s earnings.

```
1  // Fig. 11.9: fig11_09.cpp
2  // BasePlusCommissionEmployee class test program.
3  #include <iostream>
4  #include <iomanip>
5  #include "BasePlusCommissionEmployee.h"
6  using namespace std;
7
8  int main()
9  {
10    // instantiate BasePlusCommissionEmployee object
11    BasePlusCommissionEmployee
12       employee( "Bob", "Lewis", "333-33-3333", 5000, .04, 300 );
13
14    // set floating-point output formatting
15    cout << fixed << setprecision( 2 );
16
17    // get commission employee data
18    cout << "Employee information obtained by get functions: \n"
19       << "\nFirst name is " << employee.getFirstName()
20       << "\nLast name is " << employee.getLastName()
21       << "\nSocial security number is "
22       << employee.getSocialSecurityNumber()
23       << "\nGross sales is " << employee.getGrossSales()
24       << "\nCommission rate is " << employee.getCommissionRate()
25       << "\nBase salary is " << employee.getBaseSalary() << endl;
26
27    employee.setBaseSalary( 1000 ); // set base salary
28
29    cout << "\nUpdated employee information output by print function: \n"
30       << endl;
31    employee.print(); // display the new employee information
32
33    // display the employee's earnings
34    cout << "\n\nEmployee's earnings: $" << employee.earnings() << endl;
35 } // end main
```

Fig. 11.9 | `BasePlusCommissionEmployee` class test program. (Part 1 of 2.)

```
Employee information obtained by get functions:

First name is Bob
Last name is Lewis
Social security number is 333-33-3333
Gross sales is 5000.00
Commission rate is 0.04
Base salary is 300.00

Updated employee information output by print function:

base-salaried commission employee: Bob Lewis
social security number: 333-33-3333
gross sales: 5000.00
commission rate: 0.04
base salary: 1000.00

Employee's earnings: $1200.00
```

Fig. 11.9 | `BasePlusCommissionEmployee` class test program. (Part 2 of 2.)

Exploring the Similarities Between Class `BasePlusCommissionEmployee` *and Class* `CommissionEmployee`

Most of the code for class `BasePlusCommissionEmployee` (Figs. 11.7–11.8) is *similar, if not identical*, to the code for class `CommissionEmployee` (Figs. 11.4–11.5). For example, in class `BasePlusCommissionEmployee`, `private` data members `firstName` and `lastName` and member functions `setFirstName`, `getFirstName`, `setLastName` and `getLastName` are identical to those of class `CommissionEmployee`. Classes `CommissionEmployee` and `BasePlusCommissionEmployee` also both contain `private` data members `socialSecurityNumber`, `commissionRate` and `grossSales`, as well as *get* and *set* functions to manipulate these members. In addition, the `BasePlusCommissionEmployee` constructor is *almost* identical to that of class `CommissionEmployee`, except that `BasePlusCommissionEmployee`'s constructor *also* sets the `baseSalary`. The other additions to class `BasePlusCommissionEmployee` are `private` data member `baseSalary` *and* member functions `setBaseSalary` and `getBaseSalary`. Class `BasePlusCommissionEmployee`'s `print` member function is *nearly identical* to that of class `CommissionEmployee`, except that `BasePlusCommissionEmployee`'s `print` *also* outputs the value of data member `baseSalary`.

We literally *copied* code from class `CommissionEmployee` and *pasted* it into class `BasePlusCommissionEmployee`, then modified class `BasePlusCommissionEmployee` to include a base salary and member functions that manipulate the base salary. This *copy-and-paste approach* is error prone and time consuming.

Software Engineering Observation 11.1

Copying and pasting code *from one class to another can spread many physical* copies of the same code *and can spread* errors *throughout a system, creating a code-maintenance nightmare. To avoid duplicating code (and possibly errors), use* inheritance, *rather than the "copy-and-paste" approach, in situations where you want one class to "absorb" the data members and member functions of another class.*

Software Engineering Observation 11.2

With inheritance, the common data members and member functions of all the classes in the hierarchy are declared in a base class. When changes are required for these common features, you need to make the changes only *in the base class—derived classes then inherit the changes. Without inheritance, changes would need to be made to* all *the source code files that contain a copy of the code in question.*

11.3.3 Creating a CommissionEmployee–BasePlusCommissionEmployee Inheritance Hierarchy

Now we create and test a new BasePlusCommissionEmployee class (Figs. 11.10–11.11) that *derives from* class CommissionEmployee (Figs. 11.4–11.5). In this example, a BasePlusCommissionEmployee object *is a* CommissionEmployee (because inheritance passes on the capabilities of class CommissionEmployee), but class BasePlusCommissionEmployee *also* has data member baseSalary (Fig. 11.10, line 22). The *colon (:)* in line 10 of the class definition indicates inheritance. Keyword public indicates the *type of inheritance.* As a derived class (formed with public inheritance), BasePlusCommissionEmployee inherits *all* the members of class CommissionEmployee, *except* for the constructor—each class provides its *own* constructors that are specific to the class. (Destructors, too, are not inherited.) Thus, the public services of BasePlusCommissionEmployee include its constructor (lines 13–14) and the public member functions inherited from class CommissionEmployee—*although we cannot see these inherited member functions* in BasePlusCommissionEmployee's source code, they're nevertheless a part of derived class BasePlusCommissionEmployee. The derived class's public services also include member functions setBaseSalary, getBaseSalary, earnings and print (lines 16–20).

```
1  // Fig. 11.10: BasePlusCommissionEmployee.h
2  // BasePlusCommissionEmployee class derived from class
3  // CommissionEmployee.
4  #ifndef BASEPLUS_H
5  #define BASEPLUS_H
6
7  #include <string> // C++ standard string class
8  #include "CommissionEmployee.h" // CommissionEmployee class declaration
9
10 class BasePlusCommissionEmployee : public CommissionEmployee
11 {
12 public:
13    BasePlusCommissionEmployee( const std::string &, const std::string &,
14       const std::string &, double = 0.0, double = 0.0, double = 0.0 );
15
16    void setBaseSalary( double ); // set base salary
17    double getBaseSalary() const; // return base salary
18
19    double earnings() const; // calculate earnings
20    void print() const; // print BasePlusCommissionEmployee object
```

Fig. 11.10 | BasePlusCommissionEmployee class definition indicating inheritance relationship with class CommissionEmployee. (Part 1 of 2.)

```
private:
   double baseSalary; // base salary
}; // end class BasePlusCommissionEmployee

#endif
```

Fig. 11.10 | BasePlusCommissionEmployee class definition indicating inheritance relationship with class CommissionEmployee. (Part 2 of 2.)

```
// Fig. 11.11: BasePlusCommissionEmployee.cpp
// Class BasePlusCommissionEmployee member-function definitions.
#include <iostream>
#include <stdexcept>
#include "BasePlusCommissionEmployee.h"
using namespace std;

// constructor
BasePlusCommissionEmployee::BasePlusCommissionEmployee(
   const string &first, const string &last, const string &ssn,
   double sales, double rate, double salary )
   // explicitly call base-class constructor
   : CommissionEmployee( first, last, ssn, sales, rate )
{
   setBaseSalary( salary ); // validate and store base salary
} // end BasePlusCommissionEmployee constructor

// set base salary
void BasePlusCommissionEmployee::setBaseSalary( double salary )
{
   if ( salary >= 0.0 )
      baseSalary = salary;
   else
      throw invalid_argument( "Salary must be >= 0.0" );
} // end function setBaseSalary

// return base salary
double BasePlusCommissionEmployee::getBaseSalary() const
{
   return baseSalary;
} // end function getBaseSalary

// calculate earnings
double BasePlusCommissionEmployee::earnings() const
{
   // derived class cannot access the base class's private data
   return baseSalary + ( commissionRate * grossSales );
} // end function earnings

```

Fig. 11.11 | BasePlusCommissionEmployee implementation file: private base-class data cannot be accessed from derived class. (Part 1 of 2.)

```
40 // print BasePlusCommissionEmployee object
41 void BasePlusCommissionEmployee::print() const
42 {
43    // derived class cannot access the base class's private data
44    cout << "base-salaried commission employee: " << firstName << ' '
45       << lastName << "\nsocial security number: " << socialSecurityNumber
46       << "\ngross sales: " << grossSales
47       << "\ncommission rate: " << commissionRate
48       << "\nbase salary: " << baseSalary;
49 } // end function print
```

Compilation Errors from the LLVM Compiler in Xcode 4.5

```
BasePlusCommissionEmployee.cpp:37:26:
   'commissionRate' is a private member of 'CommissionEmployee'
BasePlusCommissionEmployee.cpp:37:43:
   'grossSales' is a private member of 'CommissionEmployee'
BasePlusCommissionEmployee.cpp:44:53:
   'firstName' is a private member of 'CommissionEmployee'
BasePlusCommissionEmployee.cpp:45:10:
   'lastName' is a private member of 'CommissionEmployee'
BasePlusCommissionEmployee.cpp:45:54:
   'socialSecurityNumber' is a private member of 'CommissionEmployee'
BasePlusCommissionEmployee.cpp:46:31:
   'grossSales' is a private member of 'CommissionEmployee'
BasePlusCommissionEmployee.cpp:47:35:
   'commissionRate' is a private member of 'CommissionEmployee'
```

Fig. 11.11 | `BasePlusCommissionEmployee` implementation file: `private` base-class data cannot be accessed from derived class. (Part 2 of 2.)

Figure 11.11 shows `BasePlusCommissionEmployee`'s member-function implementations. The constructor (lines 9–16) introduces **base-class initializer syntax** (line 13), which uses a member initializer to pass arguments to the base-class (`CommissionEmployee`) constructor. C++ requires that a derived-class constructor call its base-class constructor to initialize the base-class data members that are inherited into the derived class. Line 13 does this by *explicitly* invoking the `CommissionEmployee` constructor by name, passing the constructor's parameters `first`, `last`, `ssn`, `sales` and `rate` as arguments to initialize the base-class data members `firstName`, `lastName`, `socialSecurityNumber`, `grossSales` and `commissionRate`, respectively. If `BasePlusCommissionEmployee`'s constructor did *not* invoke class `CommissionEmployee`'s constructor *explicitly*, C++ would attempt to invoke class `CommissionEmployee`'s default constructor implicitly—but the class does *not* have such a constructor, so the compiler would issue an *error*. Recall from Chapter 3 that the compiler provides a default constructor with no parameters in any class that does *not* explicitly include a constructor. However, `CommissionEmployee` *does* explicitly include a constructor, so a default constructor is *not* provided.

Common Programming Error 11.1

When a derived-class constructor calls a base-class constructor, the arguments passed to the base-class constructor must be consistent with the number and types of parameters specified in one of the base-class constructors; otherwise, a compilation error occurs.

Performance Tip 11.1

In a derived-class constructor, invoking base-class constructors and initializing member objects explicitly in the member initializer list prevents duplicate initialization in which a default constructor is called, then data members are modified again in the derived-class constructor's body.

Compilation Errors from Accessing Base-Class `private` *Members*

The compiler generates errors for line 37 of Fig. 11.11 because base class `CommissionEmployee`'s data members `commissionRate` and `grossSales` are `private`—derived class `BasePlusCommissionEmployee`'s member functions are *not* allowed to access base class `CommissionEmployee`'s `private` data. The compiler issues additional errors in lines 44–47 of `BasePlusCommissionEmployee`'s `print` member function for the same reason. As you can see, C++ rigidly enforces restrictions on accessing `private` data members, so that *even a derived class (which is intimately related to its base class) cannot access the base class's* `private` *data.*

Preventing the Errors in `BasePlusCommissionEmployee`

We purposely included the erroneous code in Fig. 11.11 to emphasize that a derived class's member functions *cannot* access its base class's `private` data. The errors in `BasePlusCommissionEmployee` could have been prevented by using the *get* member functions inherited from class `CommissionEmployee`. For example, line 37 could have invoked `getCommissionRate` and `getGrossSales` to access `CommissionEmployee`'s `private` data members `commissionRate` and `grossSales`, respectively. Similarly, lines 44–47 could have used appropriate *get* member functions to retrieve the values of the base class's data members. In the next example, we show how using `protected` data *also* allows us to avoid the errors encountered in this example.

Including the Base-Class Header in the Derived-Class Header with `#include`

Notice that we `#include` the base class's header in the derived class's header (line 8 of Fig. 11.10). This is necessary for three reasons. First, for the derived class to use the base class's name in line 10, we must tell the compiler that the base class exists—the class definition in `CommissionEmployee.h` does exactly that.

The second reason is that the compiler uses a class definition to determine the *size* of an object of that class (as we discussed in Section 3.6). A client program that creates an object of a class `#include`s the class definition to enable the compiler to reserve the proper amount of memory for the object. When using inheritance, a derived-class object's size depends on the data members declared explicitly in its class definition *and* the data members *inherited* from its direct and indirect base classes. Including the base class's definition in line 8 allows the compiler to determine the memory requirements for the base class's data members that become part of a derived-class object and thus contribute to the total size of the derived-class object.

The last reason for line 8 is to allow the compiler to determine whether the derived class uses the base class's inherited members properly. For example, in the program of Figs. 11.10–11.11, the compiler uses the base-class header to determine that the data members being accessed by the derived class are `private` in the base class. Since these are *inaccessible* to the derived class, the compiler generates errors. The compiler also uses the base class's *function prototypes* to *validate* function calls made by the derived class to the inherited base-class functions.

Linking Process in an Inheritance Hierarchy

In Section 3.7, we discussed the linking process for creating an executable GradeBook application. In that example, you saw that the client's object code was linked with the object code for class GradeBook, as well as the object code for any C++ Standard Library classes used in either the client code or in class GradeBook.

The linking process is similar for a program that uses classes in an inheritance hierarchy. The process requires the object code for all classes used in the program and the object code for the direct and indirect base classes of any derived classes used by the program. Suppose a client wants to create an application that uses class BasePlusCommissionEmployee, which is a derived class of CommissionEmployee (we'll see an example of this in Section 11.3.4). When compiling the client application, the client's object code must be linked with the object code for classes BasePlusCommissionEmployee and CommissionEmployee, because BasePlusCommissionEmployee inherits member functions from its base class CommissionEmployee. The code is also linked with the object code for any C++ Standard Library classes used in class CommissionEmployee, class BasePlusCommissionEmployee or the client code. This provides the program with access to the implementations of all of the functionality that the program may use.

11.3.4 CommissionEmployee–BasePlusCommissionEmployee Inheritance Hierarchy Using protected Data

Chapter 3 introduced access specifiers public and private. A base class's public members are accessible within its body and anywhere that the program has a handle (i.e., a name, reference or pointer) to an object of that class or one of its derived classes. A base class's private members are accessible only within its body and to the friends of that base class. In this section, we introduce the access specifier **protected**.

Using protected access offers an intermediate level of protection between public and private access. To enable class BasePlusCommissionEmployee to *directly access* CommissionEmployee data members firstName, lastName, socialSecurityNumber, grossSales and commissionRate, we can declare those members as protected in the base class. A base class's protected members *can* be accessed within the body of that base class, by members and friends of that base class, and by members and friends of any classes derived from that base class.

*Defining Base Class **CommissionEmployee** with **protected** Data*

Class CommissionEmployee (Fig. 11.12) now declares data members firstName, lastName, socialSecurityNumber, grossSales and commissionRate as protected (lines 31–36) rather than private. The member-function implementations are identical to those in Fig. 11.5, so CommissionEmployee.cpp is not shown here.

```
1  // Fig. 11.12: CommissionEmployee.h
2  // CommissionEmployee class definition with protected data.
3  #ifndef COMMISSION_H
4  #define COMMISSION_H
5
```

Fig. 11.12 | CommissionEmployee class definition that declares protected data to allow access by derived classes. (Part 1 of 2.)

```
#include <string> // C++ standard string class

class CommissionEmployee
{
public:
   CommissionEmployee( const std::string &, const std::string &,
      const std::string &, double = 0.0, double = 0.0 );

   void setFirstName( const std::string & ); // set first name
   std::string getFirstName() const; // return first name

   void setLastName( const std::string & ); // set last name
   std::string getLastName() const; // return last name

   void setSocialSecurityNumber( const std::string & ); // set SSN
   std::string getSocialSecurityNumber() const; // return SSN

   void setGrossSales( double ); // set gross sales amount
   double getGrossSales() const; // return gross sales amount

   void setCommissionRate( double ); // set commission rate
   double getCommissionRate() const; // return commission rate

   double earnings() const; // calculate earnings
   void print() const; // print CommissionEmployee object
protected:
   std::string firstName;
   std::string lastName;
   std::string socialSecurityNumber;
   double grossSales; // gross weekly sales
   double commissionRate; // commission percentage
}; // end class CommissionEmployee

#endif
```

Fig. 11.12 | CommissionEmployee class definition that declares protected data to allow access by derived classes. (Part 2 of 2.)

Class BasePlusCommissionEmployee

The definition of class BasePlusCommissionEmployee from Figs. 11.10–11.11 remains *unchanged*, so we do *not* show it again here. Now that BasePlusCommissionEmployee inherits from the updated class CommissionEmployee (Fig. 11.12), BasePlusCommissionEmployee objects *can* access inherited data members that are declared protected in class CommissionEmployee (i.e., data members firstName, lastName, socialSecurityNumber, grossSales and commissionRate). As a result, the compiler does *not* generate errors when compiling the BasePlusCommissionEmployee earnings and print member-function definitions in Fig. 11.11 (lines 34–38 and 41–49, respectively). This shows the special privileges that a derived class is granted to access protected base-class data members. Objects of a derived class also can access protected members in *any* of that derived class's *indirect* base classes.

Class BasePlusCommissionEmployee does *not* inherit class CommissionEmployee's constructor. However, class BasePlusCommissionEmployee's constructor (Fig. 11.11, lines 9–16) calls class CommissionEmployee's constructor explicitly with member initializer syntax (line 13). Recall that BasePlusCommissionEmployee's constructor must *explicitly* call the constructor of class CommissionEmployee, because CommissionEmployee does *not* contain a default constructor that could be invoked implicitly.

Testing the Modified BasePlusCommissionEmployee *Class*

To test the updated class hierarchy, we reused the test program from Fig. 11.9. As shown in Fig. 11.13, the output is identical to that of Fig. 11.9. We created the first class BasePlusCommissionEmployee *without using inheritance* and created this version of BasePlusCommissionEmployee *using inheritance*; however, both classes provide the *same* functionality. The code for class BasePlusCommissionEmployee (i.e., the header and implementation files), which is 74 lines, is considerably *shorter* than the code for the noninherited version of the class, which is 161 lines, because the inherited version absorbs part of its functionality from CommissionEmployee, whereas the noninherited version does not absorb any functionality. Also, there is now only *one* copy of the CommissionEmployee functionality declared and defined in class CommissionEmployee. This makes the source code easier to maintain, modify and debug, because the source code related to a CommissionEmployee exists only in the files CommissionEmployee.h and CommissionEmployee.cpp.

```
Employee information obtained by get functions:

First name is Bob
Last name is Lewis
Social security number is 333-33-3333
Gross sales is 5000.00
Commission rate is 0.04
Base salary is 300.00

Updated employee information output by print function:

base-salaried commission employee: Bob Lewis
social security number: 333-33-3333
gross sales: 5000.00
commission rate: 0.04
base salary: 1000.00

Employee's earnings: $1200.00
```

Fig. 11.13 | protected base-class data can be accessed from derived class.

Notes on Using protected *Data*

In this example, we declared base-class data members as protected, so derived classes can modify the data directly. Inheriting protected data members slightly improves performance, because we can directly access the members without incurring the overhead of calls to *set* or *get* member functions.

Software Engineering Observation 11.3

In most cases, it's better to use private *data members to encourage proper software engineering, and leave code optimization issues to the compiler. Your code will be easier to maintain, modify and debug.*

Using protected data members creates two serious problems. First, the derived-class object does *not* have to use a member function to set the value of the base class's protected data member. An *invalid* value can easily be assigned to the protected data member, thus leaving the object in an *inconsistent* state—e.g., with CommissionEmployee's data member grossSales declared as protected, a derived-class object can assign a negative value to grossSales. The second problem with using protected data members is that derived-class member functions are more likely to be written so that they *depend on the base-class implementation*. Derived classes should depend only on the base-class services (i.e., non-private member functions) and *not* on the base-class implementation. With protected data members in the base class, if the base-class implementation changes, we may need to modify *all* derived classes of that base class. For example, if for some reason we were to change the names of data members firstName and lastName to first and last, then we'd have to do so for all occurrences in which a derived class references these base-class data members directly. Such software is said to be **fragile** or **brittle**, because a small change in the base class can "break" derived-class implementation. You should be able to change the base-class implementation while still providing the *same* services to derived classes. Of course, if the base-class services change, we must reimplement our derived classes—good object-oriented design attempts to prevent this.

Software Engineering Observation 11.4

It's appropriate to use the protected access specifier when a base class should provide a service (i.e., a non-private member function) only to its derived classes and friends.

Software Engineering Observation 11.5

Declaring base-class data members private (as opposed to declaring them protected) enables you to change the base-class implementation without having to change derived-class implementations.

11.3.5 CommissionEmployee–BasePlusCommissionEmployee Inheritance Hierarchy Using private Data

We now reexamine our hierarchy once more, this time using the *best software engineering practices*. Class CommissionEmployee now declares data members firstName, lastName, socialSecurityNumber, grossSales and commissionRate as private as shown previously in lines 31–36 of Fig. 11.4.

Changes to Class CommissionEmployee's Member Function Definitions

In the CommissionEmployee constructor implementation (Fig. 11.14, lines 9–16), we use member initializers (line 12) to set the values of the members firstName, lastName and socialSecurityNumber. We show how the derived-class BasePlusCommissionEmployee (Fig. 11.15) can invoke non-private base-class member functions (setFirstName, getFirstName, setLastName, getLastName, setSocialSecurityNumber and getSocialSecurityNumber) to manipulate these data members.

In the body of the constructor and in the bodies of member function's earnings (Fig. 11.14, lines 85–88) and print (lines 91–98), we call the class's *set* and *get* member functions to access the class's private data members. If we decide to change the data member names, the earnings and print definitions will *not* require modification—only the definitions of the *get* and *set* member functions that directly manipulate the data members will need to change. *These changes occur solely within the base class—no changes to the derived class are needed.* Localizing the effects of changes like this is a good software engineering practice.

```
// Fig. 11.14: CommissionEmployee.cpp
// Class CommissionEmployee member-function definitions.
#include <iostream>
#include <stdexcept>
#include "CommissionEmployee.h" // CommissionEmployee class definition
using namespace std;

// constructor
CommissionEmployee::CommissionEmployee(
   const string &first, const string &last, const string &ssn,
   double sales, double rate )
   : firstName( first ), lastName( last ), socialSecurityNumber( ssn )
{
   setGrossSales( sales ); // validate and store gross sales
   setCommissionRate( rate ); // validate and store commission rate
} // end CommissionEmployee constructor

// set first name
void CommissionEmployee::setFirstName( const string &first )
{
   firstName = first; // should validate
} // end function setFirstName

// return first name
string CommissionEmployee::getFirstName() const
{
   return firstName;
} // end function getFirstName

// set last name
void CommissionEmployee::setLastName( const string &last )
{
   lastName = last; // should validate
} // end function setLastName

// return last name
string CommissionEmployee::getLastName() const
{
   return lastName;
} // end function getLastName

// set social security number
void CommissionEmployee::setSocialSecurityNumber( const string &ssn )
{
   socialSecurityNumber = ssn; // should validate
} // end function setSocialSecurityNumber

```

Fig. 11.14 | CommissionEmployee class implementation file: CommissionEmployee class uses member functions to manipulate its private data. (Part 1 of 2.)

```
// return social security number
string CommissionEmployee::getSocialSecurityNumber() const
{
   return socialSecurityNumber;
} // end function getSocialSecurityNumber

// set gross sales amount
void CommissionEmployee::setGrossSales( double sales )
{
   if ( sales >= 0.0 )
      grossSales = sales;
   else
      throw invalid_argument( "Gross sales must be >= 0.0" );
} // end function setGrossSales

// return gross sales amount
double CommissionEmployee::getGrossSales() const
{
   return grossSales;
} // end function getGrossSales

// set commission rate
void CommissionEmployee::setCommissionRate( double rate )
{
   if ( rate > 0.0 && rate < 1.0 )
      commissionRate = rate;
   else
      throw invalid_argument( "Commission rate must be > 0.0 and < 1.0" );
} // end function setCommissionRate

// return commission rate
double CommissionEmployee::getCommissionRate() const
{
   return commissionRate;
} // end function getCommissionRate

// calculate earnings
double CommissionEmployee::earnings() const
{
   return getCommissionRate() * getGrossSales();
} // end function earnings

// print CommissionEmployee object
void CommissionEmployee::print() const
{
   cout << "commission employee: "
      << getFirstName() << ' ' << getLastName()
      << "\nsocial security number: " << getSocialSecurityNumber()
      << "\ngross sales: " << getGrossSales()
      << "\ncommission rate: " << getCommissionRate();
} // end function print
```

Fig. 11.14 | CommissionEmployee class implementation file: CommissionEmployee class uses member functions to manipulate its private data. (Part 2 of 2.)

Performance Tip 11.2

Using a member function to access a data member's value can be slightly slower than accessing the data directly. However, today's optimizing compilers are carefully designed to perform many optimizations implicitly (such as inlining set *and* get *member-function calls). You should write code that adheres to proper software engineering principles, and leave optimization to the compiler. A good rule is, "Do not second-guess the compiler."*

Changes to Class `BasePlusCommissionEmployee`'s Member Function Definitions

Class `BasePlusCommissionEmployee` inherits `CommissionEmployee`'s `public` member functions and can access the `private` base-class members via the inherited member functions. The class's header remains unchanged from Fig. 11.10. The class has several changes to its member-function implementations (Fig. 11.15) that distinguish it from the previous version of the class (Figs. 11.10–11.11). Member functions `earnings` (Fig. 11.15, lines 34–37) and `print` (lines 40–48) each invoke member function `getBaseSalary` to obtain the base salary value, rather than accessing `baseSalary` directly. This insulates `earnings` and `print` from potential changes to the implementation of data member `baseSalary`. For example, if we decide to rename data member `baseSalary` or change its type, only member functions `setBaseSalary` and `getBaseSalary` will need to change.

```
1  // Fig. 11.15: BasePlusCommissionEmployee.cpp
2  // Class BasePlusCommissionEmployee member-function definitions.
3  #include <iostream>
4  #include <stdexcept>
5  #include "BasePlusCommissionEmployee.h"
6  using namespace std;
7
8  // constructor
9  BasePlusCommissionEmployee::BasePlusCommissionEmployee(
10    const string &first, const string &last, const string &ssn,
11    double sales, double rate, double salary )
12    // explicitly call base-class constructor
13    : CommissionEmployee( first, last, ssn, sales, rate )
14 {
15    setBaseSalary( salary ); // validate and store base salary
16 } // end BasePlusCommissionEmployee constructor
17
18 // set base salary
19 void BasePlusCommissionEmployee::setBaseSalary( double salary )
20 {
21    if ( salary >= 0.0 )
22       baseSalary = salary;
23    else
24       throw invalid_argument( "Salary must be >= 0.0" );
25 } // end function setBaseSalary
26
27 // return base salary
28 double BasePlusCommissionEmployee::getBaseSalary() const
29 {
```

Fig. 11.15 | `BasePlusCommissionEmployee` class that inherits from class `CommissionEmployee` but cannot directly access the class's `private` data. (Part 1 of 2.)

```
30       return baseSalary;
31    } // end function getBaseSalary
32
33    // calculate earnings
34    double BasePlusCommissionEmployee::earnings() const
35    {
36       return getBaseSalary() + CommissionEmployee::earnings();
37    } // end function earnings
38
39    // print BasePlusCommissionEmployee object
40    void BasePlusCommissionEmployee::print() const
41    {
42       cout << "base-salaried ";
43
44       // invoke CommissionEmployee's print function
45       CommissionEmployee::print();
46
47       cout << "\nbase salary: " << getBaseSalary();
48    } // end function print
```

Fig. 11.15 | `BasePlusCommissionEmployee` class that inherits from class `CommissionEmployee` but cannot directly access the class's `private` data. (Part 2 of 2.)

`BasePlusCommissionEmployee` Member Function `earnings`

Class `BasePlusCommissionEmployee`'s `earnings` function (Fig. 11.15, lines 34–37) redefines class `CommissionEmployee`'s `earnings` member function (Fig. 11.14, lines 85–88) to calculate the earnings of a base-salaried commission employee. Class `BasePlusCommissionEmployee`'s version of `earnings` obtains the portion of the employee's earnings based on commission alone by calling base-class `CommissionEmployee`'s `earnings` function with the expression `CommissionEmployee::earnings()` (Fig. 11.15, line 36). `BasePlusCommissionEmployee`'s `earnings` function then adds the base salary to this value to calculate the total earnings of the employee. Note the syntax used to invoke a redefined base-class member function from a derived class—place the base-class name and the scope resolution operator (`::`) before the base-class member-function name. This member-function invocation is a good software engineering practice: Recall from Chapter 9 that, if an object's member function performs the actions needed by another object, we should call that member function rather than duplicating its code body. By having `BasePlusCommissionEmployee`'s `earnings` function invoke `CommissionEmployee`'s `earnings` function to calculate part of a `BasePlusCommissionEmployee` object's earnings, we avoid duplicating the code and reduce code-maintenance problems.

Common Programming Error 11.2

When a base-class member function is redefined in a derived class, the derived-class version often calls the base-class version to do additional work. Failure to use the `::` operator prefixed with the name of the base class when referencing the base class's member function causes infinite recursion, because the derived-class member function would then call itself.

BasePlusCommissionEmployee Member Function print

Similarly, BasePlusCommissionEmployee's print function (Fig. 11.15, lines 40–48) redefines class CommissionEmployee's print function (Fig. 11.14, lines 91–98) to output the appropriate base-salaried commission employee information. The new version displays part of a BasePlusCommissionEmployee object's information (i.e., the string "commission employee" and the values of class CommissionEmployee's private data members) by calling CommissionEmployee's print member function with the qualified name CommissionEmployee::print() (Fig. 11.15, line 45). BasePlusCommissionEmployee's print function then outputs the remainder of a BasePlusCommissionEmployee object's information (i.e., the value of class BasePlusCommissionEmployee's base salary).

Testing the Modified Class Hierarchy

Once again, this example uses the BasePlusCommissionEmployee test program from Fig. 11.9 and produces the same output. Although each "base-salaried commission employee" class behaves identically, the version in this example is the best engineered. *By using inheritance and by calling member functions that hide the data and ensure consistency, we've efficiently and effectively constructed a well-engineered class.*

Summary of the CommissionEmployee–BasePlusCommissionEmployee Examples

In this section, you saw an evolutionary set of examples that was carefully designed to teach key capabilities for good software engineering with inheritance. You learned how to create a derived class using inheritance, how to use protected base-class members to enable a derived class to access inherited base-class data members and how to redefine base-class functions to provide versions that are more appropriate for derived-class objects. In addition, you learned how to apply software engineering techniques from Chapter 9 and this chapter to create classes that are easy to maintain, modify and debug.

11.4 Constructors and Destructors in Derived Classes

As we explained in the preceding section, instantiating a derived-class object begins a *chain* of constructor calls in which the derived-class constructor, before performing its own tasks, invokes its direct base class's constructor either explicitly (via a base-class member initializer) or implicitly (calling the base class's default constructor). Similarly, if the base class is derived from another class, the base-class constructor is required to invoke the constructor of the next class up in the hierarchy, and so on. The last constructor called in this chain is the one of the class at the base of the hierarchy, whose body actually finishes executing *first*. The most derived-class constructor's body finishes executing *last*. Each base-class constructor initializes the base-class data members that the derived-class object inherits. In the CommissionEmployee/BasePlusCommissionEmployee hierarchy that we've been studying, when a program creates a BasePlusCommissionEmployee object, the CommissionEmployee constructor is called. Since class CommissionEmployee is at the base of the hierarchy, its constructor executes, initializing the private CommissionEmployee data members that are part of the BasePlusCommissionEmployee object. When CommissionEmployee's constructor completes execution, it returns control to BasePlusCommissionEmployee's constructor, which initializes the BasePlusCommissionEmployee object's baseSalary.

Software Engineering Observation 11.6

When a program creates a derived-class object, the derived-class constructor immediately calls the base-class constructor, the base-class constructor's body executes, then the derived class's member initializers *execute and finally the derived-class constructor's body executes. This process cascades up the hierarchy if it contains more than two levels.*

When a derived-class object is destroyed, the program calls that object's destructor. This begins a chain (or cascade) of destructor calls in which the derived-class destructor and the destructors of the direct and indirect base classes and the classes' members execute in *reverse* of the order in which the constructors executed. When a derived-class object's destructor is called, the destructor performs its task, then invokes the destructor of the next base class up the hierarchy. This process repeats until the destructor of the final base class at the top of the hierarchy is called. Then the object is removed from memory.

Software Engineering Observation 11.7

Suppose that we create an object of a derived class where both the base class and the derived class contain (via composition) objects of other classes. When an object of that derived class is created, first the constructors for the base class's member objects execute, then the base-class constructor body executes, then the constructors for the derived class's member objects execute, then the derived class's constructor body executes. Destructors for derived-class objects are called in the reverse of the order in which their corresponding constructors are called.

Base-class constructors, destructors and overloaded assignment operators (Chapter 10) are *not* inherited by derived classes. Derived-class constructors, destructors and overloaded assignment operators, however, can call base-class versions.

C++11: Inheriting Base Class Constructors

Sometimes a derived class's constructors simply mimic the base class's constructors. A frequently requested convenience feature for C++11 was the ability to *inherit* a base class's constructors. You can now do this by *explicitly* including a `using` declaration of the form

```
using BaseClass::BaseClass;
```

anywhere in the derived-class definition. In the preceding declaration, *BaseClass* is the base class's name. With a few exceptions (listed below), for each constructor in the base class, the compiler generates a derived-class constructor that calls the corresponding base-class constructor. The generated constructors perform only *default initialization* for the derived class's additional data members. When you inherit constructors:

- By default, each inherited constructor has the *same* access level (`public`, `protected` or `private`) as its corresponding base-class constructor.
- The default, copy and move constructors are *not* inherited.
- If a constructor is *deleted* in the base class by placing `= delete` in its prototype, the corresponding constructor in the derived class is *also* deleted.
- If the derived class does not *explicitly* define constructors, the compiler generates a default constructor in the derived class—*even* if it inherits other constructors from its base class.
- If a constructor that you *explicitly* define in a derived class has the *same* parameter list as a base-class constructor, then the base-class constructor is *not* inherited.

- A base-class constructor's default arguments are *not* inherited. Instead, the compiler generates *overloaded constructors* in the derived class. For example, if the base class declares the constructor

```
BaseClass( int = 0, double = 0.0 );
```

the compiler generates the following *two* derived-class constructors *without* default arguments

```
DerivedClass( int );
DerivedClass( int, double );
```

These each call the *BaseClass* constructor that specifies the default arguments.

11.5 public, protected and private Inheritance

When deriving a class from a base class, the base class may be inherited through `public`, `protected` or `private` inheritance. We normally use `public` inheritance in this book. Use of `protected` inheritance is rare. Figure 11.16 summarizes for each type of inheritance the accessibility of base-class members in a derived class. The first column contains the base-class access specifiers.

Base-class member-access specifier	Type of inheritance		
	`public` inheritance	`protected` inheritance	`private` inheritance
`public`	`public` in derived class. Can be accessed directly by member functions, `friend` functions and nonmember functions.	`protected` in derived class. Can be accessed directly by member functions and `friend` functions.	`private` in derived class. Can be accessed directly by member functions and `friend` functions.
`protected`	`protected` in derived class. Can be accessed directly by member functions and `friend` functions.	`protected` in derived class. Can be accessed directly by member functions and `friend` functions.	`private` in derived class. Can be accessed directly by member functions and `friend` functions.
`private`	Hidden in derived class. Can be accessed by member functions and `friend` functions through `public` or `protected` member functions of the base class.	Hidden in derived class. Can be accessed by member functions and `friend` functions through `public` or `protected` member functions of the base class.	Hidden in derived class. Can be accessed by member functions and `friend` functions through `public` or `protected` member functions of the base class.

Fig. 11.16 | Summary of base-class member accessibility in a derived class.

When deriving a class with `public` inheritance, `public` members of the base class become `public` members of the derived class, and `protected` members of the base class become `protected` members of the derived class. A base class's `private` members are *never* accessible directly from a derived class, but can be accessed through calls to the `public` and `protected` members of the base class.

When deriving a class with `protected` inheritance, `public` and `protected` members of the base class become `protected` members of the derived class. When deriving a class with `private` inheritance, `public` and `protected` members of the base class become `private` members (e.g., the functions become utility functions) of the derived class. `Private` and `protected` inheritance are not *is-a* relationships.

11.6 Software Engineering with Inheritance

Sometimes it's difficult to appreciate the scope of problems faced by designers who work on large-scale software projects in industry. People experienced with such projects say that effective software reuse improves the software development process. Object-oriented programming facilitates software reuse, thus shortening development times and enhancing software quality.

When we use inheritance to create a new class from an existing one, the new class inherits the data members and member functions of the existing class, as described in Fig. 11.16. We can customize the new class to meet our needs by redefining base-class members and by including additional members. The derived-class programmer does this in C++ *without* accessing the base class's source code (the derived class must be able to *link* to the base class's object code). This powerful capability is attractive to software developers. They can develop proprietary classes for sale or license and make these classes available to users in object-code format. Users then can derive new classes from these library classes rapidly and without accessing the proprietary source code. The software developers need to supply the headers along with the object code

The availability of substantial and useful class libraries delivers the maximum benefits of software reuse through inheritance. The standard C++ libraries tend to be general purpose and limited in scope. There is a worldwide commitment to the development of class libraries for a huge variety of application arenas.

Software Engineering Observation 11.8

At the design stage in an object-oriented system, the designer often determines that certain classes are closely related. The designer should "factor out" common attributes and behaviors and place these in a base class, then use inheritance to form derived classes.

Software Engineering Observation 11.9

Creating a derived class does not affect its base class's source code. Inheritance preserves the integrity of the base class.

11.7 Wrap-Up

This chapter introduced inheritance—the ability to create a class by absorbing an existing class's data members and member functions and embellishing them with new capabilities. Through a series of examples using an employee inheritance hierarchy, you learned the notions of base classes and derived classes and used `public` inheritance to create a derived class that inherits members from a base class. The chapter introduced the access specifier `protected`—derived-class member functions can access `protected` base-class members. You learned how to access redefined base-class members by qualifying their names with the base-class name and scope resolution operator (`::`). You also saw the order in which constructors and destructors are called for objects of classes that are part of an inheritance hierarchy. Finally, we explained the three types of inheritance—`public`, `protected` and `private`—and the accessibility of base-class members in a derived class when using each type.

In Chapter 12, Object-Oriented Programming: Polymorphism, we build on our discussion of inheritance by introducing polymorphism—an object-oriented concept that enables us to write programs that handle, in a more general manner, objects of a wide variety of classes related by inheritance. After studying Chapter 12, you'll be familiar with classes, objects, encapsulation, inheritance and polymorphism—the essential concepts of object-oriented programming.

12

Object-Oriented Programming: Polymorphism

Objectives

In this chapter you'll:

- Learn how polymorphism makes programming more convenient and systems more extensible.
- Learn the distinction between abstract and concrete classes and how to create abstract classes.
- Use runtime type information (RTTI).
- Learn how C++ implements `virtual` functions and dynamic binding.
- Understand how `virtual` destructors ensure that all appropriate destructors run on an object.

Outline

12.1 Introduction

We now continue our study of OOP by explaining and demonstrating **polymorphism** with inheritance hierarchies. Polymorphism enables you to "program in the *general*" rather than "program in the *specific*." In particular, polymorphism enables you to write programs that process objects of classes that are part of the *same* class hierarchy as if they were all objects of the hierarchy's base class. As we'll soon see, polymorphism works off base-class *pointer handles* and base-class *reference handles*, but *not* off name handles.

Implementing for Extensibility

With polymorphism, you can design and implement systems that are easily *extensible*—new classes can be added with little or no modification to the general portions of the program, as long as the new classes are part of the inheritance hierarchy that the program processes generally. The only parts of a program that must be altered to accommodate new classes are those that require direct knowledge of the new classes that you add to the hierarchy. For example, if we create class `Tortoise` that inherits from class `Animal` (which might respond to a `move` message by crawling one inch), we need to write only the `Tortoise` class and the part of the simulation that instantiates a `Tortoise` object. The portions of the simulation that process each `Animal` generally can remain the same.

Optional Discussion of Polymorphism "Under the Hood"

A key feature of this chapter is its (optional) detailed discussion of polymorphism, `virtual` functions and dynamic binding "under the hood," which uses a detailed diagram to explain how polymorphism can be implemented in C++.

12.2 Introduction to Polymorphism: Polymorphic Video Game

Suppose that we design a video game that manipulates objects of many *different* types, including objects of classes `Martian`, `Venutian`, `Plutonian`, `SpaceShip` and `LaserBeam`. Imagine that each of these classes inherits from the common base class `SpaceObject`, which contains the member function `draw`. Each derived class implements this function in a manner appropriate for that class. A screen-manager program maintains a container (e.g., a `vector`) that holds `SpaceObject` *pointers* to objects of the various classes. To refresh the screen, the screen manager periodically sends each object the *same* message—namely, `draw`. Each type of object responds in a unique way. For example, a `Martian` object might draw itself in red with the appropriate number of antennae, a `SpaceShip` object might draw itself as a silver flying saucer, and a `LaserBeam` object might draw itself as a bright red beam across the screen. The *same* message (in this case, `draw`) sent to a *variety* of objects has *many forms* of results—hence the term polymorphism.

A polymorphic screen manager facilitates adding new classes to a system with minimal modifications to its code. Suppose that we want to add objects of class `Mercurian` to our video game. To do so, we must build a class `Mercurian` that inherits from `SpaceObject`, but provides its own definition of member function `draw`. Then, when *pointers* to objects of class `Mercurian` appear in the container, you do not need to modify the code for the screen manager. The screen manager invokes member function `draw` on *every* object in the container, *regardless* of the object's type, so the new `Mercurian` objects simply "plug right in." Thus, without modifying the system (other than to build and include the classes themselves), you can use polymorphism to accommodate additional classes, including ones that were *not even envisioned* when the system was created.

Software Engineering Observation 12.1

Polymorphism enables you to deal in generalities *and let the execution-time environment concern itself with the* specifics. *You can direct a variety of objects to behave in manners appropriate to those objects* without even knowing their types—*as long as those objects belong to the same inheritance hierarchy and are being accessed off a common base-class pointer or a common base-class reference.*

Software Engineering Observation 12.2

Polymorphism promotes extensibility: *Software written to invoke polymorphic behavior is written* independently *of the specific types of the objects to which messages are sent. Thus,* new *types of objects that can respond to* existing *messages can be incorporated into such a system without modifying the base system. Only client code that instantiates new objects must be modified to accommodate new types.*

12.3 Relationships Among Objects in an Inheritance Hierarchy

Section 11.3 created an employee class hierarchy, in which class `BasePlusCommissionEmployee` inherited from class `CommissionEmployee`. The Chapter 11 examples manipulated `CommissionEmployee` and `BasePlusCommissionEmployee` objects by using the objects' names to invoke their member functions. We now examine the relationships among classes in a hierarchy more closely. The next several sections present a series of examples that demonstrate how base-class and derived-class *pointers* can be aimed at base-class and derived-class objects, and how those pointers can be used to invoke member functions that manipulate those objects.

- In Section 12.3.1, we assign the address of a derived-class object to a base-class pointer, then show that invoking a function via the base-class pointer invokes the *base-class functionality* in the derived-class object—i.e., the *type of the handle determines which function is called.*
- In Section 12.3.2, we assign the address of a base-class object to a derived-class pointer, which results in a compilation error. We discuss the error message and investigate why the compiler does *not* allow such an assignment.
- In Section 12.3.3, we assign the address of a derived-class object to a base-class pointer, then examine how the base-class pointer can be used to invoke only the base-class functionality—*when we attempt to invoke derived-class member functions through the base-class pointer, compilation errors occur.*
- Finally, in Section 12.3.4, we demonstrate how to get polymorphic behavior from base-class pointers aimed at derived-class objects. We introduce `virtual` functions and polymorphism by declaring a base-class function as `virtual`. We then assign the address of a derived-class object to the base-class pointer and use that pointer to invoke derived-class functionality—*precisely the capability we need to achieve polymorphic behavior.*

A key concept in these examples is to demonstrate that with `public` inheritance *an object of a derived class can be treated as an object of its base class.* This enables various interesting manipulations. For example, a program can create an array of base-class pointers that point to objects of many derived-class types. Despite the fact that the derived-class objects are of *different types*, the compiler allows this because each derived-class object *is an* object of its base class. However, *we cannot treat a base-class object as an object of any of its derived classes.* For example, a `CommissionEmployee` is not a `BasePlusCommissionEmployee` in the hierarchy defined in Chapter 11—a `CommissionEmployee` does *not* have a `baseSalary` data member and does *not* have member functions `setBaseSalary` and `getBaseSalary`. The *is-a* relationship applies only from a *derived class* to its *direct and indirect base classes.*

12.3.1 Invoking Base-Class Functions from Derived-Class Objects

The example in Fig. 12.1 reuses the final versions of classes `CommissionEmployee` and `BasePlusCommissionEmployee` from Section 11.3.5. The example demonstrates three ways to aim base- and derived-class pointers at base- and derived-class objects. The first two are natural and straightforward—we aim a base-class pointer at a base-class object and invoke base-class functionality, and we aim a derived-class pointer at a derived-class object and invoke derived-class functionality. Then, we demonstrate the relationship between derived classes and base classes (i.e., the *is-a* relationship of inheritance) by aiming a base-class pointer at a derived-class object and showing that the base-class functionality is indeed available in the derived-class object.

```
// Fig. 12.1: fig12_01.cpp
// Aiming base-class and derived-class pointers at base-class
// and derived-class objects, respectively.
#include <iostream>
#include <iomanip>
#include "CommissionEmployee.h"
#include "BasePlusCommissionEmployee.h"
using namespace std;

int main()
{
   // create base-class object
   CommissionEmployee commissionEmployee(
      "Sue", "Jones", "222-22-2222", 10000, .06 );

   // create base-class pointer
   CommissionEmployee *commissionEmployeePtr = nullptr;

   // create derived-class object
   BasePlusCommissionEmployee basePlusCommissionEmployee(
      "Bob", "Lewis", "333-33-3333", 5000, .04, 300 );

   // create derived-class pointer
   BasePlusCommissionEmployee *basePlusCommissionEmployeePtr = nullptr;

   // set floating-point output formatting
   cout << fixed << setprecision( 2 );

   // output objects commissionEmployee and basePlusCommissionEmployee
   cout << "Print base-class and derived-class objects:\n\n";
   commissionEmployee.print(); // invokes base-class print
   cout << "\n\n";
   basePlusCommissionEmployee.print(); // invokes derived-class print

   // aim base-class pointer at base-class object and print
   commissionEmployeePtr = &commissionEmployee; // perfectly natural
   cout << "\n\n\nCalling print with base-class pointer to "
      << "\nbase-class object invokes base-class print function:\n\n";
   commissionEmployeePtr->print(); // invokes base-class print

   // aim derived-class pointer at derived-class object and print
   basePlusCommissionEmployeePtr = &basePlusCommissionEmployee; // natural
   cout << "\n\n\nCalling print with derived-class pointer to "
      << "\nderived-class object invokes derived-class "
      << "print function:\n\n";
   basePlusCommissionEmployeePtr->print(); // invokes derived-class print

   // aim base-class pointer at derived-class object and print
   commissionEmployeePtr = &basePlusCommissionEmployee;
   cout << "\n\n\nCalling print with base-class pointer to "
      << "derived-class object\ninvokes base-class print "
```

Fig. 12.1 | Assigning addresses of base-class and derived-class objects to base-class and derived-class pointers. (Part 1 of 2.)

```
        << "function on that derived-class object:\n\n";
    commissionEmployeePtr->print(); // invokes base-class print
    cout << endl;
} // end main
```

```
Print base-class and derived-class objects:

commission employee: Sue Jones
social security number: 222-22-2222
gross sales: 10000.00
commission rate: 0.06

base-salaried commission employee: Bob Lewis
social security number: 333-33-3333
gross sales: 5000.00
commission rate: 0.04
base salary: 300.00


Calling print with base-class pointer to
base-class object invokes base-class print function:

commission employee: Sue Jones
social security number: 222-22-2222
gross sales: 10000.00
commission rate: 0.06


Calling print with derived-class pointer to
derived-class object invokes derived-class print function:

base-salaried commission employee: Bob Lewis
social security number: 333-33-3333
gross sales: 5000.00
commission rate: 0.04
base salary: 300.00


Calling print with base-class pointer to derived-class object
invokes base-class print function on that derived-class object:

commission employee: Bob Lewis
social security number: 333-33-3333
gross sales: 5000.00
commission rate: 0.04
```

Notice that the base salary is *not* displayed

Fig. 12.1 | Assigning addresses of base-class and derived-class objects to base-class and derived-class pointers. (Part 2 of 2.)

Recall that each `BasePlusCommissionEmployee` object *is a* `CommissionEmployee` that *also* has a base salary. Class `BasePlusCommissionEmployee`'s `earnings` member function (lines 34–37 of Fig. 11.15) redefines class `CommissionEmployee`'s `earnings` member function (lines 85–88 of Fig. 11.14) to include the object's base salary. Class `BasePlusCommissionEmployee`'s `print` member function (lines 40–48 of Fig. 11.15) redefines class `CommissionEmployee`'s `version` (lines 91–98 of Fig. 11.14) to display the same information *plus* the employee's base salary.

Creating Objects and Displaying Their Contents

In Fig. 12.1, lines 13–14 create a `CommissionEmployee` object and line 17 creates a pointer to a `CommissionEmployee` object; lines 20–21 create a `BasePlusCommissionEmployee` object and line 24 creates a pointer to a `BasePlusCommissionEmployee` object. Lines 31 and 33 use each object's name to invoke its `print` member function.

Aiming a Base-Class Pointer at a Base-Class Object

Line 36 assigns the address of base-class object `commissionEmployee` to base-class pointer `commissionEmployeePtr`, which line 39 uses to invoke member function `print` on that `CommissionEmployee` object. This invokes the version of `print` defined in base class `CommissionEmployee`.

Aiming a Derived-Class Pointer at a Derived-Class Object

Similarly, line 42 assigns the address of derived-class object `basePlusCommissionEmployee` to derived-class pointer `basePlusCommissionEmployeePtr`, which line 46 uses to invoke member function `print` on that `BasePlusCommissionEmployee` object. This invokes the version of `print` defined in derived class `BasePlusCommissionEmployee`.

Aiming a Base-Class Pointer at a Derived-Class Object

Line 49 then assigns the address of derived-class object `basePlusCommissionEmployee` to base-class pointer `commissionEmployeePtr`, which line 53 uses to invoke member function `print`. This "crossover" is allowed because an object of a derived class *is an* object of its base class. Despite the fact that the base class `CommissionEmployee` pointer points to a *derived class* `BasePlusCommissionEmployee` object, the *base class* `CommissionEmployee`'s `print` member function is invoked (rather than `BasePlusCommissionEmployee`'s `print` function). The output of each `print` member-function invocation in this program reveals that *the invoked functionality depends on the type of the pointer (or reference) used to invoke the function, not the type of the object for which the member function is called.* In Section 12.3.4, when we introduce `virtual` functions, we demonstrate that it's possible to invoke the object type's functionality, *rather than* invoke the handle type's functionality. We'll see that this is crucial to implementing polymorphic behavior—the key topic of this chapter.

12.3.2 Aiming Derived-Class Pointers at Base-Class Objects

In Section 12.3.1, we assigned the address of a derived-class object to a base-class pointer and explained that the C++ compiler allows this assignment, because a derived-class object *is a* base-class object. We take the opposite approach in Fig. 12.2, as we aim a derived-class pointer at a base-class object. [*Note:* This program reuses the final versions of classes `CommissionEmployee` and `BasePlusCommissionEmployee` from Section 11.3.5.] Lines 8–9 of Fig. 12.2 create a `CommissionEmployee` object, and line 10 creates a `BasePlusCommissionEmployee` pointer. Line 14 attempts to assign the address of base-class object `commissionEmployee` to derived-class pointer `basePlusCommissionEmployeePtr`, but the compiler generates an error. The compiler prevents this assignment, because a `CommissionEmployee` is *not* a `BasePlusCommissionEmployee`.

Consider the consequences if the compiler were to allow this assignment. Through a `BasePlusCommissionEmployee` pointer, we can invoke *every* `BasePlusCommissionEmployee` member function, including `setBaseSalary`, for the object to which the pointer points (i.e., the base-class object `commissionEmployee`). However, the `CommissionEm-`

ployee object does *not* provide a setBaseSalary member function, *nor* does it provide a baseSalary data member to set. This could lead to problems, because member function setBaseSalary would assume that there is a baseSalary data member to set at its "usual location" in a BasePlusCommissionEmployee object. This memory does not belong to the CommissionEmployee object, so member function setBaseSalary might overwrite other important data in memory, possibly data that belongs to a different object.

```
// Fig. 12.2: fig12_02.cpp
// Aiming a derived-class pointer at a base-class object.
#include "CommissionEmployee.h"
#include "BasePlusCommissionEmployee.h"

int main()
{
   CommissionEmployee commissionEmployee(
      "Sue", "Jones", "222-22-2222", 10000, .06 );
   BasePlusCommissionEmployee *basePlusCommissionEmployeePtr = nullptr;

   // aim derived-class pointer at base-class object
   // Error: a CommissionEmployee is not a BasePlusCommissionEmployee
   basePlusCommissionEmployeePtr = &commissionEmployee;
} // end main
```

Microsoft Visual C++ compiler error message:

```
C:\cpphtp8_examples\ch12\Fig12_02\fig12_02.cpp(14): error C2440: '=' :
   cannot convert from 'CommissionEmployee *' to 'BasePlusCommissionEmployee
*'
         Cast from base to derived requires dynamic_cast or static_cast
```

Fig. 12.2 | Aiming a derived-class pointer at a base-class object.

12.3.3 Derived-Class Member-Function Calls via Base-Class Pointers

Off a base-class pointer, the compiler allows us to invoke *only* base-class member functions. Thus, if a base-class pointer is aimed at a derived-class object, and an attempt is made to access a *derived-class-only member function*, a compilation error will occur.

Figure 12.3 shows the consequences of attempting to invoke a derived-class member function off a base-class pointer. [*Note:* We're again reusing the versions of classes CommissionEmployee and BasePlusCommissionEmployee from Section 11.3.5.] Line 11 creates commissionEmployeePtr—a pointer to a CommissionEmployee object—and lines 12–13 create a BasePlusCommissionEmployee object. Line 16 aims the base-class commissionEmployeePtr at derived-class object basePlusCommissionEmployee. Recall from Section 12.3.1 that this is allowed, because a BasePlusCommissionEmployee *is a* CommissionEmployee (in the sense that a BasePlusCommissionEmployee object contains all the functionality of a CommissionEmployee object). Lines 20–24 invoke base-class member functions getFirstName, getLastName, getSocialSecurityNumber, getGrossSales and getCommissionRate off the base-class pointer. All of these calls are allowed, because BasePlusCommissionEmployee *inherits* these member functions from CommissionEmployee. We know that commissionEmployeePtr is aimed at a BasePlusCommissionEmployee object, so in lines 28–29 we attempt to invoke `BasePlusCommissionEmployee` member functions `getBaseSalary` and `setBaseSalary`. The compiler generates errors on both of these calls, because they're *not* made to member functions of base-class `CommissionEmployee`. The handle can be used to invoke *only* those functions that are members of that handle's associated class type. (In this case, off a `CommissionEmployee *`, we can invoke only `CommissionEmployee` member functions `setFirstName`, `getFirstName`, `setLastName`, `getLastName`, `setSocialSecurityNumber`, `getSocialSecurityNumber`, `setGrossSales`, `getGrossSales`, `setCommissionRate`, `getCommissionRate`, `earnings` and `print`.)

```
1  // Fig. 12.3: fig12_03.cpp
2  // Attempting to invoke derived-class-only member functions
3  // via a base-class pointer.
4  #include <string>
5  #include "CommissionEmployee.h"
6  #include "BasePlusCommissionEmployee.h"
7  using namespace std;
8
9  int main()
10 {
11    CommissionEmployee *commissionEmployeePtr = nullptr; // base class ptr
12    BasePlusCommissionEmployee basePlusCommissionEmployee(
13       "Bob", "Lewis", "333-33-3333", 5000, .04, 300 ); // derived class
14
15    // aim base-class pointer at derived-class object (allowed)
16    commissionEmployeePtr = &basePlusCommissionEmployee;
17
18    // invoke base-class member functions on derived-class
19    // object through base-class pointer (allowed)
20    string firstName = commissionEmployeePtr->getFirstName();
21    string lastName = commissionEmployeePtr->getLastName();
22    string ssn = commissionEmployeePtr->getSocialSecurityNumber();
23    double grossSales = commissionEmployeePtr->getGrossSales();
24    double commissionRate = commissionEmployeePtr->getCommissionRate();
25
26    // attempt to invoke derived-class-only member functions
27    // on derived-class object through base-class pointer (disallowed)
28    double baseSalary = commissionEmployeePtr->getBaseSalary();
29    commissionEmployeePtr->setBaseSalary( 500 );
30 } // end main
```

GNU C++ compiler error messages:

```
fig12_03.cpp:28:47: error: 'class CommissionEmployee' has no member named
   'getBaseSalary'
fig12_03.cpp:29:27: error: 'class CommissionEmployee' has no member named
   'setBaseSalary'
```

Fig. 12.3 | Attempting to invoke derived-class-only functions via a base-class pointer.

Downcasting

The compiler will allow access to derived-class-only members from a base-class pointer that's aimed at a derived-class object *if* we explicitly cast the base-class pointer to a derived-class pointer—this is known as **downcasting.** As you know, it's possible to aim a base-class pointer at a derived-class object. However, as we demonstrated in Fig. 12.3, a base-class pointer can be used to invoke *only* the functions declared in the base class. Downcasting allows a derived-class-specific operation on a derived-class object pointed to by a base-class pointer. After a downcast, the program *can* invoke derived-class functions that are not in the base class. Downcasting is a potentially dangerous operation. Section 12.8 demonstrates how to *safely* use downcasting.

Software Engineering Observation 12.3

If the address of a derived-class object has been assigned to a pointer of one of its direct or indirect base classes, it's acceptable to cast that base-class pointer back to a pointer of the derived-class type. In fact, this must *be done to call derived-class member functions that do not appear in the base class.*

12.3.4 Virtual Functions and Virtual Destructors

In Section 12.3.1, we aimed a base-class `CommissionEmployee` pointer at a derived-class `BasePlusCommissionEmployee` object, then invoked member function `print` through that pointer. Recall that the *type of the handle* determined which class's functionality to invoke. In that case, the `CommissionEmployee` pointer invoked the `CommissionEmployee` member function `print` on the `BasePlusCommissionEmployee` object, even though the pointer was aimed at a `BasePlusCommissionEmployee` object that has its own custom `print` function.

Software Engineering Observation 12.4

With `virtual` functions, the type of the object, not *the type of the handle used to invoke the member function, determines which version of a `virtual` function to invoke.*

Why `virtual` Functions Are Useful

First, we consider why `virtual` functions are useful. Suppose that shape classes such as `Circle`, `Triangle`, `Rectangle` and `Square` are all derived from base class `Shape`. Each of these classes might be endowed with the ability to *draw itself* via a member function `draw`, but the function for each shape is quite different. In a program that draws a set of shapes, it would be useful to be able to treat all the shapes generally as objects of the base class `Shape`. Then, to draw any shape, we could simply use a base-class `Shape` pointer to invoke function `draw` and let the program determine *dynamically* (i.e., at runtime) which derived-class `draw` function to use, based on the type of the object to which the base-class `Shape` pointer points at any given time. This is *polymorphic behavior.*

Declaring `virtual` Functions

To enable this behavior, we declare `draw` in the base class as a **`virtual` function**, and we **override** `draw` in *each* of the derived classes to draw the appropriate shape. From an implementation perspective, *overriding* a function is no different than *redefining* one (which is the approach we've been using until now). An overridden function in a derived class has the *same signature and return type* (i.e., *prototype*) as the function it overrides in its base class. If we do not declare the base-class function as `virtual`, we can *redefine* that function. By contrast, if we declare the base-class function as `virtual`, we can *override* that function to enable *polymorphic behavior.* We declare a `virtual` function by preceding the function's prototype with the keyword `virtual` in the base class. For example,

```
virtual void draw() const;
```

would appear in base class `Shape`. The preceding prototype declares that function `draw` is a `virtual` function that takes no arguments and returns nothing. This function is declared `const` because a `draw` function typically would not make changes to the `Shape` object on which it's invoked—virtual functions do *not* have to be `const` functions.

Software Engineering Observation 12.5

Once a function is declared `virtual`, it remains `virtual` all the way down the inheritance hierarchy from that point, even if that function is not explicitly declared `virtual` when a derived class overrides it.

Good Programming Practice 12.1

Even though certain functions are implicitly `virtual` because of a declaration made higher in the class hierarchy, explicitly declare these functions `virtual` at every level of the class hierarchy to promote program clarity.

Software Engineering Observation 12.6

When a derived class chooses not *to override a `virtual` function from its base class, the derived class simply inherits its base class's `virtual` function implementation.*

Invoking a `virtual` Function Through a Base-Class Pointer or Reference

If a program invokes a `virtual` function through a base-class pointer to a derived-class object (e.g., `shapePtr->draw()`) or a base-class reference to a derived-class object (e.g., `shapeRef.draw()`), the program will choose the correct derived-class `draw` function *dynamically* (i.e., at execution time) *based on the object type—not the pointer or reference type.* Choosing the appropriate function to call at execution time (rather than at compile time) is known as **dynamic binding** or **late binding**.

Invoking a `virtual` Function Through an Object's Name

When a `virtual` function is called by referencing a specific object by *name* and using the dot member-selection operator (e.g., `squareObject.draw()`), the function invocation is *resolved at compile time* (this is called **static binding**) and the `virtual` function that's called is the one defined for (or inherited by) the class of that particular object—this is *not* polymorphic behavior. Thus, dynamic binding with `virtual` functions occurs only off pointers (and, as we'll soon see, references).

`virtual` Functions in the `CommissionEmployee` Hierarchy

Now let's see how `virtual` functions can enable polymorphic behavior in our employee hierarchy. Figures 12.4–12.5 are the headers for classes `CommissionEmployee` and `BasePlusCommissionEmployee`, respectively. We modified these to declare each class's `earnings` and `print` member functions as `virtual` (lines 29–30 of Fig. 12.4 and lines 19–20 of Fig. 12.5). Because functions `earnings` and `print` are `virtual` in class `CommissionEmployee`, class `BasePlusCommissionEmployee`'s `earnings` and `print` functions *override* class `CommissionEmployee`'s. In addition, class `BasePlusCommissionEmployee`'s `earnings` and `print` functions are declared **`override`**.

11

Error-Prevention Tip 12.1

Apply C++11's `override` *keyword to every overridden function in a derived-class. This forces the compiler to check whether the base class has a member function with the same name and parameter list (i.e., the same signature). If not, the compiler generates an error.*

Now, if we aim a base-class `CommissionEmployee` pointer at a derived-class `BasePlusCommissionEmployee` object, and the program uses that pointer to call either function `earnings` or `print`, the `BasePlusCommissionEmployee` object's corresponding function will be invoked. There were *no* changes to the member-function implementations of classes `CommissionEmployee` and `BasePlusCommissionEmployee`, so we reuse the versions of Figs. 11.14 and 11.15.

```
// Fig. 12.4: CommissionEmployee.h
// CommissionEmployee class header declares earnings and print as virtual.
#ifndef COMMISSION_H
#define COMMISSION_H

#include <string> // C++ standard string class

class CommissionEmployee
{
public:
   CommissionEmployee( const std::string &, const std::string &,
      const std::string &, double = 0.0, double = 0.0 );

   void setFirstName( const std::string & ); // set first name
   std::string getFirstName() const; // return first name

   void setLastName( const std::string & ); // set last name
   std::string getLastName() const; // return last name

   void setSocialSecurityNumber( const std::string & ); // set SSN
   std::string getSocialSecurityNumber() const; // return SSN

   void setGrossSales( double ); // set gross sales amount
   double getGrossSales() const; // return gross sales amount

   void setCommissionRate( double ); // set commission rate
   double getCommissionRate() const; // return commission rate

   virtual double earnings() const; // calculate earnings
   virtual void print() const; // print object
private:
   std::string firstName;
   std::string lastName;
   std::string socialSecurityNumber;
   double grossSales; // gross weekly sales
   double commissionRate; // commission percentage
}; // end class CommissionEmployee

#endif
```

Fig. 12.4 | `CommissionEmployee` class header declares `earnings` and `print` as `virtual`.

```
// Fig. 12.5: BasePlusCommissionEmployee.h
// BasePlusCommissionEmployee class derived from class
// CommissionEmployee.
#ifndef BASEPLUS_H
#define BASEPLUS_H

#include <string> // C++ standard string class
#include "CommissionEmployee.h" // CommissionEmployee class declaration

class BasePlusCommissionEmployee : public CommissionEmployee
{
public:
   BasePlusCommissionEmployee( const std::string &, const std::string &,
      const std::string &, double = 0.0, double = 0.0, double = 0.0 );

   void setBaseSalary( double ); // set base salary
   double getBaseSalary() const; // return base salary

   virtual double earnings() const override; // calculate earnings
   virtual void print() const override; // print object
private:
   double baseSalary; // base salary
}; // end class BasePlusCommissionEmployee

#endif
```

Fig. 12.5 | `BasePlusCommissionEmployee` class header declares `earnings` and `print` functions as `virtual` and `override`.

We modified Fig. 12.1 to create the program of Fig. 12.6. Lines 40–51 of Fig. 12.6 demonstrate again that a `CommissionEmployee` pointer aimed at a `CommissionEmployee` object can be used to invoke `CommissionEmployee` functionality, and a `BasePlusCommissionEmployee` pointer aimed at a `BasePlusCommissionEmployee` object can be used to invoke `BasePlusCommissionEmployee` functionality. Line 54 aims the base-class pointer `commissionEmployeePtr` at derived-class object `basePlusCommissionEmployee`. Note that when line 61 invokes member function `print` off the base-class pointer, the derived-class `BasePlusCommissionEmployee`'s `print` member function is invoked, so line 61 outputs different text than line 53 does in Fig. 12.1 (when member function `print` was *not* declared `virtual`). We see that declaring a member function `virtual` causes the program to dynamically determine which function to invoke *based on the type of object to which the handle points, rather than on the type of the handle.* Note again that when `commissionEmployeePtr` points to a `CommissionEmployee` object, class `CommissionEmployee`'s `print` function is invoked (Fig. 12.6, line 40), and when `CommissionEmployeePtr` points to a `BasePlusCommissionEmployee` object, class `BasePlusCommissionEmployee`'s `print` function is invoked (line 61). Thus, the same message—`print`, in this case—sent (off a base-class pointer) to a variety of objects related by inheritance to that base class, takes on many forms—this is polymorphic behavior.

```
// Fig. 12.6: fig12_06.cpp
// Introducing polymorphism, virtual functions and dynamic binding.
#include <iostream>
#include <iomanip>
#include "CommissionEmployee.h"
#include "BasePlusCommissionEmployee.h"
using namespace std;

int main()
{
   // create base-class object
   CommissionEmployee commissionEmployee(
      "Sue", "Jones", "222-22-2222", 10000, .06 );

   // create base-class pointer
   CommissionEmployee *commissionEmployeePtr = nullptr;

   // create derived-class object
   BasePlusCommissionEmployee basePlusCommissionEmployee(
      "Bob", "Lewis", "333-33-3333", 5000, .04, 300 );

   // create derived-class pointer
   BasePlusCommissionEmployee *basePlusCommissionEmployeePtr = nullptr;

   // set floating-point output formatting
   cout << fixed << setprecision( 2 );

   // output objects using static binding
   cout << "Invoking print function on base-class and derived-class "
      << "\nobjects with static binding\n\n";
   commissionEmployee.print(); // static binding
   cout << "\n\n";
   basePlusCommissionEmployee.print(); // static binding

   // output objects using dynamic binding
   cout << "\n\n\nInvoking print function on base-class and "
      << "derived-class \nobjects with dynamic binding";

   // aim base-class pointer at base-class object and print
   commissionEmployeePtr = &commissionEmployee;
   cout << "\n\nCalling virtual function print with base-class pointer"
      << "\nto base-class object invokes base-class "
      << "print function:\n\n";
   commissionEmployeePtr->print(); // invokes base-class print

   // aim derived-class pointer at derived-class object and print
   basePlusCommissionEmployeePtr = &basePlusCommissionEmployee;
   cout << "\n\nCalling virtual function print with derived-class "
      << "pointer\nto derived-class object invokes derived-class "
      << "print function:\n\n";
   basePlusCommissionEmployeePtr->print(); // invokes derived-class print
```

Fig. 12.6 | Demonstrating polymorphism by invoking a derived-class `virtual` function via a base-class pointer to a derived-class object. (Part 1 of 2.)

```

   // aim base-class pointer at derived-class object and print
   commissionEmployeePtr = &basePlusCommissionEmployee;
   cout << "\n\nCalling virtual function print with base-class pointer"
      << "\nto derived-class object invokes derived-class "
      << "print function:\n\n";

   // polymorphism; invokes BasePlusCommissionEmployee's print;
   // base-class pointer to derived-class object
   commissionEmployeePtr->print();
   cout << endl;
} // end main
```

```
Invoking print function on base-class and derived-class
objects with static binding

commission employee: Sue Jones
social security number: 222-22-2222
gross sales: 10000.00
commission rate: 0.06

base-salaried commission employee: Bob Lewis
social security number: 333-33-3333
gross sales: 5000.00
commission rate: 0.04
base salary: 300.00


Invoking print function on base-class and derived-class
objects with dynamic binding

Calling virtual function print with base-class pointer
to base-class object invokes base-class print function:

commission employee: Sue Jones
social security number: 222-22-2222
gross sales: 10000.00
commission rate: 0.06

Calling virtual function print with derived-class pointer
to derived-class object invokes derived-class print function:

base-salaried commission employee: Bob Lewis
social security number: 333-33-3333
gross sales: 5000.00
commission rate: 0.04
base salary: 300.00

Calling virtual function print with base-class pointer
to derived-class object invokes derived-class print function:

base-salaried commission employee: Bob Lewis
social security number: 333-33-3333
gross sales: 5000.00
commission rate: 0.04
base salary: 300.00
```

Notice that the base salary *is* now displayed

Fig. 12.6 | Demonstrating polymorphism by invoking a derived-class `virtual` function via a base-class pointer to a derived-class object. (Part 2 of 2.)

`virtual` Destructors

A problem can occur when using polymorphism to process dynamically allocated objects of a class hierarchy. So far you've seen destructors that are not declared with keyword `virtual`. If a derived-class object with a non-`virtual` destructor is destroyed by applying the `delete` operator to a *base-class pointer* to the object, the C++ standard specifies that the behavior is *undefined.*

The simple solution to this problem is to create a `public` **`virtual` destructor** in the base class. If a base class destructor is declared `virtual`, the destructors of any derived classes are *also* `virtual` and they *override* the base class destructor. For example, in class `CommissionEmployee`'s definition, we can define the `virtual` destructor as follows:

```
virtual ~CommissionEmployee() { }
```

Now, if an object in the hierarchy is destroyed explicitly by applying the `delete` operator to a *base-class pointer,* the destructor for the *appropriate class* is called based on the object to which the base-class pointer points. Remember, when a derived-class object is destroyed, the base-class part of the derived-class object is also destroyed, so it's important for the destructors of *both* the derived and base classes to execute. The base-class destructor automatically executes after the derived-class destructor. From this point forward, we'll include a `virtual` destructor in *every* class that contains `virtual` functions.

Error-Prevention Tip 12.2

If a class has `virtual` functions, always *provide a `virtual` destructor, even if one is not required for the class. This ensures that a custom derived-class destructor (if there is one) will be invoked when a derived-class object is deleted via a base class pointer.*

Common Programming Error 12.1

Constructors cannot be `virtual`. Declaring a constructor `virtual` is a compilation error.

C++11: `final` Member Functions and Classes

Prior to C++11, a derived class could override *any* of its base class's `virtual` functions. In C++11, a base-class `virtual` function that's declared **`final`** in its prototype, as in 11

```
virtual someFunction( parameters ) final;
```

cannot be overridden in any derived class—this guarantees that the base class's `final` member function definition will be used by all base-class objects and by all objects of the base class's direct *and* indirect derived classes. Similarly, prior to C++11, *any* existing class could be used as a base class in a hierarchy. As of C++11, you can declare a class as `final` to prevent it from being used as a base class, as in

```
class MyClass final // this class cannot be a base class
{
   // class body
};
```

Attempting to override a `final` member function or inherit from a `final` base class results in a compilation error.

12.4 Type Fields and switch Statements

One way to determine the type of an object is to use a switch statement to check the value of a field in the object. This allows us to distinguish among object types, then invoke an appropriate action for a particular object. For example, in a hierarchy of shapes in which each shape object has a shapeType attribute, a switch statement could check the object's shapeType to determine which print function to call.

Using switch logic exposes programs to a variety of potential problems. For example, you might forget to include a type test when one is warranted, or might forget to test all possible cases in a switch statement. When modifying a switch-based system by adding new types, you might forget to insert the new cases in *all* relevant switch statements. Every addition or deletion of a class requires the modification of every switch statement in the system; tracking these statements down can be time consuming and error prone.

Software Engineering Observation 12.7

Polymorphic programming can eliminate the need for switch *logic. By using the polymorphism mechanism to perform the equivalent logic, you can avoid the kinds of errors typically associated with* switch *logic.*

Software Engineering Observation 12.8

An interesting consequence of using polymorphism is that programs take on a simplified appearance. They contain less branching logic and simpler sequential code.

12.5 Abstract Classes and Pure virtual Functions

When we think of a class as a type, we assume that programs will create objects of that type. However, there are cases in which it's useful to define *classes from which you never intend to instantiate any objects*. Such classes are called **abstract classes**. Because these classes normally are used as base classes in inheritance hierarchies, we refer to them as **abstract base classes**. These classes cannot be used to instantiate objects, because, as we'll soon see, abstract classes are *incomplete*—derived classes must define the "missing pieces" before objects of these classes can be instantiated. We build programs with abstract classes in Section 12.6.

An abstract class is a base class from which other classes can inherit. Classes that can be used to instantiate objects are called **concrete classes**. Such classes define or inherit implementations for *every* member function they declare. We could have an *abstract* base class TwoDimensionalShape and derive such *concrete* classes as Square, Circle and Triangle. We could also have an *abstract* base class ThreeDimensionalShape and derive such *concrete* classes as Cube, Sphere and Cylinder. Abstract base classes are *too generic* to define real objects; we need to be *more specific* before we can think of instantiating objects. For example, if someone tells you to "draw the two-dimensional shape," what shape would you draw? Concrete classes provide the *specifics* that make it possible to instantiate objects.

An inheritance hierarchy does *not* need to contain any abstract classes, but many object-oriented systems have class hierarchies headed by abstract base classes. In some cases, abstract classes constitute the top few levels of the hierarchy. A good example of this is the shape hierarchy in Fig. 11.3, which begins with abstract base class Shape. On the next level of the hierarchy we have two more abstract base classes—TwoDimensionalShape and ThreeDimensionalShape. The next level of the hierarchy defines *concrete* classes for two-dimensional shapes (namely, Circle, Square and Triangle) and for three-dimensional shapes (namely, Sphere, Cube and Tetrahedron).

Pure Virtual Functions

A class is made abstract by declaring one or more of its virtual functions to be "pure." A **pure virtual function** is specified by placing "= 0" in its declaration, as in

```
virtual void draw() const = 0; // pure virtual function
```

The "= 0" is a **pure specifier.** Pure virtual functions typically do *not* provide implementations, though they can. Each *concrete* derived class *must override all* base-class pure virtual functions with concrete implementations of those functions; otherwise, the derived class is also abstract. The difference between a virtual function and a pure virtual function is that a virtual function *has* an implementation and gives the derived class the *option* of overriding the function; by contrast, a pure virtual function does *not* have an implementation and *requires* the derived class to override the function for that derived class to be concrete; otherwise the derived class remains *abstract.*

Pure virtual functions are used when it does *not* make sense for the base class to have an implementation of a function, but you want all concrete derived classes to implement the function. Returning to our earlier example of space objects, it does not make sense for the base class SpaceObject to have an implementation for function draw (as there is no way to draw a generic space object without having more information about what type of space object is being drawn). An example of a function that would be defined as virtual (and not pure virtual) would be one that returns a name for the object. We can name a generic SpaceObject (for instance, as "space object"), so a default implementation for this function can be provided, and the function does not need to be *pure* virtual. The function is still declared virtual, however, because it's expected that derived classes will override this function to provide *more specific* names for the derived-class objects.

Software Engineering Observation 12.9

An abstract class defines a common public interface for the various classes in a class hierarchy. An abstract class contains one or more pure virtual *functions that concrete derived classes* must *override.*

Common Programming Error 12.2

Failure to override a pure virtual *function in a derived class makes that class abstract. Attempting to instantiate an object of an abstract class causes a compilation error.*

Software Engineering Observation 12.10

An abstract class has at least one pure virtual *function. An abstract class also can have data members and concrete functions (including constructors and destructors), which are subject to the normal rules of inheritance by derived classes.*

Although we *cannot* instantiate objects of an abstract base class, we *can* use the abstract base class to declare *pointers* and *references* that can refer to objects of any *concrete* classes derived from the abstract class. Programs typically use such pointers and references to manipulate derived-class objects polymorphically.

Device Drivers and Polymorphism

Polymorphism is particularly effective for implementing *layered software systems*. In operating systems, for example, each type of physical device could operate quite differently from the others. Even so, commands to *read* or *write* data from and to devices may have a certain uniformity. The *write* message sent to a *device-driver* object needs to be interpreted specifically in the context of that device driver and how that device driver manipulates devices of a specific type. However, the *write* call itself really is no different from the *write* to any other device in the system—place some number of *bytes* from memory onto that device. An object-oriented operating system could use an abstract base class to provide an interface appropriate for all device drivers. Then, through inheritance from that abstract base class, derived classes are formed that all operate similarly. The capabilities (i.e., the `public` functions) offered by the device drivers are provided as pure `virtual` functions in the abstract base class. The implementations of these pure `virtual` functions are provided in the derived classes that correspond to the specific types of device drivers. This architecture also allows new devices to be *added* to a system easily. The user can just plug in the device and install its new device driver. The operating system "talks" to this new device through its device driver, which has the same `public` member functions as all other device drivers—those defined in the device driver abstract base class.

12.6 Case Study: Payroll System Using Polymorphism

This section reexamines the `CommissionEmployee`–`BasePlusCommissionEmployee` hierarchy that we explored throughout Section 11.3. In this example, we use an abstract class and polymorphism to perform payroll calculations based on the type of employee. We create an enhanced employee hierarchy to solve the following problem:

> *A company pays its employees weekly. The employees are of three types:* Salaried employees *are paid a fixed weekly salary regardless of the number of hours worked,* commission employees *are paid a percentage of their sales and* base-salary-plus-commission employees *receive a base salary plus a percentage of their sales. For the current pay period, the company has decided to reward base-salary-plus-commission employees by adding 10 percent to their base salaries. The company wants to implement a C++ program that performs its payroll calculations polymorphically.*

We use abstract class `Employee` to represent the general concept of an employee. The classes that derive directly from `Employee` are `SalariedEmployee` and `CommissionEmployee`. Class `BasePlusCommissionEmployee`—derived from `CommissionEmployee`—represents the last employee type. The UML class diagram in Fig. 12.7 shows the inheritance hierarchy for our polymorphic employee payroll application. The abstract class name `Employee` is *italicized*, as per the convention of the UML.

Abstract base class `Employee` declares the "interface" to the hierarchy—that is, the set of member functions that a program can invoke on all `Employee` objects. Each employee, regardless of the way his or her earnings are calculated, has a first name, a last name and a social security number, so `private` data members `firstName`, `lastName` and `socialSecurityNumber` appear in abstract base class `Employee`.

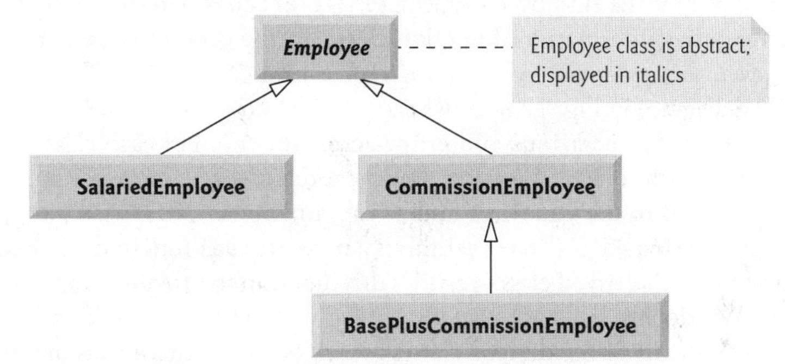

Fig. 12.7 | `Employee` hierarchy UML class diagram.

Software Engineering Observation 12.11

A derived class can inherit interface and/or implementation from a base class. Hierarchies designed for ***implementation inheritance*** *tend to have their functionality high in the hierarchy—each new derived class inherits one or more member functions that were defined in a base class, and the derived class uses the base-class definitions. Hierarchies designed for* ***interface inheritance*** *tend to have their functionality lower in the hierarchy—a base class specifies one or more functions that should be defined for each class in the hierarchy (i.e., they have the same prototype), but the individual derived classes provide their own implementations of the function(s).*

The following sections implement the `Employee` class hierarchy. The first five each implement one of the abstract or concrete classes. The last section implements a test program that builds objects of all these classes and processes the objects polymorphically.

12.6.1 Creating Abstract Base Class `Employee`

Class `Employee` (Figs. 12.9–12.10, discussed in further detail shortly) provides functions `earnings` and `print`, in addition to various *get* and *set* functions that manipulate `Employee`'s data members. An `earnings` function certainly applies generally to all employees, but each earnings calculation depends on the employee's class. So we declare `earnings` as pure `virtual` in base class `Employee` because *a default implementation does not make sense* for that function—there is not enough information to determine what amount `earnings` should return. Each derived class *overrides* `earnings` with an appropriate implementation. To calculate an employee's earnings, the program assigns the address of an employee's object to a base class `Employee` *pointer*, then invokes the `earnings` function on that object. We maintain a `vector` of `Employee` pointers, each of which points to an `Employee` object. *Of course, there cannot be `Employee` objects, because `Employee` is an abstract class—because of inheritance, however, all objects of all concrete derived classes of `Employee` may nevertheless be thought of as `Employee` objects.* The program iterates through the `vector` and calls function `earnings` for each `Employee` object. C++ processes these function calls *polymorphically*. Including `earnings` as a pure `virtual` function in `Employee` *forces* every direct derived class of `Employee` that wishes to be a *concrete* class to *override* `earnings`.

Function `print` in class `Employee` displays the first name, last name and social security number of the employee. As we'll see, each derived class of `Employee` overrides function `print` to output the employee's type (e.g., `"salaried employee:"`) followed by the rest of the employee's information. Function `print` in the derived classes could also call `earnings`, even though `earnings` is a pure-`virtual` function in base class `Employee`.

The diagram in Fig. 12.8 shows each of the four classes in the hierarchy down the left side and functions `earnings` and `print` across the top. For each class, the diagram shows the desired results of each function. Italic text represents where the values from a particular object are used in the `earnings` and `print` functions. Class `Employee` specifies "`= 0`" for function `earnings` to indicate that this is a pure `virtual` function and hence has *no* implementation. Each derived class overrides this function to provide an appropriate implementation. We do *not* list base class `Employee`'s *get* and *set* functions because they're *not* overridden in any of the derived classes—each of these functions is inherited and used "as is" by each of the derived classes.

	earnings	print
Employee	= 0	*firstName lastName* social security number: *SSN*
Salaried-Employee	*weeklySalary*	salaried employee: *firstName lastName* social security number: *SSN* weekly salary: *weeklySalary*
Commission-Employee	*commissionRate* * *grossSales*	commission employee: *firstName lastName* social security number: *SSN* gross sales: *grossSales*; commission rate: *commissionRate*
BasePlus-Commission-Employee	(*commissionRate* * *grossSales*) + *baseSalary*	base-salaried commission employee: *firstName lastName* social security number: *SSN* gross sales: *grossSales*; commission rate: *commissionRate*; base salary: *baseSalary*

Fig. 12.8 | Polymorphic interface for the `Employee` hierarchy classes.

`Employee` Class Header

Let's consider class `Employee`'s header (Fig. 12.9). The `public` member functions include a constructor that takes the first name, last name and social security number as arguments (lines 11–12); a virtual destructor (line 13); *set* functions that set the first name, last name and social security number (lines 15, 18 and 21, respectively); *get* functions that return the first name, last name and social security number (lines 16, 19 and 22, respectively); pure `virtual` function `earnings` (line 25) and `virtual` function `print` (line 26).

```
1  // Fig. 12.9: Employee.h
2  // Employee abstract base class.
3  #ifndef EMPLOYEE_H
```

Fig. 12.9 | `Employee` abstract base class. (Part 1 of 2.)

```
#define EMPLOYEE_H

#include <string> // C++ standard string class

class Employee
{
public:
   Employee( const std::string &, const std::string &,
      const std::string & );
   virtual ~Employee() { } // virtual destructor

   void setFirstName( const std::string & ); // set first name
   std::string getFirstName() const; // return first name

   void setLastName( const std::string & ); // set last name
   std::string getLastName() const; // return last name

   void setSocialSecurityNumber( const std::string & ); // set SSN
   std::string getSocialSecurityNumber() const; // return SSN

   // pure virtual function makes Employee an abstract base class
   virtual double earnings() const = 0; // pure virtual
   virtual void print() const; // virtual
private:
   std::string firstName;
   std::string lastName;
   std::string socialSecurityNumber;
}; // end class Employee

#endif // EMPLOYEE_H
```

Fig. 12.9 | Employee abstract base class. (Part 2 of 2.)

Recall that we declared `earnings` as a pure `virtual` function because first we must know the *specific* `Employee` type to determine the appropriate `earnings` calculations. Declaring this function as pure `virtual` indicates that each concrete derived class *must* provide an `earnings` implementation and that a program can use base-class `Employee` pointers to invoke function `earnings` *polymorphically* for *any* type of `Employee`.

`Employee` Class Member-Function Definitions

Figure 12.10 contains the member-function definitions for class `Employee`. No implementation is provided for `virtual` function `earnings`. The `Employee` constructor (lines 9–14) does not validate the social security number. Normally, such validation should be provided.

```
1 // Fig. 12.10: Employee.cpp
2 // Abstract-base-class Employee member-function definitions.
3 // Note: No definitions are given for pure virtual functions.
4 #include <iostream>
5 #include "Employee.h" // Employee class definition
6 using namespace std;
```

Fig. 12.10 | Employee class implementation file. (Part 1 of 2.)

```

// constructor
Employee::Employee( const string &first, const string &last,
   const string &ssn )
   : firstName( first ), lastName( last ), socialSecurityNumber( ssn )
{
   // empty body
} // end Employee constructor

// set first name
void Employee::setFirstName( const string &first )
{
   firstName = first;
} // end function setFirstName

// return first name
string Employee::getFirstName() const
{
   return firstName;
} // end function getFirstName

// set last name
void Employee::setLastName( const string &last )
{
   lastName = last;
} // end function setLastName

// return last name
string Employee::getLastName() const
{
   return lastName;
} // end function getLastName

// set social security number
void Employee::setSocialSecurityNumber( const string &ssn )
{
   socialSecurityNumber = ssn; // should validate
} // end function setSocialSecurityNumber

// return social security number
string Employee::getSocialSecurityNumber() const
{
   return socialSecurityNumber;
} // end function getSocialSecurityNumber

// print Employee's information (virtual, but not pure virtual)
void Employee::print() const
{
   cout << getFirstName() << ' ' << getLastName()
      << "\nsocial security number: " << getSocialSecurityNumber();
} // end function print
```

Fig. 12.10 | Employee class implementation file. (Part 2 of 2.)

The virtual function print (lines 53–57) provides an *implementation* that will be *overridden* in *each* of the derived classes. Each of these functions will, however, use the abstract class's version of print to print information *common to all classes* in the Employee hierarchy.

12.6.2 Creating Concrete Derived Class SalariedEmployee

Class SalariedEmployee (Figs. 12.11–12.12) derives from class Employee (line 9 of Fig. 12.11). The public member functions include a constructor that takes a first name, a last name, a social security number and a weekly salary as arguments (lines 12–13); a virtual destructor (line 14); a *set* function to assign a new nonnegative value to data member weeklySalary (line 16); a *get* function to return weeklySalary's value (line 17); a virtual function earnings that calculates a SalariedEmployee's earnings (line 20) and a virtual function print (line 21) that outputs the employee's type, namely, "salaried employee: " followed by employee-specific information produced by base class Employee's print function and SalariedEmployee's getWeeklySalary function.

```
1  // Fig. 12.11: SalariedEmployee.h
2  // SalariedEmployee class derived from Employee.
3  #ifndef SALARIED_H
4  #define SALARIED_H
5
6  #include <string> // C++ standard string class
7  #include "Employee.h" // Employee class definition
8
9  class SalariedEmployee : public Employee
10 {
11 public:
12    SalariedEmployee( const std::string &, const std::string &,
13       const std::string &, double = 0.0 );
14    virtual ~SalariedEmployee() { } // virtual destructor
15
16    void setWeeklySalary( double ); // set weekly salary
17    double getWeeklySalary() const; // return weekly salary
18
19    // keyword virtual signals intent to override
20    virtual double earnings() const override; // calculate earnings
21    virtual void print() const override; // print object
22 private:
23    double weeklySalary; // salary per week
24 }; // end class SalariedEmployee
25
26 #endif // SALARIED_H
```

Fig. 12.11 | SalariedEmployee class header.

SalariedEmployee Class Member-Function Definitions

Figure 12.12 contains the member-function definitions for SalariedEmployee. The class's constructor passes the first name, last name and social security number to the Employee constructor (line 11) to initialize the private data members that are inherited from the base class, but not directly accessible in the derived class. Function earnings (lines 33–36) overrides pure virtual function earnings in Employee to provide a *concrete* implementation that returns the SalariedEmployee's weekly salary. If we did not define earnings, class SalariedEmployee would be an *abstract* class, and any attempt to instantiate a SalariedEmployee object would cause a compilation error. In class SalariedEmployee's header, we declared member functions earnings and print as virtual (lines 20–21 of Fig. 12.11)—actually, placing the virtual keyword before these member functions is *redundant*. We defined them as virtual in base class Employee, so they remain virtual functions throughout the class hierarchy. Explicitly declaring such functions virtual at every level of the hierarchy promotes program clarity. Not declaring earnings as pure virtual signals our intent to provide an implementation in this concrete class.

```
1  // Fig. 12.12: SalariedEmployee.cpp
2  // SalariedEmployee class member-function definitions.
3  #include <iostream>
4  #include <stdexcept>
5  #include "SalariedEmployee.h" // SalariedEmployee class definition
6  using namespace std;
7
8  // constructor
9  SalariedEmployee::SalariedEmployee( const string &first,
10    const string &last, const string &ssn, double salary )
11    : Employee( first, last, ssn )
12 {
13    setWeeklySalary( salary );
14 } // end SalariedEmployee constructor
15
16 // set salary
17 void SalariedEmployee::setWeeklySalary( double salary )
18 {
19    if ( salary >= 0.0 )
20       weeklySalary = salary;
21    else
22       throw invalid_argument( "Weekly salary must be >= 0.0" );
23 } // end function setWeeklySalary
24
25 // return salary
26 double SalariedEmployee::getWeeklySalary() const
27 {
28    return weeklySalary;
29 } // end function getWeeklySalary
30
31 // calculate earnings;
32 // override pure virtual function earnings in Employee
33 double SalariedEmployee::earnings() const
34 {
35    return getWeeklySalary();
36 } // end function earnings
37
38 // print SalariedEmployee's information
39 void SalariedEmployee::print() const
40 {
```

Fig. 12.12 | SalariedEmployee class implementation file. (Part 1 of 2.)

```
41      cout << "salaried employee: ";
42      Employee::print(); // reuse abstract base-class print function
43      cout << "\nweekly salary: " << getWeeklySalary();
44   } // end function print
```

Fig. 12.12 | SalariedEmployee class implementation file. (Part 2 of 2.)

Function print of class SalariedEmployee (lines 39–44 of Fig. 12.12) overrides Employee function print. If class SalariedEmployee did not override print, SalariedEmployee would inherit the Employee version of print. In that case, SalariedEmployee's print function would simply return the employee's full name and social security number, which does not adequately represent a SalariedEmployee. To print a SalariedEmployee's complete information, the derived class's print function outputs "salaried employee: " followed by the base-class Employee-specific information (i.e., first name, last name and social security number) printed by *invoking the base class's* print *function* using the scope resolution operator (line 42)—this is a nice example of code reuse. Without the scope resolution operator, the print call would cause *infinite recursion.* The output produced by SalariedEmployee's print function also contains the employee's weekly salary obtained by invoking the class's getWeeklySalary function.

12.6.3 Creating Concrete Derived Class CommissionEmployee

Class CommissionEmployee (Figs. 12.13–12.14) derives from Employee (Fig. 12.13, line 9). The member-function implementations (Fig. 12.14) include a constructor (lines 9–15) that takes a first name, last name, social security number, sales amount and commission rate; *set* functions (lines 18–24 and 33–39) to assign new values to data members commissionRate and grossSales, respectively; *get* functions (lines 27–30 and 42–45) that retrieve their values; function earnings (lines 48–51) to calculate a CommissionEmployee's earnings; and function print (lines 54–60) to output the employee's type, namely, "commission employee: " and employee-specific information. The constructor passes the first name, last name and social security number to the Employee constructor (line 11) to initialize Employee's private data members. Function print calls base-class function print (line 57) to display the Employee-specific information.

```
1   // Fig. 12.13: CommissionEmployee.h
2   // CommissionEmployee class derived from Employee.
3   #ifndef COMMISSION_H
4   #define COMMISSION_H
5
6   #include <string> // C++ standard string class
7   #include "Employee.h" // Employee class definition
8
9   class CommissionEmployee : public Employee
10  {
11  public:
12     CommissionEmployee( const std::string &, const std::string &,
13        const std::string &, double = 0.0, double = 0.0 );
```

Fig. 12.13 | CommissionEmployee class header. (Part 1 of 2.)

```
   virtual ~CommissionEmployee() { } // virtual destructor

   void setCommissionRate( double ); // set commission rate
   double getCommissionRate() const; // return commission rate

   void setGrossSales( double ); // set gross sales amount
   double getGrossSales() const; // return gross sales amount

   // keyword virtual signals intent to override
   virtual double earnings() const override; // calculate earnings
   virtual void print() const override; // print object
private:
   double grossSales; // gross weekly sales
   double commissionRate; // commission percentage
}; // end class CommissionEmployee

#endif // COMMISSION_H
```

Fig. 12.13 | CommissionEmployee class header. (Part 2 of 2.)

```
// Fig. 12.14: CommissionEmployee.cpp
// CommissionEmployee class member-function definitions.
#include <iostream>
#include <stdexcept>
#include "CommissionEmployee.h" // CommissionEmployee class definition
using namespace std;

// constructor
CommissionEmployee::CommissionEmployee( const string &first,
   const string &last, const string &ssn, double sales, double rate )
   : Employee( first, last, ssn )
{
   setGrossSales( sales );
   setCommissionRate( rate );
} // end CommissionEmployee constructor

// set gross sales amount
void CommissionEmployee::setGrossSales( double sales )
{
   if ( sales >= 0.0 )
      grossSales = sales;
   else
      throw invalid_argument( "Gross sales must be >= 0.0" );
} // end function setGrossSales

// return gross sales amount
double CommissionEmployee::getGrossSales() const
{
   return grossSales;
} // end function getGrossSales

```

Fig. 12.14 | CommissionEmployee class implementation file. (Part 1 of 2.)

```
// set commission rate
void CommissionEmployee::setCommissionRate( double rate )
{
   if ( rate > 0.0 && rate < 1.0 )
      commissionRate = rate;
   else
      throw invalid_argument( "Commission rate must be > 0.0 and < 1.0" );
} // end function setCommissionRate

// return commission rate
double CommissionEmployee::getCommissionRate() const
{
   return commissionRate;
} // end function getCommissionRate

// calculate earnings; override pure virtual function earnings in Employee
double CommissionEmployee::earnings() const
{
   return getCommissionRate() * getGrossSales();
} // end function earnings

// print CommissionEmployee's information
void CommissionEmployee::print() const
{
   cout << "commission employee: ";
   Employee::print(); // code reuse
   cout << "\ngross sales: " << getGrossSales()
      << "; commission rate: " << getCommissionRate();
} // end function print
```

Fig. 12.14 | `CommissionEmployee` class implementation file. (Part 2 of 2.)

12.6.4 Creating Indirect Concrete Derived Class `BasePlusCommissionEmployee`

Class `BasePlusCommissionEmployee` (Figs. 12.15–12.16) directly inherits from class `CommissionEmployee` (line 9 of Fig. 12.15) and therefore is an *indirect* derived class of class `Employee`. Class `BasePlusCommissionEmployee`'s member-function implementations include a constructor (lines 9–15 of Fig. 12.16) that takes as arguments a first name, a last name, a social security number, a sales amount, a commission rate *and* a base salary. It then passes the first name, last name, social security number, sales amount and commission rate to the `CommissionEmployee` constructor (line 12) to initialize the inherited members. `BasePlusCommissionEmployee` also contains a *set* function (lines 18–24) to assign a new value to data member `baseSalary` and a *get* function (lines 27–30) to return `baseSalary`'s value. Function `earnings` (lines 34–37) calculates a `BasePlusCommissionEmployee`'s earnings. Line 36 in function `earnings` calls base-class `CommissionEmployee`'s `earnings` function to calculate the commission-based portion of the employee's earnings. This is another nice example of code reuse. `BasePlusCommissionEmployee`'s `print` function (lines 40–45) outputs `"base-salaried"`, followed by the output of base-class `CommissionEmployee`'s `print` function (another example of code reuse), then the base salary. The resulting output begins with `"base-salaried commission employee: "` followed by the rest of the `Base-`

PlusCommissionEmployee's information. Recall that CommissionEmployee's print displays the employee's first name, last name and social security number by invoking the print function of its base class (i.e., Employee)—yet another example of code reuse. BasePlusCommissionEmployee's print initiates a chain of functions calls that spans *all three levels* of the Employee hierarchy.

```
// Fig. 12.15: BasePlusCommissionEmployee.h
// BasePlusCommissionEmployee class derived from CommissionEmployee.
#ifndef BASEPLUS_H
#define BASEPLUS_H

#include <string> // C++ standard string class
#include "CommissionEmployee.h" // CommissionEmployee class definition

class BasePlusCommissionEmployee : public CommissionEmployee
{
public:
   BasePlusCommissionEmployee( const std::string &, const std::string &,
      const std::string &, double = 0.0, double = 0.0, double = 0.0 );
   virtual ~CommissionEmployee() { } // virtual destructor

   void setBaseSalary( double ); // set base salary
   double getBaseSalary() const; // return base salary

   // keyword virtual signals intent to override
   virtual double earnings() const override; // calculate earnings
   virtual void print() const override; // print object
private:
   double baseSalary; // base salary per week
}; // end class BasePlusCommissionEmployee

#endif // BASEPLUS_H
```

Fig. 12.15 | BasePlusCommissionEmployee class header.

```
// Fig. 12.16: BasePlusCommissionEmployee.cpp
// BasePlusCommissionEmployee member-function definitions.
#include <iostream>
#include <stdexcept>
#include "BasePlusCommissionEmployee.h"
using namespace std;

// constructor
BasePlusCommissionEmployee::BasePlusCommissionEmployee(
   const string &first, const string &last, const string &ssn,
   double sales, double rate, double salary )
   : CommissionEmployee( first, last, ssn, sales, rate )
{
   setBaseSalary( salary ); // validate and store base salary
} // end BasePlusCommissionEmployee constructor

```

Fig. 12.16 | BasePlusCommissionEmployee class implementation file. (Part 1 of 2.)

```
// set base salary
void BasePlusCommissionEmployee::setBaseSalary( double salary )
{
   if ( salary >= 0.0 )
      baseSalary = salary;
   else
      throw invalid_argument( "Salary must be >= 0.0" );
} // end function setBaseSalary

// return base salary
double BasePlusCommissionEmployee::getBaseSalary() const
{
    return baseSalary;
} // end function getBaseSalary

// calculate earnings;
// override virtual function earnings in CommissionEmployee
double BasePlusCommissionEmployee::earnings() const
{
    return getBaseSalary() + CommissionEmployee::earnings();
} // end function earnings

// print BasePlusCommissionEmployee's information
void BasePlusCommissionEmployee::print() const
{
   cout << "base-salaried ";
   CommissionEmployee::print(); // code reuse
   cout << "; base salary: " << getBaseSalary();
} // end function print
```

Fig. 12.16 | `BasePlusCommissionEmployee` class implementation file. (Part 2 of 2.)

12.6.5 Demonstrating Polymorphic Processing

To test our `Employee` hierarchy, the program in Fig. 12.17 creates an object of each of the three concrete classes `SalariedEmployee`, `CommissionEmployee` and `BasePlusCommissionEmployee`. The program manipulates these objects, first with *static binding*, then *polymorphically*, using a `vector` of `Employee` pointers. Lines 22–27 create objects of each of the three concrete `Employee` derived classes. Lines 32–38 output each `Employee`'s information and earnings. Each member-function invocation in lines 32–37 is an example of *static binding*—at *compile time*, because we are using *name handles* (not *pointers* or *references* that could be set at *execution time*), the *compiler* can identify each object's type to determine which `print` and `earnings` functions are called.

```
1  // Fig. 12.17: fig12_17.cpp
2  // Processing Employee derived-class objects individually
3  // and polymorphically using dynamic binding.
4  #include <iostream>
5  #include <iomanip>
6  #include <vector>
```

Fig. 12.17 | `Employee` class hierarchy driver program. (Part 1 of 4.)

```
#include "Employee.h"
#include "SalariedEmployee.h"
#include "CommissionEmployee.h"
#include "BasePlusCommissionEmployee.h"
using namespace std;

void virtualViaPointer( const Employee * const ); // prototype
void virtualViaReference( const Employee & ); // prototype

int main()
{
   // set floating-point output formatting
   cout << fixed << setprecision( 2 );

   // create derived-class objects
   SalariedEmployee salariedEmployee(
      "John", "Smith", "111-11-1111", 800 );
   CommissionEmployee commissionEmployee(
      "Sue", "Jones", "333-33-3333", 10000, .06 );
   BasePlusCommissionEmployee basePlusCommissionEmployee(
      "Bob", "Lewis", "444-44-4444", 5000, .04, 300 );

   cout << "Employees processed individually using static binding:\n\n";

   // output each Employee's information and earnings using static binding
   salariedEmployee.print();
   cout << "\nearned $" << salariedEmployee.earnings() << "\n\n";
   commissionEmployee.print();
   cout << "\nearned $" << commissionEmployee.earnings() << "\n\n";
   basePlusCommissionEmployee.print();
   cout << "\nearned $" << basePlusCommissionEmployee.earnings()
      << "\n\n";

   // create vector of three base-class pointers
   vector< Employee * > employees( 3 );

   // initialize vector with pointers to Employees
   employees[ 0 ] = &salariedEmployee;
   employees[ 1 ] = &commissionEmployee;
   employees[ 2 ] = &basePlusCommissionEmployee;

   cout << "Employees processed polymorphically via dynamic binding:\n\n";

   // call virtualViaPointer to print each Employee's information
   // and earnings using dynamic binding
   cout << "Virtual function calls made off base-class pointers:\n\n";

   for ( const Employee *employeePtr : employees )
      virtualViaPointer( employeePtr );

   // call virtualViaReference to print each Employee's information
   // and earnings using dynamic binding
   cout << "Virtual function calls made off base-class references:\n\n";
```

Fig. 12.17 | Employee class hierarchy driver program. (Part 2 of 4.)

```
   for ( const Employee *employeePtr : employees )
      virtualViaReference( *employeePtr ); // note dereferencing
} // end main

// call Employee virtual functions print and earnings off a
// base-class pointer using dynamic binding
void virtualViaPointer( const Employee * const baseClassPtr )
{
   baseClassPtr->print();
   cout << "\nearned $" << baseClassPtr->earnings() << "\n\n";
} // end function virtualViaPointer

// call Employee virtual functions print and earnings off a
// base-class reference using dynamic binding
void virtualViaReference( const Employee &baseClassRef )
{
   baseClassRef.print();
   cout << "\nearned $" << baseClassRef.earnings() << "\n\n";
} // end function virtualViaReference
```

```
Employees processed individually using static binding:

salaried employee: John Smith
social security number: 111-11-1111
weekly salary: 800.00
earned $800.00

commission employee: Sue Jones
social security number: 333-33-3333
gross sales: 10000.00; commission rate: 0.06
earned $600.00

base-salaried commission employee: Bob Lewis
social security number: 444-44-4444
gross sales: 5000.00; commission rate: 0.04; base salary: 300.00
earned $500.00

Employees processed polymorphically using dynamic binding:

Virtual function calls made off base-class pointers:

salaried employee: John Smith
social security number: 111-11-1111
weekly salary: 800.00
earned $800.00

commission employee: Sue Jones
social security number: 333-33-3333
gross sales: 10000.00; commission rate: 0.06
earned $600.00

base-salaried commission employee: Bob Lewis
social security number: 444-44-4444
gross sales: 5000.00; commission rate: 0.04; base salary: 300.00
earned $500.00
```

Fig. 12.17 | Employee class hierarchy driver program. (Part 3 of 4.)

```
Virtual function calls made off base-class references:

salaried employee: John Smith
social security number: 111-11-1111
weekly salary: 800.00
earned $800.00

commission employee: Sue Jones
social security number: 333-33-3333
gross sales: 10000.00; commission rate: 0.06
earned $600.00

base-salaried commission employee: Bob Lewis
social security number: 444-44-4444
gross sales: 5000.00; commission rate: 0.04; base salary: 300.00
earned $500.00
```

Fig. 12.17 | `Employee` class hierarchy driver program. (Part 4 of 4.)

Line 41 creates the `vector employees`, which contains three `Employee` pointers. Line 44 aims `employees[0]` at object `salariedEmployee`. Line 45 aims `employees[1]` at object `commissionEmployee`. Line 46 aims `employee[2]` at object `basePlusCommissionEmployee`. The compiler allows these assignments, because a `SalariedEmployee` *is an* `Employee`, a `CommissionEmployee` *is an* `Employee` and a `BasePlusCommissionEmployee` *is an* `Employee`. Therefore, we can assign the addresses of `SalariedEmployee`, `CommissionEmployee` and `BasePlusCommissionEmployee` objects to base-class `Employee` pointers, even though `Employee` is an *abstract* class.

Lines 54–55 traverse `vector employees` and invoke function `virtualViaPointer` (lines 67–71) for each element in `employees`. Function `virtualViaPointer` receives in parameter `baseClassPtr` the address stored in an `employees` element. Each call to `virtualViaPointer` uses `baseClassPtr` to invoke `virtual` functions `print` (line 69) and `earnings` (line 70). Function `virtualViaPointer` does *not* contain *any* `SalariedEmployee`, `CommissionEmployee` or `BasePlusCommissionEmployee` type information. The function knows *only* about base-class type `Employee`. Therefore, the compiler *cannot know* which concrete class's functions to call through `baseClassPtr`. Yet at execution time, each virtual-function invocation *correctly* calls the function on the object to which `baseClassPtr` currently points. The output illustrates that *the appropriate functions for each class are indeed invoked* and that each object's proper information is displayed. For instance, the weekly salary is displayed for the `SalariedEmployee`, and the gross sales are displayed for the `CommissionEmployee` and `BasePlusCommissionEmployee`. Also, obtaining the earnings of each `Employee` polymorphically in line 70 produces the same results as obtaining these employees' earnings via *static binding* in lines 33, 35 and 37. All `virtual` function calls to `print` and `earnings` are resolved at *runtime* with *dynamic binding*.

Finally, lines 61–62 traverse `employees` and invoke function `virtualViaReference` (lines 75–79) for each `vector` element. Function `virtualViaReference` receives in its parameter `baseClassRef` (of type `const Employee &`) a *reference* to the object obtained by *dereferencing the pointer* stored in each `employees` element (line 62). Each call to `virtualViaReference` invokes `virtual` functions `print` (line 77) and `earnings` (line 78) via `baseClassRef` to demonstrate that *polymorphic processing occurs with base-class references as well.*

Each `virtual`-function invocation calls the function on the object to which `baseClassRef` refers at runtime. This is another example of *dynamic binding*. The output produced using base-class references is identical to the output produced using base-class pointers.

12.7 (Optional) Polymorphism, Virtual Functions and Dynamic Binding "Under the Hood"

C++ makes polymorphism easy to program. It's certainly possible to program for polymorphism in non-object-oriented languages such as C, but doing so requires complex and potentially dangerous pointer manipulations. This section discusses how C++ can implement polymorphism, `virtual` functions and dynamic binding internally. This will give you a solid understanding of how these capabilities really work. More importantly, it will help you appreciate the *overhead* of polymorphism—in terms of additional *memory consumption* and *processor time*. This can help you determine when to use polymorphism and when to avoid it. C++ Standard Library classes like `array` and `vector` are implemented *without* polymorphism and `virtual` functions to avoid the associated execution-time overhead and achieve optimal performance.

First, we'll explain the data structures that the compiler builds at *compile time* to support polymorphism at execution time. You'll see that polymorphism is accomplished through three levels of pointers, i.e., *triple indirection*. Then we'll show how an executing program uses these data structures to execute `virtual` functions and achieve the *dynamic binding* associated with polymorphism. Our discussion explains one *possible* implementation; this is not a language requirement.

When C++ compiles a class that has one or more `virtual` functions, it builds a **virtual function table** (*vtable*) for that class. The *vtable* contains pointers to the class's `virtual` functions. Just as the name of a built-in array contains the address in memory of the array's first element, a **pointer to a function** contains the starting address in memory of the code that performs the function's task. An executing program uses the *vtable* to select the proper function implementation each time a `virtual` function of that class is called. The leftmost column of Fig. 12.18 illustrates the *vtables* for the classes `Employee`, `SalariedEmployee`, `CommissionEmployee` and `BasePlusCommissionEmployee`.

`Employee` Class vtable

In the `Employee` class *vtable*, the first function pointer is set to `0` (i.e., `nullptr`), because function `earnings` is a *pure* `virtual` function and therefore *lacks an implementation*. The second function pointer points to function `print`, which displays the employee's full name and social security number. [*Note:* We've abbreviated the output of each `print` function in this figure to conserve space.] Any class that has one or more null pointers in its *vtable* is an *abstract* class. Classes without any null *vtable* pointers (such as `SalariedEmployee`, `CommissionEmployee` and `BasePlusCommissionEmployee`) are *concrete* classes.

`SalariedEmployee` Class vtable

Class `SalariedEmployee` overrides function `earnings` to return the employee's weekly salary, so the function pointer points to the `earnings` function of class `SalariedEmployee`. `SalariedEmployee` also overrides `print`, so the corresponding function pointer points to the `SalariedEmployee` member function that prints `"salaried employee: "` followed by the employee's name, social security number and weekly salary.

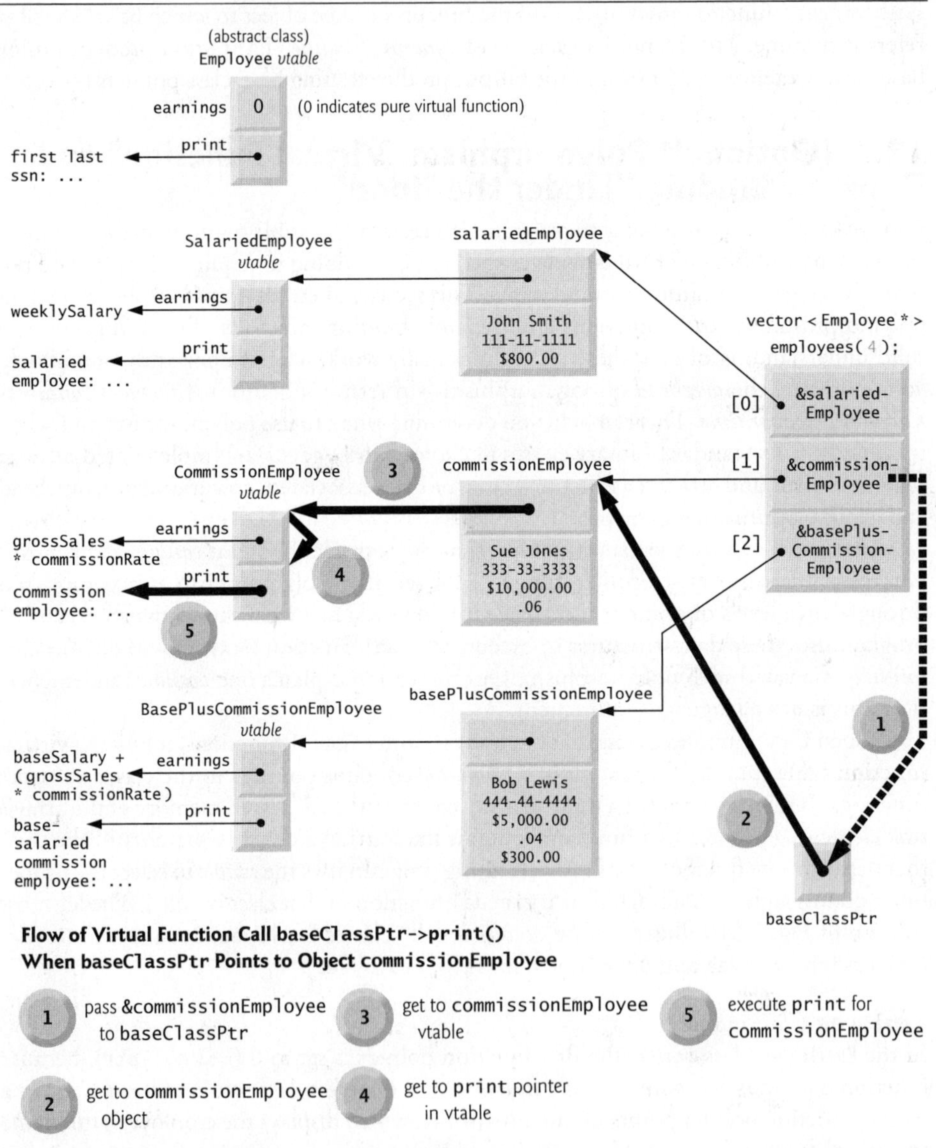

Fig. 12.18 | How virtual function calls work.

CommissionEmployee Class vtable

The earnings function pointer in the *vtable* for class CommissionEmployee points to CommissionEmployee's earnings function that returns the employee's gross sales multiplied by the commission rate. The print function pointer points to the CommissionEmployee version of the function, which prints the employee's type, name, social security number, commission rate and gross sales. As in class HourlyEmployee, both functions override the functions in class Employee.

`BasePlusCommissionEmployee` Class vtable

The `earnings` function pointer in the *vtable* for class `BasePlusCommissionEmployee` points to the `BasePlusCommissionEmployee`'s `earnings` function, which returns the employee's base salary plus gross sales multiplied by commission rate. The `print` function pointer points to the `BasePlusCommissionEmployee` version of the function, which prints the employee's base salary plus the type, name, social security number, commission rate and gross sales. Both functions override the functions in class `CommissionEmployee`.

Inheriting Concrete `virtual` Functions

In our `Employee` case study, each *concrete* class provides its own implementation for `virtual` functions `earnings` and `print`. You've learned that each class which inherits *directly* from abstract base class `Employee` *must implement* `earnings` in order to be a *concrete* class, because `earnings` is a pure `virtual` function. These classes do *not* need to implement function `print`, however, to be considered concrete—`print` is *not* a *pure* `virtual` function and derived classes can inherit class `Employee`'s implementation of `print`. Furthermore, class `BasePlusCommissionEmployee` does *not* have to implement either function `print` or `earnings`—both function implementations can be inherited from concrete class `CommissionEmployee`. If a class in our hierarchy were to inherit function implementations in this manner, the *vtable* pointers for these functions would simply point to the function implementation that was being inherited. For example, if `BasePlusCommissionEmployee` did not override `earnings`, the `earnings` function pointer in the *vtable* for class `BasePlusCommissionEmployee` would point to the same `earnings` function as the *vtable* for class `CommissionEmployee` points to.

Three Levels of Pointers to Implement Polymorphism

Polymorphism is accomplished through an elegant data structure involving *three levels of pointers*. We've discussed one level—the function pointers in the *vtable*. These point to the actual functions that execute when a `virtual` function is invoked.

Now we consider the second level of pointers. *Whenever an object of a class with one or more `virtual` functions is instantiated, the compiler attaches to the object a pointer to the* vtable *for that class.* This pointer is normally at the front of the object, but it isn't required to be implemented that way. In Fig. 12.18, these pointers are associated with the objects created in Fig. 12.17 (one object for each of the types `SalariedEmployee`, `CommissionEmployee` and `BasePlusCommissionEmployee`). The diagram displays each of the object's data member values. For example, the `salariedEmployee` object contains a pointer to the `SalariedEmployee` *vtable*; the object also contains the values `John Smith`, `111-11-1111` and `$800.00`.

The third level of pointers simply contains the handles to the objects that receive the `virtual` function calls. The handles in this level may also be *references*. Fig. 12.18 depicts the `vector employees` that contains `Employee` *pointers*.

Now let's see how a typical `virtual` function call executes. Consider the call `baseClassPtr->print()` in function `virtualViaPointer` (line 69 of Fig. 12.17). Assume that `baseClassPtr` contains `employees[ 1 ]` (i.e., the address of object `commissionEmployee` in `employees`). When the compiler compiles this statement, it determines that the call is indeed being made via a *base-class pointer* and that `print` is a `virtual` function.

The compiler determines that `print` is the *second* entry in each of the *vtables*. To locate this entry, the compiler notes that it will need to skip the first entry. Thus, the compiler compiles an **offset** or **displacement** into the table of machine-language object-code pointers to find the code that will execute the `virtual` function call. The size in bytes of the offset depends on the number of bytes used to represent a function pointer on an individual platform. For example, on a 32-bit platform, a pointer is typically stored in four bytes, whereas on a 64-bit platform, a pointer is typically stored in eight bytes. We assume four bytes for this discussion.

The compiler generates code that performs the following operations [*Note:* The numbers in the list correspond to the circled numbers in Fig. 12.18]:

1. Select the ith entry of `employees` (in this case, the address of object `commissionEmployee`), and pass it as an argument to function `virtualViaPointer`. This sets parameter `baseClassPtr` to point to `commissionEmployee`.
2. *Dereference* that pointer to get to the `commissionEmployee` object—which, as you recall, begins with a pointer to the `CommissionEmployee` *vtable*.
3. *Dereference* `commissionEmployee`'s *vtable* pointer to get to the `CommissionEmployee` *vtable*.
4. Skip the offset of four bytes to select the `print` function pointer.
5. *Dereference* the `print` function pointer to form the "name" of the actual function to execute, and use the function call operator `()` to execute the appropriate `print` function, which in this case prints the employee's type, name, social security number, gross sales and commission rate.

Fig. 12.18's data structures may appear to be complex, but this complexity is managed by the compiler and *hidden* from you, making polymorphic programming straightforward. The pointer dereferencing operations and memory accesses that occur on every `virtual` function call require some additional execution time. The *vtables* and the *vtable* pointers added to the objects require some additional memory.

Performance Tip 12.1

Polymorphism, as typically implemented with `virtual` functions and dynamic binding in C++, is efficient. You can use these capabilities with nominal impact on performance.

Performance Tip 12.2

Virtual functions and dynamic binding enable polymorphic programming as an alternative to `switch` logic programming. Optimizing compilers normally generate polymorphic code that's nearly as efficient as hand-coded `switch`-based logic. Polymorphism's overhead is acceptable for most applications. In some situations—such as real-time applications with stringent performance requirements—polymorphism's overhead may be too high.

12.8 Case Study: Payroll System Using Polymorphism and Runtime Type Information with Downcasting, `dynamic_cast`, `typeid` and `type_info`

Recall from the problem statement at the beginning of Section 12.6 that, for the current pay period, our fictitious company has decided to reward `BasePlusCommissionEmployees` by adding 10 percent to their base salaries. When processing `Employee` objects polymorphically in Section 12.6.5, we did not need to worry about the "specifics." Now, however, to adjust the base salaries of BasePlusCommissionEmployees, we have to determine the *specific type* of each Employee object *at execution time*, then act appropriately. This section demonstrates the powerful capabilities of **runtime type information (RTTI)** and **dynamic casting**, which enable a program to determine an object's type at execution time and act on that object accordingly.[1]

Figure 12.19 uses the Employee hierarchy developed in Section 12.6 and increases by 10 percent the base salary of each BasePlusCommissionEmployee. Line 21 declares three-element vector employees that stores pointers to Employee objects. Lines 24–29 populate the vector with the *addresses* of *dynamically allocated* objects of classes SalariedEmployee (Figs. 12.11–12.12), CommissionEmployee (Figs. 12.13–12.14) and BasePlusCommissionEmployee (Figs. 12.15–12.16). Lines 32–52 iterate through the employees vector and display each Employee's information by invoking member function print (line 34). Recall that because print is declared virtual in *base class* Employee, the system invokes the appropriate *derived-class* object's print function.

```
1  // Fig. 12.19: fig12_19.cpp
2  // Demonstrating downcasting and runtime type information.
3  // NOTE: You may need to enable RTTI on your compiler
4  // before you can compile this application.
5  #include <iostream>
6  #include <iomanip>
7  #include <vector>
8  #include <typeinfo>
9  #include "Employee.h"
10 #include "SalariedEmployee.h"
11 #include "CommissionEmployee.h"
12 #include "BasePlusCommissionEmployee.h"
13 using namespace std;
14
15 int main()
16 {
17    // set floating-point output formatting
18    cout << fixed << setprecision( 2 );
19
20    // create vector of three base-class pointers
21    vector < Employee * > employees( 3 );
22
23    // initialize vector with various kinds of Employees
24    employees[ 0 ] = new SalariedEmployee(
25       "John", "Smith", "111-11-1111", 800 );
26    employees[ 1 ] = new CommissionEmployee(
27       "Sue", "Jones", "333-33-3333", 10000, .06 );
28    employees[ 2 ] = new BasePlusCommissionEmployee(
29       "Bob", "Lewis", "444-44-4444", 5000, .04, 300 );
30
```

Fig. 12.19 | Demonstrating downcasting and runtime type information. (Part 1 of 2.)

1. Some compilers require that RTTI be enabled before it can be used in a program. The compilers we used for testing this book's examples—GNU C++ 4.7, Visual C++ 2012 and Xcode 4.5 LLVM—each enable RTTI by default.

```
   // polymorphically process each element in vector employees
   for ( Employee *employeePtr : employees )
   {
      employeePtr->print(); // output employee information
      cout << endl;

      // attempt to downcast pointer
      BasePlusCommissionEmployee *derivedPtr =
         dynamic_cast < BasePlusCommissionEmployee * >( employeePtr );

      // determine whether element points to a BasePlusCommissionEmployee
      if ( derivedPtr != nullptr ) // true for "is a" relationship
      {
         double oldBaseSalary = derivedPtr->getBaseSalary();
         cout << "old base salary: $" << oldBaseSalary << endl;
         derivedPtr->setBaseSalary( 1.10 * oldBaseSalary );
         cout << "new base salary with 10% increase is: $"
            << derivedPtr->getBaseSalary() << endl;
      } // end if

      cout << "earned $" << employeePtr->earnings() << "\n\n";
   } // end for

   // release objects pointed to by vector's elements
   for ( const Employee *employeePtr : employees )
   {
      // output class name
      cout << "deleting object of "
         << typeid( *employeePtr ).name() << endl;

      delete employeePtr;
   } // end for
} // end main
```

```
salaried employee: John Smith
social security number: 111-11-1111
weekly salary: 800.00
earned $800.00

commission employee: Sue Jones
social security number: 333-33-3333
gross sales: 10000.00; commission rate: 0.06
earned $600.00

base-salaried commission employee: Bob Lewis
social security number: 444-44-4444
gross sales: 5000.00; commission rate: 0.04; base salary: 300.00
old base salary: $300.00
new base salary with 10% increase is: $330.00
earned $530.00

deleting object of class SalariedEmployee
deleting object of class CommissionEmployee
deleting object of class BasePlusCommissionEmployee
```

Fig. 12.19 | Demonstrating downcasting and runtime type information. (Part 2 of 2.)

Determining an Object's Type with dynamic_cast

In this example, as we encounter a BasePlusCommissionEmployee object, we wish to increase its base salary by 10 percent. Since we process the Employees polymorphically, we cannot (with the techniques you've learned so far) be certain as to which type of Employee is being manipulated at any given time. This creates a problem, because BasePlusCommissionEmployee employees *must* be identified when we encounter them so they can receive the 10 percent salary increase. To accomplish this, we use operator **dynamic_cast** (line 39) to determine whether the current Employee's type is BasePlusCommissionEmployee. This is the *downcast* operation we referred to in Section 12.3.3. Lines 38–39 *dynamically downcast* employeePtr from type Employee * to type BasePlusCommissionEmployee *. If employeePtr points to an object that *is a* BasePlusCommissionEmployee object, then that object's *address* is assigned to derived-class pointer derivedPtr; otherwise, nullptr is assigned to derivedPtr. Note that dynamic_cast rather than static_cast is *required* here to perform type checking on the underlying object—a static_cast would simply cast the Employee * to a BasePlusCommissionEmployee * regardless of the underlying object's type. With a static_cast, the program would attempt to increase *every* Employee's base salary, resulting in undefined behavior for each object that is not a BasePlusCommissionEmployee.

If the value returned by the dynamic_cast operator in lines 38–39 *is not* nullptr, the object *is* the correct type, and the if statement (lines 42–49) performs the special processing required for the BasePlusCommissionEmployee object. Lines 44, 46 and 48 invoke BasePlusCommissionEmployee functions getBaseSalary and setBaseSalary to retrieve and update the employee's salary.

Calculating the Current **Employee***'s Earnings*

Line 51 invokes member function earnings on the object to which employeePtr points. Recall that earnings is declared virtual in the base class, so the program invokes the derived-class object's earnings function—another example of *dynamic binding*.

Displaying an **Employee***'s Type*

Lines 55–62 display each employee's *object type* and uses the delete operator to deallocate the dynamic memory to which each vector element points. Operator **typeid** (line 59) returns a *reference* to an object of class **type_info** that contains the information about the type of its operand, including the name of that type. When invoked, type_info member function **name** (line 59) returns a pointer-based string containing the typeid argument's *type name* (e.g., "class BasePlusCommissionEmployee"). To use typeid, the program must include header **<typeinfo>** (line 8).

Portability Tip 12.1

The string returned by type_info *member function* name *may vary by compiler.*

Compilation Errors That We Avoided By Using **dynamic_cast**

We avoid several compilation errors in this example by *downcasting* an Employee pointer to a BasePlusCommissionEmployee pointer (lines 38–39). If we remove the dynamic_cast from line 39 and attempt to assign the current Employee pointer directly to BasePlusCommissionEmployee pointer derivedPtr, we'll receive a compilation error. C++ does *not* allow a program to assign a base-class pointer to a derived-class pointer because the *is-a* relationship does *not* apply—a `CommissionEmployee` is *not* a `BasePlusCommissionEmployee`. The *is-a* relationship applies only between the derived class and its base classes, not vice versa.

Similarly, if lines 44, 46 and 48 used the current base-class pointer from `employees`, rather than derived-class pointer `derivedPtr`, to invoke derived-class-only functions `getBaseSalary` and `setBaseSalary`, we would receive a compilation error at each of these lines. As you learned in Section 12.3.3, attempting to invoke *derived-class-only functions* through a *base-class pointer* is *not* allowed. Although lines 44, 46 and 48 execute only if `commissionPtr` is not `nullptr` (i.e., if the cast *can* be performed), we *cannot* attempt to invoke derived-class `BasePlusCommissionEmployee` functions `getBaseSalary` and `setBaseSalary` on the base-class `Employee` pointer. Recall that, using a base class `Employee` pointer, we can invoke only functions found in base class `Employee`—`earnings`, `print` and `Employee`'s *get* and *set* functions.

12.9 Wrap-Up

In this chapter we discussed polymorphism, which enables us to "program in the general" rather than "program in the specific," and we showed how this makes programs more extensible. We began with an example of how polymorphism would allow a screen manager to display several "space" objects. We then demonstrated how base-class and derived-class pointers can be aimed at base-class and derived-class objects. We said that aiming base-class pointers at base-class objects is natural, as is aiming derived-class pointers at derived-class objects. Aiming base-class pointers at derived-class objects is also natural because a derived-class object *is an* object of its base class. You learned why aiming derived-class pointers at base-class objects is dangerous and why the compiler disallows such assignments. We introduced `virtual` functions, which enable the proper functions to be called when objects at various levels of an inheritance hierarchy are referenced (at execution time) via base-class pointers or references. This is known as dynamic binding or late binding. We discussed `virtual` destructors, and how they ensure that all appropriate destructors in an inheritance hierarchy run on a derived-class object when that object is deleted via a base-class pointer or reference. We then discussed pure `virtual` functions and abstract classes (classes with one or more pure `virtual` functions). You learned that abstract classes cannot be used to instantiate objects, while concrete classes can. We then demonstrated using abstract classes in an inheritance hierarchy. You learned how polymorphism works "under the hood" with *vtables* that are created by the compiler. We used runtime type information (RTTI) and dynamic casting to determine the type of an object at execution time and act on that object accordingly. We also used the `typeid` operator to get a `type_info` object containing a given object's type information.

In the next chapter, we discuss many of C++'s I/O capabilities and demonstrate several stream manipulators that perform various formatting tasks.

13

Stream Input/Output: A Deeper Look

Objectives

In this chapter you'll:

- Use C++ object-oriented stream input/output.
- Format input and output.
- Learn about the stream-I/O class hierarchy.
- Use stream manipulators.
- Control justification and padding.
- Determine the success or failure of input/output operations.
- Learn to tie output streams to input streams.

Outline

13.1 Introduction

This chapter discusses a range of capabilities sufficient for performing most common I/O operations and overviews the remaining capabilities. We discussed some of these features earlier in the text; now we provide a more complete treatment. Many of the I/O features that we'll discuss are object oriented. This style of I/O makes use of other C++ features, such as references, function overloading and operator overloading.

C++ uses *type-safe I/O.* Each I/O operation is executed in a manner sensitive to the data type. If an I/O function has been defined to handle a particular data type, then that member function is called to handle that data type. If there is no match between the type of the actual data and a function for handling that data type, the compiler generates an error. Thus, improper data cannot "sneak" through the system (as can occur in C, allowing for some subtle and bizarre errors).

Users can specify how to perform I/O for objects of user-defined types by overloading the stream insertion operator (<<) and the stream extraction operator (>>). This **extensibility** is one of C++'s most valuable features.

Software Engineering Observation 13.1

Use the C++-style I/O exclusively in C++ programs, even though C-style I/O is available to C++ programmers.

Error-Prevention Tip 13.1

C++ I/O is type safe.

Software Engineering Observation 13.2

C++ enables a common treatment of I/O for predefined types and user-defined types. This commonality facilitates software development and reuse.

13.2 Streams

C++ I/O occurs in **streams**, which are sequences of bytes. In input operations, the bytes flow from a device (e.g., a keyboard, a disk drive, a network connection, etc.) to main memory. In output operations, bytes flow from main memory to a device (e.g., a display screen, a printer, a disk drive, a network connection, etc.).

An application associates meaning with bytes. The bytes could represent characters, raw data, graphics images, digital speech, digital video or any other information an application may require. The system I/O mechanisms should transfer bytes from devices to memory (and vice versa) consistently and reliably. Such transfers often involve some mechanical motion, such as the rotation of a disk or a tape, or the typing of keystrokes at a keyboard. The time these transfers take typically is far greater than the time the processor requires to manipulate data internally. Thus, I/O operations require careful planning and tuning to ensure optimal performance.

C++ provides both "low-level" and "high-level" I/O capabilities. Low-level I/O capabilities (i.e., **unformatted I/O**) specify that some number of bytes should be transferred device-to-memory or memory-to-device. In such transfers, the individual byte is the item of interest. Such low-level capabilities provide high-speed, high-volume transfers but are not particularly convenient.

Programmers generally prefer a higher-level view of I/O (i.e., **formatted I/O**), in which bytes are grouped into meaningful units, such as integers, floating-point numbers, characters, strings and user-defined types. These type-oriented capabilities are satisfactory for most I/O other than high-volume file processing.

Performance Tip 13.1

Use unformatted I/O for the best performance in high-volume file processing.

Portability Tip 13.1

Unformatted I/O is not portable across all platforms.

13.2.1 Classic Streams vs. Standard Streams

In the past, the C++ **classic stream libraries** enabled input and output of `char`s. Because a `char` normally occupies *one* byte, it can represent only a limited set of characters (such as those in the ASCII character set used by most readers of this book, or other popular character sets). However, many languages use alphabets that contain more characters than a single-byte `char` can represent. The ASCII character set does not provide these characters; the **Unicode® character set** does. Unicode is an extensive international character set that represents the majority of the world's "commercially viable" languages, mathematical symbols and much more. For more information on Unicode, visit www.unicode.org.

C++ includes the **standard stream libraries**, which enable developers to build systems capable of performing I/O operations with Unicode characters. For this purpose, C++ includes the type **wchar_t**, which among other uses can store Unicode characters. The C++ standard also redesigned the classic C++ stream classes, which processed only chars, as class templates with specializations for processing characters of types char and wchar_t, respectively. We use the char specializations. The size of type wchar_t is not specified by the standard. C++11's new char16_t and char32_t types for representing Unicode characters were added to provide character types with explicitly specified sizes.

13.2.2 iostream Library Headers

The C++ iostream library provides hundreds of I/O capabilities. Several headers contain portions of the library interface.

Most C++ programs include the <iostream> header, which declares basic services required for all stream-I/O operations. The <iostream> header defines the cin, cout, cerr and clog objects, which correspond to the standard input stream, the standard output stream, the unbuffered standard error stream and the buffered standard error stream, respectively. (cerr and clog are discussed in Section 13.2.3.) Both unformatted- and formatted-I/O services are provided.

The <iomanip> header declares services useful for performing formatted I/O with so-called **parameterized stream manipulators**, such as setw and setprecision.

The <fstream> header declares services for file processing. We use this header in the file-processing programs of Chapter 14.

13.2.3 Stream Input/Output Classes and Objects

The iostream library provides many templates for handling common I/O operations. For example, class template **basic_istream** supports stream-input operations, class template **basic_ostream** supports stream-output operations, and class template **basic_iostream** supports both stream-input and stream-output operations. Each template has a predefined template specialization that enables char I/O. In addition, the iostream library provides a set of typedefs that provide aliases for these template specializations. The **typedef** specifier declares synonyms (aliases) for data types. You'll sometimes use typedef to create shorter or more readable type names. For example, the statement

```
typedef Card *CardPtr;
```

defines an additional type name, CardPtr, as a *synonym* for type Card *. Creating a name using typedef does *not* create a data type; it creates only a new type name. Section 20.3 discusses typedef in detail. The typedef **istream** represents a basic_istream<char> that enables char input. Similarly, the typedef **ostream** represents a basic_ostream<char> that enables char output. Also, the typedef **iostream** represents a basic_iostream<char> that enables both char input and output. We use these typedefs throughout this chapter.

Stream-I/O Template Hierarchy and Operator Overloading

Templates basic_istream and basic_ostream both derive through single inheritance from base template **basic_ios**.[1] Template basic_iostream derives through *multiple in-*

heritance[2] from templates `basic_istream` and `basic_ostream`. The UML class diagram of Fig. 13.1 summarizes these inheritance relationships.

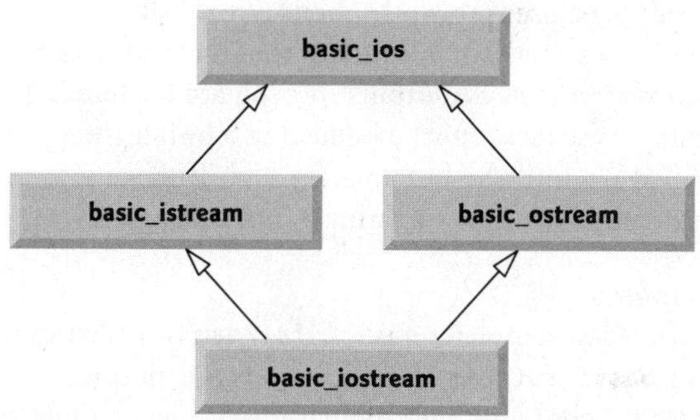

Fig. 13.1 | Stream-I/O template hierarchy portion.

Operator overloading provides a convenient notation for performing input/output. The *left-shift operator (<<)* is overloaded to designate stream output and is referred to as the *stream insertion operator*. The *right-shift operator (>>)* is overloaded to designate stream input and is referred to as the *stream extraction operator*. These operators are used with the standard stream objects `cin`, `cout`, `cerr` and `clog` and, commonly, with stream objects you create in your own code.

Standard Stream Objects `cin`*,* `cout`*,* `cerr` *and* `clog`

Predefined object `cin` is an `istream` instance and is said to be "connected to" (or attached to) the *standard input device*, which usually is the keyboard. The stream extraction operator (>>) as used in the following statement causes a value for integer variable `grade` (assuming that `grade` has been declared as an `int` variable) to be input from `cin` to memory:

```
cin >> grade; // data "flows" in the direction of the arrows
```

The compiler determines the data type of `grade` and selects the appropriate overloaded stream extraction operator. Assuming that `grade` has been declared properly, the stream extraction operator does not require additional type information (as is the case, for example, in C-style I/O). The >> operator is overloaded to input data items of fundamental types, strings and pointer values.

The predefined object `cout` is an `ostream` instance and is said to be "connected to" the *standard output device*, which usually is the display screen. The stream insertion operator (<<), as used in the following statement, causes the value of variable `grade` to be output from memory to the standard output device:

```
cout << grade; // data "flows" in the direction of the arrows
```

The compiler determines the data type of `grade` (assuming `grade` has been declared properly) and selects the appropriate stream insertion operator. The << operator is overloaded to output data items of fundamental types, strings and pointer values.

---

1. This chapter discusses templates only in the context of the template specializations for `char` I/O.
2. Multiple inheritance is discussed in Chapter 21, Other Topics.

The predefined object `cerr` is an `ostream` instance and is said to be "connected to" the *standard error device,* normally the screen. Outputs to object `cerr` are **unbuffered,** implying that each stream insertion to `cerr` causes its output to appear *immediately*—this is appropriate for notifying a user promptly about errors.

The predefined object `clog` is an instance of the `ostream` class and is said to be "connected to" the *standard error device.* Outputs to `clog` are **buffered.** This means that each insertion to `clog` could cause its output to be held in a buffer (that is, an area in memory) until the buffer is filled or until the buffer is flushed. Buffering is an I/O performance-enhancement technique discussed in operating-systems courses.

File-Processing Templates

C++ file processing uses class templates **`basic_ifstream`** (for file input), **`basic_ofstream`** (for file output) and **`basic_fstream`** (for file input and output). As with the standard streams, C++ provides `typedef`s for working with these class templates. For example, the `typedef` **`ifstream`** represents a `basic_ifstream<char>` that enables `char` input from a file. Similarly, `typedef` **`ofstream`** represents a `basic_ofstream<char>` that enables `char` output to a file. Also, `typedef` **`fstream`** represents a `basic_fstream<char>` that enables `char` input from, and output to, a file. Template `basic_ifstream` inherits from `basic_istream`, `basic_ofstream` inherits from `basic_ostream` and `basic_fstream` inherits from `basic_iostream`. The UML class diagram of Fig. 13.2 summarizes the various inheritance relationships of the I/O-related classes. The full stream-I/O class hierarchy provides most of the capabilities that you need. Consult the class-library reference for your C++ system for additional file-processing information.

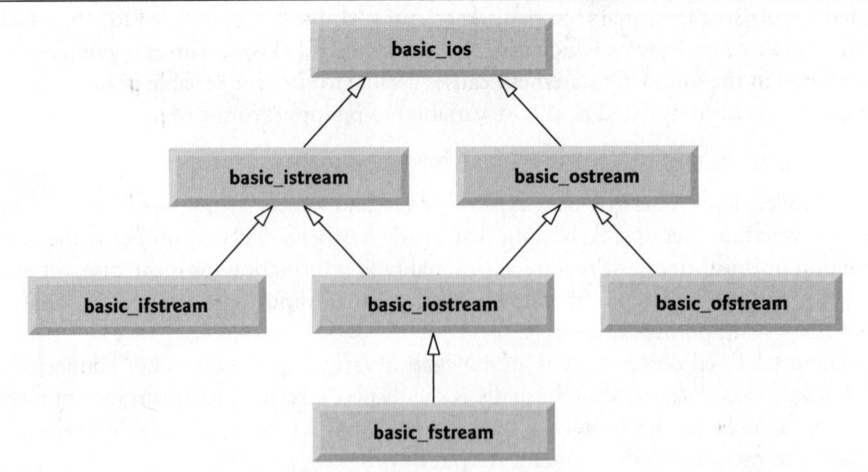

Fig. 13.2 | Stream-I/O template hierarchy portion showing the main file-processing templates.

13.3 Stream Output

Formatted and unformatted output capabilities are provided by `ostream`. Capabilities include output of standard data types with the stream insertion operator (<<); output of characters via the `put` member function; unformatted output via the `write` member function; output of integers in decimal, octal and hexadecimal formats; output of floating-point values with various precision, with forced decimal points, in scientific notation and in fixed notation; output of data justified in fields of designated widths; output of data in fields padded with specified characters; and output of uppercase letters in scientific notation and hexadecimal notation.

13.3.1 Output of char * Variables

C++ determines data types automatically—an improvement over C, but this feature sometimes "gets in the way." For example, suppose we want to print the address stored in a `char *` pointer. The << operator has been overloaded to output a `char *` as a *null-terminated C-style string*. To output the *address*, you can cast the `char *` to a `void *` (this can be done to any pointer variable). Figure 13.3 demonstrates printing a `char *` variable in both string and address formats. The address prints here as a hexadecimal (base-16) number—in general, the way addresses print is *implementation dependent*. To learn more about hexadecimal numbers, see Appendix D. We say more about controlling the bases of numbers in Section 13.6.1 and Section 13.7.4.

```cpp
// Fig. 13.3: fig13_03.cpp
// Printing the address stored in a char * variable.
#include <iostream>
using namespace std;

int main()
{
   const char *const word = "again";

   // display value of char *, then display value of char *
   // after a static_cast to void *
   cout << "Value of word is: " << word << endl
      << "Value of static_cast< const void * >( word ) is: "
      << static_cast< const void * >( word ) << endl;
} // end main
```

```
Value of word is: again
Value of static_cast< const void * >( word ) is: 0135CC70
```

Fig. 13.3 | Printing the address stored in a `char *` variable.

13.3.2 Character Output Using Member Function put

We can use the `put` member function to output characters. For example, the statement

```cpp
cout.put( 'A' );
```

displays a single character `A`. Calls to `put` may be *cascaded*, as in the statement

```cpp
cout.put( 'A' ).put( '\n' );
```

which outputs the letter `A` followed by a newline character. As with <<, the preceding statement executes in this manner, because the dot operator (.) associates from left to right, and the put member function returns a reference to the ostream object (cout) that received the put call. The put function also may be called with a numeric expression that represents an ASCII value, as in the following statement, which also outputs A:

```
cout.put( 65 );
```

13.4 Stream Input

Now let's consider stream input. Formatted and unformatted input capabilities are provided by istream. The stream extraction operator (>>) normally skips **white-space characters** (such as blanks, tabs and newlines) in the input stream; later we'll see how to change this behavior. After each input, the stream extraction operator returns a *reference* to the stream object that received the extraction message (e.g., cin in the expression cin >> grade). If that reference is used as a condition (e.g., in a while statement's loop-continuation condition), the stream's overloaded void * cast operator function is implicitly invoked to convert the reference into a non-null pointer value or the null pointer based on the success or failure, respectively, of the last input operation. A non-null pointer converts to the bool value true to indicate success and the null pointer converts to the bool value false to indicate failure. When an attempt is made to read past the end of a stream, the stream's overloaded void * cast operator returns the *null pointer* to indicate *end-of-file*.

Each stream object contains a set of **state bits** used to control the stream's state (i.e., formatting, setting error states, etc.). These bits are used by the stream's overloaded void * cast operator to determine whether to return a non-null pointer or the null pointer. Stream extraction causes the stream's **failbit** to be set if data of the wrong type is input and causes the stream's **badbit** to be set if the operation fails. Sections 13.7–13.8 discuss stream state bits in detail, then show how to test these bits after an I/O operation.

13.4.1 get and getline Member Functions

The **get** member function with *no arguments* inputs *one* character from the designated stream (including white-space characters and other nongraphic characters, such as the key sequence that represents end-of-file) and returns it as the value of the function call. This version of get returns EOF when *end-of-file* is encountered on the stream.

Using Member Functions eof*,* get *and* put

Figure 13.4 demonstrates the use of member functions eof and get on input stream cin and member function put on output stream cout. Recall from Chapter 5 that EOF is represented as an int. This program reads characters into the int variable character, so that we can test each character entered to see if it's EOF. The program first prints the value of cin.eof()—i.e., false (0 on the output)—to show that *end-of-file* has *not* occurred on cin. The user enters a line of text and presses *Enter* followed by end-of-file (*<Ctrl> z* on Microsoft Windows systems, *<Ctrl> d* on Linux and Mac systems). Line 15 reads each character, which line 16 outputs to cout using member function put. When end-of-file is encountered, the while statement ends, and line 20 displays the value of cin.eof(), which is now true (1 on the output), to show that end-of-file has been set on cin. This program uses the version of istream member function get that takes no arguments and returns the character being input (line 15). Function eof returns true only after the program attempts to read past the last character in the stream.

```
// Fig. 13.4: fig13_04.cpp
// get, put and eof member functions.
#include <iostream>
using namespace std;

int main()
{
   int character; // use int, because char cannot represent EOF

   // prompt user to enter line of text
   cout << "Before input, cin.eof() is " << cin.eof() << endl
      << "Enter a sentence followed by end-of-file:" << endl;

   // use get to read each character; use put to display it
   while ( ( character = cin.get() ) != EOF )
      cout.put( character );

   // display end-of-file character
   cout << "\nEOF in this system is: " << character << endl;
   cout << "After input of EOF, cin.eof() is " << cin.eof() << endl;
} // end main
```

```
Before input, cin.eof() is 0
Enter a sentence followed by end-of-file:
Testing the get and put member functions
Testing the get and put member functions
^Z

EOF in this system is: -1
After input of EOF, cin.eof() is 1
```

Fig. 13.4 | get, put and eof member functions.

The get member function with a character-reference argument inputs the next character from the input stream (even if this is a *white-space character*) and stores it in the character argument. This version of get returns a reference to the istream object for which the get member function is being invoked.

A third version of get takes three arguments—a built-in array of chars, a size limit and a delimiter (with default value '\n'). This version reads characters from the input stream. It either reads *one fewer* than the specified maximum number of characters and terminates or terminates as soon as the *delimiter* is read. A null character is inserted to terminate the input string in the character array used as a buffer by the program. The delimiter is not placed in the character array but *does remain in the input stream* (the delimiter will be the next character read). Thus, the result of a second consecutive get is an empty line, unless the delimiter character is removed from the input stream (possibly with cin.ignore()).

Comparing cin *and* cin.get

Figure 13.5 compares input using stream extraction with cin (which reads characters until a white-space character is encountered) and input using cin.get. The call to cin.get (line 22) does *not* specify a delimiter, so the *default* '\n' character is used.

```
// Fig. 13.5: fig13_05.cpp
// Contrasting input of a string via cin and cin.get.
#include <iostream>
using namespace std;

int main()
{
   // create two char arrays, each with 80 elements
   const int SIZE = 80;
   char buffer1[ SIZE ];
   char buffer2[ SIZE ];

   // use cin to input characters into buffer1
   cout << "Enter a sentence:" << endl;
   cin >> buffer1;

   // display buffer1 contents
   cout << "\nThe string read with cin was:" << endl
      << buffer1 << endl << endl;

   // use cin.get to input characters into buffer2
   cin.get( buffer2, SIZE );

   // display buffer2 contents
   cout << "The string read with cin.get was:" << endl
      << buffer2 << endl;
} // end main
```

```
Enter a sentence:
Contrasting string input with cin and cin.get

The string read with cin was:
Contrasting

The string read with cin.get was:
 string input with cin and cin.get
```

Fig. 13.5 | Contrasting input of a string via `cin` and `cin.get`.

Using Member Function `getline`

Member function **`getline`** operates similarly to the third version of the `get` member function and *inserts a null character* after the line in the built-in array of `char`s. The `getline` function removes the delimiter from the stream (i.e., reads the character and discards it), but does *not* store it in the character array. The program of Fig. 13.6 demonstrates the use of the `getline` member function to input a line of text (line 13).

```
1 // Fig. 13.6: fig13_06.cpp
2 // Inputting characters using cin member function getline.
3 #include <iostream>
4 using namespace std;
```

Fig. 13.6 | Inputting characters using `cin` member function `getline`. (Part 1 of 2.)

```
int main()
{
   const int SIZE = 80;
   char buffer[ SIZE ]; // create array of 80 characters

   // input characters in buffer via cin function getline
   cout << "Enter a sentence:" << endl;
   cin.getline( buffer, SIZE );

   // display buffer contents
   cout << "\nThe sentence entered is:" << endl << buffer << endl;
} // end main
```

```
Enter a sentence:
Using the getline member function

The sentence entered is:
Using the getline member function
```

Fig. 13.6 | Inputting characters using `cin` member function `getline`. (Part 2 of 2.)

13.4.2 `istream` Member Functions `peek`, `putback` and `ignore`

The **`ignore`** member function of `istream` reads and discards a designated number of characters (the default is *one*) or terminates upon encountering a designated delimiter (the default is `EOF`, which causes `ignore` to skip to the end of the file when reading from a file).

The **`putback`** member function places the previous character obtained by a `get` from an input stream back into that stream. This function is useful for applications that scan an input stream looking for a field beginning with a specific character. When that character is input, the application returns the character to the stream, so the character can be included in the input data.

The **`peek`** member function returns the next character from an input stream but does not remove the character from the stream.

13.4.3 Type-Safe I/O

C++ offers **type-safe I/O**. The << and >> operators are overloaded to accept data items of *specific* types. If unexpected data is processed, various error bits are set, which the user may test to determine whether an I/O operation succeeded or failed. If operators << and >> have not been overloaded for a user-defined type and you attempt to input into or output the contents of an object of that user-defined type, the compiler reports an error. This enables the program to "stay in control." We discuss these error states in Section 13.8.

13.5 Unformatted I/O Using `read`, `write` and `gcount`

Unformatted input/output is performed using the **`read`** and **`write`** member functions of `istream` and `ostream`, respectively. Member function `read` inputs *bytes* to a built-in array of `char`s in memory; member function `write` outputs bytes from a built-in array of `char`s. These bytes are *not formatted* in any way. They're input or output as raw bytes. For example, the call

```
char buffer[] = "HAPPY BIRTHDAY";
cout.write( buffer, 10 );
```

outputs the first 10 bytes of `buffer` (including null characters, if any, that would cause output with `cout` and `<<` to terminate). The call

```
cout.write( "ABCDEFGHIJKLMNOPQRSTUVWXYZ", 10 );
```

displays the first 10 characters of the alphabet.

The `read` member function inputs a designated number of characters into a built-in array of `char`s. If *fewer* than the designated number of characters are read, `failbit` is set. Section 13.8 shows how to determine whether `failbit` has been set. Member function **`gcount`** reports the number of characters read by the last input operation.

Figure 13.7 demonstrates `istream` member functions `read` and `gcount`, and `ostream` member function `write`. The program inputs 20 characters (from a longer input sequence) into the array `buffer` with `read` (line 13), determines the number of characters input with `gcount` (line 17) and outputs the characters in `buffer` with `write` (line 17).

```
1  // Fig. 13.7: fig13_07.cpp
2  // Unformatted I/O using read, gcount and write.
3  #include <iostream>
4  using namespace std;
5
6  int main()
7  {
8     const int SIZE = 80;
9     char buffer[ SIZE ]; // create array of 80 characters
10
11    // use function read to input characters into buffer
12    cout << "Enter a sentence:" << endl;
13    cin.read( buffer, 20 );
14
15    // use functions write and gcount to display buffer characters
16    cout << endl << "The sentence entered was:" << endl;
17    cout.write( buffer, cin.gcount() );
18    cout << endl;
19 } // end main
```

```
Enter a sentence:
Using the read, write, and gcount member functions
The sentence entered was:
Using the read, writ
```

Fig. 13.7 | Unformatted I/O using `read`, `gcount` and `write`.

13.6 Introduction to Stream Manipulators

C++ provides various **stream manipulators** that perform formatting tasks. The stream manipulators provide capabilities such as setting field widths, setting precision, setting and unsetting format state, setting the fill character in fields, flushing streams, inserting a newline into the output stream (and flushing the stream), inserting a null character into the output stream and skipping white space in the input stream. These features are described in the following sections.

13.6.1 Integral Stream Base: dec, oct, hex and setbase

Integers are interpreted normally as decimal (base-10) values. To change the base in which integers are interpreted on a stream, insert the **hex** manipulator to set the base to hexadecimal (base 16) or insert the **oct** manipulator to set the base to octal (base 8). Insert the **dec** manipulator to reset the stream base to decimal. These are all *sticky* manipulators.

A stream's base also may be changed by the **setbase** stream manipulator, which takes an `int` argument of `10`, `8`, or `16` to set the base to decimal, octal or hexadecimal, respectively. Because `setbase` takes an argument, it's called a *parameterized stream manipulator.* Parameterized stream manipulators like `setbase` require the header `<iomanip>`. The stream base value remains the same until changed explicitly; `setbase` settings are sticky. Figure 13.8 demonstrates stream manipulators `hex`, `oct`, `dec` and `setbase`. For more information on decimal, octal and hexadecimal numbers, see Appendix D.

```
// Fig. 13.8: fig13_08.cpp
// Using stream manipulators hex, oct, dec and setbase.
#include <iostream>
#include <iomanip>
using namespace std;

int main()
{
   int number;

   cout << "Enter a decimal number: ";
   cin >> number; // input number

   // use hex stream manipulator to show hexadecimal number
   cout << number << " in hexadecimal is: " << hex
      << number << endl;

   // use oct stream manipulator to show octal number
   cout << dec << number << " in octal is: "
      << oct << number << endl;

   // use setbase stream manipulator to show decimal number
   cout << setbase( 10 ) << number << " in decimal is: "
      << number << endl;
} // end main
```

```
Enter a decimal number: 20
20 in hexadecimal is: 14
20 in octal is: 24
20 in decimal is: 20
```

Fig. 13.8 | Using stream manipulators `hex`, `oct`, `dec` and `setbase`.

13.6.2 Floating-Point Precision (precision, setprecision)

We can control the **precision** of floating-point numbers (i.e., the number of digits to the right of the decimal point) by using either the `setprecision` stream manipulator or the **`precision`** member function of `ios_base`. A call to either of these sets the precision for all subsequent output operations until the next precision-setting call. A call to member function `precision` with no argument returns the current precision setting (this is what you need to use so that you can *restore the original precision* eventually after a sticky setting is no longer needed). The program of Fig. 13.9 uses both member function `precision` (line 22) and the `setprecision` manipulator (line 31) to print a table that shows the square root of 2, with precision varying from 0 to 9.

```
1  // Fig. 13.9: fig13_09.cpp
2  // Controlling precision of floating-point values.
3  #include <iostream>
4  #include <iomanip>
5  #include <cmath>
6  using namespace std;
7
8  int main()
9  {
10    double root2 = sqrt( 2.0 ); // calculate square root of 2
11    int places; // precision, vary from 0-9
12
13    cout << "Square root of 2 with precisions 0-9." << endl
14       << "Precision set by ios_base member function "
15       << "precision:" << endl;
16
17    cout << fixed; // use fixed-point notation
18
19    // display square root using ios_base function precision
20    for ( places = 0; places <= 9; ++places )
21    {
22       cout.precision( places );
23       cout << root2 << endl;
24    } // end for
25
26    cout << "\nPrecision set by stream manipulator "
27       << "setprecision:" << endl;
28
29    // set precision for each digit, then display square root
30    for ( places = 0; places <= 9; ++places )
31       cout << setprecision( places ) << root2 << endl;
32 } // end main
```

```
Square root of 2 with precisions 0-9.
Precision set by ios_base member function precision:
1
1.4
1.41
1.414
1.4142
1.41421
1.414214
1.4142136
1.41421356
1.414213562
```

Fig. 13.9 | Controlling precision of floating-point values. (Part 1 of 2.)

```
Precision set by stream manipulator setprecision:
1
1.4
1.41
1.414
1.4142
1.41421
1.414214
1.4142136
1.41421356
1.414213562
```

Fig. 13.9 | Controlling precision of floating-point values. (Part 2 of 2.)

13.6.3 Field Width (`width`, `setw`)

The **`width`** member function (of base class `ios_base`) sets the *field width* (i.e., the number of character positions in which a value should be output or the maximum number of characters that should be input) and *returns the previous width*. If values output are narrower than the field width, **fill characters** are inserted as **padding.** A value wider than the designated width will *not* be truncated—the *full number* will be printed. The `width` function with no argument returns the current setting.

Common Programming Error 13.1

The width setting applies only for the next insertion or extraction (i.e., the width setting is not sticky); afterward, the width is set implicitly to `0` *(that is,* input and output will be performed with default settings*). Assuming that the width setting applies to all subsequent outputs is a logic error.*

Common Programming Error 13.2

When a field is not *sufficiently wide to handle outputs, the outputs print as wide as necessary, which can yield confusing outputs.*

Figure 13.10 demonstrates the use of the `width` member function on both input and output. On input into a `char` array, *a maximum of one fewer characters than the width will be read,* because provision is made for the null character to be placed in the input string. Remember that stream extraction *terminates* when *nonleading white space* is encountered. The `setw` stream manipulator also may be used to set the field width. [*Note:* When prompted for input in Fig. 13.10, the user should enter a line of text and press *Enter* followed by end-of-file (<*Ctrl*> *z* on Microsoft Windows systems and <*Ctrl*> *d* on Linux and OS X systems).]

```
// Fig. 13.10: fig13_10.cpp
// width member function of class ios_base.
#include <iostream>
using namespace std;

```

Fig. 13.10 | `width` member function of class `ios_base`. (Part 1 of 2.)

```
int main()
{
   int widthValue = 4;
   char sentence[ 10 ];

   cout << "Enter a sentence:" << endl;
   cin.width( 5 ); // input only 5 characters from sentence

   // set field width, then display characters based on that width
   while ( cin >> sentence )
   {
      cout.width( widthValue++ );
      cout << sentence << endl;
      cin.width( 5 ); // input 5 more characters from sentence
   } // end while
} // end main
```

```
Enter a sentence:
This is a test of the width member function
This
   is
     a
   test
      of
      the
      widt
          h
        memb
           er
          func
           tion
```

Fig. 13.10 | `width` member function of class `ios_base`. (Part 2 of 2.)

13.6.4 User-Defined Output Stream Manipulators

You can create your own stream manipulators. Figure 13.11 shows how to create and use *new* nonparameterized stream manipulators `bell` (lines 8–11), `carriageReturn` (lines 14–17), `tab` (lines 20–23) and `endLine` (lines 27–30). For output stream manipulators, the return type and parameter must be of type `ostream &`. When line 35 inserts the `endLine` manipulator in the output stream, function `endLine` is called and line 29 outputs the escape sequence `\n` and the `flush` manipulator (which flushes the output buffer) to the standard output stream `cout`. Similarly, when lines 35–44 insert the manipulators `tab`, `bell` and `carriageReturn` in the output stream, their corresponding functions—`tab` (line 20), `bell` (line 8) and `carriageReturn` (line 14) are called, which in turn output various escape sequences.

```
1  // Fig. 13.11: fig13_11.cpp
2  // Creating and testing user-defined, nonparameterized
3  // stream manipulators.
4  #include <iostream>
5  using namespace std;
```

Fig. 13.11 | User-defined, nonparameterized stream manipulators. (Part 1 of 2.)

```

// bell manipulator (using escape sequence \a)
ostream& bell( ostream& output )
{
   return output << '\a'; // issue system beep
} // end bell manipulator

// carriageReturn manipulator (using escape sequence \r)
ostream& carriageReturn( ostream& output )
{
   return output << '\r'; // issue carriage return
} // end carriageReturn manipulator

// tab manipulator (using escape sequence \t)
ostream& tab( ostream& output )
{
   return output << '\t'; // issue tab
} // end tab manipulator

// endLine manipulator (using escape sequence \n and flush stream
// manipulator to simulate endl)
ostream& endLine( ostream& output )
{
   return output << '\n' << flush; // issue endl-like end of line
} // end endLine manipulator

int main()
{
   // use tab and endLine manipulators
   cout << "Testing the tab manipulator:" << endLine
      << 'a' << tab << 'b' << tab << 'c' << endLine;

   cout << "Testing the carriageReturn and bell manipulators:"
      << endLine << "..........";

   cout << bell; // use bell manipulator

   // use carriageReturn and endLine manipulators
   cout << carriageReturn << "-----" << endLine;
} // end main
```

```
Testing the tab manipulator:
a       b       c
Testing the carriageReturn and bell manipulators:
-----.....
```

Fig. 13.11 | User-defined, nonparameterized stream manipulators. (Part 2 of 2.)

13.7 Stream Format States and Stream Manipulators

Various stream manipulators can be used to specify the kinds of formatting to be performed during stream-I/O operations. Stream manipulators control the output's format settings. Figure 13.12 lists each stream manipulator that controls a given stream's format state. All these manipulators belong to class `ios_base`. We show examples of most of these stream manipulators in the next several sections.

Manipulator	Description
`skipws`	*Skip white-space characters* on an input stream. This setting is reset with stream manipulator `noskipws`.
`left`	*Left justify* output in a field. *Padding* characters appear to the *right* if necessary.
`right`	*Right justify* output in a field. Padding characters appear to the *left* if necessary.
`internal`	Indicate that a number's *sign* should be *left justified* in a field and a number's *magnitude* should be *right justified* in that same field (i.e., *padding* characters appear *between* the sign and the number).
`boolalpha`	Specify that `bool` *values* should be displayed as the word `true` or `false`. The manipulator `noboolalpha` sets the stream back to displaying bool values as 1 (true) and 0 (false).
`dec`	Specify that integers should be treated as *decimal* (base 10) values.
`oct`	Specify that integers should be treated as *octal* (base 8) values.
`hex`	Specify that integers should be treated as *hexadecimal* (base 16) values.
`showbase`	Specify that the *base* of a number is to be output *ahead* of the number (a leading `0` for octals; a leading `0x` or `0X` for hexadecimals). This setting is reset with stream manipulator `noshowbase`.
`showpoint`	Specify that floating-point numbers should be output with a *decimal point*. This is used normally with `fixed` to *guarantee* a certain number of digits to the *right* of the decimal point, even if they're zeros. This setting is reset with stream manipulator `noshowpoint`.
`uppercase`	Specify that *uppercase letters* (i.e., `X` and `A` through `F`) should be used in a *hexadecimal* integer and that *uppercase* `E` should be used when representing a floating-point value in *scientific notation*. This setting is reset with stream manipulator `nouppercase`.
`showpos`	Specify that *positive* numbers should be preceded by a plus sign (`+`). This setting is reset with stream manipulator `noshowpos`.
`scientific`	Specify output of a floating-point value in *scientific notation*.
`fixed`	Specify output of a floating-point value in *fixed-point notation* with a specific number of digits to the *right* of the decimal point.

Fig. 13.12 | Format state stream manipulators from `<iostream>`.

13.7.1 Trailing Zeros and Decimal Points (`showpoint`)

Stream manipulator **`showpoint`** is a sticky setting that forces a floating-point number to be output with its *decimal point* and *trailing zeros*. For example, the floating-point value `79.0` prints as `79` without using `showpoint` and prints as `79.000000` (or as many trailing zeros as are specified by the current *precision*) using `showpoint`. To reset the `showpoint` setting, output the stream manipulator **`noshowpoint`**. The program in Fig. 13.13 shows how to use stream manipulator `showpoint` to control the printing of *trailing zeros* and *decimal points* for floating-point values. Recall that the *default precision* of a floating-point number is 6. When neither the `fixed` nor the `scientific` stream manipulator is used, the precision represents the number of significant digits to display (i.e., the total number of digits to display), *not* the number of digits to display after decimal point.

```
// Fig. 13.13: fig13_13.cpp
// Controlling the printing of trailing zeros and
// decimal points in floating-point values.
#include <iostream>
using namespace std;

int main()
{
   // display double values with default stream format
   cout << "Before using showpoint" << endl
      << "9.9900 prints as: " << 9.9900 << endl
      << "9.9000 prints as: " << 9.9000 << endl
      << "9.0000 prints as: " << 9.0000 << endl << endl;

   // display double value after showpoint
   cout << showpoint
      << "After using showpoint" << endl
      << "9.9900 prints as: " << 9.9900 << endl
      << "9.9000 prints as: " << 9.9000 << endl
      << "9.0000 prints as: " << 9.0000 << endl;
} // end main
```

```
Before using showpoint
9.9900 prints as: 9.99
9.9000 prints as: 9.9
9.0000 prints as: 9

After using showpoint
9.9900 prints as: 9.99000
9.9000 prints as: 9.90000
9.0000 prints as: 9.00000
```

Fig. 13.13 | Controlling the printing of trailing zeros and decimal points in floating-point values.

13.7.2 Justification (`left`, `right` and `internal`)

Stream manipulators **`left`** and **`right`** enable fields to be *left justified* with *padding* characters to the *right* or *right justified* with *padding* characters to the *left*, respectively. The padding character is specified by the `fill` member function or the `setfill` parameterized stream manipulator (which we discuss in Section 13.7.3). Figure 13.14 uses the `setw`, `left` and `right` manipulators to left justify and right justify integer data in a field.

```
// Fig. 13.14: fig13_14.cpp
// Left and right justification with stream manipulators left and right.
#include <iostream>
```

Fig. 13.14 | Left and right justification with stream manipulators `left` and `right`. (Part 1 of 2.)

```
#include <iomanip>
using namespace std;

int main()
{
   int x = 12345;

   // display x right justified (default)
   cout << "Default is right justified:" << endl
      << setw( 10 ) << x;

   // use left manipulator to display x left justified
   cout << "\n\nUse std::left to left justify x:\n"
      << left << setw( 10 ) << x;

   // use right manipulator to display x right justified
   cout << "\n\nUse std::right to right justify x:\n"
      << right << setw( 10 ) << x << endl;
} // end main
```

```
Default is right justified:
     12345

Use std::left to left justify x:
12345

Use std::right to right justify x:
     12345
```

Fig. 13.14 | Left and right justification with stream manipulators `left` and `right`. (Part 2 of 2.)

Stream manipulator **`internal`** indicates that a number's *sign* (or *base* when using stream manipulator showbase) should be *left justified* within a field, that the number's *magnitude* should be *right justified* and that *intervening spaces* should be *padded* with the *fill character*. Figure 13.15 shows the `internal` stream manipulator specifying internal spacing (line 10). Note that **showpos** forces the plus sign to print (line 10). To reset the showpos setting, output the stream manipulator **noshowpos**.

```
1  // Fig. 13.15: fig13_15.cpp
2  // Printing an integer with internal spacing and plus sign.
3  #include <iostream>
4  #include <iomanip>
5  using namespace std;
6
7  int main()
8  {
9     // display value with internal spacing and plus sign
10    cout << internal << showpos << setw( 10 ) << 123 << endl;
11 } // end main
```

Fig. 13.15 | Printing an integer with internal spacing and plus sign. (Part 1 of 2.)

```
+      123
```

Fig. 13.15 | Printing an integer with internal spacing and plus sign. (Part 2 of 2.)

13.7.3 Padding (`fill`, `setfill`)

The `fill` **member function** specifies the *fill character* to be used with justified fields; *spaces* are used for padding by *default*. The function returns the prior padding character. The `setfill` **manipulator** also sets the *padding character*. Figure 13.16 demonstrates function `fill` (line 30) and stream manipulator `setfill` (lines 34 and 37) to set the fill character.

```
1  // Fig. 13.16: fig13_16.cpp
2  // Using member function fill and stream manipulator setfill to change
3  // the padding character for fields larger than the printed value.
4  #include <iostream>
5  #include <iomanip>
6  using namespace std;
7
8  int main()
9  {
10    int x = 10000;
11
12    // display x
13    cout << x << " printed as int right and left justified\n"
14       << "and as hex with internal justification.\n"
15       << "Using the default pad character (space):" << endl;
16
17    // display x with base
18    cout << showbase << setw( 10 ) << x << endl;
19
20    // display x with left justification
21    cout << left << setw( 10 ) << x << endl;
22
23    // display x as hex with internal justification
24    cout << internal << setw( 10 ) << hex << x << endl << endl;
25
26    cout << "Using various padding characters:" << endl;
27
28    // display x using padded characters (right justification)
29    cout << right;
30    cout.fill( '*' );
31    cout << setw( 10 ) << dec << x << endl;
32
33    // display x using padded characters (left justification)
34    cout << left << setw( 10 ) << setfill( '%' ) << x << endl;
35
36    // display x using padded characters (internal justification)
37    cout << internal << setw( 10 ) << setfill( '^' ) << hex
38       << x << endl;
39 } // end main
```

Fig. 13.16 | Using member function `fill` and stream manipulator `setfill` to change the padding character for fields larger than the printed values. (Part 1 of 2.)

```
10000 printed as int right and left justified
and as hex with internal justification.
Using the default pad character (space):
     10000
10000
0x    2710

Using various padding characters:
*****10000
10000%%%%%
0x^^^^2710
```

Fig. 13.16 | Using member function `fill` and stream manipulator `setfill` to change the padding character for fields larger than the printed values. (Part 2 of 2.)

13.7.4 Integral Stream Base (dec, oct, hex, showbase)

C++ provides stream manipulators **`dec`**, **`hex`** and **`oct`** to specify that integers are to be displayed as decimal, hexadecimal and octal values, respectively. Stream insertions *default* to *decimal* if none of these manipulators is used. With stream extraction, integers prefixed with `0` (zero) are treated as *octal* values, integers prefixed with `0x` or `0X` are treated as *hexadecimal* values, and all other integers are treated as *decimal* values. Once a particular base is specified for a stream, all integers on that stream are processed using that base until a different base is specified or until the program terminates.

Stream manipulator **`showbase`** forces the *base* of an integral value to be output. Decimal numbers are output by default, octal numbers are output with a leading `0`, and hexadecimal numbers are output with either a leading `0x` or a leading `0X` (as we discuss in Section 13.7.6, stream manipulator `uppercase` determines which option is chosen). Figure 13.17 demonstrates the use of stream manipulator `showbase` to force an integer to print in decimal, octal and hexadecimal formats. To reset the `showbase` setting, output the stream manipulator **`noshowbase`**.

```cpp
// Fig. 13.17: fig13_17.cpp
// Stream manipulator showbase.
#include <iostream>
using namespace std;

int main()
{
   int x = 100;

   // use showbase to show number base
   cout << "Printing integers preceded by their base:" << endl
      << showbase;

   cout << x << endl; // print decimal value
   cout << oct << x << endl; // print octal value
   cout << hex << x << endl; // print hexadecimal value
} // end main
```

Fig. 13.17 | Stream manipulator `showbase`. (Part 1 of 2.)

```
Printing integers preceded by their base:
100
0144
0x64
```

Fig. 13.17 | Stream manipulator showbase. (Part 2 of 2.)

13.7.5 Floating-Point Numbers; Scientific and Fixed Notation (scientific, fixed)

The sticky stream manipulators `scientific` and `fixed` control the output format of floating-point numbers. Stream manipulator **`scientific`** forces the output of a floating-point number to display in scientific format. Stream manipulator **`fixed`** forces a floating-point number to display a specific number of digits (as specified by member function `precision` or stream manipulator `setprecision`) to the right of the decimal point. Without using another manipulator, the floating-point-number value determines the output format.

Figure 13.18 demonstrates displaying floating-point numbers in fixed and scientific formats using stream manipulators `scientific` (line 18) and `fixed` (line 22). The exponent format in scientific notation might differ across different compilers.

```
1  // Fig. 13.18: fig13_18.cpp
2  // Floating-point values displayed in system default,
3  // scientific and fixed formats.
4  #include <iostream>
5  using namespace std;
6
7  int main()
8  {
9     double x = 0.001234567;
10    double y = 1.946e9;
11
12    // display x and y in default format
13    cout << "Displayed in default format:" << endl
14       << x << '\t' << y << endl;
15
16    // display x and y in scientific format
17    cout << "\nDisplayed in scientific format:" << endl
18       << scientific << x << '\t' << y << endl;
19
20    // display x and y in fixed format
21    cout << "\nDisplayed in fixed format:" << endl
22       << fixed << x << '\t' << y << endl;
23 } // end main
```

```
Displayed in default format:
0.00123457      1.946e+009

Displayed in scientific format:
1.234567e-003   1.946000e+009
```

Fig. 13.18 | Floating-point values displayed in default, scientific and fixed formats. (Part 1 of 2.)

```
Displayed in fixed format:
0.001235        1946000000.000000
```

Fig. 13.18 | Floating-point values displayed in default, scientific and fixed formats. (Part 2 of 2.)

13.7.6 Uppercase/Lowercase Control (uppercase)

Stream manipulator **uppercase** outputs an uppercase X or E with hexadecimal-integer values or with scientific notation floating-point values, respectively (Fig. 13.19). Using stream manipulator uppercase also causes all letters in a hexadecimal value to be uppercase. By *default*, the letters for hexadecimal values and the exponents in scientific notation floating-point values appear in *lowercase*. To reset the uppercase setting, output the stream manipulator **nouppercase**.

```cpp
// Fig. 13.19: fig13_19.cpp
// Stream manipulator uppercase.
#include <iostream>
using namespace std;

int main()
{
   cout << "Printing uppercase letters in scientific" << endl
      << "notation exponents and hexadecimal values:" << endl;

   // use std:uppercase to display uppercase letters; use std::hex and
   // std::showbase to display hexadecimal value and its base
   cout << uppercase << 4.345e10 << endl
      << hex << showbase << 123456789 << endl;
} // end main
```

```
Printing uppercase letters in scientific
notation exponents and hexadecimal values:
4.345E+010
0X75BCD15
```

Fig. 13.19 | Stream manipulator uppercase.

13.7.7 Specifying Boolean Format (boolalpha)

C++ provides data type bool, whose values may be false or true, as a preferred alternative to the old style of using 0 to indicate false and nonzero to indicate true. A bool variable outputs as 0 or 1 by *default*. However, we can use stream manipulator **boolalpha** to set the output stream to display bool values as the strings "true" and "false". Use stream manipulator **noboolalpha** to set the output stream to display bool values as integers (i.e., the default setting). The program of Fig. 13.20 demonstrates these stream manipulators. Line 11 displays the bool value, which line 8 sets to true, as an integer. Line 15 uses manipulator boolalpha to display the bool value as a string. Lines 18–19 then change the bool's value and use manipulator noboolalpha, so line 22 can display the bool value as an integer. Line 26 uses manipulator boolalpha to display the bool value as a string. Both boolalpha and noboolalpha are sticky settings.

Good Programming Practice 13.1

Displaying `bool` *values as* `true` *or* `false`*, rather than nonzero or 0, respectively, makes program outputs clearer.*

```
// Fig. 13.20: fig13_20.cpp
// Stream manipulators boolalpha and noboolalpha.
#include <iostream>
using namespace std;

int main()
{
   bool booleanValue = true;

   // display default true booleanValue
   cout << "booleanValue is " << booleanValue << endl;

   // display booleanValue after using boolalpha
   cout << "booleanValue (after using boolalpha) is "
      << boolalpha << booleanValue << endl << endl;

   cout << "switch booleanValue and use noboolalpha" << endl;
   booleanValue = false; // change booleanValue
   cout << noboolalpha << endl; // use noboolalpha

   // display default false booleanValue after using noboolalpha
   cout << "booleanValue is " << booleanValue << endl;

   // display booleanValue after using boolalpha again
   cout << "booleanValue (after using boolalpha) is "
      << boolalpha << booleanValue << endl;
} // end main
```

```
booleanValue is 1
booleanValue (after using boolalpha) is true

switch booleanValue and use noboolalpha

booleanValue is 0
booleanValue (after using boolalpha) is false
```

Fig. 13.20 | Stream manipulators `boolalpha` and `noboolalpha`.

13.7.8 Setting and Resetting the Format State via Member Function `flags`

Throughout Section 13.7, we've been using stream manipulators to change output format characteristics. We now discuss how to return an output stream's format to its default state after having applied several manipulations. Member function **`flags`** without an argument returns the current format settings as an **`fmtflags`** data type (of class `ios_base`), which represents the **format state**. Member function `flags` with an `fmtflags` argument sets the format state as specified by the argument and returns the prior state settings. The initial settings of the value that `flags` returns might differ across several systems. The program of Fig. 13.21 uses member function `flags` to save the stream's original format state (line 17), then restore the original format settings (line 25).

```
1  // Fig. 13.21: fig13_21.cpp
2  // flags member function.
3  #include <iostream>
4  using namespace std;
5
6  int main()
7  {
8     int integerValue = 1000;
9     double doubleValue = 0.0947628;
10
11    // display flags value, int and double values (original format)
12    cout << "The value of the flags variable is: " << cout.flags()
13       << "\nPrint int and double in original format:\n"
14       << integerValue << '\t' << doubleValue << endl << endl;
15
16    // use cout flags function to save original format
17    ios_base::fmtflags originalFormat = cout.flags();
18    cout << showbase << oct << scientific; // change format
19
20    // display flags value, int and double values (new format)
21    cout << "The value of the flags variable is: " << cout.flags()
22       << "\nPrint int and double in a new format:\n"
23       << integerValue << '\t' << doubleValue << endl << endl;
24
25    cout.flags( originalFormat ); // restore format
26
27    // display flags value, int and double values (original format)
28    cout << "The restored value of the flags variable is: "
29       << cout.flags()
30       << "\nPrint values in original format again:\n"
31       << integerValue << '\t' << doubleValue << endl;
32 } // end main
```

```
The value of the flags variable is: 513
Print int and double in original format:
1000    0.0947628

The value of the flags variable is: 012011
Print int and double in a new format:
01750   9.476280e-002

The restored value of the flags variable is: 513
Print values in original format again:
1000    0.0947628
```

Fig. 13.21 | `flags` member function.

13.8 Stream Error States

The state of a stream may be tested through bits in class `ios_base`. Earlier in the book, we indicated that you can test, for example, whether an input was successful. Figure 13.22

shows how to test these state bits. In industrial-strength code, you'll want to perform similar tests on your I/O operations.

```cpp
// Fig. 13.22: fig13_22.cpp
// Testing error states.
#include <iostream>
using namespace std;

int main()
{
   int integerValue;

   // display results of cin functions
   cout << "Before a bad input operation:"
      << "\ncin.rdstate(): " << cin.rdstate()
      << "\n    cin.eof(): " << cin.eof()
      << "\n   cin.fail(): " << cin.fail()
      << "\n    cin.bad(): " << cin.bad()
      << "\n   cin.good(): " << cin.good()
      << "\n\nExpects an integer, but enter a character: ";

   cin >> integerValue; // enter character value
   cout << endl;

   // display results of cin functions after bad input
   cout << "After a bad input operation:"
      << "\ncin.rdstate(): " << cin.rdstate()
      << "\n    cin.eof(): " << cin.eof()
      << "\n   cin.fail(): " << cin.fail()
      << "\n    cin.bad(): " << cin.bad()
      << "\n   cin.good(): " << cin.good() << endl << endl;

   cin.clear(); // clear stream

   // display results of cin functions after clearing cin
   cout << "After cin.clear()" << "\ncin.fail(): " << cin.fail()
      << "\ncin.good(): " << cin.good() << endl;
} // end main
```

```
Before a bad input operation:
cin.rdstate(): 0
    cin.eof(): 0
   cin.fail(): 0
    cin.bad(): 0
   cin.good(): 1

Expects an integer, but enter a character: A

After a bad input operation:
cin.rdstate(): 2
    cin.eof(): 0
   cin.fail(): 1
```

Fig. 13.22 | Testing error states. (Part 1 of 2.)

```
   cin.bad(): 0
  cin.good(): 0

After cin.clear()
cin.fail(): 0
cin.good(): 1
```

Fig. 13.22 | Testing error states. (Part 2 of 2.)

The **eofbit** is set for an input stream after *end-of-file* is encountered. A program can use member function **eof** to determine whether end-of-file has been encountered on a stream after an attempt to extract data *beyond* the end of the stream. The call

```
cin.eof()
```

returns `true` if end-of-file has been encountered on `cin` and `false` otherwise.

The `failbit` is set for a stream when a *format error* occurs on the stream and no characters are input (e.g., when you attempt to read a *number* and the user enters a *string*). When such an error occurs, the characters are *not* lost. The **fail** member function reports whether a stream operation has failed. Usually, recovering from such errors is possible.

The `badbit` is set for a stream when an error occurs that results in the *loss of data*. The **bad** member function reports whether a stream operation *failed*. Generally, such serious failures are nonrecoverable.

The **goodbit** is set for a stream if *none* of the bits `eofbit`, `failbit` or `badbit` is set for the stream.

The **good** member function returns `true` if the `bad`, `fail` and `eof` functions would *all* return `false`. I/O operations should be performed only on "good" streams.

The **rdstate** member function returns the stream's *error state*. Calling `cout.rdstate`, for example, would return the stream's state, which then could be tested by a `switch` statement that examines `eofbit`, `badbit`, `failbit` and `goodbit`. The *preferred* means of testing the state of a stream is to use member functions `eof`, `bad`, `fail` and `good`—using these functions does not require you to be familiar with particular status bits.

The **clear** member function is used to *restore* a stream's state to "good," so that I/O may proceed on that stream. The default argument for `clear` is `goodbit`, so the statement

```
cin.clear();
```

clears `cin` and sets `goodbit` for the stream. The statement

```
cin.clear( ios::failbit )
```

sets the `failbit`. You might want to do this when performing input on `cin` with a user-defined type and encountering a problem. The name `clear` might seem inappropriate in this context, but it's correct.

The program of Fig. 13.22 demonstrates member functions `rdstate`, `eof`, `fail`, `bad`, `good` and `clear`. The actual values output may differ across different compilers.

The `operator!` member function of `basic_ios` returns `true` if the `badbit` is set, the `failbit` is set or *both* are set. The `operator void *` member function returns `false` (`0`) if the `badbit` is set, the `failbit` is set or both are set. These functions are useful in file processing when a `true`/`false` condition is being tested under the control of a selection statement or repetition statement.

13.9 Tying an Output Stream to an Input Stream

Interactive applications generally involve an `istream` for input *and* an `ostream` for output. When a prompting message appears on the screen, the user responds by entering the appropriate data. Obviously, the prompt needs to appear *before* the input operation proceeds. With output buffering, outputs appear only when the buffer *fills*, when outputs are *flushed* explicitly by the program or automatically at the end of the program. C++ provides member function **`tie`** to synchronize (i.e., "tie together") the operation of an `istream` and an `ostream` to ensure that outputs appear *before* their subsequent inputs. The call

```
cin.tie( &cout );
```

ties `cout` (an `ostream`) to `cin` (an `istream`). Actually, this particular call is redundant, because C++ performs this operation automatically to create a user's standard input/output environment. However, the user would tie other `istream`/`ostream` pairs explicitly. To untie an input stream, `inputStream`, from an output stream, use the call

```
inputStream.tie( 0 );
```

13.10 Wrap-Up

This chapter summarized how C++ performs input/output using streams. You learned about the stream-I/O classes and objects, as well as the stream I/O template class hierarchy. We discussed `ostream`'s formatted and unformatted output capabilities performed by the `put` and `write` functions. You learned about `istream`'s formatted and unformatted input capabilities performed by the `eof`, `get`, `getline`, `peek`, `putback`, `ignore` and `read` functions. We discussed stream manipulators and member functions that perform formatting tasks—`dec`, `oct`, `hex` and `setbase` for displaying integers; `precision` and `setprecision` for controlling floating-point precision; and `width` and `setw` for setting field width. You also learned additional formatting `iostream` manipulators and member functions—`showpoint` for displaying decimal point and trailing zeros; `left`, `right` and `internal` for justification; `fill` and `setfill` for padding; `scientific` and `fixed` for displaying floating-point numbers in scientific and fixed notation; `uppercase` for uppercase/lowercase control; `boolalpha` for specifying boolean format; and `flags` and `fmtflags` for resetting the format state.

In the next chapter, you'll learn about file processing, including how persistent data is stored and how to manipulate it.

14

File Processing

Objectives

In this chapter you'll:

- Create, read, write and update files.
- Use sequential file processing.
- Use random-access file processing.
- Use high-performance unformatted I/O operations.
- Learn the differences between formatted-data and raw-data file processing.
- Build a transaction-processing program using random-access file processing.
- Understand the concept of object serialization.

Outline

14.1 Introduction

Storage of data in memory is *temporary*. **Files** are used for **data persistence**—*permanent* retention of data. Computers store files on **secondary storage devices**, such as hard disks, CDs, DVDs, flash drives and tapes. In this chapter, we explain how to build C++ programs that create, update and process data files. We consider both *sequential files* and *random-access files*. We compare *formatted-data* file processing and *raw-data* file processing. We examine techniques for input of data from, and output of data to, `string` streams rather than files in Chapter 19.

14.2 Files and Streams

C++ views each file simply as *a sequence of bytes* (Fig. 14.1). Each file ends either with an **end-of-file marker** or at a specific byte number recorded in an operating-system-maintained, administrative data structure. When a file is *opened*, an object is created, and a stream is associated with the object. In Chapter 13, we saw that objects `cin`, `cout`, `cerr` and `clog` are created when `<iostream>` is included. The streams associated with these objects provide communication channels between a program and a particular file or device. For example, the `cin` object (standard input stream object) enables a program to input data from the keyboard or from other devices, the `cout` object (standard output stream object) enables a program to output data to the screen or other devices, and the `cerr` and `clog` objects (standard error stream objects) enable a program to output error messages to the screen or other devices.

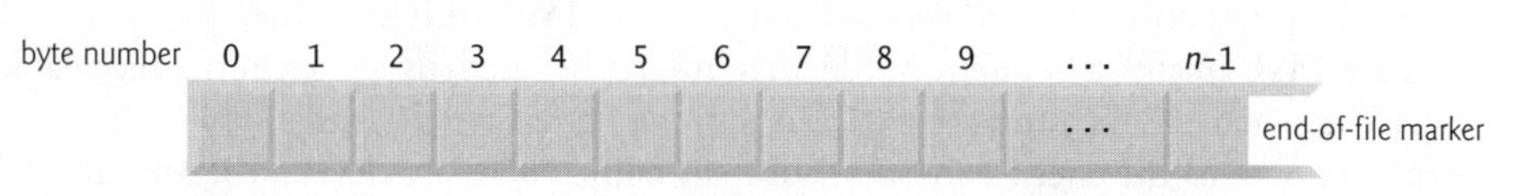

Fig. 14.1 | C++'s simple view of a file of *n* bytes.

File-Processing Class Templates

To perform file processing in C++, headers `<iostream>` and `<fstream>` must be included. Header `<fstream>` includes the definitions for the stream class templates `basic_ifstream` (for file input), `basic_ofstream` (for file output) and `basic_fstream` (for file input *and* output). Each class template has a predefined template specialization that enables `char` I/O. In addition, the `<fstream>` library provides `typedef` aliases for these template specializations. For example, the `typedef ifstream` represents a specialization of `basic_ifstream` that enables `char` input from a file. Similarly, `typedef ofstream` represents a specialization of `basic_ofstream` that enables `char` output to files. Also, `typedef fstream` represents a specialization of `basic_fstream` that enables `char` input from, *and* output to, files.

These templates derive from the class templates `basic_istream`, `basic_ostream` and `basic_iostream`, respectively. Thus, all member functions, operators and manipulators that belong to these templates (which we described in Chapter 13) also can be applied to file streams. Figure 14.2 summarizes the inheritance relationships of the I/O classes that we've discussed to this point.

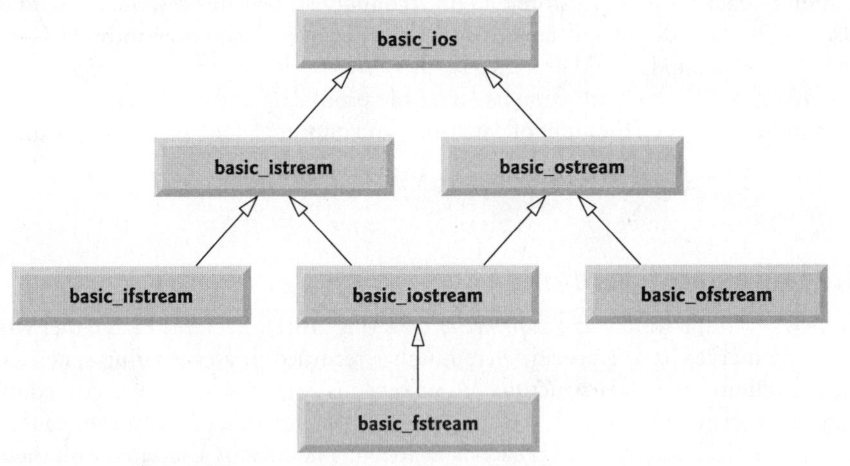

Fig. 14.2 | Portion of stream I/O template hierarchy.

14.3 Creating a Sequential File

C++ imposes no structure on a file. Thus, a concept like that of a "record" does not exist in a C++ file. You must structure files to meet the application's requirements. The following example shows how you can impose a simple record structure on a file.

Figure 14.3 creates a sequential file that might be used in an accounts-receivable system to help manage the money owed to a company by its credit clients. For each client, the program obtains the client's account number, name and balance (i.e., the amount the client owes the company for goods and services received in the past). The data obtained for each client constitutes a *record* for that client. The account number serves as the *record key*; that is, the program creates and maintains the records of the file in account number order. This program assumes the user enters the records in account number order. In a comprehensive accounts receivable system, a sorting capability would be provided for the user to enter records *in any* order—the records then would be *sorted* and written to the file.

```
1  // Fig. 14.3: Fig14_03.cpp
2  // Create a sequential file.
3  #include <iostream>
4  #include <string>
5  #include <fstream> // contains file stream processing types
6  #include <cstdlib> // exit function prototype
7  using namespace std;
8
9  int main()
10 {
11    // ofstream constructor opens file
12    ofstream outClientFile( "clients.txt", ios::out );
13
14    // exit program if unable to create file
15    if ( !outClientFile ) // overloaded ! operator
16    {
17       cerr << "File could not be opened" << endl;
18       exit( EXIT_FAILURE );
19    } // end if
20
21    cout << "Enter the account, name, and balance." << endl
22       << "Enter end-of-file to end input.\n? ";
23
24    int account; // the account number
25    string name; // the account owner's name
26    double balance; // the account balance
27
28    // read account, name and balance from cin, then place in file
29    while ( cin >> account >> name >> balance )
30    {
31       outClientFile << account << ' ' << name << ' ' << balance << endl;
32       cout << "? ";
33    } // end while
34 } // end main
```

```
Enter the account, name, and balance.
Enter end-of-file to end input.
? 100 Jones 24.98
? 200 Doe 345.67
? 300 White 0.00
? 400 Stone -42.16
? 500 Rich 224.62
? ^Z
```

Fig. 14.3 | Create a sequential file.

Opening a File

Figure 14.3 writes data to a file, so we open the file for output by creating an `ofstream` object. Two arguments are passed to the object's constructor—the **filename** and the **file-open mode** (line 12). For an `ofstream` object, the file-open mode can be either **`ios::out`** (the default) to *output* data to a file or **`ios::app`** to *append* data to the end of a file (without modifying any data already in the file). Since `ios::out` is the default, the second constructor argument in line 12 is not required. Existing files opened with mode `ios::out` are

truncated—all data in the file is *discarded*. If the specified file does *not* yet exist, then the `ofstream` object *creates* the file, using that filename. Prior to C++11, the filename was specified as a pointer-based string—as of C++11, it can also be specified as a `string` object.

Error-Prevention Tip 14.1

Use caution when opening an existing file for output (`ios::out`), especially when you want to preserve the file's contents, which will be discarded without warning.

Line 12 creates an `ofstream` object named `outClientFile` associated with the file `clients.txt` that's opened for output. The arguments `"clients.txt"` and `ios::out` are passed to the `ofstream` constructor, which opens the file—this establishes a "line of communication" with the file. By *default*, `ofstream` objects are opened for *output*, so line 12 could have used the alternate statement

```
ofstream outClientFile( "clients.txt" );
```

to open `clients.txt` for output. Figure 14.4 lists the file-open modes. These modes can also be combined, as we discuss in Section 14.8.

Mode	Description
`ios::app`	*Append* all output to the end of the file.
`ios::ate`	Open a file for output and move to the end of the file (normally used to append data to a file). Data can be written *anywhere* in the file.
`ios::in`	Open a file for *input*.
`ios::out`	Open a file for *output*.
`ios::trunc`	*Discard* the file's contents (this also is the default action for `ios::out`).
`ios::binary`	Open a file for binary, i.e., *nontext*, input or output.

Fig. 14.4 | File open modes.

Opening a File via the **open** *Member Function*

You can create an `ofstream` object *without* opening a specific file—in this case, a file can be attached to the object later. For example, the statement

```
ofstream outClientFile;
```

creates an `ofstream` object that's not yet associated with a file. The `ofstream` member function **open** opens a file and attaches it to an *existing* `ofstream` object as follows:

```
outClientFile.open( "clients.txt", ios::out );
```

Error-Prevention Tip 14.2

Some operating systems allow you to open the same file multiple times simultaneously. Avoid doing this because it can lead to subtle problems.

Testing Whether a File Was Opened Successfully

After creating an `ofstream` object and *attempting* to open it, the program tests whether the open operation was *successful*. The `if` statement in lines 15–19 uses the *overloaded* `ios` member function operator! to determine whether the open operation succeeded. The condition returns a true value if either the failbit or the badbit (see Chapter 13) is set for the stream on the open operation. Some possible errors are attempting to open a *non-existent* file for reading, attempting to open a file for reading or writing from a directory that you don't have permission to access, and opening a file for writing when no disk space is available.

If the condition indicates an unsuccessful attempt to open the file, line 17 outputs the error message "File could not be opened", and line 18 invokes function exit to terminate the program. The argument to exit is returned to the environment from which the program was invoked. Passing EXIT_SUCCESS (also defined in <cstdlib>) to exit indicates that the program terminated *normally*; passing any other value (in this case EXIT_FAILURE) indicates that the program terminated due to an *error*.

The Overloaded void * *Operator*

Another *overloaded* ios member function—operator void *—converts the stream to a pointer, so it can be tested as 0 (i.e., the null pointer) or nonzero (i.e., any other pointer value). When a pointer value is used as a condition, C++ interprets a null pointer in a condition as the bool value false and interprets a non-null pointer as the bool value true. If the failbit or badbit has been set for the stream, 0 (false) is returned. The condition in the while statement of lines 29–33 invokes the operator void * member function on cin *implicitly*. The condition remains true as long as neither the failbit nor the badbit has been set for cin. Entering the *end-of-file* indicator sets the failbit for cin. The operator void * function can be used to test an input object for end-of-file, but you can also call member function eof on the input object.

Processing Data

If line 12 opens the file successfully, the program begins processing data. Lines 21–22 prompt the user to enter either the various fields for each record or the end-of-file indicator when data entry is complete. Figure 14.5 lists the keyboard combinations for entering end-of-file for various computer systems.

Computer system	Keyboard combination
UNIX/Linux/Mac OS X	*<Ctrl-d>* (on a line by itself)
Microsoft Windows	*<Ctrl-z>* (sometimes followed by pressing *Enter*)

Fig. 14.5 | End-of-file key combinations.

Line 29 extracts each set of data and determines whether end-of-file has been entered. When end-of-file is encountered or bad data is entered, operator void * returns the null pointer (which converts to the bool value false) and the while statement terminates. The user enters end-of-file to inform the program to process no additional data. The end-of-file indicator is set when the user enters the end-of-file key combination. The while statement loops until the end-of-file indicator is set (or bad data is entered).

Line 31 writes a set of data to the file clients.txt, using the stream insertion operator << and the outClientFile object associated with the file at the beginning of the program. The data may be retrieved by a program designed to read the file (see Section 14.4). The file created in Fig. 14.3 is simply a *text file*, so it can be viewed by any text editor.

Closing a File

Once the user enters the end-of-file indicator, `main` terminates. This implicitly invokes `outClientFile`'s destructor, which *closes* the `clients.txt` file. You also can close the `ofstream` object *explicitly*, using member function **`close`** as follows:

```
outClientFile.close();
```

Error-Prevention Tip 14.3

Always close a file as soon as it's no longer needed in a program

The Sample Execution

In the sample execution for the program of Fig. 14.3, the user enters information for five accounts, then signals that data entry is complete by entering end-of-file (`^Z` is displayed for Microsoft Windows). This dialog window does *not* show how the data records appear in the file. To verify that the program created the file successfully, the next section shows how to create a program that reads this file and prints its contents.

14.4 Reading Data from a Sequential File

Files store data so it may be *retrieved* for processing when needed. The previous section demonstrated how to create a file for sequential access. We now discuss how to *read* data sequentially from a file. Figure 14.6 reads and displays the records from the `clients.txt` file that we created using the program of Fig. 14.3. Creating an `ifstream` object opens a file for *input*. The `ifstream` constructor can receive the filename and the file open mode as arguments. Line 15 creates an `ifstream` object called `inClientFile` and associates it with the `clients.txt` file. The arguments in parentheses are passed to the `ifstream` constructor, which opens the file and establishes a "line of communication" with the file.

Good Programming Practice 14.1

If a file's contents should not *be modified, use* **`ios::in`** *to open it* only *for input. This prevents unintentional modification of the file's contents and is another example of the principle of least privilege.*

```
1  // Fig. 14.6: Fig14_06.cpp
2  // Reading and printing a sequential file.
3  #include <iostream>
4  #include <fstream> // file stream
5  #include <iomanip>
6  #include <string>
7  #include <cstdlib>
8  using namespace std;
9
10 void outputLine( int, const string &, double ); // prototype
```

Fig. 14.6 | Reading and printing a sequential file. (Part 1 of 2.)

```

int main()
{
   // ifstream constructor opens the file
   ifstream inClientFile( "clients.txt", ios::in );

   // exit program if ifstream could not open file
   if ( !inClientFile )
   {
      cerr << "File could not be opened" << endl;
      exit( EXIT_FAILURE );
   } // end if

   int account; // the account number
   string name; // the account owner's name
   double balance; // the account balance

   cout << left << setw( 10 ) << "Account" << setw( 13 )
      << "Name" << "Balance" << endl << fixed << showpoint;

   // display each record in file
   while ( inClientFile >> account >> name >> balance )
      outputLine( account, name, balance );
} // end main

// display single record from file
void outputLine( int account, const string &name, double balance )
{
   cout << left << setw( 10 ) << account << setw( 13 ) << name
      << setw( 7 ) << setprecision( 2 ) << right << balance << endl;
} // end function outputLine
```

```
Account   Name         Balance
100       Jones          24.98
200       Doe           345.67
300       White           0.00
400       Stone         -42.16
500       Rich          224.62
```

Fig. 14.6 | Reading and printing a sequential file. (Part 2 of 2.)

Opening a File for Input

Objects of class `ifstream` are opened for *input* by default, so the statement

```
ifstream inClientFile( "clients.txt" );
```

opens `clients.txt` for input. Just as with an `ofstream` object, an `ifstream` object can be created without opening a specific file, because a file can be attached to it later.

Ensuring That the File Was Opened

Before attempting to retrieve data from the file, the program uses the condition `!inClientFile` to determine whether the file was opened successfully.

Reading from the File

Line 32 reads a set of data (i.e., a record) from the file. After line 32 executes the first time, `account` has the value `100`, `name` has the value `"Jones"` and `balance` has the value `24.98`. Each time line 32 executes, it reads another record from the file into the variables `account`, `name` and `balance`. Line 33 displays the records, using function `outputLine` (lines 37–41), which uses parameterized stream manipulators to format the data for display. When the end of file has been reached, the *implicit call to* `operator void *` *in the* `while` *condition* returns the null pointer (which converts to the `bool` value `false`), the `ifstream` destructor closes the file and the program terminates.

File Position Pointers

To retrieve data sequentially from a file, programs normally start reading from the beginning of the file and read all the data consecutively until the desired data is found. It might be necessary to process the file sequentially several times (from the beginning of the file) during the execution of a program. Both `istream` and `ostream` provide member functions for *repositioning the file-position pointer* (the byte number of the next byte in the file to be read or written). These member functions are **`seekg`** ("seek get") for `istream` and **`seekp`** ("seek put") for `ostream`. Each `istream` object has a *get pointer*, which indicates the byte number in the file from which the next *input* is to occur, and each `ostream` object has a *put pointer*, which indicates the byte number in the file at which the next *output* should be placed. The statement

```
inClientFile.seekg( 0 );
```

repositions the file-position pointer to the *beginning* of the file (location `0`) attached to `inClientFile`. The argument to `seekg` is a `long` integer. A second argument can be specified to indicate the **seek direction**, which can be **`ios::beg`** (the default) for positioning relative to the *beginning* of a stream, **`ios::cur`** for positioning relative to the *current position* in a stream or **`ios::end`** for positioning relative to the *end* of a stream. The file-position pointer is an integer value that specifies the location in the file as a number of bytes from the file's starting location (this is also referred to as the **offset** from the beginning of the file). Some examples of positioning the *get* file-position pointer are

```
// position to the nth byte of fileObject (assumes ios::beg)
fileObject.seekg( n );

// position n bytes forward in fileObject
fileObject.seekg( n, ios::cur );

// position n bytes back from end of fileObject
fileObject.seekg( n, ios::end );

// position at end of fileObject
fileObject.seekg( 0, ios::end );
```

The same operations can be performed using `ostream` member function `seekp`. Member functions **`tellg`** and **`tellp`** are provided to return the current locations of the *get* and *put* pointers, respectively. The following statement assigns the *get* file-position pointer value to variable `location` of type `long`:

```
location = fileObject.tellg();
```

Credit Inquiry Program

Figure 14.7 enables a credit manager to display the account information for those customers with zero balances (i.e., customers who do not owe the company any money), credit (negative) balances (i.e., customers to whom the company owes money), and debit (positive) balances (i.e., customers who owe the company money for goods and services received in the past). The program displays a menu and allows the credit manager to enter one of three options to obtain credit information. Option 1 produces a list of accounts with zero balances. Option 2 produces a list of accounts with credit balances. Option 3 produces a list of accounts with debit balances. Option 4 terminates program execution. Entering an invalid option displays the prompt to enter another choice. Lines 64–65 enable the program to read from the beginning of the file after end-of-file has been read.

```
1   // Fig. 14.7: Fig14_07.cpp
2   // Credit inquiry program.
3   #include <iostream>
4   #include <fstream>
5   #include <iomanip>
6   #include <string>
7   #include <cstdlib>
8   using namespace std;
9
10  enum RequestType { ZERO_BALANCE = 1, CREDIT_BALANCE, DEBIT_BALANCE, END };
11  int getRequest();
12  bool shouldDisplay( int, double );
13  void outputLine( int, const string &, double );
14
15  int main()
16  {
17     // ifstream constructor opens the file
18     ifstream inClientFile( "clients.txt", ios::in );
19
20     // exit program if ifstream could not open file
21     if ( !inClientFile )
22     {
23        cerr << "File could not be opened" << endl;
24        exit( EXIT_FAILURE );
25     } // end if
26
27     int account; // the account number
28     string name; // the account owner's name
29     double balance; // the account balance
30
31     // get user's request (e.g., zero, credit or debit balance)
32     int request = getRequest();
33
34     // process user's request
35     while ( request != END )
36     {
37        switch ( request )
38        {
```

Fig. 14.7 | Credit inquiry program. (Part 1 of 4.)

```
         case ZERO_BALANCE:
            cout << "\nAccounts with zero balances:\n";
            break;
         case CREDIT_BALANCE:
            cout << "\nAccounts with credit balances:\n";
            break;
         case DEBIT_BALANCE:
            cout << "\nAccounts with debit balances:\n";
            break;
      } // end switch

      // read account, name and balance from file
      inClientFile >> account >> name >> balance;

      // display file contents (until eof)
      while ( !inClientFile.eof() )
      {
         // display record
         if ( shouldDisplay( request, balance ) )
            outputLine( account, name, balance );

         // read account, name and balance from file
         inClientFile >> account >> name >> balance;
      } // end inner while

      inClientFile.clear(); // reset eof for next input
      inClientFile.seekg( 0 ); // reposition to beginning of file
      request = getRequest(); // get additional request from user
   } // end outer while

   cout << "End of run." << endl;
} // end main

// obtain request from user
int getRequest()
{
   int request; // request from user

   // display request options
   cout << "\nEnter request" << endl
      << " 1 - List accounts with zero balances" << endl
      << " 2 - List accounts with credit balances" << endl
      << " 3 - List accounts with debit balances" << endl
      << " 4 - End of run" << fixed << showpoint;

   do // input user request
   {
      cout << "\n? ";
      cin >> request;
   } while ( request < ZERO_BALANCE && request > END );

   return request;
} // end function getRequest
```

Fig. 14.7 | Credit inquiry program. (Part 2 of 4.)

```

// determine whether to display given record
bool shouldDisplay( int type, double balance )
{
   // determine whether to display zero balances
   if ( type == ZERO_BALANCE && balance == 0 )
      return true;

   // determine whether to display credit balances
   if ( type == CREDIT_BALANCE && balance < 0 )
      return true;

   // determine whether to display debit balances
   if ( type == DEBIT_BALANCE && balance > 0 )
      return true;

   return false;
} // end function shouldDisplay

// display single record from file
void outputLine( int account, const string &name, double balance )
{
   cout << left << setw( 10 ) << account << setw( 13 ) << name
      << setw( 7 ) << setprecision( 2 ) << right << balance << endl;
} // end function outputLine
```

```
Enter request
 1 - List accounts with zero balances
 2 - List accounts with credit balances
 3 - List accounts with debit balances
 4 - End of run
? 1

Accounts with zero balances:
300       White           0.00

Enter request
 1 - List accounts with zero balances
 2 - List accounts with credit balances
 3 - List accounts with debit balances
 4 - End of run
? 2

Accounts with credit balances:
400       Stone         -42.16

Enter request
 1 - List accounts with zero balances
 2 - List accounts with credit balances
 3 - List accounts with debit balances
 4 - End of run
? 3

Accounts with debit balances:
100       Jones          24.98
200       Doe           345.67
500       Rich          224.62
```

Fig. 14.7 | Credit inquiry program. (Part 3 of 4.)

```
Enter request
 1 - List accounts with zero balances
 2 - List accounts with credit balances
 3 - List accounts with debit balances
 4 - End of run
? 4
End of run.
```

Fig. 14.7 | Credit inquiry program. (Part 4 of 4.)

14.5 Updating Sequential Files

Data that is formatted and written to a sequential file as shown in Section 14.3 cannot be modified without the risk of destroying other data in the file. For example, if the name "`White`" needs to be changed to "`Worthington`," the old name cannot be overwritten without corrupting the file. The record for `White` was written to the file as

```
300 White 0.00
```

If this record were rewritten beginning at the same location in the file using the longer name, the record would be

```
300 Worthington 0.00
```

The new record contains six more characters than the original one. Therefore, the characters beyond the second "`o`" in "`Worthington`" would overwrite the beginning of the next sequential record in the file. The problem is that, in the formatted input/output model using the stream insertion operator << and the stream extraction operator >>, fields—and hence records—can vary in size. For example, values 7, 14, –117, 2074, and 27383 are all `int`s, which store the same number of "raw data" bytes internally (typically four bytes on 32-bit machines and eight bytes on 64-bit machines). However, these integers become different-sized fields, depending on their actual values, when output as formatted text (character sequences). So, the formatted input/output model usually is not used to update records *in place*. Sections 14.6–14.10 show how to perform in-place updates with fixed-length records.

Such updating can be done awkwardly. For example, to make the preceding name change, the records before `300 White 0.00` in a sequential file could be *copied* to a new file, the updated record then written to the new file, and the records after `300 White 0.00` copied to the new file. Then the old file could be deleted and the new file renamed. This requires processing *every* record in the file to update one record. If many records are being updated in one pass of the file, though, this technique can be acceptable.

14.6 Random-Access Files

So far, we've seen how to create sequential files and search them to locate information. Sequential files are inappropriate for **instant-access applications**, in which a particular record must be located immediately. Common instant-access applications are airline reservation systems, banking systems, point-of-sale systems, automated teller machines and other kinds of **transaction-processing systems** that require rapid access to specific data. A bank might have hundreds of thousands (or even millions) of other customers, yet, when a customer uses an automated teller machine, the program checks that customer's account in a few seconds or less for sufficient funds. This kind of instant access is made possible with **random-access files.** Individual records of a random-access file can be accessed directly (and quickly) without having to search other records.

As we've said, C++ does not impose structure on a file. So the application that wants to use random-access files must create them. A variety of techniques can be used. Perhaps the easiest method is to require that all records in a file be of the *same fixed length*. Using same-size, fixed-length records makes it easy for a program to quickly calculate (as a function of the record size and the record key) the exact location of any record relative to the beginning of the file. We'll soon see how this facilitates *immediate access* to specific records, even in large files.

Figure 14.8 illustrates C++'s view of a random-access file composed of fixed-length records (each record, in this case, is 100 bytes long). A random-access file is like a railroad train with many same-size cars—some empty and some with contents.

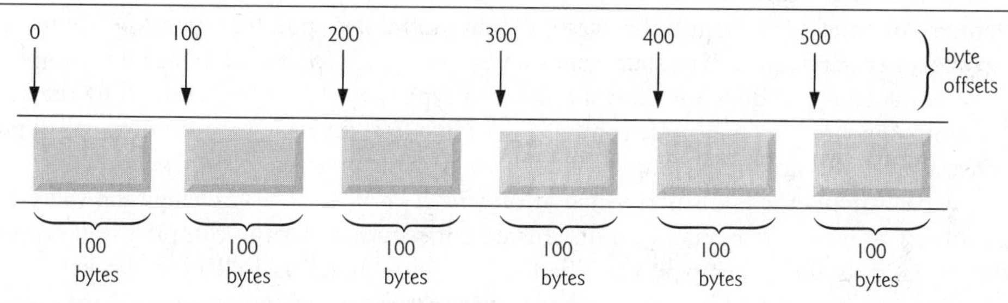

Fig. 14.8 | C++ view of a random-access file.

Data can be inserted into a random-access file without destroying other data in the file. Data stored previously also can be updated or deleted without rewriting the entire file. In the following sections, we explain how to create a random-access file, enter data into the file, read the data both sequentially and randomly, update the data and delete data that is no longer needed.

14.7 Creating a Random-Access File

The `ostream` member function `write` outputs to the specified stream a fixed number of bytes, beginning at a specific location in memory. When the stream is associated with a file, function `write` writes the data *at the location in the file specified by the put file-position pointer.* The `istream` member function **`read`** inputs a fixed number of bytes from the specified stream to an area in memory beginning at a specified address. If the stream is associated with a file, function `read` inputs bytes at the location in the file specified by the "get" file-position pointer.

Writing Bytes with `ostream` Member Function `write`

When writing the integer `number` to a file, instead of using the statement

```
outFile << number;
```

which for a four-byte integer could print as few digits as one or as many as 11 (10 digits plus a sign, each requiring a single byte of storage), we can use the statement

```
outFile.write( reinterpret_cast< const char * >( &number ),
   sizeof( number ) );
```

which always writes the *binary* version of the integer number's *four* bytes (on a machine with four-byte integers). Function write treats its first argument as a group of bytes by viewing the object in memory as a const char *, which is a pointer to a byte. Starting from that location, function write outputs the number of bytes specified by its second argument—an integer of type size_t. As we'll see, istream function read can subsequently be used to read the four bytes back into integer variable number.

Converting Between Pointer Types with the reinterpret_cast *Operator*

Unfortunately, most pointers that we pass to function write as the first argument are *not* of type const char *. To output objects of other types, we must convert the pointers to those objects to type const char *; otherwise, the compiler will not compile calls to function write. C++ provides the **reinterpret_cast** operator for cases like this in which a pointer of one type must be cast to an *unrelated* pointer type. Without a reinterpret_cast, the write statement that outputs the integer number will not compile because the compiler does *not* allow a pointer of type int * (the type returned by the expression &number) to be passed to a function that expects an argument of type const char *—as far as the compiler is concerned, these types are *inconsistent.*

A reinterpret_cast is performed at *compile time* and does *not* change the value of the object to which its operand points. Instead, it requests that the compiler reinterpret the operand as the target type (specified in the angle brackets following the keyword reinterpret_cast). In Fig. 14.11, we use reinterpret_cast to convert a ClientData pointer to a const char *, which reinterprets a ClientData object as bytes to be output to a file. Random-access file-processing programs rarely write a single field to a file. Typically, they write one object of a class at a time, as we show in the following examples.

Error-Prevention Tip 14.4

It's easy to use reinterpret_cast *to perform dangerous manipulations that could lead to serious execution-time errors.*

Portability Tip 14.1

reinterpret_cast *is compiler dependent and can cause programs to behave differently on different platforms. Use this operator only if it's absolutely necessary.*

Portability Tip 14.2

A program that reads unformatted data (written by write*) must be compiled and executed on a system compatible with the program that wrote the data, because different systems may represent internal data differently.*

Credit Processing Program

Consider the following problem statement:

> *Create a credit-processing program capable of storing at most 100 fixed-length records for a company that can have up to 100 customers. Each record should consist of an account number that acts as the record key, a last name, a first name and a balance. The program should be able to update an account, insert a new account, delete an account and insert all the account records into a formatted text file for printing.*

The next few sections create this credit-processing program. Figure 14.11 illustrates opening a random-access file, defining the record format using an object of class `ClientData` (Figs. 14.9–14.10) and writing data to the disk in *binary* format. This program initializes all 100 records of the file `credit.dat` with *empty* objects, using function `write`. Each empty object contains the account number `0`, emptylast and first name strings and the balance `0.0`. Each record is initialized with the space in which the account data will be stored.

```
// Fig. 14.9: ClientData.h
// Class ClientData definition used in Fig. 14.11-Fig. 14.14.
#ifndef CLIENTDATA_H
#define CLIENTDATA_H

#include <string>

class ClientData
{
public:
   // default ClientData constructor
   ClientData( int = 0, const std::string & = "",
      const std::string & = "", double = 0.0 );

   // accessor functions for accountNumber
   void setAccountNumber( int );
   int getAccountNumber() const;

   // accessor functions for lastName
   void setLastName( const std::string & );
   std::string getLastName() const;

   // accessor functions for firstName
   void setFirstName( const std::string & );
   std::string getFirstName() const;

   // accessor functions for balance
   void setBalance( double );
   double getBalance() const;
private:
   int accountNumber;
   char lastName[ 15 ];
   char firstName[ 10 ];
   double balance;
}; // end class ClientData

#endif
```

Fig. 14.9 | `ClientData` class header.

```
// Fig. 14.10: ClientData.cpp
// Class ClientData stores customer's credit information.
#include <string>
```

Fig. 14.10 | `ClientData` class represents a customer's credit information. (Part 1 of 3.)

```
#include "ClientData.h"
using namespace std;

// default ClientData constructor
ClientData::ClientData( int accountNumberValue, const string &lastName,
   const string &firstName, double balanceValue )
   : accountNumber( accountNumberValue ), balance( balanceValue )
{
   setLastName( lastNameValue );
   setFirstName( firstNameValue );
} // end ClientData constructor

// get account-number value
int ClientData::getAccountNumber() const
{
   return accountNumber;
} // end function getAccountNumber

// set account-number value
void ClientData::setAccountNumber( int accountNumberValue )
{
   accountNumber = accountNumberValue; // should validate
} // end function setAccountNumber

// get last-name value
string ClientData::getLastName() const
{
   return lastName;
} // end function getLastName

// set last-name value
void ClientData::setLastName( const string &lastNameString )
{
   // copy at most 15 characters from string to lastName
   int length = lastNameString.size();
   length = ( length < 15 ? length : 14 );
   lastNameString.copy( lastName, length );
   lastName[ length ] = '\0'; // append null character to lastName
} // end function setLastName

// get first-name value
string ClientData::getFirstName() const
{
   return firstName;
} // end function getFirstName

// set first-name value
void ClientData::setFirstName( const string &firstNameString )
{
   // copy at most 10 characters from string to firstName
   int length = firstNameString.size();
```

Fig. 14.10 | ClientData class represents a customer's credit information. (Part 2 of 3.)

```
55       length = ( length < 10 ? length : 9 );
56       firstNameString.copy( firstName, length );
57       firstName[ length ] = '\0'; // append null character to firstName
58    } // end function setFirstName
59
60    // get balance value
61    double ClientData::getBalance() const
62    {
63       return balance;
64    } // end function getBalance
65
66    // set balance value
67    void ClientData::setBalance( double balanceValue )
68    {
69       balance = balanceValue;
70    } // end function setBalance
```

Fig. 14.10 | `ClientData` class represents a customer's credit information. (Part 3 of 3.)

Objects of class `string` *do not have uniform size*, rather they use dynamically allocated memory to accommodate strings of various lengths. We must maintain fixed-length records, so class `ClientData` stores the client's first and last name in fixed-length `char` arrays (declared in Fig. 14.9, lines 32–33). Member functions `setLastName` (Fig. 14.10, lines 35–42) and `setFirstName` (Fig. 14.10, lines 51–58) each copy the characters of a `string` object into the corresponding `char` array. Consider function `setLastName`. Line 38 invokes `string` member function **`size`** to get the length of `lastNameString`. Line 39 ensures that `length` is fewer than 15 characters, then line 40 copies `length` characters from `lastNameString` into the `char` array `lastName` using `string` member function `copy`. Member function `setFirstName` performs the same steps for the first name.

Opening a File for Output in Binary Mode

In Fig. 14.11, line 11 creates an `ofstream` object for the file `credit.dat`. The second argument to the constructor—`ios::out | `**`ios::binary`**—indicates that we are opening the file for output in *binary mode*, which is *required* if we are to write *fixed-length records*. Multiple file-open modes are combined by separating each open mode from the next with the `|` operator, which is known as the *bitwise inclusive OR operator*. (Chapter 20 discusses this operator in detail.) Lines 24–25 cause the `blankClient` (which was constructed with default arguments at line 20) to be written to the `credit.dat` file associated with `ofstream` object `outCredit`. Remember that operator `sizeof` returns the size in bytes of the object contained in parentheses (see Chapter 8). The first argument to function `write` at line 24 must be of type `const char *`. However, the data type of `&blankClient` is `ClientData *`. To convert `&blankClient` to `const char *`, line 24 uses the cast operator `reinterpret_cast`, so the call to `write` compiles without issuing a compilation error.

```
1    // Fig. 14.11: Fig14_11.cpp
2    // Creating a randomly accessed file.
3    #include <iostream>
```

Fig. 14.11 | Creating a random-access file with 100 blank records sequentially. (Part 1 of 2.)

```
#include <fstream>
#include <cstdlib>
#include "ClientData.h" // ClientData class definition
using namespace std;

int main()
{
   ofstream outCredit( "credit.dat", ios::out | ios::binary );

   // exit program if ofstream could not open file
   if ( !outCredit )
   {
      cerr << "File could not be opened." << endl;
      exit( EXIT_FAILURE );
   } // end if

   ClientData blankClient; // constructor zeros out each data member

   // output 100 blank records to file
   for ( int i = 0; i < 100; ++i )
      outCredit.write( reinterpret_cast< const char * >( &blankClient ),
         sizeof( ClientData ) );
} // end main
```

Fig. 14.11 | Creating a random-access file with 100 blank records sequentially. (Part 2 of 2.)

14.8 Writing Data Randomly to a Random-Access File

Figure 14.12 writes data to the file `credit.dat` and uses the combination of `fstream` functions `seekp` and `write` to store data at *exact* locations in the file. Function `seekp` sets the *put* file-position pointer to a specific position in the file, then function `write` outputs the data. Line 6 includes the header `ClientData.h` defined in Fig. 14.9, so the program can use `ClientData` objects.

```
1  // Fig. 14.12: Fig14_12.cpp
2  // Writing to a random-access file.
3  #include <iostream>
4  #include <fstream>
5  #include <cstdlib>
6  #include "ClientData.h" // ClientData class definition
7  using namespace std;
8
9  int main()
10 {
11    int accountNumber;
12    string lastName;
13    string firstName;
14    double balance;
15
16    fstream outCredit( "credit.dat", ios::in | ios::out | ios::binary );
```

Fig. 14.12 | Writing to a random-access file. (Part 1 of 3.)

```

   // exit program if fstream cannot open file
   if ( !outCredit )
   {
      cerr << "File could not be opened." << endl;
      exit( EXIT_FAILURE );
   } // end if

   cout << "Enter account number (1 to 100, 0 to end input)\n? ";

   // require user to specify account number
   ClientData client;
   cin >> accountNumber;

   // user enters information, which is copied into file
   while ( accountNumber > 0 && accountNumber <= 100 )
   {
      // user enters last name, first name and balance
      cout << "Enter lastname, firstname, balance\n? ";
      cin >> lastName;
      cin >> firstName;
      cin >> balance;

      // set record accountNumber, lastName, firstName and balance values
      client.setAccountNumber( accountNumber );
      client.setLastName( lastName );
      client.setFirstName( firstName );
      client.setBalance( balance );

      // seek position in file of user-specified record
      outCredit.seekp( ( client.getAccountNumber() - 1 ) *
         sizeof( ClientData ) );

      // write user-specified information in file
      outCredit.write( reinterpret_cast< const char * >( &client ),
         sizeof( ClientData ) );

      // enable user to enter another account
      cout << "Enter account number\n? ";
      cin >> accountNumber;
   } // end while
} // end main
```

```
Enter account number (1 to 100, 0 to end input)
? 37
Enter lastname, firstname, balance
? Barker Doug 0.00
Enter account number
? 29
Enter lastname, firstname, balance
? Brown Nancy -24.54
Enter account number
? 96
```

Fig. 14.12 | Writing to a random-access file. (Part 2 of 3.)

```
Enter lastname, firstname, balance
? Stone Sam 34.98
Enter account number
? 88
Enter lastname, firstname, balance
? Smith Dave 258.34
Enter account number
? 33
Enter lastname, firstname, balance
? Dunn Stacey 314.33
Enter account number
? 0
```

Fig. 14.12 | Writing to a random-access file. (Part 3 of 3.)

Opening a File for Input and Output in Binary Mode

Line 16 uses the `fstream` object `outCredit` to open the existing `credit.dat` file. The file is opened for input and output in *binary mode* by combining the file-open modes `ios::in`, `ios::out` and `ios::binary`. Opening the existing `credit.dat` file in this manner ensures that this program can manipulate the records written to the file by the program of Fig. 14.11, rather than creating the file from scratch.

Positioning the File Position Pointer

Lines 47–48 position the *put* file-position pointer for object `outCredit` to the byte location calculated by

```
( client.getAccountNumber() - 1 ) * sizeof( ClientData )
```

Because the account number is between 1 and 100, 1 is subtracted from the account number when calculating the byte location of the record. Thus, for record 1, the file-position pointer is set to byte 0 of the file.

14.9 Reading from a Random-Access File Sequentially

In the previous sections, we created a random-access file and wrote data to that file. In this section, we develop a program that reads the file sequentially and prints only those records that contain data. These programs produce an additional benefit. See if you can determine what it is; we'll reveal it at the end of this section.

The `istream` function `read` inputs a specified number of bytes from the current position in the specified stream into an object. For example, lines 31–32 from Fig. 14.13 read the number of bytes specified by `sizeof(ClientData)` from the file associated with `ifstream` object `inCredit` and store the data in the `client` record. Function `read` requires a first argument of type `char *`. Since `&client` is of type `ClientData *`, `&client` must be cast to `char *` using the cast operator `reinterpret_cast`.

```
1 // Fig. 14.13: Fig14_13.cpp
2 // Reading a random-access file sequentially.
3 #include <iostream>
```

Fig. 14.13 | Reading a random-access file sequentially. (Part 1 of 3.)

```
#include <iomanip>
#include <fstream>
#include <cstdlib>
#include "ClientData.h" // ClientData class definition
using namespace std;

void outputLine( ostream&, const ClientData & ); // prototype

int main()
{
   ifstream inCredit( "credit.dat", ios::in | ios::binary );

   // exit program if ifstream cannot open file
   if ( !inCredit )
   {
      cerr << "File could not be opened." << endl;
      exit( EXIT_FAILURE );
   } // end if

   // output column heads
   cout << left << setw( 10 ) << "Account" << setw( 16 )
      << "Last Name" << setw( 11 ) << "First Name" << left
      << setw( 10 ) << right << "Balance" << endl;

   ClientData client; // create record

   // read first record from file
   inCredit.read( reinterpret_cast< char * >( &client ),
      sizeof( ClientData ) );

   // read all records from file
   while ( inCredit && !inCredit.eof() )
   {
      // display record
      if ( client.getAccountNumber() != 0 )
         outputLine( cout, client );

      // read next from file
      inCredit.read( reinterpret_cast< char * >( &client ),
         sizeof( ClientData ) );
   } // end while
} // end main

// display single record
void outputLine( ostream &output, const ClientData &record )
{
   output << left << setw( 10 ) << record.getAccountNumber()
      << setw( 16 ) << record.getLastName()
      << setw( 11 ) << record.getFirstName()
      << setw( 10 ) << setprecision( 2 ) << right << fixed
      << showpoint << record.getBalance() << endl;
} // end function outputLine
```

Fig. 14.13 | Reading a random-access file sequentially. (Part 2 of 3.)

```
Account   Last Name        First Name      Balance
29        Brown            Nancy            -24.54
33        Dunn             Stacey           314.33
37        Barker           Doug               0.00
88        Smith            Dave             258.34
96        Stone            Sam               34.98
```

Fig. 14.13 | Reading a random-access file sequentially. (Part 3 of 3.)

Figure 14.13 reads every record in the `credit.dat` file sequentially, checks each record to determine whether it contains data, and displays formatted outputs for records containing data. The condition in line 35 uses the `ios` member function `eof` to determine when the end of file is reached and causes execution of the `while` statement to terminate. Also, if an error occurs when reading from the file, the loop terminates, because `inCredit` evaluates to `false`. The data input from the file is output by function `outputLine` (lines 48–55), which takes two arguments—an `ostream` object and a `clientData` structure to be output. The `ostream` parameter type is interesting, because any `ostream` object (such as `cout`) or any object of a derived class of `ostream` (such as an object of type `ofstream`) can be supplied as the argument. This means that the *same* function can be used, for example, to perform output to the standard-output stream and to a file stream without writing separate functions.

What about that additional benefit we promised? If you examine the output window, you'll notice that the records are listed in *sorted order* (by account number). This is a consequence of how we stored these records in the file, using direct-access techniques. Sorting using direct-access techniques is relatively fast. *The speed is achieved by making the file large enough to hold every possible record that might be created.* This, of course, means that the file could be occupied *sparsely* most of the time, resulting in a waste of storage. This is an example of the *space-time trade-off:* By using *large amounts of space*, we can develop *a much faster sorting algorithm*. Fortunately, the continuous reduction in price of storage units has made this less of an issue.

14.10 Case Study: A Transaction-Processing Program

We now present a substantial transaction-processing program (Fig. 14.14) using a random-access file to achieve instant-access processing. The program maintains a bank's account information. It updates existing accounts, adds new accounts, deletes accounts and stores a formatted listing of all current accounts in a text file. We assume that the program of Fig. 14.11 has been executed to create the file `credit.dat` and that the program of Fig. 14.12 has been executed to insert the initial data. Line 25 opens the `credit.dat` file by creating an `fstream` object for both reading and writing in binary format.

```
1  // Fig. 14.14: Fig14_14.cpp
2  // This program reads a random-access file sequentially, updates
3  // data previously written to the file, creates data to be placed
4  // in the file, and deletes data previously stored in the file.
```

Fig. 14.14 | Bank account program. (Part 1 of 6.)

```
#include <iostream>
#include <fstream>
#include <iomanip>
#include <cstdlib>
#include "ClientData.h" // ClientData class definition
using namespace std;

int enterChoice();
void createTextFile( fstream& );
void updateRecord( fstream& );
void newRecord( fstream& );
void deleteRecord( fstream& );
void outputLine( ostream&, const ClientData & );
int getAccount( const char * const );

enum Choices { PRINT = 1, UPDATE, NEW, DELETE, END };

int main()
{
   // open file for reading and writing
   fstream inOutCredit( "credit.dat", ios::in | ios::out | ios::binary );

   // exit program if fstream cannot open file
   if ( !inOutCredit )
   {
      cerr << "File could not be opened." << endl;
      exit ( EXIT_FAILURE );
   } // end if

   int choice; // store user choice

   // enable user to specify action
   while ( ( choice = enterChoice() ) != END )
   {
      switch ( choice )
      {
         case PRINT: // create text file from record file
            createTextFile( inOutCredit );
            break;
         case UPDATE: // update record
            updateRecord( inOutCredit );
            break;
         case NEW: // create record
            newRecord( inOutCredit );
            break;
         case DELETE: // delete existing record
            deleteRecord( inOutCredit );
            break;
         default: // display error if user does not select valid choice
            cerr << "Incorrect choice" << endl;
            break;
      } // end switch

```

Fig. 14.14 | Bank account program. (Part 2 of 6.)

```
      inOutCredit.clear(); // reset end-of-file indicator
   } // end while
} // end main

// enable user to input menu choice
int enterChoice()
{
   // display available options
   cout << "\nEnter your choice" << endl
      << "1 - store a formatted text file of accounts" << endl
      << "    called \"print.txt\" for printing" << endl
      << "2 - update an account" << endl
      << "3 - add a new account" << endl
      << "4 - delete an account" << endl
      << "5 - end program\n? ";

   int menuChoice;
   cin >> menuChoice; // input menu selection from user
   return menuChoice;
} // end function enterChoice

// create formatted text file for printing
void createTextFile( fstream &readFromFile )
{
   // create text file
   ofstream outPrintFile( "print.txt", ios::out );

   // exit program if ofstream cannot create file
   if ( !outPrintFile )
   {
      cerr << "File could not be created." << endl;
      exit( EXIT_FAILURE );
   } // end if

   // output column heads
   outPrintFile << left << setw( 10 ) << "Account" << setw( 16 )
      << "Last Name" << setw( 11 ) << "First Name" << right
      << setw( 10 ) << "Balance" << endl;

   // set file-position pointer to beginning of readFromFile
   readFromFile.seekg( 0 );

   // read first record from record file
   ClientData client;
   readFromFile.read( reinterpret_cast< char * >( &client ),
      sizeof( ClientData ) );

   // copy all records from record file into text file
   while ( !readFromFile.eof() )
   {
      // write single record to text file
      if ( client.getAccountNumber() != 0 ) // skip empty records
         outputLine( outPrintFile, client );
```

Fig. 14.14 | Bank account program. (Part 3 of 6.)

```

      // read next record from record file
      readFromFile.read( reinterpret_cast< char * >( &client ),
         sizeof( ClientData ) );
   } // end while
} // end function createTextFile

// update balance in record
void updateRecord( fstream &updateFile )
{
   // obtain number of account to update
   int accountNumber = getAccount( "Enter account to update" );

   // move file-position pointer to correct record in file
   updateFile.seekg( ( accountNumber - 1 ) * sizeof( ClientData ) );

   // read first record from file
   ClientData client;
   updateFile.read( reinterpret_cast< char * >( &client ),
      sizeof( ClientData ) );

   // update record
   if ( client.getAccountNumber() != 0 )
   {
      outputLine( cout, client ); // display the record

      // request user to specify transaction
      cout << "\nEnter charge (+) or payment (-): ";
      double transaction; // charge or payment
      cin >> transaction;

      // update record balance
      double oldBalance = client.getBalance();
      client.setBalance( oldBalance + transaction );
      outputLine( cout, client ); // display the record

      // move file-position pointer to correct record in file
      updateFile.seekp( ( accountNumber - 1 ) * sizeof( ClientData ) );

      // write updated record over old record in file
      updateFile.write( reinterpret_cast< const char * >( &client ),
         sizeof( ClientData ) );
   } // end if
   else // display error if account does not exist
      cerr << "Account #" << accountNumber
         << " has no information." << endl;
} // end function updateRecord

// create and insert record
void newRecord( fstream &insertInFile )
{
   // obtain number of account to create
   int accountNumber = getAccount( "Enter new account number" );
```

Fig. 14.14 | Bank account program. (Part 4 of 6.)

```

   // move file-position pointer to correct record in file
   insertInFile.seekg( ( accountNumber - 1 ) * sizeof( ClientData ) );

   // read record from file
   ClientData client;
   insertInFile.read( reinterpret_cast< char * >( &client ),
      sizeof( ClientData ) );

   // create record, if record does not previously exist
   if ( client.getAccountNumber() == 0 )
   {
      string lastName;
      string firstName;
      double balance;

      // user enters last name, first name and balance
      cout << "Enter lastname, firstname, balance\n? ";
      cin >> setw( 15 ) >> lastName;
      cin >> setw( 10 ) >> firstName;
      cin >> balance;

      // use values to populate account values
      client.setLastName( lastName );
      client.setFirstName( firstName );
      client.setBalance( balance );
      client.setAccountNumber( accountNumber );

      // move file-position pointer to correct record in file
      insertInFile.seekp( ( accountNumber - 1 ) * sizeof( ClientData ) );

      // insert record in file
      insertInFile.write( reinterpret_cast< const char * >( &client ),
         sizeof( ClientData ) );
   } // end if
   else // display error if account already exists
      cerr << "Account #" << accountNumber
         << " already contains information." << endl;
} // end function newRecord

// delete an existing record
void deleteRecord( fstream &deleteFromFile )
{
   // obtain number of account to delete
   int accountNumber = getAccount( "Enter account to delete" );

   // move file-position pointer to correct record in file
   deleteFromFile.seekg( ( accountNumber - 1 ) * sizeof( ClientData ) );

   // read record from file
   ClientData client;
   deleteFromFile.read( reinterpret_cast< char * >( &client ),
      sizeof( ClientData ) );
```

Fig. 14.14 | Bank account program. (Part 5 of 6.)

```
217
218    // delete record, if record exists in file
219    if ( client.getAccountNumber() != 0 )
220    {
221       ClientData blankClient; // create blank record
222
223       // move file-position pointer to correct record in file
224       deleteFromFile.seekp( ( accountNumber - 1 ) *
225          sizeof( ClientData ) );
226
227       // replace existing record with blank record
228       deleteFromFile.write(
229          reinterpret_cast< const char * >( &blankClient ),
230          sizeof( ClientData ) );
231
232       cout << "Account #" << accountNumber << " deleted.\n";
233    } // end if
234    else // display error if record does not exist
235       cerr << "Account #" << accountNumber << " is empty.\n";
236 } // end deleteRecord
237
238 // display single record
239 void outputLine( ostream &output, const ClientData &record )
240 {
241    output << left << setw( 10 ) << record.getAccountNumber()
242       << setw( 16 ) << record.getLastName()
243       << setw( 11 ) << record.getFirstName()
244       << setw( 10 ) << setprecision( 2 ) << right << fixed
245       << showpoint << record.getBalance() << endl;
246 } // end function outputLine
247
248 // obtain account-number value from user
249 int getAccount( const char * const prompt )
250 {
251    int accountNumber;
252
253    // obtain account-number value
254    do
255    {
256       cout << prompt << " (1 - 100): ";
257       cin >> accountNumber;
258    } while ( accountNumber < 1 || accountNumber > 100 );
259
260    return accountNumber;
261 } // end function getAccount
```

Fig. 14.14 | Bank account program. (Part 6 of 6.)

The program has five options (Option 5 is for terminating the program). Option 1 calls function `createTextFile` to store a formatted list of all the account information in a text file called `print.txt` that may be printed. Function `createTextFile` (lines 80–116) takes an `fstream` object as an argument to be used to input data from the `credit.dat` file. Function `createTextFile` invokes `istream` member function `read` (lines 102–103) and uses the sequential-file-access techniques of Fig. 14.13 to input data from `credit.dat`. Function `outputLine`, discussed in Section 14.9, outputs the data to file `print.txt`. Note that function `createTextFile` uses `istream` member function `seekg` (line 98) to ensure that the file-position pointer is at the beginning of the file. After choosing Option 1, the `print.txt` file contains

```
Account   Last Name        First Name    Balance
29        Brown            Nancy          -24.54
33        Dunn             Stacey         314.33
37        Barker           Doug             0.00
88        Smith            Dave           258.34
96        Stone            Sam             34.98
```

Option 2 calls `updateRecord` (lines 119–157) to update an account. This function updates only an *existing* record, so the function first determines whether the specified record is *empty*. Lines 129–130 read data into object `client`, using `istream` member function `read`. Then line 133 compares the value returned by `getAccountNumber` of the `client` object to zero to determine whether the record contains information. If this value is zero, lines 155–156 print an error message indicating that the record is empty. If the record contains information, line 135 displays the record, using function `outputLine`, line 140 inputs the transaction amount and lines 143–152 calculate the new balance and rewrite the record to the file. A typical execution for Option 2 is

```
Enter account to update (1 - 100): 37
37        Barker           Doug             0.00

Enter charge (+) or payment (-): +87.99
37        Barker           Doug            87.99
```

Option 3 calls function `newRecord` (lines 160–202) to add a new account to the file. If the user enters an account number for an *existing* account, `newRecord` displays an error message indicating that the account exists (lines 200–201). This function adds a new account in the same manner as the program of Fig. 14.12. A typical execution for Option 3 is

```
Enter new account number (1 - 100): 22
Enter lastname, firstname, balance
? Johnston Sarah 247.45
```

Option 4 calls function `deleteRecord` (lines 205–236) to delete a record from the file. Line 208 prompts the user to enter the account number. Only an *existing* record may be deleted, so, if the specified account is empty, line 235 displays an error message. If the account exists, lines 221–230 reinitialize that account by copying an empty record (`blankClient`) to the file. Line 232 displays a message to inform the user that the record has been deleted. A typical execution for Option 4 is

```
Enter account to delete (1 - 100): 29
Account #29 deleted.
```

14.11 Object Serialization

This chapter and Chapter 13 introduced the object-oriented style of input/output. However, our examples concentrated on I/O of fundamental types rather than objects of user-defined types. In Chapter 10, we showed how to input and output objects using operator overloading. We accomplished object input by overloading the stream extraction operator, >>, for the appropriate `istream`. We accomplished object output by overloading the stream insertion operator, <<, for the appropriate `ostream`. In both cases, only an object's data members were input or output, and, in each case, they were in a format meaningful only for objects of that particular type. An object's member functions are *not* input or output with the object's data; rather, *one copy of the class's member functions remains available internally and is shared by all objects of the class.*

When object data members are output to a disk file, we *lose* the object's type information. We store only the values of the object's attributes, not type information, on the disk. If the program that reads this data knows the object type to which the data corresponds, the program can read the data into an object of that type as we did in our random-access file examples.

An interesting problem occurs when we store objects of different types in the same file. How can we distinguish them (or their collections of data members) as we read them into a program? The problem is that objects typically do *not* have type fields (we discussed this issue in Chapter 12).

One approach used by several programming languages is called **object serialization**. A so-called **serialized object** is an object represented as a sequence of bytes that includes the object's *data* as well as information about the object's *type* and the *types of data stored in the object*. After a serialized object has been written to a file, it can be read from the file and **deserialized**—that is, the type information and bytes that represent the object and its data can be used to *recreate* the object in memory. C++ does *not* provide a built-in serialization mechanism; however, there are third party and open source C++ libraries that support object serialization. The open source Boost C++ Libraries (`www.boost.org`) provide support for serializing objects in text, binary and extensible markup language (XML) formats (`www.boost.org/libs/serialization/doc/index.html`).

14.12 Wrap-Up

In this chapter, we presented various file-processing techniques to manipulate persistent data. You were introduced to the differences between character-based and byte-based streams, and to several file-processing class templates in header `<fstream>`. Then, you learned how to use sequential file processing to manipulate records stored in order, by a record-key field. You also learned how to use random-access files to "instantly" retrieve and manipulate fixed-length records. We presented a substantial transaction-processing program using a random-access file to achieve "instant-access" processing. Finally, we discussed the basic concepts of object serialization. We introduced the Standard Library `array` and `vector` classes in Chapter 7. In the next chapter, you'll learn about the Standard Library's other predefined data structures (known as containers) as well as the basics of iterators, which are used to manipulate container elements.

15

Standard Library Containers and Iterators

Objectives

In this chapter you'll:

- Introduce the Standard Library containers, iterators and algorithms.
- Use the `vector`, `list` and `deque` sequence containers.
- Use the `set`, `multiset`, `map` and `multimap` associative containers.
- Use the `stack`, `queue` and `priority_queue` container adapters.
- Use iterators to access container elements.
- Use the `copy` algorithm and `ostream_iterator`s to output a container.
- Use the `bitset` "near container" to implement the Sieve of Eratosthenes for determining prime numbers.

Outline

15.1 Introduction

The Standard Library defines powerful, template-based, reusable components that implement many common data structures and algorithms used to process those data structures. We began introducing templates in Chapters 6–7 and use them extensively here and in Chapter 16. Historically, the features presented in this chapter were often referred to as the *Standard Template Library* or *STL*.[1] We'll occasionally refer to these features as the STL. In the C++ standard document, these features are simply referred to as part of the C++ Standard Library.

Containers, Iterators and Algorithms

This chapter introduces three key components of the Standard Library—**containers** (*templatized* data structures), iterators and algorithms. Containers are data structures capable of storing objects of *almost* any data type (there are some restrictions). We'll see that there are three styles of container classes—*first-class containers*, *container adapters* and *near containers*.

Common Member Functions Among Containers

Each container has associated member functions—a subset of these is defined in *all* containers. We illustrate most of this common functionality in our examples of `array` (which was introduced in Chapter 7), `vector` (which was introduced in Chapter 7 and we cover in more depth here), `list` (Section 15.5.2) and `deque` (Section 15.5.3).

Iterators

Iterators, which have properties similar to those of *pointers*, are used to manipulate container elements. *Built-in arrays* also can be manipulated by Standard Library algorithms, using pointers as iterators. We'll see that manipulating containers with iterators is convenient and provides tremendous expressive power when combined with Standard Library algorithms—in some cases, reducing many lines of code to a single statement.

---

1. The STL was developed by Alexander Stepanov and Meng Lee at Hewlett-Packard and is based on their generic programming research, with significant contributions from David Musser.

Algorithms

Standard Library **algorithms** are function templates that perform such common data manipulations as *searching*, *sorting* and *comparing elements or entire containers*. The Standard Library provides *many* algorithms. Most of them use iterators to access container elements. Each algorithm has *minimum requirements* for the types of iterators that can be used with it. We'll see that containers support specific iterator types, some more powerful than others. A *container's* supported iterator type determines whether the container can be used with a specific algorithm. Iterators encapsulate the mechanisms used to access container elements. This encapsulation enables many of the algorithms to be applied to various containers *independently* of the underlying container implementation. This also enables you to create new algorithms that can process the elements of *multiple* container types.

Custom Templatized Data Structures

It's possible to build your own *custom* templatized data structures, including linked lists, queues, stacks and trees. Typically these are implemented with objects that are linked together via pointers. Such code is complex and error-prone—the slightest omissions or oversights can lead to serious *memory-access violations* and *memory-leak* errors with no forewarning from the compiler. If many programmers on a large project implement custom containers and algorithms for different tasks, the code becomes difficult to modify, maintain and debug.

Software Engineering Observation 15.1

Avoid reinventing the wheel; program with the components of the C++ Standard Library.

Error-Prevention Tip 15.1

The prepackaged, templatized Standard Library containers are sufficient for most applications. Using the Standard Library helps you reduce testing and debugging time.

Performance Tip 15.1

The Standard Library was conceived and designed for performance and flexibility.

15.2 Introduction to Containers

The Standard Library container types are shown in Fig. 15.1. The containers are divided into four major categories—**sequence containers**, **ordered associative containers**, **unordered associative containers** and **container adapters**.

Container class	Description
Sequence containers	
`array`	Fixed size. Direct access to any element.
`deque`	Rapid insertions and deletions at front or back. Direct access to any element.
`forward_list`	Singly linked list, rapid insertion and deletion anywhere. New in C++11.

Fig. 15.1 | Standard Library container classes and container adapters. (Part 1 of 2.)

Container class	Description
`list`	Doubly linked list, rapid insertion and deletion anywhere.
`vector`	Rapid insertions and deletions at back. Direct access to any element.
Ordered associative containers—keys are maintained in sorted order	
`set`	Rapid lookup, no duplicates allowed.
`multiset`	Rapid lookup, duplicates allowed.
`map`	One-to-one mapping, no duplicates allowed, rapid key-based lookup.
`multimap`	One-to-many mapping, duplicates allowed, rapid key-based lookup.
Unordered associative containers	
`unordered_set`	Rapid lookup, no duplicates allowed.
`unordered_multiset`	Rapid lookup, duplicates allowed.
`unordered_map`	One-to-one mapping, no duplicates allowed, rapid key-based lookup.
`unordered_multimap`	One-to-many mapping, duplicates allowed, rapid key-based lookup.
Container adapters	
`stack`	Last-in, first-out (LIFO).
`queue`	First-in, first-out (FIFO).
`priority_queue`	Highest-priority element is always the first element out.

Fig. 15.1 | Standard Library container classes and container adapters. (Part 2 of 2.)

Containers Overview

The *sequence containers* represent *linear* data structures (i.e., all of their elements are conceptually "lined up in a row"), such as `array`s, `vector`s and linked lists. *Associative containers* are *nonlinear* data structures that typically can locate elements stored in the containers quickly. Such containers can store sets of values or **key–value pairs**. As of C++11, the keys in associative containers are *immutable* (they cannot be modified). The sequence containers and associative containers are collectively referred to as the **first-class containers**. Stacks and queues are typically constrained versions of sequence containers. For this reason, the Standard Library implements class templates `stack`, `queue` and `priority_queue` as **container adapters** that enable a program to view a sequence container in a constrained manner. Class `string` supports the same functionality as a *sequence container*, but stores only character data.

Near Containers

There are other container types that are considered **near containers**—built-in arrays, `bitset`s for maintaining sets of flag values and `valarray`s for performing high-speed *mathematical vector* (not to be confused with the `vector` container) operations. These types are considered *near containers* because they exhibit some, but not all, capabilities of the *first-class containers*.

Common Container Functions

Most containers provide similar functionality. Many operations apply to all containers, and other operations apply to subsets of similar containers. Figure 15.2 describes the many functions that are commonly available in most Standard Library containers. Overloaded operators <, <=, >, >=, == and != are *not* provided for `priority_queue`s. Overloaded operators <, <=, > and >= are *not* provided for the *unordered associative containers*. Member functions `rbegin`, `rend`, `crbegin` and `crend` are *not* available in a `forward_list`. Before using any container, you should study its capabilities.

Member function	Description
default constructor	A constructor that *initializes an empty container*. Normally, each container has several constructors that provide different ways to initialize the container.
copy constructor	A constructor that initializes the container to be a *copy of an existing container* of the same type.
11 move constructor	A move constructor (new in C++11 and discussed in Chapter 24) moves the contents of an existing container of the same type into a new container. This avoids the overhead of copying each element of the argument container.
destructor	Destructor function for cleanup after a container is no longer needed.
`empty`	Returns `true` if there are *no* elements in the container; otherwise, returns `false`.
`insert`	Inserts an item in the container.
`size`	Returns the number of elements currently in the container.
copy `operator=`	Copies the elements of one container into another.
11 move `operator=`	The move assignment operator (new in C++11 and discussed in Chapter 24) moves the elements of one container into another. This avoids the overhead of copying each element of the argument container.
`operator<`	Returns `true` if the contents of the first container are *less than* the second; otherwise, returns `false`.
`operator<=`	Returns `true` if the contents of the first container are *less than or equal to* the second; otherwise, returns `false`.
`operator>`	Returns `true` if the contents of the first container are *greater than* the second; otherwise, returns `false`.
`operator>=`	Returns `true` if the contents of the first container are *greater than or equal to* the second; otherwise, returns `false`.
`operator==`	Returns `true` if the contents of the first container are *equal to* the contents of the second; otherwise, returns `false`.
`operator!=`	Returns `true` if the contents of the first container are *not equal to* the contents of the second; otherwise, returns `false`.
11 `swap`	Swaps the elements of two containers. As of C++11, there is now a non-member function version of swap that swaps the contents of its two arguments (which must be of the same container type) using move operations rather than copy operations.
`max_size`	Returns the *maximum number of elements* for a container.

Fig. 15.2 | Common member functions for most Standard Library containers. (Part 1 of 2.)

Member function	Description
`begin`	Overloaded to return either an `iterator` or a `const_iterator` that refers to the *first element* of the container.
`end`	Overloaded to return either an `iterator` or a `const_iterator` that refers to the *next position after the end* of the container.
`cbegin` (C++11)	Returns a `const_iterator` that refers to the container's *first element.*
`cend` (C++11)	Returns a `const_iterator` that refers to the *next position after the end* of the container.
`rbegin`	The two versions of this function return either a `reverse_iterator` or a `const_reverse_iterator` that refers to the *last element* of the container.
`rend`	The two versions of this function return either a `reverse_iterator` or a `const_reverse_iterator` that refers to the *position before the first element* of the container.
`crbegin` (C++11)	Returns a `const_reverse_iterator` that refers to the *last element* of the container.
`crend` (C++11)	Returns a `const_reverse_iterator` that refers to the *position before the first element* of the container.
`erase`	Removes *one or more* elements from the container.
`clear`	Removes *all* elements from the container.

Fig. 15.2 | Common member functions for most Standard Library containers. (Part 2 of 2.)

First-Class Container Common Nested Types

Figure 15.3 shows the common first-class container *nested types* (types defined inside each container class definition). These are used in template-based declarations of variables, parameters to functions and return values from functions (as you'll see in this chapter and Chapter 16). For example, `value_type` in each container always represents the type of elements stored in the container. The types `reverse_iterator` and `const_reverse_iterator` are not provided by class `forward_list`.

`typedef`	Description
`allocator_type`	The type of the object used to allocate the container's memory—not included in class template `array`.
`value_type`	The type of element stored in the container.
`reference`	A reference for the container's element type.
`const_reference`	A reference for the container's element type that can be used only to *read* elements in the container and to perform `const` operations.
`pointer`	A pointer for the container's element type.
`const_pointer`	A pointer for the container's element type that can be used only to *read* elements and to perform `const` operations.

Fig. 15.3 | Nested types found in first-class containers. (Part 1 of 2.)

typedef	Description
`iterator`	An iterator that points to an element of the container's element type.
`const_iterator`	An iterator that points to an element of the container's element type. Used only only to *read* elements and to perform `const` operations.
`reverse_iterator`	A reverse iterator that points to an element of the container's element type. Used to iterate through a container in reverse.
`const_reverse_iterator`	A reverse iterator that points to an element of the container's element type and can be used only to *read* elements and to perform `const` operations. Used to iterate through a container in reverse.
`difference_type`	The type of the result of subtracting two iterators that refer to the same container (`operator-` is not defined for iterators of `list`s and associative containers).
`size_type`	The type used to count items in a container and index through a sequence container (cannot index through a `list`).

Fig. 15.3 | Nested types found in first-class containers. (Part 2 of 2.)

Requirements for Container Elements

Before using a Standard Library container, it's important to ensure that the type of objects being stored in the container supports a *minimum* set of functionality. When an object is inserted into a container, a *copy* of the object is made. For this reason, the object type should provide a *copy constructor* and *copy assignment operator* (custom or default versions, depending on whether the class uses dynamic memory). Also, the *ordered associative containers* and many algorithms require elements to be *compared*—for this reason, the object type should provide *less-than (<)* and *equality (==) operators*. As of C++11, objects can also be *moved* into container elements, in which case the object type needs a *move constructor* and *move assignment operator*—Chapter 24 discusses *move semantics*.

15.3 Introduction to Iterators

Iterators have many similarities to *pointers* and are used to point to *first-class container* elements and for other purposes. Iterators hold *state* information sensitive to the particular containers on which they operate; thus, iterators are implemented for each type of container. Certain iterator operations are uniform across containers. For example, the *dereferencing operator (*)* dereferences an iterator so that you can use the element to which it points. The *++ operation on an iterator* moves it to the container's *next element* (much as incrementing a pointer into a built-in array aims the pointer at the next array element).

First-class containers provide member functions `begin` and `end`. Function **`begin`** returns an iterator pointing to the *first* element of the container. Function **`end`** returns an iterator pointing to the *first element past the end of the container* (one past the end)—a nonexistent element that's frequently used to determine when the end of a container is reached. If iterator `i` points to a particular element, then `++i` points to the "next" element and `*i` refers to the element pointed to by `i`. The iterator resulting from `end` is typically used in an equality or inequality comparison to determine whether the "moving iterator" (`i` in this case) has reached the end of the container.

An object of a container's iterator type refers to a container element that *can* be modified. An object of a container's const_iterator type refers to a container element that *cannot* be modified.

Using **istream_iterator** *for Input and* **ostream_iterator** *for Output*

We use iterators with **sequences** (also called **ranges**). These sequences can be in containers, or they can be **input sequences** or **output sequences**. The program of Fig. 15.4 demonstrates input from the standard input (a sequence of data for input into a program), using an **istream_iterator**, and output to the standard output (a sequence of data for output from a program), using an **ostream_iterator**. The program inputs two integers from the user at the keyboard and displays the sum of the integers. As you'll see later in this chapter, istream_iterators and ostream_iterators can be used with the Standard Library algorithms to create powerful statements. For example, you can use an ostream_iterator with the copy algorithm to copy a container's *entire* contents to the standard output stream with a single statement.

```
1  // Fig. 15.4: fig15_04.cpp
2  // Demonstrating input and output with iterators.
3  #include <iostream>
4  #include <iterator> // ostream_iterator and istream_iterator
5  using namespace std;
6
7  int main()
8  {
9     cout << "Enter two integers: ";
10
11    // create istream_iterator for reading int values from cin
12    istream_iterator< int > inputInt( cin );
13
14    int number1 = *inputInt; // read int from standard input
15    ++inputInt; // move iterator to next input value
16    int number2 = *inputInt; // read int from standard input
17
18    // create ostream_iterator for writing int values to cout
19    ostream_iterator< int > outputInt( cout );
20
21    cout << "The sum is: ";
22    *outputInt = number1 + number2; // output result to cout
23    cout << endl;
24 } // end main
```

```
Enter two integers: 12 25
The sum is: 37
```

Fig. 15.4 | Demonstrating input and output with iterators.

istream_iterator

Line 12 creates an istream_iterator that's capable of *extracting* (inputting) int values from the standard input object cin. Line 14 *dereferences* iterator inputInt to read the first integer from cin and assigns that integer to number1. The dereferencing operator * applied to iterator `inputInt` gets the value from the stream associated with `inputInt`; this is similar to *dereferencing a pointer*. Line 15 positions iterator `inputInt` to the next value in the input stream. Line 16 inputs the next integer from `inputInt` and assigns it to `number2`.

`ostream_iterator`

Line 19 creates an `ostream_iterator` that's capable of inserting (outputting) `int` values in the standard output object `cout`. Line 22 outputs an integer to `cout` by assigning to `*outputInt` the sum of `number1` and `number2`. Notice that we use the dereferenced `outputInt` iterator as an *lvalue* in the assignment statement. If you want to output another value using `outputInt`, the iterator must be incremented with ++ first. Either the prefix or postfix increment can be used—we use the prefix form for *performance* reasons because it does not create a temporary object.

Error-Prevention Tip 15.2

*The * (dereferencing) operator when applied to a `const` iterator returns a reference to `const` for the container element, disallowing the use of non-`const` member functions.*

Iterator Categories and Iterator Category Hierarchy

Figure 15.5 shows the iterator categories. Each category provides a specific set of functionality. Figure 15.6 illustrates the hierarchy of iterator categories. As you follow the hierarchy from bottom to top, each iterator category supports all the functionality of the categories *below* it in the figure. Thus the "weakest" iterator types are at the bottom and the most powerful one is at the top. Note that this is *not* an inheritance hierarchy.

Category	Description
random access	Combines the capabilities of a *bidirectional iterator* with the ability to *directly* access *any* element of the container, i.e., to jump forward or backward by an arbitrary number of elements. These can also be compared with relational operators.
bidirectional	Combines the capabilities of a *forward iterator* with the ability to move in the *backward* direction (i.e., from the end of the container toward the beginning). Bidirectional iterators support multipass algorithms.
forward	Combines the capabilities of *input and output iterators* and retains their position in the container (as state information). Such iterators can be used to pass through a sequence more than once (for so-called multipass algorithms).
output	Used to write an element to a container. An output iterator can move only in the *forward* direction one element at a time. Output iterators support *only* one-pass algorithms—the same output iterator *cannot* be used to pass through a sequence twice.
input	Used to read an element from a container. An input iterator can move only in the *forward* direction (i.e., from the beginning of the container to the end) one element at a time. Input iterators support *only* one-pass algorithms—the same input iterator *cannot* be used to pass through a sequence twice.

Fig. 15.5 | Iterator categories.

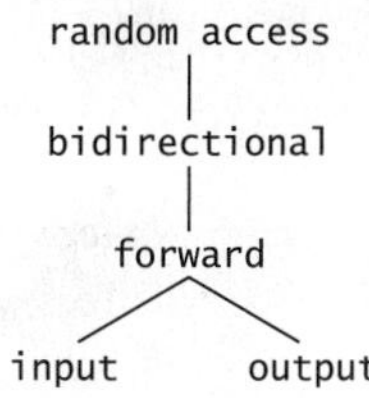

Fig. 15.6 | Iterator category hierarchy.

Container Support for Iterators

The iterator category that each container supports determines whether that container can be used with specific algorithms. *Containers that support random-access iterators can be used with all Standard Library algorithms*—with the exception that if an algorithm requires changes to a container's size, the algorithm can't be used on built-in arrays or `array` objects. Pointers into *built-in* arrays can be used in place of iterators with most algorithms. Figure 15.7 shows the iterator category of each container. The first-class containers, `string`s and built-in arrays are all traversable with iterators.

Container	Iterator type	Container	Iterator type
Sequence containers (first class)		*Unordered associative containers (first class)*	
`vector`	random access	`unordered_set`	bidirectional
`array`	random access	`unordered_multiset`	bidirectional
`deque`	random access	`unordered_map`	bidirectional
`list`	bidirectional	`unordered_multimap`	bidirectional
`forward_list`	forward		
Ordered associative containers (first class)		*Container adapters*	
`set`	bidirectional	`stack`	none
`multiset`	bidirectional	`queue`	none
`map`	bidirectional	`priority_queue`	none
`multimap`	bidirectional		

Fig. 15.7 | Iterator types supported by each container.

Predefined Iterator `typedef`*s*

Figure 15.8 shows the predefined iterator `typedef`s that are found in the Standard Library container class definitions. Not every `typedef` is defined for every container. We use `const` versions of the iterators for traversing `const` *containers* or non-`const` containers that should not be modified. We use *reverse iterators* to traverse containers in the *reverse* direction.

Error-Prevention Tip 15.3

Operations performed on a `const_iterator` *return references to* `const` *to prevent modification to elements of the container being manipulated. Using* `const_iterator`*s where appropriate is another example of the principle of least privilege.*

Predefined typedefs for iterator types	Direction of ++	Capability
`iterator`	forward	read/write
`const_iterator`	forward	read
`reverse_iterator`	backward	read/write
`const_reverse_iterator`	backward	read

Fig. 15.8 | Iterator `typedef`s.

Iterator Operations

Figure 15.9 shows operations that can be performed on each iterator type. In addition to the operators shown for all iterators, iterators must provide default constructors, copy constructors and copy assignment operators. A *forward* iterator supports ++ and all of the *input* and *output* iterator capabilities. A *bidirectional* iterator supports `--` and all the capabilities of *forward* iterators. A *random access* iterator supports all of the operations shown in the table. For input iterators and output iterators, it's not possible to save the iterator then use the saved value later.

Iterator operation	Description
All iterators	
`++p`	Preincrement an iterator.
`p++`	Postincrement an iterator.
`p = p1`	Assign one iterator to another.
Input iterators	
`*p`	Dereference an iterator as an *rvalue*.
`p->m`	Use the iterator to read the element `m`.
`p == p1`	Compare iterators for equality.
`p != p1`	Compare iterators for inequality.
Output iterators	
`*p`	Dereference an iterator as an *lvalue*.
`p = p1`	Assign one iterator to another.
Forward iterators	Forward iterators provide all the functionality of both input iterators and output iterators.
Bidirectional iterators	
`--p`	Predecrement an iterator.
`p--`	Postdecrement an iterator.
Random-access iterators	
`p += i`	Increment the iterator `p` by `i` positions.
`p -= i`	Decrement the iterator `p` by `i` positions.

Fig. 15.9 | Iterator operations for each type of iterator. (Part 1 of 2.)

Iterator operation	Description
`p + i` *or* `i + p`	Expression value is an iterator positioned at `p` incremented by `i` positions.
`p - i`	Expression value is an iterator positioned at `p` decremented by `i` positions.
`p - p1`	Expression value is an integer representing the distance between two elements in the same container.
`p[ i ]`	Return a reference to the element offset from `p` by `i` positions
`p < p1`	Return `true` if iterator `p` is *less than* iterator `p1` (i.e., iterator `p` is *before* iterator `p1` in the container); otherwise, return `false`.
`p <= p1`	Return `true` if iterator `p` is *less than or equal to* iterator `p1` (i.e., iterator `p` is *before* iterator `p1` or *at the same location* as iterator `p1` in the container); otherwise, return `false`.
`p > p1`	Return `true` if iterator `p` is *greater than* iterator `p1` (i.e., iterator `p` is *after* iterator `p1` in the container); otherwise, return `false`.
`p >= p1`	Return `true` if iterator `p` is *greater than or equal to* iterator `p1` (i.e., iterator `p` is *after* iterator `p1` or *at the same location* as iterator `p1` in the container); otherwise, return `false`.

Fig. 15.9 | Iterator operations for each type of iterator. (Part 2 of 2.)

15.4 Introduction to Algorithms

The Standard Library provides scores of *algorithms* you'll use frequently to manipulate a variety of containers. *Inserting, deleting, searching, sorting* and others are appropriate for some or all of the sequence and associative containers. *The algorithms operate on container elements only indirectly through iterators.* Many algorithms operate on sequences of elements defined by iterators pointing to the *first element* of the sequence and to *one element past the last element.* It's also possible to *create your own new algorithms* that operate in a similar fashion so they can be used with the Standard Library containers and iterators. In this chapter, we'll use the `copy` algorithm in many examples to copy a container's contents to the standard output. We discuss many Standard Library algorithms in Chapter 16.

15.5 Sequence Containers

The C++ Standard Template Library provides five *sequence containers*—`array`, `vector`, `deque`, `list` and `forward_list`. Class templates `array`, `vector` and `deque` are based on built-in arrays. Class templates `list` and `forward_list` implement linked-list data structures. We've already discussed and used class template `array` extensively, so we do not cover it again here.

Performance and Choosing the Appropriate Container

Figure 15.2 presented the operations common to *most* of the Standard Library containers. Beyond these operations, each container typically provides a variety of other capabilities. Many of these are common to several containers, but they're not always equally efficient for each container.

Software Engineering Observation 15.2

It's usually preferable to reuse Standard Library containers rather than developing customized templatized data structures. For novices, `vector` *is typically satisfactory for most applications.*

Performance Tip 15.2

Insertion at the back of a `vector` *is efficient. The* `vector` *simply grows, if necessary, to accommodate the new item. It's expensive to insert (or delete) an element in the middle of a* `vector`*—the entire portion of the* `vector` after *the insertion (or deletion) point must be moved, because* `vector` *elements occupy contiguous cells in memory.*

Performance Tip 15.3

Applications that require frequent insertions and deletions at both ends of a container normally use a `deque` *rather than a* `vector`*. Although we can insert and delete elements at the front and back of both a* `vector` *and a* `deque`*, class* `deque` *is more efficient than* `vector` *for doing insertions and deletions at the front.*

Performance Tip 15.4

Applications with frequent insertions and deletions in the middle and/or at the extremes of a container normally use a `list`*, due to its efficient implementation of insertion and deletion anywhere in the data structure.*

15.5.1 `vector` Sequence Container

Class template `vector`, which we introduced in Section 7.10, provides a data structure with *contiguous* memory locations. This enables efficient, direct access to any element of a `vector` via the subscript operator `[]`, exactly as with a built-in array. Like class template `array`, template `vector` is most commonly used when the data in the container must be easily accessible via a subscript or will be sorted, and when the number of elements may need to grow. When a `vector`'s memory is exhausted, the `vector` *allocates* a larger built-in array, *copies* (or *moves*; Chapter 24) the original elements into the new built-in array and *deallocates* the old built-in array. .

Performance Tip 15.5

Choose the `vector` *container for the best random-access performance in a container that can grow.*

Performance Tip 15.6

Objects of class template `vector` *provide rapid indexed access with the overloaded subscript operator* `[]` *because they're stored in* contiguous memory *like a built-in array or an* `array` *object.*

Using `vector`*s and Iterators*

Figure 15.10 illustrates several functions of the `vector` class template. Many of these functions are available in every *first-class container*. You must include header `<vector>` to use class template `vector`.

```cpp
// Fig. 15.10: Fig15_10.cpp
// Standard Library vector class template.
#include <iostream>
#include <vector> // vector class-template definition
using namespace std;

// prototype for function template printVector
template < typename T > void printVector( const vector< T > &integers2 );

int main()
{
   const size_t SIZE = 6; // define array size
   int values[ SIZE ] = { 1, 2, 3, 4, 5, 6 }; // initialize values
   vector< int > integers; // create vector of ints

   cout << "The initial size of integers is: " << integers.size()
      << "\nThe initial capacity of integers is: " << integers.capacity();

   // function push_back is in vector, deque and list
   integers.push_back( 2 );
   integers.push_back( 3 );
   integers.push_back( 4 );

   cout << "\nThe size of integers is: " << integers.size()
      << "\nThe capacity of integers is: " << integers.capacity();
   cout << "\n\nOutput built-in array using pointer notation: ";

   // display array using pointer notation
   for ( const int *ptr = begin( values ); ptr != end( values ); ++ptr )
      cout << *ptr << ' ';

   cout << "\nOutput vector using iterator notation: ";
   printVector( integers );
   cout << "\nReversed contents of vector integers: ";

   // display vector in reverse order using const_reverse_iterator
   for ( auto reverseIterator = integers.crbegin();
      reverseIterator!= integers.crend(); ++reverseIterator )
      cout << *reverseIterator << ' ';

   cout << endl;
} // end main

// function template for outputting vector elements
template < typename T > void printVector( const vector< T > &integers2 )
{
   // display vector elements using const_iterator
   for ( auto constIterator = integers2.cbegin();
      constIterator != integers2.cend(); ++constIterator )
      cout << *constIterator << ' ';
} // end function printVector
```

Fig. 15.10 | Standard Library vector class template. (Part 1 of 2.)

```
The initial size of integers is: 0
The initial capacity of integers is: 0
The size of integers is: 3
The capacity of integers is: 4

Output built-in array using pointer notation: 1 2 3 4 5 6
Output vector using iterator notation: 2 3 4
Reversed contents of vector integers: 4 3 2
```

Fig. 15.10 | Standard Library `vector` class template. (Part 2 of 2.)

Creating a `vector`

Line 14 defines an instance called `integers` of class template `vector` that stores `int` values. When this object is instantiated, an empty `vector` is created with size 0 (i.e., the number of elements stored in the `vector`) and capacity 0 (i.e., the number of elements that can be stored without allocating more memory to the `vector`).

`vector` *Member Functions* `size` *and* `capacity`

Lines 16 and 17 demonstrate the `size` and `capacity` functions; each initially returns 0 for `vector v` in this example. Function `size`—available in *every* container except `forward_List`—returns the number of elements currently stored in the container. Function **`capacity`** (specific to `vector` and `deque`) returns the number of elements that can be stored in the `vector` before the `vector` needs to *dynamically resize itself* to accommodate more elements.

`vector` *Member Function* `push_back`

Lines 20–22 use function **`push_back`**—available in *sequence containers* other than `array` and `forward_list`—to add an element to the end of the `vector`. If an element is added to a full `vector`, the `vector` increases its size—some implementations have the `vector` *double* its capacity. Sequence containers other than `array` and `vector` also provide a **`push_front`** function.

Performance Tip 15.7

It can be wasteful to double a `vector`'s size when more space is needed. For example, a full `vector` of 1,000,000 elements resizes to accommodate 2,000,000 elements when a new element is added. This leaves 999,999 unused elements. You can use `resize` and `reserve` to control space usage better.

Updated `size` *and* `capacity` *After Modifying a* `vector`

Lines 24 and 25 use `size` and `capacity` to illustrate the new size and capacity of the `vector` after the three `push_back` operations. Function `size` returns 3—the number of elements added to the `vector`. Function `capacity` returns 4 (though this could vary by compiler), indicating that we can add one more element before the `vector` needs to add more memory. When we added the first element, the `vector` allocated space for one element, and the size became 1 to indicate that the `vector` contained only one element. When we added the second element, the capacity *doubled* to 2 and the size became 2 as well. When we added the third element, the capacity doubled again to 4. So we can actually add another element before the `vector` needs to allocate more space. When the `vector` eventually fills its allocated capacity and the program attempts to add one more element to the vector, the vector will double its capacity to eight elements.

vector *Growth*

The manner in which a vector grows to accommodate more elements—a time consuming operation—is *not* specified by the C++ Standard. C++ library implementers use various clever schemes to minimize the overhead of *resizing* a vector. Hence, the output of this program may vary, depending on the version of vector that comes with your compiler. Some library implementers allocate a large initial capacity. If a vector stores a small number of elements, such capacity may be a waste of space. However, it can greatly improve performance if a program adds many elements to a vector and does not have to reallocate memory to accommodate those elements. This is a classic *space–time trade-off*. Library implementors must balance the amount of memory used against the amount of time required to perform various vector operations.

Outputting Built-in Array Contents with Pointers

Lines 29–30 demonstrate how to output the contents of the built-in array values using pointers and pointer arithmetic. Pointers into a built-in array can be used as iterators. Recall from Section 8.5 that C++11 functions begin and end (line 29) from the <iterator> header each take a built-in array as an argument. Function begin returns an iterator pointing to the built-in array's first element and function end returns an iterator representing the position one element *after* the end of the built-in array. Functions begin and end may *also* receive container objects as arguments. Note that we use the != operator in the loop-continuation condition. When iterating using pointers to built-in array elements, it's common for the loop-continuation condition to test whether the pointer has reached the end of the built-in array. This technique is commonly used by the standard library algorithms. 11

Outputting vector *Contents with Iterators*

Line 33 calls function printVector (defined in lines 45–51) to output the contents of a vector using iterators. The function receives a reference to a const vector. The for statement in lines 48–50 initializes control variable constIterator using vector member function **cbegin** (new in C++11), which returns a const_iterator to the vector's first element. We infer the control variable's type (vector<int>::const_iterator) using the auto keyword. Prior to C++11, you would have used the overloaded begin member function to get the const_iterator—when called on a const container, begin returns a const_iterator. The other version of begin returns an iterator that can be used for non-const containers. 11

The loop continues as long as constIterator has not reached the end of the vector. This is determined by comparing constIterator to the result of calling the vector's **cend** member function (also new in C++11), which returns a const_iterator indicating the *location past the last element* of the vector. If constIterator is equal to this value, the end of the vector has been reached. Prior to C++11, you would have used the overloaded end member function to get the const_iterator. Functions cbegin, begin, cend and end are available for all first-class containers. 11

The body of the loop dereferences constIterator to get the current element's value. Remember that the iterator acts like a pointer to the element and that operator * is overloaded to return a reference to the element. The expression ++constIterator (line 49) positions the iterator to the vector's next element. Note that lines 48–50 could have been replaced with the following range-based for statement:

```
for ( auto const &item : integers2 )
   cout << item << ' ';
```

Common Programming Error 15.1

Attempting to dereference an iterator positioned outside its container is a runtime logic error. In particular, the iterator returned by end should not be dereferenced or incremented.

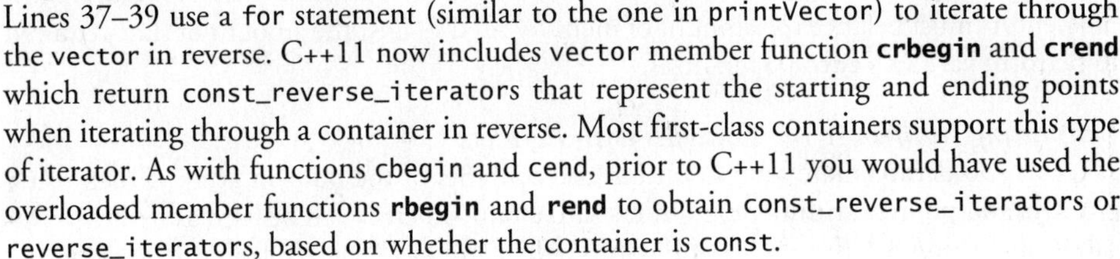

Displaying the **vector***'s Contents in Reverse with* **const_reverse_iterators**

Lines 37–39 use a for statement (similar to the one in printVector) to iterate through the vector in reverse. C++11 now includes vector member function **crbegin** and **crend** which return const_reverse_iterators that represent the starting and ending points when iterating through a container in reverse. Most first-class containers support this type of iterator. As with functions cbegin and cend, prior to C++11 you would have used the overloaded member functions **rbegin** and **rend** to obtain const_reverse_iterators or reverse_iterators, based on whether the container is const.

C++11: **shrink_to_fit**

As of C++11, you can ask a vector or deque to return unneeded memory to the system by calling member function **shrink_to_fit**. This *requests* that the container reduce its capacity to the number of elements in the container. According to the C++ standard, implementations can *ignore* this request so that they can perform implementation-specific optimizations.

vector *Element-Manipulation Functions*

Figure 15.11 illustrates functions for retrieving and manipulating vector elements. Line 16 uses an overloaded vector constructor that takes two iterators as arguments to initialize integers. Line 16 initializes integers with the contents of the array values from beginning of values up to—but not including—values.cend() (which points to the element *after* the end of values). In C++11, you can use list initializers to initialize vectors as in

```
vector< int > integers{ 1, 2, 3, 4, 5, 6 };
```

or

```
vector< int > integers = { 1, 2, 3, 4, 5, 6 };
```

However, these are not fully supported across compilers yet. For this reason, this chapter's examples frequently initialize other containers with array contents as in line 16.

```
1  // Fig. 15.11: fig15_15.cpp
2  // Testing Standard Library vector class template
3  // element-manipulation functions.
4  #include <iostream>
```

Fig. 15.11 | vector class template element-manipulation functions. (Part 1 of 3.)

```
#include <array> // array class-template definition
#include <vector> // vector class-template definition
#include <algorithm> // copy algorithm
#include <iterator> // ostream_iterator iterator
#include <stdexcept> // out_of_range exception
using namespace std;

int main()
{
   const size_t SIZE = 6;
   array< int, SIZE > values = { 1, 2, 3, 4, 5, 6 };
   vector< int > integers( values.cbegin(), values.cend() );
   ostream_iterator< int > output( cout, " " );

   cout << "Vector integers contains: ";
   copy( integers.cbegin(), integers.cend(), output );

   cout << "\nFirst element of integers: " << integers.front()
      << "\nLast element of integers: " << integers.back();

   integers[ 0 ] = 7; // set first element to 7
   integers.at( 2 ) = 10; // set element at position 2 to 10

   // insert 22 as 2nd element
   integers.insert( integers.cbegin() + 1, 22 );

   cout << "\n\nContents of vector integers after changes: ";
   copy( integers.cbegin(), integers.cend(), output );

   // access out-of-range element
   try
   {
      integers.at( 100 ) = 777;
   } // end try
   catch ( out_of_range &outOfRange ) // out_of_range exception
   {
      cout << "\n\nException: " << outOfRange.what();
   } // end catch

   // erase first element
   integers.erase( integers.cbegin() );
   cout << "\n\nVector integers after erasing first element: ";
   copy( integers.cbegin(), integers.cend(), output );

   // erase remaining elements
   integers.erase( integers.cbegin(), integers.cend() );
   cout << "\nAfter erasing all elements, vector integers "
      << ( integers.empty() ? "is" : "is not" ) << " empty";

   // insert elements from the array values
   integers.insert( integers.cbegin(), values.cbegin(), values.cend() );
   cout << "\n\nContents of vector integers before clear: ";
   copy( integers.cbegin(), integers.cend(), output );
```

Fig. 15.11 | vector class template element-manipulation functions. (Part 2 of 3.)

```
58
59      // empty integers; clear calls erase to empty a collection
60      integers.clear();
61      cout << "\nAfter clear, vector integers "
62         << ( integers.empty() ? "is" : "is not" ) << " empty" << endl;
63   } // end main
```

```
Vector integers contains: 1 2 3 4 5 6
First element of integers: 1
Last element of integers: 6

Contents of vector integers after changes: 7 22 2 10 4 5 6

Exception: invalid vector<T> subscript

Vector integers after erasing first element: 22 2 10 4 5 6
After erasing all elements, vector integers is empty

Contents of vector integers before clear: 1 2 3 4 5 6
After clear, vector integers is empty
```

Fig. 15.11 | vector class template element-manipulation functions. (Part 3 of 3.)

ostream_iterator

Line 17 defines an ostream_iterator called output that can be used to output integers separated by single spaces via cout. An ostream_iterator<int> outputs only values of type int or a compatible type. The first argument to the constructor specifies the output stream, and the second argument is a string specifying the separator for the values output—in this case, the string contains a space character. We use the ostream_iterator (defined in header <iterator>) to output the contents of the vector in this example.

copy Algorithm

Line 20 uses Standard Library algorithm **copy** (from header **<algorithm>**) to output the entire contents of integers to the standard output. The algorithm copies each element in a range from the location specified by the iterator in its first argument and up to, but *not* including, the location specified by the iterator in its second argument. These two arguments must satisfy *input iterator* requirements—they must be iterators through which values can be read from a container, such as const_iterators. They must also represent a range of elements—applying ++ to the first iterator must eventually cause it to reach the second iterator argument in the range. The elements are copied to the location specified by the *output iterator* (i.e., an iterator through which a value can be stored or output) specified as the last argument. In this case, the *output iterator* is an ostream_iterator that's attached to cout, so the elements are copied to the standard output.

vector Member Functions front and back

Lines 22–23 use functions **front** and **back** (available for most *sequence containers*) to determine the vector's first and last elements, respectively. Notice the difference between functions front and begin. Function front returns a reference to the first element in the vector, while function begin returns a *random access iterator* pointing to the first element in the vector. Also notice the difference between functions back and end. Function back returns a reference to the `vector`'s last element, whereas function `end` returns a *random access iterator* pointing to the location *after* the last element.

Common Programming Error 15.2

The `vector` *must not be empty; otherwise, the results of* `front` *and* `back` *are undefined.*

Accessing `vector` *Elements*

Lines 25–26 illustrate two ways to access `vector` elements. These can also be used with `deque` containers. Line 25 uses the subscript operator that's overloaded to return either a reference to the value at the specified location or a reference to that `const` value, depending on whether the container is `const`. Function `at` (line 26) performs the same operation, but with *bounds checking*. Function `at` first checks the value supplied as an argument and determines whether it's in the `vector`'s bounds. If not, function `at` throws an `out_of_range` exception (as demonstrated in lines 35–42). Figure 15.12 shows some of the Standard Library exception types. (The Standard Library exception types are discussed in Chapter 17.)

Exception type	Description
`out_of_range`	Indicates when subscript is out of range—e.g., when an invalid subscript is specified to `vector` member function `at`.
`invalid_argument`	Indicates an invalid argument was passed to a function.
`length_error`	Indicates an attempt to create too long a container, `string`, etc.
`bad_alloc`	Indicates that an attempt to allocate memory with `new` (or with an allocator) failed because not enough memory was available.

Fig. 15.12 | Some exception types in header `<stdexcept>`.

`vector` *Member Function* `insert`

Line 29 uses one of the several overloaded **`insert`** functions provided by each *sequence container* (except `array`, which has a fixed size, and `forward_list`, which has the function `insert_after` instead). Line 29 inserts the value 22 before the element at the location specified by the iterator in the first argument. In this example, the iterator is pointing to the `vector`'s second element, so 22 is inserted as the second element and the original second element becomes the third element. Other versions of `insert` allow inserting multiple copies of the same value starting at a particular position, or inserting a range of values from another container, starting at a particular position. As of C++11, this version of member function `insert` returns an iterator pointing to the item that was inserted. 11

`vector` *Member Function* `erase`

Lines 45 and 50 use the two **`erase`** functions that are available in all *first-class containers* (except `array`, which has a fixed size, and `forward_list`, which has the function `erase_after` instead). Line 45 erases the element at the location specified by the iterator argument (in this example, the first element). Line 50 specifies that all elements in the range specified by the two iterator arguments should be erased. In this example, all the elements are erased. Line 52 uses function **`empty`** (available for all containers and adapters) to confirm that the `vector` is empty.

Common Programming Error 15.3

Normally `erase` *destroys the objects that are erased from a container. However, erasing an element that contains a pointer to a dynamically allocated object does* not `delete` *the dynamically allocated memory—this can lead to a memory leak. If the element is a* `unique_ptr`*, the* `unique_ptr` *would be destroyed and the dynamically allocated memory* would *be deleted. If the element is a* `shared_ptr`*, the reference count to the dynamically allocated object would be decremented and the memory would be deleted* only *if the reference count reached* `0`*.*

`vector` *Member Function* `insert` *with Three Arguments (Range* `insert`*)*

Line 55 demonstrates the version of function `insert` that uses the second and third arguments to specify the starting location and ending location in a sequence of values (in this case, from the `array` `values`) that should be inserted into the `vector`. Remember that the ending location specifies the position in the sequence *after* the last element to be inserted; copying occurs up to, but *not* including, this location. As of C++11, this version of member function `insert` returns an iterator pointing to the first item that was inserted—if nothing was inserted, the function returns its first argument.

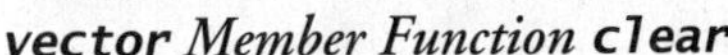

`vector` *Member Function* `clear`

Finally, line 60 uses function **`clear`** (found in all *first-class containers* except `array`) to empty the `vector`—this does not necessarily return any of the `vector`'s memory to the system. [*Note:* We'll cover many common container member functions in the next few sections. We'll also cover many functions that are specific to each container.]

15.5.2 `list` Sequence Container

The **`list`** *sequence container* (from header `<list>`) allows insertion and deletion operations at *any* location in the container. If most of the insertions and deletions occur at the *ends* of the container, the `deque` data structure (Section 15.5.3) provides a more efficient implementation. Class template `list` is implemented as a *doubly linked list*—every node in the `list` contains a pointer to the previous node in the `list` and to the next node in the `list`. This enables class template `list` to support *bidirectional iterators* that allow the container to be traversed both forward and backward. Any algorithm that requires *input, output, forward* or *bidirectional iterators* can operate on a `list`. Many `list` member functions manipulate the elements of the container as an ordered set of elements.

C++11: `forward_list` *Container*

C++11 now includes the new **`forward_list`** sequence container (header `<forward_list>`), which is implemented as a *singly linked list*—every node in the `list` contains a pointer to the next node in the `list`. This enables class template `list` to support *forward iterators* that allow the container to be traversed in the forward direction. Any algorithm that requires *input, output* or *forward iterators* can operate on a `forward_list`.

`list` *Member Functions*

In addition to the member functions in Fig. 15.2 and the common member functions of all *sequence containers* discussed in Section 15.5, class template `list` provides other member functions, including `splice`, `push_front`, `pop_front`, `remove`, `remove_if`, `unique`, `merge`, `reverse` and `sort`. Several of these member functions are `list`-optimized implementations of the Standard Library algorithms presented in Chapter 16. Both `push_front` and `pop_front` are also supported by `forward_list` and `deque`. Figure 15.13 demonstrates several features of class `list`. Remember that many of the functions presented in Figs. 15.10–15.11 can be used with class `list`, so we focus on the new features in this example's discussion.

```
// Fig. 15.13: fig15_13.cpp
// Standard library list class template.
#include <iostream>
#include <array>
#include <list> // list class-template definition
#include <algorithm> // copy algorithm
#include <iterator> // ostream_iterator
using namespace std;

// prototype for function template printList
template < typename T > void printList( const list< T > &listRef );

int main()
{
   const size_t SIZE = 4;
   array< int, SIZE > ints = { 2, 6, 4, 8 };
   list< int > values; // create list of ints
   list< int > otherValues; // create list of ints

   // insert items in values
   values.push_front( 1 );
   values.push_front( 2 );
   values.push_back( 4 );
   values.push_back( 3 );

   cout << "values contains: ";
   printList( values );

   values.sort(); // sort values
   cout << "\nvalues after sorting contains: ";
   printList( values );

   // insert elements of ints into otherValues
   otherValues.insert( otherValues.cbegin(), ints.cbegin(), ints.cend() );
   cout << "\nAfter insert, otherValues contains: ";
   printList( otherValues );

   // remove otherValues elements and insert at end of values
   values.splice( values.cend(), otherValues );
   cout << "\nAfter splice, values contains: ";
   printList( values );

   values.sort(); // sort values
   cout << "\nAfter sort, values contains: ";
   printList( values );

```

Fig. 15.13 | Standard Library `list` class template. (Part 1 of 3.)

```
   // insert elements of ints into otherValues
   otherValues.insert( otherValues.cbegin(), ints.cbegin(), ints.cend() );
   otherValues.sort(); // sort the list
   cout << "\nAfter insert and sort, otherValues contains: ";
   printList( otherValues );

   // remove otherValues elements and insert into values in sorted order
   values.merge( otherValues );
   cout << "\nAfter merge:\n   values contains: ";
   printList( values );
   cout << "\n   otherValues contains: ";
   printList( otherValues );

   values.pop_front(); // remove element from front
   values.pop_back(); // remove element from back
   cout << "\nAfter pop_front and pop_back:\n   values contains: "
   printList( values );

   values.unique(); // remove duplicate elements
   cout << "\nAfter unique, values contains: ";
   printList( values );

   // swap elements of values and otherValues
   values.swap( otherValues );
   cout << "\nAfter swap:\n   values contains: ";
   printList( values );
   cout << "\n   otherValues contains: ";
   printList( otherValues );

   // replace contents of values with elements of otherValues
   values.assign( otherValues.cbegin(), otherValues.cend() );
   cout << "\nAfter assign, values contains: ";
   printList( values );

   // remove otherValues elements and insert into values in sorted order
   values.merge( otherValues );
   cout << "\nAfter merge, values contains: ";
   printList( values );

   values.remove( 4 ); // remove all 4s
   cout << "\nAfter remove( 4 ), values contains: ";
   printList( values );
   cout << endl;
} // end main

// printList function template definition; uses
// ostream_iterator and copy algorithm to output list elements
template < typename T > void printList( const list< T > &listRef )
{
   if ( listRef.empty() ) // list is empty
      cout << "List is empty";
   else
   {
```

Fig. 15.13 | Standard Library `list` class template. (Part 2 of 3.)

```
100         ostream_iterator< T > output( cout, " " );
101         copy( listRef.cbegin(), listRef.cend(), output );
102      } // end else
103   } // end function printList
```

```
values contains: 2 1 4 3
values after sorting contains: 1 2 3 4
After insert, otherValues contains: 2 6 4 8
After splice, values contains: 1 2 3 4 2 6 4 8
After sort, values contains: 1 2 2 3 4 4 6 8
After insert and sort, otherValues contains: 2 4 6 8
After merge:
   values contains: 1 2 2 2 3 4 4 4 6 6 8 8
   otherValues contains: List is empty
After pop_front and pop_back:
   values contains: 2 2 2 3 4 4 4 6 6 8r
After unique, values contains: 2 3 4 6 8
After swap:
   values contains: List is empty
   otherValues contains: 2 3 4 6 8
After assign, values contains: 2 3 4 6 8
After merge, values contains: 2 2 3 3 4 4 6 6 8 8
After remove( 4 ), values contains: 2 2 3 3 6 6 8 8
```

Fig. 15.13 | Standard Library `list` class template. (Part 3 of 3.)

Creating `list` Objects

Lines 17–18 instantiate two `list` objects capable of storing `int`s. Lines 21–22 use function **`push_front`** to insert integers at the beginning of `values`. Function `push_front` is specific to classes `forward_list`, `list` and `deque`. Lines 23–24 use function `push_back` to insert integers at the end of `values`. *Function `push_back` is common to all sequence containers*, except `array` and `forward_list`.

`list` Member Function `sort`

Line 29 uses `list` member function **`sort`** to arrange the elements in the `list` in *ascending order*. [*Note:* This is different from the `sort` in the Standard Library algorithms.] A second version of function `sort` allows you to supply a *binary predicate function* that takes two arguments (values in the list), performs a comparison and returns a `bool` value indicating whether the first argument should come before the second in the sorted contents. This function determines the order in which the elements of the `list` are sorted. This version could be particularly useful for a `list` that stores pointers rather than values. [*Note:* We demonstrate a *unary predicate function* in Fig. 16.3. A unary predicate function takes a single argument, performs a comparison using that argument and returns a `bool` value indicating the result.]

`list` Member Function `splice`

Line 39 uses `list` function **`splice`** to remove the elements in `otherValues` and insert them into `values` before the iterator position specified as the first argument. There are two other versions of this function. Function `splice` with three arguments allows one element to be removed from the container specified as the second argument from the location specified by the iterator in the third argument. Function `splice` with four arguments uses the last two arguments to specify a range of locations that should be removed from the container in the second argument and placed at the location specified in the first argument. Class template `forward_list` provides a similar member function named `splice_after`.

`list` *Member Function* `merge`

After inserting more elements in `otherValues` and *sorting* both `values` and `otherValues`, line 54 uses `list` member function **`merge`** to remove all elements of `otherValues` and insert them in sorted order into `values`. Both `list`s *must* be *sorted* in the *same* order before this operation is performed. A second version of `merge` enables you to supply a *binary predicate function* that takes two arguments (values in the list) and returns a `bool` value. The predicate function specifies the sorting order used by `merge`.

`list` *Member Function* `pop_front`

Line 60 uses `list` function **`pop_front`** to remove the first element in the `list`. Line 60 uses function **`pop_back`** (available for *sequence containers* other than `array` and `forward_list`) to remove the last element in the `list`.

`list` *Member Function* `unique`

Line 65 uses `list` function **`unique`** to *remove duplicate elements* in the `list`. The `list` should be in *sorted* order (so that all duplicates are side by side) before this operation is performed, to guarantee that all duplicates are eliminated. A second version of `unique` enables you to supply a *predicate function* that takes two arguments (values in the list) and returns a `bool` value specifying whether two elements are equal.

`list` *Member Function* `swap`

Line 70 uses function **`swap`** (available to all *first-class containers*) to exchange the contents of `values` with the contents of `otherValues`.

`list` *Member Functions* `assign` *and* `remove`

Line 77 uses `list` function **`assign`** (available to all *sequence containers*) to replace the contents of `values` with the contents of `otherValues` in the range specified by the two iterator arguments. A second version of `assign` replaces the original contents with copies of the value specified in the second argument. The first argument of the function specifies the number of copies. Line 86 uses `list` function **`remove`** to delete all copies of the value `4` from the `list`.

15.5.3 deque Sequence Container

Class **`deque`** provides many of the benefits of a `vector` and a `list` in one container. The term `deque` is short for "double-ended queue." Class `deque` is implemented to provide efficient indexed access (using subscripting) for reading and modifying its elements, much like a `vector`. Class `deque` is also implemented for *efficient insertion and deletion operations at its front and back*, much like a `list` (although a `list` is also capable of efficient insertions and deletions in the *middle* of the `list`). Class `deque` provides support for random-access iterators, so `deque`s can be used with all Standard Library algorithms. One of the most common uses of a `deque` is to maintain a *first-in, first-out queue* of elements. In fact, a `deque` is the default underlying implementation for the `queue` adaptor (Section 15.7.2).

Additional storage for a `deque` can be allocated at either end of the `deque` in blocks of memory that are typically maintained as a built-in array of pointers to those blocks.[2] Due to the *noncontiguous memory layout* of a deque, a deque iterator must be more "intelligent" than the pointers that are used to iterate through vectors, arrays or built-in arrays.

Performance Tip 15.8

In general, deque *has higher overhead than* vector*.*

Performance Tip 15.9

Insertions and deletions in the middle of a deque *are optimized to minimize the number of elements copied, so it's more efficient than a* vector *but less efficient than a* list *for this kind of modification.*

Class deque provides the same basic operations as class vector, but like list adds member functions **push_front** and **pop_front** to allow insertion and deletion at the beginning of the deque, respectively.

Figure 15.14 demonstrates features of class deque. Remember that many of the functions presented in Fig. 15.10, Fig. 15.11 and Fig. 15.13 also can be used with class deque. Header **<deque>** must be included to use class deque.

```
// Fig. 15.14: fig15_14.cpp
// Standard Library deque class template.
#include <iostream>
#include <deque> // deque class-template definition
#include <algorithm> // copy algorithm
#include <iterator> // ostream_iterator
using namespace std;

int main()
{
   deque< double > values; // create deque of doubles
   ostream_iterator< double > output( cout, " " );

   // insert elements in values
   values.push_front( 2.2 );
   values.push_front( 3.5 );
   values.push_back( 1.1 );

   cout << "values contains: ";

   // use subscript operator to obtain elements of values
   for ( size_t i = 0; i < values.size(); ++i )
      cout << values[ i ] << ' ';

   values.pop_front(); // remove first element
   cout << "\nAfter pop_front, values contains: ";
   copy( values.cbegin(), values.cend(), output );

```

Fig. 15.14 | Standard Library deque class template. (Part 1 of 2.)

2. This is an implementation-specific detail, not a requirement of the C++ standard.

```
29      // use subscript operator to modify element at location 1
30      values[ 1 ] = 5.4;
31      cout << "\nAfter values[ 1 ] = 5.4, values contains: ";
32      copy( values.cbegin(), values.cend(), output );
33      cout << endl;
34   } // end main
```

```
values contains: 3.5 2.2 1.1
After pop_front, values contains: 2.2 1.1
After values[ 1 ] = 5.4, values contains: 2.2 5.4
```

Fig. 15.14 | Standard Library deque class template. (Part 2 of 2.)

Line 11 instantiates a deque that can store double values. Lines 15–17 use functions push_front and push_back to insert elements at the beginning and end of the deque.

The for statement in lines 22–23 uses the subscript operator to retrieve the value in each element of the deque for output. The condition uses function size to ensure that we do not attempt to access an element *outside* the bounds of the deque.

Line 25 uses function pop_front to demonstrate removing the first element of the deque. Line 30 uses the subscript operator to obtain an *lvalue*. This enables values to be assigned directly to any element of the deque.

15.6 Associative Containers

The *associative containers* provide *direct access* to store and retrieve elements via **keys** (often called **search keys**). The four *ordered associative containers* are multiset, set, multimap and map. Each of these maintains its keys in *sorted order*. There are also four corresponding *unordered associative containers*—unordered_multiset, unordered_set, unordered_multimap and unordered_map—that offer the most of the same capabilities as their ordered counterparts. The primary difference between the ordered and unordered associative containers is that the unordered ones do *not* maintain their keys in *sorted* order. In this section, we focus on the *ordered associative containers.*

Performance Tip 15.10

The unordered associative containers might offer better performance for cases in which it's not necessary to maintain keys in sorted order.

Iterating through an *ordered associative container* traverses it in the sort order for that container. Classes **multiset** and **set** provide operations for manipulating sets of values where the values are the keys—there is *not* a separate value associated with each key. The primary difference between a multiset and a set is that a multiset *allows duplicate keys* and a set does not. Classes **multimap** and **map** provide operations for manipulating values associated with keys (these values are sometimes referred to as **mapped values**). The primary difference between a multimap and a map is that a multimap allows *duplicate keys* with associated values to be stored and a map allows only *unique keys* with associated values. In addition to the common container member functions, *ordered associative containers* also support several other member functions that are specific to associative containers. Examples of each of the *ordered associative containers* and their common member functions are presented in the next several subsections.

15.6.1 multiset Associative Container

The multiset *ordered associative container* (from header **<set>**) provides fast storage and retrieval of keys and allows duplicate keys. The elements' ordering is determined by a so-called **comparator function object**. For example, in an integer multiset, elements can be sorted in *ascending order* by ordering the keys with **comparator function object less<int>**. We discuss function objects in detail in Section 16.4. For this chapter, we'll simply show how to use less<int> when declaring ordered associative containers. The data type of the keys in all *ordered associative containers* must support comparison based on the comparator function object—keys sorted with less<T> must support comparison with operator<. If the keys used in the *ordered associative containers* are of user-defined data types, those types must supply the appropriate comparison operators. A multiset supports *bidirectional iterators* (but not *random-access iterators*). In if the order of the keys is not important, you can use unordered_multiset (header <unordered_set>) instead.

Figure 15.15 demonstrates the multiset *ordered associative container* for a multiset of ints with keys that are sorted in *ascending order*. Containers multiset and set (Section 15.6.2) provide the same basic functionality.

```
// Fig. 15.15: fig15_15.cpp
// Standard Library multiset class template
#include <array>
#include <iostream>
#include <set> // multiset class-template definition
#include <algorithm> // copy algorithm
#include <iterator> // ostream_iterator
using namespace std;

int main()
{
   const size_t SIZE = 10;
   array< int, SIZE > a = { 7, 22, 9, 1, 18, 30, 100, 22, 85, 13 };
   multiset< int, less< int > > intMultiset; // multiset of ints
   ostream_iterator< int > output( cout, " " );

   cout << "There are currently " << intMultiset.count( 15 )
      << " values of 15 in the multiset\n";

   intMultiset.insert( 15 ); // insert 15 in intMultiset
   intMultiset.insert( 15 ); // insert 15 in intMultiset
   cout << "After inserts, there are " << intMultiset.count( 15 )
      << " values of 15 in the multiset\n\n";

   // find 15 in intMultiset; find returns iterator
   auto result = intMultiset.find( 15 );

   if ( result != intMultiset.end() ) // if iterator not at end
      cout << "Found value 15\n"; // found search value 15
```

Fig. 15.15 | Standard Library multiset class template. (Part 1 of 2.)

```
30
31       // find 20 in intMultiset; find returns iterator
32       result = intMultiset.find( 20 );
33
34       if ( result == intMultiset.end() ) // will be true hence
35          cout << "Did not find value 20\n"; // did not find 20
36
37       // insert elements of array a into intMultiset
38       intMultiset.insert( a.cbegin(), a.cend() );
39       cout << "\nAfter insert, intMultiset contains:\n";
40       copy( intMultiset.begin(), intMultiset.end(), output );
41
42       // determine lower and upper bound of 22 in intMultiset
43       cout << "\n\nLower bound of 22: "
44          << *( intMultiset.lower_bound( 22 ) );
45       cout << "\nUpper bound of 22: " << *( intMultiset.upper_bound( 22 ) );
46
47       // use equal_range to determine lower and upper bound
48       // of 22 in intMultiset
49       auto p = intMultiset.equal_range( 22 );
50
51       cout << "\n\nequal_range of 22:" << "\n   Lower bound: "
52          << *( p.first ) << "\n   Upper bound: " << *( p.second );
53       cout << endl;
54    } // end main
```

```
There are currently 0 values of 15 in the multiset
After inserts, there are 2 values of 15 in the multiset

Found value 15
Did not find value 20

After insert, intMultiset contains:
1 7 9 13 15 15 18 22 22 30 85 100

Lower bound of 22: 22
Upper bound of 22: 30

equal_range of 22:
   Lower bound: 22
   Upper bound: 30
```

Fig. 15.15 | Standard Library `multiset` class template. (Part 2 of 2.)

Creating a `multiset`

Line 14 creates a `multiset` of `int`s ordered in *ascending order*, using the function object `less<int>`. *Ascending order* is the default for a `multiset`, so `less<int>` can be omitted. C++11 fixes a compiler issue with spacing between the closing > of `less<int>` and the closing > of the `multiset` type. Before C++11, if you specified this `multiset`'s type as

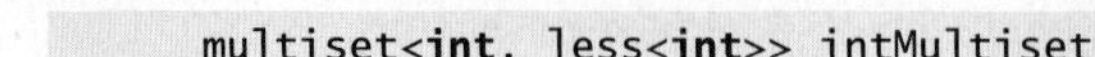

```
multiset<int, less<int>> intMultiset;
```

the compiler would treat >> at the end of the type as the >> operator and generate a compilation error. For this reason, you were required to put a space between the closing > of less<int> and the closing > of the multiset type (or any other similar template type, such as vector<vector<int>>). As of C++11, the preceding declaration compiles correctly.

multiset Member Function count

Line 17 uses function **count** (available to all *associative containers*) to count the number of occurrences of the value 15 currently in the multiset.

multiset Member Function insert

Lines 20–21 use one of the several overloaded versions of function insert to add the value 15 to the multiset twice. A second version of insert takes an iterator and a value as arguments and begins the search for the insertion point from the iterator position specified. A third version of insert takes two iterators as arguments that specify a range of values to add to the multiset from another container.

multiset Member Function find

Line 26 uses function **find** (available to all *associative containers*) to locate the value 15 in the multiset. Function find returns an iterator or a const_iterator pointing to the location at which the value is found. If the value is *not* found, find returns an iterator or a const_iterator equal to the value returned by calling end on the container. Line 32 demonstrates this case.

Inserting Elements of Another Container into a multiset

Line 38 uses function **insert** to insert the elements of array a into the multiset. In line 40, the copy algorithm copies the elements of the multiset to the standard output in *ascending order.*

multiset Member Functions lower_bound *and* upper_bound

Lines 44 and 45 use functions **lower_bound** and **upper_bound** (available in all *associative containers*) to locate the earliest occurrence of the value 22 in the multiset and the element *after* the last occurrence of the value 22 in the multiset. Both functions return iterators or const_iterators pointing to the appropriate location or the iterator returned by end if the value is not in the multiset.

pair *Objects and* multiset *Member Function* equal_range

Line 49 creates and intializes a pair object called p. Once again, we use C++11's auto keyword to infer the variable's type from its initializer—in this case, the return value of multiset member function equal_range, which is a pair object. Such objects associate pairs of values. The contents of a p will be two const_iterators for our multiset of ints. The multiset function **equal_range** returns a pair containing the results of calling both lower_bound and upper_bound. Type pair contains two public data members called **first** and **second**. Line 49 uses function equal_range to determine the lower_bound and upper_bound of 22 in the multiset. Line 52 uses p.first and p.second to access the lower_bound and upper_bound. We *dereferenced* the iterators to output the values at the locations returned from equal_range. Though we did not do so here, you should always ensure that the iterators returned by lower_bound, upper_bound and equal_range are not equal to the container's *end* iterator before dereferencing the iterators.

C++11: Variadic Class Template **`tuple`**

C++ also includes class template `tuple`, which is similar to `pair`, but can hold any number of items of various types. As of C++11, class template `tuple` has been reimplemented using *variadic templates*—templates that can receive a *variable* number of arguments. We discuss `tuple` and variadic templates in Chapter 24, C++11: Additional Features.

15.6.2 set Associative Container

The `set` *associative container* (from header <set>) is used for fast storage and retrieval of *unique* keys. The implementation of a `set` is identical to that of a `multiset`, except that a `set` must have unique keys. Therefore, if an attempt is made to insert a *duplicate* key into a `set`, the duplicate is ignored; because this is the intended mathematical behavior of a set, we do not identify it as a common programming error. A `set` supports *bidirectional iterators* (but not *random-access iterators*). If the order of the keys is not important, you can use `unordered_set` (header <unordered_set>) instead. Figure 15.16 demonstrates a `set` of `double`s.

```
// Fig. 15.16: fig15_16.cpp
// Standard Library set class template.
#include <iostream>
#include <array>
#include <set>
#include <algorithm>
#include <iterator> // ostream_iterator
using namespace std;

int main()
{
   const size_t SIZE = 5;
   array< double, SIZE > a = { 2.1, 4.2, 9.5, 2.1, 3.7 };
   set< double, less< double > > doubleSet( a.begin(), a.end() );
   ostream_iterator< double > output( cout, " " );

   cout << "doubleSet contains: ";
   copy( doubleSet.begin(), doubleSet.end(), output );

   // insert 13.8 in doubleSet; insert returns pair in which
   // p.first represents location of 13.8 in doubleSet and
   // p.second represents whether 13.8 was inserted
   auto p = doubleSet.insert( 13.8 ); // value not in set
   cout << "\n\n" << *( p.first )
      << ( p.second ? " was" : " was not" ) << " inserted";
   cout << "\ndoubleSet contains: ";
   copy( doubleSet.begin(), doubleSet.end(), output );

   // insert 9.5 in doubleSet
   p = doubleSet.insert( 9.5 ); // value already in set
   cout << "\n\n" << *( p.first )
      << ( p.second ? " was" : " was not" ) << " inserted";
   cout << "\ndoubleSet contains: ";
```

Fig. 15.16 | Standard Library `set` class template. (Part 1 of 2.)

```
34      copy( doubleSet.begin(), doubleSet.end(), output );
35      cout << endl;
36   } // end main
```

```
doubleSet contains: 2.1 3.7 4.2 9.5

13.8 was inserted
doubleSet contains: 2.1 3.7 4.2 9.5 13.8

9.5 was not inserted
doubleSet contains: 2.1 3.7 4.2 9.5 13.8
```

Fig. 15.16 | Standard Library set class template. (Part 2 of 2.)

Line 14 creates a set of doubles ordered in *ascending order*, using the function object less<double>. The constructor call takes all the elements in array a and inserts them into the set. Line 18 uses algorithm copy to output the contents of the set. Notice that the value 2.1—which appeared twice in array—appears only *once* in doubleSet. This is because container set does *not* allow duplicates.

Line 23 defines and initializes a pair to store the result of a call to set function insert. The pair returned consists of a const_iterator pointing to the item in the set inserted and a bool value indicating whether the item was inserted—true if the item was not in the set; false if it was.

Line 23 uses function insert to place the value 13.8 in the set. The returned pair, p, contains an iterator p.first pointing to the value 13.8 in the set and a bool value that's true because the value was inserted. Line 30 attempts to insert 9.5, which is already in the set. The output shows that 9.5 was not inserted again because sets don't allow duplicate keys. In this case, p.first in the returned pair points to the existing 9.5 in the set.

15.6.3 multimap Associative Container

The *multimap associative container* is used for fast storage and retrieval of keys and associated values (often called key–value pairs). Many of the functions used with multisets and sets are also used with multimaps and maps. The elements of multimaps and maps are pairs of keys and values instead of individual values. When inserting into a multimap or map, a pair object that contains the key and the value is used. The ordering of the keys is determined by a *comparator function object*. For example, in a multimap that uses integers as the key type, keys can be sorted in *ascending order* by ordering them with *comparator function object* less<int>. Duplicate keys are allowed in a multimap, so multiple values can be associated with a single key. This is called a **one-to-many relationship**. For example, in a credit-card transaction-processing system, one credit-card account can have many associated transactions; in a university, one student can take many courses, and one professor can teach many students; in the military, one rank (like "private") has many people. A multimap supports *bidirectional iterators*, but not *random-access iterators*. Figure 15.17 demonstrates the *multimap associative container*. Header **<map>** must be included to use class multimap. If the order of the keys is not important, you can use unordered_multimap (header <unordered_map>) instead.

Performance Tip 15.11

A `multimap` is implemented to efficiently locate all values paired with a given key.

```
// Fig. 15.17: fig15_17.cpp
// Standard Library multimap class template.
#include <iostream>
#include <map> // multimap class-template definition
using namespace std;

int main()
{
   multimap< int, double, less< int > > pairs; // create multimap

   cout << "There are currently " << pairs.count( 15 )
      << " pairs with key 15 in the multimap\n";

   // insert two value_type objects in pairs
   pairs.insert( make_pair( 15, 2.7 ) );
   pairs.insert( make_pair( 15, 99.3 ) );

   cout << "After inserts, there are " << pairs.count( 15 )
      << " pairs with key 15\n\n";

   // insert five value_type objects in pairs
   pairs.insert( make_pair( 30, 111.11 ) );
   pairs.insert( make_pair( 10, 22.22 ) );
   pairs.insert( make_pair( 25, 33.333 ) );
   pairs.insert( make_pair( 20, 9.345 ) );
   pairs.insert( make_pair( 5, 77.54 ) );

   cout << "Multimap pairs contains:\nKey\tValue\n";

   // walk through elements of pairs
   for ( auto mapItem : pairs )
      cout << mapItem.first << '\t' << mapItem.second << '\n';

   cout << endl;
} // end main
```

```
There are currently 0 pairs with key 15 in the multimap
After inserts, there are 2 pairs with key 15

Multimap pairs contains:
Key     Value
5       77.54
10      22.22
15      2.7
15      99.3
20      9.345
25      33.333
30      111.11
```

Fig. 15.17 | Standard Library `multimap` class template.

Line 9 creates a `multimap` in which the key type is `int`, the type of a key's associated value is `double` and the elements are ordered in *ascending order*. Line 11 uses function `count` to determine the number of key–value pairs with a key of `15` (none yet, since the container is currently empty).

Line 15 uses function `insert` to add a new key–value pair to the `multimap`. The expression `make_pair( 15, 2.7 )` creates a `pair` object in which `first` is the key (`15`) of type `int` and `second` is the value (`2.7`) of type `double`. Function `make_pair` automatically uses the types that you specified for the keys and values in the `multimap`'s declaration (line 9). Line 16 inserts another `pair` object with the key `15` and the value `99.3`. Then lines 18–19 output the number of pairs with key `15`. As of C++11, you can use list initalization for `pair` objects, so line 15 can be simplified as

```
pairs.insert( { 15, 2.7 } );
```

Similarly, C++11 enables you to use list initialization to initialize an object being returned from a function. For example, if a function returns a `pair` containing an `int` and a `double`, you could write:

```
return { 15, 2.7 };
```

Lines 22–26 insert five additional `pairs` into the `multimap`. The range-based `for` statement in lines 31–32 outputs the contents of the `multimap`, including both keys and values. We infer the type of the loop's control variable (a `pair` containing an `int` key and a `double` value) with keyword `auto`. Line 32 accesses the members of the current `pair` in each element of the `multimap`. Notice in the output that the keys appear in *ascending order*.

C++11: List Initializing a Key–Value Pair Container

In this example, we used separate calls to member function insert to place key–value pairs in a `multimap`. If you know the key–value pairs in advance, you can use list initialization when you create the `multimap`. For example, the following statement initializes a `multimap` with three key–value pairs that are represented by the sublists in the main intializer list:

```
multimap< int, double, less< int > > pairs =
   { { 10, 22.22 }, { 20, 9.345 }, { 5, 77.54 } };
```

15.6.4 map Associative Container

The *`map` associative container* (from header `<map>`) performs fast storage and retrieval of *unique keys* and *associated values*. Duplicate keys are *not* allowed—a single value can be associated with each key. This is called a **one-to-one mapping**. For example, a company that uses unique employee numbers, such as 100, 200 and 300, might have a `map` that associates employee numbers with their telephone extensions—4321, 4115 and 5217, respectively. With a `map` you specify the key and get back the associated data quickly. Providing the key in a `map`'s subscript operator `[]` locates the value associated with that key in the `map`. Insertions and deletions can be made *anywhere* in a `map`. If the order of the keys is not important, you can use `unordered_map` (header `<unordered_map>`) instead.

Figure 15.18 demonstrates a `map` and uses the same features as Fig. 15.17 to demonstrate the subscript operator. Lines 27–28 use the subscript operator of class `map`. When the subscript is a key that's already in the `map` (line 27), the operator returns a reference to the associated value. When the subscript is a key that's *not* in the `map` (line 18), the operator inserts the key in the map and returns a reference that can be used to associate a value with that key. Line 27 replaces the value for the key 25 (previously 33.333 as specified in line 16) with a new value, 9999.99. Line 28 inserts a new key–value pair in the map (called **creating an association**).

```
1  // Fig. 15.18: fig15_18.cpp
2  // Standard Library class map class template.
3  #include <iostream>
4  #include <map> // map class-template definition
5  using namespace std;
6
7  int main()
8  {
9     map< int, double, less< int > > pairs;
10
11    // insert eight value_type objects in pairs
12    pairs.insert( make_pair( 15, 2.7 ) );
13    pairs.insert( make_pair( 30, 111.11 ) );
14    pairs.insert( make_pair( 5, 1010.1 ) );
15    pairs.insert( make_pair( 10, 22.22 ) );
16    pairs.insert( make_pair( 25, 33.333 ) );
17    pairs.insert( make_pair( 5, 77.54 ) ); // dup ignored
18    pairs.insert( make_pair( 20, 9.345 ) );
19    pairs.insert( make_pair( 15, 99.3 ) ); // dup ignored
20
21    cout << "pairs contains:\nKey\tValue\n";
22
23    // walk through elements of pairs
24    for ( auto mapItem : pairs )
25       cout << mapItem.first << '\t' << mapItem.second << '\n';
26
27    pairs[ 25 ] = 9999.99; // use subscripting to change value for key 25
28    pairs[ 40 ] = 8765.43; // use subscripting to insert value for key 40
29
30    cout << "\nAfter subscript operations, pairs contains:\nKey\tValue\n";
31
32    // use const_iterator to walk through elements of pairs
33    for ( auto mapItem : pairs )
34       cout << mapItem.first << '\t' << mapItem.second << '\n';
35
36    cout << endl;
37 } // end main
```

```
pairs contains:
Key     Value
5       1010.1
10      22.22
15      2.7
20      9.345
25      33.333
30      111.11
```

Fig. 15.18 | Standard Library map class template. (Part 1 of 2.)

```
After subscript operations, pairs contains:
Key     Value
5       1010.1
10      22.22
15      2.7
20      9.345
25      9999.99
30      111.11
40      8765.43
```

Fig. 15.18 | Standard Library map class template. (Part 2 of 2.)

15.7 Container Adapters

The three **container adapters** are stack, queue and priority_queue. Container adapters are *not first-class containers*, because they do *not* provide the actual data-structure implementation in which elements can be stored and because adapters do *not* support iterators. The benefit of an *adapter class* is that you can choose an appropriate underlying data structure. All three *adapter classes* provide member functions **push** and **pop** that properly insert an element into each adapter data structure and properly remove an element from each adapter data structure. The next several subsections provide examples of the adapter classes.

15.7.1 stack Adapter

Class **stack** (from header **<stack>**) enables insertions into and deletions from the underlying container at one end called the *top*, so a stack is commonly referred to as a *last-in, first-out* data structure. We introduced stacks in our discussion of the function-call stack in Section 6.11. A stack can be implemented with vector, list or deque. This example creates three integer stacks, using vector, list and deque as the underlying data structure to represent the stack. By default, a stack is implemented with a deque. The stack operations are push to insert an element at the *top* of the stack (implemented by calling function push_back of the underlying container), pop to remove the *top* element of the stack (implemented by calling function pop_back of the underlying container), **top** to get a reference to the top element of the stack (implemented by calling function back of the underlying container), empty to determine whether the stack is empty (implemented by calling function empty of the underlying container) and size to get the number of elements in the stack (implemented by calling function size of the underlying container).

Figure 15.19 demonstrates the stack adapter class. Lines 18, 21 and 24 instantiate three integer stacks. Line 18 specifies a stack of integers that uses the default deque container as its underlying data structure. Line 21 specifies a stack of integers that uses a vector of integers as its underlying data structure. Line 24 specifies a stack of integers that uses a list of integers as its underlying data structure.

```
1  // Fig. 15.19: fig15_19.cpp
2  // Standard Library stack adapter class.
3  #include <iostream>
```

Fig. 15.19 | Standard Library stack adapter class. (Part 1 of 3.)

```
#include <stack> // stack adapter definition
#include <vector> // vector class-template definition
#include <list> // list class-template definition
using namespace std;

// pushElements function-template prototype
template< typename T > void pushElements( T &stackRef );

// popElements function-template prototype
template< typename T > void popElements( T &stackRef );

int main()
{
   // stack with default underlying deque
   stack< int > intDequeStack;

   // stack with underlying vector
   stack< int, vector< int > > intVectorStack;

   // stack with underlying list
   stack< int, list< int > > intListStack;

   // push the values 0-9 onto each stack
   cout << "Pushing onto intDequeStack: ";
   pushElements( intDequeStack );
   cout << "\nPushing onto intVectorStack: ";
   pushElements( intVectorStack );
   cout << "\nPushing onto intListStack: ";
   pushElements( intListStack );
   cout << endl << endl;

   // display and remove elements from each stack
   cout << "Popping from intDequeStack: ";
   popElements( intDequeStack );
   cout << "\nPopping from intVectorStack: ";
   popElements( intVectorStack );
   cout << "\nPopping from intListStack: ";
   popElements( intListStack );
   cout << endl;
} // end main

// push elements onto stack object to which stackRef refers
template< typename T > void pushElements( T &stackRef )
{
   for ( int i = 0; i < 10; ++i )
   {
      stackRef.push( i ); // push element onto stack
      cout << stackRef.top() << ' '; // view (and display) top element
   } // end for
} // end function pushElements

```

Fig. 15.19 | Standard Library `stack` adapter class. (Part 2 of 3.)

```
55 // pop elements from stack object to which stackRef refers
56 template< typename T > void popElements( T &stackRef )
57 {
58    while ( !stackRef.empty() )
59    {
60       cout << stackRef.top() << ' '; // view (and display) top element
61       stackRef.pop(); // remove top element
62    } // end while
63 } // end function popElements
```

```
Pushing onto intDequeStack: 0 1 2 3 4 5 6 7 8 9
Pushing onto intVectorStack: 0 1 2 3 4 5 6 7 8 9
Pushing onto intListStack: 0 1 2 3 4 5 6 7 8 9

Popping from intDequeStack: 9 8 7 6 5 4 3 2 1 0
Popping from intVectorStack: 9 8 7 6 5 4 3 2 1 0
Popping from intListStack: 9 8 7 6 5 4 3 2 1 0
```

Fig. 15.19 | Standard Library `stack` adapter class. (Part 3 of 3.)

Function `pushElements` (lines 46–53) pushes the elements onto each `stack`. Line 50 uses function `push` (available in each *adapter class*) to place an integer on top of the `stack`. Line 51 uses `stack` function `top` to retrieve the *top* element of the `stack` for output. *Function* `top` *does not remove the top element.*

Function `popElements` (lines 56–63) pops the elements off each `stack`. Line 60 uses `stack` function `top` to retrieve the top element of the `stack` for output. Line 61 uses function `pop` (available in each *adapter class*) to remove the *top* element of the `stack`. Function `pop` does *not* return a value.

15.7.2 queue Adapter

A queue is similar to a *waiting line*. The item that has been in the queue the *longest* is the *next* one removed—so a queue is referred to as a **first-in, first-out** (FIFO) data structure. Class **`queue`** (from header **`<queue>`**) enables insertions at the *back* of the underlying data structure and deletions from the *front*. A `queue` can store its elements in objects of the Standard Library's `list` or `deque` containers. By default, a `queue` is implemented with a `deque`. The common `queue` operations are `push` to insert an element at the back of the `queue` (implemented by calling function `push_back` of the underlying container), `pop` to remove the element at the front of the `queue` (implemented by calling function `pop_front` of the underlying container), **`front`** to get a reference to the *first* element in the `queue` (implemented by calling function `front` of the underlying container), **`back`** to get a reference to the *last* element in the `queue` (implemented by calling function `back` of the underlying container), `empty` to determine whether the `queue` is *empty* (implemented by calling function `empty` of the underlying container) and `size` to get the number of elements in the `queue` (implemented by calling function `size` of the underlying container).

Figure 15.20 demonstrates the `queue` adapter class. Line 9 instantiates a `queue` of `doubles`. Lines 12–14 use function `push` to add elements to the `queue`. The `while` statement in lines 19–23 uses function `empty` (available in *all* containers) to determine whether the `queue` is empty (line 19). While there are more elements in the `queue`, line 21 uses `queue` function front to read (but not remove) the first element in the queue for output. Line 22 removes the first element in the queue with function pop (available in all *adapter classes*).

```
1  // Fig. 15.20: fig15_20.cpp
2  // Standard Library queue adapter class template.
3  #include <iostream>
4  #include <queue> // queue adapter definition
5  using namespace std;
6
7  int main()
8  {
9     queue< double > values; // queue with doubles
10
11    // push elements onto queue values
12    values.push( 3.2 );
13    values.push( 9.8 );
14    values.push( 5.4 );
15
16    cout << "Popping from values: ";
17
18    // pop elements from queue
19    while ( !values.empty() )
20    {
21       cout << values.front() << ' '; // view front element
22       values.pop(); // remove element
23    } // end while
24
25    cout << endl;
26 } // end main
```

```
Popping from values: 3.2 9.8 5.4
```

Fig. 15.20 | Standard Library queue adapter class templates.

15.7.3 priority_queue Adapter

Class **priority_queue** (from header <queue>) provides functionality that enables *insertions* in *sorted order* into the underlying data structure and deletions from the *front* of the underlying data structure. By default, a priority_queue's elements are stored in a vector. When elements are added to a priority_queue, they're inserted in *priority order*, such that the highest-priority element (i.e., the *largest* value) will be the first element removed from the priority_queue. This is usually accomplished by arranging the elements in a data structure called a **heap** (not to be confused with the heap for dynamically allocated memory) that always maintains the largest value (i.e., highest-priority element) at the front of the data structure. We use the Standard Library's *heap algorithms* in Section 16.3.12. The comparison of elements is performed with *comparator function object* less<T> by default, but you can supply a different comparator.

There are several common priority_queue operations. Function push inserts an element at the appropriate location based on *priority order* of the priority_queue (implemented by calling function push_back of the underlying container, which then reorders the elements in priority order. Function pop removes the *highest-priority* element of the priority_queue (implemented by calling function pop_back of the underlying container after removing the top element of the heap). **top** gets a reference to the *top* element of the priority_queue (implemented by calling function front of the underlying container). empty determines whether the priority_queue is *empty* (implemented by calling function empty of the underlying container). size gets the number of elements in the priority_queue (implemented by calling function size of the underlying container).

Figure 15.21 demonstrates the priority_queue adapter class. Line 9 instantiates a priority_queue that stores double values and uses a vector as the underlying data structure. Lines 12–14 use function push to add elements to the priority_queue. The while statement in lines 19–23 uses function empty (available in *all* containers) to determine whether the priority_queue is empty (line 19). While there are more elements, line 21 uses priority_queue function top to retrieve the *highest-priority* element (i.e., the largest value) in the priority_queue for output. Line 22 removes the *highest-priority* element in the priority_queue with function pop (available in all adapter classes).

```
1  // Fig. 15.21: fig15_21.cpp
2  // Standard Library priority_queue adapter class.
3  #include <iostream>
4  #include <queue> // priority_queue adapter definition
5  using namespace std;
6
7  int main()
8  {
9     priority_queue< double > priorities; // create priority_queue
10
11    // push elements onto priorities
12    priorities.push( 3.2 );
13    priorities.push( 9.8 );
14    priorities.push( 5.4 );
15
16    cout << "Popping from priorities: ";
17
18    // pop element from priority_queue
19    while ( !priorities.empty() )
20    {
21       cout << priorities.top() << ' '; // view top element
22       priorities.pop(); // remove top element
23    } // end while
24
25    cout << endl;
26 } // end main
```

```
Popping from priorities: 9.8 5.4 3.2
```

Fig. 15.21 | Standard Library priority_queue adapter class.

15.8 Class bitset

Class **bitset** makes it easy to create and manipulate **bit sets**, which are useful for representing a set of bit flags. bitsets are fixed in size at compile time. Class bitset is an alternate tool for *bit manipulation*, discussed in Chapter 20.

The declaration

```
bitset< size > b;
```

creates `bitset` `b`, in which every on of the `size` bits is initially `0` ("off").

The statement

```
b.set( bitNumber );
```

sets bit `bitNumber` of `bitset` `b` "on." The expression `b.set()` sets all bits in `b` "on."

The statement

```
b.reset( bitNumber );
```

sets bit `bitNumber` of `bitset` `b` "off." The expression `b.reset()` sets all bits in `b` "off."

The statement

```
b.flip( bitNumber );
```

"flips" bit `bitNumber` of `bitset` `b` (e.g., if the bit is "on", `flip` sets it "off"). The expression `b.flip()` flips all bits in `b`.

The statement

```
b[ bitNumber ];
```

returns a reference to the bit `bitNumber` of `bitset` `b`. Similarly,

```
b.at( bitNumber );
```

performs range checking on `bitNumber` first. Then, if `bitNumber` is in range, `at` returns a reference to the bit. Otherwise, `at` throws an `out_of_range` exception.

The statement

```
b.test( bitNumber );
```

performs *range checking* on `bitNumber` first. If `bitNumber` is in range, `test` returns `true` if the bit is on, `false` it's off. Otherwise, `test` throws an `out_of_range` exception.

The expression

```
b.size()
```

returns the number of bits in `bitset` `b`.

The expression

```
b.count()
```

returns the number of bits that are set in `bitset` `b`.

The expression

```
b.any()
```

returns `true` if any bit is set in `bitset` `b`.

The expression

11

```
b.all()
```

returns `true` if all of the bits are set in `bitset` `b`.

The expression

```
b.none()
```

returns `true` if none of the bits is set in `bitset` `b`.

The expressions

```
b == b1
b != b1
```

compare the two `bitsets` for equality and inequality, respectively.

Each of the bitwise assignment operators `&=`, `|=` and `^=` (discussed in detail in Section 20.5) can be used to combine `bitsets`. For example,

```
b &= b1;
```

performs a bit-by-bit logical AND between `bitsets` `b` and `b1`. The result is stored in `b`. Bitwise logical OR and bitwise logical XOR are performed by

```
b |= b1;
b ^= b2;
```

The expression

```
b >>= n;
```

shifts the bits in `bitset` `b` right by `n` positions.

The expression

```
b <<= n;
```

shifts the bits in `bitset` `b` left by `n` positions.

The expressions

```
b.to_string()
b.to_ulong()
```

convert `bitset` `b` to a `string` and an `unsigned long`, respectively.

15.9 Wrap-Up

In this chapter, we introduced three key components of the Standard Library—containers, iterators and algorithms. You learned about the linear *sequence containers*, `array` (Chapter 7), `vector`, `deque`, `forward_list` and `list`, which all represent linear data structures. We discussed the nonlinear *associative containers*, `set`, `multiset`, `map` and `multimap` and their unordered versions. You also saw that the *container adapters* `stack`, `queue` and `priority_queue` can be used to restrict the operations of the sequence containers `vector`, `deque` and `list` for the purpose of implementing the specialized data structures represented by the container adapters. You learned the categories of iterators and that each algorithm can be used with any container that supports the minimum iterator functionality that the algorithm requires. You also learned class `bitset`, which makes it easy to create and manipulate bit sets as a container.

The next chapter continues our discussion of the Standard Library's containers, iterators and algorithms with a detailed treatment of algorithms. You'll also learn about function pointers, function objects and C++11's new lambda expressions.

Recommended Reading

Abrahams, D., and A. Gurtovoy. *C++ Template Metaprogramming: Concepts, Tools, and Techniques from Boost and Beyond.* Boston: Addison-Wesley Professional, 2004.

Ammeraal, L. *STL for C++ Programmers*. New York: John Wiley & Sons, 1997.

Austern, M. H. *Generic Programming and the STL: Using and Extending the C++ Standard Template Library.* Boston: Addison-Wesley, 2000.

Becker, P. *The C++ Standard Library Extensions: A Tutorial and Reference*. Boston: Addison-Wesley Professional, 2006.

Glass, G., and B. Schuchert. *The STL <Primer>*. Upper Saddle River, NJ: Prentice Hall PTR, 1995.

Heller, S., and Chrysalis Software Corp., *C++: A Dialog: Programming with the C++ Standard Library.* New York, Prentice Hall PTR, 2002.

Josuttis, N. *The C++ Standard Library: A Tutorial and Reference (2nd edition)*. Boston: Addison-Wesley Professional, 2012.

Josuttis, N. *The C++ Standard Library: A Tutorial and Handbook*. Boston: Addison-Wesley, 2000.

Karlsson, B. Beyond *the C++ Standard Library: An Introduction to Boost*. Boston: Addison-Wesley Professional, 2005.

Koenig, A., and B. Moo. *Ruminations on C++*. Boston: Addison-Wesley, 1997.

Lippman, S., J. Lajoie, and B. Moo. *C++ Primer (Fifth Edition)*. Boston: Addison-Wesley Professional, 2012.

Meyers, S. *Effective STL: 50 Specific Ways to Improve Your Use of the Standard Template Library.* Boston: Addison-Wesley, 2001.

Musser, D. R., G. Derge and A. Saini. *STL Tutorial and Reference Guide: C++ Programming with the Standard Template Library, Second Edition.* Boston: Addison-Wesley, 2010.

Musser, D. R., and A. A. Stepanov. "Algorithm-Oriented Generic Libraries," *Software Practice and Experience,* Vol. 24, No. 7, July 1994.

Nelson, M. *C++ Programmer's Guide to the Standard Template Library.* Foster City, CA: Programmer's Press, 1995.

Pohl, I. *C++ Distilled: A Concise ANSI/ISO Reference and Style Guide.* Boston: Addison-Wesley, 1997.

Reese, G. *C++ Standard Library Practical Tips.* Hingham, MA: Charles River Media, 2005.

Robson, R. *Using the STL: The C++ Standard Template Library, Second Edition.* New York: Springer, 2000.

Schildt, H. *STL Programming from the Ground Up, Third Edition.* New York: McGraw-Hill Osborne Media, 2003.

Schildt, H. *STL Programming from the Ground Up*. New York: Osborne McGraw-Hill, 1999.

Stepanov, A., and M. Lee. "The Standard Template Library," *Internet Distribution* 31 October 1995 `<www.cs.rpi.edu/~musser/doc.ps>`.

Stroustrup, B. "C++11—the New ISO C++ Standard" `<www.stroustrup.com/C++11FAQ.html>`.

Stroustrup, B. "Making a `vector` Fit for a Standard," *The C++ Report,* October 1994.

Stroustrup, B. *The Design and Evolution of C++*. Boston: Addison-Wesley, 1994.

Stroustrup, B. T*he C++ Programming Language, Fourth Edition*. Boston: Addison-Wesley Professional, 2013.

Stroustrup, B. *The C++ Programming Language, Third Edition.* Boston: Addison-Wesley, 2000.

Vandevoorde, D., and N. Josuttis. *C++ Templates: The Complete Guide.* Boston: Addison-Wesley, 2003.

Vilot, M. J., "An Introduction to the Standard Template Library," *The C++ Report,* Vol. 6, No. 8, October 1994.

Wilson, M. *Extended STL, Volume 1: Collections and Iterators.* Boston: Addison-Wesley, 2007.

16

Standard Library Algorithms

Objectives

In this chapter you'll:

- Program with many of the dozens of Standard Library algorithms.
- Use iterators with algorithms to access and manipulate the elements of Standard Library containers.
- Pass function pointers, function objects and lambda expressions into Standard Library algorithms.

Outline

16.1 Introduction

This chapter continues our discussion of the Standard Library's containers, iterators and algorithms by focusing on algorithms that perform common data manipulations such as *searching, sorting* and *comparing elements or entire containers.* The Standard Library provides over 90 algorithms, many of which are new in C++11. The complete list can be found in Sections 25 and 26.7 of the C++ standard document and there are various online references where you can learn about each algorithm, such as `en.cppreference.com/w/cpp/algorithm`. Most of them use iterators to access container elements. As you'll see, various algorithms can receive a *function pointer* (a pointer to a function's code) as an argument. Such algorithms use the pointer to call the function—typically with one or two container elements as arguments. We'll introduce function pointers in more detail in this chapter. Later in the chapter we'll present the concept of a *function object*, which is similar to a function pointer but is implemented as an object of a class that has an overloaded function-call operator (`operator()`) so that the object can be used like a function name. Finally, we'll introduce *lambda expressions*—C++11's new shorthand mechanism for creating *anonymous function objects* (that is, function objects that do not have names).

16.2 Minimum Iterator Requirements

With few exceptions, the Standard Library separates algorithms from containers. This makes it much easier to add new algorithms. An important part of every container is the *type of iterator* it supports (Fig. 15.7). This determines which algorithms can be applied to the container. For example, both `vector`s and `array`s support *random-access iterators* that provide *all* of the iterator operations shown in Fig. 15.9. *All* Standard Library algorithms can operate on `vector`s and the ones that do not modify a container's size can also operate on `array`s. Each Standard Library algorithm that takes iterator arguments requires those iterators to provide a minimum level of functionality. If an algorithm requires a *forward iterator*, for example, that algorithm can operate on any container that supports *forward iterators, bidirectional iterators* or *random-access iterators*.

Software Engineering Observation 16.1

Standard Library algorithms do not *depend on the implementation details of the containers on which they operate. As long as a container's (or built-in array's) iterators satisfy the requirements of an algorithm, the algorithm can work on the container.*

Portability Tip 16.1

Because Standard Library algorithms process containers only indirectly *through iterators, one algorithm can often be used with* many *different containers.*

Software Engineering Observation 16.2

The Standard Library containers are implemented concisely. The algorithms are separated *from the containers and operate on elements of the containers only* indirectly *through iterators. This separation makes it easier to write generic algorithms applicable to a variety of container classes.*

Software Engineering Observation 16.3

Using the "weakest iterator" that yields acceptable performance helps produce maximally reusable components. For example, if an algorithm requires only forward iterators, it can be used with any container that supports forward iterators, bidirectional iterators or random-access iterators. However, an algorithm that requires random-access iterators can be used only with containers that have random-access iterators.

Iterator Invalidation

Iterators simply *point* to container elements, so it's possible for iterators to become *invalid* when certain container modifications occur. For example, if you invoke `clear` on a `vector`, *all* of its elements are *removed.* If a program had any iterators that pointed to that `vector`'s elements before `clear` was called, those iterators would now be *invalid.* Section 23 of the C++ standard discusses all the cases in which iterators (and pointers and references) are invalidated for each Standard Library container. Here we summarize when iterators are invalidated during *insert* and *erase* operations.

When *inserting* into a:

- `vector`—If the `vector` is reallocated, all iterators pointing to that `vector` are invalidated. Otherwise, iterators from the insertion point to the end of the `vector` are invalidated.
- `deque`—All iterators are invalidated.
- `list` or `forward_list`—All iterators *remain valid.*
- Ordered associative container—All iterators *remain valid.*
- Unordered associative container—All iterators are invalidated if the containers need to be reallocated.

When *erasing* from a container, iterators to the *erased* elements are invalidated. In addition:

- `vector`—Iterators from the erased element to the end of the `vector` are invalidated.
- `deque`—If an element in the middle of the deque is erased, all iterators are invalidated.

16.3 Algorithms

Sections 16.3.1–16.3.13 demonstrate many of the Standard Library algorithms.

16.3.1 fill, fill_n, generate and generate_n

Figure 16.1 demonstrates algorithms `fill`, `fill_n`, `generate` and `generate_n`. Algorithms **`fill`** and **`fill_n`** set every element in a range of container elements to a specific value. Algorithms **`generate`** and **`generate_n`** use a **generator function** to create values for every element in a *range* of container elements. The *generator function* takes no arguments and returns a value that can be placed in an element of the container.

```
// Fig. 16.1: fig16_01.cpp
// Algorithms fill, fill_n, generate and generate_n.
#include <iostream>
#include <algorithm> // algorithm definitions
#include <array> // array class-template definition
#include <iterator> // ostream_iterator
using namespace std;

char nextLetter(); // prototype of generator function

int main()
{
   array< char, 10 > chars;
   ostream_iterator< char > output( cout, " " );
   fill( chars.begin(), chars.end(), '5' ); // fill chars with 5s

   cout << "chars after filling with 5s:\n";
   copy( chars.cbegin(), chars.cend(), output );

   // fill first five elements of chars with As
   fill_n( chars.begin(), 5, 'A' );

   cout << "\n\nchars after filling five elements with As:\n";
   copy( chars.cbegin(), chars.cend(), output );

   // generate values for all elements of chars with nextLetter
   generate( chars.begin(), chars.end(), nextLetter );

   cout << "\n\nchars after generating letters A-J:\n";
   copy( chars.cbegin(), chars.cend(), output );

   // generate values for first five elements of chars with nextLetter
   generate_n( chars.begin(), 5, nextLetter );

   cout << "\n\nchars after generating K-O for the"
      << " first five elements:\n";
   copy( chars.cbegin(), chars.cend(), output );
   cout << endl;
} // end main

```

Fig. 16.1 | Algorithms `fill`, `fill_n`, `generate` and `generate_n`. (Part 1 of 2.)

```
41  // generator function returns next letter (starts with A)
42  char nextLetter()
43  {
44     static char letter = 'A';
45     return letter++;
46  } // end function nextLetter
```

```
chars after filling with 5s:
5 5 5 5 5 5 5 5 5 5

chars after filling five elements with As:
A A A A A 5 5 5 5 5

chars after generating letters A-J:
A B C D E F G H I J

chars after generating K-O for the first five elements:
K L M N O F G H I J
```

Fig. 16.1 | Algorithms `fill`, `fill_n`, `generate` and `generate_n`. (Part 2 of 2.)

`fill` *Algorithm*

Line 13 defines a 10-element `array` of `char` values. Line 15 uses the `fill` algorithm to place the character `'5'` in every element of `chars` from `chars.begin()` up to, but *not* including, `chars.end()`. The iterators supplied as the first and second argument must be at least *forward iterators* (i.e., they can be used for both input from a container and output to a container in the *forward* direction).

`fill_n` *Algorithm*

Line 21 uses the `fill_n` algorithm to place the character `'A'` in the first five elements of `chars`. The iterator supplied as the first argument must be at least an *output iterator* (i.e., it can be used to *write* into a container in the *forward* direction). The second argument specifies the number of elements to fill. The third argument specifies the value to place in each element.

`generate` *Algorithm*

Line 27 uses the `generate` algorithm to place the result of a call to *generator function* `nextLetter` in every element of `chars` from `chars.begin()` up to, but *not* including, `chars.end()`. The iterators supplied as the first and second arguments must be at least *forward iterators*. Function `nextLetter` (lines 42–46) begins with the character `'A'` maintained in a `static` local variable. The statement in line 45 postincrements the value of `letter` and returns the old value of `letter` each time `nextLetter` is called.

`generate_n` *Algorithm*

Line 33 uses the `generate_n` algorithm to place the result of a call to *generator function* `nextLetter` in five elements of `chars`, starting from `chars.begin()`. The iterator supplied as the first argument must be at least an *output iterator*.

A Note About Reading Standard Library Algorithm Documentation

When you look at the Standard Library algorithms documentation for algorithms that can receive function pointers as arguments, you'll notice in the documentation that the corresponding parameters do *not* show pointer declarations. Such parameters can actually receive as arguments *function pointers*, *function objects* (Section 16.4) or *lambda expressions* (Section 16.5). For this reason, the Standard Library declares such parameters using more generic names.

For example, the generate algorithm's prototype is listed in the C++ standard document as:

```
template<class ForwardIterator, class Generator>
void generate(ForwardIterator first, ForwardIterator last,
   Generator gen);
```

indicating that generate expects as arguments *ForwardIterators* representing the range of elements to process and a *Generator function*. The standard explains that the algorithm calls the Generator function to obtain a value for each element in the range specified by the *ForwardIterators*. The standard also specifies that the Generator must take no arguments and return a value of the element type.

Similar documentation is provided for each algorithm that can receive a function pointer, function object or lambda expression. In most of this chapter's examples, as we present each algorithm, we specify the requirements for such parameters. We typically do so in the context of functions, and pass function pointers into the algorithms. In Sections 16.4–16.5, we discuss how to create and use function objects and lambda expressions that you can pass to algorithms.

16.3.2 equal, mismatch and lexicographical_compare

Figure 16.2 demonstrates comparing sequences of values for equality using algorithms equal, mismatch and lexicographical_compare.

```
// Fig. 16.2: fig16_02.cpp
// Algorithms equal, mismatch and lexicographical_compare.
#include <iostream>
#include <algorithm> // algorithm definitions
#include <array> // array class-template definition
#include <iterator> // ostream_iterator
using namespace std;

int main()
{
   const size_t SIZE = 10;
   array< int, SIZE > a1 = { 1, 2, 3, 4, 5, 6, 7, 8, 9, 10 };
   array< int, SIZE > a2( a1 ); // initializes a2 with copy of a1
   array< int, SIZE > a3 = { 1, 2, 3, 4, 1000, 6, 7, 8, 9, 10 };
   ostream_iterator< int > output( cout, " " );

   cout << "a1 contains: ";
   copy( a1.cbegin(), a1.cend(), output );
   cout << "\na2 contains: ";
   copy( a2.cbegin(), a2.cend(), output );
   cout << "\na3 contains: ";
   copy( a3.cbegin(), a3.cend(), output );
```

Fig. 16.2 | Algorithms equal, mismatch and lexicographical_compare. (Part 1 of 2.)

```
23
24      // compare a1 and a2 for equality
25      bool result = equal( a1.cbegin(), a1.cend(), a2.cbegin() );
26      cout << "\n\na1 " << ( result ? "is" : "is not" )
27         << " equal to a2.\n";
28
29      // compare a1 and a3 for equality
30      result = equal( a1.cbegin(), a1.cend(), a3.cbegin() );
31      cout << "a1 " << ( result ? "is" : "is not" ) << " equal to a3.\n";
32
33      // check for mismatch between a1 and a3
34      auto location = mismatch( a1.cbegin(), a1.cend(), a3.cbegin() );
35      cout << "\nThere is a mismatch between a1 and a3 at location "
36         << ( location.first - a1.begin() ) << "\nwhere a1 contains "
37         << *location.first << " and a3 contains " << *location.second
38         << "\n\n";
39
40      char c1[ SIZE ] = "HELLO";
41      char c2[ SIZE ] = "BYE BYE";
42
43      // perform lexicographical comparison of c1 and c2
44      result = lexicographical_compare(
45         begin( c1 ), end( c1 ), begin( c2 ), end( c2 ) );
46      cout << c1 << ( result ? " is less than " :
47         " is greater than or equal to " ) << c2 << endl;
48   } // end main
```

```
a1 contains: 1 2 3 4 5 6 7 8 9 10
a2 contains: 1 2 3 4 5 6 7 8 9 10
a3 contains: 1 2 3 4 1000 6 7 8 9 10

a1 is equal to a2.
a1 is not equal to a3.

There is a mismatch between a1 and a3 at location 4
where a1 contains 5 and a3 contains 1000

HELLO is greater than or equal to BYE BYE
```

Fig. 16.2 | Algorithms `equal`, `mismatch` and `lexicographical_compare`. (Part 2 of 2.)

`equal` Algorithm

Line 25 uses the **`equal`** algorithm to compare two sequences of values for equality. The second sequence must contain at least as many elements as the first—`equal` returns `false` if the sequences are *not* of the same length. The `== operator` (whether built-in or overloaded) performs the element comparisons. In this example, the elements in `a1` from `a1.cbegin()` up to, but *not* including, `a1.cend()` are compared to the elements in `a2` starting from `a2.cbegin()`. In this example, `a1` and `a2` are equal. The three iterator arguments must be at least *input iterators* (i.e., they can be used for input from a sequence in the *forward* direction). Line 30 uses function `equal` to compare `a1` and `a3`, which are *not* equal.

`equal` Algorithm with Binary Predicate Function

Another version of `equal` takes a *binary predicate function* as a fourth parameter. The binary predicate function receives the two elements being compared and returns a `bool` value indicating whether the elements are equal. This can be useful in sequences that store objects or pointers to values rather than actual values, because you can define one or more comparisons. For example, you can compare `Employee` objects for age, social security number, or location rather than comparing entire objects. You can compare what pointers refer to rather than comparing the pointer values (i.e., the addresses stored in the pointers).

`mismatch` *Algorithm*

Lines 34 calls the **`mismatch`** algorithm to compare two sequences of values. The algorithm returns a `pair` of iterators indicating the location in each sequence of the *mismatched* elements. If all the elements match, the two iterators in the `pair` are equal to the end iterator for each sequence. The three iterator arguments must be at least *input iterators*. We *infer* the type of the `pair` object `location` with C++11's `auto` keyword (line 34). Line 36 determines the actual location of the mismatch in the `array`s with the expression `location.first - a1.begin()`, which evaluates to the number of elements between the iterators (this is analogous to pointer arithmetic; Chapter 8). This corresponds to the element number in this example, because the comparison is performed from the beginning of each `array`. As with `equal`, there is another version of `mismatch` that takes a *binary predicate function* as a fourth parameter.

`lexicographical_compare` *Algorithm*

Lines 44–45 use the **`lexicographical_compare`** algorithm to compare the contents of two `char` built-in arrays. This algorithm's four iterator arguments must be at least *input iterators*. As you know, pointers into built-in arrays are *random-access iterators*. The first two iterator arguments specify the range of locations in the first sequence. The last two specify the range of locations in the second sequence. Once again, we use the C++11 `begin` and `end` functions to determine the range of elements for each built-in array. While iterating through the sequences, the `lexicographical_compare` checks if the element in the first sequence is less than the corresponding element in the second sequence. If so, the algorithm returns `true`. If the element in the first sequence is greater than or equal to the element in the second sequence, the algorithm returns `false`. This algorithm can be used to arrange sequences *lexicographically*. Typically, such sequences contain strings.

16.3.3 `remove`, `remove_if`, `remove_copy` and `remove_copy_if`

Figure 16.3 demonstrates removing values from a sequence with algorithms `remove`, `remove_if`, `remove_copy` and `remove_copy_if`.

```
// Fig. 16.3: fig16_03.cpp
// Algorithms remove, remove_if, remove_copy and remove_copy_if.
#include <iostream>
#include <algorithm> // algorithm definitions
#include <array> // array class-template definition
#include <iterator> // ostream_iterator
using namespace std;

bool greater9( int ); // prototype

```

Fig. 16.3 | Algorithms `remove`, `remove_if`, `remove_copy` and `remove_copy_if`. (Part 1 of 3.)

```
int main()
{
   const size_t SIZE = 10;
   array< int, SIZE > init = { 10, 2, 10, 4, 16, 6, 14, 8, 12, 10 };
   ostream_iterator< int > output( cout, " " );

   array< int, SIZE > a1( init ); // initialize with copy of init
   cout << "a1 before removing all 10s:\n   ";
   copy( a1.cbegin(), a1.cend(), output );

   // remove all 10s from a1
   auto newLastElement = remove( a1.begin(), a1.end(), 10 );
   cout << "\na1 after removing all 10s:\n   ";
   copy( a1.begin(), newLastElement, output );

   array< int, SIZE > a2( init ); // initialize with copy of init
   array< int, SIZE > c = { 0 }; // initialize to 0s
   cout << "\n\na2 before removing all 10s and copying:\n   ";
   copy( a2.cbegin(), a2.cend(), output );

   // copy from a2 to c, removing 10s in the process
   remove_copy( a2.cbegin(), a2.cend(), c.begin(), 10 );
   cout << "\nc after removing all 10s from a2:\n   ";
   copy( c.cbegin(), c.cend(), output );

   array< int, SIZE > a3( init ); // initialize with copy of init
   cout << "\n\na3 before removing all elements greater than 9:\n   ";
   copy( a3.cbegin(), a3.cend(), output );

   // remove elements greater than 9 from a3
   newLastElement = remove_if( a3.begin(), a3.end(), greater9 );
   cout << "\na3 after removing all elements greater than 9:\n   ";
   copy( a3.begin(), newLastElement, output );

   array< int, SIZE > a4( init ); // initialize with copy of init
   array< int, SIZE > c2 = { 0 }; // initialize to 0s
   cout << "\n\na4 before removing all elements"
      << "\ngreater than 9 and copying:\n   ";
   copy( a4.cbegin(), a4.cend(), output );

   // copy elements from a4 to c2, removing elements greater
   // than 9 in the process
   remove_copy_if( a4.cbegin(), a4.cend(), c2.begin(), greater9 );
   cout << "\nc2 after removing all elements"
      << "\ngreater than 9 from a4:\n   ";
   copy( c2.cbegin(), c2.cend(), output );
   cout << endl;
} // end main

// determine whether argument is greater than 9
bool greater9( int x )
{
```

Fig. 16.3 | Algorithms remove, remove_if, remove_copy and remove_copy_if. (Part 2 of 3.)

```
63      return x > 9;
64   } // end function greater9
```

```
a1 before removing all 10s:
   10 2 10 4 16 6 14 8 12 10
a1 after removing all 10s:
   2 4 16 6 14 8 12

a2 before removing all 10s and copying:
   10 2 10 4 16 6 14 8 12 10
c after removing all 10s from a2:
   2 4 16 6 14 8 12 0 0 0

a3 before removing all elements greater than 9:
   10 2 10 4 16 6 14 8 12 10
a3 after removing all elements greater than 9:
   2 4 6 8

a4 before removing all elements
greater than 9 and copying:
   10 2 10 4 16 6 14 8 12 10
c2 after removing all elements
greater than 9 from a4:
   2 4 6 8 0 0 0 0 0 0
```

Fig. 16.3 | Algorithms `remove`, `remove_if`, `remove_copy` and `remove_copy_if`. (Part 3 of 3.)

`remove` Algorithm

Line 22 uses the **`remove`** algorithm to eliminate from `a1` *all* elements with the value `10` in the range from `a1.begin()` up to, but *not* including, `a1.end()`. The first two iterator arguments must be *forward iterators*. This algorithm does *not* modify the number of elements in the container or destroy the eliminated elements, but it does move *all* elements that are *not* eliminated toward the *beginning* of the container. The algorithm returns an iterator positioned after the last element that was not removed. Elements from the iterator position to the end of the container have *unspecified* values.

`remove_copy` Algorithm

Line 32 uses the **`remove_copy`** algorithm to copy *all* elements from `a2` that do *not* have the value `10` in the range from `a2.cbegin()` up to, but *not* including, `a2.cend()`. The elements are placed in `c`, starting at position `c.begin()`. The iterators supplied as the first two arguments must be *input iterators*. The iterator supplied as the third argument must be an *output iterator* so that the element being copied can be *inserted* into the copy location. This algorithm returns an iterator positioned after the last element copied into `vector c`.

`remove_if` Algorithm

Line 41 uses the **`remove_if`** algorithm to delete from `a3` *all* those elements in the range from `a3.begin()` up to, but *not* including, `a3.end()` for which our user-defined unary *predicate function* `greater9` returns `true`. Function `greater9` (defined in lines 61–64) returns `true` if the value passed to it is greater than 9; otherwise, it returns `false`. The iterators supplied as the first two arguments must be *forward iterators*. This algorithm does *not* modify the number of elements in the container, but it does move to the *beginning* of the container *all* elements that are *not* removed. This algorithm returns an iterator positioned after the last element that was *not* removed. All elements from the iterator position to the end of the container have *undefined* values.

remove_copy_if Algorithm

Line 53 uses the **remove_copy_if** algorithm to copy all those elements from a4 in the range from a4.cbegin() up to, but *not* including, a4.cend() for which the *unary predicate function* greater9 returns true. The elements are placed in c2, starting at c2.begin(). The iterators supplied as the first two arguments must be *input iterators*. The iterator supplied as the third argument must be an *output iterator* so that the element being copied can be *assigned* to the copy location. This algorithm returns an iterator positioned after the *last* element copied into c2.

16.3.4 replace, replace_if, replace_copy and replace_copy_if

Figure 16.4 demonstrates replacing values from a sequence using algorithms replace, replace_if, replace_copy and replace_copy_if.

```
// Fig. 16.4: fig16_04.cpp
// Algorithms replace, replace_if, replace_copy and replace_copy_if.
#include <iostream>
#include <algorithm>
#include <array>
#include <iterator> // ostream_iterator
using namespace std;

bool greater9( int ); // predicate function prototype

int main()
{
   const size_t SIZE = 10;
   array< int, SIZE > init =  = { 10, 2, 10, 4, 16, 6, 14, 8, 12, 10 };
   ostream_iterator< int > output( cout, " " );

   array< int, SIZE >  a1( init ); // initialize with copy of init
   cout << "a1 before replacing all 10s:\n   ";
   copy( a1.cbegin(), a1.cend(), output );

   // replace all 10s in a1 with 100
   replace( a1.begin(), a1.end(), 10, 100 );
   cout << "\na1 after replacing 10s with 100s:\n   ";
   copy( a1.cbegin(), a1.cend(), output );

   array< int, SIZE > a2( init ); // initialize with copy of init
   array< int, SIZE > c1; // instantiate c1
   cout << "\n\na2 before replacing all 10s and copying:\n   ";
   copy( a2.cbegin(), a2.cend(), output );

   // copy from a2 to c1, replacing 10s with 100s
   replace_copy( a2.cbegin(), a2.cend(), c1.begin(), 10, 100 );
```

Fig. 16.4 | Algorithms replace, replace_if, replace_copy and replace_copy_if. (Part 1 of 2.)

```
    cout << "\nc1 after replacing all 10s in a2:\n   ";
    copy( c1.cbegin(), c1.cend(), output );

    array< int, SIZE > a3( init ); // initialize with copy of init
    cout << "\n\na3 before replacing values greater than 9:\n   ";
    copy( a3.cbegin(), a3.cend(), output );

    // replace values greater than 9 in a3 with 100
    replace_if( a3.begin(), a3.end(), greater9, 100 );
    cout << "\na3 after replacing all values greater"
       << "\nthan 9 with 100s:\n   ";
    copy( a3.cbegin(), a3.cend(), output );

    array< int, SIZE > a4( init ); // initialize with copy of init
    array< int, SIZE > c2; // instantiate c2‘
    cout << "\n\na4 before replacing all values greater "
       << "than 9 and copying:\n   ";
    copy( a4.cbegin(), a4.cend(), output );

    // copy a4 to c2, replacing elements greater than 9 with 100
    replace_copy_if( a4.cbegin(), a4.cend(), c2.begin(), greater9, 100 );
    cout << "\nc2 after replacing all values greater than 9 in v4:\n   ";
    copy( c2.begin(), c2.end(), output );
    cout << endl;
} // end main

// determine whether argument is greater than 9
bool greater9( int x )
{
    return x > 9;
} // end function greater9
```

```
a1 before replacing all 10s:
   10 2 10 4 16 6 14 8 12 10
a1 after replacing 10s with 100s:
   100 2 100 4 16 6 14 8 12 100

a2 before replacing all 10s and copying:
   10 2 10 4 16 6 14 8 12 10
c1 after replacing all 10s in a2:
   100 2 100 4 16 6 14 8 12 100

a3 before replacing values greater than 9:
   10 2 10 4 16 6 14 8 12 10
a3 after replacing all values greater
than 9 with 100s:
   100 2 100 4 100 6 100 8 100 100

a4 before replacing all values greater than 9 and copying:
   10 2 10 4 16 6 14 8 12 10
c2 after replacing all values greater than 9 in a4:
   100 2 100 4 100 6 100 8 100 100
```

Fig. 16.4 | Algorithms `replace`, `replace_if`, `replace_copy` and `replace_copy_if`. (Part 2 of 2.)

`replace` *Algorithm*

Line 22 uses the **`replace`** algorithm to replace *all* elements with the value `10` in the range `a1.begin()` up to, but *not* including, `a1.end()` with the new value `100`. The iterators supplied as the first two arguments must be *forward iterators* so that the algorithm can *modify* the elements in the sequence.

`replace_copy` *Algorithm*

Line 32 uses the **`replace_copy`** algorithm to copy *all* elements in the range `a2.cbegin()` up to, but *not* including, `a2.cend()`, replacing *all* elements with the value `10` with the new value `100`. The elements are copied into `c1`, starting at position `c1.begin()`. The iterators supplied as the first two arguments must be *input iterators*. The iterator supplied as the third argument must be an *output iterator* so that the element being copied can be *assigned* to the copy location. This function returns an iterator positioned after the *last* element copied into `c1`.

`replace_if` *Algorithm*

Line 41 uses the **`replace_if`** algorithm to replace *all* those elements from `a3.begin()` up to, but *not* including, `a3.end()` for which the *unary predicate function* `greater9` returns `true`. Function `greater9` (defined in lines 60–63) returns `true` if the value passed to it is greater than 9; otherwise, it returns `false`. The value `100` replaces each value greater than 9. The iterators supplied as the first two arguments must be *forward iterators*.

`replace_copy_if` *Algorithm*

Line 53 uses the **`replace_copy_if`** algorithm to copy *all* elements from `a4.cbegin()` up to, but *not* including, `a4.cend()`. Elements for which the *unary predicate function* `greater9` returns `true` are replaced with the value `100`. The elements are placed in `c2`, starting at position `c2.begin()`. The iterators supplied as the first two arguments must be *input iterators*. The iterator supplied as the third argument must be an *output iterator* so that the element being copied can be *assigned* to the copy location. This algorithm returns an iterator positioned after the *last* element copied into `c2`.

16.3.5 Mathematical Algorithms

Figure 16.5 demonstrates several common mathematical algorithms, including `random_shuffle`, `count`, `count_if`, `min_element`, `max_element`, `minmax_element`, `accumulate`, `for_each` and `transform`.

```
// Fig. 16.5: fig16_05.cpp
// Mathematical algorithms of the Standard Library.
#include <iostream>
#include <algorithm> // algorithm definitions
#include <numeric> // accumulate is defined here
#include <array>
#include <iterator>
using namespace std;

bool greater9( int ); // predicate function prototype
```

Fig. 16.5 | Mathematical algorithms of the Standard Library. (Part 1 of 3.)

```
void outputSquare( int ); // output square of a value
int calculateCube( int ); // calculate cube of a value

int main()
{
   const size_t SIZE = 10;
   array< int, SIZE > a1 = { 1, 2, 3, 4, 5, 6, 7, 8, 9, 10 };
   ostream_iterator< int > output( cout, " " );

   cout << "a1 before random_shuffle: ";
   copy( a1.cbegin(), a1.cend(), output );

   random_shuffle( a1.begin(), a1.end() ); // shuffle elements of a1
   cout << "\na1 after random_shuffle: ";
   copy( a1.cbegin(), a1.cend(), output );

   array< int, SIZE > a2 = { 100, 2, 8, 1, 50, 3, 8, 8, 9, 10 };
   cout << "\n\na2 contains: ";
   copy( a2.cbegin(), a2.cend(), output );

   // count number of elements in a2 with value 8
   int result = count( a2.cbegin(), a2.cend(), 8 );
   cout << "\nNumber of elements matching 8: " << result;

   // count number of elements in a2 that are greater than 9
   result = count_if( a2.cbegin(), a2.cend(), greater9 );
   cout << "\nNumber of elements greater than 9: " << result;

   // locate minimum element in a2
   cout << "\n\nMinimum element in a2 is: "
      << *( min_element( a2.cbegin(), a2.cend() ) );

   // locate maximum element in a2
   cout << "\nMaximum element in a2 is: "
      << *( max_element( a2.cbegin(), a2.cend() ) );

   // locate minimum and maximum elements in a2
   auto minAndMax = minmax_element( a2.cbegin(), a2.cend() );
   cout << "\nThe minimum and maximum elements in a2 are "
      << *minAndMax.first << " and " << *minAndMax.second
      << ", respectively";

   // calculate sum of elements in a1
   cout << "\n\nThe total of the elements in a1 is: "
      << accumulate( a1.cbegin(), a1.cend(), 0 );

   // output square of every element in a1
   cout << "\n\nThe square of every integer in a1 is:\n";
   for_each( a1.cbegin(), a1.cend(), outputSquare );

   array< int, SIZE > cubes; // instantiate cubes

```

Fig. 16.5 | Mathematical algorithms of the Standard Library. (Part 2 of 3.)

```
63    // calculate cube of each element in a1; place results in cubes
64    transform( a1.cbegin(), a1.cend(), cubes.begin(), calculateCube );
65    cout << "\n\nThe cube of every integer in a1 is:\n";
66    copy( cubes.cbegin(), cubes.cend(), output );
67    cout << endl;
68 } // end main
69
70 // determine whether argument is greater than 9
71 bool greater9( int value )
72 {
73    return value > 9;
74 } // end function greater9
75
76 // output square of argument
77 void outputSquare( int value )
78 {
79    cout << value * value << ' ';
80 } // end function outputSquare
81
82 // return cube of argument
83 int calculateCube( int value )
84 {
85    return value * value * value;
86 } // end function calculateCube
```

```
a1 before random_shuffle: 1 2 3 4 5 6 7 8 9 10
a1 after random_shuffle: 9 2 10 3 1 6 8 4 5 7

a2 contains: 100 2 8 1 50 3 8 8 9 10
Number of elements matching 8: 3
Number of elements greater than 9: 3

Minimum element in a2 is: 1
Maximum element in a2 is: 100
The minimum and maximum elements in a2 are 1 and 100, respectively

The total of the elements in a1 is: 55

The square of every integer in a1 is:
81 4 100 9 1 36 64 16 25 49

The cube of every integer in a1 is:
729 8 1000 27 1 216 512 64 125 343
```

Fig. 16.5 | Mathematical algorithms of the Standard Library. (Part 3 of 3.)

random_shuffle *Algorithm*

Line 23 uses the **random_shuffle** algorithm to reorder randomly the elements in the range a1.begin() up to, but *not* including, a1.end(). This algorithm takes *two random-access iterator* arguments. This version of random_shuffle uses rand for randomization and produces the same results each time you run the program unless you seed the random-number generator with srand. Another version of random_shuffle receives as its third argument a C++11 uniform random-number generator.

`count` *Algorithm*

Line 32 uses the **`count`** algorithm to count the elements with the value `8` in the range `a2.cbegin()` up to, but *not* including, `a2.cend()`. This algorithm requires its two iterator arguments to be at least *input iterators*.

`count_if` *Algorithm*

Line 36 uses the **`count_if`** algorithm to count elements in the range from `a2.cbegin()` up to, but *not* including, `a2.cend()` for which the *predicate function* `greater9` returns `true`. Algorithm `count_if` requires its two iterator arguments to be at least *input iterators*.

`min_element` *Algorithm*

Line 41 uses the **`min_element`** algorithm to locate the *smallest* element in the range from `a2.cbegin()` up to, but *not* including, `a2.cend()`. The algorithm returns a *forward iterator* located at the *first* smallest element, or `a2.end()` if the range is *empty*. The algorithm's two iterator arguments must be at least *forward iterators*. A second version of this algorithm takes as its third argument a binary function that compares two elements in the sequence. This algorithm returns the `bool` value `true` if the first argument is *less than* the second.

Error-Prevention Tip 16.1

It's a good practice to check that the range specified in a call to `min_element` *is not empty and that the return value is not the "past the end" iterator.*

`max_element` *Algorithm*

Line 45 uses the **`max_element`** algorithm to locate the *largest* element in the range from `a2.cbegin()` up to, but *not* including, `a2.cend()`. The algorithm returns a *forward iterator* located at the *first* largest element. The algorithm's two iterator arguments must be at least *forward iterators*. A second version of this algorithm takes as its third argument a *binary predicate function* that compares the elements in the sequence. The binary function takes two arguments and returns the `bool` value `true` if the first argument is *less than* the second.

C++11: `minmax_element` *Algorithm*

Line 48 uses the new C++11 **`minmax_element`** algorithm to locate both the *smallest* and *largest* elements in the range from `a2.cbegin()` up to, but *not* including, `a2.cend()`. The algorithm returns a pair of *forward iterators* located at the smallest and largest elements, respectively. If there are duplicate smallest or largest elements, the iterators are located at the first smallest and last largest values. The algorithm's two iterator arguments must be at least *forward iterators*. A second version of this algorithm takes as its third argument a *binary predicate function* that compares the elements in the sequence. The binary function takes two arguments and returns the `bool` value `true` if the first argument is *less than* the second.

`accumulate` *Algorithm*

Line 55 uses the **`accumulate`** algorithm (the template of which is in header `<numeric>`) to sum the values in the range from `a1.cbegin()` up to, but *not* including, `a1.cend()`. The algorithm's two iterator arguments must be at least *input iterators* and its third argument represents the initial value of the total. A second version of this algorithm takes as its fourth argument a general function that determines how elements are accumulated. The general function must take *two* arguments and return a result. The first argument to this function is the current value of the accumulation. The second argument is the value of the current element in the sequence being accumulated.

for_each Algorithm

Line 59 uses the **for_each** algorithm to apply a general function to every element in the range from a1.cbegin() up to, but *not* including, a1.cend(). The general function takes the current element as an argument and may modify that element (if it's received by reference and is not const). Algorithm for_each requires its two iterator arguments to be at least *input iterators*.

transform Algorithm

Line 63 uses the **transform** algorithm to apply a general function to *every* element in the range from a1.cbegin() up to, but *not* including, a1.cend(). The general function (the fourth argument) should take the current element as an argument, must *not* modify the element and should return the transformed value. Algorithm transform requires its first two iterator arguments to be at least *input iterators* and its third argument to be at least an *output iterator*. The third argument specifies where the transformed values should be placed. Note that the third argument can equal the first. Another version of transform accepts five arguments—the first two arguments are *input iterators* that specify a range of elements from one source container, the third argument is an *input iterator* that specifies the first element in another source container, the fourth argument is an *output iterator* that specifies where the transformed values should be placed and the last argument is a general function that takes two arguments. This version of transform takes one element from each of the two input sources and applies the general function to that pair of elements, then places the transformed value at the location specified by the fourth argument.

16.3.6 Basic Searching and Sorting Algorithms

Figure 16.6 demonstrates some basic searching and sorting Standard Library algorithms, including find, find_if, sort, binary_search, all_of, any_of, none_of and find_if_not.

```
// Fig. 16.6: fig16_06.cpp
// Standard Library search and sort algorithms.
#include <iostream>
#include <algorithm> // algorithm definitions
#include <array> // array class-template definition
#include <iterator>
using namespace std;

bool greater10( int value ); // predicate function prototype

int main()
{
   const size_t SIZE = 10;
   array< int, SIZE > a = { 10, 2, 17, 5, 16, 8, 13, 11, 20, 7 };
   ostream_iterator< int > output( cout, " " );
```

Fig. 16.6 | Standard Library search and sort algorithms. (Part 1 of 3.)

```
    cout << "array a contains: ";
    copy( a.cbegin(), a.cend(), output ); // display output vector

    // locate first occurrence of 16 in a
    auto location = find( a.cbegin(), a.cend(), 16 );

    if ( location != a.cend() ) // found 16
       cout << "\n\nFound 16 at location " << ( location - a.cbegin() );
    else // 16 not found
       cout << "\n\n16 not found";

    // locate first occurrence of 100 in a
    location = find( a.cbegin(), a.cend(), 100 );

    if ( location != a.cend() ) // found 100
       cout << "\nFound 100 at location " << ( location - a.cbegin() );
    else // 100 not found
       cout << "\n100 not found";

    // locate first occurrence of value greater than 10 in a
    location = find_if( a.cbegin(), a.cend(), greater10 );

    if ( location != a.cend() ) // found value greater than 10
       cout << "\n\nThe first value greater than 10 is " << *location
          << "\nfound at location " << ( location - a.cbegin() );
    else // value greater than 10 not found
       cout << "\n\nNo values greater than 10 were found";

    // sort elements of a
    sort( a.begin(), a.end() );
    cout << "\n\narray a after sort: ";
    copy( a.cbegin(), a.cend(), output );

    // use binary_search to locate 13 in a
    if ( binary_search( a.cbegin(), a.cend(), 13 ) )
       cout << "\n\n13 was found in a";
    else
       cout << "\n\n13 was not found in a";

    // use binary_search to locate 100 in a
    if ( binary_search( a.cbegin(), a.cend(), 100 ) )
       cout << "\n100 was found in a";
    else
       cout << "\n100 was not found in a";

    // determine whether all of the elements of a are greater than 10
    if ( all_of( a.cbegin(), a.cend(), greater10 ) )
       cout << "\n\nAll the elements in a are greater than 10";
    else
       cout << "\n\nSome elements in a are not greater than 10";

```

Fig. 16.6 | Standard Library search and sort algorithms. (Part 2 of 3.)

```
68       // determine whether any of the elements of a are greater than 10
69       if ( any_of( a.cbegin(), a.cend(), greater10 ) )
70          cout << "\n\nSome of the elements in a are greater than 10";
71       else
72          cout << "\n\nNone of the elements in a are greater than 10";
73
74       // determine whether none of the elements of a are greater than 10
75       if ( none_of( a.cbegin(), a.cend(), greater10 ) )
76          cout << "\n\nNone of the elements in a are greater than 10";
77       else
78          cout << "\n\nSome of the elements in a are greater than 10";
79
80       // locate first occurrence of value that's not greater than 10 in a
81       location = find_if_not( a.cbegin(), a.cend(), greater10 );
82
83       if ( location != a.cend() ) // found a value less than or eqaul to 10
84          cout << "\n\nThe first value not greater than 10 is " << *location
85             << "\nfound at location " << ( location - a.cbegin() );
86       else // no values less than or equal to 10 were found
87          cout << "\n\nOnly values greater than 10 were found";
88
89       cout << endl;
90    } // end main
91
92    // determine whether argument is greater than 10
93    bool greater10( int value )
94    {
95       return value > 10;
96    } // end function greater10
```

```
array a contains: 10 2 17 5 16 8 13 11 20 7

Found 16 at location 4
100 not found

The first value greater than 10 is 17
found at location 2

array a after sort: 2 5 7 8 10 11 13 16 17 20

13 was found in a
100 was not found in a

Some elements in a are not greater than 10

Some of the elements in a are greater than 10

Some of the elements in a are greater than 10

The first value not greater than 10 is 2
found at location 0
```

Fig. 16.6 | Standard Library search and sort algorithms. (Part 3 of 3.)

`find` *Algorithm*

Line 21 uses the **`find`** algorithm to locate the value `16` in the range from `a.cbegin()` up to, but not including, `a.cend()`. The algorithm requires its two iterator arguments to be at least *input iterators* and returns an *input iterator* that either is positioned at the first element containing the value or indicates the end of the sequence (as is the case in line 29).

`find_if` *Algorithm*

Line 37 uses the **`find_if`** algorithm (a linear search) to locate the first value in the range from `a.cbegin()` up to, but *not* including, `a.cend()` for which the *unary predicate function* `greater10` returns `true`. Function `greater10` (defined in lines 93–96) takes an integer and returns a `bool` value indicating whether the integer argument is *greater than* 10. Algorithm `find_if` requires its two iterator arguments to be at least *input iterators*. The algorithm returns an *input iterator* that either is positioned at the first element containing a value for which the predicate function returns `true` or indicates the end of the sequence.

`sort` *Algorithm*

Line 46 uses **`sort`** algorithm to arrange the elements in the range from `a.begin()` up to, but *not* including, `a.end()` in *ascending order*. The algorithm requires its two iterator arguments to be *random-access iterators*. A second version of this algorithm takes a third argument that's a *binary predicate function* taking two arguments that are values in the sequence and returning a `bool` indicating the *sorting order*—if the return value is `true`, the two elements being compared are in *sorted order*.

`binary_search` *Algorithm*

Line 51 uses the **`binary_search`** algorithm to determine whether the value 13 is in the range from `a.cbegin()` up to, but *not* including, `a.cend()`. The values must be sorted in *ascending order*. Algorithm `binary_search` requires its two iterator arguments to be at least *forward iterators*. The algorithm returns a `bool` indicating whether the value was found in the sequence. Line 57 demonstrates a call to `binary_search` in which the value is *not* found. A second version of this algorithm takes a fourth argument that's a *binary predicate function* taking two arguments that are values in the sequence and returning a `bool`. The predicate function returns `true` if the two elements being compared are in *sorted order*. To obtain the *location* of the search key in the container, use the `lower_bound` or `find` algorithms.

11

C++11: `all_of` *Algorithm*

Line 63 uses the **`all_of`** algorithm to determine whether the *unary predicate function* `greater10` returns `true` for *all* of the elements in the range from `a.cbegin()` up to, but *not* including, `a.cend()`. Algorithm `all_of` requires its two iterator arguments to be at least *input iterators*.

11

C++11: `any_of` *Algorithm*

Line 69 uses the **`any_of`** algorithm to determine whether the *unary predicate function* `greater10` returns `true` for *at least one* of the elements in the range from `a.cbegin()` up to, but *not* including, `a.cend()`. Algorithm `any_of` requires its two iterator arguments to be at least *input iterators*.

11

C++11: `none_of` *Algorithm*

Line 75 uses the **`none_of`** algorithm to determine whether the *unary predicate function* `greater10` returns `false` for *all* of the elements in the range from `a.cbegin()` up to, but *not* including, `a.cend()`. Algorithm `none_of` requires its two iterator arguments to be at least *input iterators*.

C++11: **find_if_not** *Algorithm*

Line 81 uses the **find_if_not** algorithm to locate the first value in the range from a.cbegin() up to, but *not* including, a.cend() for which the *unary predicate function* greater10 returns false. Algorithm find_if requires its two iterator arguments to be at least *input iterators*. The algorithm returns an *input iterator* that either is positioned at the first element containing a value for which the predicate function returns false or indicates the end of the sequence.

16.3.7 swap, iter_swap and swap_ranges

Figure 16.7 demonstrates algorithms swap, iter_swap and swap_ranges for *swapping* elements.

```
// Fig. 16.7: fig16_07.cpp
// Algorithms iter_swap, swap and swap_ranges.
#include <iostream>
#include <array>
#include <algorithm> // algorithm definitions
#include <iterator>
using namespace std;

int main()
{
   const size_t SIZE = 10;
   array< int, SIZE > a = { 1, 2, 3, 4, 5, 6, 7, 8, 9, 10 };
   ostream_iterator< int > output( cout, " " );

   cout << "Array a contains:\n   ";
   copy( a.cbegin(), a.cend(), output ); // display array a

   swap( a[ 0 ], a[ 1 ] ); // swap elements at locations 0 and 1 of a

   cout << "\nArray a after swapping a[0] and a[1] using swap:\n   ";
   copy( a.cbegin(), a.cend(), output ); // display array a

   // use iterators to swap elements at locations 0 and 1 of array a
   iter_swap( a.begin(), a.begin() + 1 ); // swap with iterators
   cout << "\nArray a after swapping a[0] and a[1] using iter_swap:\n   ";
   copy( a.cbegin(), a.cend(), output );

   // swap elements in first five elements of array a with
   // elements in last five elements of array a
   swap_ranges( a.begin(), a.begin() + 5, a.begin() + 5  );

   cout << "\nArray a after swapping the first five elements\n"
        << "with the last five elements:\n   ";
   copy( a.cbegin(), a.cend(), output );
   cout << endl;
} // end main
```

Fig. 16.7 | Algorithms iter_swap, swap and swap_ranges. (Part 1 of 2.)

```
Array a contains:
   1 2 3 4 5 6 7 8 9 10
Array a after swapping a[0] and a[1] using swap:
   2 1 3 4 5 6 7 8 9 10
Array a after swapping a[0] and a[1] using iter_swap:
   1 2 3 4 5 6 7 8 9 10
Array a after swapping the first five elements
with the last five elements:
   6 7 8 9 10 1 2 3 4 5
```

Fig. 16.7 | Algorithms `iter_swap`, `swap` and `swap_ranges`. (Part 2 of 2.)

`swap` Algorithm

Line 18 uses the **`swap`** algorithm to exchange two values. In this example, the first and second elements of `array a` are exchanged. The function takes as arguments references to the two values being exchanged.

`iter_swap` Algorithm

Line 24 uses function **`iter_swap`** to exchange the two elements. The function takes two *forward iterator* arguments (in this case, iterators to elements of an `array`) and exchanges the values in the elements to which the iterators refer.

`swap_ranges` Algorithm

Line 30 uses function **`swap_ranges`** to exchange the elements from `a.begin()` up to, but not including, `a.begin() + 5` with the elements beginning at position `a.begin() + 5`. The function requires three *forward iterator* arguments. The first two arguments specify the range of elements in the first sequence that will be exchanged with the elements in the second sequence starting from the iterator in the third argument. In this example, the two sequences of values are in the same `array`, but the sequences can be from different arrays or containers. The sequences must not overlap. The destination sequence must be large enough to contain all the elements of the ranges being swapped.

16.3.8 `copy_backward`, `merge`, `unique` and `reverse`

Figure 16.8 demonstrates algorithms `copy_backward`, `merge`, `unique` and `reverse`.

```
// Fig. 16.8: fig16_08.cpp
// Algorithms copy_backward, merge, unique and reverse.
#include <iostream>
#include <algorithm> // algorithm definitions
#include <array> // array class-template definition
#include <iterator> // ostream_iterator
using namespace std;

int main()
{
   const size_t SIZE = 5;
   array< int, SIZE > a1 = { 1, 3, 5, 7, 9 };
```

Fig. 16.8 | Algorithms `copy_backward`, `merge`, `unique` and `reverse`. (Part 1 of 2.)

```
13      array< int, SIZE > a2 = { 2, 4, 5, 7, 9 };
14      ostream_iterator< int > output( cout, " " );
15
16      cout << "array a1 contains: ";
17      copy( a1.cbegin(), a1.cend(), output ); // display a1
18      cout << "\narray a2 contains: ";
19      copy( a2.cbegin(), a2.cend(), output ); // display a2
20
21      array< int, SIZE > results;
22
23      // place elements of a1 into results in reverse order
24      copy_backward( a1.cbegin(), a1.cend(), results.end() );
25      cout << "\n\nAfter copy_backward, results contains: ";
26      copy( results.cbegin(), results.cend(), output );
27
28      array< int, SIZE + SIZE >  results2;
29
30      // merge elements of a1 and a2 into results2 in sorted order
31      merge( a1.cbegin(), a1.cend(), a2.cbegin(), a2.cend(),
32         results2.begin() );
33
34      cout << "\n\nAfter merge of a1 and a2 results2 contains: ";
35      copy( results2.cbegin(), results2.cend(), output );
36
37      // eliminate duplicate values from results2
38      auto endLocation = unique( results2.begin(), results2.end() );
39
40      cout << "\n\nAfter unique results2 contains: ";
41      copy( results2.begin(), endLocation, output );
42
43      cout << "\n\narray a1 after reverse: ";
44      reverse( a1.begin(), a1.end() ); // reverse elements of a1
45      copy( a1.cbegin(), a1.cend(), output );
46      cout << endl;
47   } // end main
```

```
array a1 contains: 1 3 5 7 9
array a2 contains: 2 4 5 7 9

After copy_backward, results contains: 1 3 5 7 9

After merge of a1 and a2 results2 contains: 1 2 3 4 5 5 7 7 9 9

After unique results2 contains: 1 2 3 4 5 7 9

array a1 after reverse: 9 7 5 3 1
```

Fig. 16.8 | Algorithms copy_backward, merge, unique and reverse. (Part 2 of 2.)

copy_backward Algorithm

Line 24 uses the **copy_backward** algorithm to copy elements in the range from a1.cbegin() up to, but *not* including, a1.cend(), placing the elements in results by starting from the element before results.end() and working toward the beginning of the array. The algorithm returns an iterator positioned at the *last* element copied into the results (i.e., the beginning of results, because of the backward copy). The elements are placed in results in the same order as a1. This algorithm requires three *bidirectional iterator* arguments (iterators that can be *incremented* and *decremented* to iterate *forward* and *backward* through a sequence, respectively). One difference between copy_backward and copy is that the iterator returned from copy is positioned *after* the last element copied and the one returned from copy_backward is positioned *at* the last element copied (i.e., the first element in the sequence). Also, copy_backward *can* manipulate *overlapping* ranges of elements in a container as long as the first element to copy is *not* in the destination range of elements.

11 In addition to the copy and copy_backward algorithms, C++11 now includes the **move** and **move_backward** algorithms. These use C++11's new move semantics (discussed in Chapter 24, C++11: Additional Features) to move, rather than copy, objects from one container to another.

merge *Algorithm*

Lines 31–32 use the **merge** algorithm to combine two *sorted ascending sequences* of values into a third sorted ascending sequence. The algorithm requires five iterator arguments. The first four must be at least *input iterators* and the last must be at least an *output iterator*. The first two arguments specify the range of elements in the first sorted sequence (a1), the second two arguments specify the range of elements in the second sorted sequence (a2) and the last argument specifies the starting location in the third sequence (results2) where the elements will be merged. A second version of this algorithm takes as its sixth argument a *binary predicate function* that specifies the *sorting order*.

back_inserter, front_inserter *and* inserter *Iterator Adapters*

Line 28 creates the array results2 with the number of elements in a1 and a2. Using the merge algorithm requires that the sequence where the results are stored be at least the size of the sequences being merged. If you do not want to allocate the number of elements for the resulting sequence before the merge operation, you can use the following statements:

```
vector< int > results2;
merge( a1.begin(), a1.end(), a2.begin(), a2.end(),
   back_inserter( results2 ) );
```

The argument back_inserter(results2) uses function template **back_inserter** (header <iterator>) for the vector results2. A back_inserter calls the container's default push_back function to insert an element at the *end* of the container. If an element is inserted into a container that has no more space available, *the container grows in size*—which is why we used a vector in the preceding statements, because arrays are fixed size. Thus, the number of elements in the container does *not* have to be known in advance. There are two other inserters—**front_inserter** (uses push_front to insert an element at the *beginning* of a container specified as its argument) and **inserter** (uses insert to insert an element *at* the iterator supplied as its second argument in the container supplied as its first argument).

unique *Algorithm*

Line 38 uses the **unique** algorithm on the *sorted* sequence of elements in the range from results2.begin() up to, but *not* including, results2.end(). After this algorithm is applied to a sorted sequence with *duplicate* values, only a *single* copy of each value remains in the sequence. The algorithm takes two arguments that must be at least *forward iterators*.

The algorithm returns an iterator positioned *after the last element* in the sequence of unique values. The values of all elements in the container after the last unique value are *undefined*. A second version of this algorithm takes as a third argument a *binary predicate function* specifying how to compare two elements for *equality*.

`reverse` *Algorithm*

Line 44 uses the **`reverse`** algorithm to reverse all the elements in the range from `a1.begin()` up to, but *not* including, `a1.end()`. The algorithm takes two arguments that must be at least *bidirectional iterators*.

C++11: `copy_if` *and* `copy_n` *Algorithms*

C++11 now includes the new copy algorithms `copy_if` and `copy_n`. The **`copy_if`** algorithm copies each element from a range if the *unary predicate function* in its fourth argument returns `true` for that element. The iterators supplied as the first two arguments must be *input iterators*. The iterator supplied as the third argument must be an *output iterator* so that the element being copied can be *assigned* to the copy location. This algorithm returns an iterator positioned after the *last* element copied.

The **`copy_n`** algorithm copies the number of elements specified by its second argument from the location specified by its first argument (an *input iterator*). The elements are output to the location specified by its third argument (an *output iterator*).

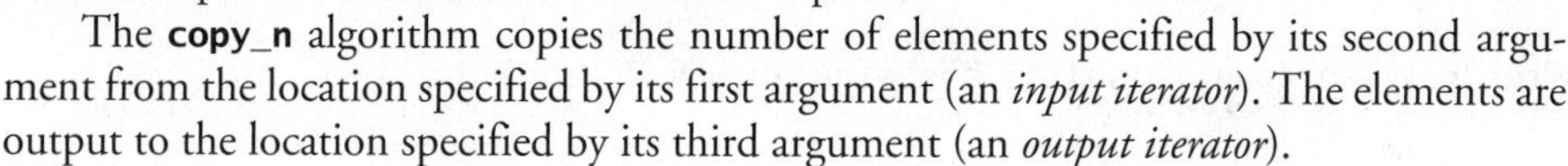

16.3.9 `inplace_merge`, `unique_copy` and `reverse_copy`

Figure 16.9 demonstrates algorithms `inplace_merge`, `unique_copy` and `reverse_copy`.

```
// Fig. 16.9: fig16_09.cpp
// Algorithms inplace_merge, reverse_copy and unique_copy.
#include <iostream>
#include <algorithm> // algorithm definitions
#include <array> // array class-template definition
#include <vector> // vector class-template definition
#include <iterator> // back_inserter definition
using namespace std;

int main()
{
   const int SIZE = 10;
   array< int, SIZE > a1 = { 1, 3, 5, 7, 9, 1, 3, 5, 7, 9 };
   ostream_iterator< int > output( cout, " " );

   cout << "array a1 contains: ";
   copy( a1.cbegin(), a1.cend(), output );

   // merge first half of a1 with second half of a1 such that
   // a1 contains sorted set of elements after merge
   inplace_merge( a1.begin(), a1.begin() + 5, a1.end() );

   cout << "\nAfter inplace_merge, a1 contains: ";
   copy( a1.cbegin(), a1.cend(), output );
```

Fig. 16.9 | Algorithms `inplace_merge`, `reverse_copy` and `unique_copy`. (Part 1 of 2.)

```
25
26      vector< int > results1;
27
28      // copy only unique elements of a1 into results1
29      unique_copy( a1.cbegin(), a1.cend(), back_inserter( results1 ) );
30      cout << "\nAfter unique_copy results1 contains: ";
31      copy( results1.cbegin(), results1.cend(), output );
32
33      vector< int > results2;
34
35      // copy elements of a1 into results2 in reverse order
36      reverse_copy( a1.cbegin(), a1.cend(), back_inserter( results2 ) );
37      cout << "\nAfter reverse_copy, results2 contains: ";
38      copy( results2.cbegin(), results2.cend(), output );
39      cout << endl;
40   } // end main
```

```
array a1 contains: 1 3 5 7 9 1 3 5 7 9
After inplace_merge, a1 contains: 1 1 3 3 5 5 7 7 9 9
After unique_copy results1 contains: 1 3 5 7 9
After reverse_copy, results2 contains: 9 9 7 7 5 5 3 3 1 1
```

Fig. 16.9 | Algorithms `inplace_merge`, `reverse_copy` and `unique_copy`. (Part 2 of 2.)

`inplace_merge` *Algorithm*

Line 21 uses the **`inplace_merge`** algorithm to merge two *sorted sequences* of elements in the *same* container. In this example, the elements from `a1.begin()` up to, but *not* including, `a1.begin() + 5` are merged with the elements from `a1.begin() + 5` up to, but *not* including, `a1.end()`. This algorithm requires its three iterator arguments to be at least *bidirectional iterators*. A second version of this algorithm takes as a fourth argument a *binary predicate function* for comparing elements in the two sequences.

`unique_copy` *Algorithm*

Line 29 uses the **`unique_copy`** algorithm to make a copy of all the unique elements in the sorted sequence of values from `a1.cbegin()` up to, but *not* including, `a1.cend()`. The copied elements are placed into `vector` `results1`. The first two arguments must be at least *input iterators* and the last must be at least an *output iterator*. In this example, we did *not* preallocate enough elements in `results1` to store *all* the elements copied from `a1`. Instead, we use function `back_inserter` (defined in header `<iterator>`) to add elements to the end of `results1`. The `back_inserter` uses `vector`'s `push_back` member function to insert elements at the end of the `vector`. Because the `back_inserter` *inserts* an element *rather than replacing* an existing element's value, the `vector` is able to grow to accommodate additional elements. A second version of the `unique_copy` algorithm takes as a fourth argument a *binary predicate function* for comparing elements for *equality*.

`reverse_copy` *Algorithm*

Line 36 uses the **`reverse_copy`** algorithm to make a reversed copy of the elements in the range from `a1.cbegin()` up to, but *not* including, `a1.cend()`. The copied elements are inserted into `results2` using a `back_inserter` object to ensure that the `vector` can *grow* to accommodate the appropriate number of elements copied. Algorithm reverse_copy requires its first two iterator arguments to be at least *bidirectional iterators* and its third to be at least an *output iterator.*

16.3.10 Set Operations

Figure 16.10 demonstrates algorithms includes, set_difference, set_intersection, set_symmetric_difference and set_union for manipulating *sets of sorted values.*

```
// Fig. 16.10: fig16_10.cpp
// Algorithms includes, set_difference, set_intersection,
// set_symmetric_difference and set_union.
#include <iostream>
#include <array>
#include <algorithm> // algorithm definitions
#include <iterator> // ostream_iterator
using namespace std;

int main()
{
   const size_t SIZE1 = 10, SIZE2 = 5, SIZE3 = 20;
   array< int, SIZE1 > a1 = { 1, 2, 3, 4, 5, 6, 7, 8, 9, 10 };
   array< int, SIZE2 > a2 = { 4, 5, 6, 7, 8 };
   array< int, SIZE2 > a3 = { 4, 5, 6, 11, 15 };
   ostream_iterator< int > output( cout, " " );

   cout << "a1 contains: ";
   copy( a1.cbegin(), a1.cend(), output ); // display array a1
   cout << "\na2 contains: ";
   copy( a2.cbegin(), a2.cend(), output ); // display array a2
   cout << "\na3 contains: ";
   copy( a3.cbegin(), a3.cend(), output ); // display array a3

   // determine whether a2 is completely contained in a1
   if ( includes( a1.cbegin(), a1.cend(), a2.cbegin(), a2.cend() ) )
      cout << "\n\na1 includes a2";
   else
      cout << "\n\na1 does not include a2";

   // determine whether a3 is completely contained in a1
   if ( includes( a1.cbegin(), a1.cend(), a3.cbegin(), a3.cend() ) )
      cout << "\na1 includes a3";
   else
      cout << "\na1 does not include a3";

   array< int, SIZE1 > difference;

   // determine elements of a1 not in a2
   auto result1 = set_difference( a1.cbegin(), a1.cend(),
      a2.cbegin(), a2.cend(), difference.begin() );
```

Fig. 16.10 | Algorithms includes, set_difference, set_intersection, set_symmetric_difference and set_union. (Part 1 of 2.)

```
42       cout << "\n\nset_difference of a1 and a2 is: ";
43       copy( difference.begin(), result1, output );
44
45       array< int, SIZE1 > intersection;
46
47       // determine elements in both a1 and a2
48       auto result2 = set_intersection( a1.cbegin(), a1.cend(),
49          a2.cbegin(), a2.cend(), intersection.begin() );
50       cout << "\n\nset_intersection of a1 and a2 is: ";
51       copy( intersection.begin(), result2, output );
52
53       array< int, SIZE1 + SIZE2 > symmetric_difference;
54
55       // determine elements of a1 that are not in a2 and
56       // elements of a2 that are not in a1
57       auto result3 = set_symmetric_difference( a1.cbegin(), a1.cend(),
58          a3.cbegin(), a3.cend(), symmetric_difference.begin() );
59       cout << "\n\nset_symmetric_difference of a1 and a3 is: ";
60       copy( symmetric_difference.begin(), result3, output );
61
62       array< int, SIZE3 > unionSet;
63
64       // determine elements that are in either or both sets
65       auto result4 = set_union( a1.cbegin(), a1.cend(),
66          a3.cbegin(), a3.cend(), unionSet.begin() );
67       cout << "\n\nset_union of a1 and a3 is: ";
68       copy( unionSet.begin(), result4, output );
69       cout << endl;
70    } // end main
```

```
a1 contains: 1 2 3 4 5 6 7 8 9 10
a2 contains: 4 5 6 7 8
a3 contains: 4 5 6 11 15

a1 includes a2
a1 does not include a3

set_difference of a1 and a2 is: 1 2 3 9 10

set_intersection of a1 and a2 is: 4 5 6 7 8

set_symmetric_difference of a1 and a3 is: 1 2 3 7 8 9 10 11 15

set_union of a1 and a3 is: 1 2 3 4 5 6 7 8 9 10 11 15
```

Fig. 16.10 | Algorithms `includes`, `set_difference`, `set_intersection`, `set_symmetric_difference` and `set_union`. (Part 2 of 2.)

`includes` *Algorithm*

Lines 26 and 32 call the **`includes`** algorithm, which compares two sets of *sorted* values to determine whether *every* element of the second set is in the first set. If so, `includes` returns `true`; otherwise, it returns `false`. The first two iterator arguments must be at least *input iterators* and must describe the first set of values. In line 26, the first set consists of the elements from a1.cbegin() up to, but *not* including, a1.cend(). The last two iterator arguments must be at least *input iterators* and must describe the second set of values. In this example, the second set consists of the elements from a2.cbegin() up to, but *not* including, a2.cend(). A second version of algorithm includes takes a fifth argument that's a *binary predicate function* indicating the order in which the elements were originally sorted. The two sequences must be sorted using the *same comparison function.*

set_difference *Algorithm*

Lines 40–41 use the **set_difference** algorithm to find the elements from the first set of sorted values that are *not* in the second set of sorted values (both sets of values must be in *ascending order*). The elements that are *different* are copied into the fifth argument (in this case, the array difference). The first two iterator arguments must be at least *input iterators* for the first set of values. The next two iterator arguments must be at least *input iterators* for the second set of values. The fifth argument must be at least an *output iterator* indicating where to store a copy of the values that are *different.* The algorithm returns an *output iterator* positioned immediately after the *last* value copied into the set to which the fifth argument points. A second version of set_difference takes a sixth argument that's a *binary predicate function* indicating the *order* in which the elements were *originally sorted.* The two sequences must be sorted using the *same comparison function.*

set_intersection *Algorithm*

Lines 48–49 use the **set_intersection** algorithm to determine the elements from the first set of sorted values that *are* in the second set of sorted values (both sets of values must be in *ascending* order). The elements *common to both sets* are copied into the fifth argument (in this case, array intersection). The first two iterator arguments must be at least *input iterators* for the first set of values. The next two iterator arguments must be at least *input iterators* for the second set of values. The fifth argument must be at least an *output iterator* indicating where to store a copy of the values that are the same. The algorithm returns an *output iterator* positioned immediately after the last value copied into the set to which the fifth argument points. A second version of set_intersection takes a sixth argument that's a *binary predicate function* indicating the order in which the elements were *originally* sorted. The two sequences must be sorted using the *same comparison function.*

set_symmetric_difference *Algorithm*

Lines 57–58 use the **set_symmetric_difference** algorithm to determine the elements in the first set that are *not* in the second set and the elements in the second set that are *not* in the first set (both sets must be in *ascending order*). The elements that are *different* are copied from both sets into the fifth argument (the array symmetric_difference). The first two iterator arguments must be at least *input iterators* for the first set of values. The next two iterator arguments must be at least *input iterators* for the second set of values. The fifth argument must be at least an *output iterator* indicating where to store a copy of the values that are different. The algorithm returns an *output iterator* positioned immediately after the *last* value copied into the set to which the fifth argument points. A second version of set_symmetric_difference takes a sixth argument that's a *binary predicate function* indicating the order in which the elements were originally sorted. The two sequences must be sorted using the *same comparison function.*

`set_union` *Algorithm*

Lines 65–66 use the **`set_union`** algorithm to create a set of all the elements that are in *either or both* of the two sorted sets (both sets of values must be in *ascending order*). The elements are copied from both sets into the fifth argument (in this case the array `unionSet`). Elements that appear in *both* sets are only copied from the first set. The first two iterator arguments must be at least *input iterators* for the first set of values. The next two iterator arguments must be at least *input iterators* for the second set of values. The fifth argument must be at least an *output iterator* indicating where to store the copied elements. The algorithm returns an *output iterator* positioned immediately after the *last* value copied into the set to which the fifth argument points. A second version of `set_union` takes a sixth argument that's a *binary predicate function* indicating the order in which the elements were *originally* sorted. The two sequences must be sorted using the *same comparison function.*

16.3.11 `lower_bound`, `upper_bound` and `equal_range`

Figure 16.11 demonstrates algorithms `lower_bound`, `upper_bound` and `equal_range`.

```
// Fig. 16.11: fig16_11.cpp
// Algorithms lower_bound, upper_bound and
// equal_range for a sorted sequence of values.
#include <iostream>
#include <algorithm> // algorithm definitions
#include <array> // aray class-template definition
#include <iterator> // ostream_iterator
using namespace std;

int main()
{
   const size_t SIZE = 10;
   array< int, SIZE > a = { 2, 2, 4, 4, 4, 6, 6, 6, 6, 8 };
   ostream_iterator< int > output( cout, " " );

   cout << "array a contains:\n";
   copy( a.cbegin(), a.cend(), output );

   // determine lower-bound insertion point for 6 in a
   auto lower = lower_bound( a.cbegin(), a.cend(), 6 );
   cout << "\n\nLower bound of 6 is element "
      << ( lower - a.cbegin() ) << " of array a";

   // determine upper-bound insertion point for 6 in a
   auto upper = upper_bound( a.cbegin(), a.cend(), 6 );
   cout << "\nUpper bound of 6 is element "
      << ( upper - a.cbegin() ) << " of array a";

   // use equal_range to determine both the lower- and
   // upper-bound insertion points for 6
   auto eq = equal_range( a.cbegin(), a.cend(), 6 );
```

Fig. 16.11 | Algorithms `lower_bound`, `upper_bound` and `equal_range` for a sorted sequence of values. (Part 1 of 2.)

```
   cout << "\nUsing equal_range:\n   Lower bound of 6 is element "
        << ( eq.first - a.cbegin() ) << " of array a";
   cout << "\n   Upper bound of 6 is element "
      << ( eq.second - a.cbegin() ) << " of array a";
   cout << "\n\nUse lower_bound to locate the first point\n"
      << "at which 5 can be inserted in order";

   // determine lower-bound insertion point for 5 in a
   lower = lower_bound( a.cbegin(), a.cend(), 5 );
   cout << "\n   Lower bound of 5 is element "
      << ( lower - a.cbegin() ) << " of array a";
   cout << "\n\nUse upper_bound to locate the last point\n"
      << "at which 7 can be inserted in order";

   // determine upper-bound insertion point for 7 in a
   upper = upper_bound( a.cbegin(), a.cend(), 7 );
   cout << "\n   Upper bound of 7 is element "
      << ( upper - a.cbegin() ) << " of array a";
   cout << "\n\nUse equal_range to locate the first and\n"
      << "last point at which 5 can be inserted in order";

   // use equal_range to determine both the lower- and
   // upper-bound insertion points for 5
   eq = equal_range( a.cbegin(), a.cend(), 5 );
   cout << "\n   Lower bound of 5 is element "
      << ( eq.first - a.cbegin() ) << " of array a";
   cout << "\n   Upper bound of 5 is element "
      << ( eq.second - a.cbegin() ) << " of array a" << endl;
} // end main
```

```
Array a contains:
2 2 4 4 4 6 6 6 6 8

Lower bound of 6 is element 5 of array a
Upper bound of 6 is element 9 of array a
Using equal_range:
   Lower bound of 6 is element 5 of array a
   Upper bound of 6 is element 9 of array a

Use lower_bound to locate the first point
at which 5 can be inserted in order
   Lower bound of 5 is element 5 of array a

Use upper_bound to locate the last point
at which 7 can be inserted in order
   Upper bound of 7 is element 9 of array a

Use equal_range to locate the first and
last point at which 5 can be inserted in order
   Lower bound of 5 is element 5 of array a
   Upper bound of 5 is element 5 of array a
```

Fig. 16.11 | Algorithms `lower_bound`, `upper_bound` and `equal_range` for a sorted sequence of values. (Part 2 of 2.)

`lower_bound` *Algorithm*

Line 20 uses the **`lower_bound`** algorithm to find the first location in a sorted sequence of values at which the third argument could be inserted in the sequence such that the sequence would still be *sorted in ascending order*. The first two iterator arguments must be at least *forward iterators*. The third argument is the value for which to determine the lower bound. The algorithm returns a *forward iterator* pointing to the position at which the insert can occur. A second version of `lower_bound` takes as a fourth argument a *binary predicate function* indicating the order in which the elements were *originally* sorted.

`upper_bound` *Algorithm*

Line 25 uses the **`upper_bound`** algorithm to find the last location in a sorted sequence of values at which the third argument could be inserted in the sequence such that the sequence would still be sorted in *ascending order*. The first two iterator arguments must be at least *forward iterators*. The third argument is the value for which to determine the upper bound. The algorithm returns a *forward iterator* pointing to the position at which the insert can occur. A second version of `upper_bound` takes as a fourth argument a *binary predicate function* indicating the order in which the elements were *originally* sorted.

`equal_range` *Algorithm*

Line 31 uses the **`equal_range`** algorithm to return a `pair` of *forward iterators* containing the results of performing both a `lower_bound` and an `upper_bound` operation. The first two arguments must be at least *forward iterators*. The third is the value for which to locate the equal range. The algorithm returns a `pair` of *forward iterators* for the lower bound (`eq.first`) and upper bound (`eq.second`), respectively.

Locating Insertion Points in Sorted Sequences

Algorithms `lower_bound`, `upper_bound` and `equal_range` are often used to locate *insertion points* in sorted sequences. Line 40 uses `lower_bound` to locate the first point at which `5` can be inserted in order in `a`. Line 47 uses `upper_bound` to locate the last point at which `7` can be inserted in order in `a`. Line 55 uses `equal_range` to locate the first and last points at which `5` can be inserted in order in `a`.

16.3.12 Heapsort

Figure 16.12 demonstrates the Standard Library algorithms for performing the **heapsort sorting algorithm**, in which an array of elements is arranged into a data structure called a *heap*. For more information on Heapsort and for additional resources, see:

```
en.wikipedia.org/wiki/Heapsort
```

```
// Fig. 16.12: fig16_12.cpp
// Algorithms push_heap, pop_heap, make_heap and sort_heap.
#include <iostream>
#include <algorithm>
#include <array>
```

Fig. 16.12 | Algorithms `push_heap`, `pop_heap`, `make_heap` and `sort_heap`. (Part 1 of 3.)

```
#include <vector>
#include <iterator>
using namespace std;

int main()
{
   const size_t SIZE = 10;
   array< int, SIZE > init = { 3, 100, 52, 77, 22, 31, 1, 98, 13, 40 };
   array< int, SIZE > a( init ); // copy of init
   ostream_iterator< int > output( cout, " " );

   cout << "Array a before make_heap:\n";
   copy( a.cbegin(), a.cend(), output );

   make_heap( a.begin(), a.end() ); // create heap from array a
   cout << "\Array a after make_heap:\n";
   copy( a.cbegin(), a.cend(), output );

   sort_heap( a.begin(), a.end() ); // sort elements with sort_heap
   cout << "\Array a after sort_heap:\n";
   copy( a.cbegin(), a.cend(), output );

   // perform the heapsort with push_heap and pop_heap
   cout << "\n\nArray init contains: ";
   copy( init.cbegin(), init.cend(), output ); // display array init
   cout << endl;

   vector< int > v;

   // place elements of array init into v and
   // maintain elements of v in heap
   for ( size_t i = 0; i < SIZE; ++i )
   {
      v.push_back( init[ i ] );
      push_heap( v.begin(), v.end() );
      cout << "\nv after push_heap(init[" << i << "]): ";
      copy( v.cbegin(), v.cend(), output );
   } // end for

   cout << endl;

   // remove elements from heap in sorted order
   for ( size_t  j = 0; j < v.size(); ++j )
   {
      cout << "\nv after " << v[ 0 ] << " popped from heap\n";
      pop_heap( v.begin(), v.end() - j );
      copy( v.cbegin(), v.cend(), output );
   } // end for

   cout << endl;
} // end main
```

Fig. 16.12 | Algorithms push_heap, pop_heap, make_heap and sort_heap. (Part 2 of 3.)

```
Array a before make_heap:
3 100 52 77 22 31 1 98 13 40
Array a after make_heap:
100 98 52 77 40 31 1 3 13 22
Array a after sort_heap:
1 3 13 22 31 40 52 77 98 100

Array init contains: 3 100 52 77 22 31 1 98 13 40

v after push_heap(init[0]): 3
v after push_heap(init[1]): 100 3
v after push_heap(init[2]): 100 3 52
v after push_heap(init[3]): 100 77 52 3
v after push_heap(init[4]): 100 77 52 3 22
v after push_heap(init[5]): 100 77 52 3 22 31
v after push_heap(init[6]): 100 77 52 3 22 31 1
v after push_heap(init[7]): 100 98 52 77 22 31 1 3
v after push_heap(init[8]): 100 98 52 77 22 31 1 3 13
v after push_heap(init[9]): 100 98 52 77 40 31 1 3 13 22

v after 100 popped from heap
98 77 52 22 40 31 1 3 13 100
v after 98 popped from heap
77 40 52 22 13 31 1 3 98 100
v after 77 popped from heap
52 40 31 22 13 3 1 77 98 100
v after 52 popped from heap
40 22 31 1 13 3 52 77 98 100
v after 40 popped from heap
31 22 3 1 13 40 52 77 98 100
v after 31 popped from heap
22 13 3 1 31 40 52 77 98 100
v after 22 popped from heap
13 1 3 22 31 40 52 77 98 100
v after 13 popped from heap
3 1 13 22 31 40 52 77 98 100
v after 3 popped from heap
1 3 13 22 31 40 52 77 98 100
v after 1 popped from heap
1 3 13 22 31 40 52 77 98 100
```

Fig. 16.12 | Algorithms push_heap, pop_heap, make_heap and sort_heap. (Part 3 of 3.)

make_heap Algorithm

Line 20 uses the **make_heap** algorithm to take a sequence of values in the range from a.begin() up to, but *not* including, a.end() and *create a heap* that can be used to produce a *sorted sequence*. The two iterator arguments must be *random-access iterators*, so this algorithm will work only with arrays, vectors and deques. A second version of this algorithm takes as a third argument a *binary predicate function* for *comparing* values.

sort_heap Algorithm

Line 24 uses the **sort_heap** algorithm to *sort a sequence of values* in the range from a.begin() up to, but *not* including, a.end() that are already arranged in a heap. The two iterator arguments must be *random-access iterators*. A second version of this algorithm takes as a third argument a *binary predicate function* for *comparing* values.

push_heap Algorithm

Line 40 uses the **push_heap** algorithm to *add a new value into a heap*. We take one element of array init at a time, *append it* to the *end* of vector v and perform the push_heap operation. If the appended element is the *only* element in the vector, the vector is *already* a heap. Otherwise, push_heap rearranges the vector elements into a heap. Each time push_heap is called, it assumes that the *last* element currently in the vector (i.e., the one that's appended before the push_heap call) is the element being added to the heap and that all other elements in the vector are already arranged as a heap. The two iterator arguments to push_heap must be *random-access iterators*. A second version of this algorithm takes as a third argument a *binary predicate function* for *comparing* values.

pop_heap Algorithm

Line 51 uses **pop_heap** to remove the *top* heap element. This algorithm assumes that the elements in the range specified by its two *random-access iterator* arguments are already a heap. Repeatedly removing the *top* heap element results in a sorted sequence of values. Algorithm pop_heap *swaps* the *first* heap element (v.begin()) with the *last* heap element (the element before v.end() - j), then ensures that the elements up to, but *not* including, the last element still form a heap. Notice in the output that, after the pop_heap operations, the vector is *sorted* in *ascending order*. A second version of this algorithm takes as a third argument a *binary predicate function* for comparing values.

C++11: is_heap and is_heap_until Algorithms

In addition to the make_heap, sort_heap, push_heap and pop_heap algorithms presented in Fig. 16.12, C++11 now includes the new algorithms is_heap and is_heap_until. The **is_heap** algorithm returns true if the elements in the specified range represent a heap. A second version of this algorithm takes as a third argument a *binary predicate function* for comparing values.

The **is_heap_until** algorithm checks the specified range of values and returns an iterator pointing to the last item in the range for which the elements up to, but not including, that iterator represent a heap.

16.3.13 min, max, minmax and minmax_element

Figure 16.13 demonstrates algorithms min, max, minmax and minmax_element.

```
// Fig. 16.13: fig16_13.cpp
// Algorithms min, max, minmax and minmax_element.
#include <iostream>
#include <array>
#include <algorithm>
using namespace std;

int main()
{
   cout << "The minimum of 12 and 7 is: " << min( 12, 7 );
   cout << "\nThe maximum of 12 and 7 is: " << max( 12, 7 );
   cout << "\nThe minimum of 'G' and 'Z' is: " << min( 'G', 'Z' );
```

Fig. 16.13 | Algorithms min, max, minmax and minmax_element. (Part 1 of 2.)

```
13      cout << "\nThe maximum of 'G' and 'Z' is: " << max( 'G', 'Z' );
14
15      // determine which argument is the min and which is the max
16      auto result1 = minmax( 12, 7 );
17      cout << "\n\nThe minimum of 12 and 7 is: " << result1.first
18         << "\nThe maximum of 12 and 7 is: " << result1.second;
19
20      array< int, 10 > items = { 3, 100, 52, 77, 22, 31, 1, 98, 13, 40 };
21      ostream_iterator< int > output( cout, " " );
22
23      cout << "\n\nArray items contains: ";
24      copy( items.cbegin(), items.cend(), output );
25
26      auto result2 = minmax_element( items.cbegin(), items.cend() );
27      cout << "\nThe minimum element in items is: " << *result2.first
28         << "\nThe maximum element in items is: " << *result2.second
29         << endl;
30   } // end main
```

```
The minimum of 12 and 7 is: 7
The maximum of 12 and 7 is: 12
The minimum of 'G' and 'Z' is: G
The maximum of 'G' and 'Z' is: Z

The minimum of 12 and 7 is: 7
The maximum of 12 and 7 is: 12

Array items contains: 3 100 52 77 22 31 1 98 13 40
The minimum element in items is: 1
The maximum element in items is: 100
```

Fig. 16.13 | Algorithms `min`, `max`, `minmax` and `minmax_element`. (Part 2 of 2.)

Algorithms `min` and `max` with Two Parameters

Algorithms **`min`** and **`max`** (demonstrated in lines 10–13) determine the minimum and the maximum of two elements, respectively.

C++11: `min` and `max` Algorithms with `initializer_list` Parameters

C++11 now includes overloaded versions of the algorithms `min` and `max` that each receive an `initializer_list` parameter and return the smallest or largest item in the list initializer that's passed as an argument. For example, the following statement returns 7:

```
int minumum = min( { 10, 7, 14, 21, 17 } );
```

Each of these new `min` and `max` algorithms is overloaded with a version that takes as a second argument a *binary predicate function* for comparing values.

C++11: `minmax` Algorithm

C++11 now includes the **`minmax`** algorithm (line 16) that receives two items and returns a `pair` in which the smaller item is stored in `first` and the larger item is stored in `second`. A second version of this algorithm takes as a third argument a *binary predicate function* for comparing values.

C++11: `minmax_element` Algorithm

C++11 now includes the **`minmax_element`** algorithm (line 26) that receives two *input iterators* representing a range of elements and returns a `pair` of iterators in which `first` points to the smallest element in the range and `second` points to the largest. A second version of this algorithm takes as a third argument a *binary predicate function* for comparing values.

16.4 Function Objects

Many Standard Library algorithms allow you to pass a *function pointer* into the algorithm to help the algorithm perform its task. For example, the `binary_search` algorithm that we discussed in Section 16.3.6 is overloaded with a version that requires as its fourth parameter a *function pointer* that takes two arguments and returns a `bool` value. The algorithm uses this function to compare the search key to an element in the collection. The function returns `true` if the search key and element being compared are equal; otherwise, the function returns `false`. This enables `binary_search` to search a collection of elements for which the element type does *not* provide an overloaded equality < operator.

Any algorithm that can receive a *function pointer* can also receive an object of a class that overloads the function-call operator (parentheses) with a function named `operator()`, provided that the overloaded operator meets the requirements of the algorithm—in the case of `binary_search`, it must receive two arguments and return a `bool`. An object of such a class is known as a **function object** and can be used syntactically and semantically like a function or *function pointer*—the overloaded parentheses operator is invoked by using a function object's name followed by parentheses containing the arguments to the function. Most algorithms can use function objects and functions interchangeably. As you'll learn in Section 16.5, C++11's lambda expressions can also be used where function pointers and function objects are used.

Advantages of Function Objects Over Function Pointers

Function objects provide several advantages over *function pointers*. The compiler can inline a *function object's* overloaded `operator()` to improve performance. Also, since they're objects of classes, *function objects* can have data members that `operator()` can use to perform its task.

Predefined Function Objects of the Standard Template Library

Many predefined *function objects* can be found in the header **`<functional>`**. Figure 16.14 lists several of the dozens of Standard Library *function objects*, which are all implemented as class templates. Section 20.8 of the C++ standard contains the complete list of function objects. We used the *function object* `less<T>` in the `set`, `multiset` and `priority_queue` examples, to specify the sorting order for elements in a container.

Using the `accumulate` Algorithm

Figure 16.15 uses the `accumulate` numeric algorithm (introduced in Fig. 16.5) to calculate the sum of the squares of the elements in an `array`. The fourth argument to `accumulate` is a **binary function object** (that is, a *function object* for which `operator()` takes two arguments) or a *function pointer* to a **binary function** (that is, a function that takes two arguments). Function `accumulate` is demonstrated twice—once with a *function pointer* and once with a *function object*.

Function object	Type	Function object	Type
`divides< T >`	arithmetic	`logical_or< T >`	logical
`equal_to< T >`	relational	`minus< T >`	arithmetic
`greater< T >`	relational	`modulus< T >`	arithmetic
`greater_equal< T >`	relational	`negate< T >`	arithmetic
`less< T >`	relational	`not_equal_to< T >`	relational
`less_equal< T >`	relational	`plus< T >`	arithmetic
`logical_and< T >`	logical	`multiplies< T >`	arithmetic
`logical_not< T >`	logical		

Fig. 16.14 | Function objects in the Standard Library.

```
// Fig. 16.15: fig16_15.cpp
// Demonstrating function objects.
#include <iostream>
#include <array> // array class-template definition
#include <algorithm> // copy algorithm
#include <numeric> // accumulate algorithm
#include <functional> // binary_function definition
#include <iterator> // ostream_iterator
using namespace std;

// binary function adds square of its second argument and the
// running total in its first argument, then returns the sum
int sumSquares( int total, int value )
{
   return total + value * value;
} // end function sumSquares

// Class template SumSquaresClass defines overloaded operator()
// that adds the square of its second argument and running
// total in its first argument, then returns sum
template< typename T >
class SumSquaresClass
{
public:
   // add square of value to total and return result
   T operator()( const T &total, const T &value )
   {
      return total + value * value;
   } // end function operator()
}; // end class SumSquaresClass

int main()
{
   const size_t SIZE = 10;
   array< int, SIZE > integers = { 1, 2, 3, 4, 5, 6, 7, 8, 9, 10 };
```

Fig. 16.15 | Binary function object. (Part 1 of 2.)

```
36      ostream_iterator< int > output( cout, " " );
37
38      cout << "array integers contains:\n";
39      copy( integers.cbegin(), integers.cend(), output );
40
41      // calculate sum of squares of elements of array integers
42      // using binary function sumSquares
43      int result = accumulate( integers.cbegin(), integers.cend(),
44         0, sumSquares );
45
46      cout << "\n\nSum of squares of elements in integers using "
47         << "binary\nfunction sumSquares: " << result;
48
49      // calculate sum of squares of elements of array integers
50      // using binary function object
51      result = accumulate( integers.cbegin(), integers.cend(),
52         0, SumSquaresClass< int >() );
53
54      cout << "\n\nSum of squares of elements in integers using "
55         << "binary\nfunction object of type "
56         << "SumSquaresClass< int >: " << result << endl;
57   } // end main
```

```
array integers contains:
1 2 3 4 5 6 7 8 9 10

Sum of squares of elements in integers using binary
function sumSquares: 385

Sum of squares of elements in integers using binary
function object of type SumSquaresClass< int >: 385
```

Fig. 16.15 | Binary function object. (Part 2 of 2.)

Function `sumSquares`

Lines 13–16 define a function `sumSquares` that squares its second argument `value`, adds that square and its first argument `total` and returns the sum. Function `accumulate` will pass each of the elements of the sequence over which it iterates as the second argument to `sumSquares` in the example. On the first call to `sumSquares`, the first argument will be the initial value of the `total` (which is supplied as the third argument to `accumulate`; `0` in this program). All subsequent calls to `sumSquares` receive as the first argument the running sum returned by the previous call to `sumSquares`. When `accumulate` completes, it returns the sum of the squares of all the elements in the sequence.

Class `SumSquaresClass`

Lines 21–30 define the class template `SumSquaresClass` with an overloaded `operator()` that has two parameters and returns a value—the requirements for a binary function object. On the first call to the *function object*, the first argument will be the initial value of the `total` (which is supplied as the third argument to `accumulate`; `0` in this program) and the second argument will be the first element in `array integers`. All subsequent calls to `operator` receive as the first argument the result returned by the previous call to the *func-*

tion object, and the second argument will be the next element in the `array`. When `accumulate` completes, it returns the sum of the squares of all the elements in the `array`.

Passing Function Pointers and Function Objects to Algorithm `accumulate`

Lines 43–44 call function `accumulate` with a *pointer to function* `sumSquares` as its last argument. Similarly, the statement in lines 51–52 calls `accumulate` with an object of class `SumSquaresClass` as the last argument. The expression `SumSquaresClass<int>()` creates (and calls the default constructor for) an instance of class `SumSquaresClass` (a *function object*) that's passed to `accumulate`, which invokes the function `operator()`. Lines 51–52 could be written as two separate statements, as follows:

```
SumSquaresClass< int > sumSquaresObject;
result = accumulate( integers.cbegin(), integers.cend(),
   0, sumSquaresObject );
```

The first line defines an object of class `SumSquaresClass`. That object is then passed to `accumulate`.

16.5 Lambda Expressions

As you've seen in this chapter, many algorithms can receive function pointers or function objects as parameters. Before you can pass a function pointer or function object to an algorithm, the corresponding function or class must have been declared.

C++11's **Lambda expressions** (or **lambda functions**) enable you to define anonymous function objects *where they're passed* to a function. They're defined locally inside functions and can "capture" (by value or by reference) the local variables of the enclosing function then manipulate these variables in the lambda's body. Figure 16.16 demonstrates a simple lambda expression example that doubles the value of each element in an `int` array.

```
// Fig. 16.16: fig16_16.cpp
// Lambda expressions.
#include <iostream>
#include <array>
#include <algorithm>
using namespace std;

int main()
{
   const size_t SIZE = 4; // size of array values
   array< int, SIZE >  values = { 1, 2, 3, 4 }; // initialize values

   // output each element multiplied by two
   for_each( values.cbegin(), values.cend(),
      []( int i ) { cout << i * 2 << endl; } );

   int sum = 0; // initialize sum to zero

   // add each element to sum
   for_each( values.cbegin(), values.cend(),
      [ &sum ]( int i ) { sum += i; } );
```

Fig. 16.16 | Lambda expressions. (Part 1 of 2.)

```
22
23      cout << "sum is " << sum << endl; // output sum
24   } // end main
```

```
2
4
6
8
sum is 10
```

Fig. 16.16 | Lambda expressions. (Part 2 of 2.)

Lines 10 and 11 declare and initialize a small `array` of `int`s named `values`. Lines 14–15 call the `for_each` algorithm on the elements of `values`. The third argument (line 15) to `for_each` is a *lambda expression*. Lambdas begin with *lambda introducer* (`[]`), followed by a parameter list and function body. Return types can be inferred automatically if the body is a single statement of the form `return` *expression*`;`—otherwise, the return type is `void` by default or you can explicitly use a *trailing return type* (introduced in Section 6.18). The compiler converts the lambda expression into a function object. The lambda expression in line 15 receives an `int`, multiplies it by 2 and displays the result. The `for_each` algorithm passes each element of the `array` to the lambda.

The second call to the `for_each` algorithm (lines 20–21) calculates the sum of the `array` elements. The lambda introducer `[&sum]` indicates that this lambda expression *captures* the local variable `sum` *by reference* (note the use of the ampersand), so that the lambda can modify `sum`'s value. Without the ampersand, `sum` would be captured by value and the local variable outside the lambda expression would *not* be updated. The `for_each` algorithm passes each element of `values` to the lambda, which adds the value to the `sum`. Line 23 then displays the value of `sum`.

You can assign lambda expressions to variables, which can then be used to invoke the lambda expression or pass it to other functions. For example, you can assign the lambda expression in line 15 to a variable as follows:

```
auto myLambda = []( int i ) { cout << i * 2 << endl; };
```

You can then use the variable name as a function name to invoke the lambda as in:

```
myLambda( 10 ); // outputs 20
```

16.6 Standard Library Algorithm Summary

The C++ standard specifies over 90 algorithms—many overloaded with two or more versions. The standard separates the algorithms into several categories—*mutating sequence algorithms, nonmodifying sequence algorithms, sorting and related algorithms* and *generalized numeric operations*. To learn about the algorithms that we did not present in this chapter, see your compiler's documentation or visit sites such as

```
en.cppreference.com/w/cpp/algorithm
msdn.microsoft.com/en-us/library/yah1y2x8.aspx
```

Mutating Sequence Algorithms

Figure 16.17 shows many of the **mutating-sequence algorithms**—i.e., algorithms that modify the containers they operate on. Algorithms new in C++11 are marked with an * in Figs. 16.17–16.20. Algorithms presented in this chapter are shown in **bold**.

Mutating sequence algorithms from header <algorithm>			
copy	**copy_n***	**copy_if***	**copy_backward**
move*	move_backward*	**swap**	**swap_ranges**
iter_swap	**transform**	**replace**	**replace_if**
replace_copy	**replace_copy_if**	**fill**	**fill_n**
generate	**generate_n**	**remove**	**remove_if**
remove_copy	**remove_copy_if**	**unique**	**unique_copy**
reverse	**reverse_copy**	rotate	rotate_copy
random_shuffle	shuffle*	is_partitioned*	partition
stable_partition	partition_copy*	partition_point*	

Fig. 16.17 | Mutating-sequence algorithms from header <algorithm>.

Nonmodifying Sequence Algorithms

Figure 16.18 shows the **nonmodifying sequence algorithms**—i.e., algorithms that do *not* modify the containers they operate on.

Nonmodifying sequence algorithms from header <algorithm>			
all_of*	**any_of***	**none_of***	**for_each**
find	**find_if**	**find_if_not***	find_end
find_first_of	adjacent_find	**count**	**count_if**
mismatch	**equal**	is_permutation*	search
search_n			

Fig. 16.18 | Nonmodifying sequence algorithms from header <algorithm>.

Sorting and Related Algorithms

Figure 16.19 shows the *sorting and related algorithms.*

Sorting and related algorithms from header <algorithm>			
sort	stable_sort	partial_sort	partial_sort_copy
is_sorted*	is_sorted_until*	nth_element	**lower_bound**
upper_bound	**equal_range**	**binary_search**	**merge**

Fig. 16.19 | Sorting and related algorithms from header <algorithm>. (Part 1 of 2.)

Sorting and related algorithms from header <algorithm>			
inplace_merge	includes	set_union	set_intersection
set_difference	set_symmetric_difference		push_heap
pop_heap	make_heap	sort_heap	is_heap*
is_heap_until*	min	max	minmax*
min_element	max_element	minmax_element*	lexicographical_compare
next_permutation	prev_permutation		

Fig. 16.19 | Sorting and related algorithms from header <algorithm>. (Part 2 of 2.)

Numerical Algorithms
Figure 16.20 shows the numerical algorithms of the header **<numeric>**.

Numerical algorithms from header <numeric>		
accumulate	partial_sum	iota*
inner_product	adjacent_difference	

Fig. 16.20 | Numerical algorithms from header <numeric>.

16.7 Wrap-Up

In this chapter, we demonstrated many of the Standard Library algorithms, including mathematical algorithms, basic searching and sorting algorithms and set operations. You learned the types of iterators each algorithm requires and that each algorithm can be used with any container that supports the minimum iterator functionality the algorithm requires. We introduced function objects that work syntactically and semantically like ordinary functions, but offer advantages such as performance and the ability to store data. Finally, you used lambda expressions to create function objects inline then passed them to Standard Library algorithms.

We introduced exception handling earlier in the book in our discussion of arrays. In the next chapter, we take a deeper look at C++'s rich set of exception handling capabilities.

17

Exception Handling: A Deeper Look

Objectives

In this chapter you'll:

- Use `try`, `catch` and `throw` to detect, handle and indicate exceptions, respectively.
- Declare new exception classes.
- Understand how stack unwinding enables exceptions not caught in one scope to be caught in another.
- Handle `new` failures.
- Use `unique_ptr` to prevent memory leaks.
- Understand the standard exception hierarchy.

Outline

17.1 Introduction

As you know from Section 7.10, an **exception** is an indication of a problem that occurs during a program's execution. **Exception handling** enables you to create applications that can resolve (or handle) exceptions. In many cases, this allows a program to continue executing as if no problem had been encountered. The features presented in this chapter enable you to write **robust** and **fault-tolerant programs** that can deal with problems and continue executing or terminate gracefully.

We begin with a review of exception-handling concepts via an example that demonstrates handling an exception that occurs when a function attempts to divide by zero. We show how to handle exceptions that occur in a constructor or destructor and exceptions that occur if operator `new` fails to allocate memory for an object. We introduce several C++ Standard Library exception handling classes and show you how to create your own.

Software Engineering Observation 17.1

Exception handling provides a standard *mechanism for processing errors. This is especially important when working on a project with a large team of programmers.*

Software Engineering Observation 17.2

Incorporate your exception-handling strategy into your system from its inception. Including effective exception handling after a system has been implemented can be difficult.

Error-Prevention Tip 17.1

Without exception handling, it's common for a function to calculate and return a value on success or return an error indicator on failure. A common problem with this achitecture is using the return value in a subsequent calculation without first checking whether the value is the error indicator. Exception handling eliminates this problem.

17.2 Example: Handling an Attempt to Divide by Zero

Let's consider a simple example of exception handling (Figs. 17.1–17.2). We show how to deal with a common arithmetic problem—*division by zero*. Division by zero using integer arithmetic typically causes a program to terminate prematurely. In floating-point arithmetic, many C++ implementations allow division by zero, in which case a result of positive or negative infinity is displayed as `INF` or `-INF`, respectively.

In this example, we define a function named `quotient` that receives two integers input by the user and divides its first `int` parameter by its second `int` parameter. Before performing the division, the function casts the first `int` parameter's value to type `double`. Then, the second `int` parameter's value is (implicitly) promoted to type `double` for the calculation. So function `quotient` actually performs the division using two `double` values and returns a `double` result.

Although division by zero is often allowed in floating-point arithmetic, for the purpose of this example we treat any attempt to divide by zero as an error. Thus, function `quotient` tests its second parameter to ensure that it isn't zero before allowing the division to proceed. If the second parameter is zero, the function *throws an exception* to indicate to the caller that a problem occurred. The caller (`main` in this example) can then process the exception and allow the user to type two new values before calling function `quotient` again. In this way, the program can continue executing even after an improper value is entered, thus making the program more robust.

The example consists of two files. `DivideByZeroException.h` (Fig. 17.1) defines an *exception class* that represents the type of the problem that might occur in the example, and `fig17_02.cpp` (Fig. 17.2) defines the `quotient` function and the `main` function that calls it. Function `main` contains the code that demonstrates exception handling.

Defining an Exception Class to Represent the Type of Problem That Might Occur

Figure 17.1 defines class `DivideByZeroException` as a derived class of Standard Library class **`runtime_error`** (from header **`<stdexcept>`**). Class `runtime_error`—a derived class of **`exception`** (from header **`<exception>`**)—is the C++ standard base class for representing runtime errors. Class `exception` is the standard C++ base class for exception in the C++ Standard Library. (Section 17.10 discusses class `exception` and its derived classes in detail.) A typical exception class that derives from the `runtime_error` class defines only a constructor (e.g., lines 11–12) that passes an error-message string to the base-class `runtime_error` constructor. Every exception class that derives directly or indirectly from `exception` contains the `virtual` function **`what`**, which returns an exception object's error message. You're not required to derive a custom exception class, such as `DivideByZeroException`, from the standard exception classes provided by C++. However, doing so allows you to use the `virtual` function `what` to obtain an appropriate error message. We use an object of this `DivideByZeroException` class in Fig. 17.2 to indicate when an attempt is made to divide by zero.

```
1  // Fig. 17.1: DivideByZeroException.h
2  // Class DivideByZeroException definition.
3  #include <stdexcept> // stdexcept header contains runtime_error
4
5  // DivideByZeroException objects should be thrown by functions
6  // upon detecting division-by-zero exceptions
7  class DivideByZeroException : public std::runtime_error
8  {
9  public:
10    // constructor specifies default error message
11    DivideByZeroException()
12       : std::runtime_error( "attempted to divide by zero" ) {}
13 }; // end class DivideByZeroException
```

Fig. 17.1 | Class `DivideByZeroException` definition.

Demonstrating Exception Handling

Figure 17.2 uses exception handling to wrap code that might throw a `DivideByZeroException` and to handle that exception, should one occur. The user enters two integers, which are passed as arguments to function `quotient` (lines 10–18). This function divides its first parameter (`numerator`) by its second parameter (`denominator`). Assuming that the user does not specify `0` as the denominator for the division, function `quotient` returns the division result. If the user inputs `0` for the denominator, `quotient` throws an exception. In the sample output, the first two lines show a successful calculation, and the next two show a failure due to an attempt to divide by zero. When the exception occurs, the program informs the user of the mistake and prompts the user to input two new integers. After we discuss the code, we'll consider the user inputs and flow of program control that yield *these outputs.*

```
1  // Fig. 17.2: fig17_02.cpp
2  // Example that throws exceptions on
3  // attempts to divide by zero.
4  #include <iostream>
5  #include "DivideByZeroException.h" // DivideByZeroException class
6  using namespace std;
7
8  // perform division and throw DivideByZeroException object if
9  // divide-by-zero exception occurs
10 double quotient( int numerator, int denominator )
11 {
12    // throw DivideByZeroException if trying to divide by zero
13    if ( denominator == 0 )
14       throw DivideByZeroException(); // terminate function
15
16    // return division result
17    return static_cast< double >( numerator ) / denominator;
18 } // end function quotient
19
20 int main()
21 {
22    int number1; // user-specified numerator
23    int number2; // user-specified denominator
24
25    cout << "Enter two integers (end-of-file to end): ";
26
27    // enable user to enter two integers to divide
28    while ( cin >> number1 >> number2 )
29    {
30       // try block contains code that might throw exception
31       // and code that will not execute if an exception occurs
32       try
33       {
34          double result = quotient( number1, number2 );
35          cout << "The quotient is: " << result << endl;
36       } // end try
37       catch ( DivideByZeroException &divideByZeroException )
38       {
```

Fig. 17.2 | Example that throws exceptions on attempts to divide by zero. (Part 1 of 2.)

```
39            cout << "Exception occurred: "
40               << divideByZeroException.what() << endl;
41         } // end catch
42
43         cout << "\nEnter two integers (end-of-file to end): ";
44      } // end while
45
46      cout << endl;
47   } // end main
```

```
Enter two integers (end-of-file to end): 100 7
The quotient is: 14.2857

Enter two integers (end-of-file to end): 100 0
Exception occurred: attempted to divide by zero

Enter two integers (end-of-file to end): ^Z
```

Fig. 17.2 | Example that throws exceptions on attempts to divide by zero. (Part 2 of 2.)

Enclosing Code in a `try` *Block*

The program begins by prompting the user to enter two integers. The integers are input in the condition of the `while` loop (line 28). Line 34 passes the values to function `quotient` (lines 10–18), which either divides the integers and returns a result, or **throws an exception** (i.e., indicates that an error occurred) on an attempt to divide by zero. Exception handling is geared to situations in which the function that detects an error is unable to handle it.

As you learned in Section 7.10, `try` blocks enable exception handling, enclosing statements that might cause exceptions and statements that should be skipped if an exception occurs. The `try` block in lines 32–36 encloses the invocation of function `quotient` and the statement that displays the division result. In this example, because the invocation of function `quotient` (line 34) can *throw* an exception, we enclose this function invocation in a `try` block. Enclosing the output statement (line 35) in the `try` block ensures that the output will occur *only* if function `quotient` returns a result.

Software Engineering Observation 17.3

Exceptions may surface through explicitly mentioned code in a `try` *block, through calls to other functions and through deeply nested function calls initiated by code in a* `try` *block.*

Defining a `catch` *Handler to Process a* `DivideByZeroException`

You saw in Section 7.10 that exceptions are processed by `catch` handlers. At least one `catch` handler (lines 37–41) *must* immediately follow each `try` block. An exception parameter should *always* be declared as a *reference* to the type of exception the `catch` handler can process (`DivideByZeroException` in this case)—this prevents copying the exception object when it's caught and allows a catch handler to properly catch derived-class exceptions as well. When an exception occurs in a `try` block, the `catch` handler that executes is the first one whose type *matches* the type of the exception that occurred (i.e., the type in the `catch` block matches the thrown exception type exactly or is a *direct or indirect* base class of it). If an exception parameter includes an *optional* parameter name, the `catch` handler can use that parameter name to interact with the caught exception in the body of the `catch` handler, which is delimited by braces ({ and }). A `catch` handler typically reports the error to the user, logs it to a file, terminates the program gracefully or tries an alternate strategy to accomplish the failed task. In this example, the `catch` handler simply reports that the user attempted to divide by zero. Then the program prompts the user to enter two new integer values.

Common Programming Error 17.1

It's a syntax error to place code between a `try` *block and its corresponding* `catch` *handlers or between its* `catch` *handlers.*

Common Programming Error 17.2

Each `catch` *handler can have only a single parameter—specifying a comma-separated list of exception parameters is a syntax error.*

Common Programming Error 17.3

It's a compilation error to catch the same *type in multiple* `catch` *handlers following a single* `try` *block.*

Termination Model of Exception Handling

If an exception occurs as the result of a statement in a `try` block, the `try` block expires (i.e., terminates immediately). Next, the program searches for the first `catch` handler that can process the type of exception that occurred. The program locates the matching `catch` by comparing the thrown exception's type to each `catch`'s exception-parameter type until the program finds a match. A match occurs if the types are *identical* or if the thrown exception's type is a *derived class* of the exception-parameter type. When a match occurs, the code in the matching `catch` handler executes. When a `catch` handler finishes processing by reaching its closing right brace (}), the exception is considered handled and the local variables defined within the `catch` handler (including the `catch` parameter) go out of scope. Program control does *not* return to the point at which the exception occurred (known as the **throw point**), because the `try` block has *expired*. Rather, control resumes with the first statement (line 43) after the last `catch` handler following the `try` block. This is known as the **termination model of exception handling**. Some languages use the **resumption model of exception handling**, in which, after an exception is handled, control resumes just after the throw point. As with any other block of code, *when a* `try` *block terminates, local variables defined in the block go out of scope.*

Common Programming Error 17.4

Logic errors can occur if you assume that after an exception is handled, control will return to the first statement after the throw point.

Error-Prevention Tip 17.2

With exception handling, a program can continue executing (rather than terminating) after dealing with a problem. This helps ensure the kind of robust applications that contribute to what's called mission-critical computing or business-critical computing.

If the `try` block completes its execution successfully (i.e., no exceptions occur in the `try` block), then the program ignores the `catch` handlers and program control continues with the first statement after the last `catch` following that `try` block.

If an exception that occurs in a `try` block has *no* matching `catch` handler, or if an exception occurs in a statement that is *not* in a `try` block, the function that contains the statement terminates immediately, and the program attempts to locate an enclosing `try` block in the calling function. This process is called **stack unwinding** and is discussed in Section 17.4.

Flow of Program Control When the User Enters a Nonzero Denominator

Consider the flow of control when the user inputs the numerator `100` and the denominator `7`. In line 13, function `quotient` determines that the `denominator` is not zero, so line 17 performs the division and returns the result (`14.2857`) to line 34 as a `double`. Program control then continues sequentially from line 34, so line 35 displays the division result—line 36 ends the `try` block. Because the `try` block completed successfully and did *not* throw an exception, the program does *not* execute the statements contained in the `catch` handler (lines 37–41), and control continues to line 43 (the first line of code after the `catch` handler), which prompts the user to enter two more integers.

Flow of Program Control When the User Enters a Denominator of Zero

Now consider the case in which the user inputs the numerator `100` and the denominator `0`. In line 13, `quotient` determines that the `denominator` is zero, which indicates an attempt to divide by zero. Line 14 throws an exception, which we represent as an object of class `DivideByZeroException` (Fig. 17.1).

To throw an exception, line 14 in Fig. 17.2 uses keyword **`throw`** followed by an operand of the type of exception to throw. Normally, a `throw` statement specifies *one* operand. (In Section 17.3, we discuss how to use a `throw` statement with *no* operand.) The operand of a `throw` can be of *any* type (but it must be copy constructable). If the operand is an object, we call it an **exception object**—in this example, the exception object is of type `DivideByZeroException`. However, a `throw` operand also can assume other values, such as the value of an expression that does *not* result in an object of a class (e.g., `throw x > 5`) or the value of an `int` (e.g., `throw 5`). The examples in this chapter focus exclusively on throwing objects of exception classes.

Error-Prevention Tip 17.3

In general, you should throw only objects of exception class types.

As part of throwing an exception, the `throw` operand is created and used to initialize the parameter in the `catch` handler, which we discuss momentarily. The `throw` statement in line 14 creates a `DivideByZeroException` object. When line 14 throws the exception, function `quotient` exits immediately. So, line 14 throws the exception *before* function `quotient` can perform the division in line 17. This is a central characteristic of exception handling: *If your program explicitly throws an exception, it should do so before the error has an opportunity to occur.*

Because we enclosed the call to `quotient` (line 34) in a `try` block, program control enters the `catch` handler (lines 37–41) that immediately follows the `try` block. This `catch` handler serves as the exception handler for the divide-by-zero exception. In general, when an exception is thrown within a `try` block, the exception is caught by a `catch` handler that specifies the type matching the thrown exception. In this program, the `catch` handler specifies that it catches `DivideByZeroException` objects—this type matches the object type thrown in function `quotient`. Actually, the `catch` handler catches a *reference* to the `DivideByZeroException` object created by function `quotient`'s `throw` statement (line 14), so that the `catch` handler does *not* make a copy of the exception object.

The `catch`'s body (lines 39–40) prints the error message returned by function `what` of base-class `runtime_error`—i.e., the string that the `DivideByZeroException` constructor (lines 11–12 in Fig. 17.1) passed to the `runtime_error` base-class constructor.

Good Programming Practice 17.1

Associating each type of runtime error with an appropriately named exception type improves program clarity.

17.3 Rethrowing an Exception

A function might use a resource—like a file—and might want to release the resource (i.e., close the file) if an exception occurs. An exception handler, upon receiving an exception, can release the resource then notify its caller than an exception occurred by **rethrowing the exception** via the statement

```
throw;
```

Regardless of whether a handler can process an exception, the handler can *rethrow* the exception for further processing outside the handler. The next enclosing `try` block detects the rethrown exception, which a `catch` handler listed after that enclosing `try` block attempts to handle.

Common Programming Error 17.5

Executing an empty `throw` *statement outside a* `catch` *handler abandons exception processing and terminates the program immediately.*

The program of Fig. 17.3 demonstrates rethrowing an exception. In `main`'s `try` block (lines 29–34), line 32 calls function `throwException` (lines 8–24). The `throwException` function also contains a `try` block (lines 11–15), from which the `throw` statement in line 14 `throw`s an instance of standard-library-class `exception`. Function `throwException`'s `catch` handler (lines 16–21) catches this exception, prints an error message (lines 18–19) and rethrows the exception (line 20). This terminates function `throwException` and returns control to line 32 in the `try...catch` block in `main`. The `try` block *terminates* (so line 33 does *not* execute), and the `catch` handler in `main` (lines 35–38) catches this exception and prints an error message (line 37). Since we do not use the exception parameters in the `catch` handlers of this example, we omit the exception parameter names and specify only the type of exception to catch (lines 16 and 35).

```
1  // Fig. 17.3: fig17_03.cpp
2  // Rethrowing an exception.
3  #include <iostream>
4  #include <exception>
5  using namespace std;
6
```

Fig. 17.3 | Rethrowing an exception. (Part 1 of 2.)

```
// throw, catch and rethrow exception
void throwException()
{
   // throw exception and catch it immediately
   try
   {
      cout << "  Function throwException throws an exception\n";
      throw exception(); // generate exception
   } // end try
   catch ( exception & ) // handle exception
   {
      cout << "  Exception handled in function throwException"
         << "\n  Function throwException rethrows exception";
      throw; // rethrow exception for further processing
   } // end catch

   cout << "This also should not print\n";
} // end function throwException

int main()
{
   // throw exception
   try
   {
      cout << "\nmain invokes function throwException\n";
      throwException();
      cout << "This should not print\n";
   } // end try
   catch ( exception & ) // handle exception
   {
      cout << "\n\nException handled in main\n";
   } // end catch

   cout << "Program control continues after catch in main\n";
} // end main
```

```
main invokes function throwException
  Function throwException throws an exception
  Exception handled in function throwException
  Function throwException rethrows exception

Exception handled in main
Program control continues after catch in main
```

Fig. 17.3 | Rethrowing an exception. (Part 2 of 2.)

17.4 Stack Unwinding

When an exception is thrown but not caught in a particular scope, the function call stack is "unwound," and an attempt is made to catch the exception in the next outer try...catch block. Unwinding the function call stack means that the function in which the exception was not caught terminates, all local variables that have completed intitialization in that function are destroyed and control returns to the statement that originally invoked that function. If a try block encloses that statement, an attempt is made to catch the exception. If a try block does *not* enclose that statement, stack unwinding occurs again. If no catch handler ever catches this exception, the program terminates. The program of Fig. 17.4 demonstrates stack unwinding.

```
// Fig. 17.4: fig17_04.cpp
// Demonstrating stack unwinding.
#include <iostream>
#include <stdexcept>
using namespace std;

// function3 throws runtime error
void function3()
{
   cout << "In function 3" << endl;

   // no try block, stack unwinding occurs, return control to function2
   throw runtime_error( "runtime_error in function3" ); // no print
} // end function3

// function2 invokes function3
void function2()
{
   cout << "function3 is called inside function2" << endl;
   function3(); // stack unwinding occurs, return control to function1
} // end function2

// function1 invokes function2
void function1()
{
   cout << "function2 is called inside function1" << endl;
   function2(); // stack unwinding occurs, return control to main
} // end function1

// demonstrate stack unwinding
int main()
{
   // invoke function1
   try
   {
      cout << "function1 is called inside main" << endl;
      function1(); // call function1 which throws runtime_error
   } // end try
   catch ( runtime_error &error ) // handle runtime error
   {
      cout << "Exception occurred: " << error.what() << endl;
      cout << "Exception handled in main" << endl;
   } // end catch
} // end main
```

Fig. 17.4 | Stack unwinding. (Part 1 of 2.)

```
function1 is called inside main
function2 is called inside function1
function3 is called inside function2
In function 3
Exception occurred: runtime_error in function3
Exception handled in main
```

Fig. 17.4 | Stack unwinding. (Part 2 of 2.)

In `main`, the `try` block (lines 34–38) calls `function1` (lines 24–28). Next, `function1` calls `function2` (lines 17–21), which in turn calls `function3` (lines 8–14). Line 13 of `function3` throws a `runtime_error` object. However, because no `try` block encloses the `throw` statement in line 13, stack unwinding occurs—`function3` terminates at line 13, then returns control to the statement in `function2` that invoked `function3` (i.e., line 20). Because no `try` block encloses line 20, stack unwinding occurs again—`function2` terminates at line 20 and returns control to the statement in `function1` that invoked `function2` (i.e., line 27). Because no `try` block encloses line 27, stack unwinding occurs one more time—`function1` terminates at line 27 and returns control to the statement in `main` that invoked `function1` (i.e., line 37). The `try` block of lines 34–38 encloses this statement, so the first matching `catch` handler located after this `try` block (line 39–43) catches and processes the exception. Line 41 uses function `what` to display the exception message.

17.5 When to Use Exception Handling

Exception handling is designed to process **synchronous errors**, which occur when a statement executes, such as *out-of-range array subscripts*, *arithmetic overflow* (i.e., a value outside the representable range of values), *division by zero*, *invalid function parameters* and *unsuccessful memory allocation* (due to lack of memory). Exception handling is not designed to process errors associated with **asynchronous events** (e.g., disk I/O completions, network message arrivals, mouse clicks and keystrokes), which occur in parallel with, and independent of, the program's flow of control.

Software Engineering Observation 17.4

Exception handling provides a single, uniform technique for processing problems. This helps programmers on large projects understand each other's error-processing code.

Software Engineering Observation 17.5

Exception handling enables predefined software components to communicate problems to application-specific components, which can then process the problems in an application-specific manner.

Exception handling also is useful for processing problems that occur when a program interacts with software elements, such as member functions, constructors, destructors and classes. Such software elements often use exceptions to notify programs when problems occur. This enables you to implement *customized error handling* for each application.

Software Engineering Observation 17.6

Functions with common error conditions should return `nullptr`, `0` or other appropriate values, such as `bool`s, rather than throw exceptions. A program calling such a function can check the return value to determine success or failure of the function call.

Complex applications normally consist of predefined software components and application-specific components that use the predefined components. When a predefined component encounters a problem, that component needs a mechanism to communicate the problem to the application-specific component—the *predefined component cannot know in advance how each application processes a problem that occurs.*

C++11: Declaring Functions That Do Not Throw Exceptions

11

As of C++11, if a function does not throw any exceptions *and* does not call any functions that throw exceptions, you should explicitly state that a function *does not* throw exceptions. This indicates to client-code programmers that there's no need to place calls to the function in a `try` block. Simply add **`noexcept`** to the right of the function's parameter list in both the prototype and the definition. For a `const` member function, place `noexcept` after `const`. If a function that's declared `noexcept` calls another function that throws an exception or executes a `throw` statement, the program terminates. We'll say more about `noexcept` in Chapter 24.

17.6 Constructors, Destructors and Exception Handling

First, let's discuss an issue that we've mentioned but not yet resolved satisfactorily: What happens when an error is detected in a *constructor*? For example, how should an object's constructor respond when it receives invalid data? Because the constructor *cannot return a value* to indicate an error, we must choose an alternative means of indicating that the object has not been constructed properly. One scheme is to return the improperly constructed object and hope that anyone using it would make appropriate tests to determine that it's in an inconsistent state. Another scheme is to set some variable outside the constructor. The preferred alternative is to require the constructor to `throw` an exception that contains the error information, thus offering an opportunity for the program to handle the failure.

Before an exception is thrown by a constructor, destructors are called for any member objects whose constructors have run to completion as part of the object being constructed. Destructors are called for every automatic object constructed in a `try` block before the exception is caught. Stack unwinding is guaranteed to have been completed at the point that an exception handler begins executing. If a destructor invoked as a result of stack unwinding throws an exception, the program terminates. This has been linked to various security attacks.

Error-Prevention Tip 17.4

Destructors should catch exceptions to prevent program termination.

Error-Prevention Tip 17.5

Do not throw exceptions from the constructor of an object with static storage duration. Such exceptions cannot be caught.

If an object has member objects, and if an exception is thrown before the outer object is fully constructed, then destructors will be executed for the member objects that have been constructed prior to the occurrence of the exception. If an array of objects has been partially constructed when an exception occurs, only the destructors for the constructed objects in the array will be called.

Error-Prevention Tip 17.6

When an exception is thrown from the constructor for an object that's created in a `new` *expression, the dynamically allocated memory for that object is released.*

Error-Prevention Tip 17.7

A constructor should throw an exception if a problem occurs while initializing an object. Before doing so, the constructor should release any memory that it dynamically allocated.

Initializing Local Objects to Acquire Resources

An exception could preclude the operation of code that would normally *release a resource* (such as memory or a file), thus causing a **resource leak** that prevents other programs from acquiring the resource. One technique to resolve this problem is to initialize a local object to acquire the resource. When an exception occurs, the destructor for that object will be invoked and can free the resource.

17.7 Exceptions and Inheritance

Various exception classes can be derived from a common base class, as we discussed in Section 17.2, when we created class `DivideByZeroException` as a derived class of class `exception`. If a `catch` handler catches a reference to an exception object of a base-class type, it also can `catch` a reference to all objects of classes publicly derived from that base class—this allows for polymorphic processing of related exceptions.

Error-Prevention Tip 17.8

Using inheritance with exceptions enables an exception handler to `catch` *related errors with concise notation. One approach is to* `catch` *each type of reference to a derived-class exception object individually, but a more concise approach is to* `catch` *pointers or references to base-class exception objects instead. Also, catching pointers or references to derived-class exception objects individually is error prone, especially if you forget to test explicitly for one or more of the derived-class reference types.*

17.8 Processing new Failures

When operator `new` fails, it `throw`s a **`bad_alloc`** exception (defined in header `<new>`).In this section, we present two examples of `new` failing. The first uses the version of `new` that `throw`s a `bad_alloc` exception when `new` fails. The second uses function **`set_new_handler`** to handle `new` failures. [*Note:* The examples in Figs. 17.5–17.6 allocate large amounts of dynamic memory, which could cause your computer to become sluggish.]

new Throwing bad_alloc on Failure

Figure 17.5 demonstrates `new` *implicitly* throwing `bad_alloc` on failure to allocate the requested memory. The `for` statement (lines 16–20) inside the `try` block should loop 50 times and, on each pass, allocate an array of 50,000,000 `double` values. If `new` fails and throws a `bad_alloc` exception, the loop terminates, and the program continues in line 22, where the `catch` handler catches and processes the exception. Lines 24–25 print the message `"Exception occurred:"` followed by the message returned from the base-class-exception version of function `what` (i.e., an implementation-defined exception-specific message, such as `"bad allocation"` in Microsoft Visual C++). The output shows that the program performed only four iterations of the loop before `new` failed and threw the `bad_alloc` exception. Your output might differ based on the physical memory, disk space available for virtual memory on your system and the compiler you're using.

```
1  // Fig. 17.5: fig17_05.cpp
2  // Demonstrating standard new throwing bad_alloc when memory
3  // cannot be allocated.
4  #include <iostream>
5  #include <new> // bad_alloc class is defined here
6  using namespace std;
7
8  int main()
9  {
10    double *ptr[ 50 ];
11
12    // aim each ptr[i] at a big block of memory
13    try
14    {
15       // allocate memory for ptr[ i ]; new throws bad_alloc on failure
16       for ( size_t i = 0; i < 50; ++i )
17       {
18          ptr[ i ] = new double[ 50000000 ]; // may throw exception
19          cout << "ptr[" << i << "] points to 50,000,000 new doubles\n";
20       } // end for
21    } // end try
22    catch ( bad_alloc &memoryAllocationException )
23    {
24       cerr << "Exception occurred: "
25          << memoryAllocationException.what() << endl;
26    } // end catch
27 } // end main
```

```
ptr[0] points to 50,000,000 new doubles
ptr[1] points to 50,000,000 new doubles
ptr[2] points to 50,000,000 new doubles
ptr[3] points to 50,000,000 new doubles
Exception occurred: bad allocation
```

Fig. 17.5 | `new` throwing `bad_alloc` on failure.

`new` Returning `nullptr` on Failure

The C++ standard specifies that programmers can use an older version of `new` that returns `nullptr` upon failure. For this purpose, header `<new>` defines object **`nothrow`** (of type `nothrow_t`), which is used as follows:

```
double *ptr = new( nothrow ) double[ 50000000 ];
```

The preceding statement uses the version of new that does *not* throw bad_alloc exceptions (i.e., nothrow) to allocate an array of 50,000,000 doubles.

Software Engineering Observation 17.7

To make programs more robust, use the version of new that throws bad_alloc exceptions on failure.

Handling new *Failures Using Function* set_new_handler

An additional feature for handling new failures is function set_new_handler (prototyped in standard header <new>). This function takes as its argument a pointer to a function that takes no arguments and returns void. This pointer points to the function that will be called if new fails. This provides you with a uniform approach to handling all new failures, regardless of where a failure occurs in the program. Once set_new_handler registers a **new handler** in the program, operator new does *not* throw bad_alloc on failure; rather, it defers the error handling to the new-handler function.

If new allocates memory successfully, it returns a pointer to that memory. If new fails to allocate memory and set_new_handler did not register a new-handler function, new throws a bad_alloc exception. If new fails to allocate memory and a new-handler function has been registered, the new-handler function is called. The new-handler function should perform one of the following tasks:

1. Make more memory available by deleting other dynamically allocated memory (or telling the user to close other applications) and return to operator new to attempt to allocate memory again.
2. Throw an exception of type bad_alloc.
3. Call function abort or exit (both found in header <cstdlib>) to terminate the program. These were introduced in Section 9.7.

Figure 17.6 demonstrates set_new_handler. Function customNewHandler (lines 9–13) prints an error message (line 11), then calls abort (line 12) to terminate the program. The output shows that the loop iterated four times before new failed and invoked function customNewHandler. Your output might differ based on the physical memory, disk space available for virtual memory on your system and your compiler.

```
1  // Fig. 17.6: fig17_06.cpp
2  // Demonstrating set_new_handler.
3  #include <iostream>
4  #include <new> // set_new_handler function prototype
5  #include <cstdlib> // abort function prototype
6  using namespace std;
7
8  // handle memory allocation failure
9  void customNewHandler()
10 {
11    cerr << "customNewHandler was called";
12    abort();
13 } // end function customNewHandler
```

Fig. 17.6 | set_new_handler specifying the function to call when new fails. (Part 1 of 2.)

```

// using set_new_handler to handle failed memory allocation
int main()
{
   double *ptr[ 50 ];

   // specify that customNewHandler should be called on
   // memory allocation failure
   set_new_handler( customNewHandler );

   // aim each ptr[i] at a big block of memory; customNewHandler will be
   // called on failed memory allocation
   for ( size_t i = 0; i < 50; ++i )
   {
      ptr[ i ] = new double[ 50000000 ]; // may throw exception
      cout << "ptr[" << i << "] points to 50,000,000 new doubles\n";
   } // end for
} // end main
```

```
ptr[0] points to 50,000,000 new doubles
ptr[1] points to 50,000,000 new doubles
ptr[2] points to 50,000,000 new doubles
ptr[3] points to 50,000,000 new doubles
customNewHandler was called
```

Fig. 17.6 | `set_new_handler` specifying the function to call when new fails. (Part 2 of 2.)

17.9 Class unique_ptr and Dynamic Memory Allocation

A common programming practice is to *allocate* dynamic memory, assign the address of that memory to a pointer, use the pointer to manipulate the memory and *deallocate* the memory with `delete` when the memory is no longer needed. If an exception occurs after successful memory allocation but *before* the `delete` statement executes, a *memory leak* could occur. C++11 provides class template **`unique_ptr`** in header **`<memory>`** to deal with this situation.

An object of class `unique_ptr` maintains a pointer to dynamically allocated memory. When a `unique_ptr` object destructor is called (for example, when a `unique_ptr` object goes out of scope), it performs a `delete` operation on its pointer data member. Class template `unique_ptr` provides overloaded operators `*` and `->` so that a `unique_ptr` object can be used just as a regular pointer variable is. Figure 17.9 demonstrates a `unique_ptr` object that points to a dynamically allocated object of class `Integer` (Figs. 17.7–17.8).

```
// Fig. 17.7: Integer.h
// Integer class definition.

class Integer
{
```

Fig. 17.7 | `Integer` class definition. (Part 1 of 2.)

```
public:
   Integer( int i = 0 ); // Integer default constructor
   ~Integer(); // Integer destructor
   void setInteger( int i ); // set Integer value
   int getInteger() const; // return Integer value
private:
   int value;
}; // end class Integer
```

Fig. 17.7 | `Integer` class definition. (Part 2 of 2.)

```
// Fig. 17.8: Integer.cpp
// Integer member function definitions.
#include <iostream>
#include "Integer.h"
using namespace std;

// Integer default constructor
Integer::Integer( int i )
   : value( i )
{
   cout << "Constructor for Integer " << value << endl;
} // end Integer constructor

// Integer destructor
Integer::~Integer()
{
   cout << "Destructor for Integer " << value << endl;
} // end Integer destructor

// set Integer value
void Integer::setInteger( int i )
{
   value = i;
} // end function setInteger

// return Integer value
int Integer::getInteger() const
{
   return value;
} // end function getInteger
```

Fig. 17.8 | Member function definitions of class `Integer`.

Line 15 of Fig. 17.9 creates `unique_ptr` object `ptrToInteger` and initializes it with a pointer to a dynamically allocated `Integer` object that contains the value 7. Line 18 uses the `unique_ptr` overloaded `->` operator to invoke function `setInteger` on the `Integer` object that `ptrToInteger` manages. Line 21 uses the `unique_ptr` overloaded `*` operator to dereference `ptrToInteger`, then uses the dot (`.`) operator to invoke function `getInteger` on the `Integer` object. Like a regular pointer, a `unique_ptr`'s `->` and `*` overloaded operators can be used to access the object to which the `unique_ptr` points.

```cpp
// Fig. 17.9: fig17_09.cpp
// Demonstrating unique_ptr.
#include <iostream>
#include <memory>
using namespace std;

#include "Integer.h"

// use unique_ptr to manipulate Integer object
int main()
{
   cout << "Creating a unique_ptr object that points to an Integer\n";

   // "aim" unique_ptr at Integer object
   unique_ptr< Integer > ptrToInteger( new Integer( 7 ) );

   cout << "\nUsing the unique_ptr to manipulate the Integer\n";
   ptrToInteger->setInteger( 99 ); // use unique_ptr to set Integer value

   // use unique_ptr to get Integer value
   cout << "Integer after setInteger: " << ( *ptrToInteger ).getInteger()
      << "\n\nTerminating program" << endl;
} // end main
```

```
Creating a unique_ptr object that points to an Integer
Constructor for Integer 7

Using the unique_ptr to manipulate the Integer
Integer after setInteger: 99

Terminating program
Destructor for Integer 99
```

Fig. 17.9 | `unique_ptr` object manages dynamically allocated memory.

Because `ptrToInteger` is a local automatic variable in `main`, `ptrToInteger` is destroyed when `main` terminates. The `unique_ptr` destructor forces a `delete` of the `Integer` object pointed to by `ptrToInteger`, which in turn calls the `Integer` class destructor. The memory that `Integer` occupies is released, regardless of how control leaves the block (e.g., by a `return` statement or by an exception). Most importantly, using this technique can *prevent memory leaks*. For example, suppose a function returns a pointer aimed at some object. Unfortunately, the function caller that receives this pointer might not `delete` the object, thus resulting in *a memory leak*. However, if the function returns a `unique_ptr` to the object, the object will be deleted automatically when the `unique_ptr` object's destructor gets called.

`unique_ptr` *Notes*

The class is called `unique_ptr` because only *one* `unique_ptr` at a time can own a dynamically allocated object. By using its overloaded assignment operator or copy constructor, a `unique_ptr` can *transfer ownership* of the dynamic memory it manages. The *last* `unique_ptr` object that maintains the pointer to the dynamic memory will delete the memory. This makes `unique_ptr` an ideal mechanism for returning dynamically allocated memory to client code. When the unique_ptr goes out of scope in the *client* code, the unique_ptr's destructor destroys the dynamically allocated object and deletes its memory.

unique_ptr to a Built-In Array

You can also use a unique_ptr to manage a dynamically allocated built-in array. For example, consider the statement

```
unique_ptr< string[] > ptr( new string[ 10 ] );
```

which dynamically allocates an array of 10 strings managed by ptr. The type string[] indicates that the managed memory is a built-in array containing strings. When a unique_ptr that manages an array goes out of scope it deletes the memory with delete [] so that every element of the array receives a destructor call.

A unique_ptr that manages an array provides an overloaded [] operator for accessing the array's elements. For example, the statement

```
ptr[ 2 ] = "hello";
```

assigns "hello" to the string at ptr[2] and the statement

```
cout << ptr[ 2 ] << endl;
```

displays that string.

17.10 Standard Library Exception Hierarchy

Experience has shown that exceptions fall nicely into a number of categories. The C++ Standard Library includes a hierarchy of exception classes, some of which are shown in Fig. 17.10. As we first discussed in Section 17.2, this hierarchy is headed by base-class exception (defined in header <exception>), which contains virtual function what that derived classes can override to issue appropriate error messages.

Immediate derived classes of base-class exception include runtime_error and **logic_error** (both defined in header <stdexcept>), each of which has several derived classes. Also derived from exception are the exceptions thrown by C++ operators—for example, bad_alloc is thrown by new (Section 17.8), **bad_cast** is thrown by dynamic_cast (Chapter 12) and **bad_typeid** is thrown by typeid (Chapter 12).

Common Programming Error 17.6

Placing a catch handler that catches a base-class object before a catch that catches an object of a class derived from that base class is a logic error. The base-class catch catches all objects of classes derived from that base class, so the derived-class catch will never execute.

Class logic_error is the base class of several standard exception classes that indicate errors in program logic. For example, class **invalid_argument** indicates that a function received an invalid argument. (Proper coding can, of course, prevent invalid arguments from reaching a function.) Class **length_error** indicates that a length larger than the maximum size allowed for the object being manipulated was used for that object. Class **out_of_range** indicates that a value, such as a subscript into an array, exceeded its allowed range of values.

Class runtime_error, which we used briefly in Section 17.4, is the base class of several other standard exception classes that indicate execution-time errors. For example, class

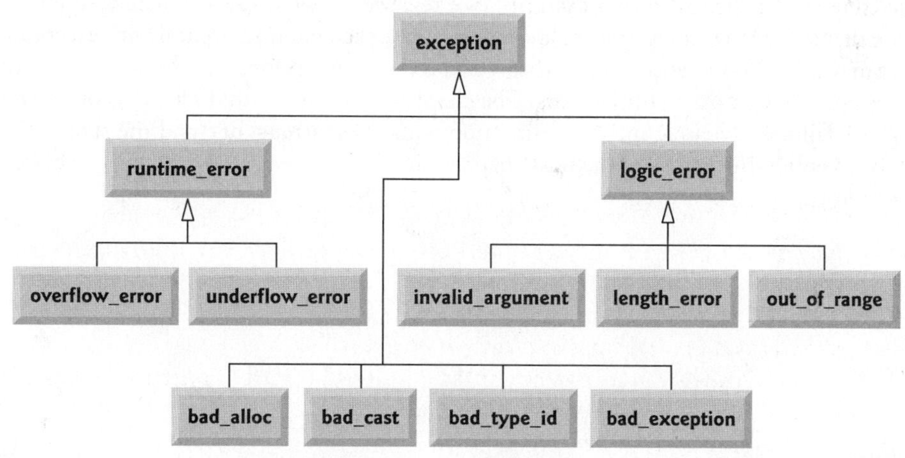

Fig. 17.10 | Some of the Standard Library exception classes.

`overflow_error` describes an **arithmetic overflow error** (i.e., the result of an arithmetic operation is larger than the largest number that can be stored in the computer) and class `underflow_error` describes an **arithmetic underflow error** (i.e., the result of an arithmetic operation is smaller than the smallest number that can be stored in the computer).

Common Programming Error 17.7

Exception classes need not be derived from class `exception`*, so catching type* `exception` *is not guaranteed to* `catch` *all exceptions a program could encounter.*

Error-Prevention Tip 17.9

To `catch` *all exceptions potentially thrown in a* `try` *block, use* `catch(...)`*. One weakness with catching exceptions in this way is that the type of the caught exception is unknown. Another weakness is that, without a named parameter, there's no way to refer to the exception object inside the exception handler.*

Software Engineering Observation 17.8

The standard `exception` *hierarchy is a good starting point for creating exceptions. You can build programs that can* `throw` *standard exceptions,* `throw` *exceptions derived from the standard exceptions or* `throw` *your own exceptions not derived from the standard exceptions.*

Software Engineering Observation 17.9

Use `catch(...)` *to perform recovery that does not depend on the exception type (e.g., releasing common resources). The exception can be rethrown to alert more specific enclosing* `catch` *handlers.*

17.11 Wrap-Up

In this chapter, you learned how to use exception handling to deal with errors in a program. You learned that exception handling enables you to remove error-handling code from the "main line" of the program's execution. We demonstrated exception handling in the context of a divide-by-zero example. We reviewed how to use `try` blocks to enclose code that may throw an exception, and how to use `catch` handlers to deal with exceptions that may arise. You learned how to throw and rethrow exceptions, and how to handle the exceptions that occur in constructors. The chapter continued with discussions of processing `new` failures, dynamic memory allocation with class `unique_ptr` and the standard library exception hierarchy. In the next chapter, you'll learn how to build your own custom class templates.

18

Introduction to Custom Templates

Objectives

In this chapter you'll:

- Use class templates to create groups of related classes.
- Distinguish between class templates and class-template specializations.
- Learn about nontype template parameters.
- Learn about default template arguments.
- Learn about overloading function templates.

18.1 Introduction

In Chapters 7, 15 and 16, you used many of the Standard Library's *prepackaged* templatized containers and algorithms. Function templates (which were introduced in Chapter 6) and **class templates** enable you to conveniently specify a variety of related (overloaded) functions—called **function-template specializations**—or a variety of related classes—called **class-template specializations**, respectively. This is called **generic programming**. Function templates and class templates are like *stencils* out of which we trace shapes; function-template specializations and class-template specializations are like the separate tracings that all have the same shape, but could, for example, be drawn in different colors and textures. In this chapter, we demonstrate how to create a custom class template and a function template that manipulates objects of our class-template specializations.

18.2 Class Templates

It's possible to *understand* the concept of a stack (a data structure into which we insert items *only* at the *top* and retrieve those items *only* from the *top* in *last-in, first-out order*) *independent of the type of the items* being placed in the stack. However, to *instantiate* a stack, a data type must be specified. This creates a nice opportunity for software reusability—as you already saw with the `stack` container adapter in Section 15.7.1. Here, we define a stack *generically* then use *type-specific* versions of this generic stack class.

Software Engineering Observation 18.1

Class templates encourage software reusability by enabling a variety of type-specific class-template specializations to be instantiated from a single class template.

Class templates are called **parameterized types**, because they require one or more *type parameters* to specify how to customize a generic class template to form a *class-template specialization*. To produce many specializations you write only one class-template definition (as we'll do shortly). When a particular specialization is needed, you use a concise, simple notation, and the compiler writes the specialization source code. One `Stack` class template, for example, could thus become the basis for creating many `Stack` class-template specializations (such as "`Stack` of `double`s," "`Stack` of `int`s," "`Stack` of `Employee`s," "`Stack` of `Bill`s," etc.) used in a program.

Common Programming Error 18.1

To create a template specialization with a user-defined type, the user-defined type must meet the template's requirements. For example, the template might compare objects of the user-defined type with < to determine sorting order, or the template might call a specific member function on an object of the user-defined type. If the user-defined type does not overload the required operator or provide the required functions, compilation errors occur.

Creating Class Template **Stack<T>**

The `Stack` class-template definition in Fig. 18.1 looks like a conventional class definition, with a few key differences. First, it's preceded by line 7

```
template< typename T >
```

All class templates begin with keyword **`template`** followed by a list of **template parameters** enclosed in **angle brackets** (< and >); each template parameter that represents a type *must* be preceded by either of the *interchangeable* keywords **`typename`** or `class`. The type parameter `T` acts as a placeholder for the `Stack`'s element type. The names of type parameters must be *unique* inside a template definition. You need not specifically use identifier `T`—any valid identifier can be used. The element type is mentioned generically throughout the `Stack` class-template definition as `T` (lines 12, 18 and 42). The type parameter becomes associated with a specific type when you create an object using the class template—at that point, the compiler generates a copy of the class template in which all occurrences of the type parameter are replaced with the specified type. Another key difference is that we did *not* separate the class template's interface from its implementation.

Software Engineering Observation 18.2

Templates are typically defined in headers, which are then `#include`d in the appropriate client source-code files. For class templates, this means that the member functions are also defined in the header—typically inside the class definition's body, as we do in Fig. 18.1.

```
1  // Fig. 18.1: Stack.h
2  // Stack class template.
3  #ifndef STACK_H
4  #define STACK_H
5  #include <deque>
6
7  template< typename T >
8  class Stack
9  {
10 public:
11    // return the top element of the Stack
12    T& top()
13    {
14       return stack.front();
15    } // end function template top
16
17    // push an element onto the Stack
18    void push( const T &pushValue )
19    {
20       stack.push_front( pushValue );
21    } // end function template push
22
23    // pop an element from the stack
24    void pop()
25    {
26       stack.pop_front();
27    } // end function template pop
```

Fig. 18.1 | `Stack` class template. (Part 1 of 2.)

```
28
29       // determine whether Stack is empty
30       bool isEmpty() const
31       {
32          return stack.empty();
33       } // end function template isEmpty
34
35       // return size of Stack
36       size_t size() const
37       {
38          return stack.size();
39       } // end function template size
40
41    private:
42       std::deque< T > stack; // internal representation of the Stack
43    }; // end class template Stack
44
45    #endif
```

Fig. 18.1 | `Stack` class template. (Part 2 of 2.)

Class Template **Stack<T>***'s Data Representation*

Section 15.7.1 showed that the Standard Library's `stack` adapter class can use various containers to store its elements. Of course, a `stack` requires insertions and deletions *only* at its *top*. So, for example, a `vector` or a `deque` could be used to store the `stack`'s elements. A `vector` supports fast insertions and deletions at its *back*. A `deque` supports fast insertions and deletions at its *front* and its *back*. A `deque` is the default representation for the Standard Library's `stack` adapter because a `deque` grows more efficiently than a `vector`. A `vector` is maintained as a *contiguous* block of memory—when that block is full and a new element is added, the `vector` allocates a larger contiguous block of memory and *copies* the old elements into that new block. A `deque`, on the other hand, is typically implemented as list of fixed-size, built-in arrays—new fixed-size built-in arrays are added as necessary and none of the existing elements are copied when new items are added to the front or back. For these reasons, we use a `deque` (line 42) as the underlying container for our `Stack` class.

Class Template **Stack<T>***'s Member Functions*

The member-function definitions of a class template are *function templates*, but are not preceded with the `template` keyword and template parameters in angle brackets (< and >) when they're defined within the class template's body. As you can see, however, they do use the class template's template parameter `T` to represent the element type. Our `Stack` class template does *not* define it's own constructors—the *default constructor* provided by the compiler will invoke the `deque`'s default constructor. We also provide the following member functions in Fig. 18.1:

- `top` (lines 12–15) returns a reference to the `Stack`'s top element.
- `push` (lines 18–21) places a new element on the top of the `Stack`.
- `pop` (lines 24–27) removes the `Stack`'s top element.

- isEmpty (lines 30–33) returns a bool value—true if the Stack is empty and false otherwise.
- size (lines 36–39) returns the number if elements in the Stack.

Each of these member functions *delegates* its responsibility to the appropriate member function of class template deque.

Declaring a Class Template's Member Functions Outside the Class Template Definition

Though we did *not* do so in our Stack class template, member-function definitions can appear *outside* a class template definition. If you do this, each must begin with the template keyword followed by the *same* set of template parameters as the class template. In addition, the member functions must be qualified with the class name and scope resolution operator. For example, you can define the pop function outside the class-template definition as follows:

```
template< typename T >
inline void Stack<T>::pop()
{
   stack.pop_front();
} // end function template pop
```

Stack<T>:: indicates that pop is in the scope of class Stack<T>. The Standard Library's container classes tend to define all their member functions *inside* their class definitions.

Testing Class Template **Stack<T>**

Now, let's consider the driver (Fig. 18.2) that exercises the Stack class template. The driver begins by instantiating object doubleStack (line 9). This object is declared as a Stack<double> (pronounced "Stack of double"). The compiler associates type double with type parameter T in the class template to produce the source code for a Stack class with elements of type double that actually stores its elements in a deque<double>.

```
1  // Fig. 18.2: fig18_02.cpp
2  // Stack class template test program.
3  #include <iostream>
4  #include "Stack.h" // Stack class template definition
5  using namespace std;
6
7  int main()
8  {
9     Stack< double > doubleStack; // create a Stack of double
10    const size_t doubleStackSize = 5; // stack size
11    double doubleValue = 1.1; // first value to push
12
13    cout << "Pushing elements onto doubleStack\n";
14
15    // push 5 doubles onto doubleStack
16    for ( size_t i = 0; i < doubleStackSize; ++i )
17    {
```

Fig. 18.2 | Stack class template test program. (Part 1 of 2.)

```
      doubleStack.push( doubleValue );
      cout << doubleValue << ' ';
      doubleValue += 1.1;
   } // end while

   cout << "\n\nPopping elements from doubleStack\n";

   // pop elements from doubleStack
   while ( !doubleStack.isEmpty() ) // loop while Stack is not empty
   {
      cout << doubleStack.top() << ' '; // display top element
      doubleStack.pop(); // remove top element
   } // end while

   cout << "\nStack is empty, cannot pop.\n";

   Stack< int > intStack; // create a Stack of int
   const size_t intStackSize = 10; // stack size
   int intValue = 1; // first value to push

   cout << "\nPushing elements onto intStack\n";

   // push 10 integers onto intStack
   for ( size_t i = 0; i < intStackSize; ++i )
   {
      intStack.push( intValue );
      cout << intValue++ << ' ';
   } // end while

   cout << "\n\nPopping elements from intStack\n";

   // pop elements from intStack
   while ( !intStack.isEmpty() ) // loop while Stack is not empty
   {
      cout << intStack.top() << ' '; // display top element
      intStack.pop(); // remove top element
   } // end while

   cout << "\nStack is empty, cannot pop." << endl;
} // end main
```

```
Pushing elements onto doubleStack
1.1 2.2 3.3 4.4 5.5

Popping elements from doubleStack
5.5 4.4 3.3 2.2 1.1
Stack is empty, cannot pop

Pushing elements onto intStack
1 2 3 4 5 6 7 8 9 10

Popping elements from intStack
10 9 8 7 6 5 4 3 2 1
Stack is empty, cannot pop
```

Fig. 18.2 | Stack class template test program. (Part 2 of 2.)

Lines 16–21 invoke push (line 18) to place the double values 1.1, 2.2, 3.3, 4.4 and 5.5 onto doubleStack. Next, lines 26–30 invoke top and pop in a while loop to remove the five values from the stack. Notice in the output of Fig. 18.2, that the values do pop off in *last-in, first-out order*. When doubleStack is empty, the pop loop terminates.

Line 34 instantiates int stack intStack with the declaration

```
Stack< int > intStack;
```

(pronounced "intStack is a Stack of int"). Lines 41–45 repeatedly invoke push (line 43) to place values onto intStack, then lines 50–54 repeatedly invoke top and pop to remove values from intStack until it's empty. Once again, notice in the output that the values pop off in last-in, first-out order.

18.3 Function Template to Manipulate a Class-Template Specialization Object

Notice that the code in function main of Fig. 18.2 is *almost identical* for both the doubleStack manipulations in lines 9–32 and the intStack manipulations in lines 34–56. This presents another opportunity to use a function template. Figure 18.3 defines function template testStack (lines 10–39) to perform the same tasks as main in Fig. 18.2—push a series of values onto a Stack<T> and pop the values off a Stack<T>.

```
1  // Fig. 18.3: fig18_03.cpp
2  // Passing a Stack template object
3  // to a function template.
4  #include <iostream>
5  #include <string>
6  #include "Stack.h" // Stack class template definition
7  using namespace std;
8
9  // function template to manipulate Stack< T >
10 template< typename T >
11 void testStack(
12    Stack< T > &theStack, // reference to Stack< T >
13    const T &value, // initial value to push
14    const T &increment, // increment for subsequent values
15    size_t size, // number of items to push
16    const string &stackName ) // name of the Stack< T > object
17 {
18    cout << "\nPushing elements onto " << stackName << '\n';
19    T pushValue = value;
20
21    // push element onto Stack
22    for ( size_t i = 0; i < size; ++i )
23    {
24       theStack.push( pushValue ); // push element onto Stack
25       cout << pushValue << ' ';
26       pushValue += increment;
27    } // end while
28
```

Fig. 18.3 | Passing a Stack template object to a function template. (Part 1 of 2.)

```
29    cout << "\n\nPopping elements from " << stackName << '\n';
30
31    // pop elements from Stack
32    while ( !theStack.isEmpty() ) // loop while Stack is not empty
33    {
34       cout << theStack.top() << ' ';
35       theStack.pop(); // remove top element
36    } // end while
37
38    cout << "\nStack is empty. Cannot pop." << endl;
39 } // end function template testStack
40
41 int main()
42 {
43    Stack< double > doubleStack;
44    const size_t doubleStackSize = 5;
45    testStack( doubleStack, 1.1, 1.1, doubleStackSize, "doubleStack" );
46
47    Stack< int > intStack;
48    const size_t intStackSize = 10;
49    testStack( intStack, 1, 1, intStackSize, "intStack" );
50 } // end main
```

```
Pushing elements onto doubleStack
1.1 2.2 3.3 4.4 5.5

Popping elements from doubleStack
5.5 4.4 3.3 2.2 1.1
Stack is empty, cannot pop

Pushing elements onto intStack
1 2 3 4 5 6 7 8 9 10

Popping elements from intStack
10 9 8 7 6 5 4 3 2 1
Stack is empty, cannot pop
```

Fig. 18.3 | Passing a Stack template object to a function template. (Part 2 of 2.)

Function template testStack uses T (specified at line 10) to represent the data type stored in the Stack<T>. The function template takes five arguments (lines 12–16):

- the Stack<T> to manipulate
- a value of type T that will be the first value pushed onto the Stack<T>
- a value of type T used to increment the values pushed onto the Stack<T>
- the number of elements to push onto the Stack<T>
- a string that represents the name of the Stack<T> object for output purposes

Function main (lines 41–50) instantiates an object of type Stack<double> called doubleStack (line 43) and an object of type Stack<int> called intStack (line 47) and uses these objects in lines 45 and 49. The compiler infers the type of T for testStack from the type used to instantiate the function's first argument (i.e., the type used to instantiate doubleStack or intStack).

18.4 Nontype Parameters

Class template Stack of Section 18.2 used only a type parameter (Fig. 18.1, line 7) in its template declaration. It's also possible to use **nontype template parameters**, which can have default arguments and are treated as constants. For example, the C++ standard's array class template begins with the template declaration:

```
template < class T, size_t N >
```

(Recall that keywords class and typename are *interchangeable* in template declarations.) So, a declaration such as

```
array< double, 100 > salesFigures;
```

creates a 100-element array of doubles class-template specialization, then uses it to instantiate the object salesFigures. The array class template encapsulates a *built-in array*. When you create an array class-template specialization, the array's built-in array data member has the type and size specified in the declaration—in the preceding example, it would be a built-in array of double values with 100 elements.

18.5 Default Arguments for Template Type Parameters

In addition, a type parameter can specify a **default type argument**. For example, the C++ standard's stack *container adapter* class template begins with:

```
template < class T, class Container = deque< T > >
```

which specifies that a stack uses a deque *by default* to store the stack's elements of type T. The declaration

```
stack< int > values;
```

creates a stack of ints class-template specialization (behind the scenes) and uses it to instantiate the object named values. The stack's elements are stored in a deque<int>.

Default type parameters must be the *rightmost* (trailing) parameters in a template's type-parameter list. When you instantiate a template with two or more default arguments, if an omitted argument is not the rightmost, then all type parameters to the right of it also must be omitted. As of C++11, you can now use default type arguments for template type parameters in function templates.

18.6 Overloading Function Templates

Function templates and overloading are intimately related. In Section 6.18, you learned that when overloaded functions perform *identical* operations on *different* types of data, they can be expressed more compactly and conveniently using function templates. You can then write function calls with different types of arguments and let the compiler generate separate *function-template specializations* to handle each function call appropriately. The function-template specializations generated from a given function template all have the same name, so the compiler uses overload resolution to invoke the proper function.

You may also *overload* function templates. For example, you can provide other function templates that specify the *same* function name but *different* function parameters. A function template also can be overloaded by providing nontemplate functions with the same function name but different function parameters.

Matching Process for Overloaded Functions

The compiler performs a matching process to determine what function to call when a function is invoked. It looks at both existing functions and function templates to locate a function or generate a function-template specialization whose function name and argument types are consistent with those of the function call. If there are no matches, the compiler issues an error message. If there are multiple matches for the function call, the compiler attempts to determine the *best* match. If there's *more than one* best match, the call is *ambiguous* and the compiler issues an error message.[1]

18.7 Wrap-Up

This chapter discussed class templates and class-template specializations. We used a class template to create a group of related class-template specializations that each perform identical processing on different data types. We discussed nontype template parameters. We also discussed how to overload a function template to create a customized version that handles a particular data type's processing in a manner that differs from the other function-template specializations. In the next chapter, we present the features of C++'s `string` class and introduce `string` stream processing.

1. The compiler's process for resolving function calls is complex. The complete details are discussed in Section 13.3.3 of the C++ standard.

19

Class `string` and String Stream Processing: A Deeper Look

Objectives

In this chapter you'll:

- Manipulate `string` objects.
- Determine `string` characteristics.
- Find, replace and insert characters in `string`s.
- Convert `string` objects to pointer-based strings and vice versa.
- Use `string` iterators.
- Perform input from and output to `string`s in memory.
- Use C++11 numeric conversion functions.

Outline

19.1 Introduction

The class template **basic_string** provides typical string-manipulation operations such as copying, searching, etc. The template definition and all support facilities are defined in namespace std; these include the typedef statement

```
typedef basic_string< char > string;
```

that creates the alias type string for **basic_string<char>**. A typedef is also provided for the **wchar_t** type (wstring). Type wchar_t[1] stores characters (e.g., two-byte characters, four-byte characters, etc.) for supporting other character sets. We use string exclusively throughout this chapter. To use strings, include header <string>.

Initializing a string *Object*

A string object can be initialized with a constructor argument as in

```
string text( "Hello" ); // creates a string from a const char *
```

which creates a string containing the characters in "Hello", or with two constructor arguments as in

```
string name( 8, 'x' ); // string of 8 'x' characters
```

which creates a string containing eight 'x' characters. Class string also provides a *default constructor* (which creates an *empty* string) and a *copy constructor*. A string also can be initialized in its definition as in

```
string month = "March"; // same as: string month( "March" );
```

Remember that = in the preceding declaration is *not* an assignment; rather it's an *implicit call to the* string *class constructor*, which does the conversion.

1. Type wchar_t commonly is used to represent Unicode®, but wchar_t's size is not specified by the standard. C++11 also has types char16_t and char32_t for Unicode support. The Unicode Standard outlines a specification to produce consistent encoding of the world's characters and *symbols*. To learn more about the Unicode Standard, visit www.unicode.org.

`string`s Are Not Necessarily Null Terminated

Unlike pointer-based `char *` strings, `string` objects are not necessarily null terminated. [*Note:* The C++ standard document provides only a description of the capabilities of class `string`—implementation is platform dependent.]

Length of a `string`

The length of a `string` can be retrieved with member function **`size`** and with member function **`length`**. The subscript operator, `[]` (which does not perform bounds checking), can be used with `string`s to access and modify individual characters. A `string` object has a first subscript of `0` and a last subscript of `size() - 1`.

Processing `string`s

Most `string` member functions take as arguments a *starting subscript location* and the number of characters on which to operate.

`string` I/O

The stream extraction operator (>>) is overloaded to support `string`s. The statements

```
string stringObject;
cin >> stringObject;
```

declare a `string` object and read a `string` from `cin`. Input is delimited by whitespace characters. When a delimiter is encountered, the input operation is terminated. Function **`getline`** also is overloaded for `string`s. Assuming `string1` is a `string`, the statement

```
getline( cin, string1 );
```

reads a `string` from the keyboard into `string1`. Input is delimited by a newline (`'\n'`), so `getLine` can read a line of text into a `string` object. You can specify an *alternate delimiter* as the optional third argument to `getline`.

Validating Input

In earlier chapters, we mentioned the importance of validating user input in industrial-strength code. The capabilities presented in this chapter—and the regular-expression capabilities shown in Section 24.5—are frequently used to perform validation. 11

19.2 `string` Assignment and Concatenation

Figure 19.1 demonstrates *`string` assignment* and *concatenation*. Line 4 includes header `<string>` for class `string`. The `string`s `string1`, `string2` and `string3` are created in lines 9–11. Line 13 assigns the value of `string1` to `string2`. After the assignment takes place, `string2` is a copy of `string1`. Line 14 uses member function **`assign`** to copy `string1` into `string3`. A separate copy is made (i.e., `string1` and `string3` are independent objects). Class `string` also provides an overloaded version of member function `assign` that copies a specified number of characters, as in

```
targetString.assign( sourceString, start, numberOfCharacters );
```

where `sourceString` is the `string` to be copied, `start` is the starting subscript and `numberOfCharacters` is the number of characters to copy.

Line 19 uses the subscript operator to assign `'r'` to `string3[ 2 ]` (forming `"car"`) and to assign `'r'` to `string2[ 0 ]` (forming `"rat"`). The `string`s are then output.

```cpp
// Fig. 19.1: Fig19_01.cpp
// Demonstrating string assignment and concatenation.
#include <iostream>
#include <string>
using namespace std;

int main()
{
   string string1( "cat" );
   string string2; // initialized to the empty string
   string string3; // initialized to the empty string

   string2 = string1; // assign string1 to string2
   string3.assign( string1 ); // assign string1 to string3
   cout << "string1: " << string1 << "\nstring2: " << string2
      << "\nstring3: " << string3 << "\n\n";

   // modify string2 and string3
   string2[ 0 ] = string3[ 2 ] = 'r';

   cout << "After modification of string2 and string3:\n" << "string1: "
      << string1 << "\nstring2: " << string2 << "\nstring3: ";

   // demonstrating member function at
   for ( size_t i = 0; i < string3.size(); ++i )
      cout << string3.at( i ); // can throw out_of_range exception

   // declare string4 and string5
   string string4( string1 + "apult" ); // concatenation
   string string5; // initialized to the empty string

   // overloaded +=
   string3 += "pet"; // create "carpet"
   string1.append( "acomb" ); // create "catacomb"

   // append subscript locations 4 through end of string1 to
   // create string "comb" (string5 was initially empty)
   string5.append( string1, 4, string1.size() - 4 );

   cout << "\n\nAfter concatenation:\nstring1: " << string1
      << "\nstring2: " << string2 << "\nstring3: " << string3
      << "\nstring4: " << string4 << "\nstring5: " << string5 << endl;
} // end main
```

```
string1: cat
string2: cat
string3: cat

After modification of string2 and string3:
string1: cat
string2: rat
string3: car
```

Fig. 19.1 | Demonstrating string assignment and concatenation. (Part 1 of 2.)

```
After concatenation:
string1: catacomb
string2: rat
string3: carpet
string4: catapult
string5: comb
```

Fig. 19.1 | Demonstrating `string` assignment and concatenation. (Part 2 of 2.)

Lines 25–26 output the contents of `string3` one character at a time using member function **`at`**. Member function `at` provides **checked access** (or **range checking**); i.e., going past the end of the `string` throws an `out_of_range` exception. *The subscript operator,* `[]`*, does not provide checked access.* This is consistent with its use on arrays. Note that you can also iterate through the characters in a string using C++11's range-based `for` as in

```
for ( char c : string3 )
   cout << c;
```

which ensures that you do not access any elements outside the `string`'s bounds.

Common Programming Error 19.1

Accessing an element beyond the size of the `string` *using the subscript operator is an unreported logic error.*

String `string4` is declared (line 29) and initialized to the result of concatenating `string1` and `"apult"` using the *overloaded* `+` *operator*, which for class `string` denotes *concatenation*. Line 33 uses the *overloaded addition assignment operator,* `+=`, to concatenate `string3` and `"pet"`. Line 34 uses member function **`append`** to concatenate `string1` and `"acomb"`.

Line 38 appends the string `"comb"` to empty `string` `string5`. This member function is passed the `string` (`string1`) to retrieve characters from, the starting subscript in the `string` (`4`) and the number of characters to append (the value returned by `string1.size() - 4`).

19.3 Comparing strings

Class `string` provides member functions for comparing `strings`. Figure 19.2 demonstrates class `string`'s comparison capabilities.

```
// Fig. 19.2: Fig19_02.cpp
// Comparing strings.
#include <iostream>
#include <string>
using namespace std;

int main()
{
   string string1( "Testing the comparison functions." );
```

Fig. 19.2 | Comparing `strings`. (Part 1 of 3.)

```
   string string2( "Hello" );
   string string3( "stinger" );
   string string4( string2 ); // "Hello"

   cout << "string1: " << string1 << "\nstring2: " << string2
      << "\nstring3: " << string3 << "\nstring4: " << string4 << "\n\n";

   // comparing string1 and string4
   if ( string1 == string4 )
      cout << "string1 == string4\n";
   else if ( string1 > string4 )
         cout << "string1 > string4\n";
   else // string1 < string4
      cout << "string1 < string4\n";

   // comparing string1 and string2
   int result = string1.compare( string2 );

   if ( result == 0 )
      cout << "string1.compare( string2 ) == 0\n";
   else if ( result > 0 )
      cout << "string1.compare( string2 ) > 0\n";
   else // result < 0
      cout << "string1.compare( string2 ) < 0\n";

   // comparing string1 (elements 2-5) and string3 (elements 0-5)
   result = string1.compare( 2, 5, string3, 0, 5 );

   if ( result == 0 )
      cout << "string1.compare( 2, 5, string3, 0, 5 ) == 0\n";
   else if ( result > 0 )
      cout << "string1.compare( 2, 5, string3, 0, 5 ) > 0\n";
   else // result < 0
      cout << "string1.compare( 2, 5, string3, 0, 5 ) < 0\n";

   // comparing string2 and string4
   result = string4.compare( 0, string2.size(), string2 );

   if ( result == 0 )
      cout << "string4.compare( 0, string2.size(), "
         << "string2 ) == 0" << endl;
   else if ( result > 0 )
      cout << "string4.compare( 0, string2.size(), "
         << "string2 ) > 0" << endl;
   else // result < 0
      cout << "string4.compare( 0, string2.size(), "
           << "string2 ) < 0" << endl;

   // comparing string2 and string4
   result = string2.compare( 0, 3, string4 );

   if ( result == 0 )
      cout << "string2.compare( 0, 3, string4 ) == 0" << endl;
```

Fig. 19.2 | Comparing strings. (Part 2 of 3.)

```
63      else if ( result > 0 )
64         cout << "string2.compare( 0, 3, string4 ) > 0" << endl;
65      else // result < 0
66         cout << "string2.compare( 0, 3, string4 ) < 0" << endl;
67   } // end main
```

```
string1: Testing the comparison functions.
string2: Hello
string3: stinger
string4: Hello

string1 > string4
string1.compare( string2 ) > 0
string1.compare( 2, 5, string3, 0, 5 ) == 0
string4.compare( 0, string2.size(), string2 ) == 0
string2.compare( 0, 3, string4 ) < 0
```

Fig. 19.2 | Comparing `strings`. (Part 3 of 3.)

The program declares four `strings` (lines 9–12) and outputs each (lines 14–15). Line 18 tests `string1` against `string4` for equality using the *overloaded equality operator*. If the condition is `true`, `"string1 == string4"` is output. If the condition is `false`, the condition in line 20 is tested. All the `string` class overloaded relational and equality operator functions return `bool` values.

Line 26 uses `string` member function **`compare`** to compare `string1` to `string2`. Variable `result` is assigned `0` if the `strings` are equivalent, a *positive number* if `string1` is **lexicographically** greater than `string2` or a *negative number* if `string1` is *lexicographically* less than `string2`. When we say that a `string` is *lexicographically* less than another, we mean that the `compare` method uses the numerical values of the characters (see Appendix B, ASCII Character Set) in each `string` to determine that the first `string` is less than the second. Because a `string` starting with `'T'` is considered lexicographically greater than a string starting with `'H'`, `result` is assigned a value greater than `0`, as confirmed by the output. A lexicon is a dictionary.

Line 36 compares portions of `string1` and `string3` using an *overloaded* version of member function `compare`. The first two arguments (`2` and `5`) specify the *starting subscript* and *length* of the portion of `string1` (`"sting"`) to compare with `string3`. The third argument is the comparison `string`. The last two arguments (`0` and `5`) are the *starting subscript* and *length* of the portion of the comparison `string` being compared (also `"sting"`). The value assigned to `result` is `0` for equality, a positive number if `string1` is *lexicographically* greater than `string3` or a negative number if `string1` is *lexicographically* less than `string3`. The two pieces being compared here are identical, so `result` is assigned `0`.

Line 46 uses another *overloaded* version of function `compare` to compare `string4` and `string2`. The first two arguments are the same—the *starting subscript* and *length*. The last argument is the comparison `string`. The value returned is also the same—`0` for equality, a positive number if `string4` is *lexicographically* greater than `string2` or a negative number if `string4` is *lexicographically* less than `string2`. Because the two pieces of `strings` being compared here are identical, `result` is assigned `0`.

Line 59 calls member function `compare` to compare the first `3` characters in `string2` to `string4`. Because `"Hel"` is less than `"Hello"`, a value less than zero is returned.

19.4 Substrings

Class string provides member function **substr** for retrieving a substring from a string. The result is a new string object that's copied from the source string. Figure 19.3 demonstrates substr. The program declares and initializes a string at line 9. Line 13 uses member function substr to retrieve a substring from string1. The first argument specifies the *beginning subscript* of the desired substring; the second argument specifies the substring's *length*.

```
1  // Fig. 19.3: Fig19_03.cpp
2  // Demonstrating string member function substr.
3  #include <iostream>
4  #include <string>
5  using namespace std;
6
7  int main()
8  {
9     string string1( "The airplane landed on time." );
10
11    // retrieve substring "plane" which
12    // begins at subscript 7 and consists of 5 characters
13    cout << string1.substr( 7, 5 ) << endl;
14 } // end main
```

```
plane
```

Fig. 19.3 | Demonstrating string member function substr.

19.5 Swapping strings

Class string provides member function **swap** for swapping strings. Figure 19.4 swaps two strings. Lines 9–10 declare and initialize strings first and second. Each string is then output. Line 15 uses string member function swap to swap the values of first and second. The two strings are printed again to confirm that they were indeed swapped. The string member function swap is useful for implementing programs that sort strings.

```
1  // Fig. 19.4: Fig19_04.cpp
2  // Using the swap function to swap two strings.
3  #include <iostream>
4  #include <string>
5  using namespace std;
6
7  int main()
8  {
9     string first( "one" );
10    string second( "two" );
11
12    // output strings
13    cout << "Before swap:\n first: " << first << "\nsecond: " << second;
```

Fig. 19.4 | Using the swap function to swap two strings. (Part 1 of 2.)

```
   
   first.swap( second ); // swap strings

   cout << "\n\nAfter swap:\n first: " << first
      << "\nsecond: " << second << endl;
} // end main
```

```
Before swap:
 first: one
second: two

After swap:
 first: two
second: one
```

Fig. 19.4 | Using the swap function to swap two `string`s. (Part 2 of 2.)

19.6 `string` Characteristics

Class `string` provides member functions for gathering information about a `string`'s *size*, *length*, *capacity*, *maximum length* and other characteristics. A `string`'s *size* or *length* is the number of characters currently stored in the `string`. A `string`'s **capacity** is the number of characters that can be stored in the `string` without allocating more memory. The capacity of a `string` must be at least equal to the current size of the `string`, though it can be greater. The exact capacity of a `string` depends on the implementation. The **maximum size** is the largest possible size a `string` can have. If this value is exceeded, a `length_error` exception is thrown. Figure 19.5 demonstrates `string` class member functions for determining various characteristics of `string`s.

```
// Fig. 19.5: Fig19_05.cpp
// Printing string characteristics.
#include <iostream>
#include <string>
using namespace std;

void printStatistics( const string & );

int main()
{
   string string1; // empty string

   cout << "Statistics before input:\n" << boolalpha;
   printStatistics( string1 );

   // read in only "tomato" from "tomato soup"
   cout << "\n\nEnter a string: ";
   cin >> string1; // delimited by whitespace
   cout << "The string entered was: " << string1;

```

Fig. 19.5 | Printing `string` characteristics. (Part 1 of 3.)

```
   cout << "\nStatistics after input:\n";
   printStatistics( string1 );

   // read in "soup"
   cin >> string1; // delimited by whitespace
   cout << "\n\nThe remaining string is: " << string1 << endl;
   printStatistics( string1 );

   // append 46 characters to string1
   string1 += "1234567890abcdefghijklmnopqrstuvwxyz1234567890";
   cout << "\n\nstring1 is now: " << string1 << endl;
   printStatistics( string1 );

   // add 10 elements to string1
   string1.resize( string1.size() + 10 );
   cout << "\n\nStats after resizing by (length + 10):\n";
   printStatistics( string1 );
   cout << endl;
} // end main

// display string statistics
void printStatistics( const string &stringRef )
{
   cout << "capacity: " << stringRef.capacity() << "\nmax size: "
      << stringRef.max_size() << "\nsize: " << stringRef.size()
      << "\nlength: " << stringRef.size()
      << "\nempty: " << stringRef.empty();
} // end printStatistics
```

```
Statistics before input:
capacity: 15
max size: 4294967294
size: 0
length: 0
empty: true

Enter a string: tomato soup
The string entered was: tomato
Statistics after input:
capacity: 15
max size: 4294967294
size: 6
length: 6
empty: false

The remaining string is: soup
capacity: 15
max size: 4294967294
size: 4
length: 4
empty: false

string1 is now: soup1234567890abcdefghijklmnopqrstuvwxyz1234567890
capacity: 63
max size: 4294967294
```

Fig. 19.5 | Printing string characteristics. (Part 2 of 3.)

```
size: 50
length: 50
empty: false

Stats after resizing by (length + 10):
capacity: 63
max size: 4294967294
size: 60
length: 60
empty: false
```

Fig. 19.5 | Printing `string` characteristics. (Part 3 of 3.)

The program declares empty `string` `string1` (line 11) and passes it to function `printStatistics` (line 14). Function `printStatistics` (lines 42–48) takes a reference to a `const string` as an argument and outputs the capacity (using member function **`capacity`**), maximum size (using member function **`max_size`**), size (using member function `size`), length (using member function `size`) and whether the `string` is empty (using member function `empty`). The initial call to `printStatistics` indicates that the initial values for the size and length of `string1` are `0`.

The size and length of `0` indicate that there are no characters stored in `string`. Recall that the *size* and *length* are always identical. In this implementation, the maximum size is 4,294,967,294. Object `string1` is an empty `string`, so function `empty` returns `true`.

Line 18 inputs a string. In this example, `"tomato soup"` is input. Because a space character is a delimiter, only `"tomato"` is stored in `string1`; however, `"soup"` remains in the input buffer. Line 22 calls function `printStatistics` to output statistics for `string1`. Notice in the output that the length is `6` and the capacity is `15`.

Line 25 reads `"soup"` from the input buffer and stores it in `string1`, thereby replacing `"tomato"`. Line 27 passes `string1` to `printStatistics`.

Line 30 uses the *overloaded* += operator to concatenate a 46-character-long string to `string1`. Line 32 passes `string1` to `printStatistics`. The capacity has increased to `63` elements and the length is now `50`.

Line 35 uses member function **`resize`** to increase the length of `string1` by `10` characters. The additional elements are set to null characters. The output shows that the capacity has *not* changed and the length is now `60`.

19.7 Finding Substrings and Characters in a `string`

Class `string` provides `const` member functions for finding substrings and characters in a `string`. Figure 19.6 demonstrates the `find` functions.

```
// Fig. 19.6: Fig19_06.cpp
// Demonstrating the string find member functions.
#include <iostream>
#include <string>
```

Fig. 19.6 | Demonstrating the `string` `find` member functions. (Part 1 of 2.)

```
using namespace std;

int main()
{
   string string1( "noon is 12 pm; midnight is not." );
   int location;

   // find "is" at location 5 and 24
   cout << "Original string:\n" << string1
      << "\n\n(find) \"is\" was found at: " << string1.find( "is" )
      << "\n(rfind) \"is\" was found at: " << string1.rfind( "is" );

   // find 'o' at location 1
   location = string1.find_first_of( "misop" );
   cout << "\n\n(find_first_of) found '" << string1[ location ]
      << "' from the group \"misop\" at: " << location;

   // find 'o' at location 28
   location = string1.find_last_of( "misop" );
   cout << "\n\n(find_last_of) found '" << string1[ location ]
      << "' from the group \"misop\" at: " << location;

   // find '1' at location 8
   location = string1.find_first_not_of( "noi spm" );
   cout << "\n\n(find_first_not_of) '" << string1[ location ]
      << "' is not contained in \"noi spm\" and was found at: "
      << location;

   // find '.' at location 13
   location = string1.find_first_not_of( "12noi spm" );
   cout << "\n\n(find_first_not_of) '" << string1[ location ]
      << "' is not contained in \"12noi spm\" and was "
      << "found at: " << location << endl;

   // search for characters not in string1
   location = string1.find_first_not_of(
      "noon is 12 pm; midnight is not." );
   cout << "\nfind_first_not_of(\"noon is 12 pm; midnight is not.\")"
      << " returned: " << location << endl;
} // end main
```

```
Original string:
noon is 12 pm; midnight is not.

(find) "is" was found at: 5
(rfind) "is" was found at: 24

(find_first_of) found 'o' from the group "misop" at: 1

(find_last_of) found 'o' from the group "misop" at: 28

(find_first_not_of) '1' is not contained in "noi spm" and was found at: 8

(find_first_not_of) '.' is not contained in "12noi spm" and was found at: 13

find_first_not_of("noon is 12 pm; midnight is not.") returned: -1
```

Fig. 19.6 | Demonstrating the string find member functions. (Part 2 of 2.)

String string1 is declared and initialized in line 9. Line 14 attempts to find "is" in string1 using function **find**. If "is" is found, the subscript of the starting location of that string is returned. If the string is not found, the value **string::npos** (a public static constant defined in class string) is returned. This value is returned by the string find-related functions to indicate that a substring or character was not found in the string.

Line 15 uses member function **rfind** to search string1 *backward* (i.e., *right-to-left*). If "is" is found, the subscript location is returned. If the string is not found, string::npos is returned. [*Note:* The rest of the find functions presented in this section return the same type unless otherwise noted.]

Line 18 uses member function **find_first_of** to locate the *first* occurrence in string1 of any character in "misop". The searching is done from the beginning of string1. The character 'o' is found in element 1.

Line 23 uses member function **find_last_of** to find the *last* occurrence in string1 of any character in "misop". The searching is done from the end of string1. The character 'o' is found in element 28.

Line 28 uses member function **find_first_not_of** to find the *first* character in string1 *not* contained in "noi spm". The character '1' is found in element 8. Searching is done from the beginning of string1.

Line 34 uses member function find_first_not_of to find the *first* character *not* contained in "12noi spm". The character '.' is found in element 13. Searching is done from the beginning of string1.

Lines 40–41 use member function find_first_not_of to find the *first* character *not* contained in "noon is 12 pm; midnight is not.". In this case, the string being searched contains every character specified in the string argument. Because a character was not found, string::npos (which has the value -1 in this case) is returned.

19.8 Replacing Characters in a string

Figure 19.7 demonstrates string member functions for *replacing* and *erasing* characters. Lines 10–14 declare and initialize string string1. Line 20 uses string member function **erase** to erase everything from (and including) the character in position 62 to the end of string1. [*Note:* Each newline character occupies one character in the string.]

```
1  // Fig. 19.7: Fig19_07.cpp
2  // Demonstrating string member functions erase and replace.
3  #include <iostream>
4  #include <string>
5  using namespace std;
6
7  int main()
8  {
9     // compiler concatenates all parts into one string
10    string string1( "The values in any left subtree"
11       "\nare less than the value in the"
12       "\nparent node and the values in"
13       "\nany right subtree are greater"
14       "\nthan the value in the parent node" );
```

Fig. 19.7 | Demonstrating string member functions erase and replace. (Part 1 of 2.)

```

   cout << "Original string:\n" << string1 << endl << endl;

   // remove all characters from (and including) location 62
   // through the end of string1
   string1.erase( 62 );

   // output new string
   cout << "Original string after erase:\n" << string1
      << "\nAfter first replacement:\n";

   size_t position = string1.find( " " ); // find first space

   // replace all spaces with period
   while ( position != string::npos )
   {
      string1.replace( position, 1, "." );
      position = string1.find( " ", position + 1 );
   } // end while

   cout << string1 << "\nAfter second replacement:\n";

   position = string1.find( "." ); // find first period

   // replace all periods with two semicolons
   // NOTE: this will overwrite characters
   while ( position != string::npos )
   {
      string1.replace( position, 2, "xxxxx;;yyy", 5, 2 );
      position = string1.find( ".", position + 1 );
   } // end while

   cout << string1 << endl;
} // end main
```

```
Original string:
The values in any left subtree
are less than the value in the
parent node and the values in
any right subtree are greater
than the value in the parent node

Original string after erase:
The values in any left subtree
are less than the value in the

After first replacement:
The.values.in.any.left.subtree
are.less.than.the.value.in.the

After second replacement:
The;;alues;;n;;ny;;eft;;ubtree
are;;ess;;han;;he;;alue;;n;;he
```

Fig. 19.7 | Demonstrating string member functions erase and replace. (Part 2 of 2.)

Lines 26–33 use find to locate each occurrence of the space character. Each space is then *replaced* with a period by a call to string member function **replace**. Function replace takes three arguments: the *subscript* of the character in the string at which replacement should *begin*, the *number of characters to replace* and the *replacement string*. Member function find returns string::npos when the search character is *not found*. In line 32, 1 is added to position to continue searching at the location of the *next* character.

Lines 37–45 use function find to find every period and another overloaded function replace to replace every period and its following character with two semicolons. The arguments passed to this version of replace are the subscript of the element where the replace operation begins, the number of characters to replace, a replacement character string from which a *substring* is selected to use as replacement characters, the element in the character string where the replacement substring begins and the number of characters in the replacement character string to use.

19.9 Inserting Characters into a string

Class string provides member functions for *inserting* characters into a string. Figure 19.8 demonstrates the string insert capabilities.

The program declares, initializes then outputs strings string1, string2, string3 and string4. Line 19 uses string member function **insert** to insert string2's content before element 10 of string1.

Line 22 uses insert to insert string4 before string3's element 3. The last two arguments specify the *starting* and *last* element of string4 that should be inserted. Using string::npos causes the *entire* string to be inserted.

```
1  // Fig. 19.8: Fig19_08.cpp
2  // Demonstrating class string insert member functions.
3  #include <iostream>
4  #include <string>
5  using namespace std;
6
7  int main()
8  {
9     string string1( "beginning end" );
10    string string2( "middle " );
11    string string3( "12345678" );
12    string string4( "xx" );
13
14    cout << "Initial strings:\nstring1: " << string1
15       << "\nstring2: " << string2 << "\nstring3: " << string3
16       << "\nstring4: " << string4 << "\n\n";
17
18    // insert "middle" at location 10 in string1
19    string1.insert( 10, string2 );
20
21    // insert "xx" at location 3 in string3
22    string3.insert( 3, string4, 0, string::npos );
23
```

Fig. 19.8 | Demonstrating class string insert member functions. (Part 1 of 2.)

```
   cout << "Strings after insert:\nstring1: " << string1
      << "\nstring2: " << string2 << "\nstring3: " << string3
      << "\nstring4: " << string4 << endl;
} // end main
```

```
Initial strings:
string1: beginning end
string2: middle
string3: 12345678
string4: xx

Strings after insert:
string1: beginning middle end
string2: middle
string3: 123xx45678
string4: xx
```

Fig. 19.8 | Demonstrating class `string` `insert` member functions. (Part 2 of 2.)

19.10 Conversion to Pointer-Based char * Strings

You can convert `string` class objects to pointer-based strings. As mentioned earlier, unlike pointer-based strings, `string`s are *not necessarily null terminated.* These conversion functions are useful when a given function takes a pointer-based string as an argument. Figure 19.9 demonstrates conversion of `string`s to pointer-based strings.

```
// Fig. 19.9: Fig19_09.cpp
// Converting strings to pointer-based strings and character arrays.
#include <iostream>
#include <string>
using namespace std;

int main()
{
   string string1( "STRINGS" ); // string constructor with char * arg
   const char *ptr1 = nullptr; // initialize *ptr1
   size_t length = string1.size();
   char *ptr2 = new char[ length + 1 ]; // including null

   // copy characters from string1 into allocated memory
   string1.copy( ptr2, length, 0 ); // copy string1 to ptr2 char *
   ptr2[ length ] = '\0'; // add null terminator

   cout << "string string1 is " << string1
      << "\nstring1 converted to a pointer-based string is "
      << string1.c_str() << "\nptr1 is ";

   // Assign to pointer ptr1 the const char * returned by
   // function data(). NOTE: this is a potentially dangerous
```

Fig. 19.9 | Converting `string`s to pointer-based strings and character arrays. (Part 1 of 2.)

```
24       // assignment. If string1 is modified, pointer ptr1 can
25       // become invalid.
26       ptr1 = string1.data(); // non-null terminated char array
27
28       // output each character using pointer
29       for ( size_t i = 0; i < length; ++i )
30          cout << *( ptr1 + i ); // use pointer arithmetic
31
32       cout << "\nptr2 is " << ptr2 << endl;
33       delete [] ptr2; // reclaim dynamically allocated memory
34    } // end main
```

```
string string1 is STRINGS
string1 converted to a pointer-based string is STRINGS
ptr1 is STRINGS
ptr2 is STRINGS
```

Fig. 19.9 | Converting `strings` to pointer-based strings and character arrays. (Part 2 of 2.)

The program declares a `string`, a `size_t` and two `char` pointers (lines 9–12). The `string string1` is initialized to `"STRINGS"`, `ptr1` is initialized to `nullptr` and `length` is initialized to the length of `string1`. Memory of sufficient size to hold a pointer-based string equivalent of `string string1` is allocated dynamically and attached to `char` pointer `ptr2`.

Line 15 uses `string` member function **copy** to copy object `string1` into the `char` array pointed to by `ptr2`. Line 16 places a terminating null character in the array pointed to by `ptr2`.

Line 20 uses function **`c_str`** to obtain a `const char *` that points to a null terminated pointer-based string with the same content as `string1`. The pointer is passed to the stream insertion operator for output.

Line 26 assigns the `const char * ptr1` a pointer returned by class `string` member function **data**. This member function returns a *non-null-terminated* built-in character array. We do *not* modify `string string1` in this example. If `string1` were to be modified (e.g., the `string`'s dynamic memory changes its address due to a member function call such as `string1.insert( 0, "abcd" );`), `ptr1` could become invalid—which could lead to unpredictable results.

Lines 29–30 use pointer arithmetic to output the character array pointed to by `ptr1`. In lines 32–33, the pointer-based string `ptr2` is output and the memory allocated for `ptr2` is `delete`d to avoid a memory leak.

Common Programming Error 19.2

Not terminating the character array returned by `data` *with a null character can lead to execution-time errors.*

19.11 Iterators

Class `string` provides *iterators* (introduced in Chapter 15) for forward and backward *traversal* of `strings`. Iterators provide access to individual characters with a syntax that's similar to pointer operations. *Iterators are not range checked.* Figure 19.10 demonstrates iterators.

```
1  // Fig. 19.10: Fig19_10.cpp
2  // Using an iterator to output a string.
3  #include <iostream>
4  #include <string>
5  using namespace std;
6
7  int main()
8  {
9     string string1( "Testing iterators" );
10    string::const_iterator iterator1 = string1.begin();
11
12    cout << "string1 = " << string1
13       << "\n(Using iterator iterator1) string1 is: ";
14
15    // iterate through string
16    while ( iterator1 != string1.end() )
17    {
18       cout << *iterator1; // dereference iterator to get char
19       ++iterator1; // advance iterator to next char
20    } // end while
21
22    cout << endl;
23 } // end main
```

```
string1 = Testing iterators
(Using iterator iterator1) string1 is: Testing iterators
```

Fig. 19.10 | Using an iterator to output a string.

Lines 9–10 declare string string1 and **string::const_iterator** iterator1. Recall that a const_iterator *cannot* be used to modify the data that you're iterating through—in this case the string. Iterator iterator1 is initialized to the beginning of string1 with the string class member function **begin**. Two versions of begin exist—one that returns an iterator for iterating through a non-const string and a const version that returns a const_iterator for iterating through a const string. Line 12 outputs string1.

Lines 16–20 use iterator iterator1 to "walk through" string1. Class string member function **end** returns an iterator (or a const_iterator) for the position past the last element of string1. Each element is printed by *dereferencing the iterator* much as you'd dereference a pointer, and the iterator is advanced one position using operator ++. In C++11, lines 10 and 16–20 can be replaced with a range-based for, as in

```
for ( char c : string1 )
   cout << c;
```

Class string provides member functions **rend** and **rbegin** for accessing individual string characters in reverse from the end of a string toward the beginning. Member functions rend and rbegin return **reverse_iterators** or **const_reverse_iterators** (based on whether the string is non-const or const).

Good Programming Practice 19.1

When the operations involving the iterator should not modify the data being processed, use a `const_iterator`. This is another example of employing the principle of least privilege.

19.12 String Stream Processing

In addition to standard stream I/O and file stream I/O, C++ stream I/O includes capabilities for inputting from, and outputting to, `string`s in memory. These capabilities often are referred to as **in-memory I/O** or **string stream processing.**

Input from a `string` is supported by class **`istringstream`**. Output to a `string` is supported by class **`ostringstream`**. The class names `istringstream` and `ostringstream` are actually *aliases* defined by the `typedef`s

```
typedef basic_istringstream< char > istringstream;
typedef basic_ostringstream< char > ostringstream;
```

Class templates `basic_istringstream` and `basic_ostringstream` provide the same functionality as classes `istream` and `ostream` plus other member functions specific to *in-memory formatting*. Programs that use in-memory formatting must include the **`<sstream>`** and `<iostream>` headers.

Error-Prevention Tip 19.1

One application of these techniques is data validation. *A program can read an entire line at a time from the input stream into a `string`. Next, a validation routine can scrutinize the contents of the `string` and correct (or repair) the data, if necessary. Then the program can proceed to input from the `string`, knowing that the input data is in the proper format.*

Error-Prevention Tip 19.2

To assist with data validation, C++11 provides powerful regular-expression *capabilities. For example, if a program requires a user to enter a U.S. format telephone number (e.g., `(800) 555-1212`), you can use a regular-expression pattern to confirm that the user's input matches the expected format. Many websites provide regular expressions for validating email addresses, URLs, phone numbers, addresses and other popular kinds of data. We introduce regular expressions and provide several examples in Chapter 24.*

Software Engineering Observation 19.1

Outputting to a `string` is a nice way to take advantage of the powerful output formatting capabilities of C++ streams. Data can be prepared in a `string` to mimic the edited screen format. That `string` could be written to a disk file to preserve the screen image.

An `ostringstream` object uses a `string` object to store the output data. The **`str`** member function of class `ostringstream` returns a copy of that `string`.

Demonstrating `ostringstream`

Figure 19.11 demonstrates an `ostringstream` object. The program creates `ostringstream` object `outputString` (line 10) and uses the stream insertion operator to output a series of `string`s and numerical values to the object.

```
1  // Fig. 19.11: Fig19_11.cpp
2  // Using an ostringstream object.
3  #include <iostream>
4  #include <string>
5  #include <sstream> // header for string stream processing
6  using namespace std;
7
8  int main()
9  {
10    ostringstream outputString; // create ostringstream instance
11
12    string string1( "Output of several data types " );
13    string string2( "to an ostringstream object:" );
14    string string3( "\n        double: " );
15    string string4( "\n           int: " );
16    string string5( "\naddress of int: " );
17
18    double double1 = 123.4567;
19    int integer = 22;
20
21    // output strings, double and int to ostringstream outputString
22    outputString << string1 << string2 << string3 << double1
23       << string4 << integer << string5 << &integer;
24
25    // call str to obtain string contents of the ostringstream
26    cout << "outputString contains:\n" << outputString.str();
27
28    // add additional characters and call str to output string
29    outputString << "\nmore characters added";
30    cout << "\n\nafter additional stream insertions,\n"
31       << "outputString contains:\n" << outputString.str() << endl;
32  } // end main
```

```
outputString contains:
Output of several data types to an ostringstream object:
        double: 123.457
           int: 22
address of int: 0012F540

after additional stream insertions,
outputString contains:
Output of several data types to an ostringstream object:
        double: 123.457
           int: 22
address of int: 0012F540
more characters added
```

Fig. 19.11 | Using an ostringstream object.

Lines 22–23 output string string1, string string2, string string3, double double1, string string4, int integer, string string5 and the address of int integer—all to outputString in memory. Line 26 uses the stream insertion operator and the call outputString.str() to display a copy of the string created in lines 22–23. Line 29 demonstrates that more data can be *appended* to the string in memory by simply issuing another stream insertion operation to `outputString`. Lines 30–31 display `string` `outputString` after appending additional characters.

An `istringstream` object inputs data from a `string` in memory to program variables. Data is stored in an `istringstream` object as characters. Input from the `istringstream` object works identically to input from any file. The end of the `string` is interpreted by the `istringstream` object as *end-of-file*.

Demonstrating `istringstream`

Figure 19.12 demonstrates input from an `istringstream` object. Lines 10–11 create `string` `input` containing the data and `istringstream` object `inputString` constructed to contain the data in `string` `input`. The `string` `input` contains the data

```
Input test 123 4.7 A
```

which, when read as input to the program, consist of two strings (`"Input"` and `"test"`), an `int` (`123`), a `double` (`4.7`) and a `char` (`'A'`). These characters are extracted to variables `string1`, `string2`, `integer`, `double1` and `character` in line 18.

```
1  // Fig. 19.12: Fig19_12.cpp
2  // Demonstrating input from an istringstream object.
3  #include <iostream>
4  #include <string>
5  #include <sstream>
6  using namespace std;
7
8  int main()
9  {
10    string input( "Input test 123 4.7 A" );
11    istringstream inputString( input );
12    string string1;
13    string string2;
14    int integer;
15    double double1;
16    char character;
17
18    inputString >> string1 >> string2 >> integer >> double1 >> character;
19
20    cout << "The following items were extracted\n"
21       << "from the istringstream object:" << "\nstring: " << string1
22       << "\nstring: " << string2 << "\n   int: " << integer
23       << "\ndouble: " << double1 << "\n  char: " << character;
24
25    // attempt to read from empty stream
26    long value;
27    inputString >> value;
28
29    // test stream results
30    if ( inputString.good() )
31       cout << "\n\nlong value is: " << value << endl;
32    else
33       cout << "\n\ninputString is empty" << endl;
34 } // end main
```

Fig. 19.12 | Demonstrating input from an `istringstream` object. (Part 1 of 2.)

```
The following items were extracted
from the istringstream object:
string: Input
string: test
   int: 123
double: 4.7
  char: A

inputString is empty
```

Fig. 19.12 | Demonstrating input from an `istringstream` object. (Part 2 of 2.)

The data is then output in lines 20–23. The program attempts to read from `inputString` again in line 27. The `if` condition in line 30 uses function `good` (Section 13.8) to test if any data remains. Because no data remains, the function returns `false` and the `else` part of the `if...else` statement is executed.

19.13 C++11 Numeric Conversion Functions

C++11 now contains functions for converting from numeric values to `string`s and from `string`s to numeric values. Though you could previously perform such conversions using other techniques, the functions presented in this section were added for convenience.

Converting Numeric Values to `string` *Objects*

C++11's **`to_string`** function (from the `<string>` header) returns the `string` representation of its numeric argument. The function is overloaded for types `int`, `unsigned int`, `long`, `unsigned long`, `long long`, `unsigned long long`, `float`, `double` and `long double`.

Converting `string` *Objects to Numeric Values*

C++11 provides eight functions (Fig. 19.13; from the `<string>` header) for converting `string` objects to numeric values. Each function attempts to convert the *beginning* of its `string` argument to a numeric value. If no conversion can be performed, each function throws an `invalid_argument` exception. If the result of the conversion is out of range for the function's return type, each function throws an `out_of_range` exception.

Function	Return type	Function	Return type
Functions that convert to integral types		*Functions that convert to floating-point types*	
`stoi`	`int`	`stof`	`float`
`stol`	`long`	`stod`	`double`
`stoul`	`unsigned long`	`stold`	`long double`
`stoll`	`long long`		
`stoull`	`unsigned long long`		

Fig. 19.13 | C++11 functions that convert from `string`s to numeric types.

Functions That Convert `string`*s to Integral Types*

Consider an example of converting a `string` to an integral value. Assuming the `string`:

```
string s( "100hello" );
```

the following statement converts the beginning of the string to the `int` value `100` and stores that value in `convertedInt`:

```
int convertedInt = stoi( s );
```

Each function that converts a `string` to an integral type actually receives *three* parameters—the last two have default arguments. The parameters are:

- A `string` containing the characters to convert.
- A pointer to a `size_t` variable. The function uses this pointer to store the index of the first character that was *not* converted. The default argument is a null pointer, in which case the function does *not* store the index.
- An `int` from 2 to 36 representing the number's base—the default is base 10.

So, the preceding statement is equivalent to

```
int convertedInt = stoi( s, nullptr, 10 );
```

Given a `size_t` variable named `index`, the statement:

```
int convertedInt = stoi( s, &index, 2 );
```

converts the binary number `"100"` (base 2) to an `int` (100 in binary is the `int` value 4) and stores in `index` the location of the string's letter `"h"` (the first character that was not converted).

Functions That Convert `string`*s to Floating-Point Types*

The functions that convert `string`s to floating-point types each receive two parameters:

- A `string` containing the characters to convert.
- A pointer to a `size_t` variable where the function stores the index of the first character that was *not* converted. The default argument is a null pointer, in which case the function does *not* store the index.

Consider an example of converting a `string` to an floating-point value. Assuming the `string`:

```
string s( "123.45hello" );
```

the following statement converts the beginning of the `string` to the `double` value `123.45` and stores that value in `convertedDouble`:

```
double convertedDouble = stod( s );
```

Again, the second argument is a null pointer by default.

19.14 Wrap-Up

This chapter discussed the details of C++ Standard Library class `string`. We discussed assigning, concatenating, comparing, searching and swapping strings. We also introduced a number of methods to determine string characteristics, to find, replace and insert characters in a string, and to convert strings to pointer-based strings and vice versa. You learned about string iterators and performing input from and output to strings in memory. Finally, we introduced C++11's new functions for converting numeric values to strings and for converting strings to numeric values. In the next chapter, we introduce structs, which are similar to classes, and discuss the manipulation of bits, characters and C strings.

20

Bits, Characters, C Strings and `structs`

Objectives

In this chapter you'll:

- Create and use `structs` and to understand their near equivalence with classes.
- Use `typedef` to create aliases for data types.
- Manipulate data with the bitwise operators and to create bit fields for storing data compactly.
- Use the functions of the character-handling library `<cctype>`.
- Use the string-conversion functions of the general-utilities library `<cstdlib>`.
- Use the string-processing functions of the string-handling library `<cstring>`.

Outline

20.1 Introduction

We now discuss structures, their near equivalence with classes, and the manipulation of bits, characters and C strings. Many of the techniques we present here are included for the benefit of those who will work with legacy C and C++ code.

Like classes, C++ structures may contain access specifiers, member functions, constructors and destructors. In fact, *the only differences between structures and classes in C++ is that structure members default to `public` access and class members default to `private` access when no access specifiers are used, and that structures default to `public` inheritance, whereas classes default to `private` inheritance.* Our presentation of structures here is typical of the legacy C code and early C++ code you'll see in industry.

We present a high-performance card shuffling and dealing simulation in which we use structure objects containing C++ `string` objects to represent the cards. We discuss the *bitwise operators* that allow you to access and manipulate the *individual bits* in bytes of data. We also present *bitfields*—special structures that can be used to specify the exact number of bits a variable occupies in memory. These bit-manipulation techniques are common in programs that interact directly with hardware devices that have limited memory. The chapter finishes with examples of many character and C string-manipulation functions—some of which are designed to process blocks of memory as arrays of bytes. The detailed C string treatment in this chapter is mostly for reasons of legacy code support and because there are still remnants of C string use in C++, such as command-line arguments (Appendix F). *New development should use C++ `string` objects rather than C strings.*

20.2 Structure Definitions

Consider the following structure definition:

```
struct Card
{
   string face;
   string suit;
}; // end struct Card
```

Keyword **`struct`** introduces the definition for structure `Card`. The identifier `Card` is the **structure name** and is used in C++ to declare variables of the **structure type** (in C, the type name of the preceding structure is `struct Card`). `Card`'s definition contains two `string` members—`face` and `suit`.

The following declarations

```
Card oneCard;
Card deck[ 52 ];
Card *cardPtr;
```

declare `oneCard` to be a structure variable of type `Card`, `deck` to be an array with 52 elements of type `Card` and `cardPtr` to be a pointer to a `Card` structure. Variables of a given structure type can also be declared by placing a comma-separated list of the variable names between the closing brace of the structure definition and the semicolon that ends the structure definition. For example, the preceding declarations could have been incorporated into the `Card` structure definition as follows:

```
struct Card
{
   string face;
   string suit;
} oneCard, deck[ 52 ], *cardPtr;
```

As with classes, structure members are *not* necessarily stored in *consecutive* bytes of memory. Sometimes there are "holes" in a structure, because some computers store specific data types only on certain memory boundaries for performance reasons, such as half-word, word or double-word boundaries. A word is a standard memory unit used to store data in a computer—usually two, four or eight bytes and typically eight bytes on today's popular 64-bit systems. Consider the following structure definition in which structure objects `sample1` and `sample2` of type `Example` are declared:

```
struct Example
{
   char c;
   int i;
} sample1, sample2;
```

A computer with two-byte words might require that each of the members of `Example` be aligned on a word boundary (i.e., at the beginning of a word—this is *machine dependent*). Figure 20.1 shows a sample storage alignment for an object of type `Example` that's been assigned the character `'a'` and the integer `97` (the bit representations of the values are shown). If the members are stored beginning at word boundaries, there is a one-byte hole (byte `1` in the figure) in the storage for objects of type `Example`. The value in the one-byte hole is *undefined*. If the values in `sample1` and `sample2` are in fact equal, the structure objects might *not* be equal, because the *undefined* one-byte holes are not likely to contain identical values.

Common Programming Error 20.1

Comparing variables of structure types is a compilation error.

Portability Tip 20.1

Because the size of data items of a particular type is machine dependent, and because storage alignment considerations are machine dependent, so too is the representation of a structure.

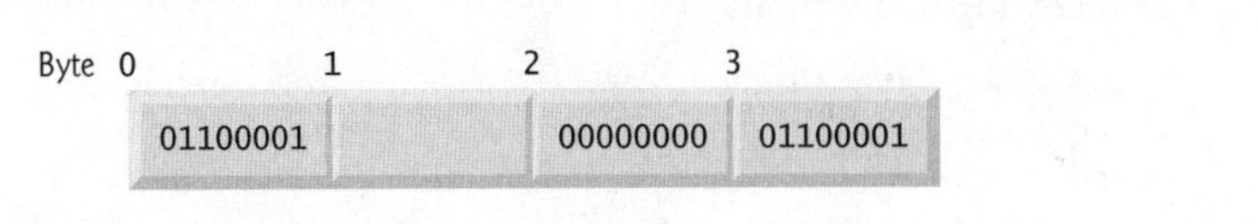

Fig. 20.1 | Possible storage alignment for an `Example` object, showing an undefined byte.

20.3 typedef

Keyword **`typedef`** provides a mechanism for creating *synonyms* (or *aliases*) for previously defined data types. Names for structure types are often defined with `typedef` to more readable type names. For example, the statement

```
typedef Card *CardPtr;
```

defines the new type name `CardPtr` as a synonym for type `Card *`.

Creating a new name with `typedef` does *not* create a new type; `typedef` simply creates a *new type name* that can then be used in the program as an alias for an existing type name.

20.4 Example: Card Shuffling and Dealing Simulation

The card shuffling and dealing program in Figs. 20.2–20.4 represents the deck of cards as an `array` of structures.

```
// Fig. 20.2: DeckOfCards.h
// Definition of class DeckOfCards that
// represents a deck of playing cards.
#include <string>
#include <array>

// Card structure definition
struct Card
{
   std::string face;
   std::string suit;
}; // end structure Card

// DeckOfCards class definition
class DeckOfCards
{
public:
   static const int numberOfCards = 52;
   static const int faces = 13;
   static const int suits = 4;

   DeckOfCards(); // constructor initializes deck
   void shuffle(); // shuffles cards in deck
   void deal() const; // deals cards in deck

```

Fig. 20.2 | Definition of class `DeckOfCards` that represents a deck of playing cards. (Part 1 of 2.)

```
private:
   std::array< Card, numberOfCards > deck; // represents deck of cards
}; // end class DeckOfCards
```

Fig. 20.2 | Definition of class `DeckOfCards` that represents a deck of playing cards. (Part 2 of 2.)

The constructor (lines 12–31 of Fig. 20.3) initializes the `array` in order with character strings representing Ace through King of each suit. Function `shuffle` implements the shuffling algorithm. The function loops through all 52 cards (subscripts 0 to 51). For each card, a number between 0 and 51 is picked randomly. Next, the current `Card` and the randomly selected `Card` are swapped in the `array`. A total of 52 swaps are made in a single pass of the entire `array`, and the `array` is shuffled. Because the `Card` structures were swapped in place in the `array`, the dealing algorithm implemented in function `deal` requires only one pass of the `array` to deal the shuffled cards.

```
1  // Fig. 20.3: DeckOfCards.cpp
2  // Member-function definitions for class DeckOfCards that simulates
3  // the shuffling and dealing of a deck of playing cards.
4  #include <iostream>
5  #include <iomanip>
6  #include <cstdlib> // prototypes for rand and srand
7  #include <ctime> // prototype for time
8  #include "DeckOfCards.h" // DeckOfCards class definition
9  using namespace std;
10
11 // no-argument DeckOfCards constructor intializes deck
12 DeckOfCards::DeckOfCards()
13 {
14    // initialize suit array
15    static string suit[ suits ] =
16       { "Hearts", "Diamonds", "Clubs", "Spades" };
17
18    // initialize face array
19    static string face[ faces ] =
20       { "Ace", "Deuce", "Three", "Four", "Five", "Six", "Seven",
21       "Eight", "Nine", "Ten", "Jack", "Queen", "King" };
22
23    // set values for deck of 52 Cards
24    for ( size_t i = 0; i < deck.size(); ++i )
25    {
26       deck[ i ].face = face[ i % faces ];
27       deck[ i ].suit = suit[ i / faces ];
28    } // end for
29
30    srand( static_cast< size_t >( time( nullptr ) ) ); // seed
31 } // end no-argument DeckOfCards constructor
32
33 // shuffle cards in deck
34 void DeckOfCards::shuffle()
35 {
```

Fig. 20.3 | Member-function definitions for class `DeckOfCards`. (Part 1 of 2.)

```
   // shuffle cards randomly
   for ( size_t i = 0; i < deck.size(); ++i )
   {
      int j = rand() % numberOfCards;
      Card temp = deck[ i ];
      deck[ i ] = deck[ j ];
      deck[ j ] = temp;
   } // end for
} // end function shuffle

// deal cards in deck
void DeckOfCards::deal() const
{
   // display each card's face and suit
   for ( size_t i = 0; i < deck.size(); ++i )
      cout << right << setw( 5 ) << deck[ i ].face << " of "
         << left << setw( 8 ) << deck[ i ].suit
         << ( ( i + 1 ) % 2 ? '\t' : '\n' );
} // end function deal
```

Fig. 20.3 | Member-function definitions for class DeckOfCards. (Part 2 of 2.)

```
// Fig. 20.4: fig20_04.cpp
// Card shuffling and dealing program.
#include "DeckOfCards.h" // DeckOfCards class definition

int main()
{
   DeckOfCards deckOfCards; // create DeckOfCards object
   deckOfCards.shuffle(); // shuffle the cards in the deck
   deckOfCards.deal(); // deal the cards in the deck
} // end main
```

```
 King of Clubs           Ten of Diamonds
 Five of Diamonds       Jack of Clubs
Seven of Spades         Five of Clubs
Three of Spades         King of Hearts
  Ten of Clubs         Eight of Spades
Eight of Hearts          Six of Hearts
 Nine of Diamonds       Nine of Clubs
Three of Diamonds      Queen of Hearts
  Six of Clubs         Seven of Hearts
Seven of Diamonds       Jack of Diamonds
 Jack of Spades         King of Diamonds
Deuce of Diamonds       Four of Clubs
Three of Clubs          Five of Hearts
Eight of Clubs           Ace of Hearts
Deuce of Spades          Ace of Clubs
  Ten of Spades        Eight of Diamonds
  Ten of Hearts          Six of Spades
Queen of Diamonds       Nine of Hearts
Seven of Clubs         Queen of Clubs
```

Fig. 20.4 | Card shuffling and dealing program. (Part 1 of 2.)

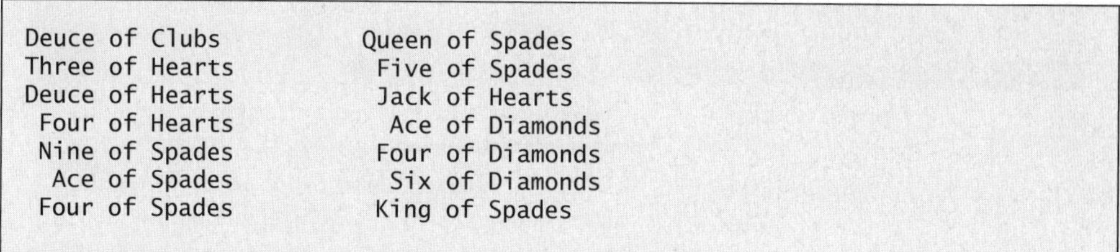

```
Deuce of Clubs          Queen of Spades
Three of Hearts          Five of Spades
Deuce of Hearts          Jack of Hearts
 Four of Hearts           Ace of Diamonds
 Nine of Spades          Four of Diamonds
  Ace of Spades           Six of Diamonds
 Four of Spades          King of Spades
```

Fig. 20.4 | Card shuffling and dealing program. (Part 2 of 2.)

20.5 Bitwise Operators

C++ provides extensive *bit-manipulation* capabilities for getting down to the so-called "bits-and-bytes" level. Operating systems, test-equipment software, networking software and many other kinds of software require that you communicate "directly with the hardware." We introduce each of the *bitwise operators*, and we discuss how to save memory by using *bit fields*.

All data is represented internally by computers as sequences of bits. Each bit can assume the value `0` or the value `1`. On most systems, a sequence of eight bits, each of which forms a byte—the standard storage unit for a variable of type `char`. Other data types are stored in larger numbers of bytes. Bitwise operators are used to manipulate the bits of integral operands (`char`, `short`, `int` and `long`; both `signed` and `unsigned`). Normally the bitwise operators are used with unsigned integers.

Portability Tip 20.2

Bitwise data manipulations are machine dependent.

The bitwise operator discussions in this section show the binary representations of the integer operands. For a detailed explanation of the binary (also called base-2) number system, see Appendix D. Because of the machine-dependent nature of bitwise manipulations, some of these programs might not work on your system without modification.

The bitwise operators are: **bitwise AND (`&`)**, **bitwise inclusive OR (`|`)**, **bitwise exclusive OR (`^`)**, **left shift (`<<`)**, **right shift (`>>`)** and **bitwise complement (`~`)**—also known as the **one's complement**. We've been using `&`, `<<` and `>>` for other purposes—this is a classic example of *operator overloading*. The *bitwise AND*, *bitwise inclusive OR* and *bitwise exclusive OR* operators compare their two operands bit by bit. The *bitwise AND* operator sets each bit in the result to 1 if the corresponding bit in *both* operands is 1. The *bitwise inclusive OR* operator sets each bit in the result to 1 if the corresponding bit in *either (or both)* operand(s) is 1. The *bitwise exclusive OR* operator sets each bit in the result to 1 if the corresponding bit in *either* operand—*but not both*—is 1. The *left-shift* operator shifts the bits of its left operand to the left by the number of bits specified in its right operand. The *right-shift* operator shifts the bits in its left operand to the right by the number of bits specified in its right operand. The *bitwise complement* operator sets all `0` bits in its operand to `1` in the result and sets all `1` bits in its operand to `0` in the result. Detailed discussions of each bitwise operator appear in the following examples. The bitwise operators are summarized in Fig. 20.5.

<table>
<tr><th>Operator</th><th>Name</th><th>Description</th></tr>
<tr><td>&</td><td>bitwise AND</td><td>The bits in the result are set to 1 if the corresponding bits in the two operands are both 1.</td></tr>
<tr><td>|</td><td>bitwise inclusive OR</td><td>The bits in the result are set to 1 if one or both of the corresponding bits in the two operands is 1.</td></tr>
<tr><td>^</td><td>bitwise exclusive OR</td><td>The bits in the result are set to 1 if exactly one of the corresponding bits in the two operands is 1.</td></tr>
<tr><td><<</td><td>left shift</td><td>Shifts the bits of the first operand left by the number of bits specified by the second operand; fill from right with 0 bits.</td></tr>
<tr><td>>></td><td>right shift with sign extension</td><td>Shifts the bits of the first operand right by the number of bits specified by the second operand; the method of filling from the left is machine dependent.</td></tr>
<tr><td>~</td><td>bitwise complement</td><td>All 0 bits are set to 1 and all 1 bits are set to 0.</td></tr>
</table>

Fig. 20.5 | Bitwise operators.

Printing a Binary Representation of an Integral Value

When using the bitwise operators, it's useful to illustrate their precise effects by printing values in their binary representation. The program of Fig. 20.6 prints an unsigned integer in its binary representation in groups of eight bits each.

```
// Fig. 20.6: fig20_06.cpp
// Printing an unsigned integer in bits.
#include <iostream>
#include <iomanip>
using namespace std;

void displayBits( unsigned ); // prototype

int main()
{
   unsigned inputValue = 0; // integral value to print in binary

   cout << "Enter an unsigned integer: ";
   cin >> inputValue;
   displayBits( inputValue );
} // end main

// display bits of an unsigned integer value
void displayBits( unsigned value )
{
   const int SHIFT = 8 * sizeof( unsigned ) - 1;
   const unsigned MASK = 1 << SHIFT;

   cout << setw( 10 ) << value << " = ";
```

Fig. 20.6 | Printing an unsigned integer in bits. (Part 1 of 2.)

```
25
26       // display bits
27       for ( unsigned i = 1; i <= SHIFT + 1; ++i )
28       {
29          cout << ( value & MASK ? '1' : '0' );
30          value <<= 1; // shift value left by 1
31
32          if ( i % 8 == 0 ) // output a space after 8 bits
33             cout << ' ';
34       } // end for
35
36       cout << endl;
37    } // end function displayBits
```

```
Enter an unsigned integer: 65000
     65000 = 00000000 00000000 11111101 11101000
```

```
Enter an unsigned integer: 29
        29 = 00000000 00000000 00000000 00011101
```

Fig. 20.6 | Printing an unsigned integer in bits. (Part 2 of 2.)

Function `displayBits` (lines 19–37) uses the *bitwise AND* operator to combine variable `value` with constant `MASK`. Often, the *bitwise AND* operator is used with an operand called a **mask**—an integer value with specific bits set to 1. Masks are used to *hide* some bits in a value while *selecting* other bits. In `displayBits`, line 22 assigns constant `MASK` the value `1 << SHIFT`. The value of constant `SHIFT` was calculated in line 21 with the expression

```
8 * sizeof( unsigned ) - 1
```

which multiplies the number of bytes an `unsigned` object requires in memory by 8 (the number of bits in a byte) to get the total number of bits required to store an `unsigned` object, then subtracts 1. The bit representation of `1 << SHIFT` on a computer that represents `unsigned` objects in four bytes of memory is

```
10000000 00000000 00000000 00000000
```

The *left-shift operator* shifts the value `1` from the low-order (rightmost) bit to the high-order (leftmost) bit in `MASK`, and fills in `0` bits from the right. Line 29 prints a `1` or a `0` for the current leftmost bit of variable `value`. Assume that variable `value` contains `65000` (`00000000 00000000 11111101 11101000`). When `value` and `MASK` are combined using `&`, all the bits except the high-order bit in variable `value` are "masked off" (hidden), because any bit "ANDed" with `0` yields `0`. If the leftmost bit is `1`, `value & MASK` evaluates to

```
00000000 00000000 11111101 11101000   (value)
10000000 00000000 00000000 00000000   (MASK)
-----------------------------------
00000000 00000000 00000000 00000000   (value & MASK)
```

which is interpreted as `false`, and `0` is printed. Then line 30 shifts variable `value` left by one bit with the expression `value <<= 1` (i.e., `value = value << 1`). These steps are repeated for each bit variable `value`. Eventually, a bit with a value of `1` is shifted into the leftmost bit position, and the bit manipulation is as follows:

```
11111101 11101000 00000000 00000000    (value)
10000000 00000000 00000000 00000000    (MASK)
-----------------------------------
10000000 00000000 00000000 00000000    (value & MASK)
```

Because both left bits are `1`s, the expression's result is nonzero (true) and `1` is printed. Figure 20.7 summarizes the results of combining two bits with the bitwise AND operator.

Bit 1	Bit 2	Bit 1 & Bit 2
0	0	0
1	0	0
0	1	0
1	1	1

Fig. 20.7 | Results of combining two bits with the bitwise AND operator (&).

Common Programming Error 20.2

Using the logical AND operator (&&) for the bitwise AND operator (&) and vice versa is a logic error.

The program of Fig. 20.8 demonstrates the *bitwise AND operator*, the *bitwise inclusive OR* operator, the *bitwise exclusive OR* operator and the *bitwise complement operator*. Function `displayBits` (lines 48–66) prints the `unsigned` integer values.

```
1  // Fig. 20.8: fig20_08.cpp
2  // Bitwise AND, inclusive OR,
3  // exclusive OR and complement operators.
4  #include <iostream>
5  #include <iomanip>
6  using namespace std;
7
8  void displayBits( unsigned ); // prototype
9
10 int main()
11 {
12    // demonstrate bitwise &
13    unsigned number1 = 2179876355;
14    unsigned mask = 1;
15    cout << "The result of combining the following\n";
16    displayBits( number1 );
17    displayBits( mask );
18    cout << "using the bitwise AND operator & is\n";
19    displayBits( number1 & mask );
```

Fig. 20.8 | Bitwise AND, inclusive OR, exclusive OR and complement operators. (Part 1 of 3.)

```

   // demonstrate bitwise |
   number1 = 15;
   unsigned setBits = 241;
   cout << "\nThe result of combining the following\n";
   displayBits( number1 );
   displayBits( setBits );
   cout << "using the bitwise inclusive OR operator | is\n";
   displayBits( number1 | setBits );

   // demonstrate bitwise exclusive OR
   number1 = 139;
   unsigned number2 = 199;
   cout << "\nThe result of combining the following\n";
   displayBits( number1 );
   displayBits( number2 );
   cout << "using the bitwise exclusive OR operator ^ is\n";
   displayBits( number1 ^ number2 );

   // demonstrate bitwise complement
   number1 = 21845;
   cout << "\nThe one's complement of\n";
   displayBits( number1 );
   cout << "is" << endl;
   displayBits( ~number1 );
} // end main

// display bits of an unsigned integer value
void displayBits( unsigned value )
{
   const int SHIFT = 8 * sizeof( unsigned ) - 1;
   const unsigned MASK = 1 << SHIFT;

   cout << setw( 10 ) << value << " = ";

   // display bits
   for ( unsigned i = 1; i <= SHIFT + 1; ++i )
   {
      cout << ( value & MASK ? '1' : '0' );
      value <<= 1; // shift value left by 1

      if ( i % 8 == 0 ) // output a space after 8 bits
         cout << ' ';
   } // end for

   cout << endl;
} // end function displayBits
```

```
The result of combining the following
2179876355 = 10000001 11101110 01000110 00000011
         1 = 00000000 00000000 00000000 00000001
using the bitwise AND operator & is
         1 = 00000000 00000000 00000000 00000001
```

Fig. 20.8 | Bitwise AND, inclusive OR, exclusive OR and complement operators. (Part 2 of 3.)

```
The result of combining the following
       15 = 00000000 00000000 00000000 00001111
      241 = 00000000 00000000 00000000 11110001
using the bitwise inclusive OR operator | is
      255 = 00000000 00000000 00000000 11111111

The result of combining the following
      139 = 00000000 00000000 00000000 10001011
      199 = 00000000 00000000 00000000 11000111
using the bitwise exclusive OR operator ^ is
       76 = 00000000 00000000 00000000 01001100

The one's complement of
    21845 = 00000000 00000000 01010101 01010101
is
4294945450 = 11111111 11111111 10101010 10101010
```

Fig. 20.8 | Bitwise AND, inclusive OR, exclusive OR and complement operators. (Part 3 of 3.)

Bitwise AND Operator (&)

In Fig. 20.8, line 13 assigns 2179876355 (10000001 11101110 01000110 00000011) to variable `number1`, and line 14 assigns 1 (00000000 00000000 00000000 00000001) to variable `mask`. When `mask` and `number1` are combined using the *bitwise AND operator (&)* in the expression `number1 & mask` (line 19), the result is 00000000 00000000 00000000 00000001. All the bits except the low-order bit in variable `number1` are "masked off" (hidden) by "ANDing" with constant `MASK`.

Bitwise Inclusive OR Operator (|)

The *bitwise inclusive OR operator* is used to set specific bits to 1 in an operand. In Fig. 20.8, line 22 assigns 15 (00000000 00000000 00000000 00001111) to variable `number1`, and line 23 assigns 241 (00000000 00000000 00000000 11110001) to variable `setBits`. When `number1` and `setBits` are combined using the *bitwise inclusive OR operator* in the expression `number1 | setBits` (line 28), the result is 255 (00000000 00000000 00000000 11111111). Figure 20.9 summarizes the results of combining two bits with the *bitwise inclusive-OR operator.*

Common Programming Error 20.3

Using the logical OR operator (||) for the bitwise OR operator (|) and vice versa is a logic error.

Bit 1	Bit 2	Bit 1 | Bit 2
0	0	0
1	0	1
0	1	1
1	1	1

Fig. 20.9 | Combining two bits with the bitwise inclusive-OR operator (|).

Bitwise Exclusive OR (^)

The *bitwise exclusive OR operator (^)* sets each bit in the result to 1 if *exactly* one of the corresponding bits in its two operands is 1. In Fig. 20.8, lines 31–32 assign variables `number1` and `number2` the values `139` (`00000000 00000000 00000000 10001011`) and `199` (`00000000 00000000 00000000 11000111`), respectively. When these variables are combined with the *bitwise exclusive OR operator* in the expression `number1 ^ number2` (line 37), the result is `00000000 00000000 00000000 01001100`. Figure 20.10 summarizes the results of combining two bits with the *bitwise exclusive OR operator*.

Bit 1	Bit 2	Bit 1 ^ Bit 2
0	0	0
1	0	1
0	1	1
1	1	0

Fig. 20.10 | Combining two bits with the bitwise exclusive OR operator (^).

Bitwise Complement (~)

The *bitwise complement operator (~)* sets all `1` bits in its operand to `0` in the result and sets all `0` bits to `1` in the result—otherwise referred to as "taking the *one's complement* of the value." In Fig. 20.8, line 40 assigns variable `number1` the value `21845` (`00000000 00000000 01010101 01010101`). When the expression `~number1` evaluates, the result is (`11111111 11111111 10101010 10101010`).

Bitwise Shift Operators

Figure 20.11 demonstrates the *left-shift operator (<<)* and the *right-shift operator (>>)*. Function `displayBits` (lines 27–45) prints the `unsigned` integer values.

```
1  // Fig. 20.11: fig20_11.cpp
2  // Using the bitwise shift operators.
3  #include <iostream>
4  #include <iomanip>
5  using namespace std;
6
7  void displayBits( unsigned ); // prototype
8
9  int main()
10 {
11    unsigned number1 = 960;
12
13    // demonstrate bitwise left shift
14    cout << "The result of left shifting\n";
15    displayBits( number1 );
16    cout << "8 bit positions using the left-shift operator is\n";
```

Fig. 20.11 | Bitwise shift operators. (Part 1 of 2.)

```
17       displayBits( number1 << 8 );
18
19       // demonstrate bitwise right shift
20       cout << "\nThe result of right shifting\n";
21       displayBits( number1 );
22       cout << "8 bit positions using the right-shift operator is\n";
23       displayBits( number1 >> 8 );
24    } // end main
25
26    // display bits of an unsigned integer value
27    void displayBits( unsigned value )
28    {
29       const int SHIFT = 8 * sizeof( unsigned ) - 1;
30       const unsigned MASK = 1 << SHIFT;
31
32       cout << setw( 10 ) << value << " = ";
33
34       // display bits
35       for ( unsigned i = 1; i <= SHIFT + 1; ++i )
36       {
37          cout << ( value & MASK ? '1' : '0' );
38          value <<= 1; // shift value left by 1
39
40          if ( i % 8 == 0 ) // output a space after 8 bits
41             cout << ' ';
42       } // end for
43
44       cout << endl;
45    } // end function displayBits
```

```
The result of left shifting
       960 = 00000000 00000000 00000011 11000000
8 bit positions using the left-shift operator is
    245760 = 00000000 00000011 11000000 00000000

The result of right shifting
       960 = 00000000 00000000 00000011 11000000
8 bit positions using the right-shift operator is
         3 = 00000000 00000000 00000000 00000011
```

Fig. 20.11 | Bitwise shift operators. (Part 2 of 2.)

Left-Shift Operator

The *left-shift operator (<<)* shifts the bits of its left operand to the left by the number of bits specified in its right operand. Bits vacated to the right are replaced with 0s; bits shifted off the left are lost. In Fig. 20.11, line 11 assigns variable `number1` the value 960 (00000000 00000000 00000011 11000000). The result of left-shifting variable `number1` eight bits in the expression `number1 << 8` (line 17) is 245760 (00000000 00000011 11000000 00000000).

Right-Shift Operator

The *right-shift operator (>>)* shifts the bits of its left operand to the right by the number of bits specified in its right operand. Performing a right shift on an `unsigned` integer causes the vacated bits at the left to be replaced by 0s; bits shifted off the right are lost. In the program of Fig. 20.11, the result of right-shifting `number1` in the expression `number1 >> 8` (line 23) is `3` (`00000000 00000000 00000000 00000011`).

Common Programming Error 20.4

The result of shifting a value is undefined *if the right operand is negative or if the right operand is greater than or equal to the number of bits in which the left operand is stored.*

Portability Tip 20.3

The result of right-shifting a signed value is machine dependent. *Some machines fill with zeros and others use the sign bit.*

Bitwise Assignment Operators

Each bitwise operator (except the bitwise complement operator) has a corresponding assignment operator. These **bitwise assignment operators** are shown in Fig. 20.12; they're used in a similar manner to the arithmetic assignment operators introduced in Chapter 4.

Bitwise assignment operators	
`&=`	Bitwise AND assignment operator.
`|=`	Bitwise inclusive OR assignment operator.
`^=`	Bitwise exclusive OR assignment operator.
`<<=`	Left-shift assignment operator.
`>>=`	Right-shift with sign extension assignment operator.

Fig. 20.12 | Bitwise assignment operators.

Figure 20.13 shows the precedence and associativity of the operators introduced up to this point in the text. They're shown top to bottom in decreasing order of precedence.

Operators	Associativity	Type
`::` (unary; right to left) `::` (binary; left to right) `()` (grouping parentheses)	left to right *[See caution in Fig. 2.7 regarding grouping parentheses.]*	primary
`()` `[]` `.` `->` `++` `--` `static_cast`<*type*>`()`	left to right	postfix
`++` `--` `+` `-` `!` `delete` `sizeof` `*` `~` `&` `new`	right to left	prefix
`*` `/` `%`	left to right	multiplicative
`+` `-`	left to right	additive
`<<` `>>`	left to right	shifting
`<` `<=` `>` `>=`	left to right	relational

Fig. 20.13 | Operator precedence and associativity. (Part 1 of 2.)

Operators	Associativity	Type
`==` `!=`	left to right	equality
`&`	left to right	bitwise AND
`^`	left to right	bitwise XOR
`|`	left to right	bitwise OR
`&&`	left to right	logical AND
`||`	left to right	logical OR
`?:`	right to left	conditional
`=` `+=` `-=` `*=` `/=` `%=` `&=` `|=` `^=` `<<=` `>>=`	right to left	assignment
`,`	left to right	comma

Fig. 20.13 | Operator precedence and associativity. (Part 2 of 2.)

20.6 Bit Fields

C++ provides the ability to specify the number of bits in which an integral type or `enum` type member of a class or a structure is stored. Such a member is referred to as a **bit field.** Bit fields enable *better memory utilization* by storing data in the minimum number of bits required. Bit field members *must* be declared as an integral or `enum` type.

Performance Tip 20.1
Bit fields help conserve storage.

Consider the following structure definition:

```
struct BitCard
{
   unsigned face : 4;
   unsigned suit : 2;
   unsigned color : 1;
}; // end struct BitCard
```

The definition contains three `unsigned` bit fields—`face`, `suit` and `color`—used to represent a card from a deck of 52 cards. A bit field is declared by following an integral type or `enum` type member with a colon (`:`) and an integer constant representing the **width of the bit field** (i.e., the number of bits in which the member is stored). The width must be an integer constant.

The preceding structure definition indicates that member `face` is stored in four bits, member `suit` in 2 bits and member `color` in one bit. The number of bits is based on the desired range of values for each structure member. Member `face` stores values between `0` (Ace) and `12` (King)—four bits can store a value between 0 and 15. Member `suit` stores values between `0` and `3` (`0` = Diamonds, `1` = Hearts, `2` = Clubs, `3` = Spades)—two bits can store a value between `0` and `3`. Finally, member `color` stores either `0` (Red) or `1` (Black)—one bit can store either `0` or `1`.

The program in Figs. 20.14–20.16 creates `array` `deck` containing `BitCard` structures (line 25 of Fig. 20.14). The constructor inserts the 52 cards in the `deck` `array`, and function deal prints the 52 cards. Notice that bit fields are accessed exactly as any other structure member is (lines 14–16 and 25–30 of Fig. 20.15). The member color is included as a means of indicating the card color.

```cpp
// Fig. 20.14: DeckOfCards.h
// Definition of class DeckOfCards that
// represents a deck of playing cards.
#include <array>

// BitCard structure definition with bit fields
struct BitCard
{
   unsigned face : 4; // 4 bits; 0-15
   unsigned suit : 2; // 2 bits; 0-3
   unsigned color : 1; // 1 bit; 0-1
}; // end struct BitCard

// DeckOfCards class definition
class DeckOfCards
{
public:
   static const int faces = 13;
   static const int colors = 2; // black and red
   static const int numberOfCards = 52;

   DeckOfCards(); // constructor initializes deck
   void deal() const; // deals cards in deck
private:
   std::array< BitCard, numberOfCards > deck; // represents deck of cards
}; // end class DeckOfCards
```

Fig. 20.14 | Definition of class DeckOfCards that represents a deck of playing cards.

```cpp
1  // Fig. 20.15: DeckOfCards.cpp
2  // Member-function definitions for class DeckOfCards that simulates
3  // the shuffling and dealing of a deck of playing cards.
4  #include <iostream>
5  #include <iomanip>
6  #include "DeckOfCards.h" // DeckOfCards class definition
7  using namespace std;
8
9  // no-argument DeckOfCards constructor intializes deck
10 DeckOfCards::DeckOfCards()
11 {
12    for ( size_t i = 0; i < deck.size(); ++i )
13    {
14       deck[ i ].face = i % faces; // faces in order
15       deck[ i ].suit = i / faces; // suits in order
16       deck[ i ].color = i / ( faces * colors ); // colors in order
17    } // end for
18 } // end no-argument DeckOfCards constructor
```

Fig. 20.15 | Member-function definitions for class DeckOfCards. (Part 1 of 2.)

```

// deal cards in deck
void DeckOfCards::deal() const
{
   for ( size_t k1 = 0, k2 = k1 + deck.size() / 2;
      k1 < deck.size() / 2 - 1; ++k1, ++k2 )
      cout << "Card:" << setw( 3 ) << deck[ k1 ].face
         << "  Suit:" << setw( 2 ) << deck[ k1 ].suit
         << "  Color:" << setw( 2 ) << deck[ k1 ].color
         << "   " << "Card:" << setw( 3 ) << deck[ k2 ].face
         << "  Suit:" << setw( 2 ) << deck[ k2 ].suit
         << "  Color:" << setw( 2 ) << deck[ k2 ].color << endl;
} // end function deal
```

Fig. 20.15 | Member-function definitions for class DeckOfCards. (Part 2 of 2.)

```
// Fig. 20.16: fig20_16.cpp
// Card shuffling and dealing program.
#include "DeckOfCards.h" // DeckOfCards class definition

int main()
{
   DeckOfCards deckOfCards; // create DeckOfCards object
   deckOfCards.deal(); // deal the cards in the deck
} // end main
```

```
Card:  0  Suit: 0  Color: 0   Card:  0  Suit: 2  Color: 1
Card:  1  Suit: 0  Color: 0   Card:  1  Suit: 2  Color: 1
Card:  2  Suit: 0  Color: 0   Card:  2  Suit: 2  Color: 1
Card:  3  Suit: 0  Color: 0   Card:  3  Suit: 2  Color: 1
Card:  4  Suit: 0  Color: 0   Card:  4  Suit: 2  Color: 1
Card:  5  Suit: 0  Color: 0   Card:  5  Suit: 2  Color: 1
Card:  6  Suit: 0  Color: 0   Card:  6  Suit: 2  Color: 1
Card:  7  Suit: 0  Color: 0   Card:  7  Suit: 2  Color: 1
Card:  8  Suit: 0  Color: 0   Card:  8  Suit: 2  Color: 1
Card:  9  Suit: 0  Color: 0   Card:  9  Suit: 2  Color: 1
Card: 10  Suit: 0  Color: 0   Card: 10  Suit: 2  Color: 1
Card: 11  Suit: 0  Color: 0   Card: 11  Suit: 2  Color: 1
Card: 12  Suit: 0  Color: 0   Card: 12  Suit: 2  Color: 1
Card:  0  Suit: 1  Color: 0   Card:  0  Suit: 3  Color: 1
Card:  1  Suit: 1  Color: 0   Card:  1  Suit: 3  Color: 1
Card:  2  Suit: 1  Color: 0   Card:  2  Suit: 3  Color: 1
Card:  3  Suit: 1  Color: 0   Card:  3  Suit: 3  Color: 1
Card:  4  Suit: 1  Color: 0   Card:  4  Suit: 3  Color: 1
Card:  5  Suit: 1  Color: 0   Card:  5  Suit: 3  Color: 1
Card:  6  Suit: 1  Color: 0   Card:  6  Suit: 3  Color: 1
Card:  7  Suit: 1  Color: 0   Card:  7  Suit: 3  Color: 1
Card:  8  Suit: 1  Color: 0   Card:  8  Suit: 3  Color: 1
Card:  9  Suit: 1  Color: 0   Card:  9  Suit: 3  Color: 1
Card: 10  Suit: 1  Color: 0   Card: 10  Suit: 3  Color: 1
Card: 11  Suit: 1  Color: 0   Card: 11  Suit: 3  Color: 1
Card: 12  Suit: 1  Color: 0   Card: 12  Suit: 3  Color: 1
```

Fig. 20.16 | Bit fields used to store a deck of cards.

It's possible to specify an **unnamed bit field**, in which case the field is used as **padding** in the structure. For example, the structure definition uses an unnamed three-bit field as padding—nothing can be stored in those three bits. Member b is stored in another storage unit.

```
struct Example
{
   unsigned a : 13;
   unsigned   : 3; // align to next storage-unit boundary
   unsigned b : 4;
}; // end struct Example
```

An **unnamed bit field with a zero width** is used to align the next bit field on a new storage-unit boundary. For example, the structure definition

```
struct Example
{
   unsigned a : 13;
   unsigned   : 0; // align to next storage-unit boundary
   unsigned b : 4;
}; // end struct Example
```

uses an unnamed 0-bit field to *skip* the remaining bits (as many as there are) of the storage unit in which a is stored and align b on the *next storage-unit boundary.*

Portability Tip 20.4

Bit-field manipulations are machine dependent. For example, some computers allow bit fields to cross word boundaries, whereas others do not.

Common Programming Error 20.5

Attempting to access individual bits of a bit field with subscripting as if they were elements of an array is a compilation error. Bit fields are not *"arrays of bits."*

Common Programming Error 20.6

Attempting to take the address of a bit field (the & operator may not be used with bit fields because a pointer can designate only a particular byte in memory and bit fields can start in the middle of a byte) is a compilation error.

Performance Tip 20.2

Although bit fields save space, using them can cause the compiler to generate slower-executing machine-language code. This occurs because it takes extra machine-language operations to access only portions of an addressable storage unit. This is one of many examples of the space–time trade-offs *that occur in computer science.*

20.7 Character-Handling Library

Most data is entered into computers as *characters*—including letters, digits and various special symbols. In this section, we discuss C++'s capabilities for examining and manipulating individual characters. In the remainder of the chapter, we continue the discussion of *character-string manipulation* that we began in Chapter 8.

The character-handling library includes several functions that perform useful tests and manipulations of character data. Each function receives a character—represented as an int—or EOF as an argument. *Characters are often manipulated as integers.* Remember that EOF normally has the value -1 and that some hardware architectures do not allow negative values to be stored in char variables. Therefore, the character-handling functions manipulate characters as integers. Figure 20.17 summarizes the functions of the character-handling library. When using functions from the character-handling library, include the <cctype> header.

Prototype	Description
`int isdigit( int c )`	Returns 1 if c is a *digit* and 0 otherwise.
`int isalpha( int c )`	Returns 1 if c is a *letter* and 0 otherwise.
`int isalnum( int c )`	Returns 1 if c is a *digit or a letter* and 0 otherwise.
`int isxdigit( int c )`	Returns 1 if c is a *hexadecimal digit* character and 0 otherwise. (See Appendix D for a detailed explanation of binary, octal, decimal and hexadecimal numbers.)
`int islower( int c )`	Returns 1 if c is a *lowercase letter* and 0 otherwise.
`int isupper( int c )`	Returns 1 if c is an *uppercase letter*; 0 otherwise.
`int tolower( int c )`	If c is an *uppercase letter*, tolower returns c as a *lowercase letter*. Otherwise, tolower returns the argument *unchanged*.
`int toupper( int c )`	If c is a *lowercase letter*, toupper returns c as an *uppercase letter*. Otherwise, toupper returns the argument *unchanged*.
`int isspace( int c )`	Returns 1 if c is a *whitespace character*—newline ('\n'), space (' '), form feed ('\f'), carriage return ('\r'), horizontal tab ('\t'), or vertical tab ('\v')—and 0 otherwise.
`int iscntrl( int c )`	Returns 1 if c is a *control character*, such as newline ('\n'), form feed ('\f'), carriage return ('\r'), horizontal tab ('\t'), vertical tab ('\v'), alert ('\a'), or backspace ('\b')—and 0 otherwise.
`int ispunct( int c )`	Returns 1 if c is a *printing character other than a space*, a *digit*, or a *letter* and 0 otherwise.
`int isprint( int c )`	Returns 1 if c is a *printing character including space* (' ') and 0 otherwise.
`int isgraph( int c )`	Returns 1 if c is a *printing character other than space* (' ') and 0 otherwise.

Fig. 20.17 | Character-handling library functions.

Figure 20.18 demonstrates functions **isdigit**, **isalpha**, **isalnum** and **isxdigit**. Function isdigit determines whether its argument is a *digit* (0–9). Function isalpha determines whether its argument is an *uppercase letter* (A-Z) or a *lowercase letter* (a–z). Function isalnum determines whether its argument is an *uppercase letter, a lowercase letter or a digit*. Function isxdigit determines whether its argument is a *hexadecimal digit* (A–F, a–f, 0–9).

```
// Fig. 20.18: fig20_18.cpp
// Character-handling functions isdigit, isalpha, isalnum and isxdigit.
#include <iostream>
#include <cctype> // character-handling function prototypes
using namespace std;

int main()
{
   cout << "According to isdigit:\n"
      << ( isdigit( '8' ) ? "8 is a" : "8 is not a" ) << " digit\n"
      << ( isdigit( '#' ) ? "# is a" : "# is not a" ) << " digit\n";

   cout << "\nAccording to isalpha:\n"
      << ( isalpha( 'A' ) ? "A is a" : "A is not a" ) << " letter\n"
      << ( isalpha( 'b' ) ? "b is a" : "b is not a" ) << " letter\n"
      << ( isalpha( '&' ) ? "& is a" : "& is not a" ) << " letter\n"
      << ( isalpha( '4' ) ? "4 is a" : "4 is not a" ) << " letter\n";

   cout << "\nAccording to isalnum:\n"
      << ( isalnum( 'A' ) ? "A is a" : "A is not a" )
      << " digit or a letter\n"
      << ( isalnum( '8' ) ? "8 is a" : "8 is not a" )
      << " digit or a letter\n"
      << ( isalnum( '#' ) ? "# is a" : "# is not a" )
      << " digit or a letter\n";

   cout << "\nAccording to isxdigit:\n"
      << ( isxdigit( 'F' ) ? "F is a" : "F is not a" )
      << " hexadecimal digit\n"
      << ( isxdigit( 'J' ) ? "J is a" : "J is not a" )
      << " hexadecimal digit\n"
      << ( isxdigit( '7' ) ? "7 is a" : "7 is not a" )
      << " hexadecimal digit\n"
      << ( isxdigit( '$' ) ? "$ is a" : "$ is not a" )
      << " hexadecimal digit\n"
      << ( isxdigit( 'f' ) ? "f is a" : "f is not a" )
      << " hexadecimal digit" << endl;
} // end main
```

```
According to isdigit:
8 is a digit
# is not a digi

According to isalpha:
A is a letter
b is a letter
& is not a letter
4 is not a letter

According to isalnum:
A is a digit or a letter
8 is a digit or a letter
# is not a digit or a letter
```

Fig. 20.18 | Character-handling functions `isdigit`, `isalpha`, `isalnum` and `isxdigit`. (Part 1 of 2.)

```
According to isxdigit:
F is a hexadecimal digit
J is not a hexadecimal digit
7 is a hexadecimal digit
$ is not a hexadecimal digit
f is a hexadecimal digit
```

Fig. 20.18 | Character-handling functions `isdigit`, `isalpha`, `isalnum` and `isxdigit`. (Part 2 of 2.)

Figure 20.18 uses the *conditional operator (?:)* with each function to determine whether the string `" is a "` or the string `" is not a "` should be printed in the output for each character tested. For example, line 10 indicates that if `'8'` is a digit—i.e., if `isdigit` returns a true (nonzero) value—the string `"8 is a "` is printed. If `'8'` is not a digit (i.e., if `isdigit` returns 0), the string `"8 is not a "` is printed.

Figure 20.19 demonstrates functions **`islower`**, **`isupper`**, **`tolower`** and **`toupper`**. Function `islower` determines whether its argument is a *lowercase letter* (`a-z`). Function `isupper` determines whether its argument is an *uppercase letter* (`A-Z`). Function `tolower` converts an uppercase letter to lowercase and returns the lowercase letter—if the argument is not an uppercase letter, `tolower` returns the argument value unchanged. Function `toupper` converts a lowercase letter to uppercase and returns the uppercase letter—if the argument is *not* a lowercase letter, `toupper` returns the argument value *unchanged*.

```
// Fig. 20.19: fig20_19.cpp
// Character-handling functions islower, isupper, tolower and toupper.
#include <iostream>
#include <cctype> // character-handling function prototypes
using namespace std;

int main()
{
   cout << "According to islower:\n"
      << ( islower( 'p' ) ? "p is a" : "p is not a" )
      << " lowercase letter\n"
      << ( islower( 'P' ) ? "P is a" : "P is not a" )
      << " lowercase letter\n"
      << ( islower( '5' ) ? "5 is a" : "5 is not a" )
      << " lowercase letter\n"
      << ( islower( '!' ) ? "! is a" : "! is not a" )
      << " lowercase letter\n";

   cout << "\nAccording to isupper:\n"
      << ( isupper( 'D' ) ? "D is an" : "D is not an" )
      << " uppercase letter\n"
      << ( isupper( 'd' ) ? "d is an" : "d is not an" )
      << " uppercase letter\n"
      << ( isupper( '8' ) ? "8 is an" : "8 is not an" )
```

Fig. 20.19 | Character-handling functions `islower`, `isupper`, `tolower` and `toupper`. (Part 1 of 2.)

```
         << " uppercase letter\n"
         << ( isupper( '$' ) ? "$ is an" : "$ is not an" )
         << " uppercase letter\n";

      cout << "\nu converted to uppercase is "
         << static_cast< char >( toupper( 'u' ) )
         << "\n7 converted to uppercase is "
         << static_cast< char >( toupper( '7' ) )
         << "\n$ converted to uppercase is "
         << static_cast< char >( toupper( '$' ) )
         << "\nL converted to lowercase is "
         << static_cast< char >( tolower( 'L' ) ) << endl;
   } // end main
```

```
According to islower:
p is a lowercase letter
P is not a lowercase letter
5 is not a lowercase letter
! is not a lowercase letter

According to isupper:
D is an uppercase letter
d is not an uppercase letter
8 is not an uppercase letter
$ is not an uppercase letter

u converted to uppercase is U
7 converted to uppercase is 7
$ converted to uppercase is $
L converted to lowercase is l
```

Fig. 20.19 | Character-handling functions `islower`, `isupper`, `tolower` and `toupper`. (Part 2 of 2.)

Figure 20.20 demonstrates functions **`isspace`**, **`iscntrl`**, **`ispunct`**, **`isprint`** and **`isgraph`**. Function `isspace` determines whether its argument is a *whitespace character*, such as space (`' '`), form feed (`'\f'`), newline (`'\n'`), carriage return (`'\r'`), horizontal tab (`'\t'`) or vertical tab (`'\v'`). Function `iscntrl` determines whether its argument is a *control character* such as horizontal tab (`'\t'`), vertical tab (`'\v'`), form feed (`'\f'`), alert (`'\a'`), backspace (`'\b'`), carriage return (`'\r'`) or newline (`'\n'`). Function `ispunct` determines whether its argument is a *printing character other than a space, digit or letter*, such as `$`, `#`, `(`, `)`, `[`, `]`, `{`, `}`, `;`, `:` or `%`. Function `isprint` determines whether its argument is a character that can be *displayed on the screen* (including the space character). Function `isgraph` tests for the same characters as `isprint`, but the space character is *not* included.

```
// Fig. 20.20: fig20_20.cpp
// Using functions isspace, iscntrl, ispunct, isprint and isgraph.
#include <iostream>
```

Fig. 20.20 | Character-handling functions `isspace`, `iscntrl`, `ispunct`, `isprint` and `isgraph`. (Part 1 of 3.)

```
#include <cctype> // character-handling function prototypes
using namespace std;

int main()
{
   cout << "According to isspace:\nNewline "
      << ( isspace( '\n' ) ? "is a" : "is not a" )
      << " whitespace character\nHorizontal tab "
      << ( isspace( '\t' ) ? "is a" : "is not a" )
      << " whitespace character\n"
      << ( isspace( '%' ) ? "% is a" : "% is not a" )
      << " whitespace character\n";

   cout << "\nAccording to iscntrl:\nNewline "
      << ( iscntrl( '\n' ) ? "is a" : "is not a" )
      << " control character\n"
      << ( iscntrl( '$' ) ? "$ is a" : "$ is not a" )
      << " control character\n";

   cout << "\nAccording to ispunct:\n"
      << ( ispunct( ';' ) ? "; is a" : "; is not a" )
      << " punctuation character\n"
      << ( ispunct( 'Y' ) ? "Y is a" : "Y is not a" )
      << " punctuation character\n"
      << ( ispunct( '#' ) ? "# is a" : "# is not a" )
      << " punctuation character\n";

   cout << "\nAccording to isprint:\n"
      << ( isprint( '$' ) ? "$ is a" : "$ is not a" )
      << " printing character\nAlert "
      << ( isprint( '\a' ) ? "is a" : "is not a" )
      << " printing character\nSpace "
      << ( isprint( ' ' ) ? "is a" : "is not a" )
      << " printing character\n";

   cout << "\nAccording to isgraph:\n"
      << ( isgraph( 'Q' ) ? "Q is a" : "Q is not a" )
      << " printing character other than a space\nSpace "
      << ( isgraph( ' ' ) ? "is a" : "is not a" )
      << " printing character other than a space" << endl;
} // end main
```

```
According to isspace:
Newline is a whitespace character
Horizontal tab is a whitespace character
% is not a whitespace character

According to iscntrl:
Newline is a control character
$ is not a control character
```

Fig. 20.20 | Character-handling functions isspace, iscntrl, ispunct, isprint and isgraph. (Part 2 of 3.)

```
According to ispunct:
; is a punctuation character
Y is not a punctuation character
# is a punctuation character

According to isprint:
$ is a printing character
Alert is not a printing character
Space is a printing character

According to isgraph:
Q is a printing character other than a space
Space is not a printing character other than a space
```

Fig. 20.20 | Character-handling functions `isspace`, `iscntrl`, `ispunct`, `isprint` and `isgraph`. (Part 3 of 3.)

20.8 C String-Manipulation Functions

The string-handling library provides any useful functions for manipulating string data, *comparing* strings, *searching* strings for characters and other strings, *tokenizing* strings (separating strings into logical pieces such as the separate words in a sentence) and determining the *length* of strings. This section presents some common string-manipulation functions of the string-handling library (from the *C++ standard library*). The functions are summarized in Fig. 20.21; then each is used in a live-code example. The prototypes for these functions are located in header `<cstring>`.

Function prototype	Function description
`char *strcpy( char *s1, const char *s2 );`	
	Copies the string `s2` into the character array `s1`. The value of `s1` is returned.
`char *strncpy( char *s1, const char *s2, size_t n );`	
	Copies at most `n` characters of the string `s2` into the character array `s1`. The value of `s1` is returned.
`char *strcat( char *s1, const char *s2 );`	
	Appends the string `s2` to `s1`. The first character of `s2` overwrites the terminating null character of `s1`. The value of `s1` is returned.
`char *strncat( char *s1, const char *s2, size_t n );`	
	Appends at most `n` characters of string `s2` to string `s1`. The first character of `s2` overwrites the terminating null character of `s1`. The value of `s1` is returned.
`int strcmp( const char *s1, const char *s2 );`	
	Compares the string `s1` with the string `s2`. The function returns a value of zero, less than zero or greater than zero if `s1` is equal to, less than or greater than `s2`, respectively.

Fig. 20.21 | String-manipulation functions of the string-handling library. (Part 1 of 2.)

Function prototype	Function description
`int strncmp( const char *s1, const char *s2, size_t n );`	
	Compares up to `n` characters of the string `s1` with the string `s2`. The function returns zero, less than zero or greater than zero if the `n`-character portion of `s1` is equal to, less than or greater than the corresponding `n`-character portion of `s2`, respectively.
`char *strtok( char *s1, const char *s2 );`	
	A sequence of calls to `strtok` breaks string `s1` into *tokens*—logical pieces such as words in a line of text. The string is broken up based on the characters contained in string `s2`. For instance, if we were to break the string `"this:is:a:string"` into tokens based on the character `':'`, the resulting tokens would be `"this"`, `"is"`, `"a"` and `"string"`. Function `strtok` returns only one token at a time—the first call contains `s1` as the first argument, and subsequent calls to continue tokenizing the same string contain `NULL` as the first argument. A pointer to the current token is returned by each call. If there are no more tokens when the function is called, `NULL` is returned.
`size_t strlen( const char *s );`	
	Determines the length of string `s`. The number of characters preceding the terminating null character is returned.

Fig. 20.21 | String-manipulation functions of the string-handling library. (Part 2 of 2.)

Several functions in Fig. 20.21 contain parameters with data type `size_t`. This type is defined in the header `<cstring>` to be an unsigned integral type such as `unsigned int` or `unsigned long`.

Common Programming Error 20.7

Forgetting to include the `<cstring>` header when using functions from the string-handling library causes compilation errors.

Copying Strings with `strcpy` and `strncpy`

Function **`strcpy`** copies its second argument—a string—into its first argument—a character array that must be large enough to store the string *and* its *terminating null character*, (which is also copied). Function **`strncpy`** is much like `strcpy`, except that `strncpy` specifies the number of characters to be copied from the string into the array. Function `strncpy` does *not* necessarily copy the terminating null character of its second argument—a terminating null character is written only if the number of characters to be copied is at least one more than the length of the string. For example, if `"test"` is the second argument, a terminating null character is written *only* if the third argument to `strncpy` is at least `5` (four characters in `"test"` plus one terminating null character). If the third argument is larger than `5`, null characters are appended to the array until the total number of characters specified by the third argument is written.

Common Programming Error 20.8

When using `strncpy`*, the terminating null character of the second argument (a* `char *` *string) will not be copied if the number of characters specified by* `strncpy`*'s third argument is not greater than the second argument's length. In that case, a fatal error may occur if you do not manually terminate the resulting* `char *` *string with a null character.*

Figure 20.22 uses `strcpy` (line 13) to copy the entire string in array `x` into array `y` and uses `strncpy` (line 19) to copy the first `14` characters of array `x` into array `z`. Line 20 appends a null character (`'\0'`) to array `z`, because the call to `strncpy` in the program does not write a terminating null character. (The third argument is less than the string length of the second argument plus one.)

```
1  // Fig. 20.22: fig20_22.cpp
2  // Using strcpy and strncpy.
3  #include <iostream>
4  #include <cstring> // prototypes for strcpy and strncpy
5  using namespace std;
6
7  int main()
8  {
9     char x[] = "Happy Birthday to You"; // string length 21
10    char y[ 25 ];
11    char z[ 15 ];
12
13    strcpy( y, x ); // copy contents of x into y
14
15    cout << "The string in array x is: " << x
16       << "\nThe string in array y is: " << y << '\n';
17
18    // copy first 14 characters of x into z
19    strncpy( z, x, 14 ); // does not copy null character
20    z[ 14 ] = '\0'; // append '\0' to z's contents
21
22    cout << "The string in array z is: " << z << endl;
23 } // end main
```

```
The string in array x is: Happy Birthday to You
The string in array y is: Happy Birthday to You
The string in array z is: Happy Birthday
```

Fig. 20.22 | `strcpy` and `strncpy`.

Concatenating Strings with `strcat` *and* `strncat`

Function **`strcat`** appends its second argument (a string) to its first argument (a character array containing a string). The first character of the second argument replaces the null character (`'\0'`) that terminates the string in the first argument. You must ensure that the array used to store the first string is *large enough* to store the combination of the first string, the second string and the terminating null character (copied from the second string). Function **`strncat`** appends a specified number of characters from the second string to the first string and appends a terminating null character to the result. The program of Fig. 20.23 demonstrates function `strcat` (lines 15 and 25) and function `strncat` (line 20).

```
// Fig. 20.23: fig20_23.cpp
// Using strcat and strncat.
#include <iostream>
#include <cstring> // prototypes for strcat and strncat
using namespace std;

int main()
{
   char s1[ 20 ] = "Happy "; // length 6
   char s2[] = "New Year "; // length 9
   char s3[ 40 ] = "";

   cout << "s1 = " << s1 << "\ns2 = " << s2;

   strcat( s1, s2 ); // concatenate s2 to s1 (length 15)

   cout << "\n\nAfter strcat(s1, s2):\ns1 = " << s1 << "\ns2 = " << s2;

   // concatenate first 6 characters of s1 to s3
   strncat( s3, s1, 6 ); // places '\0' after last character

   cout << "\n\nAfter strncat(s3, s1, 6):\ns1 = " << s1
      << "\ns3 = " << s3;

   strcat( s3, s1 ); // concatenate s1 to s3
   cout << "\n\nAfter strcat(s3, s1):\ns1 = " << s1
      << "\ns3 = " << s3 << endl;
} // end main
```

```
s1 = Happy
s2 = New Year

After strcat(s1, s2):
s1 = Happy New Year
s2 = New Year

After strncat(s3, s1, 6):
s1 = Happy New Year
s3 = Happy

After strcat(s3, s1):
s1 = Happy New Year
s3 = Happy Happy New Year
```

Fig. 20.23 | strcat and strncat.

Comparing Strings with strcmp and strncmp

Figure 20.24 compares three strings using strcmp (lines 15–17) and strncmp (lines 20–22). Function strcmp compares its first string argument with its second string argument character by character. The function returns zero if the strings are equal, a negative value if the first string is less than the second string and a positive value if the first string is greater than the second string. Function strncmp is equivalent to strcmp, except that strncmp compares up to a specified number of characters. Function strncmp stops comparing characters if it reaches the null character in one of its string arguments. The program prints the integer value returned by each function call.

Common Programming Error 20.9

Assuming that `strcmp` *and* `strncmp` *return one (a true value) when their arguments are equal is a logic error. Both functions return zero (C++'s false value) for equality. Therefore, when testing two strings for equality, the result of the* `strcmp` *or* `strncmp` *function should be compared with zero to determine whether the strings are equal.*

```
// Fig. 20.24: fig20_24.cpp
// Using strcmp and strncmp.
#include <iostream>
#include <iomanip>
#include <cstring> // prototypes for strcmp and strncmp
using namespace std;

int main()
{
   const char *s1 = "Happy New Year";
   const char *s2 = "Happy New Year";
   const char *s3 = "Happy Holidays";

   cout << "s1 = " << s1 << "\ns2 = " << s2 << "\ns3 = " << s3
      << "\n\nstrcmp(s1, s2) = " << setw( 2 ) << strcmp( s1, s2 )
      << "\nstrcmp(s1, s3) = " << setw( 2 ) << strcmp( s1, s3 )
      << "\nstrcmp(s3, s1) = " << setw( 2 ) << strcmp( s3, s1 );

   cout << "\n\nstrncmp(s1, s3, 6) = " << setw( 2 )
      << strncmp( s1, s3, 6 ) << "\nstrncmp(s1, s3, 7) = " << setw( 2 )
      << strncmp( s1, s3, 7 ) << "\nstrncmp(s3, s1, 7) = " << setw( 2 )
      << strncmp( s3, s1, 7 ) << endl;
} // end main
```

```
s1 = Happy New Year
s2 = Happy New Year
s3 = Happy Holidays

strcmp(s1, s2) =  0
strcmp(s1, s3) =  1
strcmp(s3, s1) = -1

strncmp(s1, s3, 6) =  0
strncmp(s1, s3, 7) =  1
strncmp(s3, s1, 7) = -1
```

Fig. 20.24 | `strcmp` and `strncmp`.

To understand what it means for one string to be "greater than" or "less than" another, consider the process of alphabetizing last names. You'd, no doubt, place "Jones" before "Smith," because the first letter of "Jones" comes before the first letter of "Smith" in the alphabet. But the alphabet is more than just a list of 26 letters—it's an *ordered* list of characters. Each letter occurs in a specific position within the list. "Z" is more than just a letter of the alphabet; "Z" is specifically the 26th letter of the alphabet.

How does the computer know that one letter "comes before" another? All characters are represented inside the computer as numeric codes; when the computer compares two strings, it actually compares the numeric codes of the characters in the strings.

[*Note:* With some compilers, functions `strcmp` and `strncmp` always return `-1`, `0` or `1`, as in the sample output of Fig. 20.24. With other compilers, these functions return `0` or the difference between the numeric codes of the first characters that differ in the strings being compared. For example, when `s1` and `s3` are compared, the first characters that differ between them are the first character of the second word in each string—`N` (numeric code 78) in `s1` and `H` (numeric code 72) in `s3`, respectively. In this case, the return value will be `6` (or `-6` if `s3` is compared to `s1`).]

Tokenizing a String with `strtok`

Function **`strtok`** breaks a string into a series of **tokens.** A token is a sequence of characters separated by **delimiting characters** (usually spaces or punctuation marks). For example, in a line of text, each word can be considered a token, and the spaces separating the words can be considered delimiters. Multiple calls to `strtok` are required to break a string into tokens (assuming that the string contains more than one token). The first call to `strtok` contains two arguments, a string to be tokenized and a string containing characters that separate the tokens (i.e., delimiters). Line 15 in Fig. 20.25 assigns to `tokenPtr` a pointer to the first token in `sentence`. The second argument, `" "`, indicates that tokens in `sentence` are separated by spaces. Function `strtok` searches for the first character in `sentence` that's not a delimiting character (space). This begins the first token. The function then finds the next delimiting character in the string and replaces it with a null (`'\0'`) character. This terminates the current token. Function `strtok` saves (in a `static` variable) a pointer to the next character following the token in `sentence` and returns a pointer to the current token.

```
1  // Fig. 20.25: fig20_25.cpp
2  // Using strtok to tokenize a string.
3  #include <iostream>
4  #include <cstring> // prototype for strtok
5  using namespace std;
6
7  int main()
8  {
9     char sentence[] = "This is a sentence with 7 tokens";
10
11    cout << "The string to be tokenized is:\n" << sentence
12       << "\n\nThe tokens are:\n\n";
13
14    // begin tokenization of sentence
15    char *tokenPtr = strtok( sentence, " " );
16
17    // continue tokenizing sentence until tokenPtr becomes NULL
18    while ( tokenPtr != NULL )
19    {
20       cout << tokenPtr << '\n';
21       tokenPtr = strtok( NULL, " " ); // get next token
22    } // end while
```

Fig. 20.25 | Using `strtok` to tokenize a string. (Part 1 of 2.)

```
23
24      cout << "\nAfter strtok, sentence = " << sentence << endl;
25   } // end main
```

```
The string to be tokenized is:
This is a sentence with 7 tokens

The tokens are:

This
is
a
sentence
with
7
tokens

After strtok, sentence = This
```

Fig. 20.25 | Using `strtok` to tokenize a string. (Part 2 of 2.)

Subsequent calls to `strtok` to continue tokenizing `sentence` contain `NULL` as the first argument (line 21). The `NULL` argument indicates that the call to `strtok` should continue tokenizing from the location in `sentence` saved by the last call to `strtok`. Function `strtok` maintains this saved information in a manner that's not visible to you. If no tokens remain when `strtok` is called, `strtok` returns `NULL`. The program of Fig. 20.25 uses `strtok` to tokenize the string `"This is a sentence with 7 tokens"`. The program prints each token on a separate line. Line 24 outputs `sentence` after tokenization. Note that *`strtok` modifies the input string*; therefore, a copy of the string should be made if the program requires the original after the calls to `strtok`. When `sentence` is output after tokenization, only the word "`This`" prints, because `strtok` replaced each blank in `sentence` with a null character (`'\0'`) during the tokenization process.

Common Programming Error 20.10

Not realizing that `strtok` modifies *the string being tokenized, then attempting to use that string as if it were the original unmodified string is a logic error.*

Determining String Lengths

Function **`strlen`** takes a string as an argument and returns the number of characters in the string—the terminating null character is not included in the length. The length is also the index of the null character. The program of Fig. 20.26 demonstrates function `strlen`.

```
// Fig. 20.26: fig20_26.cpp
// Using strlen.
#include <iostream>
#include <cstring> // prototype for strlen
using namespace std;

```

Fig. 20.26 | `strlen` returns the length of a `char *` string. (Part 1 of 2.)

```
int main()
{
   const char *string1 = "abcdefghijklmnopqrstuvwxyz";
   const char *string2 = "four";
   const char *string3 = "Boston";

   cout << "The length of \"" << string1 << "\" is " << strlen( string1 )
      << "\nThe length of \"" << string2 << "\" is " << strlen( string2 )
      << "\nThe length of \"" << string3 << "\" is " << strlen( string3 )
      << endl;
} // end main
```

```
The length of "abcdefghijklmnopqrstuvwxyz" is 26
The length of "four" is 4
The length of "Boston" is 6
```

Fig. 20.26 | `strlen` returns the length of a `char *` string. (Part 2 of 2.)

20.9 C String-Conversion Functions

In Section 20.8, we discussed several of C++'s most popular C string-manipulation functions. In the next several sections, we cover the remaining functions, including functions for converting strings to numeric values, functions for searching strings and functions for manipulating, comparing and searching blocks of memory.

This section presents the C **string-conversion functions** from the **general-utilities library `<cstdlib>`**. These functions convert C strings to integer and floating-point values. In new code, C++ programmers typically use the string stream processing capabilities (Chapter 19) to perform such conversions. Figure 20.27 summarizes the C string-conversion functions. When using functions from the general-utilities library, include the `<cstdlib>` header.

Prototype	Description
`double atof( const char *nPtr )`	Converts the string `nPtr` to `double`. If the string cannot be converted, `0` is returned.
`int atoi( const char *nPtr )`	Converts the string `nPtr` to `int`. If the string cannot be converted, `0` is returned.
`long atol( const char *nPtr )`	Converts the string `nPtr` to `long int`. If the string cannot be converted, `0` is returned.
`double strtod( const char *nPtr, char **endPtr )`	Converts the string `nPtr` to `double`. `endPtr` is the address of a pointer to the rest of the string after the `double`. If the string cannot be converted, `0` is returned.

Fig. 20.27 | C string-conversion functions of the general-utilities library. (Part 1 of 2.)

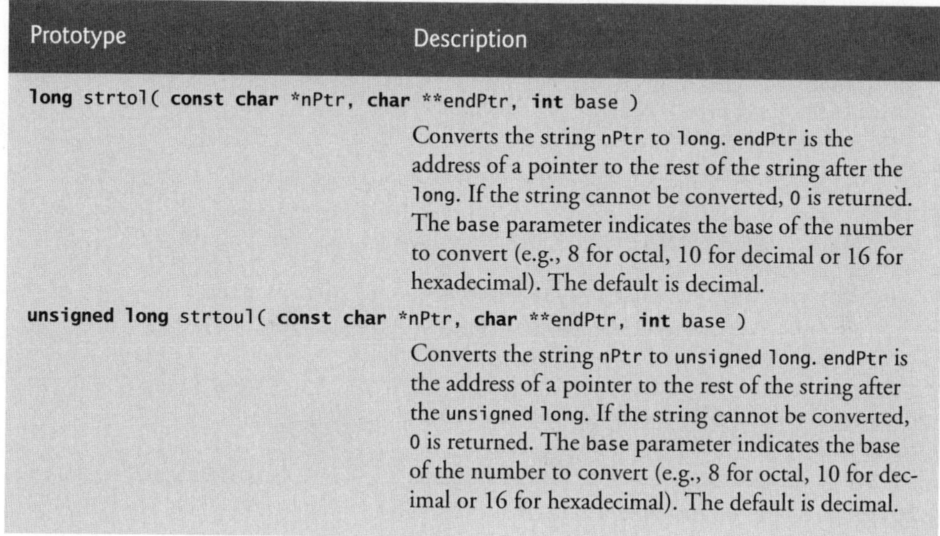

Prototype	Description
`long strtol( const char *nPtr, char **endPtr, int base )`	
	Converts the string `nPtr` to `long`. `endPtr` is the address of a pointer to the rest of the string after the `long`. If the string cannot be converted, `0` is returned. The `base` parameter indicates the base of the number to convert (e.g., 8 for octal, 10 for decimal or 16 for hexadecimal). The default is decimal.
`unsigned long strtoul( const char *nPtr, char **endPtr, int base )`	
	Converts the string `nPtr` to `unsigned long`. `endPtr` is the address of a pointer to the rest of the string after the `unsigned long`. If the string cannot be converted, `0` is returned. The `base` parameter indicates the base of the number to convert (e.g., 8 for octal, 10 for decimal or 16 for hexadecimal). The default is decimal.

Fig. 20.27 | C string-conversion functions of the general-utilities library. (Part 2 of 2.)

Function **atof** (Fig. 20.28, line 9) converts its argument—a string that represents a floating-point number—to a `double` value. The function returns the `double` value. If the string cannot be converted—for example, if the first character of the string is not a digit—function `atof` returns zero.

```
1  // Fig. 20.28: fig20_28.cpp
2  // Using atof.
3  #include <iostream>
4  #include <cstdlib> // atof prototype
5  using namespace std;
6
7  int main()
8  {
9     double d = atof( "99.0" ); // convert string to double
10
11    cout << "The string \"99.0\" converted to double is " << d
12       << "\nThe converted value divided by 2 is " << d / 2.0 << endl;
13 } // end main
```

```
The string "99.0" converted to double is 99
The converted value divided by 2 is 49.5
```

Fig. 20.28 | String-conversion function `atof`.

Function **atoi** (Fig. 20.29, line 9) converts its argument—a string of digits that represents an integer—to an `int` value. The function returns the `int` value. If the string cannot be converted, function `atoi` returns zero.

```
// Fig. 20.29: fig20_29.cpp
// Using atoi.
#include <iostream>
#include <cstdlib> // atoi prototype
using namespace std;

int main()
{
   int i = atoi( "2593" ); // convert string to int

   cout << "The string \"2593\" converted to int is " << i
      << "\nThe converted value minus 593 is " << i - 593 << endl;
} // end main
```

```
The string "2593" converted to int is 2593
The converted value minus 593 is 2000
```

Fig. 20.29 | String-conversion function `atoi`.

Function **atol** (Fig. 20.30, line 9) converts its argument—a string of digits representing a long integer—to a `long` value. The function returns the `long` value. If the string cannot be converted, function `atol` returns zero. If `int` and `long` are both stored in four bytes, function `atoi` and function `atol` work identically.

```
1  // Fig. 20.30: fig20_30.cpp
2  // Using atol.
3  #include <iostream>
4  #include <cstdlib> // atol prototype
5  using namespace std;
6
7  int main()
8  {
9     long x = atol( "1000000" ); // convert string to long
10
11    cout << "The string \"1000000\" converted to long is " << x
12       << "\nThe converted value divided by 2 is " << x / 2 << endl;
13 } // end main
```

```
The string "1000000" converted to long int is 1000000
The converted value divided by 2 is 500000
```

Fig. 20.30 | String-conversion function `atol`.

Function **strtod** (Fig. 20.31) converts a sequence of characters representing a floating-point value to `double`. Function `strtod` receives two arguments—a string (`char *`) and the address of a `char *` pointer (i.e., a `char **`). The string contains the character sequence to be converted to `double`. The second argument enables `strtod` to modify a `char *` pointer in the calling function, such that the pointer points to the location of the first character after the converted portion of the string. Line 12 indicates that `d` is assigned the `double` value converted from `string` and that `stringPtr` is assigned the location of the first character after the converted value (`51.2`) in `string`.

```
// Fig. 20.31: fig20_31.cpp
// Using strtod.
#include <iostream>
#include <cstdlib> // strtod prototype
using namespace std;

int main()
{
   const char *string1 = "51.2% are admitted";
   char *stringPtr = nullptr;

   double d = strtod( string1, &stringPtr ); // convert to double

   cout << "The string \"" << string1
      << "\" is converted to the\ndouble value " << d
      << " and the string \"" << stringPtr << "\"" << endl;
} // end main
```

```
The string "51.2% are admitted" is converted to the
double value 51.2 and the string "% are admitted"
```

Fig. 20.31 | String-conversion function `strtod`.

Function **`strtol`** (Fig. 20.32) converts to `long` a sequence of characters representing an integer. The function receives a string (`char *`), the address of a `char *` pointer and an integer. The string contains the character sequence to convert. The second argument is assigned the location of the first character after the converted portion of the string. The integer specifies the *base* of the value being converted. Line 12 indicates that `x` is assigned the `long` value converted from `string` and that `remainderPtr` is assigned the location of the first character after the converted value (`-1234567`) in `string1`. Using a null pointer for the second argument causes the remainder of the string to be ignored. The third argument, `0`, indicates that the value to be converted can be in octal (base 8), decimal (base 10) or hexadecimal (base 16). This is determined by the initial characters in the string—`0` indicates an octal number, `0x` indicates hexadecimal and a number from `1` to `9` indicates decimal.

```
1  // Fig. 20.32: fig20_32.cpp
2  // Using strtol.
3  #include <iostream>
4  #include <cstdlib> // strtol prototype
5  using namespace std;
6
7  int main()
8  {
9     const char *string1 = "-1234567abc";
10    char *remainderPtr = nullptr;
```

Fig. 20.32 | String-conversion function `strtol`. (Part 1 of 2.)

```

   long x = strtol( string1, &remainderPtr, 0 ); // convert to long

   cout << "The original string is \"" << string1
      << "\"\nThe converted value is " << x
      << "\nThe remainder of the original string is \"" << remainderPtr
      << "\"\nThe converted value plus 567 is " << x + 567 << endl;
} // end main
```

```
The original string is "-1234567abc"
The converted value is -1234567
The remainder of the original string is "abc"
The converted value plus 567 is -1234000
```

Fig. 20.32 | String-conversion function `strtol`. (Part 2 of 2.)

In a call to function `strtol`, the base can be specified as zero or as any value between 2 and 36. (See Appendix D for a detailed explanation of the octal, decimal, hexadecimal and binary number systems.) Numeric representations of integers from base 11 to base 36 use the characters A–Z to represent the values 10 to 35. For example, hexadecimal values can consist of the digits 0–9 and the characters A–F. A base-11 integer can consist of the digits 0–9 and the character A. A base-24 integer can consist of the digits 0–9 and the characters A–N. A base-36 integer can consist of the digits 0–9 and the characters A–Z. [*Note:* The case of the letter used is ignored.]

Function **`strtoul`** (Fig. 20.33) converts to `unsigned long` a sequence of characters representing an `unsigned long` integer. The function works identically to `strtol`. Line 13 indicates that `x` is assigned the `unsigned long` value converted from `string` and that `remainderPtr` is assigned the location of the first character after the converted value (`1234567`) in `string1`. The third argument, `0`, indicates that the value to be converted can be in octal, decimal or hexadecimal format, depending on the initial characters.

```
1  // Fig. 20.33: fig20_33.cpp
2  // Using strtoul.
3  #include <iostream>
4  #include <cstdlib> // strtoul prototype
5  using namespace std;
6
7  int main()
8  {
9     const char *string1 = "1234567abc";
10    char *remainderPtr = nullptr;
11
12    // convert a sequence of characters to unsigned long
13    unsigned long x = strtoul( string1, &remainderPtr, 0 );
14
15    cout << "The original string is \"" << string1
16       << "\"\nThe converted value is " << x
17       << "\nThe remainder of the original string is \"" << remainderPtr
```

Fig. 20.33 | String-conversion function `strtoul`. (Part 1 of 2.)

```
        << "\"\nThe converted value minus 567 is " << x - 567 << endl;
} // end main
```

```
The original string is "1234567abc"
The converted value is 1234567
The remainder of the original string is "abc"
The converted value minus 567 is 1234000
```

Fig. 20.33 | String-conversion function `strtoul`. (Part 2 of 2.)

20.10 Search Functions of the C String-Handling Library

This section presents the functions of the string-handling library used to search strings for characters and other strings. The functions are summarized in Fig. 20.34. Functions `strcspn` and `strspn` specify return type `size_t`. Type `size_t` is a type defined by the standard as the integral type of the value returned by operator `sizeof`.

Function **`strchr`** searches for the first occurrence of a character in a string. If the character is found, `strchr` returns a pointer to the character in the string; otherwise, `strchr` returns a null pointer. The program of Fig. 20.35 uses `strchr` (lines 14 and 22) to search for the first occurrences of `'a'` and `'z'` in the string `"This is a test"`.

Prototype	Description
`char *strchr( const char *s, int c )`	
	Locates the first occurrence of character `c` in string `s`. If `c` is found, a pointer to `c` in `s` is returned. Otherwise, a null pointer is returned.
`char *strrchr( const char *s, int c )`	
	Searches from the end of string `s` and locates the last occurrence of character `c` in string `s`. If `c` is found, a pointer to `c` in string `s` is returned. Otherwise, a null pointer is returned.
`size_t strspn( const char *s1, const char *s2 )`	
	Determines and returns the length of the initial segment of string `s1` consisting only of characters contained in string `s2`.
`char *strpbrk( const char *s1, const char *s2 )`	
	Locates the first occurrence in string `s1` of any character in string `s2`. If a character from string `s2` is found, a pointer to the character in string `s1` is returned. Otherwise, a null pointer is returned.
`size_t strcspn( const char *s1, const char *s2 )`	
	Determines and returns the length of the initial segment of string `s1` consisting of characters not contained in string `s2`.
`char *strstr( const char *s1, const char *s2 )`	
	Locates the first occurrence in string `s1` of string `s2`. If the string is found, a pointer to the string in `s1` is returned. Otherwise, a null pointer is returned.

Fig. 20.34 | Search functions of the C string-handling library.

```
// Fig. 20.35: fig20_35.cpp
// Using strchr.
#include <iostream>
#include <cstring> // strchr prototype
using namespace std;

int main()
{
   const char *string1 = "This is a test";
   char character1 = 'a';
   char character2 = 'z';

   // search for character1 in string1
   if ( strchr( string1, character1 ) != NULL )
      cout << '\'' << character1 << "' was found in \""
         << string1 << "\".\n";
   else
      cout << '\'' << character1 << "' was not found in \""
         << string1 << "\".\n";

   // search for character2 in string1
   if ( strchr( string1, character2 ) != NULL )
      cout << '\'' << character2 << "' was found in \""
         << string1 << "\".\n";
   else
      cout << '\'' << character2 << "' was not found in \""
         << string1 << "\"." << endl;
} // end main
```

```
'a' was found in "This is a test".
'z' was not found in "This is a test".
```

Fig. 20.35 | String-search function `strchr`.

Function **`strcspn`** (Fig. 20.36, line 15) determines the length of the initial part of the string in its first argument that does not contain any characters from the string in its second argument. The function returns the length of the segment.

```
1  // Fig. 20.36: fig20_36.cpp
2  // Using strcspn.
3  #include <iostream>
4  #include <cstring> // strcspn prototype
5  using namespace std;
6
7  int main()
8  {
9     const char *string1 = "The value is 3.14159";
10    const char *string2 = "1234567890";
11
12    cout << "string1 = " << string1 << "\nstring2 = " << string2
13       << "\n\nThe length of the initial segment of string1"
```

Fig. 20.36 | String-search function `strcspn`. (Part 1 of 2.)

```
        << "\ncontaining no characters from string2 = "
        << strcspn( string1, string2 ) << endl;
} // end main
```

```
string1 = The value is 3.14159
string2 = 1234567890

The length of the initial segment of string1
containing no characters from string2 = 13
```

Fig. 20.36 | String-search function `strcspn`. (Part 2 of 2.)

Function **`strpbrk`** searches for the first occurrence in its first string argument of any character in its second string argument. If a character from the second argument is found, `strpbrk` returns a pointer to the character in the first argument; otherwise, `strpbrk` returns a null pointer. Line 13 of Fig. 20.37 locates the first occurrence in `string1` of any character from `string2`.

```
1  // Fig. 20.37: fig20_37.cpp
2  // Using strpbrk.
3  #include <iostream>
4  #include <cstring> // strpbrk prototype
5  using namespace std;
6
7  int main()
8  {
9     const char *string1 = "This is a test";
10    const char *string2 = "beware";
11
12    cout << "Of the characters in \"" << string2 << "\"\n'"
13       << *strpbrk( string1, string2 ) << "\' is the first character "
14       << "to appear in\n\"" << string1 << '\"' << endl;
15 } // end main
```

```
Of the characters in "beware"
'a' is the first character to appear in
"This is a test"
```

Fig. 20.37 | String-search function `strpbrk`.

Function **`strrchr`** searches for the last occurrence of the specified character in a string. If the character is found, `strrchr` returns a pointer to the character in the string; otherwise, `strrchr` returns 0. Line 15 of Fig. 20.38 searches for the last occurrence of the character `'z'` in the string `"A zoo has many animals including zebras"`.

```
1  // Fig. 20.38: fig20_38.cpp
2  // Using strrchr.
3  #include <iostream>
4  #include <cstring> // strrchr prototype
```

Fig. 20.38 | String-search function `strrchr`. (Part 1 of 2.)

```
using namespace std;

int main()
{
   const char *string1 = "A zoo has many animals including zebras";
   char c = 'z';

   cout << "string1 = " << string1 << "\n" << endl;
   cout << "The remainder of string1 beginning with the\n"
      << "last occurrence of character '"
      << c << "' is: \"" << strrchr( string1, c ) << '\"' << endl;
} // end main
```

```
string1 = A zoo has many animals including zebras

The remainder of string1 beginning with the
last occurrence of character 'z' is: "zebras"
```

Fig. 20.38 | String-search function `strrchr`. (Part 2 of 2.)

Function **`strspn`** (Fig. 20.39, line 15) determines the length of the initial part of the string in its first argument that contains only characters from the string in its second argument. The function returns the length of the segment.

```
1  // Fig. 20.39: fig20_39.cpp
2  // Using strspn.
3  #include <iostream>
4  #include <cstring> // strspn prototype
5  using namespace std;
6
7  int main()
8  {
9     const char *string1 = "The value is 3.14159";
10    const char *string2 = "aehils Tuv";
11
12    cout << "string1 = " << string1 << "\nstring2 = " << string2
13       << "\n\nThe length of the initial segment of string1\n"
14       << "containing only characters from string2 = "
15       << strspn( string1, string2 ) << endl;
16 } // end main
```

```
string1 = The value is 3.14159
string2 = aehils Tuv

The length of the initial segment of string1
containing only characters from string2 = 13
```

Fig. 20.39 | String-search function `strspn`.

Function **`strstr`** searches for the first occurrence of its second string argument in its first string argument. If the second string is found in the first string, a pointer to the location of the string in the first argument is returned; otherwise, it returns 0. Line 15 of Fig. 20.40 uses `strstr` to find the string `"def"` in the string `"abcdefabcdef"`.

```
1  // Fig. 20.40: fig20_40.cpp
2  // Using strstr.
3  #include <iostream>
4  #include <cstring> // strstr prototype
5  using namespace std;
6
7  int main()
8  {
9     const char *string1 = "abcdefabcdef";
10    const char *string2 = "def";
11
12    cout << "string1 = " << string1 << "\nstring2 = " << string2
13       << "\n\nThe remainder of string1 beginning with the\n"
14       << "first occurrence of string2 is: "
15       << strstr( string1, string2 ) << endl;
16 } // end main
```

```
string1 = abcdefabcdef
string2 = def

The remainder of string1 beginning with the
first occurrence of string2 is: defabcdef
```

Fig. 20.40 | String-search function `strstr`.

20.11 Memory Functions of the C String-Handling Library

The string-handling library functions presented in this section facilitate manipulating, comparing and searching blocks of memory. The functions treat blocks of memory as arrays of bytes. These functions can manipulate any block of data. Figure 20.41 summarizes the memory functions of the string-handling library. In the function discussions, "object" refers to a block of data. [*Note:* The string-processing functions in prior sections operate on null-terminated strings. The functions in this section operate on arrays of bytes. The null-character value (i.e., a byte containing 0) has *no* significance with the functions in this section.]

Prototype	Description
`void *memcpy( void *s1, const void *s2, size_t n )`	
	Copies `n` characters from the object pointed to by `s2` into the object pointed to by `s1`. A pointer to the resulting object is returned. The area from which characters are copied is not allowed to overlap the area to which characters are copied.

Fig. 20.41 | Memory functions of the string-handling library. (Part 1 of 2.)

Prototype	Description
`void *memmove( void *s1, const void *s2, size_t n )`	
	Copies n characters from the object pointed to by s2 into the object pointed to by s1. The copy is performed as if the characters were first copied from the object pointed to by s2 into a temporary array, then copied from the temporary array into the object pointed to by s1. A pointer to the resulting object is returned. The area from which characters are copied is allowed to overlap the area to which characters are copied.
`int memcmp( const void *s1, const void *s2, size_t n )`	
	Compares the first n characters of the objects pointed to by s1 and s2. The function returns 0, less than 0, or greater than 0 if s1 is equal to, less than or greater than s2, respectively.
`void *memchr( const void *s, int c, size_t n )`	
	Locates the first occurrence of c (converted to unsigned char) in the first n characters of the object pointed to by s. If c is found, a pointer to c in the object is returned. Otherwise, 0 is returned.
`void *memset( void *s, int c, size_t n )`	
	Copies c (converted to unsigned char) into the first n characters of the object pointed to by s. A pointer to the result is returned.

Fig. 20.41 | Memory functions of the string-handling library. (Part 2 of 2.)

The pointer parameters to these functions are declared void *. In Chapter 8, we saw that *a pointer to any data type can be assigned directly to a pointer of type* void *. For this reason, these functions can receive pointers to any data type. Remember that *a pointer of type* void * *cannot be assigned directly to a pointer of any other data type.* Because a void * pointer cannot be dereferenced, each function receives a size argument that specifies the number of characters (bytes) the function will process. For simplicity, the examples in this section manipulate character arrays (blocks of characters).

Function **memcpy** copies a specified number of characters (bytes) from the object pointed to by its second argument into the object pointed to by its first argument. The function can receive a pointer to any type of object. The result of this function is undefined if the two objects overlap in memory (i.e., are parts of the same object). The program of Fig. 20.42 uses memcpy (line 14) to copy the string in array s2 to array s1.

```
1  // Fig. 20.42: fig20_42.cpp
2  // Using memcpy.
3  #include <iostream>
4  #include <cstring> // memcpy prototype
5  using namespace std;
6
7  int main()
8  {
9     char s1[ 17 ] = {};
```

Fig. 20.42 | Memory-handling function memcpy. (Part 1 of 2.)

```

   // 17 total characters (includes terminating null)
   char s2[] = "Copy this string";

   memcpy( s1, s2, 17 ); // copy 17 characters from s2 to s1

   cout << "After s2 is copied into s1 with memcpy,\n"
      << "s1 contains \"" << s1 << '\"' << endl;
} // end main
```

```
After s2 is copied into s1 with memcpy,
s1 contains "Copy this string"
```

Fig. 20.42 | Memory-handling function memcpy. (Part 2 of 2.)

Function **memmove**, like memcpy, copies a specified number of bytes from the object pointed to by its second argument into the object pointed to by its first argument. Copying is performed as if the bytes were copied from the second argument to a temporary array of characters, then copied from the temporary array to the first argument. This allows characters from one part of a string to be copied into another part of the same string.

Common Programming Error 20.11

String-manipulation functions other than memmove that copy characters have undefined results when copying takes place between parts of the same string.

The program in Fig. 20.43 uses memmove (line 13) to copy the last 10 bytes of array x into the first 10 bytes of array x.

```
1  // Fig. 20.43: fig20_43.cpp
2  // Using memmove.
3  #include <iostream>
4  #include <cstring> // memmove prototype
5  using namespace std;
6
7  int main()
8  {
9     char x[] = "Home Sweet Home";
10
11    cout << "The string in array x before memmove is: " << x;
12    cout << "\nThe string in array x after memmove is:  "
13       << static_cast< char * >( memmove( x, &x[ 5 ], 10 ) ) << endl;
14 } // end main
```

```
The string in array x before memmove is: Home Sweet Home
The string in array x after memmove is:  Sweet Home Home
```

Fig. 20.43 | Memory-handling function memmove.

Function **memcmp** (Fig. 20.44, lines 14–16) compares the specified number of characters of its first argument with the corresponding characters of its second argument. The function returns a value greater than zero if the first argument is greater than the second argument, zero if the arguments are equal, and a value less than zero if the first argument is less than the second argument. [*Note:* With some compilers, function memcmp returns -1, 0 or 1, as in the sample output of Fig. 20.44. With other compilers, this function returns 0 or the difference between the numeric codes of the first characters that differ in the strings being compared. For example, when s1 and s2 are compared, the first character that differs between them is the fifth character of each string—E (numeric code 69) for s1 and X (numeric code 72) for s2. In this case, the return value will be 19 (or -19 when s2 is compared to s1).]

```
// Fig. 20.44: fig20_44.cpp
// Using memcmp.
#include <iostream>
#include <iomanip>
#include <cstring> // memcmp prototype
using namespace std;

int main()
{
   char s1[] = "ABCDEFG";
   char s2[] = "ABCDXYZ";

   cout << "s1 = " << s1 << "\ns2 = " << s2 << endl
      << "\nmemcmp(s1, s2, 4) = " << setw( 3 ) << memcmp( s1, s2, 4 )
      << "\nmemcmp(s1, s2, 7) = " << setw( 3 ) << memcmp( s1, s2, 7 )
      << "\nmemcmp(s2, s1, 7) = " << setw( 3 ) << memcmp( s2, s1, 7 )
      << endl;
} // end main
```

```
s1 = ABCDEFG
s2 = ABCDXYZ

memcmp(s1, s2, 4) =   0
memcmp(s1, s2, 7) =  -1
memcmp(s2, s1, 7) =   1
```

Fig. 20.44 | Memory-handling function memcmp.

Function **memchr** searches for the first occurrence of a byte, represented as unsigned char, in the specified number of bytes of an object. If the byte is found in the object, a pointer to it is returned; otherwise, the function returns a null pointer. Line 13 of Fig. 20.45 searches for the character (byte) 'r' in the string "This is a string".

```
1 // Fig. 20.45: fig20_45.cpp
2 // Using memchr.
3 #include <iostream>
4 #include <cstring> // memchr prototype
5 using namespace std;
```

Fig. 20.45 | Memory-handling function memchr. (Part 1 of 2.)

```

int main()
{
   char s[] = "This is a string";

   cout << "s = " << s << "\n" << endl;
   cout << "The remainder of s after character 'r' is found is \""
      << static_cast< char * >( memchr( s, 'r', 16 ) ) << '\"' << endl;
} // end main
```

```
s = This is a string

The remainder of s after character 'r' is found is "ring"
```

Fig. 20.45 | Memory-handling function `memchr`. (Part 2 of 2.)

Function **`memset`** copies the value of the byte in its second argument into a specified number of bytes of the object pointed to by its first argument. Line 13 in Fig. 20.46 uses `memset` to copy `'b'` into the first 7 bytes of `string1`.

```
1  // Fig. 20.46: fig20_46.cpp
2  // Using memset.
3  #include <iostream>
4  #include <cstring> // memset prototype
5  using namespace std;
6
7  int main()
8  {
9     char string1[ 15 ] = "BBBBBBBBBBBBBB";
10
11    cout << "string1 = " << string1 << endl;
12    cout << "string1 after memset = "
13       << static_cast< char * >( memset( string1, 'b', 7 ) ) << endl;
14 } // end main
```

```
string1 = BBBBBBBBBBBBBB
string1 after memset = bbbbbbbBBBBBBB
```

Fig. 20.46 | Memory-handling function `memset`.

20.12 Wrap-Up

This chapter introduced `struct` definitions, initializing `structs` and using them with functions. We discussed `typedef`, using it to create aliases to help promote portability. We also introduced bitwise operators to manipulate data and bit fields for storing data compactly. You learned about the string-conversion functions in `<cstlib>` and the string-processing functions in `<cstring>`. The next chapter covers various additional C++ topics.

21

Other Topics

Objectives

In this chapter you'll:

- Use `const_cast` to temporarily treat a `const` object as a non-`const` object.
- Use `namespaces`
- Use operator keywords.
- Use `mutable` members in `const` objects.
- Use class-member pointer operators `.*` and `->*`.
- Use multiple inheritance.
- Understand the role of `virtual` base classes in multiple inheritance.

Outline

21.1 Introduction

We now consider additional C++ features. First, we discuss the `const_cast` operator, which allows you to add or remove the `const` qualification of a variable. Next, we discuss `namespaces`, which can be used to ensure that every identifier in a program has a *unique* name and can help resolve naming conflicts caused by using libraries that have the same variable, function or class names. We then present several *operator keywords* that are useful for programmers who have keyboards that do not support certain characters used in operator symbols, such as `!`, `&`, `^`, `~` and `|`. We continue our discussion with the `mutable` storage-class specifier, which enables you to indicate that a data member should *always be modifiable*, even when it appears in an object that's currently being treated as a `const` object by the program. Next we introduce two special operators that you can use with pointers to class members to access a data member or member function *without knowing its name* in advance. Finally, we introduce *multiple inheritance*, which enables a derived class to inherit the members of *several* base classes. As part of this introduction, we discuss potential problems with multiple inheritance and how `virtual` *inheritance* can be used to solve them.

21.2 const_cast Operator

C++ provides the **`const_cast`** operator for casting away `const` or `volatile` qualification. You declare a variable with the **`volatile`** qualifier when you expect the variable to be modified by hardware or other programs not known to the compiler. Declaring a variable `volatile` indicates that the compiler should *not optimize* the use of that variable because doing so could affect the ability of those other programs to access and modify the `volatile` variable.

In general, it's dangerous to use the `const_cast` operator, because it allows a program to modify a variable that was declared `const`. There are cases in which it's desirable, or even necessary, to cast away `const`-ness. For example, older C and C++ libraries might provide functions that have non-`const` parameters and that do not modify their parameters—if you wish to pass `const` data to such a function, you'd need to cast away the data's `const`-ness; otherwise, the compiler would report error messages.

Similarly, you could pass non-`const` data to a function that treats the data as if it were constant, then returns that data as a constant. In such cases, you might need to cast away the `const`-ness of the returned data, as we demonstrate in Fig. 21.1.

```
1  // Fig. 21.1: fig21_01.cpp
2  // Demonstrating const_cast.
3  #include <iostream>
4  #include <cstring> // contains prototypes for functions strcmp and strlen
5  #include <cctype> // contains prototype for function toupper
6  using namespace std;
7
8  // returns the larger of two C strings
9  const char *maximum( const char *first, const char *second )
10 {
11    return ( strcmp( first, second ) >= 0 ? first : second );
12 } // end function maximum
13
14 int main()
15 {
16    char s1[] = "hello"; // modifiable array of characters
17    char s2[] = "goodbye"; // modifiable array of characters
18
19    // const_cast required to allow the const char * returned by maximum
20    // to be assigned to the char * variable maxPtr
21    char *maxPtr = const_cast< char * >( maximum( s1, s2 ) );
22
23    cout << "The larger string is: " << maxPtr << endl;
24
25    for ( size_t i = 0; i < strlen( maxPtr ); ++i )
26       maxPtr[ i ] = toupper( maxPtr[ i ] );
27
28    cout << "The larger string capitalized is: " << maxPtr << endl;
29 } // end main
```

```
The larger string is: hello
The larger string capitalized is: HELLO
```

Fig. 21.1 | Demonstrating operator `const_cast`.

In this program, function `maximum` (lines 9–12) receives two C strings as `const char *` parameters and returns a `const char *` that points to the larger of the two strings. Function `main` declares the two C strings as non-`const` `char` arrays (lines 16–17); thus, these arrays are modifiable. In `main`, we wish to output the larger of the two C strings, then modify that C string by converting it to uppercase letters.

Function `maximum`'s two parameters are of type `const char *`, so the function's return type also must be declared as `const char *`. If the return type is specified as only `char *`, the compiler issues an error message indicating that the value being returned *cannot* be converted from `const char *` to `char *`—a dangerous conversion, because it attempts to treat data that the function believes to be `const` as if it were non-`const` data.

Even though function `maximum` *believes* the data to be constant, we know that the original arrays in `main` do *not* contain constant data. Therefore, `main` *should* be able to modify the contents of those arrays as necessary. Since we know these arrays *are* modifiable, we use `const_cast` (line 21) to *cast away the* `const`*-ness* of the pointer returned by `maximum`, so we can then modify the data in the array representing the larger of the two C strings. We can then use the pointer as the name of a character array in the for statement (lines 25–26) to convert the contents of the larger string to uppercase letters. Without the const_cast in line 21, this program will *not* compile, because you are *not* allowed to assign a pointer of type const char * to a pointer of type char *.

Error-Prevention Tip 21.1

In general, a const_cast should be used only when it is known in advance that the original data is not constant. Otherwise, unexpected results may occur.

21.3 mutable Class Members

In Section 21.2, we introduced the const_cast operator, which allowed us to remove the "const-ness" of a type. A const_cast operation can also be applied to a data member of a const object from the body of a const member function of that object's class. This enables the const member function to modify the data member, even though the object is considered to be const in the body of that function. Such an operation might be performed when most of an object's data members should be considered const, but a particular data member still needs to be modified.

As an example, consider a linked list that maintains its contents in sorted order. Searching through the linked list does not require modifications to the data of the linked list, so the search function could be a const member function of the linked-list class. However, it's conceivable that a linked-list object, in an effort to make future searches more efficient, might keep track of the location of the last successful match. If the next search operation attempts to locate an item that appears later in the list, the search could begin from the location of the last successful match, rather than from the beginning of the list. To do this, the const member function that performs the search must be able to modify the data member that keeps track of the last successful search.

If a data member such as the one described above should *always* be modifiable, C++ provides the storage-class specifier **mutable** as an alternative to const_cast. A mutable data member is always modifiable, even in a const member function or const object.

Portability Tip 21.1

The effect of attempting to modify an object that was defined as constant, regardless of whether that modification was made possible by a const_cast or C-style cast, varies among compilers.

mutable and const_cast are used in different contexts. For a const object with no mutable data members, operator const_cast *must* be used every time a member is to be modified. This greatly reduces the chance of a member being accidentally modified because the member is not permanently modifiable. Operations involving const_cast are typically *hidden* in a member function's implementation. The user of a class might not be aware that a member is being modified.

Software Engineering Observation 21.1

mutable members are useful in classes that have "secret" implementation details that do not contribute to a client's use of an object of the class.

Mechanical Demonstration of a `mutable` *Data Member*

Figure 21.2 demonstrates using a `mutable` member. The program defines class `TestMutable` (lines 7–21), which contains a constructor, function `getValue` and a `private` data member `value` that's declared `mutable`. Lines 15–18 define function `getValue` as a `const` member function that returns a copy of `value`. Notice that the function increments `mutable` data member `value` in the `return` statement. Normally, a `const` member function *cannot* modify data members unless the object on which the function operates—i.e., the one to which `this` points—is *cast* (using `const_cast`) to a non-`const` type. Because `value` is `mutable`, this `const` function *can* modify the data.

```
1  // Fig. 21.2: fig21_02.cpp
2  // Demonstrating storage-class specifier mutable.
3  #include <iostream>
4  using namespace std;
5
6  // class TestMutable definition
7  class TestMutable
8  {
9  public:
10    TestMutable( int v = 0 )
11    {
12       value = v;
13    } // end TestMutable constructor
14
15    int getValue() const
16    {
17       return ++value; // increments value
18    } // end function getValue
19 private:
20    mutable int value; // mutable member
21 }; // end class TestMutable
22
23 int main()
24 {
25    const TestMutable test( 99 );
26
27    cout << "Initial value: " << test.getValue();
28    cout << "\nModified value: " << test.getValue() << endl;
29 } // end main
```

```
Initial value: 99
Modified value: 100
```

Fig. 21.2 | Demonstrating a `mutable` data member.

Line 25 declares `const TestMutable` object `test` and initializes it to 99. Line 27 calls the `const` member function `getValue`, which adds one to `value` and returns its previous contents. Notice that the compiler *allows* the call to member function `getValue` on the object `test` because it's a `const` object and `getValue` is a `const` member function. However, `getValue` *modifies* variable `value`. Thus, when line 28 invokes `getValue` again, the new `value` (100) is output to prove that the `mutable` data member was indeed *modified*.

21.4 namespaces

A program may include many identifiers defined in different scopes. Sometimes a variable of one scope will "overlap" (i.e., collide) with a variable of the *same* name in a *different* scope, possibly creating a *naming conflict*. Such overlapping can occur at many levels. Identifier overlapping occurs frequently in third-party libraries that happen to use the same names for global identifiers (such as functions). This can cause compilation errors.

C++ solves this problem with **namespaces**. Each namespace defines a scope in which identifiers and variables are placed. To use a **namespace member**, either the member's name must be qualified with the namespace name and the *scope resolution operator* (`::`), as in

```
MyNameSpace::member
```

or a `using` directive must appear *before* the name is used in the program. Typically, such `using` statements are placed at the beginning of the file in which members of the `namespace` are used. For example, placing the following `using` directive at the beginning of a source-code file

```
using namespace MyNameSpace;
```

specifies that members of namespace *MyNameSpace* can be used in the file without preceding each member with *MyNameSpace* and the scope resolution operator (`::`).

A `using` directive of the form

```
using std::cout;
```

brings *one* name into the scope where the directive appears. A `using` directive of the form

```
using namespace std;
```

brings *all* the names from the specified `namespace` (`std`) into the scope where the directive appears.

Error-Prevention Tip 21.2

Precede a member with its namespace *name and the scope resolution operator* (`::`) *if the possibility exists of a naming conflict.*

Not all namespace*s are guaranteed to be unique.* Two third-party vendors might inadvertently use the same identifiers for their `namespace` names. Figure 21.3 demonstrates the use of `namespace`s.

```
// Fig. 21.3: fig21_03.cpp
// Demonstrating namespaces.
#include <iostream>
using namespace std;

int integer1 = 98; // global variable

// create namespace Example
namespace Example
{
```

Fig. 21.3 | Demonstrating the use of `namespace`s. (Part 1 of 3.)

```
   // declare two constants and one variable
   const double PI = 3.14159;
   const double E = 2.71828;
   int integer1 = 8;

   void printValues(); // prototype

   // nested namespace
   namespace Inner
   {
      // define enumeration
      enum Years { FISCAL1 = 1990, FISCAL2, FISCAL3 };
   } // end Inner namespace
} // end Example namespace

// create unnamed namespace
namespace
{
   double doubleInUnnamed = 88.22; // declare variable
} // end unnamed namespace

int main()
{
   // output value doubleInUnnamed of unnamed namespace
   cout << "doubleInUnnamed = " << doubleInUnnamed;

   // output global variable
   cout << "\n(global) integer1 = " << integer1;

   // output values of Example namespace
   cout << "\nPI = " << Example::PI << "\nE = " << Example::E
      << "\ninteger1 = " << Example::integer1 << "\nFISCAL3 = "
      << Example::Inner::FISCAL3 << endl;

   Example::printValues(); // invoke printValues function
} // end main

// display variable and constant values
void Example::printValues()
{
   cout << "\nIn printValues:\ninteger1 = " << integer1 << "\nPI = "
      << PI << "\nE = " << E << "\ndoubleInUnnamed = "
      << doubleInUnnamed << "\n(global) integer1 = " << ::integer1
      << "\nFISCAL3 = " << Inner::FISCAL3 << endl;
} // end printValues
```

```
doubleInUnnamed = 88.22
(global) integer1 = 98
PI = 3.14159
E = 2.71828
integer1 = 8
FISCAL3 = 1992
```

Fig. 21.3 | Demonstrating the use of namespaces. (Part 2 of 3.)

```
In printValues:
integer1 = 8
PI = 3.14159
E = 2.71828
doubleInUnnamed = 88.22
(global) integer1 = 98
FISCAL3 = 1992
```

Fig. 21.3 | Demonstrating the use of namespaces. (Part 3 of 3.)

Defining namespaces

Lines 9–24 use the keyword namespace to define namespace Example. The body of a namespace is delimited by braces ({}). The namespace Example's members consist of two constants (PI and E in lines 12–13), an int (integer1 in line 14), a function (printValues in line 16) and a **nested namespace** (Inner in lines 19–23). Notice that member integer1 has the same name as global variable integer1 (line 6). *Variables that have the same name must have different scopes*—otherwise compilation errors occur. A namespace can contain constants, data, classes, nested namespaces, functions, etc. Definitions of namespaces must occupy the *global scope* or be *nested* within other namespaces. Unlike classes, different namespace members can be defined in separate namespace blocks—each standard library header has a namespace block placing its contents in namespace std.

Lines 27–30 create an **unnamed namespace** containing the member doubleInUnnamed. Variables, classes and functions in an *unnamed namespace* are accessible only in the current **translation unit** (a .cpp file and the files it includes). However, unlike variables, classes or functions with static linkage, those in the *unnamed namespace* may be used as template arguments. The unnamed namespace has an implicit using directive, so its members appear to occupy the **global namespace**, are accessible directly and *do not have to be qualified with a namespace name*. Global variables are also part of the global namespace and are accessible in all scopes following the declaration in the file.

Software Engineering Observation 21.2

Each separate compilation unit has its own unique unnamed namespace; i.e., the unnamed namespace replaces the static linkage specifier.

Accessing namespace *Members with Qualified Names*

Line 35 outputs the value of variable doubleInUnnamed, which is directly accessible as part of the *unnamed namespace*. Line 38 outputs the value of global variable integer1. For both of these variables, the compiler first attempts to locate a *local* declaration of the variables in main. Since there are no local declarations, the compiler assumes those variables are in the global namespace.

Lines 41–43 output the values of PI, E, integer1 and FISCAL3 from namespace Example. Notice that each must be *qualified* with Example:: because the program does not provide any using directive or declarations indicating that it will use members of namespace Example. In addition, member integer1 must be qualified, because a global variable has the same name. Otherwise, the global variable's value is output. FISCAL3 is a member of nested namespace Inner, so it must be *qualified* with Example::Inner::.

Function `printValues` (defined in lines 49–55) is a member of `Example`, so it can access other members of the `Example` `namespace` directly *without using a* `namespace` *qualifier*. The output statement in lines 51–54 outputs `integer1`, `PI`, `E`, `doubleInUnnamed`, global variable `integer1` and `FISCAL3`. Notice that `PI` and `E` are *not qualified* with `Example`. Variable `doubleInUnnamed` is still *accessible*, because it's in the *unnamed* `namespace` and the variable name does *not conflict* with any other members of `namespace` `Example`. The global version of `integer1` must be *qualified* with the scope resolution operator (`::`), because its name *conflicts* with a member of `namespace` `Example`. Also, `FISCAL3` must be *qualified* with `Inner::`. When accessing members of a *nested* `namespace`, the members must be qualified with the `namespace` name (unless the member is being used inside the nested `namespace`).

Common Programming Error 21.1

Placing `main` *in a* `namespace` *is a compilation error.*

`using` *Directives Should* Not *Be Placed in Headers*

`namespace`s are particularly useful in large-scale applications that use many class libraries. In such cases, there's a higher likelihood of naming conflicts. When working on such projects, there should *never* be a `using` directive in a header. Having one brings the corresponding names into any file that includes the header. This could result in name collisions and subtle, hard-to-find errors. Instead, use only fully qualified names in headers (for example, `std::cout` or `std::string`).

Aliases for `namespace` *Names*

`namespace`s can be *aliased*. For example the statement

```
namespace CPPHTP = CPlusPlusHowToProgram;
```

creates the **namespace alias** `CPPHTP` for `CPlusPlusHowToProgram`.

21.5 Operator Keywords

The C++ standard provides **operator keywords** (Fig. 21.4) that can be used in place of several C++ operators. You can use operator keywords if you have keyboards that do not support certain characters such as `!`, `&`, `^`, `~`, `|`, etc.

Operator	Operator keyword	Description
Logical operator keywords		
`&&`	`and`	logical AND
`||`	`or`	logical OR
`!`	`not`	logical NOT
Inequality operator keyword		
`!=`	`not_eq`	inequality

Fig. 21.4 | Operator keyword alternatives to operator symbols. (Part 1 of 2.)

Operator	Operator keyword	Description
Bitwise operator keywords		
&	**bitand**	bitwise AND
|	**bitor**	bitwise inclusive OR
^	**xor**	bitwise exclusive OR
~	**compl**	bitwise complement
Bitwise assignment operator keywords		
&=	**and_eq**	bitwise AND assignment
|=	**or_eq**	bitwise inclusive OR assignment
^=	**xor_eq**	bitwise exclusive OR assignment

Fig. 21.4 | Operator keyword alternatives to operator symbols. (Part 2 of 2.)

Figure 21.5 demonstrates the operator keywords. Microsoft Visual C++ 2010 requires the header `<ciso646>` (line 4) to use the operator keywords. In GNU C++ and LLVM, the operator keywords are always defined and this header is not required.

```
1  // Fig. 21.5: fig21_05.cpp
2  // Demonstrating operator keywords.
3  #include <iostream>
4  #include <ciso646> // enables operator keywords in Microsoft Visual C++
5  using namespace std;
6
7  int main()
8  {
9     bool a = true;
10    bool b = false;
11    int c = 2;
12    int d = 3;
13
14    // sticky setting that causes bool values to display as true or false
15    cout << boolalpha;
16
17    cout << "a = " << a << "; b = " << b
18       << "; c = " << c << "; d = " << d;
19
20    cout << "\n\nLogical operator keywords:";
21    cout << "\n   a and a: " << ( a and a );
22    cout << "\n   a and b: " << ( a and b );
23    cout << "\n    a or a: " << ( a or a );
24    cout << "\n    a or b: " << ( a or b );
25    cout << "\n     not a: " << ( not a );
26    cout << "\n     not b: " << ( not b );
27    cout << "\na not_eq b: " << ( a not_eq b );
28
```

Fig. 21.5 | Demonstrating operator keywords. (Part 1 of 2.)

```
29      cout << "\n\nBitwise operator keywords:";
30      cout << "\nc bitand d: " << ( c bitand d );
31      cout << "\n c bitor d: " << ( c bitor d );
32      cout << "\n   c xor d: " << ( c xor d );
33      cout << "\n   compl c: " << ( compl c );
34      cout << "\nc and_eq d: " << ( c and_eq d );
35      cout << "\n c or_eq d: " << ( c or_eq d );
36      cout << "\nc xor_eq d: " << ( c xor_eq d ) << endl;
37   } // end main
```

```
a = true; b = false; c = 2; d = 3

Logical operator keywords:
   a and a: true
   a and b: false
    a or a: true
    a or b: true
     not a: false
     not b: true
a not_eq b: true

Bitwise operator keywords:
c bitand d: 2
 c bitor d: 3
   c xor d: 1
   compl c: -3
c and_eq d: 2
 c or_eq d: 3
c xor_eq d: 0
```

Fig. 21.5 | Demonstrating operator keywords. (Part 2 of 2.)

The program declares and initializes two `bool` variables and two integer variables (lines 9–12). Logical operations (lines 21–27) are performed with `bool` variables `a` and `b` using the various logical operator keywords. Bitwise operations (lines 30–36) are performed with the `int` variables `c` and `d` using the various bitwise operator keywords. The result of each operation is output.

21.6 Pointers to Class Members (.* and ->*)

C++ provides the `.*` and `->*` operators for accessing class members via pointers. This is a rarely used capability, primarily for advanced C++ programmers. We provide only a mechanical example of using pointers to class members here. Figure 21.6 demonstrates the pointer-to-class-member operators.

```
// Fig. 21.6: fig21_06.cpp
// Demonstrating operators .* and ->*.
#include <iostream>
using namespace std;

```

Fig. 21.6 | Demonstrating operators `.*` and `->*`. (Part 1 of 2.)

```
6  // class Test definition
7  class Test
8  {
9  public:
10    void func()
11    {
12       cout << "In func\n";
13    } // end function func
14
15    int value; // public data member
16 }; // end class Test
17
18 void arrowStar( Test * ); // prototype
19 void dotStar( Test * ); // prototype
20
21 int main()
22 {
23    Test test;
24    test.value = 8; // assign value 8
25    arrowStar( &test ); // pass address to arrowStar
26    dotStar( &test ); // pass address to dotStar
27 } // end main
28
29 // access member function of Test object using ->*
30 void arrowStar( Test *testPtr )
31 {
32    void ( Test::*memberPtr )() = &Test::func; // declare function pointer
33    ( testPtr->*memberPtr )(); // invoke function indirectly
34 } // end arrowStar
35
36 // access members of Test object data member using .*
37 void dotStar( Test *testPtr2 )
38 {
39    int Test::*vPtr = &Test::value; // declare pointer
40    cout << ( *testPtr2 ).*vPtr << endl; // access value
41 } // end dotStar
```

```
In test function
8
```

Fig. 21.6 | Demonstrating operators .* and ->*. (Part 2 of 2.)

The program declares class `Test` (lines 7–16), which provides `public` member function `test` and `public` data member `value`. Lines 18–19 provide prototypes for the functions `arrowStar` (defined in lines 30–34) and `dotStar` (defined in lines 37–41), which demonstrate the ->* and .* operators, respectively. Line 23 creates object `test`, and line 24 assigns 8 to its data member `value`. Lines 25–26 call functions `arrowStar` and `dotStar` with the address of the object `test`.

Line 32 in function `arrowStar` declares and initializes variable `memPtr` as a *pointer to a member function*. In this declaration, `Test::*` indicates that the variable `memPtr` is a *pointer to a member* of class `Test`. To declare a *pointer to a function*, enclose the pointer name preceded by * in parentheses, as in `(Test::*memPtr)`. A *pointer to a function* must specify, as part of its type, both the *return type* of the *function it points to* and the *parameter list* of that function. The function's *return type* appears to the left of the left parenthesis and the *parameter list* appears in a separate set of parentheses to the right of the pointer declaration. In this case, the function has a `void` return type and no parameters. The pointer `memPtr` is initialized with the address of class `Test`'s member function named `test`. The header of the function must match the *function pointer's declaration*—i.e., function `test` must have a `void` return type and no parameters. Notice that the right side of the assignment uses the *address operator (&)* to get the address of the member function `test`. Also, notice that *neither the left side nor the right side of the assignment in line 32 refers to a specific object of class* `Test`. Only the class name is used with the scope resolution operator (`::`). Line 33 invokes the member function stored in `memPtr` (i.e., `test`), using the `->*` operator. Because `memPtr` is a pointer to a member of a class, the `->*` operator must be used rather than the `->` operator to invoke the function.

Line 39 declares and initializes `vPtr` as a pointer to an `int` data member of class `Test`. The right side of the assignment specifies the address of the data member `value`. Line 40 dereferences the pointer `testPtr2`, then uses the `.*` operator to access the member to which `vPtr` points. *The client code can create pointers to class members for only those class members that are accessible to the client code.* In this example, both member function `test` and data member `value` are publicly accessible.

Common Programming Error 21.2

Declaring a member-function pointer without enclosing the pointer name in parentheses is a syntax error.

Common Programming Error 21.3

Declaring a member-function pointer without preceding the pointer name with a class name followed by the scope resolution operator (`::`) is a syntax error.

Common Programming Error 21.4

Attempting to use the `->` or `*` operator with a pointer to a class member generates syntax errors.

21.7 Multiple Inheritance

In Chapters 11 and 12, we discussed *single inheritance, in which each class is derived from exactly one base class.* In C++, a class may be derived from *more than one* base class—a technique known as **multiple inheritance** in which a derived class inherits the members of two or more base classes. This powerful capability encourages interesting forms of software reuse but can cause a variety of ambiguity problems. *Multiple inheritance is a difficult concept that should be used only by experienced programmers.* In fact, some of the problems associated with multiple inheritance are so subtle that newer programming languages, such as Java and C#, do not enable a class to derive from more than one base class.

Software Engineering Observation 21.3

Great care is required in the design of a system to use multiple inheritance properly; it should not be used when single inheritance and/or composition will do the job.

A common problem with multiple inheritance is that each of the base classes might contain data members or member functions that have the *same name*. This can lead to ambiguity problems when you attempt to compile. Consider the multiple-inheritance example (Figs. 21.7–21.11). Class `Base1` (Fig. 21.7) contains one `protected` `int` data member—`value` (line 20), a constructor (lines 10–13) that sets `value` and `public` member function `getData` (lines 15–18) that returns `value`.

```
1  // Fig. 21.7: Base1.h
2  // Definition of class Base1
3  #ifndef BASE1_H
4  #define BASE1_H
5
6  // class Base1 definition
7  class Base1
8  {
9  public:
10    Base1( int parameterValue )
11       : value( parameterValue )
12    {
13    } // end Base1 constructor
14
15    int getData() const
16    {
17       return value;
18    } // end function getData
19 protected: // accessible to derived classes
20    int value; // inherited by derived class
21 }; // end class Base1
22
23 #endif // BASE1_H
```

Fig. 21.7 | Demonstrating multiple inheritance—`Base1.h`.

Class `Base2` (Fig. 21.8) is similar to class `Base1`, except that its `protected` data is a `char` named `letter` (line 20). Like class `Base1`, `Base2` has a `public` member function `getData`, but this function returns the value of `char` data member `letter`.

```
1  // Fig. 21.8: Base2.h
2  // Definition of class Base2
3  #ifndef BASE2_H
4  #define BASE2_H
5
6  // class Base2 definition
7  class Base2
8  {
9  public:
10    Base2( char characterData )
11       : letter( characterData )
12    {
13    } // end Base2 constructor
```

Fig. 21.8 | Demonstrating multiple inheritance—`Base2.h`. (Part 1 of 2.)

```

   char getData() const
   {
      return letter;
   } // end function getData
protected: // accessible to derived classes
   char letter; // inherited by derived class
}; // end class Base2

#endif // BASE2_H
```

Fig. 21.8 | Demonstrating multiple inheritance—`Base2.h`. (Part 2 of 2.)

Class `Derived` (Figs. 21.9–21.10) inherits from both class `Base1` and class `Base2` through *multiple inheritance*. Class `Derived` has a `private` data member of type `double` named `real` (Fig. 21.9, line 20), a constructor to initialize all the data of class `Derived` and a `public` member function `getReal` that returns the value of `double` variable `real`.

```
1  // Fig. 21.9: Derived.h
2  // Definition of class Derived which inherits
3  // multiple base classes (Base1 and Base2).
4  #ifndef DERIVED_H
5  #define DERIVED_H
6
7  #include <iostream>
8  #include "Base1.h"
9  #include "Base2.h"
10 using namespace std;
11
12 // class Derived definition
13 class Derived : public Base1, public Base2
14 {
15    friend ostream &operator<<( ostream &, const Derived & );
16 public:
17    Derived( int, char, double );
18    double getReal() const;
19 private:
20    double real; // derived class's private data
21 }; // end class Derived
22
23 #endif // DERIVED_H
```

Fig. 21.9 | Demonstrating multiple inheritance—`Derived.h`.

```
// Fig. 21.10: Derived.cpp
// Member-function definitions for class Derived
#include "Derived.h"

// constructor for Derived calls constructors for
// class Base1 and class Base2.
```

Fig. 21.10 | Demonstrating multiple inheritance—`Derived.cpp`. (Part 1 of 2.)

```
7  // use member initializers to call base-class constructors
8  Derived::Derived( int integer, char character, double double1 )
9     : Base1( integer ), Base2( character ), real( double1 ) { }
10
11 // return real
12 double Derived::getReal() const
13 {
14    return real;
15 } // end function getReal
16
17 // display all data members of Derived
18 ostream &operator<<( ostream &output, const Derived &derived )
19 {
20    output << "    Integer: " << derived.value << "\n  Character: "
21         << derived.letter << "\nReal number: " << derived.real;
22    return output; // enables cascaded calls
23 } // end operator<<
```

Fig. 21.10 | Demonstrating multiple inheritance—`Derived.cpp`. (Part 2 of 2.)

To indicate *multiple inheritance* (in Fig. 21.9) we follow the colon (`:`) after `class Derived` with a comma-separated list of base classes (line 13). In Fig. 21.10, notice that constructor `Derived` explicitly calls base-class constructors for each of its base classes—`Base1` and `Base2`—using the member-initializer syntax (line 9). The *base-class constructors are called in the order that the inheritance is specified, not in the order in which their constructors are mentioned.* Also, *if the base-class constructors are not explicitly called in the member-initializer list, their default constructors will be called implicitly.*

The overloaded stream insertion operator (Fig. 21.10, lines 18–23) uses its second parameter—a reference to a `Derived` object—to display a `Derived` object's data. This operator function is a `friend` of `Derived`, so `operator<<` can directly access *all* of class `Derived`'s `protected` and `private` members, including the `protected` data member `value` (inherited from class `Base1`), `protected` data member `letter` (inherited from class `Base2`) and `private` data member `real` (declared in class `Derived`).

Now let's examine the `main` function (Fig. 21.11) that tests the classes in Figs. 21.7–21.10. Line 11 creates `Base1` object `base1` and initializes it to the `int` value `10`. Line 12 creates `Base2` object `base2` and initializes it to the `char` value `'Z'`. Line 13 creates `Derived` object `derived` and initializes it to contain the `int` value `7`, the `char` value `'A'` and the `double` value `3.5`.

```
1  // Fig. 21.11: fig21_11.cpp
2  // Driver for multiple-inheritance example.
3  #include <iostream>
4  #include "Base1.h"
5  #include "Base2.h"
6  #include "Derived.h"
7  using namespace std;
```

Fig. 21.11 | Demonstrating multiple inheritance. (Part 1 of 2.)

```
8
9   int main()
10  {
11     Base1 base1( 10 ); // create Base1 object
12     Base2 base2( 'Z' ); // create Base2 object
13     Derived derived( 7, 'A', 3.5 ); // create Derived object
14
15     // print data members of base-class objects
16     cout << "Object base1 contains integer " << base1.getData()
17        << "\nObject base2 contains character " << base2.getData()
18        << "\nObject derived contains:\n" << derived << "\n\n";
19
20     // print data members of derived-class object
21     // scope resolution operator resolves getData ambiguity
22     cout << "Data members of Derived can be accessed individually:"
23        << "\n    Integer: " << derived.Base1::getData()
24        << "\n  Character: " << derived.Base2::getData()
25        << "\nReal number: " << derived.getReal() << "\n\n";
26     cout << "Derived can be treated as an object of either base class:\n";
27
28     // treat Derived as a Base1 object
29     Base1 *base1Ptr = &derived;
30     cout << "base1Ptr->getData() yields " << base1Ptr->getData() << '\n';
31
32     // treat Derived as a Base2 object
33     Base2 *base2Ptr = &derived;
34     cout << "base2Ptr->getData() yields " << base2Ptr->getData() << endl;
35  } // end main
```

```
Object base1 contains integer 10
Object base2 contains character Z
Object derived contains:
    Integer: 7
  Character: A
Real number: 3.5

Data members of Derived can be accessed individually:
    Integer: 7
  Character: A
Real number: 3.5

Derived can be treated as an object of either base class:
base1Ptr->getData() yields 7
base2Ptr->getData() yields A
```

Fig. 21.11 | Demonstrating multiple inheritance. (Part 2 of 2.)

Lines 16–18 display each object's data values. For objects `base1` and `base2`, we invoke each object's `getData` member function. Even though there are *two* `getData` functions in this example, the calls are *not ambiguous*. In line 16, the compiler knows that `base1` is an object of class `Base1`, so class `Base1`'s `getData` is called. In line 17, the compiler knows that `base2` is an object of class `Base2`, so class `Base2`'s `getData` is called. Line 18 displays the contents of object `derived` using the overloaded stream insertion operator.

Resolving Ambiguity Issues That Arise When a Derived Class Inherits Member Functions of the Same Name from Multiple Base Classes

Lines 22–25 output the contents of object `derived` again by using the *get* member functions of class `Derived`. However, there is an *ambiguity* problem, because this object contains two `getData` functions, one inherited from class `Base1` and one inherited from class `Base2`. This problem is easy to solve by using the scope resolution operator. The expression `derived.Base1::getData()` gets the value of the variable inherited from class `Base1` (i.e., the `int` variable named `value`) and `derived.Base2::getData()` gets the value of the variable inherited from class `Base2` (i.e., the `char` variable named `letter`). The `double` value in `real` is printed *without ambiguity* with the call `derived.getReal()`—there are no other member functions with that name in the hierarchy.

Demonstrating the Is-A *Relationships in Multiple Inheritance*

The *is-a* relationships of *single inheritance* also apply in *multiple-inheritance* relationships. To demonstrate this, line 29 assigns the address of object `derived` to the `Base1` pointer `base1Ptr`. This is allowed because an object of class `Derived` *is an* object of class `Base1`. Line 30 invokes `Base1` member function `getData` via `base1Ptr` to obtain the value of only the `Base1` part of the object `derived`. Line 33 assigns the address of object `derived` to the `Base2` pointer `base2Ptr`. This is allowed because an object of class `Derived` *is an* object of class `Base2`. Line 34 invokes `Base2` member function `getData` via `base2Ptr` to obtain the value of only the `Base2` part of the object `derived`.

21.8 Multiple Inheritance and virtual Base Classes

In Section 21.7, we discussed *multiple inheritance*, the process by which one class inherits from *two or more* classes. Multiple inheritance is used, for example, in the C++ standard library to form class `basic_iostream` (Fig. 21.12).

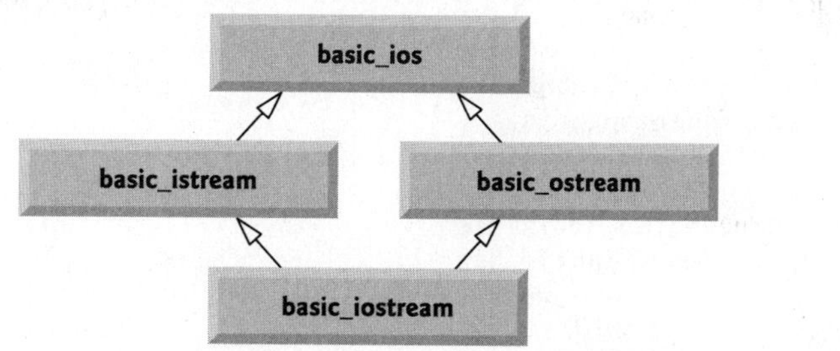

Fig. 21.12 | Multiple inheritance to form class `basic_iostream`.

Class `basic_ios` is the base class for both `basic_istream` and `basic_ostream`, each of which is formed with *single inheritance*. Class `basic_iostream` inherits from both `basic_istream` and `basic_ostream`. This enables class `basic_iostream` objects to provide the functionality of `basic_istream`s and `basic_ostream`s. In multiple-inheritance hierarchies, the inheritance described in Fig. 21.12 is referred to as **diamond inheritance**

Because classes `basic_istream` and `basic_ostream` each inherit from `basic_ios`, a potential problem exists for `basic_iostream`. Class `basic_iostream` could contain *two* copies of the members of class `basic_ios`—one inherited via class `basic_istream` and one inherited via class `basic_ostream`). Such a situation would be *ambiguous* and would result in a compilation error, because the compiler would not know which version of the members from class `basic_ios` to use. In this section, you'll see how using `virtual` base classes solves the problem of inheriting duplicate copies of an indirect base class.

Compilation Errors Produced When Ambiguity Arises in Diamond Inheritance

Figure 21.13 demonstrates the *ambiguity* that can occur in *diamond inheritance.* Class `Base` (lines 8–12) contains pure `virtual` function `print` (line 11). Classes `DerivedOne` (lines 15–23) and `DerivedTwo` (lines 26–34) each publicly inherit from `Base` and override function `print`. Class `DerivedOne` and class `DerivedTwo` each contain a **base-class subobject**—i.e., the members of class `Base` in this example.

```
1  // Fig. 21.13: fig21_13.cpp
2  // Attempting to polymorphically call a function that is
3  // multiply inherited from two base classes.
4  #include <iostream>
5  using namespace std;
6
7  // class Base definition
8  class Base
9  {
10 public:
11    virtual void print() const = 0; // pure virtual
12 }; // end class Base
13
14 // class DerivedOne definition
15 class DerivedOne : public Base
16 {
17 public:
18    // override print function
19    void print() const
20    {
21       cout << "DerivedOne\n";
22    } // end function print
23 }; // end class DerivedOne
24
25 // class DerivedTwo definition
26 class DerivedTwo : public Base
27 {
28 public:
29    // override print function
30    void print() const
31    {
32       cout << "DerivedTwo\n";
33    } // end function print
34 }; // end class DerivedTwo
35
36 // class Multiple definition
37 class Multiple : public DerivedOne, public DerivedTwo
38 {
```

Fig. 21.13 | Attempting to call a multiply inherited function polymorphically. (Part 1 of 2.)

```
39 public:
40    // qualify which version of function print
41    void print() const
42    {
43       DerivedTwo::print();
44    } // end function print
45 }; // end class Multiple
46
47 int main()
48 {
49    Multiple both; // instantiate Multiple object
50    DerivedOne one; // instantiate DerivedOne object
51    DerivedTwo two; // instantiate DerivedTwo object
52    Base *array[ 3 ]; // create array of base-class pointers
53
54    array[ 0 ] = &both; // ERROR--ambiguous
55    array[ 1 ] = &one;
56    array[ 2 ] = &two;
57
58    // polymorphically invoke print
59    for ( int i = 0; i < 3; ++i )
60       array[ i ] -> print();
61 } // end main
```

Microsoft Visual C++ compiler error message:

```
c:\cpphtp9_examples\ch23\fig21_13\fig21_13.cpp(54) : error C2594: '=' :
   ambiguous conversions from 'Multiple *' to 'Base *'
```

Fig. 21.13 | Attempting to call a multiply inherited function polymorphically. (Part 2 of 2.)

Class `Multiple` (lines 37–45) inherits from *both* class `DerivedOne` and class `DerivedTwo`. In class `Multiple`, function `print` is overridden to call `DerivedTwo`'s `print` (line 43). Notice that we must *qualify* the `print` call with the class name `DerivedTwo` to specify which version of `print` to call.

Function `main` (lines 47–61) declares objects of classes `Multiple` (line 49), `DerivedOne` (line 50) and `DerivedTwo` (line 51). Line 52 declares an array of `Base *` pointers. Each array element is initialized with the address of an object (lines 54–56). An error occurs when the address of `both`—an object of class `Multiple`—is assigned to `array[ 0 ]`. The object `both` actually contains two subobjects of type `Base`, so the compiler does not know which subobject the pointer `array[ 0 ]` should point to, and it generates a compilation error indicating an *ambiguous conversion*.

Eliminating Duplicate Subobjects with `virtual` *Base-Class Inheritance*

The problem of *duplicate subobjects* is resolved with `virtual` inheritance. When a base class is inherited as `virtual`, only *one* subobject will appear in the derived class—a process called **`virtual` base-class inheritance**. Figure 21.14 revises the program of Fig. 21.13 to use a `virtual` base class.

```
// Fig. 21.14: fig21_14.cpp
// Using virtual base classes.
#include <iostream>
using namespace std;

// class Base definition
class Base
{
public:
   virtual void print() const = 0; // pure virtual
}; // end class Base

// class DerivedOne definition
class DerivedOne : virtual public Base
{
public:
   // override print function
   void print() const
   {
      cout << "DerivedOne\n";
   } // end function print
}; // end DerivedOne class

// class DerivedTwo definition
class DerivedTwo : virtual public Base
{
public:
   // override print function
   void print() const
   {
      cout << "DerivedTwo\n";
   } // end function print
}; // end DerivedTwo class

// class Multiple definition
class Multiple : public DerivedOne, public DerivedTwo
{
public:
   // qualify which version of function print
   void print() const
   {
      DerivedTwo::print();
   } // end function print
}; // end Multiple class

int main()
{
   Multiple both; // instantiate Multiple object
   DerivedOne one; // instantiate DerivedOne object
   DerivedTwo two; // instantiate DerivedTwo object

   // declare array of base-class pointers and initialize
   // each element to a derived-class type
```

Fig. 21.14 | Using `virtual` base classes. (Part 1 of 2.)

```
54      Base *array[ 3 ];
55      array[ 0 ] = &both;
56      array[ 1 ] = &one;
57      array[ 2 ] = &two;
58
59      // polymorphically invoke function print
60      for ( int i = 0; i < 3; ++i )
61         array[ i ]->print();
62   } // end main
```

```
DerivedTwo
DerivedOne
DerivedTwo
```

Fig. 21.14 | Using `virtual` base classes. (Part 2 of 2.)

The key change is that classes `DerivedOne` (line 14) and `DerivedTwo` (line 25) each inherit from `Base` by specifying `virtual public Base`. Since both classes inherit from `Base`, they each contain a *`Base` subobject.* The benefit of *`virtual` inheritance* is not clear until class `Multiple` inherits from `DerivedOne` and `DerivedTwo` (line 36). Since each of the base classes used *`virtual` inheritance* to inherit class `Base`'s members, the compiler ensures that only *one* `Base` subobject is inherited into class `Multiple`. This eliminates the ambiguity error generated by the compiler in Fig. 21.13. The compiler now allows the implicit conversion of the derived-class pointer (`&both`) to the base-class pointer `array[ 0 ]` in line 55 in `main`. The `for` statement in lines 60–61 polymorphically calls `print` for each object.

Constructors in Multiple-Inheritance Hierarchies with `virtual` Base Classes
Implementing hierarchies with `virtual` base classes is simpler if *default constructors* are used for the base classes. Figures 21.13 and 21.14 use compiler-generated *default constructors.* If a `virtual` base class provides a constructor that requires arguments, the derived-class implementations become more complicated, because the **most derived class** must explicitly invoke the `virtual` base class's constructor. *Providing a default constructor for `virtual` base classes simplifies hierarchy design.*

21.9 Wrap-Up

In this chapter, you learned how to use the `const_cast` operator to remove the `const` qualification of a variable. We showed how to use `namespaces` to ensure that every identifier in a program has a unique name and explained how `namespaces` can help resolve naming conflicts. You saw several operator keywords to use if your keyboards do not support certain characters used in operator symbols, such as `!`, `&`, `^`, `~` and `|`. We showed how the `mutable` storage-class specifier enables you to indicate that a data member should always be modifiable, even when it appears in an object that's currently being treated as a `const`. We also showed the mechanics of using pointers to class members and the `->*` and `.*` operators. Finally, we introduced multiple inheritance and discussed problems associated with allowing a derived class to inherit the members of several base classes. As part of this discussion, we demonstrated how `virtual` inheritance can be used to solve those problems. In the next chapter, we begin our object-oriented design and implementation case study.

22

ATM Case Study, Part 1: Object-Oriented Design with the UML

Objectives

In this chapter you'll:

- Learn a simple object-oriented design methodology.
- Learn what a requirements document is.
- Identify classes and class attributes from a requirements document.
- Identify objects' states, activities and operations from a requirements document.
- Determine the collaborations among objects in a system.
- Work with the UML's use case, class, state, activity, communication and sequence diagrams to graphically model an object-oriented system.

Outline

22.1 Introduction

Now we begin the optional portion of our object-oriented design and implementation case study. In this chapter and Chapter 23, you'll design and implement an object-oriented automated teller machine (ATM) software system. The case study provides you with a concise, carefully paced, complete design and implementation experience. You'll perform the steps of an object-oriented design (OOD) process using the UML while relating them to the object-oriented concepts discussed in Chapters 2–12. In this chapter, you'll work with six popular types of UML diagrams to graphically represent the design. In Chapter 23, you'll tune the design with inheritance and polymorphism, then fully implement the ATM in an 850-line C++ application (Section 23.4).

This is *not* an exercise; rather, it's an end-to-end learning experience that concludes with a detailed walkthrough of the *complete* C++ code that implements our design.

22.2 Introduction to Object-Oriented Analysis and Design

What if you were asked to create a software system to control thousands of automated teller machines for a major bank? Or suppose you were asked to work on a team of 1000 software developers building the next U.S. air traffic control system. For projects so large and complex, you cannot simply sit down and start writing programs.

To create the best solutions, you should follow a process for **analyzing** your project's **requirements** (i.e., determining *what* the system should do) and developing a **design** that satisfies them (i.e., deciding *how* the system should do it). Ideally, you'd go through this process and carefully review the design (or have your design reviewed by other software professionals) before writing any code. If this process involves analyzing and designing your system from an object-oriented point of view, it's called an **object-oriented analysis and design (OOAD) process**. Analysis and design can save many hours by helping you to avoid an ill-planned system-development approach that has to be abandoned part of the way through its implementation, possibly wasting considerable time, money and effort. Small problems do not require an exhaustive OOAD process. It may be sufficient to write pseudocode before you begin writing C++ code.

As problems and the groups of people solving them increase in size, the methods of OOAD become more appropriate than pseudocode. Ideally, members of a group should agree on a strictly defined process for solving their problem and a uniform way of communicating the results of that process to one another. Although many different OOAD processes exist, a single graphical language for communicating the results of *any* OOAD process has come into wide use. This language, known as the Unified Modeling Language (UML), was developed in the mid-1990s under the initial direction of three software methodologists—Grady Booch, James Rumbaugh and Ivar Jacobson.

22.3 Examining the ATM Requirements Document

We begin our design process by presenting a **requirements document** that specifies the ATM system's overall purpose and *what* it must do. Throughout the case study, we refer to the requirements document to determine what functionality the system must include.

Requirements Document

A local bank intends to install a new automated teller machine (ATM) to allow users (i.e., bank customers) to perform basic financial transactions (Fig. 22.1). Each user can have only one account at the bank. ATM users should be able to *view their account balance*, *withdraw cash* (i.e., take money out of an account) and *deposit funds* (i.e., place money into an account).

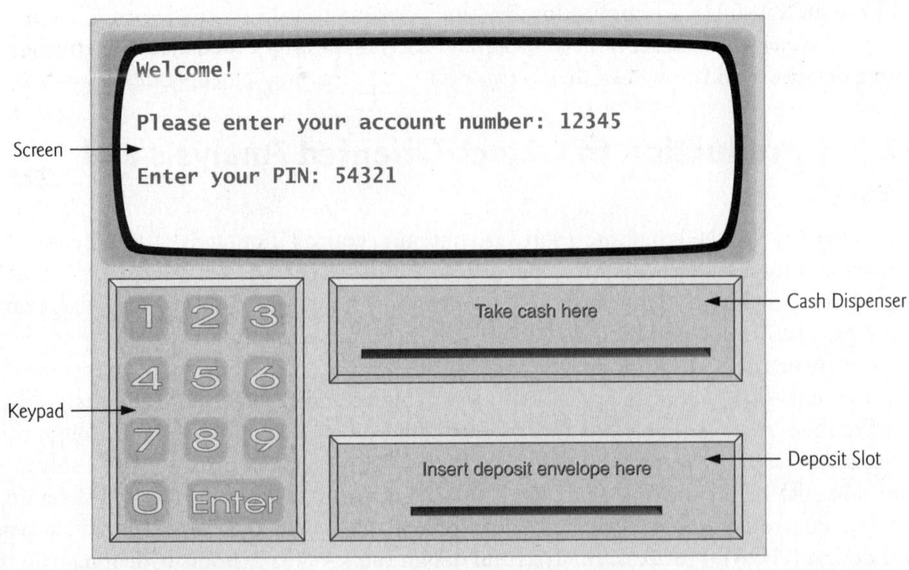

Fig. 22.1 | Automated teller machine user interface.

The user interface of the automated teller machine contains the following hardware components:

- a screen that displays messages to the user
- a keypad that receives numeric input from the user
- a cash dispenser that dispenses cash to the user and
- a deposit slot that receives deposit envelopes from the user.

The cash dispenser begins each day loaded with 500 $20 bills. [*Note:* Owing to the limited scope of this case study, certain elements of the ATM described here do not accurately mimic those of a real ATM. For example, a real ATM typically contains a device that reads a user's account number from an ATM card, whereas this ATM asks the user to type an account number using the keypad. A real ATM also usually prints a receipt at the end of a session, but all output from this ATM appears on the screen.]

The bank wants you to develop software to perform the financial transactions initiated by bank customers through the ATM. The bank will integrate the software with the ATM's hardware at a later time. The software should encapsulate the functionality of the hardware devices (e.g., cash dispenser, deposit slot) within software components, but it need not concern itself with how these devices perform their duties. The ATM hardware has not been developed yet, so instead of writing your software to run on the ATM, you should develop a first version of the software to run on a personal computer. This version should use the computer's monitor to simulate the ATM's screen, and the computer's keyboard to simulate the ATM's keypad.

An ATM session consists of authenticating a user (i.e., proving the user's identity) based on an account number and personal identification number (PIN), followed by creating and executing financial transactions. To authenticate a user and perform transactions, the ATM must interact with the bank's account information database. [*Note:* A database is an organized collection of data stored on a computer.] For each bank account, the database stores an account number, a PIN and a balance indicating the amount of money in the account. [*Note:* For simplicity, we assume that *the bank plans to build only one ATM, so we do not need to worry about multiple ATMs accessing this database at the same time. Furthermore, we assume that the bank does not make any changes to the information in the database while a user is accessing the ATM.* Also, any business system like an ATM faces reasonably complicated security issues that go well beyond the scope of this book. We make the simplifying assumption, however, that the bank trusts the ATM to access and manipulate the information in the database without significant security measures.]

Upon first approaching the ATM, the user should experience the following sequence of events (shown in Fig. 22.1):

1. The screen displays a welcome message and prompts the user to enter an account number.
2. The user enters a five-digit account number, using the keypad.
3. The screen prompts the user to enter the PIN (personal identification number) associated with the specified account number.
4. The user enters a five-digit PIN, using the keypad.
5. If the user enters a valid account number and the correct PIN for that account, the screen displays the main menu (Fig. 22.2). If the user enters an invalid ac-

count number or an incorrect PIN, the screen displays an appropriate message, then the ATM returns to *Step 1* to restart the authentication process.

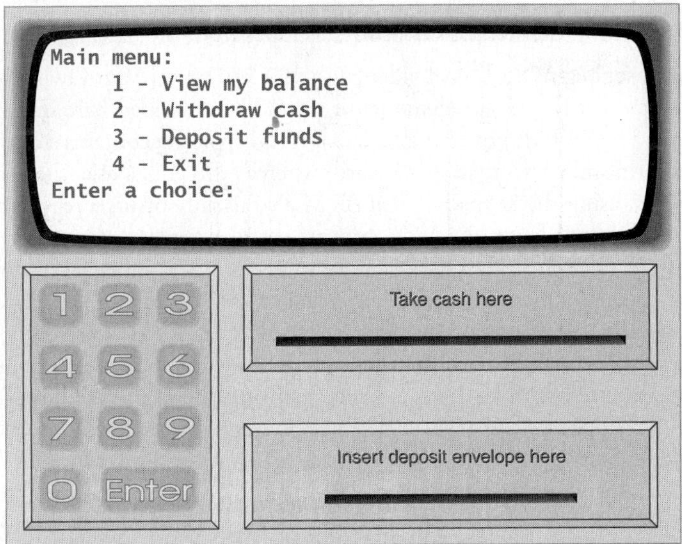

Fig. 22.2 | ATM main menu.

After the ATM authenticates the user, the main menu (Fig. 22.2) displays a numbered option for each of the three types of transactions: balance inquiry (option 1), withdrawal (option 2) and deposit (option 3). The main menu also displays an option that allows the user to exit the system (option 4). The user then chooses either to perform a transaction (by entering 1, 2 or 3) or to exit the system (by entering 4). If the user enters an invalid option, the screen displays an error message, then redisplays to the main menu.

If the user enters 1 to make a balance inquiry, the screen displays the user's account balance. To do so, the ATM must retrieve the balance from the bank's database.

The following actions occur when the user enters 2 to make a withdrawal:

1. The screen displays a menu (shown in Fig. 22.3) containing standard withdrawal amounts: $20 (option 1), $40 (option 2), $60 (option 3), $100 (option 4) and $200 (option 5). The menu also contains an option to allow the user to cancel the transaction (option 6).
2. The user enters a menu selection (1–6) using the keypad.
3. If the withdrawal amount chosen is greater than the user's account balance, the screen displays a message stating this and telling the user to choose a smaller amount. The ATM then returns to *Step 1*. If the withdrawal amount chosen is less than or equal to the user's account balance (i.e., an acceptable withdrawal amount), the ATM proceeds to *Step 4*. If the user chooses to cancel the transaction (option 6), the ATM displays the main menu (Fig. 22.2) and waits for user input.
4. If the cash dispenser contains enough cash to satisfy the request, the ATM proceeds to *Step 5*. Otherwise, the screen displays a message indicating the problem

and telling the user to choose a smaller withdrawal amount. The ATM then returns to *Step 1.*

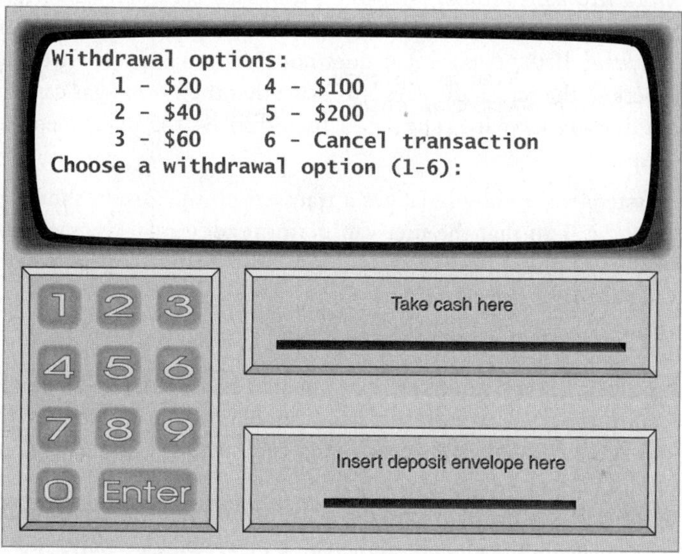

Fig. 22.3 | ATM withdrawal menu.

5. The ATM debits (i.e., subtracts) the withdrawal amount from the user's account balance in the bank's database.
6. The cash dispenser dispenses the desired amount of money to the user.
7. The screen displays a message reminding the user to take the money.

The following actions occur when the user enters 3 (while the main menu is displayed) to make a deposit:

1. The screen prompts the user to enter a deposit amount or to type 0 (zero) to cancel the transaction.
2. The user enters a deposit amount or 0, using the keypad. [*Note:* The keypad does not contain a decimal point or a dollar sign, so the user cannot type a real dollar amount (e.g., $1.25). Instead, the user must enter a deposit amount as a number of cents (e.g., 125). The ATM then divides this number by 100 to obtain a number representing a dollar amount (e.g., 125 ÷ 100 = 1.25).]
3. If the user specifies a deposit amount, the ATM proceeds to *Step 4.* If the user chooses to cancel the transaction (by entering 0), the ATM displays the main menu (Fig. 22.2) and waits for user input.
4. The screen displays a message telling the user to insert a deposit envelope into the deposit slot.
5. If the deposit slot receives a deposit envelope within two minutes, the ATM credits (i.e., adds) the deposit amount to the user's account balance in the bank's da-

tabase. *This money is not immediately available for withdrawal. The bank first must physically verify the amount of cash in the deposit envelope, and any checks in the envelope must clear (i.e., money must be transferred from the check writer's account to the check recipient's account). When either of these events occurs, the bank appropriately updates the user's balance stored in its database. This occurs independently of the ATM system.* If the deposit slot does not receive a deposit envelope within this time period, the screen displays a message that the system has canceled the transaction due to inactivity. The ATM then displays the main menu and waits for user input.

After the system successfully executes a transaction, the system should redisplay the main menu (Fig. 22.2) so that the user can perform additional transactions. If the user chooses to exit the system (option 4), the screen should display a thank you message, then display the welcome message for the next user.

Analyzing the ATM System

The preceding statement is a simplified example of a requirements document. Typically, such a document is the result of a detailed **requirements gathering** process that might include interviews with potential users of the system and specialists in fields related to the system. For example, a systems analyst who is hired to prepare a requirements document for banking software (e.g., the ATM system described here) might interview financial experts to gain a better understanding of *what* the software must do. The analyst would use the information gained to compile a list of **system requirements** to guide systems designers.

The process of requirements gathering is a key task of the first stage of the software life cycle. The **software life cycle** specifies the stages through which software evolves from the time it's first conceived to the time it's retired from use. These stages typically include: analysis, design, implementation, testing and debugging, deployment, maintenance and retirement. Several software life-cycle models exist, each with its own preferences and specifications for when and how often software engineers should perform each of these stages. **Waterfall models** perform each stage once in succession, whereas **iterative models** may repeat one or more stages several times throughout a product's life cycle.

The analysis stage of the software life cycle focuses on defining the problem to be solved. When designing any system, one must certainly *solve the problem right*, but of equal importance, one must *solve the right problem*. Systems analysts collect the requirements that indicate the specific problem to solve. Our requirements document describes our ATM system in sufficient detail that you do not need to go through an extensive analysis stage—it has been done for you.

To capture what a proposed system should do, developers often employ a technique known as **use case modeling**. This process identifies the **use cases** of the system, each of which represents a different capability that the system provides to its clients. For example, ATMs typically have several use cases, such as "View Account Balance," "Withdraw Cash," "Deposit Funds," "Transfer Funds Between Accounts" and "Buy Postage Stamps." The simplified ATM system we build in this case study allows only the first three of these use cases (Fig. 22.4).

Each use case describes a typical scenario in which the user uses the system. You've already read descriptions of the ATM system's use cases in the requirements document; the lists of steps required to perform each type of transaction (i.e., balance inquiry, withdrawal and deposit) actually described the three use cases of our ATM—"View Account Balance," "Withdraw Cash" and "Deposit Funds."

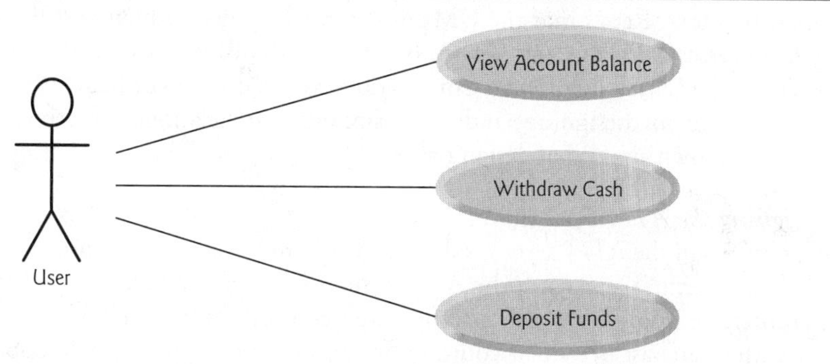

Fig. 22.4 | Use case diagram for the ATM system from the User's perspective.

Use Case Diagrams

We now introduce the first of several UML diagrams in our ATM case study. We create a **use case diagram** to model the interactions between a system's clients (in this case study, bank customers) and the system. The goal is to show the kinds of interactions users have with a system without providing the details—these are provided in other UML diagrams (which we present throughout the case study). Use case diagrams are often accompanied by informal text that describes the use cases in more detail—like the text that appears in the requirements document. Use case diagrams are produced during the analysis stage of the software life cycle. In larger systems, use case diagrams are simple but indispensable tools that help system designers remain focused on satisfying the users' needs.

Figure 22.4 shows the use case diagram for our ATM system. The stick figure represents an **actor**, which defines the roles that an external entity—such as a person or another system—plays when interacting with the system. For our automated teller machine, the actor is a User who can view an account balance, withdraw cash and deposit funds from the ATM. The User is not an actual person, but instead comprises the roles that a real person—when playing the part of a User—can play while interacting with the ATM. Note that a use case diagram can include multiple actors. For example, the use case diagram for a real bank's ATM system might also include an actor named Administrator who refills the cash dispenser each day.

We identify the actor in our system by examining the requirements document, which states, "ATM users should be able to view their account balance, withdraw cash and deposit funds." So, the actor in each of the three use cases is the User who interacts with the ATM. An external entity—a real person—plays the part of the User to perform financial transactions. Figure 22.4 shows one actor, whose name, User, appears below the actor in the diagram. The UML models each use case as an oval connected to an actor with a solid line.

Software engineers (more precisely, systems analysts) must analyze the requirements document or a set of use cases and design the system before programmers implement it. During the analysis stage, systems analysts focus on understanding the requirements document to produce a high-level specification that describes *what* the system is supposed to do. The output of the design stage—a **design specification**—should specify clearly *how* the system should be constructed to satisfy these requirements. In the next several sections, we perform the steps of a simple object-oriented design (OOD) process on the ATM system to produce a design specification containing a collection of UML diagrams and supporting text. Recall that the UML is designed for use with any OOD process. Many such processes exist, the best known of which is the Rational Unified Process™ (RUP) developed by Rational Software Corporation (now a division of IBM). RUP is a rich process intended for designing "industrial strength" applications. For this case study, we present our own simplified design process.

Designing the ATM System

We now begin the ATM system's design. A **system** is a set of components that interact to solve a problem. To perform the ATM system's designated tasks, our ATM system has a user interface (Fig. 22.1), contains software that executes financial transactions and interacts with a database of bank account information. **System structure** describes the system's objects and their interrelationships. **System behavior** describes how the system changes as its objects interact with one another. Every system has both structure and behavior—designers must specify both. There are several distinct types of system structures and behaviors. For example, the interactions among objects in the system differ from those between the user and the system, yet both constitute a portion of the system behavior.

The UML 2 specifies 13 diagram types for documenting the models of systems. Each models a distinct characteristic of a system's structure or behavior—six diagrams relate to system structure; the remaining seven relate to system behavior. We list here only the six types of diagrams used in our case study—one of these (class diagrams) models system structure—the remaining five model system behavior. We overview the remaining seven UML diagram types in Appendix G, UML 2: Additional Diagram Types.

1. **Use case diagrams**, such as the one in Fig. 22.4, model the interactions between a system and its external entities (actors) in terms of use cases (system capabilities, such as "View Account Balance," "Withdraw Cash" and "Deposit Funds").
2. **Class diagrams**, which you'll study in Section 22.4, model the classes, or "building blocks," used in a system. Each noun or "thing" described in the requirements document is a candidate to be a class in the system (e.g., "account," "keypad"). Class diagrams help us specify the structural relationships between parts of the system. For example, the ATM system class diagram will specify that the ATM is physically composed of a screen, a keypad, a cash dispenser and a deposit slot.
3. **State machine diagrams**, which you'll study in Section 22.6, model the ways in which an object changes state. An object's **state** is indicated by the values of all the object's attributes at a given time. When an object changes state, that object may behave differently in the system. For example, after validating a user's PIN, the ATM transitions from the "user not authenticated" state to the "user authenticated" state, at which point the ATM allows the user to perform financial transactions (e.g., view account balance, withdraw cash, deposit funds).
4. **Activity diagrams**, which you'll also study in Section 22.6, model an object's **activity**—the object's workflow (sequence of events) during program execution. An activity diagram models the actions the object performs and specifies the order in which it performs these actions. For example, an activity diagram shows that the

ATM must obtain the balance of the user's account (from the bank's account information database) before the screen can display the balance to the user.

5. **Communication diagrams** (called **collaboration diagrams** in earlier versions of the UML) model the interactions among objects in a system, with an emphasis on *what* interactions occur. You'll learn in Section 22.8 that these diagrams show which objects must interact to perform an ATM transaction. For example, the ATM must communicate with the bank's account information database to retrieve an account balance.
6. **Sequence diagrams** also model the interactions among the objects in a system, but unlike communication diagrams, they emphasize *when* interactions occur. You'll learn in Section 22.8 that these diagrams help show the order in which interactions occur in executing a financial transaction. For example, the screen prompts the user to enter a withdrawal amount before cash is dispensed.

In Section 22.4, we continue designing our ATM system by identifying the classes from the requirements document. We accomplish this by extracting key nouns and noun phrases from the requirements document. Using these classes, we develop our first draft of the class diagram that models the structure of our ATM system.

Web Resources

We've created an extensive UML Resource Center (`www.deitel.com/UML/`) that contains many links to additional information, including introductions, tutorials, blogs, books, certification, conferences, developer tools, documentation, e-books, FAQs, forums, groups, UML in C++, podcasts, security, tools, downloads, training courses, videos and more.

Self-Review Exercises for Section 22.3

22.1 Suppose we enabled a user of our ATM system to transfer money between two bank accounts. Modify the use case diagram of Fig. 22.4 to reflect this change.

22.2 ________ model the interactions among objects in a system with an emphasis on *when* these interactions occur.

a) Class diagrams
b) Sequence diagrams
c) Communication diagrams
d) Activity diagrams

22.3 Which of the following choices lists stages of a typical software life cycle in sequential order?

a) design, analysis, implementation, testing
b) design, analysis, testing, implementation
c) analysis, design, testing, implementation
d) analysis, design, implementation, testing

22.4 Identifying the Classes in the ATM Requirements Document

Now we begin designing the ATM system that we introduced in Section 22.3. In this section, we identify the classes that are needed to build the ATM system by analyzing the nouns and noun phrases that appear in the requirements document. We introduce UML class diagrams to model the relationships between these classes. This is an important first step in defining the structure of our system.

Identifying the Classes in a System

We begin our OOD process by identifying the classes required to build the ATM system. We'll eventually describe these classes using UML class diagrams and implement these classes in C++. First, we review the requirements document of Section 22.3 and find key nouns and noun phrases to help us identify classes that comprise the ATM system. We may decide that some of these nouns and noun phrases are attributes of other classes in the system. We may also conclude that some of the nouns do *not* correspond to parts of the system and thus should *not* be modeled at all. Additional classes may become apparent to us as we proceed through the design process.

Figure 22.5 lists the nouns and noun phrases in the requirements document. We list them from left to right in the order in which they appear in the requirements document. We list only the singular form of each noun or noun phrase.

Nouns and noun phrases in the requirements document			
bank	money / fund	account number	ATM
screen	PIN	user	keypad
bank database	customer	cash dispenser	balance inquiry
transaction	$20 bill / cash	withdrawal	account
deposit slot	deposit	balance	deposit envelope

Fig. 22.5 | Nouns and noun phrases in the requirements document.

We create classes only for the nouns and noun phrases that have significance in the ATM system. We don't need to model "bank" as a class, because it'is not a part of the ATM system—the bank simply wants us to build the ATM. "Customer" and "user" also represent outside entities—they are important because they interact with our ATM system, but we do not need to model them as classes in the ATM software. Recall that we modeled an ATM user (i.e., a bank customer) as the actor in the use case diagram of Fig. 22.4.

We do not model "$20 bill" or "deposit envelope" as classes. These are physical objects in the real world, but they are *not* part of what's being automated. We can adequately represent the presence of bills in the system using an attribute of the class that models the cash dispenser. (We assign attributes to classes in Section 22.5.) For example, the cash dispenser maintains a count of the number of bills it contains. The requirements document doesn't say anything about what the system should do with deposit envelopes after it receives them. We can assume that acknowledging the receipt of an envelope—an operation performed by the class that models the deposit slot—is sufficient to represent the presence of an envelope in the system. (We assign operations to classes in Section 22.7.)

In our simplified ATM system, representing various amounts of "money," including an account's "balance," as attributes of other classes seems most appropriate. Likewise, the nouns "account number" and "PIN" represent significant information in the ATM system. They are important attributes of a bank account. They do *not*, however, exhibit behaviors. Thus, we can most appropriately model them as attributes of an account class.

Though the requirements document frequently describes a "transaction" in a general sense, we do not model the broad notion of a financial transaction at this time. Instead, we model the three types of transactions (i.e., "balance inquiry," "withdrawal" and "deposit") as individual classes. These classes possess specific attributes needed for executing the transactions they represent. For example, a withdrawal needs to know the amount of money the user wants to withdraw. A balance inquiry, however, does not require any additional data. Furthermore, the three transaction classes exhibit unique behaviors. A withdrawal includes dispensing cash to the user, whereas a deposit involves receiving deposit envelopes from the user. *In Section 23.3, we "factor out" common features of all transactions into a general "transaction" class using the object-oriented concepts of abstract classes and inheritance.*

We determine the classes for our system based on the remaining nouns and noun phrases from Fig. 22.5. Each of these refers to one or more of the following:

- ATM
- screen
- keypad
- cash dispenser
- deposit slot
- account
- bank database
- balance inquiry
- withdrawal
- deposit

The elements of this list are likely to be classes we'll need to implement our system.

We can now model the classes in our system based on the list we've created. We capitalize class names in the design process—a UML convention—as we'll do when we write the actual C++ code that implements our design. If the name of a class contains more than one word, we run the words together and capitalize the first letter of each word (e.g., `MultipleWordName`). Using this convention, we create classes `ATM`, `Screen`, `Keypad`, `CashDispenser`, `DepositSlot`, `Account`, `BankDatabase`, `BalanceInquiry`, `Withdrawal` and `Deposit`. We construct our system using all of these classes as building blocks. Before we begin building the system, however, we must gain a better understanding of how the classes relate to one another.

Modeling Classes

The UML enables us to model, via **class diagrams**, the ATM system's classes and their interrelationships. Figure 22.6 represents class `ATM`. Each class is modeled as a rectangle with three compartments. The top compartment contains the name of the class, centered horizontally and in boldface. The middle compartment contains the class's attributes. (We discuss attributes in Section 22.5 and Section 22.6.) The bottom compartment contains the class's operations (discussed in Section 22.7). In Fig. 22.6 the middle and bottom compartments are empty, because we've not yet determined this class's attributes and operations.

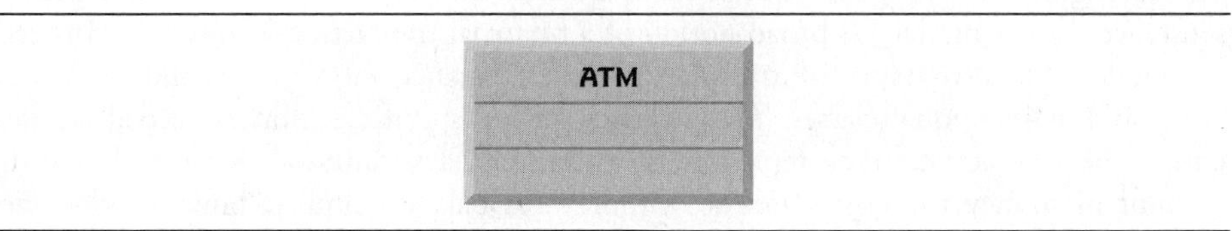

Fig. 22.6 | Representing a class in the UML using a class diagram.

Class diagrams also show the relationships among the classes of the system. Figure 22.7 shows how our classes `ATM` and `Withdrawal` relate to one another. For the moment, we choose to model only this subset of classes for simplicity; we present a more complete class diagram later in this section. Notice that the rectangles representing classes in this diagram are not subdivided into compartments. The UML allows the suppression of class attributes and operations in this manner, when appropriate, to create more readable diagrams. Such a diagram is said to be an **elided diagram**—one in which some information, such as the contents of the second and third compartments, is not modeled. We'll place information in these compartments in Section 22.5 and Section 22.7.

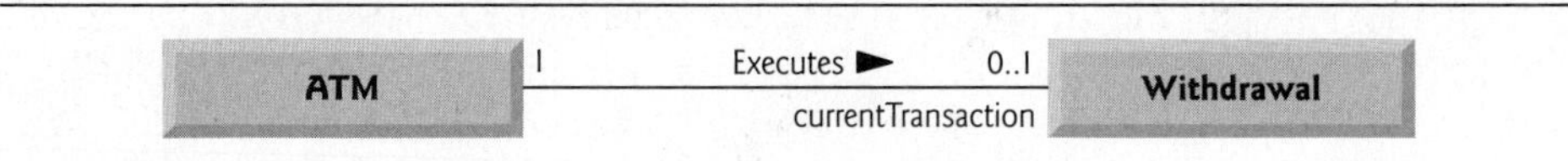

Fig. 22.7 | Class diagram showing an association among classes.

In Fig. 22.7, the solid line that connects the two classes represents an **association**—a relationship between classes. The numbers near each end of the line are **multiplicity** values, which indicate how many objects of each class participate in the association. In this case, following the line from one end to the other reveals that, at any given moment, one `ATM` object participates in an association with either zero or one `Withdrawal` objects—zero if the current user is not currently performing a transaction or has requested a different type of transaction, and one if the user has requested a withdrawal. The UML can model many types of multiplicity. Figure 22.8 lists and explains the multiplicity types.

Symbol	Meaning
0	None
1	One
m	An integer value
0..1	Zero or one
m, *n*	*m* or *n*

Fig. 22.8 | Multiplicity types. (Part 1 of 2.)

Symbol	Meaning
m..n	At least *m*, but not more than *n*
*	Any nonnegative integer (zero or more)
0..*	Zero or more (identical to *)
1..*	One or more

Fig. 22.8 | Multiplicity types. (Part 2 of 2.)

An association can be named. For example, the word `Executes` above the line connecting classes `ATM` and `Withdrawal` in Fig. 22.7 indicates the name of that association. This part of the diagram reads "one object of class `ATM` executes zero or one objects of class `Withdrawal`." Association names are directional, as indicated by the filled arrowhead—so it would be improper, for example, to read the preceding association from right to left as "zero or one objects of class `Withdrawal` execute one object of class `ATM`."

The word `currentTransaction` at the `Withdrawal` end of the association line in Fig. 22.7 is a **role name**, which identifies the role the `Withdrawal` object plays in its relationship with the `ATM`. A role name adds meaning to an association between classes by identifying the role a class plays in the context of an association. A class can play several roles in the same system. For example, in a school personnel system, a person may play the role of "professor" when relating to students. The same person may take on the role of "colleague" when participating in a relationship with another professor, and "coach" when coaching student athletes. In Fig. 22.7, the role name `currentTransaction` indicates that the `Withdrawal` object participating in the `Executes` association with an object of class `ATM` represents the transaction currently being processed by the ATM. In other contexts, a `Withdrawal` object may take on other roles (e.g., the previous transaction). Notice that we do *not* specify a role name for the `ATM` end of the `Executes` association. Role names in class diagrams are often omitted when the meaning of an association is clear without them.

In addition to indicating simple relationships, associations can specify more complex relationships, such as objects of one class being composed of objects of other classes. Consider a real-world automated teller machine. What "pieces" does a manufacturer put together to build a working ATM? Our requirements document tells us that the ATM is composed of a screen, a keypad, a cash dispenser and a deposit slot.

In Fig. 22.9, the **solid diamonds** attached to the association lines of class `ATM` indicate that class `ATM` has a **composition** relationship with classes `Screen`, `Keypad`, `CashDispenser` and `DepositSlot`. Composition implies a whole/part relationship. The class that has the *composition symbol* (the solid diamond) on its end of the association line is the whole (in this case, `ATM`), and the classes on the other end of the association lines are the parts—in this case, classes `Screen`, `Keypad`, `CashDispenser` and `DepositSlot`. The compositions in Fig. 22.9 indicate that an object of class `ATM` is formed from one object of class `Screen`, one object of class `CashDispenser`, one object of class `Keypad` and one object of class `DepositSlot`. The ATM *has a* screen, a keypad, a cash dispenser and a deposit slot. The ***has-a* relationship** defines composition. (We'll see in Section 23.3 that the *is-a* relationship defines inheritance.)

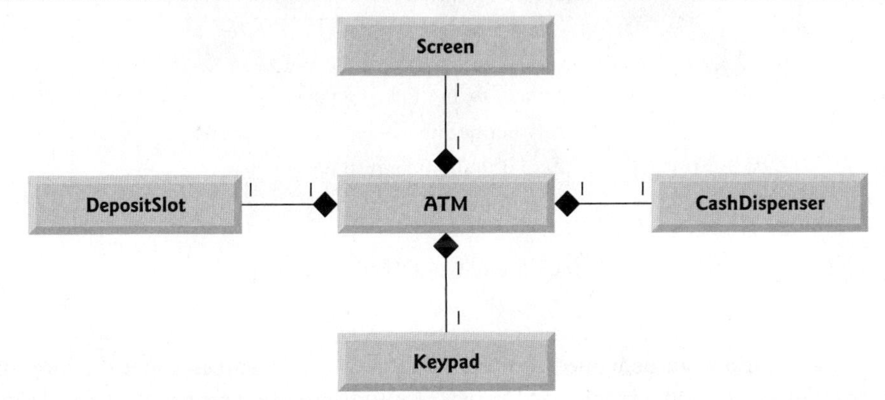

Fig. 22.9 | Class diagram showing composition relationships.

According to the UML specification, composition relationships have the following properties:

1. Only one class in the relationship can represent the whole (i.e., the diamond can be placed on only one end of the association line). For example, either the screen is part of the ATM or the ATM is part of the screen, but the screen and the ATM cannot both represent the whole in the relationship.
2. The parts in a composition relationship exist only as long as the whole, and the whole is responsible for creating and destroying its parts. For example, the act of constructing an ATM includes manufacturing its parts. Furthermore, if the ATM is destroyed, its screen, keypad, cash dispenser and deposit slot are also destroyed.
3. A part may belong to only one whole at a time, although the part may be removed and attached to another whole, which then assumes responsibility for the part.

The solid diamonds in our class diagrams indicate composition relationships that fulfill these three properties. If a *has-a* relationship does not satisfy one or more of these criteria, the UML specifies that hollow diamonds be attached to the ends of association lines to indicate **aggregation**—a weaker form of composition. For example, a personal computer and a computer monitor participate in an aggregation relationship—the computer *has a* monitor, but the two parts can exist independently, and the same monitor can be attached to multiple computers at once, thus violating the second and third properties of composition.

Figure 22.10 shows a class diagram for the ATM system. This diagram models most of the classes that we identified earlier in this section, as well as the associations between them that we can infer from the requirements document. [*Note:* Classes `BalanceInquiry` and `Deposit` participate in associations similar to those of class `Withdrawal`, so we've chosen to omit them from this diagram to keep it simple. In Section 23.3, we expand our class diagram to include all the classes in the ATM system.]

Figure 22.10 presents a graphical model of the structure of the ATM system. This class diagram includes classes `BankDatabase` and `Account` and several associations that were not present in either Fig. 22.7 or Fig. 22.9. The class diagram shows that class `ATM`

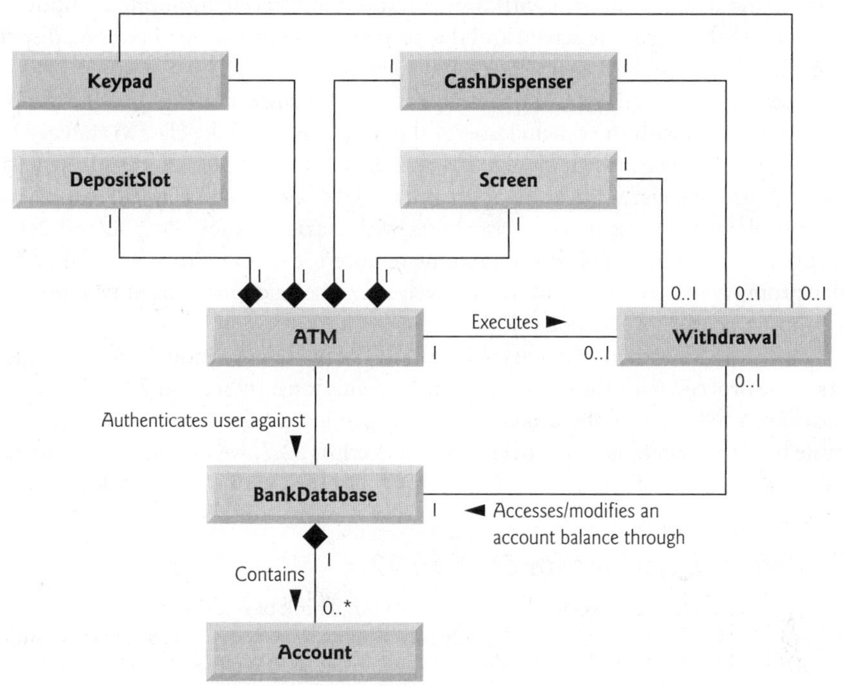

Fig. 22.10 | Class diagram for the ATM system model.

has a **one-to-one relationship** with class `BankDatabase`—one `ATM` object authenticates users against one `BankDatabase` object. In Fig. 22.10, we also model the fact that the bank's database contains information about many accounts—one object of class `BankDatabase` participates in a composition relationship with zero or more objects of class `Account`. Recall from Fig. 22.8 that the multiplicity value 0..* at the `Account` end of the association between class `BankDatabase` and class `Account` indicates that zero or more objects of class `Account` take part in the association. Class `BankDatabase` has a **one-to-many relationship** with class `Account`—the `BankDatabase` contains many `Accounts`. Similarly, class `Account` has a **many-to-one relationship** with class `BankDatabase`—there can be many `Accounts` contained in the `BankDatabase`. [*Note:* Recall from Fig. 22.8 that the multiplicity value * is identical to 0..*. We include 0..* in our class diagrams for clarity.]

Figure 22.10 also indicates that if the user is performing a withdrawal, "one object of class `Withdrawal` accesses/modifies an account balance through one object of class `BankDatabase`." We could have created an association directly between class `Withdrawal` and class `Account`. The requirements document, however, states that the "ATM must interact with the bank's account information database" to perform transactions. A bank account contains sensitive information, and systems engineers must always consider the security of personal data when designing a system. Thus, only the `BankDatabase` can access and manipulate an account directly. All other parts of the system must interact with the database to retrieve or update account information (e.g., an account balance).

The class diagram in Fig. 22.10 also models associations between class `Withdrawal` and classes `Screen`, `CashDispenser` and `Keypad`. A withdrawal transaction includes prompting the user to choose a withdrawal amount and receiving numeric input. These actions require the use of the screen and the keypad, respectively. Furthermore, dispensing cash to the user requires access to the cash dispenser.

Classes `BalanceInquiry` and `Deposit`, though not shown in Fig. 22.10, take part in several associations with the other classes of the ATM system. Like class `Withdrawal`, each of these classes associates with classes `ATM` and `BankDatabase`. An object of class `BalanceInquiry` also associates with an object of class `Screen` to display the balance of an account to the user. Class `Deposit` associates with classes `Screen`, `Keypad` and `DepositSlot`. Like withdrawals, deposit transactions require use of the screen and the keypad to display prompts and receive input, respectively. To receive deposit envelopes, an object of class `Deposit` accesses the deposit slot.

We've now identified the classes in our ATM system (although we may discover others as we proceed with the design and implementation). In Section 22.5, we determine the attributes for each of these classes, and in Section 22.6, we use these attributes to examine how the system changes over time. In Section 22.7, we determine the operations of the classes in our system.

Self-Review Exercises for Section 22.4

22.4 Suppose we have a class `Car` that represents a car. Think of some of the different pieces that a manufacturer would put together to produce a whole car. Create a class diagram (similar to Fig. 22.9) that models some of the composition relationships of class `Car`.

22.5 Suppose we have a class `File` that represents an electronic document in a stand-alone, non-networked computer represented by class `Computer`. What sort of association exists between class `Computer` and class `File`?

a) Class `Computer` has a *one-to-one* relationship with class `File`.
b) Class `Computer` has a *many-to-one* relationship with class `File`.
c) Class `Computer` has a *one-to-many* relationship with class `File`.
d) Class `Computer` has a *many-to-many* relationship with class `File`.

22.6 State whether the following statement is *true* or *false*, and if *false*, explain why: A UML diagram in which a class's second and third compartments are not modeled is said to be an elided diagram.

22.7 Modify the class diagram of Fig. 22.10 to include class `Deposit` instead of class `Withdrawal`.

22.5 Identifying Class Attributes

In Section 22.4, we began the first stage of an object-oriented design (OOD) for our ATM system—analyzing the requirements document and identifying the classes needed to implement the system. We listed the *nouns* and *noun phrases* in the requirements document and identified a separate class for each one that plays a significant role in the ATM system. We then modeled the classes and their relationships in a UML class diagram (Fig. 22.10).

Classes have attributes (data) and operations (behaviors). Class attributes are implemented in C++ programs as data members, and class operations are implemented as member functions. In this section, we determine many of the attributes needed in the ATM system. In Section 22.6, we examine how these attributes represent an object's state. In Section 22.7, we determine class operations.

Identifying Attributes

Consider the attributes of some real-world objects: A person's attributes include height, weight and whether the person is left-handed, right-handed or ambidextrous. A radio's attributes include its station setting, its volume setting and its AM or FM setting. A car's attributes include its speedometer and odometer readings, the amount of gas in its tank and what gear it's in. A personal computer's attributes include its manufacturer (e.g., Dell, HP, Apple or IBM), type of screen (e.g., LCD or CRT), main memory size and hard disk size.

We can identify many attributes of the classes in our system by looking for descriptive words and phrases in the requirements document. For each one we find that plays a significant role in the ATM system, we create an attribute and assign it to one or more of the classes identified in Section 22.4. We also create attributes to represent any additional data that a class may need, as such needs become apparent throughout the design process.

Figure 22.11 lists the words or phrases from the requirements document that describe each class. We formed this list by reading the requirements document and identifying any words or phrases that refer to characteristics of the classes in the system. For example, the requirements document describes the steps taken to obtain a "withdrawal amount," so we list "amount" next to class `Withdrawal`.

Class	Descriptive words and phrases
`ATM`	user is authenticated
`BalanceInquiry`	account number
`Withdrawal`	account number amount
`Deposit`	account number amount
`BankDatabase`	[no descriptive words or phrases]
`Account`	account number PIN balance
`Screen`	[no descriptive words or phrases]
`Keypad`	[no descriptive words or phrases]
`CashDispenser`	begins each day loaded with 500 $20 bills
`DepositSlot`	[no descriptive words or phrases]

Fig. 22.11 | Descriptive words and phrases from the ATM requirements.

Figure 22.11 leads us to create one attribute of class `ATM`. Class `ATM` maintains information about the state of the ATM. The phrase "user is authenticated" describes a state of the ATM (we introduce states in Section 22.6), so we include `userAuthenticated` as a **`Boolean` attribute** (i.e., an attribute that has a value of either `true` or `false`). The UML `Boolean` type is equivalent to the `bool` type in C++. This attribute indicates whether the

ATM has successfully authenticated the current user—`userAuthenticated` must be `true` for the system to allow the user to perform transactions and access account information. This attribute helps ensure the security of the data in the system.

Classes `BalanceInquiry`, `Withdrawal` and `Deposit` share one attribute. Each transaction involves an "account number" that corresponds to the account of the user making the transaction. We assign an integer attribute `accountNumber` to each transaction class to identify the account to which an object of the class applies.

Descriptive words and phrases in the requirements document also suggest some differences in the attributes required by each transaction class. The requirements document indicates that to withdraw cash or deposit funds, users must enter a specific "amount" of money to be withdrawn or deposited, respectively. Thus, we assign to classes `Withdrawal` and `Deposit` an attribute `amount` to store the value supplied by the user. The amounts of money related to a withdrawal and a deposit are defining characteristics of these transactions that the system requires for them to take place. Class `BalanceInquiry`, however, needs no additional data to perform its task—it requires only an account number to indicate the account whose balance should be retrieved.

Class `Account` has several attributes. The requirements document states that each bank account has an "account number" and "PIN," which the system uses for identifying accounts and authenticating users. We assign to class `Account` two integer attributes: `accountNumber` and `pin`. The requirements document also specifies that an account maintains a "balance" of the amount of money in the account and that money the user deposits does not become available for a withdrawal until the bank verifies the amount of cash in the deposit envelope, and any checks in the envelope clear. An account must still record the amount of money that a user deposits, however. Therefore, we decide that an account should represent a balance using two attributes of UML type `Double`: `availableBalance` and `totalBalance`. Attribute `availableBalance` tracks the amount of money that a user can withdraw from the account. Attribute `totalBalance` refers to the total amount of money that the user has "on deposit" (i.e., the amount of money available, plus the amount waiting to be verified or cleared). For example, suppose an ATM user deposits $50.00 into an empty account. The `totalBalance` attribute would increase to $50.00 to record the deposit, but the `availableBalance` would remain at $0. [*Note:* We assume that the bank updates the `availableBalance` attribute of an `Account` soon after the ATM transaction occurs, in response to confirming that $50 worth of cash or checks was found in the deposit envelope. We assume that this update occurs through a transaction that a bank employee performs using some piece of bank software other than the ATM. Thus, we do not discuss this transaction in our case study.]

Class `CashDispenser` has one attribute. The requirements document states that the cash dispenser "begins each day loaded with 500 $20 bills." The cash dispenser must keep track of the number of bills it contains to determine whether enough cash is on hand to satisfy withdrawal requests. We assign to class `CashDispenser` an integer attribute `count`, which is initially set to `500`.

For real problems in industry, there is no guarantee that requirements specifications will be rich enough and precise enough for the object-oriented systems designer to determine all the attributes or even all the classes. The need for additional (or fewer) classes, attributes and behaviors may become clear as the design process proceeds. As we progress through this case study, we too will continue to add, modify and delete information about the classes in our system.

Modeling Attributes

The class diagram in Fig. 22.12 lists some of the attributes for the classes in our system—the descriptive words and phrases in Fig. 22.11 helped us identify these attributes. For simplicity, Fig. 22.12 does not show the associations among classes—we showed these in Fig. 22.10. This is a common practice of systems designers when designs are being developed. Recall from Section 22.4 that in the UML, a class's attributes are placed in the middle compartment of the class's rectangle. We list each attribute's name and type separated by a colon (:), followed in some cases by an equal sign (=) and an initial value.

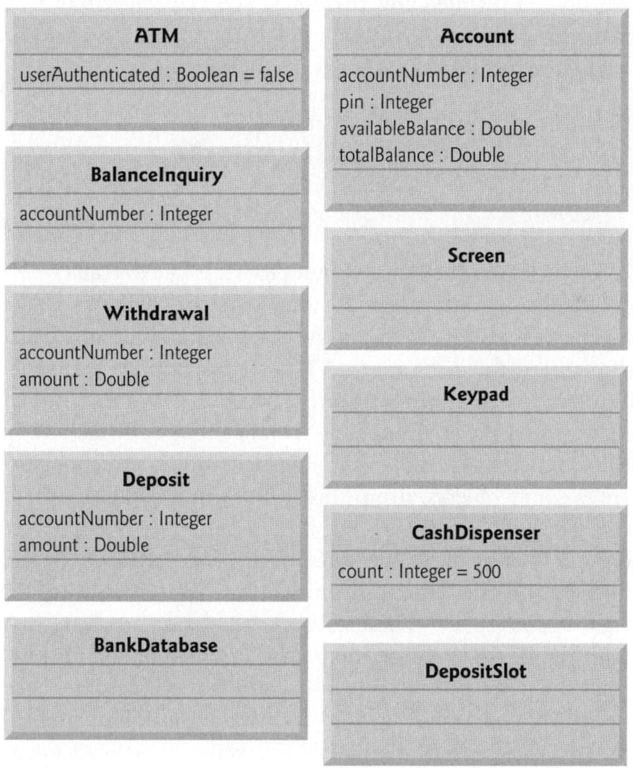

Fig. 22.12 | Classes with attributes.

Consider the `userAuthenticated` attribute of class `ATM`:

```
userAuthenticated : Boolean = false
```

This attribute declaration contains three pieces of information about the attribute. The **attribute name** is `userAuthenticated`. The **attribute type** is `Boolean`. In C++, an attribute can be represented by a fundamental type, such as `bool`, `int` or `double`, or a class type. We've chosen to model only primitive-type attributes in Fig. 22.12—we discuss the reasoning behind this decision shortly. [*Note:* Figure 22.12 lists UML data types for the attributes. When we implement the system, we'll associate the UML types `Boolean`, `Integer` and `Double` with the C++ fundamental types `bool`, `int` and `double`, respectively.]

We can also indicate an *initial value* for an attribute. The `userAuthenticated` attribute in class `ATM` has an initial value of `false`. This indicates that the system initially does not consider the user to be authenticated. If an attribute has no initial value specified, only its name and type (separated by a colon) are shown. For example, the `accountNumber` attribute of class `BalanceInquiry` is an `Integer`. Here we show no initial value, because the value of this attribute is a number that we do not yet know—it will be determined at execution time based on the account number entered by the current ATM user.

Figure 22.12 does not include any attributes for classes `Screen`, `Keypad` and `DepositSlot`. These are important components of our system, for which our design process simply has not yet revealed any attributes. We may still discover some, however, in the remaining design phases or when we implement these classes in C++. This is perfectly normal for the iterative process of software engineering.

Software Engineering Observation 22.1

At the early stages in the design process, classes often lack attributes (and operations). Such classes should not *be eliminated, however, because attributes (and operations) may become evident in the later phases of design and implementation.*

Figure 22.12 also does not include attributes for class `BankDatabase`. Recall that attributes can be represented by either fundamental types or class types. We've chosen to include only fundamental-type attributes in the class diagram in Fig. 22.12 (and in similar class diagrams throughout the case study). A class-type attribute is modeled more clearly as an association (in particular, a composition) between the class with the attribute and the class of the object of which the attribute is an instance. For example, the class diagram in Fig. 22.10 indicates that class `BankDatabase` participates in a composition relationship with zero or more `Account` objects. From this composition, we can determine that when we implement the ATM system in C++, we'll be required to create an attribute of class `BankDatabase` to hold zero or more `Account` objects. Similarly, we'll assign attributes to class `ATM` that correspond to its composition relationships with classes `Screen`, `Keypad`, `CashDispenser` and `DepositSlot`. These composition-based attributes would be redundant if modeled in Fig. 22.12, because the compositions modeled in Fig. 22.10 already convey the fact that the database contains information about zero or more accounts and that an ATM is composed of a screen, keypad, cash dispenser and deposit slot. Software developers typically model these whole/part relationships as compositions rather than as attributes required to implement the relationships.

The class diagram in Fig. 22.12 provides a solid basis for the structure of our model, but the diagram is not complete. In Section 22.6, we identify the states and activities of the objects in the model, and in Section 22.7 we identify the operations that the objects perform. As we present more of the UML and object-oriented design, we'll continue to strengthen the structure of our model.

Self-Review Exercises for Section 22.5

22.8 We typically identify the attributes of the classes in our system by analyzing the in the requirements document.

a) nouns and noun phrases
b) descriptive words and phrases

c) verbs and verb phrases
d) All of the above.

22.9 Which of the following is *not* an attribute of an airplane?
a) length
b) wingspan
c) fly
d) number of seats

22.10 Describe the meaning of the following attribute declaration of class `CashDispenser` in the class diagram in Fig. 22.12:

```
count : Integer = 500
```

22.6 Identifying Objects' States and Activities

In Section 22.5, we identified many of the class attributes needed to implement the ATM system and added them to the class diagram in Fig. 22.12. In this section, we show how these attributes represent an object's *state*. We identify some key states that our objects may occupy and discuss how objects change state in response to various events occurring in the system. We also discuss the workflow, or **activities**, that objects perform in the ATM system. We present the activities of `BalanceInquiry` and `Withdrawal` transaction objects in this section, as they represent two of the key activities in the ATM system.

State Machine Diagrams

Each object in a system goes through a series of discrete states. An object's current state is indicated by the values of the object's attributes at a given time. **State machine diagrams** (commonly called **state diagrams**) model key states of an object and show under what circumstances the object changes state. Unlike the class diagrams presented in earlier case study sections, which focused primarily on the *structure* of the system, state diagrams model some of the *behavior* of the system.

Figure 22.13 is a simple state diagram that models some of the states of an object of class `ATM`. The UML represents each state in a state diagram as a **rounded rectangle** with the name of the state placed inside it. A **solid circle** with an attached stick arrowhead designates the **initial state.** Recall that we modeled this state information as the `Boolean` attribute `userAuthenticated` in the class diagram of Fig. 22.12. This attribute is initialized to `false`, or the "User not authenticated" state, according to the state diagram.

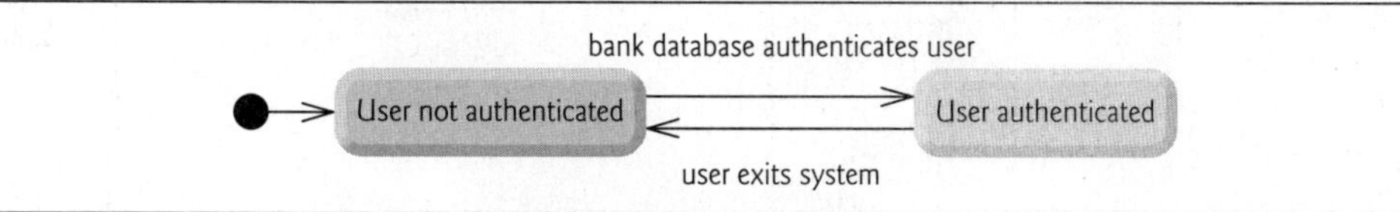

Fig. 22.13 | State diagram for the `ATM` object.

The arrows with stick arrowheads indicate **transitions** between states. An object can transition from one state to another in response to various *events* that occur in the system. The name or description of the event that causes a transition is written near the line that corresponds to the transition. For example, the `ATM` object changes from the "User not authenticated" state to the "User authenticated" state *after* the database authenticates the user. Recall from the requirements document that the database authenticates a user by comparing the account number and PIN entered by the user with those of the corresponding account in the database. If the database indicates that the user has entered a valid account number and the correct PIN, the `ATM` object transitions to the "User authenticated" state and changes its `userAuthenticated` attribute to a value of `true`. When the user exits the system by choosing the "exit" option from the main menu, the `ATM` object returns to the "User not authenticated" state in preparation for the next ATM user.

Software Engineering Observation 22.2

Software designers do not generally create state diagrams showing every possible state and state transition for all attributes—there are simply too many of them. State diagrams typically show only the most important or complex states and state transitions.

Activity Diagrams

Like a state diagram, an activity diagram models aspects of system *behavior*. Unlike a state diagram, an activity diagram models an object's workflow (sequence of events) during program execution. An activity diagram models the actions the object will perform and in what order. Recall that we used UML activity diagrams to illustrate the flow of control for the control statements presented in Chapters 4 and 5.

Figure 22.14 models the actions involved in executing a `BalanceInquiry` transaction. We assume that a `BalanceInquiry` object has been initialized and assigned a valid account number (that of the current user), so the object knows which balance to retrieve. The diagram includes the actions that occur after the user selects a balance inquiry from the main menu and before the ATM returns the user to the main menu—a `BalanceInquiry` object does not perform or initiate these actions, so we do not model them here. The diagram begins with retrieving the available balance of the user's account from the database. Next, the `BalanceInquiry` retrieves the total balance of the account. Finally, the transaction displays the balances on the screen. This action completes the execution of the transaction.

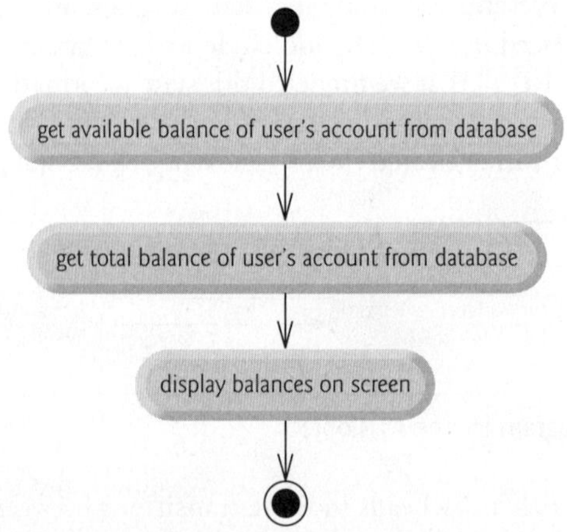

Fig. 22.14 | Activity diagram for a `BalanceInquiry` transaction.

The UML represents an action in an activity diagram as an action state modeled by a rectangle with its left and right sides replaced by arcs curving outward. Each action state contains an action expression—for example, "get available balance of user's account from database"—that specifies an action to be performed. An arrow with a stick arrowhead connects two action states, indicating the order in which the actions represented by the action states occur. The solid circle (at the top of Fig. 22.14) represents the activity's initial state—the beginning of the workflow before the object performs the modeled actions. In this case, the transaction first executes the "get available balance of user's account from database" action expression. Second, the transaction retrieves the total balance. Finally, the transaction displays both balances on the screen. The solid circle enclosed in an open circle (at the bottom of Fig. 22.14) represents the final state—the end of the workflow after the object performs the modeled actions.

Figure 22.15 shows an activity diagram for a `Withdrawal` transaction. We assume that a `Withdrawal` object has been assigned a valid account number. We do not model the user selecting a withdrawal from the main menu or the ATM returning the user to the main menu because these are not actions performed by a `Withdrawal` object. The transaction first displays a menu of standard withdrawal amounts (Fig. 22.3) and an option to cancel the transaction. The transaction then inputs a menu selection from the user. The activity flow now arrives at a decision symbol. This point determines the next action based on the associated guard conditions. If the user cancels the transaction, the system displays an appropriate message. Next, the cancellation flow reaches a merge symbol, where this activity flow joins the transaction's other possible activity flows (which we discuss shortly). A merge can have *any* number of incoming transition arrows, but only *one* outgoing transition arrow. The decision at the bottom of the diagram determines whether the transaction should repeat from the beginning. When the user has canceled the transaction, the guard condition "cash dispensed or user canceled transaction" is true, so control transitions to the activity's final state.

If the user selects a withdrawal amount from the menu, the transaction sets `amount` (an attribute of class `Withdrawal` originally modeled in Fig. 22.12) to the value chosen by the user. The transaction next gets the available balance of the user's account (i.e., the `availableBalance` attribute of the user's `Account` object) from the database. The activity flow then arrives at another decision. If the requested withdrawal amount exceeds the user's available balance, the system displays an appropriate error message informing the user of the problem. Control then merges with the other activity flows before reaching the decision at the bottom of the diagram. The guard decision "cash not dispensed and user did not cancel" is true, so the activity flow returns to the top of the diagram, and the transaction prompts the user to input a new amount.

If the requested withdrawal amount is less than or equal to the user's available balance, the transaction tests whether the cash dispenser has enough cash to satisfy the withdrawal request. If it does not, the transaction displays an appropriate error message and passes through the merge before reaching the final decision. Cash was not dispensed, so the activity flow returns to the beginning of the activity diagram, and the transaction prompts the user to choose a new amount. If sufficient cash is available, the transaction interacts with the database to debit the withdrawal amount from the user's account (i.e., subtract the amount from both the `availableBalance` and `totalBalance` attributes of the user's

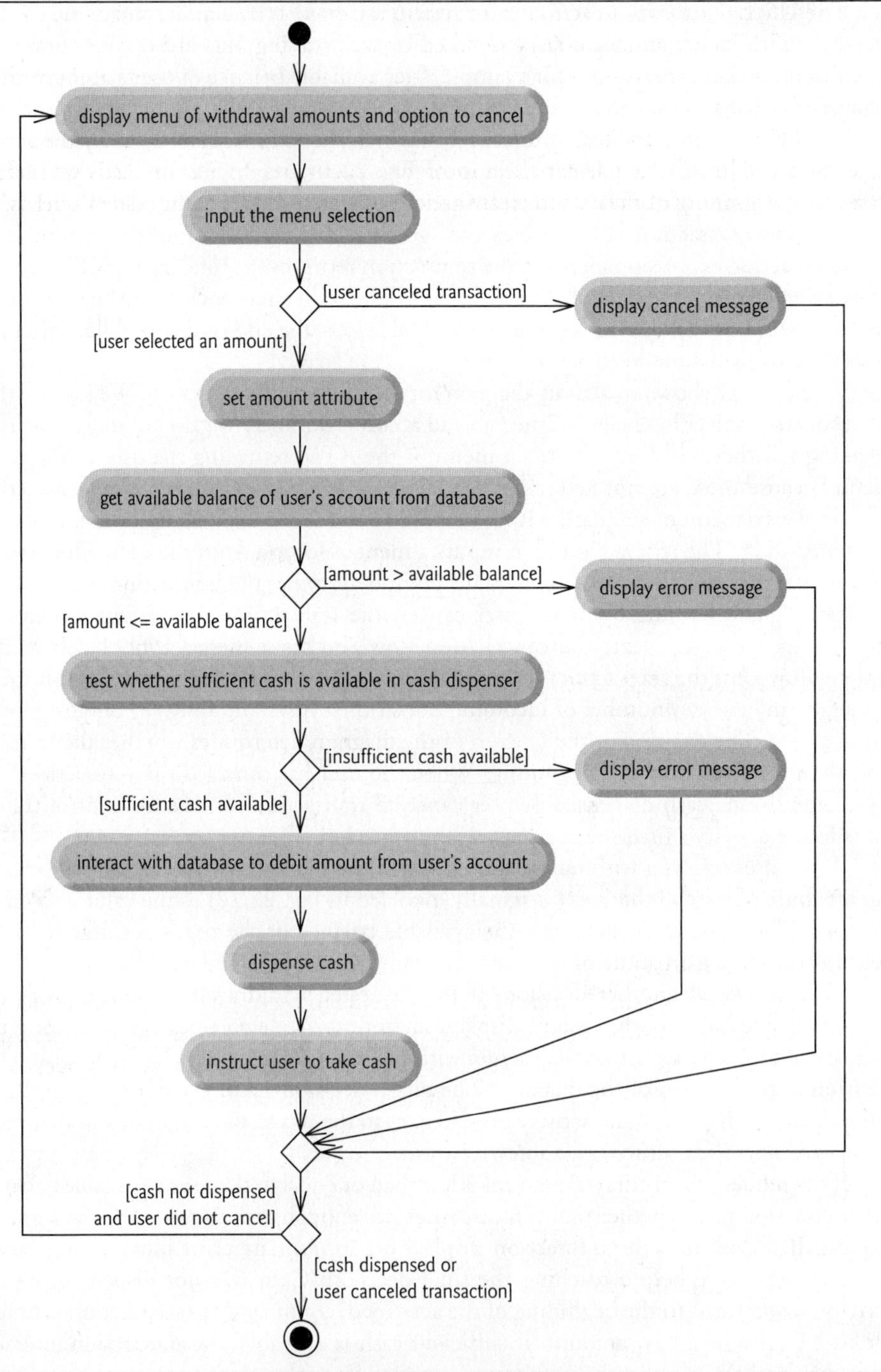

Fig. 22.15 | Activity diagram for a `Withdrawal` transaction.

`Account` object). The transaction then dispenses the desired amount of cash and instructs the user to take the cash that is dispensed. The main flow of activity next merges with the two error flows and the cancellation flow. In this case, cash was dispensed, so the activity flow reaches the final state.

We've taken the first steps in modeling the ATM system's behavior and have shown how an object's attributes participate in the object's activities. In Section 22.7, we investigate the operations of our classes to create a more complete model of the system's behavior.

Self-Review Exercises for Section 22.6

22.11 State whether the following statement is *true* or *false*, and if *false*, explain why: State diagrams model structural aspects of a system.

22.12 An activity diagram models the __________ that an object performs and the order in which it performs them.

a) actions
b) attributes
c) states
d) state transitions

22.13 Based on the requirements document, create an activity diagram for a deposit transaction.

22.7 Identifying Class Operations

In Sections 22.4—22.6, we performed the first few steps in the object-oriented design of our ATM system. In Section 22.4, we identified the classes that we'll need to implement and we created our first class diagram. In Section 22.5, we described some attributes of our classes. In Section 22.6, we examined object states and modeled object state transitions and activities. Now, we determine some of the class operations (or behaviors) needed to implement the ATM system.

Identifying Operations

An *operation* is a service that objects of a class provide to clients of the class. Consider the operations of some real-world objects. A radio's operations include setting its station and volume (typically invoked by a person adjusting the radio's controls). A car's operations include accelerating (invoked by the driver pressing the accelerator pedal), decelerating (invoked by the driver pressing the brake pedal or releasing the gas pedal), turning and shifting gears. Software objects can offer operations as well—for example, a software graphics object might offer operations for drawing a circle, drawing a line, drawing a square and the like. A spreadsheet software object might offer operations like printing the spreadsheet, totaling the elements in a row or column and graphing information in the spreadsheet as a bar chart or pie chart.

We can derive many of the operations of each class by examining the key verbs and verb phrases in the requirements document. We then relate each of these to particular classes in our system (Fig. 22.16). The verb phrases in Fig. 22.16 help us determine the operations of each class.

Class	Verbs and verb phrases
`ATM`	executes financial transactions
`BalanceInquiry`	[none in the requirements document]
`Withdrawal`	[none in the requirements document]
`Deposit`	[none in the requirements document]
`BankDatabase`	authenticates a user, retrieves an account balance, credits a deposit amount to an account, debits a withdrawal amount from an account
`Account`	retrieves an account balance, credits a deposit amount to an account, debits a withdrawal amount from an account
`Screen`	displays a message to the user
`Keypad`	receives numeric input from the user
`CashDispenser`	dispenses cash, indicates whether it contains enough cash to satisfy a withdrawal request
`DepositSlot`	receives a deposit envelope

Fig. 22.16 | Verbs and verb phrases for each class in the ATM system.

Modeling Operations

To identify operations, we examine the verb phrases listed for each class in Fig. 22.16. The "executes financial transactions" phrase associated with class `ATM` implies that class `ATM` instructs transactions to execute. Therefore, classes `BalanceInquiry`, `Withdrawal` and `Deposit` each need an operation to provide this service to the ATM. We place this operation (which we've named `execute`) in the third compartment of the three transaction classes in the updated class diagram of Fig. 22.17. During an ATM session, the `ATM` object will invoke the `execute` operation of each transaction object to tell it to execute.

The UML represents operations (which are implemented as member functions in C++) by listing the operation name, followed by a comma-separated list of parameters in parentheses, a colon and the return type:

operationName(*parameter1*, *parameter2*, ..., *parameterN*) : *return type*

Each parameter in the comma-separated parameter list consists of a parameter name, followed by a colon and the parameter type:

parameterName : *parameterType*

For the moment, we do not list the operations' parameters—we'll identify and model the parameters of some of the operations shortly. For some, we do not yet know the return types, so we also omit them from the diagram. These omissions are perfectly normal at this point. As our design and implementation proceed, we'll add the remaining return types.

Operations of Class `BankDatabase` *and Class* `Account`

Figure 22.16 lists the phrase "authenticates a user" next to class `BankDatabase`—the database is the object that contains the account information necessary to determine whether the account number and PIN entered by a user match those of an account held at the bank. Therefore, class `BankDatabase` needs an operation that provides an authentication

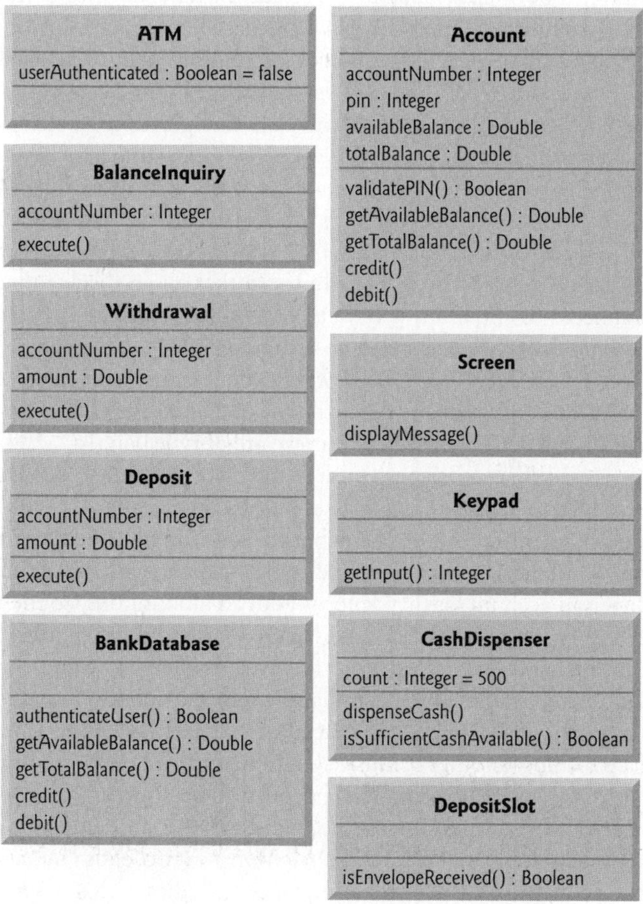

Fig. 22.17 | Classes in the ATM system with attributes and operations.

service to the ATM. We place the operation `authenticateUser` in the third compartment of class `BankDatabase` (Fig. 22.17). However, an object of class `Account`, not class `BankDatabase`, stores the account number and PIN that must be accessed to authenticate a user, so class `Account` must provide a service to validate a PIN obtained through user input against a PIN stored in an `Account` object. Therefore, we add a `validatePIN` operation to class `Account`. We specify return type `Boolean` for the `authenticateUser` and `validatePIN` operations. Each operation returns a value indicating either that the operation was successful in performing its task (i.e., a return value of `true`) or that it was not (i.e., a return value of `false`).

Figure 22.16 lists several additional verb phrases for class `BankDatabase`: "retrieves an account balance," "credits a deposit amount to an account" and "debits a withdrawal amount from an account." Like "authenticates a user," these remaining phrases refer to services that the database must provide to the ATM, because the database holds all the account data used to authenticate a user and perform ATM transactions. However, objects of class `Account` actually perform the operations to which these phrases refer. Thus, we assign an operation to both class `BankDatabase` and class `Account` to correspond to each of these phrases. Recall from Section 22.4 that, because a bank account contains sensitive information, we do *not* allow the ATM to access accounts directly. The database acts as an intermediary between the ATM and the account data, thus preventing unauthorized access. As we'll see in Section 22.8, class `ATM` invokes the operations of class `BankDatabase`, each of which in turn invokes the operation with the same name in class `Account`.

The phrase "retrieves an account balance" suggests that classes `BankDatabase` and `Account` each need a `getBalance` operation. However, recall that we created two attributes in class `Account` to represent a balance—`availableBalance` and `totalBalance`. A balance inquiry requires access to both balance attributes so that it can display them to the user, but a withdrawal needs to check only the value of `availableBalance`. To allow objects in the system to obtain each balance attribute individually, we add operations `getAvailableBalance` and `getTotalBalance` to the third compartment of classes `BankDatabase` and `Account` (Fig. 22.17). We specify a return type of `Double` for each of these operations, because the balance attributes which they retrieve are of type `Double`.

The phrases "credits a deposit amount to an account" and "debits a withdrawal amount from an account" indicate that classes `BankDatabase` and `Account` must perform operations to update an account during a deposit and withdrawal, respectively. We therefore assign `credit` and `debit` operations to classes `BankDatabase` and `Account`. You may recall that crediting an account (as in a deposit) adds an amount only to the `totalBalance` attribute. Debiting an account (as in a withdrawal), on the other hand, subtracts the amount from both balance attributes. We hide these implementation details inside class `Account`. This is a good example of encapsulation and information hiding.

If this were a real ATM system, classes `BankDatabase` and `Account` would also provide a set of operations to allow another banking system to update a user's account balance after either confirming or rejecting all or part of a deposit. Operation `confirmDepositAmount`, for example, would add an amount to the `availableBalance` attribute, thus making deposited funds available for withdrawal. Operation `rejectDepositAmount` would subtract an amount from the `totalBalance` attribute to indicate that a specified amount, which had recently been deposited through the ATM and added to the `totalBalance`, was not found in the deposit envelope. The bank would invoke this operation after determining either that the user failed to include the correct amount of cash or that any checks did not clear (i.e, they "bounced"). While adding these operations would make our system more complete, we do not include them in our class diagrams or our implementation because they are beyond the scope of the case study.

Operations of Class `Screen`

Class `Screen` "displays a message to the user" at various times in an ATM session. All visual output occurs through the screen of the ATM. The requirements document describes many types of messages (e.g., a welcome message, an error message, a thank you message) that the screen displays to the user. The requirements document also indicates that the screen displays prompts and menus to the user. However, a prompt is really just a message describing what the user should input next, and a menu is essentially a type of prompt consisting of a series of messages (i.e., menu options) displayed consecutively. Therefore, rather than assign class `Screen` an individual operation to display each type of message, prompt and menu, we simply create one operation that can display any message specified by a parameter. We place this operation (`displayMessage`) in the third compartment of class `Screen` in our class diagram (Fig. 22.17). We do not worry about the parameter of this operation at this time—we model the parameter later in this section.

Operations of Class `Keypad`

From the phrase "receives numeric input from the user" listed by class `Keypad` in Fig. 22.16, we conclude that class `Keypad` should perform a `getInput` operation. Because the ATM's keypad, unlike a computer keyboard, contains only the numbers 0–9, we specify that this operation returns an integer value. Recall from the requirements document that in different situations the user may be required to enter a different type of number (e.g., an account number, a PIN, the number of a menu option, a deposit amount as a number of cents). Class `Keypad` simply obtains a numeric value for a client of the class—it does *not* determine whether the value meets any specific criteria. Any class that uses this operation must verify that the user enters appropriate numbers, and if not, display error messages via class `Screen`). [*Note:* When we implement the system, we simulate the ATM's keypad with a computer keyboard, and for simplicity we assume that the user does not enter nonnumeric input using keys on the computer keyboard that do not appear on the ATM's keypad.]

Operations of Class `CashDispenser` *and Class* `DepositSlot`

Figure 22.16 lists "dispenses cash" for class `CashDispenser`. Therefore, we create operation `dispenseCash` and list it under class `CashDispenser` in Fig. 22.17. Class `CashDispenser` also "indicates whether it contains enough cash to satisfy a withdrawal request." Thus, we include `isSufficientCashAvailable`, an operation that returns a value of UML type `Boolean`, in class `CashDispenser`. Figure 22.16 also lists "receives a deposit envelope" for class `DepositSlot`. The deposit slot must indicate whether it received an envelope, so we place an operation `isEnvelopeReceived`, which returns a `Boolean` value, in the third compartment of class `DepositSlot`. [*Note:* A real hardware deposit slot would most likely send the ATM a signal to indicate that an envelope was received. We simulate this behavior, however, with an operation in class `DepositSlot` that class `ATM` can invoke to find out whether the deposit slot received an envelope.]

Operations of Class `ATM`

We do not list any operations for class `ATM` at this time. We are not yet aware of any services that class `ATM` provides to other classes in the system. When we implement the system with C++ code, however, operations of this class, and additional operations of the other classes in the system, may emerge.

Identifying and Modeling Operation Parameters

So far, we've not been concerned with the parameters of our operations—we've attempted to gain only a basic understanding of the operations of each class. Let's now take a closer look at some operation parameters. We identify an operation's parameters by examining what data the operation requires to perform its assigned task.

Consider the `authenticateUser` operation of class `BankDatabase`. To authenticate a user, this operation must know the account number and PIN supplied by the user. Thus we specify that operation `authenticateUser` takes integer parameters `userAccountNumber` and `userPIN`, which the operation must compare to the account number and PIN of an `Account` object in the database. We prefix these parameter names with "user" to avoid confusion between the operation's parameter names and the attribute names that belong to class `Account`. We list these parameters in the class diagram in Fig. 22.18 that models only class `BankDatabase`. [*Note:* It's perfectly normal to model only one class in a class diagram. In this case, we are most concerned with examining the parameters of this one class in particular, so we omit the other classes. In class diagrams later in the case study, in which parameters are no longer the focus of our attention, we omit the parameters to save space. Remember, however, that the operations listed in these diagrams still have parameters.]

Recall that the UML models each parameter in an operation's comma-separated parameter list by listing the parameter name, followed by a colon and the parameter type (in UML notation). Figure 22.18 thus specifies that operation `authenticateUser` takes two parameters—`userAccountNumber` and `userPIN`, both of type `Integer`. When we implement the system in C++, we'll represent these parameters with `int` values.

BankDatabase
authenticateUser(userAccountNumber : Integer, userPIN : Integer) : Boolean getAvailableBalance(userAccountNumber : Integer) : Double getTotalBalance(userAccountNumber : Integer) : Double credit(userAccountNumber : Integer, amount : Double) debit(userAccountNumber : Integer, amount : Double)

Fig. 22.18 | Class `BankDatabase` with operation parameters.

Class `BankDatabase` operations `getAvailableBalance`, `getTotalBalance`, `credit` and `debit` also each require a `userAccountNumber` parameter to identify the account to which the database must apply the operations, so we include these parameters in the class diagram of Fig. 22.18. In addition, operations `credit` and `debit` each require a `Double` parameter `amount` to specify the amount of money to be credited or debited, respectively.

The class diagram in Fig. 22.19 models the parameters of class `Account`'s operations. Operation `validatePIN` requires only a `userPIN` parameter, which contains the user-specified PIN to be compared with the PIN associated with the account. Like their counterparts in class `BankDatabase`, operations `credit` and `debit` in class `Account` each require a `Double` parameter `amount` that indicates the amount of money involved in the operation. Operations `getAvailableBalance` and `getTotalBalance` in class `Account` require no additional data to perform their tasks. Class `Account`'s operations do not require an account number parameter—each of these operations can be invoked only on a specific `Account` object, so including a parameter to specify an `Account` is unnecessary.

Figure 22.20 models class `Screen` with a parameter specified for operation `displayMessage`. This operation requires only a `String` parameter `message` that indicates the text to be displayed. Recall that the parameter types listed in our class diagrams are in UML notation, so the `String` type listed in Fig. 22.20 refers to the UML type. When we implement the system in C++, we'll in fact use a C++ `string` object to represent this parameter.

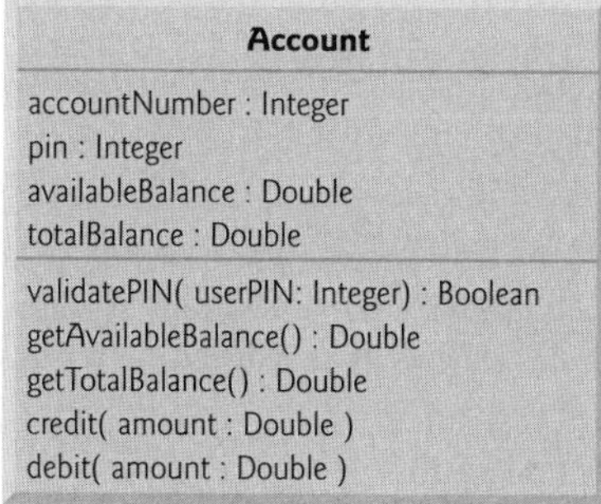

Fig. 22.19 | Class `Account` with operation parameters.

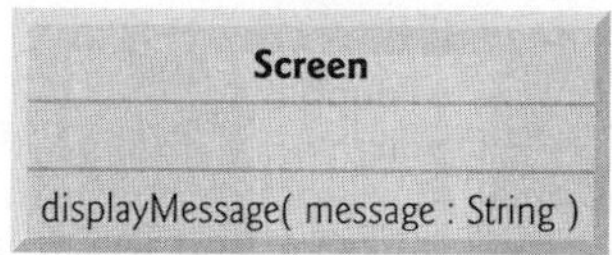

Fig. 22.20 | Class `Screen` with operation parameters.

The class diagram in Fig. 22.21 specifies that operation `dispenseCash` of class `CashDispenser` takes a `Double` parameter `amount` to indicate the amount of cash (in dollars) to be dispensed. Operation `isSufficientCashAvailable` also takes a `Double` parameter `amount` to indicate the amount of cash in question.

CashDispenser
count : Integer = 500
dispenseCash(amount : Double) isSufficientCashAvailable(amount : Double) : Boolean

Fig. 22.21 | Class `CashDispenser` with operation parameters.

We do not discuss parameters for operation `execute` of classes `BalanceInquiry`, `Withdrawal` and `Deposit`, operation `getInput` of class `Keypad` and operation `isEnvelopeReceived` of class `DepositSlot`. At this point in our design process, we cannot determine whether these operations require additional data to perform their tasks, so we leave their parameter lists empty. As we progress through the case study, we may decide to add parameters to these operations.

In this section, we've determined many of the operations performed by the classes in the ATM system. We've identified the parameters and return types of some of the operations. As we continue our design process, the number of operations belonging to each class may vary—we might find that new operations are needed or that some current operations are unnecessary—and we might determine that some of our class operations need additional parameters and different return types.

Self-Review Exercises for Section 22.7

22.14 Which of the following is not a behavior?
a) reading data from a file
b) printing output
c) text output
d) obtaining input from the user

22.15 If you were to add to the ATM system an operation that returns the `amount` attribute of class `Withdrawal`, how and where would you specify this operation in the class diagram of Fig. 22.17?

22.16 Describe the meaning of the following operation listing that might appear in a class diagram for an object-oriented design of a calculator:

```
add( x : Integer, y : Integer ) : Integer
```

22.8 Indicating Collaboration Among Objects

In this section, we concentrate on the collaborations (interactions) among objects in our ATM system. When two objects communicate with each other to accomplish a task, they are said to **collaborate**—they do this by invoking one another's operations. A **collaboration** consists of an object of one class sending a **message** to an object of another class. Messages are sent in C++ via member-function calls.

In Section 22.7, we determined many of the *operations* of the system's classes. Next, we concentrate on the *messages* that invoke these operations. To identify the collaborations, we return to the requirements document in Section 22.3. Recall that this document specifies the range of activities that occur during an ATM session (e.g., authenticating a user, performing transactions). The steps used to describe how the system must perform each of these tasks are our first indication of the collaborations in our system. As we proceed through this and the remaining sections, we may discover additional collaborations.

Identifying the Collaborations in a System

We identify the collaborations in the system by carefully reading the requirements document sections that specify what the ATM should do to authenticate a user and to perform each transaction type. For each action or step described, we decide which objects in our system must interact to achieve the desired result. We identify one object as the *sending object* (i.e., the object that sends the message) and another as the *receiving object* (i.e., the object that offers that operation to clients of the class). We then select one of the receiving object's operations (identified in Section 22.7) that must be invoked by the sending object to produce the proper behavior. For example, the ATM displays a welcome message when idle. We know that an object of class `Screen` displays a message to the user via its `displayMessage` operation. Thus, we decide that the system can display a welcome message by employing a collaboration between the `ATM` and the `Screen` in which the `ATM` sends a `displayMessage` message to the `Screen` by invoking the `displayMessage` operation of class `Screen`. [*Note:* To avoid repeating the phrase "an object of class...," we refer to each object simply by using its class name preceded by an article ("a," "an" or "the")—for example, "the `ATM`" refers to an object of class `ATM`.]

Figure 22.22 lists the collaborations that can be derived from the requirements document. For each sending object, we list the collaborations in the order in which they are discussed in the requirements document. We list each collaboration involving a unique sender, message and recipient only once, even though the collaboration may occur several times during an ATM session. For example, the first row in Fig. 22.22 indicates that the ATM collaborates with the Screen whenever the ATM needs to display a message to the user.

An object of class...	sends the message...	to an object of class...
ATM	displayMessage	Screen
	getInput	Keypad
	authenticateUser	BankDatabase
	execute	BalanceInquiry
	execute	Withdrawal
	execute	Deposit
BalanceInquiry	getAvailableBalance	BankDatabase
	getTotalBalance	BankDatabase
	displayMessage	Screen
Withdrawal	displayMessage	Screen
	getInput	Keypad
	getAvailableBalance	BankDatabase
	isSufficientCashAvailable	CashDispenser
	debit	BankDatabase
	dispenseCash	CashDispenser
Deposit	displayMessage	Screen
	getInput	Keypad
	isEnvelopeReceived	DepositSlot
	credit	BankDatabase
BankDatabase	validatePIN	Account
	getAvailableBalance	Account
	getTotalBalance	Account
	debit	Account
	credit	Account

Fig. 22.22 | Collaborations in the ATM system.

Let's consider the collaborations in Fig. 22.22. Before allowing a user to perform any transactions, the ATM must prompt the user to enter an account number, then to enter a PIN. It accomplishes each of these tasks by sending a displayMessage message to the Screen. Both of these actions refer to the same collaboration between the ATM and the Screen, which is already listed in Fig. 22.22. The ATM obtains input in response to a prompt by sending a getInput message to the Keypad. Next, the ATM must determine whether the user-specified account number and PIN match those of an account in the database. It does so by sending an authenticateUser message to the BankDatabase. Recall that the BankDatabase cannot authenticate a user directly—only the user's Account (i.e., the Account that contains the account number specified by the user) can access the user's PIN to authenticate the user. Figure 22.22 therefore lists a collaboration in which the BankDatabase sends a validatePIN message to an Account.

After the user is authenticated, the ATM displays the main menu by sending a series of displayMessage messages to the Screen and obtains input containing a menu selection by sending a getInput message to the Keypad. We've already accounted for these collaborations. After the user chooses a type of transaction to perform, the ATM executes the transaction by sending an execute message to an object of the appropriate transaction class (i.e., a BalanceInquiry, a Withdrawal or a Deposit). For example, if the user chooses to perform a balance inquiry, the ATM sends an execute message to a BalanceInquiry.

Further examination of the requirements document reveals the collaborations involved in executing each transaction type. A BalanceInquiry retrieves the amount of money available in the user's account by sending a getAvailableBalance message to the BankDatabase, which responds by sending a getAvailableBalance message to the user's Account. Similarly, the BalanceInquiry retrieves the amount of money on deposit by sending a getTotalBalance message to the BankDatabase, which sends the same message to the user's Account. To display both measures of the user's balance at the same time, the BalanceInquiry sends a displayMessage message to the Screen.

A Withdrawal sends the Screen several displayMessage messages to display a menu of standard withdrawal amounts (i.e., $20, $40, $60, $100, $200). The Withdrawal sends the Keypad a getInput message to obtain the user's menu selection, then determines whether the requested withdrawal amount is less than or equal to the user's account balance. The Withdrawal can obtain the amount of money available in the account by sending the BankDatabase a getAvailableBalance message. The Withdrawal then tests whether the cash dispenser contains enough cash by sending the CashDispenser an isSufficientCashAvailable message. A Withdrawal sends the BankDatabase a debit message to decrease the user's account balance. The BankDatabase sends the same message to the appropriate Account. Recall that debiting funds from an Account decreases both the totalBalance and the availableBalance. To dispense the requested amount of cash, the Withdrawal sends the CashDispenser a dispenseCash message. Finally, the Withdrawal sends a displayMessage message to the Screen, instructing the user to take the cash.

A Deposit responds to an execute message first by sending a displayMessage message to the Screen to prompt the user for a deposit amount. The Deposit sends a getInput message to the Keypad to obtain the user's input. The Deposit then sends a displayMessage message to the Screen to tell the user to insert a deposit envelope. To determine whether the deposit slot received an incoming deposit envelope, the Deposit sends an isEnvelopeReceived message to the DepositSlot. The Deposit updates the user's account by sending a credit message to the BankDatabase, which subsequently sends a credit message to the user's Account. Recall that crediting funds to an Account increases the totalBalance but not the availableBalance.

Interaction Diagrams

Now that we've identified possible collaborations between the objects in our ATM system, let's graphically model these interactions using the UML. Several types of **interaction diagrams** model the behavior of a system by showing how objects interact with one another. The **communication diagram** emphasizes which objects participate in collaborations. [*Note:* Communication diagrams were called **collaboration diagrams** in earlier versions of the UML.] Like the communication diagram, the **sequence diagram** shows collaborations among objects, but it emphasizes *when* messages are sent between objects *over time*.

Communication Diagrams

Figure 22.23 shows a communication diagram that models the ATM executing a BalanceInquiry. Objects are modeled in the UML as rectangles containing names in the form objectName : ClassName. In this example, which involves only one object of each type, we disregard the object name and list only a colon followed by the class name. [*Note:* Specifying the name of each object in a communication diagram is recommended when modeling multiple objects of the same type.] Communicating objects are connected with solid lines, and messages are passed between objects along these lines in the direction shown by arrows. The name of the message, which appears next to the arrow, is the name of an operation (i.e., a member function) belonging to the receiving object—think of the name as a service that the receiving object provides to sending objects (its "clients").

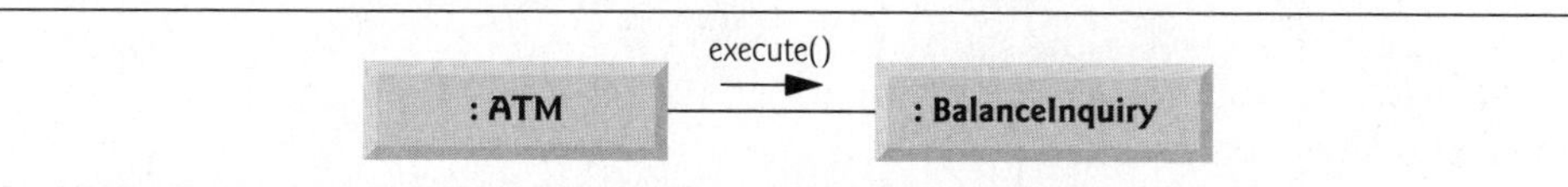

Fig. 22.23 | Communication diagram of the ATM executing a balance inquiry.

The solid filled arrow in Fig. 22.23 represents a message—or **synchronous call**—in the UML and a function call in C++. This arrow indicates that the flow of control is from the sending object (the ATM) to the receiving object (a BalanceInquiry). *Since this is a synchronous call, the sending object may not send another message, or do anything at all, until the receiving object processes the message and returns control to the sending object—the sender just waits.* For example, in Fig. 22.23, the ATM calls member function execute of a BalanceInquiry and may not send another message until execute has finished and returns control to the ATM. [*Note:* If this were an **asynchronous call**, represented by a stick arrowhead, the sending object would not have to wait for the receiving object to return control—it would continue sending additional messages immediately following the asynchronous call. Asynchronous calls often can be implemented in C++ using platform-specific libraries provided with your compiler. Such techniques are beyond the scope of this book.]

Sequence of Messages in a Communication Diagram

Figure 22.24 shows a communication diagram that models the interactions among objects in the system when an object of class BalanceInquiry executes. We assume that the object's accountNumber attribute contains the account number of the current user. The collaborations in Fig. 22.24 begin after the ATM sends an execute message to a BalanceInquiry (i.e., the interaction modeled in Fig. 22.23). The number to the left of a message name indicates the order in which the message is passed. The **sequence of messages** in a communication diagram progresses in numerical order from least to greatest. In this diagram, the numbering starts with message 1 and ends with message 3. The BalanceInquiry first sends a getAvailableBalance message to the BankDatabase (message 1), then sends a getTotalBalance message to the BankDatabase (message 2). Within the parentheses following a message name, we can specify a comma-separated list of the names of the parameters sent with the message (i.e., arguments in a C++ function call)—the BalanceInquiry passes attribute accountNumber with its messages to the BankDatabase to indicate which Account's balance information to retrieve. Recall from Fig. 22.18 that operations getAvailableBalance and getTotalBalance of class BankDatabase each require a parameter to identify an account. The BalanceInquiry next displays the availableBalance and the totalBalance to the user by passing a displayMessage message to the Screen (message 3) that includes a parameter indicating the message to be displayed.

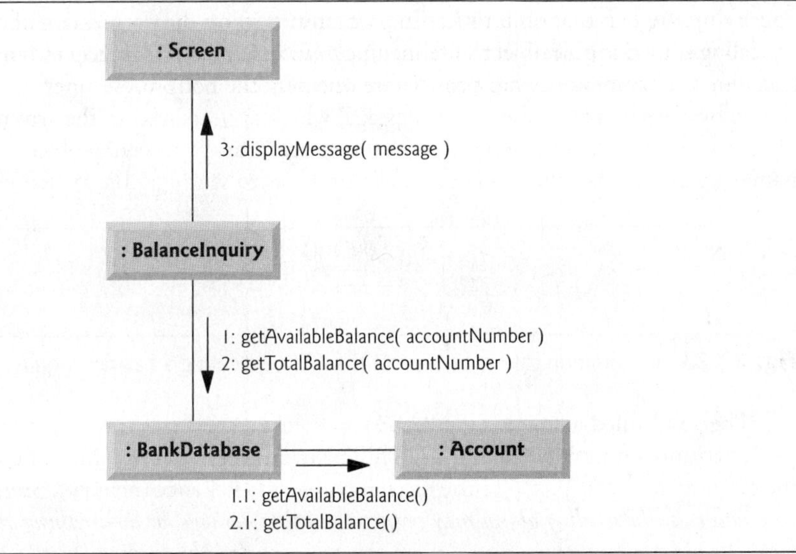

Fig. 22.24 | Communication diagram for executing a balance inquiry.

Figure 22.24 models two additional messages passing from the BankDatabase to an Account (message 1.1 and message 2.1). To provide the ATM with the two balances of the user's Account (as requested by messages 1 and 2), the BankDatabase must pass a getAvailableBalance and a getTotalBalance message to the user's Account. Messages passed within the handling of another message are called **nested messages**. The UML recommends using a decimal numbering scheme to indicate nested messages. For example, message 1.1 is the first message nested in message 1—the BankDatabase passes a getAvailableBalance message while processing BankDatabase's message of the same name. [*Note:* If the BankDatabase needed to pass a second nested message while processing message 1, the second message would be numbered 1.2.] A message may be passed only when all the nested messages from the previous message have been passed—e.g., the BalanceInquiry passes message 3 only after messages 2 and 2.1 have been passed, in that order.

The nested numbering scheme used in communication diagrams helps clarify precisely when and in what context each message is passed. For example, if we numbered the messages in Fig. 22.24 using a flat numbering scheme (i.e., 1, 2, 3, 4, 5), someone looking at the diagram might not be able to determine that BankDatabase passes the getAvailableBalance message (message 1.1) to an Account *during* the BankDatabase's processing of message 1, as opposed to *after* completing the processing of message 1. The nested decimal numbers make it clear that the second getAvailableBalance message (message 1.1) is passed to an Account within the handling of the first getAvailableBalance message (message 1) by the BankDatabase.

Sequence Diagrams

Communication diagrams emphasize the participants in collaborations but model their timing a bit awkwardly. A sequence diagram helps model the timing of collaborations more clearly. Figure 22.25 shows a sequence diagram modeling the sequence of interactions that occur when a `Withdrawal` executes. The dotted line extending down from an object's rectangle is that object's **lifeline**, which represents the progression of time. Actions typically occur along an object's lifeline in *chronological order* from top to bottom—an action near the top typically happens before one near the bottom.

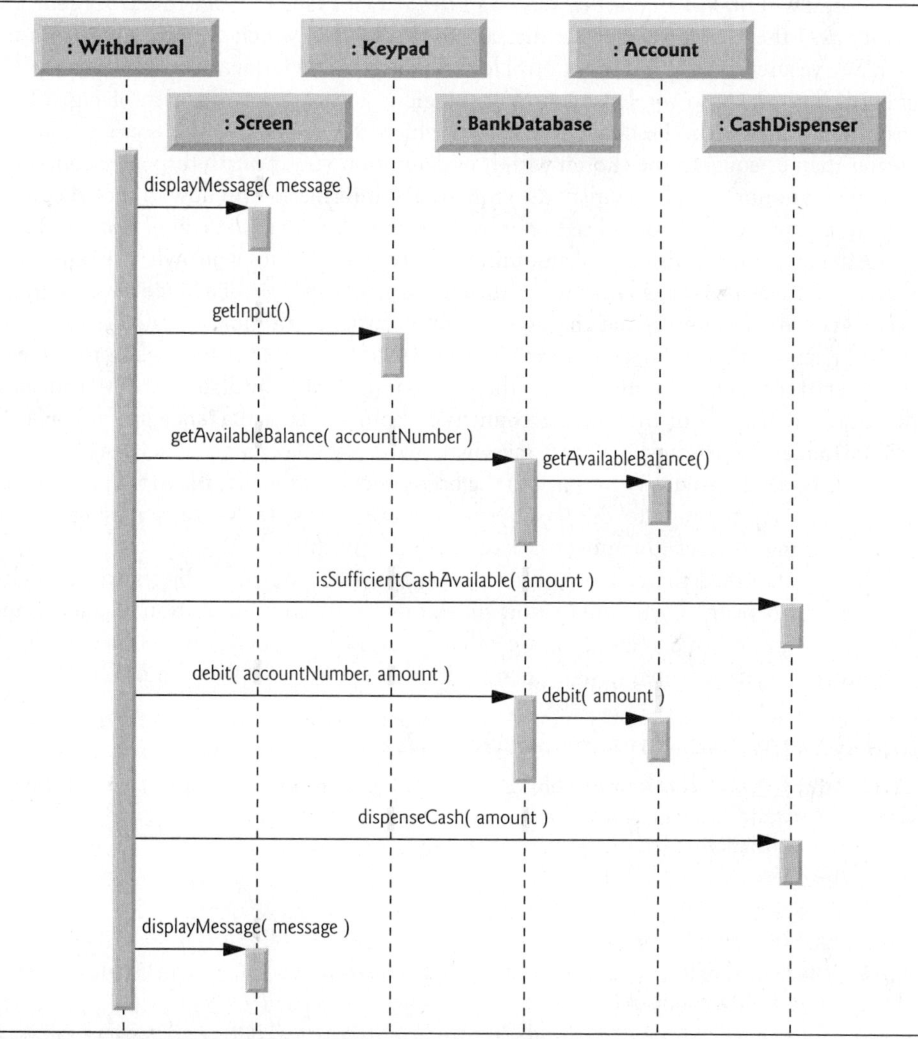

Fig. 22.25 | Sequence diagram that models a `Withdrawal` executing.

Message passing in sequence diagrams is similar to message passing in communication diagrams. A solid arrow with a filled arrowhead extending from the sending object to the receiving object represents a message between two objects. The arrowhead points to an activation on the receiving object's lifeline. An **activation**, shown as a thin vertical rectangle, indicates that an object is executing. When an object returns control, a return message, represented as a dashed line with a stick arrowhead, extends from the activation of the object returning control to the activation of the object that initially sent the message. To eliminate clutter, we omit the return-message arrows—the UML allows this practice to make diagrams more readable. Like communication diagrams, sequence diagrams can indicate message parameters between the parentheses following a message name.

The sequence of messages in Fig. 22.25 begins when a `Withdrawal` prompts the user to choose a withdrawal amount by sending a `displayMessage` message to the `Screen`. The `Withdrawal` then sends a `getInput` message to the `Keypad`, which obtains input from the user. We've already modeled the control logic involved in a `Withdrawal` in the activity diagram of Fig. 22.15, so we do not show this logic in the sequence diagram of Fig. 22.25. Instead, we model the best-case scenario in which the balance of the user's account is greater than or equal to the chosen withdrawal amount, and the cash dispenser contains a sufficient amount of cash to satisfy the request. For information on how to model control logic in a sequence diagram, please refer to the web resources at the end of Section 22.3.

After obtaining a withdrawal amount, the `Withdrawal` sends a `getAvailableBalance` message to the `BankDatabase`, which in turn sends a `getAvailableBalance` message to the user's `Account`. Assuming that the user's account has enough money available to permit the transaction, the `Withdrawal` next sends an `isSufficientCashAvailable` message to the `CashDispenser`. Assuming that there is enough cash available, the `Withdrawal` decreases the balance of the user's account (i.e., both the `totalBalance` and the `availableBalance`) by sending a `debit` message to the `BankDatabase`. The `BankDatabase` responds by sending a `debit` message to the user's `Account`. Finally, the `Withdrawal` sends a `dispenseCash` message to the `CashDispenser` and a `displayMessage` message to the `Screen`, telling the user to remove the cash from the machine.

We've identified the collaborations among the ATM system's objects and modeled some of them using UML interaction diagrams—both communication diagrams and sequence diagrams. In Section 23.2, we enhance the structure of our model to complete a preliminary object-oriented design, then we implement the ATM system in C++.

Self-Review Exercises for Section 22.8

22.17 A(n) ________ consists of an object of one class sending a message to an object of another class.

a) association
b) aggregation
c) collaboration
d) composition

22.18 Which form of interaction diagram emphasizes *what* collaborations occur? Which form emphasizes *when* collaborations occur?

22.19 Create a sequence diagram that models the interactions among objects in the ATM system that occur when a `Deposit` executes successfully, and explain the sequence of messages modeled by the diagram.

22.9 Wrap-Up

In this chapter, you learned how to work from a detailed requirements document to develop an object-oriented design. You worked with six popular types of UML diagrams to graphically model an object-oriented automated teller machine software system. In Section 23.3, we tune the design using inheritance, then in Section 23.4, we completely implement the design in an 850-line C++ application.

Answers to Self-Review Exercises

22.1 Figure 22.26 shows a use case diagram for a modified version of our ATM system that also allows users to transfer money between accounts.

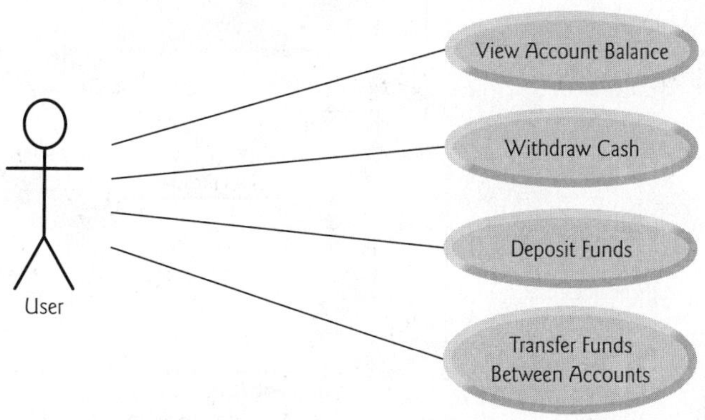

Fig. 22.26 | Use case diagram for a modified version of our ATM system that also allows users to transfer money between accounts.

22.2 b.

22.3 d.

22.4 [*Note:* Answers may vary.] Figure 22.27 presents a class diagram that shows some of the composition relationships of a class `Car`.

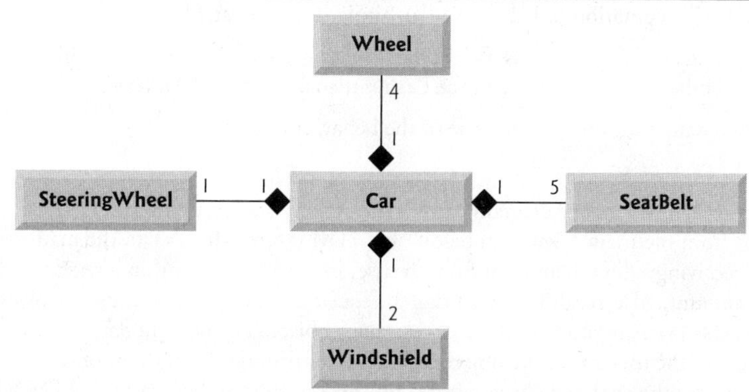

Fig. 22.27 | Class diagram showing composition relationships of a class `Car`.

22.5 c. [*Note:* In a computer network, this relationship could be many-to-many.]

22.6 True.

22.7 Figure 22.28 presents an ATM class diagram including class `Deposit` instead of class `Withdrawal`. Note that `Deposit` does not access `CashDispenser`, but does access `DepositSlot`.

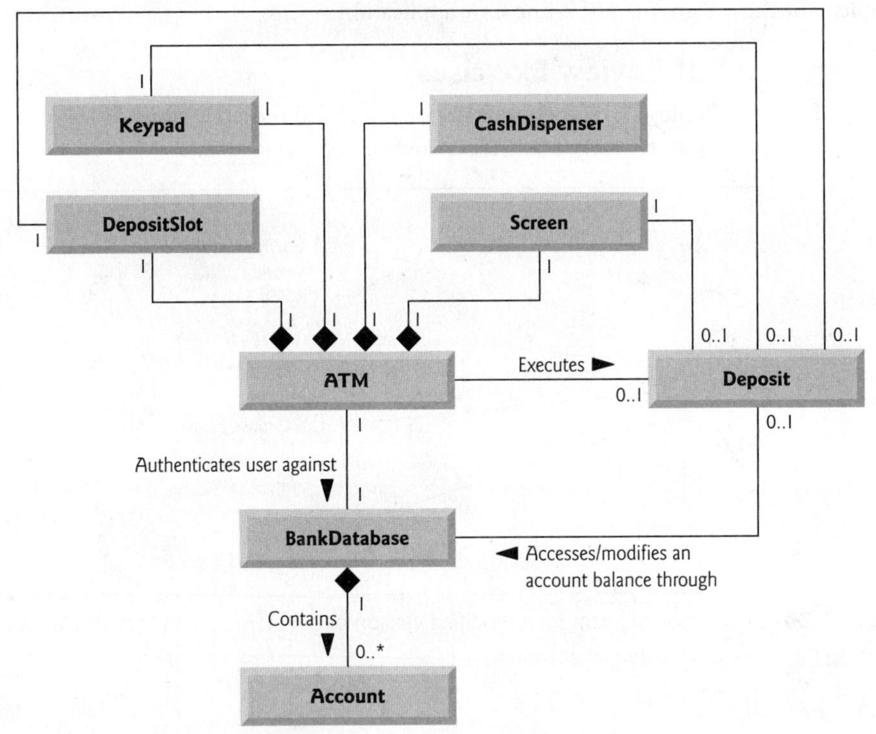

Fig. 22.28 | Class diagram for the ATM system model including class `Deposit`.

22.8 b.

22.9 c. Fly is an operation or behavior of an airplane, not an attribute.

22.10 This indicates that `count` is an `Integer` with an initial value of `500`. This attribute keeps track of the number of bills available in the `CashDispenser` at any given time.

22.11 False. State diagrams model some of the behavior of a system.

22.12 a.

22.13 Figure 22.29's activity diagram models the actions that occur after the user chooses the deposit option from the main menu and before the ATM returns the user to the main menu. Recall that part of receiving a deposit amount from the user involves converting an integer number of cents to a dollar amount. Also recall that crediting a deposit amount to an account involves increasing only the `totalBalance` attribute of the user's `Account` object. The bank updates the `availableBalance` attribute of the user's `Account` object only after confirming the amount of cash in the deposit envelope and after the enclosed checks clear—this occurs independently of the ATM system.

22.14 c.

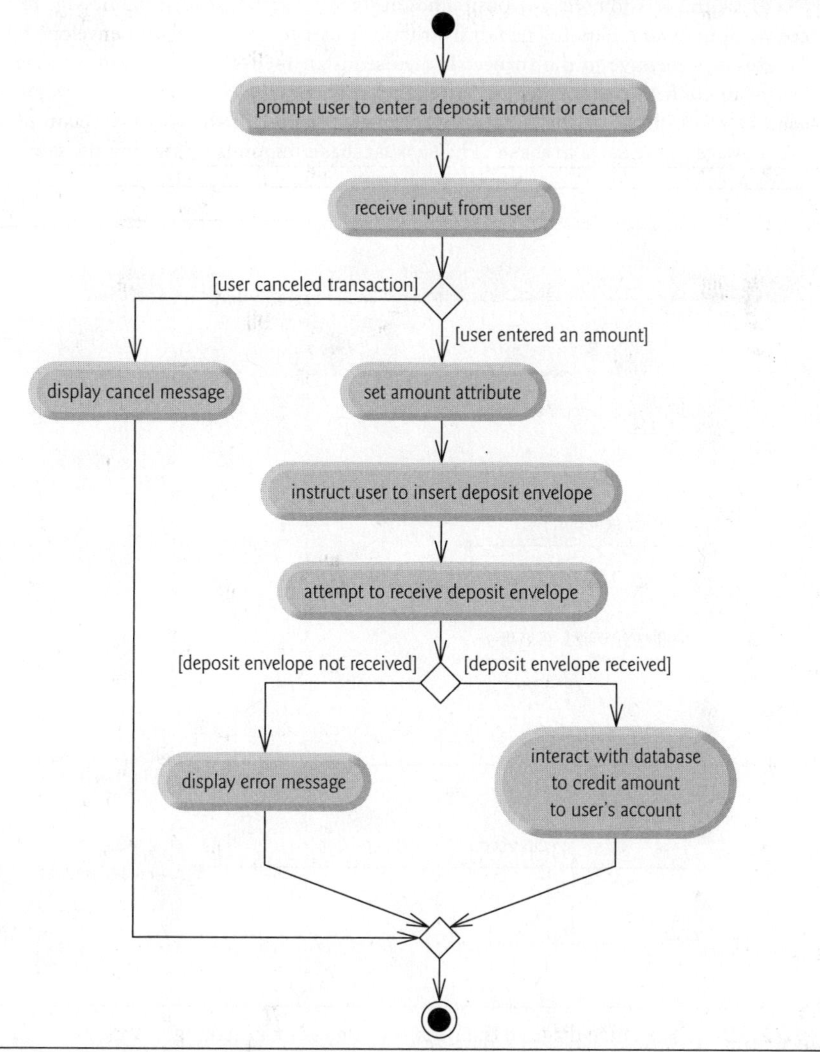

Fig. 22.29 | Activity diagram for a `Deposit` transaction.

22.15 To specify an operation that retrieves the `amount` attribute of class `Withdrawal`, the following operation would be placed in the operation (i.e., third) compartment of class `Withdrawal`:

```
getAmount( ) : Double
```

22.16 This is an operation named `add` that takes integers `x` and `y` as parameters and returns an integer value.

22.17 c.

22.18 Communication diagrams emphasize *what* collaborations occur. Sequence diagrams emphasize *when* collaborations occur.

22.19 Figure 22.30 presents a sequence diagram that models the interactions between objects that occur when a `Deposit` executes successfully. A `Deposit` first sends a `displayMessage` message to the

`Screen` to ask the user to enter a deposit amount. Next, it sends a `getInput` message to the `Keypad` to receive input from the user. Then, it instructs the user to insert a deposit envelope by sending a `displayMessage` message to the `Screen`. It then sends an `isEnvelopeReceived` message to the `DepositSlot` to confirm that the deposit envelope has been received. Finally, it increases the `totalBalance` attribute (but not the `availableBalance` attribute) of the user's `Account` by sending a `credit` message to the `BankDatabase`. The `BankDatabase` responds by sending the same message to the user's `Account`.

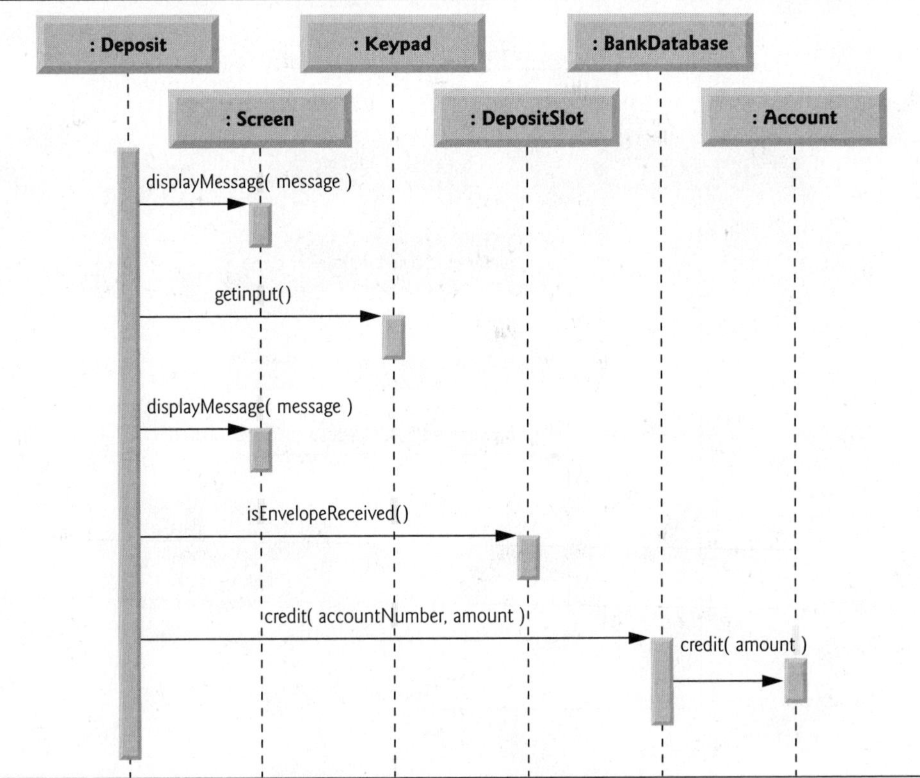

Fig. 22.30 | Sequence diagram that models a `Deposit` executing.

23

ATM Case Study, Part 2: Implementing an Object-Oriented Design

Objectives

In this chapter you'll:

- Incorporate inheritance into the design of the ATM.
- Incorporate polymorphism into the design of the ATM.
- Fully implement in C++ the UML-based object-oriented design of the ATM software.
- Study a detailed code walkthrough of the ATM software system that explains the implementation issues.

Outline

23.1 Introduction

In Chapter 22, we developed an object-oriented design for our ATM system. We now begin implementing our object-oriented design in C++. In Section 23.2, we show how to convert class diagrams to C++ code. In Section 23.3, we tune the design with inheritance and polymorphism. Then we present a full C++ code implementation of the ATM software in Section 23.4. The code is carefully commented and the discussions of the implementation are thorough and precise. Studying this application provides the opportunity for you to see a more substantial application of the kind you're likely to encounter in industry.

23.2 Starting to Program the Classes of the ATM System

Visibility

We now apply access specifiers to the members of our classes. Access specifiers `public` and `private` determine the **visibility** or accessibility of an object's attributes and operations to other objects. Before we can begin implementing our design, we must consider which attributes and operations of our classes should be `public` and which should be `private`.

Previously, we observed that data members normally should be `private` and that member functions invoked by clients of a given class should be `public`. Member functions that are called only by other member functions of the class as "utility functions," however, normally should be `private`. The UML employs **visibility markers** for modeling the visibility of attributes and operations. Public visibility is indicated by placing a plus sign (+) before an operation or an attribute; a minus sign (–) indicates private visibility. Figure 23.1 shows our updated class diagram with visibility markers included. [*Note:* We do not include any operation parameters in Fig. 23.1. This is perfectly normal. Adding visibility markers does not affect the parameters already modeled in the class diagrams of Figs. 22.18–22.21.]

Navigability

Before we begin implementing our design in C++, we introduce an additional UML notation. The class diagram in Fig. 23.2 further refines the relationships among classes in the ATM system by adding navigability arrows to the association lines. **Navigability arrows** (represented as arrows with stick arrowheads in the class diagram) indicate in which direction an association can be traversed and are based on the collaborations modeled in communica-

Fig. 23.1 | Class diagram with visibility markers.

tion and sequence diagrams (see Section 22.8). When implementing a system designed using the UML, you use navigability arrows to help determine which objects need references or pointers to other objects. For example, the navigability arrow pointing from class `ATM` to class `BankDatabase` indicates that we can navigate from the former to the latter, thereby enabling the `ATM` to invoke the `BankDatabase`'s operations. However, since Fig. 23.2 does not contain a navigability arrow pointing from class `BankDatabase` to class `ATM`, the `BankDatabase` cannot access the `ATM`'s operations. Associations in a class diagram that have navigability arrows at both ends or do not have navigability arrows at all indicate **bidirectional navigability**—navigation can proceed in either direction across the association.

Like the class diagram of Fig. 22.10, the class diagram of Fig. 23.2 omits classes `BalanceInquiry` and `Deposit` to keep the diagram simple. The navigability of the associations in which these classes participate closely parallels the navigability of class `Withdrawal`'s associations. Recall from Section 22.4 that `BalanceInquiry` has an association with class `Screen`. We can navigate from class `BalanceInquiry` to class `Screen` along this association, but we cannot navigate from class `Screen` to class `BalanceInquiry`. Thus, if we were to

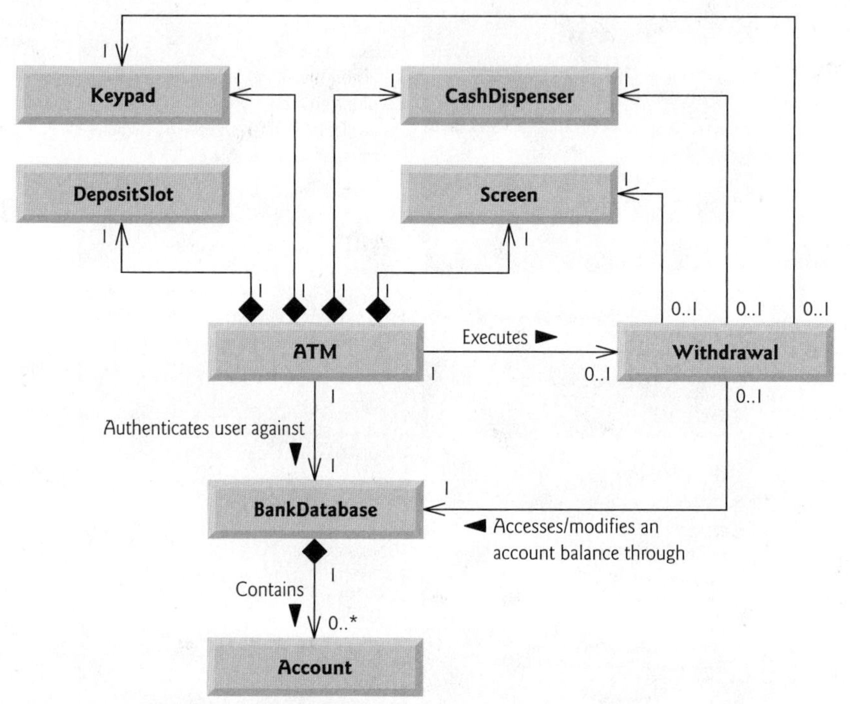

Fig. 23.2 | Class diagram with navigability arrows.

model class BalanceInquiry in Fig. 23.2, we would place a navigability arrow at class Screen's end of this association. Also recall that class Deposit associates with classes Screen, Keypad and DepositSlot. We can navigate from class Deposit to each of these classes, but not vice versa. We therefore would place navigability arrows at the Screen, Keypad and DepositSlot ends of these associations. [*Note:* We model these additional classes and associations in our final class diagram in Section 23.3, after we have simplified the structure of our system by incorporating the object-oriented concept of inheritance.]

Implementing the ATM System from Its UML Design

We are now ready to begin implementing the ATM system. We first convert the classes in the diagrams of Fig. 23.1 and Fig. 23.2 into C++ header files. This code will represent the "skeleton" of the system. In Section 23.3, we modify the header files to incorporate the object-oriented concept of inheritance. In Section 23.4, we present the complete working C++ code for our model.

As an example, we begin to develop the header file for class Withdrawal from our design of class Withdrawal in Fig. 23.1. We use this figure to determine the attributes and operations of the class. We use the UML model in Fig. 23.2 to determine the associations among classes. We follow the following five guidelines for each class:

1. Use the name in the first compartment of a class in a class diagram to define the class in a header file (Fig. 23.3). Use #ifndef, #define and #endif preprocessor directives to prevent the header from being included more than once in a program.

```
// Fig. 23.3: Withdrawal.h
// Definition of class Withdrawal that represents a withdrawal transaction
#ifndef WITHDRAWAL_H
#define WITHDRAWAL_H

class Withdrawal
{
}; // end class Withdrawal

#endif // WITHDRAWAL_H
```

Fig. 23.3 | Definition of class `Withdrawal` enclosed in preprocessor wrappers.

2. Use the attributes located in the class's second compartment to declare the data members. For example, the `private` attributes `accountNumber` and `amount` of class `Withdrawal` yield the code in Fig. 23.4.

```
// Fig. 23.4: Withdrawal.h
// Definition of class Withdrawal that represents a withdrawal transaction
#ifndef WITHDRAWAL_H
#define WITHDRAWAL_H

class Withdrawal
{
private:
   // attributes
   int accountNumber; // account to withdraw funds from
   double amount; // amount to withdraw
}; // end class Withdrawal

#endif // WITHDRAWAL_H
```

Fig. 23.4 | Adding attributes to the `Withdrawal` class header file.

3. Use the associations described in the class diagram to declare references (or pointers, where appropriate) to other objects. For example, according to Fig. 23.2, `Withdrawal` can access one object of class `Screen`, one object of class `Keypad`, one object of class `CashDispenser` and one object of class `BankDatabase`. Class `Withdrawal` must maintain handles on these objects to send messages to them, so lines 19–22 of Fig. 23.5 declare four references as `private` data members. In the implementation of class `Withdrawal` in Section 23.4, a constructor initializes these data members with references to actual objects. Lines 6–9 `#include` the header files containing the definitions of classes `Screen`, `Keypad`, `CashDispenser` and `BankDatabase` so that we can declare references to objects of these classes in lines 19–22.

4. It turns out that including the header files for classes `Screen`, `Keypad`, `CashDispenser` and `BankDatabase` in Fig. 23.5 does more than is necessary. Class `Withdrawal` contains *references* to objects of these classes—it does not contain actual objects—and the amount of information required by the compiler to create a reference differs from that which is required to create an object. Recall that creating an object requires that you provide the compiler with a definition of the class that

```
1  // Fig. 23.5: Withdrawal.h
2  // Definition of class Withdrawal that represents a withdrawal transaction
3  #ifndef WITHDRAWAL_H
4  #define WITHDRAWAL_H
5
6  #include "Screen.h" // include definition of class Screen
7  #include "Keypad.h" // include definition of class Keypad
8  #include "CashDispenser.h" // include definition of class CashDispenser
9  #include "BankDatabase.h" // include definition of class BankDatabase
10
11 class Withdrawal
12 {
13 private:
14    // attributes
15    int accountNumber; // account to withdraw funds from
16    double amount; // amount to withdraw
17
18    // references to associated objects
19    Screen &screen; // reference to ATM's screen
20    Keypad &keypad; // reference to ATM's keypad
21    CashDispenser &cashDispenser; // reference to ATM's cash dispenser
22    BankDatabase &bankDatabase; // reference to the account info database
23 }; // end class Withdrawal
24
25 #endif // WITHDRAWAL_H
```

Fig. 23.5 | Declaring references to objects associated with class `Withdrawal`.

introduces the name of the class as a new user-defined type and indicates the data members that determine how much memory is required to store the object. Declaring a *reference* (or pointer) to an object, however, requires only that the compiler knows that the object's class exists—it does not need to know the size of the object. Any reference (or pointer), regardless of the class of the object to which it refers, contains only the memory address of the actual object. The amount of memory required to store an address is a physical characteristic of the computer's hardware. The compiler thus knows the size of any reference (or pointer). As a result, including a class's full header file when declaring only a reference to an object of that class is unnecessary—we need to introduce the name of the class, but we do not need to provide the data layout of the object, because the compiler already knows the size of all references. C++ provides a statement called a **forward declaration** that signifies that a header file contains references or pointers to a class, but that the class definition lies outside the header file. We can replace the `#includes` in the `Withdrawal` class definition of Fig. 23.5 with forward declarations of classes `Screen`, `Keypad`, `CashDispenser` and `BankDatabase` (lines 6–9 in Fig. 23.6). Rather than `#include` the entire header file for each of these classes, we place only a forward declaration of each class in the header file for class `Withdrawal`. If class `Withdrawal` contained actual objects instead of references (i.e., if the ampersands in lines 19–22 were omitted), then we'd need to `#include` the full header files.

Using a forward declaration (where possible) instead of including a full header file helps avoid a preprocessor problem called a **circular include**. This problem occurs when the header file for a class A `#includes` the header file for a class B and vice versa. Some preprocessors are not be able to resolve such `#include` directives, causing a compilation error. If class A, for example, uses only a reference to an object of class B, then the `#include` in class A's header file can be replaced by a forward declaration of class B to prevent the circular include.

```
// Fig. 23.6: Withdrawal.h
// Definition of class Withdrawal that represents a withdrawal transaction
#ifndef WITHDRAWAL_H
#define WITHDRAWAL_H

class Screen; // forward declaration of class Screen
class Keypad; // forward declaration of class Keypad
class CashDispenser; // forward declaration of class CashDispenser
class BankDatabase; // forward declaration of class BankDatabase

class Withdrawal
{
private:
   // attributes
   int accountNumber; // account to withdraw funds from
   double amount; // amount to withdraw

   // references to associated objects
   Screen &screen; // reference to ATM's screen
   Keypad &keypad; // reference to ATM's keypad
   CashDispenser &cashDispenser; // reference to ATM's cash dispenser
   BankDatabase &bankDatabase; // reference to the account info database
}; // end class Withdrawal

#endif // WITHDRAWAL_H
```

Fig. 23.6 | Using forward declarations in place of `#include` directives.

5. Use the operations located in the third compartment of Fig. 23.1 to write the function prototypes of the class's member functions. If we've not yet specified a return type for an operation, we declare the member function with return type `void`. Refer to the class diagrams of Figs. 6.20–6.23 to declare any necessary parameters. For example, adding the `public` operation `execute` in class `Withdrawal`, which has an empty parameter list, yields the prototype in line 15 of Fig. 23.7. [*Note:* We code the definitions of member functions in `.cpp` files when we implement the complete ATM system in Section 23.4.]

Software Engineering Observation 23.1

Several UML modeling tools can convert UML-based designs into C++ code, considerably speeding the implementation process. For more information on these "automatic" code generators, refer to our UML Resource Center at `www.deitel.com/UML/`.

This concludes our discussion of the basics of generating class header files from UML diagrams. In Section 23.3, we demonstrate how to modify the header files to incorporate the object-oriented concept of inheritance.

```
// Fig. 23.7: Withdrawal.h
// Definition of class Withdrawal that represents a withdrawal transaction
#ifndef WITHDRAWAL_H
#define WITHDRAWAL_H

class Screen; // forward declaration of class Screen
class Keypad; // forward declaration of class Keypad
class CashDispenser; // forward declaration of class CashDispenser
class BankDatabase; // forward declaration of class BankDatabase

class Withdrawal
{
public:
   // operations
   void execute(); // perform the transaction
private:
   // attributes
   int accountNumber; // account to withdraw funds from
   double amount; // amount to withdraw

   // references to associated objects
   Screen &screen; // reference to ATM's screen
   Keypad &keypad; // reference to ATM's keypad
   CashDispenser &cashDispenser; // reference to ATM's cash dispenser
   BankDatabase &bankDatabase; // reference to the account info database
}; // end class Withdrawal

#endif // WITHDRAWAL_H
```

Fig. 23.7 | Adding operations to the `Withdrawal` class header file.

Self-Review Exercises for Section 23.2

23.1 State whether the following statement is *true* or *false*, and if *false*, explain why: If an attribute of a class is marked with a minus sign (-) in a class diagram, the attribute is not directly accessible outside of the class.

23.2 In Fig. 23.2, the association between the `ATM` and the `Screen` indicates that:
a) we can navigate from the `Screen` to the `ATM`
b) we can navigate from the `ATM` to the `Screen`
c) Both a and b; the association is bidirectional
d) None of the above

23.3 Write C++ code to begin implementing the design for class `Account`.

23.3 Incorporating Inheritance into the ATM System

We now revisit our ATM system design to see how it might benefit from inheritance. To apply inheritance, we first look for *commonality* among classes in the system. We create an inheritance hierarchy to model similar (yet not identical) classes in a more efficient and elegant manner that enables us to process objects of these classes polymorphically. We then modify our class diagram to incorporate the new inheritance relationships. Finally, we demonstrate how our updated design is translated into C++ header files.

In Section 22.4, we encountered the problem of representing a financial transaction in the system. Rather than create one class to represent all transaction types, we decided to create three individual transaction classes—`BalanceInquiry`, `Withdrawal` and `Deposit`—to represent the transactions that the ATM system can perform. Figure 23.8 shows the attributes and operations of these classes, which have one attribute (`accountNumber`) and one operation (`execute`) in common. Each class requires attribute `accountNumber` to specify the account to which the transaction applies. Each class contains operation `execute`, which the `ATM` invokes to perform the transaction. Clearly, `BalanceInquiry`, `Withdrawal` and `Deposit` represent *types of* transactions. Figure 23.8 reveals commonality among the transaction classes, so using inheritance to factor out the common features seems appropriate for designing these classes. We place the common functionality in base class `Transaction` and derive classes `BalanceInquiry`, `Withdrawal` and `Deposit` from `Transaction` (Fig. 23.9).

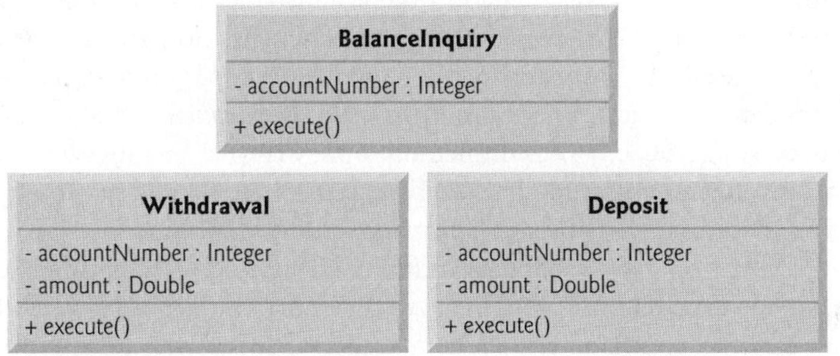

Fig. 23.8 | Attributes and operations of classes `BalanceInquiry`, `Withdrawal` and `Deposit`.

The UML specifies a relationship called a **generalization** to model inheritance. Figure 23.9 is the class diagram that models the inheritance relationship between base class `Transaction` and its three derived classes. The arrows with triangular hollow arrowheads indicate that classes `BalanceInquiry`, `Withdrawal` and `Deposit` are derived from class

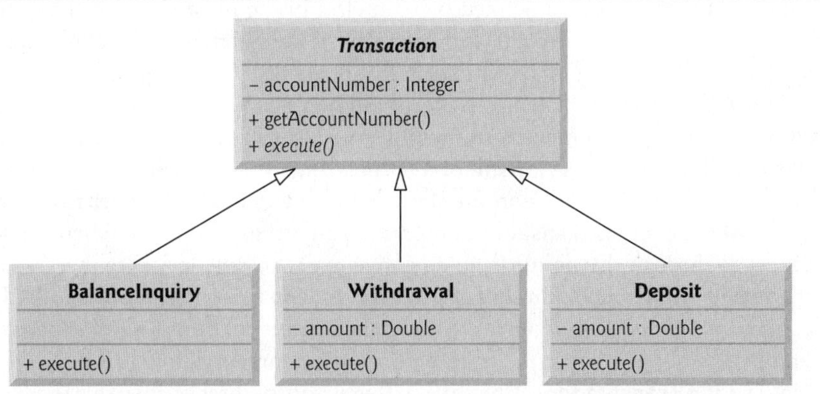

Fig. 23.9 | Class diagram modeling generalization relations\hip between base class `Transaction` and derived classes `BalanceInquiry`, `Withdrawal` and `Deposit`.

Transaction. Class Transaction is said to be a generalization of its derived classes. The derived classes are said to be **specializations** of class Transaction.

Classes BalanceInquiry, Withdrawal and Deposit share integer attribute accountNumber, so we factor out this common attribute and place it in base class Transaction. We no longer list accountNumber in the second compartment of each derived class, because the three derived classes inherit this attribute from Transaction. Recall, however, that derived classes cannot access private attributes of a base class. We therefore include public member function getAccountNumber in class Transaction. Each derived class inherits this member function, enabling the derived class to access its accountNumber as needed to execute a transaction.

According to Fig. 23.8, classes BalanceInquiry, Withdrawal and Deposit also share operation execute, so base class Transaction should contain public member function execute. However, it does not make sense to implement execute in class Transaction, because the functionality that this member function provides depends on the specific type of the actual transaction. We therefore declare member function execute as a pure virtual function in base class Transaction. This makes Transaction an *abstract class* and forces any class derived from Transaction that must be a *concrete class* (i.e., BalanceInquiry, Withdrawal and Deposit) to implement pure virtual member function execute to make the derived class concrete. The UML requires that we place abstract class names (and pure virtual functions—**abstract operations** in the UML) in italics, so Transaction and its member function execute appear in italics in Fig. 23.9. Operation execute is not italicized in derived classes BalanceInquiry, Withdrawal and Deposit. Each derived class overrides base class Transaction's execute member function with an appropriate implementation. Figure 23.9 includes operation execute in the third compartment of classes BalanceInquiry, Withdrawal and Deposit, because each class has a different concrete implementation of the overridden member function.

Processing Transactions *Polymorphically*

A derived class can inherit interface and/or implementation from a base class. Compared to a hierarchy designed for implementation inheritance, one designed for interface inheritance tends to have its functionality lower in the hierarchy—a base class signifies one or more functions that should be defined by each class in the hierarchy, but the individual derived classes provide their own implementations of the function(s). The inheritance hierarchy designed for the ATM system takes advantage of this type of inheritance, which provides the ATM with an elegant way to execute all transactions "in the general." Each class derived from Transaction inherits some implementation details (e.g., data member accountNumber), but the primary benefit of incorporating inheritance into our system is that the derived classes share a common interface (e.g., pure virtual member function execute). The ATM can aim a Transaction pointer at any transaction, and when the ATM invokes execute through this pointer, the version of execute appropriate to that transaction (i.e., the version implemented in that derived class's .cpp file) runs automatically. For example, suppose a user chooses to perform a balance inquiry. The ATM aims a Transaction pointer at a new object of class BalanceInquiry; the compiler allows this because a BalanceInquiry *is a* Transaction. When the ATM uses this pointer to invoke execute, BalanceInquiry's version of execute is called.

This polymorphic approach also makes the system easily *extensible*. Should we wish to create a new transaction type (e.g., funds transfer or bill payment), we would just create an additional `Transaction` derived class that overrides the `execute` member function with a version appropriate for the new transaction type. We would need to make only minimal changes to the system code to allow users to choose the new transaction type from the main menu and for the `ATM` to instantiate and execute objects of the new derived class. The `ATM` could execute transactions of the new type using the current code, because it executes all transactions identically.

As you learned earlier in the chapter, an abstract class like `Transaction` is one for which you never intend to instantiate objects. An abstract class simply declares common attributes and behaviors for its derived classes in an inheritance hierarchy. Class `Transaction` defines the concept of what it means to be a transaction that has an account number and executes. You may wonder why we bother to include pure `virtual` member function `execute` in class `Transaction` if `execute` lacks a concrete implementation. Conceptually, we include this member function because it's the defining behavior of all transactions—executing. Technically, we must include member function `execute` in base class `Transaction` so that the `ATM` (or any other class) can polymorphically invoke each derived class's overridden version of this function through a `Transaction` pointer or reference.

Additional Attribute of Classes `Withdrawal` and `Deposit`

Derived classes `BalanceInquiry`, `Withdrawal` and `Deposit` inherit attribute `accountNumber` from base class `Transaction`, but classes `Withdrawal` and `Deposit` contain the additional attribute `amount` that distinguishes them from class `BalanceInquiry`. Classes `Withdrawal` and `Deposit` require this additional attribute to store the amount of money that the user wishes to withdraw or deposit. Class `BalanceInquiry` has no need for such an attribute and requires only an account number to execute. Even though two of the three `Transaction` derived classes share this attribute, we do not place it in base class `Transaction`—we place only features common to *all* the derived classes in the base class, so derived classes do not inherit unnecessary attributes (and operations).

Class Diagram with `Transaction` Hierarchy Incorporated

Figure 23.10 presents an updated class diagram of our model that incorporates inheritance and introduces class `Transaction`. We model an association between class `ATM` and class `Transaction` to show that the `ATM`, at any given moment, either is executing a transaction or is not (i.e., zero or one objects of type `Transaction` exist in the system at a time). Because a `Withdrawal` is a type of `Transaction`, we no longer draw an association line directly between class `ATM` and class `Withdrawal`—derived class `Withdrawal` inherits base class `Transaction`'s association with class `ATM`. Derived classes `BalanceInquiry` and `Deposit` also inherit this association, which replaces the previously omitted associations between classes `BalanceInquiry` and `Deposit` and class `ATM`. Note again the use of triangular hollow arrowheads to indicate the specializations of class `Transaction`, as indicated in Fig. 23.9.

We also add an association between class `Transaction` and the `BankDatabase` (Fig. 23.10). All `Transactions` require a reference to the `BankDatabase` so they can access and modify account information. Each `Transaction` derived class inherits this reference, so we no longer model the association between class `Withdrawal` and the `BankDatabase`. The association between class `Transaction` and the `BankDatabase` replaces the previously omitted associations between classes `BalanceInquiry` and `Deposit` and the `BankDatabase`.

We include an association between class `Transaction` and the `Screen` because all `Transactions` display output to the user via the `Screen`. Each derived class inherits this

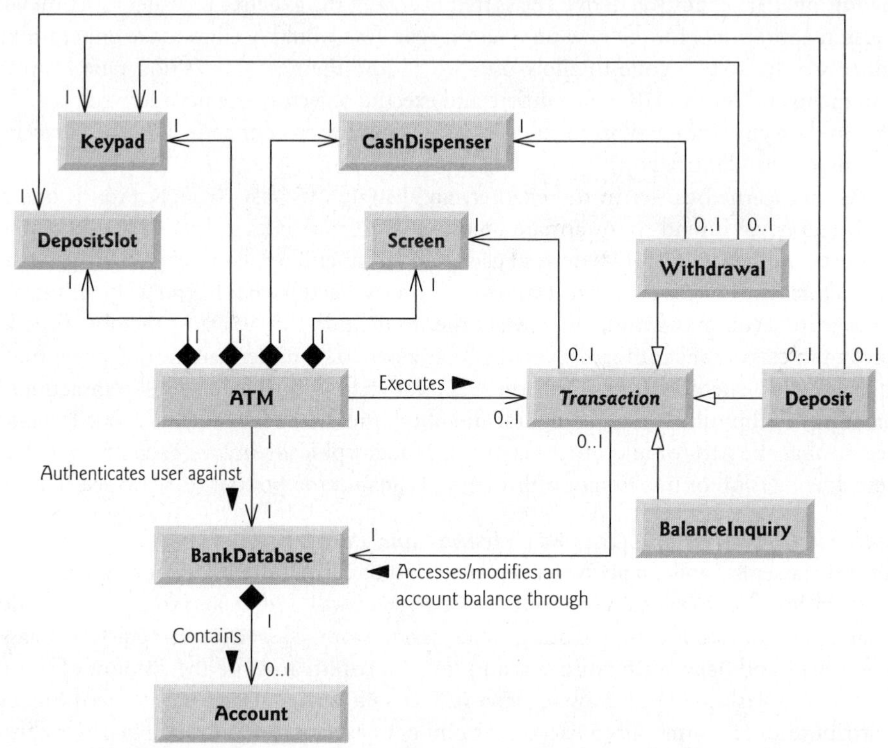

Fig. 23.10 | Class diagram of the ATM system (incorporating inheritance). Note that abstract class name `Transaction` appears in italics.

association. Therefore, we no longer include the association previously modeled between `Withdrawal` and the `Screen`. Class `Withdrawal` still participates in associations with the `CashDispenser` and the `Keypad`. We do not move these associations to base class `Transaction`, because the association with the `Keypad` applies only to classes `Withdrawal` and `Deposit`, and the association with the `CashDispenser` applies only to class `Withdrawal`.

Our class diagram incorporating inheritance (Fig. 23.10) also models `Deposit` and `BalanceInquiry`. We show associations between `Deposit` and both the `DepositSlot` and the `Keypad`. `BalanceInquiry` takes part in no associations other than those inherited from class `Transaction`—a `BalanceInquiry` interacts only with the `BankDatabase` and the `Screen`.

Figure 23.1 showed attributes and operations with visibility markers. Now we present a modified class diagram in Fig. 23.11 that includes abstract base class `Transaction`. This abbreviated diagram does not show inheritance relationships (these appear in Fig. 23.10), but instead shows the attributes and operations after we've employed inheritance in our system. Abstract class name `Transaction` and abstract operation name `execute` in class `Transaction` appear in *italics*. To save space, we do not include those attributes shown by associations in Fig. 23.10—we do, however, include them in the C++ implementation. We also omit all operation parameters, as we did in Fig. 23.1—incorporating inheritance does not affect the parameters already modeled in Figs. 22.18–22.21.

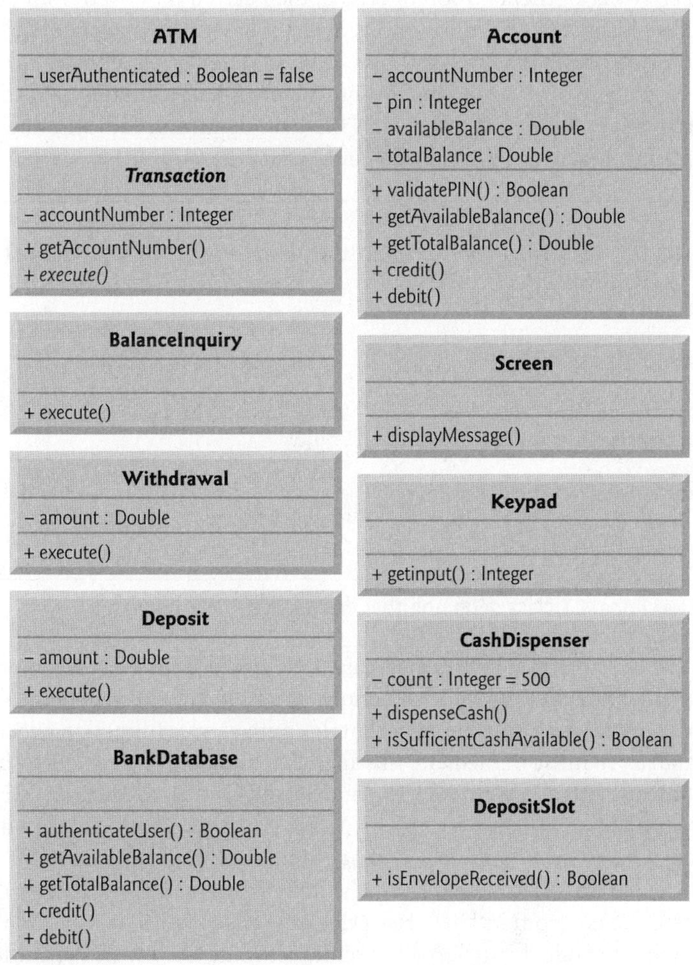

Fig. 23.11 | Class diagram after incorporating inheritance into the system.

Software Engineering Observation 23.2

A complete class diagram shows all the associations among classes and all the attributes and operations for each class. When the number of class attributes, operations and associations is substantial (as in Fig. 23.10 and Fig. 23.11), a good practice that promotes readability is to divide this information between two class diagrams—one focusing on associations and the other on attributes and operations. However, when examining classes modeled in this fashion, it's crucial to consider both class diagrams to get a complete view of the classes. For example, one must refer to Fig. 23.10 to observe the inheritance relationship between `Transaction` and its derived classes that is omitted from Fig. 23.11.

Implementing the ATM System Design Incorporating Inheritance

We now modify our implementation to incorporate inheritance, using class `Withdrawal` as an example.

1. If a class A is a generalization of class B, then class B is derived from (and is a specialization of) class A. For example, abstract base class Transaction is a generalization of class Withdrawal. Thus, class Withdrawal is derived from (and is a specialization of) class Transaction. Figure 23.12 contains a portion of class Withdrawal's header file, in which the class definition indicates the inheritance relationship between Withdrawal and Transaction (line 9).

```
1  // Fig. 23.12: Withdrawal.h
2  // Definition of class Withdrawal that represents a withdrawal transaction
3  #ifndef WITHDRAWAL_H
4  #define WITHDRAWAL_H
5
6  #include "Transaction.h" // Transaction class definition
7
8  // class Withdrawal derives from base class Transaction
9  class Withdrawal : public Transaction
10 {
11 }; // end class Withdrawal
12
13 #endif // WITHDRAWAL_H
```

Fig. 23.12 | Withdrawal class definition that derives from Transaction.

2. If class A is an abstract class and class B is derived from class A, then class B must implement the pure virtual functions of class A if class B is to be a concrete class. For example, class Transaction contains pure virtual function execute, so class Withdrawal must implement this member function if we want to instantiate a Withdrawal object. Figure 23.13 contains the C++ header file for class Withdrawal from Fig. 23.10 and Fig. 23.11. Class Withdrawal inherits data member accountNumber from base class Transaction, so Withdrawal does not declare this data member. Class Withdrawal also inherits references to the Screen and the BankDatabase from its base class Transaction, so we do not include these references in our code. Figure 23.11 specifies attribute amount and operation execute for class Withdrawal. Line 19 of Fig. 23.13 declares a data member for attribute amount. Line 16 contains the function prototype for operation execute. Recall that, to be a concrete class, derived class Withdrawal must provide a concrete implementation of the pure virtual function execute in base class Transaction. The prototype in line 16 signals your intent to override the base class pure virtual function. You must provide this prototype if you'll provide an implementation in the .cpp file. We present this implementation in Section 23.4. The keypad and cashDispenser references (lines 20–21) are data members derived from Withdrawal's associations in Fig. 23.10. In the implementation of this class in Section 23.4, a constructor initializes these references to actual objects. Once again, to be able to compile the declarations of the references in lines 20–21, we include the forward declarations in lines 8–9.

ATM Case Study Wrap-Up

This concludes our object-oriented design of the ATM system. A complete C++ implementation of the ATM system in 850 lines of code appears in Section 23.4. This working

```
// Fig. 23.13: Withdrawal.h
// Definition of class Withdrawal that represents a withdrawal transaction
#ifndef WITHDRAWAL_H
#define WITHDRAWAL_H

#include "Transaction.h" // Transaction class definition

class Keypad; // forward declaration of class Keypad
class CashDispenser; // forward declaration of class CashDispenser

// class Withdrawal derives from base class Transaction
class Withdrawal : public Transaction
{
public:
   // member function overriding execute in base class Transaction
   virtual void execute(); // perform the transaction
private:
   // attributes
   double amount; // amount to withdraw
   Keypad &keypad; // reference to ATM's keypad
   CashDispenser &cashDispenser; // reference to ATM's cash dispenser
}; // end class Withdrawal

#endif // WITHDRAWAL_H
```

Fig. 23.13 | `Withdrawal` class header file based on Figs. 23.10 and 23.11.

implementation uses key programming notions, including classes, objects, encapsulation, visibility, composition, inheritance and polymorphism. The code is abundantly commented and conforms to the coding practices you've learned. Mastering this code is a wonderful capstone experience.

Self-Review Exercises for Section 23.3

23.4 The UML uses an arrow with a ________ to indicate a generalization relationship.

a) solid filled arrowhead
b) triangular hollow arrowhead
c) diamond-shaped hollow arrowhead
d) stick arrowhead

23.5 State whether the following statement is *true* or *false*, and if *false*, explain why: The UML requires that we underline abstract class names and operation names.

23.6 Write a C++ header file to begin implementing the design for class `Transaction` specified in Fig. 23.10 and Fig. 23.11. Be sure to include `private` references based on class `Transaction`'s associations. Also be sure to include `public` *get* functions for any of the `private` data members that the derived classes must access to perform their tasks.

23.4 ATM Case Study Implementation

This section contains the complete working implementation of the ATM system that we designed in Chapter 22 and this chapter. We consider the classes in the order in which we identified them in Section 22.4:

- ATM
- Screen
- Keypad
- CashDispenser
- DepositSlot
- Account
- BankDatabase
- Transaction
- BalanceInquiry
- Withdrawal
- Deposit

We apply the guidelines discussed in Sections 23.2– and 23.3 to code these classes based on how we modeled them in the UML class diagrams of Figs. 23.10 and 23.11. To develop the definitions of classes' member functions, we refer to the activity diagrams presented in Section 22.6 and the communication and sequence diagrams presented in Section 22.8. Note that our ATM design does not specify all the program logic and may not specify all the attributes and operations required to complete the ATM implementation. This is a normal part of the object-oriented design process. As we implement the system, we complete the program logic and add attributes and behaviors as necessary to construct the ATM system specified by the requirements specification in Section 22.3.

We conclude the discussion by presenting a C++ program (ATMCaseStudy.cpp) that starts the ATM and puts the other classes in the system in use. Recall that we're developing a first version of the ATM system that runs on a personal computer and uses the computer's keyboard and monitor to approximate the ATM's keypad and screen. We also only simulate the actions of the ATM's cash dispenser and deposit slot. We attempt to implement the system, however, so that real hardware versions of these devices could be integrated without significant changes in the code.

23.4.1 Class ATM

Class ATM (Figs. 23.14–23.15) represents the ATM as a whole. Figure 23.14 contains the ATM class definition, enclosed in #ifndef, #define and #endif preprocessor directives to ensure that this definition gets included only once in a program. We discuss lines 6–11 shortly. Lines 16–17 contain the function prototypes for the class's public member functions. The class diagram of Fig. 23.11 does not list any operations for class ATM, but we now declare a public member function run (line 17) in class ATM that allows an external client of the class (i.e., ATMCaseStudy.cpp) to tell the ATM to run. We also include a function prototype for a default constructor (line 16), which we discuss shortly.

```
1  // ATM.h
2  // ATM class definition. Represents an automated teller machine.
3  #ifndef ATM_H
```

Fig. 23.14 | Definition of class ATM, which represents the ATM. (Part 1 of 2.)

```
4  #define ATM_H
5
6  #include "Screen.h" // Screen class definition
7  #include "Keypad.h" // Keypad class definition
8  #include "CashDispenser.h" // CashDispenser class definition
9  #include "DepositSlot.h" // DepositSlot class definition
10 #include "BankDatabase.h" // BankDatabase class definition
11 class Transaction; // forward declaration of class Transaction
12
13 class ATM
14 {
15 public:
16    ATM(); // constructor initializes data members
17    void run(); // start the ATM
18 private:
19    bool userAuthenticated; // whether user is authenticated
20    int currentAccountNumber; // current user's account number
21    Screen screen; // ATM's screen
22    Keypad keypad; // ATM's keypad
23    CashDispenser cashDispenser; // ATM's cash dispenser
24    DepositSlot depositSlot; // ATM's deposit slot
25    BankDatabase bankDatabase; // account information database
26
27    // private utility functions
28    void authenticateUser(); // attempts to authenticate user
29    void performTransactions(); // performs transactions
30    int displayMainMenu() const; // displays main menu
31
32    // return object of specified Transaction derived class
33    Transaction *createTransaction( int );
34 }; // end class ATM
35
36 #endif // ATM_H
```

Fig. 23.14 | Definition of class ATM, which represents the ATM. (Part 2 of 2.)

Lines 19–25 of Fig. 23.14 implement the class's attributes as `private` data members. We determine all but one of these attributes from the class diagrams of Figs. 23.10– 23.11. We implement the UML `Boolean` attribute `userAuthenticated` in Fig. 23.11 as a `bool` data member in C++ (line 19). Line 20 declares a data member not found in our UML design—an `int` data member `currentAccountNumber` that keeps track of the account number of the current authenticated user. We'll soon see how the class uses this data member.

Lines 21–24 create objects to represent the parts of the ATM. Recall from the class diagram of Fig. 23.10 that class `ATM` has composition relationships with classes `Screen`, `Keypad`, `CashDispenser` and `DepositSlot`, so class `ATM` is responsible for their creation. Line 25 creates a `BankDatabase`, with which the `ATM` interacts to access and manipulate bank account information. [*Note:* If this were a real ATM system, the `ATM` class would receive a reference to an existing database object created by the bank. However, in this implementation we are only simulating the bank's database, so class `ATM` creates the `BankDatabase` object with which it interacts.] Lines 6–10 `#include` the class definitions of `Screen`, `Keypad`, `CashDispenser`, `DepositSlot` and `BankDatabase` so that the `ATM` can store objects of these classes.

Lines 28–30 and 33 contain function prototypes for `private` utility functions that the class uses to perform its tasks. We'll see how these functions serve the class shortly. Member function `createTransaction` (line 33) returns a `Transaction` pointer. To include the class name `Transaction` in this file, we must at least include a forward declaration of class `Transaction` (line 11). Recall that a forward declaration tells the compiler that a class exists, but that the class is defined elsewhere. A forward declaration is sufficient here, as we are using a `Transaction` pointer as a return type—if we were creating or returning an actual `Transaction` object, we would need to `#include` the full `Transaction` header file.

ATM Class Member-Function Definitions

Figure 23.15 contains the member-function definitions for class `ATM`. Lines 3–7 `#include` the header files required by the implementation file `ATM.cpp`. Including the `ATM` header file allows the compiler to ensure that the class's member functions are defined correctly. This also allows the member functions to use the class's data members.

```
1  // ATM.cpp
2  // Member-function definitions for class ATM.
3  #include "ATM.h" // ATM class definition
4  #include "Transaction.h" // Transaction class definition
5  #include "BalanceInquiry.h" // BalanceInquiry class definition
6  #include "Withdrawal.h" // Withdrawal class definition
7  #include "Deposit.h" // Deposit class definition
8
9  // enumeration constants represent main menu options
10 enum MenuOption { BALANCE_INQUIRY = 1, WITHDRAWAL, DEPOSIT, EXIT };
11
12 // ATM default constructor initializes data members
13 ATM::ATM()
14    : userAuthenticated ( false ), // user is not authenticated to start
15      currentAccountNumber( 0 ) // no current account number to start
16 {
17    // empty body
18 } // end ATM default constructor
19
20 // start ATM
21 void ATM::run()
22 {
23    // welcome and authenticate user; perform transactions
24    while ( true )
25    {
26       // loop while user is not yet authenticated
27       while ( !userAuthenticated )
28       {
29          screen.displayMessageLine( "\nWelcome!" );
30          authenticateUser(); // authenticate user
31       } // end while
32
```

Fig. 23.15 | `ATM` class member-function definitions. (Part 1 of 4.)

```
         performTransactions(); // user is now authenticated
         userAuthenticated = false; // reset before next ATM session
         currentAccountNumber = 0; // reset before next ATM session
         screen.displayMessageLine( "\nThank you! Goodbye!" );
      } // end while
   } // end function run

   // attempt to authenticate user against database
   void ATM::authenticateUser()
   {
      screen.displayMessage( "\nPlease enter your account number: " );
      int accountNumber = keypad.getInput(); // input account number
      screen.displayMessage( "\nEnter your PIN: " ); // prompt for PIN
      int pin = keypad.getInput(); // input PIN

      // set userAuthenticated to bool value returned by database
      userAuthenticated =
         bankDatabase.authenticateUser( accountNumber, pin );

      // check whether authentication succeeded
      if ( userAuthenticated )
      {
         currentAccountNumber = accountNumber; // save user's account #
      } // end if
      else
         screen.displayMessageLine(
            "Invalid account number or PIN. Please try again." );
   } // end function authenticateUser

   // display the main menu and perform transactions
   void ATM::performTransactions()
   {
      // local pointer to store transaction currently being processed
      Transaction *currentTransactionPtr;

      bool userExited = false; // user has not chosen to exit

      // loop while user has not chosen option to exit system
      while ( !userExited )
      {
         // show main menu and get user selection
         int mainMenuSelection = displayMainMenu();

         // decide how to proceed based on user's menu selection
         switch ( mainMenuSelection )
         {
            // user chose to perform one of three transaction types
            case BALANCE_INQUIRY:
            case WITHDRAWAL:
            case DEPOSIT:
               // initialize as new object of chosen type
               currentTransactionPtr =
                  createTransaction( mainMenuSelection );
```

Fig. 23.15 | ATM class member-function definitions. (Part 2 of 4.)

```

            currentTransactionPtr->execute(); // execute transaction

            // free the space for the dynamically allocated Transaction
            delete currentTransactionPtr;

            break;
         case EXIT: // user chose to terminate session
            screen.displayMessageLine( "\nExiting the system..." );
            userExited = true; // this ATM session should end
            break;
         default: // user did not enter an integer from 1-4
            screen.displayMessageLine(
               "\nYou did not enter a valid selection. Try again." );
            break;
      } // end switch
   } // end while
} // end function performTransactions

// display the main menu and return an input selection
int ATM::displayMainMenu() const
{
   screen.displayMessageLine( "\nMain menu:" );
   screen.displayMessageLine( "1 - View my balance" );
   screen.displayMessageLine( "2 - Withdraw cash" );
   screen.displayMessageLine( "3 - Deposit funds" );
   screen.displayMessageLine( "4 - Exit\n" );
   screen.displayMessage( "Enter a choice: " );
   return keypad.getInput(); // return user's selection
} // end function displayMainMenu

// return object of specified Transaction derived class
Transaction *ATM::createTransaction( int type )
{
   Transaction *tempPtr; // temporary Transaction pointer

   // determine which type of Transaction to create
   switch ( type )
   {
      case BALANCE_INQUIRY: // create new BalanceInquiry transaction
         tempPtr = new BalanceInquiry(
            currentAccountNumber, screen, bankDatabase );
         break;
      case WITHDRAWAL: // create new Withdrawal transaction
         tempPtr = new Withdrawal( currentAccountNumber, screen,
            bankDatabase, keypad, cashDispenser );
         break;
      case DEPOSIT: // create new Deposit transaction
         tempPtr = new Deposit( currentAccountNumber, screen,
            bankDatabase, keypad, depositSlot );
         break;
   } // end switch

```

Fig. 23.15 | ATM class member-function definitions. (Part 3 of 4.)

```
139     return tempPtr; // return the newly created object
140  } // end function createTransaction
```

Fig. 23.15 | ATM class member-function definitions. (Part 4 of 4.)

Line 10 declares an enum named MenuOption that contains constants corresponding to the four options in the ATM's main menu (i.e., balance inquiry, withdrawal, deposit and exit). Note that setting BALANCE_INQUIRY to 1 causes the subsequent enumeration constants to be assigned the values 2, 3 and 4, as enumeration constant values increment by 1.

Lines 13–18 define class ATM's constructor, which initializes the class's data members. When an ATM object is first created, no user is authenticated, so line 14 uses a member initializer to set userAuthenticated to false. Likewise, line 15 initializes currentAccountNumber to 0 because there is no current user yet.

ATM Member Function run

ATM member function run (lines 21–38) uses an infinite loop (lines 24–37) to repeatedly welcome a user, attempt to authenticate the user and, if authentication succeeds, allow the user to perform transactions. After an authenticated user performs the desired transactions and chooses to exit, the ATM resets itself, displays a goodbye message to the user and restarts the process. We use an infinite loop here to simulate the fact that an ATM appears to run continuously until the bank turns it off (an action beyond the user's control). An ATM user has the option to exit the system, but does not have the ability to turn off the ATM completely.

Authenticating a User

Inside member function run's infinite loop, lines 27–31 cause the ATM to repeatedly welcome and attempt to authenticate the user as long as the user has not been authenticated (i.e., !userAuthenticated is true). Line 29 invokes member function displayMessageLine of the ATM's screen to display a welcome message. Like Screen member function displayMessage designed in the case study, member function displayMessageLine (declared in line 13 of Fig. 23.16 and defined in lines 20–23 of Fig. 23.17) displays a message to the user, but this member function also outputs a newline after displaying the message. We've added this member function during implementation to give class Screen's clients more control over the placement of displayed messages. Line 30 of Fig. 23.15 invokes class ATM's private utility function authenticateUser (lines 41–60) to attempt to authenticate the user.

We refer to the requirements specification to determine the steps necessary to authenticate the user before allowing transactions to occur. Line 43 of member function authenticateUser invokes member function displayMessage of the ATM's screen to prompt the user to enter an account number. Line 44 invokes member function getInput of the ATM's keypad to obtain the user's input, then stores the integer value entered by the user in a local variable accountNumber. Member function authenticateUser next prompts the user to enter a PIN (line 45), and stores the PIN input by the user in a local variable pin (line 46). Next, lines 49–50 attempt to authenticate the user by passing the accountNumber and pin entered by the user to the bankDatabase's authenticateUser member function. Class ATM sets its userAuthenticated data member to the bool value returned by this function—userAuthenticated becomes true if authentication succeeds (i.e., accountNumber and pin match those of an existing Account in bankDatabase) and remains false otherwise. If userAuthenticated is true, line 55 saves the account number entered by the user (i.e., accountNumber) in the ATM data member currentAccountNumber. The other member functions of class ATM use this variable whenever an ATM session requires access to the user's account number. If userAuthenticated is false, lines 58–59 use the screen's displayMessageLine member function to indicate that an invalid account number and/or PIN was entered and the user must try again. Note that we set currentAccountNumber only after authenticating the user's account number and the associated PIN—if the database could not authenticate the user, currentAccountNumber remains 0.

After member function run attempts to authenticate the user (line 30), if userAuthenticated is still false, the while loop in lines 27–31 executes again. If userAuthenticated is now true, the loop terminates and control continues with line 33, which calls class ATM's utility function performTransactions.

Performing Transactions

Member function performTransactions (lines 63–103) carries out an ATM session for an authenticated user. Line 66 declares a local Transaction pointer, which we aim at a BalanceInquiry, Withdrawal or Deposit object representing the ATM transaction currently being processed. We use a Transaction pointer here to allow us to take advantage of polymorphism. Also, we use the role name included in the class diagram of Fig. 22.7—currentTransaction—in naming this pointer. As per our pointer-naming convention, we append "Ptr" to the role name to form the variable name currentTransactionPtr. Line 68 declares another local variable—a bool called userExited that keeps track of whether the user has chosen to exit. This variable controls a while loop (lines 71–102) that allows the user to execute an unlimited number of transactions before choosing to exit. Within this loop, line 74 displays the main menu and obtains the user's menu selection by calling an ATM utility function displayMainMenu (defined in lines 106–115). This member function displays the main menu by invoking member functions of the ATM's screen and returns a menu selection obtained from the user through the ATM's keypad. Note that this member function is const because it does not modify the contents of the object. Line 74 stores the user's selection returned by displayMainMenu in local variable mainMenuSelection.

After obtaining a main menu selection, member function performTransactions uses a switch statement (lines 77–101) to respond to the selection appropriately. If mainMenuSelection is equal to any of the three enumeration constants representing transaction types (i.e., if the user chose to perform a transaction), lines 84–85 call utility function createTransaction (defined in lines 118–140) to return a pointer to a newly instantiated object of the type that corresponds to the selected transaction. Pointer currentTransactionPtr is assigned the pointer returned by createTransaction. Line 87 then uses currentTransactionPtr to invoke the new object's execute member function to execute the transaction. We'll discuss Transaction member function execute and the three Transaction derived classes shortly. Finally, when the Transaction derived class object is no longer needed, line 90 releases the memory dynamically allocated for it.

We aim the Transaction pointer currentTransactionPtr at an object of one of the three Transaction derived classes so that we can execute transactions *polymorphically*. For example, if the user chooses to perform a balance inquiry, mainMenuSelection equals BALANCE_INQUIRY, leading createTransaction to return a pointer to a BalanceInquiry object. Thus, currentTransactionPtr points to a BalanceInquiry, and invoking currentTransactionPtr->execute() results in BalanceInquiry's version of execute being called.

Creating a Transaction

Member function createTransaction (lines 118–140) uses a switch statement (lines 123–137) to instantiate a new Transaction derived class object of the type indicated by the parameter type. Recall that member function performTransactions passes mainMenuSelection to this member function only when mainMenuSelection contains a value corresponding to one of the three transaction types. Therefore type equals either BALANCE_INQUIRY, WITHDRAWAL or DEPOSIT. Each case in the switch statement aims the temporary pointer tempPtr at a newly created object of the appropriate Transaction derived class. Each constructor has a unique parameter list, based on the specific data required to initialize the derived class object. A BalanceInquiry requires only the account number of the current user and references to the ATM's screen and the bankDatabase. In addition to these parameters, a Withdrawal requires references to the ATM's keypad and cashDispenser, and a Deposit requires references to the ATM's keypad and depositSlot. As you'll soon see, the BalanceInquiry, Withdrawal and Deposit constructors each specify reference parameters to receive the objects representing the required parts of the ATM. Thus, when member function createTransaction passes objects in the ATM (e.g., screen and keypad) to the initializer for each newly created Transaction derived class object, the new object actually receives *references* to the ATM's composite objects. We discuss the transaction classes in more detail in Sections 23.4.8—23.4.11.

Exiting the Main Menu and Processing Invalid Selections

After executing a transaction (line 87 in performTransactions), userExited remains false and the while loop in lines 71–102 repeats, returning the user to the main menu. However, if a user does not perform a transaction and instead selects the main menu option to exit, line 95 sets userExited to true, causing the condition of the while loop (!userExited) to become false. This while is the final statement of member function performTransactions, so control returns to the calling function run. If the user enters an invalid main menu selection (i.e., not an integer from 1–4), lines 98–99 display an appropriate error message, userExited remains false and the user returns to the main menu to try again.

Awaiting the Next ATM User

When performTransactions returns control to member function run, the user has chosen to exit the system, so lines 34–35 reset the ATM's data members userAuthenticated and currentAccountNumber to prepare for the next ATM user. Line 36 displays a goodbye message before the ATM starts over and welcomes the next user.

23.4.2 Class Screen

Class Screen (Figs. 23.16–23.17) represents the screen of the ATM and encapsulates all aspects of displaying output to the user. Class Screen approximates a real ATM's screen with a computer monitor and outputs text messages using cout and the stream insertion operator (<<). In this case study, we designed class Screen to have one operation—displayMessage. For greater flexibility in displaying messages to the Screen, we now declare three Screen member functions—displayMessage, displayMessageLine and displayDollarAmount. The prototypes for these member functions appear in lines 12–14 of Fig. 23.16.

```
// Screen.h
// Screen class definition. Represents the screen of the ATM.
#ifndef SCREEN_H
#define SCREEN_H

#include <string>
using namespace std;

class Screen
{
public:
   void displayMessage( string ) const; // output a message
   void displayMessageLine( string ) const; // output message with newline
   void displayDollarAmount( double ) const; // output a dollar amount
}; // end class Screen

#endif // SCREEN_H
```

Fig. 23.16 | Screen class definition.

```
1  // Screen.cpp
2  // Member-function definitions for class Screen.
3  #include <iostream>
4  #include <iomanip>
5  #include "Screen.h" // Screen class definition
6  using namespace std;
7
8  // output a message without a newline
9  void Screen::displayMessage( string message ) const
10 {
11    cout << message;
12 } // end function displayMessage
13
14 // output a message with a newline
15 void Screen::displayMessageLine( string message ) const
16 {
17    cout << message << endl;
18 } // end function displayMessageLine
19
20 // output a dollar amount
21 void Screen::displayDollarAmount( double amount ) const
22 {
23    cout << fixed << setprecision( 2 ) << "$" << amount;
24 } // end function displayDollarAmount
```

Fig. 23.17 | Screen class member-function definitions.

Screen Class Member-Function Definitions

Figure 23.17 contains the member-function definitions for class `Screen`. Line 5 `#includes` the `Screen` class definition. Member function `displayMessage` (lines 9–12) takes a `string` as an argument and prints it to the console using `cout` and the stream insertion operator (<<). The cursor stays on the same line, making this member function appropriate for displaying prompts to the user. Member function `displayMessageLine` (lines 15–18) also prints a `string`, but outputs a newline to move the cursor to the next line. Finally, member function `displayDollarAmount` (lines 21–24) outputs a properly formatted dollar amount (e.g., `$123.45`). Line 23 uses stream manipulators `fixed` and `setprecision` to output a value formatted with two decimal places.

23.4.3 Class Keypad

Class `Keypad` (Figs. 23.18–23.19) represents the keypad of the ATM and is responsible for receiving all user input. Recall that we are simulating this hardware, so we use the computer's keyboard to approximate the keypad. A computer keyboard contains many keys not found on the ATM's keypad. However, we assume that the user presses only the keys on the computer keyboard that also appear on the keypad—the keys numbered 0–9 and the *Enter* key. Line 9 of Fig. 23.18 contains the function prototype for class `Keypad`'s one member function `getInput`. This member function is declared `const` because it does not change the object.

```
1  // Keypad.h
2  // Keypad class definition. Represents the keypad of the ATM.
3  #ifndef KEYPAD_H
4  #define KEYPAD_H
5
6  class Keypad
7  {
8  public:
9     int getInput() const; // return an integer value entered by user
10 }; // end class Keypad
11
12 #endif // KEYPAD_H
```

Fig. 23.18 | Keypad class definition.

Keypad Class Member-Function Definition

In the `Keypad` implementation file (Fig. 23.19), member function `getInput` (defined in lines 9–14) uses the standard input stream `cin` and the stream extraction operator (>>) to obtain input from the user. Line 11 declares a local variable to store the user's input. Line 12 reads input into local variable `input`, then line 13 returns this value. Recall that `getInput` obtains all the input used by the ATM. `Keypad`'s `getInput` member function simply returns the integer input by the user. If a client of class `Keypad` requires input that satisfies some particular criteria (i.e., a number corresponding to a valid menu option), the client must perform the appropriate error checking. [*Note:* Using the standard input stream `cin` and the stream extraction operator (>>) allows noninteger input to be read from the user. Because the real ATM's keypad permits only integer input, however, we assume that the user enters an integer and do not attempt to fix problems caused by noninteger input.]

```
1  // Keypad.cpp
2  // Member-function definition for class Keypad (the ATM's keypad).
3  #include <iostream>
```

Fig. 23.19 | Keypad class member-function definition. (Part 1 of 2.)

```
using namespace std;

#include "Keypad.h" // Keypad class definition

// return an integer value entered by user
int Keypad::getInput() const
{
   int input; // variable to store the input
   cin >> input; // we assume that user enters an integer
   return input; // return the value entered by user
} // end function getInput
```

Fig. 23.19 | Keypad class member-function definition. (Part 2 of 2.)

23.4.4 Class CashDispenser

Class `CashDispenser` (Figs. 23.20–23.21) represents the cash dispenser. Figure 23.20 contains the function prototype for a default constructor (line 9). Class `CashDispenser` declares two additional `public` member functions—`dispenseCash` (line 12) and `isSufficientCashAvailable` (line 15). The class trusts that a client (i.e., `Withdrawal`) calls `dispenseCash` only after establishing that sufficient cash is available by calling `isSufficientCashAvailable`. Thus, `dispenseCash` simply simulates dispensing the requested amount without checking whether sufficient cash is available. Line 17 declares `private` constant `INITIAL_COUNT`, which indicates the initial count of bills in the cash dispenser when the ATM starts (i.e., 500). Line 18 implements attribute `count` (modeled in Fig. 23.11), which keeps track of the number of bills remaining in the `CashDispenser` at any time.

```
1  // CashDispenser.h
2  // CashDispenser class definition. Represents the ATM's cash dispenser.
3  #ifndef CASH_DISPENSER_H
4  #define CASH_DISPENSER_H
5
6  class CashDispenser
7  {
8  public:
9     CashDispenser(); // constructor initializes bill count to 500
10
11    // simulates dispensing of specified amount of cash
12    void dispenseCash( int );
13
14    // indicates whether cash dispenser can dispense desired amount
15    bool isSufficientCashAvailable( int ) const;
16 private:
17    static const int INITIAL_COUNT = 500;
18    int count; // number of $20 bills remaining
19 }; // end class CashDispenser
20
21 #endif // CASH_DISPENSER_H
```

Fig. 23.20 | `CashDispenser` class definition.

CashDispenser Class Member-Function Definitions

Figure 23.21 contains the definitions of class CashDispenser's member functions. The constructor (lines 6–9) sets count to the initial count (i.e., 500). Member function dispenseCash (lines 13–17) simulates cash dispensing. If our system were hooked up to a real hardware cash dispenser, this member function would interact with the hardware device to physically dispense cash. Our simulated version of the member function simply decreases the count of bills remaining by the number required to dispense the specified amount (line 16). Line 15 calculates the number of $20 bills required to dispense the specified amount. The ATM allows the user to choose only withdrawal amounts that are multiples of $20, so we divide amount by 20 to obtain the number of billsRequired. Also, it's the responsibility of the class's client (i.e., Withdrawal) to inform the user that cash has been dispensed—CashDispenser cannot interact directly with Screen.

```
1  // CashDispenser.cpp
2  // Member-function definitions for class CashDispenser.
3  #include "CashDispenser.h" // CashDispenser class definition
4
5  // CashDispenser default constructor initializes count to default
6  CashDispenser::CashDispenser()
7  {
8     count = INITIAL_COUNT; // set count attribute to default
9  } // end CashDispenser default constructor
10
11 // simulates dispensing of specified amount of cash; assumes enough cash
12 // is available (previous call to isSufficientCashAvailable returned true)
13 void CashDispenser::dispenseCash( int amount )
14 {
15    int billsRequired = amount / 20; // number of $20 bills required
16    count -= billsRequired; // update the count of bills
17 } // end function dispenseCash
18
19 // indicates whether cash dispenser can dispense desired amount
20 bool CashDispenser::isSufficientCashAvailable( int amount ) const
21 {
22    int billsRequired = amount / 20; // number of $20 bills required
23
24    if ( count >= billsRequired )
25       return true; // enough bills are available
26    else
27       return false; // not enough bills are available
28 } // end function isSufficientCashAvailable
```

Fig. 23.21 | CashDispenser class member-function definitions.

Member function isSufficientCashAvailable (lines 20–28) has a parameter amount that specifies the amount of cash in question. Lines 24–27 return true if the CashDispenser's count is greater than or equal to billsRequired (i.e., enough bills are available) and false otherwise (i.e., not enough bills). For example, if a user wishes to withdraw $80 (i.e., billsRequired is 4), but only three bills remain (i.e., count is 3), the member function returns false.

23.4.5 Class DepositSlot

Class DepositSlot (Figs. 23.22–23.23) represents the deposit slot of the ATM. Like the version of class CashDispenser presented here, this version of class DepositSlot merely simulates the functionality of a real hardware deposit slot. DepositSlot has no data members and only one member function—isEnvelopeReceived (declared in line 9 of Fig. 23.22 and defined in lines 7–10 of Fig. 23.23)—that indicates whether a deposit envelope was received.

```
1  // DepositSlot.h
2  // DepositSlot class definition. Represents the ATM's deposit slot.
3  #ifndef DEPOSIT_SLOT_H
4  #define DEPOSIT_SLOT_H
5
6  class DepositSlot
7  {
8  public:
9     bool isEnvelopeReceived() const; // tells whether envelope was received
10 }; // end class DepositSlot
11
12 #endif // DEPOSIT_SLOT_H
```

Fig. 23.22 | DepositSlot class definition.

```
1  // DepositSlot.cpp
2  // Member-function definition for class DepositSlot.
3  #include "DepositSlot.h" // DepositSlot class definiton
4
5  // indicates whether envelope was received (always returns true,
6  // because this is only a software simulation of a real deposit slot)
7  bool DepositSlot::isEnvelopeReceived() const
8  {
9     return true; // deposit envelope was received
10 } // end function isEnvelopeReceived
```

Fig. 23.23 | DepositSlot class member-function definition.

Recall from the requirements specification that the ATM allows the user up to two minutes to insert an envelope. The current version of member function isEnvelopeReceived simply returns true immediately (line 9 of Fig. 23.23), because this is only a software simulation, and we assume that the user has inserted an envelope within the required time frame. If an actual hardware deposit slot were connected to our system, member function isEnvelopeReceived might be implemented to wait for a maximum of two minutes to receive a signal from the hardware deposit slot indicating that the user has indeed inserted a deposit envelope. If isEnvelopeReceived were to receive such a signal within two minutes, the member function would return true. If two minutes elapsed and the member function still had not received a signal, then the member function would return false.

23.4.6 Class Account

Class `Account` (Figs. 23.24–23.25) represents a bank account. Lines 9–15 in the class definition (Fig. 23.24) contain function prototypes for the class's constructor and six member functions, which we discuss shortly. Each `Account` has four attributes (modeled in Fig. 23.11)—`accountNumber`, `pin`, `availableBalance` and `totalBalance`. Lines 17–20 implement these attributes as `private` data members. Data member `availableBalance` represents the amount of funds available for withdrawal. Data member `totalBalance` represents the amount of funds available, plus the amount of deposited funds still pending confirmation or clearance.

```
1  // Account.h
2  // Account class definition. Represents a bank account.
3  #ifndef ACCOUNT_H
4  #define ACCOUNT_H
5
6  class Account
7  {
8  public:
9     Account( int, int, double, double ); // constructor sets attributes
10    bool validatePIN( int ) const; // is user-specified PIN correct?
11    double getAvailableBalance() const; // returns available balance
12    double getTotalBalance() const; // returns total balance
13    void credit( double ); // adds an amount to the Account balance
14    void debit( double ); // subtracts an amount from the Account balance
15    int getAccountNumber() const; // returns account number
16 private:
17    int accountNumber; // account number
18    int pin; // PIN for authentication
19    double availableBalance; // funds available for withdrawal
20    double totalBalance; // funds available + funds waiting to clear
21 }; // end class Account
22
23 #endif // ACCOUNT_H
```

Fig. 23.24 | `Account` class definition.

`Account` Class Member-Function Definitions

Figure 23.25 presents the definitions of class `Account`'s member functions. The class's constructor (lines 6–14) takes an account number, the PIN established for the account, the initial available balance and the initial total balance as arguments. Lines 8–11 assign these values to the class's data members using member initializers.

Member function `validatePIN` (lines 17–23) determines whether a user-specified PIN (i.e., parameter `userPIN`) matches the PIN associated with the account (i.e., data member `pin`). Recall that we modeled this member function's parameter `userPIN` in the UML class diagram of Fig. 22.19. If the two PINs match, the member function returns `true` (line 20); otherwise, it returns `false` (line 22).

Member functions `getAvailableBalance` (lines 26–29) and `getTotalBalance` (lines 32–35) are *get* functions that return the values of `double` data members `availableBalance` and `totalBalance`, respectively.

Member function `credit` (lines 38–41) adds an amount of money (i.e., parameter `amount`) to an `Account` as part of a deposit transaction. Note that this member function adds the `amount` only to data member `totalBalance` (line 40). The money credited to an account during a deposit does not become available immediately, so we modify only the total balance. We assume that the bank updates the available balance appropriately at a later time. Our implementation of class `Account` includes only member functions required for carrying out ATM transactions. Therefore, we omit the member functions that some other bank system would invoke to add to data member `availableBalance` (to confirm a deposit) or subtract from data member `totalBalance` (to reject a deposit).

```
1  // Account.cpp
2  // Member-function definitions for class Account.
3  #include "Account.h" // Account class definition
4
5  // Account constructor initializes attributes
6  Account::Account( int theAccountNumber, int thePIN,
7     double theAvailableBalance, double theTotalBalance )
8     : accountNumber( theAccountNumber ),
9       pin( thePIN ),
10      availableBalance( theAvailableBalance ),
11      totalBalance( theTotalBalance )
12 {
13    // empty body
14 } // end Account constructor
15
16 // determines whether a user-specified PIN matches PIN in Account
17 bool Account::validatePIN( int userPIN ) const
18 {
19    if ( userPIN == pin )
20       return true;
21    else
22       return false;
23 } // end function validatePIN
24
25 // returns available balance
26 double Account::getAvailableBalance() const
27 {
28    return availableBalance;
29 } // end function getAvailableBalance
30
31 // returns the total balance
32 double Account::getTotalBalance() const
33 {
34    return totalBalance;
35 } // end function getTotalBalance
36
37 // credits an amount to the account
38 void Account::credit( double amount )
39 {
40    totalBalance += amount; // add to total balance
41 } // end function credit
```

Fig. 23.25 | `Account` class member-function definitions. (Part 1 of 2.)

```
42
43 // debits an amount from the account
44 void Account::debit( double amount )
45 {
46    availableBalance -= amount; // subtract from available balance
47    totalBalance -= amount; // subtract from total balance
48 } // end function debit
49
50 // returns account number
51 int Account::getAccountNumber() const
52 {
53    return accountNumber;
54 } // end function getAccountNumber
```

Fig. 23.25 | `Account` class member-function definitions. (Part 2 of 2.)

Member function `debit` (lines 44–48) subtracts an amount of money (i.e., parameter `amount`) from an `Account` as part of a withdrawal transaction. This member function subtracts the `amount` from both data member `availableBalance` (line 46) and data member `totalBalance` (line 47), because a withdrawal affects both measures of an account balance.

Member function `getAccountNumber` (lines 51–54) provides access to an `Account`'s `accountNumber`. We include this member function in our implementation so that a client of the class (i.e., `BankDatabase`) can identify a particular `Account`. For example, `BankDatabase` contains many `Account` objects, and it can invoke this member function on each of its `Account` objects to locate the one with a specific account number.

23.4.7 Class BankDatabase

Class `BankDatabase` (Figs. 23.26–23.27) models the bank's database with which the ATM interacts to access and modify a user's account information. The class definition (Fig. 23.26) declares function prototypes for the class's constructor and several member functions. We discuss these momentarily. The class definition also declares the `BankDatabase`'s data members. We determine one data member for class `BankDatabase` based on its composition relationship with class `Account`. Recall from Fig. 23.10 that a `BankDatabase` is composed of zero or more objects of class `Account`. Line 24 of Fig. 23.26 implements data member `accounts`—a `vector` of `Account` objects—to implement this composition relationship. Lines 6–7 allow us to use `vector` in this file. Line 27 contains the function prototype for a `private` utility function `getAccount` that allows the member functions of the class to obtain a pointer to a specific `Account` in the `accounts` `vector`.

```
1 // BankDatabase.h
2 // BankDatabase class definition. Represents the bank's database.
3 #ifndef BANK_DATABASE_H
4 #define BANK_DATABASE_H
5
6 #include <vector> // class uses vector to store Account objects
7 using namespace std;
```

Fig. 23.26 | `BankDatabase` class definition. (Part 1 of 2.)

```

#include "Account.h" // Account class definition

class BankDatabase
{
public:
   BankDatabase(); // constructor initializes accounts

   // determine whether account number and PIN match those of an Account
   bool authenticateUser( int, int ); // returns true if Account authentic

   double getAvailableBalance( int ); // get an available balance
   double getTotalBalance( int ); // get an Account's total balance
   void credit( int, double ); // add amount to Account balance
   void debit( int, double ); // subtract amount from Account balance
private:
   vector< Account > accounts; // vector of the bank's Accounts

   // private utility function
   Account * getAccount( int ); // get pointer to Account object
}; // end class BankDatabase

#endif // BANK_DATABASE_H
```

Fig. 23.26 | BankDatabase class definition. (Part 2 of 2.)

BankDatabase Class Member-Function Definitions

Figure 23.27 contains the member-function definitions for class BankDatabase. We implement the class with a default constructor (lines 6–15) that adds Account objects to data member accounts. For the sake of testing the system, we create two new Account objects with test data (lines 9–10), then add them to the end of the vector (lines 13–14). The Account constructor has four parameters—the account number, the PIN assigned to the account, the initial available balance and the initial total balance.

```
1  // BankDatabase.cpp
2  // Member-function definitions for class BankDatabase.
3  #include "BankDatabase.h" // BankDatabase class definition
4
5  // BankDatabase default constructor initializes accounts
6  BankDatabase::BankDatabase()
7  {
8     // create two Account objects for testing
9     Account account1( 12345, 54321, 1000.0, 1200.0 );
10    Account account2( 98765, 56789, 200.0, 200.0 );
11
12    // add the Account objects to the vector accounts
13    accounts.push_back( account1 ); // add account1 to end of vector
14    accounts.push_back( account2 ); // add account2 to end of vector
15 } // end BankDatabase default constructor
16
```

Fig. 23.27 | BankDatabase class member-function definitions. (Part 1 of 3.)

```
// retrieve Account object containing specified account number
Account * BankDatabase::getAccount( int accountNumber )
{
   // loop through accounts searching for matching account number
   for ( size_t i = 0; i < accounts.size(); i++ )
   {
      // return current account if match found
      if ( accounts[ i ].getAccountNumber() == accountNumber )
         return &accounts[ i ];
   } // end for

   return NULL; // if no matching account was found, return NULL
} // end function getAccount

// determine whether user-specified account number and PIN match
// those of an account in the database
bool BankDatabase::authenticateUser( int userAccountNumber,
   int userPIN )
{
   // attempt to retrieve the account with the account number
   Account * const userAccountPtr = getAccount( userAccountNumber );

   // if account exists, return result of Account function validatePIN
   if ( userAccountPtr != NULL )
      return userAccountPtr->validatePIN( userPIN );
   else
      return false; // account number not found, so return false
} // end function authenticateUser

// return available balance of Account with specified account number
double BankDatabase::getAvailableBalance( int userAccountNumber )
{
   Account * const userAccountPtr = getAccount( userAccountNumber );
   return userAccountPtr->getAvailableBalance();
} // end function getAvailableBalance

// return total balance of Account with specified account number
double BankDatabase::getTotalBalance( int userAccountNumber )
{
   Account * const userAccountPtr = getAccount( userAccountNumber );
   return userAccountPtr->getTotalBalance();
} // end function getTotalBalance

// credit an amount to Account with specified account number
void BankDatabase::credit( int userAccountNumber, double amount )
{
   Account * const userAccountPtr = getAccount( userAccountNumber );
   userAccountPtr->credit( amount );
} // end function credit

// debit an amount from Account with specified account number
void BankDatabase::debit( int userAccountNumber, double amount )
{
```

Fig. 23.27 | BankDatabase class member-function definitions. (Part 2 of 3.)

```
70      Account * const userAccountPtr = getAccount( userAccountNumber );
71      userAccountPtr->debit( amount );
72   } // end function debit
```

Fig. 23.27 | BankDatabase class member-function definitions. (Part 3 of 3.)

Recall that class BankDatabase serves as an intermediary between class ATM and the actual Account objects that contain users' account information. Thus, the member functions of class BankDatabase do nothing more than invoke the corresponding member functions of the Account object belonging to the current ATM user.

We include *private utility function* getAccount (lines 18–29) to allow the BankDatabase to obtain a pointer to a particular Account within vector accounts. To locate the user's Account, the BankDatabase compares the value returned by member function getAccountNumber for each element of accounts to a specified account number until it finds a match. Lines 21–26 traverse the accounts vector. If the account number of the current Account (i.e., accounts[i]) equals the value of parameter accountNumber, the member function immediately returns the address of the current Account (i.e., a pointer to the current Account). If no account has the given account number, then line 28 returns NULL. Note that this member function must return a pointer, as opposed to a reference, because there is the possibility that the return value could be NULL—*a reference cannot be NULL, but a pointer can.*

Note that vector function size (invoked in the loop-continuation condition in line 21) returns the number of elements in a vector as a value of type size_t (which is usually unsigned int). As a result, we declare the control variable i to be of type size_t, too. On some compilers, declaring i as an int would cause the compiler to issue a warning message, because the loop-continuation condition would compare a signed value (i.e., an int) and an unsigned value (i.e., a value of type size_t).

Member function authenticateUser (lines 33–44) proves or disproves the an ATM user's identity. This function takes a user-specified account number and user-specified PIN as arguments and indicates whether they match the account number and PIN of an Account in the database. Line 37 calls utility function getAccount, which returns either a pointer to an Account with userAccountNumber as its account number or NULL to indicate that userAccountNumber is invalid. We declare userAccountPtr to be a const pointer because, once the member function aims this pointer at the user's Account, the pointer should not change. If getAccount returns a pointer to an Account object, line 41 returns the bool value returned by that object's validatePIN member function. BankDatabase's authenticateUser member function does not perform the PIN comparison itself—rather, it forwards userPIN to the Account object's validatePIN member function to do so. The value returned by Account member function validatePIN indicates whether the user-specified PIN matches the PIN of the user's Account, so member function authenticateUser simply returns this value to the client of the class (i.e., ATM).

BankDatabase trusts the ATM to invoke member function authenticateUser and receive a return value of true before allowing the user to perform transactions. BankDatabase also trusts that each Transaction object created by the ATM contains the valid account number of the current authenticated user and that this is the account number passed to the remaining BankDatabase member functions as argument userAccountNumber.

Member functions `getAvailableBalance` (lines 47–51), `getTotalBalance` (lines 54–58), `credit` (lines 61–65) and `debit` (lines 68–72) therefore simply retrieve a pointer to the user's `Account` object with utility function `getAccount`, then use this pointer to invoke the appropriate `Account` member function on the user's `Account` object. We know that the calls to `getAccount` within these member functions will never return `NULL`, because `userAccountNumber` must refer to an existing `Account`. Note that `getAvailableBalance` and `getTotalBalance` return the values returned by the corresponding `Account` member functions. Also, `credit` and `debit` simply redirect parameter `amount` to the `Account` member functions they invoke.

23.4.8 Class Transaction

Class `Transaction` (Figs. 23.28–23.29) is an *abstract base class* that represents the notion of an ATM transaction. It contains the common features of derived classes `BalanceInquiry`, `Withdrawal` and `Deposit`. Figure 23.28 expands upon the `Transaction` header file first developed in Section 23.3. Lines 13, 17–19 and 22 contain function prototypes for the class's constructor and four member functions, which we discuss shortly. Line 15 defines a *`virtual` destructor* with an empty body—this makes all derived-class destructors `virtual` (even those defined implicitly by the compiler) and ensures that dynamically allocated derived-class objects get destroyed properly when they are deleted via a base-class pointer. Lines 24–26 declare the class's `private` data members. Recall from the class diagram of Fig. 23.11 that class `Transaction` contains an attribute `accountNumber` (implemented in line 24) that indicates the account involved in the `Transaction`. We derive data members `screen` (line 25) and `bankDatabase` (line 26) from class `Transaction`'s associations modeled in Fig. 23.10—all transactions require access to the ATM's screen and the bank's database, so we include references to a `Screen` and a `BankDatabase` as data members of class `Transaction`. As you'll soon see, `Transaction`'s constructor initializes these references. The forward declarations in lines 6–7 signify that the header file contains references to objects of classes `Screen` and `BankDatabase`, but that the definitions of these classes lie outside the header file.

```
1  // Transaction.h
2  // Transaction abstract base class definition.
3  #ifndef TRANSACTION_H
4  #define TRANSACTION_H
5
6  class Screen; // forward declaration of class Screen
7  class BankDatabase; // forward declaration of class BankDatabase
8
9  class Transaction
10 {
11 public:
12    // constructor initializes common features of all Transactions
13    Transaction( int, Screen &, BankDatabase & );
14
15    virtual ~Transaction() { } // virtual destructor with empty body
16
```

Fig. 23.28 | `Transaction` class definition. (Part 1 of 2.)

```
   int getAccountNumber() const; // return account number
   Screen &getScreen() const; // return reference to screen
   BankDatabase &getBankDatabase() const; // return reference to database

   // pure virtual function to perform the transaction
   virtual void execute() = 0; // overridden in derived classes
private:
   int accountNumber; // indicates account involved
   Screen &screen; // reference to the screen of the ATM
   BankDatabase &bankDatabase; // reference to the account info database
}; // end class Transaction

#endif // TRANSACTION_H
```

Fig. 23.28 | Transaction class definition. (Part 2 of 2.)

```
// Transaction.cpp
// Member-function definitions for class Transaction.
#include "Transaction.h" // Transaction class definition
#include "Screen.h" // Screen class definition
#include "BankDatabase.h" // BankDatabase class definition

// constructor initializes common features of all Transactions
Transaction::Transaction( int userAccountNumber, Screen &atmScreen,
   BankDatabase &atmBankDatabase )
   : accountNumber( userAccountNumber ),
     screen( atmScreen ),
     bankDatabase( atmBankDatabase )
{
   // empty body
} // end Transaction constructor

// return account number
int Transaction::getAccountNumber() const
{
   return accountNumber;
} // end function getAccountNumber

// return reference to screen
Screen &Transaction::getScreen() const
{
   return screen;
} // end function getScreen

// return reference to bank database
BankDatabase &Transaction::getBankDatabase() const
{
   return bankDatabase;
} // end function getBankDatabase
```

Fig. 23.29 | Transaction class member-function definitions.

Class `Transaction` has a constructor (declared in line 13 of Fig. 23.28 and defined in lines 8–15 of Fig. 23.29) that takes the current user's account number and references to the ATM's screen and the bank's database as arguments. Because `Transaction` is an abstract class, this constructor will never be called directly to instantiate `Transaction` objects. Instead, the constructors of the `Transaction` derived classes will use *base-class initializer syntax* to invoke this constructor.

Class `Transaction` has three `public` *get* functions—`getAccountNumber` (declared in line 17 of Fig. 23.28 and defined in lines 18–21 of Fig. 23.29), `getScreen` (declared in line 18 of Fig. 23.28 and defined in lines 24–27 of Fig. 23.29) and `getBankDatabase` (declared in line 19 of Fig. 23.28 and defined in lines 30–33 of Fig. 23.29). `Transaction` derived classes inherit these member functions from `Transaction` and use them to gain access to class `Transaction`'s `private` data members.

Class `Transaction` also declares a pure `virtual` function `execute` (line 22 of Fig. 23.28). It does not make sense to provide an implementation for this member function, because a generic transaction cannot be executed. Thus, we declare this member function to be a pure `virtual` function and force each `Transaction` derived class to provide its own concrete implementation that executes that particular type of transaction.

23.4.9 Class BalanceInquiry

Class `BalanceInquiry` (Figs. 23.30–23.31) derives from abstract base class `Transaction` and represents a balance-inquiry ATM transaction. `BalanceInquiry` does not have any data members of its own, but it inherits `Transaction` data members `accountNumber`, `screen` and `bankDatabase`, which are accessible through `Transaction`'s `public` *get* functions. Line 6 `#include`s the definition of base class `Transaction`. The `BalanceInquiry` constructor (declared in line 11 of Fig. 23.30 and defined in lines 8–13 of Fig. 23.31) takes arguments corresponding to the `Transaction` data members and simply forwards them to `Transaction`'s constructor, using *base-class initializer syntax* (line 10 of Fig. 23.31). Line 12 of Fig. 23.30 contains the function prototype for member function `execute`, which is required to indicate the intention to override the base class's pure `virtual` function of the same name.

```
1  // BalanceInquiry.h
2  // BalanceInquiry class definition. Represents a balance inquiry.
3  #ifndef BALANCE_INQUIRY_H
4  #define BALANCE_INQUIRY_H
5
6  #include "Transaction.h" // Transaction class definition
7
8  class BalanceInquiry : public Transaction
9  {
10 public:
11    BalanceInquiry( int, Screen &, BankDatabase & ); // constructor
12    virtual void execute(); // perform the transaction
13 }; // end class BalanceInquiry
14
15 #endif // BALANCE_INQUIRY_H
```

Fig. 23.30 | `BalanceInquiry` class definition.

```
1  // BalanceInquiry.cpp
2  // Member-function definitions for class BalanceInquiry.
3  #include "BalanceInquiry.h" // BalanceInquiry class definition
4  #include "Screen.h" // Screen class definition
5  #include "BankDatabase.h" // BankDatabase class definition
6
7  // BalanceInquiry constructor initializes base-class data members
8  BalanceInquiry:: BalanceInquiry( int userAccountNumber, Screen &atmScreen,
9     BankDatabase &atmBankDatabase )
10    : Transaction( userAccountNumber, atmScreen, atmBankDatabase )
11 {
12    // empty body
13 } // end BalanceInquiry constructor
14
15 // performs transaction; overrides Transaction's pure virtual function
16 void BalanceInquiry::execute()
17 {
18    // get references to bank database and screen
19    BankDatabase &bankDatabase = getBankDatabase();
20    Screen &screen = getScreen();
21
22    // get the available balance for the current user's Account
23    double availableBalance =
24       bankDatabase.getAvailableBalance( getAccountNumber() );
25
26    // get the total balance for the current user's Account
27    double totalBalance =
28       bankDatabase.getTotalBalance( getAccountNumber() );
29
30    // display the balance information on the screen
31    screen.displayMessageLine( "\nBalance Information:" );
32    screen.displayMessage( " - Available balance: " );
33    screen.displayDollarAmount( availableBalance );
34    screen.displayMessage( "\n - Total balance:     " );
35    screen.displayDollarAmount( totalBalance );
36    screen.displayMessageLine( "" );
37 } // end function execute
```

Fig. 23.31 | BalanceInquiry class member-function definitions.

Class BalanceInquiry overrides Transaction's pure virtual function execute to provide a concrete implementation (lines 16–37 of Fig. 23.31) that performs the steps involved in a balance inquiry. Lines 19–20 get references to the bank database and the ATM's screen by invoking member functions inherited from base class Transaction. Lines 23–24 retrieve the available balance of the account involved by invoking member function getAvailableBalance of bankDatabase. Line 24 uses inherited member function getAccountNumber to get the account number of the current user, which it then passes to getAvailableBalance. Lines 27–28 retrieve the total balance of the current user's account. Lines 31–36 display the balance information on the ATM's screen. Recall that displayDollarAmount takes a double argument and outputs it to the screen formatted as a dollar amount. For example, if a user's availableBalance is 700.5, line 33 outputs $700.50. Line 36 inserts a blank line of output to separate the balance information from subsequent output (i.e., the main menu repeated by class `ATM` after executing the `BalanceInquiry`).

23.4.10 Class `Withdrawal`

Class `Withdrawal` (Figs. 23.32–23.33) derives from `Transaction` and represents a withdrawal ATM transaction. Figure 23.32 expands upon the header file for this class developed in Fig. 23.13. Class `Withdrawal` has a constructor and one member function `execute`, which we discuss shortly. Recall from the class diagram of Fig. 23.11 that class `Withdrawal` has one attribute, `amount`, which line 16 implements as an `int` data member. Figure 23.10 models associations between class `Withdrawal` and classes `Keypad` and `CashDispenser`, for which lines 17–18 implement references `keypad` and `cashDispenser`, respectively. Line 19 is the function prototype of a `private` utility function that we soon discuss.

```
1   // Withdrawal.h
2   // Withdrawal class definition. Represents a withdrawal transaction.
3   #ifndef WITHDRAWAL_H
4   #define WITHDRAWAL_H
5
6   #include "Transaction.h" // Transaction class definition
7   class Keypad; // forward declaration of class Keypad
8   class CashDispenser; // forward declaration of class CashDispenser
9
10  class Withdrawal : public Transaction
11  {
12  public:
13     Withdrawal( int, Screen &, BankDatabase &, Keypad &, CashDispenser & );
14     virtual void execute(); // perform the transaction
15  private:
16     int amount; // amount to withdraw
17     Keypad &keypad; // reference to ATM's keypad
18     CashDispenser &cashDispenser; // reference to ATM's cash dispenser
19     int displayMenuOfAmounts() const; // display the withdrawal menu
20  }; // end class Withdrawal
21
22  #endif // WITHDRAWAL_H
```

Fig. 23.32 | `Withdrawal` class definition.

`Withdrawal` Class Member-Function Definitions

Figure 23.33 contains the member-function definitions for class `Withdrawal`. Line 3 `#include`s the class's definition, and lines 4–7 `#include` the definitions of the other classes used in `Withdrawal`'s member functions. Line 11 declares a global constant corresponding to the cancel option on the withdrawal menu. We'll soon discuss how the class uses this constant.

```
1   // Withdrawal.cpp
2   // Member-function definitions for class Withdrawal.
3   #include "Withdrawal.h" // Withdrawal class definition
```

Fig. 23.33 | `Withdrawal` class member-function definitions. (Part 1 of 4.)

```
#include "Screen.h" // Screen class definition
#include "BankDatabase.h" // BankDatabase class definition
#include "Keypad.h" // Keypad class definition
#include "CashDispenser.h" // CashDispenser class definition

// global constant that corresponds to menu option to cancel
static const int CANCELED = 6;

// Withdrawal constructor initialize class's data members
Withdrawal::Withdrawal( int userAccountNumber, Screen &atmScreen,
   BankDatabase &atmBankDatabase, Keypad &atmKeypad,
   CashDispenser &atmCashDispenser )
   : Transaction( userAccountNumber, atmScreen, atmBankDatabase ),
     keypad( atmKeypad ), cashDispenser( atmCashDispenser )
{
   // empty body
} // end Withdrawal constructor

// perform transaction; overrides Transaction's pure virtual function
void Withdrawal::execute()
{
   bool cashDispensed = false; // cash was not dispensed yet
   bool transactionCanceled = false; // transaction was not canceled yet

   // get references to bank database and screen
   BankDatabase &bankDatabase = getBankDatabase();
   Screen &screen = getScreen();

   // loop until cash is dispensed or the user cancels
   do
   {
      // obtain the chosen withdrawal amount from the user
      int selection = displayMenuOfAmounts();

      // check whether user chose a withdrawal amount or canceled
      if ( selection != CANCELED )
      {
         amount = selection; // set amount to the selected dollar amount

         // get available balance of account involved
         double availableBalance =
            bankDatabase.getAvailableBalance( getAccountNumber() );

         // check whether the user has enough money in the account
         if ( amount <= availableBalance )
         {
            // check whether the cash dispenser has enough money
            if ( cashDispenser.isSufficientCashAvailable( amount ) )
            {
               // update the account involved to reflect withdrawal
               bankDatabase.debit( getAccountNumber(), amount );

               cashDispenser.dispenseCash( amount ); // dispense cash
```

Fig. 23.33 | `Withdrawal` class member-function definitions. (Part 2 of 4.)

```
               cashDispensed = true; // cash was dispensed

               // instruct user to take cash
               screen.displayMessageLine(
                  "\nPlease take your cash from the cash dispenser." );
            } // end if
            else // cash dispenser does not have enough cash
               screen.displayMessageLine(
                  "\nInsufficient cash available in the ATM."
                  "\n\nPlease choose a smaller amount." );
         } // end if
         else // not enough money available in user's account
         {
            screen.displayMessageLine(
               "\nInsufficient funds in your account."
               "\n\nPlease choose a smaller amount." );
         } // end else
      } // end if
      else // user chose cancel menu option
      {
         screen.displayMessageLine( "\nCanceling transaction..." );
         transactionCanceled = true; // user canceled the transaction
      } // end else
   } while ( !cashDispensed && !transactionCanceled ); // end do...while
} // end function execute

// display a menu of withdrawal amounts and the option to cancel;
// return the chosen amount or 0 if the user chooses to cancel
int Withdrawal::displayMenuOfAmounts() const
{
   int userChoice = 0; // local variable to store return value

   Screen &screen = getScreen(); // get screen reference

   // array of amounts to correspond to menu numbers
   int amounts[] = { 0, 20, 40, 60, 100, 200 };

   // loop while no valid choice has been made
   while ( userChoice == 0 )
   {
      // display the menu
      screen.displayMessageLine( "\nWithdrawal options:" );
      screen.displayMessageLine( "1 - $20" );
      screen.displayMessageLine( "2 - $40" );
      screen.displayMessageLine( "3 - $60" );
      screen.displayMessageLine( "4 - $100" );
      screen.displayMessageLine( "5 - $200" );
      screen.displayMessageLine( "6 - Cancel transaction" );
      screen.displayMessage( "\nChoose a withdrawal option (1-6): " );

      int input = keypad.getInput(); // get user input through keypad

```

Fig. 23.33 | Withdrawal class member-function definitions. (Part 3 of 4.)

```
109        // determine how to proceed based on the input value
110        switch ( input )
111        {
112           case 1: // if the user chose a withdrawal amount
113           case 2: // (i.e., chose option 1, 2, 3, 4 or 5), return the
114           case 3: // corresponding amount from amounts array
115           case 4:
116           case 5:
117              userChoice = amounts[ input ]; // save user's choice
118              break;
119           case CANCELED: // the user chose to cancel
120              userChoice = CANCELED; // save user's choice
121              break;
122           default: // the user did not enter a value from 1-6
123              screen.displayMessageLine(
124                 "\nIvalid selection. Try again." );
125        } // end switch
126     } // end while
127
128     return userChoice; // return withdrawal amount or CANCELED
129  } // end function displayMenuOfAmounts
```

Fig. 23.33 | `Withdrawal` class member-function definitions. (Part 4 of 4.)

Class `Withdrawal`'s constructor (defined in lines 13–20 of Fig. 23.33) has five parameters. It uses a base-class initializer in line 16 to pass parameters `userAccountNumber`, `atmScreen` and `atmBankDatabase` to base class `Transaction`'s constructor to set the data members that `Withdrawal` inherits from `Transaction`. The constructor also takes references `atmKeypad` and `atmCashDispenser` as parameters and assigns them to reference data members `keypad` and `cashDispenser` using member initializers (line 17).

Class `Withdrawal` overrides `Transaction`'s pure `virtual` function `execute` with a concrete implementation (lines 23–81) that performs the steps involved in a withdrawal. Line 25 declares and initializes a local `bool` variable `cashDispensed`. This variable indicates whether cash has been dispensed (i.e., whether the transaction has completed successfully) and is initially `false`. Line 26 declares and initializes to `false` a `bool` variable `transactionCanceled` that indicates whether the transaction has been canceled by the user. Lines 29–30 get references to the bank database and the ATM's screen by invoking member functions inherited from base class `Transaction`.

Lines 33–80 contain a `do...while` statement that executes its body until cash is dispensed (i.e., until `cashDispensed` becomes `true`) or until the user chooses to cancel (i.e., until `transactionCanceled` becomes `true`). This loop continuously returns the user to the start of the transaction if an error occurs (i.e., the requested withdrawal amount is greater than the user's available balance or greater than the amount of cash in the cash dispenser). Line 36 displays a menu of withdrawal amounts and obtains a user selection by calling `private` utility function `displayMenuOfAmounts` (defined in lines 85–129). This function displays the menu of amounts and returns either an `int` withdrawal amount or the `int` constant `CANCELED` to indicate that the user has chosen to cancel the transaction.

Member function `displayMenuOfAmounts` (lines 85–129) first declares local variable `userChoice` (initially 0) to store the value that the member function will return (line 87).

Line 89 gets a reference to the screen by calling member function getScreen inherited from base class Transaction. Line 92 declares an integer array of withdrawal amounts that correspond to the amounts displayed in the withdrawal menu. We ignore the first element in the array (index 0) because the menu has no option 0. The while statement in lines 95–126 repeats until userChoice takes on a value other than 0. We'll see shortly that this occurs when the user makes a valid selection from the menu. Lines 98–105 display the withdrawal menu on the screen and prompt the user to enter a choice. Line 107 obtains integer input through the keypad. The switch statement in lines 110–125 determines how to proceed based on the user's input. If the user selects a number between 1 and 5, line 117 sets userChoice to the value of the element in amounts at index input. For example, if the user enters 3 to withdraw $60, line 117 sets userChoice to the value of amounts[3] (i.e., 60). Line 118 terminates the switch. Variable userChoice no longer equals 0, so the while in lines 95–126 terminates and line 128 returns userChoice. If the user selects the cancel menu option, lines 120–121 execute, setting userChoice to CANCELED and causing the member function to return this value. If the user does not enter a valid menu selection, lines 123–124 display an error message and the user is returned to the withdrawal menu.

The if statement in line 39 in member function execute determines whether the user has selected a withdrawal amount or chosen to cancel. If the user cancels, lines 77–78 execute to display an appropriate message to the user and set transactionCanceled to true. This causes the loop-continuation test in line 80 to fail and control to return to the calling member function (i.e., ATM member function performTransactions). If the user has chosen a withdrawal amount, line 41 assigns local variable selection to data member amount. Lines 44–45 retrieve the available balance of the current user's Account and store it in a local double variable availableBalance. Next, the if statement in line 48 determines whether the selected amount is less than or equal to the user's available balance. If it isn't, lines 70–72 display an appropriate error message. Control then continues to the end of the do...while, and the loop repeats because both cashDispensed and transactionCanceled are still false. If the user's balance is high enough, the if statement in line 51 determines whether the cash dispenser has enough money to satisfy the withdrawal request by invoking the cashDispenser's isSufficientCashAvailable member function. If this member function returns false, lines 64–66 display an appropriate error message and the do...while repeats. If sufficient cash is available, then the requirements for the withdrawal are satisfied, and line 54 debits amount from the user's account in the database. Lines 56–57 then instruct the cash dispenser to dispense the cash to the user and set cashDispensed to true. Finally, lines 60–61 display a message to the user that cash has been dispensed. Because cashDispensed is now true, control continues after the do...while. No additional statements appear below the loop, so the member function returns control to class ATM.

In the function calls in lines 64–66 and lines 70–72, we divide the argument to Screen member function displayMessageLine into two string literals, each placed on a separate line in the program. We do so because each argument is too long to fit on a single line. *C++ concatenates (i.e., combines) string literals adjacent to each other, even if they are on separate lines.* For example, if you write "Happy " "Birthday" in a program, C++ will view these two adjacent string literals as the single string literal "Happy Birthday". As a result, when lines 64–66 execute, displayMessageLine receives a single string as a parameter, even though the argument in the function call appears as two string literals.

23.4.11 Class Deposit

Class Deposit (Figs. 23.34–23.35) derives from Transaction and represents a deposit ATM transaction. Figure 23.34 contains the Deposit class definition. Like derived classes BalanceInquiry and Withdrawal, Deposit declares a constructor (line 13) and member function execute (line 14)—we discuss these momentarily. Recall from the class diagram of Fig. 23.11 that class Deposit has one attribute amount, which line 16 implements as an int data member. Lines 17–18 create reference data members keypad and depositSlot that implement the associations between class Deposit and classes Keypad and DepositSlot modeled in Fig. 23.10. Line 19 contains the function prototype for a private utility function promptForDepositAmount that we'll discuss shortly.

```
1  // Deposit.h
2  // Deposit class definition. Represents a deposit transaction.
3  #ifndef DEPOSIT_H
4  #define DEPOSIT_H
5
6  #include "Transaction.h" // Transaction class definition
7  class Keypad; // forward declaration of class Keypad
8  class DepositSlot; // forward declaration of class DepositSlot
9
10 class Deposit : public Transaction
11 {
12 public:
13    Deposit( int, Screen &, BankDatabase &, Keypad &, DepositSlot & );
14    virtual void execute(); // perform the transaction
15 private:
16    double amount; // amount to deposit
17    Keypad &keypad; // reference to ATM's keypad
18    DepositSlot &depositSlot; // reference to ATM's deposit slot
19    double promptForDepositAmount() const; // get deposit amount from user
20 }; // end class Deposit
21
22 #endif // DEPOSIT_H
```

Fig. 23.34 | Deposit class definition.

Deposit Class Member-Function Definitions

Figure 23.35 presents the Deposit class implementation. Line 3 #includes the Deposit class definition, and lines 4–7 #include the class definitions of the other classes used in Deposit's member functions. Line 9 declares a constant CANCELED that corresponds to the value a user enters to cancel a deposit. We'll soon discuss how the class uses this constant.

```
1  // Deposit.cpp
2  // Member-function definitions for class Deposit.
3  #include "Deposit.h" // Deposit class definition
4  #include "Screen.h" // Screen class definition
5  #include "BankDatabase.h" // BankDatabase class definition
6  #include "Keypad.h" // Keypad class definition
```

Fig. 23.35 | Deposit class member-function definitions. (Part 1 of 3.)

```
#include "DepositSlot.h" // DepositSlot class definition

static const int CANCELED = 0; // constant representing cancel option

// Deposit constructor initializes class's data members
Deposit::Deposit( int userAccountNumber, Screen &atmScreen,
   BankDatabase &atmBankDatabase, Keypad &atmKeypad,
   DepositSlot &atmDepositSlot )
   : Transaction( userAccountNumber, atmScreen, atmBankDatabase ),
     keypad( atmKeypad ), depositSlot( atmDepositSlot )
{
   // empty body
} // end Deposit constructor

// performs transaction; overrides Transaction's pure virtual function
void Deposit::execute()
{
   BankDatabase &bankDatabase = getBankDatabase(); // get reference
   Screen &screen = getScreen(); // get reference

   amount = promptForDepositAmount(); // get deposit amount from user

   // check whether user entered a deposit amount or canceled
   if ( amount != CANCELED )
   {
      // request deposit envelope containing specified amount
      screen.displayMessage(
         "\nPlease insert a deposit envelope containing " );
      screen.displayDollarAmount( amount );
      screen.displayMessageLine( " in the deposit slot." );

      // receive deposit envelope
      bool envelopeReceived = depositSlot.isEnvelopeReceived();

      // check whether deposit envelope was received
      if ( envelopeReceived )
      {
         screen.displayMessageLine( "\nYour envelope has been received."
            "\nNOTE: The money deposited will not be available until we"
            "\nverify the amount of any enclosed cash, and any enclosed "
            "checks clear." );

         // credit account to reflect the deposit
         bankDatabase.credit( getAccountNumber(), amount );
      } // end if
      else // deposit envelope not received
      {
         screen.displayMessageLine( "\nYou did not insert an "
            "envelope, so the ATM has canceled your transaction." );
      } // end else
   } // end if
   else // user canceled instead of entering amount
   {
```

Fig. 23.35 | Deposit class member-function definitions. (Part 2 of 3.)

```
60         screen.displayMessageLine( "\nCanceling transaction..." );
61      } // end else
62   } // end function execute
63
64   // prompt user to enter a deposit amount in cents
65   double Deposit::promptForDepositAmount() const
66   {
67      Screen &screen = getScreen(); // get reference to screen
68
69      // display the prompt and receive input
70      screen.displayMessage( "\nPlease enter a deposit amount in "
71         "CENTS (or 0 to cancel): " );
72      int input = keypad.getInput(); // receive input of deposit amount
73
74      // check whether the user canceled or entered a valid amount
75      if ( input == CANCELED )
76         return CANCELED;
77      else
78      {
79         return static_cast< double >( input ) / 100; // return dollar amount
80      } // end else
81   } // end function promptForDepositAmount
```

Fig. 23.35 | `Deposit` class member-function definitions. (Part 3 of 3.)

Like class `Withdrawal`, class `Deposit` contains a constructor (lines 12–19) that passes three parameters to base class `Transaction`'s constructor using a base-class initializer (line 15). The constructor also has parameters `atmKeypad` and `atmDepositSlot`, which it assigns to its corresponding data members (line 16).

Member function `execute` (lines 22–62) overrides pure `virtual` function `execute` in base class `Transaction` with a concrete implementation that performs the steps required in a deposit transaction. Lines 24–25 get references to the database and the screen. Line 27 prompts the user to enter a deposit amount by invoking `private` utility function `promptForDepositAmount` (defined in lines 65–81) and sets data member `amount` to the value returned. Member function `promptForDepositAmount` asks the user to enter a deposit amount as an integer number of cents (because the ATM's keypad does not contain a decimal point; this is consistent with many real ATMs) and returns the `double` value representing the dollar amount to be deposited.

Line 67 in member function `promptForDepositAmount` gets a reference to the ATM's screen. Lines 70–71 display a message on the screen asking the user to input a deposit amount as a number of cents or "0" to cancel the transaction. Line 72 receives the user's input from the keypad. The `if` statement in lines 75–80 determines whether the user has entered a real deposit amount or chosen to cancel. If the user chooses to cancel, line 76 returns the constant `CANCELED`. Otherwise, line 79 returns the deposit amount after converting from the number of cents to a dollar amount by casting `input` to a `double`, then dividing by `100`. For example, if the user enters `125` as the number of cents, line 79 returns `125.0` divided by `100`, or `1.25`—125 cents is $1.25.

The `if` statement in lines 30–61 in member function `execute` determines whether the user has chosen to cancel the transaction instead of entering a deposit amount. If the user cancels, line 60 displays an appropriate message, and the member function returns. If the user enters a deposit amount, lines 33–36 instruct the user to insert a deposit envelope with the correct amount. Recall that `Screen` member function `displayDollarAmount` outputs a `double` formatted as a dollar amount.

Line 39 sets a local `bool` variable to the value returned by `depositSlot`'s `isEnvelopeReceived` member function, indicating whether a deposit envelope has been received. Recall that we coded `isEnvelopeReceived` (lines 7–10 of Fig. 23.23) to always return `true`, because we are simulating the functionality of the deposit slot and assume that the user always inserts an envelope. However, we code member function `execute` of class `Deposit` to test for the possibility that the user does not insert an envelope—good software engineering demands that programs account for all possible return values. Thus, class `Deposit` is prepared for future versions of `isEnvelopeReceived` that could return `false`. Lines 44–50 execute if the deposit slot receives an envelope. Lines 44–47 display an appropriate message to the user. Line 50 then credits the deposit amount to the user's account in the database. Lines 54–55 will execute if the deposit slot does not receive a deposit envelope. In this case, we display a message to the user stating that the ATM has canceled the transaction. The member function then returns without modifying the user's account.

23.4.12 Test Program ATMCaseStudy.cpp

`ATMCaseStudy.cpp` (Fig. 23.36) is a simple C++ program that allows us to start, or "turn on," the ATM and test the implementation of our ATM system model. The program's `main` function (lines 6–11) does nothing more than instantiate a new `ATM` object named `atm` (line 8) and invoke its `run` member function (line 9) to start the ATM.

```
1  // ATMCaseStudy.cpp
2  // Driver program for the ATM case study.
3  #include "ATM.h" // ATM class definition
4
5  // main function creates and runs the ATM
6  int main()
7  {
8     ATM atm; // create an ATM object
9     atm.run(); // tell the ATM to start
10 } // end main
```

Fig. 23.36 | `ATMCaseStudy.cpp` starts the ATM system.

23.5 Wrap-Up

In this chapter, you used inheritance to tune the design of the ATM software system, and you fully implemented the ATM in C++. Congratulations on completing the entire ATM case study! We hope you found this experience to be valuable and that it reinforced many of the object-oriented programming concepts that you've learned.

Answers to Self-Review Exercises

23.1 True. The minus sign (-) indicates private visibility. We've mentioned "friendship" as an exception to private visibility. Friendship is discussed in Chapter 9.

23.2 b.

23.3 The design for class `Account` yields the header file in Fig. 23.37.

```
// Fig. 23.37: Account.h
// Account class definition. Represents a bank account.
#ifndef ACCOUNT_H
#define ACCOUNT_H

class Account
{
public:
   bool validatePIN( int ); // is user-specified PIN correct?
   double getAvailableBalance(); // returns available balance
   double getTotalBalance(); // returns total balance
   void credit( double ); // adds an amount to the Account
   void debit( double ); // subtracts an amount from the Account
private:
   int accountNumber; // account number
   int pin; // PIN for authentication
   double availableBalance; // funds available for withdrawal
   double totalBalance; // funds available + funds waiting to clear
}; // end class Account

#endif // ACCOUNT_H
```

Fig. 23.37 | `Account` class header file based on Figs. 23.1 and 23.2.

23.4 b.

23.5 False. The UML requires that we italicize abstract class names and operation names.

23.6 The design for class `Transaction` yields the header file in Fig. 23.38. In the implementation, a constructor initializes `private` reference attributes `screen` and `bankDatabase` to actual objects, and member functions `getScreen` and `getBankDatabase` access these attributes. These member functions allow classes derived from `Transaction` to access the ATM's screen and interact with the bank's database.

```
// Fig. 36.38: Transaction.h
// Transaction abstract base class definition.
#ifndef TRANSACTION_H
#define TRANSACTION_H

class Screen; // forward declaration of class Screen
class BankDatabase; // forward declaration of class BankDatabase

class Transaction
{
public:
   int getAccountNumber(); // return account number
   Screen &getScreen(); // return reference to screen
   BankDatabase &getBankDatabase(); // return reference to bank database
```

Fig. 23.38 | `Transaction` class header file based on Figs. 23.10 and 23.11. (Part 1 of 2.)

```

   // pure virtual function to perform the transaction
   virtual void execute() = 0; // overridden in derived classes
private:
   int accountNumber; // indicates account involved
   Screen &screen; // reference to the screen of the ATM
   BankDatabase &bankDatabase; // reference to the account info database
}; // end class Transaction

#endif // TRANSACTION_H
```

Fig. 23.38 | `Transaction` class header file based on Figs. 23.10 and 23.11. (Part 2 of 2.)

Operator Precedence and Associativity

Operators are shown in decreasing order of precedence from top to bottom (Fig. A.1).

Operator	Type	Associativity
::	binary scope resolution	left to right
::	unary scope resolution	
()	grouping parentheses *[See caution in Fig. 2.7 regarding grouping parentheses.]*	
()	function call	left to right
[]	array subscript	
.	member selection via object	
->	member selection via pointer	
++	unary postfix increment	
--	unary postfix decrement	
typeid	runtime type information	
dynamic_cast < *type* >	runtime type-checked cast	
static_cast< *type* >	compile-time type-checked cast	
reinterpret_cast< *type* >	cast for nonstandard conversions	
const_cast< *type* >	cast away const-ness	

Fig. A.1 | Operator precedence and associativity chart. (Part 1 of 3.)

Operator	Type	Associativity

`++`
`--`
`+`
`-`
`!`
`~`
`sizeof`
`&`
`*`
`new`
`new[]`
`delete`
`delete[]`
	unary prefix increment
	unary prefix decrement
	unary plus
	unary minus
	unary logical negation
	unary bitwise complement
	determine size in bytes
	address
	dereference
	dynamic memory allocation
	dynamic array allocation
	dynamic memory deallocation
	dynamic array deallocation
		right to left

`(` *type* `)`	C-style unary cast	right to left
`.*` `->*`	pointer to member via object pointer to member via pointer	left to right

`*`
`/`
`%`
	multiplication
	division
	modulus
		left to right

`+` `-`	addition subtraction	left to right
`<<` `>>`	bitwise left shift bitwise right shift	left to right

`<`
`<=`
`>`
`>=`
	relational less than
	relational less than opr equal to
	relational greater than
	relational greater than or equal to
		left to right

`==` `!=`	relational is equal to relational is not equal to	left to right
`&`	bitwise AND	left to right
`^`	bitwise exclusive OR	left to right
`|`	bitwise inclusive OR	left to right
`&&`	logical AND	left to right
`||`	logical OR	left to right
`?:`	ternary conditional	right to left

Fig. A.1 | Operator precedence and associativity chart. (Part 2 of 3.)

<table>
<tr><th>Operator</th><th>Type</th><th>Associativity</th></tr>
<tr><td>=</td><td>assignment</td><td>right to left</td></tr>
<tr><td>+=</td><td>addition assignment</td><td></td></tr>
<tr><td>-=</td><td>subtraction assignment</td><td></td></tr>
<tr><td>*=</td><td>multiplication assignment</td><td></td></tr>
<tr><td>/=</td><td>division assignment</td><td></td></tr>
<tr><td>%=</td><td>modulus assignment</td><td></td></tr>
<tr><td>&=</td><td>bitwise AND assignment</td><td></td></tr>
<tr><td>^=</td><td>bitwise exclusive OR assignment</td><td></td></tr>
<tr><td>|=</td><td>bitwise inclusive OR assignment</td><td></td></tr>
<tr><td><<=</td><td>bitwise left-shift assignment</td><td></td></tr>
<tr><td>>>=</td><td>bitwise right-shift assignment</td><td></td></tr>
<tr><td>,</td><td>comma</td><td>left to right</td></tr>
</table>

Fig. A.1 | Operator precedence and associativity chart. (Part 3 of 3.)

B

ASCII Character Set

ASCII Character Set

	0	1	2	3	4	5	6	7	8	9
0	nul	soh	stx	etx	eot	enq	ack	bel	bs	ht
1	nl	vt	ff	cr	so	si	dle	dc1	dc2	dc3
2	dc4	nak	syn	etb	can	em	sub	esc	fs	gs
3	rs	us	sp	!	"	#	$	%	&	'
4	(	)	*	+	,	-	.	/	0	1
5	2	3	4	5	6	7	8	9	:	;
6	<	=	>	?	@	A	B	C	D	E
7	F	G	H	I	J	K	L	M	N	O
8	P	Q	R	S	T	U	V	W	X	Y
9	Z	[	\	]	^	_	`	a	b	c
10	d	e	f	g	h	i	j	k	l	m
11	n	o	p	q	r	s	t	u	v	w
12	x	y	z	{	|	}	~	del		

Fig. B.1 | ASCII character set.

The digits at the left of the table are the left digits of the decimal equivalents (0–127) of the character codes, and the digits at the top of the table are the right digits of the character codes. For example, the character code for "F" is 70, and the character code for "&" is 38.

Fundamental Types

Figure C.1 lists C++'s fundamental types. The C++ Standard Document does not provide the exact number of bytes required to store variables of these types in memory. However, the C++ Standard Document does indicate how the memory requirements for fundamental types relate to one another. By order of increasing memory requirements, the signed integer types are `signed char`, `short int`, `int`, `long int` and `long long int`. This means that a `short int` must provide at least as much storage as a `signed char`; an `int` must provide at least as much storage as a `short int`; a `long int` must provide at least as much storage as an `int`; and a `long long int` must provide at least as much storage as a `long int`. Each signed integer type has a corresponding unsigned integer type that has the same memory requirements. Unsigned types cannot represent negative values, but can represent approximately twice as many positive values as their associated signed types. By order of increasing memory requirements, the floating-point types are `float`, `double` and `long double`. Like integer types, a `double` must provide at least as much storage as a `float` and a `long double` must provide at least as much storage as a `double`.

The exact sizes and ranges of values for the fundamental types are implementation dependent. The header files `<climits>` (for the integral types) and `<cfloat>` (for the floating-point types) specify the ranges of values supported on your system.

The range of values a type supports depends on the number of bytes that are used to represent that type. For example, consider a system with 4 byte (32 bit) `int`s. For the signed `int` type, the nonnegative values are in the range 0 to 2,147,483,647 ($2^{31} - 1$). The negative values are in the range –1 to –2,147,483,647 ($-2^{31} - 1$). This is a total of 2^{32} possible values. An `unsigned int` on the same system would use the same number of bits to represent data, but would not represent any negative values. This results in values in the range 0 to 4,294,967,295 ($2^{32} - 1$). On the same system, a `short int` could not use more than 32 bits to represent its data and a `long int` must use at least 32 bits.

C++ provides the data type `bool` for variables that can hold only the values `true` and `false`. C++11 introduced the types `long long int` and `unsigned long long int`—typically for 64-bit integer values (though this is not required by the standard). C++11 also introduced the new character types `char16_t` and `char32_t` for representing Unicode characters.

Integral types	Floating-point types
bool	float
char	double
signed char	long double
unsigned char	
short int	
unsigned short int	
int	
unsigned int	
long int	
unsigned long int	
long long int	
unsigned long long int	
char16_t	
char32_t	
wchar_t	

Fig. C.1 | C++ fundamental types.

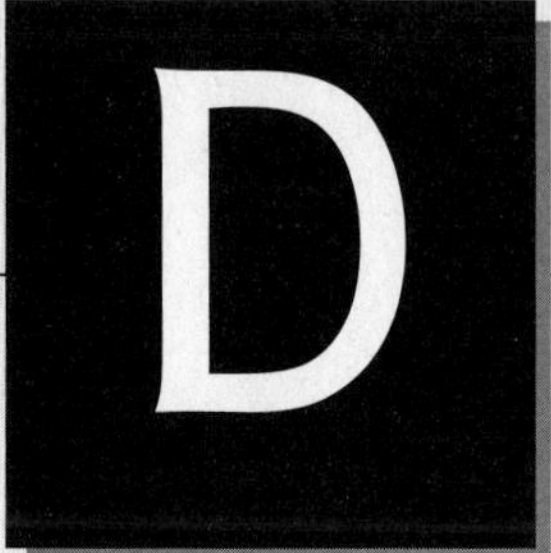

Number Systems

Objectives

In this chapter you'll:

- Understand basic number systems concepts, such as base, positional value and symbol value.
- Work with numbers in the binary, octal and hexadecimal number systems.
- Abbreviate binary numbers as octal numbers or hexadecimal numbers.
- Convert octal numbers and hexadecimal numbers to binary numbers.
- Convert back and forth between decimal numbers and their binary, octal and hexadecimal equivalents.
- Understand binary arithmetic and how negative binary numbers are represented using two's complement notation.

Outline

D.1 Introduction

In this appendix, we introduce the key number systems that C++ programmers use, especially when they are working on software projects that require close interaction with machine-level hardware. Projects like this include operating systems, computer networking software, compilers, database systems and applications requiring high performance.

When we write an integer such as 227 or –63 in a C++ program, the number is assumed to be in the **decimal (base 10) number system**. The **digits** in the decimal number system are 0, 1, 2, 3, 4, 5, 6, 7, 8 and 9. The lowest digit is 0 and the highest is 9—one less than the base of 10. Internally, computers use the **binary (base 2) number system**. The binary number system has only two digits, namely 0 and 1. Its lowest digit is 0 and its highest is 1—one less than the base of 2.

As we'll see, binary numbers tend to be much longer than their decimal equivalents. Programmers who work in assembly languages, and in high-level languages like C++ that enable them to reach down to the machine level, find it cumbersome to work with binary numbers. So two other number systems—the **octal number system (base 8)** and the **hexadecimal number system (base 16)**—are popular, primarily because they make it convenient to abbreviate binary numbers.

In the octal number system, the digits range from 0 to 7. Because both the binary and the octal number systems have fewer digits than the decimal number system, their digits are the same as the corresponding digits in decimal.

The hexadecimal number system poses a problem because it requires 16 digits—a lowest digit of 0 and a highest digit with a value equivalent to decimal 15 (one less than the base of 16). By convention, we use the letters A through F to represent the hexadecimal digits corresponding to decimal values 10 through 15. Thus in hexadecimal we can have numbers like 876 consisting solely of decimal-like digits, numbers like 8A55F consisting of digits and letters and numbers like FFE consisting solely of letters. Occasionally, a hexadecimal number spells a common word such as FACE or FEED—this can appear strange to programmers accustomed to working with numbers. The digits of the binary, octal, decimal and hexadecimal number systems are summarized in Figs. D.1–D.2.

Each of these number systems uses **positional notation**—each position in which a digit is written has a different **positional value**. For example, in the decimal number 937 (the 9, the 3 and the 7 are referred to as **symbol values**), we say that the 7 is written in the ones position, the 3 is written in the tens position and the 9 is written in the hundreds position. Note that each of these positions is a power of the base (base 10) and that these powers begin at 0 and increase by 1 as we move left in the number (Fig. D.3).

Binary digit	Octal digit	Decimal digit	Hexadecimal digit
0	0	0	0
1	1	1	1
	2	2	2
	3	3	3
	4	4	4
	5	5	5
	6	6	6
	7	7	7
		8	8
		9	9
			A (decimal value of 10)
			B (decimal value of 11)
			C (decimal value of 12)
			D (decimal value of 13)
			E (decimal value of 14)
			F (decimal value of 15)

Fig. D.1 | Digits of the binary, octal, decimal and hexadecimal number systems.

Attribute	Binary	Octal	Decimal	Hexadecimal
Base	2	8	10	16
Lowest digit	0	0	0	0
Highest digit	1	7	9	F

Fig. D.2 | Comparing the binary, octal, decimal and hexadecimal number systems.

Positional values in the decimal number system			
Decimal digit	9	3	7
Position name	Hundreds	Tens	Ones
Positional value	100	10	1
Positional value as a power of the base (10)	10^2	10^1	10^0

Fig. D.3 | Positional values in the decimal number system.

For longer decimal numbers, the next positions to the left would be the thousands position (10 to the 3rd power), the ten-thousands position (10 to the 4th power), the hundred-thousands position (10 to the 5th power), the millions position (10 to the 6th power), the ten-millions position (10 to the 7th power) and so on.

In the binary number 101, the rightmost 1 is written in the ones position, the 0 is written in the twos position and the leftmost 1 is written in the fours position. Note that each position is a power of the base (base 2) and that these powers begin at 0 and increase by 1 as we move left in the number (Fig. D.4). So, $101 = 2^2 + 2^0 = 4 + 1 = 5$.

Positional values in the binary number system			
Binary digit	1	0	1
Position name	Fours	Twos	Ones
Positional value	4	2	1
Positional value as a power of the base (2)	2^2	2^1	2^0

Fig. D.4 | Positional values in the binary number system.

For longer binary numbers, the next positions to the left would be the eights position (2 to the 3rd power), the sixteens position (2 to the 4th power), the thirty-twos position (2 to the 5th power), the sixty-fours position (2 to the 6th power) and so on.

In the octal number 425, we say that the 5 is written in the ones position, the 2 is written in the eights position and the 4 is written in the sixty-fours position. Note that each of these positions is a power of the base (base 8) and that these powers begin at 0 and increase by 1 as we move left in the number (Fig. D.5).

Positional values in the octal number system			
Decimal digit	4	2	5
Position name	Sixty-fours	Eights	Ones
Positional value	64	8	1
Positional value as a power of the base (8)	8^2	8^1	8^0

Fig. D.5 | Positional values in the octal number system.

For longer octal numbers, the next positions to the left would be the five-hundred-and-twelves position (8 to the 3rd power), the four-thousand-and-ninety-sixes position (8 to the 4th power), the thirty-two-thousand-seven-hundred-and-sixty-eights position (8 to the 5th power) and so on.

In the hexadecimal number 3DA, we say that the A is written in the ones position, the D is written in the sixteens position and the 3 is written in the two-hundred-and-fifty-sixes position. Note that each of these positions is a power of the base (base 16) and that these powers begin at 0 and increase by 1 as we move left in the number (Fig. D.6).

For longer hexadecimal numbers, the next positions to the left would be the four-thousand-and-ninety-sixes position (16 to the 3rd power), the sixty-five-thousand-five-hundred-and-thirty-sixes position (16 to the 4th power) and so on.

Positional values in the hexadecimal number system			
Decimal digit	3	D	A
Position name	Two-hundred-and-fifty-sixes	Sixteens	Ones
Positional value	256	16	1
Positional value as a power of the base (16)	16^2	16^1	16^0

Fig. D.6 | Positional values in the hexadecimal number system.

D.2 Abbreviating Binary Numbers as Octal and Hexadecimal Numbers

The main use for octal and hexadecimal numbers in computing is for abbreviating lengthy binary representations. Figure D.7 highlights the fact that lengthy binary numbers can be expressed concisely in number systems with higher bases than the binary number system.

Decimal number	Binary representation	Octal representation	Hexadecimal representation
0	0	0	0
1	1	1	1
2	10	2	2
3	11	3	3
4	100	4	4
5	101	5	5
6	110	6	6
7	111	7	7
8	1000	10	8
9	1001	11	9
10	1010	12	A
11	1011	13	B
12	1100	14	C
13	1101	15	D
14	1110	16	E
15	1111	17	F
16	10000	20	10

Fig. D.7 | Decimal, binary, octal and hexadecimal equivalents.

A particularly important relationship that both the octal number system and the hexadecimal number system have to the binary system is that the bases of octal and hexadecimal (8 and 16 respectively) are powers of the base of the binary number system (base 2). Consider the following 12-digit binary number and its octal and hexadecimal equivalents. See if you can determine how this relationship makes it convenient to abbreviate binary numbers in octal or hexadecimal. The answers follow the numbers.

Binary number	Octal equivalent	Hexadecimal equivalent
`100011010001`	`4321`	`8D1`

To see how the binary number converts easily to octal, simply break the 12-digit binary number into groups of three consecutive bits each, starting from the right, and write those groups over the corresponding digits of the octal number as follows:

```
100   011   010   001
4     3     2     1
```

Note that the octal digit you've written under each group of three bits corresponds precisely to the octal equivalent of that 3-digit binary number, as shown in Fig. D.7.

The same kind of relationship can be observed in converting from binary to hexadecimal. Break the 12-digit binary number into groups of four consecutive bits each, starting from the right, and write those groups over the corresponding digits of the hexadecimal number as follows:

```
1000   1101   0001
8      D      1
```

Notice that the hexadecimal digit you wrote under each group of four bits corresponds precisely to the hexadecimal equivalent of that 4-digit binary number as shown in Fig. D.7.

D.3 Converting Octal and Hexadecimal Numbers to Binary Numbers

In the previous section, we saw how to convert binary numbers to their octal and hexadecimal equivalents by forming groups of binary digits and simply rewriting them as their equivalent octal digit values or hexadecimal digit values. This process may be used in reverse to produce the binary equivalent of a given octal or hexadecimal number.

For example, the octal number 653 is converted to binary simply by writing the 6 as its 3-digit binary equivalent 110, the 5 as its 3-digit binary equivalent 101 and the 3 as its 3-digit binary equivalent 011 to form the 9-digit binary number 110101011.

The hexadecimal number FAD5 is converted to binary simply by writing the F as its 4-digit binary equivalent 1111, the A as its 4-digit binary equivalent 1010, the D as its 4-digit binary equivalent 1101 and the 5 as its 4-digit binary equivalent 0101 to form the 16-digit 1111101011010101.

D.4 Converting from Binary, Octal or Hexadecimal to Decimal

We are accustomed to working in decimal, and therefore it is often convenient to convert a binary, octal, or hexadecimal number to decimal to get a sense of what the number is "really" worth. Our diagrams in Section D.1 express the positional values in decimal. To convert a number to decimal from another base, multiply the decimal equivalent of each digit by its positional value and sum these products. For example, the binary number 110101 is converted to decimal 53 as shown in Fig. D.8.

Converting a binary number to decimal						
Positional values:	32	16	8	4	2	1
Symbol values:	1	1	0	1	0	1
Products:	1*32=32	1*16=16	0*8=0	1*4=4	0*2=0	1*1=1
Sum:	= 32 + 16 + 0 + 4 + 0s + 1 = 53					

Fig. D.8 | Converting a binary number to decimal.

To convert octal 7614 to decimal 3980, we use the same technique, this time using appropriate octal positional values, as shown in Fig. D.9.

Converting an octal number to decimal				
Positional values:	512	64	8	1
Symbol values:	7	6	1	4
Products	7*512=3584	6*64=384	1*8=8	4*1=4
Sum:	= 3584 + 384 + 8 + 4 = 3980			

Fig. D.9 | Converting an octal number to decimal.

To convert hexadecimal AD3B to decimal 44347, we use the same technique, this time using appropriate hexadecimal positional values, as shown in Fig. D.10.

Converting a hexadecimal number to decimal				
Positional values:	4096	256	16	1
Symbol values:	A	D	3	B
Products	A*4096=40960	D*256=3328	3*16=48	B*1=11
Sum:	= 40960 + 3328 + 48 + 11 = 44347			

Fig. D.10 | Converting a hexadecimal number to decimal.

D.5 Converting from Decimal to Binary, Octal or Hexadecimal

The conversions in Section D.4 follow naturally from the positional notation conventions. Converting from decimal to binary, octal, or hexadecimal also follows these conventions.

Suppose we wish to convert decimal 57 to binary. We begin by writing the positional values of the columns right to left until we reach a column whose positional value is greater than the decimal number. We do not need that column, so we discard it. Thus, we first write:

Positional values:	64	32	16	8	4	2	1

Then we discard the column with positional value 64, leaving:

Positional values:	32	16	8	4	2	1

Next we work from the leftmost column to the right. We divide 32 into 57 and observe that there is one 32 in 57 with a remainder of 25, so we write 1 in the 32 column. We divide 16 into 25 and observe that there is one 16 in 25 with a remainder of 9 and write 1 in the 16 column. We divide 8 into 9 and observe that there is one 8 in 9 with a remainder of 1. The next two columns each produce quotients of 0 when their positional values are divided into 1, so we write 0s in the 4 and 2 columns. Finally, 1 into 1 is 1, so we write 1 in the 1 column. This yields:

Positional values:	32	16	8	4	2	1
Symbol values:	1	1	1	0	0	1

and thus decimal 57 is equivalent to binary 111001.

To convert decimal 103 to octal, we begin by writing the positional values of the columns until we reach a column whose positional value is greater than the decimal number. We do not need that column, so we discard it. Thus, we first write:

Positional values:	512	64	8	1

Then we discard the column with positional value 512, yielding:

Positional values:	64	8	1

Next we work from the leftmost column to the right. We divide 64 into 103 and observe that there is one 64 in 103 with a remainder of 39, so we write 1 in the 64 column. We divide 8 into 39 and observe that there are four 8s in 39 with a remainder of 7 and write 4 in the 8 column. Finally, we divide 1 into 7 and observe that there are seven 1s in 7 with no remainder, so we write 7 in the 1 column. This yields:

Positional values:	64	8	1
Symbol values:	1	4	7

and thus decimal 103 is equivalent to octal 147.

To convert decimal 375 to hexadecimal, we begin by writing the positional values of the columns until we reach a column whose positional value is greater than the decimal number. We do not need that column, so we discard it. Thus, we first write:

Positional values:	4096	256	16	1

Then we discard the column with positional value 4096, yielding:

Positional values:	256	16	1

Next we work from the leftmost column to the right. We divide 256 into 375 and observe that there is one 256 in 375 with a remainder of 119, so we write 1 in the 256 column. We divide 16 into 119 and observe that there are seven 16s in 119 with a remainder of 7 and write 7 in the 16 column. Finally, we divide 1 into 7 and observe that there are seven 1s in 7 with no remainder, so we write 7 in the 1 column. This yields:

Positional values:	256	16	1
Symbol values:	1	7	7

and thus decimal 375 is equivalent to hexadecimal 177.

D.6 Negative Binary Numbers: Two's Complement Notation

The discussion so far in this appendix has focused on positive numbers. In this section, we explain how computers represent negative numbers using **two's complement notation.** First we explain how the two's complement of a binary number is formed, then we show why it represents the negative value of the given binary number.

Consider a machine with 32-bit integers. Suppose

```
int value = 13;
```

The 32-bit representation of `value` is

```
00000000 00000000 00000000 00001101
```

To form the negative of `value` we first form its **one's complement** by applying C++'s **bitwise complement operator** (~):

```
onesComplementOfValue = ~value;
```

Internally, `~value` is now `value` with each of its bits reversed—ones become zeros and zeros become ones, as follows:

```
value:
00000000 00000000 00000000 00001101

~value (i.e., value's one's complement):
11111111 11111111 11111111 11110010
```

To form the two's complement of `value`, we simply add 1 to `value`'s one's complement. Thus

```
Two's complement of value:
11111111 11111111 11111111 11110011
```

Now if this is in fact equal to –13, we should be able to add it to binary 13 and obtain a result of 0. Let's try this:

```
 00000000 00000000 00000000 00001101
+11111111 11111111 11111111 11110011
------------------------------------
 00000000 00000000 00000000 00000000
```

The carry bit coming out of the leftmost column is discarded and we indeed get 0 as a result. If we add the one's complement of a number to the number, the result will be all 1s. The key to getting a result of all zeros is that the two's complement is one more than the one's complement. The addition of 1 causes each column to add to 0 with a carry of 1. The carry keeps moving leftward until it is discarded from the leftmost bit, and thus the resulting number is all zeros.

Computers actually perform a subtraction, such as

```
x = a - value;
```

by adding the two's complement of `value` to a, as follows:

```
x = a + (~value + 1);
```

Suppose a is 27 and `value` is 13 as before. If the two's complement of `value` is actually the negative of `value`, then adding the two's complement of value to a should produce the result 14. Let's try this:

```
a (i.e., 27)         00000000 00000000 00000000 00011011
+(~value + 1)       +11111111 11111111 11111111 11110011
                    -----------------------------------
                     00000000 00000000 00000000 00001110
```

which is indeed equal to 14.

Preprocessor

Objectives

In this chapter you'll:

- Use `#include` for developing large programs.
- Use `#define` to create macros and macros with arguments.
- Understand conditional compilation.
- Display error messages during conditional compilation.
- Use assertions to test if the values of expressions are correct.

Outline

E.1 Introduction

This chapter introduces the **preprocessor**. Preprocessing occurs before a program is compiled. Some possible actions are inclusion of other files in the file being compiled, definition of **symbolic constants** and **macros, conditional compilation** of program code and **conditional execution of preprocessing directives.** All preprocessing directives begin with `#`, and only whitespace characters may appear before a preprocessing directive on a line. Preprocessing directives are not C++ statements, so they do not end in a semicolon (`;`). Preprocessing directives are processed fully before compilation begins.

Common Programming Error E.1

Placing a semicolon at the end of a preprocessing directive can lead to a variety of errors, depending on the type of preprocessing directive.

Software Engineering Observation E.1

Many preprocessor features (especially macros) are more appropriate for C programmers than for C++ programmers. C++ programmers should familiarize themselves with the preprocessor, because they might need to work with C legacy code.

E.2 #include Preprocessing Directive

The **`#include` preprocessing directive** has been used throughout this text. The `#include` directive causes a copy of a specified file to be included in place of the directive. The two forms of the `#include` directive are

```
#include <filename>
#include "filename"
```

The difference between these is the location the preprocessor searches for the file to be included. If the filename is enclosed in angle brackets (< and >)—used for standard library header files—the preprocessor searches for the specified file in an implementation-dependent manner, normally through predesignated directories. If the file name is enclosed in quotes, the preprocessor searches first in the same directory as the file being compiled, then in the same implementation-dependent manner as for a file name enclosed in angle brackets. This method is normally used to include programmer-defined header files.

The `#include` directive is used to include standard header files such as `<iostream>` and `<iomanip>`. The `#include` directive is also used with programs consisting of several source files that are to be compiled together. A header file containing declarations and definitions common to the separate program files is often created and included in the file.

Examples of such declarations and definitions are classes, structures, unions, enumerations, function prototypes, constants and stream objects (e.g., `cin`).

E.3 `#define` Preprocessing Directive: Symbolic Constants

The **`#define` preprocessing directive** creates **symbolic constants**—constants represented as symbols—and macros—operations defined as symbols. The `#define` preprocessing directive format is

```
#define identifier replacement-text
```

When this line appears in a file, all subsequent occurrences (except those inside a string) of *identifier* in that file will be replaced by *replacement-text* before the program is compiled. For example,

```
#define PI 3.14159
```

replaces all subsequent occurrences of the symbolic constant `PI` with the numeric constant `3.14159`. Symbolic constants enable you to create a name for a constant and use the name throughout the program. Later, if the constant needs to be modified throughout the program, it can be modified once in the `#define` preprocessing directive—and when the program is recompiled, all occurrences of the constant in the program will be modified. [*Note:* Everything to the right of the symbolic constant name replaces the symbolic constant. For example, `#define PI = 3.14159` causes the preprocessor to replace every occurrence of `PI` with `= 3.14159`. Such replacement is the cause of many subtle logic and syntax errors.] Redefining a symbolic constant with a new value without first undefining it is also an error. Note that `const` variables in C++ are preferred over symbolic constants. Constant variables have a specific data type and are visible by name to a debugger. Once a symbolic constant is replaced with its replacement text, only the replacement text is visible to a debugger. A disadvantage of `const` variables is that they might require a memory location of their data type size—symbolic constants do not require any additional memory.

Common Programming Error E.2

Using symbolic constants in a file other than the file in which the symbolic constants are defined is a compilation error (unless they are `#include`*d from a header file).*

Good Programming Practice E.1

Using meaningful names for symbolic constants makes programs more self-documenting.

E.4 `#define` Preprocessing Directive: Macros

[*Note:* This section is included for the benefit of C++ programmers who will need to work with C legacy code. In C++, macros can often be replaced by templates and inline functions.] A macro is an operation defined in a `#define` preprocessing directive. As with symbolic constants, the ***macro-identifier*** is replaced with the ***replacement-text*** before the program is compiled. Macros may be defined with or without ***arguments***. A macro without arguments is processed like a symbolic constant. In a macro with arguments, the arguments are substituted in the *replacement-text*, then the macro is expanded—i.e., the *replacement-text* replaces the macro-identifier and argument list in the program. There is no data type checking for macro arguments. A macro is used simply for text substitution.

Consider the following macro definition with one argument for the area of a circle:

```
#define CIRCLE_AREA( x ) ( PI * ( x ) * ( x ) )
```

Wherever `CIRCLE_AREA( y )` appears in the file, the value of `y` is substituted for `x` in the replacement text, the symbolic constant `PI` is replaced by its value (defined previously) and the macro is expanded in the program. For example, the statement

```
area = CIRCLE_AREA( 4 );
```

is expanded to

```
area = ( 3.14159 * ( 4 ) * ( 4 ) );
```

Because the expression consists only of constants, at compile time the value of the expression can be evaluated, and the result is assigned to `area` at runtime. The parentheses around each `x` in the replacement text and around the entire expression force the proper order of evaluation when the macro argument is an expression. For example, the statement

```
area = CIRCLE_AREA( c + 2 );
```

is expanded to

```
area = ( 3.14159 * ( c + 2 ) * ( c + 2 ) );
```

which evaluates correctly, because the parentheses force the proper order of evaluation. If the parentheses are omitted, the macro expansion is

```
area = 3.14159 * c + 2 * c + 2;
```

which evaluates incorrectly as

```
area = ( 3.14159 * c ) + ( 2 * c ) + 2;
```

because of the rules of operator precedence.

Common Programming Error E.3

Forgetting to enclose macro arguments in parentheses in the replacement text is an error.

Macro `CIRCLE_AREA` could be defined as a function. Function `circleArea`, as in

```
double circleArea( double x ) { return 3.14159 * x * x; }
```

performs the same calculation as `CIRCLE_AREA`, but the overhead of a function call is associated with function `circleArea`. The advantages of `CIRCLE_AREA` are that macros insert code directly in the program—avoiding function overhead—and the program remains readable because `CIRCLE_AREA` is defined separately and named meaningfully. A disadvantage is that its argument is evaluated twice. Also, every time a macro appears in a program, the macro is expanded. If the macro is large, this produces an increase in program size. Thus, there is a trade-off between execution speed and program size (if disk space is low). Note that `inline` functions (see Chapter 6) are preferred to obtain the performance of macros and the software engineering benefits of functions.

Performance Tip E.1

Macros can sometimes be used to replace a function call with `inline` *code prior to execution time. This eliminates the overhead of a function call. Inline functions are preferable to macros because they offer the type-checking services of functions.*

The following is a macro definition with two arguments for the area of a rectangle:

```
#define RECTANGLE_AREA( x, y )  ( ( x ) * ( y ) )
```

Wherever `RECTANGLE_AREA( a, b )` appears in the program, the values of `a` and `b` are substituted in the macro replacement text, and the macro is expanded in place of the macro name. For example, the statement

```
rectArea = RECTANGLE_AREA( a + 4, b + 7 );
```

is expanded to

```
rectArea = ( ( a + 4 ) * ( b + 7 ) );
```

The value of the expression is evaluated and assigned to variable `rectArea`.

The replacement text for a macro or symbolic constant is normally any text on the line after the identifier in the `#define` directive. If the replacement text for a macro or symbolic constant is longer than the remainder of the line, a backslash (\) must be placed at the end of each line of the macro (except the last line), indicating that the replacement text continues on the next line.

Symbolic constants and macros can be discarded using the **`#undef` preprocessing directive**. Directive `#undef` "undefines" a symbolic constant or macro name. The scope of a symbolic constant or macro is from its definition until it is either undefined with `#undef` or the end of the file is reached. Once undefined, a name can be redefined with `#define`.

Note that expressions with side effects (e.g., variable values are modified) should not be passed to a macro, because macro arguments may be evaluated more than once.

Common Programming Error E.4

Macros often replace a name that wasn't intended to be a use of the macro but just happened to be spelled the same. This can lead to exceptionally mysterious compilation and syntax errors.

E.5 Conditional Compilation

Conditional compilation enables you to control the execution of preprocessing directives and the compilation of program code. Each of the conditional preprocessing directives evaluates a constant integer expression that will determine whether the code will be compiled. Cast expressions, `sizeof` expressions and enumeration constants cannot be evaluated in preprocessing directives because these are all determined by the compiler and preprocessing happens before compilation.

The conditional preprocessor construct is much like the `if` selection structure. Consider the following preprocessor code:

```
#ifndef NULL
   #define NULL 0
#endif
```

which determines whether the symbolic constant NULL is already defined. The expression #ifndef NULL includes the code up to #endif if NULL is not defined, and skips the code if NULL is defined. Every **#if** construct ends with **#endif**. Directives **#ifdef** and **#ifndef** are shorthand for #if defined(*name*) and #if !defined(*name*). A multiple-part conditional preprocessor construct may be tested using the #elif (the equivalent of else if in an if structure) and the #else (the equivalent of else in an if structure) directives.

During program development, programmers often find it helpful to "comment out" large portions of code to prevent it from being compiled. If the code contains C-style comments, /* and */ cannot be used to accomplish this task, because the first */ encountered would terminate the comment. Instead, you can use the following preprocessor construct:

```
#if 0
   code prevented from compiling
#endif
```

To enable the code to be compiled, simply replace the value 0 in the preceding construct with the value 1.

Conditional compilation is commonly used as a debugging aid. Output statements are often used to print variable values and to confirm the flow of control. These output statements can be enclosed in conditional preprocessing directives so that the statements are compiled only until the debugging process is completed. For example,

```
#ifdef DEBUG
   cerr << "Variable x = " << x << endl;
#endif
```

causes the cerr statement to be compiled in the program if the symbolic constant DEBUG has been defined before directive #ifdef DEBUG. This symbolic constant is normally set by a command-line compiler or by settings in the IDE (e.g., Visual Studio) and not by an explicit #define definition. When debugging is completed, the #define directive is removed from the source file, and the output statements inserted for debugging purposes are ignored during compilation. In larger programs, it might be desirable to define several different symbolic constants that control the conditional compilation in separate sections of the source file.

Common Programming Error E.5

Inserting conditionally compiled output statements for debugging purposes in locations where C++ currently expects a single statement can lead to syntax errors and logic errors. In this case, the conditionally compiled statement should be enclosed in a compound statement. Thus, when the program is compiled with debugging statements, the flow of control of the program is not altered.

E.6 #error and #pragma Preprocessing Directives

The **#error directive**

```
#error tokens
```

prints an implementation-dependent message including the *tokens* specified in the directive. The tokens are sequences of characters separated by spaces. For example,

```
#error 1 - Out of range error
```

contains six tokens. In one popular C++ compiler, for example, when a #error directive is processed, the tokens in the directive are displayed as an error message, preprocessing stops and the program does not compile.

The **#pragma directive**

```
#pragma tokens
```

causes an implementation-defined action. A pragma not recognized by the implementation is ignored. A particular C++ compiler, for example, might recognize pragmas that enable you to take advantage of that compiler's specific capabilities. For more information on #error and #pragma, see the documentation for your C++ implementation.

E.7 Operators # and

The # and ## preprocessor operators are available in C++ and ANSI/ISO C. The # operator causes a replacement-text token to be converted to a string surrounded by quotes. Consider the following macro definition:

```
#define HELLO( x ) cout << "Hello, " #x << endl;
```

When HELLO(John) appears in a program file, it is expanded to

```
cout << "Hello, " "John" << endl;
```

The string "John" replaces #x in the replacement text. Strings separated by white space are concatenated during preprocessing, so the above statement is equivalent to

```
cout << "Hello, John" << endl;
```

The # operator must be used in a macro with arguments, because the operand of # refers to an argument of the macro.

The ## operator concatenates two tokens. Consider the following macro definition:

```
cout << "Hello, John" << endl;
#define TOKENCONCAT( x, y )  x ## y
```

When TOKENCONCAT appears in the program, its arguments are concatenated and used to replace the macro, so TOKENCONCAT(O, K) is replaced by OK in the program. The ## operator must have two operands.

E.8 Predefined Symbolic Constants

There are six **predefined symbolic constants** (Fig. E.1). The identifiers for each of these begin and (except for __cplusplus) end with *two* underscores. These identifiers and preprocessor operator defined (Section E.5) cannot be used in #define or #undef directives.

Symbolic constant	Description
__LINE__	The line number of the current source-code line (an integer constant).
__FILE__	The presumed name of the source file (a string).

Fig. E.1 | The predefined symbolic constants. (Part 1 of 2.)

Symbolic constant	Description
`__DATE__`	The date the source file is compiled (a string of the form "Mmm dd yyyy" such as "Aug 19 2002").
`__STDC__`	Indicates whether the program conforms to the ANSI/ISO C standard. Contains value 1 if there is full conformance and is undefined otherwise.
`__TIME__`	The time the source file is compiled (a string literal of the form "hh:mm:ss").
`__cplusplus`	Contains the value 199711L (the date the ISO C++ standard was approved) if the file is being compiled by a C++ compiler, undefined otherwise. Allows a file to be set up to be compiled as either C or C++.

Fig. E.1 | The predefined symbolic constants. (Part 2 of 2.)

E.9 Assertions

The **assert macro**—defined in the **<cassert>** header file—tests the value of an expression. If the value of the expression is 0 (false), then assert prints an error message and calls function **abort** (of the general utilities library—<cstdlib>) to terminate program execution. This is a useful debugging tool for testing whether a variable has a correct value. For example, suppose variable x should never be larger than 10 in a program. An assertion may be used to test the value of x and print an error message if the value of x is incorrect. The statement would be

```
assert( x <= 10 );
```

If x is greater than 10 when the preceding statement is encountered in a program, an error message containing the line number and file name is printed, and the program terminates. You may then concentrate on this area of the code to find the error. If the symbolic constant NDEBUG is defined, subsequent assertions will be ignored. Thus, when assertions are no longer needed (i.e., when debugging is complete), we insert the line

```
#define NDEBUG
```

in the program file rather than deleting each assertion manually. As with the DEBUG symbolic constant, NDEBUG is often set by compiler command-line options or through a setting in the IDE.

Most C++ compilers now include exception handling. C++ programmers prefer using exceptions rather than assertions. But assertions are still valuable for C++ programmers who work with C legacy code.

E.10 Wrap-Up

This appendix discussed the #include directive, which is used to develop larger programs. You also learned about the #define directive, which is used to create macros. We introduced conditional compilation, displaying error messages and using assertions.

Index

Symbols

Numerics

A

E

G

H

O

P

Q

R

S